Names through the Ages

Names through the Ages

T E R E S A   N O R M A N

BERKLEY BOOKS, NEW YORK

This book is an original publication of The Berkley Publishing Group.

NAMES THROUGH THE AGES

A Berkley Book / published by arrangement with
the author

PRINTING HISTORY
Berkley trade paperback edition / August 1999

The Penguin Putnam Inc. World Wide Web site address is
http://www.penguinputnam.com

ISBN: 0-425-16877-8

BERKLEY®
Berkley Books are published by The Berkley Publishing Group,
a division of Penguin Putnam Inc.,
375 Hudson Street, New York, New York 10014.
BERKLEY and the ''B'' design are trademarks
belonging to Penguin Putnam Inc.

PRINTED IN THE UNITED STATES OF AMERICA

10 9 8 7 6 5 4 3 2

[FOR MY HUSBAND, JOHN]

[CONTENTS]

VIII

[CONTENTS]

PART FOUR: IRELAND

PART FIVE: FRANCE

PART SIX: THE UNITED STATES

Part One

[ENGLAND]

[CONTENTS]

[RULERS OF ENGLAND]

Edward the Confessor (1042–1066)
William the Conqueror (1066–1087)
William II (1087–1100)
Henry I (1100–1135)
Stephen (1135–1154)
Henry II (1154–1189)
Richard I (1189–1199)
John (1199–1216)
Henry III (1216–1272)
Edward I (1272–1307)
Edward II (1307–1327)
Edward III (1327–1377)
Richard II (1377–1399)
Henry IV (1399–1413)
Henry V (1413–1422)
Henry VI (1422–1471)
Edward IV (1461–1483)
Richard III (1483–1485)
Henry VII (1485–1509)
Henry VIII (1509–1547)
Edward VI (1547–1553)

Mary I (1553–1558)
Elizabeth I (1558–1603)
James I (1603–1625)
Charles I (1625–1649)
The Commonwealth (1649–1660)
Charles II (1660–1685)
James II (1685–1688)
William and Mary (1688–1694)
William (alone) (1694–1702)
Anne (1702–1714)
George I (1714–1727)
George II (1727–1760)
George III (1760–1820)
George IV (1820–1830)
William IV (1830–1837)
Victoria (1837–1901)
Edward VII (1901–1910)
George V (1910–1936)
Edward VIII (1936)
George VI (1936–1952)
Elizabeth II (1952–Present)

Chapter One

THE DARK AGES TO THE NORMAN CONQUEST
[5 A.D.–1066]

POLITICS

BY THE TIME of the Roman invasion of Britain in 43 A.D., Celtic immigrants from the mainland were long established, and their Celtic language had become the language of the land. After the Romans set up government, the use of Latin was encouraged, as was the adoption of the behaviors and benefits of civilized Roman society. By the second or third centuries, all but those of the lowest classes and those in the farthest reaches spoke Latin and had adopted the Christian religion.

During the reign of Honorius (395–423), Roman troops were withdrawn to defend Italy from Alaric's invading Goths, and Britain's inhabitants were left to fend for themselves. With Britain now lacking an organized defense, tribes from the mainland looked upon the island with predatory interest. Saxons from Germany invaded and established settlements, and the Picts from the north of Hadrian's Wall mounted brutal excursions into British territory.

A fifth-century British ruler, Vortigern, asked for Saxon help in mounting a resistance against the Picts. The Saxons, long independent fighters, soon tired of being under Vortigern's authority. They mutinied, took control of the land, and brought its people under their own rule. Saxon settlement continued, and 200 years later, the Saxons held most of the land; the Celts who had not been assimilated into Anglo-Saxon society were pushed far into the hills, and nearly all traces of four centuries of Roman civilization were gone.

The eighth century was a period of peace and culture, yet it was not to last. Viking raids brought turmoil and the disintegration of Saxon kingdoms. York was taken, and the spiritual center of Lindisfarne was sacked. Sanctuaries were desecrated and destroyed; monks were mercilessly killed. Following the Norwegian Vikings were the Danes, who invaded and conquered Mercia, Northumbria, and East Anglia.

Alfred (849–901) was the first Saxon king able to withstand invading forces. In 865, he managed to fight the Danes to a standstill and kept them confined to a large region of their own called the Danelaw. Alfred then established a powerful West Saxon dynasty in Wessex and became the undisputed leader of all the English. He set about establishing strongholds, or burghs, which became part of a new national system of defense. Towns were created in the strongholds, setting the pattern for the early urbanization of England. The shire structure took shape, and boundaries were drawn that remained unchanged until 1974. Not only did Alfred see to the safety of his people, he made a point of undertaking their cultural and intellectual regeneration as well. Scholars and noblemen were expected to learn their country's history in their native tongue, Anglo-Saxon art flourished, and the Church experienced a surge in monasticism.

Edgar the Peaceable (959–975) continued Alfred's capable leadership. Strongly attracted to Christianity, he waited until reaching the age of twenty-nine to be crowned, the same age Christ was when he began his public ministry. Under Edgar's rule, the monastic ideal flourished, and soon more than thirty Benedictine monasteries and no fewer than six nunneries existed in the kingdom.

In 981, the Vikings began another series of attacks and invasions, and in 1017, the Danish king Cnut (1017–1035) took over the whole country. Cnut's family ruled until 1042, when his son, Harthacnut, died childless.

Edward the Confessor (1042–1066), Harthacnut's half-brother, was recalled from Normandy to assume the throne. Having been raised in Normandy, Edward introduced the French language and culture to England and liberally bestowed lands and titles upon his friends and retainers, thus paving the way for the Conquest of 1066.

SOCIETY

IN EARLY ENGLAND, a person's position in society was determined by the law as well as by local custom. Aelfric, a tenth-century monk and Abbot of Eynsham, explained that the social structure consisted of three supports of the throne: the *laboratores*, the *oratores*, and the *bellatores*. The *laboratores* consisted of those who provided the sustenance: the ploughmen and husbandmen whose sole task was to produce food to sustain the community. The *oratores* were those who promoted Christianity and served to intercede between the people and God: those who toiled solely in spirituality and the service of God. The *bellatores* were the guardians of the land, the towns, and the country. These three divisions lasted as such for centuries. Later generations would simply distinguish between the *eorls* (men with authority) and the *ceorls* (those without authority), though each of those divisions also had many levels.

The lowest level of the *laboratores* was made up of the unfree: slaves who were victims of misfortune or descendants of pre-Saxon peoples. The half-free people made up the next level. These were the unpaid cottagers who toiled and worked the land for their lord.

During this period of time, the relationship between man and lord was of paramount importance. In fact, men were more dependent upon their lords than upon their own kinsmen. If a man was without a lord, and was not a lord himself, he was outside the basic social structure. Ninth-century laws of Alfred said that a man could fight for his lord without incurring a vendetta from his kinsmen, and a man could fight for his kinsmen if the kinsmen were wrongly attacked, but under no circumstances was a man to fight against his lord; that simply was not allowed. Pursuits such as hunting for game or hawking were reserved for the ruling classes, and this privilege was strictly guarded. No man who worked with his hands was allowed to hunt.

Women occupied a significant place in society as well as in the system of work. Not only did they perform traditional household chores such as cleaning, cooking, and making clothing, women were also in charge of such tasks as shearing the sheep and milking the cows and goats. In spite of the amount of work they were obligated to perform, the women were quite privileged compared to those of later eras. She could not be compelled to marry a man not of her own choosing, and getting out of a bad marriage through divorce was quite easy. A woman could own land and personal property, and she could dispose of her property as she wished. Aethelbert of Kent (c. 600) allowed for a widow's compensation by establishing a law entitling a widow, if she had a living child, to half the goods left by her deceased husband.

RELIGION

THOUGH THE SAXONS were a pagan people who worshiped the old Germanic gods, Christianity managed to persevere. Aethelbert of Kent (d. 597) married a Christian princess and was himself converted to the Christian religion. Soon, Celtic Christian missionaries from Wales, Iona, and Ireland arrived and began to spread the Gospel. Monasteries and nunneries were established, and within 100 years, most Anglo-Saxons had been converted to the new religion. They did, however, remain strongly aware of their pagan roots and even incorporated many elements of the old religion into their new faith.

NAMING

THE SAXONS WERE a Germanic people, and they brought their Germanic system of nomenclature with them when they crossed the channel. A child was given only one name at birth. This was most commonly a compound formed from a select pool of word elements used to make names. Certain roots, such as *Ælf-* (elf), *Æthel-* (noble), and *Ēad-* (wealth), were used as first elements in compound names. Others, such as *-gifu* (gift), *-helm* (helmet, protection), and *-mund* (hand, protection) formed the second element. Yet another set, such as *ræd* (counsel), *rīc* (king, ruler), and *wulf* (wolf), was considered acceptable for either position. It is apparent that the meanings of the names were no longer of great importance, for little attention was paid to the combined meanings of the elements. Wulfstān (wolf-stone) is an example of a name whose elements were combined without much thought to meaning.

The most common initial elements of names of the royal family of Kent were *Æthel-* (noble) and *Eormen-* (strength). In Bernicia, the royal family used the element *Ōs-* (god). *Sige-* (victory) was the common initial element among East Saxon royalty, and in Wessex, *Æthel-* (noble), *Ælf-* (elf), and *Ēad-* (wealth, prosperity) were the most common. With the exception of *Æthel-*, these elements were also found in the names of commoners. *Æthel-* seems to have been reserved for royalty.

Single element names in use were either pet forms of compound names, such as Sigge from Sigmund, or names derived from a single root word. These names often originated as nicknames based on physical characteristics such as baldness, corpulence, tallness, or complexion. A few names based on occupation were also used.

Surnames were practically unknown, so familial ties were shown in a different way. A common method was alliteration. Similar to the way parents of today give their children names beginning with the same initial letter, Anglo-Saxon parents often used names beginning with the same initial element or sound. Another practice was to give the child a name formed from the first element of the father's or the mother's name along with an unrelated element. For example, the children of Ēadwine might have been named Ēadweard, Ēadmund, and Ēadgyth. Using an element from the name of each parent was less common. The most famous of these was Saint Wulfstān, the son of Æthelstān and Wulfgifu.

A third way to show familial association consisted of naming a male child after his grandfather and a female child after her grandmother. This method was rarely practiced before the tenth century, leading some scholars to the assumption that it was prohibited, perhaps on religious grounds, before that time.

When Saint Augustine and his missionaries arrived in the isles in 597 to convert the Anglo-Saxons to Christianity, Latin was again introduced, and names from the Christian religion came into occasional use by clergy. They were very rarely used among the general population. Instead, compound names such as Ōswine (friend of God) and Godfrith (God's peace) were used, thus keeping the Anglo-Saxon system of nomenclature intact yet acknowledging the importance of God in their lives.

The Danish invasion of the eighth century had more of an impact on place names than personal names outside the Danelaw. This was perhaps due to the fact that many of the Scandinavian names had cognates in the Old English tongue. In the Danelaw, however, Scandinavian names were common as were compounds formed from Anglo-Saxon and Scandinavian names. Thorgifu (Thor's gift), Ketelbeort (cauldron + bright), and Cylferth (cauldron + peace) are examples of names formed from both languages.

The second Danish invasion was headed by a Christian king, Cnut (1017–1035), who made Latin the language of diplomacy, the law, and learning in the Danelaw and the rest of England. Christian names found their way into Danish nomenclature at this time.

The following are common Anglo-Saxon elements used in name-making. Some letters in the Old English alphabet differ from those found in Modern English. For ease in understanding, the *ae* ligature, *Æ* or *æ*, is represented in this work as *Ae* and *ae*. The thorn, *Þ* or *þ*, and the eth, *Ð* or *ð*, are both written as *Th* and *th*. Diacritical marks have been retained, but it is acceptable to disregard them when making character names.

Aelf-, Elf- (elf)
Aethel-, Ethel- (noble)
Cūth- (famous)
Cwēn- (queen)
Ēad- (wealth, prosperity)
Eald- (old)
Eastre- (goddess of the rising sun)
Eormen-, Ermen-, Irmen- (strength)
God- (god, God)
Heah- (high)
Milde- (mild)
Od- (riches)
Ōs- (god, God)
Sig-, Sige-, Sigu- (victory)
Willeo- (will)

-burg,-burh (fortress)
-flaed (beauty)
-gifu (gift)
-gyth (war, strife)
-heard (hard)
-helm (helmet, protection)
-lind (serpent)
-mund (hand, protection)
-swith (strength)
-thryth (strength)
-weald (power)
-weard (guardian, protector)
-wine (friend)

beald (bold)
beorht, beort (bright)
frith (peace)
hild (battle, strife)
gār (spear)
raed (counsel)
rīc (ruler, king)
stān (stone)
wulf (wolf)

As Old English is now a dead language, the meanings of many names from that period have been lost. Others of uncertain or debated meaning and etymology are listed with their supposed meanings.

FEMALE NAMES

Acha (?)
Aelfgifu (elf gift) **Aelfgiva, Alfgifu, Elfgifu**
Aelflaed (elf beauty) **Aelfflaed, Aelffled, Aelfled, Aelfleda**
Aelfreda (elf strength) **Aelfrida, Elfreda, Elfrida**
Aethelburh (noble fortress) **Aethelburg, Ethelberga, Ethelburg, Ethelburga, Ethelburh**
Aetheldaeg (noble day)
Aetheldreda (noble strength) **Etheldreda, Etheldred**
Aethelflaed (noble beauty) **Alfled, Alfleda, Alflet, Elfled, Elfeda, Elflet, Ethelfled, Ethelfleda**

Aethelfrith (noble peace) **Ethelfrith**
Aethelgifu (noble gift) **Elgifu, Ethelgifu**
Aethelgyth (noble war, strife) **Ethelgyth**
Aethelhildr (noble battle) **Aethelhild, Aethelhilda, Ethelhild, Ethelhilda**
Aethelind (noble serpent)
Aethelswith (noble strength) **Aethylswith, Aethylswyth, Ethelswith**
Aethelthryth (noble strength) **Ethelthryd, Ethelthryth**
Aethelu (noble)

Aethelwine (noble friend) **Ethelwine**
Agatha (pure, chaste)
Alchflaed (?, perhaps *hall* + beauty) **Alchfled**
Baldhild (bold battle) **Bealdhild, Bealdhildr**
Bealdgyth (bold war, strife)
Beatrice (bringer of happiness) **Beatrix**
Bebba (?)
Bega (life; prayer)
Beorhtwine (bright friend) **Beortwine**
Beorhtwynn (bright delight) **Beortwynn**
Bertca (bright, famous)
Bertha (bright, famous)
Biedlufu (command + love, beloved)
Breguswith (? + strength)
Clotichilda (loud battle) **Clotilda**
Coenburg (bold fortress)
Cuthburh (famous fortress) **Cuthburg**
Cwēnburh (queen's fortress) **Cwēnburg**
Cwēnhild (battle queen)
Cyneburh (wise, proud; famous; family + fortress) **Cyneburg, Cyniburg**
Cynethryth (wise, proud; famous; family + strength)
Cynwise (wise, proud; famous; family + battle)
Dēorwynn (dear delight)
Eabae (?)
Ēadburh (wealthy fortress) **Eadburg, Eadburga, Eadburgh**
Ēadgifu (wealthy gift)
Ēadgyth (wealthy battle) **Eadita, Edged, Edgida, Edid, Edied, Ediet, Edit**
Ēadu (wealth)
Eald (old, venerable)
Ealdgyth (venerable strength) **Adelid, Aeldid, Aeldiet, Aeldit, Alded, Aldgid, Aldid, Aldiet, Eldid, Eldit**
Eanflaed (? + beauty) **Eanfled**
Earcongota (genuine god) **Eorcongota**
Ebba (strong as a wild boar)
Edith (wealthy battle)
Emma (strength)
Eormengard (strength + strength) **Ermengard, Irmengard**
Eormengild (strong in battle) **Ermengild, Irmengild**
Eormenthryth (strength + strength) **Ermenthryth, Irmenthryth**
Ethelinda (noble serpent)
Everild (boar battle) **Everilda**
Freawaru (peace protector)
Frigyth (peace war)
Frithuswith (peace strength) **Frithswide, Frithswith, Frithswyth**
Gautelen (from the tribe of the Gauts) **Gauzelen**
Geretrudis (spear strength) **Gertrude**
Gisilthryth (hostage strength)
Gode (good)
Godgifu (God's gift) **Godefe, Godeva**
Godgyth (God's war)
Godlēofu (God's love)
Goldburh (gold fortress) **Goldburg**

Golde (gold)
Grimhildr (helmet battle) **Grimhild**
Gunnhildr (war battle) **Gunhild, Gunnhild**
Guthfrith (war peace) **Guthfrid**
Gytha (war) **Githa**
Heahburh (tall fortress) **Heahburg**
Heahhildr (tall battle) **Heahhild**
Heiu (?, perhaps *heart, mind, soul*)
Helewis (hale, hearty and wide)
Hereswith (army strength)
Heriburg (army fortress)
Hild (battle) **Hilda, Hilde, Hylde**
Hildegard (battle protector)
Hildilid (battle)
Hulda (sweet, lovable)
Hygbald (? + bold)
Hygd (?)
Ingrede (Ing, a byname of the Norse fertility god Frey + beautiful)
Ingrith (beautiful Ing)
Isold (?, possibly *ruler of the ice*) **Isolde, Isolt**
Kyneburg (royal fortress)
Langgifu (tall gift)
Leuerune (love, beloved)
Magge (pearl)
Margaret (pearl)
Merewald (merry ruler)
Mildburh (mild fortress) **Mildburg**
Mildgyth (mild war)
Muriel (sea bright)
Ōsgifu (God's gift)
Ōsthryth (God's strength) **Osthryd**
Plectrude (lightning strength; lightning maiden) **Plecthryth**
Radagundis (counsel war) **Radegund**
Saefaru (sea passage)
Saelēofu (sea love) **Saelufu**
Saethryth (sea strength) **Saethryd**
Sexburg (?, perhaps *sickle* + fortress)
Sigeflaed (beautiful victory)
Sigga (victory)
Sigrithr (beautiful victory)
Stānburh (stone fortress) **Stanburg**
Stānhildr (stone battle) **Stanhild**
Svanhild (battle swan) **Svanhild, Swanhildr, Swanhild**
Swēte (sweet)
Swētleofu (sweet love) **Swetlufu**
Swidbert (strong and bright)
Thēode (people, nation)
Thorgifu (Thor's gift)
Thorhildr (Thor's battle) **Thorhild**
Thruidred (strength counsel)
Thrythwulf (strength wolf) **Thrydwulf**
Tofa (beautiful Thor)
Tofa-Hildr (beautiful Thor's battle)
Tortgyth (Thor's war)
Tūnhild (village battle)

Utta (wealthy)
Waecerhild (watchful in battle)
Wealhtheow (?, perhaps *foreign thief*)
Wīgburh (war fortress)
Withburga (person fortress)

Wlanchild (proud battle) **Wlanchil**
Wulfgifu (wolf gift)
Wulfthryth (wolf strength)
Wynflaed (fair and beautiful)

MALE NAMES

Adalhard (noble and hard)
Adhelm (noble helmet)
Aelfgār (elf spear) **Aelgar**
Aelfraed (elf counsel)
Aelfrīc (elf ruler)
Aelfstān (elf stone)
Aelfweard (elf guardian)
Aelfwine (elf friend)
Aethelbeorht (noble bright) **Aethelbeort, Aethelbert, Aethelbyrht, Ethelbert**
Aethelfrith (noble peace) **Aethelfrid**
Aethelheard (noble and hard)
Aethelmaer (noble famous)
Aethelraed (noble counsel) **Adelred, Adred, Aethelred, Ailred, Alret, Edred, Ethelred**
Aethelstān (noble stone) **Ethelstan**
Aethelwine (noble friend)
Aethelwulf (noble wolf)
Artor (?) **Artur**
Asketil (god's sacrificial cauldron) **Asketel**
Bealdwine (bold friend) **Baldewine, Baldewyn, Baldewyne**
Becca (pickax, mattock)
Beorhtwulf (bright wolf) **Berhtwulf**
Beorn (warrior; brave; bear)
Beornheard (bear; bold as a bear + hard, severe)
Bil (sword; a bil, a halberd)
Blitha (gentle, merry)
Boda (herald, messenger)
Brūn (brown)
Budda (beetle)
Bynni (manger, bin)
Cada (a short, lumpish person; an orphaned animal; a lamb)
Cēne (wise, bold, brave, proud) **Cyne**
Cēnweard (wise guardian)
Cēnwīg (brave in battle)
Ceolman (ship protection)
Cniht (knight, servant)
Cola (coal, black, dark, swarthy)
Creoda (creed)
Cūtha (famous)
Cūthbeorht (famous and bright) **Cuthbert**
Cūthwulf (famous wolf) **Cuthwolf**
Cwēnraed (queen counsel)
Cylferth (sacrificial cauldron of peace)
Cynebeald (royal and bold)
Cynemaer (royal and famous)

Cynerīc (royal ruler)
Cyneweard (royal guardian)
Cynewīg (royal war)
Cyng (king)
Cyppe (to be swollen; a fat or rotund person)
Cytelrīc (sacrificial cauldron + ruler, king)
Dēora (beloved; brave, bold; deer)
Dūnstān (hill stone)
Ēadgar (wealthy spear)
Ēadmund (wealthy protection)
Ēadred (wealthy counsel) **Eadraed**
Ēadrīc (wealthy ruler, king)
Ēadulf (wealthy wolf)
Ealdfrith (venerable peace)
Ealdhelm (venerable helmet)
Ealdred (venerable counsel) **Eldred**
Earnweald (eagle power)
Ecgbeorht (sword bright) **Egbeorht, Egberht, Egbert**
Eoforheard (boar hard)
Eorconbeald (genuinely bold) **Eorconbald, Eorkonbeald**
Eorconweald (genuine power) **Eorkonweald**
Eric (eternal ruler)
Estmund (beauty protection)
Flint (rock, hard as a rock)
Freodhoric (peaceful ruler)
Fugol (fowl, bird)
Gamel (old)
Gaufrid (a district of land + peace) **Gosfrid**
Gisilbeorht (pledge bright) **Gisilbeort, Gisilberht**
Glaed (glade; a short form of Glaedwine)
Glaedwine (glade friend)
Gleaw (wise, prudent)
Goda (good)
Godcild (God's child)
Godfrith (God's peace)
Godrīc (God's ruler)
Godwine (God's friend)
Golda (gold)
Goldwine (gold friend) **Goldwin**
Grante (great) **Grente**
Grēne (green)
Grimbeald (savage, fierce; a mask + bold) **Grimbald, Grimbold**
Hacon (useful, handy) **Hakon**
Hand (hand)
Harald (ruler of an army) **Harold**

Heafoc (hawk) **Hafoc**
Heaha (high, tall)
Heahbeorht (tall and bright) **Heahbeort, Heahberht**
Heahsige (tall victory)
Heahstān (tall stone)
Heard (hard, severe)
Herebeorht (army bright) **Hereberht**
Hereweald (army power)
Hereweard (army guardian) **Hereward**
Hunfrith (Old German folk name, possibly *giant + peace*)
Hwita (white, pale)
Hygebeorht (heart, mind + bright) **Hygeberht**
Ketelbern (sacrificial cauldron + bear)
Lemma (people famous; beloved and famous)
Lēodmaer (people famous)
Lēof (dear, beloved) **Leofa**
Lēofmaer (beloved and famous)
Lēofrīc (beloved ruler)
Lēofsige (beloved victory)
Lēofwine (beloved friend)
Leppe (lip)
Mann (man, servant)
Meaw (a gull)
Ōsbeald (God bold)
Ōsbeorht (God bright) **Osberht**
Ōsmund (God's protection)

Ōsweald (God's power) **Osveald**
Ōswine (God's friend)
Raedwine (counsel friend)
Saethryth (sea strength)
Sida (custom, manner; morality)
Siduwine (custom, manner; morality + friend)
Sigge (victory)
Sigmund (victory protection)
Sigweard (victory guardian)
Snel (smart, active, bold)
Sprott (sprout, shoot)
Swan (herdsman, swineheard, peasant; swan; boy, servant)
Swēta (sweet)
Swift (swift, fleet of foot)
Thorbert (Thor bright) **Thurbert**
Thorsteinn (Thor stone) **Thorstein**
Tunna (village, town)
Tūnraed (town counsel)
Tūnrīc (town ruler)
Tūnwulf (town wolf)
Wada (to go; from the popular tale of Wade, a sea serpent both feared and honored by the coastal tribes of the North and Baltic seas)
Wilfrith (resolute, will + peace)
Wine (friend)

SURNAMES

It should be remembered that surnames were not in general use during this time period. Secondary names were merely additional identifiers and were descriptive of place of residence, occupation, personal characteristics, and familial connections. The following are examples of words used as additional descriptive names.

Characteristic: These names were often used with the article *sé* or *the* (ðe). They are one of the largest groups of Anglo-Saxon "surnames."

Batoc (the stout man)
Beald (the bald; the bold)
Blaca (the black)
Brodeheved (big head)
Cada (the short, fat person)
Cild (the child)
Cola (the dark one)
Cyppe (the fat one)

Ealda (the old one)
Geonga (the young)
Grim (the savage)
Heaha (the tall)
Hoga (the wise)
Hwita (the white)
Reada (the red)
Swift (the swift)

Local: These names were not as common and used the prepositions *aet, on, de, atte, in,* and *apud.*

in Brothortun (from Brothortun)
aet Dentune (from Dentune)

de Lamburnan (from Lamburnan)
on Lundene (from Lundene)

Relationship: Usually, these were patronymics formed by adding the suffixes *suna, sune, sunu* (son of), *dohter* (daughter of), and *ing* to the genitive case of the father's name or after the father's name. Less common were formations based on the mother's name or other familial connections, such as brother, father, wife, brother-in-law, servant, or stepson of another person.

Aedesdohter (daughter of Aed *fire*)
Aelfrices suna (son of Aelfric)
Brune stepsune (stepson of Brun *brown*)
Dudding (son of Dudda)
Eadricssunu (son of Eadric *wealthy ruler*)

Eadwinesbroder (brother of Eadwine *wealthy friend*)
pater Alwin (father of Alwin *noble friend*)
Rolfes sune (son of Rolf *counsel wolf*)
Wynflaede sunu (son of Wynflaed *fair and beautiful*)

Occupation: These made up the smallest group of additional Anglo-Saxon names.

Boda (the messenger)
Cniht (the servant)

Mann (the servant)
Swan (the swineherd)

Chapter Two

THE NORMAN PERIOD
WILLIAM THE CONQUEROR TO STEPHEN
[1066–1154]

POLITICS

EDWARD THE CONFESSOR, the son of Ethelred II the Unready and Emma of Normandy, was in a Continental monastery when he was chosen to succeed his half-brother, Harthacnut, as king of England. Having been in France for thirty years, Edward had become, as sixteenth-century historian Camden put it, "all Frenchified." He had acquired the French culture, the French language, French friends, and French ideas.

Because Edward had no heir, in 1051 he named his distant cousin, William of Normandy, as his successor. It's possible Edward's choice was made as a means of garnering Norman support in the event his quarrel with his powerful father-in-law, Godwin of Essex, led to an armed confrontation. Whatever the reason, the nomination of William had unforeseeable consequences that changed the course of English history. Edward eventually reconciled with his wife's family and on his deathbed, designated Harold, his English brother-in-law, as his successor. That selection was confirmed by the Witan, the Anglo-Saxon council of kings, and on January 6, 1066, Harold took the throne.

William felt as if he had been cheated. Harold himself had sworn an oath to William in 1064 to support William's accession, so William believed Harold to be not only an usurper but a liar as well. The Norman duke wasted no time in preparing to fight for the throne he saw as rightfully his.

It has been said that the English were good at everything but government and warfare. At a time when continental armies relied on mounted, well-armored knights, the English had yet to learn to fight on horseback. Harold's army consisted of a small number of archers and a shield wall. That army, already exhausted from fighting a bloody battle against the Norwegians in Yorkshire, had to then march the length of England to engage the Normans at Hastings. They stood little chance when confronted with William's powerful army of bowmen, mounted warriors, and mercenaries from Flanders and Brittany. William's victory at Hastings was a triumph of eleventh-century military methods over those of the seventh century. On Christmas Day, with the backing of the papacy, William was crowned at Westminster Abbey and the social, political, and religious institutions of England were forever changed.

William quickly declared all the land of England to be his, then parceled out much of it to his tenants-in-chief. Norman bishops and abbots received 26 percent of the land, and Norman barons received 49 percent. Those portions were then divided among undertenants who owed allegiance and knightly service to the lords. The Anglo-Saxon nobility who weren't killed at Hastings were deposed of their lands and were probably forced to become serfs. Of all the land covered by Domesday Book, a census in England commissioned by William the Conqueror, it appears that only two English landowners retained their estates. The old English *thegnhood*, then, not only lost its land, but also its influence as Norman aristocracy took its place.

Subordinate to the great lords were the English masses, two and a half million strong and embittered by the loss of their country. William ordered strongholds and castles built to protect his interests, to quash English resistance, and to control the countryside. Five years later, William had a secure hold on the country. By 1100, there were 500 new Norman castles throughout England; the English were held firmly in check.

William was kept occupied by duties in Normandy, had to suffer through the intrigues of his eldest son, Robert, and had to deal with the aggression of the Counts of Anjou and Flanders and the king of France. In July 1087, William made a surprise attack on the French in a disputed territory between Rouen and Paris. Though victorious, he suffered a serious injury from which he died in September of the same year.

His burial was a sordid and grisly affair. He had gained a great deal of weight in his last years, and was quite obese at the time of his death. As his attendants were stuffing him into his too-small sarcophagus, his body burst, filling the church with a foul, repulsive stench. Fortunately for William, his life was much better than his death, and it is his success as a leader and his amazing accomplishments by which we remember him.

William and his wife, Matilda, had four sons and five or six daughters. In spite of the disloyalty and machinations of the eldest son, Robert, William willed Normandy to him and gave the third son, William Rufus, the English crown (second son Richard had died in a hunting accident). This soon proved an impractical arrangement, for many Norman lords held lands on both sides of the channel and weren't sure which man to support. Though the popular vote was in Robert's favor, he was swayed by the Pope's call to Crusade and sold Normandy to William Rufus in 1096 for 10,000 marks to finance his expedition to the Holy Land. William Rufus made a pact with his elder brother that if one should die without an heir, he would be succeeded by the other. This was done to disinherit their younger brother, Henry, whom both William and Robert thoroughly distrusted.

In 1100, William II Rufus was shot by an arrow while hunting and killed. Whether it was accidental or murder, no one now knows, but the ambitious Henry just happened to be hunting in the same forest at the same time. As Robert was away on Crusade, and as William had no heir, Henry took advantage of the situation and immediately had himself crowned king.

Robert returned victorious from Jerusalem, only to find his brother firmly entrenched in power. Though he initially sought to dethrone his brother, he eventually signed a treaty whereby he allowed Henry to keep England in exchange for an annual pension of £2,000.

Henry wasn't satisfied with leaving it at that. Angered that his brother and others had opposed him, he set about capturing Robert's strongholds in Wales. For several years, the brothers fought one another for the lands of England and Normandy. The battle of Tinchebrai in 1106 decided the situation: Henry was victorious and Robert spent the last twenty-eight years of his life as his brother's prisoner. Thereafter, Henry was ruthless in putting down insurrections by Norman and English alike, taking away lands and resorting to other, more brutal means of obtaining compliance.

Henry acknowledged more than twenty children, but had only two legitimate offspring: William and Matilda. William was drowned in a shipwreck in 1120, so Matilda became heir to the crown. In 1114, at the age of eleven, she was married to the Holy Roman Emperor. She was widowed in 1125, and three years later, her father married her to sixteen-year-old Geoffrey of Anjou to continue the alliance with that country. Norman lords did not like the thought of eventually being ruled by Henry's daughter and her Angevin husband, and in the summer of 1135, war broke out.

Henry died in December 1135. He had not been a flamboyant king and his policy of putting down insurrection had been brutal, but he had been an effective ruler who managed to keep England at peace for more than thirty years.

Matilda was out of the country when her father died, so Stephen, the son of William the Conqueror's daughter Adela, claimed the throne with the approval of the Norman lords. Matilda refused to renounce her rights, and in 1138, her husband invaded Normandy from Anjou; her uncle, King David of Scotland, invaded England from the north; and her half-brother, Robert of Gloucester, led the revolt in the west. The ensuing civil war lasted ten years, during which time Stephen was captured and later exchanged for Robert of Gloucester after the Londoners refused to accept Matilda as Queen. Matilda escaped from Oxford Castle and fled for the Continent. Her husband, meantime, had taken advantage of Stephen's initial capture and had taken control of Normandy.

In 1153, Matilda's son, Henry of Anjou, arrived in England. A powerful man, Henry was now duke of both Normandy and Anjou, and through his wife, Eleanor, he was also ruler of Aquitaine. In August 1153, Stephen's eldest son died, and the way was now opened for serious peace negotiations between Stephen and Henry. The Treaty of Westminster allowed Stephen to retain the crown for his lifetime on the condition that he adopt Henry as his son and heir; all Stephen's baronial lands were given to his youngest son, William. Steven wasn't given the opportunity to enjoy ruling in peace for long. He died a year later.

SOCIETY

A FEW YEARS after the Conquest, William was in need of funds to finance another campaign on the Continent. He looked to England as a source of revenue and commissioned what was to become known as Domesday Book, a census of the land, landholders, and other classes of people. It is the first known record of its kind. It quickly became apparent that English society was much as it had been for hundreds of years. Whole areas of the country were engaged in only one activity: raising food. And the food that was raised was usually just enough to meet individual needs with little left over to trade for even the simplest of tools.

William realized the English economy needed drastic reform if he were to profit from it. After offering inducements to skilled craftsmen to cross the channel and establish themselves in England, thousands of smiths, coopers, potters, tanners, weavers, and dyers spread over the land to establish shops in villages where before nothing had been except the occasional farm cottage. Soon, craftsmen were trading their products for food the farmers raised. Although food production continued to be the primary occupation, within a couple of generations of the Conquest, 40 percent of the population was engaged in some type of skill or occupation other than farming. This brought about a balance of economy that was the beginning of England's ability to prosper.

Not surprisingly, a language gap existed between the new ruling class and the native population, and little was done by either side to change that. The Normans held the English in utter contempt and displayed disdain for Anglo-Saxon culture. The defeated and humiliated English viewed their new masters as hated intruders and made no attempt to learn the tongue of their conquerors. Norman French was now the language of the law and authority, and Old English was relegated to the language of the peasant and the downtrodden.

For the most part, life in the villages continued to dictate the pace of life throughout most of England. There were no rigid divisions between villeins and nonvilleins, but status and social standing was nonetheless highly developed. Some historians have been able to identify at least twenty-one different status terms, and these divisions in personal status must have had significant impact on society.

As before the Conquest, a man still had no legal recourse against his lord unless the latter's actions were especially brutal, as in killing or maiming. The courts were unable to afford the villein protection from eviction nor award him damages for wrongs commited against him.

Intermarriage between the races became common, and third and fourth generations of Anglo-Normans were bilingual. English continued to be spoken by the masses, but it was now strongly influenced by both French and Latin. And, as it no longer had the strict constraints of a written language, Old English rapidly changed and evolved into Middle English.

As the years passed, the feudalism of England was completed. The trading base increased, and foreign communities arose in the larger towns and ports. Bristol, for example, flourished and became a port of call for Norwegian traders as well as a depot for wine and agricultural products flowing between England, Bordeaux, and Aquitane.

RELIGION

IN SPITE OF the losses to Anglo-Saxon literature and art, England's new ties to the Continent enabled the country to participate in the intellectual, religious, and artistic renaissance that thrived in eleventh- and twelfth-century France. At the time of the Conquest, William replaced most of the Saxon bishops with Norman ones and reorganized the English Church to bring it in line with the rest of Europe. Lanfranc, an Italian monk and a former teacher of the Pope, was appointed Archbishop of Canterbury in 1070.

Benedictine ''black monks'' from the reformed abbeys of Normandy arrived in his wake and established themselves in English towns. The black monks were landlords on a large scale, possessing manors that were set aside for ministering to the poor or as places of refuge and succor for travelers. In the twelfth century, the Benedictines controlled as many as twenty boroughs. English society became one where the rites of the Church encompased all major events in the life of the individual. Birth, baptism, marriage, and death had their own rituals governed by the Church.

NAMING

ALL THESE EVENTS conspired to change the type of names used in England. The Conquest brought a large number of foreign names into the country, and as the old Celtic names had given way to those of the Saxon and Norse invaders, so now did Anglo-Saxon names give way to those of the new arrivals. It is safe to say that after two or three generations, most of the old compound names had largely disappeared. Those that survived did so for one of two reasons: They were the names of saints (Edmund and Mildred for example) or they were the names of the former kings of the house of Wessex (Edgar, Alfred). There is also reason to believe that the simpler, uncompounded Old English names continued to be in popular use among the peasantry, though they too became uncommon past the thirteenth century.

Old names that did survive underwent a Gallicizing process. Several English letters and sounds caused problems for the French-speaking populace, and were dealt with in a few ways. The Æ ligature was changed to an A or an E. The *eth*, Ð, ð and the thorn Þ or þ, which basically had a *th* sound, were either omitted or turned into a *t*, or a *d* when the letter came in the middle of a name or at the end of it. Æðelwine became Aldwyne and Aylwin; Þorbeorht became Torbett and Turbert; Æðelheard became Adelard; and Æðelfrīð became Alfred. The ending *-eald* was usually changed to *-auld*, *-aud*, or *-all*. Ōsweald became Oswald, for example, and Beald became Bald, Bauld, and Baud. The letter *w* was changed into a *v* before *a, e,* and *i,* and dropped before *o* and *u*. The letter *g* was often changed to *y*, and a final *h* was replaced by *k* or *ch*. The name Ælfheah, for example, evolved into both Alfech and Elphick.

The nomenclature changed much more rapidly in London than it did in the country. However, in the first several years after the Conquest, those with Norman names were most likely Norman by birth, as those with Old English names were English natives. Very few examples exist of Norman parents bestowing English names upon their children, but it appears that as early as 1100, English parents were beginning to give their children Norman names. Not long after that time, it became something of a fashion to give English children Norman names and most of the Old English names rapidly fell into disuse. Ailwin, Alfred, Edmund, Edward, Godric, and Godwin were among the old names that continued to be used, but Edith was the only English female name to retain any type of popularity.

The Normans were fond of using diminutive forms of their names, and this propensity extended to the English population as well. The suffixes *-el,-et,-in,-on,* and *-ot* were used both singly and in combination. Bartelot, Philipot, Pennel, and Mariot are examples of names with diminutive suffixes.

Though the Church held sway over the life of the individual for several hundred years before the Conquest, Christian names had only just begun to be used in England during this time period. For example, the names Andrew, John, Matthew, and Peter occur only once in the 1086 Domesday Book, and are rare after that time until the end of the following century when other biblical names were first recorded.

William was by far the most popular male name and accounted for at least 15 percent of recorded names. Robert and Ralph follow with 11 percent and 10 percent respectively. Among the women, biblical names were not used until the very end of the twelfth or the beginning of the thirteenth century. And though the use of nonbiblical names of saints was encouraged by the Church, these names aren't recorded until the same time as the biblical ones.

The large Breton contingent who fought with William at Hastings were rewarded with English lands. Earl Alan of Richmond, the most important, was given lands in many areas. He went on to establish several Breton settlements, and the settlers in these villages were as determined to keep their own system of nomenclature as the Saxons had when they first arrived. Alan, Conan, Constantine, Justin, and Tengi are examples of Breton names used in England during the twelfth and thirteenth centuries.

In addition to the large numbers of Normans, Bretons, and Frenchmen who arrived after the Conquest, immigrants from the Netherlands began arriving as well. The natives of Flanders brought names such as Alard, Baudouin, Eude, Gerbaud, Hugue, Josce, Renouf, and Walter.

It should be noted that many of the names below were found throughout France and other European countries. Though many are ultimately of Greek, Latin, or German origin, they are listed to show to which cultural group they belonged.

FEMALE NAMES

Adelaide (nobility) **Adelheid** Norman.
Adele (nobility) Norman.
Agnes (chaste) Norman.
Alice (nobility) **Alicia** Norman.
Anabilla (?, perhaps *eagle hearth*; *lovable*; *joy*)
Annis (chaste) Norman.
Arlette (eagle) Norman.
Aveline (?) Norman.
Avis (?) Norman.
Beatrice (she who brings happiness) Norman.
Blanche (white) Norman.
Cecilia (blind, dim-sighted) Norman.
Cristina (a Christian) Norman.
Elena (light, a torch) Norman.

Laurencia (woman from Laurentum) Norman.
Mabila (lovable) Norman.
Margery (a pearl) Norman.
Marie (sea of bitterness or sorrow) Norman.
Marion (little Marie *sea of bitterness or sorrow*) **Marian** Norman.
Matilda (powerful in battle) Norman.
Maud (a pearl) Norman.
Philippa (lover of horses) Norman.
Svanhildr (battle swan) Scandinavian.
Swanilda (battle swan) Norman.
Wolveva (wolf gift)
Ysabelle (God is my oath) Norman.

MALE NAMES

Adam (man of the red earth) Norman.
Ældred (noble counsel)
Ælfheah (elf high) **AElfec, Ælfech, Elphick**
Ælfgar (elf spear) **Ælgar, Aelgar**
Ælsi (?, possibly *elf*)
Ailof (immortal) Scandinavian.
Alain (?) **Alein, Aleyns** Norman.
Alan (?) Breton.
Albert (noble and bright) Norman, Flemish.
Alelm (noble protection) Norman.
Alexander (defender of mankind) Norman.
Arthur (?)
Augustine (great, venerable) Norman.
Austin (great, venerable) Norman.
Balduin (bold friend) Flemish.
Baldwin (bold friend) **Baudwin** French.
Bealdwine (bold friend)
Beorhtsige (bright victory) **Brixi**
Bot (butt)
Brungar (brown spear)
Burgheard (fortress hard) **Burchard**
Camp (soldier)
Colbeorht (cool and bright)
David (beloved) Norman.

Doda (something rounded; a round, lumpish person) **Dodda, Dodde, Dudda, Dudde**
Donninc (the dark, swarthy one) **Donning, Dunning**
Drogo (burden bearer) Flemish, Norman.
Durand (obstinant) **Doraunt, Durant, Duraund** Norman.
Eli (high, ascent) Norman.
Erenbald (genuinely bold) Flemish.
Eudo (child) Norman.
Euing (?, possibly *well-born, noble*)
Ewen (lamb; youth; well-born)
Fulcher (people army) **Fulker**
Geoffrey (peaceful district; pledge of peace; traveler of peace) Norman.
Gerard (brave with a spear) Norman.
Gerbodo (brave with a spear) Flemish.
Godebert (God bright) **Godberd, Godbert**
Godefrid (God's peace) **Godfrid, Godfray, Godfrey**
Godeman (good man) **Godman, Goddman, Goodman, Gudman**
Godric (God ruler)
Godwine (friend of God) **Godwin**
Goisbert (God bright)
Grifin (monstrous, like a griffin)
Halden (half Dane) **Haldane, Haldein** Scandinavian.

Haerviu (battle worthy) **Aeruiu, Herevi Herui, Herveus, Hervi, Hervici** Breton.

Hamon (home) **Haim, Hamun, Heimes** Norman.

Hearding (hard, severe) **Arding, Harding**

Henric (home ruler) **Haimric, Henrie, Henry** Norman.

Herebert (army bright) **Hereberd, Herberd, Herbert, Herbelott**

Herman (soldier, army man) **Hereman, Heremond**

Hugo (heart, mind) Norman.

Ilbert (battle famous, bright) **Hilbert, Hildeberd, Hildebert** Norman.

Isac (laughter) Norman.

Iving (archer) Norman.

Ivo (archer) Norman.

Joseph (he shall add) Norman.

Juing (?)

Lambe (a lamb)

Lambert (land bright) Norman.

Lanbert (land bright) Flemish.

Landbeorht (land bright)

Laurentius (man from Laurentum) **Laurencius, Lorence, Laurens, Laurenz** Norman.

Leodagar (people spear) Norman.

Leofdaeg (love day)

Madoch (beneficent)

Manasse (forgetting) Norman.

Manbodo (man + ?) Flemish.

Martel (of Mars, warlike) Norman.

Martin (of Mars; warlike) Norman.

Maurice (dark, swarthy) Norman.

Merefin (sea hill, eminent marrow)

Morgan (bright seas)

Morganau (bright seas) Breton.

Owen (lamb; youth; well-born) **Ouen, Ouuin, Owein, Uwen**

Pagan (villager, rustic, heathen) Norman.

Philip (lover of horses) **Felipe, Phelip** Norman.

Piers (a rock, a stone) **Peris, Pieres** Norman.

Radulf (counsel + wolf) **Radolf, Raulf** Norman.

Raedwulf (counsel wolf)

Raefen (raven)

Rainbertus (bright guardian) **Rainbert, Reinberd, Reinbert, Renberd** Flemish.

Rauf (counsel wolf) **Rolf** Norman.

Raulf (counsel wolf)

Rees (ardor)

Reginald (ruler of decision) Norman.

Richard (stern king) Norman.

Riset (stern king)

Roger (famous with the spear) Norman.

Salomon (peaceful) Norman.

Seward (sea guardian) **Sauuard, Seuuard, Sewarde, Siuuart**

Sparhauoc (sparrow hawk) **Sperhauoc**

Suetman (sweet man) **Swētmann**

Swein (boy, servant) **Suein, Swain, Swayn** Scandinavian.

Tedbald (people bold) Flemish.

Teobald (people bold) **Tetbald, Tybaud** Norman.

Theoda (people)

Thurbert (Thor bright) **Torbert, Turbert** Anglo-Scandinavian.

Tuder (territorial ruler)

Tunne (town, village)

Wada (to go) **Wade**

Walter (ruler of the army) Norman.

Wazelin (from the tribe of the Gauts) Flemish.

Wazo (from the tribe of the Gauts) Flemish.

Wihomarc (?)

Wlsi (wolf victory)

Wulfsige (wolf victory) Scandinavian.

SURNAMES

During the Middle Ages, surnames were primarily used as additional identifiers, were very unstable, and were not hereditary. A study of the names of tenants-in-chief during the reign of Henry I (1100–1135) shows that only 33 percent were recorded as single names; 67 percent were recorded with additional descriptions or forms of address. Among the English undertenants, the opposite held true: 38 percent of the names had descriptions attached and 62 percent were recorded as single names. During the reign of Stephen (1135–1154), the number of people with additional names increased to more than 75 percent.

Rather than a mark of genealogy, the secondary name merely served to identify between people having the same first name. It wasn't long before the upper classes began to use secondary names as marks of distinction and a way to boast of their power and their possession of lands. According to British historian, William Camden (1551–1623), it was quite a disgrace to have but a single name. No person of consequence would have only one, yet that didn't mean that they handed a secondary name down to their children or that other family members would use the same term. Surnames, in general, had yet to become hereditary, though there is evidence that hereditary surnames existed among the Norman aristocracy in the early twelfth century.

The four types of additional names in use by the Normans echoed those of the Anglo-Saxon: characteristic, genealogical, occupational, and locational. Characteristic ''surnames'' were by far the smallest group, accounting for only 1 percent to 3 percent of the total, but these are probably the most interesting. Such names were given both as a reflection of the characteristic, such as Rufus for someone with red hair, or in direct opposition to the name's meaning. A particularly large man, for example, might be called Small, and a bald man might be called Curly or Hairy.

Genealogical ''surnames'' consisted of two types: one expressing relationship in Latin or in French, and one in which just the personal name of the father was added. Willelmus filius Turstingi, Serlus filius Alveredi, and Gauslinus frater are examples of the first type; Galterius Tyrrellus is an example of the second.

Due to the large influx of skilled craftsmen, occupational descriptions was naturally one of the largest categories. Faber (a smith), Potarius (a potter), and Parmenter (a tailor) are examples of occupational names. Locational names and territorial designations were also quite common, and with England being a feudal state, it was natural for a tenant-in-chief or even his tenants to be known by the name of the fief in which they lived. The preposition de (of) replaced the Anglo-Saxon æt. Not until the fourteenth century did the English preposition of come into use.

One particular custom lasting until the fourteenth century was the bestowal of the father's name as a secondary appellative to the firstborn legitimate son. Younger sons then took the names of the lands allotted to them.

People of Norman descent were more apt to use a genealogical name than were the English. And it should be noted that single names remained in effect much longer in the north and in the south. Also, for many, additional identifiers were used only for official documents and were not used on a daily basis.

Aedesdohter (daughter of Aed *fire*)
Aelfricessun (son of Aelfric *elf friend*)
Alwins (son of Alwin *elf friend*)
de Anjou (from Anjou) Norman.
le Archer (the archer) Norman.
de Artois (from Artois) Norman.
Batoc (the stout man)
Beald (the bald; the bold)
Blaca (the black)
Boda (the messenger)
Bouvier (cattle drover) Norman.
Brodeheved (big head)
de Brothortun (from Brothortun)
Brune (the brown) **Brun**
le Beau (the fair) Norman.
la Belle (the beautiful) Norman.
Bertran (bright raven) Norman.
le Blanc (the white) Norman.
de Brieuse (from Brus *brushwood thicket*) **de Brus** Norman.
Cada (the short, fat person)
de Champagne (from Champagne *field*) Norman.
de Chanteloup (from Chanteloup *singing wolves*) Norman.
de Chartres (from Chartres) Norman.
Cild (the child)
Cniht (the servant)
Cola (the dark one)
de Colleville (from Colleville *Col's estate*) Norman.
le Corbet (the raven) Norman.

de Coucy (from Coucy) Norman.
de Courtenay (from Courtenay *Courtenay's homestead*) Norman.
Cyppe (the fat one)
de Dentune (of Dentune)
Dubois (dweller in the woods) Norman.
Dudding (son of Dudda)
Durand (enduring, lasting) Norman.
Eadricssun (son of Eadric *wealthy ruler*)
Eadwinesbroder (brother of Eadwine *wealthy friend*)
Ealda (the old one)
Fauchet (crooked legs) Norman.
Geonga (the young)
Giffard (chubby-cheeked) Norman.
Gilbert (bright pledge) Norman.
de Glanville (from Glanville *oak tree estate*) Norman.
le Grand (the tall, the large) Norman.
le Gros (the fat) Norman.
de Harcourt (from Harcourt *army house*) Norman.
Heaha (the tall)
Hoga (the wise)
Hwita (the white)
le Jeune (the young) Norman.
de Laci (from Laci *Latius's estate*) Norman.
de Lamburnan (from Lamburnan)
de Lorris (from Lorris) Norman.
Lovett (little wolf) Norman.
de Lundene (from Lundene)

de Maci (from Maci *Matheus's estate*) Norman.
de Malleville (from Malleville) Norman.
Mann (the servant)
de Marle (blackbird) Norman.
de Meran (from Meran) Norman.
de Montfort (from Montfort *fortified hill*) Norman.
de Perci (from Perci *destroyer of cities*) Norman.
de Poitiers (from Poitiers) Norman.
de Provence (from Provence) Norman.
Reada (the red)
de Rochefort (from Rochefort *fortified rock*) Norman.
Rolfessun (son of Rolf *counsel wolf*)
le Simple (the simple-minded) Norman.

Swan (the swineherd)
Swift (the swift)
Talbot (pillager, bandit; lampblack) Norman.
Tillet (dweller near the lime trees) Norman.
de Tilly (from the lime tree grove) Norman.
Tirel (Thor rule) Norman.
de Venables (from Venables *vineyard*) Norman.
de Warenne (from Warenne) Norman.
le Warner (the warrener, a game warren) Norman.
de Warre (of the war, a warrior) Norman.
Wasket (the little Gascon) Norman.
le Werre (the warrior)
Yungwin (young friend)

Chapter Three

THE MIDDLE AGES
HENRY II TO RICHARD II
[1154–1399]

POLITICS

THE PLANTAGENET DYNASTY began with the ascension of Henry II (1154–1189) and saw England enduring a long period of struggle and unrest. Perpetual turmoil lasting more than 150 years shook the feudal system to its foundations, resulting in a change in political institutions, laws, and the habits and customs of English society.

After the death of Henry I in 1135, a bitter clash broke out between rival claimants to the throne. For the populace, it was a time of great hardship as ''devils and evil men'' took control and ''unspeakable tortures'' became common ways to obtain exactions. According to early chroniclers, it was a time when ''all was dissention, and evil, and rapine.'' The country was in such a state of anarchy that contemporary opinion was that ''Christ and his saints were asleep.'' By the time Henry II took the throne, the treasury was seriously depleted, and the barons were firmly entrenched in power.

His first order of business was to reduce the barons' power, reestablish royal control, and increase royal revenue. Through skilled leadership, Henry managed to bring about much-needed social and political reforms to the betterment of the people, though duties in his other possessions of Normandy, Maine, Anjou, Touraine, and Aquitaine kept him out of the country for all but a third of his thirty-five-year reign. He died in July 1189, leaving his possessions to Richard, his second surviving son.

Richard I (1189–1199) spent only the first six months of his ten-year reign in England. Since most of his time was spent defending other possessions and waging the Third Crusade, his absence and the heavy taxation imposed to cover his military expenses angered his English subjects.

Conditions did not improve much with Richard's brother John (1199–1216), a cruel and tyrannical king who ruled with an iron hand. After John's loss of Normandy in 1204, Philip II of France refused to accept as his tenants those who held lands on both sides of the channel. With Norman links to France severed, the nobility was further insulated and forced into accepting an English identity. For the first time since the Conquest, the ruling class was thought of as English.

John's overriding goal became the recovery of lost possessions and the opportunity to face the French king directly. Knowing he would need great resources to accomplish this, John levied heavy taxes against his subjects. Scutage, which had been levied a total of eleven times during the reigns of Henry II and Richard I, was levied eleven more times from 1199 to 1215, years that experienced an uncertain economy, prices increasing at a rate never before seen, and families facing serious financial difficulties. After a serious fallout with Pope Innocent III, John seized Church property and the Pope responded with the Interdict of 1208. For the next six years, no church services were allowed to be performed in England: no public worship, no baptisms, no death services, no sacraments. John's excommunication followed in 1209. This didn't seem to bother him in the least. His reaction was to use the Church's wealth to aid his own financial problems.

After John lost the Battle of Bouvines to Philip II of France, discontent at home turned into rebellion. In June 1215, John met with his rebel lords and agreed to terms laid out in a document that would later become known as the Magna Carta. John neither believed in the document nor had any intention of abiding by it, and the barons, having lost all patience with John, elected Louis, the son of King Philip II of France, as their antiking.

After John's death, nine-year-old Henry III ascended the throne of a country torn by chaos and civil war. His advisors went to work, and within three years, the Magna Carta had been restored, Louis of France defeated, and some semblance of order was brought to the land.

Once the young king reached his majority, he found himself at odds with his advisers and insisted on taking over the reins of government. Twenty-six years of misrule followed, during which time foreigners, fellow countrymen of the king's Poitevin mentor, and relatives of the queen flooded the country to take advantage of positions and privileges that normally would have gone to Englishmen. Civil war raged again as Henry tried to maintain his control and the barons tried to make him come under the law. Henry spent the last seven years of his reign attending to his loves of architecture and art, leaving his son, Edward, to run the country.

Edward I is considered by many to be the finest of the Plantagenets. He was a noble character who worked hard to rectify the wrongs commited during his father's reign. He stopped the transference of land to the Church, gave policing duties to the commoners, protected merchants from creditors, and preserved the great estates by making the eldest sons the inheritors of all. He succeeded in bringing Wales under the subjugation of the crown in 1284 and managed to subject the king of Scotland in 1296. Upon his death, he left his weak and foolish son, Edward II, to deal with an unresolved situation with Scotland and a country deeply in debt and with constitutional troubles.

Edward II made it clear he preferred the company of young men to that of his wife or to the important business of running the country. He made a habit of antagonizing the barons, avoiding his counselors, and bestowing gifts and titles upon favorite companions. After Edward made his beloved Piers Gaveston earl of Cornwall, a position and title reserved for the sons of kings, the barons had enough. They forced the king to exile Gaveston and accept reforms that would undermine royal prerogative. Edward did not honor the agreement. Within two months, Gaveston had brazenly returned to court and was murdered shortly thereafter.

A serious opposition movement began, and when Edward summoned his barons to military service against Scotland, several refused to go. It was probably a wise choice, for the English were soundly beaten at Bannockburn by Robert Bruce and an army that was a third the size of the king's. After that disaster, Edward gave up any pretense of running the country. England lost its overlordship of Scotland, the Scots ravaged northern England, and warfare broke out in several other parts of the kingdom.

Edward soon found new favorites in the Despensers, father and son. The younger Hugh le Despenser quickly took Gaveston's former place in companionship to the king, and together they succeeded in breaking the opposition movement and took control of the land.

Queen Isabella, humiliated and angry for having her position usurped by Hugh le Despenser, returned to France. The French court soon became a haven for exiles determined to see the end of the hated regime. A year later, to the delight of the English people, Isabella, her son, her lover Roger Mortimer, and a body of mercenaries, entered England. The Despensers were captured and executed, and the king was made to renounce the crown in favor of his son, fourteen-year-old Edward III. Keeping the deposed king alive, however, was perceived by Isabella as both an embarrassment and a threat to the new monarch. Edward II was sent to the dungeons of Berkeley Castle, where his jailers shamefully thrust a red-hot poker into his bowels, thereby satisfying their orders to kill him without leaving a mark upon his body.

Fortunately, Edward III was nothing like his father. In 1330, three years after he was crowned, he assumed personal rule and made a concerted effort to restore the dignity of the monarchy. Mortimer was convicted of an array of crimes, most of which he was quite guilty, and executed; the queen mother was forgiven and allowed to live a quiet life at Castle Rising in Norfolk. Edward restored the barons' faith in the crown and became a respected ruler.

He avenged the military losses of his father by achieving victory over the Scots. In 1337, he promoted his rightful claim to the French crown after Philip VI confiscated England's French holdings over a legal dispute. Two years later, Edward took the offensive and invaded France from the Low Countries, beginning what was to become the Hundred Years' War. By 1360, all of Edward's claims were satisfied. In return for renouncing his claim to the French throne, he won sovereignty over Calais, Aquitaine, and nearly a quarter of France.

The Hundred Years' War began again in 1369 when Gascon lords rebelled against high taxes the English imposed to cover military expenses in Spain. Edward renewed his claim to the French crown but soon lost all French conquests except Calais and a strip of the Gascon coast. Edward III died in 1377, leaving his ten-year-old grandson, Richard II, in possession of the crown.

Because of Richard's young age, a regency council was appointed and supervised by John of Gaunt. From the beginning, they were beset with problems stemming from French raids, revenue shortfalls, and social unrest. The Peasants' Revolt of 1381 was in response to yet another tax levied to offset the problem of chronic revenue shortages. This tax, instituted in 1377 and tripled in 1380, was levied on the head of each individual. It fell especially hard on the peasantry, for even the humblest person was required to pay the same amount as the richest.

In 1385, at the age of seventeen, Richard made his first attempt at personal rule; he did little to win respect and confidence. He allowed himself to be influenced by favorites and factions and failed miserably at military ventures. His first major military expedition to Scotland was such a poorly handled affair that he returned home after two weeks, tired of the whole business and never encountering the Scottish army. Two years later, the English were soundly beaten by the Scots at the Battle of Otterburn. The only thing that kept Richard in control was the presence of the respected John of Gaunt.

When John of Gaunt left to place a claim on the throne of Castile in 1386, the king's critics wasted no time impeaching Chancellor Michael de la Pole and putting government in the hands of a thirteen-member commission dominated by five opposition leaders. In 1388, the Merciless Parliament launched an attack on the king's household and many members of the court party were killed, including the king's old tutor. Richard chose to bide his time in getting his revenge.

He began to rule as a monarch of age, and the next six years passed peaceably. He created a magnificent court in which the knightly image of chivalry was exemplified. Secretly, Richard was preparing for battle by building his base of power and recruiting a private army in Wales, Cheshire, and Ireland.

In 1397, he struck without warning, arresting three old opposition lords: Gloucester, Arundel, and Warwick. Arundel was executed, Warwick was banished to the Isle of Man, and Gloucester was sent to Calais, where he was strangled. Two others, Henry of Bolingbroke (son of John of Gaunt) and Thomas Mowbray, were banished: Henry for ten years and Thomas for life. With his old enemies gone and a huge army backing him, Richard was now free to act as he chose. Those who offended him were forced to pay for pardons or risk being branded as traitors. He became somewhat of a megalomaniac, spending lavishly and setting himself above others.

After John of Gaunt's death in February 1399, Richard could have pardoned Henry of Bolingbroke to garner more support for the crown. Instead, he seized Bolingbroke's inheritance and extended his banishment to life. It was a poor choice, for the majority of the lords no longer trusted him and only awaited a leader for their resistance. Henry of Bolingbroke stepped into the role. As he progressed across the country to reclaim his inheritance, he was joined by numerous lords who were eager to support him.

Richard, meanwhile, confident of his power, had traveled to Ireland to put down a rebellion there. He took with him his most loyal supporters and left his incompetent uncle, Edmund, in charge of the realm. After hearing of developments at home, Richard left Ireland for North Wales, hoping to garner support there. Finding none, he was forced to surrender to Bolingbroke, was imprisoned in the Tower, and later removed to Pontefract Castle. Thus, with the support of the nobility and the approval of parliament, Henry of Bolingbroke won the crown, becoming the first of the Lancastrian kings. A year later, Richard was secretly put to death at Pontefract after a group of his friends made an attempt on the new king's life.

SOCIETY

POLITICS WAS NOT the only area during the later Middle Ages that was unstable and chaotic. Society as a whole was deeply disturbed. This was a calamitous time during which the people suffered under heavy taxation, social inequality, intermittent warfare, and starvation and disease.

Feudalism attained its height at the beginning of this time period, and at the end, began its fall. Feudal society was, above all, a system of overlordship and vassalage in which all authority was granted as a right to those who held the fiefs. It was a society of status, and seldom were those not born to nobility allowed to advance themselves. The exceptions were those granted special dispensations for exceptional service to the king.

The feudal aristocracy came to embrace new concepts and ideals and the knightly image, as illustrated by the cults of Saint George and King Arthur. Knights began to act with chivalry, courtesy, and even kindness, though that behavior was reserved for those of the same class or of higher social standing. Women were idealized as never before, and courtly love was pursued in earnest. This refinement of manners quickly began to displace the older notion that loyalty, honor, and virtues on the battlefield were the most important means to glory and respect. Edward III, a big fan of the Arthurian romances, did much to promote the knightly image. One way in which he did so was in the establishment of the Knights of the Garter, a very select brotherhood of twenty-six men who supported one another in war and peace.

The songs of the troubadours were the first literary works to reflect this change in ideals and attitude. The troubadours originated in southern France in one of the most highly civilized areas of feudal Europe. From there, they wandered across Europe and England, singing their songs, telling their stories, and spreading news from one area to the next. The central theme of a great number of their songs was romantic love and the idealization of women. This was quite a new and important development, for until this time, the female gender was roundly condemned by monks and Church leaders as the incarnation of evil and the reason for the downfall of man. The troubadours extolled the fairer sex and sang their praises high. Their songs also encouraged gentleness and protection of the weak, placed great value on truthfulness, and reinforced the values of honor and loyalty.

Few books were written for pleasure during this time period, but many of those that were used the same themes as the troubadours. The popular twelfth-century French writer Chrétien de Troyes regularly used Arthurian-inspired chivalry in his writings. Another medieval writer to illustrate the chivalric ideal was Marie de France. Both authors encouraged gentlemanly behavior toward females, glorified adventure, held that experience was the true road to wisdom, and promoted the traditional knightly values of honesty, loyalty, and honor.

While the romances of the Arthurian cycle were very popular with the upper classes, literature soon emerged that was geared for the entertainment of urban elite who had risen to positions of power and influence equal, if not superior, to the feudal nobles. Known as the *fabliaux*, these short stories were usually satires of the feudal nobility and their obsession with chivalry, romantic love, and the determined pursuit of adventure. They were written with an aim to amuse, they poked fun at the nobility, made clergy the butt of their jokes, and were spiced with indecency and humor. Their style and content illustrate the growing worldliness of the urban classes as well as their growing disillusionment with Church leaders.

In spite of the political and social unrest of the fourteenth century, and in spite of the prevalence of disease and its attending degree of misery, this was also a time when English culture began to flower again. Around the year 1348, Edward III had an English motto embroidered on his tunic. In 1353, legal proceedings were allowed to be conducted in English rather than French; in 1362, it was enacted that all such proceedings be conducted in English; and in 1363, the chancellor opened parliament in English. The change from French to English statutes occurred in 1377, and soon afterward, parliamentary petitions began to be written in English.

In the 1360s, a London clerk named William Langland wrote *Piers Plowman*, the first major literary work to be written in English. Richard II was an enthusiastic patron of the arts, and his diligence in promoting English culture ensured the reemergence of English as a language of learning and literature. It was during Richard's reign that Geoffrey Chaucer produced most of his work, including the *Canterbury Tales*. John Trevisa translated the encyclopedia *De Proprietatibus Rerum* and the massive historical work *Polychronicon*, marking the entry of English into the world of education. For the first time in 300 years, it was no longer necessary to know a foreign tongue to participate in learned and literary culture.

Over 97 percent of the population, those who were neither aristocrats nor clergy, were lumped together in a category called the *commons*. The commons were subdivided into two groups: those of the country and those of the town. Those of the country accounted for 95 percent of the population and fell into four categories: villeins, serfs, cottars, and slaves. The villein was a person who voluntarily surrendered his land to a wealthy landholder, and after working out a contract, became a perpetual tenant. The serfs, on the other hand, were bought and sold with the land to which they were attached and could be exploited by the landholder in any way. By the thirteenth century, many of the differences disappeared and the serfs rose in status to that of the villeins. The cottars, also known as crofters, were extremely poor and lived in the most desperate of circumstances. Having no strips of land to plant or make a living from, they usually hired themselves out to the more fortunate villeins or tried to do odd jobs for the lord of the manor. Though slavery was quite rare, those who were slaves usually ended up as household servants and quite possibly were in better circumstances than the cottars.

The medieval town was not bound by feudal structure. What few feudal responsibilities it did have were owed to its overlord who, in most cases, was the king. Therefore, townsmen enjoyed a measure of freedom not available to country dwellers. Towns and cities did have a hierarchy of their own, however. The upper class was known as *citizens* or *burgesses*. These citizens had full rights and a say in the town's governance. The rest of the town's dwellers were apprentices, servants, laborers, and aliens from outside the country of England. Though these people had none of the special rights or privileges of the citizens, advancement was possible. Citizenship could be either purchased or acquired by rising through the hierarcy of a trade to the level of master.

In both city and country life, society was very much a male-dominated one. In principle, every female was supposed to be under the authority of a man: A girl was subject to her father; a woman was subject to her husband. A female did not normally inherit land unless her father died without sons. Additionally, women never held official positions, never officially participated in governmental activities, had only limited standing under the law, and were rarely allowed to become citizens of a town. Among the upper classes and the nobility, women married in their early teens. Among the commoners, women usually waited until their early twenties to be married.

Some women were able to achieve a measure of independence in widowhood, which was quite common in this age of disease and warfare. Under the law, a widow was entitled to a share of her husband's estate for support for the duration of her lifetime. If her husband had practiced a trade and owned a business, it was possible for her to take the business over. In a few instances, women were even admitted into the guild that covered their deceased husbands' trade.

Another way a woman could achieve independence was to travel to a town and seek employment. The number of professions ending in *-ster*, which designated a female worker, illustrates the variety of jobs available to women. Among them are brewster (brewer of ale) and baxster (a baker). In the wool industry there were cardster (a carder of wool); kempster (a comber of wool); spinster (a spinner of thread); fullester (a fuller); dreyster (a dryer of wool after it was washed); blackster (a dyer); webster (a weaver of thread); seamster (a seamstress); and wollester (a wool merchant). A ropster made rope; a tapster made tapestries. In spite of the availability of work in the towns, women rarely ventured out on their own to seek their fortunes. This was a time of hardship, and most women had to rely on some type of male protection.

As the economy became more market-oriented, feudalism became less viable and quickly began to wane. No longer was subsistence farming the rule. People now produced crops for sale, undertook the raising of sheep for wool, and many country workers went to the cities to establish themselves in trades. Once the tenants or cottars had left, it was very difficult to find them and force their return. As more people left the fiefs, the feudal power of the barons was undermined, and it became necessary to pay people to work the manorial lands. The manorial system was so weakened that it became nearly impossible to operate.

Another factor to hasten the end of feudalism was nature itself. The early part of the fourteenth century experienced a significant change in climate. There was such a drop in temperature that some refer to the time as a "little ice age." Not only was there serious devastation of crops, freezing temperatures triggered severe floods in 1315 to 1317, and people feared they were witnessing a repeat of the biblical Flood. To make matters worse, starting in the year 1313, several episodes of sheep and cattle plagues succeeded in killing off much of the livestock. This was by far the worst agrarian crisis the island had seen since the coming of the Normans.

With the crops damaged and so many animals dead, malnutrition and starvation were common both in the country and in the towns. Wheat rose ten times its normal price and men risked execution by hunting in the forests to provide for their stricken families. In such grim circumstances, few had anything extra for the needy. Many of the charities vanished. One historical chronicle reports of people forced to eat dogs, cats, the dung of doves, and those in the most desperate of circumstances, even the bodies of those who had died.

Perhaps the greatest social calamity of all happened during the reign of Edward III: the black death. Known then as the "great mortality" or "the pestilence," the plague, carried by fleas on black rats, crossed from the continent and entered England via Southampton and Bristol. From there it worked its way across the country, killing 90 percent of its victims. Whole villages were decimated. After the great mortality of 1348–1349, more plagues followed in 1361 and 1368–1369. The plague of 1361 was known as the "pestilence of the children," as youngsters were the ones particularly vulnerable. The population, which has been estimated as being between 4.5 and 5 million, fell to around 2 million by the end of the century.

For the masses, it was a life of great hardship. Inadequate nutrition, unsanitary conditions, and a lifetime of hard work took its toll. Severe overcrowding, sickness and disease, and inadequate sanitation made living conditions in the larger towns and cities appallingly bad. Rats were common; fleas and lice infested everything and everyone.

These conditions made childhood a time of great danger and resulted in an extremely high rate of child mortality. Nearly 300 out of 1,000 children died in their first year. After ten years, half would still be living, and at the age of twenty, only 300 would have survived. Life expectancy at birth was seventeen years. Once a person survived childhood, however, the mortality rate among the general population rose to forty-two years, and it was not uncommon for people to live into their sixties. The knights, whose lives were marked by hazard, had a life span of a mere thirty to thirty-five years. The leading cause of death among women was childbirth.

As industry continued to expand, trade increased between England, the Continent, and the Near East, and there was an accompanying stimulation in the economy. New jobs were plentiful, and agricultural and material products were in high demand. Yet, with the population cut so drastically, there was a corresponding cut in the number of available workers. The increased demand for workers, tenants, and produce resulted in higher wages, making it possible for the underclasses to rise in rank and circumstance.

RELIGION

THE CHURCH CONTINUED to play a significant role in society. Like government, the Church had its own hierarchy. At its head were the powerful bishops and other leaders who combined spiritual authority with administrative and political power. Next were the clergy, the underpaid and overworked priests and deacons who had to answer to their superiors. The priests were in what was known as the major orders: the regular clergy, composed of monks and those who were subject to religious orders, and the secular clergy, which consisted of priests who lived in the world outside a religious order. Those of the secular clergy were recruited from all walks of life, and many had little more than a rudimentary knowledge of the doctrines of the Church. They recited the Latin service by rote and typically understood little of it, for Latin was generally unknown among the uneducated lower classes.

Many priests were quite poor, despite the land granted them by the manor and the tithes that were often grudgingly given by even poorer parishioners. Out of their meager earnings, the priests were required to pay for the upkeep of their chapels and give alms to the needy.

Though many good priests devoted their lives to helping the needy and to preaching the Gospel, early reports indicate that others didn't always follow the directives of the Church. Many lived openly with wives and children, neglected the upkeep of church buildings, embezzled funds, stayed away from their parishes for long lengths of time, had sexual relationships with their maidservants and their parishioners, were prone to drunkeness, and sold the sacraments. In the smaller villages, services were held irregularly and sermons were rare.

Friars spent much of their time preaching among the poor, often telling Bible stories on the village greens and teaching about virtue and morality. Mystery plays, which illustrated the fall and redemption of mankind, were performed in town squares and at fairs across the country.

In the towns, each craft and merchant guild had its own patron saint and chapel, and guild members regularly met to worship and celebrate the religious holidays. Eventually, the guilds took over presentation of the mystery plays. Miracle plays, which dealt with the lives and deaths of saints, were quite popular as well.

Nonetheless, people knew nothing more than the basics of their religion and then, only what was told to them. The Bible was written in Latin, chained in the church, and never found among the general population. Few people knew the prayers or scriptures in English, nor understood much of what the priest said.

With Church leaders corrupted by wealth and material possessions, and with so many of the secular clergy corrupt and incompetent, relations between the Church and the people became strained, and anticlericalism abounded. When the troubadours weren't singing about chivalry, they were delivering acid satires against the hypocrisy and rapacity of the Church, using their songs as a way of expressing public disillusionment and the general contempt men felt toward their spiritual leaders. In the fourteenth century, this disillusionment culminated in organized religious protest.

Lollardy, the first protest for reform, took place during the reign of Edward III. The first Lollard, John Wycliffe, was troubled by the lack of true Christianity among the clergy. He demanded a return to a simpler, less materialistic lifestyle, demanded the Church get rid of its wealth, questioned transubstantiation (the changing of the bread and wine at Communion into the actual body and blood of Christ), and maintained that man need confess his sins to God alone. He advocated marriage of the clergy, argued that an evil Pope had no power over Christians, and said that the Bible, the one sure foundation of the faith, should be made available in the common English language to every man. To this end, Wycliffe translated his own version of the Bible. In spite of serious efforts to supress it, many copies survived to circulate among the people. For those who were not of the clergy, this was their first look at the book upon which their religion was based. For the first time, people were not dependent upon the clergy to relate the words and stories of the Bible. Individuals were able to read for themselves the stories, parables, and words of Christ and the apostles.

The Church, afraid of losing control of the people, reacted with panic. Those who dared advocate the use of English in the churches, and those who questioned transubstantiation or the priests' role and responsibilities, were branded as heretics. John Wycliffe surely would have come to harm if it weren't for the support of his friend, John of Gaunt. In spite of such powerful protection, the Archbishop of Canterbury succeeded in ousting

Wycliffe from his position as rector at Oxford. He spent the rest of his days publishing his sermons and writings and died in December 1384. Reform did not die with Wycliffe. His ideas inspired others to speak out and stimulated the serious reform movement, which was to begin in the next century.

NAMING

THE CHRISTENING CEREMONY was the first formal event in the newborn's life and the single most vital ritual performed by the Church, for without it one could not enter the kingdom of heaven. Baptism was so important that even commoners were encouraged to learn the words of the ritual in the event of a doubtful birth. In such cases, midwives were instructed to baptize the infant as soon as the head emerged. It was preferable to know the words in Latin: *Ego baptizo te in nomine Patris et Filii et Spiritus Sancti. Amen.* However, it was also acceptable to deliver the words in English: *I crystene the (thee) in the nome of the Fader, and the Son and the Holy Gost. Amen.* If there was doubt that the child would survive the birth, the midwife quite often gave it a neuter name such as Creature, Chylde of God, or Vitalis.

Formal christening took place within the week if the child survived. The father and the godparents took the child to the church, where the ceremony was performed by the parish priest. Because the mother was not allowed to enter the church prior to her own ceremony of purification to cleanse her from the "spiritual stain" of childbirth, she was usually absent from the christening ceremony.

The child had two godparents of the same sex and one of the opposite, and their role was taken quite a bit more seriously than it is today. The godparents were expected to see to the religious education of the child, and interestingly, people related by godparentage were forbidden to marry one another. (In this age when divorce was forbidden, relationship by godparentage was sometimes used as a means of obtaining an annulment of an undesired marriage.)

It was during the christening ceremony that the child was given the most important symbol of its entry into society and the Church: a name. The child was supposed to be given the same name as the principal godparent of the same sex. However, the names found during this time indicate that this rule was not always followed. Though Christian names were rarely used before this time, by the end of the twelfth century, the growing influence of the Church is reflected in the number of names bestowed that referred to the day of birth, and in the increased use of saint's names. Names referring to a child's day of birth include Christmas, Nowell, Easter, Epiphany, Theophania, Whitsun, Loveday, and Pentecost. In the late twelfth and early thirteenth centuries, there was probably a larger percentage of spiritual names in use than in any other time until the twentieth century. Taking biblical saints first, Bartholomew, James, Luke, Michael, Paul, Philip, and Simon are first recorded between 1185 and 1200. Barnabas is first found in 1201, but Mark isn't recorded until 1303.

At the end of the twelfth century, William was still the commonest male name, accounting for 15 percent of the total. Robert follows with 11 percent, Richard with 8 percent, then John with just 2 percent. At the end of the thirteenth century, the most significant change is seen with the name John, when perhaps a third to a half of the male population was so named. William comes in second at 14 percent, Robert has 11 percent, and Richard, 10 percent. In the fourteenth century, John was still the most popular male name, and William was still second most common. Thomas and Robert run an even third place in popularity. One study indicates there were only eighty-six male names in common usage.

Some of the more popular Old English names were still in use, though they were now quite rare. A list of 800 jurors and bailiffs from Kent in 1313–1314 illustrates this point, containing only one Aylwyn, two Edmunds, one Edward, and one Hereward. Toward the end of the fourteenth century, Old English names are hardly to be found, and the ones that did survive likely did so because they were the names of saints.

A significant change also occurred in women's names. The old Germanic names that were so popular after the Conquest gave way to names from mythology and names of legendary and scriptural saints. Joan, one of the most popular names, is first found in 1189, as is Agnes and Catherine. Mary is first recorded around 1203, and Anne in 1218. Late-twelfth-century records show names such as Antigone, Camilla, Cassandra, Extranea, and Melodia. As the thirteenth century advanced, the pool of female names shrank as the more elaborate names tended to be replaced by saints' names.

In the fourteenth century, Alice was the most popular female name; Joan was the second most popular. None of the female names dominated to the extent that John did among male names, however. One reason could be the variety of names in use or the interesting trend, which began in the thirteenth century, of bestowing male names upon female children. In order to bring a female child under the protection of a male saint, the child was often given that saint's name. Though the Latin records of the thirteenth century show females bearing names with feminine Latinate endings (Alexandra, Jacoba, Nicholaa, Philippa), other records indicate that they were actually baptized as Alexander, Jacob, Nicholas, and Philip. The male names Aubrey, Basil, Edmund, Eustace, Gilbert, Giles, Reynold, Roger, Simon, Thomas, and William were also bestowed upon female children.

The use of diminutive suffixes was quite common to this time period. The French suffixes were still in use, and English suffixes -cock, -kok, and -kin are first recorded at the end of the thirteenth century. Some believe -kin to be of Flemish origin as it is found in the Low Countries in the tenth century. With a few exceptions, these suffixes are masculine and form names such as Malkin and Watkin from Mary and Walter; Hancock and Wilkok from Hans and Will. Among the lower classes, diminutive forms and rhyming diminutives of names were quite popular. Gib was from Gilbert; Daw from David; Dick and Hick from Richard; Dodge and Hodge from Roger; Dob, Hob, and Robin from Robert; Wat from Walter; Kit from Catherine; Cis from Cecily.

The following is a list of Saint's Days. Children, when not named after their godparents or their day of birth, quite typically were named after the saint on whose day they were born.

JANUARY

5 Edward the Confessor
13 Saint Hilary the Bishop
15 Saint Maure the Abbot
16 Saint Marcel the Pope and Martyr
17 Saint Supplis the Bishop; Saint Anthony
18 Saint Prisce the Virgin
19 Saint Wolston the Bishop
20 Saint Fabian; Saint Sebastian

21 Saint Annice (Agnes) the Virgin
22 Saint Vincent the Martyr
24 Saint Timothy
25 The Conversion of Saint Paul
27 Saint Julian the Bishop
30 Saint Batilde the Queen
31 Saint Ignace the Bishop and Martyr

FEBRUARY

1 Saint Bride (Bridget) the Virgin
2 The Purification of Mary
3 Saint Blase the Bishop and Martyr
4 Saint Agatha the Virgin
5 Saint Vedast the Bishop; Saint Amande the Bishop
10 Saint Scholaste the Virgin

10 Saint Valentine
14 Saint Julian the Virgin
22 The Cathedration of Saint Peter;
     Saint Matthie (Matthias) the Apostle
29 Saint Oswald the Bishop and Confessor

MARCH

1 Saint David
7 Saint Perpetua the Virgin; Saint Felice the Virgin
12 Saint Gregory
17 Saint Patrick

18 Saint Edward the King and Confessor
20 Saint Cuthbert the Bishop and Confessor
21 Saint Benet (Benedict) the Abbot and Confessor

APRIL

2 Saint Mary the Egyptian
3 Saint Richard the Bishop and Confessor
4 Saint Ambrose the Bishop and Confessor
6 Saint Sixtus
13 Saint Eufemie
14 Saint Tiburce; Saint Valerian

19 Saint Alphege the Bishop and Martyr
23 Saint George the Martyr
25 Saint Mark the Evangelist
26 Saint Clete the Pope and Martyr
28 Saint Vital the Martyr

MAY

1 Saint Philip the Apostle; Saint Jacob the Apostle
6 Saint John
10 Saint Gordian; Saint Epinache
12 Saint Nere Achille; Saint Pancras
19 Saint Dunstan the Bishop and Confessor

25 Saint Urban the Bishop; Saint Adhelm the Bishop
26 Saint Austin (Augustine) the Bishop and Confessor
28 Saint Germain the Bishop and Confessor
31 Saint Purnel the Virgin

JUNE

1 Saint Nichomede the Martyr
2 Saint Marcelin; Saint Peter
5 Saint Boniface the Bishop
8 Saint Medard; Saint Gildard
11 Saint Barnabas the Apostle
14 Saint Basil the Bishop and Confessor
15 Saint Vitus
16 Saint Cyriac

17 Saint Botulf
18 Saint Mark; Saint Marcellian
19 Saint Gervase
22 Saint Alban the Martyr
23 Saint Etheldred the Virgin and Martyr
28 Saint Leo the Pope and Confessor
29 Saint Peter; Saint Paul

JULY

2 Saint Swithun
7 Saint Thomas the Martyr
14 Saint Metheldred the Virgin and Martyr
17 Saint Kenelm the King
18 Saint Arnulf the King
20 Saint Margaret the Virgin and Martyr
22 Saint Mary Magdalene

23 Saint Appolinar the Martyr
24 Saint Christine the Virgin and Martyr
25 Saint James the Apostle
26 Saint Ann
28 Saint Sampson
29 Saint Felix; Saint Simplis; Saint Faustin
31 Saint Neot

AUGUST

2 Saint Stephen the Pope
4 Saint Dominic
5 Saint Oswald the King and Martyr
7 Saint Donate
8 Saint Cyriac
9 Saint Roman the Martyr
10 Saint Lawrence the Martyr
11 Saint Tyburce the Martyr

11 Saint Hypolite
13 Saint Oswin the King
20 Saint Timothy
23 Saint Bartholomew
24 Saint Louis
25 Saint Austin the Bishop
28 Saint Cuthbert the Virgin

SEPTEMBER

1 Saint Giles
5 Saint Bertin
16 Saint Edith the Virgin
17 Saint Lambert
20 Saint Eustace

21 Saint Matthew
22 Saint Maurice
26 Saint Justin; Saint Cyprian
29 Saint Michael the Archangel (Michaelmas)
30 Saint Jerome

OCTOBER

1 Saint Remigius
2 Saint Leodegar the Bishop and Confessor
4 Saint Francis the Confessor
6 Saint Faith the Virgin and Martyr
9 Saint Dennis

15 Saint Wolfran the Bishop and Confessor
18 Saint Luke
25 Saint Crispin; Saint Crispianus
28 Saint Simon; Saint Jude the Apostle
31 Saint Quentin the Martyr

NOVEMBER

6 Saint Leonard the Abbot and Confessor
11 Saint Martin the Bishop and Confessor
13 Saint Brice the Bishop
16 Saint Edmund the Archbishop
17 Saint Hugh the Bishop

20 Saint Edmund the King and Martyr
22 Saint Cecily the Virgin and Martyr
23 Saint Clement the Pope
25 Saint Katherine the Virgin and Martyr
20 Saint Andrew

DECEMBER

4 Saint Barbara
6 Saint Nicholas the Bishop and Confessor
7 Saint Ambrose
13 Saint Lucy the Virgin and Martyr
21 Saint Thomas

26 Saint Stephen the Martyr
27 Saint John the Apostle and Evangelist
29 Saint Thomas the Archbishop and Martyr
31 Saint Silvester the Pope and Confessor

FEMALE NAMES

Adela (noble)
Adelaide (nobility)
Agatha (good)
Agilina (formidable) **Egelina, Egeline**
Agnes (chaste, pure)
Albreda (elf counsel)
Aldith (old battle) **Aeldiet, Aeldit, Aeldid, Ailiet, Ailith, Aldid, Eldid, Eldit**
Alexander (defender of mankind)
Alexandra (defender of mankind)
Alice (nobility)
Aline (noble one) **Alina, Alyna**
Amabel (?) **Amabil, Amabilia**
Amice (friend) **Amicia**
Amphelisia (?) **Amfelice, Amphelicia, Amphelice, Anfelise**
Anastasia (resurrection) **Anestasia**
Ann (grace, full of grace, mercy) Recorded first in 1218.
Annabel (?, possibly *eagle*; *hearth*; *lovable*; or *joy*)
Annora (honor, esteem)
Antigone (contrary)
Arabella (?, perhaps *eagle*; *hearth*) **Arabel, Orabel, Oriabel**
Aude (old)
Avice (?)
Barbot (foreign woman) **Barbat, Barbata, Barbota**
Basil (kingly)
Basilie (kingly)
Beata (happy)
Beatrice (bringer of blessings or joy) **Beatriz**
Cassandra (?) **Cassander, Casse**
Cecilia (blind, dim-sighted) **Cecille, Cecelya**
Christopher (bearing Christ) **Cristofre**
Clarice (bright, clear, famous) **Claris, Clarisse**
Cristina (a Christian, follower of Christ)
Dionysia (of Dionysus, the Greek god of wine and revelry)
Edith (prosperous war)
Eleanor (light, torch, bright) **Alienor, Elianor**
Elena (light) **Elen, Ellen**
Elfleda (noble and beautiful; beautiful elf)
Elisot (God is my oath)
Elizabeth (God is my oath) **Libbe**
Ella (?, possibly *all*)
Ellota (God is my oath)
Emilia (?)
Emma (strength)
Estrild (goddess of battle)
Eugenia (nobility, excellence)
Euphemia (good speech) **Eufemia, Eufemmia**
Eustacia (steadfast, happy in harvest) **Eustace**
Felice (fortunate, lucky) **Felise**
Florence (blooming)
Frideswide (strong peace)
Gabriel (God is strength) **Gabrielle**
Gemma (a gem) Only rarely used.

Gertrude (spear strength)
Gillian (youth, downy) **Gillot, Julian, Julien, Juliet, Julyan, Jolyan; Gill, Jill**
Githa (war) **Gytha**
Godiva (God's gift) **Godeva**
Goodeth (God's war) **Goditha**
Grace (grace, mercy)
Gunilda (war battle) **Gunnilda**
Gunnora (war) **Gunora**
Helewise (hale, hearty + wide) **Helewis, Heilewis, Helevis, Elwisia**
Hilary (cheerful) **Hillary**
Hilda (war, battle) **Hilde**
Hodierna (of this day) **Odiern, Odierna**
Ida (labor)
Idonea (?, perhaps *work, labor; suitable*)
Ingrid (beautiful Ing, a Norse fertility god)
Isabel (God is my oath) **Isabele, Isabella; Belle, Biby, Ibb**
Ivette (archer)
Jaclyn (God is gracious) **Jakelin, Jakolin**
Jacob (supplanting, seizing by the heels)
Jacoba (supplanting, seizing by the heels)
Joan (God is gracious)
Johanna (God is gracious)
Joia (joy) **Joy**
Jolecia (viola)
Jolenta (viola)
Joscelin (from the tribe of the Gauts)
Judith (praised) **Judita**
Katerin (pure, unsullied) **Caterin, Katelin**
Laurette (laurel) **Lauretta, Loretta**
Lavina (?) **Lavena**
Lettice (gladness) **Leticia, Letyce**
Loveday (born on a love day)
Lucy (light) **Luce**
Mabel (lovable) **Mabil**
Madelin (from Magdala) **Maudelyn**
Margaret (a pearl) **Margareta, Magge, Mogge, Pogge**
Margery (a pearl)
Margota (a pearl)
Marina (of the sea) Used from the fourteenth century.
Marion (sea of bitterness or sorrow)
Mariot (sea of bitterness or sorrow) Not used before the thirteenth century.
Mary (sea of bitterness or sorrow) **Malle, Molle** Not used before the thirteenth century, and only rarely afterward.
Matilda (mighty in battle)
Maud (mighty in battle)
Melisent (work-strong) **Milisent**
Mildred (mild strength)
Mirabel (wonderful, glorious)
Monday (born on Monday)
Nicolas (victory of the people)

Noel (Christmas)
Nona (ninth)
Olive (olive tree)
Organa (?, possibly *organic*)
Oriel (?, perhaps *fire + strife, war*)
Osanne (hosanna) **Ozanne**
Pentecost (fiftieth day) From the beginning of the thirteenth century.
Petronil (stone) **Parnel, Pernel, Peronel, Petronell, Petronyl**
Philip (lover of horses)
Philomena (powerful friend)

Pleasance (pleasant) **Placence, Plesence** From the thirteenth century.
Prudence (prudence) From the thirteenth century.
Regina (queen) **Reine**
Roese (horse) **Rohese, Roseia, Roysia**
Rosamund (horse protection) **Rosamond**
Sabina (Sabine woman) **Sabin**
Sara (princess) **Sarra**
Scholastica (scholar)
Sibill (prophetess, fortune teller) **Sibel, Sibil, Sybil, Sybyl, Sibbe**

MALE NAMES

Abel (breath)
Abraham (father of a multitude)
Absalom (father of peace) **Absalon**
Acelin (tribe of the Gauts) **Ascelyn, Asselin**
Adam (man of the red earth)
Adrian (man from Hadrianus)
Alan (?, perhaps *handsome, rock*) **Aleyne**
Alard (noble and hard)
Aldus (old)
Aldwin (old friend) **Alduin**
Alexander (defender of mankind) **Sander**
Alfred (elf counsel)
Algar (elf spear) **Aelger, Alger**
Ambrose (immortal)
Amias (?, perhaps friendship)
Amiel (industrious)
Andrew (manly) **Dande**
Anselm (God's helmet)
Antony (?, *priceless, of inestimable worth* is a folk definition)
Arnold (eagle power) **Ernald**
Artur (?) **Artor**
Athelstan (noble stone) **Athestan**
Aubrey (elf ruler) **Aubri**
Austin (great, venerable)
Aylmer (nobly famous)
Aylwin (elf friend)
Baldric (bold ruler)
Baldwin (bold friend)
Bardolph (bright wolf)
Barnabas (son of exhortation)
Bartholomew (son of Talmai *hill, mound, furrows*)
Basil (kingly)
Berold (bear rule) **Berolt**
Bertelmeu (son of Talmai) **Bette**
Bertin (bright friend) **Bette**
Christopher (bearing Christ)
Ciprianus (from Cyprus) Used from the thirteenth century.
Clemens (gentle, mild)

Constantine (constant, steadfast) **Constans, Cuss, Cust**
Crispin (curled)
Damian (tamer)
Daniel (judged by God)
David (beloved)
Dominic (belonging to a lord; belonging to the Lord) **Dominik**
Drogo (to carry, a burden)
Durand (enduring, lasting) **Durant**
Edgar (wealthy spear)
Edmond (wealthy protection)
Edward (wealthy guardian)
Edwin (wealthy friend)
Egbert (bright sword)
Eustace (steadfast; happy in harvest)
Florian (flowery)
Francis (a Frank, a freeman)
Gabriel (God is strength)
Gamel (old)
Gaston (?, possibly *guest, stranger; from Gascony*)
Gawyne (battle hawk) **Gawyn**
Geoffrey (district, traveler, pledge + peace) **Geffrei, Geffrey**
George (earth worker, farmer)
Gerald (spear rule)
Gerbert (spear bright)
Gerbold (spear bold)
Gervais (servant of the spear) **Gervas, Gervase, Jarvis**
Giffard (give + bold, fierce)
Gilbert (bright pledge) **Gib, Gil**
Giles (goatskin shield of Zeus; a protection)
Godard (God hard)
Godfrey (God's peace)
Godric (powerful God)
Godwin (friend of God)
Gregory (vigilant, watchful)
Griffin (like a griffin, monstrous)
Gunther (bold in war)
Guy (a guide, leader)
Hardwin (hard friend)

Harold (power of the army)
Hector (holding fast)
Henry (home ruler)
Herbert (army bright)
Hereward (army guard)
Herman (warrior, soldier)
Hilary (cheerful)
Hubert (bright heart) **Hubard**
Hugh (heart, mind, soul) **Hugo**
Ives (archer) **Ivo, Yvo**
Jacob (supplanting, seizing by the heels)
James (supplanting, seizing by the heels)
Jeremiah (God will uplift) **Jeremy**
Joachim (God will establish) **Joachin**
John (God is gracious)
Jonas (dove)
Jordan (a flowing down) **Judd, Jurd**
Joseph (he shall add)
Julian (youth, downy)
Kenrick (royal rule)
Kenward (brave guardian) **Keneweard, Kenard**
Lambert (bright land)
Lancelot (?, perhaps *little land*)
Laurance (from Laurentum)
Leofric (dear ruler)
Leofwin (dear friend)
Leonard (bold as a lion)
Lewis (famous in war) **Lowis**
Lionel (little lion)
Lovell (wolf)
Luke (light; man from Loukania)
Manfred (peace of man)
Martin (of Mars, warlike)
Matheus (gift of God) **Mathiu, Mattheus**
Mauger (spear grinder)
Maynard (strong and hardy)
Michael (Who is like God?)
Milo (?, perhaps *mild, peaceful, merciful*) **Milon**
Nicholas (victory of the people) **Nicoll, Nichol, Coll**
Odo (wealth)
Ogier (rich spear)
Osbern (god bear) **Osborn**
Oscar (God's spear)

Osmond (God's protection) **Osmund**
Oswald (God's power)
Oswin (friend of God)
Paulin (small)
Pernel (a rock, a stone) **Penne, Pennel**
Peter (a rock, a stone)
Philip (lover of horses) **Fippe, Philipot, Pot**
Piers (a rock, a stone)
Quintin (fifth)
Ralph(counsel wolf)
Randulf (shield wolf)
Raymund (counsel protection) **Raimund, Reimond**
Raynold (powerful protection) **Rainald, Raynald, Renold, Reynold**
Reginald (judgment power)
Renfred (counsel might)
Reynard (counsel hard)
Richard (stern king)
Robert (bright with fame) **Dob, Dobbe, Hob, Hobbe, Nabbe, Rob, Robb**
Roger (famous with the spear)
Roland (famous land) **Rolland**
Rolf (famous wolf) **Rolft, Roulf**
Samson (the sun) **Sansom**
Simon (heard) **Simond, Symon**
Siward (victory protection)
Stephen (a crown, a garland)
Talbot (pillager, bandit; lampblack)
Theobald (bold people)
Theodoric (ruler of the people)
Thomas (a twin)
Thorold (Thor's strength) **Turold**
Thurbern (Thor-bear, Thor-warrior)
Thurstan (Thor's stone)
Tobias (God is good)
Tristram (tumult, sadness)
Ulric (wolf rule)
Urban (villager)
Valentine (healthy, strong)
Vincent (conquering)
Walter (ruler of an army)
William (resolute protector)

SURNAMES

Down to the thirteenth century, there were no set rules for the assumption of secondary names. A sample of Assize Rolls from the years 1219–1231 show no instances of people having but a single name. Fifty-three percent of locational names contain either Latin or French prepositions (usually *de*); English prepositions are not found. Because the French prepositions seem to have been adopted into the English of the time, these are expressed herein as Anglo-Norman. The majority of genealogical names express relationship. Among the characteristic and occupational names, half contain the Anglo-Norman article *le,* and half have no article at all. The unclassified names are perhaps the most interesting. Though they account for only 13 percent of the total, those who had these names were usually criminals. One possible reason could be that many of the criminals had no sure knowledge of their parentage and were rovers with no permanent residence and no occupation.

Manorial court rolls from the thirteenth century show that country dwellers were most commonly known by their place of residence. In many instances, these were people who had lived their entire lives in the same small spot, and this is reflected in such secondary names as de Birches (the birches); de Bosco (the wood); de Brueria (the heath); de Hulle (the hill); de Molendino (the mill); de Putte (the pit). Some names contained a mix of Latin and French or Anglo-Norman prefixes: de la Broke (of the brook); de la Het (of the heath); in le Put (in the pit); de la Zate (of the gate). Some English prepositions could be found: Abovethenbroc (above the brook); Attebroc (at the brook); atte Lone ende (at the lane's end).

One of the best sources for thirteenth-century names is a list called *Rotuli Hundredorum*, the Hundred Rolls. When Edward I proceeded to remedy the abuses of his father's reign, his first step was to gather evidence and make a list of all the people who had suffered from oppression and exactions. It is a huge list, covering nearly 1,500 pages and containing about 70,000 names. There are a few single names to be found, but these number at less than 1 percent and belong to the class of cottars and bondsmen.

In general, characteristic and genealogical surnames were more common among the lower servant classes, and those with trades more commonly bore occupational names. Records dating to this period show that the nobility were more often distinguished by surnames referring to their personal estates. The second most common surname to this class was genealogical.

The growth of the English language is apparent in the growing use of English prepositions. *At, atte, bi* and *by, over, under,* and *Binethe* (beneath) are examples of the English prepositions that were used. The Anglo-Norman articles *la, le,* and *li* were more frequently used in combination with English words than with French.

There is also a noticeable decline in the use of the terms *filius* (son of) and *filia* (daughter of). Instead, a surname derived from a relative was used in its nominative form. Take the names John Roger and Stephen Thomas, for example. John was the son of Roger; Stephen was the son of Thomas. Genealogical names of this period also used the genitive endings *es,-is,-s*, and-*y*. Most of the names ending in -*es* were women's names, and it stands to reason that Joan le Warneres was either the wife or widow of Ralph le Warner, that Alice Candeles was married to Walter Candel, and that Matilda Stevenes was the spouse of Stephen le Hattere. A surname like Stevens could also have been borne by a servant or person in the house of Stephen or by the son or daughter of Stephen. There seems to have been no set rule for the addition of the final letters, which is probably due to the fact that the English language itself had no set rules regarding spelling. Indeed, examples exist of the same people having their names spelled in different ways in different records.

The most important factor in the making of surnames in the fourteenth century was the growing popularity of the English language. At the beginning of the century, native tongues were freely spoken throughout the land by the commoners. Latin was used for legal records; French was the language of the courts, education, and the language in which sermons were delivered. In 1348, Edward III had an English motto embroidered on his tunic, and Richard II addressed the commons at Smithfield in English in 1381. Thus legitimized by kingly usage, English rapidly became the common language of conversation and surnames that arose from the spoken tongue were many. It is interesting that while Old English personal names were now quite rare, their preservation can be found in a large number of surnames.

On the whole, secondary names were much more common in the south than in the north. In the midland counties, 50 percent to 70 percent of the names were without articles, prepositions, or filial expression. In Cornwall, the figure rises to 83 percent. In the northern counties, the great number of entries in the tax roles using *filius* and *de* show that few of those people had common second names, and the recording clerks were constrained to identify them with a genealogical or local reference. A note of interest is the prevalent use of the filial suffix *son* in the north. This might be due to the native custom of expressing one's genealogy: John son of Roger, son of Adam, son of Edward, etc. One's pedigree was greatly prized and was usually traced back for many generations.

In general, local descriptions in the fourteenth century were usually nothing more than addresses: of the Garth house, in the lane, from the valley, at the hillock, by the water, beyond the town. By the end of the fourteenth century, occupational names were much more prevalent without an article, and genealogical names saw a decline in the employment of words denoting kinship. Secondary names based on characteristics also began to decline.

There is no agreed-upon time when surnames became hereditary. It was a slow process that was not uniform in all levels of society or areas of the country. The names do appear, however, to have started on the path to becoming hereditary during this time. If the blond-haired children have the same last name as their father, Will Rufus (red-haired), the name was likely inherited. It must be remembered, though, that after two or three generations, it was just as likely for a family member to part with tradition and decide on a different surname.

Albyn (white)
Alienor (light, torch, bright)
Alwins (son of Alwin *elf friend*)
de Anjou (from Anjou)
de Artois (from Artois)
Bacheler (young knight, novice in arms)
Bacon (side of bacon) **Bakon**
Ball (ball; bald place; the round one)
Barber (a barber, one who practiced surgery and dentistry) **Barbur**
Barnelby (son of consolation)
Baroun (a baron, a nobleman)
Basse (short, of small height)
Batoc (the stout man)
Beald (the bald; the bold)
le Beau (the fair)
Belesone (son of Bele)
la Belle (the beautiful)
Bene (pleasant, kind)
Berenger (bear spear)
Bertran (bright raven)
Berwyk (dweller at an outlying hall or grange)
de Birches (dweller by the birch trees)
Blaca (the black)
Boda (the messenger)
Bonefey (good fate)
de Bosco (dweller by the woods)
Botte (butt; toad)
Bounde (husbandman, peasant)
Bouvier (cattle drover)
Brian (force, strength; valor; high; kingly)
de Brieuse (from Brus *brushwood thicket*) **de Brus**
de la Broke (of the brook)

de Brueria (from the heath)
Brune (the brown) **Brun**
Bully (from the bull's enclosure)
Burgeis (a freeman of a borough)
Buxton (Bucca's stone)
Cada (the short, fat person)
Candeles (a maker or seller of candles) **Candel**
Castello (castle)
de Champagne (from Champagne *field*)
de Chanteloup (from Chanteloup *singing wolves*)
de Chartres (from Chartres)
Chaucer (maker of leather pants)
Cild (the child)
del Clee (dweller by the river fork, dweller by the fork in a road)
Cniht (the servant)
Cokes (a cook, a seller of cooked meats)
Cola (the dark one)
de Colleville (from Colleville *Col's estate*)
Colt (a colt; frisky, lively)
le Corbet (the raven)
de Coucy (from Coucy)
de Courtenay (from Courtenay *Courtenay's homestead*)
Cyppe (the fat one)
de Dentune (of Dentune)
Dubois (dweller in the woods)
Dudding (son of Dudda)
Duns (brown-haired)
Durand (enduring, lasting) **Durant**
Dych (dweller near the dike)
Eadricssun (son of Eadric *wealthy ruler*)
Eadwinesbroder (brother of Eadwine *wealthy friend*)
Ealda (the old one)

Fabre (a smith)
Fauchet (crooked legs)
del Fernyside (from the ferny slope)
Geonga (the young)
Giffard (chubby-cheeked)
Gilbert (bright pledge)
de Glanville (from Glanville *oak tree estate*)
le Grand (the tall, the large)
le Gronne (the large)
le Gros (the fat)
Grymbaud (helmet bold)
Hales (dweller in the remote valley)
Harald (ruler of the army)
de Harcourt (from Harcourt *army house*)
Hattere (maker or seller of hats) **Hatter**
Hayward (guardian of the fence or hedge)
Heaha (the tall)
de la Het (of the heath)
Hirde (a herdsman)
Hoga (the wise)
de Hulle (dweller near the hill)
Hwita (the white)
Jago (supplanting, seizing by the heels)
le Jeune (the young)
Kaer (fort)
Kenwrek (famous king)
Kingessone (son of the king)
de Laci (from Laci *Latius's estate*)
de Lamburnan (from Lamburnan)
Larcher (the archer)
Legge (leg)
Lighfot (light foot)
de Lorris (from Lorris)
Lovett (little wolf)
de Lundene (from Lundene)
de Maci (from Maci *Matheus' estate*)
Maggesone (son of Magge *a pearl*)
de Malleville (from Malleville)
Mann (the servant)
Mannyng (the servant)
de Marle (blackbird)
de Meran (from Meran)
Merton (from the place by the lake)
de Molendino (dweller by the mill)
de Montfort (from Montfort *fortified hill*)

Pariz (from Paris)
Pek (a peck; a maker or seller of pecks)
de Perci (from Perci *destroyer of cities*)
de Poitiers (from Poitiers)
de Ponte (dweller by the bridge)
Poore (pauper)
Porter (a porter, a doorkeeper, a carrier of burdens)
Provence (from Provence)
de Putte (dweller by the pit)
Reada (the red)
Rede (red, ruddy-complexioned)
Rees (ardor)
Robe (bright with fame)
Rochefort (from Rochefort *fortified rock*)
Roke (at the oak; dweller by the rock)
Rolfeson (son of Rolf *counsel wolf*)
Russel (red-haired) **Russell**
Simple (the simple-minded)
Skynner (the skinner)
Smalle (the small)
Stevenes (son of Steven *a crown, garland*)
Swan (the swineherd)
Swift (the swift)
Taillour (a tailor)
Talbot (pillager, bandit; lampblack)
del Thwayt (dweller at the forest clearing)
Tillet (dweller near the lime trees)
de Tilly (from the lime tree grove)
Tirel (Thor rule)
Trane (trickery; a trap)
Tyssone (son of Ty *firebrand*)
de Venables (from Venables *vineyard*)
la Verrere (a glazier)
Walworth (from the Welshman's farm)
de Warenne (from Warenne)
le Warner (the warrener, a game warren) **Warneres**
de Warre (of the war, a warrior)
Wasket (the little Gascon)
atte Watere (at the water)
le Werre (the warrior)
del Wode (dweller in the wood)
de Wylaston (from the village of Willa *resolute*)
Yungwin (young friend)
de la Zate (of the gate)

Chapter Four

THE RENAISSANCE
HENRY IV TO HENRY VII
[1399–1509]

POLITICS

THE RISE OF the House of Lancaster (1399–1471) began with the ascension of Henry IV. Born in 1367 to John of Gaunt and Blanche of Lancaster, Henry was thirty-two when he took the crown from Richard II. On the day of his coronation, he was subject to three ill omens that predicted the future of his reign. According to Adam of Usk, a Welsh councillor, the first omen was when Henry lost one of his shoes in the coronation procession. ''Whence, in the first place, the Commons who rose up against him hated him ever after his whole life long.'' The second ill omen occurred when one of his golden spurs fell off. ''Whence, in the second place, the soldiery opposed him in rebellion.'' At the coronation banquet, the third omen occurred when a sudden gust of wind blew Henry's crown from his head. ''Whence, in the last place, he was set aside from his kingdom and supplanted by Prince Henry.''

It's possible the ill omens weren't just superstition, for nearly the whole of Henry IV's reign was plagued by rebellion and unrest. Three months after he took the crown, he had to flee Windsor to escape a rebel coup led by the earls of Huntingdon, Kent, and Salisbury to restore Richard II to the throne. The attempt failed, the rebels were executed, and Richard was secretly murdered at Pontefract. Some thirty other rebels were tried and executed shortly afterward; their chopped up bodies, taken to London in sacks, bore graphic witness to Henry's merciless response. He survived another plot to overthrow him in 1405, and again, he showed no mercy to his detractors. The sudden illness that partially paralyzed him shortly afterward was said to have been God's divine punishment for his actions.

The fact that Henry was able to so easily usurp the crown and keep it is testimony to his skill as a ruler in an age where legitimacy lay at the base of political theory. Not even the commons, who were struggling under the burden of heavy taxes, saw fit to question Henry's right to the throne. Assured of his position and against all odds, Henry was able to defeat the rebel barons, neutralize threats from Scotland and France, and bring Wales back into allegiance.

In 1413, it was quite clear that Henry was dying. He suffered from heart disease and diseases of the skin that progressed to the point that his face and body were now badly disfigured. His end came at Westminster Palace on March 20, 1413. His son, Henry V, was at his side and received his blessing.

Henry V is viewed as a brilliant general and a conscientious administrator who saw to the needs of his people. He set upon his course by first righting the wrongs of his father's reign. He returned the estates of the earl of March (whose father had been Richard II's heir), brought the earl of Oxford and the earl of Huntingdon back into favor, had the body of Richard II reburied with pomp at Westminster Abbey, and stepped up persecution of the Lollards, who roundly condemned the noblemen's wealth.

In August 1415, Henry and an army of 10,000 sailed from Southampton to the Normandy coast to pursue the conquest of France. In the first two months, Harfleur surrendered, and Henry saw fantastic success at Agincourt. With such easy victories behind them, the English saw the merit of Henry's plans and united behind him. Henry promoted himself as France's rightful king and spent the next five years in conquest of the country.

By 1418, the English controlled Lower Normandy; a year later, the entire duchy. Henry signed the Treaty of Troyes in 1420. In essence, this document stated that Henry would be recognized as Charles VI's heir and that he would marry Charles's daughter, Catherine. In return, Henry was obligated to avenge the murder of the Duke of Burgundy and make war on the dauphin, who held most of France south of the Loire. During the winter of 1421–1422, Henry fell sick with an illness he could not overcome (probably dysentery). On August 31, 1422, he died at Bois de Vincennes, leaving behind his wife and infant son and an unresolved situation in France.

Henry VI was only nine months old when his father died. His uncle, the duke of Gloucester, was nominated as Regent in Henry V's will, but was allowed to serve only as protector. Charles VI died a few weeks after Henry V, and the infant's other uncle, the duke of Bedford, acted as Regent in France.

In 1431, Henry was crowned king of France in Paris and the English held their own until the death of the Duke of Bedford in 1435. Once England lost the strength and administrative ability of its French regent and the support of the Burgundians, its stronghold on France was doomed. By 1453, all but Calais was lost. The Hundred Years' War was over.

Things had not been going so well at home, either. The Duke of Gloucester managed to see Henry to adulthood, but Henry was a weak king. He was virtuous, religious, and scholarly, yet he proved himself incapable of leading his country or inspiring his people. He also allowed himself to be influenced by a small group of men, including the earl of Suffolk, the Bishop of Ayscough, and Edmund Beaufort, Duke of Somerset.

At a time when England was trying to retain its French possessions, Suffolk arranged for Henry to marry Margaret of Anjou, with the secret agreement that Henry would give up Anjou and Maine. After Suffolk's plans became known, he was under dire straits to restore his reputation and decided the way to accomplish that would be to launch an attack on France. This started a series of battles that culminated in the loss of Normandy and the loss of Aquitaine, an English possession for almost 300 years. After Normandy was taken, Suffolk was impeached in parliament. Henry banished him for five years, but Suffolk's ship was intercepted in the Channel and he was executed on the spot.

With Henry now suffering from bouts of madness, noblemen were fighting for power, government was falling apart, the economy was failing, and general lawlessness and corruption were wreaking havoc across the country. The 1450 insurrection, Cade's Rebellion, stemmed from the people's disgust with the state of affairs.

Margaret of Anjou feared that the Duke of York was plotting to destroy the royal family. She set herself against him and his followers, touching off the Wars of the Roses (1455–1485). This was a war of the nobility, and for the most part, the common people were little affected. Several years after hostilities began, York managed to rout the king's army at Northampton and submit his claim to the throne. Parliament decided to let Henry remain king until death on condition that he recognize York as his heir. Henry acquiesced; Margaret did not. She escaped to Scotland and raised a new Lancastrian force. Without waiting for reinforcements, York hurried to meet the threat and was killed in a battle at Wakefield in 1460.

Fourteen-sixty-one was the last year of Henry VI's reign. Queen Margaret and her army marched on London, yet the city refused admittance for fear of the looting that would occur if the northerners gained entrance. Warwick, the son of the earl of Salisbury and an ally of York, joined his forces with those of Edward, York's eldest son. Edward entered London in triumph and was crowned king. Henry and Margaret were forced to seek refuge in Scotland. By 1463, Margaret had returned to France with her son, leaving Henry to his own devices. He ended up wandering as a common fugitive until 1465, when he was arrested and put in the Tower. He was restored five years later, but the details of his restoration belong more to the reign of Edward IV.

Though Henry was pious and good-hearted, as a king he did little to inspire respect. Edward IV, on the other hand, was tall, handsome, brave, courageous in battle, and understood the common man's concerns with government and the country. His first order of business was to address the issues of his opposition. He worked to make the crown solvent, swearing to the people that he'd live on his own funds and not approach the commons for money except in the most serious of circumstances. To that end, he kept tight control of royal household expenditures and set about increasing his personal wealth by undertaking various overseas trading ventures. Edward also confiscated many of the lands given away by the Lancastrian kings and put crown lands in the hands of paid officials rather than dole them out to favored companions and supporters.

Edward IV spent the first part of his reign being mentored by his cousin Richard Neville, the Earl of Warwick (Warwick the Kingmaker). Neville had inherited the earldom of Salisbury and had inherited that of Warwick when he married its heiress, Anne Beauchamp. Domineering, ambitious, and fourteen years Edward's senior, it was the Kingmaker who pulled the strings in the early days of Edward's reign.

Edward eventually began to grow tired of Warwick's imperious manner, and a rift appeared in their relationship. It has been suggested that two things were at the root of their problems: sex and diplomacy. Edward was a terrible ladies' man with a penchant for older women. He made little secret of his pursuit and conquest of the ladies of his court and household, caring not whether they were highborn or servants. One woman, a Lancastrian widow named Elizabeth Grey (Woodinville), steadfastly refused to submit. Edward was intrigued by this woman who stood up to him, and in the spirit of the conquest, ended up marrying her.

Warwick, meanwhile, was in the process of negotiating a treaty of friendship with France that was to be sealed by the marriage of Edward to a French princess. After Edward married Elizabeth, Warwick, having enjoyed the attention of the French king and expecting a reward of French lands and titles, was angry and humiliated and took the marriage as a personal affront. To make matters worse, Edward made it clear he was no longer interested in being Warwick's protégé and set about pursuing his own agenda. Warwick decided that since he had made one king, he could do it again. He conspired with Clarence, Edward's own brother, and together they rose against the king.

Edward realized he could never contemplate a truce with Warwick. Not only had the man turned Clarence's loyalties, he had also executed several of Elizabeth's relatives, including her father and brother, and was busy instigating rebellions in Wales and Lincolnshire. Edward was determined to see him finished and went after him, prompting Warwick and the disloyal Clarence to flee to France.

This was just what Louis XI had been waiting for. He reconciled Warwick with Margaret of Anjou and formed an alliance between them. Warwick and a force of men reentered England, caught Edward by surprise, and forced him to flee to Burgundy. Warwick then brought Henry VI out of the Tower, cleaned him up, and put him back on the throne as a puppet king.

Louis XI and Warwick then declared war on the duke of Burgundy. The duke allied himself with Edward and lent him a fleet and troops. In 1471, Edward returned to England and took Warwick and Queen Margaret to battle. The Kingmaker was killed, Margaret's son Prince Edward was killed, the traitorous Clarence generously received a pardon, and the old befuddled Henry VI was taken back to the Tower and quietly put to death.

The rest of Edward's reign passed fairly smoothly. Trade flourished and the crown was freed from debt. Edward was able to reestablish law and order throughout the countryside, and he established a seven-year treaty of peace with France that gave him a substantial annual pension in exchange for not fighting.

Edward's health began to decline during the last years of his reign, and in April 1483, he contracted a fever and died. He left the crown to his twelve-year-old son, Prince Edward, and named his brother, Richard of Gloucester, as protector.

Just after Edward IV's death, young Edward's uncle, Anthony Woodville (Lord Rivers) and half-brother, Sir Richard Gray, escorted him to London. They were intercepted by Richard of Gloucester and the duke of Buckingham, both of whom held serious grudges against the Woodvilles. Anthony Woodville and Sir Gray were taken to prison and executed; Edward was escorted to London and the Tower. The queen mother, her daughters, and the young duke of York sought sanctuary within the walls of Westminster Abbey.

The little duke was lured away from the protection of his mother and hustled off to the Tower to join his brother. Afterward, Richard had a sermon preached at Saint Paul's Cross that declared the two youngsters to be illegitimate as their father, King Edward IV, had broken an engagement with Eleanor Butler in order to marry the queen. Once this was done, the duke of Buckingham publicly suggested that Richard was the rightful heir; after a few "modest" refusals, Richard accepted the crown and proceeded to coronation in July 1483.

History does not detail what became of the princes in the Tower, but they were never seen alive again, and the mystery became the most emotive murder investigation in English history. It is quite possible that the poor children died a natural death in the horrors of the Tower, but it is just as likely that they were killed shortly after Richard's coronation. Whatever befell them, most believed that Richard was directly responsible. After his death, his images were blackened and his personal correspondence destroyed so that no real evidence of his motives exists. Whatever the reasons and whatever the method, he clearly usurped the throne.

After Richard's coronation, the Duke of Buckingham must have been worried about his own part in Richard's rise to power, for he quickly changed roles from supporter to that of conspirator. He reconciled with both the Woodvilles and the exiled Henry Tudor and led an ill-fated insurrection against the king. Severe weather hampered his efforts, and after heavy rains pelted his army, he was taken without a fight and beheaded. Henry Tudor's small fleet returned to Brittany without attempting a landing.

Elizabeth Woodville, convinced she'd never see her young sons again, was determined to bring Richard down. She proposed the marriage of her eldest daughter, Elizabeth, to Henry Tudor. This would be politically dangerous for Richard, as Elizabeth was the eldest daughter of Edward IV and Henry was the sole surviving heir to the Lancastrian claim to the crown.

The next year of Richard's reign was one of personal tragedy and diplomatic failure. His only child, Prince Edward, died, and he failed in his attempts to extradite Henry Tudor from Brittany. Queen Anne died in March the following year, prompting rumors that Richard had poisoned her in order to marry Elizabeth of York, Henry Tudor's intended bride.

By late summer 1485, Henry Tudor, supported by disgruntled Englishmen and French soldiers, made his landing at South Wales. He met Richard at Bosworth Field and in the ensuing battle, Richard was slain.

Richard had been a capable administrator during his brother's reign, but he lacked the kingly virtues that had made Edward IV so popular. He was a bad judge of character, he had great difficulty in making friends, and he made enemies out of the friends he did have. He also did nothing to endear himself to the nobility nor was able to garner much of their support. In the end, Lord Stanley, who had been at Richard's side the past two years, cast his lot with Henry Tudor, while the Earl of Northumberland, Richard's northern supporter, stood apart from the battle and watched Richard die. Stanley reportedly retrieved Richard's crown from under a gorse bush and placed it on the head of Henry Tudor, the first of the Tudor kings.

Henry won the crown by being victorious in battle, but he won the popular vote of the people as well. They accepted him as a rightful claimant to the throne and welcomed him as the one who put an end to the tyranny of Richard's rule. Pope Innocent VIII went so far as to threaten with excommunication any who dared challenge Henry's legitimacy.

In 1486, Henry married Elizabeth of York, thus uniting the rival houses of Lancaster and York. This did not bring an end to the conspiracies and intrigues that surrounded him, however. From the beginning of his reign until the end, he was pestered by pretenders and Yorkist claimants to the throne. It also seems that Henry took a page from Richard III's book, for directly after his victory at Bosworth Field, he sent the ten-year-old earl of Warwick (son of Edward IV's brother Clarence) to the Tower, believing him to be his most serious competitor for the crown.

Once Henry successfully removed the imposters and the conspirators within his court, he substituted their places on the King's Council with members of the lesser nobility and the middle class. The new council reestablished law and order throughout the realm and brought a measure of respectability back to government. Henry stimulated the economy by encouraging foreign trade. Exports of English wool to the Flemings soared, and commercial treaties allowed special privileges to the English merchant adventurers. The king also did his bit for exploration by financing John Cabot's expedition to America.

Henry was successful on the diplomatic scene as well. The Treaty of Medina del Campo bound England to Spain; the marriage of Henry's eldest son, Arthur, to Catherine of Aragon late in 1501 strengthened the alliance, though he died but a few months later. In 1502, Margaret, his eldest daughter, was wed to James IV of Scotland, thus paving the way for unification of the kingdoms.

A year later, Queen Elizabeth died in childbed and a grief-stricken Henry became despondent and a bit of a recluse. He died in April 1509, leaving England with a full treasury, internal peace and prosperity, and a place of respect among the international community.

SOCIETY

THE SAME TUMULT and intrigue found in political life manifested itself among the lives of England's citizens. Fifteenth-century society was worldly, restless, and the masses were growing tired of being manipulated by the Church and government. Serious outbreaks of disease continued to harass England's citizens, making death a constant and very real foe.

Childhood was the most dangerous time of life, and infant mortality continued to be high. Possibly 20 percent to 30 percent of babies died before their first year, and only about 60 percent managed to make it to their tenth birthday. If they made it to age twenty, their chances of surviving subsequent bouts of illness and disease increased dramatically.

Parents invested as much love and care in their children as do most modern-day parents. Love and affection were freely given, and manners and proper grooming habits were taught. Most youngsters' lives were devoted to play, and while they were given daily chores to perform, children didn't enter the workforce until their teen years.

Among the commoners, people didn't marry until their twenties, and not until the prospective couple had suitable employment and lodgings to occupy as man and wife. The upper classes, who didn't need to worry about money or housing, tended to marry a bit younger, with the men in their mid-twenties and the women in their late teens or early twenties.

By and large, the people were much better off than they had been in a good long time. Population size still hadn't caught up to its preplague proportions, and jobs were plentiful. With wages for both farm workers and those employed in the crafts rising faster than the prices of goods produced, the people were able to enjoy a much higher standard of living. Luxury items such as pewter candlesticks and brass pots were popular and in high demand, and people were able to afford finer clothing and better quality of food.

Better wages also led to improved housing. Peasant houses were wood-framed, wattle-and-daub dwellings, normally consisting of one to three rooms and supporting a thatched roof. The outside walls were typically whitewashed with lime to keep the rain from washing them away so quickly. Some cottages had stone walls, but as stone was a very expensive building material, these kinds of cottages were only found in places where stone was naturally plentiful.

Window openings were very small and few in number, and to help conserve heat and provide privacy, wooden shutters and modest curtains were used. The front and back doors were made of wood, and floors were typically of packed earth. One room was used for living quarters, and the other was the sleeping area for the entire family. Wealthier peasants often had an extra room used for working and meal preparation. The land on which the house was built was the toft, and in addition to the principal dwelling, outbuildings for storage or housing animals were common. Behind the toft was the croft, a small patch of land dedicated to garden use.

The wealthy continued to live in grand style. The manor halls of the Middle Ages were built to last, and the great estates continued to be handed down from generation to generation. However, new construction veered away from fortified castles and manor homes surrounded by thick walls designed to resist assault. Manor homes were becoming less compact, with larger, airier rooms. Stone was still the building material of choice, though the less wealthy commonly used brick or a superior form of wattle and daub. Floors were made of wood, and roofs were made of slate or clay tile.

Only 10 percent of the population lived in the towns and cities. They were crowded, filthy, and difficult to control. Traffic laws began to be implemented to establish some sort of control over the roads. Carts with iron-clad wheels were not allowed inside the city limits of many towns, and limits on speed were also set. One such order demanded that "no carter within the liberties shall drive his cart more quickly when it is unloaded than when it is loaded." Air quality was another concern. In 1467, one town banned the building of kilns for burning brick because the attendant fumes were fouling the air and were believed to be killing the fruit trees. In London, conditions became so bad that the residents petitioned for agricultural controls within the city. "Swannes, gees, herons, and ewes and other pultrie whereof the ordure and standing of them is of grate stenche and so evel savour that it causeth grete and parlous inffecting of the people and long hath done."

Towns were also characterized by the presence of craft guilds, merchant guilds, and the new journeyman guilds. The guilds became increasingly important throughout the fifteenth century, and the divisions separating them was greater, providing fuel for a number of open conflicts. Mystery plays and miracle plays continued to be sponsored by the guilds, and late in the fifteenth century, morality plays were included in the lineup.

Urban housing consisted of tenements that were typically three and four stories high, plus a cellar and an attic. Houses were built very closely together, and the upper floors jutted out over the street to create more space. A tradesman, craftsman, or merchant usually occupied the bottom floor so his dwelling could also be used as a shop. The upper floors were rented to laborers, and in general, the poorer the person, the higher the floor he or she occupied.

Construction was basically the same as the peasant's cottage, but walls were increasingly made of plaster-covered wooden lathes. The wealthier city dwellers used brick and sometimes stone. Roofs were slate, tile, or wood covered with lead; thatched roofs were forbidden because of the danger of fire.

Sanitation was a constant problem. Common privies were located at the back of the townhouse, and quite typically served an entire block of townhouses. Most people chose to use a chamber pot, which they then emptied along with all other sorts of trash, out a window to the street below. Official rakers had the job of raking up the rubbish and carting it off, but there was no way they could keep the problem under control.

The first English books were printed in the fifteenth century by William Caxton, inventor of the printing press. His first book was *Histories of Troy*, but he was soon printing such classics as *The Canterbury Tales* by Chaucer and *Morte d'Arthur* by Malory, as well as books on morals and manners. Another of Caxton's works, *A Description of Britain*, offers an interesting glimpse at English society as a whole. "Men of the South beeth esier and more mylde; and men of the North be more unstable, more cruel and more uneasy; the myddel men beeth some dele partners with bothe." Such works as these had a strong influence among the families wealthy enough to afford them. They also, unintentionally, created yet another social division between the rich and the poor.

RELIGION

IT WASN'T UNTIL the fifteenth century that John Wycliffe's ideas on religion began to take root within a wide section of the population and set the stage for the full-blown Reformation of the sixteenth century. The Lollards were vocal in their condemnation of wealth and advocated a return to a more pious lifestyle. They also held the belief that the bread and wine of communion retained their nature and were not physically changed into the body and blood of Christ. Seeing their beliefs as subversive, dangerous, and heretical, Henry IV signed the statute *De Heretico Comburendo* in 1401, which condemned many poor souls to martyrdom. Sir William Sautre was the first to be burned at the stake for his beliefs.

Such disgusting punishment only succeeded in further alienating people from the established Church, and demand for Wycliffe's English Bible continued to grow. Though measures were taken to confiscate and destroy all copies, over 100 managed to survive.

NAMING

THE BEGINNING OF the fifteenth century saw an increase in the use of saints' names, but as the Reformation movement gained momentum, their use suffered a decline. They continued to be popular among Catholics, but those involved in protestantism tended to use names taken from the Bible.

Male names continued to be used for females, but that trend was beginning to decline as feminine forms of the names evolved. Alexander, for instance, was passed over in favor of Alexandra, and Philip was soon to give way to Philippa.

The vernacular suffixes -*cock* and -*kin* continued to be added to pet forms of names to create names such as Malkin (from Mary), Watkin from Walter, and Wilcock from William. Rhyming forms were also popular. Rob was the obvious pet form of Robert, and from it were created names like Bob and Hob. Rich, the typical pet form of Richard, gave rise to Hitch, and from Rick (Ricard) came Dick and Hick. These names, very popular in the fifteenth century, were used primarily among the lower classes, quite typically as independent names.

FEMALE NAMES

Adela (noble) **Adele**
Adeline (little noble one) **Adelina, Edelina**
Agace (good) **Agase, Agas**
Agalia (splendor)
Agneta (chaste, pure)
Albreda (elf counsel) Not used after the fifteenth century.
Aldith (old + battle, strife)
Alexandra (defender of mankind)
Alice (noble one)
Alicia (noble one) **Alesia**
Aline (noble one) **Alina, Alyna**
Alison (noble one) **Alicen, Alisceon, Allison, Alyson**
Amicia (?, possibly a linen cloth worn by a priest) **Ameis, Amis, Amisia**
Amphelicia (?) **Amfelice, Amphelice, Amphilis, Amphillis**
Amye (beloved) **Amia**
Anastasia (resurrection) **Anastase, Anestasia**
Ankerita (free from shame)
Anne (grace, full of grace, mercy) **Ann**
Annis (chaste, pure) **Annais, Annes, Anneyce, Annys**
Annora (honor)
Annot (chaste, pure)
Arabella (?, perhaps *eagle*; *hearth*) **Arabel, Arable**
Athelina (noble one)
Audrey (noble strength) **Audrye**
Aveline (?) **Avelyn**
Avice (?) **Aves, Avis Avise**
Barbary (foreign woman)
Barbata (foreign woman) **Barbota**
Basilia (kingly) **Basilie, Basilla**
Beata (happiness)
Beatrix (bringer of joy) **Beatrice, Beatricia, Beautrice, Betrys**
Benedicta (blessed)
Bennet (blessed) **Benet, Bennitt**
Bess (God is my oath) **Bessie**
Blanch (white) **Blaunch**
Bride (strength) **Bryde**
Cassandra (?) **Cassander**
Cecilia (blind, dim-sighted) **Cecelya, Cecilie, Cecille, Cecillia**
Christian (a Christian, a follower of Christ)
Christiana (a Christian, a follower of Christ) **Christiania, Cristiane**
Christina (a Christian, a follower of Christ)
Clare (bright, clear)
Clarice (bright, clear) **Claricia**
Clemencia (clement, mild) **Clementia**
Colette (victory of the people) **Colett, Coletta, Collette**
Constance (constant)

Denise (of Dionysus) **Denis**
Dennot (of Dionysus)
Dionisia (of Dionysus) **Deonysia, Dionycia**
Diot (of Dionysus)
Dominic (belonging to a lord; belonging to the Lord) **Dominick**
Dominica (belonging to a lord; belonging to the Lord)
Dowsabel (sweet) **Dowzable, Dussabel**
Elena (light, torch, bright)
Elinor (light, torch, bright) **Elianor**
Eliza (God is my oath)
Elizabella (God is my oath)
Elizabeth (God is my oath)
Ellin (light, torch, bright) **Elin**
Ellot (light, torch, bright) **Elot**
Em (strength) **Emm**
Emblin (industrious, worker) **Imblen**
Emeline (industrious, worker)
Emilia (rival)
Emlin (industrious, worker) **Emlyn**
Emmet (rival) **Emmot**
Epham (fair of voice) **Effim, Effum**
Esther (star; myrtle)
Ethelburg (noble + fortress) **Ethelburga**
Etheldred (noble strength) **Ethelred**
Eulalia (fair of speech) **Eulalie, Ulalia**
Euphemia (fair of voice) **Eufemia, Eupheme**
Eustace (steadfast; happy harvest)
Eustacia (steadfast; happy harvest)
Eve (life)
Everild (boar + favor)
Faith (faith, complete trust)
Felice (lucky) **Fillys**
Felicity (happiness) **Phelisstie**
Florence (a blooming)
Frances (a Frank, from France) **Francesse**
Frideswid (peace + strong) **Fridiswid, Fridswed**
Gabriel (God is my strength)
Gaynore (white wave) **Ganor**
Gertrude (spear strength) **Garthrite, Gartrite, Gartrude, Gethrude**
Gillian (youth)
Goodife (God's gift)
Goodeth (God's war)
Grace (grace, mercy)
Gwenore (white wave)
Gwyneth (blessed)
Hannah (grace, full of grace, mercy)
Helen (light, torch, bright)

Helena (light, torch, bright)
Hephzibah (she is my delight) **Hepzibah, Hepsie**
Hester (star; myrtle)
Hilaria (cheerful)
Hilarie (cheerful)
Honor (honor) **Honour**
Honora (honor)
Honoria (honor)
Hope (hope, expectation)
Idonia (again) **Ideny, Idonea**
Imyne (?) **Imayne**
Isabel (God is my oath) **Esabel, Issabel**
Isylte (ruler of the ice)
Jacquetta (little Jacques *God is gracious*)
Jane (God is gracious)
Janeta (God is gracious)
Jeane (God is gracious) **Jean**
Jennet (God is gracious) **Jonet**
Joan (God is gracious) **Joane, Jone**
Judith (from Judah; he will be praised)
Julian (youth) **Jelyan, Julien**
Kate (pure, unsullied)
Katherne (pure, unsullied) **Catherne**
Kerenhappuch (horn of antimony, eyelash paint) **Keren**
Keziah (cassia)
Kinburga (royal fortress)
Kitty (pure, unsullied)
Kyneburg (royal fortress)
Laetitia (happiness) **Letitia**
Lalage (to babble)
Laurana (woman from Laurentum)
Laurencia (woman from Laurentum)
Laurentia (woman from Laurentum)
Laureola (woman from Laurentum)
Lavinia (from Latium)
Leah (weary)
Lettice (happiness) **Letice**
Lillian (lily) **Lilian**
Lora (man from Laurentum)
Loretta (man from Laurentum) **Lauretta**
Lovdie (love day)
Love (love)
Luce (light)
Lucy (light)
Mabel (lovable) **Mabile, Mabill, Mable, Mabyle**
Mabella (lovable)
Madeline (from Magdala)
Madge (a pearl)
Magdalen (from Magdala) **Magdelyn**
Magge (a pearl)
Mahala (tenderness)
Marah (bitterness)
Marcella (of Mars, warlike)
Marcia (of Mars, warlike)
Margaret (a pearl)
Margery (a pearl) **Margerye**

Margyt (a pearl) **Margat, Merget**
Marion (sea of bitterness or sorrow)
Mary (sea of bitterness or sorrow) Rarely used in Elizabeth's reign.
Maud (battle strength) **Mawde**
Maudlin (from Magdala)
Mawdelyn (from Magdala)
Meraude (of the sea) **Meroud**
Mercy (mercy, compassion)
Merkeret (a pearl)
Mildred (mild + strength)
Melicent (work + strength) **Milesent**
Minerva (?)
Moll (sea of bitterness or sorrow)
Molly (sea of bitterness or sorrow)
Monday (born on Monday)
Monica (?)
Meriall (sea bright) **Meryall**
Naomi (my joy, my delight)
Nell (light, torch, bright) **Nelly**
Nicol (victory of the people)
Olive (the olive tree) **Olyff, Olyffe**
Olympia (of Olympus)
Onora (honor)
Orabell (?) **Orable, Oriabel**
Osanna (save now, save pray)
Parnell (a rock)
Patience (patience, forebearance)
Peg (a pearl) **Peggy**
Penelope (a bobbin)
Pentecost (fiftieth [day])
Persis (Persian woman)
Petronel (a rock)
Philadelphia (brotherly love)
Philip (lover of horses) **Phil**
Phillice (green, verdant) **Philles**
Phillida (green, verdant)
Phoebe (bright, shining) **Phebe**
Pleasance (pleasant)
Precilla (former, ancient)
Prisca (former, ancient)
Prothesia (?) **Prothasey**
Prudence (prudent)
Radegund (famous counsel)
Richardyne (little ruler)
Rosamond (horse protection) **Rossamond**
Ruth (friend, companion) **Ruthe**
Sabina (Sabine woman)
Salome (peace)
Sanchia (holy) **Sanche**
Sarah (princess)
Sarey (princess)
Scholastica (scholar)
Sophia (wisdom) First used in 1607 when it was given to the youngest daughter of James I.
Susanna (lily, rose)

Susanney (lily, rose)
Sybil (fortune-teller, prophetess) **Sybell**
Sybby (fortune-teller, prophetess)
Tace (hold peace, be silent)
Tacy (hold peace, be silent)
Theodora (God's gift)
Theodosia (God-given)
Theophila (God's friend)
Thomson (little Tom *a twin*) **Tomson**
Thomasin (little Tom *a twin*) **Thamasin, Thomasing**
Tiffeny (Epiphany, manifestation of God) **Tyffany**
Troth (fidelity, good faith)
Tryphena (delicate, dainty)

Tryphosa (delicate, dainty)
Ursalay (she-bear) **Urseley**
Valentine (strong, healthy)
Venetia (blessed)
Violet (violet-colored)
Vivien (alive)
Wannore (white wave) **Wannour**
Winfrith (white wave)
Wynifreed (white wave) **Winefred**
Yolande (?, possibly *violet*)
Zelina (heaven)
Zenobia (the life of Zeus) Restricted mainly to Cornwall.
Zillah (shade) A favorite gypsy name.

MALE NAMES

Aaron (the exalted one)
Abel (breath)
Abraham (father of a multitude)
Absalom (father of peace) **Absalon**
Acelin (tribe of the Gauts) **Ascelyn, Asselin**
Adam (man of the red earth)
Adelard (noble and hard)
Adrian (man from Hadrianus)
Alan (?, perhaps *handsome, rock*) **Aleyne**
Alard (noble and hard) **Alart**
Alaric (noble ruler)
Alban (from Alba)
Aldus (old)
Aldred (old counsel)
Aldwin (old friend)
Alexander (defender of mankind) **Sander**
Alfred (elf counsel)
Algar (elf spear) **Alger**
Algernon (mustached)
Alvery (elf counsel; wise counselor)
Ambrose (immortal)
Amias (?, perhaps friendship)
Amos (borne, a burden)
Andrew (manly) **Dande**
Angel (a messenger of God)
Anselm (God's helmet)
Antony (?, *priceless; of inestimable worth* is a folk definition)
Archibald (genuinely brave, genuinely bold)
Arnold (eagle power) **Ernald**
Arthur (?)
Athelstan (noble stone) **Athestan**
Aubrey (elf ruler) **Aubri**
Austin (great, venerable)
Aylmer (nobly famous)
Aylwin (elf friend)
Baldric (bold ruler)
Baldwin (bold friend)
Bardolph (bright wolf)

Barnabas (son of exhortation)
Bartholomew (son of Talmai *hill, mound, furrows*)
Basil (kingly)
Bertin (bright friend)**Bette**
Christopher (bearing Christ)
Clemens (gentle, mild)
Constantine (constant, steadfast) **Constans, Cuss, Cust**
Crispin (curled)
Damian (tamer)
Daniel (judged by God)
David (beloved)
Dominic (belonging to a lord; belonging to the Lord) **Dominik**
Drogo (to carry, a burden)
Durand (enduring, lasting) **Durant**
Edgar (wealthy spear)
Edmond (wealthy protection)
Edward (wealthy guardian)
Edwin (wealthy friend)
Eustace (steadfast; happy in harvest)
Florence (blooming)
Florian (flowery)
Francis (a Frank, a freeman)
Gabriel (God is strength)
Gaston (?, possibly *guest, stranger; from Gascony*)
Gawyne (battle hawk) **Gawyn**
Geoffrey (district, traveler, pledge + peace) **Geffrey**
George (earth worker, farmer)
Gerald (spear rule)
Gervais (servant of the spear) **Gervas, Gervase, Jarvis**
Giffard (give + bold, fierce)
Gilbert (bright pledge) **Gib, Gil**
Giles (goatskin shield of Zeus; a protection)
Godfrey (God's peace)
Godric (powerful God)
Godwin (friend of God)
Gregory (vigilant, watchful)
Griffin (like a griffin, monstrous)
Gunther (bold in war)

Guy (a guide, leader)
Hardwin (hard friend)
Harold (power of the army)
Hector (holding fast)
Henry (home ruler)
Herbert (army bright)
Hereward (army guard)
Herman (warrior, soldier)
Hilary (cheerful)
Hubert (bright heart) **Hubard**
Hugh (heart, mind, soul) **Hugo**
Ives (archer) **Ivo, Yvo**
Jacob (supplanting, seizing by the heels)
James (supplanting, seizing by the heels)
Jeremiah (God will uplift) **Jeremy**
Joachim (God will establish) **Joachin**
John (God is gracious)
Jonas (dove)
Jordan (a flowing down) **Judd, Jurd**
Joseph (he shall add)
Julian (youth, downy)
Kenrick (royal rule)
Kenward (brave guardian) **Kenard**
Lambert (bright land)
Lancelot (?, perhaps *little land*)
Laurance (from Laurentum)
Leonard (bold as a lion)
Lewis (famous in war)
Lionel (little lion)
Lovell (wolf)
Luke (light; man from Loukania)
Manfred (peace of man)
Martin (of Mars, warlike)
Matheu (gift of God) **Mathiu, Mattheu**
Maynard (strong and hardy)
Michael (Who is like God?)
Milo (?, perhaps *mild, peaceful; merciful*) **Milon**
Nicholas (victory of the people) **Nicoll, Nichol, Coll**
Odo (wealth)
Osbern (God bear) **Osborn**
Oscar (God's spear)

Osmond (God's protection) **Osmund**
Oswald (God's power)
Oswin (friend of God)
Paulin (small)
Pernel (a rock, a stone) **Pennel**
Peter (a rock, a stone)
Philip (lover of horses) **Fippe**
Piers (a rock, a stone)
Quintin (fifth)
Ralph (counsel wolf)
Randulf (shield wolf)
Raymund (counsel protection) **Raimund, Reimond**
Raynold (powerful protection) **Rainald, Raynald, Renold, Reynold**
Reginald (judgment power)
Renfred (counsel might)
Reynard (counsel hard)
Richard (stern king)
Robert (bright with fame) **Dob, Dobbe, Hob, Hobbe, Nabbe, Rob, Robb**
Roger (famous with the spear)
Roland (famous land) **Rolland**
Rolf (famous wolf) **Rolft, Roulf**
Samson (the sun) **Sansom**
Saunder (defender of mankind) **Saundre**
Simon (heard) **Simond, Symon**
Siward (victory protection)
Stephen (a crown, a garland)
Talbot (pillager, bandit; lampblack)
Theobald (bold people)
Theodoric (ruler of the people)
Thomas (a twin)
Thurstan (Thor's stone)
Tobias (God is good)
Tristram (tumult, sadness)
Ulric (wolf rule)
Urban (villager)
Valentine (healthy, strong)
Vincent (conquering)
Walter (ruler of an army)
William (resolute protector)

SURNAMES

Surnames during this time period were not always hereditary, nor were they permanent. Additionally, it appears that many surnames were used as identifiers for official purposes, rather than a personal badge of identity. During the first half of the fifteenth century, about 25 percent of the people had an occupational surname, 27 percent had a surname based on locality, 17 percent were genealogical, 6 percent were based on personal characteristics, and 25 percent were unclassified. Only about 2 percent of the names used a Latin or French preposition, and even less used an English one.

The second half of the fifteenth century was very similar, but names based on occupation and personal characteristics dropped a bit. Henry VII encouraged immigration, and a large number of foreigners from all walks of life added their names to the English.

Acheson (son of Ache, Aeche *sword*)
Acres (dweller at the acre)
Adinot (little Adam *man of the red earth*)
Agas (good)
Aitkane (little Adam *man of the red earth*)
Akerman (a farmer or ploughman)
Alardson (son of Alard *nobly brave*)
Alaway (noble war; old war)
Albin (white) **Albyn**
Albryght (nobly bright)
Aldhous (old house)
Almaund (German)
Alwins (son of Alwin *elf friend*)
Anjou (from Anjou)
Armstrong (strong arms) **Armstrang**
Atwater (dweller by the water)
Bacheler (young knight, novice in arms)
Bacon (side of bacon) **Bakon**
Baker (a baker)
Ball (ball; bald place; the round one)
Barber (a barber, one who practiced surgery and dentistry) **Barbur**
Barnelby (son of consolation)
Baron (a baron, a nobleman)
Base (short, of small height)
Beald (the bald; the bold)
Beau (the fair)
Bellson (son of Bele)
Belle (the beautiful)
Berenger (bear spear)
Bertelot (little Bartholomew *son of Talmai*)
Bertran (bright raven)
Berwyk (dweller at an outlying hall or grange)
Birche (dweller by the birch trees)
Black (the black)
Blanchard (whitish)
Boda (the messenger) **Bode**
Bonnefey (good fate)
Bosco (dweller by the woods)
Botte (butt; toad)
Bounde (husbandman, peasant)
Bouvier (cattle drover)
Bowyer (a maker or trader of bows)
Brian (force, strength; valor; high; kingly)
Broke (of the brook)
Brune (the brown) **Brun**
Bruse (from Brus *brushwood thicket*)
Bully (from the bull's enclosure)
Burgeis (a freeman of a borough)
Buxton (Bucca's stone)
Cade (the short, fat person)
Candeles (a maker or seller of candles) **Candel**
Castello (castle)

Champagne (from Champagne *field*) **Champayn**
Chanteloup (from Chanteloup *singing wolves*)
Chartres (from Chartres)
Chaucer (maker of leather pants)
Cild (the child)
del Clee (dweller by the river fork, dweller by the fork in a road)
Cokes (a cook, a seller of cooked meats)
Cola (the dark one)
Colleville (from Colleville *Col's estate*)
Colt (a colt; frisky, lively)
Colyer (a maker or seller of charcoal)
Corbet (the raven)
Cornish (a Cornish person)
Coucy (from Coucy)
Courtenay (from Courtenay *Courtenay's homestead*)
Cyppe (the fat one)
Danvers (from Anvers)
Darnel (the darnel plant; from Darnall) **Darnell**
Dentune (of Dentune)
Derwin (dear friend)
Drinkwater (one who drinks water) The name implies one so poor as to not to be able to afford ale, the most common drink.
Dubois (dweller in the woods)
Duchesman (a Dutchman)
Dudding (son of Dudda)
Dunn (brown-haired)
Duns (brown-haired)
Durand (enduring, lasting) **Durant**
Dych (dweller near the dike)
Eadricssun (son of Eadric *wealthy ruler*)
Eadwinesbroder (brother of Eadwine *wealthy friend*)
Ealda (the old one)
Edmundson (son of Edmund *wealthy protector*)
Ellis (Jehovah is God; God is salvation)
Ellyson (son of Ellis *Jehovah is God; God is salvation*)
Emson (son of Emma *strength*)
Ewen (lamb; youth; well-born)
Fabre (a smith)
Fauchet (crooked legs)
del Fernyside (from the ferny slope)
Florence (from Florence)
Florantyn (a Florentine)
Fleming (a Fleming) **Flymng**
Fort (strong)
Frenssh (a French person)
Geonga (the young)
Giffard (chubby-cheeked)
Gilbert (bright pledge)
Glanville (from Glanville *oak tree estate*)
Glasier (a glass maker)
Golding (son of Golda *gold*)

Goldsmith (a goldsmith)
Goodyer (good year) **Godeyere, Godier, Goudyer**
le Grand (the tall, the large)
Graunt (great, large)
Grene (dweller near the village green)
Gronne (the large)
le Gros (the fat)
Grymbaud (helmet bold)
Hales (dweller in the remote valley) **Hale**
Hankyn (little Hans)
Harald (ruler of the army)
de Harcourt (from Harcourt *army house*)
Hattere (maker or seller of hats) **Hatter**
Hawthorn (dweller near the hawthorn) **Hawthorne**
Hayward (guardian of the fence or hedge)
Heaha (the tall)
Heath (of the heath)
Hirde (a herdsman)
Howard (brave heart; chief warden; ewe herder) **Heward, Huward**
Hughlot (little Hugh)
de Hulle (dweller near the hill)
Ingram (Ing's raven; angel raven)
Irish (an Irish person) **Iryssh**
Irishman (an Irishman) **Irissheman**
Irishwoman (an Irishwoman)
Ives (archer)
Jagger (carter, peddler; God is gracious)
Jago (supplanting, seizing by the heels)
Jakeson (son of Jack *God is gracious)*
Jenour (engineer) **Jenoure**
le Jeune (the young)
Johnson (son of John *God is gracious)*
Jourdan (a flowing down, descend) **Jurdain**
Kaer (fort)
Keate (dweller at the animal hut) **Keat, Keates, Keats**
Kendrick (chief man, chief hero)
Kenwrek (famous king)
King (a king) **Kinge**
Kingesson (son of the king)
Knolles (dweller at the top of the hill) **Knoll**
Knyght (servant, knight)
de Laci (from Laci *Latius' estate)*
Lambert (bright land) **Lambard, Lambart, Lambarth**
Lamburnan (from Lamburnan)
Larcher (the archer)
Latimer (interpreter)
Lawless (an outlaw, licentious) **Lawelesse**
Legge (leg)
Lighfot (light foot)
Lokke (a lock of hair)
Lombard (long beard) **Lumbard**
de Lorris (from Lorris)
Lovett (little wolf)
Lundene (from Lundene)
Macey (from Maci *Matheus' estate)*

Maggesone (son of Magge *a pearl)*
Mailer (an enameler) **Mailler**
Maitland (discourteous, rude)
Malet (the unfortunate one, cursed)
Malleville (from Malleville)
Mallory (the unfortunate one, cursed)
Mann (the servant)
Mannyng (the servant)
Marchant (a merchant, a trader) **Marchand**
Marle (blackbird)
Matthews (son of Matthew *gift of God)*
de Meran (from Meran)
Merton (from the place by the lake)
Molendino (dweller by the mill)
de Montfort (from Montfort *fortified hill)*
Naismith (a knife smith) **Naysmith**
Nesbitt (from Nesbit of Nesbitt) **Naisbet, Naisbit, Nesbit**
Newman (a newcomer)
Nicoles (victory of the people) **Nicholls, Nichols**
Norman (a Norman, from Normandy)
Oaks (dweller near the oak trees) **Oak, Oake**
Oldfield (dweller by the old field)
Orchard (dweller near or worker at an orchard)
Osman (god-bear) **Osmand**
Oxnard (an ox herder)
Pariz (from Paris) **Parys**
Peck (a peck; a maker or seller of pecks)
de Perci (from Perci *destroyer of cities)*
Pikard (one from Picardy)
Plymouth (from Plymouth)
de Poitiers (from Poitiers)
de Ponte (dweller by the bridge)
Poore (pauper)
Porter (a porter, a doorkeeper, a carrier of burdens)
Prendregast (?, perhaps *dweller at the village near the castle)*
Provence (from Provence)
Putte (dweller by the pit)
Reada (the red)
Rede (red, ruddy-complexioned)
Rees (ardor)
Robe (bright with fame)
Rochefort (from Rochefort *fortified rock)*
Roke (at the oak; dweller by the rock)
Rolfeson (son of Rolf *counsel wolf)*
Russel (red-haired) **Russell**
Sadeler (a maker or seller of saddles) **Sadelier**
Sheparde (shepherd) **Shepard, Shepperde**
Simple (the simple-minded)
Skynner (the skinner)
Smalle (the small)
Stevenes (son of Steven *a crown, garland)*
Stoke (from Stoke)
Stolemaker (a maker or seller of stoles)
Sutton (from Sutton)
Swan (the swineherd)
Swift (the swift)

Tabard (a sleeveless coat)
Taillour (a tailor)
Tait (cheerful, gay)
Talbot (pillager, bandit; lampblack)
Thwayt (dweller at the forest clearing)
Tillet (dweller near the lime trees)
de Tilly (from the lime tree grove)
Tirel (Thor rule)
Tomlin (little Tom *a twin*)
Trane (trickery; a trap)
Trumble (strong-bold) **Trumbull**
Tysson (son of Ty *firebrand*)
Ullman (maker or seller of oil)
Underhill (dweller at the foot of a hill)
Unwin (young bear-friend)
Uppington (dweller up in the village)
Urban (dweller in the city)
Vale (dweller in the valley)
Valentine (strong, healthy)
Vaughan (small) **Vaughn**

Venables (from Venables *vineyard*)
Vennell (dweller at the small street or alley) **Vennall, Venel**
la Verrere (a glazier)
Vidal (vital, full of vitality) **Vidall**
Walsh (a Welsh person)
Walshman (a Welsh man)
Walworth (from the Welshman's farm)
de Warenne (from Warenne)
Warner (the warrener, a game warren) **Warneres**
de Warre (of the war, a warrior)
Wasket (the little Gascon)
Waters (at the water)
Webber (a weaver)
le Werre (the warrior)
White (white, fair-complexioned)
Williams (son of William *resolute protector*)
Woode (dweller in the wood)
Wylaston (from the village of Willa *resolute*)
Yungwin (young friend)
Zate (of the gate)

Chapter Five

THE REFORMATION
HENRY VIII TO ELIZABETH I
[1509–1603]

POLITICS

Henry VIII was seventeen when he ascended the throne. He was tall, handsome, and athletic, with an engaging personality that helped bring an air of vitality to his court that was in sharp contrast to the soberness of his father's court. Henry was also a Renaissance scholar who was determined to promote the arts and humanities. Yet the things we remember most about Henry VIII are his many marriages and the repulsive way he got rid of his unwanted wives. It was to that end that Henry severed his relationship with the Catholic Church and put the Reform movement into high gear.

In order to preserve England's alliance with Spain, Henry had been betrothed at the age of twelve to Catherine of Aragon, the widow of his brother, Arthur. Though Catherine was now twenty-three, she was still beautiful and graceful, and Henry found it easy to fulfill his father's dying wish to see the marriage through. In 1511, Catherine gave birth to a son, but to Henry's great despair, the infant lived just six short weeks. Following a series of miscarriages, Catherine gave birth to daughter Mary; after three years, it became clear she would have no more children.

In 1519, Henry VIII, Charles of Spain, and Francis I of France put themselves forward as candidates for Emperor of the Holy Roman Empire. Henry, the oldest and most experienced of the candidates, was passed over in favor of Charles V. Therein began a rivalry among the three rulers that dominated European politics for the next thirty years.

Henry's lord chancellor, Thomas Wolsey, organized the Field of Cloth of Gold, a giant fair and sporting event he hoped would bring peace to Europe and introduce the rebirth of chivalry. The event, spanning four weeks in the summer of 1520, succeeded as far as the games went, but the heads of state continued to regard one another with distrust. After the death of Pope Leo X, Henry campaigned hard for Thomas Wolsey's election, but Adrian of Utrecht won the bid. Adrian soon died, and Henry again tried and failed to see Wolsey elected.

By this time, Henry was so eager to sire a legitimate son that he was desperately seeking a way out of his marriage to Catherine. He began to believe that since he married his dead brother's wife, the marriage was against God's law. The more he thought about it, the more convinced he was that he was right. In 1527, Henry demanded that Wolsey use his influence with Rome to declare his marriage invalid so that he might marry Anne Boleyn.

That same year, Rome was sacked by imperialist troops and Pope Clement VII became a puppet of Emperor Charles V. Since Catherine was Charles' aunt, the Pope refused to annul Henry's marriage. Henry was furious. He decided a break from the Church was the only way he'd ever be rid of his wife.

In November 1530, Henry repaid Wolsey's failure in obtaining a divorce by having him arrested for treason; he died en route to London. After the Reformation, Parliament made Henry Pope of the English Church, Archbishop Cranmer declared the king's marriage to Catherine invalid and allowed him to marry the already pregnant Anne Boleyn in January 1533.

Catherine was to live out the rest of her life in the country in less than splendid surroundings with only a tiny household to assist her. Yet that was far better than the fate that befell the king's other wives. Catherine remained true to the Catholic faith and instilled the same love for the Church in her daughter, Mary. Henry celebrated her death in 1536 by dressing entirely in yellow.

When Anne gave birth to Elizabeth, Henry was less than pleased. He had been praying for a legitimate son, not another daughter. To take his mind off his family, he took personal interest in proposed legislation to modernize government and secure his position as head of both Church and state by parliamentary ratification.

Anne's downfall came with the news that Henry had been seriously injured in a riding accident. According to the Duke of Norfolk, who brought her the news, she underwent such a great shock as to miscarry a male child. Henry was furious and saw to some fairly diabolical dealings to procure yet another divorce. A lutist for the court admitted on the rack to adultery with Anne. Four other men were also implicated, including the queen's own brother, Lord Rochford. All five men and Anne were tried and found guilty. Queen Anne was executed in May 1536 on the same day that Archbishop Cranmer granted Henry's request to marry Jane Seymour.

Though Jane's coronation never took place due to an outbreak of the plague, she managed to do what all Henry's other wives could not: She produced a healthy male child. In October 1537, she brought Edward, the Prince of Wales, into the world. Unfortunately, Jane died of fever shortly thereafter, and Henry honored her by having her buried in Saint George's Chapel. Upon Henry's death, his coffin was ordered to rest next to hers.

In Europe, meanwhile, Francis I and Charles V signed a ten-year treaty of peace. Henry, whose religious reforms were now progressing more rapidly, began to fear the monarchs would join forces in support of the Pope and invade England. His search for Protestant alliances coincided with his search for another wife, and upon seeing a flattering portrait of Anne of Cleves, decided a match with her would be both politically and personally successful. The marriage was arranged without Henry ever actually seeing his intended. He paid for that oversight, for Anne was the very antithesis of beauty, spoke no English, and had no redeeming talents. The marriage was never consummated and Henry secured another divorce.

His next match was with the beautiful Catherine Howard, niece of the Duke of Norfolk. To her misfortune, she continued her affairs with at least two other lovers and was summarily executed in February 1542. A year later, Henry married educated and twice-widowed Catherine Parr. She took it upon herself to make a warm home for the king and persuaded him to unite his family by bringing his children to court where she could see to their welfare and education. Mary was twenty-one, Elizabeth was ten, and Prince Edward just six; until this time, they lived apart from one another and had almost no contact with their father.

Henry VIII died at the close of January 1547, leaving instructions for a balanced Council of Regents to take over the reins of government until Edward VI came of age. His well-laid plans came to naught. Shortly after his death, Edward's uncle, Edward Seymour, took control and overturned the Council of Regents to make himself Protector of the Realm and sole guardian of his nephew. Edward was at first but a puppet king, and Seymour was able to follow his own agenda. Though successful in the area of religious reform, he failed in the area of the economy. Prices had been rising steadily since the turn of the century, and there was large-scale unemployment in the countryside. Several agrarian revolts illustrated how dire circumstances were becoming.

Seymour was sent to the Tower for mismanaging the economy and was replaced by the duke of Northumberland, a man who used his considerable power and influence to further Protestant religious reforms. In 1552, Edward suffered bouts of measles and smallpox. Once it became apparent that the king was in seriously failing health, Northumberland began to fear the succession of Mary, a devout Catholic. In a desperate gamble to retain a Protestant on the throne, he persuaded the dying Edward to name his cousin, Lady Jane Grey, great-granddaughter of Henry VII, as his heir. In July 1553, sixteen-year-old Edward died of consumption.

When Mary heard of Edward's death, she notified the council that she would be accepting the crown. After receiving word that they had already accepted Lady Jane Grey, Mary gathered together a number of supporters and sought help from those with Protestant leanings by promising not to alter any of the religious laws set forth during the reign of Edward VI. A month later, Mary had succeeded in taking control of the crown. Lady Jane Grey, her husband Guildford Dudley, and the duke of Northumberland were immediately taken to the Tower.

The accession of thirty-seven-year-old Mary was welcomed by Englishmen who believed Northumberland and the late king had gone too far in their promotion of Protestantism. They soon had cause for regrets as the first eight months of Mary's reign brought many changes that were far from popular. In spite of her promises, Mary quickly undid the religious reforms of Edward's reign and commanded that every Englishman become Catholic. She also banished all foreigners from English soil, banned printing, banned the use of

English in the Church, forcibly divorced clergymen from their wives, and had many Protestant leaders executed. She replaced the higher clergy, had more than two dozen of England's most prominent men imprisoned in the Tower, and released those who were placed there during the previous reign. The much-feared Stephen Gardiner, a major proponent of the burning of heretics, was released and made Bishop of Winchester and Lord Chancellor of England. The depraved Stephen Bonner, another who took special delight in the burnings, was made Bishop of London.

Mary was secretly assisted in her search for a husband by French ambassador, Simon Renard. Together they narrowed a list of potential bridegrooms down to Philip II of Spain. Not only was he Catholic, he was handsome and Spanish as well, a definite plus for the half-Spanish Mary. Once her marriage plans became known, fears that a Spanish king would lead to the loss of national independence culminated in a revolt early in 1554. The leader of the rebellion, Sir Thomas Wyatt, was executed for his role in the uprising, as were the luckless Lady Jane Grey and her husband, Guildford Dudley. Mary was convinced her sister Elizabeth was involved in the plot and had her taken to the Tower. When no evidence could be found to incriminate her, she was put under house arrest at Woodstock Palace.

Mary and Philip were married in July 1554. Several months later, Mary returned to London convinced she was with child. Unfortunately, she had mistaken the symptoms of dropsy with those of pregnancy. Philip's duties kept him away from England and Mary, and parliament, fearful of the strength of the Spanish Empire, refused to crown him king of England.

By 1557, England was siding with Spain in war against France. In spite of the strength of both countries, England lost Calais in January 1558. This was the greatest national disaster since the loss of English possessions in the Hundred Years' War. The people were devastated and blamed Mary not only for the loss but for the loss of national prestige and pride as well.

Mary's illness progressively worsened, and she brought Elizabeth to Hatfield where they managed somewhat of a reconciliation. When Mary died in November 1558, her heart and bowels were interned in the Chapel Royal at Saint James Cathedral and her body at Westminster Abbey. Much symbolism can be found in this separation, as Mary was half English and half Spanish and had never really understood her English countrymen nor her mother's people.

Elizabeth, on the other hand, knew exactly how to lead her people. She saw the mending of the English spirit as her first duty and believed that religious accord would do much to further that end. Determined to avoid the extremes of her brother and sister, Elizabeth opted instead for middle ground she hoped would be less offensive to both Catholics and Protestants. She had herself declared Supreme Governor of the Church, abolished the supremacy of the Pope, and repealed the religious statutes imposed under Mary. Though the extremists on either side were not satisfied, Elizabeth succeeded in taking a great deal of emphasis off religion and ushered in an era of more happiness and contentment than had been seen in a long while.

Elizabeth had a number of problems with foreign affairs, and many of them stemmed from her cousin, Mary of Scotland. Mary, a great-granddaughter of Henry VII and the wife of Francis II of France, sought to claim the throne of England. When England made an alliance with Scotland's Protestant Lords of the Congregation and assisted them in expelling the French, the lords acknowledged Elizabeth's right to the throne and demanded Mary relinquish her claim. After Francis II died, Mary returned to Scotland to find the religious and political situation untenable. She found supporters in disaffected Catholics and thus began a rivalry with Elizabeth that was to end with her execution in 1587.

England's crisis with Spain was due largely to the marauding and buccaneering taking place among Spain's possessions in the New World. Secretly backed by the government, English ships overtook Spanish galleons and relieved them of their treasures. In response, the Spanish Armada sailed for the channel to invade England. Against the judgment of her councillors, Elizabeth personally went to meet her troops on the coast and exhorted them to victory. Under the leadership of Sir Francis Drake, the Armada was scattered, and England was victorious.

Elizabeth, the last of the Tudors, died in 1603 at the age of sixty-nine, never having named a successor to follow her. She had presided over an elegant court and actively promoted literature and exploration, and except for the Irish, she also promoted religious tolerance. In her last speech to parliament in 1601, she addressed her role as monarch by saying that though being queen was a glorious thing, she found the greatest joy in the love and loyalty of her subjects. "There will never Queen sit in my seat with more zeal to my country. And though you have had, and may have, many Princes more mighty and wise sitting in this seat, yet you never had, or shall have, any that will be more careful and loving."

SOCIETY

THIS WAS AN age when violence, intrigue, and betrayal were everyday occurrences, and such behavior was bound to leave its effect on people. It is interesting to note the strange contradictions in character of the leading people of the times. Edward IV's former constable, John Tiptoft, Earl of Worcester, is a good example. A widely traveled humanist scholar, he introduced, with Edward's approval, the practice of impalement for traitors, earning the nickname "the butcher of England." Richard III, a loving and faithful father and husband, had the little princes killed; Henry VII executed young Warwick for no reason other than his Yorkist blood; and Henry VIII, a true Renaissance man, grew up with a coarse side to him adequately illustrated by the way in which he disposed of his wives.

Perhaps people were tiring of the strictly structured society and the calloused attitudes toward life that were so prevalent, for significant social changes began occurring throughout Europe. Feudalism was supplanted by capitalism, and the Renaissance movement that had started in Italy in the beginning of the fourteenth century was soon spreading across the Continent. English students flocked to Italy to study in the relaxed, intellectual climates of Milan, Florence, and Rome. Upon returning home, they shared their new ideas and experiences, and the seeds for change began to germinate.

The Renaissance experienced in England, however, was quite different from that of Italy, which was strongly affected by Saracen and Byzantine influences, as well as its own classical traditions. The northern Europeans tended to view life from more of a religious and moral angle, and their Renaissance movement reflected that. It was more of a philosophical and literary movement as opposed to the artistic and intellectual movement the Italians enjoyed.

England's Renaissance scholars were primarily interested in a more relaxed attitude toward religion, an enlightened attitude toward education, and more civilized behavior in society. Sir Thomas More eloquently described his idea of a perfect society in his *Utopia*, Sir Francis Bacon touted the benefits of inductive reasoning, and great playwrights such as Christopher Marlowe, Beaumont and Fletcher, and William Shakespeare described the lust for fullness of life that was characteristic of the time.

Cities continued to be crowded and dirty but were relatively few in number. London was the largest, with a population of 120,000 by the time Elizabeth took the throne and 200,000 when she died. Bristol, Norwich, and York were the other large towns with populations numbering between 10,000 and 25,000. Most people lived in villages with less than 500 inhabitants.

The homes of the lower classes had changed little from the preceeding time period. They continued to be small, wood-framed, wattle-and-daub constructions with thatched roofs, packed dirt floors, and tiny, shuttered windows having panes of thin horn or oiled linen. Those who were a little better off sometimes added wooden floors and chimneys and glass-paned windows. The land on which the peasant cottage was built continued to be known as the croft, and outbuildings to house the animals and store tools, a dairy, and perhaps another small building to serve as a brewhouse or a kitchen were common.

Housing in the cities was also much like that in the previous time period. Multistoried, timber and plaster-walled tenements continued to be the most common type of dwelling for the masses; the wealthy built much finer single-family homes of brick or stone.

RELIGION

EUROPE WAS UNDERGOING rapid change during this time, both religiously and politically. With the Renaissance came the popularity of humanism, which led many to question man's purpose in nature and consequently, the authority of the Church to rule over all. In Germany, Luther launched his Protestant Reformation and Henry wrote a tract against him, *The Defence of the Seven Sacraments*, that championed the Church and explained the validity of the sacraments. Henry dedicated his best-selling book to Pope Leo X and let all know that he was ready to defend the Church by force and by ''the resources of his mind.'' Henry never originally planned on changing the Church, he merely wanted to bring it under his own authority. Mass continued to be spoken in Latin and the Catholic Act of Six Articles, which championed Catholic beliefs and allowed for severe penalties to nonbelievers, was passed in 1539.

The most significant changes occurred during the reign of Henry's son, Edward VI, who was almost fanatically Protestant. Soon after his coronation, the Catholic Act of Six Articles and all other acts of parliament and statutes regarding religion were abolished. In 1549, the English Prayer Book was issued, which allowed people to use the common language in church instead of Latin. Under Edward's reign, the Church of England became a fully Protestant church, but it would soon change again.

After Edward's death, the devoutly Catholic Mary came to the throne and set about undoing Protestant reforms to bring the Church back into the Catholic fold. Part of her motivation was loyalty toward the Church, but she also believed her marital problems were God's way of punishing her for supposed heresies practiced in England during the reigns of her father and brother. The anti-Lollard statute, *De Heretico Comburendo*, was reinstated, and in 1555, the Marian persecution of Protestants began. Nearly 300 people were burned at the stake and countless others died in prison or died prematurely as their health was broken from various tortures and exactions. Scourging became a common way of exacting punishment. In the house of Bishop Bonner, a child of eight was scourged to death. Indeed, many children died after their parents and protectors were taken from them in the persecution.

Elizabeth opted for a middle ground to bring about religious accord. She brought the Church under crown control again and repealed *De Heretico Comburendo* and other religious statutes imposed under Mary, yet retained much of the pomp and ceremony of a Catholic mass. Saints' days were reduced but not eliminated, and Church administration remained much as it had under the Catholic Church.

Through most of her reign, Elizabeth chose not to make religion a big issue, but in the spirit of uniformity, she required people to attend church every Sunday; those choosing not to worship in the Church of England were subject to a fine. In addition, public officials were required to take the Oath of Supremacy, by which the swearer upheld Elizabeth's role as supreme head of the Church.

Her attitude changed in 1570 after the Pope issued a decree deposing her from the crown. She began to execute those who supported the Pope and his policies; Jesuit missionaries were horribly tortured and executed if caught.

Not everyone was satisfied with Elizabeth's church. About 5 percent of the population remained Catholic, and many of the Protestant reformers felt the Church of England didn't go far enough in breaking from Catholic tradition. They began to form independent congregations, and Elizabeth saw such separatism as a significant threat to her authority. Like the Catholics, nonconformists were ruthlessly suppressed.

People continued to believe in magic. They were very superstitious, and fortune-tellers and others with supernatural gifts were actively sought out, as people believed their lives might be helped by special potions and magical charms. There was a very dark and dangerous side to this, however. While magic was accepted, witches were not. Accusations of witchcraft reached a peak in the last twenty years of the sixteenth century, and the common form of punishment for those convicted was death.

NAMING

THE REFORMATION HAD the greatest effect on names in England since Norman Conquest. Until now, the pool of first names was small. In fact, it was common to give the same name to more than one child. To make up for the dearth, pet forms of names came into widespread use. The -cock and -kin forms of names became rare after 1450, but shortened forms, like Will from William, Rob from Robert, Barb from Barbara, and Cath from Catherine were popular. Feminine pet names like Emmot, Philpot, Marriot, and Wilmot continued to be used through the sixteenth and seventeenth centuries.

Christian names were generally confined to the few made popular through the mystery and miracle plays, such as Abraham, Adam, Daniel, David, Jacob, and Joseph for the men, and Anna, Eve, Elizabeth, Hannah, Hester, Judith, Mary, and Sarah for the women. The remainder of the names were usually saints' names, like Basil, Blase, Crispin, Agnes, Agnetha, Barbara, Katherine, and Margaret. As discontent with the Catholic Church became more widespread, the saints' names fell from favor and were replaced by other scriptural names that became known when the Bible was made available to the masses.

The Puritans gave their children names that were a bit out of the ordinary. At first they tended toward Latin names that described virtues or godly characteristics, such as Amor, Beata, Desideratus. Later, English forms of such names as Love, Given, Grace, and Mercy came into use. A few Puritan parents even went so far as to give their children names such as Fear-not, Renewed, Safe-on-high, Dust, Ashes, Sin-denie, and Acceptance. Even whole scriptures were bestowed upon innocent babes. The most prolific time of Puritan nomenclature was between the years of 1580 to 1640. C. W. Bardsley gives an interesting and amusing look at the subject in his *Curiosities of Puritan Nomenclature*.

The same three female names held top billing for 200 years: Elizabeth, Mary, and Anne. Over 50 percent of the female population were the bearers of those names, with Elizabeth being the most popular. The same was true for men. William, John, and Thomas were the names given to more than half the males in England, with William topping the popularity poll.

FEMALE NAMES

Abigail (father of exaltation) **Abbey**
Abijah (the Lord is father)
Abishag (wise)
Adah (adornment)
Adele (noble) **Adela**
Adelin (nobility)

Agalia (splendor)
Agatha (good)
Agnes (chaste, pure)
Alexandra (defender of mankind)
Alice (noble one) **Alys**
Aline (noble)

Alison (noble one)
Amana (established)
Amata (love)
Amisia (?, possibly *friendship*) **Ameis**
Amphelicia (?) **Amfelice, Amphelice, Amphillis**
Amy (beloved)
Anastase (resurrection)
Ankerita (undisgraced, free from shame) Anglicized form of the Welsh Angharad.
Andrea (womanly)
Anne (grace, full of grace, mercy) **Ann, Anna**
Annis (chaste, pure) **Annes, Annys**
Antigone (of contrary birth)
Apeline(pertaining to Apollo)
Aphrah (dust) **Aphra**
Apphia (increasing)
Arabella (?, perhapse *eagle*; *hearth*) **Arabel, Arable**
Asenath (?, perhaps *thornbush*)
Atarah (crown)
Athalia (the Lord is exalted)
Audrey (noble strength)
Averil (boar battle) **Averell, Everild**
Avice (?) **Avis, Avise**
Azubah (forsaken)
Barbara (foreign woman)
Bathsheba (daughter of the oath, daughter of Sheba)
Bathshua (daughter of riches, daughter of Shua)
Beata (happy)
Beatrice (bringer of joy) **Bettrice**
Benedicta (blessed)
Benet (blessed) **Bennet**
Berenice (bringer of victory)
Bertha (bright)
Bess (God is my oath) **Bessie**
Beth (God is my oath)
Beulah (married)
Bilhah (bashful, faltering)
Bithiah (daughter of Jehovah)
Blanch (white)
Brilliana Coinage of Sir Edward Conway based on Brill, Holland.
Cassandra (?)
Cicely (blind, dim-sighted) **Cecily, Cycly, Sisley**
Charity (charity, benevolence)
Chloe (blooming, verdant)
Christabel (?, probably *beautiful Christ*) **Christabell**
Christiana (a Christian, a follower of Christ)
Christine (a Christian, a follower of Christ)
Christmas (born at Christmastime)
Chrysogon (golden birth)
Clare (bright, clear, famous)
Clarice (bright, clear, famous) **Claricia**
Claudia (lame)
Clemence (clement, mild)
Clemency (clement, mild) **Clemencia**
Comfort (comfort, care)

Constancy (constant) **Constance, Custance**
Cynthia (of Kynthos)
Damaris (?, possibly *heifer*)
Deborah (a bee)
Desiderata (desire)
Diana (divine)
Dina (judged) **Dinah**
Dorcas (gazelle)
Dorothea (gift of God) **Doll**
Dove (a dove)
Dowsabel (sweet) **Dowzable, Dussabel**
Drusilla (?)
Edith (prosperous in war) **Edyth**
Eleanor (light, torch, bright)
Elizabeth (God is my oath) **Bess, Bessie, Beth, Eliza**
Ellen (light, torch, bright) **Elen**
Emma (strength; work) **Em**
Emeline (strength; work) **Em**
Emmot (strength; work; rival)
Esther (myrtle; star)
Eunice (good victory)
Euphemia (fair speech)
Eustacia (steadfast; happy harvest)
Eve (life)
Faith (faith, trust)
Felice (lucky)
Felicity (happiness)
Florence (a blooming)
Frances (a Frank, a freeman)
Frideswid (strong peace)
Gabriela (God is my strength)
Gertrude (spear strength)
Goodeth (God's war)
Grace (grace, mercy)
Gwyneth (blessed)
Hannah (grace, full of grace, mercy)
Helah (rust)
Helen (light, torch, bright)
Helena (light, torch, bright)
Hephzibah (she is my delight) **Hepzibah, Hepsie**
Hester (myrtle; star)
Hilarie (cheerful)
Honor (honor, esteem) **Honour**
Honora (honor, esteem)
Hope (hope, expectation)
Ideny (work, labor)
Imyne (?)
Isabel (God is my oath) **Isabell, Isobel**
Isylte (?, perhaps *ruler of the ice*) **Isott**
Jackett (supplanting; seizing by the heels) From the French Jacquette.
Jael (mountain goat)
Jane (God is gracious)
Jean (God is gracious) **Jeane**
Jecoliah (the Lord prevails)
Jelyan (youth; downy)

Jemima (pure)
Jerioth (curtains)
Jerushah (a possession)
Joan (God is gracious)
Johanna (God is gracious)
Joy (joy, happiness)
Judith (praised)
Julia (youth, downy)
Katherine (pure, unsullied) **Catherine, Kate, Kitty**
Kerenhappuch (horn of antimony)
Keturah (incense)
Kezia (cassia)
Kinburga (royal fortress)
Laetitia (happiness) **Letitia**
Lalage (babbler)
Laura (laurel)
Laurana (woman from Laurentum)
Laurencia (woman from Laurentum)
Laurentia (woman from Laurentum)
Laureola (woman from Laurentum)
Lavinia (from Latium)
Leah (weary)
Lettice (happiness) **Letice**
Lillian (lily) **Lilian**
Lois (?)
Lora (man from Laurentum)
Loretta (man from Laurentum) **Lauretta**
Love (love)
Lucy (light)
Mabel (lovable) **Mabile, Mabill, Mable, Mabyle**
Mabella (lovable)
Madeline (from Magdala)
Madge (a pearl)
Magdalen (from Magdala) **Magdelyn**
Magge (a pearl)
Mahala (tenderness)
Mahalath (a lute, a lyre)
Marah (bitterness)
Marcella (of Mars, warlike)
Marcia (of Mars, warlike)
Margaret (a pearl)
Marion (sea of bitterness or sorrow)
Marjorie (a pearl)
Martha (lady, mistress)
Mary (sea of bitterness or sorrow) Rarely used in Elizabeth's
    reign, except among Catholics.
Maud (battle strength) **Mawde**
Maudlin (from Magdala)
Melicent (work + strength) **Milesent**
Meraude (of the sea) **Meroud**
Mercy (mercy, compassion)
Mildred (mild + strength)
Minerva (?)
Miriam (sea of bitterness or sorrow)
Moll (sea of bitterness or sorrow)
Molly (sea of bitterness or sorrow)

Monday (born on Monday)
Monica (?)
Meriall (sea bright) **Meryall**
Naamah (sweetness)
Naomi (my joy, my delight)
Nell (light, torch, bright) **Nelly**
Nicol (victory of the people)
Olive (the olive tree) **Olyff, Olyffe**
Olympia (of Olympus)
Onora (honor)
Ophrah (a fawn)
Orpah (a fawn, a forelock)
Orabell (?) **Orable, Oriabel**
Osanna (save now, save pray)
Parnell (a rock)
Patience (patience, forbearance)
Peg (a pearl) **Peggy**
Penelope (a bobbin)
Pentecost (fiftieth [day])
Persis (Persian woman)
Petronel (a rock)
Philadelphia (brotherly love)
Philip (lover of horses) **Phil**
Phillice (green, verdant) **Philles**
Phillida (green, verdant)
Phoebe (bright, shining) **Phebe**
Pleasance (pleasant)
Precilla (former, ancient) **Priscilla**
Prisca (former, ancient)
Prothesia (?) **Prothasey**
Prudence (prudent)
Rachel (ewe)
Radegund (famous counsel)
Rebekah (noose)
Rhoda (a rose)
Richardyne (little ruler)
Rosamond (horse protection) **Rossamond**
Ruth (friend, companion) **Ruthe**
Sabina (Sabine woman)
Salome (peace)
Sanchia (holy) **Sanche**
Sapphira (beautiful)
Sarah (princess)
Sarey (princess)
Scholastica (scholar)
Susanna (lily, rose)
Susanney (lily, rose)
Sybil (fortune-teller, prophetess) **Sybell**
Sybby (fortune-teller, prophetess)
Tabitha (roe, gazelle)
Tace (hold peace, be silent)
Tacy (hold peace, be silent)
Tamar (palm, a date palm)
Theodora (God's gift)
Theodosia (God-given)
Theophila (God's friend)

Thomson (little Tom *a twin*) **Tomson**
Thomasin (little Tom *a twin*) **Thamasin, Thomasing**
Tiffeny (Epiphany, manifestation of God) **Tyffany**
Tirzah (pleasantness)
Troth (fidelity, good faith)
Tryphena (delicate, dainty)
Ursula (she-bear)
Valentine (strong, healthy)

Venetia (blessed)
Violet (violet-colored)
Vivien (alive)
Wannore (white wave) **Wannour**
Zeresh (gold, splendor)
Zilpah (?)
Zipporah (a little bird)

MALE NAMES

Abel (breath)
Abner (the father is a light)
Abraham (father of a multitude)
Abram (father of exaltation)
Absalom (father of peace) **Absalon**
Adam (man of the red earth)
Adrian (man from Hadrianus)
Alan (?, perhaps *handsome, rock*) **Aleyne**
Alard (noble and hard)
Aldus (old)
Aldwin (old friend) **Alduin**
Alexander (defender of mankind) **Sander**
Alfred (elf counsel)
Algar (elf spear) **Aelger, Alger**
Ambrose (immortal)
Amias (?, perhaps friendship)
Amiel (industrious)
Amos (borne, a burden)
Andrew (manly) **Dande**
Anselm (God's helmet)
Antony (?, *priceless, of inestimable worth* is a folk definition)
Arnold (eagle power) **Ernald**
Asa (healer)
Athelstan (noble stone) **Athestan**
Aubrey (elf ruler) **Aubri**
Austin (great, venerable)
Aylmer (nobly famous)
Aylwin (elf friend)
Azariah (whom Jehovah helps)
Baldric (bold ruler)
Baldwin (bold friend)
Bardolph (bright wolf)
Barnabas (son of exhortation)
Bartholomew (son of Talmai *hill, mound, furrows*)
Basil (kingly)
Berold (bear rule) **Berolt**
Bertin (bright friend)**Bette**
Caleb (dog; faithful)
Christopher (bearing Christ)
Ciprianus (from Cyprus)
Clemens (gentle, mild)
Clement (gentle, mild)
Constantine (constant, steadfast) **Constans, Cuss, Cust**

Cornelius (a horn)
Crispin (curled)
Damian (tamer)
Daniel (judged by God)
David (beloved)
Dominic (belonging to a lord; belonging to the Lord) **Dominik**
Drogo (to carry, a burden)
Durand (enduring, lasting) **Durant**
Edgar (wealthy spear)
Edmond (wealthy protection)
Edward (wealthy guardian)
Edwin (wealthy friend)
Egbert (bright sword)
Eli (high, ascent)
Elias (Jehovah is God)
Elijah (Jehovah is God)
Elisha (God is salvation)
Elkanah (God created)
Ephraim (very fruitful)
Erastus (lovely, beloved)
Esau (hairy)
Eustace (steadfast; happy in harvest)
Ezekiel (God strengthens)
Festus (?)
Florian (flowery)
Francis (a Frank, a freeman)
Gabriel (God is strength)
Gamel (old)
Gaston (?, possibly *guest, stranger; from Gascony*)
Gavin (battle hawk)
Gedaliah (made great by Jehovah)
Geoffrey (district, traveler, pledge + peace) **Geffrei, Geffrey**
George (earth worker, farmer)
Gerald (spear rule)
Gerbert (spear bright)
Gerbold (spear bold)
Gershon (expulsion)
Gervais (servant of the spear) **Gervas, Gervase, Jarvis**
Giffard (give + bold, fierce)
Gilbert (bright pledge) **Gib, Gil**
Giles (goatskin shield of Zeus; a protection)
Godard (God hard)
Godfrey (God's peace)

Godric (powerful God)
Godwin (friend of God)
Gregory (vigilant, watchful)
Griffin (like a griffin, monstrous)
Gunther (bold in war)
Guy (a guide, leader)
Hardwin (hard friend)
Harold (power of the army)
Hector (holding fast)
Henry (home ruler)
Herbert (army bright)
Hereward (army guard)
Herman (warrior, soldier)
Hezekian (God strengthens)
Hilary (cheerful)
Hiram (exalted brother)
Hosea (salvation)
Hubert (bright heart) **Hubard**
Hugh (heart, mind, soul) **Hugo**
Ira (watchful)
Isaac (laughter)
Isaiah (God is salvation)
Ives (archer) **Ivo, Yvo**
Jacob (supplanting, seizing by the heels)
James (supplanting, seizing by the heels)
Japheth (enlargement)
Jason (healer)
Jedaiah (invoker of Jehovah)
Jedidiah (beloved of Jehovah)
Jeremiah (God will uplift) **Jeremy**
Jesimiel (God sets up)
Jesse (gift)
Jethro (excellence)
Joachim (God will establish) **Joachin**
John (God is gracious)
Jonas (dove) **Jonah**
Jordan (a flowing down) **Judd, Jurd**
Joseph (he shall add)
Joshua (God is salvation)
Josiah (the Lord supports)
Julian (youth, downy)
Kenrick (royal rule)
Kenward (brave guardian) **Keneweard, Kenard**
Laban (white)
Lambert (bright land)
Lancelot (?, perhaps *little land*)
Laurance (from Laurentum)
Leofric (dear ruler)
Leofwin (dear friend)
Leonard (bold as a lion)
Levi (joining)
Lewis (famous in war) **Lowis**
Lionel (little lion)
Lovell (wolf)
Luke (light; man from Loukania)
Malachi (my messenger)

Manfred (peace of man)
Marcus (of Mars, warlike)
Mark (of Mars, warlike)
Martin (of Mars, warlike)
Matheus (gift of God) **Mathiu, Mattheus**
Matthias (gift of God)
Mauger (spear grinder)
Maynard (strong and hardy)
Meshach (agile)
Micah (Who is like God?)
Michael (Who is like God?)
Milo (?, perhaps *mild, peaceful; merciful*) **Milon**
Mordecai (worshiper of Marduk)
Moses (drawn out of the water)
Nathan (gift)
Nathanael (gift of God) **Nathaniel**
Nehemiah (comforted by Jehovah)
Nicholas (victory of the people) **Nicoll, Nichol, Coll**
Noah (rest, comfort)
Odo (wealth)
Ogier (rich spear)
Osbern (god bear) **Osborn**
Oscar (God's spear)
Osmond (God's protection) **Osmund**
Oswald (God's power)
Oswin (friend of God)
Paul (small)
Paulin (small)
Pernel (a rock, a stone) **Penne, Pennel**
Peter (a rock, a stone)
Philip (lover of horses) **Fippe, Philipot, Pot**
Piers (a rock, a stone)
Quintin (fifth)
Ralph (counsel wolf)
Randulf (shield wolf)
Raymund (counsel protection) **Raimund, Reimond**
Reginald (judgment power)
Renfred (counsel might)
Reuben (behold, a son!)
Reynard (counsel hard)
Raynold (powerful protection) **Rainald, Raynald, Renold, Reynold**
Richard (stern king)
Robert (bright with fame) **Dob, Dobbe, Hob, Hobbe, Nabbe, Rob, Robb**
Roger (famous with the spear)
Roland (famous land) **Rolland**
Rolf (famous wolf) **Rolft, Roulf**
Samson (the sun) **Sansom**
Samuel (heard of God)
Saul (asked for)
Seth (appointed)
Shem (renowned)
Silas (ask for)
Simon (heard) **Simond, Symon**
Siward (victory protection)

Solomon (peaceful)
Stephen (a crown, a garland)
Talbot (pillager, bandit; lampblack)
Theobald (bold people)
Theodoric (ruler of the people)
Thomas (a twin)
Thurstan (Thor's stone)
Timothy (honor, respect)
Tobias (God is good)
Tristram (tumult, sadness)
Ulric (wolf rule)

Urban (villager)
Valentine (healthy, strong)
Vincent (conquering)
Walter (ruler of an army)
William (resolute protector)
Zachariah (God remembers)
Zacharias (God remembers)
Zebedee (God bestows)
Zebulun (to carry, to exalt)
Zephaniah (the Lord has hidden)

SURNAMES

Though the Reformation had a great effect on the personal names of this time period, the movement arrived too late in the development of surnames to have had much of a direct effect. Indirectly, vicious religious persecution on the Continent prompted thousands to flee to Britain in search of sanctuary. Government encouraged such immigration, and people from France, Spain, Germany, Italy, and the Low Countries added their names to the growing pool. Brywer and Ewen are examples of Breton names, Anjou and Achard are examples of French names, Broun and Blanchard are names from Normandy, and Hankyn and Pipertyn are examples of Flemish names. In many cases, the foreign surname was abandoned in favor of an English identifier based on occupation or nationality. Baker and Carpenter, and Fleming, Irishman, Norman, Champayn, and Florantyn are examples of such names.

Achard (?, perhaps *dreaded army*)
Adams (son of Adam)
Akerman (a farmer or ploughman)
Albin (white) **Albyn**
Albryght (nobly bright)
Almaund (German)
Anjou (from Anjou)
Armstrong (strong arms) **Armstrang**
Bacheler (young knight, novice in arms)
Bacon (side of bacon)
Baker (a baker)
Ball (ball; bald place; the round one)
Barber (a barber, one who practiced surgery and dentistry)
Barnelby (son of consolation)
Baron (a baron, a nobleman)
Base (the short one)
Berenger (bear spear)
Bertelot (little Bartholomew)
Blanchard (whitish)
Bowyer (a maker or trader of bows)
Brown (brown, brown-haired) **Broun**
Burgis (a freeman of a borough) **Burgeis**
Buxton (Bucca's stone)
Carpenter (a carpenter)
Champayn (from Champaign)
Chaucer (maker of leather pants)
Colyer (a maker or seller of charcoal)
Cornish (a Cornish person)

Danvers (from Anvers)
Darnel (the darnel plant; from Darnall) **Darnell**
Derwin (dear friend)
Drinkwater (one who drinks water) The name implies one so poor as to not be able to afford ale, the most common drink.
Duchesman (a Dutchman)
Dunn (brown-haired)
Edmundson (son of Edmond *wealthy protector*)
Ellis (Jehovah is God; God is salvation)
Ellyson (son of Ellis *Jehovah is God; God is salvation*)
Emson (son of Emma *strength*)
Ewen (lamb; youth; well-born)
Florence (from Florence)
Florantyn (a Florentine)
Fleming (a Fleming) **Flymng**
Fort (strong)
Frenssh (a French person)
Glasier (a glass maker)
Golding (son of Golda *gold*)
Goldsmith (a goldsmith)
Goodyer (good year) **Godeyere, Godier, Goudyer**
Graunt (great, large)
Grene (dweller near the village green)
Hale (dweller in the remote valley)
Hankyn (little Hans)
Hawthorn (dweller near the hawthorn) **Hawthorne**
Howard (brave heart; chief warden; ewe herder) **Heward, Huward**

Hughlot (little Hugh)
Ingram (Ing's raven; angel raven)
Irish (an Irish person) **Iryssh**
Irishman (an Irishman) **Irissheman**
Irishwoman (an Irishwoman)
Ives (archer)
Jagger (carter, peddler; God is gracious)
Jenour (engineer) **Jenoure**
Jakeson (son of Jack *God is gracious*)
Johnson (son of John *God is gracious*)
Jourdan (a flowing down, descend)**Jurdain**
Keate (dweller at the animal hut) **Keat, Keates, Keats**
Kendrick (chief man, chief hero)
King (a king) **Kinge**
Knolles (dweller at the top of the hill) **Knoll**
Knyght (servant, knight)
Lambert (bright land) **Lambard, Lambart, Lambarth**
Latimer (interpreter)
Lawless (an outlaw, licentious) **Lawelesse**
Legg (leg)
Lokke (a lock of hair)
Lombard (long beard) **Lumbard**
Mailer (an enameler) **Mailler**
Maitland (discourteous, rude)
Malet (the unfortunate one, cursed)
Mallory (the unfortunate one, cursed)
Marchant (a merchant, a trader) **Marchand**
Matthews (son of Matthew *gift of God*)
Naismith (a knife smith) **Naysmith**
Nesbitt (from Nesbit or Nesbitt) **Naisbet, Naisbit, Nesbit**
Newman (a newcomer)
Nicoles (victory of the people) **Nicholls, Nichols**
Norman (a Norman, from Normandy)
Oaks (dweller near the oak trees) **Oak, Oake**

Oldfield (dweller by the old field)
Orchard (dweller near or worker at an orchard)
Osman (god-bear) **Osmand**
Oxnard (an ox herder)
Parys (from Paris)
Pikard (one from Picardy)
Plymouth (from Plymouth)
Poore (pauper)
Prendregast (?, perhaps *dweller at the village near the castle*)
Sadeler (a maker or seller of saddles) **Sadelier**
Sheparde (shepherd) **Shepard, Shepperde**
Stoke (from Stoke)
Stolemaker (a maker or seller of stoles)
Sutton (from Sutton)
Tabard (a sleeveless coat)
Tait (cheerful, gay)
Talbot (lampblack)
Tomlin (little Tom *a twin*)
Trumble (strong-bold) **Trumbull**
Ullman (maker or seller of oil)
Underhill (dweller at the foot of a hill)
Unwin (young bear-friend)
Uppington (dweller up in the village)
Urban (dweller in the city)
Vale (dweller in the valley)
Valentine (strong, healthy)
Vaughan (small) **Vaughn**
Vennell (dweller at the small street or alley) **Vennall, Venel**
Vidal (vital, full of vitality) **Vidall**
Walsh (a Welsh person)
Walshman (a Welshman)
Webber (a weaver)
White (white, fair-complexioned)
Williams (son of William *resolute protector*)

Chapter Six

THE EARLY MODERN WORLD
JAMES I TO GEORGE III
[1603–1820]

POLITICS

FOLLOWING ELIZABETH'S DEATH, James I, the King of Scots, united the two countries by assuming the title King of Great Britain. He found the English throne quite different from that of Scotland where the Church still retained great influence over government and the king was considered more or less a chief among equals. In England, not only was James the supreme ruler over his subjects, he was head of the Church, as well. He also came into the possession of a great deal of hereditary wealth. His newfound fortune and stature might have corrupted him somewhat, for he became pompous and arrogant, and a lavish and frivolous spender who had to ask parliament several times for more money.

In 1604, James achieved peace with Spain. To show his goodwill, he refused to sanction the privateering that Drake and Sir Walter Raleigh had made so profitable for Elizabeth I. In 1613, James married Elizabeth, his eldest daughter, to Frederick the Elector Palatine in a bid to win Protestant allies on the Continent. Several years later, when Spain took to arms against Frederick, James thought to end the fighting by marrying his son Charles to the sister of King Philip IV of Spain. James believed the union would restore Frederick's occupied dominions and serve as a way to enter into an alliance with the most powerful country in Europe. The match never took place, and once again, the countries were at war. James I, "the wisest fool in Christendom," died in March 1625, never accomplishing much as a king and failing to aspire to any type of greatness.

Charles I, James's youngest son, succeeded to the throne, and within two months was married to Henrietta Maria, the sister of King Louis XIII of France. From the beginning, Charles was influenced by his father's personal favorite, the Marquis of Buckingham, a man who had already proven to be incompetent in foreign affairs. In spite of Charles's marriage, Buckingham soon had the king at arms with both France and Spain.

The House of Commons refused to grant both the supplies needed for war and most of the money Charles sought for personal reasons. Charles, therefore, had to resort to other means to increase his wealth. He cashed his wife's dowry, exacted forced loans from the wealthy (imprisoning those who would not comply), refused to pay for his soldiers' housing, and diverted the proceeds from customs duties to his own coffers.

When Charles's third parliament met in 1628, the members of the commons were far from happy. The aggression against Spain on behalf of France was being very poorly managed and Charles's moneymaking schemes were bitterly resented, as was his attitude toward the Church of England (he preferred Catholic ritual and rites to long sermons and extempore prayer). A Petition of Right was drawn up, which condemned forced loans, the billeting of soldiers upon the people without paying for them, arbitrary imprisonment, martial law, and a host of other unjust actions. Even Buckingham's assassination in August 1628, which ended his influence over Charles, failed to bring about a reconciliation between king and parliament.

Afterward, a period of eleven years of nonparliamentary government followed (The Eleven Years of Tyranny), during which time Charles ended his war against Spain and forced the Anglican Prayer Book on the Scots to bring the Scottish kirk (church) in line with the Church of England. Lowland Scots rebelled, and the Bishops' Wars (1639 and 1640) ended with a Scottish army camped on English soil and Charles's army soundly beaten.

The crisis necessitated the recall of parliament, and Charles had to make several concessions, including an agreement to the Triennial Act (parliament to be called every three years) and a promise not to dissolve parliament without its own consent. Two issues he refused to discuss were the reform of the Church of England (which members thought was becoming Catholicized) and control of the militia (the only permanent military force in the kingdom apart from the king's personal guard). Parliament became split in its support of the king, and in 1642, after a failed attempted to arrest five members of the House of Commons, Charles withdrew from London and both sides prepared for war. Charles steadfastly refused to yield on the issues of the church and his militia, and in August 1642, civil war began with the king raising his colors at Nottingham.

Much like the politicians of today who look for votes in every corner, Charles made many promises that he had no means nor intentions of keeping. He garnered support in Scotland by promising to implement the Presbyterian system of church government in England, made promises to English Anglicans that the Church would not be reformed, and yet other promises to Roman Catholics and to Puritan leaders of the parliamentarian army. Though Charles proved a capable commander-in-chief, parliament had much better resources and military talent at its disposal. After four years, the parliamentary army proved victorious. Charles, who had sought the support of the Scottish Covenanter army, was turned over to parliament for not keeping his promise to introduce Presbyterian religious reforms.

Events came thick and fast in the last two years of Charles's reign. In 1647, the army had a falling out with parliament over lack of pay and a fear of Presbyterian uniformity throughout the realm. Charles was kidnapped by Oliver Cromwell and Thomas Fairfax's Roundhead army and placed in honorable captivity; the king escaped, fled to the Isle of Wight where he played his enemies off one another, and once again agreed to religious concessions to garner Scottish support. In 1648, the Scots marched south in support of Charles, only to be defeated by Cromwell; the Royalists, tired of Puritan restraints and exactions, started a revolt in southeastern England and were put down by Fairfax. Parliament was then purged of its Presbyterian members and Charles was taken into captivity. Some of the navy had declared for Charles, and the king's son, Charles II, took command of a fleet and set sail to free his father. They were too late. In January 1649, a high court of justice was seated to try the king for waging war against his own people. The trial was a farce. Charles was publicly beheaded and his body was secretly buried in Windsor Castle.

For the next eleven years, Great Britain was a commonwealth governed by a council of state. The Long Parliament was dismissed, and a military council selected 129 religious members (the Saints) to replace it. The Saints, revolutionary and fanatical, were eventually persuaded to resign, and officers of the army declared Cromwell Lord Protector and put a council of state and a new parliament in place to rule with him. This parliament lasted but four months. Next, Cromwell divided the country into eleven districts governed by puritanical major-generals. Aside from stomping out militarism, this short-lived plan did little but make people's lives miserable and strip much of the joy out of living. Another parliament was seated in 1657, and Cromwell was offered the crown, yet misunderstandings saw this parliament dissolved as well. Cromwell died a year later, leaving his incompetent son, Richard (Tumbledown Dick), in charge. Within five months, England was in a state of chaos. General Monk and army marched from Scotland to London, restored parliament, and offered the crown to Charles II (the Restoration).

Though the commonwealth had problems in successfully governing Great Britain, it did have a few accomplishments. In 1651, the Act of Navigation allowed imports to enter the country only by English ships or those of the producing country and gave the English a huge advantage over trade. In 1655, Jamaica was captured from the Spanish, and with the French, the English captured Dunkirk from Spain in 1658.

When Charles II accepted the crown, he accepted parliament's land settlement and an annual stipend of £1,200,000. He married Catherine of Braganza, the daughter of the king of Portugal, which brought him a handsome dowry along with Bombay and Tangier. Charles sold Dunkirk to the French and was pressured into a two-year war with the Dutch that was primarily based on naval rivalries and trade issues. It was a disastrous time during which England endured the Great Plague (1665), the Great Fire (1666), and problems with the war that mainly stemmed from lack of proper funding. In 1667, peace was concluded with the Dutch, netting Charles New Amsterdam (New York) and New Jersey. It was at this time that Charles's chief minister, the earl of Clarendon, was dismissed, and a five-member group known as the Cabal became the king's advisers.

In 1668, Charles joined in a short-lived alliance with Holland and Sweden against French aggression, but in 1670, he secretly negotiated the Treaty of Dover in which he promised to support the French against the Dutch in exchange for monetary compensation and, at an appropriate time, openly declare himself Catholic. He kept the treaty secret from his Protestant ministers while his Catholic ones found additional sources of funding lest the House of Commons refuse to support the war. Charles issued a Declaration of Indulgence repealing all acts against Catholics and Nonconformists, and without informing parliament, entered the war. Parliament retaliated by forcing Charles to sign the Test Act, which excluded Roman Catholics from all offices. Though the king signed (prompting his brother, the duke of York, to resign his naval command), parliament still refused to fund the war, and Charles was obliged to make a separate peace with the Dutch.

In 1673, Charles replaced the Cabal with Sir Thomas Osborne, Lord Danby, who set about organizing members of Church and court into the Tory party. Ex-Cabal member, Lord Ashley, formed the Whig party to see the Catholic Duke of York excluded from the throne. With the Dutch and French still at war, Charles was pressured to take up arms against Catholic France. He married his niece, Mary, to Prince William III of Orange, securing a Dutch alliance and soothing parliament's Protestant members.

Anti-Catholic hostilites spilled forth after the notorious "Popish Plot" in 1678 incited fear and suspicion that Charles had somehow made promises to the French about making England Catholic once again. Years were spent with Charles fighting parliament over their efforts to exclude all but Anglican communicants from holding seats in parliament and to exclude the Duke of York from the throne.

In 1681, a fifth parliament was seated, and Charles had to contend with the Tories and the Whigs vying for supremacy. The Tories were aided by the Whigs' plot to assassinate both Charles and his brother James. The Whig movement was crushed, and the last four years of Charles's reign were relatively peaceful. He ended up keeping his promise to the French, and before his death in 1685, was restored into the Catholic Church.

Charles, the "Merry Monarch," had been a favorite with the commoners. His zest for life, his fun-loving nature, and his love of splendor were like a breath of fresh air after the restrictive influences of straitlaced and fire-and-brimstone Puritans who thought such excess was sinful. Charles also had a large sexual appetite, and though he steadfastly refused to divorce his barren wife, Catherine of Braganza, he did take a succession of mistresses and sired several children. As these offspring were illegitimate, James was next in line for the throne.

After James promised to preserve the Church of England, the House of Commons agreed to give him a fair chance at being king and awarded him with a generous annual stipend. As with other kings and queens before him, the subject of religion encompassed James's short three-year reign. His secret goal was to see religious and civic equality among Catholics and Protestants, and his problems began once he set out to accomplish that goal. The commons were initially very loyal to James, but after he issued a Declaration of Indulgence, suspended the Test Acts, and found a way to dispense with certain laws, they turned against him.

James published a second Declaration of Indulgence in 1688 with the order that it be read in every church. This prompted seven bishops, including the Archbishop of Canterbury, to refuse and to question James's authority to issue such an order. The seven bishops were put on trial for seditious libel and were acquitted by jury. On June 10, the king's second wife, Mary of Modena, gave birth to a son (the Old Pretender), and fears that England would be subject to a Catholic dynasty abounded. James's daughters, Mary and Anne, by wife Anne Hyde, were Protestant, and it was upon them that non-Catholics looked to save the situation. On the same day the bishops' verdict was being celebrated in the streets, six laymen and the Bishop of London, the Immortal Seven, secretly invited James' son-in-law and nephew, William III of Orange, to England to overthrow James and allow Mary to succeed her father.

When William landed with a large army in 1688, much of James's army and all of his navy went over to the other side. James sent his wife and infant to France, and after pretending to negotiate with William, secretly fled the capital. He was caught, taken back to London, and escaped to board a ship for France. On Christmas Day 1688, James II entered permanent exile.

Before William and Mary were given the crown, they had to agree to a Declaration of Rights that limited the monarchy. During the course of their reign, that declaration was turned into a bill that gave parliament control over finance and the army, withdrew the power to suspend laws, and allowed for freedom of speech and freedom in elections. An Act of Indulgence permitted Nonconformists (but not Catholics) to worship freely, but continued to reserve offices and appointments for Anglican communicants.

Several other constitutional changes took place during this reign that were to forever affect the monarchy. An Act of Succession stipulated that the monarch must not marry a Catholic, must be a member of the Church of England, and must not leave the kingdom without parliamentary permission. A Triennial Act was signed, requiring parliament to meet each year with a new parliament being summoned every three years; a Civil List Act put the king's expenditures under the control of parliament; and a Mutiny Act prevented a standing army during times of peace without parliamentary consent.

In 1689, William was successful in uniting most of Europe against French domination. Financial difficulties with the prolonged War of the League of Augsburg (1688–1697) led to the formation of the Bank of England in 1694, an event some believe to be the most important of the reign of William and Mary.

Queen Mary made it clear in the beginning that she was content to leave the running of the country to her husband, though she did lend her considerable influence over the moral climate of the court. She died of smallpox in December 1694, leaving behind a grieving William who was never to marry again and no heir to succeed him.

In 1701, an Act of Settlement provided for the crown to pass from William to Anne, Mary's younger sister, then to the Electress Sophia of Hanover, the twelfth child of Elizabeth, daughter of James I. William died a year later in March 1702.

When Anne was born to James II and Anne Hyde, it was thought that she would never ascend to the throne. She was therefore uneducated and untrained for the role of monarch, and her husband, Prince George of Denmark, was a man who preferred to stay behind the scenes. Anne gave birth to seventeen children, none of whom survived infancy. The longest-living child was the hydrocephalic William, who survived but eleven years. Anne herself was prey to ill health and was in a great deal of pain throughout her reign.

While Anne was not a remarkable queen, many notable events happened during her reign. Under the military leadership of John Churchill, Duke of Marlborough, England was part of a second Grand Alliance against France and entered into the War of the Spanish Succession. Many victories and territorial gains were achieved abroad. Gibraltar, Minorca, Nova Scotia, Newfoundland, and Hudson Bay Territory all came under Great Britain's umbrella during Anne's reign. At home, the union of England with Scotland was finalized in 1707. The two parliaments merged, but Scotland managed to keep its own church and its own laws. Queen Anne died in August 1714, after a long illness.

Sophia, Electress of Hanover and daughter of James I, died just two months before Anne. Therefore, it was her son, George, to whom the crown passed, and he did not come to England without scandal. His wife, Sophia Dorothea of Celle, had made the mistake of having an affair with a Swedish count, and George's subsequent treatment of her had shocked Europe. In 1694, Count Königsmark disappeared without a trace, and it was widely rumored that George had the count's body cut up and buried beneath the floorboards of Herrenhausen, his country house. George then divorced Sophia Dorothea, forbade her from seeing their children ever again, and had her imprisoned in the Castle of Ahlden. She was only twenty-eight at the time and was to live another thirty-two years in captivity.

George spoke no English and had no real interest in England, and he had no clue to proper kingly behavior. His propensity to make a fool of himself made him the butt of many jokes. His passion for ugly women didn't help his image, either. He brought two mistresses to court with him: the very thin Ehrengard von Schulenberg and the very corpulent Charlotte Kielmansegge. It is said that George's passion for Schulenberg had petered out (she was close to sixty years old), but he still spent most of his evenings with her, cutting out paper patterns with a pair of scissors. Schulenberg became known as "The Maypole" and Kielmansegge had the dubious title "Elephant and Castle."

As George had been previously contacted by the Whigs in Anne's cabinet and he knew he had their support, it was to them that he gave several important offices. However, many still thought the crown belonged to James, the exiled son of James II, and in September 1715, the Jacobite rebellion began.

In 1720, the crash of the South Sea Company, a finance company contracted to manage £30 million of the national debt, saw many investors ruined and led many prominent members of court to be implicated in gross fraud. Confidence in the government fell to a low, and Jacobites used the opportunity to champion their cause. In 1722, Robert Walpole was made chancellor of the exchequer and had control over patronage and the House of Commons. In effect, Robert Walpole was Great Britain's first prime minister.

Sophia Dorothea died in November 1726, and after receiving the news, George celebrated by going to the theater. He also refused to allow her burial. Story has it that a fortune-teller once told him that he would not live a year longer than his wife. Perhaps George remembered the prophecy, for it is said he was filled with foreboding. Seven months later, he set out for Hanover with "The Maypole." As the king's carriage neared Osnabrück Castle, George was struck down by a cerebral hemorrhage. His body was never brought back for burial.

George II had detested his father for the imprisonment of his mother. As a child, he had gone so far as to attempt to swim the moat around the Castle of Ahlden to see her. As an adult, his earnest and open wish was to see his father dead so his mother could be released from captivity. So great was the enmity between them that George spent a large amount of energy plotting against his father and taking every opportunity to antagonize him.

He and his wife, Caroline of Anspach, created a rival court that was much more fun and lively than the royal court, and they earnestly set about cultivating English friends and English culture. Yet, after his ascension to the throne, George II began to grow more like his father. Gone was the gaiety that marked his earlier court and gone was George's relaxed way with his friends. Court became dreadfully dull as he emphasized proper court etiquette, absolute punctuality, and talked forever about his valor on the battlefield. As his reign wore on, he grew more and more anti-English, showing rudeness and contempt toward members of his court and doing little to endear himself to his English subjects.

Perhaps most surprising was the poor relationship he and Caroline had with their eldest son, Frederick. From the moment the child was born, they seemed to detest the sight of him. Poor Frederick endured astonishing verbal abuse and other reprehensible actions from both parents and ended up returning their sentiments. Just as George II plotted against his father, so Frederick conspired against his and played Tory against Whig in an effort to undermine the stability of George II's administration. Frederick spent a great deal of time hoping for his father's death, but it was he who died first. George II remained true to character and refused to pay his deceased son's debts.

In 1743, George fought against the French, becoming the last British king to personally lead his troops into battle. He also involved the country in the Seven Years' War, and in 1759, a year before his death, the country saw some great military achievements. The English dominated in India, made conquests in Canada and the Caribbean, and ruled the seas with their superior navy.

George II did not have a dignified death. He suffered from constipation for years, and on the morning of October 25, 1760, his exertions in trying to pass an adequate stool proved too much. He died of a heart attack while sitting on the toilet.

George I and George II revealed their dislike for Great Britain and expressed their preference for Hanover, but George III, the eldest son of Frederick and Augusta of Saxe-Gotha, was born and raised in England and it was to England that his love and sympathy lay. He was a decent, religious, generous, courageous, and hardworking man who was loved by his people in spite of his later bouts of insanity. He was also a patron of the arts and founder of the Royal Academy. George was married to Charlotte of Mecklenburg-Strelitz, and they had fifteen children: nine sons (two died at a young age) and six daughters.

After ascending the throne, George III set about restoring the power lost to the monarchy through the reigns of his grandfather and great-grandfather. He recovered the royal patronage and had his prime minister, the Earl of Bute, work to achieve peace with France. The Seven Years' War ended in 1763 with the Peace of Paris. After Bute resigned his post, a succession of prime ministers followed with George eventually selecting his childhood friend, Lord Frederick North, for the position.

The Seven Years' War had left Britain with an enormous wartime debt, and it was decided that the American Colonies were obliged to pay their share for defense and for their administrative costs. The money was raised by the Sugar Act of 1764, which placed tariffs on Colonial imports of sugar, tea, coffee, and wine. This put a significant strain on the colonists' pocketbooks, and ominous rumblings began to be heard from American merchants and consumers. In 1765, parliament responded with the Stamp Act that taxed virtually every kind of printed material, from playing cards to legal documents. This prompted a boycott of English products and caused such a commotion that it was repealed a year later. Parliament failed to learn their lesson and established a set of new taxes called the Townshend Acts. The Americans boycotted again, cutting English imports in half. This time, parliament's response was to send in troops. The loss of America followed, Lord North was out as prime minister, and King George was accused of mismanagement and of wasting the blood of Englishmen.

After North's departure, Lord Rockingham became prime minister with the plan to reduce the king's influence in politics by taking away his right to choose his own ministers. He took matters to the extreme, seeking to impose all manner of restrictions and humiliations upon the king. George responded by dismissing all members of the coalition and placing his own choice, William Pitt, in the office of prime minister. Though parliament expressed their displeasure with the turn of events by making life tough for George and his young protégé, public opinion had turned in favor of the king, and a general election confirmed George's choice. William Pitt held his office for twenty-one years, leading the country to renewed national pride and prosperity and eventually through an entanglement with revolutionary France.

With the country at peace, George was able to concentrate on his love of botany and agriculture. He wrote several pamphlets on agricultural improvements under the name Ralph Robinson, prompting his subjects to refer to him as ''Farmer George.''

In November 1788, George suffered his first mental breakdown. And suffer he did, for he was put under the care of Dr. Francis Willis, the proprietor of a private mental hospital, and a Dr. Warren. Their forms of treatment were nothing short of cruel and unusual. Dr. Willis thought he'd get positive results from threats, lectures, and total body restraint usually involving a straitjacket, the king's bed, or an iron chair. Dr. Warren preferred to slather George's entire body with special poultices of Spanish fly and mustard so that the painful blisters that resulted would draw the ''evil humors'' out of his body. Despite this deplorable treatment, George managed to recover a few months later.

From the physical manifestations of George's illness (yellow or bloodshot eyes, a nasty rash, rapid pulse, swollen feet, red-colored urine, and mental affliction) some modern doctors believe that he actually might have suffered from an illness known as porphyria, whereby too much of the blood's red pigment is produced and poisons the entire nervous system. If this were the case, poor George was not insane but merely suffering the effects of a rare illness.

George suffered two other brief relapses in 1801 and 1804, but was still fit to rule. He adamantly refused to allow the Catholic Emancipation, which would again allow Roman Catholics to sit in parliament. George believed it was his duty to honor his cornation oath to uphold the Church of England and the Protestant faith and in his quest to do so, forced Pitt from office in 1801, then Grenville in 1807. In 1810, permanent insanity befell the king, and he suffered another ten years in isolation at Windsor Castle, blind, unkempt, and uncared for. He died in 1820.

George's long reign oversaw vast development that began to change the face of England. Better roads were built, canals were constructed, agricultural improvements were made, and the population increased from seven to twelve million. The increased mining of raw materials and the exploitation of coal, steam, and iron culminated in the achievement of mechanization. The Industrial Revolution had been ushered in.

SOCIETY

THE BEGINNING OF this period of time saw the common people in dire straits. Cities were crowded, filthy, and dangerous. In London, plague broke out in 1603, 1625, and 1636, killing scores of people. Nevertheless, during the first half of the seventeenth century, people leaving the countryside in search of work doubled London's population to 400,000. The economy was in poor shape; jobs were scarce and wages were very low. Buildings were crumbling, sanitation was far from adequate, and crime was rampant. The people, tired of living in such conditions, began to stand up for their rights, individual freedoms, and a measure of equality. Forced tithing to the Church of England and even private ownership of land came under attack by those who could barely afford to put food on the table, let alone pay to support the Church.

When Cromwell took over the reins of government, he was not about to tolerate such radical beliefs and such unruliness in society and attempted to exert the same kind of control over the people of England as he had over their ruler. In 1655, England was divided into districts, each with a major-general, and the districts were subdivided into parishes watched over by justices of the peace. It was the duty of the major-generals and the justices of the peace to keep a close eye on the morals and behaviors of the people.

In an effort to bring about a more harmonious and spiritual society, alehouses were closed and cockfights, duels, and races were not allowed, nor were activities such as dancing around the Maypole or celebrating Christmas. The theaters were closed for a number of years, and people were strictly censored in their speech and actions. Activities deemed immoral were expressly forbidden and poor souls caught gambling or even swearing were severely punished. The major-generals were far from popular, and the people had cause to rejoice when Charles II was restored to the crown.

England after the Commonwealth was a land of contrasts and extremes. It was an age of grinding poverty, violence, disease, filth, drunkenness, infidelity, materialism, and chaos. It was also an age of beauty, civility, intellectual development, and toleration. It was a time when workers' wages were so low that hunger was a fact of life, and a time when the wealthy dined on lavish feasts and dropped hundreds or thousands of pounds in a night of gambling.

At least 50 percent of England's inhabitants were agricultural workers, and it's been estimated that in the latter half of the seventeenth century and throughout the eighteenth century, nearly half the people were not making enough money to live on. Inflation had set in, and prices rose tremendously. A series of poor laws were enacted to help those in need, but they fell far short of meeting the needs of the people.

Nevertheless, the Restoration returned a great deal of happiness to English society. In 1662, Charles II formed The Royal Society to promote the arts and sciences. Literature was encouraged, the theaters were reopened, social clubs were established, and people's private lives were left alone.

People were also becoming more interested in the news. English newsbooks began to be printed during the early 1620s but were strictly regulated. In 1665, the *London Gazette* became the official, twice-weekly source of news. Restrictions on printing were greatly loosened, and soon, many unofficial news publications were established.

Plague hit again in June 1665 and claimed the lives of a thousand people a day by September. A year later, the "great fire" swept through the city, leaving it in ruins, and even more people were homeless and impoverished. Architecht Christopher Wren laid out a new, symmetrical design for the city, and London entered a period of grand reconstruction.

In 1696, government raised money by placing a tax on windows. In the city, tenements were assessed as single houses, rather than multiple dwellings. Thus, landlords commonly blocked off the windows to avoid paying the tax. It was a disastrous move for tenants who already lived in overcrowded and close quarters. Now they were also faced with inadequate air and light, making their living conditions impossible to bear. The tax was repeatedly increased until its repeal in 1851.

There was little change in the next century in the general state of the country. Smog was a very real problem in the larger cities, as were the mountains of garbage, dangerously rutted streets, and the filth and stench of manure, cesspits, rotting carcasses of animals, and the polluted rivers where everything was thrown. Both crime and unemployment continued to be high. Women had an especially difficult time, as they were barred from many types of jobs. More often than not, the females who went to the cities in search of employment resorted to prostitution to survive.

Perhaps because of such extremes in English society of the seventeenth and eighteenth centuries, new attitudes began to develop concerning the country's moral responsiblity to provide a decent life for all its citizens. These new attitudes were promoted by spiritual leaders working among the poor and became the focus of a new evangelical movement designed to promote reform within the Church of England itself, and to offer the people new hope for a dignified life.

RELIGION

BEFORE THE RESTORATION, Nonconformists were actively promoting their own ideas of Protestantism and were breaking off into independent sects, regardless of statutes forbidding them to do so. Congregationalists, Presbyterians, Baptists, Quakers, Unitarians, and Independents all had active and loyal congregations who were supportive in the face of persecution.

After Charles II was restored, fanaticism in religion declined. The Toleration Act of 1689 allowed freedom of worship to all Nonconformists, with the exception of the Unitarians, who rejected the doctrine of the Trinity. In spite of the relaxed attitudes of the times, people who were not members of the Church of England continued to be excluded from public office.

NAMING

THE SEVENTEENTH CENTURY saw increased usage of Bible names throughout the population. The Puritans continued to give unusual names to their children, but these were much more restrained than the strange and unwieldy names of the late sixteenth century. It's interesting to note, however, that almost any name in the Bible was considered acceptable, even ones whose original bearers had questionable reputations, such as Diana, Delilah, Cain, and Pontius Pilate.

There was also an increase in the use of surnames as first names during this time period. The trend originated among the wealthy, when the surname of the godparent was bestowed upon a child at baptism as a means of expressing love and goodwill. It was also a matter of pride to see family names raised in status. Names such as Calthorp, Grevill, Guildford, and Pickering were happily bestowed upon children at baptism, and male children weren't the only so named. It was also common to find females with names such as Essex, Hill, and Percy.

The bestowal of a middle name was popularized in the seventeenth century. It was most common to give only one middle name, but giving a child two or more secondary names in addition to the first name was by no means a rare occurrence.

Children orphaned or abandoned by their parents often ended up in foundling homes like the Foundling Hospital (opened in 1741), where they were baptized and given the names of the hospitals' wealthy patrons. (This came back to haunt many a patron when some of the grown children sought to lay claims of kinship upon them.) Once that supply of names was exhausted, names of famous religious persons were used, like John Wycliffe and Joseph Latimer. Names were also culled from other famous personalities. William Shakespeare, Geoffrey Chaucer, John Milton, and Francis Bacon are examples. Then the names of military notables were used, and infants were given names like Francis Drake and Oliver Cromwell. People from the arts lent their names: Michael Angelo, Peter Paul Rubens, and Anthony Vandyke are examples. Names were taken from popular novels, from flora and fauna, from explorers, and even from handicrafts and trades. Names based on the childrens' unfortunate circumstances, such as Forsaken, Helpless, Misericordia, and Lamentation were also used.

Throughout this time period, Elizabeth, Anne, and Mary were the three most common female names, with over 50 percent of the population being so named. For males, the top three names continued to be William, John, and Thomas.

FEMALE NAMES

Abigail (father of exaltation) **Abbey**
Abijah (the Lord is father)
Abishag (wise)
Adah (adornment)
Adele (noble) **Adela**
Adeline (nobility)
Agalia (splendor)
Agatha (good)
Agnes (chaste, pure)
Alethea (truth) **Alethea, Aletheia, Alithea**
Alexandra (defender of mankind)
Aline (noble)
Alison (noble one)
Althea (wholesome)
Amana (established)
Amanda (beloved) seventeenth-century invention.
Amata (love)
Amicia (?, possibly *friendship*) **Amice**
Amphelicia (?) **Amfelice, Amphelice, Amphillis**
Amy (beloved)
Anastasia (resurrection)
Andrea (womanly)
Angela (an angel)
Angelica (angelic) Used from the eighteenth century.
Anne (grace, full of grace, mercy) **Ann, Anna**
Annis (chaste, pure)
Anthea (flowery)
Antigone (of contrary birth)
Aphrah (dust) **Aphra**
Apphia (increasing)
Appolonia (of Apollo) **Appolina**
Arabella (?, perhaps *eagle; hearth*) **Arabel**
Arminel (strength)
Artemisia (belonging to Artemis)
Asenath (?, perhaps *thornbush*)
Aspasia (welcome)
Atarah (crown)
Athalia (the Lord is exalted)
Audrey (noble strength)
Aurelia (golden)
Aurora (the dawn)
Averil (boar battle) **Averell, Everild**
Avice (?) **Avis, Avise**
Azubah (forsaken)
Baptista (a baptiser)

Bathsheba (daughter of the oath, daughter of Sheba)
Bathshua (daughter of riches, daughter of Shua)
Beata (happy)
Beatrice (bringer of joy) **Bettrice**
Belinda (?, perhaps *snake*)
Benedicta (blessed)
Benet (blessed) **Bennet, Bennitt**
Berenice (bringer of victory)
Bertha (bright)
Bess (God is my oath) **Bessie**
Beth (God is my oath)
Beulah (married)
Bilhah (bashful, faltering)
Bithiah (daughter of Jehovah) **Bethia**
Blanch (white)
Blanchia (white)
Brilliana Coinage of Sir Edward Conway based on Brill, Holland.
Britannia (from Britain) Used in the eighteenth century.
Carmilla (?) Used in the late eighteenth century.
Carola (full-grown, a woman)
Caroletta (full-grown, a woman)
Caroline (full-grown, a woman) **Caro, Carrie, Lina**
Cassandra (?)
Catherine (pure, unsullied) **Catharine**
Cecilia (blind, dim-sighted) Used in the late eighteenth century.
Charis (grace)
Charissa (grace)
Charity (charity, benevolence)
Charlotte (full-grown, a woman) **Charlet**
Charmian (a little joy)
Chauncey (belonging to Chancey, France)
Chloe (blooming, verdant)
Chloris (green)
Christabel (?, probably *beautiful Christ*) **Christabell**
Christiana (a Christian, a follower of Christ)
Christine (a Christian, a follower of Christ) **Christina**
Christmas (born at Christmastime)
Chrysogon (golden birth)
Cicely (blind, dim-sighted) **Cecily, Sisley**
Clare (bright, clear, famous)
Clarimond (bright protection)
Clarinda (bright, clear, famous)
Clarissa (bright, clear, famous) **Clarice, Claricia**

Claudia (lame)
Clemence (clement, mild)
Clemency (clement, mild) **Clemencia**
Clorinda (green, verdant)
Comfort (comfort, care)
Constancy (constant) **Constance, Custance**
Cordelia (?, perhaps *daughter of the sea*)
Corinna (maiden)
Cornelia (a horn) Used since the eighteenth century.
Cynthia (of Kynthos)
Damaris (?, possibly *heifer*)
Deborah (a bee)
Delia (from Delos)
Delilah (delicate)
Denise (of Dionysus) **Denis**
Desiderata (desire)
Diana (divine)
Dina (judged) **Dinah**
Donnet (given)
Dorcas (gazelle)
Dorothea (gift of God) **Doll**
Douglas (dark, black + blue, green, gray)
Dove (a dove)
Drusilla (?)
Dulcibella (sweet and beautiful) **Dulcibell**
Dulcie (sweet)
Easter (born on Easter)
Eden (delight)
Edith (prosperous in war) **Edyth**
Eleanor (light, torch, bright) **Elianor, Elinor**
Elizabeth (God is my oath) **Bess, Bessie, Beth, Betty** (eighteenth century), **Eliza, Lizzie, Lizzy**
Ellen (light, torch, bright) **Elen**
Ellis (nobility)
Eloisa (hale, hearty)
Emeline (strength; work) **Emmeline**
Emeraud (an emerald)
Emerlee (strength; work)
Emilia (strength; work)
Emily (strength; work)
Emma (strength; work) **Em**
Emmot (strength; work; rival)
Esmeralda (emerald)
Essex (from Essex)
Esther (myrtle; star)
Ethel (noble)
Ethelinda (noble + tender, soft; a snake)
Eugenia (well-born, noble)
Eulalia (fair speech)
Eunice (good victory)
Euphemia (fair speech)
Eustacia (steadfast; happy harvest)
Eveline (?) **Evelina, Evelyn**
Eve (life)
Faith (faith, trust)
Felice (lucky)

Felicity (happiness)
Flavia (yellow)
Florence (a blooming)
Flower (a flower) Eighteenth-century name.
Fortunatus (fortunate)
Frances (a Frank, a freeman) **Francesse**
Frusannah (?, perhaps a blending of Frances and Susannah)
Gabriela (God is my strength) **Gabrielle**
Georgiana (earth worker, farmer) Used in the eighteenth century.
Gertrude (spear strength) **Gartrett**
Giles (kid; goatskin shield of Zeus)
Gillian (youth, downy)
Goodeth (God war) Seventeenth century.
Grace (grace, mercy)
Gwyneth (blessed)
Hannah (grace, full of grace, mercy)
Harriet (home ruler)
Helah (rust)
Helen (light, torch, bright)
Helena (light, torch, bright)
Hephzibah (she is my delight) **Hepzibah, Hepsie**
Hermia (of Hermes)
Hermione (of Hermes)
Hester (myrtle; star)
Hilarie (cheerful)
Hill (dweller at the hill)
Honor (honor, esteem) **Honour**
Honora (honor, esteem) **Honoria**
Hope (hope, expectation)
Horatia (?) Used after the seventeenth century.
Hortensia (?) Used after the seventeenth century.
Hosannah (save pray) **Hosanna**
Huldah (weasel)
Ideny (work, labor) **Idonea, Idonia, Idony**
Isabel (God is my oath) **Isabell, Isobel**
Ismenia (?)
Isylte (?, perhaps *ruler of the ice*) **Isold, Isolda, Isolt**
Jacklin (supplanting, seizing by the heels) **Jacqueline**
Jacoba (supplanting, seizing by the heels) **Jacobina**
Jael (mountain goat)
Jane (God is gracious)
Janet (God is gracious; little Jane) **Jennet**
Jean (God is gracious) **Jeane**
Jecoliah (the Lord prevails)
Jemima (pure)
Jerioth (curtains)
Jeromia (sacred name)
Jerushah (a possession)
Jessie (little Janet *God is gracious*; gift)
Joan (God is gracious)
Johanna (God is gracious) **Joanna**
Joy (joy, happiness)
Joyce (merry, happy)
Judith (praised)
Julia (youth, downy)

Juliana (youth, downy)
Juliet (youth, downy)
Justina (right, just)
Katherine (pure, unsullied) **Catherine, Kate, Kitty**
Kerenhappuch (horn of antimony)
Keturah (incense)
Kezia (cassia)
Kinburga (royal fortress)
Laetitia (happiness) **Letitia**
Lalage (babbler)
Laura (laurel)
Laurana (woman from Laurentum)
Laurencia (woman from Laurentum)
Laurentia (woman from Laurentum)
Laureola (woman from Laurentum)
Lavinia (from Latium)
Leah (weary)
Lettice (happiness) **Letice**
Lillian (lily) **Lilian**
Lois (?)
Lora (man from Laurentum)
Loretta (man from Laurentum) **Lauretta**
Louise (famous in war) Used from the late seventeenth century.
Love (love)
Lucia (light) Used from late seventeenth century.
Lucilla (light)
Lucinda (light)
Lucy (light)
Lydia (Lydian woman)
Mabel (lovable) **Mabill**
Mabella (lovable)
Madeline (from Magdala)
Madge (a pearl)
Magdalen (from Magdala) **Magdelyn**
Magge (a pearl)
Mahala (tenderness)
Mahalath (a lute, a lyre)
Marah (bitterness)
Marcella (of Mars, warlike)
Marcia (of Mars, warlike)
Margaret (a pearl)
Maria (sea of bitterness or sorrow) Used since the eighteenth century.
Marie (sea of bitterness or sorrow)
Marion (sea of bitterness or sorrow)
Marjorie (a pearl)
Martha (lady, mistress)
Mary (sea of bitterness or sorrow)
Matilda (strength in battle) From mid-eighteenth century.
Maud (battle strength)
Mehetabel (God makes happy)
Melanie (dark, black) **Melloney, Melony**
Melicent (work + strength) **Milesent**
Melissa (a bee) From the eighteenth century.
Melody (a melody) From the eighteenth century.

Meraude (of the sea)
Mercy (mercy, compassion)
Mildred (mild strength)
Millicent (work strength) **Milicent, Millesant**
Minerva (?)
Miranda (worthy to be loved)
Miriam (sea of bitterness or sorrow)
Moll (sea of bitterness or sorrow)
Molly (sea of bitterness or sorrow)
Monday (born on Monday)
Monica (?)
Meriall (sea bright) **Meryall**
Naamah (sweetness)
Naomi (my joy, my delight)
Nell (light, torch, bright) **Nelly**
Nicol (victory of the people)
Noel (born at Christmas)
Olive (the olive tree) **Olyff, Olyffe**
Olivia (the olive tree)
Olympia (of Olympus)
Onora (honor)
Ophelia (help, succor)
Ophrah (a fawn)
Orabell (?) **Orable, Oriabel**
Orpah (a fawn, a forelock)
Oriana (to rise)
Osanna (save now, save pray)
Pamela A literary coinage of poet Sir Philip Sidney (1554-1586).
Parnell (a rock)
Patience (patience, forebearance)
Peg (a pearl) **Peggy**
Penelope (a bobbin)
Pentecost (fiftieth [day])
Percy (from Percy, Normandy)
Perdita (lost)
Perpetua (perpetual, eternal)
Persis (Persian woman)
Petronel (a rock) **Peternel**
Philadelphia (brotherly love)
Philip (lover of horses) **Phelyp, Phylypp**
Phillice (green, verdant) **Phillis, Phyllis** Very rare in the eighteenth century.
Phillida (green, verdant)
Philomena (beloved)
Phoebe (bright, shining) **Phebe**
Pleasance (pleasant)
Precilla (former, ancient) **Priscilla**
Prisca (former, ancient)
Prothesia (?)
Prudence (prudent)
Rachel (ewe)
Rebekah (noose)
Renatus (reborn)
Rhoda (a rose)
Richenda (little Richard *stern king*)
Robina (bright with fame)

Rosabel (beautiful rose) Eighteenth-century invention.
Rosalie (rose garland)
Rosalind (horse or fame + gentle, tender, or serpent)
Rosamond (horse protection) **Rossamond**
Rose (a rose)
Roseanna (rose + grace, full of grace, mercy) **Roseann, Roseanne** Eighteenth-century invention.
Rosemary (rose + sea of bitterness or sorrow) Eighteenth-century invention.
Rosetta (little Rose)
Rowena (famous friend)
Ruth (friend, companion) **Ruthe**
Sabina (Sabine woman)
Salome (peace)
Sanchia (holy) **Sanche**
Sapphira (beautiful)
Sarah (princess)
Sarey (princess)
Scholast (a scholar)
Scholastica (a scholar)
Selina (the moon) **Selene, Selinah**
Sidonia (linen cloth) **Sidonie, Sidony**
Silvia (wood)
Sophia (wisdom)
Susan (lily, rose)
Susanna (lily, rose) **Susannah**
Susanney (lily, rose)
Sybil (fortune-teller, prophetess) **Sybell**
Tabitha (roe, gazelle)

Tacy (hold peace, be silent) A Quaker name.
Tamar (palm, a date palm) **Tamara**
Tess (harvester)
Tessa (harvester) **Tess**
Theodora (God's gift) **Theo**
Theodosia (God-given) **Theo**
Theophila (God's friend) **Theo**
Theresa (harvester) **Tess, Tessa**
Thermuthis (?)
Thirza (acceptance, pleasantness) **Thyrza**
Thomson (little Tom *a twin*) **Tomson**
Thomasin (little Tom *a twin*) **Thamasin**
Tiffeny (Epiphany, manifestation of God) **Tyffany**
Tirzah (acceptance, pleasantness)
Troth (fidelity, good faith)
Tryphena (delicate, dainty)
Unity (united)
Ursula (she-bear)
Valentine (strong, healthy)
Venetia (blessed)
Viola (violet)
Violet (violet-colored)
Vivien (alive)
Wilhelmina (resolute protector)
Winifred (blessed peace) **Winnifred, Winnie**
Zeresh (gold, splendor)
Zillah (shade) A favorite Gypsy name.
Zilpah (?)
Zipporah (a little bird)

MALE NAMES

Abel (breath)
Abner (the father is a light)
Abraham (father of a multitude)
Abram (father of exaltation)
Absalom (father of peace) **Absalon**
Adam (man of the red earth)
Adelulf (noble wolf)
Adrian (man from Hadrianus)
Aeneas (praiser)
Alan (?, perhaps *handsome, rock*) **Allan, Allen**
Alberic (elf ruler) Used from eighteenth century.
Aldred (old counsel)
Aldus (old)
Aldwin (old friend) **Alduin**
Alexander (defender of mankind) **Alec, Alick, Sander**
Algernon (mustached)
Aloysius (famous in war)
Ambrose (immortal)
Amias (?, perhaps friendship)
Amiel (industrious)
Amos (borne, a burden)
Amyas (?)

Anketil (god's kettle, sacrificial cauldron) **Anchitel**
Andrew (manly) **Dande, Dandy, Tandy**
Anthony (?, *priceless, of inestimable worth* is a folk definition) **Antony; Tony**
Archebald (genuinely bold, genuinely brave) **Archibald**
Asa (healer)
Athelstan (noble stone) **Athestan**
Augustus (great, venerable)
Austin (great, venerable)
Averil (boar battle)
Aylmer (nobly famous)
Aylwin (elf friend)
Azariah (whom Jehovah helps)
Baldwin (bold friend)
Balthasar (?) Seventeenth century.
Baptist (a baptiser)
Bardolph (bright wolf)
Barnabas (son of exhortation) **Barnaby**
Bartholomew (son of Talmai *hill, mound, furrows*)
Basil (kingly)
Beavis (archer) **Bevis**
Benedict (blessed) **Benedick**

Benjamin (son of the right hand) **Ben**
Bennet (blessed)
Berold (bear rule) **Berolt**
Bertin (bright friend)
Bertram (bright raven) **Bertran**
Blase (babbler) **Blaze**
Bruno (brown)
Caesar (hairy) **Cesar** Given to those born by cesarean section.
Caleb (dog; faithful)
Charles (full-grown, a man)
Chauncey (belonging to Chancey, France) **Chauncy**
Christian (a Christian, a follower of Christ)
Christmas (born at Christmas)
Christopher (bearing Christ) **Chris, Kester, Kit**
Ciprianus (from Cyprus) Seventeeth century.
Claud (lame)
Comfort (comfort, care)
Constant (constant, steadfast)
Constantine (constant, steadfast) **Constans, Cuss, Cust**
    Through the seventeenth century.
Cornelius (a horn)
Crispin (curled)
Cyriack (lordly)
Cyril (lordly)
Cyrus (lord)
Damian (tamer)
Daniel (judged by God)
Darby (from the settlement by the deer)
David (beloved)
Dennis (belonging to Dionysus) **Denis**
Dominic (belonging to a lord, belonging to the Lord) **Dominik**
Donald (world ruler)
Douglas (black, dark + blue, green, gray)
Durand (enduring, lasting) **Durant**
Easter (born at Easter)
Ebenezer (stone of help)
Eden (delight)
Edgar (wealthy spear)
Edmond (wealthy protection) **Edmund**
Edward (wealthy guardian)
Edwin (wealthy friend)
Eleazar (God has helped)
Eli (high, ascent)
Elias (Jehovah is God)
Elijah (Jehovah is God)
Elisha (God is salvation)
Elkanah (God created)
Elmer (nobly famous)
Emery (ruler of strength)
Enoch (dedicated)
Ephraim (very fruitful)
Erasmus (loved, desired)
Ernest (earnest, resolute)
Esau (hairy)
Eubule (he of good counsel)
Eugene (well-born)

Eusebius (pious)
Eustace (steadfast; happy in harvest)
Evelyn (?)
Everard (strong as a boar)
Everitt (strong as a boar) **Everit**
Ezekiel (God strengthens)
Ezra (help)
Fabian (a bean)
Felix (lucky)
Festus (?)
Florence (a blooming)
Florian (flowery)
Francis (a Frank, a freeman)
Frederick (peaceful king) **Frederic**
Fulbert (very bright)
Fulke (people) **Fulk** Seventeenth century.
Gabriel (God is strength)
Gamaliel (the Lord is recompense)
Garrett (spear rule) **Garett, Garit, Garitt**
Gaston (?)
Gavin (battle hawk)
Gedaliah (made great by Jehovah)
Geoffrey (district, traveler, pledge + peace) **Geffrei, Geffrey**
George (earth worker, farmer)
Gerald (spear rule)
Germayne (a German) **Germain**
Gershon (expulsion, stranger) **Gershom**
Gervais (servant of the spear) **Gervas, Gervase, Jarvis**
Gideon (hewer)
Giffard (give + bold, fierce)
Gilbert (bright pledge) **Gib, Gil**
Giles (goatskin shield of Zeus; a protection)
Godric (powerful God)
Godwin (friend of God)
Goldwin (friend of gold)
Gregory (vigilant, watchful)
Griffin (like a griffin, monstrous)
Gunther (bold in war)
Guy (a guide, leader)
Hamlet (little house) **Hamlett, Hamnet**
Hamon (little house)
Harry (home ruler)
Hartley (from the hart's woods) From late eighteenth century.
Hector (holding fast)
Henry (home ruler)
Herbert (army bright)
Herman (warrior, soldier)
Hezekiah (God strengthens)
Hilary (cheerful) **Hilarie**
Hiram (exalted brother)
Horatio (?)
Hosanna (save pray)
Hosea (salvation)
Hugh (heart, mind, soul) **Hugo**
Ingram (Ing's raven; angel raven)
Ira (watchful)

Isaac (laughter) **Izaak**
Isaiah (God is salvation)
Israel (contender with God)
Ives (archer) **Ivo, Yvo**
Jabez (height)
Jacob (supplanting, seizing by the heels)
James (supplanting, seizing by the heels)
Japheth (enlargement) **Japet, Japeth**
Jared (descending)
Jason (healer)
Jasper (treasure master) **Jesper**
Jedaiah (invoker of Jehovah)
Jedidiah (beloved of Jehovah)
Jeremiah (God will uplift) **Jeremy**
Jerome (holy name)
Jesimiel (God sets up)
Jesse (gift)
Jethro (excellence)
Joachim (God will establish) **Joachin**
Joel (the Lord is God)
John (God is gracious)
Jonas (dove) **Jonah**
Jonathan (God has given)
Jordan (a flowing down) **Judd, Jurd**
Joseph (he shall add) **Joe**
Joshua (God is salvation)
Josiah (the Lord supports)
Julian (youth, downy)
Julius (youth, downy)
Justin (just)
Kenrick (royal rule)
Kenward (brave guardian) **Kenard** Seventeenth century.
Laban (white)
Lambert (bright land) Rarely used.
Laurance (from Laurentum)
Lazarus (whom God helps)
Lemuel (devoted to God)
Leonard (bold as a lion)
Levi (joining)
Levin (dear friend) Seventeenth century.
Lewis (famous in war) **Louis**
Lionel (little lion)
Lucas (light, man from Loukania)
Lucian (light, man from Loukania)
Lucius (light, man from Loukania)
Luke (light; man from Loukania)
Lyell (lion) **Lyel** Seventeenth century.
Malachi (my messenger)
Manfred (peace of man)
Marcus (of Mars, warlike)
Mark (of Mars, warlike)
Martin (of Mars, warlike)
Matheus (gift of God) **Mathiu, Mattheus**
Matthias (gift of God)
Mauger (spear grinder)
Maynard (strong and hardy)

Meshach (agile)
Micah (Who is like God?)
Michael (Who is like God?)
Milo (?, perhaps *mild, peaceful; merciful*) **Milon**
Mordecai (worshiper of Marduk)
Moses (drawn out of the water)
Nathan (gift)
Nathanael (gift of God) **Nathaniel**
Nehemiah (comforted by Jehovah)
Neville (from the new town) **Nevell, Nevil**
Nicholas (victory of the people) **Nicoll, Nichol, Coll**
Noah (rest, comfort)
Obadiah (servant of God)
Odo (wealth)
Osbern (god bear) **Osborn**
Oscar (God's spear)
Osmond (God's protection) **Osmund**
Oswald (God's power)
Pascal (Easter, born at Easter)
Patrick (a patrician, an aristocrat)
Paul (small)
Paulin (small)
Percy (from Percy, Normandy)
Philip (lover of horses) Very rarely used.
Phineas (oracle)
Quintin (fifth)
Rafe (counsel wolf)
Ralph (counsel wolf) Eighteenth century.
Randulf (shield wolf)
Raymund (counsel protection) **Raimund, Reimond**
Raynold (powerful protection) **Rainald, Raynald, Renold, Reynold**
Reginald (judgment power)
Renfred (counsel might)
Reuben (behold, a son!)
Reynard (counsel hard)
Richard (stern king)
Robert (bright with fame) **Rob, Robb**
Roger (famous with the spear) Used in the sixteenth and seventeenth centuries.
Roland (famous land) **Rolland**
Samson (the sun) **Sansom**
Samuel (heard of God)
Saul (asked for)
Seth (appointed)
Shem (renowned)
Silas (ask for)
Simon (heard) **Simond, Symon**
Siward (victory protection)
Solomon (peaceful)
Stephen (a crown, a garland)
Talbot (pillager, bandit; lampblack)
Theodoric (ruler of the people)
Thomas (a twin)
Thurstan (Thor's stone)
Timothy (honor, respect)

Titus (?, possibly *to honor*)
Tobias (God is good)
Tristram (tumult, sadness)
Uriah (God is light)
Valentine (healthy, strong)
Vincent (conquering)
Walter (ruler of an army)

William (resolute protector)
Winston (from Winston *friend's town*)
Zachariah (God remembers)
Zacharias (God remembers)
Zebedee (God bestows)
Zebulun (to carry, to exalt)
Zephaniah (the Lord has hidden)

SURNAMES

Children born out of wedlock assumed the surnames of their mothers or sometimes if the fathers were known, a compounding of the names of both parents. An illegitimate child continued to be regarded as a bastard, even if the parents were wed after its birth. Until 1926, under English law, "Subsequent marriage of parents does not legitimate a child born of them before the marriage." Among the rest of the population, surnames were now hereditary, and their spellings became more regularized.

Adams (son of Adam)
Akerman (a farmer or ploughman) **Ackerman**
Albin (white) **Albyn**
Albright (nobly bright) **Allbright**
Almand (German) **Allmand**
Armstrong (strong arms) **Armstrang**
Ashburner (charcoal maker)
Ashton (dweller at the town by the ash trees)
Aston (from the east town; noble stone)
Austin (great, venerable) **Austen**
Bacheler (young knight, novice in arms)
Bacon (side of bacon)
Baker (a baker)
Ball (ball; bald place; the round one)
Barber (a barber, one who practiced surgery and dentistry)
Barnelby (son of consolation)
Baron (a baron, a nobleman)
Base (the short one)
Berenger (bear spear)
Bertelot (little Bartholomew)
Blanchard (whitish)
Bowyer (a maker or trader of bows)
Brown (brown, brown-haired) **Browne**
Burgis (a freeman of a borough)
Buxton (Bucca's stone)
Calthorp (from Calthorpe *Calla's estate*)
Calvin (bald)
Carpenter (a carpenter)
Champayn (from Champaign)
Chaucer (maker of leather pants)
Chauncey (belonging to Chancey, France)
Colyer (a maker or seller of charcoal)
Cornish (a Cornish person)
Danvers (from Anvers)
Darnel (the darnel plant; from Darnall) **Darnell**
Derwin (dear friend)
Drinkwater (one who drinks water)

Dunn (brown-haired)
Dwight (the white one)
Edmundson (son of Edmond *wealthy protector*)
Ellis (Jehovah is God; God is salvation)
Ellyson (son of Ellis *Jehovah is God; God is salvation*)
Emson (son of Emma *strength*)
Essex (from Essex)
Ewen (lamb; youth; well-born)
Florantine (a Florentine)
Florence (from Florence)
Fleming (a Fleming)
Fort (strong)
French (a French person)
Glasier (a glass maker)
Golding (son of Golda *gold*)
Goldsmith (a goldsmith)
Goodyer (good year) **Goodyear**
Grant (great, large)
Greene (dweller near the village green)
Grevill (from Gréville, La Manche)
Guildford (from Guildford *river ford near the marigolds*)
Hale (dweller in the remote valley)
Hankyn (little Hans)
Hawthorn (dweller near the hawthorn) **Hawthorne**
Hill (dweller near the hill)
Howard (brave heart; chief warden; ewe herder) **Heward, Huward**
Hughlot (little Hugh)
Ingram (angel raven)
Irish (an Irish person)
Ives (archer)
Jagger (carter, peddler; God is gracious)
Jenour (engineer) **Jenoure**
Jakeson (son of Jack *God is gracious*)
Johnson (son of John *God is gracious*)
Jordan (a flowing down, descend) **Jourdan, Jurdain**
Keate (dweller at the animal hut) **Keat, Keates, Keats**

Kendrick (chief man, chief hero)
King (a king) **Kinge**
Knight (servant, knight)
Knolles (dweller at the top of the hill) **Knoll**
Lambert (bright land) **Lambard, Lambart, Lambarth**
Latimer (interpreter)
Lawless (an outlaw, licentious) **Lawelesse**
Legg (leg)
Lombard (long beard) **Lumbard**
Mailer (an enameler) **Mailler**
Maitland (discourteous, rude)
Malet (the unfortunate one, cursed)
Mallory (the unfortunate one, cursed)
Marchant (a merchant, a trader) **Marchand**
Matthews (son of Matthew *gift of God*)
Naismith (a knife smith) **Naysmith**
Nesbitt (from Nesbit or Nesbitt) **Naisbet, Naisbit, Nesbit**
Neville (from the new town)
Newman (a newcomer)
Nicoles (victory of the people) **Nicholls, Nichols**
Norman (a Norman, from Normandy)
Oaks (dweller near the oak trees) **Oak, Oake**
Oldfield (dweller by the old field)
Orchard (dweller near or worker at an orchard)
Osman (god-bear) **Osmand**
Oxnard (an ox herder)
Percy (from Percy, La Manche)
Pickering (from Piker's meadow)
Pikard (one from Picardy)
Plymouth (from Plymouth)
Poore (pauper)
Prendregast (?, perhaps *dweller at the village near the castle*)
Ravenhill (dweller at the raven's hill)

Redford (dweller at the red ford)
Redgrave (dweller at the red grove)
Renshaw (from the raven's wood)
Richmond (from Richmond *rich mountain*)
Robertson (son of Robert *bright with fame*)
Rochester (from Rochester *Hróf's stronghold*)
Ross (dweller on the peninsula)
Russell (little red-haired one)
Sadeler (a maker or seller of saddles) **Sadelier**
Shepard (shepherd) **Shepperde**
Stoke (from Stoke)
Stolemaker (a maker or seller of stoles)
Sutton (from Sutton)
Tabard (a sleeveless coat)
Tait (cheerful, gay)
Talbot (lampblack)
Tomlin (little Tom *a twin*)
Trumble (strong-bold) **Trumbull**
Ullman (maker or seller of oil)
Underhill (dweller at the foot of a hill)
Unwin (young bear-friend)
Uppington (dweller up in the village)
Urban (dweller in the city)
Vale (dweller in the valley)
Valentine (strong, healthy)
Vaughan (small) **Vaughn**
Vennell (dweller at the small street or alley) **Vennall, Venel**
Vidal (vital, full of vitality) **Vidall**
Walsh (a Welsh person)
Walshman (a Welsh man)
Webber (a weaver)
White (white, fair complexioned)
Williams (son of William *resolute protector*)

Chapter Seven

THE MODERN WORLD
GEORGE IV TO ELIZABETH II
[1820–PRESENT]

POLITICS

GEORGE IV FUNCTIONED as regent for nine years before his mentally ill father passed away. He had been witty, energetic, and wild in his youth, and his being named regent did nothing to temper those attitudes and behaviors. The Regency period was a colorful time filled with banquets, parties, hectic lifestyles, and relaxed moral attitudes.

By the time George inherited the throne, he was fifty-seven years old. Hard living had taken its toll, and he was an old man well before his time. He slept poorly and was dependent upon the large doses of laudanum he put in his brandy. In his later years, he sometimes pretended that he had played an important part at Waterloo, causing people to be unsure whether he was playing a farce or if he was turning into a lunatic like his father had been.

After his father died, George sought to use his position to divorce his vulgar, undignified wife, Caroline of Brunswick, by means of a Bill of Pains and Penalties. The divorce was denied, and George banned her from his coronation ceremony. He should have let her attend, for she made quite a scene attempting to break into the coronation. She died shortly afterward, sparing George further humiliation and embarrassment.

Notable changes of leadership occurred when George IV ascended the throne. George Canning was made foreign secretary, and Robert Peel became home secretary. Peel revamped and humanized the penal code, and he changed the nature of the police force by disarming them and giving them a more helpful, less military mission. Other accomplishments followed. In 1828, Protestant Nonconformists were finally allowed the freedom to hold public office, and a year later, the Catholic Emancipation Act was signed.

George died in June 1830. His only child, Charlotte, had died in childbed, so it was to his brother William, the Duke of Clarence and third son of George III, that the crown went. William had been unschooled in the role of monarch and even, it seems, in the way of proper behavior. He became a midshipman in the navy at the age of thirteen and eventually became a capable officer. But he was a sailor through and through, and his colorful language and coarse manners reflected that. Though William was liked well enough by the royal family, he was nicknamed ''Silly Billy'' and was never really well-respected by them.

When it became apparent that his brother, George IV, would have no further heirs, William was determined to live to become king and show everybody that he wasn't the goof they all thought him to be. To that end, he took great pains with his health, gargling a couple of gallons of water each morning and wearing huge galoshes to keep his feet warm to prevent chills. He also spent months practicing his signature, writing ''William R'' over and over in anticipation. After notification of his brother's death, William, ecstatic at having finally achieved his goal, didn't even attempt to moderate or contain his excitement. He was seen racing about London in an open carriage, with a huge grin on his face, offering lifts to people and doffing his hat and bowing to passersby.

His seven-year reign saw a Whig government carry out parliamentary reform that assured fair representation of the people. Slavery was abolished in 1833, and to address the terrible problem of children slaving away in factories, the Factory Act of 1833 forbade the hiring of children under the age of nine and restricted the hours of employees aged nine through thirteen to forty-eight per week, and those aged thirteen through eighteen to sixty-eight hours per week.

Though great accomplishments were happening, William himself was finding that being king was not as much fun as he expected it would be. His quarrel with his sister-in-law, the duchess of Kent, was unfortunate as well. William's heir was Victoria, the daughter of the duchess and the deceased Duke of Kent. The duchess refused to allow Victoria to go to court, calling it a ''hot-bed of vice.'' This angered William, and he retaliated by spreading vulgar stories about a relationship between the duchess and the controller of her household. In 1836, the duchess infuriated the king by taking over a suite of rooms in Kensington Palace without permission. As Victoria was still a minor, her mother would act as regent if William were to die. It was a proposition the king couldn't bear to contemplate, and he directed the same determination he'd shown in outliving his brother to seeing Victoria come of age. He succeeded. He died on June 20, 1837, a month after Victoria's eighteenth birthday.

Victoria's reign lasted sixty-four years, the longest of any English monarch. She ushered in the Victorian Era, an age that oversaw the urbanization of England, great intellectual, literary, religious, and moral reawakening, several wars oversees, and parliamentary and social reform.

In her first years as monarch, she was greatly influenced by her charming and gallant prime minister, Lord Melbourne, who advised her on everything from politics to what she should or should not read. After her marriage to Prince Albert of Saxe-Coburg, she came under her husband's influence and finally came to understand the serious social problems that plagued the country's working class. The Corn Laws, which prohibited the importation of foreign corn, were repealed after the Great Potato Famine of 1846 in Ireland, the working conditions in mines and factories were improved, and there was great work done on the country's railway system. In the 1850s, Prince Albert's Great International Exhibition encouraged trade and tourism, Britain became involved in the Crimean War, and the government took over the reins of Indian government from the East India Company.

Victoria suffered her greatest personal tragedy in 1861: the death of Prince Albert. She withdrew immediately into seclusion and isolated herself for so long that some believed she did not deserve the amount of money the state was paying her. Calls for abolishing the monarchy were heard, and she eventually returned to a more visible presence. In 1876, Prime Minister Benjamin Disraeli persuaded parliament to grant her the title Empress of India.

The remaining years of her reign were occupied with the struggle between Conservatives and the Liberal Party on issues such as social reform, Irish home rule, and limitations of the power of the House of Lords. The queen's own conservative views were echoed by much of the population, and her earlier unpopularity was replaced by an almost worshipful attitude toward her by her subjects. Her Golden Jubilee in 1887 was marked by great celebration, and her Diamond Jubilee in 1897 was celebrated with even greater exuberance and pride for the greatness of an empire that spanned the globe. She came to be regarded as the "grandmother of Europe," as the marriages of her nine children to members of the royal houses of the Continent led to many multinational grandchildren and great-grandchildren.

When Victoria died in January 1901 at the age of eighty-one, a whole age had passed. She had been queen for so long that no one could remember the proper steps to take at the death of a monarch and how to prepare for the accession of the new sovereign.

The crown went to fifty-nine-year-old Edward VII, the eldest son of Victoria and Albert. As a child, his father had felt that firm discipline, a strict regimen, and constant moral exhortation were what was required to turn him into a responsible adult in preparation for his role as king. Edward rebelled against the pressure and restrictions and engaged in a lifestyle that was directly opposite from the moral one his parents believed in. While on army maneuvers in Ireland, an actress was smuggled into his tent. His father went into a rage upon hearing about it, and coincidentally died a few weeks later. Victoria blamed Edward for his father's death and thereafter set a policy of excluding him from government. Thus, his main activity became the pursuit of pleasure. In fact, his later success at foreign relations was built on the ties he made while on pleasure visits abroad.

Edward and his nephew, the German Kaiser William II, held a strong mutual dislike of one another. Germany sought an alliance with Austria and Italy, Russia and France were allies, and Britain allied itself first with Japan in 1902, with France in 1904, then with Russia in 1907.

Edward VII died in May 1910. His reign spanned only nine years, but he gave his name to an era that saw social change, progressive foreign policy, and a renewed popularity of the royal family.

Edward made sure his relationship with his children was far different from the sad one he'd had with his own parents. George V enjoyed a happy childhood and a close-knit family. Being the second son, he trained in the navy and became the commander of a torpedo boat. In January 1892, to his great dispair, his elder brother, Prince Eddy, died of pneumonia; George was now the heir to the throne. He was made the Prince of Wales and worked closely with his father in preparation for his own accession.

In 1911, a Parliament Bill to restrict the Upper House and the National Insurance Act passed. These were years when Irish civil war loomed, the women's suffrage movement was in full swing, and the working class was unsettled. Yet all rallied together when faced by World War I in 1914. In July of that year, Austria declared war on Serbia, and Russia rose to Serbia's defense. In August, Germany declared war on Russia and France, and England rose on behalf of its allies. In 1917, anti-German sentiment led to the loss of George's family name of Saxe-Coburg and Gotha: He volunteered to adopt that of Windsor.

Most of the country's problems were social and due to dire postwar conditions. The vote was given to all men over twenty-one and all women over thirty; in 1928, all over the age of twenty-one were given voting rights. In 1932, George broadcast his Christmas message by radio to his subjects in all parts of the realm, personally touching the common people as they'd never been touched by the monarchy before. When George V died in 1936, economic conditions had improved, and the outlook was optimistic.

Before his father's death, Edward VIII spent most of his time traveling on ambassadorial trips. He chafed under the constrictions imposed on his daily life and often sought refuge at his country estate. It was there that he met and fell in love with twice-married American Wallis Simpson in 1931. By 1935, her divorce to her husband was finalized, and before Edward informed his father of his affair, George V had died and Edward had become king. It was a turbulent year, during which time Edward knew he had a choice to make: the monarchy or the woman he loved. He chose the woman. In December 1936, he abdicated in favor of his brother.

George VI never believed his brother would actually go through with the abdication, but when the monarchy was thrust upon him, he was determined to do his best for his country. His was the first coronation to be broadcast by radio.

In Germany, Hitler's Nazi regime was carrying out its devious plans, and by 1939, World War II had begun. Prime Minister Winston Churchill saw England through the horrors of war; George and his wife were nearly killed in a daylight raid during the blitz in 1940. In 1942, the king's brother, the duke of Kent, was killed in active duty.

Following World War II, a postwar general election put a Labor government in place. Britain accepted the formation of the United Nations, withdrew from the Indian subcontinent, made Ceylon a dominion in 1948, granted Burma independence in 1949, made Malaya a Federation, and became a welfare state and a part of NATO. In 1951, Winston Churchill was brought back to power. In February 1952, George VI died in his sleep.

The eldest daughter of King George VI and Queen Elizabeth was Princess Elizabeth Alexandra Mary, and it was to her that the crown went. She was raised in a relaxed, loving home and was carefully schooled for her future role as queen. In 1945, at the age of nineteen, she persuaded her parents to let her join the Auxiliary Transport Service so she could do her part for the war effort. She proved a capable driver and mechanic, met men and women from all walks of life, and enjoyed interacting without the shield of royalty standing in her way. In 1947, she married her third cousin, Prince Philip of Greece. It was the first televised event of its kind in the history of the country.

Elizabeth was on a state visit in Kenya when she heard the news of her father's death. She was crowned Elizabeth II in June 1953. Under the influence of Prince Philip, the role of the monarchy was revised and modernized. All types of media were used to bring the royal family closer to their subjects, and the responsibilities of the monarchy has come to mean the combined efforts of the family as a group, not just the sovereign as an individual.

SOCIETY

WHEN ENGLAND STARTED on the road to industrialization late in the eighteenth century, British society was forever changed. Popular sentiment was that industrialization would bring about the ''conquest of nature'' and would lead to the ''betterment of the species'' and the ''civilization of the masses.''

The whole Victorian era was one of amazing growth as mechanized factories became the main units of production over the efforts of individual, skilled laborers. Fueling all that machinery led to an increased need for coal, which in turn resulted in more mines and a need for more miners.

Britain took full advantage of all its overseas possessions during this time. Cheap raw materials were brought into the country and manufactured into a variety of goods for domestic sales and foreign export. Such a wealth of goods resulted in the establishment of many more shops, markets, and even chain stores; one English grocer operated a chain of sixty shops in London alone. In 1863, the country's first department store was established in London. Brisk trade in textiles, heavy machinery, iron and steel, and munitions, and the country's expertise at ship building resulted in Britain's status as the largest and strongest empire of the nineteenth century.

But such prosperity had a dark side that was at complete contrast to the Victorian ideals of the conquest of nature, betterment of the species, and civilization of the masses. True, industrialization was the impetus for a great deal of innovation and new discoveries that benefited the human race and helped relieve the burdens of everyday living. But mechanization also required fewer human workers. And as the population had nearly tripled since the end of the eighteenth century, this meant severe unemployment. This was especially true in the area of weaving, as power looms took the place of skilled hand weavers. Whole areas were left without work, and as competition for jobs became fierce, factory owners exploited the situation by hiring women and children for a fraction of what a man would earn. Workers endured appalling hardships. Conditions in the factories and mines became so alarming that in 1842, women and children were forbidden to work in the mines. In 1847, government passed the Ten Hours Act, restricting to ten hours a day, the number of hours women and children could work in the textile mills. Such terrible conditions prompted workingmen to form protective unions. By the end of the nineteenth century, there were nearly two million trade unionists.

The ideal of the "conquest of nature" may have sounded like progress, but in reality, early industrialization was more like the "exploitation of nature" as little thought was given to the consequences of that conquest in terms of the environment and its role in nature. Mining left great slag heaps towering over towns and villages; little thought was given to runoff poisoning streams and the land. Coal-powered factories belched black soot that covered everything for miles, and their cinder heaps rose nearly as high as the slag heaps. Pollution was terrible.

The economy slowed late in the nineteenth century, partly because the English had failed to develop more efficient machinery and failed to cultivate the technological research that would lead to those improvements. It soon became apparent that a lack of education among the masses was creating a workforce with neither the skills nor the education to further progress and help the country maintain its position among the leading nations of the world. In 1870, the Education Act was passed, and grammar schools were established across England.

During the first half of the nineteenth century, railroad building reached a feverish peak. The railways revolutionized the distribution of food and consumer goods, quickly and efficiently carried mail throughout the kingdom, and promoted travel and tourism. Railroads soon became indispensable to society. In 1844, parliament set low fares to make travel affordable and passed an act requiring railway companies to run at least one train every day except Sundays, Christmas Day, and Good Friday.

Disaster came in the form of World War I. Over a million British troops lost their lives during the war, and the ones who survived came home to a crumbling economy and rampant unemployment. It wasn't until after World War II that life became easier for all segments of English society. Advancements in technology, the use of improved fuels, improved transportation systems, and new sanitation systems led to better living conditions. An aggressive building program undertaken to replace areas damaged during the war provided desperately needed jobs and helped modernize much of the country. Today, over 50 percent of the people own their own homes and enjoy the comforts modern society has to offer.

In 1947, the government established a welfare state to see to the needs of the English people. Unemployment pay and old-age benefits helped ease suffering, as did a new system of providing medical care to all.

At the beginning of this time period, the country's economy rested in the manufacture and export of textiles and products from the heavy industries. Today, Britain is a world leader in advanced coal mining technologies, it's a leader in the computer industries, and it's one of the largest chemical-producing nations in the world. London has the world's largest concentration of banks and has the largest insurance market.

Since 1944, education has been free and mandatory for children aged five through sixteen. Primary education is divided into two stages: infant and junior. The infant stage, for children aged five through ten, consists of the basic skills of reading, writing, and arithmetic. The junior stage is more formal, and the students tackle more difficult subjects such as foreign languages, math, and science. After graduation from primary school, some students choose to continue their education in the sixth form, the final two-year stage of primary education. Colleges and universities are available for advanced studies.

RELIGION

THOUGH CHURCHGOING IS still very important to many, religion no longer plays as important a role in regulating the activities of English society as in the past. The two primary church organizations remain the Church of England and the Roman Catholic Church. Other sects and religions, such as Presbyterians, Methodists, Congregationalists, Baptists, and Jews, continue to have small but loyal memberships. Hinduism and Islam are also represented as people continue to immigrate from Pakistan and India.

NAMING

DURING THE NINETEENTH century, many English parents used surnames as their children's first names. Though not an unknown trend, the practice gained special popularity during this time period. Further, some parents bestowed the mother's maiden surname upon their firstborn children. The practice is still common today, but more often the mother's maiden name is bestowed not as a first name, but as a middle name.

Many of the old biblical names that remained so popular for so many centuries were beginning to be supplanted by modern naming traditions. These include the use of nature names, flower names, names of precious gems, and names taken from popular movies, television series, and books. The bestowal of modern coinages is another modern naming trend increasing in popularity. Names from Wales, Cornwall, Scotland, and Ireland are in widespread use, and as more immigrants enter the country, the pool of names widens.

FEMALE NAMES

Abigail (father of exaltation) **Abbey**
Adah (adornment)
Adele (noble) **Adela**
Adeline (nobility)
Adria (from Hadrianus)
Adrianne (from Hadrianus) **Adriana, Adrianna, Adrienne**
Agalia (splendor)
Agnes (chaste, pure) **Aggie**
Alana (?, perhaps *handsome; rock*; O child)
Alberta (noble and bright)
Alethea (truth) **Alethea, Aletheia, Alithea**
Alexa (defender)
Alexandra (defender of mankind)
Alexis (defender)
Alice (nobility)
Alicia (nobility)
Alinda (beautiful)
Aline (noble)
Alison (noble one)
Allegra (cheerful)
Alma (soul; nourishing)
Alpha (ox; leader; first)
Althea (wholesome)
Alyssa (nobility)
Amana (established)
Amanda (beloved)
Amaranth (unfading, a flower name and the name of a shep-

herdess in Virgil's *Eclogues*. In legend, the amaranth is an imaginary flower that never fades and never dies.)
Amaryllis (?, a flower name; a conventional name for a shepherdess in pastoral poetry.)
Amber (amber, a translucent, fossil resin)
Amelia (work; rival)
Amicia (?, possibly *friendship*) **Amice**
Amity (friendship)
Amy (beloved)
Anastasia (resurrection)
Andrea (womanly)
Andriana (womanly)
Andrine (womanly)
Angela (an angel)
Angelica (angelic)
Anne (grace, full of grace, mercy) **Ann, Anna**
Annis (chaste, pure)
Anthea (flowery)
Antonia (?, *priceless, of inestimable worth* is a folk definition)
Appolonia (of Apollo) **Appolina**
April (second, latter; born during April)
Arabella (?, perhaps *eagle*; *hearth*) **Arabel**
Arlene A modern coinage.
Arlette (little eagle)
Ashley (dweller near the ash tree forest)
Audrey (noble strength)
Augusta (great, venerable)
Aurelia (golden)

Aurora (the dawn)
Ava (?)
Aveline (?)
Averil (boar battle) **Averell, Everild**
Avice (?) **Avis, Avise**
Barbara (foreign woman) **Barb**
Beatrice (bringer of joy) **Beatrix**
Becca (noose)
Becky (noose)
Belinda (?, perhaps *snake*)
Bella (beautiful) **Belle**
Benet (blessed) **Bennet, Bennitt**
Berenice (bringer of victory)
Bertha (bright)
Beryl (a green gemstone)
Bess (God is my oath) **Bessie**
Beth (God is my oath)
Bethany (house of figs)
Blanch (white) **Blanche**
Bliss (happiness, joy)
Blossom (a bloom, flower)
Blythe (cheerful)
Bobbie (bright with fame)
Bonnie (pretty, pleasant)
Brenda (the blade of a sword)
Brenna (?, possibly *force, strength; high*)
Brianne (*force, strength; high*)
Bridget (strength)
Brilliana Coinage of Sir Edward Conway based Brill, Holland.
Brooke (a brook, a stream). **Brook**
Bryony (the bryony plant)
Camilla (virgin of unblemished character)
Candace (white, pure, sincere)
Cara (beloved)
Careen (?)
Carina (a keel of a ship)
Carla (a freeman)
Carleen (a freeman) **Carlin**
Carmel (vineyard, orchard) **Carmela**
Carmilla (?)
Carol (full-grown, a woman) **Carole, Caryl**
Caroline (full-grown, a woman) **Caro, Carrie, Lina**
Casey (?)
Cassandra (?)
Cassia (cinnamon)
Cassidy (descendent of Caiside *bent, curly, lock*)
Cassie Short for Cassandra, Catherine, and Cassidy.
Catherine (pure, unsullied) **Catharine, Katherine; Cassie, Cathy, Kate, Kitty**
Cecilia (blind, dim-sighted)
Celeste (celestial, heavenly)
Celia (heaven)
Chantale (stone, boulder)
Charis (grace)
Charissa (grace)
Charity (charity, benevolence)

Charlene (full-grown)
Charlotte (full-grown, a woman) **Charlet**
Charmaine (charm, chant)
Charmian (a little joy)
Chauncey (belonging to Chancey, France)
Cherish (cherish, treasure)
Cherry (darling; a cherry)
Cheryl Modern coinage.
Cheryth Modern coinage.
Chevonne (God is gracious)
Chloe (blooming, verdant)
Chloris (green)
Christa (a Christian)
Christabel (?, probably *beautiful Christ*) **Christabell**
Christiana (a Christian, a follower of Christ)
Christine (a Christian, a follower of Christ) **Christina**
Cicely (blind, dim-sighted) **Cecily, Sisley**
Cindy (from Kynthos; light)
Clarabelle (bright, clear, famous + beautiful)
Clare (bright, clear, famous)
Clarimond (bright protection)
Clarinda (bright, clear, famous)
Clarissa (bright, clear, famous) **Clarice, Claricia**
Claudia (lame)
Clemence (clement, mild)
Clementine (clement, mild)
Cleo (glory, fame)
Clorinda (green, verdant)
Colleen (a young girl)
Constance (constant)
Cora (maiden)
Coralie (maiden)
Cordelia (?, perhaps *daughter of the sea*)
Corinna (maiden) **Corinne**
Cornelia (a horn)
Courtney (from Courtenay, France)
Cressa (?)
Cressida (?)
Crystal (crystal, clear)
Cynthia (of Kynthos)
Cyra (lord)
Dahlia (the dahlia flower)
Daisy (day's eye, a daisy)
Damaris (?, possibly *heifer*)
Dana (a Dane; judge)
Danielle (God is my judge)
Daria (?)
Darlene (darling) **Darlena**
Darrene (?)
Dawn (dawn, daybreak)
Deanna (divine)
Deborah (a bee) **Debora, Debra; Debbie**
Dee Short for any name beginning with the letter *D*.
Deirdre (young girl)
Delia (from Delos)
Delicia (delight)

Delilah (delicate)
Delwyn (pretty and blessed)
Delyth (pretty)
Denise (of Dionysus) **Denis**
Desiderata (desire)
Diana (divine)
Dilys (genuine)
Dina (judged; sea warrior) **Dinah**
Dionne (divine; of Zeus)
Dolly (gift of God; sorrows)
Donna (world ruler)
Donnet (given)
Dora (gift)
Dorcas (gazelle)
Doreen (gift)
Doria (gift; Dorian woman)
Dorinda (gift)
Dorothea (gift of God) **Doll**
Dove (a dove)
Drusilla (?)
Dulcibella (sweet and beautiful) **Dulcibell**
Dulcie (sweet)
Earlene (an earl) **Earline, Erlene, Erline**
Ebony (ebony, a hard, black wood)
Eden (delight)
Edith (prosperous in war) **Edyth**
Edna (rejuvenation, delight)
Edwina (wealthy friend)
Eileen (?) **Aileen, Aline, Ileen**
Elaine (light, torch, bright)
Eleanor (light, torch, bright) **Elianor, Elinor**
Elizabeth (God is my oath) **Bess, Bessie, Beth, Betty** (eighteenth century), **Eliza, Lizzie, Lizzy**
Elfreda (elf strength)
Elisa (God is my oath)
Eliza (God is my oath)
Ella (foreign, other; light)
Ellen (light, torch, bright) **Elen**
Ellis (nobility)
Eloisa (hale, hearty)
Elsa (God is my oath) **Else**
Emeline (strength; work) **Emmeline**
Emeny (?)
Emerald (an emerald)
Emerlee (strength; work)
Emilia (strength; work)
Emily (strength; work)
Emma (strength; work)
Emmeline (little rival)
Emmot (strength; work; rival)
Enid (?, perhaps *soul*)
Erica (eternal ruler) **Erika**
Erin (Ireland)
Esmeralda (emerald) **Esmerelda**
Essex (from Essex)
Estelle (star)

Esther (myrtle; star)
Ethel (noble)
Ethelinda (noble + tender, soft; a snake)
Eugenia (well-born, noble) **Eugenie**
Eulalia (fair speech)
Eunice (good victory)
Euphemia (fair speech)
Eustacia (steadfast; happy harvest)
Evangeline (good news, the Gospel)
Eve (life) **Eva**
Eveline (?) **Evelina, Evelyn**
Faith (faith, trust)
Felice (lucky)
Felicity (happiness)
Fern (a fern)
Fidelma (?)
Finella (white shoulders)
Fiona (fair, white, clear)
Flavia (yellow)
Fleur (a flower)
Flora (a flower)
Florence (a blooming)
Flower (a flower)
Frances (a Frank, a freeman) **Francesse**
Francesca (a Frenchwoman)
Francine (French)
Francoise (a Frenchwoman)
Frederica (peaceful ruler)
Frusannah (?, perhaps a blending of Frances and Susannah)
Gabriela (God is my strength) **Gabrielle**
Gail (father of exaltation) **Gale, Gayle**
Gay (happy, merry) **Gae, Gaye**
Gaynor (white, fair, blessed + smooth, soft)
Gemma (a gem)
Geneva (juniper berry)
Genista (a broom plant)
Georgia (earth worker, farmer) **Georgie**
Georgiana (earth worker, farmer)
Georgina (earth worker, farmer)
Geraldine (spear ruler)
Gertrude (spear strength)
Ghislain (pledge) **Ghislaine**
Gillian (youth, downy)
Gina (earthworker, farmer)
Ginger (the ginger spice; red-haired)
Giselle (pledge)
Gladys (lame)
Glenna (mountain valley)
Glenys (pure, holy)
Gloria (glory)
Goodeth (God war)
Grace (grace, mercy)
Greer (watchful, vigilant)
Guinevere (white, fair, blessed + smooth, soft)
Gwen (white, fair, blessed)
Gwyneth (blessed) **Gwenyth**

Hannah (grace, full of grace, mercy)
Harriet (home ruler)
Hayley (dweller in the remote valley; the hay meadow)
Hazel (the hazel tree)
Heather (a heather plant)
Helah (rust)
Helen (light, torch, bright)
Helena (light, torch, bright) **Helene**
Henrietta (home ruler)
Hermia (of Hermes)
Hermione (of Hermes)
Hester (myrtle; star)
Hilarie (cheerful) **Hilary, Hillarie, Hillary**
Hilda (battle)
Holly (the holly tree) **Hollie** Often given to children born near Christmas.
Honey (honey; sweet one)
Honor (honor, esteem) **Honour**
Honora (honor, esteem) **Honoria; Nora**
Hope (hope, expectation)
Horatia (?)
Hortensia (?) **Hortense**
Hosannah (save pray) **Hosanna**
Ida (work, labor)
Ideny (work, labor) **Idonea, Idonia, Idony**
Imogene (?) **Imogen**
India (from the subcontinent of India)
Iona (from the small Hebridean island of Iona)
Irene (peace)
Iris (the iris flower; the Greek goddess of the rainbow)
Isabel (God is my oath) **Isabell, Isobel**
Ismenia (?)
Isylte (?, perhaps *ruler of the ice*) **Isold, Isolda, Isolt**
Ivy (the ivy plant) **Ivey**
Jacklin (supplanting, seizing by the heels) **Jacklyn, Jacqueline; Jackie, Jacqui**
Jade (stone of the side)
Jael (mountain goat)
Jamie (supplanted, seizing by the heels) **Jaime, Jaimi, Jamey**
Jan (God is gracious)
Jane (God is gracious)
Janelle (God is gracious) **Janella**
Janet (God is gracious; little Jane) **Jennet**
Janey (little Jane *God is gracious*) **Janie, Jayney**
Janine (God is gracious) **Jeanine**
Jasmine (jasmine) **Jasmin, Jasmyn, Jazmin**
Jean (God is gracious) **Jeane**
Jeanette (little Jean *God is gracious*) **Janette, Jannette**
Jeanie (little Jean *God is gracious*) **Jeannie**
Jemima (pure)
Jennifer (white, fair, blessed + smooth, soft) **Jenifer; Jennie, Jenny**
Jerioth (curtains)
Jeromia (sacred name)
Jessica (gift; God is gracious)
Jessie (little Janet *God is gracious*; gift)
Jetta (a hard, black stone)
Jill (youth, downy)
Jo Short form of names beginning with *Jo-*.
Joan (God is gracious)
Jocelyn (from the tribe of the Gauts) **Jocelin, Joceline, Joscelin**
Jody (praised) **Jodi, Jodie**
Johanna (God is gracious) **Joanna**
Josephine (he shall add)
Josie (he shall add)
Joy (joy, happiness)
Joyce (merry, happy)
Judith (praised)
Judy (praised)
Julia (youth, downy) **Julie**
Juliana (youth, downy)
Juliet (youth, downy)
June (the sixth month; born in June)
Justina (right, just) **Justine**
Karen (pure, unsullied) **Keren**
Kat (pure, unsullied)
Kate (pure, unsullied) **Katie**
Katrina (pure, unsullied)
Kay Short form of any name beginning with the letter *K*.
Kayley (slender)
Keeley (slender)
Kelly (war, strife; wood, grove)
Kelsey (victory ship)
Kendall (spring)
Kerry (black-haired one; pure, unsullied)
Keturah (incense)
Kezia (cassia)
Kiera (little dark one)
Kim (?)
Kimberley (?) **Kimberely, Kimberly; Kim**
Kimbra Modern coinage.
Kimmie (little Kim)
Kinburga (royal fortress)
Kyla (narrow)
Laetitia (happiness) **Letitia**
Lalage (babbler)
Lana (handsome; rock; O child)
Lark (a songbird)
Laura (laurel)
Laurana (woman from Laurentum)
Laurel (a laurel bush)
Lauren (from Laurentum)
Laurencia (woman from Laurentum)
Laurentia (woman from Laurentum)
Laureola (woman from Laurentum)
Lavinia (from Latium)
Leah (weary)
Leanne (dweller by the wood or clearing + grace)
Lee (dweller by the wood or clearing) **Lea, Leigh**
Leila (dark beauty) **Leela, Leilah, Leilia**

Leona (lion) **Liona**
Leonora (light, torch, bright)
Leslie (smaller meadow, smaller clearing) **Lesley**
Lettice (happiness) **Letice, Letitia**
Lexa (defender) **Lexi, Lexie, Lexy**
Liane (sun)
Lilith (of the night) **Lillith**
Lillian (lily) **Lilian**
Lily (lily)
Linda (beautiful, pretty; tender, soft)
Linden (a lime tree)
Lindsay (from Lindsay *colony by the lake*)
Lindsey (from Lindsey *the linden tree island*)
Lindy Modern coinage.
Linnet (flax, flaxen-haired; a songbird) **Linnette**
Linnie Modern coinage. **Linnie, Linny, Lynni**
Lisa (God is my oath)
Lisabeth (God is my oath) **Lisbet; Beth, Lisa**
Lisha Modern coinage.
Lissa (a bee; nobility)
Liz (God is my oath) **Lizzie, Lizzy**
Lois (?)
Lora (man from Laurentum)
Loreen (laurel) **Lorene**
Loretta (man from Laurentum) **Lauretta**
Lori (laurel)
Lorinda Modern coinage.
Lorna Coinage of novelist R. D. Blackmore (1825–1900) for his novel *Lorna Doone* (1864).
Lorraine (territory of the people of Lothar *famous army*)
Louella (famous in war + foreign; light)
Louise (famous in war) **Louisa**
Love (love)
Lucetta (little Lucy *light*)
Lucia (light)
Lucilla (light)
Lucinda (light)
Lucy (light)
Lydia (Lydian woman)
Lynette (shapely; flaxen, flaxen-haired; little lake) **Lynn**
Lynn (lake)
Mabel (lovable) **Mabill**
Mabella (lovable)
Madeline (from Magdala)
Madge (a pearl)
Magdalen (from Magdala) **Magdelyn**
Maggie (a pearl)
Mahala (tenderness)
Mahalath (a lute, a lyre)
Mahalia (fatlings, a calf, lamb, or kid)
Mamie (a pearl)
Marah (bitterness) **Mara**
Marcella (of Mars, warlike)
Marcia (of Mars, warlike)
Margaret (a pearl)
Margery (a pearl) **Marjorie**

Margot (a pearl) **Margo**
Maria (sea of bitterness or sorrow)
Mariam (sea of bitterness or sorrow)
Marianne (sea of bitterness or sorrow + grace) **Mariann, Maryann, Maryanne.**
Marie (sea of bitterness or sorrow)
Mariella (little Maria *sea of bitterness or sorrow*)
Marilee (sea of bitterness or sorrow + a wood, clearing)
Marilyn (sea of bitterness or sorrow + lake)
Marina (of the sea)
Marion (sea of bitterness or sorrow)
Marisa Modern coinage. **Marissa, Maryssa.**
Martha (lady, mistress)
Martina (of Mars, warlike)
Mary (sea of bitterness or sorrow)
Matilda (strength in battle)
Maud (battle strength) **Maude**
Maura (great; dark-skinned)
Maureen (little Mary *sea of bitterness or sorrow*)
Mavis (songbird)
Maxie (greatest)
Maxine (greatest) **Maxi, Maxie**
May (pearl; the fifth month; born during May) **Mae**
Megan (a pearl)
Melanie (dark, black) **Melloney, Melony; Mel**
Melicent (work + strength) **Milesent**
Melinda (beautiful)
Melissa (a bee)
Melody (a melody)
Meraude (of the sea)
Mercy (mercy, compassion)
Meredith (sea protector; a lord)
Merla (sea hill; fortress by the sea)
Merle (a blackbird)
Merrielle (cheerful, happy)
Merry (cheerful, happy)
Meryl (bright sea)
Michelle (Who is like God?)
Micki (Who is like God?) **Mickie, Mikki**
Mildred (mild strength)
Millicent (work strength) **Milicent, Millesant**
Minerva (?)
Mirabelle (of greatest beauty, lovely)
Miranda (worthy to be loved)
Miriam (sea of bitterness or sorrow)
Misty (misty, foggy)
Moira (sea of bitterness or sorrow)
Molly (sea of bitterness or sorrow)
Mona (noble)
Monday (born on Monday)
Monica (?)
Morgan (lady of the sea)
Muriel (sea bright) **Meriall, Meriel, Meryall, Miriel**
Myra Coinage of poet Fulke Greville (1554–1628).
Myrna (affection, beloved)
Naamah (sweetness)

Nancy (grace, full of grace, mercy) **Nan**
Nanette (little Nan *grace*) **Nannette**
Naomi (my joy, my delight)
Natalie (natal day, Christmas)
Nell (light, torch, bright) **Nelly**
Nerissa (sea snail) A coinage of Shakespeare.
Nerys (a lord)
Nicole (victory of the people)
Nicolette (victory of the people) **Nicki, Nicky**
Nina (grace, full of grace, mercy)
Noel (born at Christmas)
Nora (light)
Noreen (little Nora *light*)
Norma (northman)
Octavia (eighth)
Olive (the olive tree)
Olivia (the olive tree)
Olympia (of Olympus)
Onora (honor)
Opal (an opal)
Ophelia (help, succor)
Ophrah (a fawn)
Orpah (a fawn, a forelock)
Orabell (?) **Orable, Oriabel**
Oriana (to rise)
Osanna (save now, save pray)
Pamela A literary coinage of Sir Philip Sidney (1554–1586).
Parnell (a rock)
Patience (patience, forebearance)
Patricia (a patrician, an aristocrat)
Pauline (small)
Pearl (a pearl)
Peg (a pearl) **Peggy**
Penelope (a bobbin)
Pentecost (fiftieth [day])
Percy (from Percy, Normandy)
Perdita (lost)
Perpetua (perpetual, eternal)
Persis (Persian woman)
Petra (a rock)
Petronel (a rock)
Petula Modern coinage.
Philippa (lover of horses) **Philipa, Phillippa**
Phillice (green, verdant) **Phillis, Phyllis** Very rare in the Eighteenth century.
Phillida (green, verdant)
Philomena (beloved)
Phoebe (bright, shining) **Phebe**
Phyllis (a leaf)
Pippa (a lover of horses)
Pleasance (pleasant)
Polly (little Mary *sea of bitterness or sorrow*)
Portia (a pig)
Precilla (former, ancient) **Priscilla**
Prisca (former, ancient)
Prudence (prudent)

Quanda (queen)
Queenie (queen)
Quilla (quill, hollow stalk)
Quinn (queen)
Rachel (ewe) **Rachael**
Rachelle (ewe)
Rae (wise protection)
Raine (queen)
Randi (shield wolf) **Randie**
Reanna Modern coinage.
Rebecca (noose) **Rebeka, Rebekah**
Regina (queen)
Renate (reborn)
Rexanne (king + grace)
Rexelle (king + light; foreign) **Rexella**
Rhiannon (great queen)
Rhoda (a rose)
Rhonda (good lance)
Richenda (little Richard *stern king*)
Rikki (little Richard *stern king*)
Rita (a pearl)
Robert (bright with fame)
Robina (bright with fame)
Rona (wise ruler)
Rosabel (beautiful rose) Eighteenth-century invention.
Rosalie (rose garland)
Rosalind (horse or fame + gentle, tender, or serpent)
Rosamond (horse protection) **Rossamond**
Rose (a rose)
Roseanna (rose + grace, full of grace, mercy) **Roseann, Roseanne** Eighteenth-century invention.
Rosemary (rose + sea of bitterness or sorrow) Eighteenth-century invention.
Rosetta (little Rose)
Rowena (famous friend)
Roxane (dawn of day)
Ruby (reddish)
Ruth (friend, companion) **Ruthe**
Sabina (Sabine woman)
Sabrina (?)
Sally (princess)
Salome (peace)
Sanchia (holy) **Sanche**
Sandra (defender of mankind) **Saundra, Sondra**
Sapphira (beautiful)
Sarah (princess)
Sasha (defender of mankind)
Selda (companion; happiness, joy)
Selina (the moon) **Selene, Selinah**
Serena (calm, peaceful)
Shan (God is gracious)
Shanee (God is gracious)
Shannah (lily, rose)
Sharon (a plain, a flat area) Middle of the twentieth century.
Sheena (God is gracious)
Sheila (blind)

Shelley (clearing on or near a slope)
Sherry (a fortified Spanish wine; darling)
Shireen Modern coinage.
Shirley (shire; bright + clearing, meadow, a wood)
Sidonia (linen cloth) **Sidonie, Sidony**
Silver (silver; precious)
Silvia (wood)
Sloan (a multitude of people, warriors)
Sonya (wisdom) **Sonja**
Sophia (wisdom) **Sophie**
Sorrel (sour)
Stacey (resurrection)
Stella (a star)
Stephanie (a crown, garland)
Sue (lily, rose)
Susan (lily, rose) **Sue, Susie, Suzy**
Susanna (lily, rose) **Susannah; Sue, Susie, Suzy**
Sybil (fortune-teller, prophetess) **Sibyl**
Tabitha (roe, gazelle)
Tacy (hold peace, be silent) A Quaker name.
Tamara (palm, a date palm) **Tamra; Tami, Tammie, Tammy**
Tamsin (a twin)
Tanya (?)
Tara (a hill)
Tawny (tanned, a soft, brownish yellow colored)
Teal (a teal, a wild duck; bluish green colored)
Terri (harvester; soft, tender) **Teri, Terie, Terry**
Terryl Modern coinage.
Tessa (harvester) **Tess**
Thea (God's gift)
Thelma Coinage of author Marie Corelli for the novel *Thelma* (1887).
Theodora (God's gift) **Theo**
Theodosia (God-given) **Theo**
Theophila (God's friend) **Theo**
Theresa (harvester) **Tess, Tessa**
Thirza (acceptance, pleasantness) **Thyrza**
Thomasina (a twin)
Thomson (little Tom *a twin*) **Tomson**
Thomasin (little Tom *a twin*) **Thamasin**
Tiffeny (Epiphany, manifestation of God) **Tiffany, Tyffany**
Tina Short form of names ending in *-tina*.
Tirzah (acceptance, pleasantness)
Toni (?)

Tonya (?)
Tracy (place of Thracius; harvester)
Tricia (a patrician)
Trina (pure, unsullied)
Troth (fidelity, good faith)
Trudie (spear strength)
Tryphena (delicate, dainty)
Unity (united)
Urania (the sky, heaven)
Ursula (she-bear)
Valda (strong, healthy)
Valentine (strong, healthy)
Vanessa Coinage of satirist Jonathan Swift (1667–1754).
Venetia (blessed)
Vera (faith)
Verena (?, perhaps *true*)
Verna (of Vernon, France)
Veronica (true image) **Ronnie**
Vicky (victory) **Vicki, Vikki**
Victoria (victory) **Tori, Torie, Tory, Vicki, Vicky, Vikki**
Viola (violet)
Violet (violet-colored)
Virginia (springlike, flourishing)
Vivian (alive) **Viviann, Vivianne, Vivien, Vivienne**
Wanda (?, perhaps *wand, stem; from the tribe of the Wends*)
Wendy Modern coinage.
Wilhelmina (resolute protector) **Willa**
Willa (resolute protector)
Willow (willow; gracefully slender)
Wilma (resolute protector)
Winifred (blessed peace) **Winnifred, Winnie**
Xenia (hospitality)
Yasmin (jasmine)
Yolanda (violet) **Yolande**
Ysanne Modern coinage.
Yvette (archer)
Yvonne (archer)
Zanna (lily, rose)
Zara (flower, blossom)
Zaylie Modern coinage.
Zelda (companion; happiness, joy)
Zoe (life)
Zula From the African tribal name Zulu.

MALE NAMES

Aaron (exalted)
Abel (breath)
Abner (the father is a light)
Abraham (father of a multitude)
Acton (from the town by the oaks)
Adam (man of the red earth)
Addison (son of Addy)

Adrian (man from Hadrianus)
Aeneas (praiser)
Alan (?, perhaps *handsome, rock*) **Allan, Allen**
Alban (from Alba)
Albert (noble and bright)
Aldred (old counsel)
Aldus (old)

Aldwin (old friend)

Alexander (defender of mankind) **Alec, Alick, Sander**

Alfred (elf counsel)

Algernon (mustached)

Aloysius (famous in war)

Alton (from the old town)

Ambrose (immortal)

Amos (borne, a burden)

Andrew (manly) **Dande, Dandy, Tandy**

Anthony (?, *priceless, of inestimable worth* is a folk definition) **Antony, Tony**

Archebald (genuinely bold, genuinely brave) **Archibald**

Art (a bear)

Arthur (?)

Asa (healer)

Ashley (dweller near the ash tree forest)

Athelstan (noble stone) **Athestan**

Aubrey (elf ruler) **Aubri**

Augustus (great, venerable)

Austin (great, venerable)

Averil (boar battle)

Aylmer (nobly famous)

Aylwin (elf friend)

Azariah (whom Jehovah helps)

Bailey (administrator, manager; the wall of the outer court of a feudal castle)

Baldric (bold ruler)

Baldwin (bold friend)

Balthasar (?)

Barclay (from the birch meadow)

Barnabas (son of exhortation) **Barnaby; Barney**

Bartholomew (son of Talmai *hill, mound, furrows*) **Bart**

Basil (kingly)

Baxter (a baker)

Beau (handsome)

Beavis (archer) **Bevis**

Benedict (blessed) **Benedick; Ben**

Benjamin (son of the right hand) **Ben**

Bennet (blessed)

Bentley (dweller near the heath or grassy meadow)

Bernard (bold as a bear)

Berold (bear rule) **Berolt**

Bertin (bright friend)

Bertram (bright raven) **Bertran**

Bill (resolute protector) **Billy**

Blaise (babbler) **Blaze**

Blake (black, dark-complexioned; bright, shining, pale)

Brad (broad)

Bradford (from the broad ford) **Brad**

Bradley (from the broad meadow or woods) **Brad**

Brent (the burnt, dweller near the burned land) Originally used as a name for a criminial who had been branded for his crimes.

Brett (a Breton)

Brian (force, strength; valor; hill, steep; kingly)

Brice (strength, valor)

Bruce (from Brus, France)

Bruno (brown)

Burgess (inhabitant or freeman of a borough)

Burton (from Burton *fortress village*)

Byron (at the cow sheds)

Cade (a young animal; a cask, barrel)

Caleb (dog; faithful)

Calvin (bald)

Carl (freeman, peasant)

Carlton (from the settlement of freemen)

Carter (a carter, one who used a cart)

Casey (watchful, vigilant)

Cecil (blind, dim-sighted)

Cedric Coinage of Sir Walter Scott (1771–1832) for a character in *Ivanhoe* (1819).

Cesar (hairy; blue gray) **Caesar**

Chad (?)

Chandler (a maker of candles)

Charles (full-grown, a man)

Charlton (settlement of freemen)

Chauncey (belonging to Chancey, France) **Chauncy**

Chester (camp of the legions)

Christian (a Christian, a follower of Christ) **Chris**

Christopher (bearing Christ) **Chris, Kester, Kit**

Clark (a clerk)

Claud (lame) **Claude**

Clayton (settlement near the clay pit)

Cliff (dweller near the cliff)

Clifford (ford at the cliff) **Cliff**

Clifton (settlement near the cliff) **Cliff**

Clint (settlement near the cliff)

Clinton (settlement near the cliff) **Clint**

Clive (cliff, slope, bank of a river)

Clyde (?)

Cole (coal; coal-black, dark; victory of the people)

Coleman (a charcoal burner, a dealer of coal) **Cole**

Colin (victory of the people)

Conrad (bold counsel)

Cornelius (a horn)

Cosmo (order, beauty)

Craig (rugged rocks, crag)

Creighton (from the town near the border)

Crispin (curled)

Curtis (courteous)

Cyprian (from Cyprus)

Cyriack (lordly)

Cyril (lordly)

Cyrus (lord)

Dale (dale, hollow, valley; dweller in the dale)

Damian (tamer)

Dane (a Dane; dweller in the valley)

Daniel (judged by God)

Darby (from the settlement by the deer)

Darcy (from D'Arcy, France)

Darius (?)

Darrell (from Airelle, France) **Darell, Darrel, Darryl, Daryll**

Darren Modern coinage.
David (beloved) **Davy**
Davy (beloved) **Davey, Davie**
Dean (a dean; dweller in the valley)
Del (ruler of the people)
Delbert (ruler of the people + bright, famous)
Dell (dweller in the dell)
Delroy (famous ruler + king; red; dweller in the dell + king; red)
Dennis (belonging to Dionysus) **Denis**
Denton (settlement near the den)
Denzell (from Denzell) **Denzil**
Derek (leader of the people) **Derick, Derrick**
Desmond (South Munster)
Dick (stern king)
Digby (settlement by the ditch)
Dominic (belonging to a lord; belonging to the Lord) **Dominik**
Donald (world ruler) **Don**
Dorian Coinage of Oscar Wilde (1854–1900).
Douglas (black, dark + blue, green, gray)
Drew (manly)
Drogo (to carry, a burden)
Duane (little dark one) **Dwayne**
Dudley (from Dudda's lea)
Duke (a duke; devotee of Maedóc)
Dunstan (dark stone)
Durand (enduring, lasting) **Durant**
Dustin (?)
Eamon (wealthy protector)
Earl (an earl)
Ebenezer (stone of help) **Ben**
Ed (wealth, prosperity)
Eden (delight)
Edgar (wealthy spear) **Ed, Eddie**
Edmond (wealthy protection) **Edmund; Ed, Eddie**
Edward (wealthy guardian) **Ed**
Edwin (wealthy friend) **Ed, Eddie**
Eldon (Ella's hill)
Eleazar (God has helped)
Eli (high, ascent)
Elias (Jehovah is God)
Elijah (Jehovah is God)
Elisha (God is salvation)
Elkanah (God created)
Ellis (Jehovah is God; God is salvation)
Elmer (nobly famous)
Elroy (the king)
Emery (ruler of strength)
Emmet (work; strength)
Enoch (dedicated)
Ephraim (very fruitful)
Erasmus (loved, desired)
Erastus (lovely, beloved)
Eric (eternal ruler)
Ernest (earnest, resolute)
Errol (?)

Esau (hairy)
Esmond (graceful protection; beautiful hand)
Ethan (strength, firmness, long-lived)
Eugene (well-born)
Eusebius (pious)
Eustace (steadfast; happy in harvest)
Evelyn (?)
Everard (strong as a boar)
Everitt (strong as a boar) **Everit**
Ezekiel (God strengthens)
Ezra (help)
Fabian (a bean)
Felix (lucky)
Fenton (settlement near the fen)
Ferdinand (peace; journey; youth, life + courage; venture, risk; ready, prepared)
Fife (from Fife, Scotland) **Fyfe**
Festus (?)
Florence (a blooming)
Florian (flowery)
Floyd (gray)
Ford (dweller by the ford)
Forrest (dweller or worker in the forest)
Foster (foster parent, nurse; officer in charge of a forest, a forest worker; a maker of scissors)
Francis (a Frank, a freeman)
Frank (a Frank)
Franklin (a freeman)
Fred (peace; counsel)
Frederick (peaceful king) **Frederic; Fred**
Fulbert (very bright)
Fulke (people) **Fulk**
Gabriel (God is strength)
Galen (calm)
Gamel (old)
Gareth (?)
Garfield (dweller near the triangular field)
Garrett (spear rule) **Garett**
Garrison (from Garriston) **Gary, Garry**
Garth (an enclosed yard or garden)
Gary (spear of battle)
Gaston (?)
Gavin (battle hawk)
Gene (well-born)
Geoffrey (district, traveler, pledge + peace) **Geffrey, Jeffrey; Geoff, Jeff**
George (earth worker, farmer)
Gerald (spear rule)
Gerbert (spear bright)
Gervais (servant of the spear) **Gervas, Gervase, Jarvis**
Gideon (hewer)
Giffard (give + bold, fierce)
Gilbert (bright pledge) **Gib, Gil**
Giles (goatskin shield of Zeus; a protection)
Glen (mountain valley, secluded valley)
Goldwin (friend of gold)

Godard (God hard)
Godfrey (God's peace)
Godric (powerful God)
Godwin (friend of God)
Gordon (?) Used late in the nineteenth century in honor of General Charles Gordon (1833–1835).
Graham (from Grantham)
Grant (great, large)
Granville (from Granville, France)
Gregory (vigilant, watchful)
Griffin (like a griffin, monstrous)
Gunther (bold in war)
Guy (a guide, leader)
Hal (home ruler)
Hale (dweller in the remote valley)
Hamlet (little house) **Hamlett, Hamnet**
Harding (bold man)
Hardwin (hard friend)
Harold (power of the army)
Harrison (son of Harry *home ruler*) **Harry**
Harry (home ruler)
Hartley (from the hart's woods)
Harvey (battle worthy)
Hector (holding fast)
Henry (home ruler)
Herbert (army bright)
Herman (warrior, soldier)
Hezekiah (God strengthens)
Hilary (cheerful)
Hiram (exalted brother)
Horatio (?)
Howard (heart brave; chief warden; ewe herder)
Hubert (bright heart) **Hubard**
Hugh (heart, mind, soul) **Hugo**
Humphrey (warrior of peace)
Ike (laughter)
Ingram (Ing's raven; angel raven)
Ira (watchful)
Isaac (laughter) **Izaak**
Isaiah (God is salvation)
Israel (contender with God)
Ives (archer) **Ivo, Yvo**
Ivor (archer)
Jack (God is gracious)
Jackson (son of Jack *God is gracious*) **Jack**
Jacob (supplanting, seizing by the heels) **Jake**
Jake (supplanting, seizing by the heels)
James (supplanting, seizing by the heels) **Jamie, Jim, Jimmy**
Jan (God is gracious)
Japheth (enlargement) **Japet, Japeth**
Jared (descending)
Jarvis (servant of the spear)
Jason (healer)
Jasper (treasure master) **Jesper**
Jay Short form of names beginning with the letter *J*.
Jedaiah (invoker of Jehovah)

Jedidiah (beloved of Jehovah)
Jefferson (son of Jeff) **Jeff**
Jeremiah (God will uplift)
Jeremy (God will uplift)
Jerome (holy name)
Jerry Short form of names beginning with *Jer-*.
Jesimiel (God sets up)
Jesse (gift)
Jethro (excellence)
Joachim (God will establish) **Joachin**
Joe (he shall add) **Joey**
Joel (the Lord is God)
John (God is gracious) **Jon; Johnny**
Jonas (dove) **Jonah**
Jonathan (God has given)
Jordan (a flowing down) **Judd**
Joseph (he shall add) **Joe**
Joshua (God is salvation)
Josiah (the Lord supports)
Judd (a flowing down)
Julian (youth, downy)
Julius (youth, downy)
Justin (just)
Keith (?, perhaps *the wind*; *wood*)
Kelly (war, strife)
Kelsey (victory ship)
Kelvin (from the River Kelvin) First used in the 1920s.
Kemp (fighter, warrior; athlete, wrestler)
Kendall (valley of the River Kent; valley of the spring) **Ken, Kenny**
Kenrick (royal rule) **Kendrick, Kendrik; Ken, Kenny**
Kenelm (brave protection) **Ken, Kenny**
Kenneth (handsome, comely) **Ken, Kenny**
Kent (?, perhaps *rim, edge, border*; *white, bright*)
Kenward (brave guardian) **Keneward, Kenard**
Kevin (handsome at birth)
Kimball (royal and bold)
Kipp (dweller near the pointed hill)
Kirk (church; dweller near the church)
Kyle (a narrow strait)
Lambert (bright land)
Lance (land; a light spear)
Laurance (from Laurentum)
Lazarus (whom God helps)
Lee (dweller near the clearing, meadow, or wood)
Leighton (homestead of the leeks; a worker in a kitchen garden)
Leland (dweller near the fallow land)
Lemuel (devoted to God)
Leo (lion)
Leon (lion)
Leonard (bold as a lion)
Leroy (the king)
Leslie (garden of hollies; the gray fort)
Lester (a dyer; from Leicester)
Levi (joining)

Levin (dear friend)
Lewis (famous in war) **Louis**
Lionel (little lion)
Lloyd (gray, gray-haired)
Lovell (wolf)
Lucas (light; man from Lucania)
Lucian (light; man from Lucania)
Lucius (light; man from Lucania)
Luke (light; man from Lucania)
Lyle (dweller on the isle)
Magnus (great, large)
Malachi (my messenger)
Malcolm (servant of Saint Columba)
Manfred (peace of man)
Marcus (of Mars, warlike) **Marc**
Mark (of Mars, warlike) **Marc**
Marmaduke (servant of Maedóc) **Duke**
Marshall (servant of the horses)
Martin (of Mars, warlike) **Marty**
Mason (a stone mason)
Matthew (gift of God) **Matt**
Matthias (gift of God) **Matt**
Mauger (spear grinder)
Maurice (dark, swarthy; a Moor) **Morrice, Morris; Maury**
Max (greatest)
Maximilian (greatest Aemilianus) **Max**
Maxwell (dweller near the stream of Maccus *great*) **Max**
Maynard (strong and hardy)
Melvin (?, perhaps *council protector*) **Melvyn; Mel**
Merlin (sea hill; sea fortress)
Mervyn (sea hill; eminent marrow)
Micah (Who is like God?)
Michael (Who is like God?) **Mike**
Miles (?, perhaps *mild, peaceful; merciful*)
Milo (?, perhaps *mild, peaceful; merciful*) **Milon**
Milton (from the mill town; from the middle town)
Mitchell (who is like God?)
Monroe (dweller at the red morass)
Montgomery (the hill of the powerful man)
Mordecai (worshiper of Marduk)
Morton (from the settlement by the moor)
Moses (drawn out of the water)
Myron (myrrh)
Nathan (gift)
Nathanael (gift of God) **Nathaniel**
Ned (wealthy guardian)
Nehemiah (comforted by Jehovah)
Neil (champion; cloud)
Nelson (son of Nel *light*; son of Neil *champion; cloud*)
Neville (from the new town)
Nicholas (victory of the people) **Nicoll, Nichol, Coll**
Nigel (champion; cloud)
Noah (rest, comfort)
Nolan (shout)
Norman (northman)
Norris (northerner; nurse)

Odo (wealth)
Ogier (rich spear)
Orson (bear cub)
Orville (?)
Osborn (god bear) **Osborne; Oz, Ozzie**
Oscar (God's spear)
Osmond (God's protection) **Osmund; Oz, Ozzie**
Oswald (God's power)
Oswin (friend of God)
Patrick (a patrician; an aristocrat) **Pat**
Paul (small)
Paulin (small)
Percy (destroyer of cities)
Pernel (a rock, a stone) **Penne, Pennel**
Peter (a rock, a stone)
Philip (lover of horses)
Piers (a rock, a stone) **Pearce, Pierce**
Quentin (fifth) **Quintin, Quinton**
Quincy (fifth)
Rafe (counsel wolf)
Ralph (counsel wolf)
Randall (shield wolf)
Randolf (shield wolf) **Randolph; Randy**
Ray (wise, judgment)
Raymund (counsel protection) **Raymond; Ray**
Rayner (warrior of judgment)
Raynold (powerful protection) **Raynald, Renold, Reynold**
Read (red-haired, ruddy-complexioned)
Rees (ardor)
Reginald (judgment power) **Reggie**
Reid (red-haired; ruddy-complexioned)
Renfred (counsel might)
Reuben (behold, a son!)
Rex (a king)
Reynard (counsel hard)
Richard (stern king) **Dick, Rick, Ricky**
Riley (dweller near the rye field)
Robert (bright with fame) **Bob, Bobbie, Rob, Robbie**
Roderick (famous ruler) **Rod, Roddy**
Rodney (from Hróda's *fame* Roda's island) **Rod**
Roger (famous with the spear)
Roland (famous land) **Rolland, Rowland**
Rolf (famous wolf) **Rolft, Roulf**
Roscoe (dweller near the roe deer's woods)
Roy (red-haired; a king)
Russell (red-haired) **Russ**
Rusty (red-haired) **Russ**
Ryan (little king)
Sam (name of God; the sun)
Samson (the sun) **Sansom; Sam**
Samuel (heard of God) **Sam**
Saul (asked for)
Scott (an Irishman, a Scot)
Seth (appointed)
Seymour (Saint Maur *a Moor*)
Shane (God is gracious)

Shaun (God is gracious)
Shaw (dweller near the woods or grove of trees)
Sheldon (shelf, ledge, crag + hill)
Sherman (a shearer of woolen cloth) **Sherm**
Sidney (dweller on or near the wide meadow or wide island)
   Sydney; Sid, Syd
Silas (ask for)
Silvester (of the woods) **Sylvester**
Simon (heard) **Simond, Symon**
Siward (victory protection)
Solomon (peaceful)
Stanley (dweller near the stony clearing)
Stephen (a crown, a garland) **Stephan, Steven; Steve**
Stuart (a steward, keeper of the animal enclosure)
Talbot (pillager, bandit; lampblack)
Taylor (a tailor)
Terence (soft, tender)
Thaddeus (God's gift; praised) **Tad**
Theodore (God's gift) **Theo**
Thomas (a twin) **Thom, Tom, Tommy**
Thurstan (Thor's stone)
Timothy (honor, respect) **Tim, Timmy**
Tobias (God is good) **Toby**
Toby (God is good)
Todd (a fox)
Tony (?, *priceless, of inestimable worth* is a folk definition)
Travis (traversing, passing through a gate or over a bridge)
Tristram (tumult, sadness) **Trystan, Trystram**

Troy (from Troyes, France)
Tyler (a maker or seller of tiles; a tiler)
Ulric (wolf rule)
Verne (dweller among the ferns)
Vernon (from Vernon, France)
Victor (victor, winner)
Vincent (conquering)
Virgil (?, perhaps *spring*; *youthful, flourishing*)
Wade (to go; a wading place)
Wallace (a Welshman) **Wally**
Walter (ruler of an army) **Wally, Walt**
Ward (guard, watchman)
Warren (dweller at or keeper of a game preserve)
Wayne (a wagoner)
Wesley (dweller at the western wood or clearing) **Wes**
Wilfred (desire for peace) **Wilfrid; Will**
Willard (resolutely brave) **Will**
William (resolute protector) **Will**
Winston (friendly town)
Woodrow (dweller at the hedgerow near the wood; dweller at the houses near the wood) **Woody**
Yorick (earthworker, farmer)
Zachariah (God remembers)
Zacharias (God remembers)
Zachary (God remembers)
Zeke (God strengthens)
Zephaniah (the Lord has hidden)

SURNAMES

Immigration has had an effect on English surnames ever since the Norman Conquest back in 1066. Large numbers of Irish arrived during the Great Famine and added their distinctive names to the mix. In recent years, immigrants from the subcontinent of India have been one of the largest groups to enter the country. As more people arrive on England's shores, the pool of surnames grows apace with the population.

Adams (son of Adam *man of the red earth*)
Addison (son of Addy)
Akerman (a farmer or ploughman) **Ackerman**
Albin (white) **Albyn**
Albright (nobly bright) **Allbright**
Almand (German) **Allmand**
Armstrong (strong arms) **Armstrang**
Ashburner (charcoal maker)
Ashley (dweller near the ash tree forest)
Ashton (dweller at the town by the ash trees)
Aston (from the east town; noble stone)
Austin (great, venerable) **Austen**
Bacheler (young knight, novice in arms)
Bacon (side of bacon)
Bailey (administrator, manager; dweller near the wall of the castle)
Baker (a baker)

Ball (ball; bald place; the round one)
Barber (a barber, one who practiced surgery and dentistry)
Barclay (from Berkeley *the birch meadow*)
Barnelby (son of consolation)
Baron (a baron, a nobleman)
Barrett (traffic, commerce; trouble, contention)
Barton (from the barley enclosure)
Base (the short one)
Baxter (a baker)
Bennett (blessed)
Bentley (dweller near the heath or grassy meadow)
Berenger (bear spear)
Bertelot (little Bartholomew)
Black (black, black-haired)
Blake (black, black-haired; bright, shining, pale)
Blanchard (whitish)
Bowyer (a maker or trader of bows)

Bradford (dweller near the broad ford)
Bradley (dweller near the broad lea)
Branton (dweller near the brushwood hill)
Brent (the burnt; dweller near the burned land)
Brett (a Breton)
Brice (force, strength; valor)
Brigham (dweller near the bridge)
Brown (brown, brown-haired) **Browne**
Bryant (force, strength; valor)
Burgis (a freeman of a borough)
Burton (settlement near the fortress)
Buxton (Bucca's stone)
Byron (dweller at the cow sheds)
Calthorp (from Calthorpe *Calla's estate*)
Calvin (bald)
Carlton (settlement of the freemen)
Carpenter (a carpenter)
Cary (movement)
Champayn (from Champaign)
Chandler (a maker or seller of candles)
Chapman (a merchant, businessman)
Charlton (settlement of the freemen)
Chaucer (maker of leather pants)
Chauncey (from Chancey, France)
Clifford (from the ford by the cliff)
Clifton (from the settlement near the cliff)
Clinton (from the settlement near the cliff)
Coleman (a charcoal burner, a dealer of coal)
Colyer (a maker or seller of charcoal)
Cornish (a Cornish person)
Craig (dweller near the crag)
Dale (dweller in the dale)
Daniels (son of Daniel *God is my judge*)
Danvers (from Anvers)
Darnel (the darnel plant; from Darnall) **Darnell**
Davidson (son of David *beloved*)
Dean (a dean)
Derwin (dear friend)
Douglass (black, dark + blue, green, gray)
Drinkwater (one who drinks water) The name implies one so poor as to not be able to afford ale, the most common drink.
Dunn (brown-haired)
Dwight (the white one)
Edmundson (son of Edmond *wealthy protector*)
Elliot (Jehovah is God)
Ellis (Jehovah is God; God is salvation)
Ellison (son of Ellis *Jehovah is God; God is salvation*)
Emson (son of Emma *strength*)
Essex (from Essex)
Ewen (lamb; youth; well-born)
Fenton (from the settlement near the fen)
Florence (from Florence)
Florantine (a Florentine)
Fleming (a Fleming)
Fletcher (a maker or seller of arrows)
Ford (dweller by the ford)

Forrest (dweller or worker in the forest)
Fort (strong)
Franklin (a freeman)
French (a French person)
Garfield (dweller near the triangular field)
Glasier (a glass maker)
Golding (son of Golda *gold*)
Goldsmith (a goldsmith)
Goodyear (good year)
Grant (great, large)
Granville (large town)
Greene (dweller near the village green)
Hale (dweller in the remote valley)
Hall (worker at the manor home)
Hankyn (little Hans)
Harding (bold man)
Haroldson (son of Harold *ruler of the army*)
Harrison (son of Harry *home ruler*)
Harry (home ruler)
Hawthorn (dweller near the hawthorn) **Hawthorne**
Henry (home ruler)
Hill (dweller near the hill)
Howard (brave heart; chief warden; ewe herder) **Huard, Huward; Hew**
Hughlot (little Hugh)
Humphrey (warrior of peace)
Ingram (angel raven)
Irish (an Irish person)
Ives (archer)
Jagger (carter, peddler; God is gracious)
Jakeson (son of Jack *God is gracious*)
James (supplanting, seizing by the heels)
Jamison (son of James *supplanting, seizing by the heels*)
Jansson (son of Jan *God is gracious*)
Jenour (engineer) **Jenoure**
Jenson (son of Jen *God is gracious*)
Johnson (son of John *God is gracious*)
Jordan (a flowing down, descend) **Jourdan, Jurdain**
Keate (dweller at the animal hut) **Keat, Keates, Keats**
Kelsey (victory ship)
Kelvin (dweller near the River Kelvin)
Kemp (fighter, warrior; athlete, wrestler)
Kendrick (chief man, chief hero)
Kent (from Kent)
Kerr (an overgrown wetland)
King (a king) **Kinge**
Knolles (dweller at the top of the hill) **Knoll**
Knight (servant, knight)
Lambert (bright land) **Lambard, Lambart, Lambarth**
Latimer (interpreter)
Lawless (an outlaw, licentious) **Lawelesse**
Lee (wood, clearing, meadow)
Legg (leg)
Leland (dweller near the fallow land)
Lombard (long beard) **Lumbard**
Mailer (an enameler) **Mailler**

Maitland (discourteous, rude)
Malet (the unfortunate one, cursed)
Mallory (the unfortunate one, cursed)
Marchant (a merchant, a trader) **Marchand**
Matthews (son of Matthew *gift of God*)
Maxwell (dweller near the stream of Maccus *great*)
Mickelson (son of Michael *Who is like God?*) **Michaelson**
Miller (a miller)
Naismith (a knife smith) **Naysmith**
Nesbitt (from Nesbit or Nesbitt) **Naisbet, Naisbit, Nesbit**
Neville (from the new town)
Newman (a newcomer)
Nicoles (victory of the people) **Nicholls, Nichols**
Norman (a Norman, from Normandy)
Oaks (dweller near the oak trees) **Oak, Oake**
Oldfield (dweller by the old field)
Orchard (dweller near or worker at an orchard)
Osman (god bear) **Osmand**
Oxnard (an ox herder)
Percy (from Percy, La Manche)
Pickering (from Piker's meadow)
Pikard (one from Picardy)
Plymouth (from Plymouth)
Poore (pauper)
Prendregast (?, perhaps *dweller at the village near the castle*)
Ravenhill (dweller at the raven's hill)
Redford (dweller at the red ford)
Redgrave (dweller at the red grove)
Renshaw (from the raven's wood)
Richmond (from Richmond *rich mountain*)
Robertson (son of Robert *bright with fame*)
Rochester (from Rochester *Hróf's stronghold*)

Ross (dweller on the peninsula)
Russell (little red-haired one)
Sadeler (a maker or seller of saddles) **Sadelier**
Shepard (shepherd) **Shepperde**
Stoke (from Stoke)
Stolemaker (a maker or seller of stoles)
Sutton (from Sutton)
Tabard (a sleeveless coat)
Tait (cheerful, gay)
Talbot (lampblack)
Tomlin (little Tom *a twin*)
Trumble (strong-bold) **Trumbull**
Ullman (maker or seller of oil)
Underhill (dweller at the foot of a hill)
Unwin (young bear-friend)
Uppington (dweller up in the village)
Urban (dweller in the city)
Vale (dweller in the valley)
Valentine (strong, healthy)
Vaughan (small) **Vaughn**
Vennell (dweller at the small street or alley) **Vennall, Venel**
Vidal (vital, full of vitality) **Vidall**
Walsh (a Welsh person)
Walshman (a Welsh man)
Webber (a weaver)
White (white, fair complexioned)
Williams (son of William *resolute protector*)
Wilson (son of Will *resolute protector*)
York (from York *yew tree*; *place of boars*)
Zimmerman (a carpenter)
Young (young, youthful)

Part Two

[SCOTLAND]

[CONTENTS]

[RULERS OF SCOTLAND]

Kenneth MacAlpin (843–860)
Donald I (860–863)
Constantine I (863–877)
Aedh (877–878)
Eocha (878–889)
Donald II (889–900)
Constantine II (900–943)
Malcolm I (943–954)
Indulphus (954–962)
Duff (962–967)
Colin (967–971)
Kenneth II (971–995)
Constantine III (995–997)
Kenneth III (997–1005)
Malcolm II (1005–1034)
Duncan I (1034–1040)
Macbeth (1040–1057)
Malcolm III (1057–1093)
Donald Bane (1093–1094)
Duncan II (1094)
Donald Bane (1094–1097)
Edgar (1097–1107)
Alexander I (1107–1124)
David I (1124–1153)
Malcolm IV (1153–1165)
William the Lion (1165–1214)
Alexander II (1214–1249)
Alexander III (1249–1286)
Margaret, the Maid of Norway (1286–1290)
First Interregnum (1290–1292)
John Balliol (1292–1296)
Second Interregnum (1296–1306)

Robert Bruce (1306–1329)
David II (1329–1371)
Robert II (1371–1390)
Robert III (1390–1406)
James I (1406–1437)
James II (1437–1460)
James III (1460–1488)
James IV (1488–1513)
James V (1513–1542)
Mary Queen of Scots (1542–1567)
James VI (James I of England) (1567–1625)
Charles I (1625–1649)
Charles II (1649–1651)
Commonwealth and Protectorate (1651–1660)
Charles II (1660–1685)
James VII (James II of England) (1685–1689)
William II (William III of England) and
    Mary (1689–1694)
William II (1694–1702) (alone)
Anne (1702–1714)
George I (1714–1727)
George II (1727–1760)
George III (1760–1820)
George IV (1820–1830)
William IV (1830–1837)
Victoria (1837–1901)
Edward VII (1901–1910)
George V (1910–1936)
Edward VIII (1936)
George VI (1936-1952)
Elizabeth (1952-Present)

Chapter One

THE DARK AGES TO DONALD BANE
[843–1093]

SCOTLAND IS A land divided geographically into three distinct parts: the Highlands, the Central Lowlands, and the Southern Uplands. The Highlands are made up of rough, rugged hills and mountains that are largely uninhabitable and able to sustain only a small amount of agriculture. The Lowlands are more hospitable and are capable of sustaining crops and supporting livestock. The area of greatest settlement has traditionally been the fertile central area known as the Midland Valley, though early immigrants also settled in the Highlands and the hills of the Southern Uplands.

Groups of Celts migrated to the island around 700 B.C. They were advanced, skilled, and aggressive, lived among the earlier peoples, and probably intermarried with them. By the time the Romans arrived, there were several groups of Celts living in Scotland. One group, the Caledonians (eventually called the Picts), occupied northern Scotland and are thought to have been superior in strength and numbers. Other groups were the Damnonii, Novantae, Selgovae, and the Votadini.

The Romans arrived at the southern border of Scotland late in the 70s A.D., and by 83 A.D. had advanced into the northern Highlands. They did not intermingle with the Celts, and except for doing battle with them, had no real effect on Celtic society. In 122, the emperor Hadrian ordered the construction of Hadrian's Wall to keep the northern Celts from raiding Roman-held territory or from joining forces with the southern Celts; in 142, another fort line known as the Antonine Wall was constructed.

At the time of the Romans' departure, Scotland was divided among four groups, three of which were Celts: the Picts, the Britons, and the Scotti, descendants of raiders from Ireland. The fourth group was the Angles, a Germanic tribe that had been raiding the eastern coast for many years.

The Picts inevitably clashed with the Scots as the latter group moved into Pict-held territory in search of farmland. The quest for land brought the ambitious, battle-hungry Angles into confrontation with the Picts, as well. The Angles' day of reckoning came in 685 when their king Ecgfrith and his large army were soundly defeated. He abandoned all further attempts to move into Pict territory.

In the late eighth and early ninth centuries, Viking attacks weakened the Picts to a point that they were no longer able to stand up to the Scots. In 843, Kenneth MacAlpin, half Scot and half Pict, successfully united the two groups under one Scottish throne to form the kingdom of Scotia. He is recognized as the first king of Scottish history.

The kings did not receive a crown but were "set upon the stone" and hailed by a seannachie who recited the new king's pedigree back to Gaythelus (the original Gael from the Mediterranean). That stone, the Stone of Destiny, was a sandstone slab believed to have originated with Gaythelus and said to have accompanied the Scots on all their journeyings. The Stone, the Scots' most treasured possession, stood for permanence and power. An old prophecy put forth that "wherever the stone should rest, a king of Scots would reign."

POLITICS

MAINTAINING CONTROL OF the Picts was not an easy task for Kenneth MacAlpin, for many were fiercely independent and opposed Kenneth's rule. Perhaps in an effort to appease them, he transferred his capital from Dunadd in Argyll to Scone in Perth, the sacred center of the Picts. He also transferred the Scots' most important symbol, the Stone of Destiny, to his new capital. Kenneth ruled for sixteen years and died in 860.

Kenneth's successor was his brother, Donald (860–862), who was in turn followed by Kenneth's son, Constantine (862–877). The method of succession differed from what had been the norm among the separate groups. Traditionally, the early kings were chosen on merit and on their popularity among the group of royal advisers. It was an imprecise system that led to multiple candidates vying for the crown. It also made it very unlikely for early kings to live out their natural life, as the primary way to change rulers was to do away with the current one.

Toward the end of the eighth century, Vikings began raiding wealthy monasteries along the Scottish coast. In the ninth century, they began to make their way inland in search of land. Due to determined Pictish and Scottish resistance, Vikings established themselves primarily along the coast. Some ventured as far south as the hills of Galloway and intermarried with the Britons, spawning a race of wild and energetic people known as the Gallgaels.

The Viking's main power base was in the Orkneys. At the end of the 800s, the Norwegian King Harald Fair-hair decided to add the islands to his empire and sent one of his earls, Rognvald, and a force of men to occupy them. With the Norwegian throne so far away, the earls of Orkney began to rule like kings themselves. The greatest was probably Thorfinn the Mighty, ruler over all Viking dominions in Scotland from the 1040s to his death in 1065. His widow, Ingiborg, married Malcolm III, Macbeth's successor.

In 900, Constantine II ascended to the Scottish throne. His attacks on Northumbria and Lothian provoked the English into retaliation. In 934, Aethelstan invaded Scotland and was victorious over the Scots, the Vikings of Northumbria, Man, and Ireland, and the Strathclyde Welsh. A beaten Constantine paid homage to Aethelstan, recognized him as overlord, and agreed to give up his war against the English. Constantine then abdicated, and the Scottish throne went to his brother, Malcolm I.

Relations between England and the Scots remained strained, and thirty years later, King Edgar took a fleet to Scotland to demand subservience from Kenneth II. This went against the grain of the fiercely independent Scots, and in 1018, Malcolm II successfully challenged the Lothian Angles and annexed the Lothian kingdom. He was helped in battle by Owain, the king of Strathclyde, and received the Strathclyde kingdom when Owain died shortly after the battle. Malcolm II died in 1034, passing his kingdom to his grandson, Duncan I.

Duncan was nothing like the aged monarch portrayed in Shakespeare's *Macbeth*. In reality, Duncan was young, spoiled, and impetuous. He invaded Northumbria against the advice of his counselors, then was forced to withdraw after a disastrous defeat. After returning to Scotland, he was faced with a revolt of his underlords, which included his cousin, Macbeth, and was henceforth killed during a fight at Bothgouanan. Duncan had ruled for six years.

At this time, Scotland was divided into seven provinces: Angus, Atholl, Caithness, Fife, Mar, Moray, and Strathearn. Each province was governed by a *mormaer,* a term used to describe a lord, viceroy, or other high official. Some mormaers were of royal blood, some were not, but they all retained great power and influence over their provinces.

Macbeth was the mormaer of Moray and a descendant of Kenneth MacAlpin, which made him a popular choice to succeed Duncan I. He was a competent ruler who managed to bring a semblance of law and order across the country and unite the various clans under his lordship. He was eventually challenged in 1057 by Malcolm Ceanmor (Great Head), one of Duncan's sons who had been in exile in England. With the help of the English Earl of Northumbria, Malcolm put together an army, invaded Scotland, and engaged Macbeth in Aberdeenshire. Macbeth was killed in battle, and Malcolm's stepson, Lulach, was chosen to succeed as king.

Having someone other than himself as king wasn't in Malcolm's plan. A few months later, he defeated Lulach during a skirmish and had him put to death. He then took the throne as Malcolm III, founding a new dynasty of Scottish kings known as the House of Canmore.

Macbeth and Lulach were the last kings of ancient Scotland. Both spoke Gaelic and both descended from Kenneth MacAlpin, thus representing both the old Pict and Scots clans. In a sense, they were chiefs of the chiefs in the clan system. Macbeth also kept a peaceful kingdom and didn't concern himself with making war with England. If he had triumphed instead of Malcolm, the country of Scotland would have proceeded on a very different course than it did.

Malcolm, however, owed a debt to the English, and as many of his supporters had ties to England, the stage was set for the English to capitalize on that debt. Malcolm and his supporters were bribed with money and other gifts to promote English causes. His wife died in the mid-1060s, and in 1069, he married Margaret, the sister of Edward the Confessor.

Margaret brought the English culture and language to the Scottish court, as well as a religiousness that was much more devout than was commonly found in Scotland. From the beginning, the marriage was viewed with a great deal of suspicion and concern by several parties.

First off, the Gaelic-speaking Highland clans and others of Scottish and Pictish descent saw the union as the beginning of the end of the Gaelic language and way of life. Their predictions became true as English replaced Gaelic as the language of court, the government, and the church. The Vikings of northern Scotland regarded the marriage as a direct threat, as the Anglo-Saxons had successfully defeated the Vikings in England. In time, the Vikings were edged out of their possessions, and many chose to integrate with the Scots. The Gallgaels of Galloway also viewed the marriage with distrust, for they feared Malcolm would bring in foreign troops to quash their independence.

Though Malcolm had lost much of the trust and respect of his people, he remained patriotic to Scotland. After the Norman Conquest, William the Conqueror held England firmly in his grasp, but his position in sparsely populated northern England was not as secure. In 1071, Malcolm took advantage of that weakness and crossed the border to harrass farms and villages and carry off people to serve as slaves in Scotland.

A furious William retaliated the next year by sending mounted, armored troops across land and a fleet of ships up the eastern coast. Malcolm's forces were defeated in Perthshire, but William's victory wasn't a decisive one, and Malcolm invaded northern England at least three more times. He was killed outside the stronghold of Alnwick on his last foray across the border in 1093. His wife, Margaret, died three weeks later in Edinburgh.

Scottish political life changed greatly during Malcolm's thirty-six-year reign. Margaret had a profound influence over her husband, and the king offended much of the Gaelic population when English culture and language were introduced into government. He also went against centuries of tradition when he decided that only the highborn should have access to the king or hold royal offices. In the traditional Gaelic political system, the chief was always available to any of his people; it was one of the reasons the people held such great loyalty and respect for their leader. And, with the exception of slaves, all classes of people had equal opportunity to serve the clan and hold higher offices. Malcolm's new attitude was in direct opposition to that tradition, and it served to alienate him from a large sector of the people.

Even Malcolm's final act was a break from centuries of Scottish tradition and symbolic of the end of the old Celtic monarchy. Rather than be buried in Iona, the spiritual homeland of the Dalriada, Malcolm chose a joint interment with Margaret at the new Benedictine Abbey of Dunfermline. After his death, an effort was made to return a Gaelic consciousness to politics by reestablishing the Gaelic language and culture in Scottish politics.

SOCIETY

THE ARRIVAL OF the Celts marked the beginning of the Iron Age in Scotland. These people buried their dead in timbered chambers, rode horses, used iron implements, and utilized wagons with spoked wheels. They were energetic raiders, so they also constructed fortified villages and large stone towers to protect themselves from other clans.

Celtic clothing was made from linen and wool. Males wore trousers of brightly colored, checkered material, knee-length, boldly colored tunics, and flowing capes. Female clothing was just as brightly colored, and long, wide skirts, belted tunics, and woolen cloaks comprised the typical costume. Both sexes adorned their clothing and their bodies with elaborately wrought jewelry, and they ornamented their weapons, as well.

The Celts were an energetic people who took great delight in hunting, playing sports, and feasting. They were hard workers, accomplished farmers, skilled craftsmen, fierce warriors, and competent traders. They lived in tightly knit family groups and had an established and rich oral tradition.

The Picts distinguished themselves by tattooing designs on their foreheads and other body parts. They were the largest group, and as they held the Highlands, they consequently held the most territory. The central feature of Highland society was the clan system. Simply put, people were divided into three classes: freemen, workers, and slaves. The freemen had full rights and were interrelated by blood or marriage. Workers, or subjects, were members of the clan and had limited rights but were not related by blood, and the last group, people captured during raids, were slaves with no rights.

The clan was a fiercely loyal, tightly knit group led by a powerful chief whose word was law. He had proprietary rights over the property and possessions of other clan members, he controlled the division of land, sent clan members on raids, and led the clan in battle. He expected, and was given, absolute loyalty. The Highland clans remained immune to outside influences and developed into extremely strong social and political organizations.

Pictish succession was different from that of the other Celtic groups. Among the Picts, succession to the chieftancy was made through the female side of the family. A new chief was the son of the old chief's daughter or sister. He would not be succeeded by his own son but by either his daughter's son or a nephew.

The Scots from Ireland were warriors, farmers, beekeepers, fishermen, and breeders and traders of livestock. Their search for quality farmland led them to the Midland Valley, where they quickly established themselves. Other Celtic clans, such as the Votadini and the Britons, lived in villages surrounded by wooden palisades.

After Malcolm III came into power, English craftsmen and merchants were encouraged to settle in the more prosperous areas of Scotland, and their way of life clashed with that of the clan. Malcolm also made

English the language of government, essentially forcing the Scottish people to learn a foreign tongue to be able to communicate with their government officials. For such an independent and patriotic people as the Scots, this was an obvious betrayal to the cause of nationalism, and steps would soon be taken to reverse this policy.

RELIGION

WHEN THE ROMANS left Britain, they left their Christian religion behind to flourish among the Celts. Many Welsh had adopted Christianity, as had the Britons; the Picts remained pagan. A British Celtic bishop, Saint Ninian, built a church and founded a school for religious teachers in Scotland around the year 400. He sent missionaries out, but made little headway with the Picts. Saint Columba arrived from Ireland 150 years later, establishing a monastery on the isle of Iona and working to spread the faith. In 597, Saint Augustine arrived and began his own missionary work. A succession of monks continued to send missions into pagan territory, and by the seventh century, much of Scotland had been converted to the new religion.

Though the Scottish Church eventually decided to come under the leadership of Rome, it evolved differently than did the Church in England and on the Continent. Not only were Scottish monks and priests allowed to marry, their offices were passed down to their sons. Churchgoing was not strictly observed, nor was Sunday regarded as a day of rest.

Margaret, the queen of Malcolm III, initiated reform. She was a very devout woman who led by example, and it was through her influence that new monastic ideals from Europe spread within the Scottish Church. It was also through Margaret's efforts that the Church and monarchy were brought closer together.

NAMING

GAELIC NAMES IN Scotland differed little from those found in Ireland. They fell into the same three main classes: compounded or dithematic, uncompounded or monothematic, and derivatives. Compounded names were comprised of two themes or elements, uncompounded names were formed from only one theme or element, and derivatives were formed from other words or names. An example of the first category is Brandubh (raven + dark, black), one from the second category is Bran (raven), and one from the third category is Bearchán (little spear).

Several Viking names from early Scotland have been preserved by way of runic inscriptions found on stones in the Orkneys and other places. The names are very similar to their Germanic cousins, including Anglo-Saxon names. As the Vikings intermarried with the Picts and Scots, Norse names came into use among the native population as did Norse/Gaelic combinations. Norse names were also translated into Gaelic, and Gaelic names found their way into the pool of Viking names. For example, Amhlaoibh is the Gaelic form of Olaf, Somhairle is the Gaelic form of the Old Norse Sumarlíðor, and Tormod is from the Old Norse þómóðr. Birgit is an example of a Norse name that has Gaelic roots. For ease in understanding, the thorn (Þ, þ) and the Icelandic eth Ð, ð have been transliterated as Th and th.

FEMALE NAMES

Aifric (pleasant)
Ailbhe (?, perhaps *white*)
Aithbhreac (new speckled one)
Alana (O child)
Alma (all-good)
Aoibh (beauty)
Aoibheann (beautiful, fair form)
Aoife (beauty)
Beatha (life)
Beathag (life)
Bebhinn (sweet, melodious lady)
Blath (flower)
Blathnait (flower)
Brighid (strength)
Brona (sorrow)
Brynhildr (armored for battle) A Viking name.
Caoilfhionn (slender and fair)
Ciannait (little ancient one)
Ciara (black-haired one)
Damhnait (little poet)
Dearbhail (poet's daughter)
Deirdre (?, perhaps *young girl* or *fear*)
Deòiridh (pilgrim)
Diorbhorguil (true oath, true testimony)
Doireann (sullen)
Dubheasa (dark beauty)
Ealga (noble)

Eimhear (swift)
Feidhelm (?)
Fiona (white, fair, clear)
Fionnaghuala (white shoulders)
Freya (lady, mistress)
Gobnait (little mouth)
Gormfhlait (blue lady)
Gráinne (grain goddess)
Ide (thirst)
Malamhín (smooth brow)
Mór (great, large)
Morainn (fair seas)
Mórín (little great one)
Muadhnait (little noble one)
Muireall (bright seas) **Muirgheal**
Muireann (long-haired)
Muirne (beloved, affection)
Niamh (bright)
Oighrig (?, perhaps *new speckled one*)
Raghnaid (battle of decision)
Rathnait (little graceful one)
Samhaoir (summer sailor, Viking)
Saraid (excellent)
Sláine (health)
Sorcha (bright)
Suibhne (goodness)
Ùna (dearth, famine, hunger)

MALE NAMES

Abbán (little abbot)
Aceard (?)
Aelfric (elf ruler)
Aidan (fire)
Ailpean (?) **Ailpein**
Alasdair (defender or helper of mankind) Scottish form of Alexander.
Amhlaidh (ancestor's relic) Scottish form of Olaf.
Amundi (fearful protector) A Viking name.
Aodán (little fiery one)
Aodh (fire)
Aodhagán (little fiery one)
Aonghus (one, choice, preeminent) **Aonghas**
Arailt (leader of the army) Scottish form of Harald.
Arnbjorn (eagle + bear)
Art (bear)
Artair (?) Scottish form of Arthur.
Artán (little bear)
Beathan (life)
Brian (force, strength; kingly)

Brúnn (brown) A Viking name.
Cailean (dove) Scottish form of Columba.
Calum (dove) Scottish form of Columba.
Cinaed (born of fire) **Cionaed**
Coinneach (handsome, comely)
Còiseam (steadfast, enduring) Scottish form of Constantine.
Comhnall (strength; wisdom; high; dog)
Conall (strength; wisdom; high; dog)
Cormag (?, perhaps *raven; son of defilement; son of the charioteer*)
Cúmhaige (hound of the plain)
Cuthbert (well-known, famous) **Cuthburt**
Diarmad (free, without injunction) **Diarmid**
Domhnall (world ruler)
Donn (brown, brown-haired)
Donnchadh (brown warrior)
Donnell (world ruler)
Dubh (dark-complexioned)
Dubhghall (dark-haired stranger)
Dùbhghlas (dark, black + blue, green, gray)

Duncan (brown warrior) **Dunecan**
Eachann (brown horse)
Eadgar (spear of prosperity)
Eairrdsidh (genuinely bold, genuinely brave)
Eallair (worker in a cellar)
Earnulf (eagle wolf)
Eilifr (immortal) A Viking name.
Einar (lone warrior) A Viking name.
Einrithi (one peace) A Viking name.
Eirìkr (eternal ruler) A Viking name.
Eóghan (lamb; youth; well-born)
Erik (eternal ruler) A Viking name.
Eysteinn (one stone) A Viking name.
Fearchar (dear man)
Fearghas (man of valor and strength)
Fionnlagh (fair warrior, white warrior) A byname for a Viking.
Frithrekr (king of peace) A Viking name.
Gunnbjorn (battle bear) A Viking name.
Gunnr (war, battle, strife) A Viking name.
Gwalchmai (battle hawk)
Hallvarthr (defender of the rock) A Viking name.
Haraldr (leader of the army) A Viking name.
Hávarthr (defender of the rock) A Viking name.
Heming (?, possibly *shape; shape-changer; a werewolf*) **Hemming**
Ìomhair (bow warrior, archer) **Ìomhar** Scottish form of Ivar.
Ivarr (bow warrior, archer) **Ivar** A Viking name.
Keir (dark-complexioned)
Kiaran (little dark-haired one) **Kieran**

Kolbjorn (?, bear) A Viking name.
Lachlan (warlike; land of the lochs) **Lachann, Lachlann**
Láki (?) A Viking name.
Leggr (leg) A Viking name.
Magnus (great, large) A Viking name.
Malcolumb (servant of Saint Columba)
Mànus (great, large) Scottish form of Magnus.
Muireadhach (sea warrior)
Murchadh (sea warrior)
Niall (champion)
Oláfr (ancestral relic) A Viking name.
Oscar (a friend of deer) Introduced from Ireland.
Raghnall (powerful judgment) Scottish form of Rögnvaldr.
Randulfr (shield wolf) A Viking name.
Ranulf (shield wolf)
Raonull (powerful judgment)
Rögnvaldr (powerful judgment) A Viking name.
Ruairí (red, ruddy-complexioned) **Ruairi, Ruairidh**
Saemundr (hand of victory) A Viking name.
Safugel (sea fowl) A Viking name.
Seaghdh (?, perhaps *hawklike; fine*)
Somhairle (Viking, summer sailor)
Tadhg (poet) **Taogh**
Teobold (brave people, bold people)
Thorfynn (Thor + beautiful, fair) Viking/Gaelic name.
Thorgeirr (Thor's warrior) A Viking name.
Thorlákr (shaped like Thor) A Viking name.
Toirdhealbhach (shaped like Thor)
Ulf (wolf)
Vinget (?)

SURNAMES

Although hereditary surnames had not yet come into existence, it was quite common for early Scots to add additional descriptions to their names. They fell into the same four categories as surnames: characteristic, local, genealogical, and occupational. Local and occupational descriptions were less common than characteristic and genealogical.

Clan members traditionally added the name of their chief to their own names, usually adding the word *Mac* (son of) in front of it. Not only was the clan name a means of identification, it was also a badge of pride, a symbol of the bearer's intense devotion to his social group, and often the word last shouted when a clansman fell in battle.

The Vikings typically used some type of additional name. Most were characteristic or genealogical, and those of the characteristic class were quite often less than complimentary. Thórarin Kyllinef (cod nose), Asbjorn Krókauga (crook eye), and Thórarin Breithmagi (broad paunch) are examples.

Boyd (yellow-haired)
Breithmagi (broad paunch) Viking name.
Buchan (small)
Cam (crooked)

Cameron (crooked nose)
Campbell (crooked mouth)
Donn (brown)
Dubh (dark, black)

Fionn (white-haired, fair-haired)
Fótr (limp-leg) Viking name.
Galinn (the silly) Viking name.
Geslíngr (gosling) Viking name.
Hausakljúfr (skull-splitter) Viking name.
Keikr (back-bent) Viking name.
Klíningr (oily tongue) Viking name.
Krókauga (crook-eye) Viking name.
Kyllinef (cod-nose) Viking name.
Mókr (the drowsy) Viking name.

Mór (great, large)
Nefja (nosy) Viking name.
Ruaraidh (red-haired, ruddy-complexioned)
Rauthi (the red) Viking name.
Saefugalasuna (son of Safugel *sea fowl*) Viking name.
Skalli (bald head) Viking name.
Slafsi (the slobberer) Viking name.
Spýtu-leggr (spindleshanks) Viking name.
Tréskeggr (tree beard)

Chapter Two

THE REIGN OF DONALD BANE TO MARGARET, THE MAID OF NORWAY
[1093–1286]

POLITICS

AFTER THE DEATH of Malcolm III, his brother, Donald Bane, was chosen as successor, according to the traditional Scottish system. Donald didn't have the same fondness for the English that Malcolm had, and he spearheaded a brief revival of the Celtic spirit. Less than a year later, Donald was deposed by Malcolm's son (by Ingiborg), Duncan II, who had the backing of the Norman William Rufus. Duncan was killed in 1094, and Donald Bane was restored to the throne. He was deposed again three years later, this time by Norman-backed Edgar, Malcolm's eldest son by Margaret.

One of Edgar's first acts was to make peace with Magnus Barelegs, the king of Norway. The terms included forfeiting the Scottish claim to the Hebrides and Kintyre. To the great despair of the Scots, their spiritual center, Iona, passed into Norse hands. Just as devastating to the common Scotsman was the rejection of their language and culture by their king. The monarch and his nobility became a French-speaking elite, and the gulf between king and commoner and between king and Highland chief was vastly widened.

After Edgar's death in 1107, he was succeeded by his brothers, Alexander, then David. David I came to the throne at a time when England was torn by civil war. By supporting one side, then the other, he succeeded in extending Scotland's southern border and obtaining a promise of all Northumbria once Henry of Anjou took the English throne.

Like his father's, David's actions were a paradox. On one hand, he was very patriotic to Scotland, and on the other, he was firm in his determination to introduce Anglo-Norman ideas into the country. He married Matilda, the daughter of Henry I, yet continued to do battle with England over possession of the northern counties. He formally acknowledged his son as his successor, thereby exchanging tanistry, the traditional Scottish method of choosing a king, to a hereditary one. He modeled the transformation of the Scottish Church after the English Church but refused to recognize the archbishop of York as the archbishop of Scotland. He encouraged his Norman friends to build castles, then founded townships near the castles, which he populated with English traders, craftsmen, merchants, and handymen, even though the lords' power became nearly as great as his own. Under David's rule, Edinburgh became the capital of Scotland and the center of his administration.

David died in 1153, leaving his twelve-year-old grandson, Malcolm IV, to succeed him. The young king was immediately surrounded by the Norman friends and advisers of his late father and grandfather, a situation that did not sit well with his Scottish subjects. Several rebellions broke out, both in protest over the youngster's succeeding as king and over Norman influence in the Scottish court. Malcolm's forces, with the help of Henry II, succeeded in putting down the rebellions, but the ill feeling remained. To make matters worse, Henry persuaded Malcolm to relinquish the Scottish claim to Northumbria.

Malcolm IV died in 1165 at the age of twenty-four. His successor was his brother, William the Lion. Though William ruled for nearly fifty years, he didn't accomplish much for Scotland. He joined Henry II's son in intrigue, was captured in 1174, then forced to sign the Treaty of Falaise, whereby he acknowledged Henry II as his feudal superior, swore to become his liegeman, and acknowledged that he held Scotland only by Henry's permission. Scottish soldiers were ousted from their positions in several castles, which were then manned with English garrisons (though Scotland had to pay all their expenses). For the next fifteen years, Scotland was forced into subservience. In 1189, Richard I of England canceled the treaty in exchange for 10,000 marks—money that would help finance his crusade to the Holy Land.

When John took the English throne, William was forced into giving him 15,000 marks for his goodwill and made to hand over his daughters, Margaret and Isabella, for marriage to John's sons (which, by the way, never happened). When Alexander II succeeded his father to the Scottish throne, he made immediate claim to the northern counties. He married Joan, the sister of Henry III, but relations soured, and Henry renewed the claim of suzerainty dating back to the time of the Conqueror. Alexander agreed to give up his claim to the northern counties in exchange for an income from certain estates there. In 1237, a settlement of lands was reached, leaving the King of Scots with lands in Northumberland and Cumberland.

Several times afterward, the Scottish kings were made to pay homage to the kings of England, though they steadfastly denied their homage was for the whole country of Scotland. The English kings, on the other hand, just as adamantly declared that they were.

Alexander also had problems with the Vikings in the north and west. He offered the Norwegian king a large sum of money in exchange for Viking-held territories in Scotland, but the king refused, saying he didn't need the money. Alexander then decided to mount an invasion on the western isles. On his way there, he became ill and died. He was fifty years old.

Alexander's son, Alexander III, was just eight when he came to the throne. He had also been promised in marriage to Margaret, a daughter of Henry III. Both circumstances worked to England's advantage and helped to tighten its control over Scotland as the young king was surrounded by English interests. Henry III declared himself to be Alexander's principal counselor, as well as overlord of Scotland. Despite the interference,

Alexander grew into a fine and patriotic king remembered for his peaceful and prosperous reign. Scotland under his patronage enjoyed a golden age.

After the death of Margaret, Alexander married Yolande de Dreux. Returning home to his new bride one stormy night, Alexander rode his horse off a cliff and was killed. His sons had preceeded him in death, so his sole heir was his three-year-old granddaughter, Margaret, the Maid of Norway. Alexander III was the last king of the House of Canmore. He was the last truly Scottish king, for all that followed him were mainly of foreign descent.

SOCIETY

SCOTTISH SOCIETY PAID the price for its royal family accepting help from the Normans, for traditional Gaelic society with its clan system and communal ownership of land was lost when the Norman-supported kings introduced the Norman feudal system. The sons of Malcolm III repaid the support of their Norman friends by granting them tracts of land usually taken from clans in the Lowlands. Later, David was to formally sponsor the establishment of Anglo-Norman families by granting them charters. Some of the most recognized names of Scottish history were of Norman descent. Robert Bruce, John Balliol, and the Stewarts, for example, all descended from Normans who were granted estates or were in the king's service.

The new lords took control of their land by building motte-and-bailey strongholds and maintaining private armies to garrison them. Agricultural improvements were introduced, and tenants and landlords operated on the same system as in England.

Between the parish churches and the castles, small towns known as burghs sprouted up and were populated by Scots, the English, and Flemings. Most were deliberate acts of town planning and were established to become centers of trade, to promote the production of crafts, and to promote a degree of public order. In time, they became vital and sustaining communities. The bartering of goods was the principal form of trade, as coinage didn't become widespread until the thirteenth century.

The actual number of newcomers was quite small, however, and the majority of land remained in the hands of the Scottish clans. Life in the country was not altered all that much and proceeded in a simple manner. Most people raised their own crops and had their own herds of cattle and sheep. Milk, cheese, oatmeal, and barley were the staple foods, though meat was also consumed.

Most of the above social changes occured in the Lowlands. It was a different story in the Highlands and the Islands. In the Western Isles, a blended Celtic/Norse civilization took hold, and they followed and kept their own traditions, regardless of whether they formally claimed allegiance to either Scotland or Norway. In the Northern Isles, the Norse earldom of Orkney ruled, and the people followed Scandinavian traditions. The Highlanders remained true to their traditional Gaelic way of life and did not make the same improvements in living conditions nor any of the societal changes that followed the establishment of the burghs in the Lowlands.

The introduction of feudalism was not taken lightly. Though it actually brought more prosperity to the Lowlands, Highland chiefs had no intention of letting the king take control of the clans, nor would they support a system that demanded fixed periods of military service. The gulf between the king and the people, which had been formed when Malcolm III was king, was forever widened after David I came to the throne.

RELIGION

THE FINAL BREAK with the old Celtic Church came with the reign of David (1124–1153). A more energetic reformer than his mother, David succeeded in bringing the Scottish Church in line with European practices.

He encouraged the formation of new monasteries for European orders like the Augustinians and the Cistercians, divided Scotland into ten sees, organized the creation of parishes within the sees, organized the system of tithe-paying, created new bishoprics, and appointed new bishops that were either Anglo-Norman or pro–Anglo-Norman in outlook. The last was done to bring the Church in line with the rest of Europe and to bring it into the feudal system that included the monarchy. Anglo-Norman bishops would be unlikely to challenge this new turn of events.

The formation of religious houses were to affect society as well as religion. The monks introduced new building and farming techniques from Europe, they were good sheep farmers and wool merchants, and were miners of coal and even producers of salt. They also organized markets and founded towns.

The Church changed from its age-old Celtic traditions to one modeled in the fashion of the English. It soon owned a great deal of the better land to be had in Scotland and attained a great deal of wealth. The religious houses became quite wealthy as well, as it was common practice for them to be the recipients of the tithes and patronages of the parish churches. The vicars of the parish churches, on the other hand, were paid very little, which usually forced them to return to nonreligious livelihoods in order to support themselves. By the reign of William the Lion, the Church was in dire need of reform.

NAMING

THE SCOTTISH NAMES in this time period were little different from those found in the previous chapter. The Gaelic language remained the language of the masses, and they retained the tradition of naming their children Gaelic names. Many of the Gaelic/Norse combination names were now common and not relegated only to those areas held by the Vikings.

There were a variety of names to be found in towns established near the Anglo-Norman estates, including Scottish, Anglo-Norman, English, and Frisian. However, except in the case of intermarriage, the names were not commonly shared among the different groups of people. Therefore, you would not find a Scot with a name like Adele or William, nor would you find an Anglo-Norman with the name Sorcha or Aonghus.

FEMALE NAMES

Ada (noble)
Adelaide (nobility)
Agnes (chaste, pure)
Ailbhe (?, perhaps *white*)
Aithbhreac (new speckled one)
Alana (O child)
Alma (all good)
Alys (noble one)
Annis (chaste, pure)
Aoibh (beauty)
Aoibheann (beautiful, fair form)
Arabella (?, perhaps *eagle; hearth*) **Arabel, Arabell**
Beatha (life)
Beathag (life; welcome)
Bebhinn (sweet, melodious lady)
Bethoc (life)
Blath (flower)
Blathnait (flower)

Brenda (?, possibly *the blade of a sword* or *sword wolf*)
Brighid (strength)
Brona (sorrow)
Caoilfhionn (slender and fair)
Ciannait (little ancient one)
Ciara (black-haired one)
Damhnait (little poet)
Deirdre (?, perhaps *young girl* or *fear*)
Diorbhail (true oath, testimony) **Dearbhail, Diorbhorguil**
Doireann (sullen)
Dubheasa (dark beauty)
Ealga (noble)
Eimhear (swift) **Eamhair**
Elen (light, torch, bright) **Ellen**
Fiona (white, fair, clear)
Fionnaghuala (white shoulders) **Fionnghuala**
Freya (lady, mistress)
Gormlaith (blue lady)

Kenna (comely; born of fire)
Lachina (land of the lochs)
Malamhìn (smooth brow)
Margareta (a pearl) **Margaret**
Mór (great, large)
Mórag (great, large)
Morainn (fair seas)
Muireall (bright seas; fair one of the sea)
Muireann (long-haired)
Muirne (beloved, affection)
Murdag (sea warrior)

Niamh (bright)
Oighrig (?, perhaps *new speckled one*)
Raghnaid (battle of decision)
Rathnait (little graceful one)
Saraid (excellent)
Sláine (health)
Sorcha (bright)
Suibhne (goodness)
Ùna (*famine, hunger, lamb*)
Ursula (she-bear)

MALE NAMES

Abbán (little abbot)
Adam (man of the red earth) Used by the English and Flemish.
Adelulf (noble wolf) A Flemish name.
Ádhamh (man of the red earth) Scottish form of Adam.
Ádhamhnán (little Adam)
Aidan (fire)
Ailpean (?) **Ailpein**
Alard (noble and brave) A Flemish name.
Alasdair (defender of mankind) **Alastair, Alisdair, Alistair** Scottish form of Alexander.
Alexander (defender of mankind)
Amhlaidh (ancestral relic) Scottish form of Olaf.
Andra (manly) Scottish form of Andrew.
Andrew (manly)
Aodán (fire)
Aodh (fire)
Aodhagán (little Aodh)
Aonghas (one, choice, preeminent)
Arailt (leader of the army) Scottish form of Harald.
Art (a bear)
Artair (?) Scottish form of Arthur.
Artán (little bear)
Baudewyn (bold friend) A Flemish name.
Beathan (life)
Cailean (dove) Scottish form of Columba.
Calum (dove) Scottish form of Columba.
Christiaen (a Christian, a follower of Christ) A Flemish name.
Cinaed (born of fire) **Cionaed**
Coinneach (handsome, comely)
Còiseam (enduring, steadfast) Scottish form of Constantine.
Collin (victory of the people) **Colyn** A Flemish name.
Comhnall (strength; wisdom; high; wolf; dog)
Conall (strength; wisdom; high; wolf; dog)
Cormag (?, perhaps *raven; son of defilement; son of the charioteer*)
Culloch (boar; cock)
Cúmhaige (hound of the plain)
Diarmid (without injunction, freeman) **Diarmad**
Domhnall (world ruler)
Donn (brown, brown-haired)
Donnchadh (brown warrior)

Donnell (world ruler)
Dubhghall (dark-haired stranger)
Dùbhghlas (black, dark + blue, green, gray)
Duncan (brown warrior)
Eachann (brown horse)
Eadgar (spear of prosperity)
Eairrdsidh (genuinely bold, genuinely brave)
Eallair (worker in a cellar)
Edward (wealthy protector)
Einar (lone warrior)
Eóghan (lamb; youth; well-born)
Erik (eternal ruler) **Eric**
Fearchar (dear man)
Fearghas (man of valor)
Fionnlagh (white warrior; fair-haired warrior)
Gillanders (servant of Saint Andrew)
Gilleonan (servant of Saint Adhamhnain)
Gilles (young goat, a kid) A Flemish name.
Gillespie (servant of the bishop)
Guillaume (resolute protector) A Flemish name.
Gwalchmai (battle hawk)
Harald (leader of the army) **Harold**
Heinri (home ruler) A Flemish name.
Heming (?, possibly *shape; shape-changer; a werewolf*)
Hugo (heart, mind, soul) A Flemish name.
Humfrey (warrior of peace)
Ìomhair (archer) Scottish form of Ivor.
Ivor (archer)
Jehan (God is gracious) A Flemish name.
John (God is gracious) Used by the English and Flemish.
Jordan (to flow down, descend) A Flemish name.
Keir (dark-complexioned)
Kenneth (born of fire; comely, handsome)
Kieran (little dark one) **Kiaran**
Lachlann (warlike; land of the lochs) **Lachlan**
Lucas (light; man from Lucania)
Magnus (great, large)
Mainard (brave strength) A Flemish name.
Malcolm (servant of Saint Columba)
Mànus (great, large) Scottish form of Magnus.
Mathys (gift of God) A Flemish name.

Michel (Who is like God?) Used by the English and Flemish.
Muireadhach (happy seas; mariner, sailor)
Murchadh (sea warrior) **Muireach**
Niall (champion; a cloud)
Obrecht (elf king) A Flemish name.
Olaf (ancestral relic)
Oscar (friend of deer)
Philip (lover of horses) Used by the English.
Philippe (lover of horses) A Flemish name.
Pierres (a rock, a stone) A Flemish name.
Pieter (a rock, a stone) A Flemish name.
Raghnall (powerful judgment)
Ranald (ruler of decision)
Randulf (shield wolf)
Ranulf (shield wolf)
Raonull (ruler of decision)
Richard (stern king) Used by the English and Flemings.

Roger Used by the English and Flemings.
Ruaraidh (red, ruddy)
Somerled (Viking, summer sailor)
Somhairle (Viking, summer sailor)
Stephen (a crown, garland) Used by the English and Flemings.
Tadhg (a poet)
Thomas (a twin)
Thorbjörn (Thor + bear) A Viking name.
Thorketil (Thor + sacrificial cauldron) A Viking name.
Thorstein (Thor + rock) **Thorsteinn**
Toirdhealbhach (shaped like Thor)
Tòmas (a twin) Scottish form of Thomas.
Walin (foreigner) A Flemish name.
Walter (ruler of an army) Used by the English and Flemings.
Wautier (ruler of an army) A Flemish name.
Willaume (resolute protector) A Flemish name.
William (resolute protector) Used by the English.

SURNAMES

In the Lowlands, an area subjected to strong Anglo-Norman influence, surnames developed among the Scots, even those with Gaelic first names, much as they did in England. Names based on occupation, location, personal characteristics, as well as patronymics and matronymics now came into being among the Scottish population. When the kings, beginning primarily with David I, encouraged foreigners to settle in Scotland, English, Norman-French, and Flemish surnames were added to the mix. Surnames during this period were not hereditary.

In the Highlands, it was a different story. To a person's first name was added his or her father's name, creating a genealogical system to differentiate one person from another. The clan was still the primary family and social group, and when a person joined a clan, he or she assumed the clan name, even if there was no familial relationship to the group. The surname usually consisted of the name of the clan's chief to which was prefixed the word *mac* (son). Highland surnames were hereditary only so long as the clan leaders' names remained the same. A change in leadership could bring about a change in surnames. Scottish ''surnames'' for this period can be formed by adding the father's name to that of the son or daughter.

Baldwin (bold friend) Used by the English and Flemish.
Balliol (war, fortification)
Bec (beak, bill of a bird) A Flemish name.
Bruce (from Brieuse, a local in France)
Buchanan (little small one)
Cameron (crooked nose)
Campbell (crooked mouth)
Flandrensis (from Flanders)
le Fleming (the Fleming) **le Flemeng**
Freskin (?) A Flemish name.
MacAodha (son of Aodh *fire*)

MacBain (son of Bain *fair, white*)
MacBeth (son of Beatha *life*)
Maclean (son of the servant of John)
McCulloch (son of Culloch *boar; cock*)
MacDiarmid (son of Diarmid *without injunction; a freeman*)
MacDonell (son of Donell *world ruler*)
MacGregor (son of Gregor *vigilant, a watchman*)
MacKay (son of Aedh *fire*)
Macleod (son of Léoid *ugly*)
Scott (a Scot)
Wallace (a Welshman, a foreigner)

Chapter Three

POLITICS

ALEXANDER III'S HEIR was his granddaughter, three-year-old Margaret, the Maid of Norway. Margaret died in 1290 without ever setting foot in Scotland, and there were no fewer than thirteen claimants to the throne. All were either legitimate or illegitimate descendants of the royal house of Canmore, but only three could be considered prime candidates: Robert de Brus (Bruce), a twice-named heir to the throne during the reigns of Alexander II and Alexander III, and a great-great-grandson of David I; John de Bailleul (Balliol), a great-great-great-grandson of David I; and John Hastings, another great-great-great-grandson of David I. With the threat of civil war looming, King Edward of England was invited to arbitrate in the selection of the king. He agreed, then with the most amazing arrogance, gave the claimants three weeks to acknowlege him as overlord of all Scotland first, and he had an army behind him to force the issue should the heirs refuse. They accepted, to the great anger and dismay of Scotland's influential families and clans.

The seven earls of Scotland put in a bid for Robert Bruce, but the Bishop of Saint Andrews asked for John Balliol. In the end, Edward chose the latter, probably because Balliol was known as a weakling and that would make it that much easier for Edward to control him, which he did to a humiliating degree.

In 1294, Edward summoned his feudal knights and lords when he went to war against France. He included John Balliol in that call and demanded the Scottish king supply both men and money for the war. By that time, Scotland had enough of the English king's contemptuous treatment. The call to arms was refused, a council of four bishops, four barons, and four earls was formed, and a treaty was made with the French instead.

A furious Edward attacked Scotland in 1296 and enjoyed a succession of victories that culminated in Balliol's surrender in July of the same year. On his way home, Edward took Scotland's precious Stone of Destiny from Scone and Saint Margaret's portion of the True Cross, carted off valuable Scottish records, held a parliament at Berwick, and set up a government staffed by English officials.

The independent and nationalist Scots rebelled. William Wallace, Scotland's most famous and beloved national hero, distinguished himself in battle and was pronounced "Guardian of the Kingdom of Scotland and Leader of its Armies in the name of John, by the Grace of God, Illustrious King of Scotland." He was beaten at Falkirk, escaped, and with a price on his head, went into hiding from where he emerged to attack

English castles or camps. Wallace was betrayed in 1305 and taken to London for trial. He was convicted of treason, hanged, drawn, and quartered. His head was put on a pike on London Bridge, and his other body parts displayed as a warning at four other points in Scotland. If Edward thought this display would make the Scots cower in submission, he was wrong, for it only served to stiffen their resolve to see all English out of Scotland.

Another patriot to take up the cause was Robert Bruce, who was pronounced king in 1306, a year before Edward I died. Edward II made an attempt to follow in his father's footsteps by invading Scotland. The whole affair was a disaster that was over before it had even begun. Bruce, encouraged by the new king's weakness, mounted a campaign to take English-held castles. In 1314, Edward II invaded again, but again was routed at the famous Battle of Bannockburn.

For the next nine years, the Scots raided the northern English until, in 1323, Edward II signed a truce. In 1328, Edward III recognized Robert Bruce as king of an independent realm by signing the Treaty of Northampton and sealing it with the betrothal of his baby sister, Joan, to Bruce's young son, David. On June 7, 1329, Robert Bruce, King of Scots died.

Bruce's successor was his five-year-old son, David. The first few years of his reign passed under the regency of the capable earl of Moray (a nephew of Bruce). After he died in 1332, the next regent was the earl of Mar, another of Bruce's nephews. He died fighting Edward Balliol, who had been encouraged by Edward III to take the crown.

Edward III then broke the Treaty of Northampton and invaded Scotland. After successfully putting down the Scots, he declared Edward Balliol to be king in 1333. In return, Balliol gave several of the southern counties to England. The young king David and his equally young queen were sent to France for protection, where they remained for almost nine years. In the Highlands, regents continued to rule in David's name.

In 1339, the pressure was taken off Scotland when Edward III put forth his claim to the French throne. Balliol was left unprotected, and that man, faced with retaliating Scots, fled the country. In 1341, David returned home to accept his crown. Unfortunately, he didn't measure up to the expectations of his countrymen. His life in France had left him without the qualifications to lead the Scottish nation, and that was never more evident than after his disastrous raid on Northumberland that ended in his capture and placement in the Tower of London for more than ten years. David was eventually ransomed back in 1357 for a declaration of Edward's overlordship and 100,000 marks, a tremendous amount of money that was supposed to be paid in ten years.

David did little for his country but cause hardship. After he returned, he neglected his government and country and lived a life of luxury and idleness. In 1363, David suggested to Edward that if he canceled payment of the ransom, David would will Scotland to him in the event David died childless. The Scottish lords refused to accept that, and when David died in 1371, his countrymen were still struggling to pay the ransom of a king who had been captured through no fault but his own, and who had prepared to give away his own country.

David's successor was his nephew, Robert the Steward, the holder of the hereditary office of high steward of Scotland, and the first of the Stewart kings. Under the Stewarts' guidance, Scotland passed from the Middle Ages into a brief renaissance, and then into modern times. It also endured a long struggle between crown and baronage during which time the crown slowly increased its power and reduced that of the clans and powerful southern families.

Robert II inherited a country deep in debt and suffering from internal conflict. He had years of administrative experience behind him and was a popular king, though advanced in years. In the 1380s, trouble brewed afresh with England. Robert reaffirmed the ''Auld Alliance'' with France, prompting the English to retaliate with border raids and skirmishes, which caused the Scots to exact their revenge upon the English. Robert II died in 1390, and power was transferred to his son John, who was given the name Robert III upon his coronation.

Unfortunately, the new king was not fit to rule. Not only had a serious accident with his horse left him with a physical impediment rendering him incapable of riding again, he was naturally weak and timid and lacked the resolve and strength of character needed to lead Scotland through such troubled times. He let his brother Robert, the earl of Fife, govern on his behalf during the beginning of his reign, but then took over the job himself in 1394. He appointed his son, David, as lieutenant of the kingdom in 1398 and created for him the first dukedom of Scotland, Rothesay. The dukedom of Albany was created for Fife as a consolation.

David was shiftless, vicious, and vindictive, and lived a debased life. He was arrested in 1401, imprisoned, and reportedly starved to death. Robert's other son, the young James, was sent to France in 1406. On the way, his ship was intercepted by the English and twelve-year-old James captured and lodged in the Tower of London. There he would remain until 1424. A devastated Robert III died shortly after receiving the news of his son's capture.

The duke of Albany was quick to step into the role of regent, but his ability to govern adequately was tempered by the great families, including his own, who wielded their power ruthlessly in the pursuit of supremacy. Some believed that Albany had deliberately dragged his feet over the negotiations for James's release because he'd set his own sights on the crown. He never attempted to take the monarchy, however, and continued as regent until his death in 1420 at more than eighty years of age.

Albany's son Murdoch succeed as regent, and in 1423, he successfully negotiated James's release. James I was finally crowned at Scone in 1424 and immediately set out to restore law and order to his country. He also embarked on a scheme of revenge against those he thought were responsible for his long incarceration. The first to suffer were his own kinfolk. Murdoch and his family were arrested, tried before a panel of lords headed by the earl of Atholl, who was the king's uncle and Albany's half-brother, and beheaded. Other families such as the Grahams and the Douglases suffered as well. At the beginning of James's reign there were fifteen earldoms and one dukedom, but by the time he was finished exacting his revenge, only eight earldoms remained. All the lands and revenues of the others had been confiscated and passed to the king.

The Highland chiefs were next on James's list. He invited all the clan chiefs to a conference at Inverness, and when they arrived, put them in irons and even had several put to death. Once James made his position as king and supreme ruler clear, those chiefs whose lives were spared were allowed to leave. The clan leaders felt dishonored, and they were bitterly angry.

Now, both the nobles and the clan chiefs plotted to eliminate the king, but the successful conspirators were Sir Robert Graham and Sir Robert Stewart, who killed James during a fight in a cellar of a monastery in Perth. Both men were eventually hunted down and tortured to death.

Scotland was time and time again put into the unfortunate position of having a child succeed as king. It was a situation that often led to anarchy as government was put into the hands of regents, or kings' widows, or great lords who were usually feuding with one another. The situation didn't change after James's death, for next in line was his six-year-old son, James II.

The General Council appointed Bishop Cameron of Glasgow as lord chancellor and Archibald, the fifth earl of Douglas, as Regent. Douglas turned out to be a dismal choice, for he had none of the legendary courage and backbone of his family and was ill-suited for the work of government. The years of James's minority saw much corruption as the powerful clans and families took advantage of Scotland's lack of a worthy leader.

Once James came of age, he chose to govern for himself. In order to establish commercial and political ties with the continent, James secured a marriage to Marie, the niece of the duke of Burgundy. Next, he turned his sights homeward and worked to curb the power of the great families. The Black Douglases were destroyed, and other families were forced into submission.

James II was killed in August 1460 when he was hit by shrapnel from an exploding cannon at the siege of Roxburgh castle. He was succeeded by his nine-year-old son, James III, and Scotland was again faced with the trials of having a child-king. His mother and Bishop Kennedy, his cousin, governed on his behalf; after their deaths, Lord Boyd was named regent. Under Boyd's leadership, a marriage was arranged between the king, who was now eighteen, and Margaret, the daughter of Christian I of Denmark and Norway. Her dowry of the Orkneys and Shetlands returned those islands to the possession of Scotland.

James III cared little for government, preferring to spend his time with a small group of gifted and intelligent favorites rather than with his nobles. His unpopularity spurred a number into plotting against him and none were more active than his brothers, the earls of Albany and Mar, Archibald Douglas, the head of the Red Douglases, and Colin Campbell, Chief of Clan Campbell. In 1488, a group of conspirators that included Douglas and Campbell kidnapped James's young son and proclaimed him King of Scots in place of his father. James was forced into a confrontation, and in June 1488, was killed during the Battle of Sauchieburn.

James IV was only fifteen at the time, but he was enough his own man to keep from being ruled by his nobles. He was also so filled with remorse at his father's death and the improper way he came to the throne that for the rest of his life he wore an iron chain around his body as penance.

James proved to be the ablest and most popular of the Stewart kings. When civil war broke out a year after he came to the throne, he took the field at the head of his troops and led them to victory over the rebels. His gifts were not limited to leadership. He went about all aspects of his life with just as much energy and enthusiasm. He was very religious, yet had many mistresses and a great number of illegitimate children. He was highly intelligent and spoke several languages, including Gaelic (which brought him closer to the Gaelic-speaking Highlanders), and was an accomplished musician. He was open-handed, friendly, courageous, and he oversaw a golden age of learning and the arts as the Renaissance reached Scotland. His was a prosperous and peaceful period. He even did something none of his predecessors had done: He made a series of visits to the islands and western Highlands to introduce himself to the various clans and encouraged them to improve their lot by fishing and shipbuilding. Nothing much came of the visits, and he changed his policy to reflect more of a feudal approach rather than a patriarchal one. His attempt to impose feudal overlords on the clans was a mistake, for they resented his interference and rose against him, forcing him to establish a number of strongholds throughout the Highlands.

In 1503, when James was twenty-eight, he married Margaret Tudor, the twelve-year-old daughter of Henry VII, to form an alliance with England. For years he worked to keep the peace between France and England, but when he turned to England to assist during a French appeal for aid, his brother-in-law, Henry VIII, insolently declined to help and even threatened James's position as king. James felt he had no choice but to fight for the survival of himself and his kingdom.

He mustered the most splendid army and invaded in August 1513. He met the English at Flodden Field, and at first it appeared as if the Scots would take the day. Unfortunately, his troops were out-armed, and the battle turned into a massacre. James was killed, and along with him, the flower of Scottish chivalry. Among the dead were James's son, Alexander, the Bishop of Caithness and the Bishop of the Isles, the Dean of Glasgow, the Provost of Edinburgh, many chiefs of the Highland clans, fourteen lords and nine earls, and thousands of Scotland's finest warriors and young men. After the battle, James's body was taken to his brother-in-law, but Henry denied it burial and no one knows what became of it.

Scotland's situation was now extremely precarious. Her king and her finest leaders were dead, her army was wiped out, and her only ally, France, was also in grave danger. Her new king, James V, was an infant, and his unintelligent mother had become regent. For the next year or two, lawlessness abounded. Margaret eventually forfeited the regency and married the head of the Red Douglases, the Earl of Angus. James III's brother, the French-educated and French-speaking Duke of Albany, succeeded as regent in 1515.

Political intrigue followed, and the young king was kept a virtual prisoner by the Douglases. In 1528, James disguised himself as a groom and escaped. "I vow that Scotland will not hold us both," he said in reference to his captors. He was sixteen and determined both to govern for himself and to bring down the Douglases. He succeeded in forcing Angus to flee across the border, then set to work to reestablish law and order.

Scotland's troubles with England resurfaced as Henry VIII defied the Pope and tried to extend Protestantism to Scotland. James resisted, and Henry crossed the border and formally declared himself to be lord-superior of Scotland. James replied by invading England, but his nobles refused to march, and his army was therefore quite small and easily defeated. The king escaped and rode to Falkland where he received the news that his wife had borne him a daughter. Remembering the way the crown came to his family through Marjorie Bruce, he uttered the prophecy, "It came with a lass and it will pass with a lass." He supposedly gave one little laugh and fell back dead. It was December 1542.

It seems history was to repeat itself. After the death of Alexander III in 1286, the nearest male kinsman of Margaret, the Maid of Norway, was her great-uncle, the king of England. Scotland had again passed to an infant girl whose nearest male kinsman just happened to be the king of England, Henry VIII. Henry knew how to exploit a situation, and he had just the son to do it with: Edward.

SOCIETY

THE BEGINNING OF this period was a time of great chivalry and also great brutality. Killings, maimings, and so forth were commonplace, yet so was more civilized behavior and more refined manners. In order to provide better defense, new castles and, later, the manor houses, were constructed of stone, though the interior buildings often continued to be made of wood or of wood and clay. Tower-houses were the dominant form of fortified residence.

Among the country folk, life continued apace, with small landowners working their farms to support their families. The women baked bread and brewed ale, and they spun wool, wove it into cloth, and made clothing from it. Houses continued to be primitive huts walled and roofed with turf. There were no windows, no chimney, and no door except for a simple hide curtain. Livestock and people alike shared the quarters. Goods could be purchased at the market, which was a weekly event except during Lady Mary Fair, when it was held daily for the week-long celebration.

In the fourteenth century, the Black Death made its appearance in Scotland. Countryside and burgh alike were ravaged by the plague, and by the time it had finished its second pass through the country in 1361, a third of the population had perished.

The plague had a devastating effect on the nation's economy, as well. Already broke from trying to meet the ransom demands for David, the country was put into even more dire straits after much of its workforce was killed off.

Another event of the fourteenth century was the disappearance of villeinage; though some of the feudal duties continued to apply, the common peasant was no longer a mere serf but a freeman who was no longer bound to one estate.

In the fifteenth century, Scotland's alliance with France resulted in Scotland gaining a bit of Continental culture. French influence could be found in Scots literature, architecture, and in the country's educational institutions. In 1450, Glasgow University was founded, giving the country's youth an opportunity to study. Both James I and II patronized the arts and crafts and encouraged their subjects to practice archery and swordsmanship rather than the more common games of golf and soccer.

The Renaissance came to Scotland during the reign of James IV. It was a golden age of learning and the arts, and in 1507, Scotland's first printing press was set up and its third university, King's College, was founded. Trade flourished with the Low Countries, and manufactured goods and luxuries from abroad were now available to more than just the nobility.

However, these improved social conditions were really limited to the Lowlands. In the Highlands, life went on much as it had for centuries and the hold of Church or state on the Highlanders was still quite tenuous. Fancy clothes, books, and education mattered little. What mattered the most to clansmen was their clan, land, and cattle. The clan chief was still regarded as a father by his people, and his people, his children. It was the chief's responsibility to help his clansmen settle their disputes, aid them when needed, and protect them from their enemies. It was the clansmen's duty to give the chief their absolute loyalty and to follow where he led. Pride of family was as deeply rooted as the clans themselves.

The Highland chiefs paid little attention to their kings in the south except to view them as either potential allies or enemies in their own struggles for power. They regarded themselves almost as independent of the rest of Scotland, and it was this very independence that prompted the kings to try to assert some control over them.

RELIGION

NEW RELIGIOUS ORDERS came to Scotland in the middle of the thirteenth century. Rather than shut themselves up in closed monasteries, the new monks chose to take their message to the people and ended up performing many of the duties of the overworked and underpaid parish priests. During the reigns of the Stewarts, religion was further expanded. James IV, in particular, encouraged a great deal of church building and sought to transplant many religious houses from rural areas to more populated ones where their service and good examples would be more effective.

The corruption that had infected the Church in Europe and England now took root in Scotland. At no other time was the Church so corrupt or degraded. Indeed, Pope Eugenius IV commented that the Scottish bishops were "Pilates rather than Prelates." Many priests and nuns had numerous children that they provided for at the expense of the Church. Appointments were often made on a whim or carried out without respect to qualifications. Alexander Stewart, for instance, the illegitimate son of James IV, was made Archbishop of Saint Andrews, the Abbot of Arbroath, and Prior of Coldingham when he was just eleven years old.

The Scottish Church was immensely wealthy, controlling more than half the nation's wealth and holding a huge amount of land. The crown enjoyed lavish ecclesiastical subsidies, but while the state benefitted from such conditions, the people did not. In spite of the Church's monetary resources, a great number of parish churches were allowed to fall into ruin, and fewer and fewer parishioners attended mass.

Statutes were passed in an attempt to correct the problems. Among them were those encouraging the clergy to learn to read and to preach at least four times a year. Others forbade the prelates and clergy from keeping their illegitimate offspring with them or promoting them to church offices.

English translations of the Bible began to be smuggled across the border early in the sixteenth century, and they had just as profound an effect in Scotland as they had in England. People were now able to read the words of the gospel and discover for themselves the true nature of Christianity and how far from the principles their priests and religious leaders were. Active discontent was everywhere, and Protestantism began to be touted in the streets. In 1528, the first Protestant martyr, Patrick Hamilton, was slowly burned at the stake outside the Chapel of Saint Salvator. His death left a lasting impression on the people of Scotland, and the new Protestant doctrine swept across a country that was begging for something other that what it had.

NAMING

ONCE THE SCOTTISH monarchs encouraged Englishmen and other foreigners to settle in the Lowlands, the names they brought with them took root as well. The most common first names of the Lowlanders were James, John, Robert, and Thomas, though John suffered for a time from bad associations with both English and Scottish kings. Among the women, the most common name by far was Margaret, but Mary was also popular. In the Highlands, traditional Gaelic names were the rule.

The intermarriage of nobility to those of other nationalities also affected the names found during this time period. James V, for example, married two French women: Madeleine, the daughter of François I, and Marie de Guise-Lorraine, bringing these names into use.

FEMALE NAMES

Ada (noble)
Adela (noble)
Adelaide (nobility)
Adeline (nobility)
Agatha (good)
Agnes (chaste, pure)
Alana (O child)
Alice (noble one)
Alicia (noble one)
Anna (grace, full of grace, mercy)
Annabel (?, perhaps *eagle; hearth; lovable;* or *joy*) **Anabel, Annabell**
Annag (grace, full of grace, mercy)
Arabella (?, perhaps *eagle; hearth*) **Arabela**
Barbara (foreign woman)
Beathag (life)
Bethoc (life)
Brenda (sword)
Brighid (strength)
Cairistiona (a Christian, a follower of Christ) Scottish form of Christine.
Cecilia (blind, dim-sighted)
Clara (clear, bright, famous)
Cristina (a Christian, a follower of Christ)
Diorbhail (true oath, true testimony)
Eamhair (?)
Edmée (beloved) **Esmée**

Efrica (pleasant) **Effririca**
Fiona (white, fair, clear)
Fionnaghuala (white shoulders) **Fionnghuala**
Freya (lady, mistress)
Gormlaith (blue lady)
Hannah (grace, full of grace, mercy)
Isabel (God is my oath)
Iseabail (God is my oath) Scottish form of Isabel.
Johanna (God is gracious)
Karistina (a Christian, a follower of Christ)
Katerina (pure, unsullied)
Kenna (born of fire; comely)
Madeleine (of Magdala)
Margaret (a pearl)
Margery (a pearl) **Marjorie**
Marie (sea of bitterness or sorrow)
Mary (sea of bitterness or sorrow)
Mór (great, large) **Mora**
Morag (great, large)
Morainn (bright seas, fair one of the sea)
Murdag (sea warrior) **Murdann, Murdina**
Nan (grace, full of grace, mercy)
Nora (a woman from the north)
Raghnaid (advice, counsel, decision + battle)
Sorcha (bright)
Ùna (?, perhaps *famine, hunger* or *lamb*)
Ursula (she-bear)

MALE NAMES

Adaidh (man of the red earth)
Adam (man of the red earth)
Ádhamh (man of the red earth) Scottish form of Adam.
Ádhamhnán (little Adam)
Aidan (fire)
Ailpean (?) **Ailpein**
Aindrea (manly) Scottish form of Andrew.
Alan (?, perhaps *handsome; rock*)
Alasdair (defender of mankind) Scottish form of Alexander.
Alexander (defender of mankind)
Andra (manly) Scottish form of Andrew.
Andrew (manly)
Angus (one, choice, preeminent)
Aodán (fire)
Aodh (fire)
Aodhagán (little Aodh)
Aonghas (one, choice, preeminent)
Arailt (leader of the army) Scottish form of Harold.
Archibald (genuinely brave, genuinely bold)
Art (bear)
Artan (little bear)
Beathan (life)
Benedict (blessed)
Benneit (blessed) Scottish form of Benedict.
Bennet (blessed)
Cailean (dove) Scottish form of Columba.
Calman (bald)
Calum (dove) Scottish form of Columba.
Campbell (crooked mouth)
Coinneach (handsome, comely)
Colin (dove) **Collin**
Comhnall (strength; wisdom; high; wolf; dog)
Conall (strength; wisdom; high; wolf; dog)
Cormag (?, perhaps *raven; son of defilement; son of the char-ioteer*)
Cúmhaige (hound of the plain)
Dàibhidh (beloved) Scottish form of David.
David (beloved)
Domhnall (world ruler)
Donald (world ruler) **Donnald**
Donn (brown, brown-haired)
Donnchadh (brown warrior)
Donnell (world ruler)
Dougal (dark-haired stranger)
Dubhghall (dark-haired stranger)
Dubhglas (black, dark + blue, green, gray)
Duncan (brown warrior) **Donkan**
Eachann (brown horse)
Eairrdsidh (genuinely bold, genuinely brave)
Eallair (worked in a cellar)
Edward (wealthy guardian)
Eideard (wealthy guardian) Scottish form of Edward.
Eóghan (lamb; youth; well-born)
Eric (eternal ruler)

Fearchar (dear man)
Fearghas (man of valor)
Fionnlagh (white warrior, fair-haired warrior)
Florence (blooming, flourishing)
Gavin (battle hawk)
Gilchrist (servant of Christ)
Gillanders (servant of Saint Andrew)
Gillemichel (servant of Saint Michael)
Gillies (servant of Jesus)
Gregor (vigilant, watchful) **Grigor**
Griogair (vigilant, watchful)
Gybbon (bright pledge)
Hamish (supplanting, seizing by the heels)
Henry (home ruler)
James (supplanting, seizing by the heels)
Jankyn (God is gracious)
Johannes (God is gracious)
John (God is gracious)
Keir (dark-complexioned)
Kenneth (born of fire; comely, handsome)
Kieran (little dark one) **Kiaran**
Labhrainn (man from Laurentum) Scottish form of Laurence.
Lachlan (warlike; land of the lochs) **Lachann, Lachlann**
Laurence (man from Laurentum)
Magnus (great, large)
Malcolm (servant of Saint Columba)
Malise (black, dark)
Mànus (great, large)
Màrtainn (of Mars, warlike) Scottish form of Martin.
Martyn (of Mars, warlike)
Muireadhach (happy seas, mariner, sailor)
Murchadh (sea warrior) **Muireach**
Murdoch (mariner)
Niall (champion; a cloud)
Nigel (cloud; champion)
Norman (northman)
Oscar (spear of God; friend of the deer) **Osgar**
Pàdraig (a patrician) **Padraic**
Patrick (a patrician)
Philip (lover of horses)
Raghnall (ruler of judgment)
Raibeart (bright with fame) Scottish form of Robert.
Ranald (ruler of decision, judgment power)
Ranulf (shield wolf)
Raonull (ruler of decision)
Reid (red, red-haired)
Richard (stern king)
Robert (bright with fame)
Ruaraidh (red, ruddy)
Ruiseart (stern king) Scottish form of Richard.
Scymynd (heard)
Simon (heard)
Somerled (Viking, summer sailor)
Somhairle (Viking, summer sailor)

Tadhg (a poet)
Thomas (a twin)
Toirdhealbhach (shaped like Thor)
Tomas (a twin) **Tòmas** Scottish form of Thomas.

Tòrmod (northman) Scottish form of Norman.
Uilleam (resolute protector) **Uilliam** Scottish form of William.
Walter (ruler of an army)
William (resolute protector)

SURNAMES

Surnames of the Highlanders continued in traditional patronymic form, but the surnames of the Lowlanders typically followed the same patterns as the English. Characteristic and genealogical descriptions and names from places or occupations were common. In the fourteenth century, the use of the preposition *de* in local names declined, and at the end of the century, occupational names were much more common without the preposition *le*.

Balliol (wall, fortification)
Boyd (yellow-haired)
Brody (dweller near the ditch)
Bruce (from Brus)
Buchanan (little small one)
Burns (from the burnt house)
Cameron (crooked nose)
Campbell (crooked mouth)
Chisholm (gravel island)
Colquhoun (the narrow wood)
Douglas (dark, black and blue, green, gray; stream)
Dubh (dark, black)
Dunbar (fort of the summit)
Elphinstone (from Elphin's estate)
Erroll (from Erroll)
Erskine (?, perhaps *height of the cleft*)
Forbes (field)
Fraser (a Frisian)
Galbraith (Welsh stranger, British stranger)
Gillebride (servant of Saint Bridget *strength*)
Gillespik (servant of the bishop)
Gordon (?, from a Scottish place name)
Graham (?, from a place name, the second element of which is *home, dwelling, manor*)
Grant (great, large)
Gray (gray)
Gunn (war, battle)
Haldane (half Dane)
Hamilton (from the town near the blunt hill)
Henryson (son of Henry *home ruler*)
Hepburn (high stream)
Homes (dweller on a river island)
Huntley (wood of the huntsman)
Innes (island)
Keith (?, possibly *wind* or *wood*)
Kennedy (ugly head, ugly helmet)
Lamont (a lawyer)
Leslie (garden of hollies; the gray fort)
Lindsay (from the settlement by the lake)
Livingstone (from Leofing's stone)
MacArthur (son of Arthur)

Macaulay (son of Olaf *ancestral relic*)
MacBain (son of Bain *fair, white*)
MacBeth (son of Beatha *life*)
Maclean (son of the servant of John)
McCowyn (son of Eoghain *youth*)
McCrystyn (son of Kristin *a Christian*)
McCulloch (son of Culloch *boar; cock*)
MacDiarmid (son of Diarmid *a freeman, without injunction*)
Macdonald (son of Donald *world ruler*)
MacDonell (son of Donell *world ruler*)
MacDougall (son of Dougall *dark-haired stranger*)
MacEwen (son of Ewen *youth*)
MacFergus (son of Fergus *man of valor or strength*)
MacGillivray (son of Gille-Brath *the servant of judgment*)
MacInnes (son of Innes *island*)
MacKay (son of Aedh *fire*)
McKee (son of Aedh *fire*)
MacLennan (son of the servant of Finnan *fair one*)
Macleod (son of Léoid *ugly*)
MacKenzie (son of Coinneach *handsome, comely*) **McKenzie**
MacKinnon (son of Fingon *fair birth*)
MacMartin (son of Martin *of Mars, warlike*)
McNeill (son of Neill *a champion; cloud*)
MacQueen (son of Suibhne *well-going, pleasant*)
MacTavish (son of Thomas *a twin*)
Malcolm (servant of Saint Columba)
Matheson (son of Matthew *gift of God*)
Mercer (storekeeper)
Moncreiffe (from Moncreiffe *hill of the trees*)
Munro (dweller at the red morass)
Murray (from Moray *beside the sea*)
Ogilvy (from Ogilvie *high hill*)
Oliphant (dealer of ivory; dweller at the sign of the elephant)
Ramsay (from the raven's island)
Ross (dweller on the promontory, dweller on the peninsula)
Scott (a Scot)
Sinclair (Saint Clair)
Spalding (from Spalding)
Stewart (a steward, keeper of the animal enclosure) **Stuart**
Strathearn (a valley)
Sutherland (from the southern land)
Wallace (a Welshman, a foreigner)

Chapter Four

MARY QUEEN OF SCOTS TO JAMES I
[1542–1603]

POLITICS

MARY QUEEN OF Scots was less than a week old when she inherited the crown in 1542. As the English king was her nearest male relative, the outlook for Scotland was bleak. Henry VIII, determined to conquer Scotland, immediately put forth a marriage proposal between his son, Edward, and little Mary. Though a treaty of marriage was negotiated with the Scots regent, the queen mother had other plans. The baby was crowned queen at Scone, and the treaty of marriage was repudiated by the lords.

A livid Henry responded by invading Scotland in the summer of 1544, laying waste to Edinburgh and the border towns and devastating the countryside. Orders given to English soldiers read, ''Put all to fyre and swoorde, burne Edinborough towne, so rased and defaced when you have sacked and gotten what ye can of it, as there may remayne forever a perpetuel memory of the vengaunce of God.'' Known as the Rough Wooing, the rampage left behind a legacy of hatred for the English that was to last for centuries.

Scotland now found itself in an extremely difficult situation. The country was torn between reaching out to its traditional ally, Catholic France, for help, or to end the hostilities and make an alliance with its traditional enemy, Protestant England. Had the Church not been so totally corrupt and the people so disillusioned with its religious leaders, the choice probably would have been a simple one. As it was, the people were more than ready to reach out toward a religious ideal that was far from what they believed the traditional Church embodied. The monarchy, however, knowing it was in great peril, chose to ally itself with France.

In 1548, Mary was taken to France and betrothed to the dauphin to further and strengthen the bond between the countries. In 1554, the queen mother, Marie de Guise, assumed the regency and saw a program of Church reform put in place.

In 1559, the dauphin, sixteen-year-old Queen Mary's Catholic husband, inherited the French throne and put claim to England and Scotland. Protestants, afraid of losing their independence and experiencing another Catholic crackdown, went on the rampage and sacked all the churches in Perth. Marie de Guise appealed to France for more aid, and the English queen opened negotiations with Scottish Protestants.

Events came to a head in 1560 when the English army confronted French forces in Scotland. In June, Marie de Guise died, thereby eliminating a powerful political force. A month later, the Treaty of Edinburgh was signed to provide for the departure of English and French troops from Scotland upon the recognition of Elizabeth as Queen of England. The treaty put an end to Scotland's historical alliance with France.

In 1561, the newly widowed Mary returned to Scotland to claim her inheritance and rule as queen. In 1565, in accordance to the rites of the Catholic Church, she married her cousin, Henry Stewart, four years her junior and with a notoriously bad reputation, and had him proclaimed king. Less than a year later, Henry became jealous of Mary's attention to her Italian secretary and murdered him in her presence. Henry was sent to his house near Edinburgh to recuperate from an unknown but supposedly disgraceful disease, and it was there that he and his house were blown up. The crime was never solved, but most believed the Protestant James Hepburn, fourth Earl of Bothwell and Lord High Admiral, had been involved. Mary seemed to overlook the fact that he had just as bad a reputation as Henry Stewart, and they were married eight weeks later in a Protestant ceremony.

Now, both Protestants and Catholics were against Mary. She was taken by a group of Protestant lords (on the pretext of saving her from Bothwell) and, in a short red petticoat, was led through the streets of Edinburg. She was forced to abdicate in favor of her infant son and imprisoned in Lochleven Castle. In 1568, Mary escaped and fled to England to throw herself on the mercy of her cousin, Queen Elizabeth. Unfortunately, Elizabeth had no mercy, and Mary was immediately imprisoned. After being held for nineteen years, Mary Queen of Scots was executed.

After Mary's abdication, her son was immediately crowned James VI and the country was again plunged into a tug of war between Protestants and Catholics and a succession of regents who were either murdered in office or forced to abdicate. In 1582, James was kidnapped by a group of Protestant nobles led by the Earl of Gowrie and was held at Ruthven. The nobles then took control of the government. A year later, the young king escaped, made his way to Saint Andrews, proclaimed himself king, and assumed power.

James continued to have problems with civil and religious strife. He was raised, and remained, Protestant, probably because it kept him on reasonably good terms with Queen Elizabeth, whom he hoped to succeed. In 1585, he established an alliance with England and made only the briefest of formal protests when his mother was executed. In March 1603, James's fondest desire was fulfilled. Queen Elizabeth of England had died and he had been named heir. The unification of the countries was at hand.

SOCIETY

CELTIC TRADITIONS AND culture persisted in the Highlands as the clans ignored most of what was happening in the south and continued to pursue their old feuds and rivalries. In the south, religious and political unrest spilled over into social unrest. To make matters worse, famine was a recurring problem in the sixteenth and early seventeenth centuries. Diseases such as typhus that went hand in hand with famine, spread into segments of the population that normally would not suffer from starvation, such as the wealthier classes and those whose jobs did not depend upon agriculture or weren't patronized primarily by the lower classes.

In the wake of the Reformation, a great deal of the wealth and lands taken from the Catholic Church were acquired by private landowners. With more money now available and the south still in turmoil, the lords and barons embarked on an extensive period of tower-house building. Such impressive homes, however, were only for the wealthy. The majority of the urban population continued to live in tightly packed tenements and buildings where social class determined the floor on which a person lived. The rich merchants lived on the ground floor, and as the number of floors went up, the class of people went down with the poorest occupying the freezing attics. In the countryside, dismal turf or turf-and-stone huts people shared with their animals were still the rule.

An interesting characteristic of Scottish society was the pervasive belief in superstition and the supernatural. The people were firmly convinced in the reality of witches and supernatural beings like ghosts, fairies, trolls, elves, and banshees. And it wasn't just the common, ignorant folk who held these beliefs. The nobility was just as wary of the unknown. Even James VI was obsessed with witches and witchcraft.

Another societal characteristic was the austere way in which the people lived their lives. Their plain living and frugality, a by-product of the equally austere way in which they practiced their Protestant religion, soon became a hallmark of Scottish society.

Every major town had a grammar school that taught the rudiments of Latin to the children of barons and freeholders. Children entered school at the age of eight or nine and took lessons for three years. The groundwork for a national education system was laid in the sixteenth century by John Knox in his *First Book of Discipline*. In theory, every parish was to have its own school for rich and poor children alike. Though the problems presented by putting a plan of that magnitude in place kept it from being fulfilled, it was to become the blueprint for Scottish education. Edinburgh University was founded in 1582 and Marischal College in Aberdeen in 1593, bringing the number of Scottish universities to five.

RELIGION

AT THE BEGINNING of this time period, the Church was extremely corrupt and its practices were probably as far from the tenets of Christianity as they could get. The English Bible, banned by parliament, was smuggled over the border and gave people their first true look at the words of God and the premise upon which their religion was based. The impact was immediate and revolutionary, prompting many to zealously embrace the cause of Protestantism.

In 1544, when religious persecution was at its height, Father John Knox entered the country. He was a forceful and eloquent man who laid the foundation for the triumph of Protestantism in Scotland. Knox was imprisoned in 1546 and released three years later.

The Protestant movement steadily gained ground, in spite of the influence of the Catholic queen mother. In 1557, a document known as the First Covenant was drawn up in which a group of noblemen calling themselves Lords of the Congregation pledged to make a break with Rome and establish a reformed national church. In 1558, the Catholic hierarchy, probably feeling as if they were losing the battle, decided to make an example of an eighty-two-year-old Protestant priest by burning him at the stake. The event had such a poor turnout that the archbishop's servants were forced to burn the old man themselves. The priest, Walter Myln, was the last Protestant to be burned in Scotland.

When news came that the Protestant Elizabeth had ascended the English throne, Marie de Guise, now most anxious to unite Scotland and France, was prepared to suppress the First Covenant by force, if necessary. In 1559, requests from Protestant noblemen prompted John Knox's return. His anti-Catholic sermons were more inflammatory and inciting than ever and served to work up mobs of disgruntled parishioners; churches were wrecked, and altars and religious icons were destroyed.

In 1560, parliament passed several statutes abolishing the authority of the Pope in Scotland and making it unlawful to celebrate the Catholic Mass. John Knox and five others were called upon to formulate the creed and constitution of a new, reformed church based on Calvinistic principles. Instead of a heirarcy of bishops and archbishops, the Church of Scotland was first governed by Kirk Sessions of lay elders, and later by district Presbyteries, which met once or twice a year in a General Assembly of the Kirk.

The early reformed church was austere, and that characteristic was only to increase with time until Christmas and Easter were no longer observed, Knox's liturgy was abandoned in favor of spontaneous prayer, and the celebration of communion practiced less and less. The churches were unadorned, and singing was unaccompanied.

When Mary returned from France, she had no intention of abandoning her own Catholic faith, though she tried her best to get along with both religions. Nevertheless, intrigues between Protestants and Catholics were common until the end of her reign. Afterward, the enmity that existed between them was overshadowed by strife between Protestant factions. James VI detested Calvinism and sought a more episcopal approach, and there were others who held the opposite view just as passionately. The conflict would continue to grow in strength and violence during the seventeenth century.

NAMING

IN THE SOUTH, the Reformation had an effect on the names found during this period. In general, many names of nonscriptural Catholic saints fell into disgrace. None of these names were Scottish, but because of the influence of the Catholic Church, many had been in common use among the people. Basil, Christopher, Denis, and Quentin are examples of saints' names that fell into disuse.

For women, religion had an even greater impact on naming, for the names that were now frowned upon had been the most popular for years. Agnes, Cecily, Katherine, and Margaret are examples of women's names that suffered a decline in use. These names, though not bestowed as often as they had been in the past, still remained viable. As in the previous time period, male names were also bestowed upon females; the practice was most common in families lacking sons. Alexander, Edmund, and Nicholas are examples of popular masculine names used for both sexes. Feminine forms of the names generally didn't appear until later.

Once the Bible became available to the Scots, there was a new pool of names from which to draw upon. Those most desired were the names from the Old Testament, since the names of the apostles had long been in use and were closely tied to the Catholic Church.

Those in the Highlands continued to draw from their pool of Gaelic names and didn't feel the need to seek out unfamiliar names that hadn't been used before. Many of the Gaelic names, however, began to change and become more simplified.

FEMALE NAMES

Adela (noble)
Adelaide (noble one)
Adeline (noble)
Agatha (good)
Agnes (chaste, pure)
Aileen (?) **Alina, Aline**
Ailie (?, pet form of Aileen)
Aimili (work)
Alana (O child; handsome; rock)
Alexander (defender of mankind)
Alexandra (defender of mankind) **Alexandria**
Alice (noble one)
Alison (little Alice)
Amelia (work)
Anna (grace, full of grace, mercy)
Annabel (?, possibly *eagle*; *hearth*; *lovable*; or *joy*) **Anabel, Annabell, Annable**
Annag (gracious, full of grace, mercy) Gaelic form of Anne.
Anne (gracious, full of grace, mercy) **Ann**

Annis (pure, chaste) **Annice, Annys**
Annot (gracious, full of grace, mercy; chaste, pure) Gaelic form of Anne and Agnes.
Arabella (?, perhaps *eagle; hearth*) **Arabela**
Aubrey (elf ruler)
Basil (kingly)
Barabal (foreign woman)
Barbara (foreign woman)
Beathag (life)
Beatrice (bringer of joy)
Beitiris (bringer of joy)
Bethoc (life)
Brenda (sword)
Brighid (strength)
Cairistiona (a Christian, a follower of Christ) Scottish form of Christine.
Cait (pure, unsullied) Scottish form of Kate.
Caitriona (pure, unsullied) **Catriona** Scottish form of Catherine.
Cecilia (blind, dim-sighted)

Ceit (pure, unsullied) Scottish form of Kate.
Ceiteag (pure, unsullied) Scottish form of Katie.
Christy (a Christian, a follower of Christ)
Clara (bright, clear, famous)
Criosaidh (a Christian, a follower of Christ) Scottish form of Chrissie.
Davida (beloved)
Deòiridh (pilgrim)
Diorbhail (true oath, true testimony)
Donalda (world ruler)
Donnag (world ruler)
Dorcas (gazelle)
Eamhair (?)
Edmée (loved) **Esmée**
Edmund (wealthy protection)
Eibhlin (?)
Elizabeth (God is my oath)
Elspeth (God is my oath)
Euphemia (well-spoken) **Eufemia, Eupheme**
Eustace (steadfast; happy in harvest)
Fiona (white, fair, clear)
Fionnaghuala (white shoulders) **Fionnghuala**
Florence (blooming, flourishing)
Freya (lady, mistress, noblewoman)
Gilbert (bright pledge)
Giles (goatskin shield of Zeus, a protection)
Gormlaith (blue lady)
Hannah (grace, full of grace, mercy)
Hester (myrtle; star)
Isabel (God is my oath)
Iseabail (God is my oath) Scottish form of Isabel.
Jacob (supplanting, seizing by the heels)
Jean (God is gracious) **Jeane, Jeanne**
Jeanie (God is gracious) **Jeannie**
Jennet (God is gracious) **Jonet**
Jenny (God is gracious)
Joan (God is gracious) **Joane, Jone**
Kate (pure, unsullied)
Katherine (pure, unsullied)
Kenna (born of fire; comely)
Lachina (land of the lochs)
Liùsaidh (famous in war) Scottish form of Lucy.
Lucy (famous in war) **Luce**
Magaidh (a pearl) Scottish form of Maggie.
Maggie (a pearl)
Maidie (a maiden, a young, unmarried woman)
Mairead (a pearl) **Maighread** Scottish form of Margaret.
Malamhìn (smooth brow)
Malcolmina (servant of Columba)

Marcella (of Mars)
Margaret (a pearl)
Marie (sea of bitterness or sorrow)
Marion (sea of bitterness or sorrow)
Marjorie (a pearl)
Marsaili (a pearl) Scottish form of Margery.
Martha (lady, mistress)
Mary (sea of bitterness or sorrow)
Maura (great; dark, swarthy, a Moor)
Mór (great, large)
Morag (great, large) **Mórag**
Morainn (fair seas; long-haired)
Morna (beloved) **Myrna**
Muireall (bright seas, fair one of the sea)
Murdag (sea warrior) **Murdann, Murdina**
Nan (grace, full of grace, mercy)
Nicholas (victory of the people)
Nora (a Norman)
Oighrig (?, perhaps *speckled* or *fair speech*)
Peigi (a pearl) Scottish form of Peggy.
Philip (lover of horses)
Rachel (ewe) Used after the Reformation.
Raghnaid (advice, counsel, decision + battle)
Raonaid (ewe) Scottish form of Rachel.
Rebecca (noose) Used after the Reformation.
Reine (queen)
Reynold (ruler of decision)
Robin (bright with fame)
Rowena (?, perhaps *famous friend; famous joy* or *blessed lance*)
Seonag (God is gracious) Scottish form of Joan.
Seònaid (God is gracious) Scottish form of Janet.
Seòrdag (earthworker, farmer)
Sibylla (fortune-teller, prophetess) **Sibyll, Sybell, Sybill**
Sidony (linen; cloth of Christ) Used by Catholics for babes born near the Feast of the Winding Sheet.
Simon (heard)
Sìne (God is gracious) Scottish form of Jane.
Siubhan (God is gracious) Scottish form of Jane.
Siùsan (lily, rose) Scottish form of Susan.
Sorcha (bright)
Susan (lily, rose)
Susanna (lily, rose)
Thomas (a twin)
Thomasia (a twin) Feminine form of Thomas.
Thomasin (a twin) **Thomasina** Feminine form of Thomas.
Ùna (?, perhaps *famine, hunger* or *lamb*)
Ursula (she bear)
Wilmot (resolute protector)

MALE NAMES

Adaidh (man of the red earth)
Adam (man of the red earth)
Àdhamh (man of the red earth) Scottish form of Adam.
Àdhamhnán (little Adam)
Adie (little Adam)
Aidan (fire)
Ailbeart (noble and bright)
Ailean (?, perhaps *handsome; rock*) Scottish form of Alan.
Ailpean (?) **Ailpein**
Aindrea (manly) Scottish form of Andrew.
Alan (?, perhaps *handsome; rock*)
Alasdair (defender of mankind) Scottish form of Alexander.
Albert (noble and bright)
Alex (defender) **Alec, Alick**
Alexander (defender of mankind)
Amhlaidh (ancestral relic) Scottish form of Olaf.
Andra (manly) Scottish form of Andrew.
Andrew (manly)
Angus (once, choice, preeminent)
Aodán (fire)
Aodh (fire)
Aodhagán (little Aodh; little fire)
Aonghas (one, choice, preeminent)
Arailt (leader of the army) Scottish form of Harold.
Archibald (genuinely bold, genuinely brave)
Archie (genuinely bold, genuinely brave)
Art (a bear)
Artair (?) Scottish form of Arthur.
Arthur (?)
Augustus (great, venerable)
Bearnard (bold as a bear)
Beathan (life)
Benedict (blessed)
Benjamin (son of the right hand) Used after the Reformation.
Benneit (blessed) Scottish form of Benedict.
Bennet (blessed)
Bernard (bold as a bear) Declined in use after the Reformation.
Bhaltair (ruler of an army) Scottish form of Walter.
Cailean (dove) Scottish form of Columba.
Calum (dove) Scottish form of Columba.
Charles (full-grown, a man) Used after 1566.
Charlie (full-grown, a man)
Christopher (bearing Christ)
Christy (bearing Christ)
Clement (gentle, mild)
Cliamain (gentle, mild) Scottish form of Clement.
Coinneach (handsome, comely)
Còiseam (constant, steadfast) Scottish form of Constantine.
Colin (dove)
Comhnall (strength; wisdom; high; wolf; dog)
Conall (strength; wisdom; high; wolf; dog) **Connell, Connull**
Constantine (constant, steadfast)
Cormag (?, perhaps *raven; son of defilement; son of the charioteer*)

Cuithbeart (well-known, famous) Scottish form of Cuthbert.
Cúmhaige (hound of the plain)
Cuthbert (well-known, famous)
Dàibhidh (beloved) Scottish form of David.
Dàniel (God is my judge) Rarely used.
David (beloved)
Deòrsa (earthworker, farmer) Scottish form of George.
Diarmid (without injunction, freeman) **Diarmad**
Domhnall (world ruler)
Donn (brown, brown-haired)
Donnchadh (brown warrior)
Donnell (world ruler)
Dougal (dark-haired stranger) **Dugal, Dugald**
Drew (manly)
Dubhghall (dark-haired stranger) **Dùghall**
Dùbhghlas (black, dark + blue, green, gray)
Duncan (brown warrior)
Eachann (brown horse)
Eairrdsidh (genuinely bold, genuinely brave) Scottish form of Archie.
Eallair (worker in a cellar)
Eanraig (home ruler) Scottish form of Henry.
Edmund (wealthy protection)
Edward (wealthy guardian)
Eideard (wealthy guardian)
Eóghan (lamb; youth; well-born)
Eòin (God is gracious) Scottish form of John.
Eric (eternal ruler)
Eustace (steadfast; happy in harvest)
Fearchar (dear man)
Fearghas (man of valor)
Fergus (man of valor)
Filib (lover of horses) Scottish form of Philip.
Fionnlagh (white warrior, fair-haired warrior)
Francis (a Frenchman)
Frang (a Frenchman) Scottish form of Francis.
Gavin (battle hawk)
Geordie (earthworker, farmer)
George (earthworker, farmer)
Gibidh (famous pledge)
Gilbert (famous pledge)
Gillanders (servant of Saint Andrew)
Gilleabart (famous pledge) Scottish form of Gilbert.
Gilleonan (servant of Saint Adhamhnain)
Gillespie (servant of the bishop)
Gillies (servant of Jesus)
Godfrey (peace of God)
Goiridh (peace of God) **Goraidh**
Graham (?, second element is *home, dwelling*)
Gregor (vigilant, watchful)
Griogair (vigilant, watchful)
Hamish (supplanting, seizing by the heels) Scottish form of James.
Harry (home ruler)

Hugh (heart, mind, soul)
Iain (God is gracious) **Ian**
Ìomhair (archer) **Ìomhear, Ìomhar** Scottish form of Ivor.
Ivor (archer)
Jack (God is gracious)
Jacob (supplanting, seizing by the heels) Not used before the Reformation except rare use among clergy.
James (supplanting, seizing by the heels)
Jamie (supplanting, seizing by the heels)
Jesse (gift) Used after the Reformation.
Jimmy (supplanting, seizing by the heels)
Jock (God is gracious)
John (God is gracious)
Jonathan (God has given) After the Reformation.
Keir (dark-complexioned)
Kenneth (born of fire; comely, handsome)
Kester (bearing Christ) Scottish form of Christopher.
Kieran (little dark one) **Kiaran**
Labhrainn (man from Laurentum) Scottish form of Laurence.
Lachlan (warlike; land of the lochs) **Lachann, Lachlann**
Laurence (man from Laurentum)
Lewis (famous in war)
Lucas (light; man from Lucania)
Luthais (famous in war)
Magnus (great, large)
Malcolm (servant of Saint Columba)
Mànus (great, large)
Màrtainn (of Mars, warlike) Scottish form of Martin.
Martin (of Mars, warlike)
Mata (gift of God)
Matthew (gift of God)
Michael (who is like God?)
Micheil (who is like God?) Scottish form of Michael.
Muireadhach (happy seas, mariner, sailor)
Murchadh (sea warrior) **Muireach**
Murdoch (mariner)
Neacal (victory of the people)
Neil (champion; a cloud) **Neal, Neill**
Niall (champion; a cloud)
Nicholas (victory of the people)
Norman (a northman)
Oilbhries (olive tree) Scottish form of Oliver.
Olghar (olive tree) Scottish form of Oliver.
Oliver (olive tree)
Oscar (spear of God; friend of the deer) **Osgar**
Pàdraig (a patrician) **Padraic**

Pàl (small)
Parlan (son of Talmai) Scottish form of Bartholomew.
Patrick (a patrician)
Paul (small)
Peader (a rock, a stone)
Peter (a rock, a stone)
Philip (lover of horses)
Raghnall (powerful judgment)
Raibeart (bright with fame) Scottish form of Robert.
Ranald (ruler of decision) **Ronald**
Ranulf (shield wolf)
Raonull (ruler of decision)
Reid (red, red-haired)
Richard (stern king)
Robert (bright with fame)
Rory (red, ruddy)
Ruaraidh (red, ruddy)
Ruiseart (stern king) Scottish form of Richard.
Sachairi (God remembers) Scottish form of Zachary.
Sandaidh (defender of mankind) Scottish form of Sandy.
Sandy (defender of mankind)
Seaghan (God is gracious) Scottish form of John.
Séamus (seizing by the heel, supplanting) Scottish form of James.
Seoc (God is gracious) Scottish form of Jock.
Seth (appointed) Used after the Reformation.
Sìm (heard) Scottish form of Simon.
Simidh (seizing by the heels, supplanting) Scottish form of Jimmy.
Simon (heard)
Somerled (Viking, mariner, sailor)
Somhairle (Viking, mariner, sailor)
Sorley (Viking, mariner, sailor)
Steaphan (a crown, a garland) Scottish form of Stephen.
Stephen (a crown, a garland)
Tadhg (a poet) **Taogh**
Teàrlach (full-grown, a man) **Tearlach**
Thomas (a twin)
Toirdhealbhach (shaped like Thor)
Tòmas (a twin) Scottish form of Thomas.
Tòrmod (northman) Scottish form of Norman.
Uilleam (resolute protector) **Uilliam** Scottish form of William.
Walter (ruler of an army)
William (resolute protector)
Zachary (God remembers)

SURNAMES

James VI was kidnapped by the earl of Gowrie (Ruthven) in 1582. Then, seventeen years later, another incident, this time with the earl's son, took place. Following the first abduction, James had the earl of Gowrie executed. Following the second incident, which James asserted was a plot to assassinate him, the next earl mysteriously met his end. James, in an effort to draw attention away from himself and promote the guilt of

Gowrie, had parliament pass an act abolishing the surname of Ruthven. The act states "that the surname of Ruthven sall now and in all tyme cumming be extinguischit and aboleissit for euir." Those who bore the name were required to renounce it and choose another surname. In 1602, all persons who had formerly borne the name were forbidden to come within ten miles of the royal residence.

In the south, surnames followed the same pattern as stated in the previous chapter, but they had even fewer prepositions, and the names were now largely inherited. In the north, patronymics and clan names were the norm.

Balliol (wall, fortification)
Boyd (yellow-haired)
Brody (dweller near the ditch)
Bruce (from Brus *brushwood thicket*)
Buchanan (little small one)
Burns (from the burnt house)
Cameron (crooked nose)
Campbell (crooked mouth)
Chisholm (gravel island)
Colquhoun (the narrow wood)
Douglas (dark, black + blue, green, gray; stream)
Dubh (dark, black)
Dunbar (fort of the summit)
Elphinstone (from Elphin's estate)
Erroll (from Erroll)
Erskine (?, perhaps *height of the cleft*)
Forbes (field)
Fraser (a Frisian)
Galbraith (Welsh stranger, British stranger)
Gillebride (servant of Saint Bridget *strength*)
Gillespie (servant of the bishop)
Gordon (?, from a Scottish place name)
Graham (?, from a place name, the second element of which is *home, dwelling, manor*)
Grant (great, large)
Gray (gray)
Gunn (war, battle)
Haldane (half Dane)
Hamilton (from the town near the blunt hill)
Henryson (son of Henry *home ruler*)
Hepburn (high stream)
Homes (dweller on a river island)
Huntley (wood of the huntsman)
Innes (island)
Keith (?, possibly *wind* or *wood*)
Kennedy (ugly head, ugly helmet)
Lamont (a lawyer)
Leslie (garden of hollies; the gray fort)
Lindsay (from the settlement by the lake)
Livingstone (from Leofing's stone)
MacArthur (son of Arthur)
Macaulay (son of Olaf *ancestral relic*)
MacBain (son of Bain *fair, white*)
MacBeth (son of Beatha *life*)

Maclean (son of the servant of John)
McCowyn (son of Eoghain *youth*)
McCrystyn (son of Kristin *a Christian*)
McCulloch (son of Culloch *boar; cock*)
MacDiarmid (son of Diarmid *a freeman, without injunction*)
Macdonald (son of Donald *world ruler*)
MacDonell (son of Donell *world ruler*)
MacDougall (son of Dougall *dark-haired stranger*)
MacEwen (son of Ewen *youth*)
MacFergus (son of Fergus *man of valor or strength*)
MacGillivray (son of Gille-Brath *the servant of judgment*)
MacInnes (son of Innes *island*)
MacKay (son of Aedh *fire*)
McKee (son of Aedh *fire*)
MacKenzie (son of Coinneach *handsome, comely*) **McKenzie**
MacKinnon (son of Fingon *fair birth*)
MacLennan (son of the servant of Finnan *fair one*)
Macleod (son of Léoid *ugly*)
MacMartin (son of Martin *of Mars, warlike*)
Macmillan (son of Maolain *the servant*)
McNeill (son of Neill *a champion; cloud*)
MacQueen (son of Suibhne *well-going, pleasant*)
MacRanald (son of Ranald *ruler of judgment*)
MacTaggart (son of the priest)
MacTavish (son of Thomas *a twin*)
Malcolm (servant of Saint Columba)
Matheson (son of Matthew *gift of God*)
Maxwell (dweller at Maccus's pool)
Mercer (storekeeper)
Moncreiffe (from Moncreiffe *hill of the trees*)
Mowbray (from Montbrai)
Munro (dweller at the red morass)
Murray (from Moray *beside the sea*)
Ogilvy (from Ogilvie *high hill*)
Oliphant (dealer of ivory; dweller at the sign of the elephant)
Ramsay (from the raven's island)
Ross (dweller on the promontory, dweller on the peninsula)
Scott (a Scot)
Sinclair (Saint Clair)
Spalding (from Spalding)
Stewart (a steward, keeper of the animal enclosure) **Stuart**
Strathearn (a valley)
Sutherland (from the southern land)
Wallace (a Welshman, a foreigner)

Chapter Five

JAMES I TO THE ACT OF UNION
[1603–1706]

POLITICS

JAMES VI OF Scotland was declared heir of the deceased Queen Elizabeth of England. In April 1603, he set out for London and his new life as James I of England. Though he continued to speak Scots for the rest of his life, he was to return to his native country only once, and that was in 1617, when he personally dealt with several issues of Church reform.

James's ultimate goal was the union of the two countries, and to further that end, he used the term *Great Britain* in reference to the entire island and named the new flag the Union Jack. In 1607, an Act of Union was put forth but was voted down. The English, it seems, had as little desire to join with the Scots as the Scots had with the English.

After James's death in 1625, Charles ascended the throne. Though born a Scot, he was taken to England when he was three and had never returned. He therefore knew little of the Scots and their culture or traditions, their divided nature, or their problems and concerns. He saw his major duty toward Scotland lay in bringing the Presbyterian Church in line with the Church of England. The Scots, however, were determined to fight for their religion and signed a document known as the National Covenant, uniting Church and state. The Covenanters went to war against their king in 1639 and again in 1640 over the issue of religion.

Soon, civil war in England had both king and the English parliament seeking help from the Scots. In 1643, Covenanters sided with the English parliament and signed the Solemn League and Covenant, under which Scottish forces would attack Royalists in return for £30,000 a month and the promise that a religious reformation based on the Scottish Kirk would take place in England and Ireland. For the next two years, Scottish Covenanters and English parliamentarians headed by Oliver Cromwell fought against Charles's royalist forces.

In 1646, Charles I surrendered to the Scots, who turned him over to Cromwell for the promise of £400,000. He was executed in 1649 and the Scots, even those who had fought against him, were deeply disturbed at the execution of their own king. They proclaimed Charles's heir, Prince Charles, King of Scots. When Charles II arrived in Scotland in 1650, Cromwell immediately invaded and occupied Edinburgh.

Cromwell had no intention of abiding by the terms of the Solemn League and Covenant, yet the Scots who had aided him still refused to admit they had been duped. It took wholesale slaughter of the Scottish people by Cromwell's army for Covenanters to realize they had thrown their lot in with the devil and turned forces against him. In one battle fought primarily by Highlanders, of 800 Macleans who stood and fought, 760 lost their lives. Cromwell pursued the Scottish army south and finally defeated them at the Battle of Worcester. Charles II escaped and fled to France.

Cromwell now controlled Scotland as lord protector, established a new system of military government, and saw to it that the last vestiges of resistance were put down. An Ordinance of Union in 1654 formally united Scotland and England to become part of the Commonwealth. The Scottish Parliament no longer met, though thirty members were sent to represent the Scottish commons in the parliament at Westminster. Efficient though Cromwell's government might have been, it was also deeply resented.

After Cromwell's death in 1660, Charles II returned to England and was restored to the monarchy. He never again returned to Scotland but governed through a privy council in Edinburgh and a secretary in London. Like his father, much of Charles's dealings with Scotland concerned religion. He had no intention of promoting Presbyterianism and saw to it that many measures his father put in place with regards to the Scottish Kirk were restored. Force was used to bring the Scots in line with Charles's wishes, but the Scots only retaliated in kind. The situation worsened, and the government's responses and measures of repression grew so severe that the 1680s became known as the Killing Time.

In 1685, Charles II was succeeded by his brother, James VII. He was the first Catholic king in 120 years, and both the Scots and English were afraid he'd try to reestablish Catholicism as the national religion. Sentiment against him was high. In 1688, Whig leaders invited James's son-in-law, William of Orange, to invade and overthrow the king; James fled to France. In 1689, William and James's daughter, Mary, were crowned king and queen of England and Ireland, and king and queen of Scotland.

Many in the Highlands continued to remain loyal to James and supported his attempts to regain his crown, but he was outmaneuvered and outmanned by William, and he abandoned his quest for the crown. The Highlanders, however, were not ready to accept William as king. Attemps to bribe the chiefs into submission met with little success, nor did they cower before the stronghold built near Inverlochy. A proclamation was therefore issued ordering clan chiefs to take the oath of allegiance to William no later than January 1, 1692. James VII, in exile in France, authorized the chiefs to take the oath, and when the deadline rolled around, only two had yet to do so: the elderly MacIan MacDonald of Glencoe and the powerful MacDonell of Glengarry.

It was the opportunity William and his secretary of state were waiting for. They chose to make an example of the MacDonalds, ostensibly to bring about Highland cooperation, but which probably was just an act of extreme vengence as MacDonald merely arrived three days late due to inclement weather. The result was a disgraceful and brutal massacre, irrespective of age and innocence, of an unsuspecting group of people asleep in their beds. William's reputation was now thoroughly destroyed in the Highlands, and public opinion of him in the Lowlands was soon to falter as well.

Unfair trading practices giving special privileges to the English effectively strangled Scottish overseas trade. To rectify the situation, William Paterson, a Scot who helped found the Bank of England and who gave Northern London a new and efficient water supply, proposed to establish The Company of Scotland Trading to Africa and the Indies, with both England and Scotland contributing to the startup costs. The plan was to gain control of the narrow isthmus of Darien linking North and South America so ships sending goods to and from India wouldn't have to go around the Cape of Good Hope or Cape Horn. It appears no one told the Scots the land was already owned by the Spanish nor of the conditions they would encounter.

The plan proceeded apace until English partners learned of William's disapproval and promptly withdrew their support, leaving Scotland to finance the entire venture. About £400,000 was raised, which is believed to have been nearly half of the available cash in Scotland. In July 1698, three ships and 1,200 emigrants set sail for Darien. Without waiting to see how the first expedition fared, two other groups of settlers ventured forth a year later.

Disaster awaited the first group in the form of disease and inadequate provisioning. Survivors approached the English colony of Jamaica for help, only to be told that King William had expressly forbidden any assistance be given them. By the time they made it back home, few had survived. The second group fared little better and had the added disaster of losing a ship to fire as it lay at anchor. The third group was also faced with disease, attacks by the Spaniards, and the loss of a ship. By all accounts, the entire undertaking had been a disaster with 2,000 lives and £400,000 lost. And as far as the Scots were concerned, the blame lay squarely on William. Anti-English sentiment was very high.

Meanwhile, Queen Anne had succeeded William. She was without an heir and the next in line was James Edward, the Catholic son of James II. The English, determined not to endure another Catholic king, passed an Act of Settlement in 1701, giving the crown to the German Electress Sophia of Hanover, a granddaughter of James I, upon Anne's death. The Scottish parliament passed its own act in 1704, giving themselves the right of announcing the successor to the Scottish throne. The successor was to be a Protestant descendant of the House of Stuart who would not occupy the English throne unless Scotland were given equal trading rights and freedom of religion. Provisions were also made for a standing Scottish army, and foreign policy was removed from the control of the monarch.

In 1705, English parliament passed the Aliens Act that treated all Scots as aliens unless they accepted the Hanoverian succession. That meant Scottish-owned lands in England would be seized, and Scottish exports of cattle, linen, and coal would not be allowed. Tensions were increasing and it appeared that war would be the likely outcome.

Yet it was against a backdrop of hostility on both sides that England and Scotland were able to come to an agreement. The outcome was the Treaty of Union, which gave the Scots £400,000 to compensate for the Darien fiasco, gave them the same trading privileges as the English, and allowed for freedom of religion and the freedom to dictate their own religious affairs. It also dissolved the Scottish parliament, though sixteen Scottish peers and forty-five members of the House of Commons joined the English parliament. The Scots were allowed to keep their own legal system, but were required to accept a share of Britain's national debt. The countries were to be known as Great Britain and would share a flag composed of elements from both existing flags. In spite of intense and open disagreement on both sides, the treaty was accepted and on March 6, 1707, received royal consent.

The crown, sword, and scepter were wrapped in linen and placed in a box in Edinburgh Castle. Scotland was no longer an independent country.

SOCIETY

UP UNTIL NOW, the Highland chiefs had always gone their own way and ignored events in the South as unimportant and of no consequence to them or their clans. Feuds, raids, and general unrest was common. Even the lords of the isles considered themselves to be independent sovereigns and not obligated to answer to the Scottish monarchy.

Once James VI became James I of England and was safely away from Scotland, he began to take a closer look at the Highlands and decided it was time to bring them under control. His method of accomplishing this was to issue Letters of Fire and Sword, which basically gave clans the authority to deal with errant neighbors as they saw fit, even to the point of annihilating one another. A prime target was the unruly Clan Gregor, which caused so much trouble in the north. Their traditional enemies were given permission to exterminate them by destroying their homes, stealing their livestock, and killing any MacGregor they came across. Another clan to suffer was the Macdonalds of Islay.

In 1608, Maclean of Duart and several other chiefs were invited aboard one of James's ships and imprisoned. They were released a year later, after they gave pledges of good behavior, promised to have their sons educated in the Lowlands, and agreed to discourage drinking, begging, and the use of firearms, and to reduce the numbers of their entourages. Highland life was quieter for a time and the lords of the isles stopped proclaiming their sovereignty. The Campbells of Argyll soon emerged as agents of the government and protectors of the Lowlands against those clans who would not abide by the king's demands.

The Highlanders still preferred their traditional ways of life. Sheep and cattle raiding was common, as was looting one another's farms. Roads were very few, and those that did exist were but rough tracks. Robbery and other types of violence made the roads dangerous, and few ventured out alone. In the sixteenth and seventeenth centuries, Highlanders were regarded with special contempt and prejudice by outsiders. They were derogatorily called "Irish," as was their language and religion.

Society was much different in the burghs, which had evolved into quite wealthy communities. Many merchants and other city dwellers were even better off in terms of finance and possessions than the lords who lived on country estates. Social stratification among the lower classes was the same as in the preceeding time period. One notable difference now was that overcrowding had led to the construction of a large number of residential buildings, some of which were ten stories in height. In these new buildings, however, the wealthier people occupied the higher floors to be away from the stench and noise of the streets. The largest cities were Aberdeen, Dundee, Edinburgh, and Glasgow.

In the 1690s, a series of disasters struck Scottish agriculture, which was already behind the times in respect to improvements and innovations. Grain prices tumbled, then disease swept through Scottish cattle in both the Lowlands and the Highlands. In the second half of the decade, widespread crop failure occurred in four of the five years. Famine following the destruction of crops and livestock was accompanied by diseases such as typhus that impacted all levels of society. And, in spite of efforts of the burghs to help the starving, nearly a quarter of the population (about 1.25 million people) had perished by the end of the decade.

RELIGION

JAMES HAD ALWAYS disliked the strict Calvinistic approach of the new reformed Church of Scotland, and he showed his disapproval of the Presbyterians by refusing to allow the General Assembly to meet. In 1606, the king summoned seven leading ministers to England, imprisoned them in the Tower for three years, and forbade them to ever return to Scotland.

The Church resisted James's efforts to change, so the monarch set out for Scotland in 1617. It was his first and last visit to his native country. He took an organ with him, which he put in the Chapel Royal of Holyrood, and he added a gowned chorus, both of which were very unpopular and viewed as frivolous. He also forced the imposition of the Five Articles in 1618, which stated that Communion should be taken while kneeling; observance of the traditional Christian festivals should be resumed; confirmation should only be administered by bishops, not by ministers; that private baptism must be allowed in cases of serious illness; and that private Communion should be offered to those seriously ill. The unpopular articles were met with opposition and led to a widespread boycott of those churches following them.

When Charles I came to the throne, he sought to bring the Presbyterian Scottish Kirk in line with the Church of England. In 1625, an Act of Revocation was passed, returning to the Church those lands and titles taken during the Reformation so the Church would have adequate provision for the maintenance of its clergy. Four years later, he demanded religious observances in Scotland conform to the English standard.

In the 1630s, Charles had a Revised Prayer Book drawn up to replace extempore prayer, one of the hallmarks of the Scottish Kirk. The book was read for the first time in 1637 to scenes of protest and wild disorder that soon became stronger and more organized. When Charles issued a proclamation demanding that nobles cease resisting the Prayer Book, the nobles and church leaders responded with the National Covenant, which encouraged Scots to maintain their true religion.

The Scots made a pact with Cromwell, giving their military support in exchange for a reformation of the Church of England based on the Scottish Kirk. Cromwell had no intention of following through with his promise, and the Scots' hope for religious reformation was crushed.

After Cromwell's death, Charles II restored the measures his father put in place, but hundreds of ministers refused to abide by the new requirements and held their own illegal worship services (conventicles) in barns, houses, and in the open air. To eliminate the conventicles, the government made it illegal not to attend the new Sunday services. Resistance was met with governmental force, which in turn, was met with more resistance and violence.

William agreed to the restoration of Scotland's Presbyterian Kirks, and later, the Treaty of Union gave the Scots one of the things they most desired: the freedom to control their own religious affairs.

NAMING

NAMING TRADITIONS IN Scotland during this time period were probably influenced by religion more than anything else. The Scots' religious practices were quite strict, and things considered popish or Catholic were frowned upon. Therefore, many of the common saints' names fell in popularity and were replaced with names taken from the biblical Old Testament. However, the most popular names for women continued to be Mary, Elizabeth, and Anne. Among men, James, John, and Andrew were popular.

Another tradition copied from the English was the propensity of the Scots to give their female children male names. Philip, Alexander, and Nicholas are examples of male names bestowed upon females.

FEMALE NAMES

Abigail (father of exaltation)
Adela (noble)
Adelaide (noble one)
Agatha (good)
Agnes (chaste, pure)
Aileen (?) **Alina, Aline**
Ailie (pet form of Aileen and Alice)
Alexander (defender of mankind)
Alexandra (defender of mankind) **Alexandria**
Alison (noble one) **Alicen, Allison**
Anna (grace, full of grace, mercy) **Ann, Anne**
Annabel (?, possibly *eagle*; *hearth*; *lovable*; or *joy*) **Annabell, Annabella**
Annag (grace, full of grace, mercy)
Annot (grace, full of grace, mercy)
Arabella (?, perhaps *eagle*; *hearth*) **Arabela**
Asenath (?, perhaps *thornbush*)

Aubrey (elf ruler)
Audrey (noble strength)
Barbara (foreign woman)
Basil (kingly)
Beathag (life)
Beatrice (bringer of joy)
Beitiris (bringer of joy)
Bethia (daughter of God)
Brenda (sword)
Cait (pure, unsullied) **Ceit** Scottish form of Kate.
Caitriona (pure, unsullied) Scottish form of Catherine.
Cassandra (?)
Cecilia (blind, dim-sighted)
Ceiteag (pure, unsullied) Scottish form of Katie.
Christy (a Christian, a follower of Christ)
Clara (bright, clear, famous)

Criosaidh (a Christian, a follower of Christ) Scottish form of
Chrissie.
Davida (beloved)
Davina (beloved)
Diorbhail (true oath, true testimony)
Donalda (world ruler)
Donnag (world ruler)
Dorcas (gazelle)
Edmund (wealthy protection)
Elizabeth (God is my oath)
Elspeth (God is my oath)
Eustace (steadfast; happy in harvest)
Finella (white shoulders)
Fiona (white, fair, clear)
Fionnghuala (white shoulders) **Fionnala, Fionnauala, Fion-
nghala, Finola**
Flora (a flower) **Florrie**
Florence (blooming, flourishing)
Gilbert (bright pledge)
Giles (goatskin shield of Zeus, a protection)
Gormlaith (blue lady)
Grace (grace, mercy)
Hannah (grace, full of grace, mercy)
Harriet (home ruler)
Hester (myrtle; star)
Isabel (God is my oath)
Iseabail (God is my oath) Scottish form of Isabel.
Jacob (supplanting, seizing by the heels)
Jane (God is gracious)
Janet (God is gracious; little Jane)
Jean (God is gracious) **Jeane, Jeanne**
Jeanie (God is gracious) **Jeannie**
Jennet (God is gracious) **Jonet**
Jenny (God is gracious)
Jessie (gift; God is gracious)
Joan (God is gracious) **Joane, Jone**
Judith (praised)
Kate (pure, unsullied)
Katherine (pure, unsullied)
Kenna (born of fire; comely)
Kirsty (Christian, a follower of Christ) **Kirstie**
Kirstin (Christian, a follower of Christ)
Liùsaidh (famous in war) Scottish form of Lucy.
Louisa (famous in war)
Lucy (famous in war) **Luce**
Magaidh (a pearl) Scottish form of Maggie.
Maggie (a pearl)
Maidie (a maiden, a young unmarried woman)
Mairead (a pearl) Scottish form of Margaret.
Mairi (sea of bitterness or sorrow) Gaelic form of Mary.
Malcolmina (servant of Saint Columba)

Marcella (of Mars)
Maretta (of Mars)
Margaret (a pearl)
Margery (a pearl)
Marie (sea of bitterness or sorrow)
Marion (sea of bitterness or sorrow)
Marsaili (a pearl) Scottish form of Margery.
Martha (lady, mistress)
Mary (sea of bitterness or sorrow)
Maura (great, large; dark-skinned, a Moor)
Mór (great, large)
Mórag (great, large) **Morag**
Morainn (fair seas; long-haired)
Morna (beloved) **Myrna**
Muireall (bright seas, fair one of the sea)
Murdag (sea warrior) **Murdann**
Nicholas (victory of the people)
Nora (a northman)
Oighrig (?, perhaps *new speckled one; fair speech*)
Peigi (a pearl) Scottish form of Peggy.
Philip (lover of horses)
Rachel (ewe)
Raghnaid (advice, counsel, decision + battle)
Raonaid (ewe) Scottish form of Rachel.
Rebecca (noose)
Rhoda (famous king)
Robin (bright with fame)
Rowena (?, perhaps *famous friend; famous joy; blessed lance*)
Seona (God is gracious) Scottish form of Janet.
Seonag (God is gracious) Scottish form of Joan.
Seònaid (God is gracious) Scottish form of Janet.
Seòrdag (earthworker, farmer)
Sheena (God is gracious)
Sibylla (fortune-teller, prophetess) **Sibyll, Sybill**
Simon (heard)
Sìne (God is gracious) Scottish form of Jane.
Siubhan (God is gracious) Scottish form of John.
Siùsan (lily, rose) Scottish form of Susan.
Sophia (wisdom, skill)
Sorcha (bright)
Susan (lily, rose)
Susanna (lily, rose) **Susannah**
Teasag (gift) Scottish form of Jessie.
Thomas (a twin)
Thomasia (a twin) Feminine form of Thomas.
Thomasin (a twin) **Thomasina** Feminine form of Thomas.
Tríona (pure, unsullied)
Ùna (dearth, famine, hunger; lamb)
Ursula (she-bear)

MALE NAMES

Adaidh (man of the red earth)
Adam (man of the red earth)
Àdhamh (man of the red earth) Scottish form of Adam.
Àdhamhnán (little Adam)
Adelulf (noble wolf)
Adie (little Adam)
Aidan (fire)
Ailbeart (noble and bright)
Ailean (?, perhaps *handsome; rock*)
Ailpean (?) **Ailpein**
Aindrea (manly) Scottish form of Andrew.
Alan (?, perhaps *handsome; rock*) **Allan**
Alard (noble and brave)
Alasdair (defender of mankind) Scottish form of Alexander.
Albert (noble and bright)
Alex (defender) **Alec, Alick**
Alexander (defender of mankind)
Allein (?, perhaps *handsome; rock*) Gaelic form of Allan.
Andra (manly) Scottish form of Andrew.
Angus (one, choice, preeminent)
Aodán (fire)
Arailt (leader of the army) Scottish form of Harold.
Archibald (genuinely bold, genuinely brave)
Archie (genuinely bold, genuinely brave)
Art (a bear)
Artair (?) Scottish form of Arthur.
Arthur (?)
Augustus (great, venerable)
Bearnard (bold as a bear)
Beathan (life)
Benedict (blessed)
Benjamin (son of the right hand)
Benneit (blessed) Scottish form of Benedict.
Bennet (blessed)
Bernard (bold as a bear)
Calum (dove) Scottish form of Columba.
Charles (full-grown, a man)
Charlie (full-grown, a man)
Christopher (bearing Christ)
Christy (bearing Christ)
Clement (gentle, mild)
Coinneach (handsome, comely)
Còiseam (constant, mild) Scottish form of Constantine.
Colin (dove)
Comhnall (strength; wisdom; high; wolf; dog)
Conall (strength; wisdom; high; wolf; dog)
Constantine (constant, steadfast)
Cormac (?, perhaps *raven; son of defilement; son of the charioteer*) **Cormag**
Dàibhidh (beloved) Scottish form of David.
Daniel (God is my judge)
David (beloved)
Deòrsa (earthworker, farmer) Scottish form of George.
Diarmid (without injunction, freeman) **Diarmad**

Donald (world ruler)
Donn (brown, brown-haired)
Donnell (world ruler)
Dougal (dark-haired stranger) **Dugal, Dugald**
Douglas (black, dark + blue, green, gray)
Drew (manly)
Duncan (brown warrior)
Eanraig (home ruler) Scottish form of Henry.
Edmund (wealthy protection)
Edward (wealthy guardian)
Edwin (wealthy friend)
Eric (eternal ruler) **Erik**
Euan (lamb; youth; well-born)
Eugene (well-born, noble)
Eumann (wealthy protection)
Eunan (little Adam)
Evan (lamb; youth; well-born)
Evander (good man; archer)
Ewan (lamb; youth; well-born)
Farquhar (dear man)
Fergus (man of valor)
Fingall (fair-haired stranger)
Finlay (fair-haired warrior)
Francis (a Frank, a freeman)
Frang (a Frank, a freeman) Scottish form of Francis.
Gavin (battle hawk)
Geordie (earth worker, farmer)
Gilbert (famous pledge)
Gillanders (servant of Saint Andrew)
Gilleabart (famous pledge) Scottish form of Gilbert.
Gilleonan (servant of Saint Adomnan)
Gillespie (servant of the bishop)
Gillies (servant of Jesus)
Godfrey (peace of God)
Goiridh (peace of God) **Goraidh** Scottish form of Godfrey.
Gregor (vigilant, a watchman) **Grigor**
Gregory (vigilant, a watchman)
Griogair (vigilant, a watchman) Scottish form of Gregory.
Hamish (supplanting, seizing by the heels) Scottish form of James.
Haral (leader of the army)
Harold (leader of the army)
Harry (leader of the army)
Hector (to restrain)
Henry (home ruler)
Hugh (heart, mind, spirit)
Hugo (heart, mind, soul)
Iagan (little fire)
Iain (God is gracious)
Ian (God is gracious)
Iòseph (may he add) Scottish form of Joseph.
Ivor (archer)
Jack (God is gracious)
Jacob (supplanting; seizing by the heels)

James (supplanting, seizing by the heels)
Jamie (supplanting, seizing by the heels)
Jesse (gift)
Jock (God is gracious)
John (God is gracious) **Johnnie**
Jonathan (God has given)
Joseph (he shall add) **Joe**
Keir (dark-complexioned)
Kenneth (born of fire; comely, handsome)
Kester (bearing Christ)
Kieran (little dark one) **Kiaran**
Labhrainn (man from Laurentum) Scottish form of Laurence.
Lachlan (warlike; land of the lochs) **Lachann, Lachlann**
Laurence (man from Laurentum)
Lewis (famous in war)
Lucas (light; man from Lucania)
Luthais (famous in war) Scottish form of Lewis.
Magnus (great, large)
Mainard (strong and brave)
Malcolm (servant of Saint Columba)
Mànus (great, large)
Martin (of Mars, warlike)
Matthew (gift of God) **Matt**
Michael (Who is like God?)
Micheil (Who is like God?) Scottish form of Michael.
Murdoch (mariner)
Neil (champion; a cloud) **Neal, Neill**
Niall (champion; a cloud)
Nicholas (victory of the people)
Norman (a northman)
Oliver (olive tree)
Oscar (spear of God; friend of the deer)
Parlan (son of Talmai) Scottish form of Bartholomew.
Patrick (patrician, aristocrat) **Pat**

Paul (small)
Peader (a rock, a stone)
Peter (a rock, a stone)
Philip (lover of horses)
Raghnall (powerful judgment)
Raibeart (bright with fame) Scottish form of Robert.
Ranald (ruler of decision) **Rannald**
Reid (red, red-haired) **Reed**
Richard (stern king)
Robert (bright with fame)
Robin (bright with fame)
Roger (spear fame)
Rory (red, ruddy)
Ruiseart (stern king) Scottish form of Richard.
Sandy (defender of mankind)
Seaghan (God is gracious) Scottish form of John.
Séamus (supplanting, seizing by the heels) Scottish form of James.
Seth (appointed)
Simon (heard)
Somerled (Viking, summer sailor)
Somhairle (Viking, summer sailor)
Sorley (Viking, summer sailor)
Steaphan (a crown, a garland) Scottish form of Stephen.
Stephen (crown, garland)
Tadhg (a poet)
Teàrlach (full-grown, a man) **Tearlach** Scottish form of Charles.
Thearlaich (full-grown, a man) Scottish form of Charlie.
Thomas (a twin) **Tommy**
Tòmas (a twin) **Tomag** Scottish form of Thomas.
Walter (ruler of an army)
William (resolute protector) **Willie**
Zachary (God remembers)

SURNAMES

Surnames were now hereditary in the Lowlands. In the Highlands, however, surnames were just coming into general use as they were now required for legal documents. Some Scots took the name of their clan chief, some chose a patronymic, and others chose surnames reflective of an occupation or personal characteristic. It was quite common for members of different clans to have the same surnames.

Early in the seventeenth century, fighting between clans was particularly intense. The McGregors received the largest part of the blame and therefore assumed the greatest penalties. In April 1603, an act was passed abolishing the surname McGregor. ''The whole persons of that clan should renounce their name and take some other name, and they nor none of their posterity should call themselves Gregor or McGregoure thereafter, under the pain of death.'' Few took heed of the warning, and in 1633, a more severe act was passed depriving the holders of the name of all their rights and forbidding ministers to baptize male children with the name Gregour. The clan lived the next several years in compliance, and in 1661, Charles II rescinded the act. It was revived again in 1693.

In 1641, an act of Charles I restored the surname Ruthven, making it lawful for the heirs of the name ''to enjoy and assume to themselves the surname of Ruthven, and to use it as if the Act of 1600 had never been made against them.''

Armstrong (strong arms) **Armstrang**
Baldwin (bold friend)
Baxter (baker)
Campbell (crooked mouth)
Duff (black, dark)
Gibbs (famous pledge)
Glas (black, dark)
Gordon (?, from a place name of uncertain etymology)
Haig (dweller at the enclosed field)
MacDiarmid (son of Diarmid *freeman, without injunction*)
Mackay (son of Aodha *fire*)
Mackenzie (son of Coinneach *comely, handsome*)
Maclachlan (son of Lachlan *land of the lochs*)

Maclean (son of the servant of Saint John)
Macleod (son of Léoid *ugly*)
Muir (dweller by the moor)
Munroe (dweller at the red morass)
Murray (from Moray *beside the sea*)
Ross (dweller on the promontory or peninsula)
Scott (a Scot)
Sinclair (from Saint Clair, Normandy)
Stewart (a steward, a keeper of the animal enclosure)
Stuart (a steward, a keeper of the animal enclosure)
Sutherland (from the south lands)
Telford (iron cleaver)
Wilson (son of Will *resolute protector*)

Chapter Six

THE ACT OF UNION TO THE INDUSTRIAL REVOLUTION
[1706–1850]

POLITICS

"WE ARE BOUGHT and sold for English gold!''

That was the Jacobite cry as the Treaty of Union was being debated in the Scottish parliament. Once the treaty passed, the reality was far from the ideal the politicians had been touting. The English expected their taxes right away but procrastinated in bequeathing the promised £400,000. The English also continued to look down on the Scots with disdain, treating them like conquered subjects, rather than as partners in the Union. More importantly, the English did not hold true to the promise of allowing Scotland to retain the administration of its church and legal affairs. Such double-dealings nearly brought about a repeal of the Union in 1713; only four votes kept it intact.

Politics were unsettled during the decade following the Act of Union, and the matter of succession was still very much under debate. Many Scots, especially the Highlanders, favored James Edward, the son of James VI. The Presbyterians wanted him only if he would change his religion, and even the English weren't happy with their selection of the German Hanovers. Both sides of the border experienced numerous uprisings and unrest.

Queen Anne died in 1714 and was succeeded by the unkingly George of Hanover. In 1715, events came to a head when Jacobite forces squared off against governmental forces. James Edward arrived from France later that year, but instead of bringing an army with him to back his claim and assist the Scots, he was accompanied by a handful of servants. His cause was clearly lost, and he returned to France after just a few weeks. That year of unrest came to be known as the "Fifteen," and government was not about to pardon the Scottish rebels. Many Jacobites were captured and executed, and still more were sent as slaves to plantations in the West Indies. Antiunion sentiment in the Highlands remained strong, and steps were taken to ensure the peace by establishing a military presence in the area. As the English continued to misinterpret the terms of the Act of Union, Scottish sentiment toward their southern neighbor continued to worsen.

Jacobite hopes were raised again in 1745, when Prince Charles Edward (Bonnie Prince Charlie) took advantage of the English war with France and entered Scotland to fight for his father's right to the crown. Perhaps if he'd had the whole country of Scotland behind him instead of just the Highlanders, the outcome would have been different. That was not the case, however, and with an army inadequate to the large number of English forces and the Lowland Scots joining them, the outcome of his campaign was not victory but defeat culminating at the battle of Culloden in April 1746.

And bitter defeat it was, for the order given to English forces was "No quarter." No one in the Highlands was to be spared. The wounded were either shot to death or burned alive; prisoners were executed. More than 100 prisoners were taken into England, tried, sentenced, and executed in flagrant violation of the Act of Union. Some prisoners and their entire families were thrown into jails where they died from either starvation or disease; more than 1,000 were sold to American plantations as slaves. Across the Highlands, precious crops were destroyed and livestock slaughtered or sold at ridiculously low prices to Lowlanders or the English. Homes were burned or otherwise destroyed. It was systematic, brutal, and total devastation of the Highlands and the clans, backed not only by the London government, but by Lowlanders and other Presbyterian Scots who reviled the Highlanders for adhering to their Catholic faith.

It didn't end there. Measures were taken to eliminate the structure of the clans and the clan relationship that was the foundation upon which all Scottish law had been built. The right of Scotland to retain its laws had been guaranteed under the Treaty of Union, and when those rights were violated by the English, the whole of Scotland found reason to feel violated.

For five months after Culloden, Bonnie Prince Charlie wandered across the Highlands with the incredible sum of £30,000 levied upon his head. With the help of those he met along the way, he made it to the coast where he was picked up by a French frigate and taken to live the rest of his life in exile. It is testimony to the Highlanders' unfailing loyalty that in spite of the monetary reward and the horrors being carried out by government troops, not one person came forward with information as to Charles's whereabouts or betrayed him to the government.

SOCIETY

THERE WERE DRAMATIC changes in Scottish life during the eighteenth century. Not only did Scotland experience the Industrial Revolution, there were a number of other revolutions in the areas of agriculture, trading, urban development, transport, architecture, and even in intellectual areas. The time is commonly referred to as the Scottish Renaissance.

Trading opportunities produced by the Union enabled traders to enter new markets, and the Industrial Revolution resulted in large amounts of goods for export. Another boost to the economy came through agricultural development. During the Improvements, foreign grasses and grains, hay-making, turnips, the potato, clover, and the English plow were all introduced. In 1723, the Honorable Society of Improvers was founded by those interested in learning new agricultural methods. The land was transformed into a series of neat, well-drained, and enclosed farms that were much more prosperous than the chaotic tangle of multiple-tenant farms that existed before. As the new methods brought forth greater harvests and larger, heavier livestock, landowners saw an increase in wealth and farm workers began to be better paid and housed. Overall, the diet of the peasantry was greatly improved, as was long-term health.

Money from the Improvements made it possible to finance change and development in urban areas. One of the most ambitious undertakings was the New Town in Edinburgh. Until now, rich and poor lived together in multistoried tenements with only the crudest sanitation. New Town drew the wealthy away from stench and filth of the inner city to beautiful Georgian homes along clean, wide streets and elegant squares. But when the rich took their wealth out of the inner city, the Old Town declined even further into a dangerously overcrowded slum.

Following the turmoil of the Fifteen, then again after the Battle of Culloden, government went to drastic lengths to eliminate the Highland "threat." The method chosen was the systematic destruction and suppression of the Gaelic way of life that had flourished for centuries. Lands were confiscated, the authority and power of the clan chiefs were stripped from them, and they lost their traditional patriarchal position. Those people who remained were forbidden to speak their Gaelic language. A Disarmament Act forbade clansmen to possess or bear weapons, and even bagpipes were forbidden as they were considered weapons of war. The Disclothing Act made it illegal to wear the traditional Highland tartans and kilts: "the Philabeg, or Little Kilt, Trowse, Shoulder-Belts or any Part whatsoever of what peculiarly belongs to the Highland Garb." The penalties attached to the acts were death or long-term imprisonment. Though the Acts were ignored in many places and were largely unenforceable, they served as a substantial warning that Gaelic traditions were not acceptable to government. The fabric of Highland society was ripped apart, leaving people with scars that went soul deep and forever altering their way of life.

Another event to change Highland society was the increase in sheep farming. Many landowners had been leasing out their lands to "tacksmen." Tacksmen (*tack* meaning lease) either farmed the land themselves or were middlemen who subleased to tenants in return for rent or produce. By the 1740s, many lairds found it more profitable to turn their lands over to sheep farming. Since sheep farming produced few jobs, that meant that the people who had been renting lands (the crofters) were forced to move elsewhere. Evictions of crofters and cottars (farmworkers) increased at an alarming rate. While some chose to go quietly, there were others who believed they had a hereditary claim to the lands in accordance with the clan system and had to be removed by force. Some moved to wilder, more inaccessible parts, others sought work in the cities, some were moved to nearly worthless lands along the coast so they could become fishermen (though they knew nothing of fishing and were given no boats or nets), and still more emigrated from a country they felt betrayed them. The evictions, known as the Clearances, left the terrorized people homeless and completely destitute, and left the Highlands empty and deserted of its lifeblood.

Some of the lands that had been confiscated after the Rising of 1745 were given to a group of trustees who were directed to use them to promote Protestantism, to establish order, and to provide education to the remaining Highlanders. To further that end, new villages were planned and built, a system of schools was established, improvements to the land were made, and handicrafts were introduced to give people a trade. Efforts to establish order were so successful that in 1782, the ban on wearing the kilt was lifted. In 1784, many of the forfeited lands were sold back to their former owners at a moderate price.

The improved educational system encouraged the speaking of English over Gaelic and led to a significant decrease in the number of people speaking the traditional language of the Highlands. After the Church discontinued preaching in Gaelic, the numbers declined even further. By the mid-nineteenth century, Gaelic still survived, but mainly among the lower classes who were not as well-educated and who clung to the old ways longer than most.

The Industrial Revolution was helped along by advances in machine technology, improved transportation, and cheap labor imported from the Highlands and places like Ireland. Shipbuilding, iron and steel industries, coal mining, armament plants, heavy engineering, and the weaving industries helped bolster the economy and provided jobs. Unfortunately, the profits seen from these ventures were rarely shared among the workers. Wages went down as the number of available workers went up. Child labor was commonplace, and youngsters typically worked the same type of day as the adults: twelve hours with a half hour off for breakfast and a half hour for dinner.

For the first half of the nineteenth century, the population of Scotland's cities grew so quickly that a tremendous burden was put on the medieval systems of refuse disposal. The crowded inner cities were breeding grounds for disease and vermin of all kinds, and outbreaks of cholera, typhus, influenza, and tuberculosis killed thousands.

RELIGION

THOUGH THE CHURCH of Scotland was regarded as the nation's church, it was not embraced by all Scots. There were still many Catholics and Episcopalians in the country, and even some Prebyterians did not agree with its structure. In 1712, the Westminster parliament turned its back on one of the terms of the Act of Union and deprived individual congregations of their right to choose their own minister.

The Episcopalians and the Presbyterians eventually drifted farther apart when they chose to support differing sides on the issue of succession. And the Presbyterian community itself was divided by several issues and began to break apart and form new sects. The United Presbyterian Church was formed in 1847 from groups of dissenters.

Under the law, Catholic mass was forbidden, and though Catholics continued to meet quietly, the number of parishioners fell during the eighteenth century. Overall, Highlanders continued to hold onto their Catholic religion longer than did the Lowland Scots. The Episcopalians were believed to have been supporters of the Jacobite cause along with the Catholics and suffered deliberate persecution as rigorous laws were passed against them. This church also experienced a decline in members and clergy during the last half of the eighteenth century.

The Presbyterian Church of Scotland stood behind the English in the quest to put down the Highlands following the Rising of 1745. The Duke of Cumberland, called the Butcher by many, was even given an official address from the General Assembly of the Scottish Kirk, which praised his conduct and valor during the turbulent time.

For the most part, Scotland continued to be a country whose religious convictions governed much of the daily lives of its citizens. Piety, hard work, thrift, truth, and honesty were the virtues parents taught their children and practiced themselves. There were those in the Kirk who held very strict views on morality and who generally viewed most forms of entertainment and pleasure as sin. These very devout people, called Evangelicals, led missionary teams to towns without churches and even to lands such as Africa, promoted Sunday schools, encouraged public condemnation of ''sinners'' during the church service, and formed prayer societies to supplement the established services of the Kirk.

Throughout the eighteenth century, services were very austere and even lacked reading from the Bible or the recitation of established readings like the Lord's Prayer and the Apostles' Creed. Long sermons and prayers delivered by the minister formed the base of the worship service, and the congregation took part only in the singing of metrical psalms.

A common event of the eighteenth century was the ''holy fair.'' The fair was a large gathering of people from a wide area who met to participate in a joint service. Poet Robert Burns's view of the holy fairs as ''jostling, promiscuous assemblies'' shows they were in reality quite different from the ideal of a gathering filled with reverent and devout people.

The most important religious issue was the schism created in the Church when liberal ideas came under attack from government and the Church's patrons. The ''Ten Years' Conflict'' as it came to be known, culminated in the ''Disruption'' of 1843 and a split in the Church. Out of 1,200 ministers, more than a third left their parishes to form the Free Church. Around a third of the members of the established Church left as well. In less than four years, 700 churches had been formed by the Free Church. Schoolteachers belonging to the Free Church were fired from their jobs, so they created their own schools and in twenty-five years' time, had established nearly 600 schools.

NAMING

THE PRACTICE OF bestowing male names upon female children decreased during this time. In its place, the Scots made up feminine forms of male names. Angusina, Adamina, and Jamesina are examples of these kinds of names. As the Gaelic language was suppressed, Gaelic names were increasingly discarded in favor of Anglicized forms.

FEMALE NAMES

Abigail (father of exaltation)
Abrahamina (father of a multitude)
Adamina (man of the red earth)
Adela (noble)
Aeneasina (?, perhaps *to praise*)
Agatha (good)
Agnes (chaste, pure)
Aileen (?) **Alina, Aline**
Alexandra (defender of mankind) **Alexandria**
Alexina (defender)
Alison (noble one) **Allison**
Angusina (one, choice, preeminent)
Anna (grace, full of grace, mercy) **Ann, Anne**
Annabel (?, perhaps *eagle; hearth; lovable*; or *joy*) **Annabel, Annabella**
Annag (grace, full of grace, mercy) Gaelic form of Anna.
Annot (grace, full of grace, mercy) Gaelic form of Anne.
Arabella (?, perhaps *eagle; hearth*) **Arabela**

Barbara (foreign woman)
Beathag (life)
Beatrice (bringer of joy)
Beitiris (bringer of joy) Scottish form of Beatrice.
Bethia (daughter of God)
Brenda (sword)
Cait (pure, unsullied) **Ceit** Scottish form of Kate.
Caitriona (pure, unsullied) Scottish form of Catherine.
Cassandra (?)
Cecilia (blind, dim-sighted)
Ceiteag (pure, unsullied) Scottish form of Katie.
Christy (a Christian, a follower of Christ) **Chrissie**
Clara (bright, clear, famous)
Clementina (gentle, mild)
Criosaidh (a Christian, a follower of Christ) Scottish form of Chrissie.
David (beloved)
Davidina (beloved)

Davina (beloved)
Donalda (world ruler)
Donnag (world ruler)
Dorcas (gazelle)
Elizabeth (God is my oath) **Elisabeth**
Finella (white shoulders)
Fiona (white, fair, clear)
Fionnala (white shoulders) **Fionnauala, Finola**
Flora (a flower)
Florence (blooming, flourishing)
Forbesia (dweller at a field)
Grace (grace, mercy)
Hannah (grace, full of grace, mercy)
Harriet (home ruler)
Hester (myrtle; star)
Isabel (God is my oath)
Iseabail (God is my oath) Scottish form of Isabel.
Jacobina (supplanting, seizing by the heels)
Jamesina (supplanting, seizing by the heels)
Jane (God is gracious)
Janet (God is gracious; little Jane)
Jean (God is gracious) **Jeane, Jeanne**
Jeanie (God is gracious) **Jeannie**
Jennet (God is gracious)
Jenny (God is gracious)
Jessie (gift; God is gracious)
Joan (God is gracious) **Joane**
Johnina (God is gracious)
Judith (praised)
Kate (pure, unsullied)
Katherine (pure, unsullied)
Kirstin (a Christian, a follower of Christ)
Kirsty (a Christian, a follower of Christ)
Louisa (famous in war)
Lucy (famous in war)
Magaidh (a pearl) Scottish form of Maggie.
Maggie (a pearl)
Maidie (a maiden, a young unmarried woman)

Mairead (a pearl) Scottish form of Margaret.
Mairi (sea of bitterness or sorrow) Scottish form of Mary.
Maretta (of Mars)
Margaret (a pearl)
Margery (a pearl)
Marie (sea of bitterness or sorrow)
Martha (lady, mistress)
Mary (sea of bitterness or sorrow)
Maura (great, large; dark-skinned, a Moor)
Mórag (great, large) **Morag**
Morainn (fair seas; long-haired)
Morna (beloved) **Myrna**
Muireall (bright seas, fair one of the sea)
Nora (a woman from the north; honor, esteem)
Peggy (a pearl)
Peigi (a pearl) Scottish form of Peggy.
Philippina (lover of horses)
Rachel (ewe)
Rebecca (noose)
Rhoda (famous king)
Roberta (bright with fame)
Robina (bright with fame)
Rowena (?, perhaps *famous friend*; *famous joy*; *blessed lance*)
Seona (God is gracious) Scottish form of Janet.
Seonag (God is gracious) Scottish form of Joan.
Seònaid (God is gracious) Scottish form of Janet.
Sheena (God is gracious)
Sophia (wisdom, skill)
Sorcha (bright)
Stewartina (a steward, keeper of the animal enclosure)
Susan (lily, rose)
Susanna (lily, rose) **Susannah**
Thomasia (a twin)
Thomasin (a twin) **Thomasina**
Tríona (pure, unsullied)
Ùna (dearth, famine, hunger; lamb)
Vallentina (healthy)
Williamina (resolute protector)

MALE NAMES

Abraham (father of a multitude)
Adaidh (man of the red earth) Scottish pet form of Adam.
Adam (man of the red earth)
Ádhamh (man of the red earth) Scottish form of Adam.
Ádhamhnán (little Adam *man of the red earth*)
Aeneas (?)
Ailbeart (bright through nobility) Scottish form of Albert.
Ailean (?, perhaps *handsome; rock*) Scottish form of Alan.
Ailpean (?) **Ailpein**
Aindrea (manly) **Anndra** Scottish form of Andrew.
Alan (?, perhaps *handsome; rock*) **Allan**
Alasdair (defender of mankind) **Alisdair, Alistair, Alister** Scottish form of Alexander.

Albert (bright through nobility)
Alex (defender, helper) **Alec, Alick**
Alexander (defender of mankind)
Andrew (manly)
Angus (one, choice, preeminent)
Antoine (?, *priceless, of inestimable worth* is a popular folk definition)
Archibald (genuinely bold, genuinely brave)
Beathan (life)
Benedict (blessed)
Benjamin (son of the right hand)
Bernard (bold as a bear)
Charles (full-grown, a man) **Charlie**

Clement (gentle, mild)
Colin (defender of mankind)
Conall (strength; wisdom; high; wolf; dog)
Constantine (constant, steadfast)
Cormac (?, perhaps *raven; son of defilement; son of the char-ioteer*)
Dàibhidh (beloved) Scottish form of David.
Daniel (God is my judge)
David (beloved)
Diarmid (without injunction, freeman) **Diarmad**
Donald (world ruler)
Donnell (world ruler)
Dougal (dark-haired stranger) **Dugal, Dugald**
Douglas (black, dark + blue, green, gray)
Drew (manly)
Duncan (brown warrior)
Edward (wealthy guardian)
Edwin (wealthy friend)
Eric (eternal ruler) **Erik**
Euan (lamb; youth; well-born)
Eugene (well-born, noble)
Eunan (little Adam)
Evan (lamb; youth; well-born)
Evander (good man; archer)
Ewan (lamb; youth; well-born)
Farquhar (dear man)
Fergus (man of valor)
Fingal (fair-haired stranger) **Fingall**
Finlay (fair-haired warrior)
Forbes (dweller at a field)
Francis (a Frank, a freeman)
Gavin (battle hawk)
Geordie (earth worker, farmer)
George (earth worker, farmer)
Gilbert (famous pledge)
Gillespie (servant of the bishop)
Godfrey (peace of God)
Gregor (vigilant, a watchman) **Grigor**
Gregory (vigilant, a watchman)
Hamish (supplanting, seizing by the heels) Scottish form of James.
Harold (leader of the army)
Henry (home ruler)
Hugh (heart, mind, spirit)
Iagan (little fire)
Iain (God is gracious) Scottish form of John.
Ian (God is gracious)
Iòseph (may he add) Scottish form of Joseph.

Ivor (archer)
Jack (God is gracious)
Jacob (supplanting, seizing by the heels)
James (supplanting, seizing by the heels)
John (God is gracious)
Joseph (he shall add)
Kenneth (comely, handsome)
Kester (bearing Christ)
Kieran (little dark one) **Kiaran**
Laurance (man from Laurentum)
Lewis (famous in war)
Luthais (famous in war) Scottish form of Lewis.
Magnus (great, large)
Malcolm (servant of Saint Columba)
Matthew (gift of God)
Michael (Who is like God?)
Micheil (Who is like God?)
Murdoch (mariner)
Neil (champion; a cloud) **Neal, Neill**
Niall (champion; a cloud)
Nicholas (victory of the people)
Oliver (olive tree)
Paul (small)
Peader (a rock, stone)
Peter (a rock, a stone)
Philip (lover of horses)
Raibert (bright with fame) Scottish form of Robert.
Ranald (ruler of decision)
Reid (red, ruddy) **Reed**
Robert (bright with fame) **Rob**
Rory (red, ruddy)
Ruaidh (red-haired)
Sandy (defender of mankind)
Seaghan (God is gracious) Scottish form of John.
Séamus (supplanting, seizing by the heels) Scottish form of James.
Somhairle (summer sailor; a Viking)
Sorley (summer sailor; a Viking)
Steaphan (a crown, a garland) Scottish form of Stephen.
Stephen (crown, garland)
Teàrlach (full-grown, a man) **Tearlach** Scottish form of Charles.
Thearlaich (full-grown, a man) Scottish form of Charlie.
Thomas (a twin)
Tòmas (a twin)
Walter (ruler of an army)
William (resolute protector)
Zachary (God remembers)

SURNAMES

By this time, surnames were hereditary. Many chose to take the name of their clan, and others chose to take their fathers' names or a name based on occupation or location.

Armstrong (strong arms)
Baldwin (bold friend)
Baxter (baker)
Cameron (crooked nose, bent nose)
Campbell (crooked mouth)
Dalrymple (from the land on the curving steam)
Fletcher (maker or seller of arrows)
Gibbs (famous pledge)
Glas (black, dark)
Gordon (?, from a place name of uncertain etymology)
Grant (great, large)
Haig (dweller at the enclosed field)
Macadam (son of Adam *man of the red earth*)
MacDhòmhnaill (son of Dhòmhnaill *world ruler*)
Macdonnell (son of Donnell *world ruler*)
McGibbon (son of Gibbon *famous pledge*)

MacGillivray (son of Gillebhrath *servant of judgment*)
McGuire (son of the pale-complexioned man)
MacIntyre (son of the carpenter)
MacIvor (son of Ivor *archer*)
Macpherson (son of the parson)
Montgomery (from Montgomerie) **Montgomerie**
Muir (dweller by the moor)
Munroe (dweller at the red morass)
Murray (from Moray *beside the sea*)
Ross (dweller on the promontory or peninsula)
Scott (a Scot)
Sinclair (from Saint Clair)
Stewart (a steward, a keeper of the animal enclosure) **Stuart**
Sutherland (from the southern lands)
Walsh (a Welshman)
Wilson (son of Will *resolute protector*)

Chapter Seven

THE INDUSTRIAL REVOLUTION TO THE PRESENT
[1850–PRESENT]

POLITICS

WHEN GEORGE IV paid a state visit to Scotland in 1822, he became the first member of the royal family to do so in nearly eighty years. But it was his niece, Queen Victoria, who paid Scotland the most attention by spending her summers in the Highlands. She was proud of her Scottish heritage and had a genuine fondness for the land and its people. It was through her patronage that the old attitudes toward Scotland began to change, and the country came to be viewed as a partner in the United Kingdom instead of just a conquered foe.

That feeling of security enabled the people to demand and receive reform in both state and Kirk. More Scottish members were added to parliament, but there remained those who believed the affairs of Scotland were not given adequate attention. The Scottish Grand Committee was formed to give special attention to Scottish bills and concerns.

In 1886, the Scottish Home Rule Association was founded to lobby for home rule. In spite of several attempts to see such legislation put in place, circumstances always seemed to return it to the back burner. In 1924, a scheme was put forth whereby Scotland would continue to be represented at Westminster yet would also have a separate Scottish parliament. Economic depression hit the country, and some called for complete severance from England. The outbreak of World War II again shelved the matter.

In 1949, there was a renewed call for a Scottish parliament within the framework of the United Kingdom, and for years the matter was considered. In 1997, nearly fifty years later, the vote was brought before the people and was passed by an overwhelming majority. For the first time since the Union with England, Scotland has its own parliament.

SOCIETY

SCOTLAND'S ECONOMIC EXPANSION continued throughout Queen Victoria's reign, but such prosperity also had an ugly side: working and living conditions. Overcrowding increased in both the cities and towns, and long hours, low wages, and unhealthy and unsafe work environments were the norm.

Model villages were established to relieve overcrowding in the towns and to offer evicted tenants from the north a place to live and work. Though some villages failed, others grew into fully developed towns, and some remain much as when they were first built.

In 1855, the Nuisances Removal Act obligated local authorities to provide adequate toilets and maintain houses and tenements in a safe and hospitable condition, to clean and whitewash unsanitary houses, and to close those that were unfit for human habitation. Large-scale urban renewal came after 1875, when whole areas were condemned and replaced with planned housing for the working class.

Scotland has always been a land of renters, and that tradition continues to this day. In spite of the government's attempts to persuade Scots to purchase their own homes, the majority continue to rent. In fact, over 58 percent of the population lives in government-owned housing projects, and there seems little incentive to do otherwise.

Before leaving the section on Scotland, it seems appropriate to talk briefly on the Scottish language. There are three languages spoken in modern Scotland: Gaelic, Scots, and English. The Gaelic was brought to Scotland by Irish immigrants in the fifth century and is still spoken in the Hebrides and along the western seaboard. The Bilingualism Project has been working within the educational system since the 1970s to make the children of those areas fluent in both Gaelic and English. Scots is the historical speech of the Lowlands and is derived from Inglis, the old English of Northern England, and influenced by French and Dutch. Though Scots has suffered from being regarded as a ''second-class'' language, the Scots Language Society has been active in promoting its use in both speech and writing. English is the official speech of the country and is taught to all.

RELIGION

IN 1900, THE Free Church joined with the United Presbyterian Church to become the United Free Church. The Church of Scotland, the "Auld Kirk," continued to remain true to its roots. It became apparent that the United Free Church differed very little from the Auld Kirk, and in 1929, the two united as the Kirk of Scotland. Dissidents formed the Continuing United Free Church. The Episcopal Church and the Roman Catholic Church survived and enjoyed an increase in numbers over the years.

In spite of the important and primary role the Kirk has played in Scottish society, it no longer has such a tight grasp on daily living as it did a century before. Society is becoming increasingly secular, and some attitudes toward morality and entertainment have relaxed as a result.

NAMING

IN THE EIGHTEENTH century, interest in Scotland's long-forgotten past led James Macpherson to gather together stories of the Fianna, the ancient Celtic ancestors and heroes of the Scots race. He composed his findings into a series of epic poems known as Ossianic poetry after the poet Ossian (Oisein), supposedly the last surviving member of the Fianna. Ancient Irish poems report Ossian as living around the time of Saint Patrick, and he is said to have been taken into one of Saint Patrick's monasteries and cared for in his old age. These epic poems led to the revival of a number of old Gaelic names, many of which were put in Anglicized form.

In the nineteenth century, many new names were coined. Plants, gemstones, vocabulary words, and place names were the primary sources of these new names. Beryl, Ruby, Garnet, Pearl, Pansy, Primrose, Iona, and Clyde are examples.

Contemporary naming practices in Scotland are much as they are in other parts of Britain and the United States. Television, films, literature, and famous personalities have more influence on the names bestowed today than either religion or familial connections. Anglicized Gaelic names are commonly used in the Lowlands and the Southern Uplands. Those living in the Highlands, where Gaelic is still widely spoken and cultural pride is strong, tend to use names in their Gaelic form.

Lately, the use of surnames as first names has been increasing among those looking for something a bit different from the traditional names. Names are now chosen primarily for ornamental reasons and the meanings are no longer of great importance.

FEMALE NAMES

Agnes (chaste, pure) Used to Anglicized Ùna (dearth, famine, hunger; lamb).
Aileen (?)
Ailie Anglicized form of Eilidh (Ellie).
Ailsa (elf victory) From the place name Ailsa Craig. Also used to Anglicize Ealasaid (Elizabeth).
Aimili (work) Scottish form of Amelia.
Aingealag (heavenly, like an angel) Scottish form of Angelica.
Ainslee (from Aene's wood or clearing) Originally a surname.
Alana (O child; ?, perhaps *handsome; rock*) **Alane, Alanna, Alannah, Alanne, Allana**
Alexandra (defender of mankind) **Lexy, Sandy**
Alexina (defender of mankind)

Alickina (defender of mankind)
Alison (nobility) **Allie**
Amelia (work)
Angela (angel)
Angelica (heavenly, like an angel)
Angie (angel, like an angel)
Angusina (one, choice, preeminent)
Annabel (?, perhaps *eagle*; *hearth*; *lovable*; or *joy*) **Annabell, Annabella, Annabelle**
Annag (grace, full of grace, mercy)
Anne (grace, full of grace, mercy) **Ann, Anna**
Annella (grace, full of grace, mercy)
Annis (pure, chaste) **Annice, Annys**

Annot (grace, full of grace, mercy)

Arabella (?, perhaps *eagle* or *hearth*) **Arabel, Arabell, Orabel**

Audra (noble strength) **Audie**

Audrey (noble strength) **Audie**

Barabal (foreign woman) Scottish form of Barbara.

Bearnas (bringer of victory; bold as a bear) Scottish form of Berenice; feminine form of Bearnard.

Beathag (life)

Beitidh (God is my oath) Scottish form of Betty.

Beitiris (bringer of happiness) Scottish form of Beatrice.

Bhictoria (victory) Scottish form of Victoria.

Bonnie (beautiful, cheerful) **Bonny** Only recently used, probably since *Gone with the Wind* (1936).

Brenda (sword)

Bride (strength) Anglicized form of Bríd.

Bridget (strength) Anglicized form of Brighid.

Brighid (strength)

Cairistìona (a Christian, a follower of Christ) **Stìneag**

Cáit (pure, unsullied) **Ceit** Scottish form of Kate.

Caitir (pure, unsullied)

Caitrìona (pure, unsullied) **Caitriana, Catriona** Scottish form of Katherine.

Calumina (dove) **Mina**

Cecily (blind, dim-sighted)

Ceiteag (pure, unsullied) Scottish form of Katie.

Charlotte (full-grown)

Christina (a Christian, a follower of Christ) **Christine**

Christy (a Christian, a follower of Christ) **Chirsty, Chrissie, Christie, Kirstie**

Clara (bright, clear, famous)

Clarissa (bright, clear, famous) **Clarisa**

Davida (beloved)

Davina (beloved)

Deòiridh (pilgrim)

Deònaid (God is gracious)

Devorgilla (true oath, true testimony) Anglicized form of Diorbhail.

Diana (divine)

Diorbhail (true oath, true testimony)

Donalda (world ruler)

Donnag (world ruler) **Donna**

Dorothy (gift of God)

Ealasaid (God is my oath) Scottish form of Elizabeth.

Eamhair (?) Scottish form of Irish Emer, a character in Irish legend.

Edmée (beloved) **Edmé, Esmée**

Effie (?) Anglicized form of Oighrig.

Eibhlín (?) Scottish form of Evelyn.

Eileen (?) Anglicized form of Eibhlín.

Eilidh (?) Scottish form of Ellie.

Elizabeth (God is my oath) **Elisabeth**

Elspeth (God is my oath)

Erica (eternal ruler)

Eubh (life) Scottish form of Eve.

Euna (dearth, famine, hunger; lamb) Anglicized form of Ùna.

Eve (life) **Eva**

Finella (white shoulders) **Fenella, Finola, Fionola** Anglicized form of Fionnaghuala.

Fiona (white, fair, clear, transparent)

Fionnaghuala (white shoulders) **Fionnaghal, Fionnala, Fionnauala, Fionnghala, Fionnghuala**

Flora (flower) Also used to Anglicize Fionnaghuala.

Frances (a Frank, freeman)

Fràngag (a Frank, a freeman) Scottish form of Frances.

Freda (blessed peace)

Freya (lady, mistress)

Gail (father of exaltation)

Georgina (earth worker, farmer)

Glenna (mountain valley)

Gormlaith (blue lady)

Gormelia (blue lady) Anglicized form of Gormlaith.

Grace (grace, mercy) **Gracie**

Greer (vigilant, watchful) Originally a surname.

Heather (plants of the heath family)

Helen (light, torch, bright)

Hughina (heart, mind, spirit)

Innes (one, choice, preeminent) From the surname (Mac)Innes.

Iona (from the isle of Iona)

Isabel (God is my oath) **Isbel, Isobel**

Iseabail (God is my oath) Scottish form of Isabel.

Isla From the name of a Scottish island.

Jamesina (supplanting, seizing by the heels) **Jamie**

Jan (God is gracious)

Jane (God is gracious)

Janet (God is gracious)

Jean (God is gracious) **Jeane, Jeanne**

Jeanie (God is gracious) **Jeannie**

Jenna (fair lady) **Jenny**

Jennifer (fair lady) **Jenny**

Jessica (gift; God is gracious) **Jessie**

Jessie (God is gracious; gift)

Joan (God is gracious)

Judith (praised) **Judi, Judie, Judy**

Kate (pure, unsullied) **Katie**

Katherine (pure, unsullied) **Catherine, Cathryn, Kathryn**

Keitha (?, perhaps *the wind* or *wood*) From the surname.

Kenna (born of fire; comely, handsome)

Lachina (land of the lochs)

Laura (laurel) **Laurie**

Leagsaidh (defender or helper of mankind) Scottish form of Lexy.

Leslie (small meadow, small clearing, small woods) From the surname.

Lexine (defender or helper of mankind)

Lexy (defender or helper of mankind)

Lindsay (from Lindum Colonia)

Lindsey (from the linden tree wetland) **Lynsey**

Liùsaidh (famous in war; light) Scottish form of Louisa and Lucy.

Lorna Nineteenth century coinage of R. D. Blackmore in *Lorna Doone* (1869).

Lorraine (territory of the people of Lothar)
Louisa (famous in war)
Lucy (light)
Magaidh (a pearl) Scottish form of Maggie.
Maggie (a pearl)
Maidie (young unmarried woman)
Mairead (a pearl) Scottish form of Margaret.
Màiri (sea of bitterness or sorrow)
Máirín (little Mary)
Malcolmina (servant of Saint Columba)
Malina (servant of Saint Columba)
Malvina (?, perhaps *smooth brow*) Coined by James Macpherson (1736–1796).
Marcella (of Mars, warlike)
Maretta (a pearl) Anglicized form of Mairead.
Margaret (a pearl)
Margery (a pearl)
Marina (of Mars; of the sea)
Marion (sea of bitterness or sorrow)
Marsaili (a pearl) Scottish form of Margery.
Martha (lady, mistress)
Mary (sea of bitterness or sorrow)
Maura (great, large; dark-skinned, a Moor)
Maureen (sea of bitterness or sorrow) **Maurene, Maurine** Anglicized form of Máirín.
Mór (great, large)
Mórag (little Mór) **Morag**
Morainn (fair seas; long-haired) **Morann**
Morna (beloved) **Myrna**
Muireall (bright seas, fair one of the sea)
Murdag (sea warrior)
Murdina (sea warrior) **Murdann**
Nan (grace, full of grace, mercy)
Neilina (champion; a cloud)
Netta (champion; a cloud)
Nora (a woman from the north; honor, esteem)
Normina (a woman from the north, a Norman)

Oighrig (?, perhaps *new speckled one*; *fair speech*) **Eithrig**
Patricia (a patrician, an aristocrat)
Peigi (a pearl) Scottish form of Peggy.
Peggy (a pearl)
Rachel (ewe)
Raghnaid (battle of decision)
Raonaid (ewe) Scottish form of Rachel.
Rebecca (noose)
Rhoda (famous king)
Robina (bright with fame) **Robena**
Rodina (famous king)
Rona (?, perhaps *wise ruler, powerful ruler*) **Rhona**
Ronalda (ruler of decision, judgment power)
Rowena (?, perhaps *famous friend, joy and fame*; *blessed lance*)
Sandy (defender of mankind)
Saundra (defender of mankind) **Sandra**
Senga Modern name, perhaps Agnes spelled backward or *slender, lanky*)
Seona (God is gracious) Scottish form of Janet.
Seonag (God is gracious) Scottish form of Joan.
Seònaid (God is gracious) Scottish form of Janet.
Seòrdag (earthworker, farmer) Scottish form of Georgia.
Sheena (God is gracious) Anglicized form of Sìne.
Sìna (God is gracious) Scottish form of Jane.
Siubhan (God is gracious) Scottish form of Irish Siobhán.
Siùsan (lily, rose)
Sophia (wisdom, skill)
Sorcha (bright)
Susan (lily, rose)
Susanna (lily, rose) **Susannah**
Teasag (gift) Scottish form of Jessie.
Tríona (pure, unsullied) **Triona** Short form of Caitrìona.
Ùna (dearth, famine, hunger; lamb)
Victoria (victory) **Tori, Torie, Tory, Vicki, Vickie, Vicky**
Winifred (blessed peace; joyful peace) **Winnie**

MALE NAMES

Adaidh (little Adam)
Adam (man of the red earth)
Ádhamh (man of the red earth) Scottish form of Adam.
Ádhamhnán (little Adam)
Aidan (fire)
Ailbeart (nobly bright) Scottish form of Albert.
Ailean (?, perhaps *handsome; rock*) Scottish form of Alan.
Ailpean (?) **Ailpein**
Aindrea (manly) Scottish form of Andrew.
Ainsley (from Aene's clearing or woods) Originally a surname.
Alan (?, perhaps *handsome; rock*) **Allan, Allen**
Alasdair (defender of mankind) **Alastair, Alaster, Alisdair, Alistair, Alister**

Albert (nobly bright)
Alex (defender) **Alec, Alick**
Alexander (defender of mankind)
Alpin (?) Anglicized form of Alpean.
Amhlaidh (ancestral relic) **Amhladh**
Andra (manly)
Andrew (manly)
Angus (one, choice, preeminent)
Aodán (little fire, little Aodh)
Aodh (fire)
Aodhagán (little Aodh)
Aonghas (one, choice, preeminent) **Aonghus**
Arailt (leader of the army) Scottish form of Harold.
Archibald (genuinely bold, genuinely brave) **Archie, Archy**

Art (a bear)
Artair (?) Scottish form of Arthur
Arthur (?)
Augustus (great, venerable) Gus
Aulay (ancestral relic) Anglicized form of Amhlaidh.
Baird (a poet)
Barclay (from Berkeley; from the birch wood) Originally a surname.
Bean (life) Anglicized form of Beathan.
Bearnard (bold as a bear)
Beathan (life)
Benedict (blessed)
Benjamin (son of the right hand)
Benneit (blessed)
Bernard (bold as a bear)
Bhaltair (ruler of an army)
Blair (dweller on the plain) Originally a surname.
Brian (force, strength; hill, high; kingly)
Bruce (from Brieuse in France) Originally a surname.
Cailean (dove)
Calum (dove)
Cameron (crooked nose) Originally a surname.
Campbell (crooked mouth) Originally a surname.
Canice (comely, handsome)
Cedric Coinage of Sir Walter Scott for a character in *Ivanhoe* (1819).
Charles (full-grown, a man) Charlie
Chris (bearing Christ)
Christopher (bearing Christ) Christie, Christy
Clement (gentle, mild)
Cliamain (gentle, mild) Scottish form of Clement.
Coinneach (handsome, comely)
Còiseam (steadfast, constant) Scottish form of Constantine.
Colin (dove) Anglicized form of Cailean.
Conall (strength; wisdom; high; wolf; dog) Connell, Connull
Constantine (steadfast, constant)
Cormag (?, perhaps *raven*; *son of defilement*; *son of the charioteer*)
Craig (dweller by the crag) Originally a surname.
Creighton (from the border village) Originally a surname.
Crisdean (Christ)
Cuithbeart (well-known, famous) Scottish form of Cuthbert.
Cúmhaige (hound of the plain)
Cuthbert (well-known, famous)
Dàibhidh (beloved)
Daniel (God is my judge)
David (beloved)
Deòrsa (earthworker, farmer) Scottish form of George.
Dermot (without injunction, a freeman) Dermid
Diarmad (without injunction, a freeman) Diarmid
Domhnall (world ruler)
Donald (world ruler) Don
Donn (brown, brown-haired)
Dougal (dark-haired stranger) Dugal, Dugald
Douglas (dark, black + blue, green, gray) Doug, Dougie
Drew (manly)

Dubhghall (dark-haired stranger)
Duff (dark, black)
Duncan (brown warrior)
Eachann (brown horse)
Eairrdsidh (genuinely bold, genuinely brave)
Eallair (worker in a cellar)
Eanraig (home ruler)
Edmund (wealthy protection)
Edward (wealthy guardian)
Eideard (wealthy guardian) Eudard
Ellar (worker in a cellar)
Eóghan (lamb; youth; well-born) Eòghann
Eòin (God is gracious) Scottish form of John.
Eric (eternal ruler) Erik
Erskine (height of the cleft) From a Scottish place name.
Euan (lamb; youth; well-born) Anglicized form of Eóghan.
Eugene (well-born, noble)
Eumann (wealthy protection) Scottish form of Edmund.
Eunan (little Adam) Anglicized form of Ádhamhnán.
Evan (lamb; youth; well-born)
Evander (good man)
Ewan (lamb; youth; well-born) Anglicized form of Eóghan.
Ewart (shepherd; a priest) Originally a surname.
Farquhar (dear man) Anglicized form of Fearchar.
Fearchar (dear man)
Fearghas (man of valor)
Fergus (man of valor)
Fife (from Fife) From the place name and surname.
Filib (lover of horses) Scottish form of Philip.
Fingall (fair-haired stranger) Fingal
Finlay (fair-haired warrior) Finley
Fionnlagh (white warrior, fair-haired warrior) Fionnla
Forbes (a field)
Francis (a Frank, a freeman) Frank
Frang (a Frank, a freeman)
Fraser (a Frisian) Frazer
Fulton (the fowl enclosure, chicken coop)
Gavin (battle hawk)
Gene (well-born, noble)
George (earth worker, farmer) Geordie
Gibidh (famous pledge) Scottish form of Gibby.
Gilbert (famous pledge) Gibby
Gillanders (servant of Saint Andrew)
Gilleabart (famous pledge)
Gilleonan (servant of Saint Adomnan)
Gillespie (servant of the bishop)
Gillies (servant of Jesus)
Gilroy (servant of the red-haired lad) From the surname.
Gladstone (stone kite) From the place name and surname.
Glenn (mountain valley) Glen
Godfrey (God's peace)
Goiridh (God's peace) Scottish form of Godfrey.
Gordon (?) From the place name and surname. Use dates to Charles Gordon (1833–1885).
Graham (?) From the place name and surname.
Grant (great, large) From the surname.

Greg (vigilant, watchful)
Gregor (vigilant, watchful) **Greg, Gregg**
Gregory (vigilant, watchful) **Greg, Gregg**
Griogair (vigilant, watchful) **Grieg**
Hamilton (from the blunt hill) From the surname.
Hamish (supplanting, seizing by the heels)
Haral (leader of the army) Scottish form of Harold.
Harold (leader of the army)
Harry (home ruler)
Hector (to restrain)
Henry (home ruler)
Hugh (heart, mind, soul)
Iagan (little fire) **Egan**
Iain (God is gracious) Scottish form of John.
Ian (God is gracious) Scottish form of John.
Innes (island) Originally a surname.
Ìomhair (archer) Scottish form of Ivor.
Ìoseph (may he add) Scottish form of Joseph.
Irving (from the west river) From the surname.
Ivor (archer)
Jack (God is gracious) **Jock**
Jacob (supplanting, seizing by the heels) **Jake**
James (supplanting, seizing by the heels) **Jamie, Jimmie, Jimmy**
Jesse (gift) **Jess**
John (God is gracious) **Johnnie**
Jonathan (God has given) **Jon**
Joseph (may he add) **Joe, Josie**
Keir (dark, swarthy)
Keith (?, perhaps *the wind* or *wood*) From the surname.
Kennedy (ugly head, ugly chief) From the surname.
Kenneth (handsome, comely) **Ken, Kenny**
Kester (bearing Christ)
Kieran (dark-haired, black-haired)
Kirk (church) From the surname.
Labhrainn (man from Laurentum) Scottish form of Laurence.
Leslie (garden of hollies; the gray fort) From the surname.
Lewis (famous in war) **Lewie**
Lindsay (from Lindum Colonia)
Luthais (famous in war) Scottish form of Lewis.
Mac (son of)
Magnus (great, large)
Malcolm (servant of Saint Columba)
Mànus (great)
Marc (of Mars, warlike; soft, tender)
Marcus (of Mars, warlike; soft, tender) **Marc**
Màrtainn (of Mars, warlike) Scottish form of Martin.
Martin (of Mars, war-like)
Mata (gift of God)
Matthew (gift of God) **Matt**
Michael (Who is like God?) **Mike**
Micheil (Who is like God?)
Muireadhach (mariner, seaman)
Murchadh (mariner, seaman)
Murdoch (mariner)
Murphy (sea warrior)

Neacal (victory of the people)
Neil (champion; a cloud) **Neal, Neill, Niel, Niell**
Niall (champion; a cloud)
Nicholas (victory of the people) **Nicolas, Nick**
Norman (a northman)
Oilbhries (olive tree)
Olghar (olive tree)
Oliver (olive tree)
Oscar (spear of God; friend of the deer) **Osgar**
Pàdraig (a patrician, an aristocrat)
Pàl (small) Scottish form of Paul.
Parlan (son of Talmai) Scottish form of Bartholomew.
Patrick (a patrician)
Paul (small)
Peader (a rock, a stone)
Peter (a rock, a stone)
Philip (lover of horses)
Quentin (fifth)
Raghnall (powerful judgment)
Raibeart (bright with fame) **Rab, Rabbie** Scottish form of Robert.
Ramsey (from Ram's island) From the surname.
Ranulf (shield wolf)
Raonull (judgment ruler)
Read (red, ruddy)
Reid (red, ruddy)
Richard (stern king)
Robert (bright with fame) **Rob**
Roderick (famous king) **Roddy**
Ronald (judgment ruler)
Roy (red-haired, ruddy-complexioned)
Ross (dweller on the promontory or peninsula; red, rust-colored)
Roy (red, ruddy)
Ruaraidh (red, ruddy)
Ruiseart (brave ruler)
Sachairi (God remembers) Scottish form of Zachary.
Sandaidh (defender of mankind) Scottish form of Sandy.
Sandy (defender of mankind) **Sawney**
Scott (an Irishman, a Scot) From the surname.
Seaghan (God is gracious)
Séamus (supplanting, seizing by the heels) Scottish form of James.
Seoc (God is gracious) Scottish form of Jock.
Seth (appointed)
Shane (God is gracious) Anglicized form of Seaghan.
Shaw (dweller at a wood or grove) From the surname.
Sìm (heard) Scottish form of Simon.
Simidh (supplanting, seizing by the heels) Scottish form of Jimmy.
Simon (heard)
Sinclair (from Saint Clair) From the surname.
Somerled (mariner, sailor)
Sorley (mariner, sailor)
Steaphan (a crown, garland) Scottish form of Stephen.
Stephen (a crown, garland)

Stewart (steward, keeper of the animal enclosure) **Stuart**
Tadhg (a poet) **Taogh**
Teague (a poet) Anglicized form of Tadhg.
Teàrlach (full-grown, a man) **Tearlach**
Thaddeus (God's gift; praised)
Thomas (a twin)
Timothy (respecting God) **Tim, Timmy**

Tòmas (a twin) Scottish form of Thomas.
Tòrmod (a northman) Scottish form of Norman.
Uilleam (resolute protector) **Uilliam** Scottish form of William.
Virgil (youthful, flourishing)
Walter (ruler of an army) **Wally, Walt**
William (resolute protector) **Will, Willy**
Zachary (God remembers)

SURNAMES

The variety found in Scottish surnames attests to the influence many different groups had on Scottish society. Surnames taken from Gaelic names form the largest group, but surnames taken from places and names brought in from other countries are also found. Scotland's alliance with France can be seen in surnames of French origin; the number of English and Flemish surnames are due to the government's policy of encouraging those groups to immigrate to the Lowlands. Viking influence upon Scottish society can be found in names such as Gunn, Kerr, and MacLeod. In the years following 1820, large numbers of Irish escaped famine by emigrating to Scotland. Their names greatly increased the pool of Gaelic names.

Anderson (son of Andrew *manly*)
Armstrong (strong in the arms)
Baird (descendant of the poet)
Barclay (dweller from the birch wood)
Brodie (son of Bruaideadh *fragment*) **Brody**
Bruce (from Brus)
Buchanan (little small one)
Burns (from the burnt house)
Cameron (crooked nose)
Campbell (crooked mouth)
Chisholm (from the gravelly island)
Colquhoun (the narrow wood)
Cunningham (from the rabbit farm; from the royal manor)
Dalrymple (from the land on the curving stream)
Davidson (son of David *beloved*)
Douglas (black, dark + blue, green, gray)
Drummond (dweller at the ridge)
Dunbar (fort of the summit)
Duncan (brown warrior)
Elphinstone (from Elphin's estate)
Erroll (from Erroll)
Erskine (?, perhaps *height of the cleft*)
Farquharson (son of Farquhar *dear man*)
Ferguson (son of Fergus *man of valor*)
Fletcher (maker or seller of arrows)
Forbes (dweller at a field)
Fraser (a Frisian)
Gibbs (famous pledge)
Gillebride (servant of Saint Bridget *strength*)
Gillespie (servant of the bishop)
Gordon (?, from a place name of uncertain etymology)
Graham (?, from a place name, the second element of which is *home, dwelling, manor*)
Grant (great, large)

Gray (gray)
Gunn (battle)
Haig (dweller at the enclosed field)
Haldane (half Dane)
Hamilton (from the town near the blunt hill)
Hepburn (high stream)
Henderson (son of Henry *home ruler*)
Innes (island)
Johnson (son of John *God is gracious*)
Keith (?, possibly *the wind* or *wood*)
Kennedy (ugly head, ugly chief)
Kerr (dweller near the brushwood or marsh)
Lamont (a lawyer)
Leslie (from the meadow of hollies)
Lindsay (from Lindsay *colony by the lake*)
Livingstone (from Leofing's stone)
Macadam (son of Adam *man of the red earth*)
MacArthur (son of Arthur)
Macaulay (son of Olaf *ancestral relic*)
MacBain (son of Bain *fair, white*)
MacBeth (son of Beatha *life*)
McCulloch (son of Culloch *boar; cock*)
MacDiarmid (son of Diarmid *freeman, without injunction*)
Macdonnell (son of Donnell *world ruler*)
MacGillivray (son of Gillebhrath *servant of judment*)
MacGregor (son of Gregor *vigilant, a watchman*)
Mackay (son of Aodha *fire*)
Mackenzie (son of Coinneach *handsome, comely*)
Maclachlan (son of Lachlan *land of the lochs*)
Maclean (son of the servant of Saint John)
MacLeod (son of Léoid *ugly*) **Macleod**
Macmillan (son of Maolain *the servant*)
MacNeill (son of Neill *a champion; cloud*)
MacQueen (son of Siubhne *well-going, pleasant*)

MacTaggart (son of the priest)
MacTavish (son of Thomas *a twin*)
Maxwell (dweller at Maccus' pool)
Muir (dweller by the moor)
Munroe (dweller at the red morass)
Murray (from Moray *beside the sea*)
Ogilvy (from Ogilvie *high hill*)
Oliphant (dweller at the sign of the elephant)
Ramsay (from the raven's island)
Robertson (son of Robert *bright with fame*)

Ross (dweller on the promontory or peninsula)
Scott (an Irishman, a Scot)
Sinclair (from Saint Clair, Normandy)
Spalding (from Spalding)
Strathearn (a valley)
Stuart (a steward, a keeper of the animal enclosure) **Steward**
Sutherland (from the south lands)
Telford (iron cleaver)
Wallace (a Welshman, foreigner)
Wilson (son of Will *resolute protector*)

Part Three

[WALES]

[Contents]

Chapter One

WALES IS THE smallest country in the British Isles, having just over 8,000 square miles of quite varied landscape. The high mountains and rugged terrain of the north give way to the rolling hills of mid-Wales, which in turn flatten out into wide plains in the south and along the coast. Most of the land is rough and unsuitable for crops, yet the earliest settlers managed to survive.

The history of the Welsh people is a story of fighting off invaders. The earliest people to settle for any length of time were hunter-gatherers from Europe who arrived somewhere between 50,000 and 10,000 years ago. Between 10,000 and 3,000 years ago, a group of small, dark-haired people arrived. They knew something about raising crops and keeping livestock, and used both stone and metal implements. The Celts, who arrived around 3,000 years ago, were well-organized warriors who fortified their villages against wild animals and intruders. Besides being ferocious and skilled in warfare, the Celts were also skilled metalworkers and had a greater knowledge of farming and raising livestock. Individual tribes usually kept to themselves and didn't unite politically. By the time the Romans arrived, five tribes had established themselves in the area of Wales: the Deceangli, the Ordovices, the Demetae, and the Silures.

Many tribes inhabited Britain, but it was probably the Catuvellauni who were the most advanced. They were also part of the confederacy of Belgic tribes from northeast Gaul who fought extensively with the Romans. After the Catuvellauni sent aid to the Belgae on the continent, Julius Caesar led retaliatory missions against them in 55 and 54 B.C. Over the next hundred years, other tribes, Belgic and non-Belgic, settled in Britain after being pushed out of Europe.

Shortly after the beginning of the Christian Era, Cunobelinus, the Catuvellauni leader, managed to conquer other tribes in southeastern Britain and united them into a single powerful kingdom with Camulodunum (Colchester) as its capital. By the second or third decade of the century, he had expanded his holdings westward.

Cunobelinus had three sons, but after his death in 40 A.D., his kingdom was divided between just two: Caratacus (Caradog) and Togodumnus. The third son, Adminius, was excluded from his inheritance. Adminius was furious at the slight and appealed to the Romans for help. As Britian had long been recognized as the granary of the north, its subjugation was very appealing to an empire needing vast quantities of food for its legions of soldiers. Adminius's appeal gave Emperor Claudius an excuse to invade.

In 43 A.D., 40,000 Roman soldiers led by Aulus Plautius reached Britain. Within three months, their hold in the southeast was firm enough for Emperor Claudius to visit. (He made a ceremonial entrance into Camulodunum on an elephant.) Four years later, the Catuvellauni had been completely subdued and Caratacus (Caradog) had fled westward into Welsh country to organize tribes for resistance.

The Romans didn't begin their advance on the tribes of Wales until four years later; Caradog was defeated in 51 A.D. It took thirty-five years and at least thirteen military campaigns to subdue the Celtic tribes. An extensive system of roads and forts helped keep the native inhabitants under control. Towns were built, and near the larger forts, villages were established by natives to provide goods and services to Roman soldiers. The Romans and Welsh began to intermingle, and soon many children were born to Roman fathers.

The west and the uplands of northern Britain constituted the military zone, and the south formed the civil zone. Wales lay almost entirely in the military zone. The exception was the southeast, where at least three Roman towns were built: Venta Silurum (Caerwent), Ariconium, and Magnis (Kenchester). Only Caerwent was situated in the boundaries of modern Wales.

Late in the third century, the Welsh coast was the target of Irish raids. By the fourth century, the raids became more frequent and were making more of an impact, for people were being taken captive and sent to Ireland as slaves. Raids were taking place by land as well, with the Picts breaking over Hadrian's Wall and making their way south to create havoc. The year 367 was particularly rough. A great deal of fighting occurred and many Roman villas were destroyed.

Such unrest was common throughout Europe, and as German tribes began to seriously threaten the Roman Empire, more Roman troops were needed on the Continent. It appears that the Roman legions had withdrawn from Wales by 390, and in 401 and 407, all troops were withdrawn from Britain to meet the Visigothic threat. They were never to return.

The fifth and sixth centuries are very important to the history of Wales, for it was then that Britain separated into its three distinct areas: The Gaelic north, the Brythonic west, and the Teutonic east. It was also the period during which the dynasties of the principle western kingdoms were formed and the language of the people evolved into the Welsh language, and the time when Christianity so pervaded the land that the people named themselves and even many of their places after the saints.

Since the withdrawal of the Roman forces from Britain was supposed to be temporary, the government continued to function on its own. But as raids, pestilence, and disease increased, government deteriorated. Without troops, order deteriorated as well. The citizens were offered some measure of protection in the walled towns, but those who lived in rural areas were completely at the mercy of the bands of raiders.

Few details of the Dark Ages of Wales exist. From oral tradition, the stories that were later written in the ninth century, it is said that a warrior, Cunedda, and his eight sons entered northern Wales from Scotland. Cunedda subdued the northern and western Welsh and the Irish who had settled there, and introduced the Brythonic (Welsh) dialect of the Celtic language. According to Celtic tradition, Cunedda's kingdom was divided between his sons Aflog, Ceredig, Dogfael, Dunawd (Donatus), Edern (Eternus), Einion Girt, Osmael, and Rumanus. Years later, regions of Wales were named after them. Ceredigion was the land of Ceredig, Dogfeiling was the land of Dogfael, Dunoding of Dunawd, Edeyrnion of Edern, Rhufoniog of Rumanus, and Osmaeliaun of Osmael. Cunedda's eldest son, Tybion, died before the invasion, and his share was given to his son, Meriaun or Meirion, which became Meirionydd. Other strong families set themselves up as kings in other parts of Wales and gave rise to dynasties of their own.

Events taking place outside the area had an impact on what was to happen in the area of Wales. In the second half of the seventh century, the Saxons spread westward and the two small Anglican kingdoms of

Deira and Bernicia united to form the kingdom of Northumbria. The Northumbrians waged war against the Celtic tribes of the kingdoms of Reged and Strathclyde, with whom the Welsh were closely linked. It was during this time that the tribes of the north began to call themselves *Cymry* (compatriots); the Welsh of Wales soon adopted the name.

In 615, the Northumbrian king Aethelfrith, succeeded in cutting the Welsh of Wales off from those of Cumbria. After Edwin of Northumbria took control of a large area including the Chester plain, the island of Anglesey, and the Isle of Man, Cadwallon of Gwynedd, fearing his territory was next on the Northumbrian hit list, allied his kingdom with that of Mercia. For a time, they held their own, but shortly after 655, the Northumbrians gained control, making the breach between Wales and Cumbria a permanent one. Wales was now isolated from the rest of the British Celts, and they were to henceforth have a separate development and a separate identity.

SOCIETY

ONCE THE ROMAN conquest had taken place, the way was opened for traders, workers, and administrators to settle. Towns were the principal places of habitation, but the more wealthy chose to build elaborate villas on rural estates. Homes were single-storied but large and spacious and built in Roman design. They were decorated with murals and mosaics, had central heating, and were surrounded by gardens, orchards, and acres of land farmed by native serfs.

The Roman way of life quickly spread to the Welsh people living in or near the towns and villages. Roman dress was adopted, as were Roman names and speech; even Roman artistic designs influenced the designs of the native Celts. They also introduced advanced methods of agriculture and new food sources. The Romans are believed to have introduced oats, apples, carrots, turnips, parsnips, leeks, cherries, vines, walnuts, and chestnuts to Britain.

In the military zone, the Welsh tended to hold themselves apart from the Romans, so their Celtic way of life was little affected by Roman civilization. Native Celts continued to live in tribal groups in dry-stone-walled huts, and they retained their traditional arts and crafts.

The departure of the Romans had a devastating effect on the Welsh who lived in the southern areas. The soldiers had not only played a vital role in the economy, they had formed family ties with the Welsh for generations. Their departure left many women and children to face uncertain circumstances by themselves. Without the continuity and strength of an established government to guide and protect the people left behind, the more civilized Roman way of life eventually gave way to the traditional Celtic way of life practiced by the majority of the Welsh.

RELIGION

UNDER ROMAN RULE, all types of religions were allowed as long as they weren't anti-Roman (which Druidism was). Both the Celts and the Romans had polytheistic religions, and it appears there was an attempt to identify Celtic gods with those of the Romans.

Christianity soon made its way to the island, and though there was a brief period of persecution, Christians were allowed freedom of worship in 313. The Emperor Constantine was baptized on his deathbed in 337, and by 378, Christianity became the state religion of the Roman Empire. Christianity soon managed to supercede the other religions in Britain, and by the year 400, all other religions were outlawed.

In Wales, the majority of which was in the military zone, Christianity had made little progress, and the

Celts living outside Roman influences continued to worship the old gods. However, it was after the Romans left that the monastic missionary movement was to take such a firm hold. Several religious institutions were established, the most famous being Llantwit Major, founded by Illtyd in the sixth century, Llancarfan, which was founded by Cadoc (Cattwg), Saint Davids by David (Dewi), and Llanbadarn, which was founded by Padarn. Unlike continental monasteries, which were places of retreat from the world, the Celtic monasteries, *clasau*, were centers of learning and bases from which the monks could venture forth to spread the gospel. Each of these institutions trained missionaries to go out and convert the Celts to Christianity, and it was through their efforts that Wales was Christianized.

The missionaries, the saints of the Welsh Church, built tiny wooden or stone chapels all over Wales. They were the first *illans* or parishes, and many still survive to this day. In fact, many Welsh place names beginning with *Llan* have their origins in these early churches.

With the spread of the pagan Germanic tribes, the Celtic Church was effectively cut off from the Mother Church, and it developed along its own lines. The customs of the early Christian Church in Britain were preserved, and several religious rituals evolved a bit differently from those of the Latin Church. In addition, the abbots and priests of the Celtic Church were allowed to marry.

In 597, Saint Augustine arrived in Britain. It was hoped that the Latin and Celtic Churches could come together in unity, but that was not to be, and the division continued.

Naming

In 400 A.D., the native people spoke a language called Brittonic, a combination of Celtic and Latin. By 700 A.D., they were speaking Welsh. Many of the names from the Roman period are Latin or Brittonic, but they were transformed when Welsh came into existence. For example, Maglocunus, a Brittonic name, was changed to Maelgwn in Welsh. These names are very old, and many of the meanings have been lost. A question mark (?) following the name signifies the meaning is unknown or uncertain. Monks that came to Wales often bore biblical names, and the adoption of those names into the Welsh culture was quicker than among the Germanic tribes in England.

As the spelling of Welsh names seems a bit unusual when compared with English, a few tips on pronunciation are in order. The letters *b, d, h, l, m, n, p,* and *t* are pronounced the same as in English. The letters *j, k, q, v, x, y,* and *z* are not found. The letters *ch, dd, ll, w,* and *y* possibly cause the most difficulty for English speakers.

Welsh Letter	Approximate English Sound
c	hard *k* as in pike
ch	guttural *ch* as in loch
dd	*th* as in this
f	*v* as in victor
ff	*f* as in fun
g	hard *g* as in get
ll	the most difficult sound, a bit like *thl*
r	trilled, as in Spanish or Scottish
s	*s* as in song

Short Vowel Sound		**Long Vowel Sound**	**Never**
a	that	ah	made
e	get	*late*	meet
i	pin	weed	line
o	got	score	ton
u	wig		thud
w	soot	school	
y	Sounds like d*id* when in the final syllable or in words of one syllable. In other cases, like *gun*.		

Every letter is sounded in Welsh. There are no silent letters, and the accent is usually on the second syllable. For example: Morganwy is pronounced Mor*gan*wee.

FEMALE NAMES

Aegle (radiance, splendor) A Roman name.
Aeliana (of the sun) A Roman name.
Aeron (battle)
Aeronwen (blessed battle)
Aeronwy (battle)
Agrona (battle)
Angharad (undisgraced, free from shame)
Aranrhod (round wheel)
Arianrhod (silver wheel)
Arianwen (silver woman)
Aurelia (golden) A Roman name.
Blodeuwedd (flower face)
Branwen (white raven, blessed raven)
Cainwen (blessed fair one)
Calida (most beautiful) A Roman name.
Calligenia (beautiful daughter) A Roman name.
Callirrhoe (beautiful stream) A Roman name.
Callisto (most beautiful) A Roman name.
Cecilia (blind, dim-sighted)
Ceridwen (blessed poetry, fair poet)
Claudia (lame) A Roman name.
Creirdyddlydd (jewel of the sea)
Creirwy (jewel, token)
Diaspad (?)
Drusilla (?, perhaps *strong*) A Roman name.
Drwg (?)
Eheubryd (?)
Eiddwen (desirous, fond + white, fair, blessed)
Elaine (light, torch, bright)
Eleri (?)
Elin (nymph)
Enid (?)
Esyllt (beautiful, fair)
Ewaedan (?)
Fabiola (a bean) A Roman name.

Felicitas (happiness, good fortune) A Roman name.
Garym (?)
Goleuddydd (?)
Gorascwrn (?)
Gwaeth (?)
Gwaethav (?)
Gwendolen (white ring, blessed ring)
Gwenfrewi (blessed peace)
Gwenhwyfar (fair lady)
Gwenllian (white, fair, blessed + linen; flood, flow)
Gwennhwyach (?)
Gwerful (completely shy)
Gwladus (lame)
Gwynach (bliss, happiness)
Gwythyr (?)
Heledd (?)
Isolde (ruler of the ice; beautiful, fair)
Julia (youth, downy) A Roman name.
Llewrwg (light)
Lucia (light) A Roman name.
Luned (shape, form)
Meinwen (slender woman, fair woman)
Melania (black, dark) A Roman name.
Morgwen (fair seas, lady of the sea)
Morwenna (?, perhaps *maiden* or *white seas, blessed seas*)
Morvudd (?)
Myfanwy (?, possibly *my fair one* or *child of the water*)
Myrddin (sea hill, fortress by the sea)
Och (?)
Olwen (white footprint, blessed footprints)
Orddu (?)
Penardun (?)
Rathtyeu (?)
Rhelemon (?)
Rhianfellt (?)

Rhiannon (?, perhaps *great queen*)
Rhianwen (fair maiden)
Rhonwen (fair-haired; blessed lance)

Sabrina (?)
Serena (clear, calm, serene) A Roman name.
Tegwen (lovely maiden)

MALE NAMES

Aaron (exalted one)
Adaon (?)
Aed (fire)
Aeddon (fire)
Aemilius (emulating, rival) A Roman name.
Aeneas (to praise) A Roman name.
Agricola (tiller of the field)
Alun (?, perhaps *rock*)
Ambrosius (immortal) A Roman name.
Anacleto (called for, invoked) A Roman name.
Anatolius (sunrise, daybreak) A Roman name.
Andras (manly)
Aneurin (noble, modest)
Anlawdd (?)
Antonius (?) A Roman name.
Arawn (?)
Arminius (soldier, warrior)
Art (a bear)
Arthur (?)
Arwystli (?, perhaps *best counsel*)
Augustinus (great, venerable) A Roman name.
Augustus (great, venerable) A Roman name.
Aurelius (golden) A Roman name.
Awst (great, venerable)
Basilius (king) A Roman name.
Bedwyr (?)
Beli (?)
Bendigaid (the blessed)
Benedictus (blessed) A Roman name.
Berwyn (fair-haired, white-haired)
Blasius (a babbler) A Roman name.
Bleddyn (a wolf's cub)
Bran (raven)
Brychan (speckled, freckled)
Bryn (hill)
Brynmor (great hill)
Brys (?)
Bwlch (?)
Cadell (small battle)
Cadfan (?)
Cadwaladr (battle leader)
Cadwallon (battle arranger)
Cadwgawn (battle glory) **Cadwgan**
Caerwyn (white fortress)
Calogerus (fair old age) A Roman name.
Caradog (beloved) **Caradoc, Caradwg**
Caswallon (?, perhaps *chief of hatred*)
Cattwg (war, battle, defense)

Cethin (dark, swarthy)
Claudius (lame) A Roman name.
Cleddyf (hard, rough)
Cledwyn (hard, rough + white, fair, blessed)
Clud (?)
Clust (?)
Constantinus (constant, steadfast) A Roman name.
Cynan (high, exalted)
Cynddelw (high, exalted or head + image, statue)
Cyndeyrn (head chief)
Cyriacus (a lord) A Roman name.
Cyrus (lordly) A Roman name.
Dai (shining)
Darius (?) A Roman name.
Deiniol (judged by God)
Dewi (beloved)
Dilwyn (blessed truth)
Donatus (given by God) A Roman name.
Drych (?)
Dylan (?, perhaps *sea*)
Dynawd (given)
Edeyrn (?)
Einion (anvil)
Emlyn (?)
Emyr (ruler, king)
Eniawn (upright)
Erim (?)
Eternus (eternal) A Roman name.
Fabianus (a bean) A Roman name.
Faustus (lucky, fortunate) A Roman name.
Flavius (fair, blond, golden) A Roman name.
Gareth (?, perhaps *civilized*)
Geraint (?, perhaps *old*)
Gildas (servant of God)
Gladus (lame)
Glewlwyd (?)
Glwyddyn (?)
Gruduen (?)
Gruffydd (reddish-brown, rust-colored)
Gwalchmai (battle hawk)
Gwallawg (?, perhaps *stammerer* or *hawk*)
Gwendoleu (white browed)
Gwevyl (?)
Gwgawn (?)
Gwiawn (sense)
Gwirydd (?)
Gwric (born on Sunday)
Gwril (lordly)

Gwrtheyrn (excelling king)
Gwyar (?)
Gwyddno (?)
Gwydion (?)
Gwydyr (wrathful)
Gwynn (white, fair, blessed) **Gwyn**
Heilyn
Henwas (?)
Hywel (eminent, prominent)
Julianus (youth, downy bearded) A Roman name.
Justinus (just, proper) A Roman name.
Kai (?)
Kynfelyn (?)
Llefelys (?)
Lleu (bright, shining)
Llew (lion)
Llwyd (gray-haired one)
Llyr (sea)
Llywarch (dear one)
Lucianus (light) A Roman name.
Mabon (son)
Macsen (greatest)
Madwg (beneficent) **Madoc, Madog**
Maelgws (chief)
Maelgwn (chief)
Manawyddan (?)
Mandurrath (man of treason)
Manogan (?)
Martinus (of Mars) A Roman name.
Math (?, perhaps *bear*)
Mathonwy (?, perhaps *bear*)
Medyr (?)
Meilyr (chief ruler)
Meirion (of Mars; manly)
Melus (black, dark) A Roman name.
Merfyn (marrow, brains or sea + eminent, prominent, hill)
Methredydd (?)

Modron (?)
Morcant (sea; circle, completion + white, bright)
Morfran (sea hill)
Morgan (sea; circle, completion + white, bright)
Muryel (?)
Myrddin (sea hill, fortress by the sea)
Nefed (?)
Nynyaw (?)
Octavius (eighth) A Roman name.
Owain (lamb; youth; well-born)
Paulus (small) A Roman name.
Pedr (rock)
Penwyn (fair-headed)
Peredur (to pierce the valley)
Philippus (lover of horses)
Pryderi (caring for, concern; trouble)
Pwyll (?)
Rhodri (wheel king)
Rhonabwy (?)
Rhydderch (reddish brown, rust-colored)
Rhys (ardor)
Saidi (?)
Sefwlch (?)
Selyf (peaceful) Welsh form of Solomon.
Sextus (sixth) A Roman name.
Stephanus (a crown, garland) A Roman name.
Tacitus (?) A Roman name.
Talfryn (high hill)
Taliesin (shining brow)
Tared (?)
Tegid (?) Welsh form of Tacitus.
Teirnyon (?)
Tiberius (of the Tiber River) A Roman name.
Twrch (?)
Urien (?, perhaps *of privileged birth; heavenly*)
Vincentius (conquering) A Roman name.
Ynyr (?, perhaps *honorable*)

SURNAMES

Surnames had not yet developed among the Welsh. Individuals were identified by their kinships. Both males and females added their father's name to their own. Occasionally, descriptive terms were added as identifiers. These could either indicate special social status or were reflective of some physical characteristic. Rhodri Mawr, for example, means Rhodri the Great, and Rhodri Hen means Rhodri the Old.

Dda (the good)
Ddrud (the bold)
Deg (?, perhaps *tenth*)
Gawr (the giant)
Genhir (long life)
Gryg (harsh)

Hen (old)
Llaw (wretched; sad; small; mean)
Mawr (the great)
Molwynog (passionate)
Mor (sea)
Uradawc (the treacherous)

Chapter Two

THE ISOLATION OF WALES TO
THE NORMAN CONQUEST
[700–1200]

POLITICS

IN THE FIRST or second century after Wales's isolation, the land was divided into several kingdoms. The North was divided between the kingdoms of Gwynedd and Powys, and the south was divided among many smaller kingdoms: Dyfed, Seisyllwg, Glywysing, Gwent, Brycheiniog, and Buellt.

In the eighth century, power shifted from the Northumbrians to the Mercians, and the Cymry soon came under attack by their one-time ally. The struggle for dominance was long and determined, but the Welsh were eventually driven back toward the foothills. Offa, the Mercian king, constructed Offa's Dyke in 784 A.D. to separate and define the territories of the Welsh and the Mercians.

During the ninth and tenth centuries, Wales came under repeated attack from Vikings. Norsemen from Irish settlements raided the coast and established several settlements to use as bases for trading. Danes attacked by sea, as well.

Rhodri Mawr (844–878) succeeded to the throne of Gwynedd by descent from his grandmother, then to the throne of Powys in 855 after the death of his uncle, and then assumed the throne of Seisyllwg in 871 after the death of his brother-in-law. For the first time, a large part of Wales was united under one ruler. The remaining tribes retained their independence.

After Rhodri Mawr's death, his territories were divided between his sons, Anarawd and Cadell. It was their pressure upon the smaller kingdoms that led the lesser kings to seek protection from King Alfred of Wessex, which eventually led to English claims of overlordship of Wales.

Cadell's son, Hywel Dda (900–950), inherited Seisyllwg, and by marriage, the kingdom of Dyfed. He then took the kingdom of Gwynedd after the death of his cousin, and added Powys, bringing much of Wales under single rule once again. Hywel took advantage of the unity by codifying the differing legal customs of various parts of Wales into a single law. He also issued the first Welsh coinage, the first to be used since the time of the Romans.

After Hywel's death, the kingdom of Gwynedd won its independence from Hywel's sons, lost it to his grandson, Maredudd (986–999), then gained it back again after Maredudd's death. Llywelyn ap Seisyll, husband of Maredudd's daughter Angharad, captured the throne of Gwynedd in 1018, and he held northern and western Wales until his death in 1023. Llywelyn's son, Gruffudd ap Llywelyn, conquered the remaining kingdoms, and for the first time, Wales was united under one ruler.

Smaller kingdoms were absorbed into larger ones until Wales was divided into four kingdoms: Gwynedd in the north, Powys in the east, and Morgannwg and Deheubarth in the south. When Gruffudd ap Llywelyn's raids into English territory prompted retaliatory attacks by the earl of Wessex, the lesser rulers of Wales abandoned Gruffudd. Deheubarth regained its independence, Gruffudd was killed, and Welsh unity was broken once again.

After William the Conqueror took control of England, he gave lands along the Welsh border to some of his most faithful followers, both as a reward for their roles in the Conquest, and as a means to curtail Welsh incursions into England. The Norman lords erected strongholds and aggressively sought to extend their holdings and increase their power with lands gained in Wales. The principle Norman lords were the earl of Chester (Hugh of Avranches), the earl of Shrewsbury (Roger of Montgomery), and the earl of Hereford (William Fitzosbern).

The Normans took advantage of the old Roman roads to carry out their raids, and by 1086, Fitzosbern in the south had established himself as far west as Caerleon in Gwent, far beyond Offa's Dyke. The earl of Shrewsbury harrassed central Wales and established a frontier castle from which he controlled parts of Powys. In the north, the Earl of Chester forced his way across northern Wales and during the exile of Gwynedd's ruler, Gruffudd ap Cynan, established a castle at Deganwy in Gwynedd and several others along the northern coast.

The Marcher Lords were not under the same political obligations or restrictions as were lords in England. The Marcher Lords had the freedom to erect castles wherever they chose and to wage war against their Welsh neighbors. They also created their own law and held their own courts.

The second stage in the Norman Conquest of Wales opened with the reign of William II in 1087. In spite of spirited resistance from the Welsh, the Norman lords were able to penetrate further into Wales. The kingdom of Brycheiniog under the leadership of Bleddyn ap Maenarch fell to Bernard de Newmarch, who also defeated Rhys ap Twedwr, king of Deheubarth, in 1093. Buellt fell to Philip de Braose, Gwent was subdued by several Norman lords, and the kingdom of Morgannwg in the west was conquered by Robert Fitzhamon, Earl of Gloucester. The entire plain of Glamorgan was brought under Norman control and divided among the followers of Fitzhamon while the hill country of the interior was left to the native Welsh rulers who were now subject to the overlordship of Fitzhamon.

The Norman lords also took control of the rest of the west coast when the earl of Shrewsbury extended his holdings by overrunning Ceredigion and conquering the kingdom of Dyfed. Shrewsbury established the lordship of Pembroke in southern Dyfed and turned it over to his brother (some say son), Arnulf of Montgomery.

Just when it appeared that all of Wales would fall to the Normans, a major Welsh revolt broke out in the north and quickly spread south. With too few Normans to hold all their conquered territory, the Welsh were able to regain much of what they had lost. In Gwynedd, the sons of Bleddyn ap Cynfin recovered their lands west of the River Conway, and Ceredigion and most of Dyfed were recovered as well, though the castle of Pembroke was able to hold out. The Welsh were close to recovering their lands in the southeast, but a royal military expedition intervened, and the Norman lords retained the lands they had won.

Gruffudd ap Cynan reestablished himself as the king of Gwynedd, and Cadwgan, Iorwerth, and Maredudd ap Bleddyn took possession of Powys and the remainder of Deheubarth. The breakup of the union between Gwynedd and Powys was to have a significant impact on the future of Wales.

William II was increasingly drawn into the situation between his lords and the Welsh, and while it was one thing to secure many of the Norman lordships, it was another to take control of the whole country. William's successor, Henry I, intervened as well, and in the early years of his reign, the boundary between the territories of the Welsh and the Marcher Lords was established.

Henry took possession of Pembroke Castle and a castle at Carmathen, thus establishing his overlordship. He also had the arrogance and the strength to do as he pleased with the territories still in the hands of the Welsh rulers. He gave Gower to the earl of Warwick, took Ceredigion from Owain ap Cadwgan and gave it to Gilbert Fitzrichard, and proceeded to do the same with Gwent Is Coed, Gwent Uwch Coed, and Brecon.

The reign of the English king Steven was filled with anarchy and chaos. The Marcher Lords both took advantage of his weakness to solidify their holds on the Welsh, then realized that without the backing of a powerful king, their situations were tenuous in the face of Welsh rebellion. By 1150, much of Dyfed had been regained by the Welsh sons of Gruffudd ap Rhys, and three years later, they had taken possession of Ceredigion as well. One of Gruffudd's sons, Owain ap Gruffudd (Owain Gwynedd), took several northern towns in Powys from the Earl of Chester, and ruled Gwynedd and northern Powys until his death in 1170.

When Henry II came to the throne, Madog ap Maredudd of Powys yielded to the English king as a means of gaining support in withstanding the ambitions of Gwynedd's king. Henry led his forces into Wales in support of the Marcher Lords, but the Welsh united under Owain Gwynedd and managed to regain their lost territories. In the face of Welsh determination, several Marcher Lords sought greener pastures in Ireland.

In 1172, Henry II appointed Rhys ap Gruffudd justice of south Wales, thereby establishing royal authority in Wales and giving Rhys superiority over the Welsh rulers and Marcher Lords. After Henry's death, Rhys attacked the Norman lordships of western Wales and brought them under his control. He also led his forces against the Normans along the eastern border, invading the lands of William de Braose, the most powerful of the Marcher Lords.

By the year 1200, eastern and southern Wales remained in the hands of the Normans. Northern and western Wales continued to be held by native kings.

SOCIETY

THERE WERE TWO main groups of people during this time: the free and the unfree. Society was organized in pyramid form. At the top was the highest ruler, the *brenin*. Beneath the brenin were the *bonheddwyr,* noblemen and landowners related to the king. Next were the *taeogion,* villeins with some rights to grazing and arable land. By and large, the *taeogion* were the serving class. Last were the unfree with no rights. The slaves, or *caethion,* guarded the livestock and tended crops. They generally did all the dirty work and could be bought and sold along with livestock.

The taeogion lived in compact settlements called *taeogdrefi.* They grew the crops necessary to supply the needs of the king and his retainers and worked under the direction of the *maer y biswail*, the mayor of the dunghill. The taeogion were also required to house the king's officials on their travels, to erect the king's buildings, to feed his hunting dogs, and to be the king's trailblazers. Every adult male *taeog* had the right to a portion of the land of his township and was bound to that land. He was not allowed to pursue any other calling, such as that of priest, poet, or smith.

While the taeogion lived in groups, the bonheddwyr lived scattered about. They were raisers of livestock and received lands through membership of a *cenedl,* a kindred group whose lands centered around the homestead of their ancestor. The bonheddwyr were required to give the king a portion of the fruits of their labor but were not required to perform physical labor for the king except to be a part of his war band.

The traditional Celtic system of gavelkind was practiced among the families. Unlike primogeniture, whereby an inheritance goes to the eldest male child, gavelkind divided the inheritance between all surviving children, thus providing for the welfare of the entire family. Since women were not allowed to own land, their portion of an inheritance was likely given in livestock.

After the abandonment of the Roman towns, no other towns were built for the next 500 years, and Welsh society was left completely rural. Some people had a winter home, the *hendref*, and a summer home, the *hafod*. Most cultivated crops and raised herds of livestock.

In early Wales, the bonds of kinship were extremely important, for it was a person's standing among kindred that determined social status. Marriage was considered a contract between a man and a woman rather than a religious sacrament that couldn't be broken, and though the man was considered the head of the household, the woman had her own rights within the law. Marriage between cousins was common, and legitimate and illegitimate children had the same rights as long as they were acknowledged by the father.

After the Norman Conquest, new elements were introduced into Welsh society. The feudal system was put in place in Norman-occupied lands, towns and villages were established close to Norman strongholds, trade was revitalized, large-scale agriculture was set in motion, and churches organized on diocesan lines were established.

When the Normans won control from the Welsh kings, they established their own system of law and their own courts and collected dues from the people for private use. The system of primogeniture, which passed inheritance to the eldest son, was also put in place. In the event there were no sons, the inheritance was divided equally among the daughters.

In each lordship, a castle was built to house the administrative offices of the lord, the court, and the jail. The earliest castles were comprised of an earthern motte (mound) upon which a bailey was constructed. Inside the bailey, wooden buildings were erected to house the lord, his retainers, and his administrative offices. Over 500 motte-and-bailey castles were erected in the early years of the Norman invasion, but by 1100, castles of stone were being built.

The Norman lords also held separate lands where they built manor houses and set serfs to work toiling in the fields. The lord's knights were granted estates in exchange for forty days of military service per year. And like the lord, each knight would build a smaller castle, establish his own court, set up his own manor, and collect dues from his tenants. Towns were established and there was a weekly market where, for a fee, people were allowed to sell or trade goods and produce. The town fair was held once or twice a year and drew traders from far away.

The remainder of the lordship, typically the more hilly areas, was held by native Welsh who continued to live in their traditional ways. They paid to the Norman lords the dues they would normally have paid to a Welsh king.

In the wake of Norman knights and those arriving to administer the governments of the Marcher Lords, a large number of English peasants arrived to work in the fields. Settlements increased in size and number, the people began to put down roots, and intermarriage with the Welsh began.

RELIGION

THROUGH THE DILIGENCE of the monks, the Welsh came to accept Christianity over their pagan Celtic religion. And, as they were isolated by Offa's Dyke, they were able to hang onto their new religion while the rest of Britain lost it under the onslaught of the pagan Germanic tribes.

The Celtic Church in Wales remained independent from Rome until late in the eighth century. At that time, it accepted the Roman system and recognized the papacy, but did not abandon its ancient customs and rites. It wasn't until after the Norman Conquest that the Church became subject to the system of dioceses and parishes and the rituals of the Latin Church.

Once the Normans had established themselves, they reorganized the Welsh Church to bring it into uniformity with the Church of Rome. It was made subject to Canon Law (which did not allow priests to marry), the wooden huts that served as churches were replaced with buildings of stone, Norman bishops were appointed, and religious houses were introduced from the Continent to lend their influence over Celtic practices. The cathedral of Saint David's was built in southwestern Wales in the twelfth century as a place of pilgrimage in honor of Saint David (Saint Dewi) the patron saint of Wales.

NAMING

THE WELSH CONTINUED to use their traditional names during this period of time. Though the Normans had successfully established themselves in Wales, they retained their traditional naming practices and did not feel the need to adopt Welsh names.

FEMALE NAMES

Aeron (battle)
Aeronwen (blessed battle)
Aeronwy (battle)
Angharad (free from shame)
Annwyl (beloved)
Aranrhod (round wheel)
Aregwydd (?)
Ariana (silver)
Arianrhod (silver wheel)
Arianwen (silver woman)
Blodeuwedd (flower face) **Blodwedd**
Blodwen (white flowers)
Branwen (white raven, blessed raven)
Buddug (victorious) **Budic**
Cainwen (fair, lovely; jewels, treasures + white, fair, blessed)
   Ceinwen
Ceridwen (blessed poetry) **Ceridwyn**
Creirdyddlydd (jewel of the sea)
Creirwy (jewel, a token)
Cristin (a Christian)
Delwen (pretty and blessed)
Dilwen (genuinely blessed)
Dwynwen (white wave)
Ealdgyth (old strife) An Old English name.
Eiddwen (desirous, fond + white, fair, blessed)
Elen (light, torch, bright)
Eleri (?)
Elin (nymph)
Enid (?, from the territory Bro Wened [in Brittany])
Eoghania (lamb; youth; well-born)

Esyllt (?, perhaps *ruler of the ice*; *beautiful, fair*)
Ffraid (strength) Welsh form of Bridget.
Flur (flower)
Gwen (white, fair, blessed)
Gwenach (white, fair, blessed)
Gwenfrewi (blessed peace)
Gwenllian (white, fair, blessed + linen or flood, flow)
Gwenyth (white, fair, blessed)
Gwladus (lame) Welsh form of Claudia.
Heledd (?) **Hyledd**
Isolde (ruler of the ice)
Luned (shape, form)
Mallt (powerful in battle) Welsh form of Maud.
Maredudd (lordly, kingly) **Meredudd**
Margaret (a pearl)
Marged (a pearl) Welsh form of Margaret.
Maud (powerful in battle)
Mawdwen (mannerly)
Medwenna (?)
Meinwen (slender and fair)
Meiriona (of Mars)
Meirionwen (of Mars + white, fair, blessed)
Mererid (a pearl) Welsh form of Margaret.
Morcant (lady of the sea, enduring seas)
Morgwen (sea lady)
Morwenna (?, perhaps *maiden*; *white seas, blessed seas*)
Myfanwy (?, perhaps *my fine one*; *child of the water*)
Myrddin (sea hill, fortress by the sea)
Nest (chaste, pure) Welsh form of Agnes.
Non (?, perhaps *queen*)

Olwen (white footprint, blessed footprint)
Rhiannon (?, perhaps *great queen*)
Rhianwen (?, second element is *white, fair, blessed*)

Rhonwen (blessed lance; fair-haired)
Sabrina (?)
Tegwen (lovely maiden)

MALE NAMES

Aed (fire)
Aeddon (fire)
Alun (?, perhaps *handsome* or *rock*)
Anarawd (?)
Andras (manly)
Art (a bear)
Arthur (?)
Arwystli (?, perhaps *best counsel*) **Arwystl**
Athrwys (?)
Aust (great, venerable) Welsh form of Augustine.
Avarddwy (?)
Awst (great, venerable) Welsh form of Augustine.
Benlli (?)
Blaidd (wolf; hero)
Bleddyn (wolf's cub; hero)
Brochwel (?)
Brychan (speckled, freckled)
Bryn (hill)
Brynmor (great hill)
Cadell (small battle)
Cadoc (war, battle, defense)
Cadwaladr (battle leader)
Cadwallon (battle arranger)
Cadwgan (glorious battle)
Caerwyn (white fortress, blessed fortress)
Caradoc (beloved) **Caradog**
Carannog (beloved)
Carvilius (friend of power)
Caswallon (?, perhaps *chief of hatred*)
Cattwg (war, battle, defense)
Ceredig (?)
Cethin (dark, swarthy)
Coel (?)
Cwrig (lord, master)
Cynan (high, exalted)
Cynddelw (high, exalted; head + statue)
Cyndeyrn (head chief)
Cyngen (king, chief)
Cynon (king, chief)
Cystenian (constant, steadfast) Welsh form of Constantinus.
Dafydd (beloved) Welsh form of David.
Dai (to shine)
Daniel (God is my judge)
David (beloved)
Deiniol (God is my judge) Welsh form of Daniel.
Dewi (beloved) Welsh form of David.
Dilwyn (genuinely blessed; blessed truth)

Dogvall (?)
Dunawd (giver) **Dynawd** Welsh form of Donatus.
Dyfrig (?)
Dylan (?, perhaps *sea*)
Edeyrn (?)
Edwin (wealthy friend)
Einion (anvil)
Einwys (anvil)
Eliffer (?)
Elised (?) **Eliseg**
Elstan (noble stone)
Emlyn (charming)
Emrys (immortal)
Emyr (ruler, king)
Enaid (soul, life)
Eniawn (upright)
Eoghan (lamb; youth; well-born)
Folant (healthy, strong) Welsh form of Valentinus.
Gareth (?, perhaps *civilized*)
Garmon (a German)
Geoffrey (a district; traveler; pledge + peace)
Geraint (?, perhaps *old*)
Gerallt (spear ruler) Welsh form of Gerald.
Giffri (?)
Gladus (lame) Welsh form of Claudius.
Glywys (?)
Gruffydd (reddish brown, rust-colored) **Gruffudd**
Gwalchmai (battle hawk)
Gwenwynwyn (?, perhaps *thrice fair*)
Gwethalyn (life)
Gwgon (?) **Gwgawn**
Gwiawn (sense)
Gwilym (resolute protector) Welsh form of William.
Gwrgant (?)
Gwriad (?)
Gwric (born on Sunday)
Gwril (lordly) Welsh form of Cyril.
Gwrtheyrn (excelling king) **Gwrtherin**
Gwydyr (wrath, vengeance)
Gwyn (white, fair, blessed) **Gwynn**
Gwyndeg (?, first part of the name is *white, fair, blessed*)
Gwynedd (white, fair, blessed)
Gwynllyw (white, fair, blessed)
Harmon (a German)
Hyfaidd (?)
Hywel (eminent, prominent) **Hywell**
Iago (supplanting, seizing by the heels)

Idwal (lord, master + wall)
Iestyn (lawful, right, just) Welsh form of Justin.
Ieuan (God is gracious) Welsh form of John.
Ifor (?)
Illtud (land of a multitude)
Iorwerth (handsome lord)
Iwrch (roe deer)
Lleu (bright, shining)
Llewelyn (bright one, shining one; lionlike)
Llwyd (gray)
Llywarch (bright horse, shining horse)
Mabon (son)
Madog (beneficent) **Madoc**
Mael (disciple)
Maenarch (?)
Manawydan (?)
Mandubrath (?, perhaps *man of treason*)
Maredudd (?, perhaps *lord*; *magnificent*)
Meilyr (chief ruler)
Meiriadwg (sea protector)
Meirion (of Mars; manly) Welsh form of Marianus.
Merddhin (sea hill)
Merfyn (marrow, brains; sea + eminent, prominent, high)
Meurig (a Moor, dark-skinned) Welsh form of Maurice.
Morgan (sea dweller)
Morven (man of the sea)
Morvren (sea raven)
Munghu (lovable) **Mungo**
Myrddin (sea hill, fortress by the sea)
Owain (lamb; warrior)
Padarn (?)

Pedair (?, perhaps *rock*)
Peredur (?, perhaps *companion of the chalice*)
Pewlin (small) Welsh form of Paulinus.
Pryderi (caring for, concern; trouble)
Pwyll (wary; forward)
Rhain (spear, lance)
Rhirid (?)
Rhiwallon (?)
Rhodri (king of the wheel)
Rhufawn (?)
Rhydderch (reddish brown, rust-colored)
Rhygyfarch (?)
Rhys (ardor)
Saithenyn (?)
Sawyl (his name is God) Welsh form of Samuel.
Seisyll (sixth) Welsh form of Sextilius.
Selyf (?)
Sioltiach (sower)
Talfryn (high hill)
Tallwch (torrent)
Tegan Euvron (golden beauty)
Teilo (?)
Tewdrig (God's gift)
Thomas (a twin)
Tomos (a twin) Welsh form of Thomas.
Trahaearn (ironlike, strong)
Tudur (ruler of the people, territorial king)
Tybiawn (?, perhaps *people's prince*)
Urien (?, perhaps *of privileged birth*)
Voeddog (victory)
Wynn (white, fair, blessed) **Wyn**
Ynyr (?, perhaps *honorable*)

SURNAMES

Surnames were not used by the Welsh during this period. People were primarily distinguished through bonds of kinship. In the naming tradition, these bonds were illustrated by the addition of a word expressing kinship and the father's name. The kinship words are *ap*, *ab* "son of," *merch* "daughter of," and *gwraig* "wife of." *Ap* and *ab* were used interchangeably. For example, Hywel, the son of Gruffudd, was Hywel ap Gruffudd. Arianwen, the daughter of Gruffudd, was Arianwen merch Gruffudd. In families where certain names were very common, a person could be distinguished by the addition of his or her father's name and grandfather's name: Gruffudd ap Gruffudd ap Hywel.

In addition to the patronymic, people were also distinguished by the town or kingdom they were from, as in Gruffudd Gwynedd. Those who were of great valor or stood out in a special way were often given an epithet much like that given to Hywell Dda (Hywell the Good). Though secondary names based on personal characteristics (not always flattering) were also used, the vast majority of secondary names were patronymics.

Bach (the small)
Bedar (the deaf)
Beisrudd (of the red cloak)
Bongam (little crooked legs)

Bras (the fat)
Brych (speckled, freckled)
Brychan (speckled, freckled)
Byr (the short)

Cadarn (the strong)
Cam (crooked)
Can (the shining one)
Chwyt (the awkward one)
Cledyfrud (of the red sword)
Cloff (the lame)
Coch (ruddy complexioned)
Cor (the dwarf)
Crach (the weakling; the little one)
Cuchwr (the frowner)
Cul (the slender one)
Dda (the good)
Ddrud (the bold)
Dw (the dark one)
Fychan (the small)
Gawn (the giant)
Gosgorduawr (of the great retinue)
Gryg (harsh) **Crug**
Gwan (the weakling)
Gwrhyt Uawr (of great manliness)
Gwynedd (white, fair, blessed)
Gyllelvawr (great knife)
Hael (generous)
Hagir (the deformed one)
Hen (old)

Hurth (the stupid one)
Hyr (the tall one)
Ieuangc (the younger)
Law-eurawc (golden hand)
Llas (the blue-eyed one)
Llawen (the merry)
Llwyd (the gray)
Llydan (the broad one)
Mawr (the great)
Melyn (yellow)
Moel (bald)
Moelwyn (white-haired)
Moelyn (bald headed)
Molwynog (the passionate) **Moelwynoc**
Off (the frail)
Penbras (fat head)
Penwyn (white-haired)
Pesrut (of the crimson cloak)
Powys (from Powys)
Suckanwr (the drunkard)
Symlen (the simple)
Syw (the smart)
Uchel (preeminent)
Ureichuras (thick arms)
Voel (the bald)

Chapter Three

THE MIDDLE AGES TO THE LOSS OF INDEPENDENCE
[1200–1283]

POLITICS

A T THE OPENING of the thirteenth century, Powys was divided between Madoc ap Gruffudd and Gwenwynwyn, and Deheubarth declined after the death of Rhys ap Gruffudd. So, it was thus from Gwynedd
that the Welsh leadership arose in the form of Llywelyn, the grandson of Owain Gwynedd. Llywelyn was
able to regain a considerable number of Welsh territories and divided the conquered land among the sons of
Rhys ap Gruffudd in 1216. Llywelyn was formally acknowledged as the overlord of independent Wales and
the independent kingdoms were now united. They would remain so until 1282.

In order to ensure the survival of independent Wales, Llywelyn put a new system of inheritance in place
among the ruling class. By exchanging the traditional system of gavelkind, the division of an inheritance
among all male heirs, for a system of single succession, he was able to eliminate the infighting that caused
so much dissention in the past. Llywelyn not only managed to unite the upper classes, he also was able to
bring together the lower classes and instill in them a sense of national and cultural pride. By the time of his
death in 1240, he was known as Llywelyn Fawr (Llywelyn the Great).

Llywelyn's successor was his son Dafydd, a man who failed to keep a firm grasp on the union in the face
of interference by Henry III. Though the English king demanded that the kingdom of Gwynedd pass to the
English crown should Dafydd fail to produce an heir, after his death in 1246, he was succeeded by Llywelyn
and Owain, the sons of his half-brother, Gruffudd. The English king wasted little time in attacking Gwynedd.
Repeated assaults left the people starving and the brothers were forced to surrender in 1247. Though the treaty
confirmed them as lords of Gwynedd Uwch Conwy, they had lost their power and the kingdom of Gwynedd.

Eight years later, a new deliverer arose in the person of Llywelyn ap Gruffudd. Llywelyn was just as
passionate about his country as was his grandfather, Llywelyn Fawr. He managed to reunite the various kings
and regain the lands lost in 1247. He also captured territories held by the English king. At a council of Welsh
kings in 1258, Llywelyn ap Gruffudd was proclaimed Prince of Wales.

Llywelyn and Henry III agreed to a truce that lasted until 1262; then they signed a treaty of peace in 1267.
Rather than consolidate his power, Llywelyn aggressively tried to wrestle additional lands away from the
Marcher Lords and the English king. Such a policy was to bring the whole of the English crown against him.

The first war of Welsh independence (1276–1277) ended in the Treaty of Aberconway, and Llywelyn was deprived of much of his power.

Discontent was widespread in the face of serious discrimination and flagrant English violations of the treaty. Dafydd ap Gruffudd, Llywelyn's brother, had sided with the English in the first war of independence in the hopes he'd be granted full sovereignty over his territories in return. When Edward didn't fulfill his promise to grant the lands, Dafydd was furious. In 1282, he joined with Llywelyn (who must have been very forgiving of his brother's disloyalty) and the second war for independence commenced.

The Welsh were determined to drive the English from their midst, and the English were just as determined to hold onto their possessions; the war continued with grave losses on both sides. In December 1282, the Welsh army, holding the line at the River Irfon in central Wales, were surprised by royal forces, and Llywelyn lost his life. So great was his influence and strength that Wales was never to recover from his loss. Llywelyn is now known as Llywelyn Ein Lyw Olas, Our Last Leader.

Dafydd did his best to assume leadership over Llywelyn's forces, but the resistance movement in southern and central Wales had all but collapsed. English forces moved north to capture Ceredigion and the northern forces moved south along the coast. Organized resistance gave way in the face of the advancing armies, and guerilla tactics had to be utilized to reduce the ranks of Edward's army. Dafydd held out for a time in a castle at Bere in southern Gwynedd. When the castle surrendered in April 1283, Dafydd fled to the mountains but was eventually captured by hostile Welsh, handed over to the English, and put to a terrible death at Shrewsbury.

SOCIETY

THE POPULATION OF Wales rose from an estimate of 160,000 at the beginning of the thirteenth century, to 300,000 at the beginning of the fourteenth century. Almost 90 percent of the people were rural dwellers, and the large increase in numbers put a tremendous strain on the land, forcing inhabitants to carve out their holdings on lands that were far from ideal.

As the population increased, the structure of Welsh society became more complex. In Gwynedd, the traditional unfree class of slaves disappeared; the *taeogion*, the lower working class, had grown smaller; the *bonheddwyr*, the freemen, constituted the majority of the population; and the upper class were fewer and far removed from the daily grind of the masses. Conditions were different in the holdings of the Marcher Lords, where the *taeogion* were still substantial in number and remained attached to the land.

The Welsh economy developed along with the increase in population. As the Welsh were unable to produce everything needed to sustain the population, imports and exports rose. More crops were raised, and more trades were practiced in the towns.

RELIGION

A GOOD DEAL of church building went on during the thirteenth century. Complex ornamentation was typical and required soft, carvable stone from English quarries. Numerous religious houses were established, including Franciscan and Dominican friaries. The Cistercians, in particular, were very sympathetic to Welsh issues.

NAMING

DURING THIS TIME period, Welsh children were given traditional Welsh names. However, the influence of the Marcher Lords and intermarriage between the Welsh and the Anglo-Normans can be seen in the few foreign names beginning to crop up. English names, such as Edmund (Edmwnd), Edward, and Agnes, and Anglo-French names, such as Alice, Cecilia, and Maud, were being bestowed upon the children of the mixed marriages. It should be remembered that this represented only a small portion of the population. The majority of names continued to be of Welsh origin.

FEMALE NAMES

Aeron (battle)
Aeronwen (battle + white, fair, blessed)
Aeronwy (battle)
Agnes (pure, chaste)
Alice (nobility)
Amabilia (lovable)
Amicia (amicable, friendly)
Angharad (undisgraced, free from shame)
Annwyl (beloved) **Anwyl**
Aranrhod (round wheel)
Ariana (silver)
Arianrhod (silver wheel)
Arianwen (silver + white, fair, blessed)
Betrys (bringer of happiness) Welsh form of Beatrice.
Blodeudd (flower face)
Blodwen (white flowers)
Branwen (white raven, blessed raven)
Cainwen (fair, lovely; jewels, treasures + white, fair, blessed)
Cecilia (blind, dim-sighted)
Ceridwen (blessed poetry, fair poet)
Creirdyddlydd (token of the sea, jewel of the sea)
Creirwy (a token, a jewel)
Delwen (pretty and blessed)
Dilwen (genuinely blessed)
Dilys (genuine, steadfast)
Dwynwen (white wave)
Eleri (?, perhaps *very bitter*)
Elin (nymph) **Elen**
Elinor (light, torch, bright)
Enid (?)
Esyllt (beautiful, fair) **Iseult, Isolde, Yseult, Ysolt**
Glenys (clean, pure, holy) **Glynis**
Gwen (white, fair, blessed)
Gwenda (white, fair, blessed + good)
Gwendolen (white, fair, blessed + ring, bow)
Gweneal (white angel, blessed angel)
Gwenfrewi (white, fair, blessed + reconciliation)
Gwenhwyfar (white, fair, blessed + smooth, soft)
Gwenllian (white, fair, blessed + linen; flow, flood)

Gwerful (circle, ring + modest, shy)
Gwladus (lame) Welsh feminine form of Claudius.
Gwyneth (white, fair, blessed)
Heledd (goodness + wound)
Helen (light, torch, bright)
Hyllaria (joy, cheerfulness)
Isabella (God is my oath)
Joan (God is gracious)
Lleulu (light)
Llewrwg (light)
Luned (shape, form)
Mallt (powerful in battle) Welsh form of Maud.
Margaret (a pearl)
Marged (a pearl) Welsh form of Margaret.
Mariota (sea of bitterness or sorrow)
Matilda (powerful in battle)
Maud (powerful in battle)
Meinwen (slender and fair)
Meiriona (of Mars; manly)
Meirionwen (of Mars; manly + white, fair, blessed)
Mererid (a pearl) Welsh form of Margaret.
Morcant (?, perhaps *lady of the sea* or *circle, completion*)
Morgwen (fair seas, lady of the sea)
Morwenna (?, perhaps *maiden* or *sea + white, fair, blessed*)
Myfanwy (?, perhaps, *my fine one, rare one* or *child of the water*)
Myrddin (sea hill, fortress by the sea)
Nest (pure, chaste) Welsh form of Agnes.
Olwen (footprint, track + white, fair, blessed)
Rhiannon (?, perhaps *great queen*)
Rhianwen (?, perhaps *fair lady*)
Rhonwen (fair-haired; blessed lance)
Roscrana (rose bush)
Sabrina (?)
Senana (?)
Tangwystl (?)
Tegwen (lovely maiden)
Tewdews (given by God)

MALE NAMES

Aedd (fire, fiery) **Aed**
Aeddon (fire, fiery)
Aedhan (little fiery one)
Alun (?, possibly *handsome; rock*) **Allan**
Andras (manly) Welsh form of Andrew.
Aneurin (noble, modest; man of excellence)
Art (a bear)
Arwystli (?, possibly *best counsel*)
Awst (great, venerable) Welsh form of August.
Awstin (great, venerable) Welsh form of Augustine.
Bathanat (son of the boar)
Bleddyn (wolf; hero)
Bran (raven)
Brithomar (the great Briton)
Brychan (speckled)
Bryn (hill)
Cadell (small battle)
Cadwaladr (leader of the battle)
Cadwallon (battle arranger)
Cadwgan (glorious battle) **Cadwgawn**
Caerwyn (white fortress; blessed fortress)
Caradog (beloved) **Caradoc**
Cattwg (war, battle, defense)
Cledwyn (hard, rough + white, fair, blessed)
Cwrig (lord, master) Welsh form of Kyriakos.
Cynan (high, exalted)
Cynddelw (?, possibly *high, exalted* or *head + image, statue*)
Cyndeyrn (head chief)
Cystenian (constant, steadfast) Welsh form of Constantine.
Dafydd (beloved) Welsh form of David.
David (beloved)
Deiniol (God is my judge) Welsh form of Daniel.
Dewi (beloved) Welsh form of David.
Dewydd (beloved) Welsh form of David.
Dilwyn (blessed truth)
Dylan (?, possibly *sea*)
Edmwnd (wealthy protection)
Ednyfed (?)
Edryd (?)
Edwin (wealthy friend)
Einion (anvil)
Emlyn (charming)
Emrys (immortal) Welsh form of Ambrose.
Emyr (ruler, king)
Gilbert (bright pledge, famous pledge)
Girioel (lordly) Welsh form of Cyril.
Gladus (lame) Welsh form of Claudius.
Goronwy (man)
Gruffudd (red, ruddy complexioned) **Gruffydd**
Gwallter (ruler of an army) Welsh form of Walter.
Gwenwynwyn (?, perhaps *thrice blessed, thrice fair*)
Gwilyn (resolute protector) Welsh form of William.
Gwyn (white, fair, blessed) **Gwynn**

Gwynedd (white, fair, blessed)
Gwythyr (victor)
Heilyn (a steward, a pourer of wine)
Henry (home ruler)
Howel (eminent)
Hu (?) **Hew**
Huw (heart, mind)
Hywel (eminent)
Idris (ardent, impulsive)
Ieuan (God is gracious)
Ifan (God is gracious) **Iefan**
Ifor (?)
Illtyd (land of the multitude)
Iorwerth (handsome lord)
Ivor (archer, bow warrior)
Jeuan (God is gracious) Welsh form of John.
Lleision (?)
Lles (light, bright, shining)
Lleu (light, bright, shining)
Lleurwg (light, bright, shining)
Llew (lion)
Llewelyn (?, perhaps *the bright or shining one; lionlike; light*)
Llewfer (light)
Llwyd (gray, gray-haired)
Llyr (sea)
Llywarch (shining horse)
Llywelyn (lightning) **Llewellyn, Llywelwyn**
Louarn (a fox)
Mabon (son)
Macsen (greatest)
Madog (beneficent) **Madawc, Madoc, Madwg**
Maelgwas (chief)
Maelgwn (chief)
Mandurrath (?, perhaps *man of black treason*)
Maredudd (great lord, large lord) **Meredudd**
Meilyr (chief ruler)
Meirion (of Mars; manly) Welsh form of Marianus.
Merfyn (marrow, brains; sea + eminent, prominent, hill, high)
Meurig (moorish, a Moor) **Meuriz**
Morcant (?, perhaps *lady of the sea* or *circle, completion*)
Myrddin (sea hill, sea fortress)
Neirin (noble, modest; man of excellence)
Owain (*lamb; youth; well-born, noble*) **Oein, Owayn, Ywain**
Pewlin (small) Welsh form of Paulinus.
Pryderi (caring for, concern; trouble)
Ralph (counsel wolf)
Rannulf (shield wolf)
Reginald (advice, counsel + ruler)
Restyn (restored)
Rhodri (king of the wheel)
Rhydderch (reddish brown, rust-colored)
Rhys (ardor)
Richard (stern king)

Robert (bright with fame)
Rodri (famous king)
Roger (spear fame, famous with the spear)
Rolant (famous land)
Ruadri (red-haired) **Ruaridh**
Sadwrn (of Saturn)
Sessylt (blind, dim-sighted) Welsh form of Cecil.
Simaith (peaceful)
Talfryn (high hill)
Taliesin (radiant brow)
Tewdur (gift of God) **Tewdwr** Welsh form of Theodore.

Thomas (a twin)
Tomos (a twin) Welsh form of Thomas.
Trahaearn (ironlike)
Trwst (proclaimer)
Tudur (ruler of the people)
Urien (?, perhaps *heavenly* or *privileged birth*)
Uthyr (terrible)
Walter (ruler of an army)
William (resolute protector)
Wynn (fair-haired, pale complexioned)
Yestin (just)
Ynyr (?, perhaps *honorable*)

SURNAMES

Surnames were not hereditary during this time period and follow the same forms as those given in the previous chapter; the majority of secondary names continued to be patronymics. One development was the blending of the word of kinship into the secondary name. Names such as Powell, from *ap Hywell,* and Bevin, from *ab Iefan,* are now being seen in official documents of the times. Additionally, when men and woman traveled to England in search of work, they were given secondary names indicating their country of origin. Domesday Book and other official registers are filled with the names Walche, Waleis, Walensis, Walseman, Walsshe, and Walys.

Bevin (son of Evan) **Beivin, Beyvin, Bovin**
Bren (the fat)
Caerleon (from Caerleon)
Cethin (dark, swarthy)
Fychan (small one)
Grey (the gray)
Griffin (red, ruddy; prince, lord)
Gwyddel (an Irishman) **Gwethel, Wydel, Wythel**
Hen (old)
de Lacy (from Lascius's estate)

Mortimer (dead sea)
Powell (son of Hywell)
Uthyr (terrible)
Walche (Welsh)
Waleis (Welsh)
Walensis (Welsh)
Walseman (Welsh)
Walsshe (Welsh)
Walys (Welsh)
de Warenne (from the warren)

Chapter Four

THE LATER MIDDLE AGES TO THE ACT OF UNION
[1283–1536]

POLITICS

THE YEARS FOLLOWING the loss of independence were very difficult on the Welsh. The lesser kings of Powys and Deheubarth were imprisoned, and all of Llywelyn's territories were confiscated by the English king, as was northern Powys. Royal hold on Wales extended across the entire north and west of the country.

Edward attempted to assert some authority over the Marcher Lords, but they were accustomed to the power and privileges their forefathers had earned by the sword, and they had no intention of giving up their positions.

Edward recalled soldiers from the royal castles to man his expedition to Gascony in 1294. The Welsh took advantage of the situation and staged a revolt. Many manor houses were destroyed, several castles were taken, and a great deal of damage was inflicted in English-held territories. Edward, forced to postpone his overseas venture, diverted 35,000 troops to Wales to put down the rebellion.

Edward's success led to another round of castle-building. The most important was Caernarfon Castle, purposefully built on a site treasured by the Welsh, for they believed their Roman hero, Macsen Wledig, had planned a fortress there and had come home there to die centuries before. Edward's first son was born at Caernarfon Castle in 1301 and was given the title Prince of Wales. Thus began the custom of bestowing that privileged rank upon the eldest male child of the rulers of England.

The years of Edward's reign passed fairly quietly. Though the higher government positions were reserved for the English, Welshmen were allowed to hold lower offices. English common law eventually superseded Welsh law, and the language of government and the courts was either Latin or Norman French.

The next and last attempt by the Welsh to throw off the English yoke wouldn't take place for over a hundred years. It began as a private land dispute between Owain Glyndŵr and Lord Grey of Ruthin in 1400, and escalated into a major rebellion against conditions under the Marcher Lords and English rule. Owain was a descendant of the royal families of all three Welsh princedoms, so he was able to command the loyalty and support of the Welsh people. A year later, the revolt had spread from northern to central and southeastern Wales, and by 1403, the entire country was involved.

Owain knew he needed men of power behind him, so he intrigued with disgruntled members of the English realm to ensure his success. Early in 1405, he joined with Edmund Mortimer (the true heir to the English throne) and Thomas Percy in an effort to bring down the king and divide Wales among the three of them.

The king got wind of the plan and took steps to prevent its success, but Owain allied himself with the French and managed to establish his authority over the whole of Wales.

The French army landed in the summer of 1405 to lend assistance, but on coming face to face with the English, it fell back without ever striking a blow. The English continued to press farther into Wales, and Owain's strong position was slowly eroded. By 1409, the English had a firm hold on the land; in 1413 that hold was complete.

In 1399, Henry of Bolingbroke, son of John of Gaunt and grandson of Edward III, took the crown from Richard II. Henry IV was succeeded by his son, Henry V (1413–1422) and his grandson, Henry VI (1422–1460). In 1431, Owain ap Maredudd, the grandson of Tudur ap Goronwy, secretly married Catherine, the widow of Henry V. Like many of the gentry of this time, Owain adopted a new surname. He chose Tudur, the name of his grandfather.

Owain's sons, Edmund and Jasper, were half-brothers of Henry VI. In 1452, Edmund became Earl of Richmond and married Margaret Beaufort, a great-granddaughter of John of Gaunt. Edmund was given the task of reestablishing royal power in western Wales. After his death in 1456, his brother Jasper, the Earl of Pembroke, continued the task.

England, meanwhile, had lost its French possessions and was in terrible financial shape. Richard, the duke of York, raised a private army from his estates in the Marches to take advantage of England's unsettled political situation. He was named successor to Henry VI, but was faced with losing that position when Henry's son was born in 1454. When Henry was sticken with a bout of insanity that same year, Richard was made protector of the realm. He was dismissed upon the king's recovery, and so took up arms to defend his right to the throne, thereby touching off a long and bitter fight for the crown known as the Wars of the Roses.

The Wars of the Roses were fought among the nobility and from the start, Wales was deeply involved. Not only were many battles between the Yorkists and Lancastrians fought on Welsh soil, Wales became the primary recruiting ground for the forces of both sides. The king was supported by Humphrey Stafford, Lord of Brecon, and by the families of the Beauforts, Mowbrays, and Talbots. He was also assisted by his half-brothers, Edmund and Jasper Tudor. Richard and his Yorkists were supported by the families of the Nevilles and the Warwicks and by William ap Thomas of Raglan, a man who had distinguished himself in the French wars.

The Wars of the Roses lasted for thirty years—years that saw the death of Richard of York; the capture and execution of Henry V; the ascension and death of Richard's son Edward IV; the usurpation and death of Edward's brother, Richard III; and the rise of the Tudors under the young Henry Tudor, the son of Edmund Tudor and Margaret Beaufort.

A sense of Welsh nationalism had been growing since the Glyndŵr Revolt, and as Henry Tudor was of Welsh stock and had the blood of Owain Glyndŵr flowing through his veins, it was behind him that the Welsh put their loyalties and support. In 1485, a Welsh army marched to London to confront royal forces. Richard III was killed on the battlefield and Henry Tudor ascended to the throne as Henry VII. He was the first Welsh-born, Welsh-speaking king of England.

Henry VII restored to the Welsh the privileges denied them under the English kings, and as the Welsh gentry saw fulfillment of their ambitions, those of the Marcher Lords were coming to an end. Under Henry VIII, the Marcher Lords were deprived of their special rights but were allowed to keep their lands as ordinary lordships. The land of Wales was divided into the English system of shires and hundreds, a new system of law and public administration of government in the English language was introduced, and in 1536, the Act of Union formally united the two countries into the State of England and Wales. The country was represented at the Westminster parliament by two people from each shire, one to represent the people and another to represent the towns.

SOCIETY

WELSH SOCIETY WAS drastically altered after the loss of independence. Traditional Welsh law, which formed the base of Welsh society, was discarded when English law became the law of the land. The development of a money economy was important, as well. Before the Norman Conquest of Wales, the *bonheddwyr* contributed to the support of their lords by means of produce or livestock. After the Conquest, all Welsh inhabitants were required to pay taxes in the form of money in ever-increasing amounts. The *bonheddwry* obligation rose by nearly 75 percent, and the *taeogion* obligation rose by an overwhelming 600 percent. Although the *taeogion* comprised just a small percentage of the population, they paid well over half the taxes. They suffered materially, as well, when their lands and livelihoods were destroyed during the wars for independence.

After Edward assumed control, the economy was stimulated by the formation of several different industries. Once the king embarked on a period of castle-building, people from all parts of England were brought in to do much of the work. In addition, a number of public works projects were initiated, and German miners were brought in to work in the mines of Tegeingl and Snowdonia.

A town was established alongside each castle to become a center of trade as well as a place to house the workers. A market was held each Saturday where the inhabitants could buy and sell their goods and produce. Annual fairs were held more often than in the past, perhaps four or five times a year instead of the original once or twice. Colonists from Ireland, Gascony, and Savoy were encouraged to settle in the towns, and many Welsh had their lands taken from them to be given to the newcomers who were granted free rent for ten years. Such preferential treatment made them the target of Welsh hatred and made them targets during Welsh uprisings.

Under the traditional Welsh system, when a person died without an heir, his lands were returned to the community as common land. Under the feudal system put in place by the English, all the land belonged to the king, and the people were regarded as feudal tenants. Therefore, if a person died without a direct heir, his land was forfeit to the king. Additionally, if a Welshman rose in revolt, his lands were confiscated and held until he surrendered and paid a fine. Such a policy greatly enlarged the lands of the English king at the expense of the Welsh communities.

The Plague hit Wales several times in the fourteenth century. The most deadly outbreaks occurred in the years 1349–1350, 1361, and 1369. Evidence concerning the plague is scarce, but it is believed to have been much worse in the Lowlands, were the majority of people lived. Perhaps as many as a quarter of the population lost their lives to the disease, and many towns were seriously impacted by the loss. Labor shortages and the decline in the economy that followed the plague led the Marcher Lords and the monastic houses to abandon direct farming of their lands. The lands were leased out instead, and ambitious members of the *bonheddwyr* were able to increase their holdings and their standard of living.

The Glyndŵr revolt also had a significant effect on Welsh society. Widespread destruction was part and parcel of the rebellion, and the country was soon impoverished. The Welsh bore the burden of Owain's failure as the English demanded compensation for years of lost rents and losses in revenue and imposed fines for the failure to hold the courts during the war. Stiff rents and the many fines imposed on the *taeogion* caused large numbers to flee to England in search of jobs to escape crushing poverty. Efforts to force the *taeogion* to return to their townships were largely unsuccessful, and many *taeogdrefi*, villein townships, were all but deserted.

The Welsh also lost many of their rights following the revolt. It was unlawful to hold public meetings; the Welsh were not allowed to hold any public office; they could not acquire land or bear arms; they were not allowed to reside in any border towns or any fortified towns; and they weren't allowed to take part in any trial involving an English person. Any Englishman who married a Welsh woman was subject to the same loss of rights.

A number of Welshmen got around the restrictions by denying their nationality and petitioning parliament to make them Englishmen. The first such petition was made in 1413 by Rhys ap Thomas, the sheriff of Carmarthenshire.

Welsh society was still sustained by an agrarian economy and would continue to be until the latter part of the eighteenth century. The old system of landholding associated with the *bonheddwyr* and the *taeogion* was replaced by the English feudal system, and that in turn disappeared with the emancipation of the *taeogion*.

In 1451, the first recorded *eisteddfod* (poetry, dance, and music competition) was held at Carmarthen. The bards spent a great deal of time reciting their verses and set down formal rules for the writing of poetry.

RELIGION

AFTER THE WARS for independence, the English king took over control of the Welsh Church. He instituted an investigation of the religious institutions in 1284 and found them to be quite different from those in England. Reforms followed, bringing the Welsh Church in line with the ways of the English Church.

Rather than bringing in English bishops and clergymen, the Church continued to be served by Welshmen who were sympathetic to their parishioners. This was something of a golden age in Welsh religious history. Many churches were built, and a fair amount of religious literature in the Welsh language was created.

The second half of the fourteenth century was quite different. The aftereffects of the plague and the pressure put upon the religious houses to help finance England's war with France put a great deal of strain on the religious community. Religious literature sharply declined, as did the number of men entering the priesthood. Though the monks continued to promote Welsh culture, they ceased to be the chroniclers of the history of the Welsh people.

This was a time when the English were busy putting down rebellions and otherwise subduing the Welsh, and they looked with disapproval at the efforts of clergy to keep the Welsh identity alive. Several attempts were made to uproot the houses that were the most aggressive in their fight for a sense of cultural continuance, with the Cistercians usually bearing the brunt of England's determination to put the Welsh in their place. By 1380, only seventy-one monks were left among the thirteen Cistercian monasteries.

Steps were taken to bring the Welsh Church into closer allegiance with Canterbury and to force church leaders into a more respectable lifestyle. To further that end, English bishops were appointed, and the wealthier benefices were also filled with Englishmen; promotion among the native clerics nearly ceased. No Welshman would again occupy the office of bishop until 1496.

The Welsh Church was vastly poorer than the Church in England, and it continued to suffer under the policy of using its income for the use of institutions and individuals in England. Even so, it had enough resources to devote to the building of new, highly decorated churches. Carved stone, frescoed walls, elaborate shrines, religious paraphernalia, and stained glass windows were quite popular and illustrated the trend in ornate religious buildings.

NAMING

THOUGH WELSH NAMES continued to be used, more English names were being bestowed throughout the population of Wales. Many of the older Welsh names had fallen by the wayside and were replaced with the names of biblical saints. John, William, Thomas, David, Madoc, Richard, and Roger were among the most common male names. Among the females, Alice, Margaret, Cecilia, Angharad, Matilda, and Gwladus were quite popular.

FEMALE NAMES

Aeron (battle)
Aeronwen (blessed battle)
Aeronwy (battle)
Agnes (chaste, pure, sacred)
Almedha (?, perhaps *shapely*)
Alys (noble one)
Angharad (free from shame) **Anarawd, Angharawd**
Anne (grace, full of grace, mercy) **Ann, Anna**
Annwyl (beloved) **Anwyl**
Aranrhod (round wheel)
Ariana (silver)
Arianrhod (silver wheel)
Arianwen (silver woman)
Bebhirn (sweet one)
Bettrys (bringer of joy) **Betrys** Welsh form of Beatrice.
Blodeuwedd (flower face) **Blodwedd**
Blodwen (white flowers)
Branwen (white raven, blessed raven)
Brocmael (?, perhaps *strong champion*)
Bronwen (white-breasted)
Buddug (victory) **Buddud**
Cain (fair, lovely; treasures, jewels) **Cein**
Cainwen (fair, lovely; jewels, treasures + white, fair, blessed) **Ceinwen**
Cathwg (pure) Welsh form of Catherine.
Catrin (pure) Welsh form of Catherine.
Ceridwen (blessed poetry, fair poet)
Creirdyddlydd (jewel of the sea)
Creirwy (jewel, token)
Delwen (pretty and blessed)
Dilwen (genuinely blessed)
Dwynwen (white wave)
Eiddwen (desirous, fond + white, fair, blessed)
Elen (light, torch, bright)
Eleri (?, perhaps *very bitter*)
Elidan (downy, youth) Welsh form of Julian.
Elin (nymph)
Elinor (light, torch, bright)
Elisa (God is my oath) **Eliza**
Elisabeth (God is my oath) **Elizabeth**
Ellen (light) **Ellin**
Eluned (shape, form) **Elined**

Enid (?, from the territory Bro Wened [in Brittany])
Eoghania (lamb; youth; well-born)
Ermin (soldier, warrior)
Essa (a nurse)
Esyllt (beautiful, fair)
Feithfailge (?, perhaps *honeysuckle ringlets*)
Ffraid (force, strength) Welsh form of Bridget.
Gelges (?, perhaps *white swan*)
Gladys (lame) Feminine form of Claudius.
Glenys (clean, pure, holy)
Gwen (white lady)
Gwenda (blessed and good)
Gwendolen (white browed)
Gweneal (white angel)
Gwenfrewi (blessed peace)
Gwenhwyfar (white wave)
Gwenllian (white, fair, blessed + flood, flow)
Gwenyth (white, fair, blessed)
Gwerful (completely shy)
Gwladus (lame) Feminine form of Claudius.
Heledd (goodness + wound) **Hyledd**
Helen (light, torch, bright)
Isolde (?, perhaps *ruler of the ice*)
Joan (God is gracious)
Kentigerna (head chief)
Lassair (flame)
Lassairfhina (flame, blush of the wine)
Ligach (pearly)
Lleulu (light)
Luanmaisi (?, perhaps *fair as the moon*)
Luned (shape, form)
Mair (sea of bitterness or sorrow) Welsh form of Mary.
Mallt (powerful in battle)
Margaret (a pearl)
Marged (a pearl) Welsh form of Margaret.
Matilda (powerful in battle)
Maud (powerful in battle)
Meinwen (slender and blessed, slender and fair)
Meiriona (of Mars)
Meirionwen (of Mars + white, fair, blessed)
Mererid (a pearl) Welsh form of Margaret.
Morgan (?, perhaps *lady of the sea; enduring seas*)

Morgwen (fair seas)
Morwenna (white seas, blessed seas)
Myfanwy (?, perhaps *my fine one; child of the water*)
Myrddin (sea hill, fortress by the sea)
Nest (pure, chaste)
Olwen (white footprint)

Rhiannon (?, perhaps *great queen*)
Rhianwen ?, second element is *white, fair, blessed*)
Rhonwen (fair-haired; blessed lance)
Sabrina (?)
Tegwen (lovely maiden)

MALE NAMES

Adam (man of the red earth)
Adda (?)
Aed (fire)
Aeddon (fire)
Andreas (manly)
Aneurin (man of excellence) **Aneirin**
Anthony (?, *priceless, of inestimable worth* is a folk definition)
Arnallt (powerful as an eagle) Welsh form of Arnold.
Arthur (?)
Arthwys (?)
Awrystli (best council)
Awst (venerable, great) Welsh form of Augustus.
Awstin (great, venerable) Welsh form of Augustine.
Baez (boar)
Balawn (strong)
Bartholomeus (son of Talmai)
Bened (blessed) Welsh form of Benedict.
Cadell (war, defense)
Cadffrawd (?, perhaps *brother's war*)
Cado (?, perhaps *battle*)
Cadvan (war horn)
Cadwallader (battle arranger) **Cadwaladyr**
Cadwallon (?, perhaps *war lord*)
Cadwgan (war)
Caradwg (beloved) **Caradoc, Caradog**
Carnhuanawc (?)
Cattwg (war, battle)
Cwrig (born on Sunday)
Cynan (high, exalted, chief)
Cynddelw (?, perhaps *high, exalted + image, statue*)
Cyndeyrn (head chief)
Cynvelin (?, possibly *lord of war*)
Cynwrig (high, exalted, chief)
Cystenian (constant, steadfast) **Cystennin** Welsh form of Constantine.
Dafydd (beloved) **Dawfydd** Welsh form of David.
David (beloved)
Deiniol (judged by God) Welsh form of Daniel.
Dewi (beloved) Welsh form of David.
Dyfan (taming) Welsh form of Damianos.
Dynawd (given) Welsh form of Donatus.
Edmund (wealthy protection)
Edmwnd (wealthy protection) **Edmwnt**
Ednyfed (?)

Edward (wealthy protector) **Edwart**
Einiawn (just) Welsh form of Justus.
Einion (anvil)
Elias (Jehovah is God)
Emrys (immortal) Welsh form of Ambrose.
Esaia (God is salvation) Welsh form of Isaiah.
Evan (God is gracious; youth; lamb; well-born)
Fychan (small)
Galath (?)
Garmon (a German)
George (earth worker, farmer)
Geraint (?, perhaps *old*)
Gerallt (spear rule) Welsh form of Gerald.
Gilbert (bright pledge, famous pledge)
Girioel (lordly) Welsh form of Cyril.
Gladus (lame) Welsh form of Claudius.
Goronwy (man)
Gruffin (red-haired, ruddy-complexioned)
Griffith (red-haired, ruddy-complexioned)
Gruffydd (red-haired, ruddy-complexioned) **Gruffudd**
Gwalchmai (battle hawk)
Gwallawg (hawk; stammerer)
Gwallter (ruler of an army) **Gwalter** Welsh form of Walter.
Gwen (white, fair, blessed)
Gwendoleu (white-browed)
Gwenwynwyn (?, possible *thrice fair, thrice blessed*)
Gwethalyn (life)
Gwiawn (sense)
Gwirydd (?)
Gwric (born on Sunday)
Gwril (lordly) Welsh form of Cyril.
Gwrtheyrn (excelling king)
Gwydyr (wrathful)
Gwyr (pure)
Henry (home ruler)
Hoel (lordly)
Hopcyn (bright with fame) Welsh form of Hopkin, a pet form of Robert.
Horas (?) Welsh form of Horace.
Hugh (heart, mind, spirit)
Hywel (eminent, prominent)
Hywgi (mind) Welsh form of Hugh.
Iago (supplanting, seizing by the heels) Welsh form of James.

Iau (of Jove, the Roman mythological supreme being) Welsh form of Jove.

Ieuan (God is gracious) **Iewan** Welsh form of John.

Ifor (?)

Ilar (cheerful) Welsh form of Hillary.

Iolo (youth, downy-bearded) Welsh form of Julius.

Iorwerth (handsome lord)

Ithel (?)

Iygnon (?)

Jasper (treasure master)

Jevan (lamb; youth; well-born)

John (God is gracious)

Jorwarth (handsome lord)

Kentigern (head chief)

Kynan (chief)

Lewys (famous in war) Welsh form of Lewis.

Lleision (?)

Llywelyn (?, possibly *bright one, shining one*; *lionlike*; *light*) **Lewelin, Lluellyn**

Madog (beneficent) **Madoc**

Maelgwn (chief)

Mathau (gift of God) Welsh form of Matthew.

Meiler (chief ruler) **Meilyr**

Meredith (lord, prince, ruler)

Meredudd (lord, prince, ruler)

Meurig (dark-skinned, a Moor) Welsh form of Maurice.

Mewrich (dark-skinned, a Moor) Welsh form of Maurice.

Myrddin (sea hill, fortress by the sea)

Nicolas (victory of the people)

Oswallt (divine power) Welsh form of Oswald.

Owain (lamb; youth; well-born)

Owen (lamb; youth; well-born)

Padrig (a patrician) Welsh form of Patrick.

Pawl (small) Welsh form of Paul.

Pedr (rock, stone) Welsh form of Peter.

Philip (lover of horses)

Phylip (lover of horses) Welsh form of Philip.

Reginald (advice, judgment, counsel + ruler)

Rheinallt (judgment ruler) Welsh form of Reginald.

Rhisiart (stern king) Welsh form of Richard.

Rhydderch (reddish brown, rust-colored)

Rhys (ardor) **Rys**

Robin (bright with fame) **Robyn**

Roger (famous with the spear)

Selyf (peaceful) Welsh form of Solomon.

Siâm (supplanting, seizing by the heels) Welsh form of James. **Siâms, Siams**

Siarl (full-grown, a man)

Sieffre (district; traveler; pledge + peace) Welsh form of Geoffrey.

Siôn (God is gracious) Welsh form of John.

Siôrs (earthworker, farmer) **Siors** Welsh form of George.

Thomas (a twin)

Timotheus (honoring God) Welsh form of Timothy.

Tomos (a twin)

Trystan (sadness, tumult) **Tristan**

Tudur (ruler of the people; territorial king)

Wiliam (resolute protector) Welsh form of William.

William (resolute protector)

SURNAMES

The majority of Welsh continued to use patronymics attached to their Christian names as a means of identification. Those who ventured forth in search of work were often designated with two or more descriptions. Examples taken from historical documents show that David ap Jeuan was also known as David Parker. Another man was listed as Maurice Flood or Lloid alias Walshman alias Apowell.

The upper classes, who were more heavily influenced by the English, began to adopt fixed and hereditary surnames in the middle of the fifteenth century. Surnames among the lower classes were not yet hereditary.

Bach (small, little)

Bevin (son of Iefan) **Bevan**

Binion (son of Einion)

Bren (kingly, royal)

Davies (son of David)

Dunn (brown)

Evans (son of Evan)

Ewin (God is gracious)

Fitzalan (son of Alan)

Fychan (small)

Gethin (the dusky one)

Glyn (a valley) **Glyne, Glynn, Glynne**

Goch (ruddy-complexioned)

Gowers (son of Gwyr)

de Grey (the gray)

Gryffin (red-haired, ruddy complexioned)

Gualter (ruler of an army)

Gwyn (white, fair, blessed) **Gwin, Gwynn, Gwynne**

Herbert (bright army, famous army)

Jankin (little John)

Jones (son of John)

de Lacy (from Lascius' estate)

Lawgoch (?)

Lewis (famous in war)

Llwyd (gray) **Lloyd**
Llywelyn (?, possibly *bright one*, *shining one*; *lionlike*; *light*)
  Lluellyn
Meredith (lord, prince, ruler)
Morice (dark-skinned, a Moor) **Morrice**
Mortimer (the dead sea)
Onion (anvil)
Owen (lamb; youth)
Powel (son of Hywel)
Price (son of Rhys)
Rhys (ardor) **Reece, Rhice, Rhyse, Rice, Ries**

Roberts (son of Robert)
Traherne (ironlike, strong)
Tudur (ruler of the people; territorial king)
Vaughan (little, small) **Vachan, Vahhan**
Voelyn (the bald one)
Wallis (a Welshman) **Waleys, Walleis**
Walsh (a Welshman)
de Warrene (dweller at or keeper of the game preserve)
Williams (son of William)
Wynn (white, fair, blessed) **Wyn, Wynne**

Chapter Five

THE ACT OF UNION AND THE RENAISSANCE TO THE INDUSTRIAL REVOLUTION
[1530–1770]

POLITICS

THE ACT OF 1536 uniting Wales to England was passed by a parliament comprised solely of English members. The main thrust of the legislation was to incorporate Wales into the country of England: "Wales is and ever hath been incorporated, annexed, united and subiecte to and unde the imperialle Crown of this Realm . . . ." In the eyes of the law, the Welsh were English, and they were granted representation in parliament.

The administration of Wales was left up to the Council of the Marches, a group accountable to the king's Privy Council. The Welsh lordships were divided into twelve shires that were divided into hundreds, then into parishes. Each shire had eight justices of the peace who acted as representatives of the crown. The justices met four times a year to deal with issues pertaining to administration of local government. They were chosen from the upper class; the common people had yet to have a hand in their country's political structure.

In 1642, civil war broke out in England between Royalists and the Parliamentarians. The majority of the Welsh people took their stand behind King Charles, but Pembroke chose to side with the Parliamentarians.

In 1644, Parliamentarians led by Oliver Cromwell invaded Wales and wreaked havoc on the grand castles and fortifications in their pursuit of the king. It was the last time fighting would take place on Welsh soil.

Even though Wales was formally united with England in 1536, the country did not lose its Welsh identity.

SOCIETY

THIS PERIOD OF time saw a great division between the wealthy landowners and the common people. The upper class participated in both local and state government, they were eligible to become members of parliament, and their sons were schooled in England or abroad. Though many could speak Welsh, English was the language of choice and the one spoken in their official lives. The commoners were far removed from the grand lifestyle of their wealthy landlords. They toiled on the land, spoke little or no English, and kept their children at home. Though the majority of the people spoke Welsh, few were literate in the language. The first Welsh book was published in 1546 by John Prys. It contained the Lord's Prayer, the Credo, and the Ten Commandments.

After the Reformation, grammar schools were established, which primarily taught Greek and Latin to those preparing for higher education. In the early 1650s, more than seventy free schools were established in the towns and villages of Wales. Although some parts of Wales were supported by industry, the country overall was still supported by an agrarian economy.

RELIGION

HENRY VIII'S BREAK with Rome caused the most important change in Welsh religion in hundreds of years. His break severed ties with the Catholic Church and caused the formation of a new church, which came under his direct authority. The Church of Wales now became part of the state Church known as the Anglican Church or the Church of England. In the latter part of the 1530s, all but three of the twenty-seven Welsh monasteries were disbanded and their lands either sold or given away.

Such actions were not welcomed by the conservative Welsh who had no history of animosity with the Catholic Church. The monks had been their neighbors and a part of Welsh society for a thousand years. Having their monasteries ruthlessly pillaged and vandalized, and in many cases utterly destroyed, must have been traumatic.

The Reformation and the ensuing Catholic Restoration were just as vicious in Wales as in England. Those who sought to turn back the clock and reestablish their traditional Catholic religion during the Reformation were in just as much danger of burning at the stake as the Protestants were during the Restoration. People wouldn't be safe from suffering such a dreadful fate until the end of the seventeenth century.

The first printed book, made in 1546, contained the Lord's Prayer, the Credo, and the Ten Commandments. The English Prayer Book was introduced in 1549, but it wasn't until 1551 that a Welsh version became available. A more Protestant version of the Prayer Book was printed two years later, and Parliament instructed that a Welsh version of the New Testament and the Prayer Book was to be available in every parish church by 1567. A complete Bible in the Welsh language wasn't finished until 1588.

When Mary ascended to the throne, she was determined to bring about a renewal of the Catholic religion. She sent a Welshman to Rome to offer the submission of her kingdom to the Pope, and it was a Welshman who became one of her closest and most zealous bishops. When Elizabeth came to the throne, the campaign to formally reestablish the Catholic religion in Wales came to an end. The Act of Uniformity set up a single Church system and a policy of mandatory attendance.

Many Welsh disagreed with Elizabeth's Anglican Church, and Wales became a home for Nonconformism. Early in the seventeenth century, separate churches were established by clergy ousted from the Anglican Church for not strictly conforming. The first Baptist church was established in 1649, and Puritanism and Quakerism were also welcomed.

During the Restoration (1660), an Act of Uniformity was again enforced. Every minister who was not an ordained Episcopalian was ordered to submit to ordination in the state Church, to state his belief in the Common Prayer, and to accept the constitution of the Church. Two thousand clergymen refused, and penal laws were enforced against both Catholics and Nonconformists. The years between 1660 and 1688 saw a great amount of persecution of the Nonconformists and Catholics, with the Quakers suffering the greatest of all. Many fled to the American colonies, but many of the wealthy and ambitious returned to the safety of the Anglican Church.

The Toleration Act of 1689 paved the way for greater freedom to worship, but neither the state Church nor the Nonconformist Churches had managed to capture the hearts and souls of the Welsh as the early Church had. It was the Methodist Revival of the eighteenth century that had the greatest affect on the Welsh. Under the direction of Griffith Jones, a system of schools was set up, and hundreds of free schools were established. Welsh Bibles and other religious books printed in the Welsh language were distributed throughout the country to be used as texts in teaching both children and adults to read and write and to provide for their religious education. Methodism started as a general evangelical movement within the state Church and its proponents didn't break away to form a separate church until the nineteenth century.

More Nonconformist groups organized, and the chapels became primary centers of church services and Welsh social life. It was there that most of the Welsh learned to read and write, and it was there that the *eisteddfodau* were held.

NAMING

THE WELSH PEOPLE were to pay dearly for rebelling against the English. The Welsh language was seen as the language of rebellion and was strongly suppressed. And, as the Welsh language fell by the wayside, so did Welsh names. Those that were popular were often used in an Anglicized form, such as Lloyd instead of Llwyd and Gladys instead of Gwladus.

For nearly all of this time period, the majority of names bestowed were those common to England. It wasn't until the Welsh Renaissance of the eighteenth century stimulated an interest in the history of Wales and promoted a renewed sense of cultural pride that the native names began to come back into style.

Religion also played a part in the bestowal of names. Once the Bible was translated into Welsh, a new source of names opened up. Nonconformists were the group most likely to bestow these new names upon their children.

FEMALE NAMES

Abigail (father of exaltation)
Agnes (pure, chaste)
Alice (noble one)
Anchoret (undisgraced, free from shame)
Anne (grace, mercy) **Ann, Anna**
Annwyl (beloved)

Antonia (?, *priceless, of inestimable worth* is a folk definition)
Arabella (?, perhaps *eagle; hearth*)
Aranrhod (round wheel)
Ariana (silver)
Arianrhod (silver wheel)
Arianwen (silver woman)

Beatrice (she who brings happiness)
Berenice (bringer of victory)
Beth (God is my oath)
Bethan (God is my oath)
Betrys (she who brings happiness) Welsh form of Beatrice.
Blanch (white) **Blanche**
Blodwen (white flowers)
Branwen (white raven, blessed raven)
Bridget (strength)
Bronwen (white breast)
Cassandra (?)
Catherine (pure, unsullied)
Cattwg (pure, unsullied) Welsh form of Catherine.
Cecilia (blind, dim-sighted) **Cecily**
Ceridwen (blessed poet, fair poet)
Charity (charity, kindness)
Christabel (?, perhaps *beautiful Christ*)
Christiana (a Christian, a follower of Christ)
Christina (a Christian, a follower of Christ)
Clarinda (bright, clear, shining)
Comfort (comfort, care)
Constancy (constant, steadfast)
Cornelia (a horn, horn of plenty)
Damaris (a calf)
Deborah (a bee)
Delwen (pretty and blessed)
Delyth (pretty, neat)
Diana (divine)
Dinah (judged)
Dorcas (a gazelle)
Dorothea (gift of God)
Drusilla (?)
Eiddwen (desirous, fond + white, fair, blessed)
Elen (light, torch, bright) **Ellen**
Elin (nymph)
Elinor (light, torch, bright) **Eleanor**
Elisa (God is my oath) **Eliza**
Elisabeth (God is my oath) **Elizabeth**
Eluned (shapely)
Emma (whole, entire)
Enid (?, from the territory Bro Wened [in Brittany])
Eoghania (lamb; youth; well-born)
Esther (myrtle; a star)
Eulalia (well-spoken)
Eunice (good victory)
Euphemia (well-spoken)
Faith (faith, complete trust)
Felicia (lucky)
Felicity (happiness)
Ffraid (strength)
Frances (a Frank) **Francis**
Gaenor (fair lady)

Gertrude (spear strength)
Glenda (clean, pure, holy + good)
Glenys (clean, pure, holy)
Grace (grace, mercy)
Gwen (white, fair, blessed)
Gwendolen (white ring) **Gwendolin, Gwendolyn**
Gweneal (white angel, blessed angel)
Gwenhwyvar (white wave) **Guenevere**
Gwenyth (white, fair, blessed)
Gwladys (lame) Feminine form of Claudius.
Hannah (grace, full of grace, mercy)
Hope (hope, desire)
Jane (God is gracious)
Janet (God is gracious; little Jane)
Jemimah (dove)
Joan (God is gracious)
Joanna (God is gracious)
Joy (joy, delight)
Judith (he will be praised)
Leah (gazelle; weary)
Lleulu (light)
Lucia (light)
Luned (shapely)
Magdalen (from Magdala) **Magdalene**
Mair (sea of bitterness or sorrow) **Meir** *Welsh form of Mary.*
Mallt (powerful in battle) Welsh form of Maud.
Margaret (a pearl)
Marged (a pearl) Welsh form of Margaret.
Mari (sea of bitterness or sorrow) Welsh form of Mary.
Martha (lady, mistress)
Mary (sea of bitterness or sorrow)
Maud (powerful in battle)
Megan (a pearl)
Meinwen (slender and fair)
Mererid (a pearl) Welsh form of Margaret.
Morgan (?, perhaps *lady of the sea; enduring seas*)
Nest (pure, chaste) Welsh form of Agnes.
Olwen (white footprint)
Priscilla (ancient, old)
Rachel (ewe)
Rebekah (noose)
Rhonwen (fair-haired; blessed lance)
Ruth (companion, friend)
Sarah (princess)
Shan (God is gracious) Welsh form of Jane.
Siân (God is gracious) Welsh form of Jane.
Sioned (God is gracious; little Jane) Welsh form of Janet.
Susannah (lily, a rose)
Tabitha (gazelle)
Tegwen (lovely maiden)
Winifred (blessed peace)
Zipporah (a little bird)

MALE NAMES

Aaron (the exalted one)
Abraham (father of a multitude)
Adam (son of the red earth)
Adda (son of the red earth) Welsh form of Adam.
Aeddon (fire)
Alexander (defender of mankind)
Alun (?, perhaps *handsome* or *rock*)
Alwyn (friend of the elves)
Andras (manly)
Andrew (manly)
Aneirin (?, perhaps *noble, modest*)
Anthony (?)
Art (a bear)
Arthur (?)
Austin (great, venerable)
Awst (great, venerable) Welsh form of Austin.
Awstin (great, venerable) Welsh form of Austin.
Berwyn (fair-haired, white-headed)
Bran (raven)
Brychan (speckled, freckled)
Bryn (hill)
Brynmor (great hill)
Cadell (small battle)
Cadogan (battle glory)
Cadwaladr (battle leader) **Cadwalader**
Cadwallon (battle arranger)
Cadwgan (glorious battle) **Cadwgawn**
Caerwyn (white fortress)
Charles (full-grown, a man)
Cyrus (a lord)
Dafydd (beloved) Welsh form of David.
Daniel (judged by God)
David (beloved)
Deiniol (judged by God) Welsh form of Daniel.
Edmund (wealthy protector)
Edmwnd (wealthy protector) Welsh form of Edward.
Edward (wealthy guardian)
Elis (Jehovah is God; God is salvation) **Ellis**
Evan (God is gracious)
Gareth (?, perhaps *civilized*)
Gavin (battle hawk)
Geoffrey (district; traveler; pledge + peace)
George (earth worker, farmer)
Geraint (?, perhaps *old*)
Gerallt (spear ruler) Welsh form of Gerald.
Gladys (lame) Welsh form of Claudius.
Glanmor (large shore)
Goronwy (man)
Gregory (vigilant, watchful)
Griffin (reddish brown, rust-colored)
Griffith (reddish brown, rust-colored)
Grigor (vigilant, watchful) Welsh form of Gregory.

Gruffydd (reddish brown, rust-colored) **Griffith, Gruffith, Gryffith**
Gwallter (ruler of an army) **Gwalter**
Gwatcyn (ruler of an army) Welsh form of Watkin.
Gwilym (resolute protector) Welsh form of William.
Gwyn (white, fair, blessed)
Henry (home ruler)
Hilary (cheerful)
Howell (eminent, prominent)
Hugh (heart, mind, soul)
Humphrey (warrior of peace)
Huw (heart, mind) Welsh form of Hugh.
Hywel (preeminent) **Howell**
Iefan (God is gracious) Welsh form of John.
Iestyn (lawful, right, just) Welsh form of Justin.
Iolo (youth, downy)
Isaac (laughter)
Ithel (bountiful, liberal)
Jacob (supplanting, seizing by the heels)
James (supplanting, seizing by the heels)
John (God is gracious)
Joseph (he shall add)
Leoline (lionlike)
Levi (joining)
Lewis (famous in war)
Llew (lion)
Llewelyn (?, perhaps *bright one, shining one; lionlike*)
Lloyd (gray)
Matthew (gift of God)
Maurice (dark, swarthy, a Moor)
Mervyn (sea hill, eminent marrow) **Mervin**
Meurig (dark, swarthy, a Moor) Welsh form of Maurice.
Michael (Who is like God?)
Morgan (sea + circle, completion; white, bright)
Morris (dark-skinned, a Moor) **Morus, Morys**
Nathan (gift)
Nathanael (gift of God)
Owen (lamb; youth; well-born)
Paul (small)
Peter (a rock, stone)
Philip (lover of horses)
Rees (ardor)
Reynold (ruler of judgment)
Rhosier (famous spear) Welsh form of Roger.
Rhys (ardor)
Richard (brave ruler)
Robert (bright with fame)
Roger (famous spear)
Roland (famous land) **Rolant, Rowland**
Samuel (name of God)
Simwnt (heard) Welsh form of Simon.
Siôn (God is gracious) Welsh form of John.
Steffan (a crown, a garland) Welsh form of Stephen.

Stephen (a crown, a garland)
Stuart (a steward, a keeper of the animal enclosure)
Theodore (God's gift)
Theophilus (friend of God)
Thomas (a twin)
Timothy (honoring God)
Tomos (a twin) Welsh form of Thomas.
Trahearn (ironlike) **Trahaearn, Trahern**

Tristan (saddness, tumult) **Tristram**
Vavasor (?)
Victor (victor, conqueror)
Walter (ruler of an army)
William (resolute protector) **Wiliam**
Wyn (white, fair, blessed) **Wynn**
Zachariah (God remembers) **Zacharias, Zechariah**

SURNAMES

Surnames were not completely hereditary until after the sixteenth century, though they were becoming hereditary among the upper classes at an earlier date. While there are several names listed below, many of these were used as additional identifiers; the patronymic remained the primary surname. Anglicized forms of Welsh names were also more common. Of the surnames that were hereditary, the most common were Davies, Evans, Howell and Powell, Hughes, Jones, Price, Rice, Roberts, and Williams.

As surnames became hereditary, the *ab* and *ap* prefixes began to be absorbed into the names. For instance, ap Howell became Powell, ap Rice became Price, and ab Evan became Bevan.

Adams (son of Adam *man of the red earth*)
Baker (the baker)
Bevan (son of Evan *God is gracious*)
Bird (a bird) **Byrd**
Bowen (son of Owain *lamb; youth; well-born*)
Brown (the brown, brown-haired)
Davies (son of David *beloved*)
Evans (son of Evan *God is gracious*)
Fychan (small)
Grey (the gray)
Griffiths (son of Griffith *reddish brown, rust-colored*)
Gruffydd (reddish brown, rust-colored)
Gwynne (white, fair, blessed)
Harris (son of Harry *home ruler*)
Harrison (son of Harry *home ruler*)
Herbert (bright army, famous army)
Hill (dweller near the hill)
Howell (preeminent)
Hughes (son of Hugh *heart, mind, soul*)
Jones (son of John *God is gracious*)
Kyffin (just, righteous)
Laurence (from Laurentum) **Lawrence**
Lee (the mute one)
Lewis (famous in war)
Lloyd (gray)
Mansel (a farmer)
Meredith (lord, prince, ruler)

Meurig (dark-skinned, a Moor)
Moore (dark-skinned, a Moor)
Morgan (sea + circle, completion; bright, white)
Morganwy (sea + circle, completion; bright, white)
Morris (dark-skinned, a Moor)
Owen (lamb; youth; well-born)
Parker (gamekeeper, keeper of the park)
Phillips (lover of horses) **Philips**
Powell (son of Hywel *eminent, prominent*) **Powel**
Price (son of Rhys *ardor*)
Pugh (son of Hugh *heart, mind, soul*)
Rice (ardor)
Roberts (son of Robert *bright with fame*)
Robertson (son of Robert *bright with fame*)
Robinson (son of Robin *bright with fame*)
Shaw (dweller in or near the woods)
Smith (a smith)
Stradling (bowlegged)
Symonds (son of Symond *heard*)
Thomas (a twin)
Thompson (son of Thomas *a twin*)
Tudur (ruler of the people; territorial king)
Vaughan (small)
Warenne (dweller at or keeper of the game preserve)
Williams (son of William *resolute protector*) **Wiliams**
Wilson (son of Will *resolute protector*)
Wynne (white, fair, blessed) **Wynn**

Chapter Six

THE INDUSTRIAL REVOLUTION TO THE PRESENT
[1770–PRESENT]

POLITICS

UNTIL NOW, POLITICS had been in the hands of the few remaining families of the gentry class. As the Industrial Revolution took the country by storm, there was a marked increase in the numbers of commoners wanting to know why they were not allowed to elect their leaders. Dreadful working conditions in the heavy industries became a pivotal issue that led to working-class solidarity and a demand for social and political reform. The liberal party and the socialist labor party were both formed and were instrumental in bringing the issues of the working class to the fore.

Welsh nationalism continued to grow. In 1925, the movement Plaid Cymru was established to promote a sense of Welsh identity and to advocate the use of the Welsh language. It also works to see that Wales is treated as an equal in its partnership with England. Its first MP was sent to London in 1966.

Wales is governed by a secretary of state for Wales in London. A Welsh office for official business exists in Cardiff, and the Welsh people are now more fairly represented in parliament then at any other time since annexation. The Welsh people enthusiastically embrace politics and they traditionally have the highest voter turnout of anyplace in Britain.

SOCIETY

THE INDUSTRIAL REVOLUTION began with the establishment of cotton mills, but it was the development of the steam engine and its use in the heavy industries that had the greatest effect on Welsh society and its economy. The demand for metal went up and large numbers of mines and metalworks were established. Zinc, copper, silver, lead ore, iron ore, and coal were all heavily mined. Wales was soon producing half the copper used worldwide; in the early 1800s, the town of Merthyr Tydfil in Gwent became the largest producer of iron in the world.

Between the years 1770 and 1851, the population of Wales doubled from half a million to over a million people. Such a drastic increase in such a short amount of time had major consequences. With less land available, people gravitated to the towns and sought work in the heavy industries. Only about a third of the population continued to live in the country.

The availability of work and what seemed to be adequate wages to those who had been starving in the countryside hid the dreadful reality of working in the pits and the ironworks. The mines were equal opportunity employers of men, women, and children, and they were extremely dangerous places to work. Respiratory diseases and carcinomas were rampant, and the youngsters who toiled in the pits or were used in place of ponies grew up stunted and had major deformities from pulling such heavy loads of coal and ore to the surface. The Factory Act of 1819 was aimed at reforming working conditions, but it fell short of expectations. After a bitter strike for improved working conditions, the miners organized themselves and formed the South Wales Miners Federation in 1898.

The economy continued to thrive, especially during the years of World War I (1914–1918). With the economic situation in hand, and as people became more secure in their livelihoods, the marriage age went down and the birth rate went up. The prosperous years were not to last, however. After World War I, the Great Depression set in and devastated the Welsh economy. By 1932, 20 percent of the people were unemployed. World War II provided some relief as large amounts of munitions and supplies were needed for the war effort, but that relief was temporary. The Welsh economy continues to be very depressed and widespread unemployment remains a significant concern.

In the late 1700s, renewed interest in the Welsh experience led to a marked increase in the number of periodicals available in Welsh and elevated the status of the language among the upper classes. Welsh began to become the language of a number of cultural activities. Poets, no longer among the cultural elite, began to rise up from all classes of people and all walks of life. The most famous now is Dylan Thomas (1914–1953).

Welsh choirs are celebrated, and some of the best have come from the mines. During the Great Depression, groups of men from the mines went to London and sang in the streets to bring an awareness to their dire situation. Many of Wales' popular brass bands also originated in the mines, and they have become a vital feature in the National Eisteddfod competition.

A formal system of education was slow to develop in Wales. In the late seventeenth and eighteenth centuries, some schools were established by the Church, and in 1833, parliament authorized a grant to assist education. But it wasn't until the Reform Act of 1867 that education was recognized as a state obligation. The Education Act of 1870 established a system of elementary education, and the Welsh Intermediate Education Act of 1889 established the system of public secondary education. Three colleges were founded in the late nineteenth century: Aberystwyth in 1872, Cardiff in 1883, and Bangor in 1884. They were later incorporated into the University of Wales in 1893.

RELIGION

IN 1770, THE majority of the Welsh were members of the Anglican Church. It was increasingly regarded as the Church of the rich landowners, judges, and lawyers. The Methodists broke away from the Church of England early in the 1800s and by the 1850s, over 80 percent had abandoned the parish church in favor of Nonconformist sects.

The number of churchgoing people are declining. Today, only 20 percent of the adult population are members of a Christian church. In spite of the Methodists' impact on society, more people belong to the Catholic, Anglican, and Presbyterian churches than to the Methodist Church.

NAMING

IN THE NINETEENTH century, biblical names were very popular among the Welsh. While many are still in use, modern naming practices reflect both a revival of traditional names and an interest in creating new coinages based on vocabulary words. Nonetheless, English names continue to be the most common found in Wales today.

FEMALE NAMES

Aeron (battle)
Aeronwen (blessed battle)
Almedha (shapely)
Angharad (undisgraced, free from shame)
Ann (gracious, full of grace, mercy) **Anna, Anne**
Annwyl (beloved)
Aranrhod (round wheel)
Ariana (silver)
Arianrhod (silver wheel)
Arianwen (silver woman)
Belle (beautiful)
Beth (God is my oath)
Bethan (God is my oath)
Blodwen (white flowers)
Branwen (white raven, blessed raven)
Bridget (strength)
Cainwen (fair, lovely; jewels, treasures + white, fair, blessed)
Carys (love)
Catherine (pure, unsullied) **Katherine; Cath, Kate, Kath, Katie**
Catrin (pure, unsullied) Welsh form of Catherine.
Ceridwen (blessed poet, fair poet)
Charlene (full-grown, a woman)
Delwen (pretty and blessed)
Delyth (pretty, neat)
Diana (divine)
Dilwen (genuinely blessed)
Dilys (genuine, steadfast, true)
Dwynwen (white wave)
Eiddwen (desirous, fond + white, fair, blessed)
Eira (snow)
Eirlys (snowdrop)
Eirwen (white snow, purity)
Elain (fawn)
Elaine (light, torch, bright)
Eleanor (light, torch, bright)
Elen (light, torch, bright) **Ellen**
Eleri (?, perhaps *very bitter*)
Elin (nymph)

Elisa (God is my oath) **Eliza**
Elisabeth (God is my oath) **Elizabeth**
Eluned (shapely)
Enfys (rainbow)
Enid (?, from the territory Bro Wened [in Brittany])
Esyllt (beautiful, fair)
Gaenor (fair lady)
Glenda (pure and good)
Glenys (clean, pure, holy) **Glenis, Glenys**
Grace (grace, mercy)
Guinevere (fair lady)
Gwen (white, fair, blessed)
Gwenda (blessed and good)
Gwendolen (eternally blessed)
Gweneal (blessed angel)
Gwenllian (white, fair, blessed + linen; flood, flow)
Gwenyth (white, fair, blessed)
Heledd (?) **Hyledd**
Helen (light, torch, bright)
Heulwen (sunshine)
Isolde (?, perhaps *ruler of the ice; beautiful, fair*)
Jane (God is gracious)
Janet (God is gracious; little Jane)
Janey (God is gracious; little Jane)
Joanna (God is gracious)
Kendall (dweller in the valley of the River Kent)
Leisa (God is my oath)
Lisa (God is my oath)
Lisbeth (God is my oath)
Luned (shapely)
Mabel (lovable)
Mabli (lovable)
Mair (sea of bitterness or sorrow)
Malvina (?)
Mared (a pearl)
Marged (a pearl)
Mari (sea of bitterness or sorrow)
Martha (lady, mistress)
Megan (a pearl) **Meaghan, Meghan**

Meinwen (slender and fair)
Meiriona (of Mars)
Meirionwen (of Mars + white, fair, blessed)
Meredith (lord, chief)
Morgan (?, possibly *lady of the sea*; *enduring seas*)
Morgwen (fair seas; lady of the sea)
Morna (beloved)
Morwenna (white seas, blessed seas)
Nerys (lord)
Nest (chaste, pure)
Olwen (white footprints)
Owena (lamb; youth; well-born)
Rhiannon (?, perhaps *great queen*)
Rhianwen (?, second element is *white, fair, blessed*)

Rhonda (good lance)
Rhonwen (fair-haired; blessed lance)
Rhosyn (a rose)
Sabrina (?)
Shan (God is gracious)
Shanee (God is gracious)
Siân (God is gracious) Welsh form of Jane.
Siani (God is gracious) Welsh form of Janey.
Siasmin (jasmine) Welsh form of Jasmine.
Sioned (God is gracious) Welsh form of Janet.
Tegwen (lovely maiden)
Teleri (your Eleri) Teleri was a maiden in King Arthur's court.
Tirion (gentle, kind)
Wendy (white-browed)
Winifred (blessed peace)

MALE NAMES

Adam (man of the red earth)
Aeddon (fire)
Alun (?, perhaps *handsome; rock*)
Alwyn (friend of the elves)
Andrew (manly)
Aneirin (?, possibly *noble, modest*)
Art (a bear)
Arthur (?)
Austin (great, venerable)
Awst (great, venerable)
Awstin (great, venerable)
Berwyn (fair-haired, white-headed)
Bleddyn (wolf cub)
Bran (raven)
Brychan (speckled, freckled)
Bryn (hill)
Brynmor (great hill)
Cadell (small battle)
Cadwgan (glorious battle)
Caerwyn (white fortress, blessed fortress)
Caradoc (beloved) **Caradog**
Carey (black, dark)
Charles (full-grown, a man)
Cledwyn (hard, rough + white, fair, blessed)
Cynan (high, exalted, chief)
Cyril (lordly)
Dafydd (beloved)
Dai (to shine)
Daniel (judged by God)
David (beloved)
Deiniol (God is judge)
Dewi (beloved)
Dilwyn (blessed truth)
Drystan (sadness, tulmult)
Dylan (?, perhaps *sea*)
Einion (anvil)

Emlyn (charming)
Emrys (immortal)
Emyr (ruler, king)
Evan (God is gracious)
Gareth (?, perhaps *civilized*)
Garth (a garden, an enclosed yard)
Gary (spear of battle)
Gavin (battle hawk)
Geoffrey (district; traveler; pledge + peace)
George (earth worker, farmer)
Geraint (?, perhaps *old*)
Gerallt (spear ruler)
Gethin (dark, swarthy)
Glyn (valley, glen) **Glynn, Glynne**
Glyndŵr (valley of water)
Gregory (vigilant, watchful)
Griffin (reddish brown, rust-colored; a prince)
Griffith (reddish brown, rust-colored; a prince)
Grigor (vigilant, watchful)
Gruffydd (reddish brown, rust-colored; a prince) **Gruffudd, Gruffydd**
Gwallter (ruler of an army)
Gwilym (resolute protector)
Gwyn (white, fair, blessed) **Gwynn, Gwynne**
Gwynedd (white, fair, blessed)
Heddwynn (blessed peace)
Hopkin (bright with fame)
Howell (eminent, prominent)
Hugh (heart, mind, soul)
Humphrey (warrior of peace)
Huw (heart, mind, soul)
Hywel (eminent, prominent) **Hywell**
Idris (ardent lord)
Iefan (God is gracious)
Ifor (?)
Ilar (cheerful)

Iolo (downy, youth)

Islwyn (below the grove)

Ivor (archer)

John (God is gracious)

Kendall (dweller in the valley of the River Kent)

Lewis (famous in war)

Llew (lion)

Llewelyn (?, perhaps *the bright one, shining one; lionlike*)

Lloyd (gray)

Llwyd (gray)

Lywarch (?)

Maurice (dark, swarthy, a Moor)

Meic (Who is like God?)

Meical (Who is like God?)

Meilyr (chief ruler)

Meirion (of Mars; manly)

Merfyn (sea hill, eminent marrow)

Merlin (sea hill, fortress by the sea)

Mervyn (sea hill, eminent marrow)

Meuriz (dark, swarthy, a Moor) **Meurig**

Michael (Who is like God?)

Morgan (white seas; eternal seas)

Mostyn (from the mossy village)

Owain (lamb; youth; well-born)

Pedr (rock, stone)

Peter (rock, stone)

Pewlin (small)

Rees (ardor)

Reynold (ruler of judgment)

Rheinallt (ruler of judgment)

Rhisiart (stern king)

Rhodri (king of the wheel)

Rhydderch (reddish brown, rust-colored)

Rhys (ardor)

Richard (stern king)

Roderick (famous king)

Rolant (famous land)

Samuel (his name is God)

Sawyl (his name is God) Welsh form of Samuel.

Siarl (full-grown, a man) Welsh form of Charles.

Sieffre (district; traveler; pledge + peace) Welsh form of Geoffrey.

Siencyn (God is gracious) Welsh form of Jenkin.

Siôn (God is gracious) Welsh form of John.

Siôr (earthworker, farmer) Welsh form of George.

Steffan (a crown, garland)

Stephen (a crown, garland)

Stuart (steward, keeper of the animal enclosure)

Talfryn (high hill)

Taliesin (shining brow)

Tewdwr (God's gift)

Theodore (God's gift)

Thomas (a twin)

Timothy (respecting God)

Tomos (a twin)

Trahaearn (ironlike) **Traherne**

Trefor (dweller at the large village)

Tristan (sadness) **Tristram, Trystan, Trystram**

Tudur

Tudor (ruler of the people)

Vaughn (small) **Vaughan**

Victor (victor, conqueror)

Walter (ruler of an army)

William (resolute protector)

Wyn (white, fair, blessed) **Wynn, Wynne**

Ynyr (honorable)

SURNAMES

Wales has the smallest number of surnames in Britain. In some smaller towns, there are so many Williamses and Joneses that identification based solely on names is difficult. In these cases, some kind of additional identifier based on a familial connection or location of residence is used.

Smith, an English name, is the most common surname in Wales today. The second and third most numerous, Jones and Williams, are Welsh. Name laws have effectively put an end to the traditional practice of a woman retaining as a surname her father's first name. Upon marriage, a woman takes her husband's surname.

Adams (son of Adam *man of the red earth*)

Baker (a baker)

Bennett (blessed)

Bevan (son of Evan *God is gracious*)

Bowen (son of Owain *lamb; youth; well-born*)

Brown (the brown, brown-haired)

Carter (a carter, a person who hauls goods on a cart)

Clark (a clerk) **Clarke**

Cook (a cook)

Cooper (a cooper, a maker or seller of barrels)

Davies (son of David *beloved*)

Davis (son of David *beloved*)

Edwards (son of Edward *wealthy guardian*)

Evans (son of Evan *God is gracious*)

Fychan (small)

Green (dweller on the village green)

Grey (the gray)

Griffiths (son of Griffith *reddish brown, rust-colored*)

Gruffydd (reddish brown, rust-colored)
Gwynne (white, fair, blessed)
Hall (dweller near or worker at the manor house)
Harris (son of Harry *home ruler*)
Harrison (son of Harry *home ruler*)
Herbert (bright army, famous army)
Hill (dweller near the hill)
Howell (preeminent)
Hughes (son of Hugh)
Jackson (son of Jack *God is gracious*)
James (supplanting, seizing by the heels)
Johnson (son of John *God is gracious*)
Jones (son of John *God is gracious*)
King (kingly)
Kyffin (just, righteous)
Laurence (from Laurentum) Lawrence
Lee (the mute one)
Lewis (famous in war)
Lloyd (gray)
Mansel (a farmer)
Martin (of Mars, warlike)
Meredith (lord, prince, ruler)
Meurig (dark-skinned, a Moor)
Moore (dark-skinned, a Moor)
Morgan (sea + circle, completion; bright, white)
Morganwy (sea + circle, completion; bright, white)
Morris (dark-skinned, a Moor)
Owen (lamb; youth; well-born)

Parker (gamekeeper, keeper of the park)
Phillips (lover of horses) **Philips**
Powell (son of Hywel *eminent, prominent*) **Powel**
Price (son of Rhys *ardor*)
Pugh (son of Hugh *heart, mind, soul*)
Rice (ardor)
Roberts (son of Robert *bright with fame*)
Robinson (son of Robin *bright with fame*)
Shaw (dweller near the woods)
Smith (a smith)
Stradling (bowlegged)
Symonds (son of Symond *heard*)
Taylor (a tailor)
Thomas (a twin)
Thompson (son of Thomas *a twin*)
Tudur (ruler of the people; territorial king)
Turner (a maker of small wooden articles, worker with a lathe)
Vaughan (small)
Walker (a fuller of cloth)
Ward (watchman, guard)
Watson (son of Wat *ruler of an army*)
White (white-haired, fair-complexioned)
Williams (son of William) **Wiliams**
Wilson (son of Will *resolute protector*)
Wood (dweller near or worker in the woods)
Wright (a carpenter)
Wynne (white, fair, blessed) **Wynn**

Part Four

[IRELAND]

[CONTENTS]

Chapter One

THE DARK AGES TO THE ANGLO-NORMAN INVASION
[3 B.C.–1175]

THE EARLIEST TRACES of man in the Emerald Isle date to around 6800 B.C. in the Mesolithic (Middle Stone Age) period. In time, other groups colonized the island. According to legend, the first of these were escaped slaves from Greece known as the Firbolgs. After the Firbolgs came the Fomorians (Fomhoire), African sea rovers who had a base on a nearby island, and after them, the Tuatha De Danann. These were the cultured and highly civilized people of the goddess Dana, and it was they who managed to subjugate the Firbolgs and keep the Fomorians at bay. Celtic Milesians from Spain followed the Tuatha De Danann and are thought to have landed around 1000 B.C. (others believe it might have been much later, possibly the fifth century B.C.). The Milesians brought with them iron weapons and implements, great artistic skill and craftsmanship, their Celtic language, a polytheistic religion, and a rich oral tradition.

POLITICS

THOUGH THE FIRBOLGS were defeated by the superior Tuatha De Danann, the Firbolg King Eochaid still managed to cut off the hand of the De Danann King Nuada. Nuada was forced to retire from his position, for none with a deformity or blemish was allowed to rule. When he left to have a silver hand made, he nominated his Fomorian champion, Breas, as king. Breas was an ungenerous and unkingly man who ignored his kin's rovings and plunderings. He managed to rule for seven years, and it was only after he committed the greatest of sins by insulting the poet Cairbre that he was overthrown and Nuada of the Silver Hand was returned to the throne. A second battle was decisively won by the De Danann, though Nuada himself was slain.

The Tuatha De Danann were defeated in battle by the Milesians. To the uncivilized Firbolg and even the powerful and victorious Milesians, the Tuatha De Danann were an amazing people. Such was the awe and respect for their ways that a great body of legend and mythology rose up about them and influenced the growth of Milesian culture. One legend relates how the Milesian poet Amergin divided the land, giving the upper part to the Milesians and the underground to the Tuatha De Danann. This gave rise to stories of fairies, leprechauns, and other enchanted folk existing under the hills.

One of the principal features of Celtic society was its decentralization. It was a rural society devoted to the cultivation of crops and the raising of animals; towns were few. The people themselves were divided into many *tuatha,* a word that can be defined as tribes, septs, or clans. The tuatha were kin groups, each with a recognized chieftain or king, a *ri,* and a collective claim to a specific area. In time, some of the tuatha allied with others to form regional kingdoms ruled by overkings.

By the sixth century, Ireland was divided into the "five-fifths of Ireland," areas that correspond to the modern provinces of Connacht, Leinster, Munster, Ulster, and a separate kingdom of Meath that is now in Leinster. The tuatha competed with one another for supremacy, and none of the kingdoms were very stable. Ulster was split between the Dál Riata in the northeast, the Airgialla in the southeast, and the northern Ui Neill (the descendants of Niall of the Nine Hostages) in the center and west. Munster was dominated by the Eóganachta, the descendants of Eogan; Connacht was ruled by the Connachta, the descendants of Conn; Leinster was divided between the Laigin in the south and the southern Ui Neill around Tara, who eventually formed the kingdom of Meath.

The chief of each tuath was elected from the *derbfine,* the small group consisting of four generations of male descendants of a common great-grandfather, all possessing royal blood. The position of ri was not hereditary from father to son but was an elected position open to all within the derbfine who possessed the qualities needed to make the best ruler. This often led to bloodshed or maiming, as a maimed chieftain was unacceptable. During the later centuries of the first millennium, a chieftain's successor was chosen within the chieftain's lifetime. The successor, the *tanaiste,* had to be without physical deformity or blemish and had to swear to uphold the ancient laws and customs or run a high risk of being deposed.

Above the chief of each tuath was the provincial chieftain, and above him, the *ard-ri,* the high king of all Ireland. Each chief paid tribute to the king above him, and in return, the higher chief paid a small courtesy tribute back to the lower chiefs. Each chief also kept about him a number of paid soldiers from his own clan, as well as a small mercenary army. From these warriors, the king chose the strongest, most powerful, and most skilled to be his champion, his *airechta.*

Some believe the position of ard-ri was established by first-century ruler Tuathal the Desired, a strong monarch who managed to bring order to the land where disorder and chaos had been the rule for generations. Tuathal enlarged the province of Meath around Tara from one tuath to eighteen and gave it the distinction of being the province of the ard-ri. He reestablished the parliament, or *feis,* of Tara and reorganized the Aonach, the great national fair that brought people together from across the land.

The feis was held every three years for three days before and three days after Samhain, the ancient Celtic festival celebrating the beginning of winter. Activities of the feis included the recital and reconfirmation of the ancient laws, the enactment of new laws, the settling of grievances and disputes, and perhaps most importantly, the recital of Irish history from the time of the ancients to present events.

Tuathal also was responsible for laying the Boru tribute on Leinster. King Eochaid of Leinster married Dairine, one of two beautiful daughters of Tuathal. Eochaid eventually tired of his bride and began thinking about her sister, Fithir. He confined Dairine in a tower, pretended that she had died, then went to Tara to seek some consolation for his loss. Tuathal pitied Eochaid and gave him his other daughter, Fithir, for a wife. After a time, Fithir discovered her sister in the tower. Humiliated, shamed, and mortified at being used so, the sisters died. Upon learning of his daughters' dishonor, an enraged Tuathal set out for Leinster. The province was saved from complete destruction only by Eochaid's promise to pay a crushing tribute every other year: 5,000 cows, 5,000 hogs, 5,000 cloaks, 5,000 brass and bronze vessels, and 5,000 ounces of silver. It was a tribute to last 500 years and was an issue over which a great deal of hardship and fighting took place.

Tuathal's successor was his son, Feidlimid Rechtmar. Nicknamed the Lawgiver, Feidlimid continued to maintain peace by making sure the laws were respected and just. He also established the Lex Talionis, the harsh law of an eye for an eye, which remained in effect until the time of Saint Patrick.

The next great ard-ri was Feidlimid's son, Conn of the Hundred Battles. Conn successfully beat his uncle, Cathair Mór, in battle and went down in Irish history as a great and celebrated warrior who managed to unite the septs of the Deagades, the Eberians, the Eremonians, and the Ithians.

Another of the great kings was the third-century Cormac Mac Art, a grandson of Conn of the Hundred Battles. Cormac, probably the most respected ruler of ancient Ireland, was renowned for his dignity, his honor, his wisdom, and his just judgments. He rebuilt the palace of Tara and added a sun house (called a *grianan*) for the women, as well as the House of the Hostages, the House of a Thousand Soldiers, and the Star of the Bards (a meeting place for poets, historians, etc.). He brought a wonderful magnificence to Tara, the likes of which had never been seen before. To this day, many regard Cormac Mac Art as Ireland's greatest king.

Niall of the Nine Hostages ruled as ard-ri between the reign of Cormac Mac Art and the coming of Saint Patrick. He founded the longest and most important Irish dynasty that ruled, almost without exception, for 600 years. Niall was above all a skilled warrior, and he excelled in raiding Britain and Gaul and bringing back hostages, livestock, and a great deal of booty. It was during one of his expeditions that a lad named Succat was captured and taken back to tend the livestock of an Irish chieftain. That teenager came to be the greatest man Ireland ever knew: its patron saint, Patrick. Niall died in the year 404, shot dead with an arrow by a son of the Leinster king who sought an end to the Boru tribute.

Great changes took place in 832 when the famous Norwegian Viking Thorgest (Turgest) made it his goal to conquer the whole of Ireland. With 120 ships and nearly 12,000 warriors supporting him, he set up his base near Lough Ree and confined his operations to the north. Thorgest made permanent settlements along the Liffey, the Boyne, and farther into the interior of the island. By 845, he'd taken control of Armagh, the holy city that housed the wooden staff of Saint Patrick (said to have been given to him by Christ) and the abbot, the spiritual leader of Ireland.

Thorgest drove out the abbot, converted the church into a pagan temple with himself as high priest, and enthroned his wife upon the altar of the church at Clonmacnois, the second holiest place in Ireland. After Thorgest was captured and drowned in Loch Owel, the Norsemen abandoned their settlements along Lough Ree, but by no means left the island altogether.

The next several years saw settlements by both the Norwegian and Danish Vikings, and the process of taking over the land was often brutal to the extreme. During the tenth and eleventh centuries, most of the invaders were of Danish stock who were successful in taking over large parts of the Irish interior. As time passed, Irish clans even allied themselves with Vikings for help in fighting one another's enemies. These alliances were usually forged through the bond of marriage. The first historical account of such a situation was the ninth-century marriage of Muirgel, the daughter of Ard-Ri Maélsechlainn (Malachy) to a Viking chieftain named Iarnkné. Alliances were also obtained through fostering out or adopting children from one side to another.

The most famous Irish leader during this time was Brían Mac Cennéidigh (son of Kennedy), who is known to most as Brian Boru. Brian's brother Mathghamhain (Mahon) succeeded their father as king of Munster in 968, at a time when they were almost always at war with the Danes and the Leinstermen. In 976, Mahon was captured and killed, and Brian Boru became king. He wasted no time avenging his brother's death. In three years' time, he was ard-ri of southern Ireland.

Brian's rival was Maélsechlainn (Malachy), the ard-ri of the north. In 998, a truce was initiated between the two groups, but fighting broke out again after a couple of years and Brian Boru emerged as the victor and king of all Ireland. He was a great statesman who reestablished law and order and ruled with a firm and steady hand. Though he spent much of his time fighting, he still saw to the building of roads, forts, and churches. He encouraged learning by building schools and bringing books back from abroad. He wasn't accepted in the north, however, and he endured a troubled relationship with the Leinstermen.

While seeking to become recognized as ard-ri in the north, Brian outfitted a fleet and manned it with his men, along with Danes from Dublin and other Norsemen from the north of Ireland. The terms of his alliance with the Norsemen guaranteed them undisputed possession of the territories they had settled upon. To reinforce the alliance, he married his daughter to the Danish King Sitric of Dublin, while Brian himself took Sitric's mother, the beautiful Gormlaith, as a second wife.

Gormlaith harbored a secret hatred for Brian, and it was through her manipulations and intrigue that Brian lost his life. Gormlaith's brother was the Leinster prince Maolmórdha (Molloy). Gormlaith threw taunts at him for allying himself with Brian and accepting gifts from him. It was something neither their father nor grandfather would have ever considered, much less done. Maolmórdha's thought that he had dishonored his clan became a festering wound. After an argument with Brian's son, Murchadh (Murrough), Maolmórdha returned home and incited his both his Leinster and his Dublin relatives to opposition.

Brian, in the meantime, had rid himself of his vexatious wife. Gormlaith approached Sigurd, Earl of the Orkneys, who agreed to help on condition that he become king of Ireland and Gormlaith's husband. Sitric sought the help of Brodar, a Viking from the Isle of Man who also wanted to be king and have Gormlaith for a wife.

Brodar assembled a great army of Norsemen from the Orkneys, the Hebrides, and the Shetlands, as well as many from Normandy, Flanders, England, and Cornwall. Leinstermen and Vikings who had settled around Dublin and Wexford joined them.

Brian had gathered together his allies in the south, along with christianized Norsemen, and a force from Scotland. He was seventy-three years old and still eager for battle, though he agreed to let his son, Murchadh, lead the fight.

On Palm Sunday, 1014, the huge northern force arrived on the shores of Clontarf, and Brian soon followed. He was reluctant to fight during such a holy time, but the pagan Danes forced the issue, and the battle began at sunrise on Good Friday. Brian's forces took a huge blow from the mail-armored Vikings, and it wasn't until later in the day, when Brian's old rival Maélsechlainn arrived to lend him a hand with fresh forces, that the battle turned in favor of the Irish. By sunset the great battle was over and the Danes were routed. It was a costly victory for the Irish, however. Brian Boru had lost his life, as had his son, Murchadh, and his grandson, Turlough. Most believe Brian Boru to have been the last great Irish king.

After Brian's death, Maélsechlainn regained the throne and managed to crush the remaining resistance. Maélsechlainn was a noble and chivalrous leader who ruled without opposition until his death in 1022. He was the last Irish king to do so.

In a surprising break from ancient custom, the position of ri and even ard-ri ceased to be an elected one. Quite often, two or more men would claim the title, and these claimants became known as "kings with opposition." Turmoil and disruption prevailed as political disunity weakened the country. It was just this infighting that left Ireland vulnerable to foreign involvement and signaled the beginning of its loss of independence.

SOCIETY

ANCIENT IRELAND CONSISTED of nearly 200 tuatha, each of which were divided into thirty or so *ballybetaighs*. Each ballybetaigh served as grazing land for 300 head of cattle and was subdivided into twelve *seasreachs*, or plowlands, of 120 acres apiece. The lands of the tuath belonged to the entire tribe, though the chief, the nobles, and some of the professional men had special privileges that gave them private use of a part of the land. Those with the privilege of private use often rented out portions of their land to tenants, or *céile,* who were from the general population, the *féine.* The céile who rented or borrowed animals were known as the unfree céile. Those who were able to afford their own stock were higher in rank and were known as the free céile. The céile contributed to the household needs of the head of the tribe and contributed a certain amount of work and military service as well.

Below the céile were two other classes of unfree people: the *bothach* and the *sencleithe,* and the *fuidir.* The bothach and the sencleithe were poor members of the tribe who made their livings at menial jobs or hired out as laborers or herdsmen. They had no voice in the tribal council nor held property rights. The fuidir were the slaves, the criminals, the strangers, and those with debts too great to pay off. With hard work and determination, individuals of both classes could prove themselves to be of worthy character and be considered for inclusion into the féine, though slaves rarely achieved that station.

Irish women of old had the distinction of being much more free and respected than the women of other cultures. From the earliest times they filled such positions as poetess, physician, druidess, and lawgiver. The women were on a footing that was almost but not quite equal to the men. Up until the time of Saint Adamnan, they even followed their husbands or brothers into battle. Though a son inherited land in preference to a daughter, she nonetheless got a portion of land upon marriage and could inherit if she had no brothers. If she did inherit, she was obliged to provide and pay for a warrior during which times such a levy was made.

Marrying was a complicated affair. After the parents agreed to the match, a dowry, the *tinnscra,* had to be paid to the husband's family. Once the marriage was consummated, the bride or her father received a kind of reverse-dowry from the groom or his family. Known as the *coibche,* it was comprised of gold, silver, jewelry, clothes, animals, or household items. According to the ancient laws, the coibche was paid in yearly installments, with the bride's father receiving the entire first year's portion, two-thirds of the next year's portion, a half of the third year's, and one-third of the fourth year's portion. To the bride went the rest of the amount. Friends presented a collective gift to the couple, the *tinol,* and of this the husband collected two-thirds right and the wife one-third right. A woman was generally treated with respect in marriage (though the man was the undisputed head of the household), and the law regarded her as a partner in the union. A married woman retained sole ownership of property she was given or had acquired before her marriage.

Most marriages consisted of a husband and one wife, but plural wives and concubines were common. Many plural wives were the result of one clan allying itself with another; the majority of the concubines likely were slaves captured in various raiding expeditions.

Legal separation was allowed for just cause, and in such an instance the wife was entitled to all of her portion of the coibche and the tinol, plus another amount for damages. Concubines, of course, had no such recourse and could be sold at any time to anyone.

Ireland was by and large an insular place, which allowed the Celtic civilization to grow without major outside interference. There were no walled towns, only a few scattered villages, and in spite of trading with other countries, the majority of the people were occupied with the simple routine of raising crops and attending livestock. Wealth was measured in animals, clothing, and jewelry.

With such a rural lifestyle, the Irish took great delight in the *aonach* or *oenach*: the fair. Many of the fairs originated as accompaniments to serious provincial and state assemblages, yet there were also a few that originated as part of a memorial to some great person. The most famous aonach was held during the feis of Tara. Other popular fairs were held at royal residences carved from the provinces surrounding Meath: the

Fair of Tlachtga, the Fair of Uisnech, the Fair of Cruachan, and the Fair of Taillte. There was also the Fair of Colmain in Kildare, the Fair of Carman in Wexford, and the Fair of Emain Macha near Armagh, which was held in commemoration of the first Milesian queen of Ireland, Macha Mong Ruad, the founder of the stronghold Emain Macha.

The fairs and assemblages were of such importance that strict laws were enacted to ensure the gatherings were properly carried out. A universal peace prevailed, and the penalty for disrupting the gatherings was death. Fugitives walked as free men, debtors could not be confronted, and all personal items such as necklaces, rings, brooches, and bracelets that had been pawned to relieve financial distress had to be returned to their owner for the duration of the festivities. Any who refused to release the ornaments received a stiff fine for the mental distress placed upon the person who was disgraced by appearing unadorned. The aonach and the feis were opportunities to see and be seen, and all attending made sure to present their best, most beautiful or handsome self.

Not only did the aonach give cause for fun and celebration, it also fulfilled an important role in Irish culture by providing the opportunity for the seanachies (historians), filidh (poets), and genealogists to recite the history and accomplishments of their forefathers, to praise the heroes and leaders of the present, to tell the legends and stories, to sing songs and play music, and to recite the genealogies of the major families back to their earliest roots. Another integral part of any fair was its markets. There were three: one for food, one for live cattle, and another called the market of the Greeks that consisted of all manner of raiment and adornment.

Some of the fairs provided the opportunity for the examination, selection, and certification of candidates for the various crafts and trades. A board composed of the king, nobles, chiefs, and doctors examined the candidates' skills before giving them the right to practice the craft or trade they applied for. The Fair of Taillte was primarily for athletic contests and, in time, was almost as well-known as a marriage mart where parents brought their children in the hopes of finding them a suitable mate. The De Danann hero Lugh is said to have first instituted the gathering as a memorial to his foster-mother, Taillte. The last Fair of Taillte was held by the order of Ard-Ri Roderic O'Connor and celebrated in 1169, the year the Normans invaded.

The first wave of Viking raiders in 795 was the beginning of a force that had deep repercussions and profound effect on Irish culture. Though the Vikings' first targets were the islands and coastal areas, by the middle of the ninth century, they had managed to make their way inland. From 830 onward, the Vikings arrived in great fleets and their brutal raids intensified. In particular, they were attracted to the monasteries and ecclesiastical centers that had grown from small religious houses into centers of population, trade, and wealth, with great storehouses and large numbers of livestock. Many were savagely and repeatedly attacked and several of the smaller ones failed to recover. In 840 and 841, a Viking contingent wintered at Lough Neagh in Ulster, and in 842, they established a settlement at Dublin. Other settlements that survive today are Cork, Limerick, Waterford, Wexford, and Wicklow. The Viking presence was now permanent instead of seasonal, and land became the objective preferred over treasure.

As Norsemen were assimilated into Irish society, intermarriage became common, and an exchange of culture took place. Walled villages and forts appeared, coin was introduced, trade increased, the Irish imitated the Vikings in armor and warfare, and before long, Norse words found their way into the Irish language. In return, Irish building styles, their distinctive metalwork, and their skill at the other arts strongly influenced those of the Norsemen. It was Irish scholars who introduced the classic literature of Greece and Rome to the Scandinavians, and Irish poets who greatly influenced the oral recountings of Viking legends and mythology. And, as the Vikings were now in a land so devoutly Christian, many were converted from their old pagan beliefs to the Christian religion of the Irish.

RELIGION

THE ANCIENT IRISH were worshipers of the sun and of a great idol called Crom Cruach. Crom Cruach stood on the plain of Magh Slech and was supposedly covered in gold and silver and surrounded by twelve other pillars or images made of brass or bronze. It is said that Saint Patrick destroyed the idol Crom Cruach when he passed through the area in the year 434. Paradise to the pagan Irish was either beneath the hills or under the ocean, and it had several names: Magh Mell, the Plain of Pleasure; I-Breasil, the Isle of the Blessed; Tir na n-Og, the Land of Perpetual Youth; and Tir-Tairnigri, the Land of Promise.

Although Saint Patrick is given the credit for bringing Christianity to Ireland, evidence exists that there were Christians in the land before his arrival, and that Irish Christians were living and spreading the message in Europe as well. Many authorities believe there were at least four Irishmen who preached to native congregations before Patrick's arrival: Saint Ailbe, Saint Ciaran, Saint Declan, and Saint Ibar.

A year before Patrick arrived, the Pope sent a missionary named Palladius to the Irish. He landed in 431 and set about establishing three churches in the southeast. Palladius supposedly left that same year, driven out by a Leinster chieftain, and died a year later in Britain. There are some who believe he stayed and worked among the people for another thirty years.

The coming of Patrick, the patron saint of Ireland, was one of the most important events in Irish history, for its effects were the most reaching, widespread, and enduring. When Patrick first came to the island, it was as a young captive from Britain named Succat. He was the sixteen-year-old son of a Roman official named Calpurnius (Calporn) and Conchessa, a niece of Saint Martin of Tours. Succat was taken in a raid by men from the fleet of King Niall, and once in Ireland, was sold to an Antrim chieftain and put to work tending sheep. After six or seven years, he escaped and traveled 200 miles to the coast, where he caught a ship for the Continent. By the time he left, Ireland and its people were firmly embedded in his soul.

Succat made his way home, then spent many years among the monasteries and religious houses of Europe. Finally, in the year 432, Pope Celestine granted his request to return to Ireland. Succat was consecrated as a bishop and given the name Patricius.

It didn't take long for Patrick to make converts, and as news of his mission was made known, he was often greeted by crowds of people. He established many churches, organized many congregations, ordained many priests, consecrated many nuns, and founded the See of Armagh that was to become, and remain, Ireland's Holy City.

During Patrick's later years, he revised Ireland's ancient code of law, the Brehon Laws. With a committee of three kings, three bishops, a poet, a philosopher, and a historian, they did away with the doctrine of an eye for an eye (the Lex Talionis), toned down the severity of some of the punishments, and took out that which wasn't consistent with the law of Christ. This great revision, the Senchus Mor, is viewed as one of Patrick's greatest accomplishments. Saint Patrick died at Down around 460. The twelve days of his wake were the Laithi na Caointe, the Days of Lamentation.

If Saint Patrick was the father of the Celtic Church, then Saint Bridget was its mother. She was born around the year 450, the daughter of a man of royal blood named Dubtach and his concubine. Before Bridget's birth, her mother was sold to a Druid, and it was in his house that Bridget was born. She grew up to be very beautiful, both in body and in spirit, and was known for her generosity to the poor and the miracles of increase that surrounded her.

After Bridget and her mother were freed from bondage, she returned to her father's house, only to suffer the indignity of his attempting to sell her into slavery after she refused to wed. Soon after, she took the veil and was consecrated as a nun. Wherever she went, people were drawn to her charity and generosity and to her kindness and faith. She was invited to Leinster and given residence at Kildare. It was there she founded the Church of the Oak, the Monastery of Kildare, and even a school. Her enclave quickly became famous and people traveled from across Ireland to receive her blessing.

At the time of her death in 525, she had nearly thirty religious houses under her leadership and her fame had stretched to the Continent. So great was the respect given her that Saint Bridget, Mary of the Gael, was interred in the same tomb as Saint Patrick. They were two of the greatest figures of Irish history.

When the Roman Empire collapsed, communication with the Mother Church nearly ceased, and the Irish church developed its own character and rites that differed from those on the Continent. Irish monasticism was even more austere than in Europe, and the simple, often primitive monasteries reflected that. Many monks chose to live alone or in very small groups, and their small, comfortless cells provided little more than a roof over their heads. Those who wanted to be part of a larger group built themselves a monastery. The first monastery to become well known was that founded by Saint Enda at the end of the fifth century. Clonard was founded in the sixth century by Saint Finnian, the "teacher of the saints of Ireland." He was so called for twelve of his students (the twelve apostles of Ireland), were founders of several famous monasteries. Included in this group were Saint Columcille (Columba), Saint Ciaran, and Saint Brendan.

Within a hundred years, the abbots had become more powerful and important than the bishops, and the monasteries became the prime centers for both religion and education, as well as food warehouses and repositories of wonderful treasures. As many of the bishops and priests were skilled in the arts and trades, workshops were an integral part of the monastery, and it was here that the beautifully ornamented books, chalices, bells, and shrines were produced. Not only were the monks skilled in the tangible arts, they were also scholars, and as such, became teachers as people flocked to listen and learn from them. The flocks often stayed, and the teachers found themselves as heads of schools. Under the guidance of centuries of saints, Christianity and learning flourished throughout the island.

NAMING

IT WAS THROUGH their great oral tradition that the Irish so proudly recited their families' descents to ancient kings and chieftains. This litany kept the old names viable and names based on past heroes have long been as common as other Celtic names based on physical characteristics and favored qualities, localities, genealogy, and occupation. Many of the ancient names are still remembered, though their meanings often are not. Ailill (sprite), Conall (high mighty), Fionn (fair), Diamaid (a freeman), Aoibhinn (beautiful, fair of form), and Gráinne (grain goddess) are examples of names taken from the legends. Flannán (little red-haired one), Dubhán (little black-haired one), Fionnbhárr (fair-haired), Cruitín (hunchback), and Órfhlaith (golden lady) are a few names based on physical characteristics. Favored qualities were represented by such names as Rathnait (grace), Sadhbh (goodness), Feidhlim (the ever-good), and Meallán (little pleasant one). Manannán (from the Isle of Man) and Deasún (from Desmond) are examples of names based on locality; Fiadmuine (treasures of the forest; a hunter) and Abbán (an abbot) are examples of names based on occupation.

Though Ireland became a very devout country, naming traditions remained typically native until the arrival of the Normans. A few saints adopted Christian names upon their ordinations, but these were few, and the trend never caught on, certainly not among the general population. One reason the names were kept out of common use for centuries was that the Irish held their saints and the characters of the Christian religion in such reverence and high regard that the names were considered too venerable to be adopted for personal use.

The names Patrick and Michael were not used until after the Normans came, and Bríghid (Bridget) and Máire were rarely used before the seventeenth century.

The Irish did, however, use some of them in combination with the words *giolla, gille* (servant of, pledge of) *mael, maol* (follower of, servant of), *ceile* (the companion or vassal of), and *cear* (the friend of) to create names showing their devotion to the respective biblical character or saint. Giollapeadair (servant of Peter), Maolcholm (servant of Columba), Giolla Chríost (the servant of Christ) are names typical to this classification.

The Vikings left a number of personal names to the Irish, many of which survive to this day. Some are readily recognizable and some evolved over the centuries. Rothrekr (Roderick), Magnus, Ivarr, and Guthfrithr (Godfrey) are examples.

In general, Irish names can be divided into three categories: names with one element, names with more than one element, and names formed from derivatives. The last classification of names is formed by the addition of prefixes and all manner of suffixes. For example: Ain-mhire (great lord), Su-ibhne (well-going), Meall-án (little pleasant one), Mainch-ín (little monk), and Muadh-nait (little noble one). This is a complicated category for English speakers, for certain suffixes are used for one sex or another. In general, most of the suffixes are male terminations, but *-nat* is a female termination: Rónán (*male,* little seal) and Rónnat (*female,* little seal).

Note: Because many Irish names are very ancient, the meanings of some have been lost or are debatable. For interest, names relating to legendary characters or characters of historical note are described as such in the lists below.

FEMALE NAMES

Aifric (pleasant)
Ailbhe (?, perhaps *white*)
Áine (joy; praise, fasting) Áine was the queen of the fairies of South Munster.
Aisling (dream, vision, daydream) **Aislinn**
Alana (O child)
Alma (?, perhaps *all-good*)
Aodhfionn (white fire)
Aodhne (*fiery*)
Aoibh (beauty)
Aoibheann (beautiful, fair form) **Aoibhinn**
Aoife (?, perhaps *beauty*) **Aoiffe** Aiofe was the wife of Cu-chullin.
Barran (little summit)
Beatha (life, livelihood)
Bébhinn (sweet, melodious lady) Bébhinn was the name of the mother and a wife of Brian Boru.
Bidelia (strength)
Blath (flower)
Bláthnaid (flower) **Bláithín, Bláthnait**
Bríghid (strength) **Brigid** Bríghid was the mythological goddess of wisdom, poetry, and song. The name was also borne by Saint Bríghid of Kildare (d. 510), a patron saint of Ireland. Out of reverence for the saint, the name ceased to be used until the seventeenth century.

Brona (sorrow)
Caoilfhionn (slender + fair, white)
Ciannait (little ancient one)
Ciara (dark one, black-haired one)
Clíodhna (?) **Clídna, Clíona**
Conchobarre (wisdom, strength, counsel + hound; aid)
Cuman (?)
Damhnait (little poet)
Dana (bold) In Irish mythology, Dana was an important goddess who gave her name to the Tuatha De Danann, one of the first groups to inhabitant the island.
Dearbhail (true desire)
Deirbhile (poet's daughter)
Deirdre (?, perhaps *young girl; fear*) Deirdre was the name of a legendary Irish princess who was betrothed to Conchobhar, the king of Ulster.
Doireann (sullen)
Dubheasa (black, dark beauty)
Dunflaith (lady of the fort)
Éadaoin (?)
Ealga (noble)
Eimhear (?, perhaps *swift*) **Emer** The name was borne by the wife of the mythological hero Cuchulainn.
Eithne (kernel) Saint Eithne, a daughter of King Laoghair, was one of Saint Patrick's first converts.

Emer (?, perhaps *swift*)
Étáin (?, perhaps *jealousy*) **Éadaoin** Étáin was a mythological sun goddess who was the lover of Midir.
Faoiltiarna (wolf lord)
Feidhelm (?) Sister to Saint Eithne, Feidhelm was one of Saint Patrick's first converts.
Fíona (fair, white, clear)
Fionnghuala (fair, white, clear + shoulder) **Fionnuala**
Gemlorg (gemlike)
Gobnait (little mouth, little beak)
Gráinne (grain goddess) Gráinne was the legendary daughter of Cormac Mac Art, a king of Ulster. She was betrothed to Finn MacCool, but eloped with Diarmaid.
Íde (thirst)
Iseult (? perhaps *ruler of the ice, beautiful, fair*) **Isolde, Yseult, Ysolte** Iseult was an Irish princess betrothed to King Mark of Cornwall, but was the beloved of Tristram.
Lassairfhina (flame or blush of the wine) **Lasairíona**
Ligach (pearly)
Luighseach (?, perhaps *light*) A feminine form of Lughaidh.
Meadhbh (?, perhaps *joy; great, large; mead*) Meadhbh was a first-century queen of Connacht who fought against Cuchulainn.
Míde (my Íde *thirst*)
Móirín (little great one)

Mór (great, large)
Muadhnait (little noble one)
Mugain (slave)
Múireann (long-haired)
Muirgheal (sea bright, fair seas)
Muirne (beloved, affection)
Niamh (bright)
Odharnait (little green one)
Órfhlaith (golden lady)
Pádraigín (patrician, an aristocrat)
Rathnait (little graceful one, little prosperous one)
Ríoghnach (queenly)
Sadhbh (goodness) **Sadbha, Sadhbha, Saidhbhe**
Saidhbhín (little Sadhbh *goodness*)
Samhaoir (?, perhaps *summer sailor*)
Saraid (excellent)
Sealbhflaith (lady of possessions)
Sláine (health)
Sorcha (bright, clear)
Tanith (estate)
Uailsi (the proud)
Uallach (the proud)
Úna (?, perhaps *famine, hunger; lamb*)
Vread (?, perhaps *pearl*)

MALE NAMES

Abbán (little abbot)
Ádhamh (man of the red earth) Gaelic form of Adam.
Adhamhnán (little Ádhamh *man of the red earth*) Saint Adhamhnán (c. 624–704) was the biographer of Saint Columba.
Ailbhe (?, perhaps *white*)
Ailill (sprite)
Ailín (?, perhaps *noble*)
Ainmire (great lord)
Anluan (great champion, great hero)
Anmcha (courageous)
Aodh (fire) **Aodha, Aoidh**
Aodhagán (little fiery one, little ardent one)
Aodhaigh (fiery)
Aodhán (little fiery one)
Aodhfin (fire + fair, white, clear) **Aodhfionn**
Árdghal (high valor)
Art (a stone; a bear)
Artúr (?) Irish form of Arthur in use since the seventh century.
Banan (white)
Banbhan (little piglet)
Baothghalach (foolish, vain and valorous)
Barra (head)
Beacán (little small one, wee one)
Beag (small)
Bearach (spearlike)

Bearchán (little spear)
Bran (raven)
Brandan (?, perhaps *raven; prince*)
Brandubh (black raven)
Bréanainn (prince)
Breandán (prince)
Bressal (war, strife) **Breasal, Breazil, Bresal**
Brian (force, strength; hill, high; kingly)
Brón (sorrow)
Buadhach (victory)
Cadhla (handsome)
Calbhach (bald)
Caoimhín (little gentle one)
Caolán (little slender one)
Cárthach (loving)
Cathal (battle mighty)
Cathaoir (warrior)
Ceallach (war, strife)
Ceallachán (small strife)
Cearbhall (champion, warrior)
Cian (ancient)
Cianán (little ancient one)
Ciarán (little black-haired one)
Ciardha (black-haired one)
Ciarrai (black)
Cinnéidid (ugly head, ugly chief)

Coileán (pup, cub)
Coinneach (handsome, comely)
Colmán (little dove)
Comhghall (copledge, hostage)
Comhghan (cobirth, twin)
Conaire (?, perhaps *hound* + *farmer*)
Conall (high-mighty) **Connell**
Conán (?, perhaps *small hound; wisdom, strength, counsel*)
Conchobhar (high will, desire; hound lover)
Conn (sense, reason, wisdom)
Dáithí (swiftness, speed, surefootedness)
Diarmaid (without injunction, a freeman) **Diarmait**
Dónal (world ruler)
Donn (brown)
Donnán (little brown one)
Donnchadh (brown warrior)
Dubh (black-haired, dark-haired)
Dubhglas (black, dark + blue, green, gray)
Eachann (master of horses)
Earna (experience, wisdom)
Éimhín (swift)
Eochaidh (horseman)
Eoghan (lamb; youth; well-born)
Fachtna (?)
Faolán (little wolf)
Fearadhach (masculine, manly)
Feardorcha (dark-complexioned man)
Fearghall (man of valor)
Fearghus (man of strength)
Feichín (little raven)
Feidhlim (the ever-good)
Fiach (raven)
Fiachra (raven)
Finghin (fair at birth)
Fionán (little fair one)
Fionn (fair, white, clear) The name of the legendary Finn MacCool, father of Ossian and the supposed builder of the Giants' Causeway.
Fionnbhárr (fair-headed)
Fionntán (little fair one)
Flann (red, ruddy)

Garbhán (little rough one)
Glaisne (?)
Godraidh (God's peace)
Haraldr (leader of the army) Introduced by the Vikings.
Iarfhlaith (tributary lord)
Íomhar (archer) Irish form of Ivor.
Lachtna (gray, dun)
Laoghaire (calf herder)
Lasairian (a flame)
Lochlainn (land of the lochs)
Lomán (little bare one)
Lorcán (little fierce one)
Maghnus (great, large)
Mainchin (little monk)
Maolbheannachta (hoper for blessing)
Maolcholm (servant of Saint Columba)
Maolmórdha (majestic chief)
Mathghamhain (a bear)
Meallán (little pleasant one)
Muireadhach (mariner, sailor)
Muirgheas (sea choice)
Murchadh (sea warrior)
Naomhán (little holy one)
Niadh (a champion)
Niall (a champion; cloud)
Odhrán (little green one)
Oisín (a fawn) The son of Finn MacCool, said to have been the last member of the Fianna.
Rádhulbh (wolf counsel)
Raghnall (powerful judgment)
Rónán (little seal)
Ruadhán (little red-haired one)
Ruairí (red, rust-colored)
Saebhreathach (noble judge)
Seanán (little ancient one)
Siadhal (sloth)
Suibhne (well-going, pleasant)
Tadhg (a poet)
Toirdealbhach (shaped like Thor)
Tuathal (people mighty)
Uaithne (green)

SURNAMES

Surnames in Ireland generally began appearing in the middle of the tenth century in the form of patronymics. The earliest of these prefixed *Ua* or *O* (grandson of; descended from) to the grandfather's name. Later, many chose to use their fathers' names and used the prefixes *Mac* (son of) and *Ni* (daughter of). A married woman prefixed her husband's name with *Ban* (wife of). Those of lesser importance assumed the surnames of their chieftains.

There are some who believe that Brian Boru (1002–1014) made surnames hereditary by way of an ordinance, but the evidence to back up this claim comes from a fragment of an ancient manuscript thought to deal with his life and might not be trustworthy. Neither Brian nor his sons had hereditary surnames, but his grandsons were the first to bear the name O'Brien, so the claim cannot be totally discounted.

It took a few centuries for surnames to become hereditary throughout the island. During this time period they were unstable and often changed after just a generation or two. Usually, when this occurred, a person would exchange his surname for one based on an ancestor that was not so distant.

MacAilín (son of Ailín *handsome; rock*)
Ó Branduibh (grandson of Brandubh *black raven*)
Ó Breasail (grandson of Bressal *strife*)
Ó Briain (grandson of Brian *force, strength; hill, high; kingly*)
MacBuadhaigh (son of Buadhach *victor*)
Ó Cathaláin (grandson of Cathal *battle mighty*)
Ó Ceallaigh (grandson of Ceallach *war, strife*)
Ó Conaill (grandson of Connall *high-mighty*)
MacConchobhair (son of Conchobhar *high will, desire; hound lover*)
MacCuilinn (son of Cuileann *holly*)

MacCuinn (son of Conn *sense, reason, wisdom*)
MacDonnchadh (son of Donnchadh *brown warrior*)
Ó Faoláin (grandson of Faolán *little wolf*)
Ó Fionnáin (grandson of Fionán *little fair one*)
Ó Lochlainn (grandson of Lachlann *land of the lochs*)
Ó Ruaìdh (grandson of Ruairí *red, ruddy*)
Ó Seanaigh (grandson of Sean *old one*)
MacShuibhne (son of Suibhne *well-going, pleasant*)
Ó Taidhg (grandson of Tadhg *poet*)
MacTighearnáin (son of Tighearnan *lord*)

Chapter Two

THE ANGLO-NORMAN INVASION TO THE RENAISSANCE
HENRY II–HENRY VIII
[1170–1536]

POLITICS

AFTER THE DEATH of Ard-Ri Maélsechlainn (Malachy) in 1022, Ireland was again rife with struggles among the kingdoms. It was this political disunity that left the island open for Norman conquest.

Early in the twelfth century, the O'Connor of Connacht wrestled power away from the descendants of Brian Boru. In 1156, the O'Connor gave way to Murchertach MacLochlainn, the king of Tir Eoghain, who recognized Diarmuid (Dermot) MacMurrough as the king of Leinster in 1161. There were several other claimants to the position of ard-ri, and after five years of difficulty in securing his position, Diarmuid set out to secure support in England. He failed to achieve active support from Henry II but succeeded in attracting the interest of the powerful Richard FitzGilbert de Clare (Strongbow) who had a stronghold in southern Wales, just sixty miles from Ireland.

In 1169, Normans began arriving on the island, and in the summer of 1170, de Clare himself invaded with an army of 1,200. The city of Waterford was taken and its citizens brutally slaughtered. Strongbow's price for supporting Diarmuid was the hand of Diarmuid's beautiful daughter, Aoife, in marriage and Diarmuid's agreement to acknowledge Strongbow as heir. This done, Strongbow and his army marched north, laying waste as they went. Diarmuid regained his throne but died less than a year later and Richard de Clare became king of Leinster.

Meanwhile, Henry II became aware of the situation, and fearing to allow De Clare such power and independence, summoned him back to England. Before returning, Strongbow managed to win a few more battles and added a few more towns to his list of conquests so as to impress upon Henry what a good prize the island would make. In October 1171, Henry landed at Waterford with an army of 4,500 mounted and foot soldiers. In the face of such a force, Ireland acceded defeat, and homage was paid to Henry.

Perhaps the Irish kings didn't realize that the difference between paying homage and tribute to one of their own, and acknowledging defeat and submitting themselves to a foreigner would mean the loss of their independence and the independence of their people. They should have, however, for it is exactly what happened. With the exception of the northern and western chiefs, the other chiefs met with Henry and paid him homage. With politeness and hospitality, Henry held court through the winter, graciously entertaining the chiefs and winning them over. He then won the support of Rome and the support of the Irish bishops. At Easter, Henry returned to England, leaving Strongbow in possession of Leinster and placing Hugh de Lacy in charge of Meath and Dublin.

After Henry and his entourage left, the Irish chiefs suddenly awoke to the fact that they had meekly allowed a foreigner to come in and take over. Determined to regain their independence, they set out to evict the invaders from their island. Although they weren't entirely successful, the Irish gave the Normans such problems that a treaty was drawn up in 1175, allowing the Normans control of Leinster, Meath, Waterford, Wexford, and the area surrounding Dublin. The Irish were given everything else, and Rory O'Connor was recognized as ard-ri under the lordship of Henry.

This didn't sit well with either the Irish or the Norman barons who were in Ireland, and the conflicts did not cease. Through the end of the century, Normans continued to take lands in ever-increasing amounts either by force, in confiscation as punishment for alleged crimes or disloyalty, or simply by royal grant, and they were quick to place defensive castles upon their newly acquired lands. The expansion increased under Henry's son, John, and reached its height in the middle of the thirteenth century. By then, almost 75 percent of Ireland was under Norman control.

During the reign of King Edward I (1272–1307), the tide began to turn in favor of the Irish. The reasons for this are disputed, and some theorize that it was due in part to a Gaelic revival in the latter part of the thirteenth century wherein many Irish families regained their strength and willingness to fight for their country and culture. Another suggestion is that too few Normans settled on the island to maintain control of all the territories they had conquered. Some believe the very disunity that had allowed the Normans in helped in keeping them from total control. Unlike in England where one king controlled all, each Irish territory was a law unto itself and did not fall if one of its neighbors did.

The Irish soon began to recruit the heavily armored *gall-oglaigh,* the gallowglasses, from the western islands of Scotland. The fierce, battle-ax swinging warriors began to win back Norman-held lands. Edward Bruce, the brother of the Scottish king, was invited to the Irish throne, and he won eighteen victories against the Anglo-Normans before being slain in 1318. Back and forth went the battles, with the Irish regaining more and more of their land, until at the end of the fourteenth century, Richard II determined to see the end of the "Irish situation."

Richard led the attack to take the Irish Ard-Ri Art MacMurrough, but MacMurrough's men had successfully fought off the huge English army by the time Richard received word that Henry of Bolingbroke was moving to take his crown. With his own throne in jeopardy, Richard II quit the island in haste. He was the last English king to attempt the conquest of Ireland for another 200 years. English rule remained isolated to the Pale, a palisaded district that covered roughly thirty miles around Dublin.

With the English penned up in the Pale, the Irish once again sought to reestablish their own leadership over the land. Three great Anglo-Irish lordships arose and came to dominate the land held by the Irish. The Butlers held the earldom of Ormond, which was comprised of Kilkenny and Tipperary. One branch of the FitzGerald family held the earldom of Desmond, comprised of Cork, Kerry, and Limerick, and another branch held the earldom of Kildare. At first, the Butlers held close ties to England and were anti-Irish in outlook, but the fourth Earl of Ormond advocated home rule for Ireland and made a point of embracing Anglo-Irish culture. The FitzGeralds, on the other hand, had renounced their English kinship and had become "more Irish than the Irish."

By now, many of the *Sean Ghalls*, the old Anglo-Normans foreigners, were completely assimilated into Irish society. They were enchanted with the Irish people and the island they now called home and had cast off their Norman names, adopted the Irish language and manner of dress, and had thrown themselves whole-heartedly into Irish culture, even to the point of living under the Brehon Laws. Just as the Vikings were assimilated into Irish society, the Irish were now assimilating the English. One Englishman from that time put it best: "If the speech is Irish the heart is also Irish."

King Edward II, aware that his subjects were changing their loyalties, established the Statutes of Kilkenny in 1367. The statutes made English-Irish marriages illegal and forbade concubinage and the fostering of children. All colonists were required to have English names, use the English language, keep English customs and the English style of dress. English churches were not allowed to receive the Irish, and colonists were not allowed to have or keep company with Irish minstrels or musicians. They could not engage in Irish pastimes or games, they were not allowed to sell their horses or any type of armor to the Irish; even the selling of food in times of war was forbidden. And the statutes were not limited to the English. Even the native Irish who lived in captured or newly formed towns were forced to abide by the statutes. The penalty for failure to comply was death or the forfeiture of a person's estate; a harsh punishment for something as harmless as wearing a mustache or not having on an English cap. Many of the statutes were simply impossible to enforce and even caused the Sean Ghalls to rebel against their own government and join the Irish quest for independence from England.

The next attempt at English domination came when Henry VII tried to obtain "whole and perfect obedience" of all the island. Garret More (Gerait Mor), the eighth Earl of Kildare and justiciar of Ireland, was dismissed in 1494, and Edward Poynings was appointed lord deputy and sent to Ireland with 400 soldiers. The aim was to counterbalance the power of the FitzGerald earls of Kildare, but the Sean Ghalls had no desire to be ruled by one who knew so little of the Irish. Garret More was soon reinstated and ruled until his death in 1513. His son, Garret Oge (Gerait Og), was appointed by Henry VIII (his cousin) to succeed him.

The ninth Earl of Kildare, even more pro-Irish than his father, continued to lobby for home rule. In 1529, Henry VIII tried to curtail FitzGerald power by dismissing Garret Oge and placing the king's son, the Duke of Richmond, in the position of lord lieutenant. Garret recovered the position three years later, but after a trumped-up bill of charges was brought against him by Dublin Castle in 1534, he was called to London. Before leaving, he appointed his son, Thomas (Silken Thomas), as vice deputy. Once in London, Garret Oge was confined to the Tower, and a fabricated story of his death was circulated in Ireland. Thomas, believing his father had been killed, initiated a rebellion against the English crown. He was joined by Irish chieftains and the Anglo-Norman-Irish, but was defeated in 1535. Garret Oge died in prison in December of the same year; Thomas and five of his uncles were sent to the Tower and, after enduring the most horrible tortures, were hanged, drawn and quartered, two years later.

The English believed they had finally erased the FitzGeralds and their calls for home rule. They were far from defeated, however. In spite of England's determined attempts over the next three years to eliminate the family, one FitzGerald child managed to survive the slaughter and was sent abroad to safety.

According to one historian, "late medieval Ireland was an island floating rudderless. There were powerful lords in both cultures able to defend their own lands and interests, but there was no single interest behind which they could all unite." The horror of the FitzGeralds' deaths provided that common ground. For the next five years, the FitzGeralds and their allies continued the fight in what is now known as the Geraldine League.

SOCIETY

NORMAN INVOLVEMENT RESULTED in a schism in Irish culture. It was a split more far-reaching than even the Viking contribution. While parts of the country remained steadfastly Celtic, other parts readily welcomed the newcomers and their continental ways. To political disunity was now added cultural disunity.

The Normans introduced the feudal system, which was much different from the traditional Irish system of the tuatha. Centralized government was also instituted. The lord lieutenant was head of the administration and was assisted by a council. From time to time, a parliament was called that was comprised of the feudal lords and the bishops and abbots of the Church. Toward the end of the thirteenth century, towns sent representatives, and these made up the Commons.

Another major Norman contribution was the establishment of towns. Before their arrival, towns were few, with the major ones being built up around the monasteries and along the coast. When the Normans took control of a parcel of land, a castle or stronghold was raised. That attracted people and trade. Before long, villages sprang up to house those who provided the castles with needed services.

In spite of the statutes against trade, Irish and English merchants formed partnerships and business alliances with one another. Not only did trade flourish between England and Ireland, it thrived between Ireland and many other countries, as well. Irish cloth and linens, woolens, furs, and leathers were all in great demand and highly prized as were Irish horses, hawks, and huge wolfhounds.

As English control and influence dwindled to within the Pale, the Irish regained their independence and returned to their Celtic ways. For more than a hundred years they lived under the old Brehon laws and celebrated their culture. This regained freedom was marked by a revival of various intellectual activities. It was a golden age for Gaelic literature, and in astronomy and medicine, the Irish were quite skilled and their services in high demand. The annalists continued to hold high positions within the clans and were regarded as next in importance to the chief. Each sept had its own annalist, a genealogist and historical chronicler whose job was to record the births and deaths of clan members and the deeds and happenings of the clan. The position was usually held by one family within the sept, with a son succeeding his father in the honored role. So seriously did the Irish regard their historians that no business ever took place without their presence. And, as truth and accuracy of the accounts were of paramount importance to the clan, the scribes traveled extensively to verify their facts and accountings.

In place of the aonach, other gatherings took place to foster the knowledge of Ireland. It was the duty of the wealthy to sponsor such assemblies, and they would call together all who were learned or read books, the chroniclers and historians, the poets, those of the Church, judges, craftsmen, and musicians.

Outside the areas of English influence, women continued to live in accordance with tradition and the Brehon laws, and took an active and often leading role in Irish society. It was through the women that many of the Anglo-Normans came to side with the Irish. History is full of the intermarryings between the two races, but Strongbow's marriage to Aoife on the bloody battlefield of Waterford was the beginning of the women's role in conquering the conquerors. Hugh de Lacy, Governor of Ireland for Henry II, married Rose O'Conor, the daughter of the King of Connacht (which resulted in de Lacy's dismissal as governor), Richard de Burgh, the Earl of Ulster, married a daughter of Hugh O'Conor, an Irish prince, and their daughter married into the Scottish royal family. William Marshall, the Earl of Pembroke, married Strongbow's daughter, and on it went until all the major Irish clans were united by blood ties to the families of the Anglo-Norman conquerors. The intermarrying continued even when forbidden by the Statutes of Kilkenny. Thomas FitzGerald, the eighth Earl of Desmond, married an Irish woman in outright defiance of the statutes. It was an act that was viewed as treasonable and hostile to the English, yet such was his love and respect for her that he refused to put her aside. FitzGerald also attempted to unite his family with that other great Anglo-Irish family, the Butlers, by marrying his daughter, Margaret (Magheen), to Piers Butler, the Earl of Ormond.

RELIGION

AT THE TIME of the Anglo-Norman conquest of Ireland, the monasteries were full of life and rich in culture. Many of the larger houses were great centers of learning and had evolved into cities that housed thousands of people. They were not always peaceful places, however. Not only had they been brutalized for centuries by Viking invaders, the religious houses also occasionally suffered at the hands of fellow countrymen as feuds and tribal battles spilled onto their lands. The Anglo-Normans continued the Viking tradition of attack. Clonmacnoise, for example, the monastery founded by Saint Ciaran, suffered six plunderings and twenty-six burnings from 834 to 1204, including an Anglo-Norman attack in 1179 during which more than 100 houses were burned to the ground. It was a victim of regular attack until an English garrison stormed the place in 1552 and took all its treasures.

The Continental reform movement of the Church made an impact on the Church in Ireland, as well. Because it had been isolated for hundreds of years, it developed differently in many respects than did the Continental churches. In an effort to bring the Irish Church in line with the rest of Europe, monks were sent in to reform the island's religious institutions. Cistercians and Augustinians, the first outsiders to establish religious houses of the Continental type, were followed by the Dominicans in 1224 and the Franciscans, until there were approximately 200 religious houses for men. As the island was divided politically and socially, so now was it divided religiously. The Irish kept to the Irish and the Anglo-Normans to the Anglo-Normans. There were several attempts to integrate, but these invariably ended in failure. Many of the Irish religious houses held very close ties to the community, and they chafed under the stern discipline and control of the Continental mother houses.

Matters were not helped when Pope Adrian IV, formerly Nicholas Breakspere, the only Englishman ever to be Pope, recognized England's claim of sovereignty over Ireland in 1155 as a way to bring its religious institutions under the control of Rome. Pope Alexander III reconfirmed Henry II's right to lordship in 1173, congratulating him for triumphing over the "disordered and undisciplined Irish," and Pope Innocent III accepted Ireland as a papal fief in 1213. It was a bitter pill for many to swallow, considering the Irish had kept Christianity alive and flourishing when other European countries were yet pagan entities. It seemed a bitter betrayal for the papacy to conspire against the Irish Church. It was an act that forever impacted the way the Irish felt about the Mother Church and the religious houses of the English.

NAMING

MANY NAMES INTRODUCED by the Anglo-Normans worked their way into the pool of names used by the Irish. Wholesale Anglicization had not yet taken place, so most native names continued to be used in their Gaelic form. Anglo-Normans who had established themselves in Ireland tended to take Irish names or Gaelicized their own names to be more like the names used by the Irish.

FEMALE NAMES

Agnes (chaste, pure)
Aifric (pleasant)
Aignéis (chaste, pure) Irish form of Agnes.
Ailbhe (?, perhaps *white*)
Áine (joy; praise, fasting)
Aisling (dream, vision, daydream) **Aislinn**
Alana (O child)
Alice (nobility)
Alicia (nobility)
Alma (?, perhaps *all-good*)
Amelia (work; rival)
Anna (grace, full of grace, mercy)
Aoibh (beauty)
Aoibheann (beautiful, fair form) **Aoibhinn**
Aoife (?, perhaps *beauty*) **Aoiffe**
Aveline (?)
Báirbre (foreign woman) Irish form of Barbara.
Barran (little summit)
Beatha (life, livelihood)
Bébhinn (sweet, melodious lady)
Bidelia (strength)
Blath (flower)
Bláthnaid (flower) **Bláithín, Bláthnait**
Brenda (sword)
Brona (sorrow)
Caitríona (pure, unsullied) Irish form of Catherine.
Caoilfhionn (slender and fair)
Cecilia (blind, dim-sighted)
Ciannait (little ancient one)
Ciara (dark one, black-haired one)
Clare (bright, clear, famous)
Clíodhna (?) **Clídna, Clíona**
Damhnait (little poet)
Dana (bold)
Dearbhail (true desire)
Deirbhile (poet's daughter)
Deirdre (?, perhaps *young girl; fear*)
Doireann (sullen)
Dubheasa (black, dark beauty)

Dunflaith (lady of the fort)
Ealga (noble)
Eileanór (light, torch, bright) Irish form of Eleanor.
Eilís (God is my oath) Irish form of Elizabeth.
Eimhear (?, perhaps *swift*) **Emer**
Eistir (myrtle; star) Irish form of Esther.
Eithne (kernel)
Elaine (light, torch, bright)
Eleanor (light, torch, bright)
Elizabeth (God is my oath)
Esther (myrtle; star)
Étáin (?, perhaps *jealousy*) **Éadaoin**
Faoiltiarna (wolf lord)
Feidhelm (?)
Fíona (fair, white, clear)
Fionnghuala (white shoulders) **Fionnuala**
Flora (a flower)
Gobnait (little mouth, little beak)
Gráinne (grain goddess)
Helen (light, torch, bright)
Honor (honor, esteem)
Íde (thirst)
Irene (peace)
Isabel (God is my oath)
Iseult (?, perhaps *ruler of the ice; beautiful, fair*) **Isolde, Yseult, Ysolte**
Isibéal (God is my oath)
Joan (God is gracious)
Lassairfhina (flame or blush of the wine) **Lasairíona**
Ligach (pearly)
Luighseach (?, perhaps *light*) A feminine form of Lughaidh.
Máda (powerful in battle) Irish form of Maud.
Maggie (a pearl)
Máirghréad (a pearl) Irish form of Margaret.
Margaret (pearl)
Maud (powerful in battle)
Meadhbh (?, perhaps *joy; great, large; mead*)
Míde (my Íde *thirst*)

Móirín (little great one)
Mór (great, large)
Muadhnait (little noble one)
Múireann (long-haired)
Muirgheal (sea bright, fair one of the sea)
Muirne (beloved, affection)
Nainsí (grace, full of grace, mercy)
Nancy (grace, full of grace, mercy)
Niamh (bright)
Nicola (victory of the people)
Odharnait (little green one)
Órfhlaith (golden lady)
Pádraigín (patrician, an aristocrat)

Rathnait (little graceful one, little prosperous one)
Ríoghnach (queenly)
Sadhbh (goodness) **Sadbha, Sadhbha, Saidhbhe**
Saidhbhín (little Sadhbh *goodness*)
Samhaoir (? summer sailor)
Saraid (excellent)
Sealbhflaith (lady of possessions)
Sisile (blind, dim-sighted) Irish form of Cecilia.
Sláine (health)
Sorcha (bright, clear)
Tanith (estate)
Treise (strength)
Úna (?, perhaps *famine, hunger; lamb*)

MALE NAMES

Abbán (little abbot)
Ádhamh (man of the red earth) Irish form of Adam.
Adhamhnán (little Ádhamh *man of the red earth*)
Águistín (great, venerable)
Ailbhe (?, perhaps *white*)
Ailill (sprite)
Ailín (?, perhaps *handsome; rock*)
Aindréas (manly) Irish form of Andrew.
Ainmire (great lord)
Alan (?, perhaps *handsome; rock*)
Alexander (defender of mankind)
Alistair (defender of mankind) Irish form of Alexander.
Andrew (manly)
Anluan (great champion)
Aodh (fire) **Aodha, Aoidh**
Aodhagán (little fiery one, little ardent one)
Aodhaigh (fiery)
Aodhán (little fiery one)
Aodhfin (white fire) **Aodhfionn**
Aralt (leader of the army) Irish form of Harold.
Árdghal (high valor)
Art (a stone; a bear)
Artúr (?)
Banan (white)
Banbhan (little piglet)
Barra (head)
Beacán (little small one, wee one)
Beag (small)
Bearach (spearlike)
Bearchán (little spear)
Benedict (blessed)
Bran (raven)
Brandan (?, raven; prince)
Brandubh (black raven)
Bréanainn (prince)
Breandán (prince)
Bressal (war, strife) **Breasal, Breazil, Bresal**
Bret (a Breton)

Brian (force, strength; hill, high; kingly)
Brón (sorrow)
Buadhach (victory)
Cadhla (handsome)
Caoimhín (little gentle one)
Caolán (little slender one)
Cárthach (loving)
Cathal (battle mighty)
Cathaoir (warrior)
Ceallach (war, strife)
Ceallachán (small strife)
Cearbhall (champion, warrior)
Cecil (blind, dim-sighted)
Cian (ancient)
Cianán (little ancient one)
Ciarán (little black-haired one)
Ciardha (black-haired one)
Ciarrai (black)
Cinnéidid (ugly head, ugly chief)
Coileán (pup, cub)
Coinneach (handsome, comely)
Colmán (little dove)
Comhghall (copledge, hostage)
Comhghan (cobirth, twin)
Conaire (?, perhaps *hound + farmer*)
Conall (high-mighty) **Connell**
Conán (?, perhaps *small hound; wisdom, strength, counsel*)
Conn (sense, reason, wisdom)
Cyril (lordly)
Dáithí (swiftness, speed, surefootedness)
David (beloved)
Diarmaid (without injunction, a freeman) **Diarmait**
Dónal (world ruler)
Donn (brown)
Donnán (little brown one)
Donnchadh (brown warrior)
Dubh (black-haired, dark-haired)
Dubhglas (black, dark + blue, green, gray)

Eachann (master of horses)
Eadbhard (wealthy guardian)
Éamonn (wealthy protection) Irish form of Edmund.
Earna (experience, wisdom)
Edmund (wealthy protection)
Edward (wealthy guardian)
Éimhín (swift)
Eochaidh (horseman)
Eoghan (lamb; youth; well-born)
Fachtna (?)
Faolán (little wolf)
Fearadhach (masculine, manly)
Fearghall (man of valor)
Fearghus (man of strength)
Feichín (little raven)
Feidhlim (the ever-good)
Fiach (raven)
Fiachra (raven)
Finghin (fair at birth)
Fionán (little fair one)
Fionn (fair, white, clear)
Fionnbhárr (fair-headed)
Fionntán (little fair one)
Flann (red, ruddy)
Garbhán (little rough one)
Gearalt (spear rule) Irish form of Gerald.
Gearárd (brave with the spear) Irish form of Gerard.
Gerald (spear rule)
Gerard (brave with the spear)
Gilbert (famous pledge)
Gilibeirt (famous pledge)
Glaisne (?)
Godraidh (God's peace)
Gréagóir (vigilant, watchful)
Gregory (vigilant, watchful)
Guy (a guide, leader)
Harold (leader of the army)
Hugh (heart, mind, soul)
Íomhar (archer) Irish form of Ivor.
Ivor (archer)
Lachtna (gray, dun)
Laoghaire (calf herder)
Lasairian (a flame)
Lochlann (land of the lochs)

Lomán (little bare one)
Lorcán (little fierce one)
Maghnus (great, large)
Mainchin (little monk)
Maolcholm (servant of Saint Columba)
Maolmórdha (majestic chief)
Meallán (little pleasant one)
Muireadhach (mariner, sailor)
Murchadh (sea warrior)
Naomhán (little holy one)
Niadh (a champion)
Niall (a champion; cloud)
Nicholas (victory of the people)
Odhrán (little green one)
Oisín (a fawn)
Philip (lover of horses)
Piers (a rock, a stone)
Pilib (lover of horses)
Raghnall (powerful judgment)
Ralph (wolf counsel)
Randolf (shield wolf)
Raymond (wise protection)
Réamonn (wise protection) Irish form of Raymond.
Robert (bright with fame)
Roderick (famous king)
Roibeárd (bright with fame) Irish form of Robert.
Rónán (little seal)
Ruadhán (little red-haired one)
Ruaidhrí (famous king) Irish form of Roderick.
Ruairí (red, rust-colored)
Seanán (little ancient one)
Suibhne (well-going, pleasant)
Tadhg (a poet)
Thomas (a twin)
Tomás (a twin)
Tuathal (people mighty)
Uaithne (green)
Ualtar (ruler of the army) Irish form of Walter.
Uilliam (resolute protector) Irish form of William.
Uinseann (conquering) Irish form of Vincent.
Úistean (heart, mind, soul) Irish form of Hugh.
Vincent (conquering)
Walter (ruler of the army)
William (resolute protector)

SURNAMES

In spite of King John's declaration in 1210 that all people in Ireland conform to the laws and customs of the English, the native Irish language, laws, customs, and names continued to be used, even to the extent that the English living in Ireland began adopting the Irish method of adding Mac to the names of their fathers or other ancestors.

In 1366, the Statutes of Kilkenny ordained that every Englishman living within the Pale use the English language and adopt an English name if he or she bore an Irish one. Those who wished to keep their Irish names had to obtain royal permission to do so. In 1465, another step to do away with the native names was taken when it was ordained that every Irishman living within the Pale "take unto himself an English surname of a town, as Sutton, Chester, Trim, Skreen, Cork, Kinsale; or a colour, as White, Black, Brown; or an art, as Smith or Carpenter; or an office, as Cook, Butler; and that he and his issue use that name under pain of forfeiture of his goods yearly."

Such statutes were designed to humiliate and degrade but were in actuality very difficult to enforce. Few Irishmen felt compelled to follow them. Those that did invariably were town dwellers engaged in some kind of craft or trade.

MacAilín (son of Ailín *handsome; rock*)
Barry (from Barri *the rampart*)
Blake (the black one)
Ó Branduibh (descendant of Brandubh *black raven*)
Ó Breasail (descendant of Bressal *strife*)
Ó Briain (descendant of Brian *force, strength; hill, high; kingly*)
MacBuadhaigh (son of Buadhach *victor*)
Burke (dweller near the stronghold)
Butler (a butler, a servant in charge of the wine cellar)
Ó Cathaláin (descendant of Cathal *battle mighty*)
Ó Ceallaigh (descendant of Ceallach *war, strife*)
Ó Conaill (descendant of Connall *high-mighty*)
MacConchobhair (son of Conchobhar *high will, desire; hound lover*)

MacCuilinn (son of Cuileann *holly*)
MacCuinn (son of Conn *sense, reason, wisdom*)
MacDonnchadh (son of Donnchadh *brown warrior*)
FitzGerald (son of Gerald *spear rule*)
Ó Faoláin (descendant of Faolán *little wolf*)
Ó Fionnáin (descendant of Fionán *little fair one*)
Joyce (joyous)
Ó Lochlainn (descendant of Lachlann *land of the lochs*)
Ó Ruaìdh (descendant of Ruairí *red, ruddy*)
Ó Seanaigh (descendant of Sean *old one*)
MacShuibhne (son of Suibhne *well-going, pleasant*)
Ó Taidhg (descendant of Tadhg *poet*)
MacTighearnáin (son of Tighearnan *lord*)
Walsh (a Welshman)

Chapter Three

THE REVOLT OF THE FITZGERALDS
TO THE CROMWELLIANS
[1535–1650]

POLITICS

Henry VIII's original plan for Ireland consisted of the English and Irish living harmoniously and peaceably under his rule. His decision to dismantle home rule by destroying the FitzGeralds and establishing English government in Ireland was one the Tudors were never able to turn back from and one that sealed the island's fate. After the execution of Silken Thomas and the elimination of the rest of the FitzGeralds, Henry and his ministers thought the Irish situation was under control. They were unaware of the existence of Gerald, the ten-year-old half-brother of Thomas, who was safely hidden away in Italy while Henry's men were laying waste to the FitzGerald clan.

Lady Eleanor FitzGerald, the widow of MacCarthy Reagh and the aunt of Gerald took up the banner in support of the Irish. Sickened by the atrocities committed against her family, she determinedly united the great families of Ireland against the English government. Even the Earl of Ormond, whose estates had greatly increased with the destruction of the FitzGeralds and the forfeiture of their lands, was horrified at the English actions and turned against the policies of Henry VIII.

Gerald, meanwhile, was well-received by the Pope and European rulers, all of whom believed Henry had usurped the English throne without right. France, at odds with Henry VIII, sought to exploit his situation with Ireland and readied a large fleet to aid the Irish. With such powerful backing behind them, the Irish proceeded to invade the English districts of Tipperary and the Pale in 1539. France ultimately decided not to help (they had come to an agreement with Henry), and the Irish were no match for the great cannons of the English army. Nonetheless, they continued their resistance movement.

Henry VIII had concerns other than the political situation with Ireland. Tangled in the mess was a serious religious issue that needed to be dealt with. After the Pope refused to grant a divorce from Catharine of Aragon, Henry decided a split between the Church and the crown was necessary. He declared himself supreme head of the Church in England and substituted his own authority in place of the papacy. The Irish Church, however, continued to be under the authority of Rome. That meant that while Princess Elizabeth was legitimate in England, she was not in Ireland. So, not only did Henry need to defeat Ireland politically, he needed to force the Irish Church to come under his authority as well.

In 1536, an Irish parliament composed entirely of Englishmen was called and passed legislation to reform the Church. A second session provided for direct rule of Ireland, and a session a year later denied all papal authority in Ireland.

As the Geraldine resistance crumbled and the Church began to yield to the king's authority, Henry called another Irish parliament. For the first time, Irish lords and representatives from the areas outside the Pale were included. In 1541, they acknowledged that Henry and his heirs would forevermore be kings of Ireland. Henry's peaceful policy of surrender and regrant was now more readily accepted. Under this arrangement, the Irish and Anglo-Irish lords gave their lands to the king, promised him allegiance, acknowleged him as head of the Church, and promised to substitute English law, language, and customs in place of their own Brehon law and their Irish culture. In return, they received the lands back as feudal grants, were usually given the title earl, and had an English lord above them in the feudal command. Indeed, one of Henry's greatest accomplishments was the submission of the rebellious and independent Ulster O'Neills. In spite of those in the far reaches who continued their staunch advocacy for Irish independence, Henry Tudor was now King of Ireland.

Few Irish realized that Henry's true aim behind the guise of surrender and regrant was to take the land and destroy Irish culture. Though the obvious effect of the surrender and regrant policy was increased support for Henry, that same policy was secretly used as a way to lessen the traditional responsibilities Irish lords had to their people. It also affected the traditional manner in which chieftains were elected. In accordance with Brehon law, the chief was elected from the derbfine. Now, English law superceded Irish tradition. Once a chieftain died, his son inherited all, and great wealth and power was kept in the hands of the one family. It was a situation that degraded the once-strong tuatha into quarreling factions across the island as the derbfine became a relic of the past.

Henry was also busy putting Englishmen into positions of power that the Irish and Anglo-Irish had held for hundreds of years. By undermining the Irish system of leadership, Henry's conquest was victorious. He kidnapped the sons of noblemen and had them raised in England where they were instructed in the ways of the English, indoctrinated in the Protestant religion, and strongly encouraged to forget their own history and culture. He backed false claimants with English soldiers until legitimate chiefs were either killed, exiled, or yielded to him. Then, when the people objected to their lands being taken away, he sent his soldiers out across the districts to lay waste to the land, kill the rebels, and send the rest of the people away from their homes. Monasteries were destroyed and their treasures stolen; the poets and historians were killed and their books of genealogy and Irish history destroyed. In this manner, Henry was able to obtain land for English settlement, and by planting his own loyal people across Ireland, he was able to plant his own will across the island as well. By the time of Henry VIII's death in 1547, the Tudor conquest of the island was in full swing.

The reign of Edward VI (1547–1553) was too brief to have had much of a political effect on Ireland, but it was at this time that the English had their revenge upon James Butler, Earl of Ormond. Unlike many of the other Sean Ghall, the Butlers had always been staunch supporters of the English. After the atrocities committed upon the Geraldines, Butler joined the FitzGerald cause and formed a strong southern alliance with the earl of Desmond. After Desmond's death, Butler added the earldom of Desmond to his own and united much of the country. This brought the wrath of England down upon him, for it was English policy to keep the major families from amassing any type of power. The earl was invited to London, and there, at a supper at Limehouse, his whole retinue was poisoned. Fifty became ill; seventeen died, including the earl himself.

The reign of Mary (1553–1558) was equally as brief, but she had more of an effect on the Irish than did her sickly brother, Edward VI. Though she reinstated the Catholic religion, she had no plans to end the conquest of Ireland. In spite of her father's policy of surrender and regrant, large areas of Ireland remained as ungovernable and intractable as ever. Mary's solution to the problem was an extension of her father's earlier attempts to force the local populations out. She had two of the most rebellious counties, Leix and Offaly, declared Queen's County and King's County, confiscated the entire territory, and brought it under the English system of government. Under the plan, the native Irish would be confined to a third of the two counties, and English settlers would be planted in the remaining two-thirds. This plantation was to continue slowly for the next 100 years.

When Elizabeth (1558–1603) came to the throne, she speared the Tudor conquest of Ireland to new heights of brutality. She had two demands of the lord deputy of Ireland: do away with Brehon Law to bring every province completely under her authority, and bring the Irish Church in line with the Church of England. To attain those goals, nothing and no one was held sacred. The elderly, the infants, the children, the priests—all were sacrificed by the sword to break the Irish spirit and obtain compliance. It was a time of butchery and desecration, of deceit and dishonor, that saw the Irish nearly destroyed; it was the beginning of 400 years of oppression and mass displacement of the Irish people. Nevertheless, they fought on, stubbornly refusing to let themselves be exterminated.

The Nine Years' War in Ulster was the culmination of Irish resistance to Elizabeth and Ireland's last stand under the Brehon Laws. As the Queen had unlimited resources at her disposal, she was the ultimate victor. In 1603, a few days after her death, Hugh O'Neill signed the Treaty of Mellifont. The Tudor conquest of Ireland was complete, and the traditional Irish form of government would never again exist.

Elizabeth's successor was James VI of Scotland (1603–1625). He continued the policy of surrender and regrant with the Ulster chiefs, but the presence of English garrisons was constant, and persecution of the natives did not diminish. It became clear that the English had won the island, and nearly 100 Ulster earls exiled themselves to the Continent. It was called the Flight of the Earls, and such a dramatic exit of so many chiefs left the Irish without any form of traditional leadership and allowed the lord deputy to confiscate their lands. Of the nine Ulster counties, six were taken by the crown. In 1609, the Articles of Plantation allowed for the settlement of 500,000 acres, upon which towns, villages, and fortified enclosures were to be raised in order to ensure a secure, profitable, and flourishing colony. A small portion of land was reserved for Irish landlords, provided they adopted English husbandry methods. Other areas were selected for plantation, and it was the eastern counties of Antrim and Down that saw the most success in the supplanting of Englishmen and Scotsmen for the native Irish.

What became of the Irish who had been displaced? Not only were they thrown off their lands and deprived of a means to make a living, they no longer had the safety and comfort of the clan to support them. Many thousands died of starvation, and thousands fled the country to enlist in Continental armies. For thirty years, a deep, bitter hatred toward the Protestant planters grew in the breasts of those who were stuggling to survive.

The main issue for both James and Charles I was the antagonism between Protestant and Catholic factions, and the endeavor to keep them from fighting with one another and disrupting government. Whereas Elizabeth had done everything she could to crush the Catholic religion and its followers, both James and Charles made more of an effort to accomodate Catholics, prompting Protestants to fear that the Catholics would become a majority. To keep that from happening, the House of Commons and the House of Lords had the lord lieutenant of Ireland, the Earl of Strafford, removed from office and beheaded. Seeing that the king could not protect even his own servants from parliament, Catholics feared another storm of Protestant persecution was about to sweep the island. Added to this fear was the bitter resentment of a people who were being destroyed; the recipe for rebellion was complete.

In the fall of 1641, rebellion under the leadership of Rory O'More broke out in Ulster. Known to history as the Irish Rising of 1641, it was less an organized military offensive than a spontaneous outbreak of aggression due to intense bitterness and anger. During the uprising, approximately 2,000 Protestant planters were killed outright and many more stripped of their clothes and possessions and driven off to seek refuge in the port cities and English-held towns. There was an undertaking by Hugh O'Neill to seize Dublin Castle, and while that failed, a number of strongholds were captured. O'Neill claimed that he was following the orders of Charles I and defending his king against a hostile parliament. It was an untrue statement that did great harm to Charles's reputation in Presbyterian Scotland and Protestant England.

Ireland became host to a number of different factions and armies, all either fighting one another or allying with one group or another. There were the Old Irish Nationalists, the New Irish Nationalists, the New Irish Royalists (who were for King Charles), Anglo-Irish Parliamentarians, Scoto-Irish Parliamentarians, and Scoto-Irish Royalists.

In spite of the number of different groups vying for supremacy, the Irish rebellion had gone so well that in the spring of 1642, a provisional Catholic government was set up in Kilkenny and the Irish Catholic Confederacy (which recognized Charles I as king) was formed. The confederation issued its own coinage, manufactured weapons and gunpowder, organized an army, and established taxes. The Papal Nuncio arrived in 1645, bringing £20,000 and enough weapons for 6,000 soldiers. The goal of the confederacy was unity of the country, but that proved elusive, and the bloody and brutal war between the Catholics and the Protestants continued for several years. Cromwell's Parliamentarians were sent to Ireland to fight against Charles. After the king met with leaders of the confederation and agreed to many of their demands, the Irish army was sent afield to fight for Charles.

In 1649, Charles I was captured and executed, and though the Irish Catholic Confederacy dissolved, they continued their resistance to English government. In late summer, Cromwell arrived to exact his revenge.

SOCIETY

THE POPULATION OF Ireland during the reign of the Tudors is believed to have been around a million people, with that number falling after the second half of the sixteenth century due to increased warfare and the displacement of the native Irish. Many Gaelic districts, especially those of Antrim, Down, and Galway, were only sparsely populated with Irish natives. The English Pale, in comparison, held over half the total population, though it comprised but a third of the area of the island. Yet it would be wrong to believe that the majority of residents of the Pale were English, for by the year 1600, those of English or Scots descent still comprised less than 2 percent of all people residing in Ireland.

Society in the Pale was much like that of Tudor England. The land within its boundaries was fertile and the ports and towns bustling and prosperous. Because of the unsettled times, there were few large, unfortified English-style manor houses. Dwellings built from native materials like wood, wattle, and thatch were the most common. The large, classic dwellings of the lordship were usually the tall, fortified towers constructed during the Anglo-Norman conquest. In the plantation areas, small stone cottages with lime-washed walls like those built in England and Scotland were the favored dwellings of the planters.

Conditions outside in the Gaelic areas were quite different from those in the Pale. Much of the Gaelic lands were either bog or covered in forest, which made it difficult to eke out an existence from the land. Society was an itinerant and pastoral one where *creaghts*, herdsmen and their escorts, led large herds of cattle and horses across the wastes from one pasture to another. Agricultural activity tended to be limited to the cultivation of small plots rather than the large, plowed fields and enclosures that were common within the

Pale. And, as the land was held by individual members of a tuath for only a year or so at a time, there was little incentive toward development or improvements. Permanent residences were uncommon. Most dwellings, even those of the chiefs and clan nobility, consisted of simple cabins or huts made of clay or branches typically covered with turf.

Apart from the creaghts who were sharecroppers, the peasants labored for landowning clans. This group of people held no property rights, had no voice in the tribal council, and were completely dependent upon the landowner they worked for. They were a highly mobile group who migrated freely across the country, much as the migrant workers of today follow the harvests and travel from state to state seeking work in the fields.

The main diet of the Irish consisted of beef, mutton, curds, buttermilk and other milk products, griddle cakes, and watercress salads. The English settlers, on the other hand, took full advantage of the abundance of wildlife found on the island by supplementing their diet with a variety of game and fish. Food was plentiful, and the people enjoyed good health.

By 1603, after nine years of warfare, Ireland was a much different place. The wholesale destruction of crops and the slaughter of animals by English soldiers resulted in a serious scarcity of food and widespread famine. The plague followed in December 1603 and wreaked havoc for another two years. Conditions were desperate, and many of Ireland's poor migrated to England and France in the hope of building a new life.

It is interesting to note that the Gaels of Ireland considered themselves to be a part of a Gaelic world that included the highlands and islands of Scotland. Gaelic consciousness and unity was more important to many than the notion of simply being Irish. They were Gaels first and inhabitants of Ireland second, and the English were viewed as foreigners invading their Gaelic world.

By the end of the sixteenth century, Anglicization of the upper classes had made some headway. They had abandoned their traditional manner of dress and adopted English fashions (though some continued to wear the distinctive Irish cloak over top) and many had also mastered the English language. When representatives of the Confederation of Kilkenny met in 1642, their business was conducted in English rather than Irish.

Anglicization of the lower classes proceeded much more slowly. In spite of the exhortations of clergy and threatened penalties, they continued in their traditional dress through the first half of the seventeenth century and clung determinedly to their language.

RELIGION

THOUGH THE REFORMATION had started some years before Henry VIII came to power, it was only during his reign that it began to affect the Irish. Henry himself was not a Protestant, and as such, his fight with Rome was based not on doctrine but on power. In order to bring the Church and its assets under his own control, he had himself declared the supreme head of the Church in England. He had to do the same in Ireland. When Henry summoned the first Irish parliament of 1536 to pass legislation declaring him head of the Irish Church, resistance came from the proctors, the representatives of the clergy. As a result, the proctors were declared a relic of the past and eliminated from the Irish parliament. A second parliament later that year had no trouble passing Henry's reform policies. While several Church appointments were given to the Irish and Anglo-Irish, many more were given to Englishmen who helped carry out the reform.

Henry also decided that the monasteries needed to be eliminated. Dissolution of the religious houses began in 1537. Ten years later, more than half of Ireland's monasteries were dissolved and their treasures carted off. Religious shrines and statues were defiled and smashed and sacred relics destroyed. Henry's policies, of course, met with Irish resistance, not only because the Irish were determined Catholics but because his intrusion into the Church was seen as yet another intrusion of foreign power into the lives of the Irish people. The monasteries had become the learning centers of the island, and their closing affected not only those that were there for an intellectual education or to learn a craft or a trade, it also affected the villages that grew up around them. But though the closings impacted the economy and education, the Church continued much as it had for centuries and resisted efforts to bring the Mass in line with the type of service held in the English Church. Recusancy (the refusal of attending the reformed church) was widespread and almost impossible to enforce.

When nine-year-old Protestant Edward VI came to the throne, the Reformation came with him, though little was initially done to foster change within the Irish Church. In 1553, the reformer John Bale attempted to introduce the new English Prayer Book—an attempt that was met with disaster when both laity and clergy revolted. Mary's accession to the throne stopped the reform movement in its tracks. Yet, in spite of the fact that she was a devout Catholic, she held little regard for either the Irish people or the Irish Church and refused to restore the monasteries.

When Elizabeth, the most aggressive of the Tudors, came to the throne, she vigorously pushed the plantation of English settlers onto Irish lands. The planters were invariably of the Protestant faith and required a Protestant church to worship in. An Act of Uniformity was passed, requiring all clergy to use the English Book of Common Prayer, even though few Irish were able to read or understand the English language it was written in; church attendance was compulsory. Elizabeth did make a concession to the Catholic Irishry and Sean Ghall by allowing them to recuse themselves from Protestant church services as long as they paid a recusancy fee and remained loyal to the crown.

Since many of the monasteries and old churches had been destroyed, the Irish Church was in quite a state of neglect. Not only had many sees been vacant for years, many of the clergy were now uneducated and their parochial duties unattended to. In 1564, a commission was formed to force reform of the Church. The commission met with a great deal of resistance outside the Pale, and in 1569, the FitzGeralds led a revolt in Munster, reportedly in defense of the Catholic faith. The English now began to believe that catholicism was the root from which all rebellion sprung, and Elizabeth's objectives began to change from simply bringing the island under the authority of the crown to complete domination, and even extermination, of a people regarded as inferior and worthless, and a religion deemed dangerous and subversive.

As the Reformation continued, means such as those used in England to bring the people within the new faith were now employed in Ireland. Torture, burnings, roastings, disbowelings, beheadings—the list of ways used to persuade the Irish to abandon their religion extended only as far as the grim imaginations of the executioners and their masters. It was enacted that every priest found preaching the Catholic religion in Ireland was to be found guilty of rebellion and henceforth hanged, then his bowels removed and burned, then beheaded and his head stuck upon a pole in a public place. Of course, that was all after suffering unspeakable tortures. The price fixed on the head of a priest was five pounds, the same as that of a wolf.

Rather than bring the flocks into the arms of the Protestant Church, such loathsome behavior by Church officials succeeded only in filling the Irish with horror, fear, and detestation. The Irish fight for political independence became wrapped in the fight for the survival of their religion and of their very race.

King James, the son of a Catholic mother and Protestant father, would have preferred to allow for liberty of conscience, but the politics of the day did not permit such a relaxed attitude. In 1605, a proclamation was issued demanding conformity to the Protestant faith and ordering all Catholic clergy evicted from the island. But, since Protestant churches and the machinery to enforce the laws of the crown were only in the Pale and in the old towns established by Anglo-Normans, the only people affected were the old English settlers.

The Church of Ireland, born from the familiar spirits of Ireland's three saints, Patrick, Brendan, and Bridget, was now a church of strangers. The Irish were pressed to seek out other places to worship. At abandoned monasteries and sacred wells, hidden away from the eyes of state officials, fugitive priests and sympathetic clergymen administered the traditional rites of the Catholic Church.

In 1641, an organization known as the Defenders rose to protect the priests. Led by Rory O'Moore, the Defenders provided fugitive priests with a way to safety. "Priest-holes" and secret hideouts were built and used to hide priests until they were smuggled out of the country. To ensure the continuation of the Catholic religion in Ireland, candidates for the priesthood were sent to French seminaries to train.

When civil war broke out in England during the reign of Charles I, Ireland was generally left to her own devices. The Catholic faith made a reemergence, and Protestants were now at the receiving end of discrimination and repression. After the war was over some eight years later and Charles had fallen to the executioner's axe, the English parliament was free to retaliate against the Catholic Irish. Late in the summer of 1649, Oliver Cromwell led an army of 30,000 to Ireland to avenge the crimes committed against Protestants and to put the rebellious Irish down once and for all.

NAMING

As THE SEAN Ghall and subsequent English settlers adopted Irish customs, their English names were often changed. Many Gaelicized their names or adopted native Gaelic ones. For example, Bartley was Gaelicized as Beartlaí, Edward became Eadbhard, and Eleanora was Gaelicized as Eileanór. To force the English to become English once again, the Statutes of Kilkenny demanded that all Englishmen born in England or Ireland readopt their English language, culture, and names. An act of parliament in 1465 took another step to stamp out Irish culture by attempting to force the Irish living within the Pale to adopt the English language and manner of dress, as well as English names. Many did so, either by changing their names altogether or by Anglicizing the spellings. Through the process of Anglicization, a number of different spellings arose from a common Irish name. For example, the masculine Éimhín (little swift one) was Anglicized as Evan, Evin, and Ewan; Eochaidh (horseman) was changed to Achaius, Aghy, Atty, and Oghie. It was also common practice to substitute the Irish name for an English one that was similar in sound. Take, for example, the name Feardorcha (dark-complexioned). The spelling was Anglicized as Fardoragh, but the English names Frederick and Ferdinand were also used to replace it. The same was true with female names. Bébhinn (sweet, melodious lady) was Anglicized as Bevin, Vivian, and Vevina. Eithne (kernel) was Anglicized as Ena, Enya, Ethna, Etna, Etney, and even Annie.

Out of reverence for the name of the mother of God, neither the name Mary nor any of its Gaelic variants were in common use before the seventeenth century. When the name began to be used, the variant Muire was reserved for the exclusive use of the Virgin Mary and was never used as a personal name.

FEMALE NAMES

Afric (pleasant) **Africa** Anglicized form of Aifric.
Aghna (chaste, pure) Irish form of Agnes.
Agnes (chaste, pure)
Aifric (pleasant)
Aignéis (chaste, pure) Irish form of Agnes.
Ailís (noble one) **Ailis, Ailíse, Ailse** Irish form of Alice.

Aimilíona (industrious; rival) Irish form of Amelina.
Áine (joy, praise; fasting)
Aisling (dream, vision, daydream) **Aislinn, Ashling, Isleen**
Alana (O child)
Alastrina (defender of mankind)

Alastríona (defender of mankind) Irish form of Alexandra and Alexandrina.

Alexandra (defender of mankind) **Alexandrina**

Alice (noble one)

Alma (?, perhaps all-good)

Amelia (industrious; rival)

Amelina (industrious; rival)

Anna (grace, mercy) **Anne** Used to Anglicize Áine, *joy, praise; fasting.*

Aoibh (beauty)

Aoibheann (beautiful, fair of form) **Aoibhinn**

Aoife (?, possibly *beauty*) **Aoiffe**

Ashling (dream, vision, daydream) Anglicized form of Aisling.

Augusteen (great, venerable)

Aveline (?)

Barran (little top, little summit)

Beatha (life, livelihood) **Betha**

Bébhinn (sweet, melodious)

Bevin (sweet, melodious) Anglicized form of Bébhinn.

Blath (flower)

Bláthnaid (flower) **Bláithín, Bláthnait**

Caiti (pure, unsullied) **Cáitín** Irish form of Katie.

Caitlín (pure, unsullied) Irish form of Catheline.

Caitríona (pure, unsullied) Irish form of Catherine.

Caoilfhionn (slender and fair)

Catheline (pure, unsullied)

Catherine (pure, unsullied) **Catharine, Catharine, Katherine**

Cathleen (pure, unsullied) Anglicized form of Caitlín.

Cecilia (blind, dim-sighted)

Christian (a Christian, a follower of Christ)

Christina (a Christian, a follower of Christ)

Chrístíona (a Christian, a follower of Christ) **Cristín** Irish form of Christine.

Ciannait (little ancient one)

Ciara (black-haired one) **Ceara**

Clár (bright, clear, famous) Irish form of Clare.

Clare (bright, clear, famous)

Clíodhna (?) **Clídna, Clíona**

Conchobarre (?, possibly *wisdom, counsel, strength + aid; hound, dog + aid; high will, desire;* or *hound lover*)

Cordelia (?, possibly *daughter of the sea* or *jewel of the sea*)

Crístíona (a Christian, a follower of Christ) Irish form of Christina.

Damhnait (poet)

Deirbhile (poet's daughter)

Deirdre (?, possibly *young girl*)

Dervila (poet) Anglicized form of Damhnait.

Doireann (sullen)

Dominica (of the Lord)

Dorren (sullen) Anglicized form of Doireann.

Éabha (life) Irish form of Eve.

Éadaoin (a mythological goddess of the sun)

Eibhlín (?) Irish form of Aveline.

Eileanór (light, torch) **Eileanóra** Irish form of Eleanor.

Eileen (?) **Aileen** Anglicized form of Eibhlín.

Eilís (God is my oath) **Eilíse** Irish form of Elizabeth.

Eimhear (?, possibly *swift*)

Eireen (peace) Irish form of Irene.

Eithne (kernel)

Elaine (light, torch, bright)

Eleanor (light, torch, bright) **Eleanora**

Elizabeth (God is my oath) **Elisabeth**

Emer (?)

Ena (kernel) Anglicized form of Eithne.

Enya (kernel) Anglicized form of Eithne.

Eve (life) **Eva** Eve was also used to Anglicize Aoife *beauty.*

Eveleen (little Eve *life*) **Evelin**

Faoiltiarna (lord of the wolves)

Feidhelm (?)

Fidelma (?) Anglicized form of Feidhelm.

Fina (fair, white, clear) **Finna** Anglicized form of Fíona.

Finola (white shoulders) **Fenella, Finella** Anglicized form of Fionnghuala.

Fíona (fair, white, clear)

Fionnghuala (white shoulders) **Fionnuala**

Gertrude (spear woman, spear strength) Used to Anglicize Gráinne *grain goddess.*

Gobnait (a mouth, a beak) **Gobinet, Gobnet**

Gráinne (grain goddess)

Grania (grain goddess) Irish form of Gráinne. Grania Mhaol Ni Mhaolmhaigh was a sixteenth century queen of the Western Isles and known to the English as Grace O'Malley.

Helena (light, torch, bright) **Helen**

Honor (honor, esteem, integrity) **Honora, Honoria**

Íde (thirst)

Irene (peace)

Isabel (God is my oath)

Iseult (?, possibly *ruler of the ice; beautiful, fair*) **Hisolda, Isolda, Isolde, Yseult, Ysolte**

Isibéal (God is my oath) Gaelic form of Isabel.

Jane (God is gracious)

Jean (God is gracious)

Joan (God is gracious)

Joanna (God is gracious) **Johanna**

Kate (pure, unsullied)

Keelin (slender, fair) Anglicized form of Caoilfhionn.

Labhaoise (famous in war) Irish form of Louisa and Louise.

Louise (famous in war) **Louisa**

Mabel (lovable)

Máda (powerful in battle) Irish form of Maud.

Maeve (?) Anglicized form of Meadhbh.

Máire (sea of bitterness or sorrow) Irish form of Mary, not used before the 17th century.

Máirín (little Mary *sea of bitterness or sorrow*)

Máirghréad (a pearl) **Máiréad, Maireád** Irish form of Margaret.

Margaret (a pearl)

Marie (sea of bitterness or sorrow)

Maude (powerful in battle)

Maura (great)

Maureen (little Mary) **Maurine** Anglicized form of Máirín.

Meadhbh (?, possibly *joy; great, large;* or *mead*)

Moina (little noble one) Anglicized form of Muadhnait.

Moira (sea of bitterness or sorrow) Anglicized form of Máire.

Móirín (little Mór *great, large*)

Mór (great, large) **Móire**

More (great, large) Anglicized form of Mór.

Moreen (little Mór) Anglicized form of Móirín.

Morrin (long-haired) Anglicized form of Múireann.

Muadhnait (little noble one) **Muadhnata, Muadhnatan**

Múireann (long-haired)

Muirgheal (sea-bright, fair one of the sea)

Muirne (beloved, affection)

Muriel (sea-bright, fair one of the sea) Anglicized form of Muirgheal.

Myrna (beloved, affection) Anglicized form of Muirne.

Níamh (bright)

Odharnait (little green one)

Ohnicio (honor, esteem) Irish form of Honor.

Órfhlaith (golden lady) **Orflath**

Orlaith (golden lady) **Orla, Orlagh** Anglicized form of Órfhlaith.

Ornat (little green one) **Orna** Anglicized form of Odharnait.

Rathnait (little prosperous one) **Ranait**

Regina (queen)

Ríoghnach (queenly)

Riona (queenly) Anglicized form of Ríoghnach.

Sabia (goodness) Anglicized form of Sadhbh.

Sabina (Sabine woman) Also used to Anglicize Sadhbhín *little Sabbath.*

Sadhbh (goodness) **Sabha, Sadbha, Sadhbha, Saidhbhe**

Sadhbhín (little Sadhbh *goodness*) **Saidhbhín**

Samhaoir (?, perhaps *summer sailor*)

Saraid (excellent)

Sheena (God is gracious) Anglicized form of Síne.

Sheila (blind, dim-sighted) **Sheela, Sheelagh** Anglicized form of Síle.

Shona (God is gracious) Anglicized form of Síne.

Siany (health) Anglicized form of Sláine.

Síle (blind, dim-sighted) Irish form of Cecilia and Cecily.

Síne (God is gracious) Irish form of Jean.

Sinéad (God is gracious) **Sinead, Sineaid** Irish form of Jane.

Siobháinín (little Siobhán *God is gracious*) **Siubháinín**

Siobhán (God is gracious) Irish form of Joan.

Sisile (blind, dim-sighted) Irish form of Cecilia and Cecily.

Sive (goodness) Irish form of Sadhbh.

Sláine (health)

Slanie (health) Anglicized form of Sláine.

Sorcha (bright, clear)

Susanne (lily, rose) **Susanna**

Súsanna (lily, rose) **Sósanna** Irish form of Susanne.

Tanith (an estate)

Treise (strength)

Úna (?, possibly *famine, hunger* or *lamb*)

MALE NAMES

Abbán (little abbot)

Abban (little abbot) Anglicized form of Abbán.

Abracham (father of a multitude) **Ábraham** Irish form of Abraham.

Abraham (father of a multitude)

Adamnan (little Adam) Anglicized form of Adhamhnán.

Ádhamh (man of the red earth) Irish form of Adam.

Adhamhnán (little Ádhamh)

Aedan (little fiery one) Anglicized form of Aodhán.

Aeneas (to praise) Brought to Ireland to Anglicize several names such as Aengus *one, choice* and Éigneachán *little death.*

Aengus (one, choice, preeminent)

Águistín (great, venerable) **Agaistin, Aghuistín** Irish form of Augustine.

Aidan (little fiery one) **Aiden** Anglicized form of Aodhán.

Ailbhe (?, perhaps *white*)

Ailill (sprite)

Ailín (?, perhaps *handsome; rock*)

Aindréas (manly) Irish form of Andrew.

Ainmire (great lord)

Alaios (famous in war) **Alabhaois** Irish form of Aloysius.

Alan (?, possibly *handsome; rock*)

Alastar (defender of mankind) **Alasdair** Irish form of Alexander.

Alastrann (defender of mankind) Irish form of Alexander.

Alexander (defender of mankind)

Alistair (defender of mankind) Anglicized form of Alastar.

Angus (one, choice, preeminent)

Anlon (great champion) Anglicized form of Anluan.

Anluan (great champion)

Antaine (?) Irish form of Anthony.

Anthony (?, *priceless, of inestimable worth*) is a folk definition.

Aodh (fire) **Aodah, Aoidh**

Aodhagán (little Aodh *fire; little fiery one*)

Aodhán (little fiery one)

Aodhfin (white fire) **Aodhfionn**

Aralt (leader of the army) Irish form of Harold.

Archibald (genuinely bold, genuinely brave)

Ardal (high valor) Anglicized form of Árdghal.

Árdghal (high valor)

Art (a bear)

Artegal (high valor) Anglicized form of Árdghal.

Arthur (?)

Artúr (?)

Banan (white)

Banbhan (little piglet)

Baothghalach (foolishly valorous)

Barry (spearlike) Anglicized form of Bearach.

Bartholomew (son of Talmai *hill, mound, furrows*)

Bartley (son of Talmai)

Basil (kingly, royal) Also used to Anglicize Breasal *war,battle, strife.*

Beacán (little one, wee one)

Beag (small, wee)

Beanón (good, well-born) **Beinean, Beineón** Irish form of Benignus.

Bearach (spearlike)

Bearchán (little spear)

Bearlaí (son of Talmai) Irish form of Bartley.

Bec (small, wee) Anglicized form of Beag.

Becan (little one, wee one) Anglicized form of Beacán.

Behellagh (foolishly valorous) Anglicized form of Baothghalach.

Benedict (blessed) Used to translate the Gaelic Maolbheannachta *hoper for blessing.*

Benen (good, well-born) Anglicized form of Beanón.

Beolagh (foolishly valorous) **Behellagh** Anglicized form of Baothghalach.

Bercan (little spear) Anglicized form of Bearchán.

Boetius (foolishly valorous) Anglicized form of Baothghalach.

Bran (raven)

Brandan (raven; prince)

Brandubh (dark raven)

Branduff (dark raven) Anglicized form of Brandubh.

Brasil (war, battle, strife) **Brazil, Bresal** Anglicized form of Breasal.

Bréanainn (prince)

Breandán (prince)

Breanie (strength, valor, kingly)

Breasal (war, battle, strife)

Brendan (prince) Anglicized form of Breandán.

Brennan (prince) Anglicized form of Breandán.

Bret (a Breton)

Brian (force, strength; valor; a hill; steep; high) **Brien**

Brón (sorrow)

Brone (sorrow) Anglicized form of Brón.

Bruaideadh (fragment)

Buadhach (victor, conqueror) **Buach**

Cadhla (handsome)

Caffar (helmet) Anglicized form of Cathbharr.

Cahal (battle mighty) Anglicized form of Cathal.

Cahir (warrior) Anglicized form of Cathaoir.

Cairbre (charioteer)

Calbhach (bald)

Callaghan (small strife) Anglicized form of Ceallachán.

Callough (bald) Anglicized form of Calbhach.

Canice (fair, handsome) Anglicized form of Coinneach.

Caoimhín (little gentle one, little kind one)

Caolán (slender)

Carbry (charioteer) Anglicized form of Cairbre.

Carlus (full-grown, a man) Irish form of Charles.

Carroll (champion, warrior) Name used to Anglicize Cearbhall.

Cárthach (loving)

Carthage (loving) **Cartagh, Carthy** Anglicized form of Cárthach.

Cathal (battle mighty) **Cahal**

Cathaoir (warrior)

Ceallach (war, battle, strife) **Keallach**

Ceallachán (little Ceallach *war, battle, strife*)

Cearbhall (champion, warrior)

Cecil (blind, dim-sighted)

Charles (full-grown, a man)

Christian (a Christian, a follower of Christ) Used to translate Giolla Chríost *servant of Christ.*

Christopher (bearer of Christ)

Cian (ancient)

Cianán (little Cian *ancient*)

Ciarán (little black-haired one)

Ciardha (black-haired one; dark one)

Ciarrai (black-haired one; dark one)

Cillian (war, strife) **Cillín, Killian**

Cinnéidid (helmeted head; ugly head) **Cinnéide, Cinnéidigh**

Coileán (pup, cub) **Cuileán**

Coinneach (fair, handsome)

Coireall (?)

Cole (victory of the people) Also used to Anglicize Comhghall *copledge, hostage.*

Colin (victory of the people) Also used to Anglicize Coileán *pup, cub.*

Colm (dove) **Colum**

Colmán (little dove)

Comhghall (copledge, hostage)

Comhghan (cobirth, twin)

Conaire (?, perhaps *hound + farmer*)

Conall (high and mighty) **Connell**

Conán (small hound; wisdom, counsel, strength)

Conchobhar (?, perhaps *wisdom, counsel, strength + aid; hound, dog + aid; high will, desire;* or *hound lover*) **Concobhar**

Conghal (valorous)

Conghalach (valorous)

Conley (chaste fire) Anglicized form of Connlaodh.

Conn (sense, reason, wisdom, high)

Connery (?) **Conary, Conrey, Conroy, Conry** Anglicized form of Conaire.

Connlaodh (chaste fire) **Connlaogh, Connlaoi, Connlaoth**

Conor (*wisdom, counsel + aid; hound*) **Connor** Anglicized form of Conchobhar.

Cowan (*cobirth, twin*) Anglicized form of Comhghan.

Críostóir (bearer of Christ) Irish form of Christopher.

Cuileann (holly)

Curran (hero, champion)

Cyril (lordly) Introduced by the English; used to Anglicize Coireall.

Dahy (nimbleness, swiftness) Anglicized form of Dáithí.

Dáibhidh (beloved) **Dáibhid** Irish form of David.

Daineal (God is my judge) **Dainial** Irish form of Daniel.

Dáithí (nimbleness, swiftness)

Dáivi (beloved) Gaelic form of Davy.

Daman (tame) Irish form of Damian.

Daniel (God is my judge)

Darby (without injunction, a freeman) Anglicized form of Diarmaid.

Darcy (of Arcy)

Dathlaoch (bright hero)

David (beloved)

Deasún (South Munster) Gaelic form of Desmond.

Dermot (without injunction, a freeman) **Dermod** Anglicized form of Diarmaid.

Devin (poet) Anglicized form of Dámh.

Diarmaid (without injunction, freeman) **Diarmid**

Dominic (belonging to a lord, belonging of the Lord)

Donagh (brown warrior) **Donaghy, Donnogh, Donogh, Donough** Anglicized form of Donnchadh.

Donahue (brown warrior) Anglicized form of Donnchadh.

Donal (world mighty) **Donall, Donnell** Anglicized form of Dónal.

Dónal (world-mighty)

Donald (world-mighty)

Donn (brown; brown-haired one)

Donnán (little Donn)

Donnchadh (brown warrior; strong warrior)

Donndubhán (little dark-haired one)

Donnghal (brown valor)

Dowan (little dark-haired one) Anglicized form of Dubhán.

Dubh (dark-haired)

Dubhán (little dark-haired one)

Dubhglas (black, dark + blue, green, gray)

Duff (black-haired) Anglicized of Dubh.

Ea (fire) Anglicized form of Aodh.

Eachann (master of horses)

Eadbhard (wealthy guardian) **Éadbárd** Irish form of Edward.

Eáin (God is gracious) Gaelic form of John.

Éamonn (wealthy protection; wealthy guardian) **Éamon, Eamon, Eamonn** Irish form of Edmund and Edward.

Earna (experience, wisdom, knowledge)

Earnán (little Earna experience, wisdom, knowledge)

Edmund (wealthy protection) **Edmond**

Edward (wealthy protection)

Egan (little fiery one) Anglicized form of Aodhagán.

Éigneachán (force person) **Eigneachán, Ighneachán**

Éimhín (swift)

Éinrí (home ruler) **Anraí, Hannraoi** Irish form of Henry.

Eochaidh (horseman)

Eoghan (well-born, noble)

Eóin (God is gracious) Irish form of John.

Euston (heart, mind, soul) Anglicized form of Úistean.

Evan (little swift one) **Ewan, Evin** Anglicized form of Éimhín.

Fachnan (?) **Faughnan** Anglicized form of Fachtna.

Fachtna (?)

Faolán (little wolf)

Fardoragh (dark-complexioned man) Anglicized form of Feardorcha.

Feagh (raven) Anglicized form of Fiach.

Fearadhach (masculine, manly)

Feardorcha (dark-complexioned man)

Fearghall (man of valor; superior valor)

Fearghus (superior strength; man of strength)

Fehin (little raven) **Fechin** Anglicized form of Feichín.

Feichín (little raven)

Feidhlim (the ever good)

Feidhlimidh (the ever good)

Felan (little wolf) **Phelan** Anglicized form of Faolán.

Felim (the ever good) **Phelim, Phellim** Anglicized form of Feidhlim.

Felimy (the ever good) **Phelimy** Anglicized form of Feidhlimidh.

Feoras (a rock, a stone) Irish form of Piers.

Fergal (man of valor; superior valor) Anglicized form of Fearghall.

Fergus (superior strength; man of strength)

Ferris (a rock, a stone) Anglicized form of Feoras.

Festus (?, perhaps *little raven*) Anglicized form of Fachnan and Feichín.

Fiach (raven)

Fiachra (raven)

Finan (little fair one) Anglicized form of Fionán.

Finbar (fair-haired) Anglicized form Fionnbhárr.

Fineen (fair at birth) Anglicized form of Finghin.

Fingal (fair)

Finghin (fair at birth) **Finín**

Finn (*fair, white, clear*) **Fynn** Anglicized form of Fionn.

Finnian (little fair one) **Finian**

Fintan (little fair one) Anglicized form of Fionntán.

Fionán (little fair one)

Fionn (fair)

Fionnbhárr (fair-haired)

Fionntán (little fair one)

Flann (red-haired, ruddy complexioned) **Flainn**

Flannán (little red-haired one; little ruddy one)

Garbhán (little rough one)

Garret (spear rule, brave with a spear) **Garrat**

Garvan (little rough one) Anglicized form of Garbhán.

Gearalt (spear rule) Irish form of Gerald.

Gearárd (brave with a spear) **Giorárd** Irish form of Gerard.

Gearóid (spear rule; brave with a spear) Irish form of Garrett.

Geoffrey (peaceful district; peaceful traveler; pledge of peace)

George (earth worker, farmer)

Gerald (spear rule)

Gerard (brave with a spear)

Gilbert (famous pledge)

Gilchrist (servant of Christ) Anglicized form of Giolla Chríost.

Gildea (servant of God) Anglicized form of Giolla Dhé.

Gilibeirt (famous pledge) Irish form of Gilbert.

Gill (servant) Anglicized form of Giolla.

Gillespie (servant of the bishop) Anglicized form of Giolla Easpuig.

Giolla Chríost (servant of Christ)

Giolla Dhé (servant of God)

Giolla Easpuig (servant of the bishop) **Giolla Easpaig**

Glaisne (?) **Glasny**

Godfrey (God's peace) Also used to Anglicize Gofraidh.

Gofraidh (God's peace) **Gothfraidh, Gothraidh** Irish form of the Old Norse Guthfrithr.

Gréagóir (vigilant, watchful) Irish form of Gregory.

Gregory (vigilant, watchful)

Harold (leader of the army)

Henry (ruler of an enclosure, home ruler)

Hewney (green) **Owney, Oynie** Anglicized form of Uaithne.

Hubert (bright heart, famous heart)

Hugh (heart, mind, soul) Also used to Anglicize Aodh *fire*.

Ian (God is gracious) Irish form of John.

Iarfhlaith (tributary lord)

Íomhar (bow warrior, archer) Irish form of Ivor.

Ion (God is gracious) Irish form of Ian.

Ionatán (God has given) Irish form of Jonathan.

Íoseph (he shall add) **Íosep, Seósamh, Seósap, Seósaph** Irish form of Joseph.

Ivor (bow warrior, archer)

Jarlath (tributary lord) Anglicized form of Iarfhlaith.

John (God is gracious)

Joseph (he shall add)

Kealan (slender) **Kelan** Anglicized form of Caolán.

Keiran (little black-haired one) **Kearn, Kern, Kerne** Anglicized form of Ciarán.

Kellagh (war, strife) Anglicized form of Cealach.

Kelly (war, strife)

Kennedy (helmeted head, ugly head) Anglicized form of Cinnéidid.

Kerill (?) Anglicized form of Coireall.

Kevin (little gentle one) **Kevan** Anglicized form of Caoimhín.

Labhrás (man from Laurentum) **Labhras** Irish form of Laurence.

Lachtna (gray, dun)

Lanty (servant of Saint Secundus) Anglicized form of Leachlainn.

Laoghaire (calf keeper, calf herder)

Laoighis (belonging to Leix)

Laoiseach (belonging to Leix)

Lasairian (little flame) **Laisrian**

Laughlin (servant of Saint Secundis; land of the lochs, Lakeland) Anglicized form of Leachlainn and Lochlainn.

Laurence (man from Laurentum)

Leachlainn (servant of Saint Secundis)

Lochlainn (Lakeland, Fiordland) **Lochlain, Lochlann**

Lomán (little bare one)

Lorcán (little fierce one)

Lúcás (light; man from Lucania) Irish form of Luke.

Lughaidh (?, perhaps *light*)

Luke (light; man from Lucania)

Lysagh (belonging to Leix) Anglicized form of Laoiseach.

Maeleachlainn (servant of Saint Secundis) **Maelsheachlainn**

Maghnus (great) **Mánus** Irish form of Magnus.

Magnus (great)

Mahon (a bear) Anglicized form of Mathghamhain.

Mainchin (little monk)

Máirtín (warlike) **Mártan** Irish form of Martin.

Malcolm (servant of Saint Columba)

Manus (great) Anglicized form of Magnus.

Maolbheannachta (hoper for blessing)

Maolcholm (servant of Saint Columba) **Maolcholuim, Maolcolm**

Maolmórdha (majestic chief)

Maolmuadh (noble chief)

Martin (warlike)

Mathghamhain (a bear)

Matthew (gift of God) Also used to Anglicize Mathghamhain *a bear*.

Meallán (little pleasant one)

Melan (little pleasant one) Anglicized form of Meallán.

Michael (Who is like God?)

Mícheál (Who is like God?) **Micheál** Gaelic form of Michael.

Muireadhach (seaman, sailor)

Muirgheas (sea choice)

Murchadh (sea warrior)

Murrough (sea warrior) Anglicized form of Murchadh.

Naomhán (little holy one)

Neil (champion; cloud) **Neal, Neale, Neill, Nyle** Anglicized form of Niall.

Nevan (little holy one) Anglicized form of Naomhán.

Niadh (a champion)

Niall (champion; cloud)

Odhrán (pale green)

Oghe (horseman) Anglicized form of Eochaidh.

Oisín (little deer, little fawn)

Oran (pale green) **Odran** Anglicized form of Odhrán.

Oscar (champion; warrior)

Ossian (little deer, little fawn) **Ossin** Anglicized form of Oisín.

Owen (well-born) Anglicized form of Eoghan.

Paddy (a patrician, an aristocrat) Pet form of Patrick.

Pádraig (a patrician, an aristocrat) **Pádraic, Pádhraic, Padhraig** Irish form of Patrick.

Padhra (a patrician, an aristocrat) **Paidi, Páidín** Irish form of Paddy.

Parlan (son of Talmai) Anglicized form of Parthalán.

Parthalon (son of Talmai) **Párthalán, Parthalán, Parthalón, Párthlán** Irish form of Bartholomew.

Patrick (a patrician, an aristocrat) **Patric**

Philip (lover of horses)

Piaras (a rock, a stone) Irish form of Piers.

Pierce (a rock, a stone)

Piers (a rock, a stone)

Pilib (lover of horses) **Filib, Filip** Irish form of Philip.

Rádhulbh (wolf counsel) Irish form of Ralph.

Raghnall (powerful judgment; ruler of judgment) Irish form of Rognvaldr and Reginald.

Ralph (counsel wolf)

Raymond (wise protection)

Réamonn (wise protection) Irish form of Raymond.

Rian (little king) **Ryan**

Richard (stern king)

Riocárd (stern king) **Riocard** Irish form of Richard.

Risteárd (stern king) Irish form of Richard.

Robert (bright with fame)

Roderick (famous king)

Roibeárd (bright with fame) **Ribeard, Ribeart, Riobárd, Riobart** Gaelic form of Robert.

Rónán (little seal)

Rory (red, ruddy-complexioned) **Rorie** Anglicized form of Ruairí.

Rowan (little red-haired one) Anglicized form of Ruadhán.

Ruadhán (little red-haired one)

Ruaidhrí (famous king) Irish form of Roderick.

Ruairí (red, ruddy-complexioned) **Ruaraidh**

Saebhreathach (noble judge)

Séafra (God's peace) **Seafraid, Séartha, Séathra**

Seaghán (God is gracious)

Seamus (supplanting, seizing by the heels) **Shamus** Anglicized form of Séamus.

Séamus (supplanting, seizing by the heels) Irish form of James.

Sean (God is gracious) **Shaun, Shawn** Anglicized spelling of Seán.

Seán (God is gracious) Irish form of Jean and Jehan.

Seanán (little old one)

Searcach (loving)

Séarlas (full-grown, a man) **Séarlus** Irish form of Charles.

Séathrún (peaceful district; peaceful traveler; pledge of peace) Gaelic form of Geoffrey.

Shane (God is gracious) Anglicized form of Seaghán and Seán.

Simon (heard) Also used to Anglicize Suibhne *well-going, pleasant.*

Síomón (heard) **Síomonn, Síomún** Irish form of Simon.

Siseal (blind, dim-sighted) Irish form of Cecil.

Sivney (well-going) Anglicized form of Suibhne.

Somhairle (summer sailor, Viking)

Sorley (summer sailor, Viking) Anglicized form of Somhairle.

Steafán (crown, garland) **Stiofán** Irish form of Stephen.

Stephen (crown, garland)

Suibhne (well-going, pleasant)

Tadhg (poet, philosopher)

Taidhgín (little poet, little philosopher)

Teige (poet, philosopher) **Teague, Teig** Anglicized form of Tadhg.

Thadeus (given by God)

Thomas (a twin)

Tiarnach (lordly) Anglicized form of Tighearnach.

Tiernan (little lord) Anglicized form of Tiarnán and Tighearnán.

Tierney (lordly) Anglicized form of Tighearnach.

Tighearnach (lordly)

Tighearnán (little lord) **Tiarnán**

Toal (people mighty) Anglicized form of Tuathal.

Toirdealbhach (shaped like Thor)

Tomáisín (little Tomás *a twin*)

Tomás (a twin) Irish form of Thomas.

Tuathal (people mighty)

Tully (people mighty) Anglicized form of Tuathal.

Turlough (shaped like Thor) **Tirloch** Anglicized form of Toirdealbhach.

Uaithne (green)

Ualtar (ruler of an army) **Ualtéir** Irish form of Walter.

Uilleóg (little Uilliam *resolute protector*) **Uilleac, Uillioc**

Uilliam (resolute protector) Gaelic form of William.

Uinseann (conquering) **Uinsionn** Gaelic form of Vincent.

Ulick (little Uilliam) Anglicized form of Uilleac and Uilleóg.

Vincent (conquering)

Walter (ruler of an army)

William (resolute protector)

SURNAMES

Once English rule extended beyond the Pale, Irish names suffered the effects of persecution along with the people. Efforts to submerge the native language are reflected in the numbers of names that underwent the process of Anglicization. Mac and O prefixes were increasingly dropped, and names were corrupted and distorted by officials with little or no knowledge of the Irish language.

Surnames underwent the same Anglicization process as did the first names. From a single Irish surname came several Anglicized forms of the name, and to confuse matters even more, a name that has evolved as an Anglicized form can come from several different Irish names. For example, Ó Cobhthaigh was Anglicized as Coffey, Coffie, Cowhey, Cowhig, and Cowie. The name Coffey, on the other hand, may have come not only from Ó Cobhthaigh, but from Ó Cathbhadha, Ó Cathbhuadhaigh, and Ó Cathmgogha. In some cases, Irish surnames were translated into English names. Mac Seáin became Johnson, for example, and Ó Bruic was translated into Badger.

An act of parliament under Queen Elizabeth abolished the surname O'Neill, and those who dared to continue with its use or adopt it in the future were to be judged of high treason and suffer forfeiture and death.

MacAbrehan (son of Abrehan *father of a multitude*)
Adair (?)
Akin (little Adam *man of the red earth*) **Aicken, Ekin**
MacArt (Anglicized form of MacAirt *a stone; a bear*) **MacArte, McArt, McArte**
Barron (a baron, a nobleman) **Baron**
Bateman (a boatman)
Bermingham (glorious and famous)
O'Birne (descendant of Bran *raven*)
Blake (black, dark)
Blaney (?)
Brady (spirited) Anglicized form of Brádaigh.
O'Brogan (descendant of Brógáin)
Brophy (descendant of Bróithe)
Burke (stronghold)
MacCahir (Anglicized form of MacCathaoir *warrior*) **MacCahier, McCahir**
Campion (a champion)
MacCartney (son of Carthannach *king*)
Chambers (an attendant, a chamberlain)
Clifford (dweller at the ford by the cliff)
MacColla (Anglicized form of MacCathail *warrior*) **McColla**
Ó Conghalaigh (descendant of Conghalach *valorous*)
McConnogher (son of Connchobhar *wisdom, council*)
O'Connor (Anglicized form of Ó Conchobhair)
Craddock (beloved) **Cradock**
O'Criane (Anglicized form of Ó Croidheáin *heart*)
Crosbie (dweller near the cross)
Ó Dathlaoich (descendant of Dathlaoch *swift hero, swift champion*)
O'Davin (Anglicized form of Ó Daimhín *little ox, little stag*)
MacDermod (Anglicized form of MacDuibhdhíorma *black troop*) **McDermod**
MacDermot (Anglicized form of MacDiarmada *a freeman, without injunction*) **McDermot**
McDonagh (Anglicized form of MacDonnchadha *brown warrior*) **McDonagh, MacDonogh**
MacDonill (Anglicized form of MacDomhnaill *world ruler*) **McDonill**
O' Dowda (Anglicized form of Ó Dubhda *dark, black one*) **O' Dowd**
O'Fahie (Anglicized form of Ó Fathaigh, possibly *foundation*)
Ferrall (Anglicized form of Ó Fearghail *man of valor*) **Farrell**
Fitz-Edmond (son of Edmond *wealthy guardian*)
Fitz-George (son of George *earth worker, farmer*)
Fitz-Hubert (son of Hubert *bright heart, bright mind*)
Fitz-Laghlin (son of Laghlin *land of the lochs*)
Fitz-Maurice (son of Maurice *Moorish, dark complexioned*)
Fitz-Nicholas (son of Nicholas *victory of the people*)
Fitz-Patrick (son of Patrick *a patrician*)

Fitz-Redmond (son of Redmond *counsel protection*)
Fitz-Thomas (son of Thomas *a twin*)
Fitz-Tirlagh (son of Tirlagh *aid + handsome; ingenious*)
Fitz-Walter (son of Walter *ruler of an army*)
Fitz-William (son of William *resolute protector*)
French (from France)
MacGerralt (son of Gerralt *mighty with a spear*) **McGerralt**
O'Harte (Anglicized form of Ó hAirt *a stone, a bear*)
O'Heyne (Anglicized form of Ó hEidhin, possibly *ivy*)
O'Hickey (Anglicized form of Ó hÍcidhe *healer*)
Hickman (servant of Richard) Common from the seventeenth century.
Hickson (son of Richard) Common from the seventeenth century.
MacHugh (Anglicized form of MacAodha *fiery, ardent*) **McHugh**
Kinshellagh (belonging to Ui Cinnsealaigh)
Linch (Anglicized form of Ó Loingsigh *sailor*)
MacMahone (Anglicized form of MacMathghamhna *bear*) **McMahone**
MacManus (Anglicized form of MacMaghnuis *great, large*)
Morishe (Moorish, dark-complexioned)
Mortogh (Anglicized form of Ó Muircheartaigh *navigator*)
MacOwen (Anglicized form of Mac Eoghan *well-born*) **McOwen, McOyn**
MacRiccard (son of Richard *stern king*) **McRiccard**
MacRorie (Anglicized form of MacRuadhri *red-haired, ruddy-complexioned*) **McRorie**
MacShane (Anglicized form of MacSeoin *God is gracious*) **McShane**
MacSwiny (Anglicized form of MacSuibhne *well-going*) **MacSwiny, McSwiny, McSwyny**
MacTeige (Anglicized form of MacTaidhg *poet*) **McTeige**
MacTirlagh (Anglicized form of MacToirdealghaigh *aid + handsome, ingenious*) **McTirlagh**
McTumultagh (Anglicized form of **MacTomaltaigh** *bulky*)
O'Higgin (Anglicized form of Ó hUigín, possibly *Viking*)
O'Kellie (Anglicized form of Ó Ceallaigh, possibly *strife*)
O'Loghlin (Anglicized form of Ó Lochlainn *land of the lochs*)
O'Maher (Anglicized form of Ó Meachair *kindly*)
Ó Maolmhuaidh (descendant of Maolmadh *noble chief*)
O'Moyle (Anglicized form of Maol *monk, disciple*)
O'Neill (Anglicized form of Ó Néill *champion; cloud* **O'Neile**
O'Relly (Anglicized form of Ó Raghallaigh *valiant, warlike*)
O'Rian (Anglicized form of Ó Maoilriain *servant of Rian* and Ó Riain *kingly*
Ó Searcaigh (descendant of Searcach *loving*)

The following list is comprised of families whose heads were considered and referred to as chiefs: MacArtan, MacAuliffe, MacAuley, O Beirne, O Boyle, O Brennan, O'Brien, O Byrne, O Cahan, O Callaghan, O Carroll, MacCarthy Mor, MacCarthy Reagh, MacClancy, O Clery, MacCoghlan, O Connell, O Connolly,

O Conor Don, O Conor Faly, O Conor Roe, O Conor Sligo, O Daly, O Dempsey, MacDermot, O Devlin, O Doherty, MacDonagh, O Donell, O Donoghue, O Donovan, O Dowd, O Driscoll, O Dunn, O Dwyer, O Farrell, O Flaherty, O Folane, O Gara, MacGeoghegan, MacGillycuddy, MacGilpatrick (Fitzpatrick), Mac-Gorman, O Grady, MacGrath, MacGuinness, MacGuire, O Hagan, O Hanlon, O Hara, O Heyne, O Keeffe, O Kelly, MacKenna, O Kennedy, MacKiernan, MacKinnane, MacLoughlin, O Loughlin, O Madden, MacMahon, O Mahony, O Malley, O Mannin, Macmanus, O Melaghlin, O Molloy, O Morchoe, O More, MacMorrough Kavanagh, O Mulryan, O Mulvey, Macnamara, O Neill, O Nolan, O Phelan, O Reilly, MacRory, O Rourke, O Shaughnessy, O Sheridan, O Sullivan Beare, O Sullivan Mór, O Toole.

Chapter Four

THE CROMWELLIANS TO THE ACT OF UNION
[1649–1800]

POLITICS

AFTER THE EXECUTION of Charles I in January 1649, English parliamentarians were now free to exact their revenge upon the Irish for their rebelliousness over the last eight years, including the rebellion of 1641, of which wildly exaggerated stories of Irish atrocities were circulated throughout England.

In August 1649, Oliver Cromwell and an army of 30,000 entered Dublin and prepared to put down the Irish. Cromwell may have seen his campaign as a kind of holy war, or he at least used religion to excuse his barbaric actions and excessive force, for he often said that all was done by the "Spirit of God." "And now give me leave to say how it comes to pass that this work is wrought," he said. "It was set upon some of our hearts that a great thing should be done, not by power or might, but by the Spirit of God. And is it not so clearly? That which caused your men to storm so courageously, it was the Spirit of God, which gave your men courage."

Cromwell began his mission in September 1649 by attacking the garrison at Drogheda. He then headed south toward Wexford. But Cromwell and his men were not satisfied with mere military victories. Unlike their battles to put down resistance in England, they showed no mercy in Ireland. Wholesale slaughter followed—infants, children, women, the elderly, those who surrendered, and even the livestock were brutally killed. Villages were burned, crops destroyed, and the land laid to waste. In less than a year's time, Cromwell had subdued the entire nation and brought many of its residents to ruin.

He departed in May 1650, leaving behind his son-in-law, Henry Ireton, as Irish commander-in-chief, and a Protestant garrison to deal with any lingering resistance and to impose the settlement that followed in 1652. It was a settlement that transfered the property of the landed Catholics who had supported the Irish rebellion and others who had not supported the parliamentarians, to the hands of Protestant settlers and the men of Cromwell's army. Catholic landowners who had not supported the rebels were allowed to keep a portion of their land holdings, provided they relocate to Connacht or Clare in the far western portion of the island by May 1, 1654. In all, eleven million acres were seized and divided between 35,000 soldiers and 1,000 planters.

One of the original interpretations behind the plantation idea was that the English planters would bring about a measure of civility to the Irish and gradually Anglicize Gaelic society by introducing English law and culture. Cromwell's wrecking of the country and the subsequent Act of Settlement, which provided for such large-scale forfeiture of land, did just the opposite. Rather than the gradual, peaceful intent of the original plantation experiment, Cromwell managed to tear Gaelic society out by its roots, leaving a legacy of bitterness toward the English and eliminating the traditional divisions between old English residents and the native Irish.

The transplantation did not go smoothly nor was it entirely successful in its mission to eliminate the Gaels and establish a Protestant population, as the new planters found they needed to keep the Irish on as tenants to work the land. Many soldiers sold the lands that were given to them so they could return to England, and still others married Irish women and allowed their children to follow the Catholic faith of their mothers. The English authorities had also overestimated the number of willing adventurers to settle Ireland. Reports of difficult conditions had tempered the enthusiasm of many would-be colonists, and authorities were forced to seek settlers from as far away as Holland. Recruiting Protestant clergymen for the Irish churches proved difficult as well, and even attempts to recruit ministers from New England were unsuccessful.

Cromwell died in the fall of 1658, and in May 1660, Charles II was restored to the English throne. With the restoration of the monarchy, Ireland's dispossessed hoped for the restoration of their own confiscated lands. In 1662, it was decided that those who could prove themselves innocent of rebelling against the English government would have their estates restored to them. Catholics were allowed to live in cities once again, though they were not allowed to be members of the corporation. They were also denied governmental positions and seats in parliament.

The Protestant Duke of Ormond was lord lieutenant of Ireland for much of Charles II's reign. After Charles's death, his Catholic brother, James II, assended to the throne; Ormond was deposed from office and James's brother-in-law, Lord Clarendon, became lord lieutenant. Richard Talbot, Earl of Tyrconnell and a leading Irish Catholic, was appointed lieutenant general of the army. He set about reorganizing the army by replacing its Protestant officers and enlisted men with Catholics. Tyrconnell soon began to dominate Clarendon, a member of the Church of England, and through his influence, Catholics were able to regain places on town councils and even hold judgeships. Catholic clergymen were allowed to freely go about their business; monasteries were reestablished, and schools were founded.

James became impatient with the slow implementation of the restoration of Catholicism, and he soon abandoned his policy of cooperation with the Church of England. Clarendon was recalled, and when Tyrconnell was appointed lord lieutenant in 1687, Protestants feared a backlash of the kind of prejudice and injustice that the Catholics had long endured. Many emigrated back to England and helped persuade the Protestant William of Orange to accept the English crown.

James's showdown with William took place in Ireland in 1690, and William's much larger army was victorious over James's French and Irish troops. James fled to France, leaving his commanders behind to cope as best they could. In 1691, the Williamite forces were successful in forcing the Irish into accepting the Treaty of Limerick. There were two parts to the treaty: military articles and civil articles. Under the military articles, the Jacobite forces were allowed to return to France or any other country except England or Scotland. Those who did not want to leave could make an oath of allegiance to William and join the English army or remain in Ireland under the civil articles. More than 11,000 chose the first option and voluntarily exiled themselves to Europe, where they formed the Irish Brigade. The exodus of soldiers, the ''Flight of the Wild Geese'' was only the beginning of Irish service in European armies. Between 1691 and 1791, half a million Irishmen joined the French army alone.

The civil articles of the Treaty of Limerick allowed for free transportation of Irish civilians to any European country besides England and Scotland, or they could remain in Ireland, provided they accept William as their king. Another plantation scheme followed, which left only one-seventh of Ireland in Catholic hands. Traditional Gaelic Ireland and the Ireland of the great Anglo-Irish baronial families was no more.

Protestant nationalism was born out of the efforts of Jonathan Swift to persuade the Protestant Irish that they were due the same rights the people of England enjoyed. The idea that the right to legislate for Ireland should belong solely to the Irish parliament found fertile ground with those who were chafing under English domination and unfair practices. When the Irish William King was passed over as archbishop of Dublin in favor of an Englishman, matters were only made worse.

It soon became apparent that the government did not have the ability to secure the country, and in 1778, both the House of Commons and the Lords of the Council agreed that a volunteer army was necessary to protect Ireland from privateers and foreign aggression. Headed by Ireland's gentry, independent companies were formed from the Protestant population, and funds were raised to purchase arms and accoutrements.

The Irish demanded compensation for carrying out the government's primary duty on their own: abolition of the trade restrictions that had destroyed Ireland's economy, and independence from the legislative authority of England's parliament. A movement was initiated to boycott the importation and use of English goods until the trade restrictions were lifted, and with the strength of a large force of armed men behind them, Ireland's leaders stood up and demanded their rights. The English were forced to recognize the gravity of the situation and accept the fact that their Irish policy had bankrupted the government in Ireland and its trade policies had backfired. English manufacturers, the ones the trade restrictions sought to protect, were now reeling from the effects of the Irish boycott. At the close of 1779, the acts restricting Irish trade were repealed, and Ireland was allowed to export and import within the same markets as the English.

In 1782, Ireland was finally given the freedom to legislate for itself. Penal laws against Catholics and Protestant dissenters were repealed, and civil liberties were extended to all, though Catholic-endowed schools and universities were still forbidden. In 1793, the Catholic Relief Bill was passed, which enabled Catholics to vote, allowed them to bear arms, opened all the trades and professions to them, and allowed them to hold many civil and military positions. Still denied were seats in parliament, judicial positions, and several other higher posts that continued to be reserved for Protestants.

In 1791, a Protestant lawyer by the name of Wolfe Tone formed a group known as the United Irishmen. Initially only Protestant, they eventually admitted Catholics and dedicated themselves to working for full independence from England. When attempts were made to suppress them in 1794, they became a secret society that did not hesitate to use force to accomplish their goal. Another group, the Protestant Orange Order, emerged around the same time with the objective of maintaining Protestant control and seeing to the safety of Protestants and their holdings. In 1798, the United Irishmen launched a rebellion, but when many members backed out at the last moment, the rebellion was quickly put down. Tone was tried and convicted of treason and sentenced to be hung, drawn, and quartered, though he managed to commit suicide before the sentence could be carried out. Even though the rebellion had been unsuccessful, Wolfe Tone left a legacy of revolutionary violence that endures to this day.

The Irish prime minister, William Pitt, came to believe that the only way to ensure peace and maintain the Protestant ascendancy was through a union with Great Britain. In 1799, parliament met and narrowly defeated the proposal. A good deal of bribery and intimidation of the members followed, as did promises for full Catholic emancipation, and when parliament met again in 1800, the measure passed. Parliamentary independence, which many had fought so hard for, had lasted only eighteen years.

SOCIETY

OLIVER CROMWELL SUCCESSFULLY butchered his way through Ireland, leaving behind a ruined country and a desperate, defeated people. He left a legacy of bitterness and famine that affected Irish society for generations. And, the economic recovery that followed his cruel methods of putting down the Irish had little effect on native Ireland, for that recovery was generally enjoyed by Protestant merchants and planters, not the Catholic masses.

It has been estimated that between the years 1641 and 1652, over 500,000 Irish were killed or had died from deprivation. This was approximately a third of the entire Irish population. Nearly 40,000 soldiers emigrated to Europe and "slave hunts" saw around 100,000 more Irish sold into slavery in the West Indies. Famine was so severe that many were forced into eating rats and mice; it even led to the occasional "Hansel and Gretel" type of situation whereby starving old women would entice children to their homes and then devour them.

The annihilation of the Catholic Irish was not relegated only to Ireland. Any Irishmen found as crewmen at sea were tied back-to-back and thrown overboard. In one instance in Scotland, eighty women and children were thrown to their deaths from a bridge simply because they were suspected of being family members of Irish soldiers.

Cromwell's confiscation of Irish lands to parcel out between his troops, English adventurers, and those who demanded land in repayment for financing Cromwell's campaign succeeding in pushing the Irish masses into a survivalist existence. With no means of supporting themselves or their families, dispossessed gangs of outlaws known as "tories" and "rapparees" began preying upon those who had been newly planted, the Protestant Anglo-Irish who had supported the English government, and even other Catholics. Many of the peasant families that did survive in Ireland often did so only because of the recent introduction of the potato, which was easily and quickly grown and not yet customarily destroyed by English forces.

King Charles's successor was his brother, James, the first Catholic king since Mary I some 130 years earlier. James set about Catholicizing the Irish establishment by replacing Protestant office holders and judges with Catholics. He allowed for the founding of Catholic schools, the reestablishment of monasteries, and allowed for people to freely practice their trades. James also suspended parliamentary statutes penalizing Catholics, and for the first time in years, Catholics were relieved of the heavy burden of oppression. Nevertheless, most of the poor continued to be poor.

After William took control, Ireland returned to pre-James conditions. Land confiscation was ongoing as the king repaid in Irish lands the money loaned to finance his war. Dispossessed Catholic landowners lost all hope of keeping their lands or regaining those that had been lost, and they usually became as destitute as the peasant population. William's Irish policy was not only designed to bring an end to the practices of the Catholic Church, it was also preoccupied with the total repression of the Catholic people.

Penal laws that were enacted to keep Catholics from achieving any position of authority or privilege assumed their worst form under Queen Anne. In contrast to other great persecutions of history that were conducted against minority groups, the English persecution of the Irish was carried out against the majority. In 1703, earlier legislation to ''exclude papists from public trust in Ireland'' was strengthened by the passage of the ''Act to prevent the further growth of Popery.'' The laws, designed to degrade and demoralize Catholics and deprive them of all civil life and advancement, succeeded in taking away nearly every means Catholics had to support themselves and reduced them to abject poverty and ignorance.

Those who sought local or national office, teachers of all levels of schooling, and practitioners of medicine or law were first required to denounce the papacy and renounce their Catholic beliefs. The act also stated that any man or woman over the age of eighteen had to appear before two judges and take an oath of allegiance to the English monarch. Failure to take the oath resulted in a fine of from two to ten pounds and a prison sentence of from three to six months. A third refusal resulted in indefinite imprisonment and the forfeiture of all property.

It was illegal for Irish Catholics to send their children to Catholic schools overseas, for a Catholic to bear arms of any type, including ceremonial dress swords, or for a Catholic to own a horse worth more than five pounds. The act also forced any Catholic, if offered five pounds for his horse, to immediately accept the offer and relinquish the animal. Catholics were not allowed to purchase land nor acquire land from a Protestant by inheritance or marriage. Those who were already landowners were required to divide their holdings equally between all sons at death. The eldest son could be sole inheritor only on the condition that he conform to the Protestant church. This nearly put an end to the old Roman Catholic gentry. Landed families were faced with the choice of having their estates broken up and subdivided with each generation or conforming to the Church of Ireland and retaining their lands. Those who wished to keep their estates intact chose the latter option; nonconformists had their estates divided with each successive generation, and their heirs sank lower and lower on the economic scale. There were families who were able to retain both faith and fortune by having a succession of only sons, but this was the exception rather than the norm, and the number of Catholic land-owners steadily declined.

Catholics were not the only group of people discriminated against in Ireland. Protestant dissenters, usually Presbyterians, also suffered religious discrimination even though they had supported William's cause. They were allowed to vote, carry arms, and retain their property, but their religion was not recognized by the government. Marriages performed by Presbyterian clergymen could be ruled illegal and the offspring of such a union could be deemed illegitimate. The 1704 Act against Popery also excluded Presbyterians from civil service and military positions. They were now also excluded from leadership positions in northern munici-palities that many of them had founded. A Toleration Act in 1719 allowed Presbyterians freedom of worship but still required them to pay tithes to the Church of Ireland. This prompted many to emigrate to the English colonies in a search for religious freedom, and they ended up playing an important role in American's quest for independence from England.

Though Ireland was part of the English Commonwealth, there was no union between the countries. Ireland had a separate executive, and free trade between the countries did not exist. It was the policy of the English government to restrict Irish trade whenever it competed with English manufacturers and merchants. The exportation of Irish cattle was prohibited; later, the export of Irish wool to any country but England was a felony. Irish manufacturers who had begun to find markets on the Continent were now confined to selling in Ireland.

The Irish brewing industry expanded until legislation confined importation of hops from England alone.

The same happened to the glass industry, which fell after the exportation of Irish glass was prohibited. In spite of such restrictions, the business of providing ships with provisions became very profitable, as did the export of butter to the Continent. High taxation and unpopular governmental policies such as these were the norm and prompted the emigration of thousands of Protestant landowners, manufacturers, and laborers. Reforms followed later in the century and, for Protestant Ireland and especially for the large-scale entrepeneur, economic prosperity returned. The masses, however, were commonly reduced to begging and continued to live in abject poverty until the last part of the eighteenth century.

Most of Ireland's estates were now owned by absentee Englishmen. The preferred practice was to live in England and lease the estates out to "squireens" who then divided the land among tenant farmers. Few improvements were made to the land, nor was there a great deal of interest in improving agricultural methods. High rents and such small holdings left little incentive and even less money for tenant farmers to make improvements, and they often lived in squalid and desperate conditions. The typical dwelling for the peasantry consisted of a one- or two-room mud cabin with a thatched roof, dirt floor, and no windows or chimney; one doorway offered the only light. It was common for a variety of livestock to live in the same small structure and wander in and out indiscriminately. The poorest were not fortunate to have even this little bit of comfort. Most were forced to squat in ditches or along the roadside in small hovels of dirt, sticks, and the occasional bit of straw. Like fragile bird nests, they were usually rebuilt once a year. Clothing was rough and scarce. Many children either did without or wore the rags handed down from their parents or siblings; shoes were extremely rare. Nationwide, about three million people depended upon the potato as their sole source of food.

With so many people living in such squalor, it is little wonder that disease was rampant and the death toll high. In 1740 and 1741, desperate conditions became even more atrocious as severe famine struck, causing mass starvation and the deaths of thousands.

When restrictions on the exportation of Irish beef were lifted in 1758, landlords were encouraged to increase their herds. To accomodate the larger number of cattle, pastures were extended, and the large common areas, on which the peasants had traditionally grazed their animals and dug peat for fuel, were fenced. Beginning in 1761, groups of men secretly met late at night and took revenge upon landowners by leveling the fences.

The mandate ordering tithes paid to the Protestant Church of Ireland prompted the formation of other secret societies, such as the Molly Maguires, the Hearts of Oak, and the Hearts of Steel. These groups widened their scope of retaliation by not only leveling fences but by ruining the landowners' crops and setting fire to barns and stacks of hay. Animals were run off, buildings were destroyed, and even kangaroo courts were held to levy justice against cruel squirees. As poor Protestant and Catholic tenants were forced into competition, they often turned against one another. A Protestant group called the Peep o'Day Boys attacked Catholic tenants at dawn, ostensibly to search for arms. The Catholics formed their own group called the Defenders, who carried out reprisals. In 1796, a major skirmish between the two gangs resulted in the deaths of twenty people and brought about the formation of the Orange Order, a defensive organization that worked to secure the safety of Protestants and their holdings from Catholic raiders.

The Irish had developed a character that was extremely complex. On one hand, they were very generous and loyal, yet on the other, the lack of work produced an amazing degree of idleness and lack of industry. They readily bowed before authority, yet they were quick to violently avenge serious wrongs. And as every city officer, every magistrate, every lawyer, every judge, and every jury was Protestant and usually anti-Catholic in outlook, it is little wonder that Catholics saw violence as the only means of protecting themselves.

Such an accounting leaves the impression of severe hardship and a dismal existence for the masses. It is an accurate assessment, but it doesn't touch on how the people coped with such an existence. Downtrodden and hungry though the masses might have been, that very existence produced in them a real spirit of charity, compassion, and hospitality. It was a special honor to share a potato and crust of bread with a visitor or traveler, and families freely offered their help to one another. The Irish were also incongruously lighthearted and cheerful. A love of poetry, music, singing, and dancing kept spirits fed, as did religious convictions that were closely and determinedly held.

RELIGION

CROMWELL'S MISSION TO Ireland was as much to bring about the downfall of the Catholic religion as it was to exact revenge on the people for siding with King Charles. He took extra measures to hunt out and execute the Catholic clergy and even set up a special concentration camp on the desolate island of Inishbofin where many were kept in squalid conditions until the Restoration in 1660. Clergymen who did escape capture usually did so by disguising themselves and working as common gardeners, coal porters, and laborers by day, then administering the rites of the church in secret meeting places. It was a dangerous occupation, as priest-catching brought out spies who infiltrated the Catholic community in order to discover the location of the meeting places so the priests could be caught and turned over to the authorities.

Charles II was the son of a Catholic mother and a Prostestant father, so he favored a policy of religious toleration. Though seventy Presbyterian ministers were forced from their parishes and replaced by Episcopalian priests from the Church of Ireland, they were allowed to organize new congregations, and no attempt was ever made to force the citizenry into attending the Church of Ireland. Restrictions on Catholics were lifted, and priests were again allowed to minister to the Irish majority. Even the Jesuits were given permission to establish a school in Drogheda. By 1673, the English public had become alarmed at the pro-Catholic policies of Charles and became even more anti-Catholic in sentiment. Charles bowed to public pressure, ordering Catholic priests to leave the country and closing the Jesuit school. Rather than abandon their posts, the priests went underground again and administered the rites of the Church in secret.

Charles's successor was his brother James II, the first Catholic to be king since the reign of Mary I almost 130 years earlier. On the religious front, King James allowed for the Catholic clergy to go freely about their work. Monasteries were reestablished and desperately needed Catholic schools were opened. Unfortunately, such freedom of religion was not to last.

William of Orange was the successful victor over King James. Under the articles of the Treaty of Limerick, William originally allowed for the same degree of religious freedom the Irish originally enjoyed under Charles II. However, when the Protestant Irish Parliament finally ratified the articles in 1697, they were in a much modified form. Several clauses were left out, including the one promising freedom of religion. Instead, all Catholic bishops, monks, nuns, and friars were banished from the island, and while some departed for the Continent, most simply went underground again.

Conditions were even worse under Anne. Not only did the Catholics suffer under harsh restrictions, so did the Scottish Presbyterian immigrants to Ireland. Their marriage and death ceremonies were not recognized as valid, they were excluded from all civil positions, and their worship and education was as restricted as the Catholics'.

In 1703, Catholic priests were required to register with the government and take an oath of allegiance to the English crown; the penalty of banishment was given to those who did not comply. A reward of twenty pounds was given to any who reported the presence of an unauthorized priest, leading to the resumption of the disreputable but popular ''profession'' of priest-catching.

Far back into the mists of history, Celtic priests held an honored position in society. After the arrival of Saint Patrick, that affection was transferred to the priests of the new Catholic religion. Now, the Catholic clergy was outlawed, and for Irish who held their priests in only the deepest of reverence, respect, and affection, the effect of having their holy men and women branded as felons was devastating to the collective Irish spirit. Being deprived of all material things was difficult enough, but now the Irish were even deprived of the beliefs that held the very fabric of their society together.

Around the latter half of the eighteenth century, religious fanaticism began to decline among the Protestants. As they became more tolerant, such rigorous persecution of the clergy began to subside, though Catholic worship continued to be celebrated less publicly than did Protestant worship. Nevertheless, the penal laws regarding religion remained in effect until the Catholic Emancipation Act of 1829.

NAMING

THE CONTINUING CONFISCATION of Irish lands brought large numbers of Scots Presbyterians and English Quakers, Baptists, and Congregationalists to Ireland. The old Gaelic world was over, and as society was radically altered, so were the names of the people within it. The new emigrants brought their own names with them, and unlike in earlier times, had no desire to Gaelicize them. On the other hand, the names of the Irish living in the English-controlled areas were speedily subjected to the process of Anglicization.

Severe oppression and prejudice led to wholesale discarding of Irish names in favor of English and biblical names. Even rural residents, who typically retain their native culture to a much greater degree than do city dwellers, abandoned their traditional names.

FEMALE NAMES

Abigail (father of exaltation)
Agnes (chaste, pure) **Agness, Agnus**
Alice (nobility)
Amelia (work)
Anabella (grace, full of grace, mercy + beautiful) **Anabelle, Annabella**
Anne (grace, full of grace, mercy) **Ann**
Annie (grace, full of grace, mercy)
Ann Mary (grace, full of grace, mercy + sea of bitterness or sorrow)
Bella (beautiful)
Bessie (God is my oath)
Betsy (God is my oath) **Betsey**
Betty (God is my oath)
Biddy (strength)
Bridget (strength) **Brigit**
Caroline (womanly)
Catherine (pure, unsullied) **Catharine**
Cecilia (blind, dim-sighted)
Cecily (blind, dim-sighted)
Celia (heaven)
Charlotte (womanly)
Cicily (blind, dim-sighted) **Sisley**
Clare (clear, bright) **Clara**
Delia (from the island of Delos)

Dorcas (gazelle)
Eleanor (light, torch, bright) **Elleanor**
Eliza (God is my oath)
Eliza Ann (God is my oath + grace, full of grace, mercy)
Elizabeth (God is my oath)
Ellen (light, torch, bright) **Elen, Elin, Ellan**
Emma (strength)
Esther (myrtle; star)
Fanny (from France, a Frank)
Florinda (a blooming)
Georgiana (earth worker, farmer)
Grace (grace, mercy)
Hannah (grace, full of grace, mercy)
Harriet (home ruler, ruler of an enclosure)
Honora (honor) **Hanora**
Isabella (God is my oath)
Jane (God is gracious)
Jane Olivia (God is gracious + olive tree)
Jennet (God is gracious)
Joanna (God is gracious) **Johanna**
Judith (from Judah; he will be praised)
Judy (from Judah; he will be praised)
Julia (youth)
Kate (pure, unsullied)
Kitty (pure, unsullied)

Lena (light, torch, bright)
Letitia (happiness, gladness)
Lily (lily)
Louisa (famous in war)
Maggie (a pearl)
Marcella (of Mars, warlike) **Marcela**
Margaret (a pearl) **Margret**
Margery (a pearl) **Margarey**
Maria (sea of bitterness or sorrow)
Martha (lady, mistress)
Mary (sea of bitterness or sorrow)
Mary Ann (sea of bitterness or sorrow + grace, full of grace, mercy) **Mariann**
Matilda (mighty in battle)
Phoebe (bright) **Phebe, Phebeus**
Prudence (prudent)
Rachel (ewe) **Rachael**

Rebecca (noose)
Rosa (rose)
Rosanna (rose + grace, full of grace, mercy)
Rose (rose)
Rose Ann (rose + full of grace, mercy)
Rosetta (little rose)
Ruth (companion, friend)
Sarah (princess)
Sarah Ann (princess + grace, full of grace, mercy)
Selina (the moon) **Silena**
Sidony (fine cloth) **Siddy**
Sophia (wisdom)
Susan (lily, rose)
Susanna (lily, rose)
Teresa (harvester) **Teressa, Theresa**
Winifred (blessed peace, fair peace) **Winnifred**

MALE NAMES

Abraham (father of a multitude)
Alex (defender of mankind)
Alexander (defender of mankind)
Andrew (manly)
Anthony (?, *priceless, of inestimable worth* is a folk definition)
Archibald (genuinely brave, genuinely bold)
Art (a stone; a bear)
Arthur (?)
Augustus (great, venerable)
Barclay (dweller at the birch meadow)
Barney (son of exhortation)
Bartholomew (son of Talmai)
Benjamin (son of the right hand)
Bernard (bold as a bear) **Barnard**
Bonaventure (good travels)
Brian (strength, kingly, high) **Bryan**
Carney (?)
Charles (a man, a freeman)
Christian (a Christian, a follower of Christ)
Christopher (bearer of Christ)
Connell (wisdom, high-mighty) **Connel**
Connor (wisdom, counsel, strength + aid; hound) **Conor**
Conway (hound of the plain)
Cornelius (a horn) **Corneleus**
Daniel (God is my judge)
Darby (a freeman, without injunction)
David (beloved)
Dennis (of Dionysus) **Denis**
Dominic (of a lord) **Dominick**
Dudley (from Dudda's lea)
Duncan (brown warrior)
Easter (born on or near Easter)
Edmund (wealthy protection) **Edmond**
Edward (wealthy guardian)
Emanuel (God with us)

Eoghan (lamb; youth; well-born)
Ephraim (very fruitful)
Eugene (well-born)
Felix (lucky)
Fergus (man of valor) **Fargus**
Francis (a Frank, from France)
Frank (a Frank, from France)
Gabriel (God is my strength)
George (an earth worker, farmer)
Giles (a protection, a goat-skin shield of Zeus)
Godfrey (peace of God)
Henry (home ruler)
Hugh (heart, mind, soul)
Humphrey (warrior of peace)
Isaac (laughter)
Jack (God is gracious) **Jackey**
James (supplanting, seizing by the heels)
Jason (healer)
Jeffrey (peaceful district; traveler of peace; pledge of peace) **Jeffery**
Jeremiah (God will uplift)
John (God is gracious) **Johnn**
Joseph (may he add, God shall add)
Kernan (little black-haired one)
Laurence (from Laurentum)
Leonard (lion-hard)
Malachi (my messenger)
Manus (great, large)
Mark (soft, tender; manly; warlike)
Martin (of Mars, warlike)
Mathias (gift of God)
Matthew (gift of God) **Mathew**
Maxwell (large spring, large stream)
Michael (Who is like God?)
Micky (Who is like God?) **Mick**

Miles (?, perhaps *mild, peaceful; merciful*) Used to Anglicize Maolmórdha *majestic chief.*
Montgomery (from Monte Goumeril)
Morgan (sea bright)
Morris (dark, swarthy, a Moor)
Moses (drawn out [of the water]; son, child)
Murphy (sea warrior)
Murray (from Moray *beside the sea*)
Nathaniel (gift of God)
Neil (champion) **Neal**
Nicholas (victory of the people)
Noel (Christmas)
Owen (well-born) **Own**
Paddy (a patrician, an aristocrat) **Pady**
Patrick (a patrician, an aristocrat)
Pat (a patrician, an aristocrat) **Patt**
Patterson (son of Peter *a rock, a stone*)
Pearse (a rock, a stone)
Peter (a rock, a stone)
Philip (lover of horses) **Phillip**

Ralph (counsel-wolf) **Ralf**
Richard (stern king)
Robert (bright with fame)
Roddy (famous with a spear)
Roger (famous with a spear) **Rodger**
Samuel (his name is God)
Silvester (a wood, a forest)
Simeon (heard)
Simon (heard)
Stephen (a crown, a garland) **Stephan, Stephane, Steven**
Stewart (a steward, a keeper of the animal enclosure)
Terrence (soft, tender) **Terance**
Thomas (a twin)
Thompson (son of Thom *a twin*)
Toal (people mighty)
Valentine (healthy, strong)
Valient (valiant, brave)
Walter (ruler of an army)
William (resolute protector)

SURNAMES

The change from Irish names to English increased after the Revolution of 1688, when the native Irish were completely subjected and suffered under a great deal of oppression. The prefixes O and Mac quickly disappeared from surnames to make them more English in character, and names continued to be Anglicized and distorted from their original forms. Spellings were changed, as were pronunciations, to be as close to English as possible. English officials, most of whom were ignorant in the Irish language, routinely translated, mistranslated, and transliterated Irish names. For instance, Mac Gabhann (son of the smith) was translated to Smith or transliterated to McGowan, and Mac Giolla Easpaig (son of the follower of the bishop) was translated to Bishop or transliterated to Gillespie. Mistranslations abounded. Perhaps one of the most ludicrous was Mac an Déaghanaigh (son of the dean). Because of its somewhat phonetical resemblance to the Irish word for bird *éan,* the name was mistranslated to Bird.

The act supressing the surname O'Neill remained on the books for this time period, and considering the anti-Gaelic policies of Cromwell and his successors, the granting of official permission to use the name was unlikely.

The primary function of Irish surnames had always been to indicate kinship to a particular group. When the English began arriving in large numbers during the seventeenth century, their surnames, such as Bird, White, Smith, and Taylor seemed absurd and were roundly mocked. Now, in an ironic turn of events, those same names were being forced on the Irish people as their own, and clan-inspired names were being taken away.

Barry (descendant of Bearach *spearlike*; dweller at the village by the border; from the rampart) Anglicized form of Ó Beargha.
Bell (dweller at the sign of the bell; beautiful, handsome; God is my oath)
Boyle (descendant of Baoghall, ?, perhaps *peril, danger* or *pledge*) Anglicized form of Ó Baoighill.

Brady (spirited)
Brennan (descendant of Braonán *little sorrowful one*) Anglicized form of Ó Braonáin.
O'Brien (descendant of Brian *force, strength*; *valor*; *high, hill*; *kingly*) Anglicized form of Ó Briain.
Brown (brown, brown-haired)

Buckley (descendant of Buachaill *boy*; dweller at the buck's or beech wood) Anglicized form of Ó Buachalla.

Burke (stronghold)

Burns (dweller at the burnt house)

Byrne (descendant of Bran *raven*) Anglicized form of Ó Broin.

Callaghan (descendant of Ceallachan *strife*) Anglicized form of Ó Ceallacháin.

Campbell (crooked mouth)

Carroll (son or descendant of Cearbhall *champion, warrior*) Anglicized form of Mac and Ó Cearbhaill.

McCarthy (son of Carthagh *loving*) Anglicized form of MacCárthaigh.

Casey (descendant of Cathasach *watchful*) **O Casey** Anglicized form of Ó Cathasaigh.

Clarke (a clerk)

Collins (descendant of Coileán *whelp, pup*) Anglicized form of Ó Coileáin.

O'Connell (descendant of Conall *wisdom, strength, desire*)

Connolly (descendant of Conghal *conflict*) **Connelly, O Connelly, O Connolly** Anglicized form of Ó Conghaile.

Connor (son or descendant of Conchobhar *wisdom, counsel, strength; hound lover*) **Mac Connor, O Connor** Anglicized form of Mac and Ó Chonchobhair.

Cullen (son or descendant of Cuileann *holly*) Anglicized form of Mac and Ó Cuilinn.

Cunningham (dweller at the royal manor)

Daly (descendant of Dálach *assembly*) Anglicized form of Ó Dálaigh.

McDermott (son of Diarmaid *without injunction, freeman*)

Doherty (descendant of Dochartach *the hurtful one*) Anglicized form of Ó Dochartaigh.

McDonald (son of Donald *world ruler*)

McDonnell (son of Donnell *world ruler*)

O'Donnell (descendant of Donnell *world ruler*)

Donnelly (descendant of Donnghal *brown + valor*) Anglicized form of Ó Donnghaile.

Donovan (descendant of Donndubhán *little dark brown one*) Anglicized form of Ó Donnabháin.

Doyle (descendant of Dubhghall *dark-haired stranger*) Anglicized form of Ó Dubhghaill.

Duffy (descendant of Dubhthach *dark-haired, dark-complexioned one*) Anglicized form of Ó Dubhthaigh.

Dunne (brown, brown-haired one) **Dunn** Anglicized form of Duinn or Doinn.

Dwyer (descendant of Dubhodhar *dark, black and dun-colored*) Anglicized form of Ó Duibhir.

Farrell (descendant of Fearghal *man of valor*) **Ferrall, O Farrell, O Ferrall** Anglicized form of Ó Fearghail.

Fitzgerald (son of Gerald *spear rule*)

Fitzpatrick (son of Patrick *a patrician, an aristocrat*)

Flanagan (descendant of Flannagán *little red one*) Anglicized form of Ó Flannagáin.

Flynn (descendant of Flann *red-haired one*) Anglicized form of Ó Flionn.

Foley (descendant of Foghlaidhe *plunderer*) Anglicized form of Ó Foghladha.

Gallagher (descendant of Gallchobhar *foreign help*) Anglicized form of Ó Gallchobhair.

Graham (dweller at the gray land or enclosure)

McGrath (son of Craith) Anglicized form of MacGraith.

Griffin (descendant of Gríobhtha *like a griffin, monsterlike; red, ruddy*) Anglicized form of Ó Gríobhtha.

Hayes (descendant of Aodha *fire*) Anglicized form of Ó hAodha.

Healy (from the high lea)

Higgins (descendant of Uigín) Anglicized form of Ó hUigín.

Hogan (descendant of Eoghain *lamb; youth; well-born*) Anglicized form of Ó hÓgáin.

Hughes (son of Hugh *heart, mind, soul*)

Johnston (son of John *God is gracious*)

Kane (descendant of Cathán *little battle*) Anglicized form of Ó Catháin.

Kavanagh (little handsome, little gentle one) Anglicized form of Caomhánach.

Keane (son of Cathán *little battle*) Anglicized form of Mac Catháin.

Keeffe (descendant of Caomh *gentle*) Anglicized form of Ó Caoimh.

Kelly (war, strife) Anglicized form of Keallagh.

McKenna (son of Cionaed *comely, handsome*) Anglicized form of Mac Cionaoith.

Kennedy (ugly head, ugly chief) Anglicized form of Cinnéidid.

Kenny (born of fire; comely, handsome) Anglicized form of Cinaed and Cionaed.

King (kingly, a monarch)

McLaughlin (son of Lochlann *land of the lochs*) Anglicized form of Mac Lochlainn.

Leary (a calf, calf herder) Anglicized form of Laoghaire.

Lynch (sailor, mariner) Anglicized form of Loingseach.

Lyons (son of ?, possibly *gray*) Anglicized form of Ó Liatháin.

Magee (son of Aodh *fire*) Anglicized form of Mag Aoidh.

Maguire (son of Uidhar *dun-colored*) Anglicized form of Mag Uidhir.

Maher (son of Meachar *kindly*) Anglicized form of Ó Meachair.

McMahon (son of Mathghamhain *a bear*) Anglicized form of Mac Mathghamhna.

Mahony (son of Mathghamhain *a bear*) **O Mahony** Anglicized form of Ó Mathghamhana.

Martin (of Mars, warlike)

Moloney (descendant of Maoldhomhnaigh *servant or devotee of the church*) **Maloney, O Maloney, O Moloney** Anglicized form of Ó Maoldhomhnaigh.

Moore (descendant of Mordha *majestic*; dweller at a moor) Anglicized form of Ó Mórdha.

Moran (descendant of Morán *little large one, little great one*) Anglicized form of Ó Moráin.

Mullan (descendant of Maolán *little bald one*) Anglicized form of Ó Maoláin.

Murphy (son or descendant of Murchadh *sea warrior*) Anglicized form of Mac Murchada and Ó Murchada.

Murray (descendant of Muireadhach *sailor*; son of the servant of Mary) Anglicized form of Ó Muireadhaigh and Mac Guilla Mhuire.

McNamara (son of Conmara *hound of the sea*) Anglicized form of Mac Conmara.

Nolan (descendant of Nuallán *little shouter*) Anglicized form of Ó Nualláin.

Power (a pauper) Anglicized form of French de Paor.

Quinn (son of Conn *sense, reason, wisdom*) Anglicized form of Mac Cuinn.

Regan (descendant of Riagán *little king*) Anglicized form of Ó Riagain.

Reid (red, ruddy)

Reilly (descendant of Raghallach *valiant, warlike*) Anglicized form of Ó Raghailligh.

Robinson (son of Robin *bright with fame*)

Rourke (descendant of Ruarc *little friend*) **O Rourke** Anglicized form of Ó Ruairc.

Ryan (descendant of Rian or Riaghan *kingly*) Anglicized form of Ó Riain and Ó Riaghain.

Scott (a Scot)

Shea (descendant of Seaghdha *hawklike, majestic*) Anglicized form of Ó Séaghdha.

Sheehan (descendant of Síodhach *peaceful*) Anglicized form of Ó Síodhacháin.

Smith (a smith)

Stewart (a steward, keeper of the animal enclosure)

Sullivan (descendant of Suileabhan ?, possibly *light eye*) **O Sullivan** Anglicized form of Ó Súileabháin.

Sweeney (son of Suibhne *pleasant, well-going*) Anglicized form of Mac Suibhne.

Thompson (son of Thomas *a twin*)

Walsh (a Welshman)

Ward (guard, watchman)

Whelan (descendant of Faolán *little wolf*) Anglicized form of Ó Faoláin.

White (white, fair complexioned)

Wilson (son of Will *resolute protector*)

Chapter Five

THE ACT OF UNION TO THE PRESENT
[1800–PRESENT]

POLITICS

AFTER SIXTEEN YEARS of civil unrest, Prime Minister William Pitt decided the time for a union between Ireland and England had arrived. The proposal was rejected by the Irish parliament in 1799, but when it met a year later, its members had been sufficiently bribed, coerced, and intimidated to accept passage of the proposal. On August 1, 1800, King George gave his assent to eliminate the Irish parliament, ending 500 years of Irish parliamentary activity and Ireland's right to self-legislate. An identical Act of Union was passed by the English parliament, and on January 1, 1801, the measures were enacted. Great Britain and Ireland became the United Kingdom of Great Britain and Ireland.

In accordance with the agreement, Ireland was given 32 seats in the House of Lords, 100 seats in the House of Commons, and the Church of Ireland was united with the Church of England to become the Established Church, or The United Church of England and Ireland. The financial systems of the islands remained separate, and existing laws remained in effect.

Irish opinion regarding the union was low from the beginning and did not change with time. Not only were the Irish underrepresented in parliament, their share of the National Debt was unfair, trade policies had wiped out Ireland's woolen and cotton industries, and taxes to pay for the war with Napoleon had skyrocketed. The marvelous economic recovery the island welcomed after trade restrictions were lifted was replaced by a depression made worse by the large flow of money to English coffers. Social unrest continued unabated and troops, which could have been used to fight against Napoleon, were deployed throughout the country to maintain order.

In July 1803, a young man named Robert Emmet tried to initiate a rebellion in the slums of Dublin. It ended up being a mere street scuffle of fifty men and was immediately broken up, but Emmet was apprehended a few days later and sentenced to death. His famous dockside speech, given just before his sentence was carried out, is still proclaimed in Irish schools: ''Let there be no inscription on my tomb. Let no man write my epitaph. . . . When my country takes her place among the nations of the earth, then, and not till then, let my epitaph be written.'' Emmet was hanged until nearly dead, then taken down, beheaded, and buried in an unmarked felon's grave. For generations afterward, Robert Emmet became a symbol for those seeking Irish independence.

Even though William Pitt had promised full emancipation for Catholics, King George firmly refused to allow it, and Catholics still were unable to sit in parliament. In 1823, Daniel O'Connell formed the Catholic Association to further Catholic interests and work for full freedoms. With the majority of the people organized behind him, O'Connell subtly warned England of what could happen if such a large number of people didn't get their way. The government was sufficiently alarmed and attempted to suppress the organization in 1825. O'Connell refused to back down and even ran for president of the board of trade. With the Catholics behind him, O'Connell won, though he was unable to take his office because of the oath of supremacy.

It became quite clear that the Catholics had found their voice in the vote, and in 1829, they finally received full emancipation as the Catholic Relief Act passed and received royal assent. The act didn't have that much of an effect on the daily lives of Ireland's Catholic citizens (Protestants still held the monopoly on the civil service jobs), but it gave them quite a pyschological boost and certainly helped their morale.

The government wasn't about to let things stand as they were, and as a way to keep the masses from exerting so much power, it raised the voting qualifications to ten pounds. The forty-shilling freeholders, then, lost their rights to vote, and the number of voters was lowered from 216,000 to just 37,000.

From the late 1820s, Liberal Clubs began organizing to provide citizens with a political education. A decade later, they were known as News Rooms, Independent Clubs, and Reading Clubs and had begun to speak out for repeal of the Union. Repeal could have meant either total separation from Great Britain or one king and two legislatures, but few groups ever stated unequivocally which choice they desired. It seemed the main idea was to force the government into a dialogue about Irish issues.

One of those issues was the increasing agrarian violence that had started as a rebellion against the forced payment of tithes to the Established Church. The ''Tithe War'' sharply escalated in the 1830s until the government decided on a one-time tax to create a general fund for clerical costs.

Another issue concerned the poor, and in 1838, the Poor Relief (Ireland) Act of 1838 extended the English welfare system to Ireland. Under the act, Ireland was divided into 130 unions, with workhouses that administered relief only to those who lived and worked within them. The system soon proved its deficiencies and didn't come close to providing relief for the masses during the 1846 famine.

Other groups, such as Young Ireland, soon began to speak out against the union. Their concept of Ireland differed from that of O'Connell's in that their visions of an independent republic included all the Irish, and O'Connell's nationalism tended to revolve around Catholics. As events of the famine unfolded in the 1840s, the Young Irelanders became increasingly Anglophobic and militant.

The famine affected every area of Irish life, including politics, and government was not up to the challenge it presented. When the potato blight reached Ireland in 1845, prime minister Sir Robert Peel purchased Indian corn and meal from the United States to be used as leverage in the case that prices on the general food rose too high. He also removed protectionist duties on grain to lower the price of bread. Both of these measures had a fatal flaw: they assumed the poor had enough money to purchase food from the market, which they didn't. He also proposed a scheme of public works projects to offer jobs to those whose potato crops had failed.

The implementation of Peel's proposals was in the hands of Charles Trevelyan, a man more concerned with the cost of the relief effort than the lives of those it was saving. It wasn't until the middle of May 1846 that government ordered the depots of Indian corn opened throughout the country. By then, people were desperate, attacking food carts on their way to market, forcing their way into flour mills, and stealing sheep and other livestock.

The amazing thing was that food of great variety was to be had in Ireland. And because Trevelyan was determined not to interfere with trade as a way to combat the famine, the foodstuffs that were desperately needed in Ireland were being exported in great quantities. The country even imported four times more wheat than it sent out. The food was there, it just wasn't made available to the poor.

In England, a new government replaced Prime Minister Peele at the end of June 1846 with Lord John Russell, and Trevelyan marked the new government's attitude toward the Irish famine by rejecting a cargo of Indian corn that was already under way for Ireland. The public works programs, which commonly took weeks to organize, were hopelessly entangled in bureaucratic red tape and delays, which kept the workers from being paid. Another failing of that scheme was that even when the workers were paid a salary, there was no existing wholesale or retail food distribution systems in place in the rural areas to make the food available for purchase.

Relief committees were organized around the country to assess the needs of the people, and it wasn't until 1847 that the public works program was abandoned in favor of direct relief. A Soup Kitchen Act was passed that allotted public funds for free soup, but unfortunately, the public works projects were terminated much more quickly than the government got around to establishing the soup kitchens, and the people had no way to obtain sustenance in the meantime. By this time, hundred of thousands had perished from starvation or the fever that accompanies such a horror.

By the summer of 1847, the ration system allotted for under the Soup Kitchen Act had taken effect and over three million Irish were receiving aid. A good summer potato harvest prompted the government to announce that all soup kitchen aid would cease at the end of September. It was a premature step, for the number of cultivators were few, the harvest was exceedingly small, and it didn't come close to feeding the people who relied upon it.

In place of the soup kitchens, new Poor Law legislation was enacted that extended the duties of the unions.

The workhouses were now liable for providing aid to those inside its walls, as well as to those outside. There was one exception: those with even as little as a quarter of an acre didn't qualify. The unions, most of which were now bankrupt, were to assume the costs of the new program. As the unions themselves were supported by the rate-payers, it was to them that all costs eventually fell. And while many of the landholders took an active part in taking care of their starving tenants, others displayed a disturbing lack of concern, even forcibly evicting those unable to pay their rents. By the end of September, two million people who had been receiving free rations were forced onto the Poor Law Unions.

As far as government was concerned, it had done all it was going to. In the words of Trevelyan, ''The only way to prevent people from becoming habitually dependent on government is to bring operations to a close . . . these things should be stopped now, or you run the risk of paralysing all private enterprise and having this country on you for an indefinite number of years. It is my opinion that too much has been done for the people. Under such treatment the people have grown worse instead of better, and we must now try what independent exertion can do. . . .''

Ireland's misery was not over. The harvests of 1848 and 1849 were almost totally blighted. Nevertheless, Lord John Russell wrote that there was nothing more government could do. ''I do not think any effort of this House would, in the present unfortunate state of Ireland, be capable of preventing the dreadful scenes of suffering and death that are now occurring in Ireland. I do not feel justified in asking the House for an additional advance of £100,000 which at least would be necessary if the House should say there should be no possible cause of starvation in Ireland.''

The leaders of Young Ireland had not missed either Trevelyan's or Russell's words nor the attitude behind them. The promise of the union in 1800 was for England and Ireland to be inseparable, with their successes in good times and failures in bad, equally shared. Now, not only had government failed dismally in its responsibility toward its citizens, it considered the Irish as unequal and undeserving of aid. The Young Irelanders capitalized on the anger the masses felt toward government and increased their antiunion activities. When rumors circulated in 1848 that the English Chartists were planning a revolt of their own, the Young Irelanders felt their own time to fight for independence had come.

Their rebellion was small and short-lived, but they continued to spread disaffection throughout the country and in 1858, founded the secret Irish Republican Brotherhood, which dedicated itself to seeking independence by any means.

In America, James Stephens and John O'Mahony, comrades from the rebellion, took advantage of the bitterness Irish immigrants felt toward Britain and formed another society known as the Fenian Brotherhood. The American group operated openly, though its true mission of providing aid for the IRB was kept a closely guarded secret.

The IRB grew slowly, and in 1864, its members began to drill and prepare for action with the help of Irish American veterans of the Civil War. The year for the rising was to be 1865, but an informant had been leaking information to the authorities, and they struck before any fighting could occur. Informants continued to betray the organization, and though subsequent risings were easily put down, the Fenians managed to sabatoge the telegraph and railway systems as well as capture smaller police barracks and coast guard stations to obtain arms.

In 1879, a Fenian named Michael Davitt began to work for a national reduction in rent rates and an end to evictions. His long-term goal was the transference of ownership from the landlord to the tenant. An aggressive new organization called the Land League was formed, and Davitt persuaded Charles Parnell, a Protestant landowner from Meath and a member of the House of Commons, to become its president. With

Parnell keeping the issue before parliament, a Land Act was passed in 1881 guaranteeing the three Fs: fair rent, fixed tenure, free sale of the tenancy at market value. The legislation fell short in protecting tenants, for there were no guidelines to establish what constituted fair rent, the fixed tenure depended upon steady payments of rents, and many tenants were already in arrears. Parnell himself spoke out so strongly against the act that he was imprisoned. He was released in 1882 on condition that further reforms would be enacted if he worked to discourage the violence. Parnell also managed to bring the cause of Irish nationalism to the forefront of British politics by demanding home rule for Ireland under the crown. To accomplish this, he organized the Irish National League to work for home rule.

The Ulster Protestants were steadfast in their opposition to home rule, knowing that because of Catholic emancipation, if home rule were ever granted, the Protestants would always be in the minority of any Irish parliament. Unionists and Conservatives formed an alliance to prevent home rule, and sectarian rioting soon broke out. Fighting was particularly bad in 1886 and 1893, after prime minister William Gladstone introduced home rule bills for the consideration of parliament.

In 1905, Ulster Unionists and the Orange Order formed the Ulster Unionist Council. Unionists in the rest of Ireland united into the Irish Unionist Alliance. A bill proposing an Irish parliament that would oversee domestic affairs was put forth in 1912, prompting the Unionists to lay plans for a provisional government. The bill passed the Commons in 1913, but was rejected by the House of Lords, and since they only had the power to delay legislation, there was still a possibility that the bill could pass. In 1914, the Unionists organized an army known as the Ulster Volunteer Force, and the Irish Republican Brotherhood countered with a military arm known as the Irish Volunteers.

World War I broke out, and government became more concerned with its war effort than with its Irish troubles. The IRB used the opportunity to secretly prepare for a rising on Easter 1916, but a series of setbacks led to a dismal failure. In retaliation, the government imposed martial law, sentenced ninety people to death, and executed fifteen before bowing to public criticism and cries of outrage.

Sinn Fein originated in 1905 as a society devoted to the reestablishment of Gaelic culture and had nothing to do with the Easter Rising, though government thought otherwise. It took political advantage of the situation and won seventy-three seats in parliament in 1918, as opposed to the Unionist's twenty-six and the parliamentary party's six. The Sinn Fein members refused to take their seats at Westminster, opting instead to assemble in Dublin as "Dail Eireann," Assembly of Ireland. Its secret military arm, led by Michael Collins, became proficient at intelligence work and carried out a successful guerrilla campaign against police, government troops, and prominent Unionists.

In 1920, the Government of Ireland Act, which provided for separate parliaments for northern and southern Ireland, was passed. In the north, the Unionists won 40 of 52 seats, while in the south, Sinn Fein won 124 of 128 seats. A truce was offered and accepted, and Ireland's War of Independence ended in July 1921.

The Anglo-Irish treaty allowed for the new Irish Free State with dominion status, provided that its parliament take an oath of allegiance to the crown and that Britain be allowed to maintain naval bases on the island. Northern Ireland had the option of remaining separate from the Irish Free State, which it chose to do. The treaty was accepted in January 1922, though nearly half the members of the Dail had voted against it. The antitreaty president of the Dail, Eamon De Valera, resigned, British troops and government administrators began to withdraw from Dublin Castle, and Ireland drifted toward civil war.

The split in the Dail was echoed by a split between members of the Irish Republican Army. Dissidents called the Irregulars repudiated the Dail, took control of several Dublin buildings, and kidnapped a protreaty general. Civil war had begun. The Irregulars set up a rival government under the leadership of De Valera in October, and the war continued until a cease-fire was negotiated in May 1923.

The Irish Free State organized its government, replacing the British administration with a new civil service and creating a new system of local government. An unarmed police force was established, as was a new judicial system. In 1925, the boundary between the Irish Free State and Northern Ireland was confirmed. De Valera broke from Sinn Fein and formed a new party, Fianna Fail (Warriors of Destiny), which became the largest opposition party.

Violence continued, and several groups, including the IRA were declared illegal. Fianna Fail was the winning party in the 1932 elections, and De Valera formed a government. The oath of allegiance to Britain was abolished, and an aggressive scheme of economic recovery was implemented. A new constitution was was endorsed in 1937 that provided for a two-chamber parliament, an elected head of state, and a cabinet government headed by a prime minister. The constitution recognized the Catholic Church as the guardian of the faith but also allowed for freedom of religion "subject to public order and morality." The family was recognized as the primary unit of nature, and to maintain its structure, divorce was forbidden.

In 1948, the Republic of Ireland Act passed, taking the country out of the British Commonwealth and making it an independent republic. Ireland was officially inaugurated on Easter Monday in 1949, and that same year, Britain declared that Northern Ireland would never cease to be a part of the United Kingdom unless the Irish parliament voted to do so.

The IRA was restored with De Valera's election, but violent activites had it declared illegal again and in 1936, it went underground. In 1939, it launched its terrorist war against England. World War II minimized IRA activites, but by the 1950s, it had begun a campaign of attacks in Northern Ireland that lasted until 1962.

The Republic of Ireland began to have a more outward look. Its prime minister met with the prime minister of Northern Ireland for the first time since the 1920s, Irish soldiers became part of the United Nations forces, a new trade agreement was made with the United Kingdom, and Ireland was accepted as part of the European Economic Community.

The story of Northern Ireland is a bit different. From the beginning, politics took place over a gun barrel as the Protestant majority sought to continue their position of ascendancy and the Catholics, resentful of the partitioning of the island, hoped the Protestants would fail. By the 1960s, a move to draw Catholics into the mainstream drew criticism from those who feared Northern Ireland would be voted into the Republic; sectarian violence continued.

The IRA established themselves as the "defenders" of the Catholic areas, and relations between Protestants and Catholics declined even further. "No-go" areas were established where neither the police nor the army would enter, but after the IRA intensified its bombing campaign against commercial establishments, government forces reentered those areas to put down the violence.

Ways were sought to bring Protestants and Catholics together in the political system, but results were predictably poor, and the country continues to be split between those who wish to remain a part of the United Kingdom and those who wish to see the British out of Ireland once and for all.

SOCIETY

RURAL SOCIETY IN the early nineteenth century was more than just that of landlord and tenant. There were large-scale farmers of more than thirty acres, middle-level farmers of fifteen to thirty acres, smallholders of one to fifteen acres, and beneath them were the cottiers, the laborers who received a small piece of land in lieu of a monetary wage.

The most glaring condition of society during the first half of the nineteenth century was the mass of people who existed in grinding poverty. While the wealthy and those with a monetary income lived as comfortably as in England, the poor were involved in a daily struggle for survival.

A large increase in population in the first forty years of the nineteenth century didn't help matters. With Dublin no longer the seat of power, wealthier citizens put their urban properties up for sale and quickly left for London. The great town houses quickly degenerated into tenements for the poor who came to the city in search of work. Apart from Ulster, Ireland failed to adequately industrialize, and even deindustrialized in some areas. Opportunities for employment, therefore, did not keep pace with population growth, and the majority were forced to live off the land.

With holdings being divided again and again to make land available, most people had to make do with very small portions of land with which to support themselves by growing cereal grains. Rents rose so high that tenants were forced to sell their entire cereal crops to pay the rent, leaving them with just the small patches of potatoes for sustenance. The cottiers, most of whom received their small pieces of land in lieu of a wage, were also reliant upon the potato patch.

By the 1830s, supplemental food was becoming scarce among the poor, and by the 1840s, the majority of the population was dependent upon that one crop, the potato. For two or three months of the year, between the time the potato stores had been exhausted and the new potatoes were ready for harvest, people were practically destitute. Casual ''pick-up work'' could bring in a little money to buy food during those ''meal months,'' but these jobs were few and far between. Only the potato patch stood between the people and starvation. The partial failures of the potato crop between the years of 1817 and 1842 brought that fact painfully to light.

The difference with the Great Famine was that the potato crop failed across the country. The blight was first noticed in England in August of 1845, and a month later it arrived in Ireland. The fungus was spread by wind, rain, and insects, and once the plant was infected, the potatoes underneath were doomed to end up as a rotten pulp. Even potatoes that had appeared sound when dug turned to rot within a few days. An over-powering stench accompanied the blight, and even potatoes that seemed normal emitted that same horrible smell when cooked. People across the island began to panic as the magnitude and seriousness of the disaster confronted them.

By February 1846, the blight had struck every county and destroyed 75 percent of the potato crop. Typhus and dysentery broke out a month later. To make matters worse, landlords began large-scale evictions of those unable to pay their rents. By October, deaths from starvation began to be reported. By December, deaths were so many that people were buried in mass graves or thrown into ditches where they were devoured by dogs and wild animals.

Horrors only increased as the potato crop continued to fail. One way out was death, and during the famine years of 1846–1849, between 1,000,000 to 1,500,000 people perished from starvation and famine-related diseases. Another way out was emigration, and about 1,500,000 people left Ireland, with about 75 percent going to the United States. In 1841, the population stood at a little more than 8,000,000. But by 1851, that number had fallen to 6,500,000, and by 1911, population sank to only 4,400,000.

Within ten years of the great famine, nearly a quarter of Ireland's population had emigrated. While that meant fewer people upon the land, life went on much as it had before. Small tenants were forced to sell their cereal crops to pay their rent, while they remained dependent upon their small plots of potatoes for survival. In 1877, a wet growing season severely impacted the potato crop, reducing the harvest to only a quarter of its normal yield. On top of this, the United States began to export vast quantities of grain to Europe, drastically lowering the market price and leaving the small Irish farmers unable to pay their rent.

Landlords were unsympathetic to the situation and began to demand rack-rents (yearly rents, which were often as much as the land was worth). They evicted those who could not afford to pay, and replaced them with tenants whose conditions were not as desperate. Those who were evicted were left without even the smallest patch of ground to grow their potatoes, leaving them in the same straits as in 1845. As famine loomed once again, a massive relief effort by Irish Americans and the English prevented disaster.

The famine impacted society not only in the number of people left but also in the classes of people. The classes most widely decimated were the rural smallholders and cottiers: those who were dependent solely upon the potato. Before the famine, they had outnumbered the farmers five to two; after the famine, they were equal in number. Those smallholders and cottiers who managed to survive now saw the need for change. Farming was diversified and early marriages, once the norm, declined in favor of obtaining a more financially secure position before wedlock. That in turn led to a decline in the birth rate and in the size of families. Education was also recognized as being of vital importance to a secure future, and school attendance was high.

Living conditions did not progress apace, however, which was glaringly obvious in the towns and cities. Most towns, and even cities such as Dublin, continued to have a nonindustrial base, and the population was reduced to dependency upon casual labor with very low wages. The majority of city dwellers were extremely poor and lived in squalid tenements and slums, many without water or sanitation devices. Diseases were common; the mortality rate was high. In fact, even in the early twentieth century, Dublin had the fifth highest adult mortality rate in the world. Conditions began to improve with the organization of workers' unions, but the fight for better wages and living conditions was ongoing.

In 1831, a government-subsidized, nondenominational elementary education system was put in place. In an effort to speed up the Anglicization process, instruction was carried out in English, and only English literature and history were taught. In the postfamine era, the Gaelic language was increasingly abandoned.

The Gaelic League was founded in 1893 by Eoin MacNeill and Douglas Hyde to de-Anglicize the Irish people. One of its primary objectives was the revival of the Irish language, and it lobbied to introduce Irish language studies into school curriculum at all levels and campaigned for bilingual street names and signs.

In 1896, Alice Milligan and Ethna Carberry (Anna Johnson), also active in the Gaelic League, founded a feminist movement through the journal *Shan Van Vocht*, and Maud Gonne founded Inghinidhe na hÉireann (Daughters of Ireland) in 1900. Members of that organization had to be of Irish birth or descent, had to be dedicated to complete independence from the United Kingdom, and were "to discourage the reading and circulation of low English literature, the singing of English songs, the attending of vulgar English entertainments at the theatre and music-hall, and to combat in every way English influence, which is doing so much injury to the artistic taste and refinement of the Irish people."

When the Irish Free State came into being, less than 18 percent of the people spoke the Gaelic language. In response, government ambitiously worked to spread the use of the native language. Irish was compulsory within the school system, and proficiency in the Irish language was required for many state jobs. Education was structured to inculcate the children with Gaelic pride and to bring about a national return to Gaelic sensibilities. However, government eventually had to admit that forcing the Irish language onto the people had failed to produce an Irish-speaking nation. In 1973, the compulsory qualifications in the Irish language were dropped for graduation certificates and entry into the civil service.

RELIGION

UNDER THE ACT of Union, the Church of Ireland united with the Church of England into a single Established Church that was also known as the United Church. At the time of the union, only 5 percent of the population were members of the Established Church. There were also Presbyterians and other Protestant dissenters, but nearly all of the remaining 95 percent were Roman Catholics.

The Catholic Relief Act of 1829 allowed for complete freedom of organization and worship, and in 1871, the Disestablishment Act went into effect. Under this act, all Irish churches, including the Established Church, were given equal legal status. Membership in the Established Church had risen, but it still amounted to less than 20 percent of the population.

After the famine, the practice of devotion in Catholic households rose, possibly as a result of the psychological trauma of the 1840s. Several religious societies formed in the 1850s, and the use of devotional aides such as the rosary, shrines, altars, and pilgrimages to holy sites became the norm in personal worship. The number of seminarians and novices increased as well. Priests increased in number by 20 percent, and nuns by 50 percent.

The Protestant Church experienced a period of revivalism, as well. Missionaries and groups such as the Society of Friends saw the famine as a great opportunity for evangelizing and often combined it with their food relief efforts.

Religion continues to play an important role in Ireland—in society as well as politics. In the Republic of Ireland, around 95 percent of the people are Catholic, but in Northern Ireland, only about a third are Catholic, with the remaining two-thirds Protestant. Many Catholics believe that if Ireland were reunited, Catholics in the north would be treated better. Protestants in the north fear reunification would mean the loss of benefits of a lifestyle secured by their place in the majority.

In 1997, Ireland's eighth president was voted into office. Mary McAleese is a Roman Catholic and the first president to come from Northern Ireland. She is determined to build bridges across the religious and political problems that divide the island. It remains to be seen if her efforts will be successful.

NAMING

AT THE BEGINNING of this time period, the vast majority of names in Ireland were the same as those found in England. A review of passenger lists from the early to later 1800s, covering all classes of people, finds that the most common female names were Anne, Biddy, Catherine, Eleanor, Eliza, Jane, Margaret, Mary, Rose, and Sarah. The most common male names were Henry, Hugh, James, John, Laurance, Mick and Michael, Patrick, Robert, Thomas, and William. Very few Irish names were recorded. Among the men, the most common Irish names were Conor, Fergus, Murphy, and Neil. For the women, only Biddy (a pet form of Bridget) was used in any number. However, it must be remembered that Irish names for both men and women were only rarely used in the 1800s.

The Gaelic League, which formed in 1893, promoted a Gaelic consciousness and encouraged people to celebrate their heritage by adopting native Irish names and bestowing them upon their children. That activity, enhanced in the 1920s by a government policy of promoting a Gaelic identity, helped to bring native names into modern use.

Nicknames are quite common in Ireland. Earlier in the century, it was estimated that at least a third of the rural population were known by a name other than the given Christian name. A study of Ulster dialect in the 1890s cited the use of odd nicknames: "Paddy Polite" was a man with good manners, "Sally Look-up" was a woman with a squint, and "Susey Fluke" was a fisherwoman.

FEMALE NAMES

Abigail (father of exhortation)
Alice (noble one)
Alley (noble one)
Amelia (industrious)
Anabella (grace, full of grace, mercy + beautiful)
Anne (grace, full of grace, mercy) **Ann**
Annie (grace, full of grace, mercy)
Bessie (God is my oath)
Betsy (God is my oath) **Betsey**
Biddy (strength)
Bridge (strength)
Bridget (strength)
Caroline (full-grown, womanly)
Catherine (pure, unsullied) **Catharine**
Cecilia (blind, dim-sighted)
Charlotte (full-grown, womanly)
Cicily (blind, dim-sighted) **Sisley**
Clara (clear, bright)
Delia (of Delos)
Dolly (gift of God)
Eleanor (light, torch, bright) **Elleanor**
Eliza (God is my oath)
Eliza Ann (God is my oath + grace, full of grace, mercy)
Ellinah (light, torch, bright)
Ellen (light, torch, bright) **Elen, Ellan, Ellin**
Elizabeth (God is my oath)
Emma (strength)
Esther (myrtlewood; star)
Fanny (from France, a Frank)
Frances (from France, a Frank)
Georgiana (earth worker, farmer)
Ginny (possible variant of Jenny *fair lady*) **Ginney**
Grace (grace)
Gracey (grace)
Harriet (ruler of an enclosure, home ruler)
Jennet (God is gracious; little Jenny)
Joanna (God is gracious) **Johanna**

Judith (from Judah; he will be praised)
Judy (from Judah; he will be praised)
Kate (pure, unsullied)
Letitia (happiness)
Lily (lily, rose)
Louisa (famous in war)
Madge (a pearl)
Maggie (a pearl)
Mandy (lovable)
Marcella (of Mars, warlike) **Marcela**
Margaret (a pearl)
Maria (sea of bitterness or sorrow)
Mary (sea of bitterness or sorrow)
Mary Ann (sea of bitterness or sorrow + grace, full of grace, mercy) **Mariann, Mary Anne**
Matilda (mighty in battle)
Nancy (grace, full of grace, mercy) **Nan**
Olivia (olive tree)
Onney (honor)
Peggy (a pearl)
Phoebe (bright) **Phebe**
Queenie (queen, queenlike) **Quenie**
Rachel (ewe) **Rachael**
Rose (a rose) **Rosa**
Rose Ann (a rose + grace, full of grace, mercy) **Rosanna**
Rosetta (little rose)
Rosie (a rose) **Rosey**
Ruth (companion)
Sarah (princess)
Sarah Ann (princess + grace, full of grace, mercy)
Sibby (God is my oath)
Sophia (wisdom)
Susan (lily, rose)
Teresa (harvester) **Theresa**
Unity (oneness, united)
Winifred (blessed peace, fair peace) **Winnifred**

MALE NAMES

Abraham (father of a multitude)
Aidan (little fiery one)
Ailín (?, perhaps *handsome; rock*) Irish form of Alan.
Aindréas (manly) **Aindrias, Aindriú** Irish form of Andrew.
Alan (?, perhaps *handsome; rock*)
Alastar (defender of mankind) **Alasdair** Irish form of Alexander.
Alex (defender of mankind)
Alexander (defender of mankind)
Alsander (defender of mankind) Irish form of Alexander.
Andrew (manly)
Angus (one, choice, preeminent)

Antaine (?) **Anntoin, Antoin, Antoine** Irish form of Anthony.
Anthony (?, *priceless*, *of inestimable worth* is a folk definition)
Aodh (fire)
Aodhán (little fiery one) **Aodhgan**
Aralt (leader of the army) Irish form of Harold.
Archibald (genuinely bold, genuinely brave)
Art (a stone; a bear)
Arthur (?)
Augustus (great, venerable)
Banbhan (little piglet)
Barclay (dweller at the birch meadow)

Barney (son of exhortation)

Barry (spearlike) Anglicized form of Bearach.

Bartholomew (son of Talmai) **Bart**

Beanón (good, well-born) **Beinean, Beineón** Irish form of Benignus.

Bearach (spearlike)

Bearchán (little spear)

Benedict (blessed)

Benen (good, well-born) Anglicized form of Beanón.

Benjamin (son of the right hand)

Bernard (bold as a bear) **Barnard**

Bram (father of a multitude)

Bran (raven)

Brandan (raven)

Brandubh (black raven)

Branduff (black raven) Anglicized form of Brandubh.

Breandán (prince)

Brendan (prince) Anglicized form of Breandán.

Bret (a Breton) **Brett, Brit, Britt**

Brian (strength, kingly, high) **Bryan**

Brody (fragment) Anglicized form of Bruaideadh.

Cadhla (handsome)

Caffar (helmet) Anglicized form of Cathbharr.

Cahal (battle mighty) **Cathal**

Cahir (warrior) Anglicized form of Cathaoir.

Cairbre (charioteer)

Callaghan (small strife) Anglicized form of Ceallachán.

Canice (fair, comely, handsome) Anglicized form of Coinneach.

Caoimhín (little gentle one)

Caolán (little slender one)

Carbry (charioteer) Anglicized form of Cairbre.

Carlin (little champion) Anglicized form of Cearbhallán.

Cassidy (curly locks; ingenious, clever, love, esteem) Anglicized form of Caiside.

Charles (a man, a freeman)

Christian (a Christian, a follower of Christ)

Christopher (bearer of Christ)

Cian (ancient)

Cianán (little ancient one)

Ciarán (little black-haired one)

Ciarrai (black)

Cillian (war, strife)

Cinnéidid (ugly head, ugly chief)

Coileán (whelp, pup)

Coinneach (fair one, handsome)

Coireall (?)

Cole (copledge, fellow hostage) Anglicized form of Comhghall.

Colin (victory of the people)

Colm (dove) Irish form of Columba.

Colmán (little dove)

Conaire (?, perhaps *hound* + *farmer*)

Conall (wisdom, high-mighty) **Connall, Connel, Connell**

Conán (wisdom, counsel, strength; small hound)

Conn (sense, reason, wisdom)

Connery (?) **Conary, Conrey, Conroy, Conry** Anglicized form of Conaire.

Conor (wisdom, counsel, strength + aid; hound) **Connor**

Conway (hound of the plain)

Corey (a cauldron, a hollow)

Cornelius (a horn) **Corneleus**

Cowan (twin) Anglicized form of Comhghan.

Críostóir (bearing Christ) Irish form of Christopher.

Cuinn (sense, wisdom, reason)

Cullen (holly) Anglicized form of Cuileann.

Curran (hero, champion)

Cyril (lordly)

Dáibhidh (beloved) **Dáibhid** Irish form of David.

Dainéal (God is my judge) Irish form of Daniel.

Dáithí (swiftness, speed, surefootedness)

Daman (tamer) Irish form of Damien.

Daniel (God is my judge)

Darby (a freeman, without injunction)

Darcy (of Arcy)

Darragh (dark oak, black oak) Anglicized form of Dubhdarach.

David (beloved)

Dennis (of Dionysus) **Denis**

Derek (ruler of the people)

Dermot (without injunction, a freeman) **Dermod** Anglicized form of Diarmaid.

Devin (poet) Anglicized form of Dámh.

Devlin (descendant of the plasterer or dauber; one who comes from Dublin *dark pool*) Anglicized form of Doibhilin.

Diarmaid (without injunction, a freeman)

Dominic (of a lord) **Dominick**

Donagh (brown warrior) **Donogh, Donough** Anglicized form of Donnchadh.

Donahue (brown warrior) Anglicized form of Donnchadh.

Donal (world ruler) **Donall** Anglicized form of Domhnall.

Donald (world ruler) Anglicized form of Domhnall.

Donn (brown)

Donnán (little brown one)

Donovan (dark brown, brown-haired) Anglicized form of Donndubhán.

Douglas (black, dark + blue, green, gray) Anglicized form of Dubhglas.

Dubh (black, dark)

Dudley (from Dudda's lea)

Duff (black, dark)

Duncan (brown warrior)

Dwyer (black, dark + sense, wisdom) Anglicized form of Dubheidir.

Éadbárd (wealthy guardian) **Eadbhard** Irish form of Edward.

Éamonn (wealthy protection) **Éamon, Eamon** Irish form of Edmund.

Edmund (wealthy protection) **Edmond**

Edward (wealthy guardian)

Egan (little fiery one) Anglicized form of Aodhagán.

Emanuel (God with us)

Emmet (strength)

Eoghan (lamb; youth; well-born)
Eóin (God is gracious) Irish form of John.
Ephraim (very fruitful)
Eugene (well-born)
Evan (little swift one) Anglicized form of imhín.
Faolán (little wolf)
Feagh (raven) Anglicized form of Fiach.
Fearghall (man of valor)
Fearghus (superior strength; man of strength)
Feidhlim (the ever good)
Felan (little wolf) Phelan Anglicized form of Faolán.
Felim (the ever good) Felimy, Phelim, Phelimy Anglicized form of Feidhlim.
Felix (lucky)
Fergal (man of valor)
Fergus (man of valor) Fargus
Fiach (raven)
Fiachra (raven)
Finan (little fair one) Fionan
Finbar (fair-haired) Anglicized form of Fionnbhárr.
Fingal (fair)
Finn (fair, white, clear) Fynn Anglicized form of Fionn.
Finnian (little fair one) Anglicized form of Fionnán.
Fintan (little fair one) Anglicized form of Fionntán.
Fionn (fair)
Fionnbhárr (fair-haired)
Francis (a Frank, from France)
Frank (a Frank, from France)
Gabriel (God is my strength)
Gannon (fair-haired man)
Garbhán (little rough one)
Garrett (brave with the spear; spear rule) Garret
Garvan (little rough one) Anglicized form of Garbhán.
Gearalt (spear rule) Irish form of Gerald.
Gearárd (brave with the spear) Irish form of Gerard.
George (an earth worker, farmer)
Gerald (spear rule)
Gerard (brave with the spear)
Gilbert (bright pledge)
Giles (a protection, a goatskin shield of Zeus)
Glenn (mountain valley)
Godfrey (peace of God)
Grady (noble, illustrious) Anglicized form of Gráda.
Gréagóir (vigilant, watchful) Irish form of Gregory.
Gregory (vigilant, watchful)
Harold (leader of the army)
Henry (home ruler)
Hugh (heart, mind, soul)
Humphrey (warrior of peace)
Ian (God is gracious)
Ióseph (he shall add) Irish form of Joseph.
Isaac (laughter)
Ivor (archer)
Jack (God is gracious) Jackey
James (supplanting, seizing by the heels) Jamie
Jason (healer)

Jeffrey (peaceful district; traveler of peace; pledge of peace) Jeffery
Jeremiah (God will uplift)
John (God is gracious) Johnn
Joseph (may he add, God shall add)
Kealan (little slender one) Anglicized form of Caolán.
Keir (little black-haired one) Anglicized form of Ciarán.
Keiran (little black-haired one) Anglicized form of Ciarán.
Keallagh (war, strife)
Kennedy (ugly head, ugly chief) Anglicized form of Cinnéi-did.
Kerill (?) Anglicized form of Coireall.
Kernan (little black-haired one)
Kevin (little gentle one) Anglicized form of Caoimhín.
Kyle (from the narrow channel)
Labhrás (man from Laurentum) Irish form of Laurence.
Laughlin (land of the lochs) Anglicized form of Leachlainn, Lochlainn and Lochlann.
Laurence (from Laurentum)
Leonard (lion-hard)
Liam (resolute protector) Short form of William.
Lochlainn (land of the lochs)
Logan (dweller at the little hollow)
Lomán (little bare one)
Lorcán (little fierce one)
Lúcás (light; man from Lucania) Irish form of Luke.
Luke (light; man from Lucania)
Magnus (great, large)
Máirtín (of Mars, warlike)
Maitiú (gift of God) Irish form of Matthew.
Malcolm (servant of Saint Columba)
Manus (great, large)
Mark (soft, tender; manly; warlike)
Martin (of Mars, warlike)
Matthew (gift of God) Mathew
Maxwell (large spring, large stream)
Michael (Who is like God?)
Micky (Who is like God?) Mick
Miles (?, perhaps mild, peaceful; merciful)
Montgomery (from Monte Goumeril)
Morgan (sea bright)
Morris (dark, swarthy, a Moor)
Murchadh (sea warrior)
Murphy (sea warrior)
Murray (from Moray beside the sea)
Murrough (sea warrior) Anglicized form of Murchadh.
Naomhán (little holy one)
Nathaniel (gift of God)
Neil (champion; cloud) Anglicized form of Niall.
Nevan (little holy one) Anglicized form of Naomhán.
Niadh (champion)
Niall (champion; cloud) Néill
Neil (champion) Neal, Neale, Neill
Nicholas (victory of the people)
Noel (Christmas)
Nolan (little proud one) Anglicized form of Nuallán.

Oran (little pale green one) Anglicized form of Odhrán.
Owen (well-born)
Paddy (a patrician, an aristocrat) **Pady**
Pádraig (a patrician, an aristocrat) **Pádraic**
Patrick (a patrician, an aristocrat), **Pat**, **Patt**
Paul (small)
Peadar (a rock, a stone) Irish form of Peter.
Pearse (a rock, a stone)
Peter (a rock, a stone)
Philip (lover of horses) **Phillip**
Pierce (a rock, a stone)
Piers (a rock, a stone)
Pól (small) Irish form of Paul.
Quinn (sense, reason, wisdom) Anglicized form of Cuinn.
Raghnall (powerful judgment)
Ralph (counsel-wolf) **Ralf**
Randall (shield wolf)
Raymond (wise protection)
Réamonn (wise protection) Irish form of Raymond.
Richard (stern king)
Riocárd (stern king) Irish form of Richard.
Robert (bright with fame)
Robin (bright with fame)
Roderick (famous with a spear) **Roddy**
Roger (famous with a spear) **Rodger**
Roibeárd (bright with fame) Irish form of Robert.
Rónán (little seal)
Rory (red, rust-colored)
Rowan (little red-haired one) Anglicized form of Ruadhán.
Roy (red)

Ruadhán (little red one)
Ruairí (red, rust-colored)
Ryan (little king)
Samuel (his name is God)
Seaghán (God is gracious) Irish form of John.
Séamus (supplanting, seizing by the heels)
Sean (God is gracious) Irish form of John.
Seanán (little ancient one)
Shane (God is gracious) Anglicized form of Seaghán.
Silvester (a wood, a forest)
Simeon (heard)
Simon (heard)
Siseal (blind, dim-sighted) Irish form of Cecil.
Sivney (well-going, pleasant) Anglicized form of Suibhne.
Steafán (a crown, a garland) Irish form of Stephen.
Stephen (a crown, a garland) **Stephan, Stephane, Steven**
Stewart (a steward, a keeper of the animal enclosure)
Suibhne (well-going, pleasant)
Terrence (soft, tender) **Terance**
Thomas (a twin)
Timothy (respecting God)
Tomás (a twin) Irish form of Thomas.
Tyrone (?, from an Irish place name)
Ualtar (ruler of an army) Irish form of Walter.
Uilliam (resolute protector) Irish form of William.
Vaughn (small) **Vaughan**
Vincent (conquering)
Walter (ruler of an army)
William (resolute protector)

SURNAMES

The use of nicknames extends even to surnames. The surname Gallagher was so common in some parts that in everyday use, other names were substituted for it. For instance, a Gallagher family living on a low-lying farm were known as the "Lowlys." One Gallagher was called "Bowers" simply because he once had a friend with him of that name; the name was eventually transfered to his son. Another method of establishing identification was to use three generations of Christian names, with the individual's name first, followed by his father's, then his grandfather's name.

The prefixes Mac and O continued to be absent from Irish names until the Gaelic League promoted their usage as a means of reestablishing a Gaelic identity. After the Republic of Ireland was formed, the government's policies to promote an Irish consciousness went even further in speeding the resumption of the Mac and O prefixes. The following is a list of 200 of the most common names found in Ireland:

Aherne (descendant of Echtighearn *horse-lord*)
Allen (?, possibly *rock*)
Armstrong (strong in the arm)
MacAuley (son of Olaf *ancestral relic*)
Barrett (bear-might)
Barry (bold as a bear)
Beatty (public victualler, inn keeper)

Bell (dweller at the sign of the bell)
Boyd (yellow-haired)
Boyle (descendant of Baoghall, ? possibly *pledge*)
Bradley (descendant of Brollach *breast*; from the broad lea)
Brady (descendant of Bradach *spirited*)
Breen (descendant of Braon *raven*)
Brennan (descendant of Braonán *little raven*)

MacBride (son of Brigit *strength*)

O'Brien (descendant of Brian *strength, virtue, kingly*)

Browne (brown one) **Brown**

Buckley (descendant of Buachalla *boy*; *dweller at the beech lea, dweller at the buck lea*)

Burke (dweller at the stronghold) **Burk**

Burns (dweller at the brook)

Butler (bottle-keeper; bottle-maker)

Byrne (descendant of Bran *raven*)

MacCabe (son of the abbot)

Cahill (descendant of Cathal *valor*)

O'Callaghan (descendant of Ceallachan *little warrior*)

Campbell (son of Cathmhaoil *battle chief; crooked mouth*)

McCann (son of Cana *whelp, pup*)

Carroll (descendant of Cearbhall *warrior, champion*)

MacCarthy (son of Carthach *friend; spear*)

Casey (descendant of Cathasach *watchful*)

Cassidy (descendant of Caiside *bent, twisted lock; clever*)

Clancy (descendant of Fhlanncaidh *red-haired one; ruddy warrior*)

Clarke (clerk)

Cleary (descendant of Cléireach *clerk, priest*) **Clery**

Coleman (descendant of Colmán *little dove*)

Collins (descendant of Coileán *pup, whelp*; son of Collin *victory of the people*)

Conlon (descendant of Conallán *little hero*)

O'Connell (descendant of Conall *high, mighty*)

Connolly (descendant of Conghal *conflict, strife*; descendant of Coingheallach) **Connelly, Conolly**

O'Connor (descendant of Conchobhar *wisdom, counsel and help, aid*)

Conway (hound of the plain)

Corcoran (descendant of Corcrán *purple*)

MacCormac (son of Cormac *chariot*)

Costello (son of Oisdealb *proud face*)

Craig (dweller at the crag)

Cronin (descendant of Crónán *little brown one, little swarthy one*) **Cronan**

Crowley (descendant of Cruadhlaoch *hard hero*)

MacCullagh (son of Culloch *boar; cock*)

Cullen (son or descendant of Cuileann *holly*) **Cullan, Cullin**

Cunningham (dweller at the royal manor)

Curran (descendant of Currán *little hero, little champion*) **Curren**

Daly (descendant of Dálach *assembly*) **Daley**

Delaney (descendant of Dubhshláine *dark, black* and *healthy, whole*)

Dempsey (descendant of Díomasach *proud*)

MacDermot (son of Diarmid *freeman, without injunction*)

Dillon (faithful, true)

Doherty (descendant of Dochartach *hurtful*)

Dolan (descendant of Dubhlan *black, dark* and *challenge*)

MacDonagh (son of Donagh or Donnchadh *brown warrior*)

MacDonald (son of Donall *world ruler*)

MacDonnell (son of Donall *world ruler*)

O'Donnell (descendant of Domhnall *world ruler*)

Donnelly (descendant of Donnghal *brown and brave*) **Donnolly**

O'Donoghue (descendant of Donnchadh *brown warrior; strong warrior*)

O'Donovan (descendant Donndubhan *little brown-haired one, little dark-haired one*)

Doran (descendant of Deoran *little stranger, an exiled person*)

Dowd (descendant of Dubhda *dark-complexioned*)

Dowling (descendant of Dúnlaing *brown spear*)

Doyle (descendant of Dubhghall *dark stranger*)

Driscoll (descendant of Eidirsceol *intermediary*)

Duffy (descendant of Dubhthach *dark-complexioned*)

Duggan (descendant of Dubhagan *little dark-complexioned one, little dark-haired one*) **Dugan**

Dunne (dark brown-haired) **Dunn**

Dwyer (descendant of Dubheidir *black, dark* and *dun-colored; wisdom, sense*)

Egan (little fiery one)

MacEvoy (son of ?, possibly Fíodhbhadhach *woodsman*)

Fahy (descendant of Fathach, ? possibly *foundation*)

Farrell (descendant of Fergal *champion, man of valor*)

Ferguson (son of Fergus *manly strength*)

Finnegan (descendant of Fionnagan *little fair-complexioned one, little fair-haired one*)

Fitzgerald (son of Gerald *spear-might*)

Fitzpatrick (son of Patrick *a patrician, an aristocrat*)

Flaherty (descendant of Flaithbheartach *rich ruler, bright hero*)

Flanagan (little ruddy-complexioned one, little red-haired one)

Fleming (from Flanders)

Flynn (descendant of Flann *red, ruddy*) **Flinn**

Foley (descendant of Foghlaidhe *a freebooter, plunderer*)

Ford (dweller at the stream crossing)

Fox (a fox)

Gallagher (descendant of Gallchobhar *eager help; foreign help*) **Gallaher**

MacGillycuddy (son of ?, possibly the *disciple of Saint Mochuda*)

Gorman (livid-complexioned, blue-complexioned)

MacGovern (son of Samhradhan *little summer*)

MacGowan (son of Gobhainn *a smith*)

O'Grady (descendant of Gráda *ugly*)

Graham (dweller at the gray land)

MacGrath (son of Rath *grace, luck*)

Greene (dweller at the green) **Green**

Griffin (debated meaning, possibly *ruddy, red* or *griffinlike; scary*)

MacGuinness (son of Aengus *one, choice*) **MacGuiness**

Hall (dweller near the hall)

Hamilton (dweller near the blunt hill)

O'Hara (descendant of Eaghra *bitter, sharp*)

Hayes (dweller near the hedge)

Healy (dweller at the high lea)

Hegarty (descendent of Eigceartach *injustice*) **Hagarty, Haggarty, Haggerty**

Hennessy (descendent of Aengus *one, choice*)

Henry (home ruler)
Hickey (little Hick [Richard] *stern king*)
Higgins (son of Higgin [Richard] *stern king*)
Hogan (descendant of Ogan *youth*)
MacHugh (son of Hugh *heart, mind, soul*; son of Aodh *fire, ardor*)
Hughes (son of Hugh *heart, mind, soul*)
Hurley (descendant of Urthaile)
Johnston (son of John *God is gracious*; from John's town)
Jones (son of John *God is gracious*)
Joyce (lord)
Kane (descendant of Cathan, ? possibly *war, warrior*)
Kavanagh (gentle, handsome)
Keane (descendant of Cian *ancient*; son of Cathan, ? possibly *war, warrior*) **Kean, Keene**
Kearney (descendant of Catharnach *warlike*; descendant of Cearnach *victorious*)
Keating (?) An Anglo-Norman family name.
O'Keeffe (descendant of Caomh *handsome, comely*)
Kelleher (Ó Céileachair *companion, dear*)
Kelly (descendant of Ceallach *war, strife*)
MacKenna (son of Cionaith *quick love*)
Kennedy (descendant of Cinnéidid *helmeted head, ugly head*)
Kenny (?, possibly *fire-sprung*)
Keogh (son of Eochaidh *horseman*)
MacKeon (son of Eoghan *well-born*)
Kerr (dweller at a fort)
Kiely (descendant of Cadhla *graceful*)
King (kingly)
Leary (descendant of Laoghaire *a calf*)
Lee (son of Laoidheach *poetic*; son of Leagha *physician*)
Lenehan (Ó Leannacháin)
Lennon (son of the servant of Finnan *little fair one*)
Long (long, tall)
MacLoughlin (son of Lochlann *land of the lochs*)
Lynch (sailor)
Lyons (descendant of Liathan *little gray one*; son of Lyon)
Madden (little hound)
Magee (son of Aodh *fire, ardor*)
Maguire (son of Odhar, *the pale-complexioned one, the dun-colored one*)
Maher (descendant of Meachair *fair, handsome*)
MacMahon (son of Mathghamhan *bear*)
O'Mahony (descendant of Mathghamhuin *the bear*) **O'Mahoney**
Malone (servant of Saint Eòin [John] *God is gracious*)
MacManus (son of Magnus *great*)
Martin (of Mars, the god of war)
Meehan (son of Miadhachan *noble, honorable*)
Molloy (servant of the noble one)
Moloney (descendant of Maoldhomhach *disciple of the church*)

Monaghan (little monk)
Mooney (hero)
Moore (dweller at a moor; Moorish, dark-complexioned)
Moran (sea warrior; tall, big)
Morgan (white sea, bright sea; mariner)
Moriarty (justice of the sea, sea-true)
Morris (Moorish, dark-complexioned)
Mullan (little bald one, little shaven one; monk, disciple) **Mullen**
Mulligan (little bald one, little shaven one; monk, disciple)
Murphy (sea warrior)
Murray (sea field)
MacNally (son of the poor man)
MacNamara (son of Cumara *hound of the sea*)
O'Neill (descendant of Niall *champion*)
Nolan (little famous one, little noble one)
Patterson (son of Patrick *patrician*)
Power (poor, pauper)
Quigley (descendant of Cuigleach *counsel, advice*)
Quinn (descendant of Conn *wise*)
Redmond (counsel-protection)
Regan (little king)
Reid (red-haired one, ruddy-complexioned)
Reilly (descendant of Raghallach *valiant, warlike*)
Riordan (little royal poet)
Robinson (son of Robin [Robert] *bright with fame*)
Roche (dweller at the rock)
Rogers (son of Roger *famous with the spear*)
Rooney (red-haired, ruddy-complexioned)
O'Rourke (descendant of Ruarc *little friend*)
Ryan (little king)
Scott (an Irishman, a Scot)
O'Shea (descendant of Seaghdha *stately, majestic*)
Sheehan (little wise one, little courteous one)
Sheridan (little wild man)
Smith (a smith)
Stewart (keeper of the animal enclosure)
O'Sullivan (descendant of Suileabhan *light eyes, white eyes*)
Sweeney (well-going)
Tobin (little Tobias *God is good*)
O'Toole (descendant of Tuathal *left-handed*)
Wallace (a Welshman)
Walsh (a Welshman)
Ward (watchman, guard)
Whelan (descendant of Faolán *little wolf*)
White (white, fair complexioned)
Woods (dweller at a wood)

The present-day "Chiefs of the Name," those who descend by primogeniture from the last formally inaugurated chiefs are:

O'Brien of Thomond
O Callaghan
O Conor Don
MacDermot of Coolavin
MacDermot Roe
O Donell of Tirconnell
O Donoghue of the Glens
O Donovan

Fox (originally surnamed Ó Catharnaigh)
MacGillycuddy of the Reeks
O Grady of Kilballyowen
O Kelly of Gallagh
O Morchoe
MacMorrough Kavanagh
O Neill of Clanaboy
O Toole of Fir Tire

Part Five

[FRANCE]

[Contents]

Chapter One

THE MEROVINGIANS
[481–768]

THE STUDY OF France can begin at several points in time, for it's difficult to say just when French history began. Some start in the distant past, when Cro-Magnon man was busy painting on cave walls. Some see the beginnings of the French nation rising with the Celts. Others begin their histories with the invasions of the Germanic tribes. But, it is generally agreed that France as a country began with the reign of the Frankish king, Clodovic (Clovis).

POLITICS

GAUL WAS UNDER the control of the Roman Empire when hordes of Germanic barbarians invaded in the fifth century. For over 200 years, the area comprising modern-day France existed in a kind of backward age as cultured Roman civilization gave way to uneducated tribal society.

In 481, Childeric, a king of the Salian Franks, died, leaving his son Clodovic (Clovis) as ruler over Tournai. Clovis was just fifteen years old but extremely ambitious. He killed off the other Salian kings, who just happened to be his close relatives, and by 486 was sole ruler of a vast amount of territory north of the Loire and the receiver of tribute from a number of southern territories.

In 491, Clovis sired a son, but instead of marrying the child's mother, he made a political match by marrying Clotilda, the daughter of Gundebaud, the Burgundian king. Clotilda gave Clovis three other sons and eventually converted him to Catholicism. At his baptism, he was pronounced king as well as leader of the new religion, a feature that would be central to the crowning of future kings and queens.

The next 300 years were ones of political intrigues and endless battles over the territories of Austrasia, Neustria, Aquitaine, and Burgundy. The heirs of Clovis held the throne of the Frankish state until 751. In the end, a succession of weak-willed kings delegated much of their authority to the governors of the palace so they could indulge themselves in more pleasurable pursuits. Those to whom the powers had been entrusted assumed control in their own right, and the Merovingian kings became but figureheads.

The greatest of the palace governors was Charles, the illegitimate son of Pepin of Heristal, who was himself a governor during the reign of Dagobert III. Charles "the Hammer" Martel was successful in many battles, but it was his defeat of the Moors at Poitiers in 733 that became his claim to fame. Though Charles did not personally aspire to the throne, he placed control of the territories of the Frankish Empire in the hands of his sons. To Carloman he gave Austrasia, Alemannia, and Thuringia. His second son, Pepin the Short, received Neustria, Burgundy, and Provence. Grifo, his illegitimate son, was given lands in Austrasia, Burgundy, and Neustria.

After Charles Martel's death in 741, Carloman and Pepin set another Merovingian figurehead on the throne (Childeric III), and set out Christianizing neighboring kingdoms. In 747, Carloman retired to a monastery, leaving Pepin to rule alone. Pepin wanted the title of king, so he sent men to the Pope to discuss the question of whether a king who did not exercise his royal power should be king. Pope Zacharias replied that it was better to give the title to the one who actually held power and recommended that Pepin assume the office. In 751, at an assembly of bishops and noblemen, Pepin the Short was lifted onto a shield and annointed King of France. The Merovingian dynasty was at an end.

The papacy had other reasons for consenting to Pepin's crowning. The Lombards had invaded and were threatening to march on Rome. The Pope hoped that Pepin would feel obligated to offer military support. In January 754, Pope Stephen approached Pepin for aid. Pepin first tried to negotiate with the Lombards, but failing at this, resigned himself to war.

He crossed the Alps, defeated the Lombards, and presented their territories to the Pope. He then proceeded to take nearly the whole of central Europe. By the end of his reign, Pepin had succeeded in taking Aquitaine and the rest of France, Gothia, Bavaria, the Rhineland, Belgium, and Holland. Pepin died in September 768, leaving his kingdom in the hands of his sons, Carloman and Carolus.

SOCIETY

THE GERMANIC INVADERS neither read nor wrote, nor had as well-developed an oral tradition as did the Celts. They had some knowledge of agriculture, but cultivating crops demanded settling in one place for an extended period of time, and that was something the Germans were reluctant to do. Most preferred hunting and foraging for foods or raiding and plundering the food stores of others to the difficult and time-consuming job of tilling the soil.

Germanic society was harsh, yet vital. Men hunted and carried out raids, and the remainder of their time was usually spent sleeping or carousing with other men of the tribe. Favored pastimes were drinking and gambling. The majority of the work of daily living was left to the women, children, and the elderly. Homes were crude timber and mud huts that were quickly and easily constructed; wealth was measured in cattle. Marriages were monogamous, except for tribal chieftains who often married more than once for political reasons. Adultery was rare and severely punished; divorce was almost nonexistent. Some tribes forbade women to remarry if their husbands died. That did not hold true for a man, however, as he required a mate to watch over his children and perform the household tasks.

The tribes eventually became more settled and developed into a feudal society. The lower orders were slaves captured during raids or those who lost their possessions through reckless gambling. The upper classes consisted of the freemen. Tribal chieftains were elected. The chief's primary function seems to have been ceremonial—a kind of father figure to promote tribal cohesion. In times of war, a military leader was elected from among the tribe's warriors. The military leader's authority was great but lasted only as long as the particular raid or battle for which he was elected. As the tribes went up against the Romans, the battles grew longer, and the military leaders assumed long-term control as kings.

Though society continued to be far from peaceful, changes were occurring. One change was in sexual morality. Relations between the sexes had been strictly regulated, but by the time Clovis assumed control, attitudes had relaxed a great deal. Mistresses, concubines, and illegitimate children were common.

Another change was the growth and advancement of feudalism. Land belonged to the king, and the people became tenants of their sovereign. The knights, who were bound to their kings by pledges of loyalty and honor, were rewarded with large estates, which were then worked by tenant farmers.

Law was basically a product of custom rather than an expression of a particular leader's will. Those who committed offenses against such custom were brought before a tribal court and subject to swift and exacting punishments. An assembly of warriors met periodically to discuss issues pertaining to war or to the welfare of the tribe. Decisions on whether to carry out a raid, for example, or to relocate the tribe to another area were typical topics addressed by the assembly.

RELIGION

THIS PERIOD OF time was one of intellectual and economic decline, but it was also one of considerable religious growth. In 511, Clovis called together a council of bishops at Orléans to discuss issues relating to the right of asylum and the recruitment of clergy. It was decided that serfs were unworthy to hold such a position, and that clergy could only be recruited from the freemen. In addition, clergy were given immunity from civil law. The monastic movement grew tremendously, and monasteries were among the most important social institutions.

NAMING

BEFORE THE FRANKISH tribes invaded Gaul, the Roman system of names was in use among the population. With the rise of the Frankish Empire, the Roman government fell away, but many of the Latin names were retained and adopted by the Franks. In the fifth century, Germanic names comprised 25 percent of the names found in Gaul. And though Pope Gregory the Great (540–604) recommended that parents give their children saints' names in recognition of their sacrifices and to perpetuate their memories, the number of Germanic names rose to nearly 50 percent in the fifth century and almost 75 percent in the seventh century. That shows that although Roman names continued to be used in the native population and were adopted by the Franks, the invaders in no way abandoned their own traditional Germanic names. These names came from the same root language as Old English names and follow the same themes. Following is a list of the most common name elements that can be used to form a great variety of names. These elements were originally combined to form names denoting strength or beauty, as Childeric (battle king) and Aethelflaed (noble beauty). As time passed, less attention was given to the meaning of the elements, and names were created with no understandable meanings. Wulfstan (wolf stone) and Mildburgh (mild fortress) are examples of names formed without regard to the meanings of the elements.

Adal- (noble)

Aelf-, Elf- (elf)

Aethel-, Ethel- (noble)

Amal- (work)

Arn- (eagle)

Bern- (bear)

Cuni- (bold)

Cuth- (famous)

Ead- (wealth, prosperity)

Eald- (old)

Eastre- (the goddess of the rising sun)

Ebur- (wild boar)

Eg- (edge)

Eormen-, Ermen-, Irmen- (strength)

Ercan- (genuine)

Folke-, Fulk-, Fulke- (folk, people)

God- (god, God)
Heah- (high, tall)
Hugu- (heart, mind, spirit)
Hun- (strength, warrior)
Milde- (mild)
Od- (riches)
Os- (god, God)
Sig-, Sige-, Sigu- (victory)
Thiuda- (folk, people)
Willeo- (will, desire)
-burg,-burgh,-burh (fortress)
-flaed (beauty)
-gifu (gift)
-gyth (war, strife)
-hard,-heard,-hart (hard, hardy, hearty, bold, brave, strong)
-helm (helmet, protection)
-lind (serpent)
-mund (hand, protection)
-swith (strength)

-thryth (strength)
-weald (power)
-weard (guardian, protector)
-wine (friend)
bald, beald (bold)
beorht, beort, beraht (bright)
brunja (breast, armor)
bruno (brown)
frith (peace)
gund (war, strife)
har (army)
hild (battle, strife, war)
man (man)
mir (fame)
raed (counsel)
ric (ruler, king)
stan (stone)
ulf, wulf (wolf)
wald (ruler, power)
wine, wini (friend)

FEMALE NAMES

Aaliz (nobility) **Aliz**
Adalgise (noble pledge)
Adalhaid (nobility) **Adalheidis, Adalheid**
Adelaïs (nobility)
Adelberg (noble fortress) **Adelburg**
Adelgonde (noble war)
Adila (nobility) **Adela**
Agiltrude (formidably strong)
Alda (old; wealthy)
Aldegonde (noble war)
Amala (work)
Amalberta (work bright)
Amalburga (labor fortress) **Amalberg, Amalberga, Amalburg**
Amalfrida (work peace)
Amalgund (work war)
Amalhilda (work battle)
Amalina (work serpent)
Amalswintha (work strength) **Amalswind**
Amaltrude (work strength)

Audofled (rich increase)
Audovère (rich guard)
Aveza (?)
Bathilda (commanding in battle)
Berchtilda (bright in battle)
Berthe (bright) **Berchte**
Berthilda (bright in battle) **Berchthilda**
Betlindis (?, second element is *serpent*)
Brunehault (armored for battle)
Brunhilda (armored for battle)
Childeberte (battle bright)
Chlodhilda (famous in battle)
Chlodosind (famous strength)
Chlodoswintha (famous strength)
Chrodehilde (famous in battle)
Chrodoswintha (famous strength)
Clotilda (famous in battle)
Dietberga (people protection)
Eberhard (boar hard)
Eberhild (boar strength) **Eburhild**

Edburg (wealthy protection)
Edelberge (noble protection) **Edelberg**
Edeline (noble cheer)
Edeltrud (noble strength) **Edeltrude**
Edila (nobility)
Emme (grandmother)
Engelberga (angel protection)
Esclairmonde (famous protection)
Evald (boar power)
Fastburg (firm fortress)
Fastrade (firm counsel)
Fredegonde (peaceful war) **Fredegund, Fredegunde, Fredegunt, Fridgund**
Fridburg (peace protection)
Fridegundis (peaceful war)
Frithswith (peace strength)
Frodberta (wise and bright)
Galswintha (?, possibly *rooster of strength*)
Geneviève (?, possibly *tribal woman*)
Gerberge (spear fortress)
Gisel (pledge)
Giselhilda (pledge battle)
Gisila (pledge)
Gismonda (pledge protection)
Godeberta (divinely bright)
Godeleva (divine gift)
Godelind (good serpent)
Gomatrude (war strength)
Griseldis (?, possibly *gray battle*) **Griselda**
Guennean (angel) A Breton name.

Guennolé (white) A Breton name.
Gweneal (white angel) A Breton name.
Hadewidis (battle wide)
Hedwig (war refuge) **Hedviga**
Helewidis (sound, healthy, and wide)
Herberga (army fortress)
Hildegard (battle protector)
Hildewig (battle war)
Hlodhild (famous battle)
Hrodny (famous and fresh)
Hrosmund (horse protection)
Hroswith (horse strength) A Lombard name.
Iduberge (happy protection)
Ingund (Ing's war) Ing was the name of a fertility god.
Isa (iron)
Iseult (ruler of the ice) **Iseulte**
Javotte (white stream)
Mahthildis (mighty in battle)
Malasintha (work strength)
Matilda (mighty in battle)
Melisenda (work strength)
Minna (memory; love; small)
Odila (wealth) **Odala, Odilia, Otila**
Plectrude (lightning strength)
Radegund (counsel war)
Raintrude (judgment strength)
Roslindis (horse serpent)
Sichilda (battle conqueror)
Swanchilda (battle swan)
Vulfégund (battle wolf)

MALE NAMES

Achille (?)
Adalbert (noble and bright)
Adalhard (noble and hard)
Agilmar (noble and famous) **Ailemar**
Alaric (ruler of all)
Albirich (elf ruler)
Amalricus (work ruler) **Amalric**
Anafrid (ancestor of peace)
Ansegisel (God's pledge)
Arnulf (eagle wolf)
Asce (from the tribe of the Gauts) **Ace**
Athalwulf (noble wolf) **Athalwolf**
Baldarich (bold rule) **Baldaric, Baldric**
Baldewin (bold friend)
Berahtram (bright raven)
Berchtiramm (bright raven)
Beringer (bear spear) **Beringaer**
Berinhard (bold as a bear) **Bernhard**
Berold (bear rule) **Berolt**
Beuves (beautiful)

Blaesus (stuttering, deformed)
Bobo (beautiful) **Bovo**
Brodulf (broad wolf)
Burchard (hard fortress)
Carloman (full-grown, a man)
Carolus (full-grown, a man)
Chainulf (home wolf)
Chararic (army ruler)
Charibert (bright army)
Chariwulf (army wolf)
Charles (full-grown, a man)
Childebert (bright in battle)
Childebrand (battle sword)
Childeric (battle king) **Childerich**
Chilperic (helping king)
Chlodio (famous)
Chlodoald (famous power)
Chlodobert (famous and bright)
Chlodomir (famous fame)
Chlodovech (famous in war) **Chlodowig**

Chloter (famous in war)
Chramne (raven)
Chrodogang (famous progress)
Chuonrath (bold counsel)
Clodomir (famous fame)
Clodovic (famous in war)
Clotaire (famous in war)
Clovis (famous in war)
Cunibert (bold and bright)
Dagobert (bright day)
Dagobrecht (bright day)
Dagolf (day wolf)
Dagrad (day counsel)
Denys (of Dionysous)
Dietberg (people protection)
Dietbert (people bright)
Dietbold (people bold, people brave)
Dietbrand (people sword)
Dietfrid (people peace)
Dietger (people spear) **Dietgar**
Diethard (people hard)
Diethelm (people helmet)
Dietmar (people fame)
Dietram (people raven)
Drogon (skillful)
Eberhard (boar hard)
Ebernund (boar protection)
Eberulf (boar wolf)
Eberwine (boar friend)
Ebles (wild boar) A Provençal name.
Ebroin (boar friend)
Ebur (wild boar)
Eburbero (boar bear)
Eburburg (boar fortress)
Ega (fearful, formidable)
Egilbert (formidable and bright)
Egilolf (formidable wolf)
Egilmar (formidable fame)
Eginhard (formidable and hard)
Egmond (formidable protection)
Eloy (the chosen)
Epurhard (boar hard)
Erchinoald (genuinely bold, genuinely brave) **Ercanbald, Erkenoald**
Erembert (public bright)
Ermenfred (peace of Ermen *strength*) Ermen was a Germanic war god.
Erulf (boar wolf)
Eudes (wealthy)
Eudon (wealthy)
Evrand (boar hard)
Evre (wild boar)
Evremond (boar protection)
Evrols (boar wolf)
Evroud (boar power)
Farabert (travel bright)

Faramond (travel protection)
Fastmann (firm man)
Fastmund (firm protection)
Ferahbald (life bold, life brave)
Ferahmund (life protection)
Ferrand (adventuring life) Provençal name.
Fiacre (eagle)
Filibert (very bright)
Flobert (wise and bright)
Folrad (people counsel)
Frederic (peace ruler)
Fridbald (peace bold)
Fridbert (peace bright)
Frideger (peace spear)
Fridhelm (peace helmet)
Fridman (peace man)
Fridmar (peace fame)
Fridmund (peace protection)
Fridolf (peace wolf)
Frithurich (peaceful ruler)
Fulcher (people guard)
Fulco (people, folk) **Fulko**
Fulrad (people counsel)
Gandolf (progress wolf)
Garalt (spear firm)
Gaubert (slaughter bright)
Gaucher (slaughter spear)
Geoffroi (peaceful district; traveler of peace; pledge of peace) **Geuffroi**
Gerald (ruler with a spear)
Gerard (spear hard) **Gerart**
Gerbert (spear bright)
Gerbold (bold with a spear, brave with a spear)
Gerlach (spear sport)
Germain (a German)
Gervase (servant of the spear)
Gerwin (spear friend)
Gevehard (give + hard, bold) **Gebehard**
Gidie (goatskin shield of Zeus, a protection) **Gide**
Gisilbert (bright pledge) **Giselbert**
Gisilfrid (pledge peace) **Giselfrid**
Gisilhard (pledge hard) **Giselhard**
Godafrid (God's peace)
Godebert (divinely bright)
Godehard (God hard)
Godegisèle (God's pledge) **Godegisel**
Godefroi (God's peace)
Godemar (good fame; God fame)
Goderic (divine king)
Godeskalk (God's servant)
Gondebaud (war bold)
Gondebert (war bright)
Gonderic (war ruler)
Gontram (war raven)
Gradlon (love) A Breton name.
Gregoire (vigilant, a watchman)

Grifo (ruddy-complexioned)
Grimaud (bold and savage)
Gualthier (powerful army)
Guarin (spear friend)
Guérin (war friend) **Guerin**
Gui (guide; sense, wisdom)
Guides (guide; sense, wisdom)
Guidon (guide; sense, wisdom)
Guillebert (bright pledge, famous pledge)
Gunthar (bold in war)
Guntram (battle raven) **Gunthram**
Guossalvo (war wolf) A Provençal name.
Guyon (guide; sense, wisdom)
Haimo (home)
Haimrich (home ruler) **Heinrich**
Hardwin (hard friend)
Harenc (army)
Haribert (army bright)
Hariman (army man, soldier)
Heimrich (home ruler) **Heinrich**
Helmar (helmet fame)
Heribert (army bright)
Herimar (army fame)
Herluin (?, perhaps *army friend*)
Heudebert (heart bright)
Hialperik (helping ruler)
Hildebert (war bright) **Hildeberht**
Hilderik (battle ruler)
Hilperik (battle ruler)
Hlod (famous)
Hlodio (famous)
Hlodheri (famous army)
Hlodmar (famous fame)
Hlodwig (famous war)
Hruodgar (famous spear)
Hruodland (famous land)
Hues (heart, mind, spirit)
Huet (heart, mind, spirit)
Hugibald (heart brave)
Hugibert (heart bright)
Hugihard (heart hard)
Hugoleik (mind sport)
Hugolin (heart, mind, spirit)
Huguenin (heart, mind, spirit)
Hugues (heart, mind, spirit)
Humbert (warrior bright)
Hunaud (warrior power)
Hunold (warrior power)
Huon (heart, mind, spirit)

Ilbert (war bright)
Imbert (iron people)
Isambaus (iron bold)
Isembert (iron bright) **Isambart, Isenbard**
Ives (archer) **Ive** A Breton form.
Ivon (archer) A Breton form.
Jaubert (good bright)
Jauffré (God's peace) A Provençal form.
Jocelin (from the tribe of the Gauts) **Josselin**
Jodetel (sportive)
Jompert (war bright)
Josse (from the tribe of the Gauts)
Judicael (sportive) **Juhel** A Breton name.
Juste (just, fair)
Lambert (land bright)
Landebert (land bright)
Lanzo (land)
Leonhard (lion hard)
Malgar (spear grinder)
Manfred (man of peace)
Milo (?, perhaps *mild, peaceful; merciful*)
Milon (? perhaps *mild, peaceful; merciful*)
Odilo (wealthy)
Ogier (wealthy spear) **Oger**
Pepin (?, possibly *chirper, whistler; a gardener*)
Radulf (counsel wolf)
Raganfrid (counsel peace)
Raginhard (counsel hard) **Raganhard**
Raginmund (counsel might)
Ragnachair (counsel hard)
Raimund (counsel might)
Richard (stern king)
Rigomer (? + famous)
Robert (bright with fame)
Rodric (famous ruler)
Roland (famous land)
Sigebert (bright victory)
Sigmund (victory protection)
Theodoric (God's gift)
Thibert (God bright)
Thorismond (Thor's protection)
Thorold (Thor's strength) **Thurold**
Turstan (Thor's stone) **Turstin**
Vincent (conquering)
Waldhar (ruler of the people)
Warinhar (protecting army)
Yves (archer)
Yvon (archer)

SURNAMES

Surnames were not in use during this time period. However, additional names were often added to the first name as a mark of distinction or as an identifier. These were usually based on physical characteristics, place of residence, or based on some other quality for which the bearer was known. The Pepins, for example, were identified by their place of residence: Pepin of Landen, Pepin of Heristal. Charles, the son of Pepin of Heristal, was famous for his military prowess and came to be known as Charles Martel (the Hammer). By today's standards, the names were not always attractive. The wife of Pepin the Short was known as Bertha of the Big Foot.

Beald (the bald; the bold) **Bald**
Cola (the dark one)
Brun (the brown)
Gleaw (the wise one)

Grim (the savage one)
Heaha (the tall one)
Martel (the hammer)

Chapter Two

THE CAROLINGIANS
[768–987]

POLITICS

PEPIN THE SHORT divided his extensive empire between his sons, Carloman and Carolus. Two weeks after his death, the brothers were crowned—Carloman at Soissons and Carolus at Noyon. In 769, Carloman incurred his brother's wrath after he refused to help him put down a rebellion in Aquitaine. Carloman didn't help the situation when a year later he chose to support Desiderius, king of the Lombards, rather than the Pope. In an effort to reunite the brothers, Desiderius offered them his daughters in marriage. Carloman married Gerbergia, and Carolus set aside his wife Himiltrude to marry Desideria.

After the marriages took place, Desiderius invaded Rome, captured the higher-ranking clergy, and tortured them to death. Both Carloman and Carolus were horrified by these events. Carolus repudiated Desideria and set out with his brother to punish the Lombards. Carloman died on the journey, and the empire was united under Carolus. He was to become Carolus Magnus: Charlemagne.

Charlemagne did more than just leave his name to the Carolingian dynasty. He ruled for forty-three years and conducted fifty-three military expeditions, the most famous of which was his intervention in Spain in 778. He had a very close relationship with the papacy, supporting the popes and offering them protection during rebellions, and seeing to the christianization of pagan tribes.

In 800, an astonishing event took place which possibly changed the fate of the western world. On Christmas day, Charlemagne was praying in the basilica of Saint Peter's when Pope Leo III placed the imperial crown of the Holy Roman Empire upon his head and proclaimed him king. Leo was strongly disliked by the people of Rome and had gone to Charlemagne at least twice for protection, so he could simply have been repaying Charlemagne for his help. Regardless, the crown of the Holy Roman Empire belonged to the senate of Byzantium and wasn't Leo's to give away. Charlemagne accepted the office anyway.

His vast empire was too much for him to manage alone, however, and he put his three sons in charge of military operations. In addition, he kept tabs on his kingdom by sending out special envoys consisting of a layman and a clergyman to the various counties to reaffirm the oaths of fealty given him by the vassals.

Charlemagne accomplished much besides simply conquering new territory. He abolished the office of mayor of the palace and eliminated the tribal dukes, and put local control in the hands of his own appointees who administered the tribal courts and kept the peace. The old system of justice was modified to include the Roman method of the sworn inquest, whereby people were brought to court and were bound by oath to tell of any illegal activities taking place in their area.

In 806, Charlemagne planned for his succession by dividing his kingdom among his sons according to Frankish custom. In 810, Charles, the eldest son, died. A year later, second son, Pepin also passed away. This left the entire empire to his youngest, Louis, and Charlemagne himself set the crown upon his son's head in 813. Less than a year later, Charlemagne contracted pleurisy while hunting and died within six days. He was seventy-two years old and had ruled for forty-six years.

Charlemagne had remarkable achievements, but he had neither the manpower nor the resources to keep it under control for long. It was too large and too diverse to keep unified, and the power and authority of the Carolingians steadily weakened.

Louis I, also known as Louis the Pious, eliminated his competition by having all his father's illegitimate sons tonsured and sent into monasteries. He had a nephew, Bernard, who held power in Italy, but Louis had him thrown into prison and had his eyes put out; he died from the complications. In spite of such behavior, Louis saw himself as a very religious person and was greatly enamored of the papacy. He called on Pope Stephen V to crown him in 816, deeming his first coronation insufficient, and in 823, had his eldest son, Lothair, crowned by the Pope as well. Louis, who suffered greatly from regret and guilt over the fate of Bernard, agreed to do public penance for the matter. This action both undermined his authority and strength and led the papacy to the conclusion that ecclesiastical power was superior to that of any government and that Louis should submit himself to the authority of the papacy.

Such an attitude was far from popular, and Louis found himself in the middle of a military revolt. He was nearly deposed, and favor had passed to his son, Lothair. He was able to regain his authority when an intense rivalry developed between his sons, Lothair, Louis, Pepin, and Charles. He partitioned his lands among them in the hopes their duties would keep them occupied. He was not to be so lucky. His sons continued their intrigues, rivalries, and attempts to gain superiority. His eldest son, Lothair, was sent into exile, and Pepin received Aquitaine and the area between the Loire and the Seine. Louis received Austrasia, Bavaria,

Frisia, and Saxony, thus earning him the nickname "the German." The youngest, Charles, was given Burgundy, Laon, Provence, Rheims, Septimania, Trier, and Woëvre.

In spite of their possessions, the children of Louis the Pious were not content. In 840, Louis the German rose to arms against his father and was henceforth defeated. Louis I became seriously ill on his return trip home. He was placed in a boat, ferried downstream, and taken to an island in the Rhine where he died at the age of sixty-two. He left a disintegrating empire in the hands of rival sons.

Louis and Charles allied themselves against their brother, Lothair, who had repeatedly acted with dishonor against them. Lothair's forces were defeated and Louis and Charles took dual oaths to support one another. The three brothers were eventually reconciled and in June 842, met and swore to live in peace.

In 843, the empire was partitioned by the treaty of Verdun, the most important treaty of French history, for it marks the beginning of France as a nation. Louis the German received the lands in the east, including the areas of Austrasia, Saxony, Bohemia, and Bavaria. Lothair took possession of the central lands, including those of Holland, eastern Belgium, Rhineland, Provence, Lombardy, Venetia, and Tuscany. His lands came to be known as Lotharingia. Charles the Bald's lands, the West Frankish Kingdom, stretched from the Atlantic to the banks of the Meuse, the Rhône, and the Saône.

Charles the Bald, the first king of France, ruled for thirty-five years. His reign was one of conflict as both his brother Louis and the Normans were intent on creating problems. On Easter day in 845, the Normans took Paris and forced Charles to pay a huge ransom. Several years later, they were responsible for carrying out numerous raids into French territory, terrorizing and pillaging several cities.

In 858, Louis the German violated the treaty of Verdun and invaded Lothair's territory, then forced his way into France. Louis's assault was stopped by Robert the Strong, an envoy of Charles's. Robert was given the office of mayor of the palace and awarded with many lands. His heirs were to become dukes of France and counts of Paris.

After the deaths of Louis the German and Lothair, Charles the Bald inherited their lands, united the empire, and ruled as emperor. In 877, he went to Rome to be crowned by the Pope but died on the return trip home. The following years saw the disintegration and decline of both the empire and the Carolingians as the crown passed quickly through the heirs of Charles the Bald to his young grandson, Charles.

Had Charles been an adult, events surely would have unfolded differently. As it was, the magnates were unwilling to give the crown to a mere child. They preferred to elect their own king than follow tradition and have a hereditary crown. Their choice was Eudes, a son of Robert the Strong who had distinguished himself in battle against the Normans. Though strong and brave in battle, Eudes was unable to rid the country of its problem with the Normans and Viking raiders.

In 893, Charles was crowned as Charles III (the Simple). In 911, the French signed a treaty with the Normans that put Normandy in their charge. Charles the Simple was attacked by Raoul, the son of the duke of Burgundy, and thrown into prison, where he died in 929. Raoul died in 935, leaving no children to inherit. His brother-in-law, Hugh the Great, led a delegation to England to bring back Louis, the son of Charles the Simple and his English wife Eadgifu, the sister of King Aethelstan.

Aethelstan was reluctant to let Louis go but did so after obtaining a guarantee that the nobles would pay Louis homage the minute he set foot on French soil. In June 936, Louis IV was crowned King of France. He was guided by Hugh the Great, the husband of Louis's aunt, Eadhild. Louis became a strong character and a capable leader but was killed in a riding accident in 954. His crown went to his thirteen-year-old son, Lothair. Hugh the Great died two years later, leaving a son, Hugh Capet, whose destiny in French history was yet to be played out.

Hugh had a second wife, Hadwig, whose brother Otto was the Germanic Roman emperor and the most powerful man in Europe. Otto the Great wasn't only the uncle of Hugh Capet, he was the guardian of Lothair as well. After Lothair reached his majority, he married Emma, the daughter of Otto's second wife, thereby tightening the bond between France and Germany. Hugh Capet became his counselor and adviser.

Lothair died in 985 at the age of forty-four. He had been complaining of a stomach ailment, and there is reason to think he may have been suffering the effects of poisoning. Lothair left the throne to his son, Louis V. The new king was nineteen, energetic, and determined to rule. Unfortunately, Louis died in a riding accident just a year later, leaving no issue. The Carolingian dynasty was at an end.

SOCIETY

SOCIETY WAS DIVIDED into three classes or estates: the clergy (the oratores), the seigneurs (the bellatores), and the workers (the laboratores). Class lines between the groups were sharply divided, and there was little equality among them. The clergy's job was to pray, to promote Christianity, and to intercede between man and God; the seigneur's job was to fight and serve as guardian of the land, the towns, and the country; the worker's job was to supply the first two groups with gold, food, and clothing—a difficult task when malnourishment and dreadful living conditions were the order of the day. There is little doubt that daily living was a struggle, especially since trade was very limited, and people had inadequate tools and little agricultural knowledge.

Charlemagne actively promoted feudalism by encouraging vassalage, whereby a knight bound himself to a seigneur by a pledge of loyalty, honor, and service. In return, the seigneur provided the knights with estates, which were then subdivided among feudal tenants. The seigneurs ruled their lands as kings and were responsible for local control and keeping the peace.

There was a great deal of cultural diversity across the Frankish Empire, and that had a great deal to do with which areas suffered the greatest impact of the Frankish invasions. Frankish influence was greater in the north, the Celts retained their culture in the west, Gallo-Roman influence was stronger in the south, the Normans brought Norse customs with them into Normandy, and a cultural mix could be found in Burgundy.

The Merovingians contributed little to society apart from some well-crafted jewelry. By the time Charlemagne took the throne, trade still had not resumed, and economic stagnation was almost complete. Roads deteriorated, urban areas were abandoned, ports were deserted, and money all but disappeared from the scene. Charlemagne promoted intellectual pursuits by establishing several schools, thereby marking a return to learning, but a return to a vital civilization and economy such as the Gallo-Romans had was still wanting.

Vikings began raiding the coastline in the ninth century and eventually made their way inland in search of monasteries and villages to pillage and slaves to carry off. The Carolingians were powerless to prevent the attacks, forcing wealthy landowners to see to their own protection. Fortified castles and strongholds were built, and private armies were retained to meet the threat.

RELIGION

CHARLEMAGNE SAW HIMSELF as a warrior for the Christian faith and to that end built many churches and saw to the restoration and expansion of several monasteries. Monastic life was thought of very highly, and monasteries became important social institutions of the time. In fact, Charlemagne and others after him rid themselves of troublemakers by having them tonsured and sent into the monasteries to live.

The institution of the Church was extremely privileged, and its bishops continued to hold great authority.

Although it played a very important role in early France, that role was mainly in the area of politics. The kings were anointed by the Pope, so they believed they were chosen by God and held their positions by divine right. The clergy, on the other hand, believed themselves to be God's representatives on earth and therefore superior to the kings. The relationship between Church and state was close, complicated, and quite often stormy.

NAMING

THIS PERIOD OF time saw a bit of a change in the names that were used. Before, the majority of the names were of Germanic origin. As Christianity and relations with other countries flourished, the Franks began using fewer of their traditional names. It's reported that in the ninth century, 50 percent or 60 percent of the names found in France were of Latin origin, 30 percent to 40 percent were biblical names, and the rest were of Germanic origin. In the latter group, the majority were compound names, though single-element names such as Berthe and Hugues were also common. Among the most common names for women were Adelaide and its various forms, Berthe, and Eleanor. For men, Charles, Louis, and Philip were popular.

FEMALE NAMES

Aaliz (nobility) **Aliz**
Adalgise (noble pledge)
Adalheid (noble one)
Adela (noble) **Adila**
Adelaide (nobility)
Adelaïs (nobility)
Adelburgh (noble fortress) **Adelburg**
Adelgonde (noble war) **Adelgund, Adelgunde**
Adelhild (noble battle)
Adeline (nobility)
Adelswinde (noble strength)
Adeltrude (noble strength)
Adriana (from Hadrianus)
Aelfgifu (elf gift)
Aethelfled (noble beauty)
Aethelhild (noble battle)
Aethelthryth (noble strength)
Agathe (good) A saint's name.
Agiltrude (formidable strength)
Agnès (chaste, pure) A saint's name.
Aida (helper, aide)
Albina (white)
Alda (wealthy; old)
Aldegonde (noble war)
Aldgitha (noble gift)
Alfhild (elf battle)
Alfreda (elf counsel)
Alienor (light)
Alswytha (hall strength)
Althaea (healer)
Amala (work)

Amalberga (work protection) **Amalburg, Amalburga, Amalburgha**
Amalberta (work bright)
Amalfrida (work peace)
Amalgund (work battle)
Amalhilda (work battle)
Amalina (work serpent)
Amalswind (work strength)
Amalswyntha (work strength) **Amalswynth**
Amaltrude (work strength)
Ancelote (servant, disciple)
Ancilée (servant)
Anne (grace, full of grace, mercy) A saint's name.
Ansgard (divine guard)
Ansgisil (divine pledge)
Arianne (very holy one)
Aude (old)
Audofled (wealthy beauty) **Audoflaed**
Auguste (great, venerable)
Aure (aura)
Aurélie (gold)
Aurore (dawn, daybreak)
Aveline (?)
Aveza (?)
Avila (?)
Baldefled (bold beauty) **Baldeflaed**
Barbara (foreign woman) A saint's name.
Béatrice (bringer of joy and happiness) **Beatrix** A saint's name.
Bénédicte (blessed) A saint's name.
Berthe (bright)

Bertille (bright battle)
Bibiane (alive) A saint's name.
Blanche (white)
Brunehault (armored for battle)
Cécile (blind, dim-sighted) A saint's name.
Céleste (heavenly)
Céline (heaven)
Christiane (a Christian, a follower of Christ)
Chrodehilde (famous battle)
Clarice (bright, clear, famous)
Claude (lame)
Clémence (mild, gentle, clement)
Clothilde (famous in battle)
Colombe (dove)
Cyrille (lordly)
Danièle (God is my judge)
Delphine (woman from Delphi) A saint's name.
Denise (of Dionysus)
Desideria (beloved, desired)
Dominique (belonging to a lord)
Dorothée (gift of God) A saint's name.
Eadgifu (wealthy gift)
Eadhild (prosperous in battle)
Eléanor (light, torch, bright)
Éliane (of the sun)
Éloise (hearty, sound, and wide; famous in war)
Émilie (emulating, trying to equal or excel)
Emma (strength)
Esther (myrtle; star)
Eugénie (well-born, noble)
Eulalie (fair speech)
Euphémie (fair speech)
Fabienne (a bean)
Fabiola (a bean) A saint's name.
Félise (lucky, happy)
Flore (a flower) A saint's name.
Florence (blooming, flourishing)
Frédérique (ruler of peace)
Geneviève (?, possibly *tribal woman*) Saint Geneviève (420—500) is the patron saint of Paris.
Gerbergia (spear fortress)
Germaine (a German)
Giselle (pledge) **Gisela**
Griselda (?, possibly *gray battle*)
Hadwig (battle strife) **Haduwig**
Hannah (grace, full of grace, mercy)
Hélène (light, torch, bright) The name of the mother of Constantine the Great.
Himiltrude (? + strength)

Honoré (honor, esteem)
Hyacinthe (hyacinth, bluebell) A saint's name.
Ida (work)
Irmengard (fortress of strength)
Jeanne (God is gracious)
Joceline (from the tribe of the Gauts) **Joscelin**
Jordane (a flowing down)
Judith (praised; from Judah)
Julitte (?, perhaps *youth, downy; praised; from Judah*) A saint's name.
Justine (just, fair)
Laure (laurel)
Léa (weary)
Luce (light)
Lucia (light) A saint's name.
Malasintha (work strength)
Marcille (of Mars, warlike) A saint's name.
Marguerite (a pearl)
Marie (sea of bitterness or sorrow)
Martine (of Mars, warlike)
Mathilde (mighty in battle)
Maude (powerful in battle)
Melisenda (work strength)
Minna (memory; love; small)
Monique (?) The name of the mother of Saint Augustine.
Nanthilda (?, the second element is *battle*)
Odila (wealth) **Odala, Odilia, Otila**
Perrine (little rock)
Philippa (lover of horses)
Plectrude (lightning strength)
Rachel (ewe)
Radegund (counsel war)
Raintrude (judgment strength)
Renée (reborn)
Romaine (a Roman)
Roslindis (horse serpent)
Sabine (Sabine woman)
Sichilda (battle conqueror)
Solange (yearly, annual; solemn, religious)
Sophie (wisdom)
Swanchilda (battle swan)
Valérie (healthy, strong)
Viole (violet)
Vivienne (alive)
Vulfégund (battle wolf)
Yolande (violet)
Yvette (archer)
Yvonne (archer)

MALE NAMES

Abel (breath)
Achille (?)
Adalard (noble and strong)
Adalbert (noble and bright) **Adelbert**
Adelar (noble eagle)
Adelbern (noble bear)
Adelgar (noble spear, noble sword)
Adelhelm (noble helmet, noble protection)
Adelhold (noble and firm)
Adelulf (noble wolf)
Adelwin (noble friend)
Adhémar (noble and great)
Adrien (man from Hadrianus)
Aelfhelm (elf helmet)
Aelfred (elf counsel)
Aethelbald (noble and brave)
Agilbert (formidably bright)
Agilo (formidable)
Agilulf (formidable wolf)
Alain (?, perhaps *rock*; *handsome*)
Aléard (noble and stern)
Alfried (elf counsel)
Alphonse (noble and ready)
Alysaundre (defender of mankind) **Alexandre**
Amalbert (bright in work)
Amalfried (work counsel)
Amalrich (work ruler)
Ambrose (immortal) A saint's name.
Anatole (sunrise, daybreak)
Ancelot (servant)
Andrieu (manly)
Anquetil (divine cauldron, divine kettle)
Anselme (divine helmet)
Ansgar (divine war)
Antoine (?, *priceless, of inestimable worth* is a folk definition) A saint's name.
Archambault (holy prince)
Aristide (best) A saint's name.
Arnhold (eagle power)
Artaud (?)
Audafrei (wealthy peace)
Audoin (wealthy friend)
Audwine (wealthy friend)
Auguste (great, venerable)
Aurèle (golden)
Ayldo (formidable and firm)
Baldegisel (bold pledge, brave pledge)
Baldewin (bold friend) **Baldwin**
Baptiste (a baptizer)
Barnabé (son of exhortation)
Barthélemy (son of Talmai)
Basile (kingly)
Baudrand (bold raven)
Baudri (bold king)

Bedrich (ruler of peace)
Benedict (blessed) A saint's name.
Benoît (blessed)
Berchtiramm (bright raven)
Bernhard (bold as a bear) **Bernard** A saint's name.
Berthold (bright power, bright and firm) **Bertold**
Blaise (deformed, stuttering) A saint's name.
Brand (sword)
Brandolf (sword wolf)
Brice (?) A saint's name.
Bruno (brown)
Carloman (full-grown, a man)
Carolus (full-grown, a man)
Cecil (blind, dim-sighted) A saint's name.
Charibert (bright warrior)
Charles (full-grown, a man)
Childebert (bright in battle)
Childebrand (battle sword)
Childerich (battle ruler)
Chilperic (helpful ruler)
Chlodio (famous)
Chlodomir (famous fame)
Chlodoweh (holy fame)
Chloter (famous warrior)
Chramne (raven)
Christian (a Christian, a follower of Christ)
Christophe (bearing Christ) A saint's name.
Chrodogang (famous progress)
Claude (lame) A saint's name.
Clément (gentle, mild) A saint's name.
Conan (wisdom)
Corin (a spear) A saint's name.
Corneille (horn) A saint's name. Saint Cornelius's relics were taken to France by Charles the Bald.
Cunibert (bold and bright)
Cyprien (from Cyprus) A saint's name.
Cyran (spear man)
Cyrille (lordly) A saint's name.
Dagobert (day bright)
Dagobrecht (day bright)
Dagolf (day wolf)
Dagrad (day counsel)
Damien (tamer) A saint's name.
Delphin (dolphin) A saint's name.
Denys (of Dionysus)
Desideratus (beloved, desired) A saint's name.
Didier (beloved, desired)
Dietberg (people fortress)
Dietbert (people bright)
Dietbold (bold people, brave people)
Dietbrand (people sword)
Dietfrid (people peace)
Dietger (people spear)
Dietmar (people fame)

Dietram (people raven)
Donatien (given by God) A saint's name.
Dunstan (hill stone)
Dunulf (hill wolf)
Ebernund (boar protection)
Eberulf (boar wolf)
Eberwine (boar friend)
Ebroin (boar friend)
Ebur (boar)
Eburberg (boar fortress)
Eburbern (boar bear)
Edelmar (noble and famous, noble and great)
Edeltrud (noble maid)
Edgard (rich spear)
Ega (formidable, awesome)
Eggert (formidable king)
Egilbert (formidable and bright)
Egilhart (formidable and hard) **Egilhard**
Egilolf (formidable wolf)
Egilmar (formidable fame)
Eginhard (formidable and hard)
Egmont (formidable protection)
Ehrenbrecht (honor bright) **Ehrenbert**
Ehrenfried (honor peace)
Eilart (formidable and hard)
Eilbert (formidable and bright)
Eilo (formidable and hard)
Eisenbert (iron bright) **Eisenbart**
Eisenbolt (iron bold, iron brave)
Eisenhart (iron hard) **Eisenhard, Eisenhardt**
Elberich (elf king)
Ellanheri (battle warrior)
Elle (battle, war)
Ello (battle, war)
Elmarik (helmeted king)
Eloi (chosen) A saint's name.
Émilien (emulating, trying to equal or excel) A saint's name.
Emmerich (work rule)
Endres (manly)
Endrikis (home ruler)
Epurhard (boar hard)
Epurhelm (boar helmet, boar protection)
Erasmus (amiable) A saint's name.
Erchenold (sacred and bold, sacred and brave, genuinely bold, genuinely brave) **Erkenoald**
Erembert (public and bright)
Erlebald (bold earl, brave earl)
Erlebert (bright earl) **Erlebryht**
Ermengild (public pledge)
Ethelmar (noble ruler)
Ethelred (noble counsel) **Ethelraed**
Eudes (rich)
Eugène (well-born, noble) A saint's name.
Evariste (satisfying) A saint's name.
Everhard (boar hard) **Everhart**
Evrand (boar hard)

Evre (boar)
Evremond (boar protection)
Fabien (a bean) A saint's name.
Fabrice (a workman, craftsman)
Farabert (travel bright)
Faramond (travel protection)
Fastmann (firm man)
Fastmund (firm protection)
Félix (happy, lucky)
Ferahbald (life bold, life brave)
Ferahmund (life protection)
Ferdinand (?, possibly *peace*; *journey*; *youth, life + courage*; *venture, risk*; *ready, prepared*)
Ferrand (?, possibly *peace*; *journey*; *youth, life + courage*; *venture, risk*; *ready, prepared*)
Firmin (steadfast)
Flobert (wise and bright)
Florentin (flourishing)
Florian (flower)
Folrad (people counsel)
Franceis (a Frank, a freeman)
Fredewolt (peace power)
Fridbald (peace bold, peace brave)
Fridbert (peace bright)
Frideger (peace spear)
Fridhelm (peace helmet, peace protection)
Fridman (peace man)
Fridmar (peace fame)
Fridmund (peace protection)
Fridolf (peace wolf)
Friedrich (ruler of peace)
Frisia (?)
Fulke (people protection) **Fulk, Fulko**
Fulrad (people counsel)
Georges (earth worker, farmer) A saint's name.
Gerbert (spear bright)
Gerhard (spear hard)
Gerlach (spear sport)
Germain (a German)
Gerwald (spear ruler)
Gerwin (spear friend)
Girairs (spear hard)
Girart (spear hard)
Girault (spear hard)
Girroald (spear hard)
Giselbert (bright pledge)
Giselberg (pledge protection)
Giselfrid (pledge peace)
Giselhard (firm pledge) **Giselhart**
Giselher (pledge army, pledge warrior)
Godard (God hard)
Godebert (God bright, divinely bright)
Godefried (God's peace)
Godegisel (God pledge, divine pledge)
Godeskalk (God's servant)
Godfroi (God's peace)

Gondebault (war bold)
Gondebert (war bright)
Gonderic (war ruler)
Gonstan (hill stone)
Gregoire (watchman) A saint's name.
Grimaud (fierce power)
Gualthier (powerful army)
Guarin (spear friend) **Guerin**
Guides (sense, wisdom)
Guillebert (bright pledge)
Gunthar (warrior)
Helmerich (helmet king)
Heruwulf (sword wolf)
Heribert (bright army, bright warrior)
Herimar (army fame, warrior fame)
Herluin (?, possibly *army friend*)
Hialperik (helping king)
Hilaire (cheerful) A saint's name.
Hildebert (battle bright)
Hilderik (battle king)
Hilperik (battle king)
Hippolyte (freer of horses) A saint's name.
Hlod (famous)
Hlodheri (famous army)
Hlodio (famous)
Hlodmar (famous fame)
Hlodwig (famous war)
Honoré (honor, esteem)
Hrodrich (famous king)
Hruodgar (famous spear)
Hruodland (famous land)
Hubert (bright heart)
Hugh (heart, mind, soul)
Hugibald (heart, mind, soul + bold, brave)
Hugoleik (heart, mind, soul + sport)
Humbert (strong and bright)
Hunaud (strong ruler)
Hunold (strong ruler)
Ivon (bow warrior, archer)
Jérôme (holy name)
Joseph (he shall add)
Jourdain (a flowing down)
Lambert (land bright)
Lance (land)
Landerik (land king) **Landerich**
Landolf (land wolf)
Landrad (land counsel)
Lanzo (land)
Laurent (from Laurentum) A saint's name.
Leander (lion man) A saint's name.
Léo (lion)
Leobhard (love hard)
Leodowald (people power, people ruler)

Leofwine (beloved friend)
Léonhard (lion hearted, brave as a lion) A saint's name.
Léopold (people bold)
Leudomir (people fame)
Leutgar (people spear)
Lothair (famous army) **Lothar**
Louis (famous in war)
Lowenhard (lion hard, stern lion)
Macaire (blessed) A saint's name.
Marc (of Mars; manly; soft, tender) A saint's name.
Marcel (of Mars; manly; soft, tender) A saint's name.
Marcellin (of Mars; manly; soft, tender) A saint's name.
Martin (of Mars, warlike) A saint's name.
Meinhard (mighty hard)
Meinrad (mighty counsel)
Nicolas (victory of the people)
Olivier (olive tree)
Otto (rich)
Pepin (?, possibly *chirper, whistler; a gardener*)
Philibert (very bright, very famous) A saint's name.
Philip (lover of horses) A saint's name.
Pierre (a rock, a stone) A saint's name.
Prosper (favorable, prosperous) A saint's name.
Radulf (counsel wolf)
Raganher (wise army)
Raimund (wise protection)
Randulf (shielf wolf)
Rémy (oarsman) A saint's name.
Richard (stern king) **Richart**
Robert (bright with fame)
Rodolphe (wolf fame)
Roger (famous spear)
Roland (famous land)
Romain (a Roman)
Sébastien (man from Sebastia) A saint's name.
Séverin (severe, strict) A saint's name.
Stéphane (a crown, a garland) A saint's name.
Sylvain (of the woods) A saint's name.
Sylvestre (of the woods) A saint's name.
Théodore (God's gift)
Théophile (beloved of God)
Ulrich (noble ruler)
Urbain (a city dweller)
Valentin (strong, healthy)
Valéry (strong, healthy)
Vincent (conquering)
Vivien (alive)
Welf (wolf)
Wilburgh (resolute fortress)
William (resolute protector)
Yves (archer)
Yvon (archer)

SURNAMES

As in the previous time period, surnames were not yet in use. Additional names were used to make distinctions within families where more than one member had the same name. Additional names were also given as nicknames relating to personal characteristics or attributes.

le **Bon** (the good)
le **Brun** (the brown)
le **Bruyant** (the boisterous)
le **Chauve** (the bald)
le **Courageux** (the courageous, the bold)

le **Fort** (the strong)
le **Hardi** (the bold)
le **Pieux** (the pious)
le **Sage** (the wise)

Secondary names were also based on locale, either one's original place of residence or a current place of residence. The following names are based on the major cities of the Frankish Kingdom in existence during the Carolingian years.

de **Aix-la-Chapelle**
de **Amiens**
de **Angoulëme**
de **Arles**
de **Barcelona**
de **Bordeaux**
de **Carnac**
de **Frankfurt**
de **Geneva**
de **Lascaux**

de **Lyons**
de **Marseilles**
de **Paris**
de **Pavia**
de **Poitiers**
de **Sémur**
de **Tours**
de **Verden**
de **Verdun**

Chapter Three

THE DIRECT CAPETIANS
[987—1328]

POLITICS

THE FRENCH NOBLES were quick to see an advantage in the end of the Carolingian dynasty. They much preferred to elect a king of their own choosing rather than see the crown pass through a hereditary line to the traitorous Charles of Lorraine. An assembly of lords was called, and Hugh Capet was placed on the throne in 987.

France of this time period was a feudal country in which the nobility ruled their own lands and only served the monarchy in time of war. It now seems apparent that the lords' motives for putting Hugh Capet on the throne wasn't because of his strength. Though Hugh had had an important role as adviser to both King Lothair and Louis V, he was not that powerful a person; his greatest desire was to be a lay abbot (his nickname Capet was based on the cape he wore as a lay abbot). By putting him on the throne, the lords believed they had elected a man who could be easily controlled. Little did they know that they had sealed the fate of France for nearly 400 years.

Little is known of Hugh Capet's personal nature other than that he wasn't the pushover many had hoped. He was a man of experience who was determined to rule in his own right and determined to see the nobility acknowledge the supremacy of the crown over their feudal holdings. He was also determined to see his own family benefit from his change in fortune. Early on, he had his son Robert associated to the throne by giving him the position of *rex designatus* (king designate). He also neutralized the Flemish threat by marrying Robert to Rozala (also known as Susanna), the daughter of King Berengar of Italy and widow of Arnulf II, Count of Flanders. After ruling for nine years, Hugh Capet contracted smallpox and died in August 996. He was the founder of a dynasty that exists to this day, a thousand years later. His descendants still occupy the thrones of Spain and the Grand Duchy of Luxembourg.

Robert, so called the Pious because of his devotion to the Church, ascended to the French throne after his father's death. More is known about Robert's character through the writings of his biographer, the monk Helgald (Helgaud) of Fleury-sur-Loire. He is said to have been tall, handsome, gentle, graceful, and well-versed in literature.

One of Robert's first acts was to repudiate his wife Rozala in favor of Bertha, the widow of the count of Blois. Pope Gregory V intervened in the marriage as there was an issue of bigamy and a question of incest as the two were closely related. Robert refused to end the relationship and was excommunicated. Robert and Bertha's only child died at birth, and after five years together, they agreed to part; his excommunication was then lifted. His third wife was Constance, the daughter of William of Provence. Four sons and two daughters were born from this marriage, but Constance was an extremely disagreeable person, and Robert attempted to have his marriage dissolved so he could marry Bertha again.

Like his father before him, Robert had his eldest son, Hugh, associated to the throne. Hugh died at the age of eighteen, and the second son, Henry, took his place in succession. Robert was given the duchy of Burgundy. Robert the Pious died in 1031. From Henry I onward, the system of primogeniture, whereby inheritance went to the eldest surviving son, went into effect and became law.

Even less is known of Henry I than of his grandfather, Hugh Capet. What is known is that his mother contested his position as king; she wanted the kingdom to go to her youngest son, Robert. War broke out between the brothers, and Henry kept the crown by renouncing French claim to Burgundy. It's also known that Henry ruled during a difficult time that saw the burning of Paris and seven years of famine.

After Henry's first wife, Matilda, died after the death of their first child, he sought a Franco-Russian alliance by marrying Anne of Kiev, the daughter of Yaroslav I, Prince of Kiev, and Ingigerd of Sweden. The marriage produced three sons and a daughter. Henry suffered from premature senility, becoming ''old and wretched'' before his time. He obtained a potion to rejuvenate himself and restore his health, but he apparently did not follow specific instructions to take the medicine without water. He died a day later, leaving the throne to his eight-year-old son, Philip, under the regency of his uncle, Baldwin V, Count of Flanders.

With the exception of a few incidents of Anglo-Norman aggression, the country was fairly peaceful during Philip's reign. His first marriage was to Bertha of Holland, who bore him five children. Twenty years later, he fell in love with Bertrade de Montfort, the wife of Fulk IV, Count of Anjou. Philip repudiated Bertha, abducted Bertrade, and found a bishop to marry them. Once Rome found out what had happened, Philip was ordered to give up his bride. He refused and was excommunicated. Only after the Pope put an interdict on the kingdom of France and closed all its churches did Philip give in. In 1104, he ceased to live with Bertrade, and he died from malaria four years later. Shortly before his death, he admitted to his personal failures and deemed himself unworthy of being buried next to his ancestors at Saint Denis. His request to be interred at the monastery of Saint Benoît-sur-Loire was granted. As for Bertrade, the beautiful young woman Philip stole away from the Count of Anjou, she took the veil after the king's death and died in 1117.

Philip's son, Louis VI the Fat, was named Thibaud at birth, but upon his baptism, was christened Louis in accordance to Carolingian tradition. By the time he gained the throne, he already had a great deal of military and life experience behind him, which served him well during his reign of twenty-nine difficult years.

Louis first married Lucienne of Rochefort but repudiated her after three childless years to marry Adelaide of Savoy, with whom he had seven sons and a daughter. Louis's eldest son, Philip, died while hunting boar, so the second son, Louis became *rex designatus*.

Louis had major achievements in the areas of foreign and domestic policy. The most important event on the foreign front took place in 1124 when England and Germany declared war on France. Louis, who was not powerful enough to resist on his own, launched an appeal to his vassals. Eight huge contingents were raised to meet the threat. His forces were so great that Emperor Henry V retreated without a fight.

At home, Louis was successful at curbing the growing power of the feudal nobility. He took military action against feudal lords and either eliminated them or forced their submission, thus returning them to dependence upon the crown. The most powerful feudal lord of the time was William, the duke of Aquitaine, who possessed nearly a quarter of French territory. In 1137, Louis obtained the hand of the duke's daughter, Eleanor, for his son in the hopes of bringing the territory of Aquitaine under the control of the crown. A lavish wedding was planned, and during the festivities, Louis was struck down by a particularly dreadful attack of dysentery. He returned home to Paris and was placed on a bed of cinders in the form of a cross. There he died at the age of fifty-six.

Louis VII the Younger and his wife Eleanor of Aquitaine were crowned on Christmas day. Eleanor was an amazing woman for her time. She was a very well-read, intelligent, lively, and forceful woman who bore Louis two daughters. However, she was also an extremely sensual woman, and Louis had his hands full from the beginning.

In 1148, Louis determined to patch relations with the Church by participating in the Crusade. Leaving France in the hands of his first minister, the monk Suger, he set out with Eleanor. After reaching Syria, scandal broke out over her relationship with her young uncle, Raymond of Poitiers, the prince of Antioch. By the time the king and queen reached Jerusalem, rumors were rampant over her intimacy with a handsome Moorish slave. Humiliated by Eleanor's scandalous behavior, Louis returned to France and began the proceedings to end his marriage. In March 1152, an annullment was granted on the grounds of consanguinity. Eleanor quickly married Henry Plantagenet, count of Anjou, who two years later became Henry II of England, thus bringing the territory of Aquitaine under English control.

Louis married Constance of Castile and had two daughters. When Constance died in 1160, the question of succession remained. A month later, Louis married Alix (also called Adèle) of Champagne. Five childless years later, a son, Philip Augustus, was born. Two more daughters followed.

After Henry of Anjou took the English crown as Henry II, Louis sought to strengthen his own country to counterbalance Henry's power. He continued his father's efforts to bring the feudal nobility back into the fold and to force his enemies into submission. Louis was so successful in strengthening his position, that Henry II had his sons pay homage to the French king, rather than attacking the county of Toulouse as they had planned. It was a triumphal moment for Louis when he received homage from the sons of the woman who'd caused him so much embarrassment.

After ruling for forty-three years, Louis VII the Young suffered a series of strokes and died in September 1180. The fleur-de-lis, the symbol of the French monarchy, is attributed to him. According to legend, an angel gave the lily to Clovis upon his conversion to Christianity in 496. Louis made the design his symbol, as did the other French kings bearing the name Louis (an evolution of the name Clovis).

The French crown was now passed to fifteen-year-old Philip II, so named Philip Augustus for the month of his birth. He'd been married just months before to Isabella of Hainault and in spite of his young age, showed an independence of spirit and was deemed mature enough to rule.

Isabella bore a son in 1187 and in 1190, lost her life giving birth to twin sons who also died. Three years later, Philip decided he needed to marry again and chose Ingeborg of Denmark. For some unexplained reason, he took a sudden and intense dislike to his bride during the wedding ceremony. Two months later, he'd repudiated her and had her shut up in a nunnery and a succession of prisons. After another three years, Philip fell in love with Agnes, the daughter of the duke of Meran, married her, and had a son and a daughter. The Church had refused to grant an annullment of Philip's marriage to Ingeborg, so they viewed this match as both adulterous and bigamous and the children as illegitimate. Yet Philip, deeply in love with Agnes, refused to part from her. He was excommunicated for his disobedience, and an interdict was placed on the kingdom. After four years, Philip bowed to pressure, giving up Agnes and reinstating Ingeborg as Queen. Agnes died a year later.

Philip more than tripled the size of his French domain. His first marriage brought him Amiens and Artois, and he took control of Normandy, Anjou, Touraine, and Poitou from the English king, John Lackland, by military conquest. He died in July 1223 of malaria, leaving a secure and greatly enlarged kingdom to his son, Louis VIII the Lion.

Before being crowned king, Louis VIII led quite an adventurous life. He was married in 1200 to Blanche of Castile, the granddaughter of Eleanor of Aquitaine, and had eleven sons and three daughters by her, the last of which was born after his death. Louis VIII had excellent military training in his youth and had led many successful military campaigns on his father's behalf. He was chosen by the English to be their king in the event they were successful in deposing King John, and was even received with royal honors in London. Though the English eventually chose John's son as successor, Louis was so highly thought of that he was given a gift of 10,000 golden marks upon his departure from England.

Once Louis VIII became king, he set his sights on Aquitaine and made several incursions into the territory. While returning from one such excursion, he became seriously ill and died of dysentery in November 1226 at the age of thirty-nine. Since his eldest surviving son, Louis IX, was just twelve years old, Blanche of Castile was designated as regent. She ruled capably for the next ten years.

Blanche wisely retained her husband's ministers (who had also served Philip Augustus) and their loyalty and support helped Blanche weather the intrigues of Philippe Hurepel (son of Philip Augustus and Agnes of Meran) and Pierre Mauclerc, duke of Brittany.

In 1234, Louis IX assumed his duties as king after his marriage to Marguerite, the daughter of Raymond Berenger IV, the count of Provence. In 1244, Louis became seriously ill and vowed to go on Crusade, should he recover his health. Four years later, he turned the kingdom over to his mother and set off with his wife and two brothers to lead the Seventh Crusade. While there, Louis was taken captive but was successfully ransomed after Marguerite gave birth to her sixth child. In 1252, they received word of Blanche of Castile's death, and the couple was obliged to return home to France; Louis's Crusade had been a failure.

The king's duties kept him home for the next fifteen years, yet Louis was devoted to the Crusades and held a burning desire to return to the Holy Land. He set out again in 1270 and was persuaded by his younger brother Charles, King of Sicily, to put down the infidels in Carthage. Unknown to Louis, plague was raging in the city. The French army was decimated, and Louis himself caught the disease. He died lying on a bed of ashes in August 1270.

Louis IX was known for his strict moral lifestyle, deep faith, piety, and integrity. It's said that he abstained from marital relations during the seasons of Advent and Lent, and when he was stirred by carnal desires, he'd get up from bed and go for a walk until the urge had passed. Louis also had great expectations of his children. He drew up a code of conduct for his eldest son and made a special point of teaching all his children to avoid the pitfalls of greed and desire. He was canonized twenty-seven years after his death by Pope Boniface VIII.

The institution of the monarchy underwent major reform during Louis's reign. The court was formed to act as both a state council and a court of appeal, over which the king presided. A treasury was established and was administrated by the Knights of the Templar. The treasury gathered the first taxes to be levied and supervised all governmental expenditure, including war and diplomatic efforts, and subsidies given to churches, hospitals, and charitable works. Local finance was left to the heads of the fiefs. The acts of court were noted in special registers called *olim,* and the treasury accounts were kept and registered by the *curia in compotis.*

Louis presided over years that saw spiritual growth, an interest in knightly chivalry, and a corresponding interest in the legends of King Arthur and the knights of the Round Table. The years also saw the birth of the legend of the Holy Grail, the discovery of the writings of Aristotle, and the works of Saint Thomas Aquinas.

Philip III the Bold was the second and eldest surviving son of Louis IX. He was married in 1262 to Isabel of Aragon and had four sons. Both he and Isabel accompanied Louis on his last Crusade, and traveled overland through Italy to bring the king's body back for burial to Saint Denis. On the journey home, Isabel was thrown from her horse and died in January 1271. Three years later, Philip married Marie of Brabant with whom he had three children.

In 1276, Philip's eldest son, nine-year-old Louis, died, and Marie was accused by the king's chamberlain, Pierre de la Brosse, of poisoning the child. It's not clear why the accusations were made, but some speculate it was because de la Brosse felt Marie was weakening his influence over the king. Whatever the case, Marie's brother, Jean of Brabant, sent a knight to defend her honor according to the custom of the times. The knight successfully defended Marie's innocence in battle and de la Brosse, unable to back his accusations with proof, was hanged.

At the end of the thirteenth century, Philip's nephew was engaged in a dispute with Peter III of Aragon over the Sicilian crown. In 1284, the crown of Aragon was offered to Philip's son, Charles de Valois. Philip accepted the offer, knowing that in order to see his son on the throne, Peter III would have to be deposed. During the military operation to further that end, Philip the Bold died of malaria in October 1285 at the age of forty.

Philip's successor was his second son, Philip IV the Fair, so called because he was regarded as "the most handsome man in the world." In spite of the pleasant connotations surrounding his name, Philip earned a bad reputation for levying heavy taxes, issuing false money that devalued the currency, for the moral laxity of his court that led to the indiscrete behavior of his daughters-in-law, for persecuting Jews, and for the brutal and fiery punishment of the Knights Templar. Nevertheless, Philip was well-liked by the common folk and was the first French king to give all three estates of society, the *oratores,* the *bellatores,* and the *laboratores,* a role in government.

Philip's acquisition of territory took a great deal of money, and as a result, he was seriously in debt. If he could be rid of the country's treasurers, the Knights Templar, he could cancel out his debts. Because the Knights were in charge of collecting taxes, they were unpopular with the people, which helped the king in his plan. He accused the Knights of the immoral acts of sodomy and swearing oaths by repudiating or spitting upon the cross. In September 1307, all the Templars were arrested, jailed, and interrogated. Confessions were exacted under severe torture and were used in court as evidence, in spite of the fact that they were all later retracted. The trial of the Templars lasted nearly five years, and all were found guilty; over fifty were burned at the stake and the order was dissolved.

Those not immediately executed were the grand master of the order, Jacques de Molay, and his assistant, Geoffroi de Charnay. They were brought out of prison two years later and taken to the square of Notre Dame for a last opportunity to confess their crimes and hear their sentences of life in prison. The two resolutely denied their guilt and were henceforth burned alive.

Before succumbing to the flames, Jacques de Molay is reported to have said, "Pope Clement, iniquitous judge and cruel executioner, I adjure you to appear in forty days' time before God's tribunal. And you, King of France, will not live to see the end of this year, and Heaven's retribution will strike down your accomplices and destroy your posterity."

De Molay's prophecies could have been but the bitter utterings of a tortured soul, but they came true, nonetheless. Forty days later, Pope Clement V became seriously ill and died, and the king's minister, who organized the whole affair, died during the summer. As for Philip IV the Fair, he suffered a stroke and died in November of the same year at just forty-six years old. His posterity was to suffer as well, for the end of the Capetians was at hand.

Philip's eldest son, Louis X the Headstrong, earned his nickname in the street riots that followed the death of the king. He had been married to Margaret of Burgundy, who was thrown into prison following accusations of adultery. After her death, Louis then married Clémence, the beautiful daughter of the king of Hungary and a member of the Capetian family. On August 19, 1315, the two were crowned king and queen at Rheims. Nine months later, after an exhausting game of indoor tennis, an overheated Louis quenched his thirst with a tankard of chilled wine. He developed a high fever and died of pneumonia a week later. His reign lasted but eighteen months.

Clémence was pregnant at the time, and hopes were pinned on her bearing a son to succeed his father. The queen was delivered of a son, Jean, but the infant lived just five days. It was rumored that the child was killed with a pin by Mahaut of Artois, his aunt and mother of Philip V's wife. And yet another rumor circulated about the little king being switched with a dead baby. Forty years later, a false John was to lay claim to the crown.

The death of the infant caused the crown to pass to Philip V the Tall, another son of Philip the Fair. Philip ruled with the assistance of his father's counselors during a time that saw a revolt of the pastoureaux, the peasant population. He suffered from tuberculosis and died in January 1322. He had been married to Jeanne of Burgundy and had three daughters and one son, who died young. His crown, therefore, was transferred to his brother, Charles IV the Fair.

Charles was married to Jeanne's sister, Blanche of Burgundy, who was also in prison for adultery. The marriage was annulled, and Charles then married Marie of Luxemburg, the daughter of Emperor Henry VII. In 1324, Marie gave birth to a stillborn son and died soon after of fever. A year later, Charles received special dispensation to marry his first cousin, Jeanne of Evreux, the granddaughter of Philip III the Bold. Jeanne had two daughters and was pregnant at the time Charles succumbed to an unexplained illness in February 1328. The king had designated his first cousin, Philip of Valois, to act as regent until Jeanne gave birth, but the queen gave birth to another girl. Under the old law of the Salian Franks, women were precluded from ascending the French throne. Therefore, the crown passed to Philip of Valois. The Capetian dynasty was finished.

SOCIETY

THE COUNTRY EXPERIENCED a period of renewal and increased vitality under the Capetians. Many of the changes to society were stimulated by growth in agriculture. Marshes were drained and forests cleared to provide more arable land, which was then marked off with hedges and farmed. The use of oxen in plowing, the use of iron in farm implements, the sowing of both spring and winter crops, and the use of windmills and water mills helped advance French agriculture and resulted in increased food production.

As these changes occurred, there was also a corresponding relaxation in the feudal system. Before, the peasants had performed work for the lord in return for the right to work their own holdings. Now, that system was giving way to wages and paid rent.

More villages were established, and larger towns and cities flourished. Towns that were well-placed held regular fairs where people came together for entertainment and the opportunity to trade and purchase items the average person was unable to produce.

As the towns grew, another class of people grew with them: the bourgeois. The citizens of the towns did not fit in well with feudal society and often found themselves at odds with many of its characteristics and customs. They found the special privileges granted to the upper classes as unfair and often clashed with the *seigneurs* who had authority over the towns.

In order to protect and further their own interests, the bourgeois formed themselves into organizations known as guilds. Each guild was united around a particular patron saint, such as Adrian for butchers, Joseph for carpenters, and Michael for grocers. The guilds not only kept an eye on the skills of its members, they also concerned themselves with the fairness of prices. Guild members commonly segregated themselves in the towns. For example, one area might be comprised of the makers of clothing, metalsmiths would locate themselves in another area, and fletchers would be grouped together in yet another section of town.

New opportunities and an adequate food supply led to a significant growth in population. By the end of the Capetian dynasty, the population of France was close to seventeen million. The majority of the people continued to live in rural areas, but the populations of the larger cities increased from around 1,000 people to 5,000 or 10,000. The most staggering increase was seen in Paris, which reached a population of 100,000 by 1328.

From the thirteenth century onward, Paris became the preferred place of residence of the French monarchy. During the reign of Philip II Augustus, many improvements were made to the city that served as the administrative center of the country. New buildings were constructed, and Saint Louis fulfilled his grandfather's architectural dreams by finishing the great Gothic cathedrals. In addition, the great crossroads of Paris were constructed, and schools were established to teach law, theology, philosophy, and the newly discovered writings of Aristotle. The Paris university was soon the most highly regarded in Europe and drew students from across the Continent.

Such a golden age was not to last. Disaster struck in the fourteenth century. In the early years of the century, a change in climate occurred. A significant drop in temperature led to widespread crop devastation and triggered severe flooding that made some people believe they were witnessing a repeat of the famous biblical Flood. To make matters worse, several sheep and cattle plagues spread through the livestock, killing off large numbers of animals. And a series of particularly nasty epidemics traveled through the human population. Severe famine ravaged the country, killing thousands and leaving others in such a weakened state that they were ill-prepared to endure the greatest calamity of all: the bubonic plague.

RELIGION

HUGH CAPET'S CORONATION oath reestablished the tie between church and state:

> I, Hugh, who am about to become king of the Franks, by divine favor, on this day of my coronation, in the presence of God and the saints, promise to each one of you to preserve for you the canonical privilege, law and justice which are due to you, to defend you with all my power with God's help, as it is just for a king to behave in his kingdom towards each bishop and towards the Church which is committed to him.

The tie with the Church remained unbroken, though relations were strained during the reigns of several Capetian kings. Philip I and Philip II were both excommunicated for illegal marriages and interdicts were placed on the kingdom to force the kings into compliance. Churches were closed, and priests were forbidden to administer the sacraments. In both cases, and only after several years had passed, did the kings give in to the pressure and repudiate their marriages so the interdicts would be lifted.

Philip IV the Fair was excommunicated on the grounds of having taxed the clergy. Only after Philip banned the export of gold and silver, which effectively kept the Holy See from obtaining the money it drew from the French Church, did the Pope reverse his decision and restore the king to the Church. Philip was again in trouble after the estates-general passed a motion affirming the king's position as sovereign and declaring that the Pope had no right to interfere in internal matters. In 1303, the Pope excommunicated the king again and attempted to annul all treaties made with France and free all provinces from their oaths of fealty. Philip's forces successfully took Pope Boniface VIII into custody, and he died insane a few days later.

Though the Pope was recognized as the leader of the Church, he had little impact on local churches. That authority was left to the bishops, the true leaders of the Church of the Gauls. The bishops continued to enjoy the same privileges and immunities from justice as they did in the previous time period, and as most of them were from wealthy, powerful families, they were also counts, dukes, and the masters of the episcopal towns.

Men from the laity were chosen to serve as rural priests. These priests lived close to the peasantry and were often miserably poor. They were supposed to live pious, chaste lives, but difficult conditions naturally led to corruption. Marriage was common among them, as was supplementing their income by toiling in the fields or filching from the coffers. Those in the monasteries were eventually seduced by the amazing number of gifts given by wealthy noblemen who wished to expiate their sins.

In time, a return to piety and devotion was encouraged and enthusiastically promoted by the efforts of such monks as Saint Bernard of Cîteaux. The monks also attempted to put an end to feudal fighting by establishing the Truce of God, which prohibited fighting four days a week, and the Peace of God, which sought a period of peace lasting several years. Such attempts were not always successful, but the Church did manage to export the lust for fighting by preaching the Crusade and persuading men to fight a holy war overseas.

NAMING

THE POOL OF names shrank a bit during this time period. Many of the old Frankish names became obsolete, as did many of the related Germanic compound names. Those that remained in use did so in altered form. For example, Chlodowig, an old Frankish name, evolved into Clodovic, Clovis, and finally, Louis. Raginmund evolved into Raimund, and Berchtilda evolved into Berthilda and Bertilda. By the end of the twelfth century, the growing influence of the Church in everyday life was reflected in the many names of saints and martyrs in use. By far the most popular names for women were Isabel, Jeanne, Marguerite, and Marie. For men, Jehan, Guillaume, Louis, Philip, and Pierre were very popular; Jehan led the pack with about 20 percent of the male population so named.

France of this time was a land of varied customs and dialects, and that variety is reflected in the variety of name forms. Take the name William, for example. In Lorraine and Franche-Comté, the *W* changes to *Vu*, thus William becomes Vuillaume, Vullième, etc. In the rest of France, the *W* becomes *Gu*: Guillaume, Guillerme, etc. Other names, such as Philip and Elaine, also took on a variety of different spellings, as do the names of today.

FEMALE NAMES

Aaliz (nobility) **Aalis, Alis, Aliz**
Adaliz (nobility)
Adele (noble) **Adela, Adèle**
Adelaide (nobility) **Adalhaid, Adalheid**

Adelais (nobility)
Adeline (nobility)
Adrienne (from Hadrianus)
Aënor (light, torch, bright)

Agathe (good)
Agilina (formidable)
Aglaë (splendor)
Agnès (chaste, pure, sacred)
Alexandra (defender of mankind)
Alia (all)
Amélie (work, labor)
Amice (friendship)
Anastasia (resurrection)
Andrée (womanly)
Anne (grace, full of grace, mercy) **Anna**
Annette (little Anne *grace, full of grace, mercy*)
Annis (chaste, pure, sacred)
Annora (honor, esteem) Norman form of Honora.
Arlette (little eagle)
Aurélie (gold)
Aveline (?)
Aveza (?)
Barbe (foreign woman)
Barbot (little Barbe *foreign woman*)
Basilie (kingly)
Batilde (commanding battle maiden) **Batilda**
Beata (happy)
Béatriz (bringer of happiness and joy) **Béatrix**
Belinda (?, second element is *serpent*)
Berthe (bright)
Bertrade (bright)
Blanche (white) **Blanch**
Cassandra (?)
Catherine (pure)
Cecilia (blind, dim-sighted)
Celeste (heavenly)
Celestine (heavenly)
Claire (bright, clear, famous)
Claremond (bright protection, famous protection)
Clarice (bright, clear, famous)
Claude (lame)
Clémence (gentle, mild, clement)
Clotilde (loud battle)
Colette (victory of the people)
Constance (constant, steadfast)
Corinne (maiden)
Corisande (?)
Cristina (a Christian, a follower of Christ)
Denise (of Dionysus)
Désirée (desired)
Douce (sweet)
Egilina (formidable)
Eglentine (prickly; sweetbrier)
Elaine (light, torch, bright)
Eleanor (light, torch, bright)
Elena (light, torch, bright)
Elisabeth (God is my oath)
Emeline (work, industrious) **Ameline**
Emilie (trying to equal or excel; rival)

Emma (strength)
Esclairmonde (bright protection, famous protection)
Etheldred (noble fame)
Eufemie (well-spoken, fair of voice)
Eugenie (nobility, excellence)
Eustacie (steadfast, happy in harvest)
Félise (felicity, goodness)
Françoise (French) From the thirteenth century.
Fridegunde (peaceful war)
Frideswide (strong peace)
Geneviève (?, perhaps *tribal woman*)
Gertrude (spear strength)
Gisela (pledge)
Gunilda (war battle) **Gunnilda**
Haueis (battle wide) **Haeis, Haouys**
Hedwig (war of contention)
Helewis (sound, hearty, and wide)
Hilde (war, battle)
Honora (honor, esteem)
Honorée (honor, esteem)
Ida (labor)
Ingeborg (Ing's fortification)
Isabelle (God is my oath) **Isabella, Ysabelle**
Iseut (ruler of the ice) **Isaut**
Jacqueline (supplanting, seizing by the heels)
Jacquette (supplanting, seizing by the heels)
Jehane (God is gracious) **Jehanne**
Joscelin (from the tribe of the Gauts)
Judith (praised; from Judah)
Julian (youth, downy)
Laure (laurel)
Laurencia (woman from Laurentum)
Laurette (laurel)
Leonie (lion)
Léonore (light, torch, bright)
Linnet (shapely)
Luce (light)
Lucette (little Luce *light*)
Lucia (light)
Lucienne (little Luce *light*)
Lucille (light)
Mabila (lovable)
Madeleine (from Magdala)
Mahaut (mighty in battle) **Mahault**
Mahhild (mighty in battle)
Marcelle (of Mars, warlike)
Margerie (a pearl)
Margot (a pearl)
Marguerite (a pearl)
Marie (sea of bitterness or sorrow)
Marthe (lady, mistress)
Martine (of Mars, warlike)
Matilda (mighty in battle)
Maud (mighty in battle)
Melisent (work strength)

Mélusine (a water nymph)
Metheldred (mild strength)
Mildred (mild strength)
Monique (?)
Muriel (sea bright) Used in Brittany and Normandy.
Nicole (victory of the people)
Nicolette (little Nicole *victory of the people*)
Noel (born at Christmas)
Odette (little Odille *wealth, prosperity*)
Odille (wealth, prosperity)
Olimpe (of Olympus)
Oriande (to rise) Oriante
Oriel (fire and strife)
Oriolt (fire and strife) Oriholt, Oriolda
Philippa (lover of horses)
Radegund (counsel fame)
Reine (queen)
Rosala (horse)

Rosamund (horse protection) Rosamond
Roslind (horse serpent)
Sabine (Sabine woman)
Sara (princess)
Sibylla (prophetess, fortune-teller)
Sidonie (fine cloth, linen)
Sophie (wisdom)
Suzanne (lily, rose)
Sylvie (of the woods)
Tifaine (Epiphany, manifestation of God)
Valérie (strong, healthy)
Véronique (?, perhaps *true image*; *bringer of victory*)
Viole (violet)
Violette (little Viole *violet*)
Willa (resolute)
Yolande (violet)
Yvette (archer)
Yvonne (archer)

MALE NAMES

Achille (?)
Adalard (noble and hard)
Adalberon (noble and bright)
Adalbert (noble and bright)
Adrian (man from Hadrianus)
Ailemar (noble and famous) Eilemar
Aimery (work ruler)
Alain (?, perhaps *handsome, rock*) Alein
Alard (noble and hard)
Alaric (ruler of all)
Alberi (elf ruler)
Algernon (mustached)
Alphonse (noble and ready)
Alveré (elf counsel)
Alysaundre (defender of mankind) Alexandre
Amande (army man, soldier)
Ambroise (immortal)
Amé (?)
Americ (work ruler) Emeric
Amfrid (ancestor of peace)
Amias (?, perhaps *friendship*)
Amiel (industrious)
Amis (friendship)
André (manly)
Anselm (God's helmet)
Antoine (?, *priceless, of inestimable worth* is a folk definition)
Armand (soldier, warrior) Armant
Arnaud (eagle power) Arnaut
Arnulf (eagle wolf)
Arthur (?)
Ascelin (from the tribe of the Gauts) Acelin
Auberi (elf ruler)

Aubert (noble and bright)
Augustus (great, venerable)
Auveré (elf counsel)
Baldri (bold ruler, brave ruler) Baudri
Baldric (bold ruler, brave ruler)
Baldwin (bold friend, brave friend) Flemish form.
Baptiste (a baptizer)
Bardolph (bright wolf) Bardolf
Barnabé (son of exhortation)
Bartelmeu (son of Talmai *hill, mound, furrows*) Bertelmeu
Basil (kingly)
Bastien (man from Sebastia)
Baudoin (bold friend, brave friend)
Benoit (blessed) Benoist, Beneoit
Beringer (bear spear)
Bernard (bold as a bear)
Berthold (bear rule) Berold, Berolt
Bertin (bright friend)
Bertrand (bright raven) Bertran
Bevis (beautiful) Beves
Blaise (babbler)
Bouchard (big mouth)
Brian (force, strength; valor; high; kingly) Used in Brittany.
Brice (?)
César (hairy; bluish gray)
Charles (full-grown, a man)
Christophe (bearing Christ)
Claud (lame)
Clemens (gentle, mild, clement)
Conan (strength, high)
Conrad (bold counsel)
Constantine (constant, steadfast)

Crispin (curled)
Cyprian (from Cyprus)
Dagobert (day bright)
Damien (tamer)
Daniel (judged by God)
David (beloved)
Delphin (a dolphin; from Delphi)
Denis (of Dionysus)
Déodat (given by God) Used in southern France.
Didier (desired)
Dieudonné (given by God) Used in northern France.
Dominique (belonging to a lord)
Donatien (given by God)
Drogo (burden bearer)
Durand (enduring, lasting)
Ector (holding fast)
Edmond (wealthy protector)
Egmont (fearful protection, awesome protection)
Eloi (chosen)
Emery (ruler of strength)
Émile (trying to equal or excel)
Emmerich (ruler of strength)
Engelrand (angel raven) **Enguerran**
Ernust (earnest, resolute) **Ernost, Ernst**
Eudes (child)
Eudon (child)
Eugène (well-born, noble)
Eustache (steadfast; happy in harvest)
Everard (boar strength)
Fabian (a bean)
Faramond (journey protection)
Félix (lucky, happy) **Felis**
Ferrand (peace; journey; youth, life + courage; venture, risk; ready)
Filbert (very bright) **Filibert, Fulbert**
Firmin (firm, steadfast)
Florian (flowery)
Fouchier (people, folk)
François (French)
Fulk (people) **Fulke**
Gabriel (God is my strength)
Gamel (old)
Garnier (protecting army)
Gascon (?, perhaps *guest, stranger; from Gascony*)
Gaspard (treasure master)
Gauvain (battle hawk)
Geoffroi (district; traveler; pledge + peace)
Georges (earth worker, farmer)
Gerald (spear rule) **Geralt**
Gerbert (bright spear)
Gerbold (spear bold, spear brave)
Germain (a German)
Gervais (servant of the spear)
Giffard (give + bold, fierce)
Gilbert (bright pledge)
Gilles (goatskin shield of Zeus; a protection) **Gile, Giles**

Godard (god hard)
Godfry (God's peace) **Godefry**
Gregoire (vigilant, watchful)
Griffin (like a griffin, monstrous)
Guillaume (resolute protector)
Guiscard (?)
Gunter (bold in war)
Guy (a guide, a leader)
Guyon (a guide, a leader)
Haerveu (battle worthy) A Breton name.
Hamo (home, house)
Hamon (home, house)
Hardwin (hard friend)
Helgaud (prosperous, hale, hearty) **Helgald**
Henry (home ruler)
Herbert (army bright)
Herman (army man, soldier)
Hernays (earnest, resolute)
Hervé (battle worthy)
Hilaire (cheerful)
Hubert (bright heart)
Hue (heart, mind, soul) Used in the south.
Hugh (heart, mind, soul)
Hugon (heart, mind, soul) Used in the north.
Hugues (heart, mind, soul) Used in the north.
Humbert (people bright)
Huon (heart, mind, soul) Used in the south.
Ignace (?, perhaps *fire*)
Ilbert (battle bright) **Ilberd**
Imbert (iron people) **Isembert**
Ingelram (angel raven)
Ives (archer) **Ive**
Ivon (archer)
Jacques (supplanting, seizing by the heels)
Jehan (God is gracious)
Jenico (?, perhaps *fire*) Provençal form of Ignace.
Jérémie (God will uplift)
Jérôme (sacred name)
Joachim (God will establish)
Joël (the Lord is God)
Joseph (he shall add)
Jourdain (a flowing down)
Judicael (sportive) **Judical** A Breton name.
Julian (youth, downy)
Juste (just, fair)
Justin (just, fair)
Lambert (bright land)
Lance (land)
Lancelin (little Lance *land*)
Lancelot (little Lance *land*)
Laurence (man from Laurentum)
Léon (lion)
Léonard (lion hard, bold as a lion)
Léopold (bold people)
Lionel (little Léon *lion*)
Louis (famous in war)

Luc (light; man from Lucania)
Magnus (great)
Manfred (man of peace)
Marc (?, perhaps *Mars; manly; soft, tender*)
Marcel (of Mars, warlike)
Marcellin (little Marcel *of Mars, warlike*)
Martin (of Mars, warlike)
Matheu (gift of God)
Mauger (spear grinder)
Maynard (strong and hardy)
Meurisse (a Moor, dark-skinned)
Michel (Who is like God?)
Miles (?, perhaps *mild, peaceful; merciful*)
Milo (?, perhaps *mild, peaceful; merciful*)
Milon (?, perhaps *mild, peaceful; merciful*)
Nicolas (victory of the people)
Noel (born at Christmas)
Odo (wealth)
Ogier (rich spear)
Olivier (olive tree)
Onfroi (people peace)
Osanne (hosannah)
Osbert (God bright)
Osmond (God protection) **Osmund**
Otho (rich)
Paulin (small)
Philip (lover of horses) **Philippe**
Philipot (little Philip *lover of horses*)
Pierre (a rock, a stone)
Piers (a rock, a stone)
Quentin (fifth)
Radulf (counsel wolf)
Raimund (counsel protection) **Reimund**
Randulf (shield wolf)
Ranfred (counsel peace)
Raoul (counsel wolf)

Reynard (counsel hard) **Rainard**
Reynaud (powerful protection) **Reinald**
Richard (stern king)
Robert (bright with fame)
Roger (famous with the spear)
Roland (famous land)
Rolf (famous wolf)
Romain (a Roman)
Samuel (name of God)
Sanson (the sun)
Sébastien (man of Sebastia)
Séverin (severe, strict)
Sigmund (victory protection)
Simon (heard)
Sylvain (of the woods)
Sylvestre (of the woods)
Talbot (pillager, bandit; lampblack)
Tancred (think counsel)
Terrick (ruler of the people)
Theobald (bold people)
Theodoric (ruler of the people)
Thierry (ruler of the people)
Thomas (a twin)
Torold (Thor's strength) **Turold**
Tristram (tumult, sadness) **Tristan**
Turstan (Thor's stone) **Turstin**
Ulric (wolf rule)
Urban (dweller in a village)
Valdemar (famous ruler)
Valentine (healthy, strong)
Valéry (foreign ruler)
Vincent (conquering)
Vivien (alive)
Willelm (resolute protector)
Yves (archer)
Yvon (archer)

SURNAMES

There is no evidence that surnames were hereditary in France before the eleventh century, and the historian Camden reaffirms that when he wrote, "About the year of our Lord 1000 surnames began to be taken up in France." After that time, the upper classes began passing their family names to their offspring. Most of the early surnames were based on place of residence, but many were also based on familial connections. Later, as the population swelled and more jobs were available, the commoners typically took secondary names based on their occupations. Appellations based on physical characteristics were in the minority. One point of interest in the study of French surnames is that unlike personal names, French surnames underwent very little change in form over the course of hundreds of years.

Surnames based on place of residence used the preposition *de* and those based on occupation or characteristic used the prepositions *le* and *la*.

Names based on familial connections:

Bertran (bright raven)
Durand (enduring, lasting)

Gilbert (bright pledge)
Tirel (Thor rule)

Surnames from places:

de Anjou
de Artois
de Brieuse
de Champagne
de Chanteloup
de Chartres
de Colleville
de Courtenay
de Coucy
de Glanville
de Harcourt
de Laci
de Lorris
de Maci
de Malleville
de Marle
de Meran

de Montfort
de Montmorency
de Nogaret
de Perci
de Poitiers
de Provence
de Puiset
de Rochefort
de Savoy
de Sorbon
de Tilly
de Venables
de Vermandois
de Vernon
Dubois (dweller in the woods)
Tillet (dweller near the lime trees)

Sunames based on physical characteristics:

la **Basse** (the short, fat one)
le **Basset** (the little short, fat one)
le **Bâtard** (the bastard)
le **Beau** (the fair; the unattractive one)
le **Begue** (the stammerer)
la **Belle** (the beautiful)
le **Blanc** (the white)
le **Bossé** (a hunchback)
Bouchard (big mouth)
le **Bruyant** (noisy, blustering)

le **Carré** (squat, thickset)
le **Corbet** (the raven)
Fauchet (crooked legs)
Giffard (chubby-cheeked)
le **Grand** (the tall; the large)
le **Gros** (the fat)
le **Jeune** (the young)
le **Libéral** (the liberal)
le **Pieux** (the pious)
le **Simple** (the simple-minded)

Names based on occupation:

le **Archer** (the archer)
Aumonier (beggar)

Babeuf (slaughterer)
Bouvier (cattle drover)

Other:

Lovvet (little wolf)
Talbot (pillager, bandit; lampblack)

Chapter Four

THE HOUSES OF VALOIS AND VALOIS-ORLÉANS
[1328—1589]

POLITICS

THE VALOIS YEARS were significant ones in which the country suffered from the plague, endured the difficulties of the Hundred Years' War, and reveled in the enlightenment of the Renaissance. The first of the Valois kings was Philip VI, the grandson of Philip III the Bold. Though Philip was as much a Capetian as others in his family, he represented the first of the line of Valois to reign as monarchs. Under Salic law, he had the right to the French crown, but he was challenged by Edward III of England, whose mother Isabelle was the sister of the last three kings. It was the pursuit of that claim that embroiled the countries in the Hundred Years' War.

Philip, brave knight and skilled horseman that he was, had not yet realized that military victory required a well-trained infantry. As was common among the nobles of his era, the infantry were despised as lowly foot soldiers, and that attitude, along with a lack of strategical and tactical knowledge, was to have dire consequences in the war. Philip suffered the loss of his naval forces at the battle of Sluys in 1340, had two horses killed from under him at Crécy in 1346, and lost Calais to the English in 1347.

Though losing Calais was hard on the French spirit, they were soon to deal with a much greater tragedy: the plague. The disease landed in the Mediterranean ports late in 1347 and by December had worked its way into Aix-en-Provence. By 1350, the entire country had been infected. In 1348, Philip's queen and mother of his eight children, Jeanne of Burgundy, contracted the disease and died. A year later, Bonne of Luxemburg, the wife of his son, Jean, also died. Philip then arranged for his son to marry Blanche of Evreaux, the daughter of the King of Navarre. When Blanche arrived at the French court, however, Philip himself fell in love with her youthful beauty and decided to keep her for himself, arranging another match for his son with Jeanne of Boulogne. A year and a half later, Philip became ill and died.

Philip VI of Valois was as determined to promote the supremacy of the monarchy as he was to living well. Following his elaborate coronation ceremony, he lived a life of great luxury that quickly put royal finances under a great deal of strain.

Philip had a few political successes in his reign. In 1347, he aquired the inheritance of the indebted Dauphiné of Viennois along with the promise that after the death of the last sovereign, the eldest sons of the

French kings would be given the title *dauphin*. And, in 1349, he bought the city of Montpellier from the king of Majorca.

Jean II the Good, the second but eldest surviving son of Philip VI, ascended to the throne in 1350, when the country was in the midst of plague. In fact, there were only three years (1403, 1419, and 1447) during the Hundred Years' War that plague was not reported somewhere in France.

Jean's nickname "the Good" is in direct opposition to his person, for historical accounts show he was a cruel and vindictive man, with a superiority complex that kept him from being concerned about the cruel realities his people were facing. On the positive side, Jean was a courageous knight who personally fought in the war with England. The low point of his reign had to be when he fell into enemy hands at the battle of Poitiers in 1356 and was taken to England as a royal captive. In exchange for his freedom, he signed the treaty of Brétigny (the Peace of 1360) whereby England was allowed to keep all the territory it had won during the war. He also agreed to pay a huge ransom amount over six years, and sent two of his sons as hostages against payment of the ransom.

Jean had inherited a love of splendor and extravagant entertainment, and immediately upon his return from London, engaged in a round of parties and festivities. It was very unfitting behavior for a monarch whose sons were now hostages and whose country was suffering hell on earth. In 1363, one of his sons escaped from captivity and returned to France. According to the rules of chivalrous behavior, Jean returned to England to take his son's place. He was received with honor and housed in Savoy Palace, but two months later, Jean II the Good became ill and died in April 1364. His body was returned to France and buried with the other kings at Saint Denis.

Jean's eldest son, the first French prince to bear the title *dauphin,* succeeded his father as Charles V. Given the nickname "The Wise" for his loves of literature and science, Charles was the finest of the Valois kings. He had acted as lieutenant-general during his father's incarceration, and therefore had the experience to assume the duties of monarch after his father's death. After the three-year truce with the English had ended, Charles went on the offensive and managed to win back all French possessions except Guyenne. Shortly before his death, Charles took stock of his country, and in an effort to ease the burden of his countrymen, abolished the penal taxes imposed by his father to replenish the treasury.

Charles was in ill health for nearly all his adult life. He was rumored to have been the victim of a poisoning attempt by his brother-in-law, Charles the Bad, and that was thought to have been at the root of all his ailments. He was very thin, prematurely bald, suffered from gout, and all his nails dried up and fell off. He obtained the services of a physician to help his nails grow again. The physician opened an ulcer in his arm to let the bad humors drain out, then ordered that it not be closed, so Charles kept a running, open wound on his arm. In addition, the king's hands became deformed and swollen by gout, he suffered terrible pain in his internal organs, and it's believed he was stricken with tuberculosis. He died in 1380 at the age of forty-three.

Charles had been married at just thirteen years of age to Jeanne of Bourbon, a woman who carried in her the seeds of madness that was inherent in her family. Charles and Jeanne had nine children, though just three, two sons and a daughter, survived to adulthood. Jeanne showed signs of instability toward the end of her life, which occurred in childbed in 1378. Her son, Charles VI was to suffer the same affliction.

When Charles V the Wise died, his eldest surviving son, Charles, was just twelve years old; a regency was established by his uncles, the dukes of Anjou, Berry, Burgundy, and Bourbon. It didn't take long for this group of men to deplete the treasury and mismanage government. They reinstated the *fouage* (hearth tax) and the *gabelle* (salt tax) and raised taxes so high that civil war broke out. In Paris, the commoners broke into the Hôtel de Ville and grabbed the lead mallets that had been stored there. They rushed the prisons and released the prisoners, murdered tax collectors, and pillaged and looted shops. The same type of activity took place in other towns and cities, and troops had to be called out. The measures taken to restore order were brutal and included beheading as many rebels as possible.

Charles cut a fine figure in his youth. He was tall, had a good physique, and was athletic, pleasant, and kind. In 1385, he was married to Isabeau of Bavaria, a young woman of charm and beauty. Charles was smitten with his bride, and it seemed the perfect beginning to a wonderful life.

He soon realized his uncles were abusing their position as regents by putting their own interests above those of France. In order to assume control in his own right, Charles staged a coup d'etat and forcefully wrestled power away from them. After sending them back to their dukedoms, he recalled the counselors of his father and reestablished law and order.

The next four years passed pleasantly for Charles and his queen. Then, in 1392, Olivier de Clisson, one of the king's counselors and the high constable, was seriously wounded by the lord Pierre de Craon, who then fled to Brittany. Charles was determined to personally bring him to justice. He called together a large army and set out. It was very hot weather in August, and as they passed through the forest of Le Mans, an old, decrepit man dressed in tatters rushed from the bushes, grabbed the bridle of the king's horse, and began screaming that he'd been betrayed. Without warning, Charles went berserk and began attacking his personal guard with a battle-ax. He'd killed four of his escort before being subdued. He was taken to the château of the Val d'Oise and diagnosed with hereditary insanity. Charles soon recovered, took back control of the government, and resumed his life of gaiety.

Just a few months later, in January 1393, a ball was held at the Hôtel de Saint Pol. A group of men dressed as ''wild men'' in costumes of feathers and thin cotton rags appeared and added a bit of fun to the evening by dancing around. Charles's brother, Louis of Orléans, sought to get a better look at the dancers by holding a torch close to them. The costumes caught fire and the men were transformed into balls of fire. For several moments, all was pandemonium as the men screamed in agony and the smell of scorched flesh circulated nauseatingly throughout the room. Someone suddenly realized that the king was among the dancers and the cry, ''Save the king!'' went up. Queen Isabeau fainted, but the queen's aunt, the duchess of Berry had the presence of mind to throw her cloak over the king and smother the flames before he was seriously injured. Shortly thereafter, Charles suffered another bout where he believed he was made of glass and was about to break into pieces. Though he recovered, he was to suffer from repeated bouts of madness for the rest of his life. He was cared for by Odette de Champdivers, a kind and gentle woman who bore him a daughter. Today, it is believed that Charles VI the Mad suffered from porphyria, the same disease that passed through royal bloodlines to strike several European rulers, including George III of Great Britain.

With Charles indisposed, his country fell into a state of chaos. A regency was established with the dukes of Burgundy and Orléans, and Isabeau took several lovers, including her brother-in-law, the duke of Orléans. The duke of Burgundy died in 1404 and was succeeded by his son, Jean the Fearless. A falling-out between Jean and the duke of Orléans ended in the latter's assassination, and Isabeau sided with Jean, even though he supported England's Henry V in a quest for the French crown. Bernard of Armagnac led the French resistance but was killed when the Burgundians seized Paris. The young dauphin, Charles, managed to escape in the confusion as the town was torn by massacre, riot, and mayhem.

In May 1420, Isabeau had Charles sign the Treaty of Troyes. Under this treaty, the dauphin Charles was dispossessed and their daughter, Catherine was married to Henry V, who would then be crowned King of France upon Charles's death. As Charles was still suffering from bouts of madness, Henry V became regent of France. Unfortunately for Henry V, he was not to realize his dream of uniting the English and French crowns. He died before Charles in August 1422, leaving his crown in the hands of his infant son, Henry VI. Charles VI the Mad died shortly afterward in October at the Hôtel de Saint Pol. While standing before the king's tomb at Saint Denis, the duke of Berry uttered the traditional words: ''Lord have mercy on the soul of the most high and excellent prince Charles, king of France, sixth of that name, our natural and sovereign lord.'' After a minute's silence, the duke then said, ''Long live King Henry, by the grace of God king of France and of England.'' It seemed as if the independent kingdom of France was at an end.

The new king, Henry VI, was the son of Henry V and Catherine of Valois, the daughter of Charles VI and Isabeau. Because the child was just ten months old, the French regency went to his English uncle John, the duke of Bedford, a capable man who believed it was necessary to conquer all of France to eliminate future problems.

The dauphin, Charles, had been banished to Bourges, but he had the support of those who were unhappy with their kingdom falling into English hands. Among them were his mother-in-law, Yolanda of Sicily (who held Anjou and Provence), and many cousins, including the duke of Bourbon, and his half-brother, Dunois. Charles wanted to regain his inheritance, but it seemed impossible. To make matters worse, because of his mother's numerous indiscretions, he was beseiged with doubts of his legitimacy.

Then, in February 1429, a young woman dressed as a man demanded and was granted an audience with the dauphin. Charles, unsure of what to expect, switched clothing with one of his courtiers and assumed a place in the crowd. The young woman entered, and ignoring the man pretending to be the dauphin, searched the crowd until she spotted the real prince. She approached and said, ''Gentle dauphin, I tell you on behalf of God my master that you are the true heir to the throne of France.'' The woman was Jean d'Arc.

By her words, she lifted the dauphin's depression and made him believe in himself and his legitimacy once again. Jean d'Arc claimed to be led by God, and indeed, she had many almost miraculous military victories against the English that led to Charles's journey to Rheims and his crowning as Charles VII by Archbishop Regnault of Chartres. The extraordinary accomplishments and faith of seventeen-year-old Jean d'Arc make her destiny as a martyr that much harder to accept.

Shamefully, Charles VII never made any attempt to save the life of the girl who had effectively handed his kingdom back to him. Perhaps he suffered guilt over the matter, for twenty-six years later, he held a rehabilitation trial to restore her reputation. She was canonized in 1920.

In 1441, Charles took advantage of English weakness following the death of the Duke of Bedford. By 1453, he'd succeeded in regaining all territories except Calais, including those held by the English for 300 years.

Charles's success was due, in part, to the military reforms he implemented. In 1445, he created the first permanent national army in France that was comprised of fully armored, paid professional men. Three years later, an infantry was added, the Compagnie des Francs-Archers (the Company of Free Archers). The archers were comprised of one-fiftieth of the men of France and were not paid but were exempt from taxation. The archers underwent regular training with the bow and crossbow and were required to report for duty should the call be made. In addition, several improvements had been made in the field of artillery. France had the finest weapons in Europe, which made fighting on the offensive more successful than ever before. Charles also surrounded himself with capable advisers who reorganized the country's finances and provided for a stable income by establishing a permanent tax structure.

Charles VII was betrothed in 1414 at the age of eleven to Marie of Anjou, and married to her in 1422. The marriage was successful, and they ended up having fourteen children together. Unfortunately for Marie, she was a plain woman and in 1443, ended up losing the affections of her husband to the young and beautiful Agnès Sorel, a maid of honor of Marie's mother. Agnès, whom Charles treated like his queen, bore the monarch three more daughters.

In 1449, Agnès accompanied Charles to Normandy, became ill with dysentery, and died. Some speculate she was poisoned. Agnès had many fine qualities, and she'd given the king a new lease on life; her death affected him deeply.

Charles suffered from general tuberculosis and developed a cancerous ulceration on his leg in 1458. He then developed some sort of dental problem that led to the necrosis of his lower jaw and rendered eating impossible. He died in July 1461, at the age of fifty-eight. He'd earned two nicknames in his lifetime: the Victorious, from winning back French possessions, and the Well Served, from surrounding himself with capable, loyal counselors.

The French crown was now in the possession of Charles VII's eldest and most difficult son, Louis XI. By all accounts, Louis was a strange character. He dressed in shabby black clothes and wore a big black hat on which was hung myriad religious tokens and charms to ward off evil spirits. He had a vicious cruel streak in him, and he enjoyed torturing his prisoners. He even forced his cousin, the duke of Orléans, to marry his daugher Jeanne, who had a hunchback and walked with a limp, in the hopes of extinguishing the duke's line.

Louis had no royal bearing and there seemed to be nothing about him to allow contemporary biographers to portray him in a favorable light. Indeed, one such chronicler described him as "a bad subject, a bad King, a dangerous enemy, a treacherous ally, and a hopelessly disappointing son." Another reported, "If you ran into him without knowing who he was you would have taken him for a buffoon or a drunkard, at any rate for a man of low condition rather than a person of distinction."

Louis was married twice, first at the age of thirteen to Margaret, the daughter of the King of Scotland. Since both were still children, Margaret lived with her mother-in-law. Louis disliked her intensely and stayed away from her. She died in 1445, while accompanying King Charles VII on a trip. Twelve years later, Louis married Charlotte of Savoy. This union produced four sons and three daughters, but in time, the king's favors went to a mistress, Marguerite de Sassenage, with whom he had two daughters. For the second half of Louis's reign, Charlotte was confined to the Château d'Amboise or to a home in Tours.

In Louis's favor, he had some diplomatic successes, and he enjoyed traveling about his kingdom rather than staying at court. His military and political goals were simple: expansion of the kingdom and absolute obedience. In his quest to accomplish both, his brutal methods gained him several enemies.

Shortly after his sixtieth birthday, Louis suffered a series of strokes. Just before his death, he put the kingdom in the hands of his eldest daughter, Anne, who would rule as regent until Louis's third and only surviving son, thirteen-year-old Charles, came of age.

Charles VIII was an unfortunate fellow. He had an enormous head, big lips, bulging eyes, and a large hook nose that nearly touched his upper lip. He was also small and quite thin, had a habit of twitching his fingers, was slow of speech, and was intellectually inferior.

In 1491, at the age of twenty-one, Charles VIII was married to Anne of Brittany, the heir to that crown. Anne was not particularly beautiful and she suffered from a slight limp, but she was a caring and devoted wife. She bore Charles three sons and a daughter, all of whom died in infancy.

Charles enjoyed the romantic ideal of war and crusade, and spent a great deal of time admiring his collection of war-related hardware. Included in his collection were Charlemagne's sword, the sword of Saint Louis, the battle-ax of the Breton warrior, DuGuesclin, and Jean d'Arc's suit of armor. In 1495, he called together his army of 30,000 men and set out to Italy to claim the kingdom of Naples (to which he had a claim through his great-grandmother), and to march on Constantinople to win the imperial Crown of Constantine, thereby becoming the first French king to initiate a war of conquest. He had a grand adventure but was forced to return home without achieving victory when it became apparent that his enemies had been waiting for France to be left defenseless. He brought back a love for Italian art, which opened the way for the Renaissance in France.

One fine spring day in 1498, Charles decided to play a game of tennis in the moat of the Château d'Amboise. On his way indoors, he fatally struck his head on a stone frame of a small door and died. Because Charles VIII had no surviving children, the crown went to his brother-in-law, Louis, the duke of Orléans. The dynasty of the House of Valois was at an end, but the bloodline was carried on through a collateral line.

Louis XII was the grandson of Charles VI's brother, Louis, who gained notoriety for his scandalous affair with his sister-in-law, Queen Isabeau. At the age of fourteen, Louis was forced into marriage with Louis XI's hunchbacked and crippled daughter, Jeanne. In spite of Jeanne's kindness and sweet disposition, Louis had refused to consummate the marriage and obtained an annulment as soon as he became king. This paved the way for him to marry Anne, the widow of Charles VIII, which ensured that Brittany was retained by the crown. It seems as if the royal couple were genuinely fond of one another. Anne gave birth to four sons, all of whom were stillborn or died in infancy, as well as two daughters, Claude and Renée. In January 1514, Anne died of a severe attack of gallstones. As Louis stood over her coffin, he prophesied his own death that same year. His prophecy came true, but not until after he'd married Mary, the daughter of Henry VII of England, in October.

The match, demanded by Henry VIII, was a condition of a treaty signed by Spain and France in 1514, shortly after Anne's death. It was not difficult for Louis to accept, for Mary was just sixteen, beautiful, and charming. Louis, on the other hand, was fifty-three. Louis was determined to prove himself a devoted and attentive husband. One chronicler reported that the king bragged of performing marvels on his wedding night. Perhaps he exhausted himself too much, for he died suddenly on New Year's Day, 1515.

Louis's crown went to his son-in-law and nephew, Francis of Angoulme. Francis was married to Louis's daughter, Claude, and had seven children with her before her death in 1524 at the age of twenty-four. He also had several mistresses and eventually contracted syphilis, from which he died in 1547.

From the beginning of his reign, the country was threatened from three sides: the north by Henry VIII, the south by Ferdinand of Aragon, and the east by the Emperor Maximilian. To make matters worse, Charles of Austria was heir to both Ferdinand and Maximilian. Francis believed he could strengthen his position by regaining the duchy of Milan, which Louis XII had won, then lost again. He accomplished that goal in 1515. Just as it seemed as if peace was at hand, Ferdinand of Aragon died, followed by the Emperor Maximilian. Charles of Austria quickly moved to claim his inheritances, becoming the most powerful man in Europe.

All three monarchs, Henry VIII, Charles V, and Francis I, put themselves forward as candidates for Holy Roman Emperor; Charles won the vote. Afterward, the Field of the Cloth of Gold was organized to facilitate a meeting between the French and English monarchs. Francis won several games against Henry and so antagonized him with his superior airs that the English king returned home and allied himself with Charles V. Francis was now the odd man out and caught between two of the most powerful rulers in the world.

Fighting, which broke out in 1521, culminated in the capture of Francis and his imprisonment in Madrid. Charles proposed restoring the old Anglo-Norman possessions to England, as well as the fief of Bourbon and the Dauphiné, but Francis' mother, Louise of Savoie, had managed to buy off Henry VIII for two million écus, and the deal never went through. Francis was released in exchange for Burgundy and his two sons as hostages. He had no intention of living up to the treaty, and entered into an alliance with the Turks. The rest of Europe believed that Charles V had abused his position of power and united against him, forcing him to sue for peace. The result was the Peace of the Ladies (1529) in which Francis gave up Milan, ransomed his sons for two million écus, and married Charles's sister, Eleanor. Peace was not to last, however. Hostilities resumed in 1536 and didn't end until 1544, when Francis agreed to give up his claim to Italy and Charles agreed to give up his claim to Burgundy.

A year later, Francis died. His eldest son, the dauphin Francis, died in 1536 at the age of nineteen, some believe from being poisoned. That left second son, Henry, to succeed as Henry II. He had been married at the age of fourteen to Catherine de Medici, who by all accounts became one of Europe's most interesting yet most sinister queens. No children were born to the couple during the first nine years of their marriage, but Henry compensated by fathering several children with ladies-in-waiting. Catherine then bore ten children in rapid succession; only seven survived childhood.

When Henry was twenty-nine, he fell in love with Diane de Poitiers, a married woman ten years his senior. Henry made her Duchess of Valentinois, and she came to hold a great deal of influence over him, much more in fact, than did his wife.

In 1552, Emperor Charles V besieged Metz, a city in northeastern France. Strong French resistance, harsh winter weather, and several epidemics combined to severely weaken Charles's troops and forced their retreat. Two years later, the worn-out emperor abdicated and retired to a Spanish monastery. He left the imperial title and Austria, Bohemia, and Hungary to his brother, Ferdinand. His son, Philip, received the Netherlands, Franche-Comté, Italy and the Mediterranean islands, Spain, and the American colonies.

When Henry tried again for the kingdom of Naples, Philip II retaliated by laying siege to Saint-Quentin. Henry took advantage of the Spaniard's preoccupation and returned Calais to the crown, a town that had been occupied by the English for the last 211 years. The victory was marked by the marriage of the dauphin to Mary Stuart in April 1558. By now, all sides were tired of war, and Henry was anxious to devote his energies to fighting Protestantism. The end of hostilities came in 1559 with the signing of the Treaty of Cateau-Cambrésis.

Henry celebrated the end of war with a round of festivals at which he personally participated in a number of tournaments. On June 30, 1559, during one such tournament, his opponent's lance splintered and a piece of it put Henry's eye out. After suffering ten days of agony, no doubt worsened by the extremely crude surgical techniques of the time, Henry II died. His kingdom was left to his eldest son, Francis II.

As Francis was fifteen, he was determined old enough to rule without a regency, though in reality, he was incapable of handling such an important position. Francis had always been delicate in health, but in November 1560, he took a turn for the worse. His left ear had festered and he suffered from headaches so severe that he had fainting spells and fits of uninterrupted screaming. He endured a horrific operation whereby his doctors attempted to relieve the pressure by drilling a hole in his head. The young king died on December 5, 1560.

His successor was his ten-year-old brother, Charles IX, with his mother, Catherine de Medici serving as regent. Her first act was to settle the religious issue. By the Ordinance of Orléans in 1561, persecution of Protestants was stopped, Protestant prisoners were set free, and in 1562, they were allowed freedom of worship.

That did not sit well with many Catholics, and the duke of Guise staged a massacre of the Protestants who were worshiping at Vassy. Protestants were outraged and spared no time in retaliating. Catherine reestablished order, but several more religious wars broke out across the nation. On the surface, Catherine allowed the Protestants their freedoms. In reality, she was behind the Massacre of Saint Bartholomew in 1572, where nearly 15,000 Protestants were slaughtered.

Though Charles IX let himself be ruled by his mother, it was he who ultimately gave his approval to her massacre plan. He seemed to suffer remorse for that act until his death from tuberculosis in 1574. In his last days, his body constantly produced a bloody sweat and in his delirium he believed he was surrounded by the blood of those he'd ordered killed.

Charles IX had just one daughter from his wife, Elizabeth of Austria, so the next king was his brother, Henry III, by all accounts, one of the strangest kings. Henry was brave, well-educated, and a very capable politician. He was also very fond of women and had affairs with many women besides being very attentive to his wife. Yet, he was also extremely effeminate. He dressed as a woman, enjoyed bedecking himself with earrings and jewelry, and surrounded himself with a troupe of handsome male followers called *mignons*. Henry loved the prestige of being king and enjoyed all the pomp and privilege that went with the monarchy. Strict etiquette was observed in his presence, and he forbade anyone to approach him too closely. The one time he lowered his guard and let someone get close to him was to be his last.

In 1587, an eighth religious war broke out over the news that Mary Stuart, now Mary Queen of Scots, had been executed. The war, known as the War of the Three Henrys, was fought by Catholic Henry III, Henry, the duke of Guise (who wanted to be king); and Henry of Navarre, the Protestant brother-in-law of the king and next in line for the throne. The Catholics formed the League of Sixteen, whose purpose was to overthrow Henry III and replace him with Henry de Guise because the former refused to eliminate Protestant Henry of Navarre from succession. Though Henry III announced that the next king would have to be Catholic, that wasn't enough to stop the duke and his league. Henry III, forced into retaliation, had Henry de Guise murdered. The league stepped up its activities, and Henry III finally called on Henry of Navarre for assistance. When the league realized their cause was lost, they sent a fanatical monk named Jacques Clément to request an audience with the king. For once, Henry III forgot to keep up royal etiquette and had the monk brought to his dressing room. It was a fatal mistake. Jacques Clément stabbed the king in the stomach and was henceforth tossed out the window by the king's guard.

The next day, a dying Henry sent for Henry of Navarre, begged him to become a Catholic, acknowledged him as successor to the French crown, and exhorted all his officers to do likewise. Henry III then passed away and with him, the house of Valois.

SOCIETY

THE FOURTEENTH CENTURY was one in which the French people must have thought they were witnessing the end of the world. The Four Horsemen of the Apocalypse—War, Famine, Pestilence, and Death—seemed to ride straight out of the Book of Revelation to deliver divine retribution. War was ongoing, and death and suffering were everywhere as severe famines and plague decimated the population. Packs of wild dogs preyed upon the dead who were often lying beside the road where they had fallen. The animals grew bolder as they lost their fear of man, and posed a serious threat to children and those caught walking without protection.

The most serious plague years, apart from the whole of the second half of the fourteenth century, were 1412, 1438–1439, 1454–1457, and 1481–1483. Outbreaks also occurred in the sixteenth century. Those who didn't die of the plague were subject to repeat epidemics of smallpox, typhus, and many other diseases.

People were desperate to find some cause for the madness that had befallen them. Some blamed the stars, others believed it was the handiwork of the devil, some believed it was divine retribution or the end of the world, and there were those who believed the Jews were behind the problems. To facilitate an end to the horror, hundreds of Jews were burned alive (a horror in itself), there were public flagellations lasting for hours to absolve people of their sins, various saints were invoked, and their relics were carried around in processions. Many simply fled from plague-infested towns, carrying their fleas with them to infect other areas.

The Peace of 1360 released large numbers of soldiers from duty, and instead of settling down and trying to find jobs, many resorted to banditry. The unemployed soldiers, known as "fleecers," went on terrible rampages that included violent robberies, massacres, the burning of villages, and the destruction of crops and livestock. Only the foolhardy or the extremely well-armed dared to venture forth. In fact, the French roads became so dangerous that the great fairs moved to Geneva and other German and Italian cities where it was safer.

During the second half of the fifteenth century, the population began to recover from the effects of plague, famine, and war. Charles VII dealt with the problem of the "fleecers" by having a number of them hanged and sending others to wage war in Switzerland and Lorraine. The better ones joined the ranks of his new standing army.

As chaos gave way under the reestablishment of law and order, the way was paved for future economic recovery. By 1500, large amounts of land had been reclaimed and long-term tenures were offered, giving farmers a sense of security and hope for the future that had been missing for so long.

Villages that been nearly wiped out were given governmental assistance in revitalization efforts. As new industries were established, new markets opened up, and the fairs gradually returned. On the coast, once great ports saw more trade coming their way and soon became involved in the spice trade.

Louis XI's domestic policies paid off in the growth of the middle class. The feudal nobility, who were first and foremost soldiers, began to be replaced by the wealthy bourgeois who'd made their fortunes through commerce and finance. Many settled on great estates in the Loire valley where the first châteaux were being constructed. A renewed interest in the arts and literature blossomed forth, and collections of books and tapestries were both a source of great pride and a symbol of status.

Francis I's captivity in Spain made him aware of Spanish discoveries in the New World. Not wanting to be left out, he commissioned his own explorers who ended up making their own discoveries in what is now the United States and Canada. Francis was also responsible for encouraging the Renaissance in France. He was a great patron of the arts and acquired a magnificent collection displayed at Fontainebleau. He also maintained several close relationships with the masters, and it was in his arms that Leonardo da Vinci died. However, it is also during the reign of Francis I that religious persecution began and led to the many civil wars fought on religious grounds over the course of the century.

The language of France was one undergoing significant change. There were two primary dialects of Old French: the *langue d'oc,* which was spoken in the south, and the *langue d'oeil,* which was spoken in the north. As travel and communications between other countries became more common, words from Latin, Greek, Spanish, and Italian worked their way into Old French. In time, the language spoken in and around Paris became the language of the royal court, government, and business, as well as the language of literature; compulsory use in official documents dates to 1539. In the latter half of the fifteenth century, the spread of French to all parts of the realm was quite rapid, and no doubt helped along by the introduction of the printing presses established in Paris and Lyons in the 1470s. The southern dialect became less widely used, but still survives as Provençal. Latin continued to be the language of the Church.

In 1470, the first printing press was built in Paris, and ten years later, the country had eight more. By the turn of the century, the number had increased threefold and continued to grow. Whereas books had been rare and possessed only by the wealthy, they were now being printed by the thousands and in the vernacular languages of the common people. It's estimated that by 1520, the shops of Parisian booksellers held as many as 50,000 to 100,000 books on all manner of subjects ranging from religious works to simple comedies and farces. It was the establishment of the printing press that was to ultimately help spread the Protestant Reformation movement.

RELIGION

DURING THE FOURTEENTH and fifteenth centuries, the Church was torn by internal strife. During the Great Schism, another papacy was established at Avignon, causing even more turmoil as the sense of unity, the "seamless garment of Christ," was disturbed. Higher church officials continued to be called from among the wealthier families and did not normally leave their accustomed lifestyle or properties behind.

The two organizations of the Church were the secular clergy, who lived in the world and had the job of leading men to salvation, and the regular clergy, the monks who lived within the walls of the monastery and took vows ranging from poverty to silence. By this point in time, the monks were also running hospitals, mills, farms, and schools.

In the secular clergy, the priests were typically recruited from among the commoners and given just enough education to perform their duties, which included performing the miracle of the Mass, baptisms, marriages, and funerals. The priest was usually the only person in a village who could read and write, and he often performed both functions for those of his parish. The priest also staged the mystery and miracle plays and directed the many spiritual pageants and processions.

The Church had much more influence over daily life than it does now, and every stage of life had its own religious rituals and ceremonies. Infants were baptized shortly after birth and were represented by godparents who took vows to see to their spiritual nourishment. Should a child make it past its first years, the ritual of confirmation signified formal membership into the Church. Marriage was also a spiritual sacrament, and when people approached death, the viaticum or last rites were administered.

In spite of all the parish priests did for their people, they were generally not too highly thought of. Some of this attitude might have sprung from abuses of position but was more likely due to the financial hardship the Church put on the people. A tithe of 10 percent was mandatory, and on top of that, priests normally charged a fee for performing nearly all their functions. They also aggressively collected monies for charities and for church repairs or expansions. One way to raise funds was the selling of indulgences which people thought would spare them time in purgatory. It was just this type of service that led Martin Luther to make his calls for widespread reform.

During the sixteenth century, parts of Germany and Switzerland, Scandinavia, and England had broken away from the Catholic Church. To some, it was a matter of royal authority versus papal authority. To others, it was a matter of religious doctrine, and they were skilled at using the printing press to further their cause. In 1517, Martin Luther attacked the selling of indulgences, and three years later, had broken away from Rome in an attempt to establish a purer form of Christianity. His writings spread across France and inspired Jean Calvin to take up the call for reform in France.

The reformers objected not only to the authority of the Pope, but to the validity of the sacraments, as well. More specifically, they believed the bread and wine of communion was merely symbolic of Christ's body and blood and did not believe it was miraculously transformed during Mass into the actual body and blood of Christ. Veneration of the saints was also rejected, as was the belief that salvation could be achieved through good works.

At first, Francis I allowed Protestant reformers their freedoms, but as the movement began to grow and became more vocal, he began repressive measures. The first Protestant martyrs were burned at the stake in 1523. By 1534, anti-Catholic posters began appearing throughout the realm. This was intolerable to Francis, and his way to eliminate the heretics was to simply burn more of them.

His son, Henry II, was an even more vicious persecutor. He established the *Chambre Ardente,* the ''Burning Chamber'' as a special court that tried people for heresy and saw to the carrying out of their sentences. Nonetheless, by the time of Henry II's death, several hundred Protestant churches had been established, and their memberships continued to grow.

NAMES

CHILDREN WERE NAMED at baptism and were named after their parents, grandparents, godparents, or some other family member the parents wished to honor. It was quite easy to make a feminine form of a male name. Usually all it took was adding an *e* on the end. Diminutive forms of names were also very popular. Another custom was to name a child for the saint appearing on the Church calendar for that baptismal day. Interestingly, a person's day of baptism and naming was celebrated rather than the day of birth.

As the Reformation movement got under way, Protestant parents began to disregard the saints' names and started choosing names from the Bible. Names such as Rachel, Ruth, and Zipporah started to make their way into the pool of names, as did those like Laban, Gédéon, and Ezéchiel. However, the most popular names continued to be Jeanne, Isabelle, and Marie for women, and Charles, Jean, Louis, and Philip for men. Anne and Marie were also used as male names during this time period, though not as regularly as traditionally male names. Countless variations in names occurred, and the few listed below are a just a fraction of the variants.

FEMALE NAMES

Adaliz (nobility)
Adèle (noble) **Adala, Adela**
Adelaide (nobility)
Adelais (nobility)
Adeline (nobility)
Adrienne (from Hadrianus)
Aënor (light, torch, bright)
Agathe (good)
Agilina (formidable)
Aglaë (splendor)
Agnès (chaste, pure, sacred)
Alberte (noble and bright)
Albertine (noble and bright)
Alexandra (defender of mankind)
Alia (all)
Alice (nobility)
Aliz (nobility)
Amélie (work, labor)
Amice (friendship)
Anastasia (resurrection)
Andrée (womanly)
Ange (angel)
Angèle (angel)
Anne (grace, full of grace, mercy) **Anna**
Annette (little Anne *grace, full of grace, mercy*)
Annis (chaste, pure, sacred)
Annora (honor, esteem) Norman form of Honora.
Antoinette (?, *priceless, of inestimable worth* is a folk definition)

Ariane (very holy one)
Arlette (little eagle)
Aurélie (gold) **Aurèle**
Aurore (dawn, daybreak)
Aveline (?)
Aveza (?)
Barbe (foreign woman)
Barbot (little Barbe *foreign woman*)
Basilie (kingly)
Batilde (commanding battle maiden) **Batilda**
Beata (happy)
Béatriz (bringer of happiness and joy) **Béatrix**
Belinda (?, second element is *serpent*)
Bernadette (bold as a bear)
Bernardine (bold as a bear)
Berthe (bright)
Bertrade (bright)
Blanche (white) **Blanch**
Brigitte (strength)
Calliste (she that is most beautiful) **Calixte, Callixte**
Caroline (full-grown)
Cassandra (?)
Caterine (pure)
Cecilia (blind, dim-sighted)
Celeste (heavenly)
Celestine (heavenly)
Céline (heaven)
Charlotte (full-grown)

Christiane (a Christian)
Christine (a Christian) **Christin, Crisinet, Cristinet**
Claire (bright, clear, famous)
Claremond (bright protection, famous protection)
Clarice (bright, clear, famous)
Claude (lame)
Claudine (lame)
Clémence (gentle, mild, clement)
Clotilde (loud battle)
Colette (victory of the people) **Collette**
Constance (constant, steadfast)
Corinne (maiden)
Corisande (?)
Cornelia (horn)
Cristina (a Christian, a follower of Christ)
Denise (of Dionysus)
Désirée (desired)
Diane (divine)
Douce (sweet)
Edma (wealthy protection)
Edmée (wealthy protection)
Egilina (formidable)
Eglentine (prickly; sweetbrier)
Elaine (light, torch, bright) **Elainne, Eleinne, Eleyne**
Elena (light, torch, bright)
Eléonore (light, torch, bright)
Elisabeth (God is my oath)
Emeline (work, industrious) **Ameline, Ammeline, Emmeline**
Emilie (trying to equal or excel; rival)
Emilienne (little Emilie)
Emma (strength)
Esclairmonde (bright protection, famous protection)
Eufemie (well-spoken, fair of voice)
Eugenie (nobility, excellence)
Eulalie (well-spoken)
Eunice (good victory)
Eustacie (steadfast, happy in harvest)
Fabienne (a bean)
Félise (felicity, goodness)
Fernande (peace; journey; youth, life + courage; venture, risk; ready, prepared)
Flavienne (yellow-haired)
Flore (a flower)
Florence (blooming, flourishing)
Françoise (French) From the thirteenth century.
Frédégonde (peaceful war)
Frédérique (ruler of peace)
Geneviève (?, perhaps *tribal woman*)
Gertrude (spear strength)
Giselle (pledge)
Gunilda (war battle) **Gunnilda**
Hedwig (battle wide)
Héloïse (sound, hearty, and wide) **Helewis**
Henriette (home ruler) **Henriet**
Hilde (war, battle) **Hilda**
Honorée (honor, esteem) **Ennoré, Enoré**

Hortense (gardener)
Huguette (heart, mind, soul)
Ida (labor)
Ingeborg (Ing's fortification)
Iphigénie (of royal birth)
Irénée (peace)
Isabelle (God is my oath) **Isabel, Ysabelle**
Iseut (ruler of the ice) **Isaut**
Jacqueline (supplanting, seizing by the heels)
Jacquette (supplanting, seizing by the heels)
Jeanne (God is gracious)
Jeannette (little Jeanne *God is gracious*)
Joscelin (from the tribe of the Gauts)
Judith (praised; from Judah)
Julian (youth, downy)
Julie (youth, downy)
Laure (laurel)
Laurencia (woman from Laurentum)
Laurette (laurel)
Leonie (lion)
Léonore (light, torch, bright)
Linnet (shapely)
Louise (famous in war)
Louisette (little Louise *famous in war*)
Louison (famous in war)
Luce (light)
Lucette (little Luce *light*)
Lucie (light) **Lucia**
Lucienne (little Luce *light*)
Lucille (light)
Mabila (lovable)
Madeleine (from Magdala)
Mahaut (mighty in battle) **Mahault**
Manon (little Marie *sea of bitterness or sorrow*)
Marcelle (of Mars, warlike)
Margerie (a pearl)
Margot (a pearl)
Margoton (a pearl)
Marguerite (a pearl)
Marianne (sea of bitterness or sorrow + grace, full of grace, mercy)
Marie (sea of bitterness or sorrow)
Mariette (little Marie *sea of bitterness or sorrow*)
Marthe (lady, mistress)
Martine (of Mars, warlike)
Matilde (mighty in battle)
Maud (mighty in battle)
Mélanie (dark, black)
Melisent (work strength)
Melissa (a bee)
Mélusine (a water nymph)
Metheldred (mild strength)
Mildred (mild strength)
Miriam (sea of bitterness or sorrow)
Monique (?)
Muriel (sea bright) Used in Brittany and Normandy.

Nanette (little Anne *grace, full of grace, mercy*) **Ninette**
Nicole (victory of the people)
Nicolette (little Nicole *victory of the people*) **Nicollet, Nicol-lette**
Ninon (little Anne *grace, full of grace, mercy*)
Noel (born at Christmas)
Odette (little Odile *wealth, prosperity*)
Odile (wealth, prosperity)
Olimpe (of Olympus)
Oriane (to rise)
Oriel (fire and strife)
Oriolt (fire and strife)
Ottilie (wealth, prosperity)
Pascale (born at Eastertime)
Paule (small)
Paulette (little Paule *small*)
Perrine (little rock, little stone)
Philippa (lover of horses)
Rachel (ewe)
Rébecca (noose)
Régine (queenly)
Reine (queen)
Renée (reborn)
Romaine (a Roman)
Rosala (horse)
Rosalie (rosalia, the annual ceremony of hanging garlands of roses on tombs)

Rosamund (horse protection) **Rosamond**
Roslind (horse serpent)
Ruth (a friend)
Sabine (Sabine woman)
Salomé (peace)
Sarah (princess)
Séraphine (burning ones)
Sibylla (prophetess, fortune-teller)
Sidonie (fine cloth, linen)
Simone (heard)
Solange (yearly, annual; solemn, religious)
Sophie (wisdom)
Stéphanie (a crown, a garland)
Suzanne (lily, rose)
Sybille (a fortune-teller, a prophetess)
Sylvie (of the woods)
Tifaine (Epiphany, manifestation of God)
Valérie (strong, healthy)
Véronique (?, perhaps *true image*; *bringer of victory*)
Viole (violet)
Violette (little Viole *violet*)
Vivienne (alive)
Willa (resolute)
Yolande (violet)
Yvette (archer)
Yvonne (archer)
Zéphyrine (the west wind)

MALE NAMES

Achille (?)
Adalard (noble and hard)
Adalbert (noble and bright) **Adelbert**
Adolphe (noble wolf)
Adrian (man from Hadrianus) **Adriane**
Agésilas (the goatskin shield of Zeus, a protection)
Ailemar (noble and famous) **Eilemar**
Aimery (work ruler) **Aimeric, Amaury, Aymery, Emery**
Aimo (home) **Aymo**
Alain (?, perhaps *handsome, rock*) **Alein**
Alard (noble and hard)
Alaric (ruler of all)
Albert (noble and bright)
Albin (white)
Alexandre (defender of mankind)
Alfred (elf counsel; wise counsel)
Algernon (mustached)
Alphonse (noble and ready)
Alphée (first)
Alveré (elf counsel)
Amalrich (work ruler) **Amalric, Amalriko, Amelric, Amel-rich, Amulric, Amulrich**
Amande (army man, soldier)
Ambroise (immortal)

Amé (?)
Amias (?, perhaps *friendship*)
Amiel (industrious)
Amis (friendship)
Anastase (resurrection) **Anastasie**
Anatole (sunrise, daybreak)
Ancelot (divine)
André (manly)
Anne (grace, full of grace, mercy)
Anselm (God's helmet)
Antoine (?, *priceless, of inestimable worth* is a folk definition)
Ara (eagle)
Ariste (best)
Armand (soldier, warrior) **Armant**
Arnaud (eagle power) **Arnaut**
Arno (eagle)
Arnold (eagle power) **Arnault, Arnould**
Arnulf (eagle wolf)
Arsène (male, virile)
Arthur (?) **Artos**
Ascelin (from the tribe of the Gauts) **Acelin**
Auberi (elf ruler)
Aubert (noble and bright)

August (great, venerable) **Auguste**
Augustin (great, venerable)
Augustus (great, venerable)
Auveré (elf counsel)
Baldri (bold ruler, brave ruler) **Baudri**
Baldric (bold ruler, brave ruler)
Baldwin (bold friend, brave friend) Flemish form.
Baptiste (a baptist)
Bardolph (bright wolf) **Bardolf**
Barnabé (son of exhortation)
Bartelmeu (son of Talmai *hill, mound, furrows*) **Bertelmeu**
Basil (kingly) **Basile**
Bastien (man from Sebastia)
Baudoin (bold friend, brave friend)
Bénédict (blessed)
Benjamin (son of the right hand)
Benoît (blessed) **Benoist, Beneoit**
Beringer (bear spear)
Bernard (bold as a bear)
Bernardin (little Bernard *bold as a bear*)
Berthold (bear rule) **Berold, Berolt**
Bertin (bright friend)
Bertrand (bright raven) **Bertran**
Bevis (beautiful) **Beves**
Blaise (babbler)
Bouchard (big mouth)
Brian (force, strength; valor; high; kingly) Used in Brittany.
Brice (?)
Célestin (heavenly)
César (hairy; bluish gray)
Charles (full-grown, a man)
Chrétien (a Christian, a follower of Christ)
Christian (a Christian, a follower of Christ) **Christen, Christin**
Christophe (bearing Christ)
Claud (lame)
Claudin (lame) **Clauden**
Clemens (gentle, mild, clement)
Cléon (glory, the glorious)
Conan (strength, high)
Conrad (bold counsel)
Constant (constant, steadfast) **Constans**
Constantine (constant, steadfast)
Crispin (curled)
Cyprian (from Cyprus)
Dagobert (day bright)
Damien (tamer)
Daniel (judged by God)
Daudet (given by God)
David (beloved)
Delphin (a dolphin; from Delphi)
Démosthène (?)
Denis (of Dionysus) **Denys**
Déodat (given by God) Used in southern France.
Didier (desired)
Dieudonné (given by God) Used in northern France.

Dion (of Zeus)
Dominique (belonging to a lord)
Donatien (given by God)
Drogo (burden bearer) **Drugo**
Dru (burden bearer)
Durand (enduring, lasting)
Ector (holding fast)
Edgar (wealthy spear)
Edmond (wealthy protector) **Edmonde, Edme**
Édouard (wealthy guardian) **Edouard**
Egmont (fearful protection, awesome protection)
Eloi (chosen)
Emery (ruler of strength)
Émile (emulating, trying to equal or excel, a rival)
Émilien (emulating, trying to equal or excel, a rival)
Emmanuel (God is with us)
Emmerich (ruler of strength)
Engelrand (angel raven) **Enguerran, Enguerrand**
Eric (eternal ruler)
Ernust (earnest, resolute) **Ernest, Ernost, Ernst**
Esmé (loved)
Esmond (beautiful hand)
Étienne (a crown, garland)
Eudes (child)
Eudon (child)
Eugène (well-born, noble)
Eustache (steadfast; happy in harvest)
Évariste (well-pleasing)
Everard (boar strength)
Fabian (a bean)
Fabrice (workman, craftsman)
Faramond (journey protection)
Félix (lucky, happy) **Felis**
Ferdinand (peace; journey; youth, life + courage; venture, risk; ready)
Ferrand (peace; journey; youth, life + courage; venture, risk; ready)
Fidèle (fidelity, faith, trush)
Filbert (very bright) **Filibert, Fulbert**
Firmin (firm, steadfast)
Flavien (yellow-haired) **Flavie**
Florent (blossoming, flourishing)
Florentin (blossoming, flourishing)
Florian (flowery)
Fouchier (people, folk)
Francis (a Frenchman, a freeman)
Franck (a Frank, a freeman)
François (French) **Francheis, Franchois, Françoys, Franzoys**
Frédéric (ruler of peace)
Fromont (free protection)
Fulk (people) **Fulke**
Gabriel (God is my strength)
Garnier (protecting army)
Gascon (?, perhaps *guest, stranger; from Gascony*)
Gaspard (treasure master)

Gaston (?, possibly *guest, stranger; from Gascony*)
Gauvain (battle hawk)
Geoffroi (district; traveler; pledge + peace)
Georges (earth worker, farmer)
Gerald (spear rule) **Geralt**
Gérard (brave with the spear) **Girard, Girardat, Girardet**
Gérardin (brave with the spear)
Gerbert (bright spear)
Germain (a German)
Gervais (servant of the spear)
Giffard (give + bold, fierce)
Gilbert (bright pledge)
Gilles (goatskin shield of Zeus; a protection) **Gile, Giles**
Godard (god hard)
Godfry (God's peace) **Godefry**
Gregoire (vigilant, watchful)
Griffin (like a griffin, monstrous)
Guillard (resolute protector)
Guillaud (resolute protector) **Guillod, Guillot, Guilloteaux**
Guillaume (resolute protector) **Guillelmus, Guillerme, Guillermaux, Guillermus**
Guillaumet (resolute protector) **Guillemet, Guillermet**
Guillon (resolute protector)
Guiscard (?)
Gunter (bold in war)
Guy (a guide, a leader)
Guyon (a guide, a leader)
Haerveu (battle worthy) Breton name.
Hamo (home, house)
Hamon (home, house)
Hardwin (hard friend)
Hector (holding fast, restraining)
Helgaud (prosperous; hearty, hale) **Helgald**
Henriot (home ruler) **Henrioud**
Henry (home ruler) **Henri**
Herbert (army bright)
Hercule (glory of Hera)
Herman (army man, soldier)
Hervé (battle worthy)
Hilaire (cheerful)
Hippolyte (freer of horses)
Hubert (bright heart)
Hue (heart, mind, soul) Used in the south.
Hugh (heart, mind, soul)
Hugo (heart, mind, soul)
Hugolin (heart, mind, soul)
Hugon (heart, mind, soul) Used in the north.
Hugot (heart, mind, soul) **Huguelet, Huguet**
Hugues (heart, mind, soul) Used in the north.
Humbert (people bright)
Huon (heart, mind, soul) Used in the south.
Ignace (?, perhaps *fire*)
Ilbert (battle bright) **Ilberd**
Imbert (iron people) **Isembert**
Ingelram (angel raven)
Isidore (gift of Isis)

Ives (archer) **Ive**
Ivon (archer)
Jacques (supplanting, seizing by the heels)
Jean (God is gracious)
Jenico (?, perhaps *fire*) Provençal form of Ignace.
Jérémie (God will uplift)
Jérôme (sacred name)
Joachim (God will establish)
Joël (the Lord is God)
Joseph (he shall add)
Jourdain (a flowing down)
Judicael (sportive) **Judical** A Breton name.
Julian (youth, downy)
Juvénal (youth)
Juste (just, fair)
Justin (just, fair)
Karl (a man, freeman, peasant)
Kaspar (treasure master)
Klemens (mild, gentle, merciful)
Konrad (wise counsel)
Konstantin (constant, steadfast)
Lambert (bright land)
Lance (land)
Lancelin (little Lance *land*)
Lancelot (little Lance *land*)
Laurence (man from Laurentum) **Laurent**
Leo (lion)
Léon (lion)
Léonard (lion hard, bold as a lion)
Léonce (lion)
Léopold (bold people)
Lionel (little Léon *lion*)
Lothar (famous warrior)
Louis (famous in war)
Luc (light; man from Lucania)
Lucien (light)
Ludwig (famous in war)
Macaire (blessed)
Magnus (great)
Manfred (man of peace)
Marc (?, perhaps *Mars; manly; soft, tender*)
Marcel (of Mars, warlike)
Marcellin (little Marcel *of Mars, warlike*)
Martin (of Mars, warlike)
Matthieu (gift of God) **Matheu**
Mauger (spear grinder)
Maynard (strong and hardy)
Meurisse (a Moor, dark-skinned)
Michel (Who is like God?)
Miles (?, perhaps *mild, peaceful; merciful*)
Milo (?, perhaps *mild, peaceful; merciful*)
Milon (?, perhaps *mild, peaceful; merciful*)
Moïse (drawn out of the water)
Nathaniel (God has given) **Nathanael**
Nicol (victory of the people) **Nicod, Nicodet, Nicoud**
Nicolas (victory of the people) **Nicollaud, Nicollier, Nicoulaz**

Nicollin (little Nicolas *victory of the people*)
Noel (born at Christmas)
Odo (wealth)
Ogier (rich spear)
Olivier (olive tree)
Onfroi (people peace)
Osanne (hosannah)
Osbert (God bright)
Osmond (God protection) **Osmund**
Paul (small) **Pol**
Paulin (little Paul *small*)
Perceval (pierce the valley) **Percevale**
Philip (lover of horses) **Phelip, Phelipe, Phelipp, Pheleppe, Philippe, Phillipe, Phillippe**
Philippes (lover of horses) **Phelipes, Phellipes, Phelippes, Philipes, Phillipes, Phillippes**
Philipot (little Philip *lover of horses*)
Pierre (a rock, a stone)
Piers (a rock, a stone)
Prosper (prosperous, favorable)
Quentin (fifth)
Raimund (counsel protection) **Raymond, Reimund, Reymond, Reymonde**
Randolf (shield wolf) **Randolph, Randulf**
Ranfred (counsel peace)
Raul (counsel wolf)
Regnault (ruler of judgment)
Rémy (oarsman)
René (rebirth)
Reynard (counsel hard) **Rainard**
Reynaud (powerful protection) **Reinald, Renaud**
Richard (stern king)
Robert (bright with fame) **Roberte**
Robin (bright with fame) **Robineaux**
Roby (bright with fame)
Roch (rest)
Rodolphe (famous wolf)
Roger (famous with the spear)
Roland (famous land) **Rolande, Rolland, Rollande**
Rolf (famous wolf)
Romain (a Roman)

Samuel (name of God)
Sanson (the sun)
Sébastien (man of Sebastia)
Séverin (severe, strict)
Sigmund (victory protection)
Simon (heard)
Spiro (to breathe, to blow)
Stéphane (a crown, garland)
Sylvain (of the woods)
Sylvestre (of the woods)
Symphorien (bearing together)
Talbot (pillager, bandit; lampblack)
Tancred (think counsel)
Terrick (ruler of the people)
Théodor (ruler of the people) **Théodore, Théodose**
Théophile (beloved of God)
Thibaut (people bold) **Thibault**
Thierry (ruler of the people)
Thomas (a twin)
Timothée (honor, respect)
Toussaint (all saints) Given to those born near All Saints' Day.
Tristan (tumult, sadness)
Turstan (Thor's stone) **Turstin**
Ulrich (wolf rule)
Urbain (dweller in a village) **Urban**
Valdemar (famous ruler)
Valentin (healthy, strong)
Valére (to be strong)
Valéry (foreign ruler) **Valéran**
Victor (victory)
Vincent (conquering)
Vivien (alive)
Vuillaume (resolute protector) **Vuillerme, Vulliamoz, Vulliamy, Vulliémoz**
Vuille (resolute protector) **Vuilliet, Vullioud**
Vuillemin (resolute protector) **Vulliemin**
Willelm (resolute protector) A Norman form of William.
Yann (God is gracious) A Breton form of John.
Yves (archer)
Yvon (archer)

SURNAMES

By this date, surnames were hereditary among a large portion of the French population. By far the largest category were those referring to place of origin or residence, and as new towns and villages were established, the pool of surnames became larger. The same held true for occupational names. Improvements and discoveries often led to the production of new jobs, and many a common person was known by his occupation or trade.

Agricola (farmer)
Albin (white) **Albine, Aubin**
de Anjou (from Anjou)

le Archer (the archer)
de Artois (from Artois)
Aymonard (little home) **Aymonod**

Aymonet (little home) **Aymonier, Emonet**
Aymonin (little home)
Barratt (bear might) **Barraud**
le Basse (the short, fat one)
le Basset (the little short, fat one)
le Beau (the handsome, the fair)
Beauchamp (fair field)
Beaufoy (beautiful beech tree)
Beaulieu (fair place)
Beaumont (fair mountain)
de Beaune (from Beaune)
Bec (mouth)
la Belle (the beautiful)
Bertran (bright raven)
le Blanc (the white)
Bouchard (big mouth)
Bouvier (cattle drover)
de Brus (from Brus *the brushwood thicket*) **de Bruis**
Bureau (bureau, desk)
Cartier (a carter)
de Champagne (from Champagne *field*)
de Champdivers (from Champdivers *diverse fields*)
Champier (from the field)
de Chanteloup (from Chanteloup *singing wolves*)
de Chartres (from Chartres)
de Clisson (from Clisson)
de Colleville (from Col's estate)
le Coq (the cock, the rooster)
le Corbet (the raven)
de Coucy (from Coucy)
de Courtenay (from Courtenay's farmstead)
de Divion (from Divion)
Dubois (of the woods)
Duprat (of the meadow)
Durand (enduring, lasting)
Fauchet (crooked legs)
de Foix (from Foix)
Giffard (chubby-cheeked)
Gilbert (bright pledge)
de Glanville (oak tree estate)
le Grand (the tall, the large)
le Gros (the fat)
de Harcourt (army house)
Jaccard (God is gracious) **Jaccaud, Jaccoud, Jacquart**
Jacolet (God is gracious)

Jacotin (God is gracious)
Jacquier (God is gracious)
Jacquinod (God is gracious) **Jacquenod, Jaquinod**
le Jeune (the young)
de Laci (Latius's estate)
le Libéral (the liberal)
de Lorris (from Lorris)
Lovvet (little wolf)
de Maci (Matheus's estate)
de Malleville (from Malleville)
Marcel (of Mars, warlike)
Margot (pearl) **Marguet**
Marguerat (pearl)
de Marle (blackbird)
de Meran (from Meran)
Monard (little house) **Monnard**
Monet (little house) **Monier, Monnet, Monnier**
de Montfort (from Montfort *fortified hill*)
de Montmorency (from Montmorency)
de Nogaret (from Nogaret)
de Perci (from Perci *destroyer of cities*)
Pernod (rock, stone) **Pernet, Perrenoud, Perrinet**
Perret (rock, stone) **Perot, Perrette, Perrot**
Perrier (rock, stone)
Perrin (rock, stone) **Pierrin**
Pierre (rock, stone)
le Pieux (the pious)
de Poitiers (from Poitiers)
de Provence (from Provence)
de Puiset (from Puiset)
de Rochefort (fortified rock)
Salmon (seller of salmon; Saint Almond)
de Savoie (from Savoie)
le Simple (the simple)
de Sorbon (from Sorbon)
Talbot (pillager, bandit; lampblack)
Tillet (dweller near the lime trees)
de Tilly (from the lime tree grove)
Tirel (Thor's rule)
de Varennes (a game preserve)
de Venables (vineyard)
de Vermandois (from Vermandois)
de Vernon (from the alder tree)
de Vienne (the white town)

Chapter Five

THE BOURBONS
[1589—1793]

POLITICS

THE PROTESTANT HENRY of Navarre ascended to the French throne after the death of Henry III. Henry's claim to the throne was through descent from the youngest son of Saint Louis, but he was also the grandson of Francis I's sister, Marguerite, and the husband of Marguerite, the daughter of Henry II and Catherine de Medici. Henry was not born into a life of wealth and luxury, but he was brought to Paris when his father, Antoine de Bourbon, became lieutenant-general of the kingdom after the death of Francis II. In 1564, Catherine de Medici took ten-year-old Henry on a tour around the kingdom and presented him to Nostradamus, who had already achieved fame as a visionary. His prophecy that Henry would someday become king and that Catherine's sons would not perpetuate their line was to be realized a quarter of a century later.

On February 27, 1594, nearly five years after Henry III's death, Henry of Navarre was crowned King Henry IV. His first act was to restore order to society by dealing with the issue of religion. He reconciled with the papacy by personally rejecting Protestantism, allowed Protestants freedom of religion, and demanded that his wishes for a peaceful society be heeded. His next act was to undo the damage caused by years of war by initiating a massive reconstruction effort. By weakening the nobility's hold on land, he made more land available to the common people. He heavily promoted agriculture, both to supply people with jobs and to supply the nation with adequate food. Other jobs were created from new manufacturing efforts such as glass, mirrors, and carpets. In addition to reforming the country's economy, new canals, roads, and bridges were constructed to facilitate transportation.

Henry's private life is a book in itself. He was a well-built man with a large hook nose, a great square beard, kind eyes, and a nice disposition. Unfortunately, he was quite lax in caring for his personal hygiene; he rarely washed and had a rank, goatlike smell about himself. His wife was Marguerite, the sister of England's Henry IV, and although they were on friendly terms, they were unsuited to one another. Henry had numerous affairs (some say he had fifty-six mistresses) and sired great families of illegitimate children whom he dearly loved and raised together as one huge family. The queen lived apart and had her own affairs.

Henry's fondest mistress was Gabrielle d'Estrées. She had borne him one son, and was pregnant a second time when Henry asked for papal permission to have his marriage annulled so he could marry Gabrielle and legitimize their children. The Pope refused, but Henry went ahead with his wedding plans. A few days later,

Gabrielle suffered an attack of eclampsia, gave birth to a stillborn son, and died the next day. Henry was devastated, especially after hearing rumors that she'd been poisoned.

He had other mistresses waiting in the wings and was ready to marry one of those when his minister arranged a marriage for him with Maria de Medici, "the fat banker." Though she could not compare to Henry's mistresses in beauty and never held the king's heart like Gabrielle had, she did her duty by him and bore three sons and three daughters. Henry continued to have numerous affairs and other children.

In 1610, Henry made plans for a military operation against the emperor Rudolf II. As his son, Louis, was only eight, he demanded that Maria be crowned so she could act as regent should the need arise. A day after the coronation, Henry set out in an open carriage to visit an ill minister. His entourage was blocked by a traffic jam (thought to have been contrived), and a man jumped from the crowded street and stabbed the king twice in the heart. Henry died within moments.

The regency of Maria nearly undid all Henry had accomplished. She replaced her husband's capable minister with Concini, the Italian husband of her foster sister. The choice was a poor one, for Concini mismanaged state funds to the extent that the treasury was ruined. Once Louis XIII became of age, he had Concini arrested, banished his mother from court, and appointed Cardinal Richelieu as his adviser.

Richelieu set to work, and the treasury was soon restored. France also allied itself with the Netherlands and Sweden against the Hapsburg monarchs. It was a move that resulted in the Thirty Years' War (1618–1648), but gained the country new territory along the Rhine. New territories were being consolidated in Canada, as well.

Louis was married at the age of fourteen to Anne of Austria. Neither was ready for marriage, and they lived separate lives for nearly twenty years. One stormy winter night, the king was forced to seek shelter at Anne's residence, and the couple slept together for the first time in decades. The result was the birth of Louis XIV; two years later, another son was born.

Louis XIII died of tuberculosis in 1643. His successor was his son, Louis XIV, *Le Roi Soleil,* the most famous of the kings of France. The reign of Louis XIV lasted seventy-two years, making it the longest in French history. He was just five years old when he assumed the crown under the regency of his mother, Anne of Austria, and was crowned on June 7, 1654, at the age of sixteen.

In the early years of his reign, power was yielded by Cardinal Mazarin, a man reputed to be having an affair with the queen mother. Trouble soon began after Mazarin reestablished the tax known as the Paulette. The parliament rose in opposition, touching off a civil war known as the Fronde parliamentaire. After Mazarin's death in 1661, Louis announced he was taking over the reins of government himself.

Louis was determined to make his kingdom the strongest and the most prosperous in the world. He started toward that goal by reforming government, establishing protective trading practices, promoting industry, and improving roads and canals to facilitate the transportation of goods. Some of his policies, however, were to work against him. He ended up draining the country's resources when he took up arms against Spain and the Netherlands in 1700 in order to expand his territory and place his grandson on the Spanish throne. The war, which lasted for twelve years, put Louis and his country in such dire straits that he was reduced to melting down his own silverware for cash.

He also deprived the Huguenots (Protestants) of their religious freedoms, prompting their wide-scale emigration to North America and other parts of Europe. The Huguenots were important merchants and traders, and their departure left the French economy much weaker. As the economy stagnated, no satisfactory methods to raise money were devised. The cost of government continued to be borne on the backs of the peasants.

Louis, always conscious of his role as absolute monarch, maintained a kingly image at all times, even in moments of ease. He was married for political reasons to Marie Thérèse, the daughter of Philip IV of Spain and Elisabeth, the eldest daughter of Henry IV, and had six children, though only one son survived childhood.

Louis was well-known for his several mistresses. The most famous were Louise de la Vallière, who gave the king five children, and Françoise Athénais de Rochechouart-Mortemart, Marquise de Montespan, who gave him eight children.

Queen Marie Thérèse died in 1683. A year later, the king secretly married Françoise Scarron, the governess of his children by the Marquise de Montespan. In 1688, Louis made her Marquise de Maintenon et du Parc, and she is known to history as Madame de Maintenon. She was never publicly acknowledged as Louis's wife, but she openly lived with him and was accorded every courtesy due to a queen.

Louis was a man of robust health and eventually outlived his son and grandson. *Le Grand Dauphin,* Louis, died of smallpox in April 1711, leaving his only son, Louis, Duke of Burgundy, to succeeded as dauphin. Louis was married to the charming and beautiful Marie Adélaïde of Savoy and had three sons by her, though the eldest died in 1705. Unfortunately, smallpox was not finished with the family. In February 1712, Marie Adélaïde contracted the disease and died. That left only their youngest, two-year-old Louis to succeed his great-grandfather. The tragic sequence of deaths prompted Louis XIV to declare that his illegimate sons could succeed to the throne if the youngster died.

Louis XIV's health failed during the last year of his life. He was overcome with bouts of gout and constipation. Gangrene set into his legs, and after two torturous weeks, *Le Roi Soleil* passed away on September 1, 1715, just four days before his seventy-seventh birthday. Madame de Maintenon, who had been at the king's bedside, retired into a religious foundation until her death in 1719.

Louis XV was only five at the time of his great-grandfather's death, so a regency was in order. The job went to Philip, Duke of Orléans, a nephew of Louis XIV and the husband of one of his daughters by Madame de Montespan.

When Louis came of age, he married Maria Leszczynska (Leczinska), the daughter of the King of Poland. The couple were well-suited, but after Maria bore the king ten children in as many years, she decided to forgo further marital relations for the sake of her health. Louis compensated by having several mistresses, the most famous being the beautiful and intelligent Jeanne Poisson, Marquise de Pompadour. She was with the king until her death nineteen years later and exercised a great deal of influence over him that affected many of his political decisions. Interestingly, their intimate relationship lasted for only five years, and it's possible she held her position as favorite by providing the king with an endless stream of young women with whom he could take his pleasures.

After Madame de Pompadour's death, Louis continued to live a life of sexual debauchery. After four years, he found another favorite in Madame de Barry, a pretty, unrefined woman who satisfied his sexual needs but refrained from interfering in politics.

Louis chose to leave government in the hands of his advisers rather than deal with problems himself. The economy was in terrible shape and a succession of poor harvests caused the price of bread to skyrocket far above the reaches of the peasants. Many starved to death. Reaction was such that Louis replaced his old adviser with Cardinal Fleury, a man who had tutored the young king. Cardinal Fleury governed capably until his death in 1743 at the age of ninety. He rehauled the system of taxation, worked to achieve financial strength, founded the Corps of Bridges and Highways, and encouraged settlement and trade in the Caribbean, Louisiana, and Canada.

War broke out in the first half of the eighteenth century, and though no fighting occurred in France, the country lost a great deal when both Canada and India went to the English. In the latter part of the century, trouble broke out in government when the parliaments made calls for a constitutional monarchy after disagreeing with the notion that absolute power belonged in the hands of the king.

By 1770, Louis felt he had to act. The parliaments were abolished, the sale of judicial offices stopped, and the king himself took over the job of appointing judges. He also took measures toward fiscal reform by lifting the tax burden off the backs of the poor and spreading them more fairly among the population. The privileged classes, upset that their taxes would be increased, immediately protested, forcing Louis to confine his new system to Paris and leaving the rest of the country to the status quo.

In 1765, the dauphin died from consumption. His wife, Marie Josèphe of Saxony, followed him in death after a year and a half; fifteen months later, his mother, Queen Marie, died. In 1774, Louis developed a high fever while spending time away with Madame du Barry. He immediately returned to Versailles and it became apparent that he'd contracted smallpox. After confessing his sins to the court chaplain, Louis XV died, leaving the crown to his grandson, Louis XVI.

In spite of the economic and political problems of the day, most of the people's disapproval stemmed from displeasure over their king's promiscuous lifestyle and his obvious lack of morals. His nickname the Well-Loved came from his reputation when he was a handsome young man, not for any loving feelings he'd engendered in his people.

The people's attitude toward the monarchy changed when Louis XVI ascended the throne. He was a fat man with a puffy face and bulging eyes, and a simple man who loved locksmithing and hunting. He did not put on artificial airs, and he was truly devoted to carrying out reforms for the benefit of his people. The beginning of the reign showed so much promise that it's hard to believe that in just twenty years the monarchy would fall.

Louis was married to Marie-Antoinette of Austria when he was sixteen and she, fifteen. Unfortunately, Louis had a physical disability that prevented the consummation of his marriage. The problem could have been fixed by circumcision, but a fear of the knife kept him from having the procedure carried out. Marie-Antoinette was a very proud woman, and it's possible her pride was wounded when her husband refused to take the action necessary to allow full marital relations. Though she probably remained loyal to the king, she often went about without him. Rumors were spread about her character and she became as unpopular as Louis XV's mistresses had been. It took seven years and a visit from his brother-in-law, the Emperor Joseph II, to persuade Louis to have the problem corrected. In 1778, the first of four children were born.

Things were not easy in Louis's political life, either. Knowing his country had serious problems, he suggested several reforms, the majority of which were never implemented due to strong opposition from the privileged classes that made up the parliament. In 1777, Louis allied France to the Americans and involved his country in the American Revolution. Though the American war was a successful one, it didn't bring France any material or financial gains. It had, in fact, put the country's finances in ruins. Public morale and faith in the government was at an all time low, and the groundwork was laid for the French Revolution.

In 1788, Louis summoned the estates-general, but unfortunately, his son became gravely ill and he was unable to grant an audience to the Third Estate. In 1789, the Third Estate took matters into their own hands by forming the National Assembly and writing a new constitution. Louis, who knew that the fate of absolute monarchy was in his hands, attempted to force the National Assembly to disband. The result was the storming of the Bastille on July 14, 1789.

The National Assembly demanded sweeping reforms in both government and society. It abolished all feudal rights and privileges of the nobility, stripping them of their vast land holdings and eliminating corrupt tax collectors and provincial judges who'd made the way easy for them. The lands of the Church were taken away, and a civil constitution was proposed for the clergy who'd never before answered to anyone but the Pope. Louis and his family were taken to Paris and ensconced in the Tuileries to remain as virtual prisoners for nearly three years.

In the beginning, Louis was hailed as the "Restorer of French Liberty." But although Louis knew many of these changes were necessary and even agreed with them, he didn't agree with a constitutional monarchy. Nonetheless, he publicly swore an oath to the constitution, and a few days later, signed the law giving a civil constitution to the clergy that made them answerable to the people. He and his family continued to be closely watched.

The first stage of the French Revolution lasted from June 1789 to August 1792. In the beginning, the National Assembly directed the course of political events and the masses had not yet achieved any political or economic clout. The masses didn't sit back, however. In the summer of 1789, many in the countryside armed themselves with pitchforks and other farm implements and attacked the homes of the nobility and clergy. Châteaux of the nobility and the homes of the upper clergy were destroyed, monasteries were pillaged, and several people were murdered.

By August, the assembly was receiving so many alarming reports of chaos in the countryside that they began to act. They abolished the remnants of serfdom, made the classes equal in the eyes of the law, granted freedom of speech, and allowed for religious toleration. In 1791, the king's authority over the army, the Church, and local government was taken away, and voting rights were granted to all men who paid a direct tax equal to three day's wages.

When the National Assembly confiscated the lands of the nobility and the Church, they had done so without thought to the consequences. Many who had their properties taken were not French citizens but foreign nobility, and they called upon their governments to intervene in the crisis. French revolutionaries thought war would be a good idea, for it would be a way to show the people that the nobility needed to be taught a lesson. France declared war on the King of Hungary and Bohemia in 1792, but it was Hapsburg armies who invaded the country and marched toward Paris. The duke of Brunswick, at the head of the Hapsburg forces, issued a warning that Paris would be destroyed if the royal family came to harm. Riots ensued, the Tuileries was ransacked, and the royal family imprisoned at the Tour du Temple. A month later, in September 1792, a national convention abolished the monarchy. That same day, Brunswick's forces retreated after suffering defeat.

The convention was not satisfied with just abolishing the monarchy, they wanted to rid themselves of the image. On January 21, 1793, Louis XVI was taken to the Place de la Concorde. Before his death, he addressed the crowd: "Frenchmen, I die innocent and I pray to God that my blood will not fall upon my people."

The convention then decided it wanted to be rid of the queen. After a farce of a trial in which she was convicted of incest with her young son, Marie-Antoinette suffered the same fate as her husband on October 16, 1793. Their two children, eight-year-old Louis and seventeen-year-old Marie Thérèse, were separated. Louis was kept in the Temple and put in the care of a cobbler named Simon. The youngster appears to have died there in June 1795, but a rumor arose that Louis was secreted away and a dead child's body put in his place. For years afterward, many pretenders came forward, claiming to be the "little Dauphin."

SOCIETY

FRENCH SOCIETY WAS still largely rural and relied on agriculture as the primary occupation and the base on which the economy was built. When Henry of Navarre ascended the throne, efforts were made to reclaim land and revitalize agriculture. During the seventeenth century, years of colder, wetter weather led to numerous crop failures and tempered economic recovery, leading to a depression and a marked increase in the prices of wheat and other staple foods. Crisis years were 1618 and 1630, with catastrophic failures occuring from 1647 to 1651. The winter of 1730, one of the coldest ever recorded, led to scores of deaths. In addition, the plague and other deadly diseases continued to attack with sinister regularity.

Toward the end of the eighteenth century, society still had not recovered. A series of bad harvests resulted in rapidly increasing prices to the extent that the price of bread alone consumed nearly half the poor person's income.

Such distresses made the gap between the wealthy and the poor that much more significant and that much harder to bear. As warfare continued to keep the government in need of revenue, the tax burden on the peasants increased. During the reign of Louis XIV, local rioting soon grew into widespread rebellion known as the Fronde.

In spite of all the problems, the age of the Bourbons, and in particular the reign of Louis XIV, was an age of cultural achievements and a golden age for the French language. Blaise Pascal, René Descartes, and Denis Diderot proved French worthy of scientific discussion, and its status was raised further by the writings of the philosophers Voltaire and Jean Jacques Rousseau, by the dramatic works of Jean Racine and Pierre Corneille, and by the popular comedies of playwright Molière.

It was also an age of architectural achievements. The splendor, magnificence, and opulence of the baroque style reached its peak in the construction of the main palaces of Versailles. The heaviness of that style gave way during the reign of Louis XV to the lighter, more refined rococo style of architecture. This style, an example of which is the Petit Trianon at Versailles, is easily recognized by its scrolls and shell designs.

While privileged society was living in such beautiful splendor, the common man was living in dire circumstance and he was growing more and more bitter with the injustice of French society and his inability to change it. His opportunity would come with the outbreak of revolution.

The French Revolution was not the result of the poverty and misery among the people, however. It was a middle-class revolt from the beginning, with objectives that were primarily for the benefit of the bourgeoisie. The middle class, having risen to a position of great affluence and prestige, was the dominant economic class in France. And yet, no matter how much wealth a merchant, banker, lawyer, or manufacturer might acquire, he had none of the political privileges granted to the upper class, none of the voting rights, and he was looked down upon as unworthy and inferior by the idle rich. It became more and more difficult for this new social group to see problems in French society yet be powerless to do anything about them. They soon began to demand a voice in politics commensurate to their economic position.

The bourgeoisie also called for economic liberties and an end to the government's protectionist policies. That policy had been of great benefit when France was just beginning to build its economy, but the country's merchants and manufacturers now believed it was hindering economic growth.

Another cause for revolution can be found in the inequitable system of taxation. There were direct taxes, which included the *taille,* the tax on real and personal property; the poll tax; and an income tax of around 10 percent. There were also indirect taxes that were added to the prices of commodities and paid by the consumer. These included tariffs on imports, tolls levied on goods shipped within France; and the tax on salt called the *gabelle*. The indirect taxes were fairly evenly distributed, as they were consumer taxes. The direct taxes, however, were not. The clergy and all Church property were exempt from all direct taxes, and the nobility used their influence and every privilege available to obtain the same exemptions. The main tax burden, therefore, was placed on the bourgeoisie and the poor.

The revolt originated among the middle class, but it needed men from the lower class to help see it through. The peasants' dismal place in society and the relics of feudalism that kept them from bettering themselves gave them a reason to follow the revolutionary leaders. Though the vast majority of the country's peasants were free men who owned their own small plots of land, they were still obligated to perform feudal obligations that had their beginnings in the Middle Ages. One such obligation was the payment of rent to the lord who had previously owned the peasant's land. Other obligations included a payment to the lord when a tract of land was sold and the payment of *banalités*—fees paid to the lord for the use of various facilities he owned, such as a baking oven, flour mill, and wine press. By this point in time, most peasants owned their own ovens and mills, yet the *banalités* continued to be collected. Another obligation was the *corvée,* whereby peasants were required to give the government several weeks of unpaid labor to maintain the nation's roadways. No other class was required to perform this service. Peasants were also supposed to turn a blind eye to the hunting privileges of the nobles that allowed them to hunt when and wherever they so chose, regardless of the damage done to peasants' crops and fields. When the bourgeoisie called upon the peasants to challenge their role in society and join the revolution, they were more than ready.

RELIGION

AT THE BEGINNING of this time period, religion was a burning issue, and Henry IV sought to relieve the tension and eliminate the religious wars. In April 1598, the Edict of Nantes was signed, guaranteeing Protestants freedom of religion, the right to hold public office, and equal rights in employment.

Saint Francis de Sales and Saint Vincent de Paul were the foremost spiritual leaders of the Catholic people. Francis de Sales, one of the most outstanding leaders of the Counter-Reformation, managed to attract thousands back to the Catholic Church. He founded several schools and taught catechetics. In 1604, he met Jane Frances de Chantal, became her spiritual adviser, and in 1610, helped her form the Order of the Visitation.

Vincent de Paul was sent to France in 1607 on a secret mission to Henry IV and eventually became the chaplain to Queen Marguerite. He devoted his life to alleviating the suffering of the poor and established several hospitals and orphanages. He also formed the Congregation of the Mission, a missionary organization that ministered to the poor across the country. He founded the Sisters of Charity with Louise de Marillac in 1633.

The clergy, the First Estate of French society, were divided in two ranks: the higher clergy who were the cardinals, archbishops, bishops, and abbots; and the lower clergy, the parish priests. The gulf between the two ranks was as great as the gulf between nobleman and peasant. The lower clergy were usually recruited from the lower classes and were often as poor as the people they served. In an effort to ease their situation, it became commonplace for priests to stray from the high ideals to which they were obligated. In contrast, the higher clergy were often from noble families and naturally moved about in those same privileged circles. Though they made up less than 1 percent of the population, the higher clergy owned 20 percent of all the land in France and had accumulated vast treasuries and wealth. There were a number of both upper and lower clergymen whose sincere love of God called them into service. But, because of the clergy's exemption from taxes and because enough paid such little attention to religious affairs, the common man was convinced the Church and its leaders were corrupt and rotten to the core.

In 1766, a Commission of Regulars was created to point out abuses and suggest reforms. Such reforms were vigorously opposed by the upper clergy and the institution of the Church remained much the same. In 1789, the people took matters into their own hands. The National Assembly confiscated all property belonging to the Catholic Church and brought its clergy under a Civil Constitution that, for the first time in French history, made them accountable to the people.

NAMING

THE MOST NOTEWORTHY comment about names from this era is the growing trend to use more than one Christian name. It is first noticed in the royal family during the reign of Francis I (1515–1547) when his daughter Marguerite married Emmanuel-Philibert of Savoy. However, it wasn't until the ascent of the house of Bourbon that the use of multiple names became a trend.

The Reformation influenced naming by establishing a number of biblical names not in use before, but the French in no way went to the extremes practiced by the English Puritans. Marie continued to be the most popular name for women, both as a single name and in combination names. It was also bestowed upon males, though most commonly as a middle name, to bring the bearer under the protection of the Virgin Mary. Joseph was used among females for the same reason. One of the most popular male names was Jean.

FEMALE NAMES

Adaliz (nobility)
Adèle (noble) **Adala, Adela**
Adelaide (nobility)
Adelais (nobility)
Adeline (nobility)
Adrienne (from Hadrianus)
Aënor (light, torch, bright)
Agathe (good)
Agilina (formidable)
Aglaë (splendor)
Agnès (chaste, pure, sacred)
Aida (aide, helper)
Alberte (noble and bright)
Albertine (noble and bright)
Alette (nobility)
Alexandra (defender of mankind)
Alexandrine (defender of mankind)
Alia (all)
Alice (nobility)
Aliz (nobility)
Amarante (unfading)
Amélie (work, labor) **Amalie**
Amice (friendship)
Anaïs (grace, full of grace, mercy) A Provençal form of Anne.
Anastasia (resurrection)
Andrée (womanly)
Ange (angel)
Angèle (angel)
Angélique (angelic)
Anne (grace, full of grace, mercy) **Anna**
Anne Elisabeth (grace, mercy + God is my oath)
Anne Henriette (grace, mercy + home ruler)
Anne Josephe (grace, mercy + he shall add)
Anne Marie (grace, mercy + sea of bitterness or sorrow)
Annette (little Anne *grace, full of grace, mercy*)
Annis (chaste, pure, sacred)
Annora (honor, esteem) Norman form of Honora.

Antoinette (?, *priceless, of inestimable worth* is a folk definition)
Ariane (very holy one)
Arlette (little eagle)
Asceline (noble)
Athénais (?, Athena the goddess of wisdom)
Athene (?, Athena the goddess of wisdom)
Aude (old)
Aure (aura)
Aurélie (gold) **Aurèle**
Aurore (dawn, daybreak)
Aveline (?)
Aveza (?)
Babette (little Barbara *foreign woman*)
Barbara (foreign woman)
Barbe (foreign woman)
Barbot (little Barbe *foreign woman*)
Basilie (kingly)
Bastienne (from Sebastia)
Batilde (commanding battle maiden) **Batilda**
Beata (happy)
Béatriz (bringer of happiness and joy) **Béatrice, Béatrix**
Belinda (?, second element is *serpent*)
Benoîte (blessed)
Bernadette (bold as a bear)
Bernardine (bold as a bear)
Bernette (bold as a bear)
Berthe (bright)
Bertrade (bright raven)
Bibiane (alive)
Blanche (white) **Blanch**
Brigitte (strength)
Calliste (she that is most beautiful) **Calixte, Callixte**
Camille (virgin of unblemished character)
Caroline (full-grown)
Cassandra (?)
Catherine (pure) **Caterine**
Cécile (blind, dim-sighted)

Ceciliane (blind, dim-sighted)
Céleste (heavenly)
Celestine (heavenly)
Céline (heaven)
Cendrine (ashes)
Chantal (stone, boulder)
Charlotte (full-grown)
Christiane (a Christian)
Christine (a Christian) **Christin, Crisinet, Cristinet**
Claire (bright, clear, famous)
Claremond (bright protection, famous protection)
Clarice (bright, clear, famous)
Claude (lame)
Claudette (little Claude *lame*)
Claudine (lame)
Clémence (gentle, mild, clement)
Clémentine (gentle, mild, clement)
Clotilde (loud battle) **Chlotilde**
Colette (victory of the people) **Collette**
Colombe (dove)
Constance (constant, steadfast)
Corinne (maiden)
Corisande (?)
Cornelia (horn)
Cristina (a Christian, a follower of Christ)
Cyrille (lordly)
Danièle (God is my judge) **Danielle**
Delphine (from Delphi)
Denise (of Dionysus)
Désirée (desired)
Diane (divine)
Dominique (belonging to a lord)
Dorothée (gift of God)
Douce (sweet)
Edma (wealthy protection)
Edmée (wealthy protection) **Esmée**
Edwige (war of contention)
Egilina (formidable)
Eglentine (prickly; sweetbrier)
Elaine (light, torch, bright) **Elainne, Eleinne, Eleyne**
Elena (light, torch, bright)
Eléonore (light, torch, bright)
Éliane (of the sun)
Elisabeth (God is my oath) **Elizabeth**
Elisabeth Angélique (God is my oath + angelic)
Elisabeth Anne (God is my oath + grace, mercy)
Elisabeth Charlotte (God is my oath + full-grown)
Elisabeth Marie (God is my oath + sea of bitterness or sorrow)
Élise (God is my oath)
Éloise (hearty and wide)
Emeline (work, industrious) **Ameline, Ammeline, Emmeline**
Emilie (trying to equal or excel; rival)
Emilienne (little Emilie)
Emma (strength)
Emmanuelle (God with us)

Esclairmonde (bright protection, famous protection)
Esther (star; myrtle)
Étiennette (crown, garland)
Eufemie (well-spoken, fair of voice) **Euphémie**
Eugénie (nobility, excellence)
Eulalie (well-spoken)
Eunice (good victory)
Eustacie (steadfast, happy in harvest)
Evangeline (good news)
Eve (life)
Fabienne (a bean)
Fabiola (a bean)
Felicienne (little Félicie *lucky, happy*)
Félicité (happiness, felicity)
Félise (lucky, happy) **Félicie**
Fernande (peace; journey; youth, life + courage; venture, risk; ready, prepared)
Flavienne (yellow-haired)
Flore (a flower)
Florence (blooming, flourishing)
Frances (a Frenchwoman)
Françoise (French)
Françoise Louise (French + famous in war)
Françoise Marie (French + sea of bitterness or sorrow)
Frédégonde (peaceful war)
Frédérique (ruler of peace)
Gabrielle (God is my strength)
Geneviève (?, perhaps *tribal woman*)
Georgette (earth worker, farmer)
Germaine (a German)
Gertrude (spear strength)
Giselle (pledge)
Gunilda (war battle) **Gunnilda**
Hannah (grace, full of grace, mercy)
Hedwig (battle wide)
Hélène (light)
Héloïse (sound, hearty, and wide) **Helewis**
Henriette (home ruler) **Henriet, Henrietta**
Hermine (army man, soldier)
Hilde (war, battle) **Hilda**
Honorée (honor, esteem) **Ennoré, Enoré, Honoré**
Hortense (gardener)
Huguette (heart, mind, soul) **Huette**
Hyacinthe (hyacinth, bluebell)
Ida (labor)
Ingeborg (Ing's fortification)
Iphigénie (of royal birth)
Irénée (peace)
Isabelle (God is my oath) **Isabel, Ysabelle**
Iseut (ruler of the ice) **Isaut**
Jacinte (hyacinth, bluebell)
Jacqueline (supplanting, seizing by the heels)
Jacquette (supplanting, seizing by the heels)
Jane (God is gracious)
Jane Frances (God is gracious + a Frenchwoman)
Jeanne (God is gracious)

Jeannette (little Jeanne *God is gracious*)
Jeannine (God is gracious)
Joëlle (the Lord is God)
Johanne (God is gracious)
Jordane (a flowing down)
Joscelin (from the tribe of the Gauts) Joceline
Josée (he shall add)
Joséphe (he shall add)
Joséphine (he shall add)
Judith (praised; from Judah)
Julie (youth, downy)
Julienne (youth, downy)
Julitte (?, perhaps *praised*; *youth, downy*)
Justine (just, lawful)
Kalliroe (beautiful stream)
Laure (laurel)
Laurence (from Laurentum) Laurencia
Laurentine (from Laurentum)
Laurette (laurel)
Léa (weary)
Léonie (lion)
Léonne (lion)
Léonore (light, torch, bright)
Léontine (lion)
Liliane (lily)
Linnet (shapely)
Lisette (God is my oath)
Louise (famous in war)
Louise Elisabeth (famous in war + God is my oath)
Louise Isabelle (famous in war + God is my oath)
Louise Marie (famous in war + sea of bitterness or sorrow)
Louisette (little Louise *famous in war*)
Louison (famous in war)
Luce (light)
Lucette (little Luce *light*)
Lucie (light) Lucia
Lucienne (little Luce *light*)
Lucille (light)
Lydie (Lydian woman)
Mabila (lovable)
Madeleine (from Magdala)
Magali (?, possibly *pearl*) A Provençal name.
Manon (little Marie *sea of bitterness or sorrow*)
Marcelle (of Mars, warlike) Marcille
Marcelline (little Marcelle *of Mars, warlike*)
Margerie (a pearl)
Margot (a pearl)
Margoton (a pearl)
Marguerite (a pearl)
Mariamne (sea of bitterness or sorrow)
Marianne (sea of bitterness or sorrow + grace, full of grace, mercy)
Marie (sea of bitterness or sorrow) Maria
Marie Adélaïde (sea of bitterness or sorrow + nobility)
Marie Amélie (sea of bitterness or sorrow + work)
Marie Ange (sea of bitterness or sorrow + angel)

Marie Anne (sea of bitterness or sorrow + grace, mercy)
Marie Caroline (sea of bitterness or sorrow + full-grown)
Marie Claire (sea of bitterness or sorrow + bright, clear, famous)
Marie Émilie (sea of bitterness or sorrow + rival)
Marie France (sea of bitterness or sorrow + French)
Marie Josèphe (sea of bitterness or sorrow + he shall add)
Marie Joséphine (sea of bitterness or sorrow + he shall add)
Marielle (little Marie *sea of bitterness or sorrow*)
Marie Louise (sea of bitterness or sorrow + famous in war)
Marie Noëlle (sea of bitterness or sorrow + Christmas child)
Marie Thérèse (sea of bitterness or sorrow + harvester)
Mariette (little Marie *sea of bitterness or sorrow*)
Marie Zéphyrine (sea of bitterness or sorrow + the west wind)
Marthe (lady, mistress)
Martine (of Mars, warlike)
Matilde (mighty in battle) Mathilde
Maud (mighty in battle)
Mélanie (dark, black)
Melisent (work strength)
Melissa (a bee)
Mélusine (a water nymph)
Metheldred (mild strength)
Michèle (Who is like God?)
Micheline (little Michèle *Who is like God?*)
Mildred (mild strength)
Mirabelle (wondrous)
Miriam (sea of bitterness or sorrow)
Monique (?)
Muriel (sea bright)
Myriam (sea of bitterness or sorrow)
Nanette (little Anne *grace, full of grace, mercy*) Ninette
Natalie (natal day, Christmas child)
Nicole (victory of the people)
Nicolette (little Nicole *victory of the people*) Nicollet, Nicollette
Ninon (little Anne *grace, full of grace, mercy*)
Noëlle (born at Christmas)
Noémie (pleasant, beautiful)
Odette (little Odile *wealth, prosperity*)
Odile (wealth, prosperity)
Olympe (of Olympus)
Ophelie (help, succor)
Oriane (to rise)
Oriel (fire and strife)
Oriolt (fire and strife)
Ornette (flowering ash tree)
Ottilie (wealth, prosperity)
Pascale (born at Eastertime)
Patrice (a patrician)
Paule (small)
Paulette (little Paule *small*)
Pauline (little Paule *small*)
Perrine (little rock, little stone)
Philippa (lover of horses)

Philoméne (lover of strength)
Pierrette (little rock)
Rachel (ewe)
Raymonde (wise protection)
Rébecca (noose)
Régine (queenly)
Reine (queen)
Renée (reborn)
Romaine (a Roman)
Rosala (horse)
Rosalie (rosalia, the annual ceremony of hanging garlands of roses on tombs)
Rosamund (horse protection) **Rosamond**
Roslind (horse serpent)
Roxane (dawn of day)
Ruth (a friend)
Sabine (Sabine woman)
Salomé (peace)
Sarah (princess)
Séraphine (burning ones)
Sibylla (prophetess, fortune-teller)
Sidonie (fine cloth, linen)
Simone (heard)

Solange (yearly, annual; solemn, religious)
Sophie (wisdom)
Sophie Béatrix (wisdom + bringer of joy)
Sophie Josèphe (wisdom + he shall add)
Sophie Marie (wisdom + sea of bitterness or sorrow)
Stéphanie (a crown, a garland)
Suzanne (lily, rose)
Sybille (a fortune-teller, a prophetess)
Sylvie (of the woods)
Thérèse (harvester)
Tifaine (Epiphany, manifestation of God)
Valérie (strong, healthy)
Véronique (?, perhaps *true image; bringer of victory*)
Viole (violet)
Violette (little Viole *violet*)
Virginie (springlike, flourishing)
Vivienne (alive)
Willa (resolute)
Yolande (violet)
Yvette (archer)
Yvonne (archer)
Zéphyrine (the west wind)
Zoë (life) **Zoé**

MALE NAMES

Achille (?)
Adalard (noble and hard)
Adalbert (noble and bright) **Adelbert**
Adolphe (noble wolf)
Adrian (man from Hadrianus) **Adriane**
Agésilas (the goatskin shield of Zeus, a protection)
Ailemar (noble and famous) **Eilemar**
Aimery (work ruler) **Aimeric, Amaury, Aymery, Emery**
Aimo (home) **Aymo**
Alain (?, perhaps *handsome, rock*) **Alein**
Alard (noble and hard)
Alaric (ruler of all)
Albert (noble and bright)
Albin (white)
Alexandre (defender of mankind)
Alfred (elf counsel; wise counsel)
Algernon (mustached)
Alliaume (noble protection)
Alphonse (noble and ready)
Alphée (first)
Alveré (elf counsel)
Amalrich (work ruler) **Amalric, Amalriko, Amelric, Amelrich**
Amande (army man, soldier) **Amand**
Ambroise (immortal)
Amadeus (lover of God)
Amé (?)
Amias (?, perhaps *friendship*)

Amiel (industrious)
Amis (friendship)
Anastase (resurrection) **Anastasie**
Anatole (sunrise, daybreak)
Ancelot (divine)
André (manly)
Anne (grace, full of grace, mercy)
Anselm (God's helmet)
Antoine (?, *priceless, of inestimable worth* is a folk definition)
Ara (eagle)
Ardouin (brave friend)
Ariste (best)
Armand (soldier, warrior) **Armant**
Arnaud (eagle power) **Arnaut**
Arno (eagle)
Arnold (eagle power) **Arnault, Arnould**
Arnulf (eagle wolf)
Arsène (male, virile)
Artaud (brave ruler)
Arthur (?) **Artos**
Ascelin (from the tribe of the Gauts) **Acelin**
Auberi (elf ruler) **Aubry**
Aubert (noble and bright)
August (great, venerable) **Auguste**
Augustin (great, venerable)
Augustus (great, venerable)
Aurèle (gold)
Aurélien (golden)

Auveré (elf counsel)
Badaud (battle rule) **Badault**
Baldri (bold ruler, brave ruler) **Baudri**
Baldric (bold ruler, brave ruler)
Baldwin (bold friend, brave friend) Flemish form.
Baptiste (a baptizer)
Bardolph (bright wolf) **Bardolf**
Barnabé (son of exhortation)
Barthélemy (son of Talmai *hill, mound, furrows*) **Bartholomé, Bertelmeu**
Basil (kingly) **Basile**
Bastien (man from Sebastia)
Baudoin (bold friend, brave friend)
Bellamy (beautiful friend)
Bénédict (blessed)
Benigne (kind)
Benjamin (son of the right hand)
Benoît (blessed) **Benoist, Beneoit**
Beringer (bear spear)
Bernard (bold as a bear)
Bernardin (little Bernard *bold as a bear*)
Berthold (bear rule) **Berold, Berolt**
Bertin (bright friend)
Bertrand (bright raven) **Bertran**
Bevis (beautiful) **Beves**
Blaise (babbler)
Bouchard (big mouth)
Brian (force, strength; valor; high; kingly) Used in Brittany.
Brice (?)
Bruno (brown)
Camille (virgin of unblemished character)
Cecil (blind, dim-sighted)
Célestin (heavenly)
César (hairy; bluish gray)
Charles (full-grown, a man)
Charles Ferdinand (full-grown + peaceful venture, youthful courage)
Charles Louis (full-grown + famous in war)
Chrétien (a Christian, a follower of Christ)
Christian (a Christian, a follower of Christ) **Christen, Christin**
Christophe (bearing Christ)
Claude (lame)
Claudin (lame) **Clauden**
Clement (gentle, mild, clement)
Cléon (glory, the glorious)
Colombain (dove)
Conan (strength, high)
Conrad (bold counsel)
Constant (constant, steadfast) **Constans**
Constantine (constant, steadfast)
Corin (a spear)
Corneille (horn)
Crispin (curled)
Curtis (courteous)
Cyprien (from Cyprus)

Cyrille (lordly)
Dagobert (day bright)
Damien (tamer)
Daniel (judged by God)
Daudet (given by God)
David (beloved)
Delphin (a dolphin; from Delphi)
Démosthène (?)
Denis (of Dionysus) **Denys**
Déodat (given by God) Used in southern France.
Didier (longing)
Dieudonné (given by God) Used in northern France.
Dimitri (of Demeter)
Dion (of Zeus)
Dominique (belonging to a lord)
Donatien (given by God)
Drogo (burden bearer) **Drugo**
Dru (burden bearer)
Durand (enduring, lasting)
Ector (holding fast)
Edgar (wealthy spear)
Edmond (wealthy protector) **Edmonde, Edme**
Édouard (wealthy guardian) **Edouard**
Egmont (fearful protection, awesome protection)
Eloi (chosen)
Emery (ruler of strength)
Émile (emulating, trying to equal or excel, a rival)
Émilien (emulating, trying to equal or excel, a rival)
Emmanuel (God is with us)
Emmanuel Philibert (God is with us + very bright)
Emmanuel Baptist (God is with us + a baptizer)
Emmerich (ruler of strength)
Engelrand (angel raven) **Enguerran, Enguerrand**
Eric (eternal ruler)
Ernest (earnest, resolute) **Ernost, Ernst**
Esmé (loved)
Esmond (beautiful hand)
Étienne (a crown, garland)
Eudes (child)
Eudon (child)
Eugène (well-born, noble)
Eustache (steadfast; happy in harvest)
Évariste (well-pleasing)
Everard (boar strength) **Evrard**
Fabien (a bean)
Fabrice (workman, craftsman)
Faramond (journey protection)
Fargeau (of iron)
Félix (lucky, happy) **Felis**
Ferdinand (peace; journey; youth, life + courage; venture, risk; ready)
Ferrand (peace; journey; youth, life + courage; venture, risk; ready)
Fidèle (fidelity, faith, trust)
Filbert (very bright) **Filibert, Fulbert, Philbert, Philibert**
Firmin (firm, steadfast)

Flavien (yellow-haired) **Flavie**
Florent (blossoming, flourishing)
Florentin (blossoming, flourishing)
Florian (flowery)
Fortuné (fortune, chance)
Fouchier (people, folk)
Francis (a Frenchman, a freeman)
Franck (a Frank, a freeman)
François (French)
Frédéric (ruler of peace)
Fromont (free protection)
Fulk (people) **Fulke**
Gabriel (God is my strength)
Garnier (protecting army)
Gascon (?, perhaps *guest, stranger; from Gascony*)
Gaspard (treasure master)
Gaston (?, possibly *guest, stranger; from Gascony*)
Gaudens (rejoicing)
Gauvain (battle hawk)
Geoffroi (district; traveler; pledge + peace)
Georges (earth worker, farmer)
Gerald (spear rule) **Geralt**
Gérard (brave with the spear) **Girard, Girardat, Girardet**
Gérardin (brave with the spear)
Gerbert (bright spear)
Germain (a German)
Gervais (servant of the spear)
Giffard (give + bold, fierce)
Gilbert (bright pledge)
Gilles (goatskin shield of Zeus; a protection) **Gile, Giles**
Godard (god hard)
Godfry (God's peace) **Godefry**
Gregoire (vigilant, watchful)
Griffin (like a griffin, monstrous)
Guillard (resolute protector)
Guillaud (resolute protector) **Guillod, Guillot, Guilloteaux**
Guillaume (resolute protector) **Guillelmus, Guillerme, Guillermaux, Guillermus**
Guillaumet (resolute protector) **Guillemet, Guillermet**
Guillon (resolute protector)
Guiscard (?)
Gunter (bold in war)
Guy (a guide, a leader)
Guyon (a guide, a leader)
Haerveu (battle worthy) Breton name.
Hamo (home, house)
Hamon (home, house)
Hardouin (hard friend)
Hector (holding fast, restraining)
Helgaud (prosperous; hearty, hale) **Helgald**
Henriot (home ruler) **Henrioud**
Henry (home ruler) **Henri**
Herbert (army bright)
Hercule (glory of Hera)
Hardouin (hard friend)
Herman (army man, soldier)

Hervé (battle worthy)
Hilaire (cheerful)
Hippolyte (freer of horses)
Hubert (bright heart)
Hue (heart, mind, soul) Used in the south.
Hugh (heart, mind, soul)
Hugo (heart, mind, soul)
Hugolin (heart, mind, soul)
Hugon (heart, mind, soul) Used in the north.
Hugot (heart, mind, soul) **Huguelet, Huguet**
Hugues (heart, mind, soul) Used in the north.
Humbert (people bright)
Huon (heart, mind, soul) Used in the south.
Ignace (?, perhaps *fire*)
Ilbert (battle bright) **Ilberd**
Imbert (iron people) **Isembert**
Ingelram (angel raven)
Isaak (laughter)
Isaïe (God is salvation)
Isidore (gift of Isis)
Ives (archer) **Ive**
Ivon (archer)
Jacques (supplanting, seizing by the heels)
Jean (God is gracious)
Jean Baptiste (God is gracious + a baptizer)
Jean Christian (God is gracious + a Christian)
Jean Claude (God is gracious + lame)
Jean Louis (God is gracious + famous in war)
Jean Luc (God is gracious + light; man from Lucania)
Jean Marc (God is gracious + of Mars, warlike)
Jean Michel (God is gracious + Who is like God?)
Jean Paul (God is gracious + small)
Jean Pierre (God is gracious + a rock)
Jenico (?, perhaps *fire*) Provençal form of Ignace.
Jérémie (God will uplift)
Jérôme (sacred name)
Joachim (God will establish)
Joël (the Lord is God)
Joseph (he shall add)
Jourdain (a flowing down)
Judicael (sportive) **Judical** A Breton name.
Julien (youth, downy)
Juste (just, fair)
Justin (just, fair)
Juvénal (youth)
Karl (a man, freeman, peasant)
Kaspar (treasure master)
Klemens (mild, gentle, merciful)
Konrad (wise counsel)
Konstantin (constant, steadfast)
Lambert (bright land)
Lance (land)
Lancelin (little Lance *land*)
Lancelot (little Lance *land*)
Laurence (man from Laurentum) **Laurent**
Leo (lion)

Léon (lion)
Léonard (lion hard, bold as a lion)
Léonce (lion)
Léopold (bold people)
Lionel (little Léon *lion*)
Lothar (famous warrior)
Louis (famous in war)
Louis Antoine (famous in war + ?, *priceless, of inestimable worth* is a folk definition)
Louis Baptiste (famous in war + a baptizer)
Louis François (famous in war + French)
Louis Joseph (famous in war + he shall add)
Louis Philip (famous in war + lover of horses)
Louis Xavier (famous in war + the new house)
Luc (light; man from Lucania)
Lucien (light)
Ludwig (famous in war)
Macaire (blessed)
Magnus (great)
Manfred (man of peace)
Marc (?, perhaps *Mars; manly; soft, tender*)
Marcel (of Mars, warlike)
Marcellin (little Marcel *of Mars, warlike*)
Martin (of Mars, warlike)
Matthieu (gift of God) **Matheu**
Mauger (spear grinder)
Maynard (strong and hardy)
Meurisse (a Moor, dark-skinned)
Michel (Who is like God?)
Miles (?, perhaps *mild, peaceful; merciful*)
Milo (?, perhaps *mild, peaceful; merciful*)
Milon (?, perhaps *mild, peaceful; merciful*)
Moïse (drawn out of the water)
Nathaniel (God has given) **Nathanael**
Nazaire (from Nazareth)
Nicodème (victory of the people)
Nicol (victory of the people) **Nicod, Nicodet, Nicoud**
Nicolas (victory of the people) **Nicollaud, Nicollier, Nicoulaz**
Nicollin (little Nicolas *victory of the people*)
Noë (rest, comfort)
Noël (born at Christmas)
Odo (wealth)
Ogier (rich spear)
Olivier (olive tree)
Onfroi (people peace)
Osanne (hosannah)
Osbert (God bright)
Osmond (God protection) **Osmund**
Pascal (born at Easter)
Patrice (a patrician)
Paul (small) **Pol**
Paulin (little Paul *small*)
Perceval (pierce the valley) **Percevale**
Peter (rock, stone)
Peter Marie (rock, stone + sea of bitterness or sorrow)
Philibert (very bright, very famous)

Philip (lover of horses) **Phelip, Phelipe, Phelipp, Philippe, Phillipe, Phillippe**
Philip Antoine (lover of horses + ?, *priceless, of inestimable worth* is a folk definition)
Philip Emmanuel (lover of horses + God is with us)
Philippes (lover of horses) **Phelipes, Phellipes, Phelippes, Philipes, Phillipes, Phillippes**
Philipot (little Philip *lover of horses*)
Pierre (a rock, a stone)
Prosper (prosperous, favorable)
Quentin (fifth)
Raimund (counsel protection) **Raymond, Reimund, Reymond, Reymonde**
Rainier (wise army)
Randolf (shield wolf) **Randolph, Randulf**
Ranfred (counsel peace)
Raoul (counsel wolf) **Raul**
Raphael (God has healed)
Regnault (ruler of judgment)
Rémy (oarsman)
René (rebirth)
Reynard (counsel hard) **Rainard**
Reynaud (powerful protection) **Reinald, Renaud**
Richard (stern king)
Robert (bright with fame) **Roberte**
Robin (bright with fame) **Robineaux**
Roby (bright with fame)
Roch (rest)
Rodolphe (famous wolf)
Roger (famous with the spear)
Roland (famous land) **Rolande, Rolland, Rollande**
Rolf (famous wolf)
Romain (a Roman)
Samuel (name of God)
Sandre (defender of mankind)
Sanson (the sun)
Saül (asked of, borrowed)
Sébastien (man of Sebastia)
Secord (hard victory)
Séverin (severe, strict)
Sigmund (victory protection)
Simon (heard)
Spiro (to breathe, to blow)
Stéphane (a crown, garland)
Sylvain (of the woods)
Sylvestre (of the woods)
Symphorien (bearing together)
Talbot (pillager, bandit; lampblack)
Tancred (think counsel)
Terrick (ruler of the people)
Théodor (ruler of the people) **Théodore, Théodose**
Théophile (beloved of God)
Thibaut (people bold) **Thibault**
Thierry (ruler of the people)
Thomas (a twin)
Timothée (honor, respect)

Toussaint (all saints) Given to those born near All Saints' Day.
Tristan (tumult, sadness)
Trudeau (Thor's power)
Turstan (Thor's stone) **Turstin**
Ulrich (wolf rule)
Urbain (dweller in a village) **Urban**
Valdemar (famous ruler)
Valentin (healthy, strong)
Valére (to be strong)
Valéry (foreign ruler) **Valéran**
Victor (victory)

Vincent (conquering)
Vivien (alive)
Vuillaume (resolute protector) **Vuillerme, Vulliamoz, Vulliamy, Vulliémoz**
Vuille (resolute protector) **Vuilliet, Vullioud**
Vuillemin (resolute protector) **Vulliemin**
Willelm (resolute protector) A Normandy form of William.
Xavier (the new house)
Yann (God is gracious) A Breton form of John.
Yves (archer)
Yvon (archer)

SURNAMES

André (manly)
Arnaud (eagle power) **Arnaut**
Aubert (noble and bright)
Auguste (great, venerable)
Ballou (from Bellou)
Barraud (bear-might) **Barratt**
Bassett (the little, short, fat one)
Bastien (from Sebasta)
Beaufort (beautiful fort, beautiful stronghold)
Beaufoy (beautiful beech tree)
Beaulieu (fair place)
de Beauchamp (from Beauchamp *fair field*)
de Beaumont (from Beaumont *beautiful mountain*)
de Beauregard (from Beauregard *beautiful place*)
Bec (mouth)
Benoît (blessed)
Berger (shephard) **Bergier**
Bertrand (bright raven) **Bertran**
Berube (dweller on the marshy ground)
Blondeau (blond, fair-complexioned)
Blondel (blond, fair-complexioned)
Blondet (blond, fair-complexioned)
Bonnin (little good one)
Bouchard (big mouth)
Bouteiller (cup-bearer, butler)
Bouvier (cattle-drover)
Brun (brown)
Brunel (little brown one)
Burnell (the dark one)
Bussy (from the thicket)
Cabot (small-headed)
Caillard (piebald; a quail) **Callard**
Castelnau (from the new castle) **Castelnau**
Cazenove (from the new house) **Cazneau**
Challoner (quilt maker, seller of quilts) **Chaloner**
Chamberlain (steward of the chamber)
Chambres (chamber attendant)
Champ (from the field)
Chandler (candle maker, seller of candles)
Chanter (singer)

Chapele (dweller at the chapel) **Chapell, Chappele, Chappelle**
Chartier (a cart driver)
Chastel (from the castle) **Chastell**
le Clerc (clerk)
Coquard (a cock, rooster)
Coudray (from the hazel grove)
Courtier (agent, broker)
D'Allemagne (from Germany) **D'Almaine**
de Fraine (of the ash tree) **Defraine**
de la Croix (of the cross) **Delacroix**
de la Rue (of the street) **Delarue**
Descartes (dweller at the outskirts of town)
Desmoulins (dweller by the mill)
De Spagne (from Spain)
de Vere (of the fishing place) **Devere**
Devereaux (from Evreux) **Devereux**
Dionne (of Dionysus)
Dorat (a gilder)
Dore (a gilder)
Doucette (little sweet one)
Du Bois (of the woods) **des Bois, Dubois, Dubos**
Du Buisson (of the thicket) **Dubuisson**
Duchêne (of the oak tree)
Duchesne (of the oak tree) **Duquesne**
Du Clos (of the enclosure) **Duclos**
Du Feu (of the beech tree) **Dufeu**
Du Lieu (of the place) **Dulieu**
Dumas (of the little farm)
Du Mont (of the mountain) **Dumont**
Du Parc (of the park) **Duparc**
Du Pont (of the bridge) **Dupont**
Du Prat (of the meadow) **Duprat**
Du Pre (of the meadow) **Dupre**
Du Puis (of the well, of the pit) **Dupuis**
Du Puy (of the high place) **Dupuy**
Durand (enduring) **Duran**
Du Val (of the valley) **Duval, Duvall**
Farge (forge)
Fargues (from Fargues *forges*)

Farjeon (little Farge *forge*)
Faudel (cattle or sheep barn)
Favre (smith, carpenter) **Faure**
Ferrand (peaceful journey)
Feuillette (dweller at the sign of the leaf [near a wine merchant])
Fleche (an archer)
Fleury (dweller by the flowers)
Fournier (oven-keeper; parish baker)
Girardin (spear hard)
Giraud (spear hard)
Grellier (slender, slim) **Grelier**
Guerrier (warrior)
Herriott (little Henry *home ruler*)
Huguelet (little Hugues *heart, mind, spirit*)
Jolie (agreeable, pleasant)
Jourdain (a flowing down)
La Cour (the short one)
La Croix (dweller near the cross)
Lafayette (dweller near a small grove of beeches)
Laffitte (dweller near the boundary stone)
Lanier (a weaver or seller of wool)
La Porte (dweller near the gate)
Larousse (red-haired, ruddy-complexioned)
La Rue (dweller on the street)
Laurent (man from Laurentum)
La Valle (dweller in the valley)
La Vigne (dweller near the vineyard)
Le Beau (the handsome one)
Le Blanc (the white-haired one, fair complexioned)
Le Grand (the large one)
Lejeune (the younger)
Lemaitre (the overseer)
Lesueur (maker or seller of shoes)
Luce (light)
Lucette (little light)
Marais (dweller near the marsh)
Marchand (a merchant)
Martel (the hammer)
Martineau (little Martin *of Mars, warlike*)
Mathieu (gift of God)
Mercier (seller of fine cloth)
Merritt (a tenant farmer)

Meserve (a surveyor of land)
Minott (measurer of goods) **Minot**
Moliere (dweller near the quarry)
Moline (from Moline *mill*)
Moreau (from Moreau *dark-skinned, a Moor*)
Moser (seller of vegetables)
Nason (small nose)
Olivier (owner of an olive grove)
Orfevre (maker and seller of golden articles)
Pasteur (a shepherd)
Petit (little)
Petitperrin (little Pierre *rock*)
Picard (from Picardy *pike men*)
Pierpont (dweller near the stone bridge)
Poincare (square fist; a strong man)
Poirier (grower and seller of pears)
Poisson (seller of fish)
Poupard (child) **Poupart**
Prévost (commander)
Regis (kingly)
Renaud (ruler of judgment)
Ricard (stern king)
Rivière (river)
Rougemont (red mountain)
Royer (wheelwright)
Saulnier (gatherer or seller of salt)
Savoy (from Savoy) **Savoie**
Séverin (severe)
Taillandier (maker or seller of iron articles)
Taillefer (cut iron)
Tailleur (a tailor)
Thibaud (people hard) **Thibault, Thibaut, Thibeau**
Thibodeau (people bold) **Thibedeau, Thibideau**
Thierry (people ruler)
Toussaint (all saints)
Trudeau (Thor's power)
Vaillant (valiant one)
Vaux (from Vaux *the valley*)
Vavasseur (under-vassal)
Verdier (a gamekeeper)
Vernier (protecting army) **Verniere**
Villiers (from Villiers *the hamlet*)
Wilmot (resolute protector)

Chapter Six

THE REVOLUTION, THE RESTORATION OF THE BOURBONS, AND THE HOUSE OF BOURBON-ORLÉANS
[1793–1848]

POLITICS

THE FRENCH REVOLUTION did not end with the execution of Louis XVI and Marie Antoinette. Instead, it moved into a second stage dominated not by the bourgeoisie but by the lower classes. The second stage was much more violent than the first and included the Reign of Terror that lasted from the summer of 1793 to 1794. The primary leaders of the extremist factions of the Revolution were Jean Paul Marat, a champion for the lower classes; Georges Jacques Danton, who provoked people to rebellion, then organized the Reign of Terror; and Maximilien Robespierre, president of the National Convention and a believer that action by any means to achieve a desired end was justifiable.

After the execution of Louis XVI, the British expelled the diplomatic representative of the French Republic. In retaliation, the revolutionaries declared war on England and Holland and announced they were ready to help the people of other nations achieve the same liberties as had the French. Their proclamation was not taken kindly by Europe's monarchs and the years from 1793 to 1815 were spent involved in wars with many countries, including Austria, Prussia, Spain, Portugal, Russia, the Kingdom of Naples, and the Kingdom of Sardinia.

In addition to those wars, the French Republic had to deal with civil unrest and rebellion. The common man who had been called into the revolution was expecting to see beneficial reforms come his way. While he was pleased to see the end of feudalism, he was not pleased to see massive amounts of confiscated lands going to the bourgeois, nor was he happy with the new municipalities and administrative units they dominated. He felt as if he had traded one master for another. There were also many royalists within the country, and others who just wanted to stay out of the whole mess. Therefore, when the government of the republic called for the conscription of 300,000 men to fight its wars, the opposition revolted.

Republican forces were viciously attacked, and they retaliated with just as much brutality. In order to put down internal unrest, harsh measures were taken that included organizing the Committee of Public Safety to identify suspected royalists and bring them to trial. The president of the National Convention, extremist leader Maximilien Robespierre, justified the measures as a necessary means to achieve civil peace and further revolutionary progress. It's estimated that approximately 20,000 people opposing the republic were beheaded during the Reign of Terror (September 1793–July 1794). During the last six weeks of Robespierre's presidency, 1,285 people lost their lives on the scaffold in Paris. Such a policy could not be tolerated. Robespierre was seized, speedily pronounced guilty, and in July 1794, he and twenty-one of his lieutenants met their fates with the guillotine.

Jean Paul Marat had died in 1793 after being stabbed in the heart by a moderate, and Georges Jacques Danton met his end at the guillotine after deciding less ruthless measures and compromise were the better ways to run the Revolution. Thus, the Revolution had devoured its own children and the Reign of Terror had come to an end.

The end of the second stage of the Revolution is known as the Thermidorian Reaction, so called from the month of Thermidor in the new calendar. During this time, the remaining leaders became increasingly conservative and repealed both the law against ''suspects'' and the law fixing maximum prices. Political prisoners were released, the Committee of Public Safety was reformed, and revolutionary extremists were forced into hiding. Priests, nobles, and royalists who had emigrated in fear of their lives began returning to their homeland and added their influence to the new conservative movement.

The third and final stage of the French Revolution began in 1795 when the National Convention adopted the Constitution of the Year III. The constitution granted voting rights to all adult males who could read and write, and it included a bill of rights and a declaration of citizens' duties. Voting was limited to the election of electors, who would then choose the members of the legislature. Only proprietors of farms and those with annual incomes equivalent to 100 days of paid labor could be electors. Executive power was given to a board (the Directory) who were chosen from the legislature.

The first two stages of the Revolution were fought by people who sincerely wanted a change in the social and political structure of France, many of whom were idealists in search of the perfect society. By contrast, the third stage was marked by cynicism and corruption as people exchanged their burning desire for reform for new opportunities to get rich. And they took advantage of every favor and privilege to accomplish that goal. The Directory was totally corrupt, and the directors' lives were ones of brazen extravagance. Graft, bribery, speculation, and gambling were everyday occurrences, and the common man was once again left with a life of grinding poverty.

Autumn of 1799 marks the coup d'état of Napoleon Bonaparte and the end of the French Revolution. The Directory had involved the country in armed conflict with Great Britain, Austria, and Russia and tried to pay for the war effort by issuing more paper money. As a result, inflation skyrocketed until the point that the paper money was worth less than 1 percent of its face value. The Directors were greatly resented for their incompetence and their indifference to the common person, so much so that Napoleon Bonaparte, a general and a war hero of the Italian campaign, was readily embraced as the country's knight in shining armor.

Napoleon became First Consul in 1799, and Consul for Life in 1802, when he obtained consent to extend his term of office from ten years to life. In 1804, he won permission to turn the republic into an empire, and in an impressive ceremony in the Cathedral of Notre Dame, he placed the crown upon his own head, becoming Napoleon I, Emperor of the French.

As leader of the French, Napoleon took the accomplishments of his predecessors and improved upon them. He centralized government, put the country on a firmer financial foundation, and put control of the currency in the hands of the private Bank of France. He saw to legal reforms and ordered the establishment of schools in every major town, brought military and technical schools under the control of the government, and founded a national university to supervise the entire education system.

Napoleon had a succession of military victories in the early years of his rule that extended the boundaries of the French Empire. By 1808, he had managed to place family members on several European thrones, thereby indirectly ruling over a great deal of Europe. He put his brother Louis on the throne of Holland, made his brother Jerome king of Westphalia, and made his brother Joseph king of Naples. From that time on, however, his personal and political life began to decay as his egotistical belief that he was a man of destiny kept him from accepting guidance from his advisers and provoked him into a continual quest for more power— a quest paid for with the lives of the finest and bravest France had to offer. It's estimated that at least 800,000 young men died in the fifteen years of Napoleon's rule.

In the spring of 1812, Napoleon took on Czar Alexander. He sent an army of 600,000 troops to Russia, but the czar refused to make a stand, and French troops were drawn further into Russia. By late October, Napoleon had accomplished nothing and decided to head for home. He had waited much too long, however, and the severe Russian winter descended upon his troops before they made it across the border. Nearly 300,000 young men died of starvation, disease, and exposure.

That disastrous campaign showed the rest of Europe that Napoleon was not invincible and they allied themselves against him. In 1813, an allied army cornered Napoleon's forces at Leipzig and the Battle of the Nations was fought. Napoleon and his forces were beaten, and his vassal states deserted him. France itself was invaded, and the allied forces marched on Paris in March 1814.

On April 12, 1814, Napoleon was forced to sign the Treaty of Fontainebleau. In exchange for renouncing all claims to the French throne, he was granted full sovereignty over the tiny island of Elba and received a yearly pension of two million francs. It was decided that the Bourbon line should be restored in the person of Louis XVIII, brother to guillotined Louis XVI, with the agreement that the monarchy be limited and constitutional.

Meanwhile, Napoleon was resenting his banishment to his tiny island kingdom and was looking for the opportunity to escape. Not everyone in France was happy with the Restoration government. Some supporters of the Empire had their jobs given to returning émigrés, a part of the army had been disbanded and its officers put on half-pay, and unemployment remained high. People were also put off by the effrontery of the returning nobles of the *ancien régime* and the lack of leadership provided by the king.

He slipped away from Elba in the spring of 1815. After reaching the French coast, he was jubilantly welcomed by the peasants and the soldiers who had been sent to intercept him. In twenty days' time, Napoleon reached Paris but was unable to confront the king; Louis XVIII and his family had already fled the city for Belgium.

The European allies declared Napoleon an outlaw and proposed to depose him by force. Napoleon assembled a large army and went after the allied forces in the hopes of defeating them before they had a chance to invade France. The result was bitter defeat at the Battle of Waterloo in Belgium. Napoleon returned to Paris, abdicated a second time, and made plans to go to America. Instead, he was forced to hide out on a British ship and was banished by the British government to the small South Atlantic island of Saint Helena. Napoleon Bonaparte died there on May 5, 1821. Louis XVIII was returned once again to the throne of France, and allied forces remained in the country to ensure that he stayed there.

Louis XVIII had been married at the age of fifteen to Marie Josephine of Saxony, a shockingly ugly young woman with huge black beetle brows. Louis had the same physical defect as his elder brother, but never went to the trouble of having his corrected, so it was quite likely the marriage was never consummated. Louis consoled himself with several close relationships, both with women and men, and Marie Josephine did the same with alcohol and girls. The queen died in England in 1810.

As an adult, Louis was extremely corpulent and suffered from gout. Because of his difficulty walking, he became the first king in French history to forgo a coronation ceremony. In 1824, his physical problems worsened, and on September 16, after weeks of agonizing pain from his gouty, ulcerated legs, Louis XVIII died. His brother, Charles X, inherited the throne.

Charles was a completely different man than his elder brothers. He was tall, well-built, and handsome. He was married at sixteen to Marie Thérèse, the sister of Louis XVIII's Marie Josephine, and had four children. Unfortunately, Marie Thérèse was nearly as ugly as her sister, and Charles was unfaithful to her until her death in 1805.

Charles organized a spectacular coronation ceremony for himself in May 1825, never knowing it was to be the last coronation of a king of France. At the beginning of his reign, he was quite popular, but once the people realized one of his goals was a return to absolutism, that popularity greatly declined. In 1830, the Chamber of Deputies presented Charles with an address stating their belief that the king was not putting the views of the people before his own. Charles responded by dissolving the chamber and ordering new elections. Of the 221 members who had opposed him, 202 were reelected. Rather than concede to the will of the people, Charles and his adviser decided a firmer hand was necessary. In July 1830, he signed four ordinances. The first put significant restrictions on the press, suppressing freedom of speech; the second illegally dissolved the chamber; the third restricted the franchise; and the fourth fixed the date for new elections. His audacity led to a three-day revolt. Charles realized his mistake and sent a representative to the opposition, telling them he would bow to their wishes. He was too late. The opposition had already offered the crown to the liberal Duke of Orléans.

Charles abdicated in favor of his young grandson, the Duke of Bordeaux (who never came to power), and left the country. He went first to Scotland, where he stayed for two years as a guest of the British crown, then moved to Prague, where he was a guest of the Austrian king. In 1836 he left for Gorizia but contracted cholera on arrival. He died soon after in November.

After Charles left, the Chamber of Deputies voted to continue the monarchy with the Duke of Orléans ruling as Louis-Philippe I, King of the French. After leading quite an adventurous life in his younger years, Louis-Philippe went to Sicily and fell in love and married the king's daughter, Marie-Amélie. The couple had ten children, seven of whom survived to distinguish themselves in one way or another. Their eldest daughter, Louise Marie, became the first Queen of the Belgians. Their youngest daughter, Clementine, married Prince Augustus of Saxe-Coburg and Gotha and became the mother of the first king of Bulgaria.

Louis-Philippe was fifty-seven years old and set in his ways when he ascended the throne of France. He had the same problem as his predesessors: the inability to accept the concept of a constitutional monarchy and the inability to understand that he ruled by will of the people, not by divine right. By 1848, opposition had grown strong enough that the king was forced to abdicate. Louis-Philippe and Marie-Amélie disguised themselves, took the false names of Mr. and Mrs. William Smith, and set out for the coast in a hackney carriage. A ship finally took them to England where they spent the remainder of their lives. Louis-Philippe died in 1850, but Marie-Amélie was to survive until 1866. So died the last king and queen of France.

SOCIETY

FRENCH SOCIETY AT the beginning of the Revolution was just as bad off as it had been under the monarchy of Louis XVI. Prices continued to rise, goods became scarce, and the republic was at war both within and without its boundaries. The government recognized the need for reforms and several were actually carried out. Among them were the prohibition of imprisonment for debt; the abolition of slavery in the French colonies; the repeal of primogeniture so inheritances could be shared; and the establishment of the metric system. In addition, prices for grain and other necessities were fixed, and the very real threat of the guillotine kept merchants from unfairly profiting at the expense of the poor.

One of the most significant achievements of Napoleon's years in office was the establishment of the Civil Code that remains to this day as the foundation of the French legal system. The code was based on the attitude of the times, and it appears to be a very archaic document by today's standards. The code established class inequality, put women forever under the guardianship of men, and reinstated slavery in the colonies. Primogeniture was reinstated, and a new class of nobility was created from wealthy businessmen.

RELIGION

ONE OF THE most interesting aspects of the Revolution had to do with religion. During the Reign of Terror, an effort was made to abolish Christianity and replace it with the worship of Reason. A new calendar was created that began the year with the birthday of the republic, September 22, 1792, and divided the months in such as way as to eliminate the Christian Sunday.

When Robespierre came to power, he replaced the cult of Reason with the cult of the Supreme Being, which allowed for the worship of a supreme being and promoted a belief in the immortality of the soul. Following that, the National Convention decided religion needed to be a private concern and that all religions not hostile to the government should be tolerated equally.

When Napoleon came to power, he reestablished the union between the Catholic Church and the state. Though the privileges the Church once enjoyed were not restored, it was given an advantage over other religions. Interestingly, Napoleon had great contempt for all religions and even treated the Pope with disrespect. He exiled Pius VII to Savonna in 1809 and kept him a virtual prisoner for four years.

NAMING

THE FRENCH REVOLUTION affected all aspects of French society—even to the extent that people were told which names could be used for their children. Acceptable names were those of famous persons in history, such as saints' names, biblical names, and the names of kings and queens. In addition, the names had to be spelled in a French way; foreign spellings or variants were not allowed. Unless a name was chosen that followed those stipulations, the public registrar would not record the birth.

FEMALE NAMES

Abelia (breath) **Abella**
Adélaïde (nobility)
Adèle (noble)
Adeline (nobility)
Adrienne (from Hadrianus)
Aënor (light, torch, bright)
Agathe (good)
Agilina (formidable)
Aglaë (splendor)
Agnès (chaste, pure, sacred)
Aida (aide, helper)
Alberte (noble and bright)
Albertine (noble and bright)

Alette (nobility)
Alexandra (defender of mankind)
Alexandrine (defender of mankind)
Alia (all)
Alice (nobility)
Aliz (nobility) **Alix**
Amarante (unfading)
Amélie (work, labor) **Amalie**
Amice (friendship)
Anaïs (grace, full of grace, mercy) A Provençal form of Anne.
Anastasia (resurrection)
Andrée (womanly)
Ange (angel)

Angèle (angel)
Angélique (angelic)
Anne (grace, full of grace, mercy) **Anna**
Anne-Elisabeth (grace, mercy + God is my oath)
Anne-Henriette (grace, mercy + home ruler)
Anne-Josephe (grace, mercy + he shall add)
Anne-Marie (grace, mercy + sea of bitterness or sorrow)
Annette (little Anne *grace, full of grace, mercy*)
Annis (chaste, pure, sacred)
Annora (honor, esteem) Norman form of Honora.
Antoinette (?, *priceless, of inestimable worth* is a folk definition)
Ariane (very holy one)
Arlette (little eagle)
Asceline (noble)
Athénais (?, Athena the goddess of wisdom)
Athene (?, Athena the goddess of wisdom)
Aude (old)
Aure (aura)
Aurélie (gold) **Aurèle**
Aurore (dawn, daybreak)
Aveline (?)
Babette (little Barbara *foreign woman*)
Barbara (foreign woman)
Barbe (foreign woman)
Basilie (kingly)
Bastienne (from Sebastia)
Beata (happy)
Béatrice (bringer of happiness and joy) **Béatriz, Béatrix**
Belinda (?, second element is *serpent*)
Benoîte (blessed)
Bernadette (bold as a bear)
Bernardine (bold as a bear)
Bernette (bold as a bear)
Berthe (bright)
Bertrade (bright raven)
Bibiane (alive)
Blanche (white) **Blanch**
Brigitte (strength)
Calliste (she that is most beautiful)
Camille (virgin of unblemished character)
Caroline (full-grown)
Cassandra (?)
Catherine (pure)
Cécile (blind, dim-sighted)
Ceciliane (blind, dim-sighted)
Céleste (heavenly)
Celestine (heavenly)
Céline (heaven)
Cendrine (ashes)
Chantal (stone, boulder)
Charlotte (full-grown)
Christelle (a Christian)
Christiane (a Christian)
Christine (a Christian) **Christin, Crisinet, Cristinet**
Claire (bright, clear, famous)

Claremond (bright protection, famous protection)
Clarice (bright, clear, famous)
Claude (lame)
Claudette (little Claude *lame*)
Claudine (lame)
Clémence (gentle, mild, clement)
Clémentine (gentle, mild, clement)
Clotilde (loud battle)
Colette (victory of the people) **Collette**
Colombe (dove)
Constance (constant, steadfast)
Corinne (maiden)
Corisande (?)
Cornelia (horn)
Cyrille (lordly)
Danièle (God is my judge) **Danielle**
Delphine (from Delphi)
Denise (of Dionysus)
Désirée (desired)
Diane (divine)
Dominique (belonging to a lord)
Dorothée (gift of God)
Douce (sweet)
Edma (wealthy protection)
Edmée (wealthy protection)
Edwige (war of contention)
Egilina (formidable)
Eglentine (prickly; sweetbrier)
Elaine (light, torch, bright)
Elena (light, torch, bright)
Eléonore (light, torch, bright)
Éliane (of the sun)
Elisabeth (God is my oath)
Elisabeth-Angélique (God is my oath + angelic)
Elisabeth-Anne (God is my oath + grace, mercy)
Elisabeth-Charlotte (God is my oath + full-grown)
Elisabeth-Marie (God is my oath + sea of bitterness or sorrow)
Élise (God is my oath)
Éloise (hearty and wide)
Emeline (work, industrious) **Ameline, Ammeline, Emmeline**
Emilie (trying to equal or excel; rival)
Emilienne (little Emilie)
Emma (strength)
Emmanuelle (God with us)
Esclairmonde (bright protection, famous protection)
Esmée (loved)
Esther (star; myrtle)
Étiennette (crown, garland)
Eugénie (nobility, excellence)
Eulalie (well-spoken)
Eunice (good victory)
Euphémie (well-spoken, fair of voice)
Eustacie (steadfast, happy in harvest)
Evangeline (good news)
Eve (life)

Fabienne (a bean)
Fabiola (a bean)
Felicienne (little Félicie *lucky, happy*)
Félicie (lucky, happy) **Félise**
Félicité (happiness, felicity)
Fernande (peace; journey; youth, life + courage; venture, risk; ready, prepared)
Flavienne (yellow-haired)
Flore (a flower)
Florence (blooming, flourishing)
Frances (a Frenchwoman)
Françoise (French)
Françoise-Louise (French + famous in war)
Françoise-Marie (French + sea of bitterness or sorrow)
Frédégonde (peaceful war)
Frédérique (ruler of peace)
Gabrielle (God is my strength)
Geneviève (?, perhaps *tribal woman*)
Georgette (earth worker, farmer)
Germaine (a German)
Gertrude (spear strength)
Ghislaine (pledge)
Gilberte (bright pledge)
Giselle (pledge)
Gunilda (war battle) **Gunnilda**
Hannah (grace, full of grace, mercy)
Hedwig (battle wide)
Hélène (light)
Héloïse (sound, hearty, and wide)
Henriette (home ruler)
Hermine (army man, soldier)
Hilde (war, battle) **Hilda**
Honorée (honor, esteem) **Ennoré, Enoré, Honoré**
Hortense (gardener)
Huguette (heart, mind, soul) **Huette**
Hyacinthe (hyacinth, bluebell)
Ida (labor)
Iphigénie (of royal birth)
Irénée (peace)
Isabelle (God is my oath) **Isabel**
Jacinte (hyacinth, bluebell)
Jacqueline (supplanting, seizing by the heels)
Jacquette (supplanting, seizing by the heels)
Jane (God is gracious)
Jane Frances (God is gracious + a Frenchwoman)
Jeanne (God is gracious)
Jeannette (little Jeanne *God is gracious*)
Jeannine (God is gracious)
Joceline (from the tribe of the Gauts)
Joëlle (the Lord is God)
Johanne (God is gracious)
Jordane (a flowing down)
Josée (he shall add)
Josèphe (he shall add)
Joséphine (he shall add)
Judith (praised; from Judah)

Julie (youth, downy)
Julienne (youth, downy)
Julitte (?, perhaps *praised; youth, downy*)
Justine (just, lawful)
Kalliroe (beautiful stream)
Laure (laurel)
Laurence (from Laurentum)
Laurentine (from Laurentum)
Laurette (laurel)
Léa (weary)
Léonie (lion)
Léonne (lion)
Léonore (light, torch, bright)
Léontine (lion)
Liliane (lily)
Linnet (shapely)
Lisette (God is my oath)
Louise (famous in war)
Louise-Elisabeth (famous in war + God is my oath)
Louise-Isabelle (famous in war + God is my oath)
Louise-Marie (famous in war + sea of bitterness or sorrow)
Louisette (little Louise *famous in war*)
Louison (famous in war)
Luce (light)
Lucette (little Luce *light*)
Lucie (light) **Lucia**
Lucienne (little Luce *light*)
Lucille (light)
Lydie (Lydian woman)
Mabila (lovable)
Madeleine (from Magdala)
Magali (?, possibly *pearl*) A Provençal name.
Manon (little Marie *sea of bitterness or sorrow*)
Marcelle (of Mars, warlike) **Marcille**
Marcelline (little Marcelle *of Mars, warlike*)
Margerie (a pearl)
Margot (a pearl)
Marguerite (a pearl)
Mariamne (sea of bitterness or sorrow)
Marianne (sea of bitterness or sorrow + grace, full of grace, mercy)
Marie (sea of bitterness or sorrow) **Maria**
Marie-Adélaïde (sea of bitterness or sorrow + nobility)
Marie-Amélie (sea of bitterness or sorrow + work)
Marie-Ange (sea of bitterness or sorrow + angel)
Marie-Anne (sea of bitterness or sorrow + grace, mercy)
Marie-Caroline (sea of bitterness or sorrow + full-grown)
Marie-Claire (sea of bitterness or sorrow + bright, clear, famous)
Marie-Émilie (sea of bitterness or sorrow + rival)
Marie-France (sea of bitterness or sorrow + French)
Marie-Josèphe (sea of bitterness or sorrow + he shall add)
Marie-Joséphine (sea of bitterness or sorrow + he shall add)
Marielle (little Marie *sea of bitterness or sorrow*)
Marie-Louise (sea of bitterness or sorrow + famous in war)
Marie-Noëlle (sea of bitterness or sorrow + Christmas child)

Marie-Thérèse (sea of bitterness or sorrow + harvester)
Mariette (little Marie *sea of bitterness or sorrow*)
Marie-Zéphyrine (sea of bitterness or sorrow + the west wind)
Marthe (lady, mistress)
Martine (of Mars, warlike)
Matilde (mighty in battle) **Mathilde**
Maud (mighty in battle)
Mélanie (dark, black)
Melisent (work strength)
Melissa (a bee)
Mélusine (a water nymph)
Michèle (Who is like God?)
Micheline (little Michèle *Who is like God?*)
Mildred (mild strength)
Mirabelle (wondrous)
Miriam (sea of bitterness or sorrow)
Monique (?)
Muriel (sea bright)
Myriam (sea of bitterness or sorrow)
Nanette (little Anne *grace, full of grace, mercy*) **Ninette**
Natalie (natal day, Christmas child)
Nicole (victory of the people)
Nicolette (little Nicole *victory of the people*) **Nicollet, Nicollette**
Ninon (little Anne *grace, full of grace, mercy*)
Noëlle (born at Christmas)
Noémie (pleasant, beautiful)
Odette (little Odile *wealth, prosperity*)
Odile (wealth, prosperity)
Olympe (of Olympus)
Ophelie (help, succor)
Oriane (to rise)
Oriel (fire and strife)
Ornette (flowering ash tree)
Ottilie (wealth, prosperity)
Pascale (born at Eastertime)
Patrice (a patrician)
Patricia (a patrician)
Patriciane (a patrician)
Paule (small)
Paulette (little Paule *small*)
Pauline (little Paule *small*)
Perrine (little rock, little stone)
Philippa (lover of horses)
Philomène (lover of strength)

Pierrette (little rock)
Rachel (ewe)
Raymonde (wise protection)
Rébecca (noose)
Régine (queenly)
Reine (queen)
Renée (reborn)
Romaine (a Roman)
Rosala (horse)
Rosalie (rosalia, the annual ceremony of hanging garlands of roses on tombs)
Rosamund (horse protection) **Rosamond**
Roslind (horse serpent)
Roxane (dawn of day)
Ruth (a friend)
Sabine (Sabine woman)
Salomé (peace)
Sarah (princess)
Séraphine (burning ones)
Sibylla (prophetess, fortune-teller)
Sidonie (fine cloth, linen)
Simone (heard)
Solange (yearly, annual; solemn, religious)
Sophie (wisdom)
Sophie-Béatrix (wisdom + bringer of joy)
Sophie-Josèphe (wisdom + he shall add)
Sophie-Marie (wisdom + sea of bitterness or sorrow)
Stéphanie (a crown, a garland)
Suzanne (lily, rose)
Sybille (a fortune-teller, a prophetess)
Sylvie (of the woods)
Thérèse (harvester)
Tifaine (Epiphany, manifestation of God)
Valérie (strong, healthy)
Véronique (?, perhaps *true image; bringer of victory*)
Viole (violet)
Violette (little Viole *violet*)
Virginie (springlike, flourishing)
Vivienne (alive)
Willa (resolute)
Yolande (violet)
Yvette (archer)
Yvonne (archer)
Zéphyrine (the west wind)
Zoë (life) **Zoé**

MALE NAMES

Achille (?)
Adalard (noble and hard)
Adalbert (noble and bright) **Adelbert**
Adolphe (noble wolf)
Adrian (man from Hadrianus) **Adriane**

Agésilas (the goatskin shield of Zeus, a protection)
Ailemar (noble and famous)
Aimery (work ruler) **Amaury, Emery**
Aimo (home) **Aymo**
Alain (?, perhaps *handsome, rock*)

Alard (noble and hard)
Alaric (ruler of all)
Albert (noble and bright)
Albin (white)
Alexandre (defender of mankind)
Alfred (elf counsel; wise counsel)
Algernon (mustached)
Alphée (first)
Alphonse (noble and ready)
Alveré (elf counsel)
Amalrich (work ruler) **Amalric, Amelric, Amelrich**
Amande (army man, soldier)
Ambroise (immortal)
Amé (?)
Amadeus (lover of God)
Amias (?, perhaps *friendship*)
Amiel (industrious)
Amis (friendship)
Anastase (resurrection) **Anastasie**
Anatole (sunrise, daybreak)
Ancelot (divine)
André (manly)
Anne (grace, full of grace, mercy)
Anselm (God's helmet)
Antoine (?, *priceless, of inestimable worth* is a folk definition)
Ara (eagle)
Ariste (best)
Armand (soldier, warrior) **Armant**
Arnaud (eagle power) **Arnaut**
Arno (eagle)
Arnold (eagle power) **Arnault, Arnould**
Arnulf (eagle wolf)
Arsène (male, virile)
Arthur (?) **Artos**
Ascelin (from the tribe of the Gauts) **Acelin**
Auberi (elf ruler)
Aubert (noble and bright)
August (great, venerable) **Auguste**
Augustin (great, venerable)
Augustus (great, venerable)
Aurèle (gold)
Aurélien (golden)
Auveré (elf counsel)
Baldri (bold ruler, brave ruler) **Baudri**
Baldric (bold ruler, brave ruler)
Baldwin (bold friend, brave friend) Flemish form.
Baptiste (a baptizer)
Bardolph (bright wolf) **Bardolf**
Barnabé (son of exhortation)
Barthélemy (son of Talmai *hill, mound, furrows*) **Bartholomé, Bertelmeu**
Basil (kingly) **Basile**
Bastien (man from Sebastia)
Baudoin (bold friend, brave friend)
Bellamy (beautiful friend)

Bénédict (blessed)
Benigne (kind)
Benjamin (son of the right hand)
Benoît (blessed)
Beringer (bear spear)
Bernard (bold as a bear)
Bernardin (little Bernard *bold as a bear*)
Berthold (bear rule) **Berold, Berolt**
Bertin (bright friend)
Bertrand (bright raven) **Bertran**
Bevis (beautiful) **Beves**
Blaise (babbler)
Bouchard (big mouth)
Brian (force, strength; valor; high; kingly) Used in Brittany.
Brice (?)
Bruno (brown)
Camille (?; virgin of unblemished character)
Cecil (blind, dim-sighted)
Célestin (heavenly)
César (hairy; bluish gray)
Charles (full-grown, a man)
Charles-Ferdinand (full-grown + peaceful venture, youthful courage)
Charles-Louis (full-grown + famous in war)
Chrétien (a Christian, a follower of Christ)
Christian (a Christian, a follower of Christ) **Christen, Christin**
Christophe (bearing Christ)
Claude (lame)
Claudin (lame) **Clauden**
Clement (gentle, mild, clement)
Cléon (glory, the glorious)
Colombain (dove)
Conan (strength, high)
Conrad (bold counsel)
Constant (constant, steadfast) **Constans**
Constantine (constant, steadfast)
Corin (a spear)
Corneille (horn)
Crispin (curled)
Curtis (courteous)
Cyprien (from Cyprus)
Cyrille (lordly)
Dagobert (day bright)
Damien (tamer)
Daniel (judged by God)
Daudet (given by God)
David (beloved)
Delphin (a dolphin; from Delphi)
Démosthène (?)
Denis (of Dionysus) **Denys**
Déodat (given by God) Used in southern France.
Didier (longing)
Dieudonné (given by God) Used in northern France.
Dimitri (of Demeter)
Dion (of Zeus)

Dominique (belonging to a lord)
Donatien (given by God)
Drogo (burden bearer) **Drugo**
Dru (burden bearer)
Durand (enduring, lasting)
Ector (holding fast)
Edgar (wealthy spear)
Edmond (wealthy protector) **Edmonde, Edme**
Édouard (wealthy guardian) **Edouard**
Egmont (fearful protection, awesome protection)
Eloi (chosen)
Emery (ruler of strength)
Émile (emulating, trying to equal or excel, a rival)
Émilien (emulating, trying to equal or excel, a rival)
Emmanuel (God is with us)
Emmanuel-Baptist (God is with us + a baptizer)
Emmanuel-Philibert (God is with us + very bright)
Emmerich (ruler of strength)
Engelrand (angel raven) **Enguerran, Enguerrand**
Eric (eternal ruler)
Ernest (earnest, resolute) **Ernost, Ernst**
Esmé (loved)
Esmond (beautiful hand)
Étienne (a crown, garland)
Eudes (child)
Eudon (child)
Eugène (well-born, noble)
Eustache (steadfast; happy in harvest)
Évariste (well-pleasing)
Everard (boar strength) **Evrard**
Fabien (a bean)
Fabrice (workman, craftsman)
Faramond (journey protection)
Fargeau (of iron)
Félix (lucky, happy) **Felis**
Ferdinand (peace; journey; youth, life + courage; venture, risk; ready)
Ferrand (peace; journey; youth, life + courage; venture, risk; ready)
Fidèle (fidelity, faith, trust)
Filbert (very bright) **Filibert, Fulbert, Philbert, Philibert**
Firmin (firm, steadfast)
Flavien (yellow-haired) **Flavie**
Florent (blossoming, flourishing)
Florentin (blossoming, flourishing)
Florian (flowery)
Fortuné (fortune, chance)
Fouchier (people, folk)
Francis (a Frenchman, a freeman)
Franck (a Frank, a freeman)
François (French)
Frédéric (ruler of peace)
Fromont (free protection)
Fulk (people) **Fulke**
Gabriel (God is my strength)
Garnier (protecting army)

Gascon (?, perhaps *guest, stranger; from Gascony*)
Gaspard (treasure master)
Gaston (?, possibly *guest, stranger; from Gascony*)
Gaudens (rejoicing)
Gauvain (battle hawk)
Geoffroi (district; traveler; pledge + peace)
Georges (earth worker, farmer)
Gérald (spear rule) **Géraud**
Gérard (brave with the spear)
Gérardin (brave with the spear)
Gerbert (bright spear)
Germain (a German)
Gervais (servant of the spear)
Giffard (give + bold, fierce)
Gilbert (bright pledge)
Gilles (goatskin shield of Zeus; a protection)
Godard (god hard)
Godfry (God's peace)
Grégoire (vigilant, watchful)
Griffin (like a griffin, monstrous)
Guillard (resolute protector)
Guillaud (resolute protector)
Guillaume (resolute protector)
Guillon (resolute protector)
Guiscard (?)
Gunter (bold in war)
Guy (a guide, a leader)
Guyon (a guide, a leader)
Haerveu (battle worthy) Breton name.
Hamon (home, house)
Hardouin (hard friend)
Hector (holding fast, restraining)
Helgaud (prosperous; hearty, hale) **Helgald**
Henri (home ruler)
Henriot (home ruler)
Herbert (army bright)
Hercule (glory of Hera)
Herman (army man, soldier)
Hervé (battle worthy)
Hilaire (cheerful)
Hippolyte (freer of horses)
Honoré (honor, esteem)
Hubert (bright heart)
Hugh (heart, mind, soul)
Hugo (heart, mind, soul)
Hugolin (heart, mind, soul)
Hugues (heart, mind, soul)
Humbert (people bright)
Ignace (?, perhaps *fire*)
Ilbert (battle bright) **Ilberd**
Imbert (iron people)
Ingelram (angel raven)
Isaak (laughter)
Isaïe (God is salvation)
Isidore (gift of Isis)
Ives (archer) **Ive**

Ivon (archer)
Jacques (supplanting, seizing by the heels)
Jacques-Louis (supplanting, seizing by the heels + famous in war)
Jean (God is gracious)
Jean-Baptiste (God is gracious + a baptizer)
Jean-Christian (God is gracious + a Christian)
Jean-Claude (God is gracious + lame)
Jean-Louis (God is gracious + famous in war)
Jean-Luc (God is gracious + light; man from Lucania)
Jean-Marc (God is gracious + of Mars, warlike)
Jean-Michel (God is gracious + Who is like God?)
Jean-Paul (God is gracious + small)
Jean-Philippe (God is gracious + lover of horses)
Jean-Pierre (God is gracious + a rock)
Jenico (?, perhaps *fire*) Provençal form of Ignace.
Jérémie (God will uplift)
Jérôme (sacred name)
Joachim (God will establish)
Joël (the Lord is God)
Joseph (he shall add)
Jourdain (a flowing down)
Judicael (sportive) **Judical** A Breton name.
Jules (youth, downy)
Julien (youth, downy)
Juvénal (youth)
Juste (just, fair)
Justin (just, fair)
Karl (a man, freeman, peasant)
Kaspar (treasure master)
Klemens (mild, gentle, merciful)
Konrad (wise counsel)
Konstantin (constant, steadfast)
Lambert (bright land)
Lance (land)
Lancelin (little Lance *land*)
Lancelot (little Lance *land*)
Laurence (man from Laurentum) **Laurent**
Léo (lion)
Léon (lion)
Léonard (lion hard, bold as a lion)
Léonce (lion)
Léopold (bold people)
Lionel (little Léon *lion*)
Lothar (famous warrior)
Louis (famous in war)
Louis-Antoine (famous in war + ?, *priceless, of inestimable worth* is a folk definition)
Louis-Baptiste (famous in war + a baptizer)
Louis-François (famous in war + French)
Louis-Joseph (famous in war + he shall add)
Louis-Philip (famous in war + lover of horses)
Louis-Xavier (famous in war + the new house)
Luc (light; man from Lucania)
Lucien (light)
Ludwig (famous in war)

Macaire (blessed)
Magnus (great)
Manfred (man of peace)
Marc (?, perhaps *Mars; manly; soft, tender*)
Marcel (of Mars, warlike)
Marcellin (little Marcel *of Mars, warlike*)
Marius (of Mars, warlike)
Martin (of Mars, warlike)
Matthieu (gift of God) **Mathieu**
Mauger (spear grinder)
Maxime (greatest)
Maximilien (greatest + rival, trying to equal or excel)
Maynard (strong and hardy)
Meurisse (a Moor, dark-skinned)
Michel (Who is like God?)
Miles (?, perhaps *mild, peaceful; merciful*)
Milo (?, perhaps *mild, peaceful; merciful*)
Milon (?, perhaps *mild, peaceful; merciful*)
Moïse (drawn out of the water)
Narcisse (?)
Nathaniel (God has given) **Nathanael**
Nazaire (from Nazareth)
Nicodème (victory of the people)
Nicol (victory of the people)
Nicolas (victory of the people)
Nicollin (little Nicolas *victory of the people*)
Noë (rest, comfort)
Noël (born at Christmas)
Odo (wealth)
Ogier (rich spear)
Olivier (olive tree)
Onfroi (people peace)
Osanne (hosannah)
Osbert (God bright)
Osmond (God protection) **Osmund**
Pascal (born at Easter)
Patrice (a patrician)
Paul (small)
Paulin (little Paul *small*)
Perceval (pierce the valley)
Philibert (very bright, very famous)
Philippe (lover of horses)
Philippe-Antoine (lover of horses + ?, *priceless, of inestimable worth* is a folk definition)
Philippe-Emmanuel (lover of horses + God is with us)
Pierre (a rock, a stone)
Pierre-August (a rock, a stone + great, venerable)
Prosper (prosperous, favorable)
Quentin (fifth)
Rainier (wise army)
Randolf (shield wolf) **Randolph, Randulf**
Ranfred (counsel peace)
Raoul (counsel wolf) **Raul**
Raphael (God has healed)
Raymond (counsel protection)
Régis (kingly)

Rémy (oarsman)
Renaud (ruler of judgment) **Regnault, Reynaud**
René (rebirth)
Reynaud (powerful protection)
Richard (stern king)
Robert (bright with fame)
Robin (bright with fame)
Roby (bright with fame)
Roch (rest)
Rodolphe (famous wolf)
Roger (famous with the spear)
Roland (famous land)
Rolf (famous wolf)
Romain (a Roman)
Samuel (name of God)
Sandre (defender of mankind)
Sanson (the sun)
Saül (asked of, borrowed)
Sébastien (man of Sebastia)
Secord (hard victory)
Séverin (severe, strict)
Sigmund (victory protection)
Simon (heard) **Siméon, Simone**
Spiro (to breathe, to blow)
Stéphane (a crown, garland)
Sylvain (of the woods)
Sylvestre (of the woods)
Symphorien (bearing together)

Talbot (pillager, bandit; lampblack)
Tancred (think counsel)
Terrick (ruler of the people)
Théodore (ruler of the people)
Théophile (beloved of God)
Thibaut (people bold) **Thibault**
Thierry (ruler of the people)
Thomas (a twin)
Timothée (honor, respect)
Toussaint (all saints) Given to those born near All Saints' Day.
Tristan (tumult, sadness)
Trudeau (Thor's power)
Turstan (Thor's stone) **Turstin**
Ulrich (wolf rule)
Urbain (dweller in a village) **Urban**
Valdemar (famous ruler)
Valentin (healthy, strong)
Valère (to be strong)
Valéry (foreign ruler) **Valéran**
Victor (victory)
Vincent (conquering)
Vivien (alive)
Willelm (resolute protector) A Normandy form of William.
Xavier (the new house)
Yann (God is gracious) A Breton form of John.
Yves (archer)
Yvon (archer)

SURNAMES

André (manly)
Arnaud (eagle power) **Arnaut**
Aubert (noble and bright)
Auguste (great, venerable)
Ballou (from Bellou)
Barraud (bear-might) **Barratt**
Bassett (the little, short, fat one)
Bastien (from Sebasta)
Beaufort (beautiful fort, beautiful stronghold)
Beaufoy (beautiful beech tree)
Beaulieu (fair place)
de Beauchamp (from Beauchamp *fair field*)
de Beaumont (from Beaumont *beautiful mountain*)
de Beauregard (from Beauregard *beautiful place*)
Bec (mouth)
Benoît (blessed)
Berger (shephard) **Bergier**
Bertrand (bright raven) **Bertran**
Berube (dweller on the marshy ground)
Blondeau (blond, fair-complexioned)
Blondel (blond, fair-complexioned)
Blondet (blond, fair-complexioned)
Bonnin (little good one)

Bouchard (big mouth)
Bouteiller (cup bearer, butler)
Bouvier (cattle drover)
Brun (brown)
Brunel (little brown one)
Burnell (the dark one)
Bussy (from the thicket)
Cabot (small-headed)
Caillard (piebald; a quail) **Callard**
Castelneau (from the new castle) **Castelnau**
Cazenove (from the new house) **Cazneau**
Challoner (quilt maker, seller of quilts) **Chaloner**
Chamberlain (steward of the chamber)
Chambres (chamber attendant)
Champ (from the field)
Chandler (candle maker, seller of candles)
Chanter (singer)
Chapele (dweller at the chapel) **Chapell, Chappele, Chappelle**
Chartier (a cart driver)
Chastel (from the castle) **Chastell**
Chatal (dweller near the livestock enclosure)
Cheftel (dweller near the livestock enclosure)

Chenal (dweller near the irrigation channel)
Chenault (dweller near the irrigation channel)
Chenaux (dweller near the irrigation channel)
Chêne (dweller near the oak tree)
Chenevier (a grower of hemp) **Chennevier**
Chénier (dweller near the oak tree)
Chenu (white-haired)
Cheptel (dweller near the livestock enclosure)
Chesne (dweller near the oak tree)
Chesnier (dweller near the oak tree)
le Clerc (clerk)
Coquard (a cock, rooster)
Coudray (from the hazel grove)
Courtier (agent, broker)
D'Allemagne (from Germany) **D'Almaine**
Dechêne (of the oak tree) **Duchêne**
Dechesne (of the oak tree) **Duchesne, Duquesne**
de Fraine (of the ash tree) **Defraine**
Delachenal (of the irrigation channel)
de la Croix (of the cross) **Delacroix**
de la Rue (of the street) **Delarue**
des Bois (of the woods)
Descartes (dweller at the outskirts of town)
Desmoulins (dweller by the mill)
De Spagne (from Spain)
de Vere (of the fishing place) **Devere**
Devereaux (from Evreux) **Devereux**
Dionne (of Dionysus)
Dorat (a gilder)
Dore (a gilder)
Doucette (little sweet one)
Du Bois (of the woods) **Dubois, Dubos**
Du Buisson (of the thicket) **Dubuisson**
Du Clos (of the enclosure) **Duclos**
Du Feu (of the beech tree) **Dufeu**
Du Lieu (of the place) **Dulieu**
Dumas (of the little farm)
Du Mont (of the mountain) **Dumont**
Du Parc (of the park) **Duparc**
Du Pont (of the bridge) **Dupont**
Du Prat (of the meadow) **Duprat**
Du Pre (of the meadow) **Dupre**
Du Puis (of the well, of the pit) **Dupuis**
Du Puy (of the high place) **Dupuy**
Durand (enduring) **Duran**
Du Val (of the valley) **Duval, Duvall**
Farge (forge)
Fargues (from Fargues *forges*)
Farjeon (little Farge *forge*)
Faudel (cattle or sheep barn)
Favre (smith, carpenter) **Faure**
Ferrand (peaceful journey)
Feuillette (dweller at the sign of the leaf [near a wine merchant])
Fleche (an archer)

Fleury (dweller by the flowers)
Fournier (oven keeper; parish baker)
Girardin (spear hard)
Giraud (spear hard)
Grellier (slender, slim) **Grelier**
Guerrier (warrior)
Herriott (little Henry *home ruler*)
Huguelet (little Hugues *heart, mind, spirit*)
Jolie (agreeable, pleasant)
Jourdain (a flowing down)
Lachenal (dweller near the irrigation channel) **Lachenaud**
La Cour (the short one)
La Croix (dweller near the cross)
Lafayette (dweller near a small grove of beeches)
Laffitte (dweller near the boundary stone)
Lanier (a weaver or seller of wool)
La Porte (dweller near the gate)
Larousse (red-haired, ruddy-complexioned)
La Rue (dweller on the street)
Laurent (man from Laurentum)
La Valle (dweller in the valley)
La Vigne (dweller near the vineyard)
Le Beau (the handsome one)
Le Blanc (the white-haired one, fair-complexioned)
Lecanu (the white-haired one) **Lecanut**
Le Grand (the large one)
Lejeune (the younger)
Lemaitre (the overseer)
Lesueur (maker or seller of shoes)
Luce (light)
Lucette (little light)
Marais (dweller near the marsh)
Marchand (a merchant)
Martel (the hammer)
Martineau (little Martin *of Mars, warlike*)
Mathieu (gift of God)
Mercier (seller of fine cloth)
Merritt (a tenant farmer)
Meserve (a surveyor of land)
Minott (measurer of goods) **Minot**
Moliere (dweller near the quarry)
Moline (from Moline *mill*)
Moreau (from Moreau *dark-skinned, a Moor*)
Moser (seller of vegetables)
Nason (small nose)
Olivier (owner of an olive grove)
Orfevre (maker and seller of golden articles)
Pasteur (a shepherd)
Petit (little)
Petitperrin (little Pierre *rock*)
Picard (from Picardy *pike men*)
Pierpont (dweller near the stone bridge)
Poincare (square fist; a strong man)
Poirier (grower and seller of pears)
Poisson (seller of fish)

Poupard (child) **Poupart**
Prévost (commander)
Quenu (dweller near the livestock enclosure)
Regis (kingly)
Renaud (ruler of judgment)
Ricard (stern king)
Rivière (river)
Rougemont (red mountain)
Royer (wheelwright)
Saulnier (gatherer or seller of salt)
Savoy (from Savoy) **Savoie**
Séverin (severe)
Taillandier (maker or seller of iron articles)
Taillefer (cut iron)

Tailleur (a tailor)
Thibaud (people hard) **Thibault, Thibaut, Thibeau**
Thibodeau (people bold) **Thibedeau, Thibideau**
Thierry (people ruler)
Toussaint (all saints)
Trudeau (Thor's power)
Vaillant (valiant one)
Vaux (from Vaux *the valley*)
Vavasseur (under-vassal)
Verdier (a gamekeeper)
Vernier (protecting army) **Verniere**
Villiers (from Villiers *the hamlet*)
Wilmot (resolute protector)

Chapter Seven

THE INDUSTRIAL REVOLUTION TO THE PRESENT
[1848–PRESENT]

POLITICS

AFTER LOUIS-PHILIPPE'S ABDICATION, the constitution was tossed out, and Republican leaders established the Second Republic. Economic depression continued, as did incidents of rioting and urban violence. A new constitution was adopted that granted suffrage to all adult male citizens. Napoleon's nephew, Louis Bonaparte, was elected president. Bonaparte didn't like the idea of having his powers restricted, and in 1851, pulled off a coup d'état. In December 1852, he suspended the constitution and proclaimed himself Emperor Napoleon III. A new constitution was drafted a year later, giving the new Emperor full authority.

Napoleon III set about encouraging economic and social reform. His most ambitious endeavors were the industrialization of the country and the public-works projects that were carried out in the cities and across the countryside. Napoleon also wished to recover his country's military prestige, and to that end, involved his troops in several major military campaigns.

Meanwhile, Prussia was uniting the German states to form a new empire. To curb the threat, Napoleon declared war against Prussia in 1870. His armies were quickly defeated, and he was forced to surrender. He was imprisoned, then sent to England where he died three years later.

With Napoleon III gone, France was left without a government. A vote of dissolution was forced upon the legislature and the Parisian deputies proclaimed the Third Republic in September 1870 and decided to continue the war. The French were outnumbered, outgunned, and outsmarted, and by January the enemy was sitting in the throne room at Versailles. Peace was bought with a war indemnity of five billion francs, partial occupation of the country for the next three years, and the cessation of the German-speaking mining provinces of Alsace and Lorraine in northeastern France. The rioting that broke out in Paris between March and May of 1871 was brutally repressed by the occupying forces, 10,000 to 30,000 revolutionaries were killed, and over the next three years, trials were held for 14,000 rebel survivors; a few were executed, most were sent to Guiana and New Caledonia. It's estimated that Paris lost 80,000 people due to the revolt, either from being killed in the fighting, from being deported, or from fleeing the city.

There was trouble with the Third Republic from the very beginning. It was divided between monarchists and those who wanted a moderate republic. In 1875, a new government was formed. Two houses formed the Congress: the Chamber, whose members were chosen by male voters, and the Senate, whose senators were chosen by a restricted electorate. The Congress elected a president to a seven-year term. In 1879, Paris was made the official seat of government, and July 14 was chosen as the national holiday. In the 1880s, several liberties were established, including freedom of the press and the right to form professional associations, such as labor unions, provided they were nonpolitical.

For the time being, France's foreign policy was one of docility in Europe but that was not the case elsewhere. The French extended their rule in Indochina and Africa, to the vast annoyance of the English, the Germans, and the Italians. France therefore settled for an alliance with Russia.

An understanding was finally achieved with England in 1904 whereby England recognized France's interests in Morocco and France recognized England's in Egypt. Efforts were then made to include Italy in the alliance by recognizing that country's intention in Tripoli. By 1907, France, Britain, and Russia had formed the alliance called the Triple Entente. Germany felt threatened and formed its own alliance with Italy and Austria.

On June 28, 1914, the crown prince of Austria, the Archduke Franz Ferdinand, was assassinated at Sarajevo. The countries of the Triple Entente encouraged Austrian restraint, but Germany sided with Austria, and Russian hostilities were heightened. The order was given to move French troops back ten kilometers from the eastern border to reduce tensions, but after Germany declared that French warplanes had violated German airspace, war was declared on August 3. German troops crossed Belgium and invaded northern France. The French, who had regained their nationalist fervor, were ready to defend themselves and recover the territories of Alsace and Lorraine. After a bloodly autumn, the armies had fought to a standstill. By the end of the year, 380,000 Frenchmen were killed and 600,000 were prisoners, wounded, or missing. The opposing forces dug in for trench warfare and it wasn't until 1918 that the combined forces of France, Britain, and the United States were able to overcome the German army and force its surrender. The armistice was signed on November 11, 1918, and a treaty of peace was signed in the Hall of Mirrors at Versailles in June 1919. Alsace and Lorraine reverted back to France, and Germany made reparations for damages caused by the war.

France went through a large period of rebuilding until 1932, when a worldwide depression hit the French economy. Meanwhile, the Nazis had come to power, and France was unable to stop the German war machine led by Adolf Hitler. In the fall of 1939, World War II began. German tanks rolled into France in May 1940. Within three weeks' time, Paris had fallen, and the French were forced to surrender and sign a truce with

Hitler. The Germans then took control of the country except for the south and southeast, which remained under a French administration that offered no resistance to the Germans.

The French general, Charles de Gaulle, had escaped the country and made it to Britain, where he formed the Free French movement. In France, an underground resistance group secretly fought German occupation, and the Germans built a series of defenses along the coast to prevent an allied invasion from the sea. In 1944, the allied forces of Canada, the United States, and Britain gathered in Britain in preparation for an attack on the French coast. On June 6, 1944, the allies landed on the beaches of Normandy. Paris was liberated in August, and the Germans were pushed back across France. Charles de Gaulle made a triumphant return and set about organizing a new government. After the Germans surrendered in May 1945, all areas of France were liberated.

In October 1945, a provisional government was established. A Constituent Assembly was elected and three-fourths of the new members were from the Communist party, the Socialist party, and the Popular Republican Movement, a new party that had formed during the war. A new constitution was voted on and new electoral laws were established that granted women suffrage. Several key industries were nationalized, as was a social security system, and a plan was drawn up for rebuilding and modernizing the country. Charles de Gaulle became the leader of this provisional government until his resignation in 1946.

The Fourth Republic had all the same problems as the Third, with the added conflicts between Communists and non-Communists, and a worsening of relations with French colonies. In 1946, Indochina revolted and the French were forced once again into war they couldn't win. In June 1954, Pierre Mendès-France told the Assembly he'd end the war within thirty days or resign. The Assembly gave him a vote of confidence, and in July, the Geneva agreement ended the war. Indochina was divided into Cambodia, Laos, and the two independent states of Vietnam, and granted self-rule.

It was then North Africa's turn to rebel. From 1956 onward, French territories in Africa (except Algeria) were granted self-rule. In 1958, Charles de Gaulle came out of retirement and formed the Fifth Republic. A new constitution was approved, and de Gaulle was voted president of the Republic. In 1962, Algeria was granted independence, and about a million French colonists and Algerians emigrated to France. Charles de Gaulle retired from politics in 1969.

In 1981, a Socialist candidate, Françoise Mitterrand, was elected president. Under his government, five major industries and most of the private banks were nationalized. Yet from 1986 on, the country began a program of privatization whereby many state-owned companies were sold. In 1991, Edith Cresson became France's first female prime minister.

SOCIETY

AT THE BEGINNING of this time period, the French economy was still based on agriculture, but unlike other European countries, few agricultural improvements had been made to increase the production and quality of crops. Other countries had already begun industrializing and expanding their economies, but France had made few attempts in that area.

Napoleon III understood the need for change, and his domestic policies were directed at eliminating the hardships of French society. His answer to the elimination of poverty was to follow the example of the United Kingdom and industrialize his country. Six railway companies were organized; the first Alpine tunnels were begun; old ports were renovated and new ports created; two large steamship companies were founded; and public works projects in Paris and other important cities were carried. In addition, Napoleon III signed a free-trade agreement with the English that forced French companies into competition. By his course of action,

Napoleon III became responsible for the greatest change ever to affect French society. In 1817, 75 percent of the people obtained their livings from the land; in 1866, 70 percent. Today, less than 7 percent of the workforce is engaged in agriculture.

The beginning of the twentieth century saw rapid industrialization, but the World Wars effectively put an end to economic and industrial growth. World War I was catastrophic to France. Not only had northern France been laid to waste and the country burdened with an enormous war debt, more than 1,300,000 of France's young men had lost their lives, over 1,100,000 were permanently disabled, and there was a marked increase in civilian deaths.

France suffered in the aftermath of World War II, as well. Much of the country was in ruins, there were severe food shortages and an inadequate rationing system, the transportation system had broken down, many ports were unable to function, and industrial production was low. Efforts to rebuild the country included a house-building program to provide housing to the 500,000 whose homes were destroyed or damaged during the occupation. Industries were given assistance in resuming production, and public works projects helped improve transportation.

Growth lasted until the 1970s, when stiff competition from overseas and higher energy costs began to affect the market and slow the economy. Smaller companies were either forced out of business or forced to merge with larger ones, and industry quickly streamlined its operations. Both actions helped reduce costs, but they also caused a rise in unemployment.

Presently, the French are much better off than ever before. In addition to having a comprehensive social-security program that provides health insurance and benefits for the disabled, retired, and unemployed, the government established a minimum wage requirement and requires employers to grant employees at least four weeks of vacation per year.

At the beginning of this time period, the Catholic Church had nearly total control over the educational system. In the 1880s, the Third Republic took education out of the Church's hands and placed it in the hands of the state. Free public education became available, and attendance was mandatory for children, including girls, between six and thirteen years of age. All instruction was secularized, which meant religious teachings were no longer allowed, and each *département* was required to maintain two teachers' colleges (one for men, one for women) to replace the thousands of teachers from the Brothers of the Christian Doctrine and the Sisters of Charity.

Today, France has one of the most comprehensive educational systems in Europe. Nursery schools are available at no cost to any child between the ages of two and six. After nursery school, children attend elementary school until eleven years of age, then attend a *collège* for four more years of standardized schooling. From fifteen to eighteen, students attend the *lycée,* a kind of high school that prepares them for vocational or technical training or for further studies in the university system. Approximately 15 percent of French children attend the private schools run by the Catholic Church.

France was a founding member of the European Community, a group of twelve nations working toward a strong European marketplace. In 1993, Germany was the final country to approve ratification of the European Community's Treaty on European Union. Under the treaty, the European Union works toward establishing common defense and foreign policies, and a common currency. It is the hope of France that it once again becomes the trading crossroads of Europe.

RELIGION

ANTICLERICALISM DURING THE Third Republic led to the separation of Church and state. In 1905, liberty of conscience was guaranteed, and Catholicism was no longer the official state religion. Church property that had been part of the public domain was returned not to the Church, but to individual Catholics who administered them through an organization called the Association for Public Worship.

Currently, about 90 percent of the people are baptized as Catholics. The largest Protestant sect is the Reformed Church, which is based on the teachings of Jean Calvin. There are also several other Protestant faiths, as well as churches for the Russian and Greek Orothodox faiths.

After World War II, many North Africans immigrated to France. They brought their Islamic religion with them, and currenty, about 2,000,000 people in France are Muslim, approximately twice the number of Protestants. In addition, there are several large Jewish communites in Paris and Marseille, and the country also has a significant number of Asian immigrants who practice the Buddhist faith.

NAMING

EARLY IN THE twentieth century, the Ballet Russe established itself in Paris. Several Russian names were introduced into the country and were eventually added to the pool of names used by the French.

In 1957, the Ministry of Justice reaffirmed that children were to be given names in accordance with to the stipulations put forth during the French Revolution. This included traditional French names, those taken from the Bible, and those from famous people in ancient history. All names were to be spelled in a French manner.

In 1966, the Ministry of Justice relaxed the rules a bit, allowing for names from mythology, variant spellings, foreign names, and the use of pet forms of names as given names. However, the registrar may use his or her discretion and not record a child's birth if the name is not in good taste or strays too far from accepted convention.

Among the most popular female names are: Marie, Michèle, Danielle, and Francine. Popular names for males are: Jean, René, and Daniel.

FEMALE NAMES

Abelia (breath) **Abella**
Adélaïde (nobility)
Adèle (noble)
Adeline (nobility) **Adelina**
Adrienne (from Hadrianus)
Aënor (light, torch, bright)
Agathe (good)
Agilina (formidable)
Aglaë (splendor)
Agnès (chaste, pure, sacred)
Aida (aide, helper)
Aimée (beloved) **Aimè, Amee**
Alberte (noble and bright)
Albertine (noble and bright)
Alette (nobility)
Alexandra (defender of mankind)
Alexandrine (defender of mankind) **Alexandrina**
Alexine (defender)
Alia (all)
Alice (nobility)
Aline (nobility)
Aliz (nobility) **Alix**

Amarante (unfading)
Amélie (work, labor) **Amalie**
Amice (friendship)
Anaïs (grace, full of grace, mercy) A Provençal form of Anne.
Anastasia (resurrection)
Andrée (womanly)
Ange (angel)
Angèle (angel)
Angeline (angel)
Angélique (angelic)
Anne (grace, full of grace, mercy) **Anna**
Anne Elisabeth (grace, mercy + God is my oath)
Anne Henriette (grace, mercy + home ruler)
Anne Josephe (grace, mercy + he shall add)
Anne Marie (grace, mercy + sea of bitterness or sorrow)
Annette (little Anne *grace, full of grace, mercy*)
Annis (chaste, pure, sacred)
Annora (honor, esteem) Norman form of Honora.
Antoinette (?, *priceless, of inestimable worth* is a folk definition)
Apolline (of Apollo)
Ariane (very holy one) **Arianne**

Arlette (little eagle)
Asceline (noble) **Aceline**
Athénais (?, Athena the goddess of wisdom)
Athene (?, Athena the goddess of wisdom)
Aude (old) **Auda**
Aure (aura)
Aurélie (gold) **Aurèle**
Aurore (dawn, daybreak) **Aurora**
Aveline (?) **Eveline, Evelyne**
Babette (little Barbara *foreign woman*)
Barbara (foreign woman)
Barbe (foreign woman)
Basilie (kingly)
Bastienne (from Sebastia)
Beata (happy)
Béatrice (bringer of happiness and joy) **Béatriz, Béatrix**
Belinda (?, second element is *serpent*)
Belle (beautiful)
Bénédicte (blessed)
Benoîte (blessed)
Bernadette (bold as a bear)
Bernardine (bold as a bear) **Bernardina**
Bernette (bold as a bear)
Berthe (bright)
Bertrade (bright raven)
Bibiane (alive)
Blanche (white) **Blanch**
Brigitte (strength)
Calliste (she that is most beautiful)
Camille (virgin of unblemished character) **Camilla**
Carole (full-grown; a joyous song)
Caroline (full-grown)
Cassandra (?)
Catherine (pure) **Katherine**
Cécile (blind, dim-sighted)
Ceciliane (blind, dim-sighted)
Céleste (heavenly)
Celestine (heavenly)
Céline (heaven) **Célina**
Cendrine (ashes)
Cerise (cherry, cherry-flavored)
Chantal (stone, boulder)
Charlotte (full-grown)
Christelle (a Christian) **Kristell, Kristelle**
Christiane (a Christian)
Christine (a Christian) **Christin, Crisinet, Cristinet, Kristina, Kristina**
Claire (bright, clear, famous) **Clair**
Claremond (bright protection, famous protection)
Clarice (bright, clear, famous) **Clarisse**
Claude (lame)
Claudette (little Claude *lame*)
Claudine (lame)
Clémence (gentle, mild, clement)
Clémentine (gentle, mild, clement)
Clotilde (loud battle) **Clothilde**

Colette (victory of the people) **Collette**
Colombe (dove)
Constance (constant, steadfast)
Corinne (maiden)
Corisande (?)
Cornelia (horn)
Cyrille (lordly)
Danièle (God is my judge) **Danielle**
Delphine (from Delphi)
Denise (of Dionysus)
Désirée (desired)
Diane (divine) **Dianne**
Dominique (belonging to a lord)
Dorothée (gift of God)
Douce (sweet)
Edith (prosperous in war)
Edma (wealthy protection)
Edmée (wealthy protection)
Edwige (war of contention)
Egilina (formidable)
Eglentine (prickly; sweetbrier)
Elaine (light, torch, bright)
Eléonore (light, torch, bright) **Éléonore**
Elena (light, torch, bright)
Éliane (of the sun)
Elisabeth (God is my oath) **Élisabeth**
Elisabeth-Angélique (God is my oath + angelic)
Elisabeth-Anne (God is my oath + grace, mercy)
Elisabeth-Charlotte (God is my oath + full-grown)
Elisabeth-Marie (God is my oath + sea of bitterness or sorrow)
Élise (God is my oath)
Éloise (hearty and wide)
Emeline (work, industrious) **Ameline, Ammeline, Emmeline**
Emilie (trying to equal or excel; rival) **Émilie**
Emilienne (little Emilie) **Émilianne, Émilienne**
Emma (strength)
Emmanuelle (God with us)
Enora (light, torch, bright)
Esclairmonde (bright protection, famous protection)
Esmée (loved)
Esther (star; myrtle)
Étiennette (crown, garland)
Eugénie (nobility, excellence)
Eulalie (well-spoken)
Eunice (good victory)
Euphémie (well-spoken, fair of voice)
Eustacie (steadfast, happy in harvest)
Evangeline (good news)
Eve (life) **Eva**
Fabienne (a bean)
Fabiola (a bean)
Félicie (lucky, happy) **Félise, Filicie**
Felicienne (little Félicie *lucky, happy*)
Félicité (happiness, felicity)
Fernande (peace; journey; youth, life + courage; venture, risk; ready, prepared)

Fifi (he shall add) Shortened form of Joséphine.

Fifine (he shall add) Shortened form of Joséphine.

Flavienne (yellow-haired)

Flore (a flower)

Florence (blooming, flourishing)

France (French, from France)

Frances (a Frenchwoman)

Franchon (French)

Francine (French)

Françoise (French)

Françoise Louise (French + famous in war)

Françoise Marie (French + sea of bitterness or sorrow)

Frédégonde (peaceful war)

Frédérique (ruler of peace)

Gabrielle (God is my strength)

Gemma (a gem, jewel)

Geneviève (?, perhaps *tribal woman*)

Georgette (earth worker, farmer)

Germaine (a German)

Gertrude (spear strength)

Ghislaine (pledge) **Ghislain**

Gilberte (bright pledge)

Giselle (pledge)

Gunilda (war battle) **Gunnilda**

Hannah (grace, full of grace, mercy)

Hedwig (battle wide)

Hélène (light)

Héloïse (sound, hearty, and wide)

Henriette (home ruler)

Hermine (army man, soldier)

Hilde (war, battle) **Hilda**

Honorée (honor, esteem) **Ennoré, Enoré, Honoré, Honore**

Honorine (honor, esteem)

Hortense (gardener)

Huguette (heart, mind, soul) **Huette**

Hyacinthe (hyacinth, bluebell)

Ida (labor)

Inès (chaste, pure)

Iphigénie (of royal birth)

Irénée (peace) **Irène**

Isabelle (God is my oath) **Isabel, Isabella**

Jacinte (hyacinth, bluebell)

Jacqueline (supplanting, seizing by the heels)

Jacquette (supplanting, seizing by the heels)

Jane (God is gracious)

Jane Frances (God is gracious + a Frenchwoman)

Janique (little Jeanne *God is gracious*)

Jeanne (God is gracious)

Jeanneton (little Jeanne *God is gracious*)

Jeannette (little Jeanne *God is gracious*) **Ginette**

Jeannine (God is gracious) **Janine**

Joceline (from the tribe of the Gauts) **Joscelin**

Joëlle (the Lord is God)

Johanne (God is gracious)

Jordane (a flowing down)

Josée (he shall add)

Josèphe (he shall add)

Joséphine (he shall add)

Josette (he shall add)

Josiane (he shall add)

Judith (praised; from Judah)

Julie (youth, downy)

Julienne (youth, downy)

Juliette (youth, downy)

Julitte (?, perhaps *praised; youth, downy*)

Justine (just, lawful)

Kalliroe (beautiful stream)

Katie (pure, unsullied)

Laure (laurel)

Laurence (from Laurentum)

Laurentine (from Laurentum)

Laurette (laurel)

Léa (weary)

Léonie (lion)

Léonne (lion)

Léonore (light, torch, bright)

Léontine (lion)

Liliane (lily)

Linnet (shapely)

Lise (God is my oath)

Lisette (God is my oath)

Louise (famous in war)

Louise-Elisabeth (famous in war + God is my oath)

Louise-Isabelle (famous in war + God is my oath)

Louise-Marie (famous in war + sea of bitterness or sorrow)

Louisette (little Louise *famous in war*)

Louisiane (famous in war)

Louison (famous in war)

Luce (light)

Lucette (little Luce *light*)

Lucie (light) **Lucia**

Lucienne (little Luce *light*)

Lucille (light)

Lucinde (light)

Lydie (Lydian woman)

Mabila (lovable)

Madeleine (from Magdala) **Madeline, Madelon**

Magali (?, possibly *pearl*) **Magalie** A Provençal name.

Manon (little Marie *sea of bitterness or sorrow*)

Marcelle (of Mars, warlike) **Marcille**

Marcelline (little Marcelle *of Mars, warlike*) **Marcelina, Marceline, Marcellina**

Margerie (a pearl)

Margot (a pearl)

Marguerite (a pearl)

Maria (sea of bitterness or sorrow)

Mariamne (sea of bitterness or sorrow)

Marianne (sea of bitterness or sorrow + grace, full of grace, mercy) **Mariane**

Marie (sea of bitterness or sorrow) **Maria**

Marie-Adélaïde (sea of bitterness or sorrow + nobility)

Marie-Amélie (sea of bitterness or sorrow + work)

Marie-Ange (sea of bitterness or sorrow + angel)
Marie-Anne (sea of bitterness or sorrow + grace, mercy)
Marie-Caroline (sea of bitterness or sorrow + full-grown)
Marie-Claire (sea of bitterness or sorrow + bright, clear, famous)
Marie-Émilie (sea of bitterness or sorrow + rival)
Marie-France (sea of bitterness or sorrow + French)
Marie-Josèphe (sea of bitterness or sorrow + he shall add)
Marie-Joséphine (sea of bitterness or sorrow + he shall add)
Marielle (little Marie *sea of bitterness or sorrow*)
Marie-Louise (sea of bitterness or sorrow + famous in war)
Marie-Noëlle (sea of bitterness or sorrow + Christmas child)
Marie-Thérèse (sea of bitterness or sorrow + harvester)
Mariette (little Marie *sea of bitterness or sorrow*)
Marie-Zéphyrine (sea of bitterness or sorrow + the west wind)
Marion (sea of bitterness or sorrow) **Marionne**
Marthe (lady, mistress)
Martine (of Mars, warlike)
Matilde (mighty in battle) **Mathilde**
Maud (mighty in battle) **Maude**
Maxine (greatest)
Mélanie (dark, black)
Melisent (work strength)
Melissa (a bee)
Mélusine (a water nymph)
Michèle (Who is like God?)
Micheline (little Michèle *Who is like God?*)
Mildred (mild strength)
Mirabelle (wondrous)
Mireio (sea of bitterness or sorrow) **Mireille** A Provençal form of Miriam.
Miriam (sea of bitterness or sorrow)
Monique (?)
Muriel (sea bright)
Myriam (sea of bitterness or sorrow)
Myriana (sea of bitterness or sorrow)
Nadette (bold as a bear)
Nadia (hope) Twentieth-century use.
Nadine (hope) Twentieth-century use.
Nanette (little Anne *grace, full of grace, mercy*) **Ninette**
Natalie (natal day, Christmas child) **Nathalie**
Nicole (victory of the people)
Nicolette (little Nicole *victory of the people*) **Nicollet, Nicollette**
Nina (grace, full of grace, mercy) Twentieth-century use.
Ninon (little Anne *grace, full of grace, mercy*)
Noëlle (born at Christmas) **Noelle**
Noémie (pleasant, beautiful)
Odette (little Odile *wealth, prosperity*)
Odile (wealth, prosperity)
Olympe (of Olympus)
Ophelie (help, succor)
Oriane (to rise) **Orianne**
Oriel (fire and strife)
Ornette (flowering ash tree)

Ottilie (wealth, prosperity)
Ottoline (wealth, prosperity)
Pascale (born at Eastertime)
Patrice (a patrician)
Patricia (a patrician)
Patriciane (a patrician)
Paule (small)
Paulette (little Paule *small*)
Pauline (little Paule *small*)
Perrine (little rock, little stone)
Philippa (lover of horses)
Philippine (lover of horses)
Philomène (lover of strength)
Pierrette (little rock)
Rachel (ewe)
Raymonde (wise protection)
Rébecca (noose)
Régine (queenly)
Reine (queen)
Renée (reborn)
Rina (pure, unsullied)
Romaine (a Roman)
Rosala (horse)
Rosalie (rosalia, the annual ceremony of hanging garlands of roses on tombs)
Rosamund (horse protection) **Rosamond**
Rose (horse; a rose)
Rose-Marie (horse; a rose + sea of bitterness or sorrow)
Roslind (horse serpent)
Roxane (dawn of day)
Ruth (a friend)
Sabine (Sabine woman)
Salomé (peace)
Sandra (defender of mankind)
Sandrine (defender of mankind)
Sarah (princess)
Sasha (defender of mankind)
Séraphine (burning ones)
Sibylla (prophetess, fortune-teller)
Sidonie (fine cloth, linen)
Simone (heard)
Solange (yearly, annual; solemn, religious)
Sophie (wisdom)
Sophie-Béatrix (wisdom + bringer of joy)
Sophie-Josèphe (wisdom + he shall add)
Sophie-Marie (wisdom + sea of bitterness or sorrow)
Stéphanie (a crown, a garland)
Suzanne (lily, rose) **Susanne**
Suzette (little Suzanne *lily, rose*)
Sybille (a fortune-teller, a prophetess)
Sylvie (of the woods)
Thérèse (harvester)
Tifaine (Epiphany, manifestation of God)
Tina (a Christian) Shortened form of Christine.
Toinette (?, *priceless, of inestimable worth* is a folk definition)
Valérie (strong, healthy)

Véronique (?, perhaps *true image; bringer of victory*)
Violaine (violet)
Viole (violet)
Violette (little Viole *violet*)
Virginie (springlike, flourishing)
Vivi (alive)
Vivienne (alive) **Vivianne**

Willa (resolute)
Yolande (violet)
Yvette (archer)
Yvonne (archer)
Zéphyrine (the west wind)
Zoë (life) **Zoé**
Zoelie (life) **Zoelle**

MALE NAMES

Abel (breath)
Abelard (noble and hard)
Achille (?)
Adalard (noble and hard)
Adalbert (noble and bright) **Adelbert**
Adam (man of the red earth)
Adolphe (noble wolf)
Adrian (man from Hadrianus) **Adriane**
Agésilas (the goatskin shield of Zeus, a protection)
Ailemar (noble and famous)
Aimé (beloved)
Aimery (work ruler) **Amaury, Emery**
Aimo (home) **Aymo**
Alain (?, perhaps *handsome, rock*) **Allain**
Alard (noble and hard) **Allard**
Alaric (ruler of all)
Albert (noble and bright) **Aubert**
Albin (white)
Alex (defender of mankind)
Alexandre (defender of mankind)
Alfred (elf counsel; wise counsel)
Algernon (mustached)
Alphée (first)
Alphonse (noble and ready)
Alveré (elf counsel)
Amadeus (lover of God)
Amalrich (work ruler) **Amalric, Amelric, Amelrich**
Amande (army man, soldier)
Ambroise (immortal)
Amé (?)
Amédée (lover of God)
Amias (?, perhaps *friendship*)
Amiel (industrious)
Amis (friendship)
Anastase (resurrection) **Anastasie**
Anatole (sunrise, daybreak)
Ancelot (divine)
André (manly)
Anne (grace, full of grace, mercy)
Anselm (God's helmet)
Antoine (?, *priceless, of inestimable worth* is a folk definition)
Ara (eagle)
Ariste (best)

Aristide (best)
Armand (soldier, warrior) **Armant, Armond**
Arnaud (eagle power) **Arnaut**
Arno (eagle)
Arnold (eagle power) **Arnault, Arnould**
Arnulf (eagle wolf)
Arsène (male, virile)
Arthur (?) **Artos**
Ascelin (from the tribe of the Gauts) **Acelin**
Auberi (elf ruler)
Aubert (noble and bright)
August (great, venerable) **Auguste**
Augustin (great, venerable)
Augustus (great, venerable)
Aurèle (gold)
Aurélien (golden)
Auveré (elf counsel)
Baldri (bold ruler, brave ruler) **Baudri**
Baldric (bold ruler, brave ruler)
Baldwin (bold friend, brave friend) Flemish form.
Baptiste (a baptizer)
Bardolph (bright wolf) **Bardolf**
Barnabé (son of exhortation)
Barthélemy (son of Talmai *hill, mound, furrows*) **Bartholomé, Bertelmeu**
Basil (kingly) **Basile**
Bastien (man from Sebastia)
Baudoin (bold friend, brave friend)
Bellamy (beautiful friend)
Bénédict (blessed)
Benigne (kind)
Benjamin (son of the right hand)
Benoît (blessed)
Beringer (bear spear)
Bernard (bold as a bear) **Barnard**
Bernardin (little Bernard *bold as a bear*)
Bernon (bold as a bear)
Berthold (bear rule) **Berold, Berolt**
Bertin (bright friend)
Bertrand (bright raven) **Bertram, Bertran**
Bevis (beautiful) **Beves**
Blaise (babbler) **Blaize**
Bouchard (big mouth)
Brian (force, strength; valor; high; kingly) Used in Brittany.

Brice (?)
Bruno (brown)
Camille (virgin of unblemished character)
Cecil (blind, dim-sighted)
Célestin (heavenly)
César (hairy; bluish gray)
Charles (full-grown, a man)
Charles-Ferdinand (full-grown + peaceful venture, youthful courage)
Charles-Louis (full-grown + famous in war)
Charlot (full-grown, a man)
Chrétien (a Christian, a follower of Christ)
Christian (a Christian, a follower of Christ) **Christen, Christin**
Christophe (bearing Christ)
Claude (lame)
Claudin (lame) **Clauden**
Clément (gentle, mild, clement) **Clement**
Cléon (glory, the glorious)
Colombain (dove)
Conan (strength, high)
Conrad (bold counsel)
Constant (constant, steadfast) **Constans**
Constantine (constant, steadfast) **Constantin**
Corin (a spear)
Corneille (horn)
Crispin (curled)
Curtis (courteous) **Curtice**
Cyprien (from Cyprus)
Cyran (a spear)
Cyrille (lordly) **Cyril**
Dagobert (day bright)
Damien (tamer) **Damyon**
Daniel (judged by God)
Daudet (given by God)
David (beloved) **Davin**
Delphin (a dolphin; from Delphi)
Démosthène (?)
Denis (of Dionysus) **Denys**
Déodat (given by God)
Didier (longing)
Dieudonné (given by God)
Dimitri (of Demeter)
Dion (of Zeus)
Dominique (belonging to a lord)
Donatien (given by God)
Drogo (burden bearer) **Drugo**
Dru (burden bearer)
Durand (enduring, lasting)
Ector (holding fast)
Edgar (wealthy spear)
Edmond (wealthy protector) **Edmonde, Edme**
Édouard (wealthy guardian) **Edouard**
Egmont (fearful protection, awesome protection)
Eloi (chosen)
Emery (ruler of strength)

Émile (emulating, trying to equal or excel, a rival) **Emile**
Émilien (emulating, trying to equal or excel, a rival)
Emmanuel (God is with us)
Emmanuel-Baptist (God is with us + a baptizer)
Emmanuel-Philibert (God is with us + very bright)
Emmerich (ruler of strength)
Engelrand (angel raven) **Enguerran, Enguerrand**
Eric (eternal ruler)
Ernest (earnest, resolute) **Ernost, Ernst**
Esmé (loved)
Esmond (beautiful hand)
Étienne (a crown, garland)
Eudes (child)
Eudon (child)
Eugène (well-born, noble)
Eustache (steadfast; happy in harvest)
Évariste (well-pleasing)
Everard (boar strength) **Evrard**
Fabien (a bean)
Fabrice (workman, craftsman)
Faramond (journey protection)
Fargeau (of iron)
Félix (lucky, happy) **Felis**
Ferdinand (peace; journey; youth, life + courage; venture, risk; ready) **Fernand**
Ferrand (peace; journey; youth, life + courage; venture, risk; ready)
Fidèle (fidelity, faith, trust)
Filbert (very bright) **Filibert, Fulbert, Philbert, Philibert**
Firmin (firm, steadfast)
Flavien (yellow-haired) **Flavie**
Florent (blossoming, flourishing)
Florentin (blossoming, flourishing)
Florian (flowery)
Fortuné (fortune, chance)
Fouchier (people, folk)
Franchot (a Frenchman)
Francis (a Frenchman, a freeman)
Francisque (a Frenchman)
Franck (a Frank, a freeman)
François (French)
Frédéric (ruler of peace)
Fromont (free protection)
Fulk (people) **Fulke**
Gabriel (God is my strength)
Garnier (protecting army)
Gascon (?, perhaps *guest, stranger; from Gascony*)
Gaspard (treasure master)
Gaston (?, possibly *guest, stranger; from Gascony*)
Gaudens (rejoicing)
Gauvain (battle hawk)
Geoffroi (district; traveler; pledge + peace) **Geoffroy, Jeoffroi**
Georges (earth worker, farmer)
Georges-Andre (earth worker + manly)
Georges-Armand (earth worker + soldier)

Georges-Emile (earth worker + rival)
Georges-Ernest (earth worker + earnest)
Gérald (spear rule) **Géraud**
Gérard (brave with the spear)
Gérardin (brave with the spear)
Gerbert (bright spear)
Germain (a German)
Gervais (servant of the spear)
Giffard (give + bold, fierce)
Gilbert (bright pledge)
Gilles (goatskin shield of Zeus; a protection)
Godard (god hard)
Godfry (God's peace) **Godefroy**
Grégoire (vigilant, watchful) **Grégorie**
Griffin (like a griffin, monstrous)
Guillard (resolute protector)
Guillaud (resolute protector)
Guillaume (resolute protector)
Guillon (resolute protector)
Guiscard (?)
Gunter (bold in war)
Guy (a guide, a leader)
Guyon (a guide, a leader)
Haerveu (battle worthy) Breton name.
Hamon (home, house)
Hardouin (hard friend)
Hector (holding fast, restraining)
Helgaud (prosperous; hearty, hale) **Helgald**
Henri (home ruler)
Henriot (home ruler)
Herbert (army bright)
Hercule (glory of Hera)
Herman (army man, soldier)
Hervé (battle worthy)
Hilaire (cheerful)
Hippolyte (freer of horses)
Honoré (honor, esteem)
Hubert (bright heart)
Hugh (heart, mind, soul)
Hugo (heart, mind, soul)
Hugolin (heart, mind, soul)
Hugues (heart, mind, soul) **Hughues**
Humbert (people bright)
Ignace (?, perhaps *fire*)
Ilbert (battle bright) **Ilberd**
Imbert (iron people)
Isaak (laughter)
Isaïe (God is salvation)
Isidore (gift of Isis)
Ives (archer) **Ive**
Ivon (archer)
Jacques (supplanting, seizing by the heels)
Jacques-Emile (supplanting + rival)
Jacques-Louis (supplanting + famous in war)
Jean (God is gracious)

Jean-Armand (God is gracious + soldier)
Jean-Baptiste (God is gracious + a baptizer)
Jean-Christian (God is gracious + a Christian)
Jean-Claude (God is gracious + lame)
Jean-Louis (God is gracious + famous in war)
Jean-Luc (God is gracious + light; man from Lucania)
Jean-Marc (God is gracious + of Mars, warlike)
Jean-Michel (God is gracious + Who is like God?)
Jean-Paul (God is gracious + small)
Jean-Pierre (God is gracious + a rock)
Jenico (?, perhaps *fire*) Provençal form of Ignace.
Jérémie (God will uplift)
Jérôme (sacred name)
Joachim (God will establish)
Joël (the Lord is God)
José (he shall add)
Joseph (he shall add)
Jourdain (a flowing down)
Judicael (sportive) **Judical** A Breton name.
Jules (youth, downy)
Julien (youth, downy)
Juvénal (youth)
Juste (just, fair)
Justin (just, fair)
Karl (a man, freeman, peasant)
Kaspar (treasure master)
Klemens (mild, gentle, merciful)
Konrad (wise counsel)
Konstantin (constant, steadfast)
Lambert (bright land)
Lance (land)
Lancelin (little Lance *land*)
Lancelot (little Lance *land*)
Laurence (man from Laurentum) **Laurent**
Léandre (lion man)
Léo (lion)
Léon (lion)
Léonard (lion hard, bold as a lion)
Léonce (lion)
Léopold (bold people)
Lionel (little Léon *lion*)
Lothar (famous warrior)
Louis (famous in war)
Louis-Antoine (famous in war + ?, *priceless, of inestimable worth* is a folk definition)
Louis-Baptiste (famous in war + a baptizer)
Louis-François (famous in war + French)
Louis-Joseph (famous in war + he shall add)
Louis-Philip (famous in war + lover of horses)
Louis-Xavier (famous in war + the new house)
Luc (light; man from Lucania)
Lucien (light)
Ludwig (famous in war)
Lyle (dweller on the isle) **Lisle**
Macaire (blessed)
Magnus (great)

Manfred (man of peace)

Marc (?, perhaps *Mars; manly; soft, tender*)

Marcel (of Mars, warlike)

Marcellin (little Marcel *of Mars, warlike*)

Marius (of Mars, warlike)

Martin (of Mars, warlike)

Matthieu (gift of God) **Mathieu**

Mauger (spear grinder)

Maxime (greatest) **Max**

Maximilien (greatest + rival, trying to equal or excel) **Max**

Maynard (strong and hardy)

Meurisse (a Moor, dark-skinned)

Michel (Who is like God?)

Miles (?, perhaps *mild, peaceful; merciful*)

Milo (?, perhaps *mild, peaceful; merciful*)

Milon (?, perhaps *mild, peaceful; merciful*)

Moïse (drawn out of the water)

Narcisse (?)

Nathaniel (God has given) **Nathanael**

Nazaire (from Nazareth)

Nicodème (victory of the people)

Nicol (victory of the people)

Nicolas (victory of the people) **Nicholas**

Nicollin (little Nicolas *victory of the people*)

Noë (rest, comfort)

Noël (born at Christmas)

Odo (wealth)

Ogier (rich spear)

Olivier (olive tree)

Onfroi (people peace)

Osanne (hosannah)

Osbert (God bright)

Osmond (God protection) **Osmund**

Pascal (born at Easter)

Patrice (a patrician)

Paul (small) **Pol**

Paulin (little Paul *small*)

Perceval (pierce the valley)

Philibert (very bright, very famous)

Philippe (lover of horses)

Philippe-Antoine (lover of horses + ?, *priceless, of inestimable worth* is a folk definition)

Philippe-Emmanuel (lover of horses + God is with us)

Pierre (a rock, a stone)

Prosper (prosperous, favorable)

Quentin (fifth)

Rainier (wise army)

Randolf (shield wolf) **Randolph, Randulf**

Ranfred (counsel peace)

Raoul (counsel wolf) **Raul**

Raphael (God has healed)

Raymond (counsel protection)

Régis (kingly)

Rémy (oarsman) **Rémi**

Renaud (ruler of judgment) **Regnault, Reynaud**

René (rebirth)

Reynaud (powerful protection) **Renaud**

Richard (stern king)

Rinaldo (ruler of judgment)

Robert (bright with fame)

Robin (bright with fame)

Roby (bright with fame)

Roch (rest)

Rodolphe (famous wolf)

Roger (famous with the spear)

Roland (famous land)

Rolf (famous wolf)

Romain (a Roman)

Sacha (defender of mankind)

Samuel (name of God)

Sandre (defender of mankind)

Sanson (the sun)

Saül (asked of, borrowed)

Sébastien (man of Sebastia)

Secord (hard victory)

Serge (?)

Séverin (severe, strict)

Sigmund (victory protection)

Simon (heard) **Siméon**

Spiro (to breathe, to blow)

Stéphane (a crown, garland)

Sylvain (of the woods) **Silvain**

Sylvestre (of the woods)

Symphorien (bearing together)

Talbot (pillager, bandit; lampblack)

Tancred (think counsel)

Terrick (ruler of the people)

Théodore (ruler of the people)

Théophile (beloved of God)

Thibaut (people bold) **Thibault**

Thierry (ruler of the people)

Thomas (a twin)

Timothée (honor, respect)

Toussaint (all saints) Given to those born near All Saints' Day.

Tristan (tumult, sadness)

Trudeau (Thor's power)

Turstan (Thor's stone) **Turstin**

Ulrich (wolf rule)

Urbain (dweller in a village) **Urban**

Valdemar (famous ruler)

Valentin (healthy, strong)

Valère (to be strong)

Valéry (foreign ruler) **Valéran**

Victor (victory)

Vincent (conquering)

Vivien (alive)

Willelm (resolute protector)

Xavier (the new house)

Yann (God is gracious) A Breton form of John.

Yannic (little Yann *God is gracious*) **Yannick**

Yves (archer)

Yvon (archer)

SURNAMES

Alleaume (noble protection) **Alliaume**

Amand (lovable) **Aman, Amann, Amman**

Ambroise (immortal) **Ambroix**

Amour (love)

Amoureaux (loving, amorous; a philanderer or an affectionate man)

Ancel (serving maid)

André (manly)

Ange (angel) **Angeau**

Antoine (?, *priceless, of inestimable worth* is a folk definition) **Anthoine**

Arnaud (eagle power) **Arnaut**

Artaud (brave rule)

Aubert (noble and bright)

Aubry (elf rule; elf counsel)

Auguste (great, venerable)

Aumonier (a beggar)

Auvray (elf rule; elf counsel) **Auffray, Aufray, Aufroix, Aufroy**

Avenier (grower or seller of oats)

Avoine (grower or seller of oats) **Avenne**

Babeuf (a slaughterer of cattle)

Badaud (battle rule; stupid, an idiot, an openmouthed idiot) **Badault**

Baine (an attendant at a bathhouse)

Ballou (from Bellou)

Barbe (the bearded one, the mustached one) **Barbé**

Barbin (the bearded one, the mustached one)

Barbot (the bearded one, the mustached one)

Barraud (bear-might) **Barratt**

Bassett (the little, short, fat one)

Bastard (a bastard, an illegitimate person) **Bastardeau, Bâtard, Bâtardeau**

Bastien (from Sebastia)

Bataille (a combative person, dweller near the battlefield) **Battaille**

Battu (a beaten servant; dweller near the beaten track) **Battut, Batu**

Bai (chestnut or auburn-haired)

Baud (bold) **Baude, Bault**

Baudel (bold; a stubborn person, mulelike) **Baudeau, Baudelier**

Béal (dweller near the millrace)

Béatrice (bringer of blessings and joy) **Béatrix, Biétrix**

Beau (handsome one) The name was also given as a nickname to an unattractive person.

Beaufort (beautiful fort, beautiful stronghold)

Beaufoy (beautiful beech tree)

Beaulieu (fair place)

Beaumarchais (fair swamp) **Beaumarchaix**

de Beaumont (from Beaumont *beautiful mountain*)

de Beauregard (from Beauregard *beautiful place*)

Beaurepaire (lovely retreat)

Bec (mouth)

Bègue (the stammerer)

Bélier (ram) A nickname for one with great sexual prowess or powerfully built.

Benjamin (son of the right hand)

Benoît (blessed)

Berger (shephard) **Bergier**

Berle (water parsnips)

Berlier (grower or seller of water parsnips)

Berlioz (little Berle *water parsnip*)

Berthier (bright army) **Bertier**

Bertrand (bright raven) **Bertran**

Berube (dweller on the marshy ground)

Bettencourt (from Betto's farm)

Bignon (bruise, swelling) Originally a nickname for one who held his head to one side.

Billard (sword brave)

Billaud (sword rule)

Bizet (unhealthy complexion)

Blanchard (white and brave) **Blancard**

Blanche (white)

Blériot (badger; a badger hunter)

Blondeau (blond, fair-complexioned)

Blondel (blond, fair-complexioned)

Blondet (blond, fair-complexioned)

Blum (flower)

Boileau (a drinker of water, a teetotaler)

Bonnevie (good life) Originally given to a womanizer or a glutton.

Bonnin (little good one)

Bontemps (good weather) Originally given to one with a good disposition.

Bonvoisin (good neighbor)

Bossut (a hunchback) **Bossé, Bossuet, Bosseux**

Bouchard (big mouth)

Bouteiller (cup bearer, butler)

Bouvier (cattle drover, a herdsman)

Briand (strength, valor; high, hill; kingly)

Brun (brown)

Brunel (little brown one)

Burnell (the dark one)

Bussy (from the thicket)

Cabot (small-headed)

Caillard (piebald; a quail) **Callard**

Calvin (bald)

Camus (snub-nosed)

Carré (a squat, thickset man)

Cartier (a carter)

Castelneau (from the new castle) **Castelnau**

Cazenove (from the new house) **Cazneau**

Challoner (quilt maker, seller of quilts) **Chaloner**

Chamberlain (steward of the chamber)

Chambres (chamber attendant)

Champ (from the field)

Chandler (candle maker, seller of candles)

Chanter (singer)

Chapele (dweller at the chapel) **Chapell, Chappele, Chappelle**

Chapuis (a carpenter) **Chapus**

Charlier (a maker or seller of carts)

Charron (a maker of carts)

Chartier (a cart driver)

Chastel (from the castle) **Chastell**

Chatal (dweller near the livestock enclosure)

Chateaubriand (the castle of Brian *force, strength; hill, high; valor*)

Chausse (maker of shoes and leggings)

Cheftel (dweller near the livestock enclosure)

Chenal (dweller near the irrigation channel)

Chenault (dweller near the irrigation channel)

Chenaux (dweller near the irrigation channel)

Chêne (dweller near the oak tree)

Chenevier (a grower of hemp) **Chennevier**

Chénier (dweller near the oak tree)

Chenu (white-haired)

Cheptel (dweller near the livestock enclosure)

Chesne (dweller near the oak tree)

Chesnier (dweller near the oak tree)

Chrétien (a Christian)

Claudd (lame)

Clemenceau (gentle, mild)

le Clerc (clerk)

Clermont (bright hill)

Cocteau (little cock)

Coquard (a cock, rooster)

Corday (from Corday *young*)

Corde (a maker of string or cord)

Cordonnier (maker or seller of cord or ribbon)

Cornier (hornblower; dweller on the corner; dweller near the dogwood tree)

Coty (dweller on the slope or riverbank)

Coudray (from the hazel grove)

Couillet (little testicle) Originally meaning a good companion.

Courtier (agent, broker)

Courvoisier (a shoemaker) **Corvisier, Crouvoisier**

Daguerre (maker or seller of daggers)

Daladier (dweller near a patch of buckthorn; a righteous person)

D'Allemagne (from Germany) **D'Almaine**

Daudet (God has given)

Daumier (a farmer who paid a tithe of produce to the lord in order to keep his land)

David (beloved)

Debussy (of the woody place)

Dechêne (of the oak tree) **Duchêne**

Dechesne (of the oak tree) **Duchesne**

de Fraine (of the ash tree) **Defraine**

Degas (a dean)

Delachenal (of the irrigation channel)

de la Croix (of the cross) **Delacroix**

de la Rue (of the street) **Delarue**

des Bois (of the woods)

Descartes (dweller at the outskirts of town)

Desmoulins (dweller by the mill)

De Spagne (from Spain)

de Vere (of the fishing place) **Devere**

Devereaux (from Evreux) **Devereux**

Diderot (desired)

Dionne (of Dionysus)

Dorat (a gilder)

Dore (a gilder)

Doucette (little sweet one)

Du Bois (of the woods) **Dubois, Dubos**

Du Buisson (of the thicket) **Dubuisson**

Du Clos (of the enclosure) **Duclos**

Du Feu (of the beech tree) **Dufeu**

Du Lieu (of the place) **Dulieu**

Dumas (of the little farm)

Du Mont (of the mountain) **Dumont**

Du Parc (of the park) **Duparc**

Du Pont (of the bridge) **Dupont**

Du Prat (of the meadow) **Duprat**

Du Pre (of the meadow) **Dupre**

Du Puis (of the well, of the pit) **Dupuis**

Du Puy (of the high place) **Dupuy**

Durand (enduring) **Duran**

Du Val (of the valley) **Duval, Duvall**

Étourneau (a bird catcher)

Farge (forge)

Fargues (from Fargues *forges*)

Farjeon (little Farge *forge*)

Faudel (cattle or sheep barn)

Favre (smith, carpenter) **Faure**

Ferrand (peaceful journey)

Feuillette (dweller at the sign of the leaf [near a wine merchant])

Fleche (an archer)

Fleury (dweller by the flowers)

Fournier (oven keeper; parish baker)

Girardin (spear hard)

Giraud (spear hard)

Grellier (slender, slim) **Grelier**

Guerrier (warrior)

Herriott (little Henry *home ruler*)

Huguelet (little Hugues *heart, mind, spirit*)

Jolie (agreeable, pleasant)

Jourdain (a flowing down)

Lachenal (dweller near the irrigation channel) **Lachenaud**

La Cour (the short one)

La Croix (dweller near the cross)

Lafayette (dweller near a small grove of beech trees)

Laffitte (dweller near the boundary stone)

L'Allemand (the German)

Landeau (famous land)
Lanier (a weaver or seller of wool)
La Porte (dweller near the gate)
L'Archer (the archer)
Larousse (red-haired, ruddy-complexioned)
La Rue (dweller on the street)
Laurent (man from Laurentum)
La Valle (dweller in the valley)
La Vigne (dweller near the vineyard)
Le Bas (the short one) **Lebas**
Le Beau (the handsome one)
Le Blanc (the white-haired one, fair-complexioned)
Lecanu (the white-haired one) **Lecanut**
Le Grand (the large one)
Lejeune (the younger)
Lemaitre (the overseer)
Le Moine (the monk) **Lemoine**
Léon (the lion)
Lesueur (maker or seller of shoes)
Luce (light)
Lucette (little light)
Marais (dweller near the marsh)
Marchand (a merchant)
Martel (the hammer)
Martineau (little Martin *of Mars, warlike*)
Mathieu (gift of God)
Menier (a miner)
Mercier (seller of fine cloth)
Merritt (a tenant farmer)
Meserve (a surveyor of land)
Meunier (a miller)
Michelet (Who is like God?)
Minott (measurer of goods) **Minot**
Moliere (dweller near the quarry)
Moline (from Moline *mill*)
Moreau (from Moreau *dark-skinned, a Moor*)
Moser (seller of vegetables)
Nason (small nose)
Olivier (owner of an olive grove)
Orfevre (maker and seller of golden articles)
Pasteur (a shepherd)

Pelletier (a furrier)
Petit (little)
Petitperrin (little Pierre *rock*)
Philippe (lover of horses)
Picard (from Picardy *pike men*) **Picquart**
Pierpont (dweller near the stone bridge)
Poincare (square fist; a strong man)
Poirier (grower and seller of pears)
Poisson (seller of fish)
Poupard (child) **Poupart**
Prévost (commander)
Quenu (dweller near the livestock enclosure)
Regis (kingly)
Renaud (ruler of judgment) **Renault, Renaut**
Ricard (stern king)
Rivière (river)
Rothschild (red shield)
Rougemont (red mountain)
Rousseau (red-haired, ruddy-complexioned)
Royer (wheelwright)
Saint-Arnauld (a follower of Saint Arnold *eagle power*)
Saint-Simon (a follower of Saint Simon *heard*)
Saulnier (gatherer or seller of salt)
Savoy (from Savoy) **Savoie**
Séverin (severe)
Taillandier (maker or seller of iron articles)
Taillefer (cut iron)
Tailleur (a tailor)
Thibaud (people hard) **Thibault, Thibaut, Thibeau**
Thibodeau (people bold) **Thibedeau, Thibideau**
Thierry (people ruler)
Toussaint (all saints)
Trudeau (Thor's power)
Vaillant (valiant one)
Vaux (from Vaux *the valley*)
Vavasseur (under-vassal)
Verdier (a gamekeeper)
Vernier (protecting army) **Verniere**
Villiers (from Villiers *the hamlet*)
Wilmot (resolute protector)

Part Six

[THE UNITED STATES]

[CONTENTS]

[THE PRESIDENTS AND VICE PRESIDENTS OF THE UNITED STATES]

President	Years in Office	Vice President
1. George Washington	1789–1797	John Adams
2. John Adams	1797–1801	Thomas Jefferson
3. Thomas Jefferson	1801–1805	Aaron Burr
	1805–1809	George Clinton
4. James Madison	1809–1813	George Clinton
	1813–1817	Elbridge Gerry
5. James Monroe	1817–1825	Daniel D. Tompkins
6. John Quincy Adams	1825–1829	John C. Calhoun
7. Andrew Jackson	1829–1833	John C. Calhoun
	1833–1837	Martin Van Buren
8. Martin Van Buren	1837–1841	Richard M. Johnson
9. William Henry Harrison	1841–1841	John Tyler
10. John Tyler	1841–1845	none
11. James K. Polk	1845–1849	George M. Dallas
12. Zachary Taylor	1849–1850	Millard Filmore
13. Millard Filmore	1850–1853	none
14. Franklin Pierce	1853–1857	William R. King
15. James Buchanan	1857–1861	John C. Breckinridge
16. Abraham Lincoln	1861–1865	Hannibal Hamlin
	1865–1865	Andrew Johnson
17. Andrew Johnson	1865–1869	none
18. Ulysses S. Grant	1869–1873	Schuyler Colfax
	1873–1877	Henry Wilson
19. Rutherford B. Hayes	1877–1881	William A. Wheeler
20. James A. Garfield	1881–1881	Chester A. Arthur
21. Chester A. Arthur	1881–1885	none
22. Grover Cleveland	1885–1889	Thomas A. Hendricks
23. Benjamin Harrison	1889–1893	Levi P. Morton
24. Grover Cleveland	1893–1897	Adlai E. Stevenson
25. William McKinley	1897–1901	Garret A. Hobart
	1901–1901	Theodore Roosevelt
26. Theodore Roosevelt	1901–1905	none
	1905–1909	Charles W. Fairbanks

27. William H. Taft	1909–1913	James S. Sherman
28. Woodrow Wilson	1913–1921	Thomas R. Marshall
29. Warren G. Harding	1921–1923	Calvin Coolidge
30. Calvin Coolidge	1923–1925	none
	1925–1929	Charles G. Dawes
31. Herbert C. Hoover	1929–1933	Charles Curtis
32. Franklin D. Roosevelt	1933–1941	John N. Garner
	1941–1945	Henry A. Wallace
	1945–1945	Harry S. Truman
33. Harry S. Truman	1945–1949	none
	1949–1953	Alben W. Barkley
34. Dwight D. Eisenhower	1953–1961	Richard M. Nixon
35. John F. Kennedy	1961–1963	Lyndon B. Johnson
36. Lyndon B. Johnson	1963–1965	none
	1965–1969	Hubert H. Humphrey
37. Richard M. Nixon	1969–1973	Spiro T. Agnew
	1973–1974	Gerald R. Ford
38. Gerald R. Ford	1974–1977	Nelson A. Rockefeller
39. Jimmy (James Earl) Carter	1977–1981	Walter F. Mondale
40. Ronald Reagan	1981–1989	George Bush
41. George Bush	1989–1993	J. Danforth Quayle
42. William Jefferson Clinton	1993–Present	Albert A. Gore, Jr.

Chapter One

COLONIZATION TO THE GREAT AWAKENING
[1620–1750]

THE FIRST PEOPLE to arrive in the Americas are believed to have crossed over a land bridge between Siberia and Alaska 50,000 years ago or more. Over the next several thousand years, these new Americans developed into hundreds of unique cultural groups and spread over the continent, adapting to flourish in many different environments. By the time the first explorers reached North America, the native population had grown to around ten million.

In 1001, the Vikings became the first Europeans to settle in North America, but they left after a dozen years. Nearly 500 years later, other Europeans began arriving to look for treasure or a shorter route to India, and in the early 1600s, several more groups left Europe for North America. Each group had its own reasons for leaving, but all were faced with the same task of building new homes for themselves in the New World. Though not all groups were successful in their ventures, there were several who managed to persevere over the hardships.

Jamestown was settled in 1607 by adventurers looking for a northern route from Europe to Asia. In 1620, a second group, the Pilgrims, set sail for Jamestown, to find a new life and freedom of religion. Heavy seas forced the *Mayflower* off course, and in December 1620, the group landed at Plymouth, far north of Jamestown. The Dutch originally came just to trade for furs, but in 1626, religious unrest in Holland prompted thirty families to emigrate to Fort Amsterdam (on the site of New York City). The fourth major group were the Swedes and the Finns who settled in the Delaware Valley in 1638.

When these groups were first starting out, they were quite small and were a great distance from one another. As supply ships returned to the mother countries with favorable news, other people decided to brave the New World and more colonies were founded. More people meant a need for government.

POLITICS

IT TOOK SEVERAL years for Jamestown to become established to the point that survival was no longer a day-to-day affair. The settlers found no gold, but they did discover tobacco. John Rolfe, the husband of Pocahontas, was able to mix the American weed with a milder Jamaican leaf to produce the country's first cash crop.

The Virginia Company was finally getting a return on its investment, but investors had expected much greater profits and began to suspect those same profits were being diverted into the pockets of the colony's provisioners. The shareholders agreed reforms were necessary, and the colonists who were working for the company were finally able to own their own land. In 1619, Governor Yeardley of Virginia appointed six councillors and arranged for the election of a legislative assembly called the House of Burgesses. Landowning males of at least seventeen years of age were allowed to vote. Two representatives of the people were elected from each private estate and two from each of the company's four estates. In 1624, the English government became sufficiently alarmed when a census showed that only 1,277 out of the 6,000 colonists had survived. The Virginia Company had its charter revoked, and Virginia became a royal colony under the royal governorship of Thomas Wyatt.

In 1620, another group set sail from England with the permission of the Virginia Company. The ship, the *Mayflower,* was supposed to land at a settlement in northern Virginia, within the bounds of the company's authority, but rough seas forced the ship to a landing farther north, near Cape Cod. Of the 102 men, women, and children aboard ship, half were Puritans; the rest were called ''strangers,'' men who dreamed of owning their own property and making their fortune in the New World. Before leaving the ship, the Puritan leaders composed a short statement regarding their intentions to establish self-government. This statement, the Mayflower Compact, is the first constitution in America:

> In the name of God, Amen. We, whose names are under-written, the Loyal Subjects of our dread Sovereign Lord, King *James* . . . Having undertaken for the Glory of God, and Advancement of the Christian Faith . . . a voyage to plant the first colony in the northern Parts of Virginia; doe by these presents solemnly and mutually in the presence of God and one of another, convenant and combine ourselves togeather into a civil Body Politick, for our better Ordering and Preservation, and Furtherance of the Ends aforesaid; And by Vertue hearof to enacte, constitute, and frame, such just and equal Lawes, Ordinances, Acts, Constitutions and Offices, from time to time, as shall be thought most meete and convenient for the Generall good of the Colonie; unto which we promise all due Submission and Obedience.

Hunger and disease took their toll that winter, and only half the pilgrims survived until spring. It was at that time that the first Indian arrived in camp. He was Squanto, a man who could speak English and understood English customs. Squanto moved in with the Pilgrims and taught them what they needed to know to survive. After three years, their success inspired a wave of Puritan immigration from England and Europe.

In 1629, seventeen ships carrying more than 1,000 people set sail for the Massachusetts Bay Colony. The colony prospered, and between 1629 to 1640, more than 20,000 colonists arrived from England. While most of the new arrivals were Puritans, some were adventurers who planned to take advantage of new opportunities to own their own land or establish themselves in business.

Some settlers did not agree with the amount of power wielded by the governors of the Massachusetts Bay Colony, believing instead that the people should have control of the government. In 1636, Reverand Thomas Hooker led a group of like-minded people away from the Colony to Connecticut, where they founded the city of Hartford. The same year, the General Court ordered Roger Williams returned to England for spreading the radical ideas of separation of Church and state, for promoting religious toleration, and for promoting the notion that the Indians should be paid for their lands. Williams managed to escape and fled to Narragansett Bay, where he wintered with a group of Indians. In the springtime, he bought land from the Indians for a settlement and founded the colony of Rhode Island. He put his ideas of religious tolerance to practice and allowed complete freedom of religion. He also granted the right to vote to all white men. It didn't take long for others who were chafing under strict Puritan rule to find their way to Rhode Island. It became such a popular place to live that the Puritan leaders took to calling it Rogue's Island, for they saw it as a haven for rogues and scoundrels.

Each colony had its own governor and its own political system. The first governor of Massachusetts was John Winthrop. He tried to govern according to the colony's charter, which stated that only shareholders in the Massachusetts Bay Company had the right to vote. This was impractical, for most of the settlers were not shareholders. Settlers were Puritans, they had had their fill of others telling them what they could and could not do and were eager to protect what they had worked so hard for. Voting privileges were therefore granted to all men who were members of the Puritan church. At first, the governor was the sole authority, but after the colonies had grown, an assembly called the General Court was instituted.

In 1655, Peter Stuyvesant, the governor of New Amsterdam, sent a fleet of vessels to occupy Fort Christina in Delaware. The Swedes and Finns surrendered without a struggle and came under the authority of the Dutch. In 1664, the Dutch were forced to surrender their colony to the English; the English flag now flew over the entire east coast of the continent.

Georgia, the last of the original thirteen colonies, was founded in 1732 by James Oglethorpe, a humanitarian who wished to grant economic opportunity to England's debtors. After convincing King George II that England's poor deserved the chance to improve their lives, and after agreeing to pay their way to America, the king agreed to charter a colony. Oglethorpe accompanied 120 people to Georgia and helped build the first settlement at Savannah. The colonists were required to have farms no larger than fifty acres, and slavery was forbidden, as was the selling of rum.

When James II came to the English throne, he attempted to take tighter control of the colonies. In 1686, he combined all the colonies from Massachusetts to New Jersey into the Dominion of New England. Individual assemblies were dismissed, and Sir Edmund Andros was appointed governor of the Dominion. Two years later, James was ousted as king in favor of William and Mary, who ended the Dominion and restored the elected assemblies of the colonies.

The governments of the colonies were alike in many ways. Each was headed by a governor, and each also had an assembly that was usually composed of an upper house (the council of advisers) and a lower house whose members were elected by the people. Each colony also had its own rules regarding who could vote. Common to all was the right granted to all property-owning white males over the age of twenty-one. In some colonies, such as in Massachusetts, only members of a particular church could vote. In some local elections, the property-owning qualification was dropped so that all white men could vote.

Blacks and Indians had almost no rights. Laws known as slave codes controlled the behaviors of slaves and denied them their human rights. White women were treated almost the same, though unmarried women and widows had a few more rights than married women who, under the law, were at the mercy of their husbands. Single women and widows could sign contracts and sue in court, and in the Carolinas and Maryland, single women who were the heads of families could purchase land on the same terms as men.

SOCIETY

THE EARLY SETTLERS to America had a very rough time of it. Lack of food and medicines and inadequate housing resulted in an alarmingly high death rate. Of the 104 people to settle in Jamestown in 1607, only 38 were alive a year later, and of the 6,000 colonists to arrive by 1624, only 1,277 had survived. Most had died of starvation, but several hundred were killed in fighting the Indians.

In 1619, a Dutch ship with twenty Africans on board arrived in Jamestown to supply tobacco growers with workers. Though its possible these first few might have worked as servants and eventually earned their freedom, by the late 1600s, after the flow of indentured servants from England had slowed, many Virginia tobacco growers had grown dependent upon slave labor to work their crops.

Most of the original settlers in Jamestown were men, and it soon became apparent to Virginia Company directors that women were needed to "make the men more settled." Since permanent settlement depended upon families, in 1619, the company sent 100 women from England to become the wives of the colonists. The price for a woman? One hundred and twenty pounds of tobacco. The women were responsible for a tremendous amount of work. Everything had to be handmade from scratch, including food, medicine, clothing, and furniture. Childbirth and hard work conspired to kill many at a young age.

The Puritan colonists suffered the same hardships. The *Mayflower* made landfall in winter, and the colonists had to build shelters to get them through until spring. Some shelters were little more than dugouts in the hillside with branches or a tarp to cover the opening; others were crude huts made of branches and sod. By the time spring rolled around, half of the 102 colonists had died from pneumonia, scurvy, and a lack of food.

After that first winter, the Pilgrims constructed small, one-room timber cottages with thatched roofs. The typical cottage had a stone-lined cellar, a sleeping loft for the children, a large fireplace, and tiny windows covered with greased paper to let in a little light. The Pilgrims brought no furniture with them, so they had to make their own furnishings. Lack of space usually limited them to a rope bed built into a corner and a bench or two. They had no table linens, silverware, glasses, or china. Food was eaten off of wooden trenchers with wooden spoons, and wooden mugs or leather bottles held the drinks.

The Dutch were among the best-prepared to start their new life. They brought cattle, milk cows, horses, sheep, and pigs from Holland. They were also able to obtain supplies from the ships of the Dutch West India Company that regularly entered the harbor to pick up loads of furs and other cargo from the traders along the Hudson. Like the others, however, daily life for the first colonists was difficult. Though their first homes were crude dugouts or huts clustered around a small palisaded fort, they soon built wooden houses and furnished them with goods and heavy furniture obtained from the trading ships. After several years, those wooden houses gave way to brick or wood-and-brick combinations constructed like the homes they'd left behind in Holland—multistoried with very steeply pitched roofs of red tile under which were two attics. One room was usually set aside to serve as a shop for trading to neighbors, the Indians, and to the trading vessels. The typical village of the Dutch immigrants included houses grouped around a church, a brewery, a windmill, and a fort. In the countryside, Dutch farmhouses were low structures built from stone or clapboard, with gently pitched roofs of thatch or shingles.

The Dutch were a much livelier group than the English Puritans. They had a great love of life and took every opportunity to throw parties where games were played and large amounts of food consumed. A number of holidays were celebrated, including First Skating Day, when the ice was officially declared safe for skaters; Sant Nikolaas Day, where gifts were left for children; New Year's Day, where everybody kept their homes open to visitors; May Day, which included dancing on the village green; and Pinkster Day, which was a time for playing practical jokes and tricks.

The Dutch exerted as much energy in work as they did in play and their homes were always spotlessly clean. So much importance was placed on utilizing every bit of time that the women wore a belt around their waists, from which hung ribbons and chains to attach keys, scissors, a small sewing kit, a knitting bag, and other small objects they liked to keep at hand.

The Dutch organized the first civilian police force in America. Known as the rattle-watch, the men patrolled the streets at night, watching for fires, thievery, or any other kind of mischief that threatened the peace. The watchmen's duties also included announcing the time and the weather. On each hour, they swung their rattles (wooden objects with a stick that clattered on a cogged wheel), then loudly called out the hour and weather conditions.

In spite of the success of New Amsterdam, it was difficult to lure additional Dutch settlers to work on the farms of the Dutch West India Company, so the company actively encouraged settlers of all nationalities. By 1640, the governor was bragging that at least fifteen languages could be heard on the streets of New Amsterdam.

The Swedes were the most organized and the most prosperous of the new settlers. They also came with the blessing of their government. King Gustavus Adolphus had tired of the continual fighting in Europe and longed for a safe place for his people, one where "the laborer should reap the fruit of his toil, where the rights of conscience should be inviolate, an asylum for the persecuted, a place of security."

King Gustavus Adolphus died before he was able to see his dream come true, but the ministers of his young heir, Christina, saw the merits of the plan. The only drawback was the Swedish people themselves. They were a contented people and had no wish to leave their orderly country for a land of unknowns. At last, in 1638, a group of twenty-three soldiers departed Sweden for America and arrived at the mouth of the Delaware in the springtime when the trees were blooming and the fish were running in the streams. They established a trading post and sent word back that the land was fertile and abundant and that settlers were desperately needed. But the Swedes still did not want to leave their homeland. The authorities then came up with a plan: criminals could either become colonists or face severe punishments. Most chose to become colonists.

Some of the criminals were accused of being weather-witches—people who could accurately forcast the weather; some were accused of being able to locate water by the aid of a peeled, forked stick. People with those abilities were believed to be in league with the devil and were unwanted in Sweden. The worst offenders, however, were the Finns. Called "the forest-destroying Finns," they were responsible for cutting down trees and burning the slash in order to plant crops in the clearings. One might think that a community of criminals would not make for a very promising start, but the crimes these men were accused of ended up being valuable skills and abilities in the New World. The first log cabins in America were constructed by the Finns and the Swedes, as were the first *bastus,* large steam bathhouses built on the riverbank.

Some of the most interesting laws of the early Swedes and Finns had to do with singing. It was one of their favorite pastimes, and they often got together in choral groups to sing folk songs from their homeland. They were very particular about their music, however, and laws were passed so they did not have to listen to any but "good" songs. Anyone whose voice was not pleasant was obligated to either sing very quietly or to keep quiet altogether. Likewise, it was forbidden to "sing as if they were calling cows." Untimely singing, such as bursting out with song in the middle of the night, had a five shilling fine.

The Swedes got along very well with their Indian neighbors and were successful in their new homes, but it was still a problem to persuade other colonists to leave Sweden. After just seventeen years, their settlement, Fort Christina, was taken over by the Dutch. Though they now came under the authority of the Dutch governor, they continued living their lives as they always had.

As religious persecution in Europe heated up, more groups emigrated to the colonies. Thirteen Mennonite and Quaker families arrived from Germany in 1688, and by the end of this period, nearly 14,000 French Huguenots had immigrated and settled in all thirteen colonies. Scots who rebelled against the British government were forcefully sent to the colonies.

In the beginning of the eighteenth century, thousands more immigrated for religious reasons. The majority established themselves in Pennsylvania, Maryland, New York, and New Jersey. The largest group by far were the Irish. During the seventeenth and eighteenth centuries, thousands were sent over as indentured servants or were Catholic refugees fleeing persecution. Many voluntarily immigrated in search of adventure and opportunity, but many arrived involuntarily when the British government shipped political prisoners over to rid the country of its rebels. When the union between Scotland and Britain took effect in 1707, large numbers of Scots left their homeland to seek political freedom. By 1750, nearly 200,000 Irish or Scots-Irish were living in the colonies.

New arrivals to the country were, of course, very conscious of their nationalities, but as groups intermarried, much of that awareness dimmed, and an American identity was forged. With such a mix of cultures, American society was bound to develop differently than society had in any of the homelands. The people were fed much better, they had liberty of conscience, and they cherished their freedom.

There was a shadow on this otherwise bright new beginning that many overlooked: the situation with the Native Americans. In 1637, the Pequots, a Mohegan clan from the Connecticut Valley, were perceived as a threat to the settlers. A trumped-up murder charge was levied against them, and the Puritans, urged on by their ministers, decided to take matters into their own hands. Several villages were attacked and burned in the middle of the night, but the worst violation happened when a stockaded Pequot village was attacked, its 600 unarmed men, women, and children murdered, and the village burned to the ground. All-out war followed, and the Pequot tribe was nearly wiped out.

The English got on well with some of the other Native American tribes, including the Wampanoag, without whose help the Pilgrims surely would have perished. But as the settlers continued to take Indian lands, the natives began to take action. In 1675, Metacom, the chief of the Wampanoag (known as King Philip for his European dress and mannerisms), retaliated. King Philip's War lasted for fifteen months and caused considerable bloodshed and devastation on both sides. Metacom was eventually captured and killed; his wife, son, and about 1,000 others were sold into slavery in the West Indies.

Conflict occurred on the Virginia frontier, as well. In the 1640s, an agreement was reached on the division of land, but when successive waves of settlers ignored the agreement, fighting began once again.

RELIGION

FREEDOM OF RELIGION was the driving force that led the first Puritan colonists to the New World, and yet once here, they showed no toleration to others with differing points of view. Everyone, even the colonists who were not separatists, were obligated to attend the community church every Sunday and follow the strict Puritan rules for behavior.

Most of the early Dutch colonists were members of the Dutch Reformed Church, but they were nowhere as strict as the Puritans, and they openly welcomed people of other faiths. New Amsterdam was soon home to Catholics, Jews, and people from various Protestant sects, and it remained so after being taken over by the English. This same sort of religious toleration was present in several of the original thirteen colonies, such as in Rhode Island, Pennsylvania, and Delaware. The first Catholic colony was Saint Mary's in the new colony of Maryland.

As the colonies prospered, religion lost some of its importance. In the 1740s, a movement called the Great Awakening challenged people to reevaluate their lives and led to a renewal of religious spirit. New England preacher Jonathan Edwards, who was famous for his fire-and-brimstone sermons, introduced the movement. George Whitefield was another charismatic preacher so popular that thousands were attracted to his outdoor meetings.

Leaders of the established churches disapproved of the movement and warned their congregations not to attend the meetings. Nevertheless, the Great Awakening did have its supporters, and those who were followers of the movement often broke away from their established churches to form new groups with others of like beliefs.

The Great Awakening did more than just encourage people to turn their lives around. It helped foster a new spirit of toleration and acceptance of other religions and helped loosen Puritan control over both religious matters and politics.

Naming

EACH SUCCESSIVE GROUP to colonize the New World brought their own naming traditions. The English adventurers brought traditional English names. The next group of colonists, the English Puritans, brought more biblical names and those unique to Puritan naming traditions, such as Mercy, Mild, Temperance, etc. The Dutch brought their Dutch names, as did the Swedes, the Finns, the French, and the Germans.

FEMALE NAMES

Abelia (breath) French.
Abelone (of Apollo) **Abellona** Scandinavian.
Abigail (father of exaltation) **Abigall, Abbey** English.
Abijah (the Lord is father) English.
Abishag (wise) English.
Adah (adornment) English.
Adalheid (nobility) German, Scandinavian.
Adelaide (nobility) German, Scandinavian.
Adele (noble) **Adela** English, French, German.
Adeline (nobility) English.
Adria (from Hadrianus) German.
Agata (good) Scandinavian.
Agatha (good) English, German.
Agathe (good) French, German.
Agna (chaste, pure) English, Scandinavian.
Agnes (chaste, pure) English, French, German, Scandinavian.
Agnethe (chaste, pure) German.
Ales (nobility) English.
Alethea (truth) **Alethea, Aletheia, Alithea** English.
Alexandra (defender of mankind) English, German, Scandinavian.
Alfreda (elf counselor) English, German.
Alice (nobility) English, French.
Alicia (nobility) English, Scandinavian.
Aline (noble) English.
Alison (noble one) English.
Althea (wholesome) English.
Amalia (work) German, Scandinavian.
Amalie (work) French.
Amana (established) English.
Amata (love) English.
Amicia (?, possibly *friendship*) **Amice** English.
Amma (grandmother) Scandinavian.
Amy (beloved) English.
Anastasia (resurrection) English, German.

Andrea (womanly) English.
Angela (an angel) English.
Angelica (angelic) English. Used from the eighteenth century.
Anguish (sorrow) English.
Anne (grace, full of grace, mercy) **Ann, Anna** English, French, German, Scandinavian.
Anneliese (grace, mercy + God is my oath) **Annelise** German and Scandinavian.
Annette (little Anne) English, French, German, Scandinavian.
Annfrid (beautiful eagle) Scandinavian.
Annis (chaste, pure) English.
Antigone (of contrary birth) English.
Anthea (flowery) English.
Antonia (?, *priceless, of inestimable* worth is a folk definition) English, French, German, Scandinavian.
Aphrah (dust) **Aphra** English.
Apphia (increasing) English.
Appolonia (of Apollo) **Appolina** English.
Arabella (?) **Arabel** English.
Arminel (strength) English.
Arna (eagle) Scandinavian.
Artemisia (belonging to Artemis) English.
Asa (a god) Scandinavian.
Asenath (?, perhaps *thornbush*) English.
Aslaug (consecrated to God) Scandinavian.
Aspasia (welcome) English.
Asta (love) Scandinavian.
Astrid (beautiful goddess) German, Scandinavian.
Atarah (crown) English.
Athalia (the Lord is exalted) English.
Aud (riches, prosperity) Scandinavian.
Audrey (noble strength) **Awdry** English.
Aurelia (golden) English.
Aurelie (golden) French.
Aurora (the dawn) English.

Aurore (the dawn) French.
Averil (boar battle) **Averell, Everild** English.
Aveza (?) German.
Avice (?) **Avis, Avise** English.
Avila (?) German.
Aymie (beloved) English.
Azubah (forsaken) English.
Baptista (a baptiser) English.
Barbera (foreign woman) English, German.
Bathsheba (daughter of the oath, daughter of Sheba) English.
Bathshua (daughter of riches, daughter of Shua) English.
Beata (happy) English, French, German, Scandinavian.
Beatrice (bringer of joy) English, French, German.
Beatrix (bringer of joy) English, French, German, Scandinavian.
Belinda (?, perhaps *snake*) English.
Benedicta (blessed) English.
Benedicte (blessed) French.
Benedikta (blessed) German, Scandinavian.
Benet (blessed) **Bennet, Bennitt** English.
Berenice (bringer of victory) English.
Bernardine (bold as a bear) German, French, Scandinavian.
Bertha (bright) English, French, German, Scandinavian.
Bess (God is my oath) **Bessie** English.
Beth (God is my oath) English.
Beulah (married) English.
Bilhah (bashful, faltering) English.
Birgit (strength) **Brigitte** German, Scandinavian.
Birgitta (strength) **Birgitte** Scandinavian.
Bithiah (daughter of Jehovah) **Bethia** English.
Blanch (white) **Blanche** English, French.
Blanchia (white) English.
Bridget (strength) English.
Carla (full-grown, a woman) German, Scandinavian.
Carol (full-grown, a woman) Scandinavian.
Carola (full-grown, a woman) English.
Carole (full-grown, a woman) French.
Caroletta (full-grown, a woman) English.
Caroline (full-grown, a woman) **Caro, Carrie, Lina** English, French, German, Scandinavian.
Cassandra (?) English, French.
Catherine (pure, unsullied) **Catharine** English, French.
Cecile (blind, dim-sighted) French.
Cecilia (blind, dim-sighted) German, Scandinavian.
Celia (blind, dim-sighted) Scandinavian.
Charis (grace) English.
Charissa (grace) English.
Charity (charity, benevolence) English.
Charlotte (full-grown, a woman) **Charlotta** English, French, German, Scandinavian.
Charmian (a little joy) English.
Chloe (blooming, verdant) English, French.
Chloris (green) English, French, German.
Christa (a Christian) Scandinavian.
Christabel (?, probably *beautiful Christ*) **Christabell, Christy** English.

Christiana (a Christian, a follower of Christ) **Christy** English, French, German, Scandinavian.
Christine (a Christian, a follower of Christ) **Christina, Christy** English, French, German, Scandinavian.
Christmas (born at Christmastime) English.
Chrysogon (golden birth) English.
Cicely (blind, dim-sighted) **Cecily, Sisley** English.
Clare (bright, clear, famous) English, French, German, Scandinavian.
Clarimond (bright protection) English.
Clarinda (bright, clear, famous) English.
Clarissa (bright, clear, famous) **Clarice, Claricia** English, French, German.
Claude (lame) French.
Claudette (little Claude *lame*) French, German.
Claudia (lame) English, German, Scandinavian.
Clemence (clement, mild) English, French.
Clemency (clement, mild) **Clemencia** English.
Clementine (clement, mild) German.
Clorinda (green, verdant) English.
Comfort (comfort, care) English.
Constancy (constant) **Constance, Constanta** English.
Constanze (constant) German.
Cordelia (?, perhaps *daughter of the sea*) English.
Cordula (?, perhaps *daughter of the sea*) German.
Corinna (maiden) English.
Corinne (maiden) French.
Cornelia (a horn) English, French, German, Scandinavian.
Cynthia (of Kynthos) English.
Dagmar (splendid day; day maid) German, Scandinavian.
Dagna (new day) Scandinavian.
Damaris (?, possibly *heifer*) English.
Dania (God is my judge) Scandinavian.
Darling (dear one) English.
Deborah (a bee) English.
Debra (a bee) German.
Delia (from Delos) English.
Delilah (delicate) English.
Denise (of Dionysus) **Denis** English, French.
Desiderata (desire) English, French.
Desire (desire) English.
Diana (divine) English.
Diane (divine) French.
Dina (judged) **Dinah** English.
Donnet (given) English.
Dorcas (gazelle) English.
Dorithe (gift of God) English.
Dorothea (gift of God) English, French, German, Scandinavian.
Dorothy (gift of God) English.
Dove (a dove) English.
Drusilla (?) English.
Dulcibella (sweet and beautiful) **Dulcibell** English.
Dulcie (sweet) English.
Easter (born on Easter) English.
Ebba (strong as a wild boar) German, Scandinavian.

Eden (delight) English.

Edith (prosperous in war) **Edyth** English, French, German, Scandinavian.

Eleanor (light, torch, bright) **Elianor, Elinor** English.

Eleonore (light, torch, bright) French, German.

Elisabet (God is my oath) **Ailsa, Betje, Eliesabet, Elsa, Liese, Lis, Lisa, Lisabet** Scandinavian.

Elisabeth (God is my oath) **Elise, Lise, Lisette** French.

Elisabeth (God is my oath) **Betti, Elsa, Elsie, Liesbeth, Liese, Lisa, Lisbeth** German.

Elizabeth (God is my oath) **Bess, Bessie, Beth, Betty** (eighteenth century), **Eliza, Lizzie, Lizzy** English.

Elke (nobility) Dutch.

Ellen (light, torch, bright) **Elen, Ellin** English.

Ellis (nobility) English.

Eloisa (hale, hearty) English.

Eloise (hale, hearty) **Heloise** French.

Elsa (God is my oath) **Else** Scandinavian.

Emelie (rival, trying to equal or excel) French, German, Scandinavian.

Emeline (strength; work) **Emmeline** English.

Emeraud (an emerald) English.

Emerlee (strength; work) English.

Emilia (strength; work) English.

Emily (strength; work) English.

Emma (strength; work) **Em** English, French, German, Scandinavian.

Emmanuelle (God is with us) French.

Emmot (strength; work; rival) English.

Erika (eternal ruler) **Erica** German, Scandinavian.

Esmeralda (emerald) English.

Ester (myrtle; star) Scandinavian.

Esther (myrtle; star) English, French, German.

Ethel (noble) English, German.

Ethelinda (noble + tender, soft; a snake) English.

Eugenia (well-born, noble) English.

Eugenie (well-born, noble) French, German, Scandinavian.

Eulalia (fair speech) English.

Eulalie (fair speech) French, German, Scandinavian.

Eunice (good victory) English, French, German, Scandinavian.

Euphemia (fair speech) English.

Euphemie (fair speech) French.

Eustacia (steadfast; happy harvest) English.

Eva (life) German, Scandinavian.

Eve (life) English, French.

Eveline (?) **Evelina, Evelyn** English, German.

Faith (faith, trust) English.

Felice (lucky, happy) English.

Felicie (lucky, happy) French, German, Scandinavian.

Felicite (happiness) French.

Felicity (happiness) English.

Flavia (yellow) English.

Flora (a flower) German, Scandinavian.

Flore (a flower) French.

Florence (a blooming) English, French.

Florenz (a blooming) German.

Frances (a Frank, a freeman) English, French, German.

Freya (lady, mistress, noblewoman) **Freja, Froja** Scandinavian.

Friede (ruler of peace; gentle peace) **Freda, Frida, Frieda** German.

Frigg (beloved) Scandinavian.

Gabriela (God is my strength) **Gabriele, Gabrielle** English, German, French.

Gerd (guarded, protected) **Gard, Gerda** Scandinavian.

Gertrude (spear strength) English, German.

Gillian (youth, downy) English.

Gisela (pledge) Scandinavian.

Gislaug (consecrated pledge) Scandinavian.

Grace (grace, mercy) English.

Gretchen (a pearl) German.

Gretel (a pearl) German.

Gudrun (secret lore of the gods) Scandinavian.

Gunilla (battle maid) Scandinavian.

Gunnhild (battle maid) **Gunhild** Scandinavian.

Gwyneth (blessed) English.

Hanna (grace, full of grace, mercy) **Hanne** English, Scandinavian.

Hannah (grace, full of grace, mercy) English, French, German.

Harriet (home ruler) English.

Hedda (war) Scandinavian.

Heidi (nobility; battle protector) German.

Helah (rust) English.

Helen (light, torch, bright) English.

Helena (light, torch, bright) English, Scandinavian.

Helene (light, torch, bright) French, German.

Helge (prosperous, successful; blessed, holy) **Helga** German, Scandinavian.

Hephzibah (she is my delight) **Hepzibah, Hepsie** English.

Hermia (of Hermes) English.

Hermione (of Hermes) English.

Hester (myrtle; star) English.

Hilarie (cheerful) English, French.

Hilda (battle, war) German, Scandinavian.

Hildagarde (battle protector) German, Scandinavian.

Honor (honor, esteem) **Honour** English

Honora (honor, esteem) **Honoria** English.

Honore (honor, esteem) French.

Hope (hope, expectation) English.

Hosannah (save pray) **Hosanna** English.

Huldah (weasel) English.

Ida (work, labor) German.

Ideny (work, labor) **Idonea, Idonia, Idony** English.

Idona (renewal; work, labor) German.

Idony (again; renewal) **Idun** Scandinavian.

Ilse (God is my oath) German, Scandinavian.

Inga (Ing, a Norse fertility god) **Inge** German, Scandinavian.

Ingeborg (Ing's fortification) Scandinavian.

Ingrid (beautiful Ing) German, Scandinavian.

Irena (peace) Scandinavian.

Irene (peace) German.

Isabel (God is my oath) **Isabell, Isobel** English, French.

Ismenia (?) English.

Jacoba (supplanting, seizing by the heels) **Jacobina** Scottlish.

Jacklin (supplanting, seizing by the heels) **Jacqueline** English.

Jael (mountain goat) English.

Jane (God is gracious) English, French.

Janet (God is gracious; little Jane) **Jennet** English.

Janna (God is gracious) Dutch.

Janne (God is gracious) Danish, Norwegian.

Jean (God is gracious) **Jeane** English, French.

Jecoliah (the Lord prevails) English.

Jemima (pure) English.

Jerioth (curtains) English.

Jeromia (sacred name) English.

Jerushah (a possession) English.

Jessie (little Janet *God is gracious*; gift) English.

Joan (God is gracious) **Jone** English.

Johanna (God is gracious) **Joanna** English, German, Scandinavian.

Jonna (God is gracious) Danish.

Josefa (he shall add) Scandinavian.

Josephe (he shall add) French.

Joy (joy, happiness) English.

Joyce (merry, happy) English.

Judith (praised) English, French, German, Scandinavian.

Julia (youth, downy) English, German, Scandinavian.

Juliana (youth, downy) English, Scandinavian.

Julie (youth, downy) French.

Juliet (youth, downy) English.

Justina (right, just) English.

Kaatje (little Katherine *pure, unsullied*) Norwegian.

Karen (pure, unsullied) Danish.

Karita (charity, affection) Scandinavian.

Karla (woman) Scandinavian.

Karolina (woman) **Karoline** Scandinavian.

Katarina (pure, unsullied) **Kajsa, Kaysa, Kata** Swedish.

Katerina (pure, unsullied) **Katharina, Kaethe, Katja** German, Scandinavian.

Katherine (pure, unsullied) **Catherine, Kathren, Kathrine; Kate, Kitty** English, Scandinavian.

Katrine (pure, unsullied) Danish.

Katryn (pure, unsullied) **Katrien, Katrijn** Dutch.

Kerenhappuch (horn of antimony) English.

Keturah (incense) English.

Kezia (cassia) English.

Kinburga (royal fortress) English.

Klara (bright, clear, famous) Scandinavian.

Kristina (a Christian) German, Scandinavian.

Laetitia (happiness) **Letitia** English.

Laila (night, dark beauty) Scandinavia.

Lalage (babbler) English.

Laufeia (leafy island) Scandinavian.

Laura (laurel) English, French, German, Scandinavian.

Laurana (from Laurentum) English.

Laurence (from Laurentum) French.

Laurencia (from Laurentum) English.

Laurentia (from Laurentum) English.

Laureola (from Laurentum) English.

Lavinia (from Latium) English.

Leah (weary) English.

Lettice (happiness) **Letice** English.

Lillian (lily) **Lilian** English, French, German.

Lisa (God is my oath) English, German, Scandinavian.

Lisabet (God is my oath) **Lisbet** English, German, Scandinavian.

Liv (life) Scandinavian.

Lois (?) English.

Lora (from Laurentum) English.

Loretta (from Laurentum) **Lauretta** English.

Louise (famous in war) **Louisa** English, French, German, Scandinavian.

Love (love) English.

Lucia (light) English, German, Scandinavian.

Lucilla (light) English.

Lucinda (light) English.

Lucy (light) English.

Lydia (Lydian woman) **Lyddia** English, German

Mabel (lovable) **Mabill** English.

Mabella (lovable) English.

Madeline (from Magdala) English, French.

Madge (a pearl) English.

Magda (from Magdala) German, Scandinavian.

Magdalen (from Magdala) **Magdelyn** English.

Magdalena (from Magdala) German, Scandinavian.

Magge (a pearl) English.

Mahala (tenderness) English.

Mahalath (a lute, a lyre) English.

Mai (sea of bitterness or sorrow; a pearl) Scandinavian.

Malene (from Magdala) Danish.

Marah (bitterness) English.

Marcella (of Mars, warlike) English, German.

Marcia (of Mars, warlike) English.

Margaret (a pearl) **Margrett** English.

Margareta (a pearl) **Margaretha, Margit** Scandinavian.

Margarethe (a pearl) **Margrethe** Danish, German.

Margery (a pearl) **Margerie** Scottish, English.

Margriet (a pearl) Dutch.

Marguerite (a pearl) French.

Maria (sea of bitterness or sorrow) English, French, German, Scandinavian.

Marie (sea of bitterness or sorrow) English, French, German.

Mariel (sea of bitterness or sorrow) French, German.

Marion (sea of bitterness or sorrow) English.

Marjorie (a pearl) English.

Marta (a pearl) Danish.

Martha (lady, mistress) English, German, Scandinavian.

Marthe (lady, mistress) French.

Martina (of Mars, warlike) Scandinavian.

Mary (sea of bitterness or sorrow) English.

Matilda (strength in battle) **Mathilda** English, French, German, Scandinavian.

Maud (battle strength) English, German.
Mehetabel (God makes happy) English.
Melanie (dark, black) English, French, German
Melicent (work + strength) **Milesent** English.
Melissa (a bee) English. From the eighteenth century.
Melody (a melody) English. From the eighteenth century.
Meraude (of the sea) English.
Mercy (mercy, compassion) English.
Meriall (sea bright) **Merriall, Meryall** English.
Mia (sea of bitterness or sorrow) Danish, Swedish.
Mikaela (who is like God?) Swedish.
Mildred (mild strength) English.
Millicent (work strength) **Melicent, Melisande, Mellicent, Milicent, Millesant** English, German.
Minerva (?) English.
Miranda (worthy to be loved) English.
Miriam (sea of bitterness or sorrow) English.
Moll (sea of bitterness or sorrow) English.
Molly (sea of bitterness or sorrow) English.
Monday (born on Monday) English.
Monica (?) English.
Monika (?) German, Scandinavian.
Monique (?) French.
Naamah (sweetness) English.
Naomi (my joy, my delight) English.
Natalie (natal day; born at Christmastime) French.
Nel (horn) Dutch.
Nell (light, torch, bright) **Nelly** English.
Nelleke (horn) Dutch.
Nellie (horn) Scandinavian.
Nicol (victory of the people) English.
Nicole (victory of the people) French, German.
Nicolette (little Nicole *victory of the people*) French.
Nilsine (victory of the people) Swedish.
Noel (born at Christmas) English.
Noelle (born at Christmas) French.
Noemie (pleasant, beautiful) French.
Oceanus (born at sea) **Oceana** English.
Oddveig (spear woman) Scandinavian.
Odette (prosperity, riches) French, German, Scandinavian.
Odile (prosperity, riches) **Odila** French, German, Scandinavian.
Ola (ancestor's relic) Scandinavian.
Olaug (dedicated to the ancestors) Scandinavian.
Olga (holy) German, Scandinavian.
Olive (the olive tree) English.
Olivia (the olive tree) English.
Olympe (of Olympus) French.
Olympia (of Olympus) English.
Onora (honor) English.
Ophelia (help, succor) English.
Ophelie (help, succor) French.
Ophrah (a fawn) English.
Oriane (to rise; golden) French.
Orpah (a fawn, a forelock) English.
Orabell (?) **Orable, Oriabel** English.

Oriana (to rise) English.
Osanna (save now, save pray) English.
Parnell (a rock) English.
Patience (patience, forbearance) English.
Peg (a pearl) **Peggy** English.
Penelope (a bobbin) English, German.
Pentecost (fiftieth [day]) English.
Percy (from Percy, Normandy) English.
Perdita (lost) English.
Pernilla (a rock) Swedish.
Pernille (a rock) Danish.
Perpetua (perpetual, eternal) English.
Persis (Persian woman) English.
Petra (a rock) German, Scandinavian.
Petronel (a rock) **Peternel** English.
Petronilla (a rock) Scandinavian.
Philadelphia (brotherly love) English.
Philip (lover of horses) English.
Philippa (lover of horses) French.
Philomena (beloved) English.
Philomene (beloved) French.
Phoebe (bright, shining) **Phebe** English.
Pia (pious, devout) Scandinavian.
Pleasance (pleasant) English.
Precilla (former, ancient) **Priscilla** English.
Prisca (former, ancient) English.
Prothesia (?) English.
Prudence (prudent) English.
Rachel (ewe) English, French, German.
Rae (doe) Scandinavian.
Ragna (advice, counsel) Scandinavian.
Ragnhild (battle decision) Scandinavian.
Rakel (ewe) Scandinavian.
Ranveig (housewife) Scandinavian.
Rebecca (noose) French.
Rebecka (noose) Scandinavian.
Rebekah (noose) **Rabecca, Rebecca** English.
Rebekka (noose) Danish, German, Norwegian.
Renate (reborn) German, Scandinavian.
Renatus (reborn) English.
Renee (reborn) French.
Rhoda (a rose) English.
Richenda (little Richard *stern king*) English.
Rinda (?) Scandinavian.
Robina (bright with fame) English, Scottish.
Rona (mighty power) Scandinavian.
Rosabel (beautiful rose) English. Eighteenth-century invention.
Rosalie (rose garland) English, French.
Rosalind (horse or fame + gentle, tender or serpent) **Rosalinde** English, German.
Rosamond (horse protection) **Rossamond** English, German.
Rose (a rose) English, French.
Roseanna (rose + grace, full of grace, mercy) **Roseann, Roseanne** English. Eighteenth-century invention.
Rosemarie (rose + sea of bitterness or sorrow; dew of the sea) Scandinavian.

Rosemary (rose + sea of bitterness or sorrow) English. Eighteenth-century invention.
Rosetta (little Rose) English.
Rowena (famous friend) English.
Roxane (dawn of day) French.
Runa (secret lore) Scandinavian.
Rut (friend, companion) Scandinavian.
Ruth (friend, companion) **Ruthe** English, French, German.
Sabina (Sabine woman) English.
Sabine (Sabine woman) French, German.
Salome (peace) English, French.
Sandra (defender of mankind) English, French, German, Scandinavian.
Sapphira (beautiful) English.
Sara (princess) German, Scandinavian.
Sarah (princess) **Sara** English, French.
Sarey (princess) English.
Saskia (?) Dutch.
Scholast (a scholar) English.
Scholastica (a scholar) English.
Selina (the moon) **Selene, Selinah** English.
Seraphine (burning ones, angels) French.
Sibylla (fortune-teller, prophetess) **Sibella, Sibilla** Scandinavian.
Sidonia (linen cloth) **Sidonie, Sidony** English.
Signy (new victory) Scandinavian.
Sigrun (victory + secret lore) Scandinavian.
Silvia (wood) English.
Simone (heard) French.
Sislye (blind, dim-sighted) English.
Sixten (victory stone) Scandinavian.
Snow (snow, fair-complexioned) English.
Sofia (wisdom) Scandinavian.
Solange (yearly; solemn, religious) French.
Solveig (house of strength) Norwegian.
Solvej (house of strength) Danish.
Solvig (house of strength) Swedish.
Sophia (wisdom) English, German.
Sophie (wisdom) French.
Stephanie (a crown, garland) French.
Sunniva (gift of the sun) Scandinavian.
Susan (lily, rose) **Suzan** English.
Susanna (lily, rose) **Susannah** English, French, German, Scandinavian.
Susanney (lily, rose) English.
Suzanna (lily, rose) English.
Suzanne (lily, rose) French.
Svanhild (battle swan) Scandinavian.
Sybil (fortune-teller, prophetess) **Sybell** English.
Sybilla (fortune-teller, prophetess) German.
Sybille (fortune-teller, prophetess) French.
Sylvia (the woods) Scandinavian.
Sylvie (the woods) French.
Synnove (gift of the sun) Danish, Swedish.
Tabitha (roe, gazelle) English.
Tacy (hold peace, be silent) A Quaker name.

Tamar (palm, a date palm) **Tamara** English.
Temperance (patience) English.
Teodora (God's gift) Scandinavian.
Tessa (harvester) **Tess** English.
Theodora (God's gift) **Theo** English.
Theodosia (God-given) **Theo** English.
Theophila (God's friend) **Theo** English.
Theresa (harvester) **Tess, Tessa** English.
Therese (harvester) French.
Thermuthis (?) English.
Thirza (acceptance, pleasantness) **Thyrza** English.
Thomasin (little Tom *a twin*) **Thamasin, Tomazin** English.
Thomson (little Tom *a twin*) **Tomson** English.
Thora (Thor) Scandinavian.
Tiffeny (Epiphany, manifestation of God) **Tyffany** English.
Tilda (battle) German, Scandinavian.
Tirzah (acceptance, pleasantness) English.
Torunn (loved by Thor) Scandinavian.
Tova (beautiful Thor) Scandinavian.
Troth (fidelity, good faith) English.
Trudie (spear strength) **Trudy** German.
Tryphena (delicate, dainty) English.
Ulla (will, determination) Scandinavian.
Ulrike (noble ruler) **Ulrika** German, Scandinavian.
Unity (united) English.
Unn (love) Scandinavian.
Ursula (she-bear) German, Scandinavian.
Valentine (strong, healthy) English.
Valerie (strong, healthy) French, German.
Vara (?) Scandinavian.
Venetia (blessed) English.
Veronika (true image) German, Scandinavian.
Veronique (true image) French.
Victoria (victory) Scandinavian.
Vigdis (goddess of war) Scandinavian.
Viktoria (victory) German.
Viola (violet) English, Scandinavian.
Viole (violet) French.
Violet (violet-colored) English.
Violette (violet-colored) French.
Vita (life) Scandinavian.
Viviane (alive) German.
Vivien (alive) English, Scandinavian.
Vivienne (alive) **Vivianne** French, Scandinavian.
Wanda (?, perhaps *stem, young tree; a Wend, an old Slavic people*) German.
Wiebke (war fortress) German, Scandinavian.
Wigburg (war fortress) Scandinavian.
Wilfreda (resolute peace) German.
Wilhelmina (resolute protector) English, German, Scandinavian.
Willa (resolute protector) German.
Wilma (resolute protector) German.
Winifred (blessed peace) **Winnifred, Winnie** English, German.
Yolande (?, possibly *violet*) French.

Yvette (little archer) French, German, Scandinavian.
Yvonne (archer) French, German, Scandinavian.
Zephyrine (the west wind) French.
Zeresh (gold, splendor) English.

Zillah (shade) English. A favorite Gypsy name.
Zilpah (?) English.
Zipporah (a little bird) English.
Zoe (live) French, German, Scandinavian.

MALE NAMES

Abel (breath) English, French, German.
Abner (the father is a light) English.
Abraham (father of a multitude) English, German, Scandinavian.
Abram (father of exaltation) English.
Absalom (father of peace) **Absalon** English.
Adalard (noble and strong) French.
Adalbert (noble and bright) **Adelbert** German.
Adalrich (noble ruler) German.
Adam (man of the red earth) English, French, German, Scandinavian.
Adelulf (noble wolf) English.
Adolphe (noble wolf) French, German, Scandinavian.
Adrian (man from Hadrianus) English, German, Scandinavian.
Adrien (man from Hadrianus) French.
Aeneas (praiser) English.
Aksel (the father is peace) Danish.
Alain (?, perhaps *handsome; rock*) **Allain** French.
Alan (?, perhaps *handsome; rock*) **Allan, Allen** English.
Alard (noble and strong) **Allard** French.
Alarik (ruler of all) Scandinavian.
Alberic (elf ruler) English. Used from eighteenth century.
Albert (bright through nobility) English, French, German, Scandinavian.
Albin (white) French.
Aldred (old counsel) English.
Alduin (old friend) French.
Aldus (old) English.
Aldwin (old friend) English.
Alex (defender, defender of mankind) English, French, German, Scandinavian.
Alexander (defender of mankind) **Alec, Alick, Sander** English, German.
Alexandre (defender of mankind) French.
Alexis (defender) German.
Algernon (mustached) English, French.
Aloysius (famous in war) English, Scandinavian.
Alphonse (noble and ready) French.
Ambroise (immortal) French.
Ambrose (immortal) English.
Amedee (love of God) French.
Amias (?, perhaps *friendship*) English, French.
Amiel (industrious) English, French.
Amos (borne, a burden) English.
Amund (awe, fear; edge, point + protector) Scandinavian.
Amyas (?) English.
Anatole (sunrise, daybreak) French.

Ancelot (divine) French.
Anders (manly) Scandinavian.
Andor (eagle + Thor) Scandinavian.
Andre (manly) French.
Andrew (manly) **Dande, Dandy, Tandy** English.
Anker (harvester) Scandinavian.
Anketil (god's kettle, sacrificial cauldron) **Anchitel** English, Scandinavian.
Anselme (divine helmet) French.
Anthony (?, *priceless, of inestimable worth* is a folk definition) **Antony, Tony** English.
Antoine (?, *priceless, of inestimable worth* is a folk definition) French.
Anton (?, *priceless, of inestimable worth* is a folk definition) German.
Antonius (?, *priceless, of inestimable worth* is a folk definition) Dutch.
Ara (eagle) French.
Archebald (genuinely bold, genuinely brave) **Archibald** English, German, Scottish.
Aren (eagle rule) Norwegian.
Arend (eagle power) Dutch, German, Norwegian.
Aristide (best) French.
Armand (soldier, warrior) **Armond** French.
Armin (soldier, warrior) German.
Arnbjorn (eagle bear) **Armbjorn** Scandinavian.
Arne (eagle) **Aren** Scandinavian.
Arno (eagle) French.
Arnold (eagle ruler) German.
Arsene (male, virile) French.
Arthur (?) English, French.
Artur (?) German.
Arvid (eagle tree) Scandinavian.
Asa (healer) English.
Asmund (God is protector) Scandinavian.
Athelstan (noble stone) **Athestan** English.
Auberi (elf ruler) **Aubry** French.
Aubert (noble and bright) French.
Auguste (great, venerable) **August** French.
Augustin (great, venerable) French.
Augustus (great, venerable) English, French.
Aurele (gold) French.
Aurelien (golden) French.
Austin (great, venerable) English.
Averil (boar battle) English.
Aylmer (nobly famous) English.
Aylwin (elf friend) English.

Azariah (whom Jehovah helps) English.
Bachelor (unmarried) English.
Baldric (bold ruler) French.
Baldwin (bold friend) English, French, German.
Balthasar (?) English.
Baptist (a baptiser) English.
Baptiste (a baptiser) French.
Bardolph (bright wolf) English, French.
Barnabas (son of exhortation) **Barnaby** English.
Barnabe (son of exhortation) French.
Bartel (son of Talmai *hill, mound, furrows*) **Bertel** Dutch, German.
Barthelemy (son of Talmai *hill, mound, furrows*) French.
Bartholomaus (son of Talmai *hill, mound, furrows*) German.
Bartholomeus (son of Talmai *hill, mound, furrows*) Dutch.
Bartholomew (son of Talmai *hill,mound, furrows*) English.
Basil (kingly) English.
Basile (kingly) French.
Bastien (man from Sebasta) French, German.
Bellamy (beautiful friend) French.
Bendt (blessed) Scandinavian.
Benedict (blessed) **Benedick, Benedicter** English.
Benedikt (blessed) Scandinavian.
Benedikte (blessed) German.
Benjamin (son of the right hand) **Ben** English, French, German, Scandinavian.
Bennet (blessed) English.
Berend (strong as a bear) **Bernd** German.
Berg (mountain) German.
Beringer (bear spear) French.
Bernhard (bold as a bear) German.
Bernt (bold as a bear) Scandinavian.
Berold (bear rule) **Berolt** English.
Bertil (bright) Scandinavian.
Bertin (bright friend) English, French.
Bertram (bright raven) **Bertran** English, French, German, Scandinavian.
Bevis (beautiful) **Beavis, Beves** English, French.
Birger (helper) Swedish.
Bjorn (bear) **Bjarne** Norwegian, Swedish.
Blaise (deformed, stuttering) **Blaize** French.
Blase (babbler) **Blaze** English.
Bo (a householder) Scandinavian.
Boston (from Boston) English.
Brice (?) French.
Broder (brother) Scandinavian. Traditionally given to younger sons.
Bruno (brown) English, French, German, Scandinavian.
Caesar (blue gray; hairy) **Cesar** Given to those born by cesarean section. English.
Caleb (dog; faithful) **Calebb** English.
Camille (?; virgin of unblemished character) French.
Carl (a man, freeman) Scandinavian.
Caspar (treasure master) **Casper, Kaspar, Kasper** Scandinavian.

Cecil (blind, dim-sighted) French.
Cesar (blue gray; hairy) French.
Charles (full-grown, a man) English, French.
Chauncey (belonging to Chancey, France) **Chauncy** English, French.
Christmas (born at Christmas) English.
Christian (a Christian, a follower of Christ) English, French, German, Scandinavian.
Christoph (bearing Christ) German.
Christophe (bearing Christ) French.
Christopher (bearing Christ) **Chris, Kester, Kit** English.
Claud (lame) English.
Claude (lame) French.
Claus (victory of the people) German.
Clement (gentle, mild) English, French.
Comfort (comfort, care) English.
Conrad (bold counsel) French, German.
Constant (constant, steadfast) English, French.
Constantine (constant, steadfast) **Constans, Cuss, Cust** English, French.
Corneille (horn) French.
Cornelis (a horn) Dutch.
Cornelius (a horn) English.
Crispin (curled) English, French.
Cyprian (from Cyprus) English.
Cyprien (from Cyprus) French.
Cyriack (lordly) English.
Cyril (lordly) English.
Cyrille (lordly) French.
Cyrus (lord) English.
Damian (tamer) English.
Damien (tamer) French.
Dana (a Dane) Scandinavian.
Daniel (judged by God) **Daniell** English, French, German, Scandinavian.
Darby (from the settlement by the deer) English.
David (beloved) English, French, German, Scandinavian.
Denis (of Dionysus) **Denys** French.
Dennis (belonging to Dionysus) **Denis** English, German.
Derek (ruler of the people) German.
Diederik (ruler of the people) Dutch.
Dierk (ruler of the people) Scandinavian.
Dieter (ruler of the people) German.
Dietrich (ruler of the people) German.
Dirk (ruler of the people) German, Scandinavian.
Dominic (belonging to a lord, belonging to the Lord) **Dominik** English, German.
Dominique (belonging to a lord, belonging to the Lord) French.
Donald (world ruler) English.
Donatien (given by God) French.
Douglas (black, dark + blue, green, gray) English.
Drue (manly) English.
Durand (enduring, lasting) **Durant** English, French.
Dyonis (of Dionysus) English.
Easter (born at Easter) English.

Ebenezer (stone of help) English.
Eberhard (strong as a wild boar) German.
Eden (delight) English.
Edgar (wealthy spear) English.
Edmond (wealthy protection) **Edmund** English, French, German, Scandinavian.
Eduard (wealthy guardian) Dutch, German.
Edvard (wealthy guardian) Scandinavian.
Edward (wealthy guardian) English.
Edwin (wealthy friend) English, German.
Edzard (brave with the spear) Scandinavian.
Egil (point of a sword) Scandinavian.
Egon (point of a sword) German.
Eilert (brave with the spear) Scandinavian.
Eilif (immortal) Norwegian.
Einar (lone warrior) Scandinavian.
Eleazar (God has helped) English.
Eli (high, ascent) English.
Elias (Jehovah is God) English.
Elijah (Jehovah is God) English.
Elisha (God is salvation) English.
Elkanah (God created) English.
Ellery (alder tree) English, German.
Ellis (Jehovah is God; God is salvation) English.
Elmer (nobly famous) English.
Elof (lone descendant) Swedish.
Emanuel (God with us) English, Scandinavian.
Emery (ruler of strength) English, French, German.
Emil (rival, trying to equal or excel) German, Scandinavian.
Emile (rival, trying to equal or excel) French.
Emilien (rival, trying to equal or excel) French.
Emmanuel (God with us) French.
Enoch (dedicated) English.
Ephraim (very fruitful) English.
Erasmus (loved, desired) English,
Erik (eternal ruler) **Eirik, Eric** French, German, Scandinavian.
Erlend (foreigner, stranger) **Erland** Scandinavian.
Ernest (earnest, resolute) English, French.
Ernst (earnest, resolute) German.
Esau (hairy) English.
Eskel (sacrificial cauldron of a god) Scandinavian.
Eubule (he of good counsel) English.
Eugene (well-born) English, French.
Eusebius (pious) English.
Eustace (steadfast; happy in harvest) English.
Eustache (steadfast, happy in harvest) French.
Evelyn (?) English.
Everard (strong as a boar) English, French.
Everhart (strong as a boar) **Evert** Dutch.
Everitt (strong as a boar) **Everit** English.
Ewould (lawful rule) Dutch.
Eyvind (island of the Wend) Scandinavian.
Ezekiel (God strengthens) English.
Ezra (help) English.
Faas (resolute counsel) Dutch.
Fabian (a bean) English, German.

Fabien (a bean) French.
Farford (from the far ford; from the fair ford) English.
Felix (lucky) English, French, German.
Ferdinand (peace; journey; youth, life + courage; venture, risk; ready) French.
Festus (?) English.
Filbert (very bright) French.
Filip (lover of horses) Scandinavian.
Finn (from Finland) Scandinavian.
Fiske (fish) Swedish.
Flemming (a Flemming) Scandinavian.
Florence (a blooming) English.
Florent (blossoming) French.
Florentin (blossoming) French.
Florian (flowery) English, French, German, Scandinavian.
Floris (blossoming) Dutch.
Francis (a Frank, a freeman) English, French.
Francois (French) French.
Frank (a Frank) German.
Franz (a Frenchman) German.
Franziskus (a Frenchman) German.
Frederic (ruler of peace) French.
Frederick (peaceful king) **Frederic** English.
Frederik (peaceful king) Scandinavian.
Fredrik (peaceful king) Swedish.
Friederich (peaceful king) **Friedrich** German.
Friedhelm (peace helmet) German.
Frode (knowing, wise) Scandinavian.
Fulbert (very bright) English.
Gabriel (God is strength) English, French, German, Scandinavian.
Gamaliel (the Lord is recompense) **Gamaliell** English.
Garrett (spear rule) **Garett, Garit, Garitt** English.
Garrick (spear; brave with the spear) **Garek** German.
Garth (yard, enclosure) Scandinavian.
Gascon (?, possibly *guest, stranger*; *from Gascony*) French.
Gaspard (treasure master) French.
Gaston (?, possibly *guest, stranger*; *from Gascony*) English, French.
Gauvain (battle hawk) French.
Gavin (battle hawk) English.
Gedaliah (made great by Jehovah) English.
Geoffrey (district; traveler; pledge + peace) **Geffrey** English.
Geoffroi (district; traveler; pledge + peace) French.
Georg (earth worker, farmer) German.
George (earth worker, farmer) English, Scandinavian.
Georges (earth worker, farmer) French.
Gerald (spear rule) English, French, German.
Gerard (brave with the spear) French, Scandinavian.
Gerhard (brave with the spear) German, Norwegian, Swedish.
Gerlach (spear sport) German, Scandinavian.
Germayne (a German) **Germain** English, French.
Gerold (spear rule) Danish.
Gerolt (spear rule) Dutch.
Gershon (expulsion, stranger) **Gershom** English
Gervais (servant of the spear) English, French.

Gideon (hewer) English.
Giffard (give + bold, fierce) English.
Gilbert (bright pledge) **Gilbart, Gib, Gil** English, French, German.
Giles (goatskin shield of Zeus; a protection) English, French.
Gillis (goatskin shield of Zeus; a protection) Scandinavian.
Godfried (peace of God) Scandinavian.
Godfry (peace of God) French.
Godric (powerful God) English.
Godwin (friend of God) English.
Goldwin (friend of gold) English.
Gottfried (peace of God) German.
Gregoire (vigilant, watchful) French.
Gregor (vigilant, watchful) German, Scandinavian.
Gregory (vigilant, watchful) English.
Griffin (like a griffin, monstrous) English.
Guillaume (resolute protector) French.
Gunnar (war, strife, battle) Scandinavian.
Gunther (bold in war) French, German, Scandinavian.
Gustaf (staff of the Goths) German, Scandinavian.
Gustav (staff of the Goths) Scandinavian.
Guy (a guide, leader) English, French, German.
Guyon (a guide, leader) French.
Haakon (chosen son) Scandinavian.
Hagen (chosen son) Danish.
Hakan (chosen son) Swedish.
Hakon (chosen son) Danish, Norwegian.
Haldor (Thor's rock) Scandinavian.
Halsten (rock stone) Swedish.
Hamlet (little house) **Hamlett, Hamnet** English.
Hamon (little house) English.
Hannes (God is gracious) Scandinavian.
Hans (God is gracious) German.
Harald (home ruler) German, Scandinavian.
Harbert (bright army) Dutch.
Hardy (tough, hard) English.
Harry (home ruler) English.
Haward (high guardian) Scandinavian.
Hector (holding fast) English, French.
Heinrich (home ruler) German.
Helmut (courageous protector) German.
Hendrik (home ruler) **Henrik** German, Scandinavian.
Henning (home ruler) Danish.
Henry (home ruler) English, French.
Herbert (army bright) English.
Heribert (army bright) German.
Herman (warrior, soldier) English.
Hermann (warrior, soldier) German.
Hilaire (cheerful) French.
Hezekiah (God strengthens) English.
Hilary (cheerful) **Hilarie** English.
Hiram (exalted brother) English.
Hjalmar (warrior's helmet) Scandinavian.
Horatio (?) English.
Hosanna (save pray) English.
Hosea (salvation) English.

Hubert (bright heart) English, French, German, Scandinavian.
Hugh (heart, mind, soul) **Hugo** English, French, German.
Hugo (heart, mind, soul) Scandinavian.
Humphrey (warrior of peace) **Humfry** English.
Ingmar (famous Ing) Ing was a Norse fertility god. Scandinavian.
Ingram (Ing's raven; angel raven) English, Scandinavian.
Ingvar (Ing + warrior) Scandinavian.
Ira (watchful) English.
Isaac (laughter) **Isaack, Isack, Izaak** English, French.
Isaiah (God is salvation) English.
Isak (laughter) Swedish.
Israel (contender with God) English.
Ivar (archer, bow warrior) **Iver** Scandinavian.
Ives (archer) **Ivo, Yvo** English.
Jabez (height) English.
Jacob (supplanting, seizing by the heels) English, Scandinavian.
Jacques (supplanting, seizing by the heels) French.
Jakob (supplanting, seizing by the heels) Scandinavian.
James (supplanting, seizing by the heels) English.
Jan (God is gracious) **Jens, Jon, Jons** Scandinavian.
Janne (God is gracious) Swedish.
Japheth (enlargement) **Japet, Japeth** English.
Jared (descending) English.
Jason (healer) English.
Jasper (treasure master) English.
Jean (God is gracious) French.
Jean-Baptiste (God is gracious + a baptizer; John the Baptist) French.
Jean-Michel (God is gracious + Who is like God?) French.
Jedaiah (invoker of Jehovah) English.
Jedidiah (beloved of Jehovah) English.
Jeremiah (God will uplift) **Jeremy** English.
Jeremias (God will uplift) Scandinavian.
Jeremie (God will uplift) French.
Jeroen (holy name) Dutch.
Jerome (holy name) English, French.
Jesimiel (God sets up) English.
Jesper (treasure master) Danish, English.
Jesse (gift) English.
Jethro (excellence) English.
Joachim (God will establish) **Joachin** English.
Joakim (God will establish) Scandinavian.
Joel (the Lord is God) English, French.
Johann (God is gracious) German.
Johannes (God is gracious) German, Scandinavian.
John (God is gracious) English.
Jonas (dove) **Jonah** English.
Jonathan (God has given) English.
Joost (just, lawful) Dutch.
Jordaan (a flowing down) Dutch.
Jordan (a flowing down) **Judd** English.
Jorg (earth worker, farmer) German.
Jorgen (earth worker, farmer) Dutch, Swedish.
Jorn (earth worker, farmer) German.

Josef (he shall add) **Joop** Dutch, German.
Joseph (he shall add) **Joe** English.
Joshua (God is salvation) English.
Josiah (the Lord supports) **Josias** English.
Jozua (the Lord supports) Scandinavian.
Julian (youth, downy) English, German.
Julien (youth, downy) French.
Julius (youth, downy) English.
Justin (just) English, French.
Justus (just) German.
Juvenal (youth) French.
Karl (man, freeman) French, German, Scandinavian.
Kaspar (treasure master) French.
Kellam (?, possibly *warrior; from Kelham*) English.
Kennet (handsome, comely) Scandinavian.
Kenrick (royal rule) English.
Kenward (brave guardian) **Kenard** English.
Klemens (gentle, mild) French, German, Scandinavian.
Knut (knot) Scandinavian.
Konrad (wise counsel) French, German, Scandinavian.
Konstantin (constant, steadfast) French, German, Scandinavian.
Kristoffer (bearing Christ) Scandinavian.
Laban (white) English.
Lambert (bright land) English, French, German, Scandinavian.
Lance (land) French.
Lars (man from Laurentum) Scandinavian.
Laurance (from Laurentum) English.
Laurence (from Laurentum) **Laurent** French.
Lazarus (whom God helps) English.
Leif (what is remaining, relic; beloved) Scandinavian.
Lemuel (devoted to God) English.
Lennart (brave as a lion) Scandinavian.
Leo (lion) English, French, German, Scandinavian.
Leon (lion) French.
Leonard (bold as a lion) English, French.
Leonhard (bold as a lion) German.
Leopold (bold people) French, German.
Levi (joining) English.
Levin (dear friend) English.
Lewis (famous in war) **Louis** English.
Lionel (little lion) English, French.
Lorens (man from Laurentum) Scandinavian.
Lorenz (man from Laurentum) German.
Louis (famous in war) French, German.
Love (love, affection) English.
Luc (light; man from Lucania) French.
Lucas (light; man from Lucania) English, Scandinavian.
Lucian (light; man from Lucania) English.
Lucien (light; man from Lucania) French.
Lucius (light; man from Lucania) English.
Ludovic (famous in war) Scandinavian.
Ludwig (famous in war) French, German.
Lukas (light; man from Lucania) German.
Luke (light; man from Lucania) English.

Lyell (lion) **Lyel** English.
Maarten (of Mars, warlike) Dutch.
Magnus (great, large) French, German, Scandinavian.
Malachi (my messenger) English.
Manfred (peace of man) English, French, German, Scandinavian.
Marc (?, perhaps *of Mars; manly; soft, tender*) French.
Marcel (of Mars, warlike) French.
Marcus (?, perhaps *of Mars; manly; soft, tender*) English, Scandinavian.
Mark (?, perhaps *of Mars; manly; soft, tender*) English.
Markus (?, perhaps *of Mars; manly; soft, tender*) German.
Marmaduke (?, perhaps *servant or devotee of Maedoc*) English.
Marten (of Mars; warlike) Swedish.
Martin (of Mars, warlike) English, French, German.
Matheu (gift of God) Dutch.
Matheus (gift of God) **Mathew, Mathewe, Mathiu, Mattheus** English.
Matteus (gift of God) Swedish.
Matthews (gift of God) **Mathies** Danish.
Matthias (gift of God) **Mathis** English, German.
Mauger (spear grinder) English.
Maurits (a Moor) Scandinavian.
Max (greatest) German.
Maynard (strong and hardy) English, French.
Meinhard (strong and hardy) German.
Meshach (agile) English.
Meurisse (a Moor) French.
Micah (Who is like God?) English.
Michael (Who is like God?) English, German, Scandinavian.
Michel (Who is like God?) French.
Michiel (Who is like God?) Dutch.
Mikael (Who is like God?) **Mikel** Swedish.
Mikkel (Who is like God?) Danish, Norwegian.
Milo (?, perhaps *mild, peaceful; merciful*) **Milon** English, French.
Moise (drawn out of the water) French.
Mordecai (worshiper of Marduk) English.
Morten (of Mars; warlike) Norwegian
Moses (drawn out of the water) **Moyses** English.
Mourning (grieving) English.
Myles (?, perhaps *mild, peaceful; merciful*) **Miles** English.
Nathan (gift) English.
Natanael (gift of God) Scandinavian.
Nathanael (gift of God) **Nathaniel, Nathaniell** English, French, German.
Nehemiah (comforted by Jehovah) English.
Neville (from the new town) **Nevell, Nevil** English.
Nicholas (victory of the people) **Nicoll, Nichol, Coll** English.
Nicol (victory of the people) French.
Nicolas (victory of the people) French.
Nikolaus (victory of the people) Scandinavian.
Noah (rest, comfort) English.
Noble (proud, noble) English.
Noe (rest, comfort) French.

Noel (born at Christmas) French.
Norbert (north bright) German.
Obadiah (servant of God) English.
Odo (wealth) English, French, German, Scandinavian.
Ola (ancestor's relic) Norwegian, Swedish.
Olaf (ancestor's relic) Scandinavian.
Olav (ancestor's relic) **Ole** Danish, Norwegian.
Oliver (olive tree) English, German.
Olivier (olive tree) French.
Olof (ancestor's relic) **Olov, Oluf** Swedish.
Osanne (hosannah) French.
Osbern (god bear) **Osborn** English, Scandinavian.
Osbert (god bright) French.
Oscar (God's spear) English.
Oskar (God's spear) German, Scandinavian.
Osmond (God's protection) **Osmund** English, French.
Oswald (God's power) English, German.
Otto (rich) German.
Over (above) English.
Owen (lamb; youth; well-born, noble) English, Welsh.
Oziell (strength of God) English.
Pascal (Easter, born at Easter) English.
Patrick (a patrician, an aristocrat) English, German.
Paul (small) English, French, German, Scandinavian.
Paulin (small) English, French, German.
Percival (pierce the valley) **Percivall** English, French.
Percy (from Percy, Normandy) English.
Peregrine (a falcon) English.
Peter (a rock, a stone) English, French, German, Scandinavian.
Philip (lover of horses) **Philipp** English, French, German.
Phineas (oracle) English.
Pierre (a rock, a stone) French.
Quintin (fifth) English.
Rafe (counsel wolf) **Raph** English.
Ragnar (warrior of decision) Scandinavian.
Rainier (wise army) French.
Ralph (counsel wolf) English, German. Eighteenth century.
Randolph (shield wolf) **Randolf** German.
Randulf (shield wolf) English, French.
Ranfred (counsel peace) French.
Raul (counsel wolf) French, German.
Raymund (counsel protection) **Raimund** English, French, German.
Raynold (powerful protection) **Rainald, Raynald, Renold, Reynold** English.
Regin (judgment, decision) Scandinavian.
Reginald (judgment power) English.
Reinhard (brave counsel) German.
Remember (to remember) English.
Renfred (counsel might) English.
Resolved (dedicated) English.
Reuben (behold, a son!) English.
Reynard (counsel hard) English, French.
Richard (stern king) English, French, German.
Rikard (stern king) Scandinavian.
River (a river) English.

Robert (bright with fame) **Rob, Robb** English, French, German, Scandinavian.
Rodolphe (wolf fame) French, German.
Roger (famous with the spear) English, French, German.
Rogier (famous with the spear) Dutch.
Roland (famous land) **Rolland** English, French, German, Scandinavian.
Rolf (famous wolf) French, German, Swedish.
Roth (famous king) Scandinavian.
Rowland (famous land) English.
Rudolf (famous wolf) German.
Rurik (famous king) Scandinavian.
Rutger (famous spear) Dutch.
Samson (the sun) **Sansom** English.
Samuel (heard of God) **Samuell** English.
Sander (defender of mankind) English, German, Scandinavian.
Sandre (defender of mankind) French.
Sanson (the sun) French.
Sapcott (dweller near the sheep shelter) English.
Saul (asked for) English, French.
Sebastiaan (man from Sebastia) Dutch.
Sebastian (man from Sebastia) Scandinavian.
Sebastien (man from Sebastia) French, German.
Seth (appointed) English.
Severin (severe, strict) French.
Shem (renowned) English.
Siegfried (powerful peace) German.
Siegmund (victorious protection) German.
Sigge (victory, conquest) Scandinavian.
Sigmund (victorious protection) French, Scandinavian.
Sigurd (guardian of victory) German, Scandinavian.
Silas (ask for) English.
Simon (heard) English, French, Scandinavian.
Siward (victory protection) English.
Solomon (peaceful) English.
Soren (apart) Danish.
Spiro (to breathe, to blow) French.
Stanislav (government is glory) German.
Steen (stone) Danish.
Stefan (a crown, a garland) **Steffen** German, Swedish.
Steffan (a crown, a garland) Swedish.
Stein (stone) Norwegian.
Steinar (stone warrior) Scandinavian.
Sten (stone) Swedish.
Stephan (a crown, a garland) Scandinavian.
Stephane (a crown, a garland) French.
Stephen (a crown, a garland) **Steven** English, Scandinavian.
Steven (a crown, a garland) Dutch.
Svein (strong, youth) **Sven** Norwegian.
Sveinn (strong, youth) Scandinavian.
Svend (strong, youth) Danish, Swedish.
Svends (strong, youth) Swedish.
Swain (stong, able, wise) Scandinavian.
Sylvester (of the woods) German.
Sylvestre (of the woods) French.

Talbot (?, pillager, bandit; lampblack) English, French.
Teodor (gift of God) Swedish.
Terrick (ruler of the people) French.
Theodoor (gift of God) Dutch.
Theodoric (ruler of the people) English.
Theophilus (lover of God) English.
Thomaas (a twin) Dutch.
Thomas (a twin) English, French, German, Scandinavian.
Thor (thunder) Scandinavian.
Thurstan (Thor's stone) English, German.
Timothee (honor, respect) French.
Timothy (honor, respect) English.
Titus (?, possibly *to honor*) English.
Tobias (God is good) **Toby** English, German.
Torsten (Thor's stone) German.
Tristan (tumult, sadness) French.
Tristram (tumult, sadness) English.
Tycho (hitting the mark) Scandinavian.
Tyge (hitting the mark) Danish.
Tyko (hitting the mark) Swedish.
Ulf (wolf) German, Scandinavian.
Uriah (God is light) English.
Valdemar (famous ruler) **Waldemar** Scandinavian.
Valentin (healthy, strong) French, German, Scandinavian.
Valentine (healthy, strong) English.
Valere (to be strong) French.
Valery (to be strong) French.
Victor (victor, winner) French, German.
Vidkun (wide experience) Scandinavian.

Viktor (victor, winner) German.
Vincens (conquering) German.
Vincent (conquering) English, French, German, Scandinavian.
Vital (vital, life-giving) German.
Vivien (alive) French.
Von (hope) Scandinavian.
Vyncent (conquering) English.
Walden (to rule) German.
Waldo (to rule) German.
Walter (ruler of an army) English, German, Scandinavian.
Wanton (one who wants everything) English.
Werner (protecting army) **Verner, Warner** German, Scandinavian.
Wilfred (desire for peace) English, German, Scandinavian.
Wilhelm (resolute protector) German.
Willelm (resolute protector) French.
Willem (resolute protector) **Vilhelm** Scandinavian.
William (resolute protector) English.
Winston (from Winston *friend's town*) English.
Wolf (wolf) German.
Wolfgang (traveling wolf) German.
Yves (archer) French.
Yvon (archer) French.
Zachariah (God remembers) English.
Zacharias (God remembers) English.
Zacheus (God remembers) English.
Zebedee (God bestows) English.
Zebulun (to carry, to exalt) English.
Zephaniah (the Lord has hidden) English.

SURNAMES

The Spanish who founded the Florida colony of Saint Augustine in 1565 were the first Europeans to settle in America. In 1598, Juan de Oñate was given the task of starting the first colony north of Mexico. Soon, many other missions and settlements were founded, and names of Hispanic origin were established throughout the American Southwest.

Likewise, the first British colonists and adventurers brought their own surnames to the New World. A little over a half of the people in the first two Jamestown contingents are known by name, but of those that are, the vast majority have British surnames.

In spite of the extremely high death rate in early Jamestown, new settlers continued to arrive, and the English government saw America as the perfect place to send its undesirables. Thosands of vagrants, prisoners, and destitute men, women, and children were rounded up and sent to Virginia to be put to work. The Bridewell, a foundation established by Queen Elizabeth for the education of destitute children, sent 200 parentless children over in 1619 and 1620.

In 1623, "Lists of the Livinge and Dead in Virginia" were prepared and contain over a thousand surnames. Most of the names are of British origin, but several French and Italian names are also listed.

In time, other settlements were founded by other cultural groups, and the pool of surnames in America widened. Among the British, French, and Germans, surnames were hereditary. That was not the case with the Scandinavians who used patronymics that changed with each generation. To the father's name, the suffixes -

sen,-son and *-datter,-dotter* were added. Thus, Karl Eriksson's son Anders was known as Anders Karlsson; his daughter Anna was Anna Karlsdotter.

There was some variation. In Norway, by this point in time, people living in the cities often had a permanent family name. A country dweller added the name of his or her farm to the first name and patronymic. Among the Dutch, surnames were largely hereditary, but in some instances, children carried on their mothers' surnames rather than their fathers'.

The following surnames are gathered from passenger lists dating from 1607 to 1750. The Spanish surnames are associated with the missions of the Southwest.

Aarsen (son of Arthur) Dutch.

Adams (son of Adam) English, Welsh.

Ackerman (a farmer or ploughman) English.

Ackermann (a farmer) German.

Albright (nobly bright) **Allbright** English.

Alden (old friend) English.

Allen (?) **Alleyn, Allin** English.

Allerton (from the alder tree farm) English.

Almond (temple protection; a German) English.

Anderson (son of Anders *manly*) English.

Andersson (son of Anders *manly*) Swedish.

Andres (manly) German.

Andrews (son of Andrew *manly*) **Andrewes, Androwes** English.

Andriesen (son of Andries *manly*) **Andriessen** Norwegian.

Appel (dweller near the apple tree) **Apfel** Dutch.

Aragón (from Aragón) Spanish.

Arents (son of Arend *eagle rule*) **Arens** Norwegian.

Arentsen (son of Aren *eagle rule*) Norwegian.

Armstrong (strong arms) **Armstrang** English.

Arnesen (son of Arne *eagle*) **Arnsen** Norwegian.

Arnold (eagle power) English.

Arrundell (little swallow) **Arundell** French.

Ashton (dweller at the town by the ash trees) English.

Askew (from Aiskew *oak woods*) **Ascue** English.

Aston (from the east town; noble stone) English.

Austin (great, venerable) **Austen** English.

Bach (dweller near the brook) German.

Bachelor (young knight, novice in arms) **Bachelour** English.

Bacon (seller of bacon) English.

Bagwell (from Bagnall *Baga's wood*) English.

Baker (a baker) English.

Baldwin (bold friend) **Baldwine, Baldwyne** English.

Ball (ball; bald place; the round one) English.

Ballentine (from Ballindean *the village by the hill*) Scottish.

Bamford (dweller near the ford by the trees) English.

Barber (a barber, one who practiced surgery and dentistry) English.

Barnett (little Bernard *bold as a bear*) **Barnet, Barnitt** English.

Baron (a baron, a nobleman) **Barran** English.

Barrett (bear ruler) **Barrat, Barratt, Barret** English.

Bassett (the little short, fat one) French.

Bauer (a farmer) German.

Baugh (poor, shabbily dressed) English.

Bayley (bailiff, steward) **Bailey, Baley, Baylie, Bayly** English.

Baylife (bailiff, steward) **Bayliff, Bayliffe**

Beale (fair, beautiful; from Beal *the bee hill; Beaga's corner*) English.

Beane (Ben *son of the right hand*) English.

Beaufort (beautiful fort) French.

Beaumont (beautiful mountain) French.

Beck (dweller near the brook) Norwegian, Swedish.

Bennet (blessed) English.

Benson (son of Ben *son of the right hand*) English.

Berenger (bear spear) English.

Berg (dweller near the mountain) Norwegian, Swedish.

Bergen (dweller near the mountain) Norwegian.

Beriston (from Beriston) English.

Berman (a bear keeper) English.

Betscomb (from Bette's valley) **Betscombs** English.

Biggs (son of Bigg *big, tall*) English.

Billington (from Billa's hill) English.

Blackman (black man; pale man) English.

Blake (fair, pale-complexioned) English.

Blanchard (whitish) English, French.

Bleecker (a fuller, a bleacher of cloth) Dutch.

Blom (flower) Swedish.

Bogaert (worker in an orchard) Dutch.

Boot (maker or seller of boots) English.

Booth (dweller near the hut or stall) English.

Boulte (bold) English.

Bouvier (cattle drover, a herdsman) French.

Bowyer (a maker or trader of bows) English.

Boys (dweller near or in the woods) **Boise, Boyce, Boyes** English, French.

Braby (dweller at the broad enclosure or farm) English.

Bradford (from the broad ford) English.

Bradshaw (dweller at the broad wood) English.

Bradway (from the broad way) **Bradwaye** English.

Branch (from Branche, Normandy) English, French.

Brewster (a brewer) English.

Britterige (bright rule) **Britteridge** English.

Brocke (a badger; dweller near the marshy land) English.

Brookes (dweller near the brook) English.

Brown (brown, brown-haired) **Browne** English.

Browning (little brown one) English.

Burger (from Burg *fortification, stronghold*)

Burges (a freeman of a borough) English.

Burnell (the dark one) French.

Burnhouse (from the burnt house) English.

Burrows (from Burrow *fort; hill*; dweller near the stronghold) **Burrowe** English.

Burtt (bright) English.

Butler (keeper of the casks of wine; maker of bottles) **Buttler** English.

Butten (from Bitton *the homestead on the River Boyd*; a maker or seller of buttons) English.

Buxton (Bucca's stone) English.

Calvert (calf herder) English.

Carman (a cart driver) English.

Carpenter (a carpenter) English.

Carter (a cart driver) English.

Carver (carver or cutter of wood) English.

Causey (from Causey *the causeway*) English.

Cazenove (from the new house) French.

Chamberlain (steward of the chamber) English, French.

Chandler (maker or seller of candles) French.

Chapele (dweller at the chapel) **Chapell, Chappelle** French.

Chaplaine (a chaplain) **Chaplin** English.

Chapman (a peddler, a merchant) English.

Chard (from Chard) English.

Chauncey (belonging to Chancey, France) English.

Chilton (the noble youth's village) English.

Chrismus (born at Christmas) English.

Christiansen (son of Christian *a Christian*) **Christianson** Norwegian.

Claes (victory of the people) **Clees** Norwegian, Swedish.

Clairborne (dweller near the stream with clay banks) English.

Clarke (a clerk) **Clark** English.

Classen (son of Clas *victory of the people*) **Claassen, Claesen, Claessen, Clasen, Clausen** Norwegian, Swedish.

Clemens (son of Clemens *gentle, mild*) Scottish.

Clement (gentle, mild) French.

le Clercq (the clerk) French.

Coltman (keeper of the colts) English.

Colyer (a maker or seller of charcoal) English.

Combs (dweller in or near the valley) **Combes** English.

Conrad (bold counsel) German.

Cooke (a cook) English.

Cooksey (from Cooksey *Cucu's island*) English.

Cooper (a maker or seller of barrels) English.

Cornille (?, possibly *horn*) French.

Cornish (a Cornish person) English.

Cotton (from Coton, Cotton; dweller in the cottage) English.

Crakston (from Crafton *place where wild saffron grew*) English.

Dalbie (from Dalby *the settlement in the dale, the farm in the valley*) English.

Damont (from up the river; from the mountain) French.

Danvers (from Anvers) English.

Davenport (from Davenport) English.

Davies (son of Davy *beloved*) **Daves, Davis** Welsh, English.

Davison (son of David *beloved*) English.

Dawson (son of Daw *beloved*) English.

Day (worker in the dairy; a female servant; a kneader of bread) English.

De Carpentier (of the carpenter) French.

Decker (a roofer) **Deckert, Dekker** Dutch.

De Graaf (the count) **De Graaff, De Graf, De Graff** Dutch.

Delacroix (of the cross) French.

de Marc (son of Marc *of Mars; manly; soft, tender*) French.

de Oñate (from Oñate) Spanish.

Derwin (dear friend) English.

Deverell (from Deverill) English.

De Vries (the Frisian) Dutch.

De Witt (white-haired, light-complexioned) Dutch.

Doty (the brave man) **Doughty** English.

Doughty (brave, strong) English.

Drinkwater (one who drinks water) The name implies one so poor as to not be able to afford ale, the most common drink. English.

Dubois (of the woods) French.

Dudley (from Dudda's wood) English.

Duffy (descendant of Dubhthach *dark, black*) Irish.

Dumont (of the mountain) French.

Dunn (brown-haired) **Dune** English.

Du Pon (of the bridge) French.

Dupre (of the meadow) French.

Durand (enduring) French.

Eames (the uncle's son) English.

Eaton (from Eaton *homestead on the river or island*) English.

Edmundson (son of Edmond *wealthy protector*) English.

Ellis (Jehovah is God; God is salvation) English.

Ellyson (son of Ellis *Jehovah is God; God is salvation*) English.

Emerson (son of Emery *work; work ruler*) **Emmerson** English.

Endecott (dweller at the end cottage) **Endicott** English.

English (an Englishman) English.

Essex (from Essex) English.

Evans (son of Evan *youth; well-born*) Welsh.

Evensen (son of Even *God is gracious*) **Evenson** Swedish.

Ewen (lamb; youth; well-born) English, Welsh.

Fairechild (beautiful child) English.

Farmer (a farmer) English.

Farnell (dweller at the fern-covered slope) English.

Farrar (friendly) Scottish.

Farrow (dweller at the sign of the boar) English.

Fischer (a fisherman; a seller of fish) German.

Fisher (a fisherman; a seller of fish) English.

Fisk (a fisherman) Swedish.

Fleming (a Fleming) **Flemming** English.

Fletcher (maker or seller of arrows) English.

Floyd (gray) Welsh.

Fossett (crooked legs) English.

Foster (a game warden, a forester) English.

Fredrickson (son of Fredrick *peaceful ruler*) **Fredricksen, Fredriksen, Fredrikson** Danish, Norwegian.

French (a French person) English.

Fuller (a cleaner and thickener of cloth) English.

Gale (dweller near the jail; cheerful, happy) English, Welsh.

Gardiner (a gardener) **Gardenar** English.

Gaspar (treasure master) French.
Gay (happy, cheerful) English.
Gerber (a worker with leather) German.
Gibbs (son of Gib *bright pledge*) English.
Gillchrist (servant of Christ) Scottish.
Gloster (?, possibly from Gloucester) English.
Golding (son of Golda *gold*) English.
Goldsmith (a goldsmith) **Gouldsmith** English.
Gonzales (a metalsmith) Spanish.
Goodman (the good man) English.
Goodyer (good year) **Goodyear** English.
Grant (great, large) English.
Graye (gray-haired) English.
Greene (dweller near the village green) English.
Gregory (vigilant, a watchman) English, Scottish.
Grimes (son of Grim *mask*) English.
Haile (dweller near the slope, dweller near the corner of land; dweller by or worker at the hall) English.
Halam (from the remote valley) **Hallam** English.
Hale (dweller in the remote valley) English.
Hall (dweller near the manor house; servant in the manor house) English.
Hansen (son of Hans *God is gracious*) **Hanson** Norwegian, Swedish, English.
Harris (son of Harry *home ruler*) Welsh, English.
Hatfield (from Hatfield *the heather field*) English.
Hawthorn (dweller near the hawthorn) **Hawthorne** English.
Haynes (dweller near the enclosures) English.
Helme (dweller near the roofed shelter; dweller near the elm tree; helmet) Dutch.
Hendriks (son of Hendrik *home ruler*) **Hendricks** Dutch.
Hendriksen (son of Hendrik *home ruler*) Danish, Swedish.
Henriksen (son of Henrik *home ruler*) **Henrichsen, Henrikson** Swedish.
Hermansen (son of Herman *soldier, warrior*) **Hermannsen** Danish, Norwegian, Swedish.
Herrott (little Henry *home ruler*) French.
Hichcocke (descendant of little Hitch *stern king*) English
Hill (dweller near the hill) **Hills** English.
Hillstrom (boulder stream) **Hellstrom** Swedish.
Hilton (from Hilton *the hill village*) English.
Hobart (mind bright) English.
Hobson (son of Hob *bright with fame*) English.
Hoff (dweller near the courtyard; from Hof *farm*) German.
Holbeck (from Holbeck *the brook in the hollow*) English.
Holland (from Holland) English.
Hollis (dweller near the holly tree) English.
Holm (dweller near the holly tree; dweller on the island) **Holme** Danish, Norwegian.
Holman (dweller on the island) Norwegian.
Hooke (dweller near the bend in the river) English.
Hooker (dweller near the bend in the river) English.
Hopkins (son of little Hob *bright with fame*) Welsh, English.
Howard (brave heart; chief warden; ewe herder) **Heward, Huward** English.
Howland (dweller near the hill) English.

Hughes (son of Hugh *heart, mind, soul*) **Huges** Welsh, English.
Hutchinson (son of Hutch *heart, mind, spirit*) English, Scottish.
Ingram (Ing's raven; angel raven) English, Scandinavian.
Irish (an Irish person) English.
Ives (archer) English.
Jackson (son of Jack *gift of God*) English.
Jacob (supplanting, seizing by the heels) English.
Jacobsen (son of Jacob *supplanting, seizing by the heels*) **Jacobsen, Jakobsen** Danish, Swedish.
Jäger (a hunter) German.
Jansen (son of Jan *God is gracious*) **Janson, Janssen, Jansson** Scandinavian.
Jensen (son of Jens *God is gracious*) **Jenson, Jenssen, Jensson** Scandinavian.
Johnson (son of John *God is gracious*) English, Scandinavian.
Jones (son of Jone *God is gracious*) English, Welsh.
Jordan (a flowing down, descend) **Jorden, Jourdan, Jurdain** English, French.
Kaufmann (a merchant) German.
Kendrick (chief man, chief hero) English.
King (a king) **Kinge** English.
Knight (servant, knight) English.
Knowles (dweller at the top of the hill) English.
Kramer (a shopkeeper, a peddler who used a small cart) German.
Lambert (bright land) **Lambard, Lambart, Lambarth,** English, French.
Landman (land man) English.
Langemore (dweller near the long moor) English.
Latham (from Latham *the barn enclosure*) English.
Latimer (interpreter) **Latimore** English.
Laurens (man from Laurentum) French.
Lawless (an outlaw, licentious) **Lawelesse** English.
Legg (leg) English.
Levet (beloved Goth) English.
Ley (dweller near the meadow or woods) English.
Lightfoote (fleet-footed) English.
Lincoln (from Lincoln *Lindum Colonia*) **Linkon** English.
Linge (dweller at the heath) English.
Litster (a dyer of cloth) English.
Lloyd (brown, gray) **Loyd** Welsh.
Longe (tall) English.
Loring (from Lorraine; dweller near the laurel tree; descendant of Loren *laurel*) English.
Ludwig (famous in war) German.
Lupo (wolf) Italian.
Lyon (lion) English.
McAllister (son of Alastair *defender of mankind*) Scottish.
McAlpine (son of Ailpean *?*) Scottish.
McArthur (son of Arthur *?*) Irish, Scottish.
McAulla (son of Amlaidh *ancestor's relic*) Irish, Scottish.
McCollum (son of Calum *dove*) Irish, Scottish.
McDonald (son of Donald *world ruler*) Irish, Scottish.
McDougald (son of Dougal *dark stranger*) **McDugald** Irish, Scottish.

McInnish (son of Innes *island*) Scottish.

McIntire (son of the carpenter) Scottish.

McKenzie (son of Coinneach *fair one, handsome*) Irish, Scottish.

McMillan (son of the monk) Scottish.

McNeil (son of Naill *champion*) Irish, Scottish.

McPhaden (son of Paddin *little Patrick*) Irish, Scottish.

Maddeson (son of Mad *gift of God*) English.

Madsen (son of Mad *gift of God*) Danish.

Mailer (an enameler) **Mailler** English.

Maitland (discourteous, rude) English.

Malaet (the unfortunate one, cursed) **Malet** English.

Mallory (the unfortunate one, cursed) English.

Manson (son of Magnus *great, large*; *son of the servant*) **Mansen** Norwegian.

Marchant (a merchant, a trader) **Marchand** English, French.

Margeson (son of Marge *a pearl*) English.

Marshall (keeper of the horses; a high official) English.

Martin (of Mars, warlike) English, French.

Martín (of Mars, warlike) Spanish.

Matheson (son of Matthew *gift of God*) **Mathewson, Mathisen, Mathison** Danish.

Matthews (son of Matthew *gift of God*) **Mathews** English.

Mercier (seller of fine cloth) French.

Metzger (a butcher) German.

Michaell (Who is like God?) English.

Michel (Who is like God?) **Michell** English, French.

Midwinter (born at Christmastime) English.

Miller (a grinder of grain) English.

Milner (a grinder of grain) English.

Minter (a minter of money) English.

Mittelberg (from the middle mountain) German.

Moises (drawn out of the water) French.

de Moone (from Mohon, France) English.

Moore (dweller near the moor) **More** English.

Moreau (from Moreau *a Moor*) French.

Morewood (dweller at the moor woods) English.

Morton (from the settlement near the moor) English.

Muhlenberg (from the mountain stream) German.

Müller (a miller) German.

Mullins (descendant of Maolan *little bald one;* from Moulines, France) **Mullines** Irish, French.

Murphy (sea warrior) Irish, Scottish.

Naylor (a maker of nails) English.

Nelson (son of Nel *victory of the people*) **Neilsen, Neilson, Nelsen** English, Scandinavian.

Nesbitt (from Nesbit or Nesbitt) **Naisbet, Naisbit, Nesbit** English.

Neville (from the new town) English.

Newman (a newcomer) English.

Nicholas (victory of the people) **Nichollas** English.

Nicoles (son of Nicol *victory of the people*) **Nicholls, Nichols** English.

Norman (a Norman, from Normandy) English.

Oake (dweller near the oak trees) **Oak** English.

O'Bryan (descendant of Brian *force, strength, valor; high, hill; kingly*)

Okley (dweller near the oak tree meadow or woods) English.

Oldfield (dweller by the old field) English.

Olives (owner of an olive grove) English.

Osborne (god-bear) **Osborn, Osbourn, Osbourne** English.

Osman (god-protection) **Osmand** English.

Pacheco (?, possibly from the name Francisco *free man*) Spanish.

Packer (a packer of wool) English.

Palmer (a palm-bearing pilgrim returning from the Holy Land) English.

Parker (a gamekeeper, keeper of the park) English, Welsh.

Parttin (from Parton *the pear orchard*) English.

Pastorius (shepherd, pastor) German.

Pattison (son of Pattie *an aristocrat, a patrician*) English.

Paulett (little Paul *small*) English, French.

Paulson (son of Paul *small*) English, Scandinavian.

Peake (dweller near the pointed hill) English.

Peck (dweller near the pointed hill) English.

Peppet (little whistler) English.

Perce (?, possibly *from Percy, La Manche; rock, stone*) **Peerse, Perse** English.

Percy (from Percy, La Manche) **Peircy, Percie** English, French.

Perkinson (son of Perkin *rock, stone*) Welsh.

Peterson (son of Peter *rock, a stone*) **Petersen** English, Scandinavian.

Petit (little) French.

Phillips (son of Philip *lover of horses*) **Philips, Phillipps** English.

Phippeny (little Philip *lover of horses*) English.

Pickering (from Piker's meadow) English.

Pierre (rock, stone) French.

Pikard (one from Picardy) English.

Plimpton (from Plympton *settlement of plum trees*) English.

Pooley (dweller near the water's edge, dweller near the island pool) English.

Poore (pauper) English.

Prendregast (?, perhaps *dweller at the village near the castle*) English.

Preston (from Preston *the priest's settlement*) English.

Price (son of Rhys *ardor*) Welsh.

Priest (a priest) **Preist** English.

Pugett (from Puget *a ridge or high place*) English.

Quackenbush (dweller near the frogs' bushes) Dutch.

Quaile (son of Paul *small;* dweller at the sign of the quail) English.

Quicke (quick, lively) English.

Quillin (descendant of Cuileann *pup, whelp*) Irish.

Quinton (from Quinton *the queen's manor*) English.

Raleigh (from the red meadow; from the roe woods) English.

Ralston (from Rolleston *settlement of Hruodwolf*) English.

Rasmussen (son of Rasmus *beloved*) **Rasmusson** Danish.

Ratclife (from the red cliff) **Ratcliffe** English.

Ravenhill (dweller at the raven's hill) English.

Rawse (son of Raw *a boor, a simpleton;* son of Rauf *shield wolf*) English.

Rawton (?, possibly *from the red town; from the roe town; from the rough town*) English.

Rayley (from Rayleigh *the roe woods*) English.

Redford (dweller at the red ford) English.

Reeve (superviser of the laborers) English.

Reid (red-haired, ruddy complexioned) English, Scottish.

Reinolds (powerful protection) English.

Renard (ruler of judgment) French.

ap Richard (son of Richard *stern king*) Welsh.

Richards (son of Richard *stern king*) English.

Rigdale (from the valley by the ridge) English.

Rittenhouse (the house near the reeds) German.

Robertson (son of Robert *bright with fame*) English.

Rochester (from Rochester *Hróf's stronghold*) English.

Rockefeller (dweller near the rye field) Dutch.

Rogers (son of Roger *famous with the spear*) Welsh, English.

Roosevelt (dweller near the rose farm) Dutch.

Rosenberger (rose mountain) Swedish.

Ross (dweller on the peninsula) **Rosse** Scottish.

Rothschild (red shield) French.

Rowsley (?, perhaps *from the rough meadow*) English.

Royall (dweller at the rye hill) English.

Russell (little red-haired one) English.

Rust (red-haired) English, Scottish.

Rutgers (son of Rutger *fame spear*) Dutch.

Sadeler (a maker or seller of saddles) **Sadler** English.

Saford (from Salford *the willow ford*; dweller near the salt ford) English.

Sanderson (son of Sander *defender of mankind*) English, Scottish.

Scarborough (from Scarborough *the castle at the gap*) English.

Scarlett (wearer of scarlet-colored clothes) English.

Schaffer (a shepherd) German.

Schenk (seller of wines; a cupbearer) **Schenck** Dutch.

Schneider (a tailor) German.

Schreiner (a maker of cabinets) German.

Schultz (an overseer; a sheriff) German.

Schumann (a maker of shoes) German.

Schuster (a cobbler) German.

Schutz (a watchman) German.

Schuyler (a schoolmaster) Dutch.

Sharpe (keen, quick-witted) English.

Sharples (from Sharples *the steep place*) English.

Shepard (shepherd) **Sheppard** English.

Sheppy (from Sheppey *the sheep's isle*) English.

Sismore (great victory) English.

Smalpage (the small, slender page) English.

Smith (a smith, a metalworker) **Smithe** English.

Snow (born during the time of snow; white-haired, very fair-complexioned) English.

Snyder (a tailor) **Snider** Dutch.

Sparshott (spear wood) English.

Spence (assistant in the provision room) English.

Spencer (dispenser of household provisions) English.

Spengler (a metalworker, a tinsmith) German.

Spurling (little sparrow) English.

Standish (from Standish *the stony enclosure*) English.

Stokes (from Stoke) English.

Stone (dweller near the stone) English.

Story (strong) English.

Strange (strange, a foreigner) **Straunge** English.

Strong (strong) English.

Sutton (from Sutton *the southern village*) English.

Symon (heard) English, Italian.

Tait (cheerful, gay) **Tate** English, Scandinavian.

Talbot (lampblack) **Talbott** English, French.

Tattam (from Tatham *Tata's homestead*) **Tatum** English.

Taylor (a tailor) English.

Temple (dweller near the temple) English.

Thimblely (?, possibly a misspelling of Thimbleby *from Thômbel's [man with a paunch] estate*) English.

Thompson (son of Thom *a twin*) **Tompson** Scottish, English.

Thorne (dweller near the thorn tree) English.

Thornegood (good thornbush) English.

Thorogood (throughly good) English.

Tillie (from Tilley *branch;* from Tilly *lime tree*) English.

Tinker (mender of pots) English.

Tomlin (little Tom *a twin*) English.

Trahern (super iron) **Trachern** Welsh.

Trevore (discreet; from the great house) Irish, English.

Trudeau (Thor's power) French.

Trumble (strong-bold) **Trumbull** English.

Trussell (from Trusley *the wood with the fallen leaves*) English.

Turner (one who makes objects with a lathe) English.

Tuthill (dweller near the toot-hill [lookout hill]) English.

Tyson (son of Ty *of Dionysus*) Dutch.

Ulman (a seller of oil) English.

Underhill (dweller at the foot of a hill) English.

Unwin (young bear-friend) English.

Updyke (dweller on the dike) **Updike** Dutch.

Uppington (dweller up in the village) English.

Usher (a doorkeeper) English, Scottish.

Vale (dweller in the valley) English.

Valentine (strong, healthy) English.

Van Buren (from the neighborhood) Dutch.

Van Camp (dweller at the field) Dutch.

Vance (dweller near the small hill) Dutch.

Van Cleve (from the city; from Cleve *cliff*) **Van Cleave, Van Cleef, Van Clief** Dutch.

Van Damme (dweller near the dam) **Van Dam, Van Damm** Dutch.

Vanderbilt (dweller near the heap or mound) Dutch.

Vanderkemp (from the field or open space) Dutch.

Vanderpool (dweller near the pond) Dutch.

Vanderveer (dweller near the ferry; a ferry operator) **Vander Veer** Dutch.

Van Dyke (dweller near the dike) **Vandyck** Dutch.

Van Holland (from Holland) Dutch.

Van Kleef (from Cleve, Germany) Dutch.

Van Patten (from Putten *well, pool*) Dutch.

Van Pelt (from Pelt *the marsh*) Dutch.
Van Winkle (shop worker; dweller near the shop) **Van Winkel** Dutch.
Vaughan (small) **Vaughn** English.
Vennell (dweller at the small street or alley) **Vennall, Venel** English.
Vincent (conquering) English.
Vroom (pious, wise) Dutch.
Vidal (vital, full of vitality) **Vidall** English.
Wagner (a wagon maker; a wagoneer) German.
Waller (a fuller of cloth) English.
Walsh (a Welsh person) English.
Walshman (a Welsh man) English.
Walton (from the homestead in the woods, from the homestead by the wall) English.
Warren (a game preserve) English.
Watson (son of Wat *ruler of an army*) **Wattson** English.
Watts (son of Watt *ruler of an army*) English.
Webber (a weaver) English.
Weber (a weaver) German.
Welder (from Weald *forest*) English.
West (from the west) English.
Weston (from the western homestead) English.
Wheelwright (a wheel maker) English.
White (white, fair-complexioned) English.
Whitehead (white-haired) English.
Whitt (white, fair-complexioned) English.
Wilder (dweller in a forest; powerful army) English.
Williams (son of William *resolute protector*) English.
Williamson (son of William *resolute protector*) English.

Wilson (son of Will *resolute protector*) **Willson** English.
Winslow (from Winslow *Wine's hill or burial mound*) English.
Winthrop (from Wina's dairy farm) **Winthropp, Wynthrop** English.
Wood (dweller in the woods) English.
Woodley (dweller at the clearing in the woods) English.
Woodson (son of Wooder *wood hard*) English.
Woodward (officer in charge of the woods; a woodsman) English.
Wyatt (little Guy *guide*) English.
Yeardley (dweller at the enclosed yard) **Yeardly** English.
Yeats (dweller near the gate or gap in the hills) **Yates** English.
Yocum (God will establish; God gives strength) **Yocom, Yokum** Dutch.
Yonkers (the young nobleman; squire) **Yonker, Younker** Dutch.
Youngberg (heather mountain) Swedish.
Youngdahl (heather valley) Swedish.
Younglove (heather leaf) Swedish.
Youngquist (heather twig) Swedish.
Zagar (a sawyer, a cutter of boards) **Zager** Dutch.
Ziegler (a mason, a maker or user of brick and tile) German.
Zimmer (a carpenter) German.
Zinzendorf (village tenant farmer) German.
Zoller (a collector of taxes on goods entering the country) German.
Zwicker (from Zwickau; maker and seller of nails; strong spear) German.
Zylstra (dweller near a drainage sluice) Dutch.

Chapter Two

THE ROAD TO REVOLUTION TO THE MEXICAN WAR
[1750–1845]

POLITICS

DURING THE EARLY years of colonization, England and the other homelands had largely left the colonies to themselves. Each had its own government with an elective assembly to pass laws and approve taxation to run government. Outside of the colonies, France claimed the lands to the north and west and protected them with a line of forts; Spain claimed lands to the south.

As the fur trade expanded, English trappers began venturing into French territory by crossing the Appalachians and making their way into the Ohio Valley in search of furs. The French, determined to protect their profitable trading arrangements with the Indians, were given orders to drive out the English and to take action to prevent their return. The French burned the cabins of English trappers and built a new line of forts in the Ohio Valley, but the English refused to be intimidated. The situation grew more serious, and both the English and the French attempted to gain the native tribes as allies. The French were supported by the Algonquins and the Hurons, but delegates from seven of the colonies were rebuffed by the Iroquois and made no alliances.

In 1754, numerous altercations in the Ohio Valley led to the French and Indian War. From the beginning, the English were hampered by a lack of unity and the French by a lack of manpower and widely dispersed settlements that were difficult to defend. The English approached the war as all wars had been fought in Europe: straightforward and in the open. The French, on the other hand, used Indian tactics that ensured several important victories.

In 1757, the tide began to turn. William Pitt became head of the British government and promised the colonists large payments for military service and supplies. Under his leadership, the strategically placed French-Canadian fort of Louisbourg was captured. The British also gained the support of the Iroquois, who convinced the Delawares to abandon their French allies. The English then captured Fort Duquesne in the Ohio Valley and renamed it Fort Pitt, from which the city of Pittsburgh grew. Two years later, the French had lost Fort Niagara, Fort Crown Point, Fort Ticonderoga, and even Quebec. In 1760, Montreal was taken, and the fate of New France was sealed.

Fighting continued in Europe among the British, French, and Spanish until the signing of the Treaty of Paris in 1763. Under the terms of the treaty, Britain gained Canada and all lands east of the Mississippi. Spain received the French lands west of the Mississippi, and France was allowed to retain only a few islands in the Caribbean.

As colonists moved into the Ohio Valley and took possession of former French lands, relations with the Indian tribes deteriorated to the point of all-out warfare. The fighting lasted only until the Treaty of Paris, but it successfully convinced the British to close the western lands to settlement. The Proclamation of 1763 was issued, forbidding people to settle west of the crest of the Appalachians and ordering those who had already established themselves west of the line to return to the colonies. Ten thousand troops were sent from Britain to enforce the proclamation, but most stayed in the coastal cities and few made it to the frontier. The colonists, angry at being forced to pay for the troops and at being told what they could and couldn't do, ignored the proclamation and continued to encroach upon Indian territory.

The Stamp Act was passed by parliament in 1764 to ensure that the colonies contributed to the costs of Britain's war effort and to the costs for their administration. Under the act, several new taxes were established, including a tax on legal documents and a tax on newspapers, almanacs, playing cards, etc. The independent colonists rejected the idea of taxation without representation, and in 1766, after a number of riots and a boycott of British goods, the act was repealed. At the same time, however, the British parliament passed the Declaratory Act that affirmed their right to make laws and raise taxes for all its possessions.

A year later, parliament passed the Townshend Acts to establish taxes on items such as glass, paper, silk, tea, and lead. Believing the colonists would resort to smuggling to avoid paying the taxes, customs officers were given writs of assistance that allowed them to inspect a ship's cargo without stating a reason for the search. Not only did this violate the law and the rights of British citizens, the primary issue remained: The British government had no right to tax those not represented in parliament.

In reaction, many merchants and planters signed nonimportation agreements whereby they agreed to stop importing the items covered under the Townshend Acts. Citizens did their part by boycotting British-made goods, by joining the patriotic groups called the Sons of Liberty and the Daughters of Liberty, and by staging protests in several port cities. British troops were soon called in to protect the customs officers and tax collectors, and their presence was a daily reminder of the British attempt to bully the colonies into compliance.

The boycott of British goods was successful in hurting enough British merchants that the British government repealed the Townshend Acts in 1770. King George III asked for the tax on tea to continue, as at least one tax had to be retained as a symbol of the right to tax the colonies. In light of the repeal of the acts, most colonists saw the tea tax as unimportant, and the next several years were peaceful ones.

Back in Britain, the British East India Company, the primary shipper of tea, found itself in serious financial troubles. The government attempted to help by passing the Tea Act of 1773, whereby the company was allowed to bypass tea merchants and sell directly to the colonists. It was hoped that lower prices would encourage people to buy more tea and allow the company to unload the massive quantities of tea being stored in British warehouses.

To parliament's great surprise, colonists protested the act because it ruined the tea merchants. In November 1773, three ships carrying tea and other cargo sailed into Boston harbor. The governor ignored the colonists' demands that the ships leave and ordered the captains to pay their taxes, and sell their cargoes within twenty days. Late one night, a group from the Sons of Liberty disguised themselves as Mohawks, boarded the ships, and quickly dumped the tea into the harbor. It was an orderly operation designed to show the colonists' resolve, and none could have predicted the ramifications of that fateful night.

The British government decided the colonists had acted with outright lawlessness and deserved to be punished. Boston harbor was closed until the colonists' paid for the tea and showed they were sorry for their actions, colonists were forbidden to hold town meetings more than once a year without permission, and a new Quartering Act was passed that required Bostonians to house British troops in their homes, rather than in tents on Boston Common. The colonists called these the Intolerable Acts because they were so harsh.

Other colonies rallied together and supported Boston through the difficult times that came as a result of the harbor being closed. Delegates from twelve colonies gathered together in Philadelphia and established the First Continental Congress to examine the situation. It was decided to continue the boycott of British goods and to ban the exportation of goods to Britain until the Intolerable Acts were repealed. In addition, each colony was encouraged to set up and train its own militia.

After the Massachusetts militia was established and the minutemen began regular training, the British government sent in more troops. Once the British commander learned the minutemen had a large cache of weapons stored in the nearby village of Concord, 700 troops set out on a sneak attack to seize the arms. What the redcoats did not know, however, was that the Sons of Liberty had been watching them and had signaled that they were on the move. Paul Revere and others rode to Concord and sounded the alarm. By the time the troops reached the village, seventy minutemen were waiting for them. A shot rang out and both sides began firing. Eight colonists were killed, and a British soldier was wounded. On the return to Boston, another confrontation occurred between British troops and 300 minutemen. With the help of colonial sharpshooters hidden in the woods, the minutemen managed to force the British into retreat. More than 200 British were missing or wounded and 73 had been killed. The colonists now knew there could be no reconciliation with Britain. Only war would decide the fate of the colonies.

The Second Continental Congress met in May 1775 and agreed to petition King George III to repeal the Intolerable Acts so a reconciliation could be made. At the same time, a Continental Army was established with George Washington as its commander. The Battle of Bunker Hill, the first major battle to be fought in the Revolutionary War, showed the British that the Americans weren't going to be an easy enemy to defeat; it also showed the Americans that they stood a chance against the military might of Britain.

By November of 1775, word came of King George's refusal to consider the petition. Two months later, Thomas Paine's pamphlet, *Common Sense,* began to circulate and led many to the conclusion that independence was the only solution to the current problem. Delegates to the Continental Congress appointed a committee to draw up a formal declaration of independence from Britain. Thomas Jefferson, one of the youngest delegates, was chosen to write the document. On July 2, 1776, the congressional delegates voted for independence, and on July 4, 1776, they accepted the Declaration of Independence and renamed the colonies the United States of America.

The war opened with the new country facing tremendous odds. Not only was the army very small and poorly trained, there was no navy. The British, on the other hand, had the full resources of the British crown behind it. By December 1776, it appeared as if the Americans would have to admit defeat. Nevertheless, the Continental Army managed to persevere, and with George Washington in charge, were victorious at the Battle of Trenton and at Princeton.

After the Americans had proven their determination to fight, other nations lent assistance. France, Britain's traditional enemy, was eager to avenge the loss of its lands and made an alliance with the Americans. Troops, a fleet of ships, and supplies were sent to aid the war effort. Also joining the cause were two Polish officers, Thaddeus Kosciusko and Casimir Pulaski, who helped train troops and build defenses; Friedrich von Steuben of Prussia, considered by many to be the finest soldier in Europe, helped train troops; and New Spain supplied the army with cattle and attacked the British in Florida.

Not allowed to help in the war effort were the African Americans. Neither free blacks nor slaves were allowed to join the army until King George offered freedom to any male slave who joined the British forces. Thousands of slaves left their masters and joined with the British; in response, Washington finally allowed blacks to serve in the Continental Army.

The Native Americans had at first remained neutral in the war for independence, but as the war progressed, most were forced into taking sides. The Algonquins supported the patriots, as did some of the Iroquois nations and the Miami Indians, but as settlers continued to move west onto Indian lands, tribes like the Cherokee sided with the British.

The end came on October 17, 1781, when British general Cornwallis surrendered his troops after being trapped on a peninsula in Chesapeake Bay. Peace talks began in Paris in 1782. Under the terms of the Treaty of Paris, Britain recognized the United States of America as an independent country. The country's boundaries stretched from the Atlantic to the Mississippi and to the southern border of Georgia; Florida was returned to New Spain. The treaty was ratified by Congress in April 1783, eight years after the first shot rang out in Concord.

Winning independence was only the first step toward the establishment of a new country, and there was still much work to be done. The years 1781 to 1789 are known as the Critical Period, for it was uncertain whether the weak central government could solve the country's political and economic problems. Though the colonies were loosely bound under the Articles of Confederation, it soon became apparent that stronger ties had to be forged.

In 1787, a special convention was called, and members drew up a new plan of government and wrote a new national constitution to create a stronger national government. Writing a document that was agreeable to all thirteen colonies proved to be very difficult, but in the end, after bitter and heated debates, the states voted for ratification of the Constitution of the United States. In January 1789, the first elections under the new government were held. George Washington was elected president and John Adams vice president. During that same year, ten amendments were added to the Constitution. Those ten are the Bill of Rights.

Late in the 1790s, Washington's secretary of state, Thomas Jefferson, clashed with the secretary of the treasury, Alexander Hamilton, over the future of the country. Each man had his supporters who formed the first political parties: the Democratic Republicans and the Federalists.

At the same time, new problems were created for the government when waves of settlers moved onto lands in the Northwest Territory in defiance of signed treaties with Indian tribes. Clashes between settlers and the natives increased, and several tribes joined together to force whites off Indian land. President Washington responded by sending in troops. In 1795, twelve Indian nations signed the Treaty of Greenville with the United States, whereby they agreed to give up 25,000 square miles of land in exchange for $20,000 and a promise of more money if the peace was kept.

In 1803, the nation doubled in size when the whole of Louisiana was purchased from the French for $15 million dollars. This brought the Mississippi and the vast territory west of the river into American hands. As few knew what these new lands included, Congress agreed to finance an army expedition to study the land and all its resources. Leading the expedition were Meriwether Lewis, Jefferson's private secretary, and William Clark, a Virginian.

France had sold Louisiana to raise money for its war against Britain. As that war progressed, ships the countries had used for trading were diverted to their war efforts. American merchants stepped into the gap and reaped great profits by hauling supplies to both sides. This, of course, was unacceptable to both sides, and both France and Britain intercepted American merchant ships on their way to Europe. Not only were hundreds of ships captured and their cargoes seized, the British navy also captured American seamen and forced them to serve on British ships.

In 1807, Jefferson persuaded Congress to boycott all foreign trade to cut off all supplies to the Europeans. While the embargo hurt Britain and France, it was even more devastating to the Americans. Many merchants were ruined, sailors and dock workers lost their jobs, and farmers lost money because their crops were not allowed to be shipped overseas. Jefferson admitted his plan had failed, and in 1809, Congress replaced the embargo with the Nonintercourse Act which allowed trade with any country except Britain and France and allowed the president to reinstate trade with either of the banned countries should they agree to stop seizing American ships.

Like Washington before him, Thomas Jefferson chose not to run for a third term in office; his friend, James Madison, won the 1808 election. More people were moving westward, and trouble between settlers and the Native Americans grew more pronounced. It was commonly believed that Britain was supplying the tribes with guns and ammunition, and people began to clamor for retaliation. Finally, in 1812, Madison felt compelled to ask Congress to declare war on Britain. The House voted seventy-nine to forty-nine in favor of war, and the Senate voted nineteen to thirteen in favor. This is the closest vote on a declaration of war in American history.

Once again, Americans were unprepared to fight a war against such a superpower as Britain. The navy had only sixteen ships in its fleet, and the army was undermanned. In order to attract more soldiers, the government agreed to give volunteers $124 and 360 acres of land for service. That was a tremendous amount of money in those days, close to a year's wages. The high pay and the prospect of gaining their own farms prompted thousands of young men to enlist. The War of 1812 raged for two years, and though neither side could declare victory, the Americans had shown the world it was capable of holding off Europe's foremost naval power.

The period following the war was one of great growth and increased prosperity. Andrew Jackson, a frontiersman from Tennessee and a hero from the War of 1812, won the popular vote in the 1824 presidential elections, but he didn't win the electoral college votes. The House chose John Quincy Adams as president.

Adams, the son of the second president, was refined and intelligent and had been admired by the people. After the election, many felt his selection had been unfairly made and his popularity dropped dramatically. Adams hoped his plans for national growth would turn public opinion around, but because those plans required the government to foot the bill, the people were even more against him. He ran for a second term in office, but was defeated in a landslide by Andrew Jackson.

There were several important events of the Jackson era, but two were to have lasting effect. The first was a crisis centering around a tariff bill passed by Congress in 1828. Under the bill, high tariffs were attached to goods imported from England. This made European goods cost more than domestic goods, and while this helped manufacturers in the North, it hurt the southern planters who sold their cotton to Europe and bought European goods in return. Jackson's vice president, John Calhoun, led the southerners in their fight against the tariff bill. The fight was so bitter and the sides so divided that Calhoun resigned his office and South Carolina threatened to secede from the Union. Over the next thirty years, the differences between the North and the South were only to worsen.

Another event to have long-term consequences was the Indian Removal Act of 1830. Cherokee land was prime cotton-growing land, and many Georgia settlers wanted it for themselves. Jackson persuaded Congress to set aside land west of the Mississippi for the Cherokee, and the state of Georgia claimed the right to seize the lands. The Cherokee, however, were well-established and prosperous farmers and had no intention of giving up their lands. They hired one of the best lawyers in the country and took the matter to the courts. They argued that signed treaties with the United States government protected their lands and that Georgia had no right to them. Supreme Court Chief Justice John Marshall agreed and upheld the treaty.

In response, Jackson refused to use government resources to enforce the court's ruling, and the tribe was left without protection. In 1830, Congress passed the Indian Removal Act, which stated that Native Americans had to move west of the Mississippi. Between 1831 and 1833, the Choctaws, the first people to be forcefully removed, were sent from Mississippi to the territory west of Arkansas.

Following the Choctaws were the Chickasaws and the Creeks. The journey was long and arduous, and many thousands died from hunger, exposure, and disease. The last stages of the removal occured between 1835 and 1838, when the United States army forced the Cherokees of Georgia to march hundreds of miles to land in Oklahoma. Like the other tribes, they were allowed to take only the clothes on their backs and were forced to leave everything they owned to the new owners of their lands. Conditions along the Trail of Tears were terrible, and of the 15,000 or so marchers, 4,000 died on the journey. Most of those who died were the sick, the elderly, and the very young who were unable to travel so far on foot. And like the other tribes, the Cherokees were sent to lands they'd never seen and where nothing awaited them. In 1835, the Seminole went to war for their lands and fought bitterly for seven long years. In the end, they too were forced away from their traditional lands, though several bands remained hidden in the Everglades and continued their fight against the United States.

In the mid-1800s, settlers steadily pushed westward into the Oregon Territory and down into Texas. In 1844, Congress declared war on Mexico in an effort to gain all of the western part of the continent.

SOCIETY

THE CONTINENTAL CONGRESS' declaration of American independence from Britain was not welcomed by all. The nation was divided by patriots who wished for liberty and loyalists who wished for a reconciliation with Britain. It was a difficult time for both, as families were torn apart by members choosing to support differing sides in the upcoming conflict. The loyalists, however, often found themselves in fear of their lives as anti-British sentiment grew. Loyalists who spoke out in favor of the monarchy ran the risk of being tarred and feathered, and many of the more vocal were forced to flee to Canada or back to England.

Women did their part to further the war effort. They took over the farms and made sure the crops were planted and the harvests brought in. They made shoes, uniforms, and blankets for the soldiers, sewed flags, and made guns and other weapons. Some followed their husbands to the front lines to cook, clean uniforms, and care for the sick and wounded. During the battles, they did anything they could to help, even to the point of taking the positions of fallen soldiers and continuing the fight.

The war also forced America into the Industrial Revolution. Because British ships had successfully block-aded the coast, the country was cut off from its European manufacturers and had to rely upon domestic production. Eli Whitney's concept of interchangeable parts markedly increased production. Other ideas, such as combining several manufacturing processes under one roof, led to a boom in the establishment of factories and led to the growth of the cities and towns. In order to attract women and children laborers, many factory owners established boardinghouses for their employees and hired housemothers to watch over the young workers. Parks, churches, and other amenities were established, and comfortable communities grew up around the factories. A typical employee worked twelve hours a day, six days a week, much like the hours one would spend working at home on the farm. Wages for women and children were half of what a man was paid, though the work was often the same.

In the beginning, factory conditions were much better than they were in Europe, and the people were grateful for the jobs and the pleasant accomodations. But as more factories were established and competition grew, employers became less interested in the welfare of their workers and conditions deteriorated. Living conditions deteriorated in the towns, as well. There were no sewers, and no sanitation measures. Garbage was usually tossed into the street and pigs were allowed to roam freely to feed on the discarded trash. The filthy, crowded conditions led to outbreaks of disease like yellow fever and cholera that were almost impossible to control.

As the country grew, the westward movement continued apace, and between the years of 1792 and 1819, eight new states joined the Union. Increased travel also brought about the need for improved roads and improved methods of transportation. In 1818, the National Road connecting Virginia and Maryland was completed, covered bridges were built, and river travel was improved by the invention of the steamboat.

Competition for land prompted Americans to look father afield toward the vast expanse of Texas. At the time, it was part of the Spanish settlement of Mexico, and Spain refused to let Americans settle there. Then, in 1821, the Spanish government gave Moses Austin a grant of land. Unfortunately, Moses Austin died before he could establish a colony. Meanwhile, Mexico gained its independence, and since only about 4,000 Mexicans lived in the Territory, it was agreed to let Austin's son, Stephen Austin complete his father's plan. Under the agreement, each settler was given a large grant of land. In return, the settlers had to become citizens of Mexico and members of the Catholic Church. Three hundred families were carefully chosen to make the move. Some became ranchers and some cotton growers. By 1830, Austin's colony had grown to 20,000.

The success of Austin's venture prompted more people to arrive in the hopes that they, too, could prosper. But these new settlers felt under no obligation to become Mexican citizens or become members of the Catholic Church, and conflicts soon arose between the Mexican officials and the Americans. The American government attempted to put an end to the conflict by twice trying to buy Texas, once in 1826, and again in 1829. In 1830, Mexico, fearing U.S. attempts to annex Texas, forbade further immigration into Texas. Mexican troops were sent in, both to discourage settling and to tighten existing laws that were being ignored by the Texans.

In 1834, General Santa Anna got rid of the Mexican constitution and set up a dictatorship. The Texans, believing they were in jeopardy of being thrown out of Texas and losing all they'd worked for, decided it was time to work for independence from Mexico. In March 1836, Texans declared their independence and called their new nation the Republic of Texas.

After the valiant fight at the Alamo in February and March 1836, Americans rushed to join Sam Houston's army. On April 21, 1836, Houston surprised Santa Anna's army and was victorious over them. The next day, Santa Anna was captured and forced to sign the treaty granting Texas its independence from Mexico. A constitution based on that of the United States was drawn up, and Sam Houston was elected president.

Troubles were not over. Mexico refused to accept the treaty signed by Santa Anna and most settlers favored annexation to the United States; the issue of slavery kept many in the northern United States from agreeing. In addition, it was feared that annexing Texas would bring about an all out war with Mexico. It was decided that things should remain as they were. Over the next several years, Texas prospered, and by the 1840s, the country had a population of nearly 140,000.

An economic crisis hit in 1837. Wild land speculation had resulted in the states printing more and more paper money that was not backed by gold or silver. In an effort to stop the craze, President Jackson ordered all future purchases be made in gold or silver, not with the paper money. People rushed to the banks to cash in their money but quickly found the banks didn't have enough gold or silver. A panic set in, and droves of people descended upon their banks demanding the exchange of their money. Hundreds of banks failed, and people were left destitute. To make matters worse, an oversupply of cotton had driven prices down to rock bottom and planters were unable to repay their loans. More banks failed, business slowed, and the country was cast into an economic depression. During the worst years, about 90 percent of the nation's factories closed, and unemployment soared. With no jobs and no money, people began to starve. Social order broke down, and crowds of hungry people broke into warehouses in search of food.

With the economy in such dire straits and no jobs to be found, many decided it was time to head west to begin anew. In 1843, the first wagon trains set out for the Oregon Territory and opened a new chapter in the development of the United States.

RELIGION

ARTICLE I OF the Bill of Rights granted freedom of religion to all residing in the United States: ''Congress shall make no law respecting an establishment of religion, or prohibiting the free exercise thereof. . . .'' Several new religious groups formed during this time period to meet the increased population and changing attitudes. Below are some of the major religious organizations active during this time period and the states in which they were formed.

African Methodist Episcopal Church (1787)
Brethren in Christ Church (1778) Pennsylvania
Christian Church (Disciples of Christ) (1809) Indiana
Church of Jesus Christ of Latter-day Saints (Mormon) (1830) New York
Cumberland Presbyterian Church (1810) Tennessee
Episcopal Church (1789) New York

Lutheran Church—Missouri Synod (1847) Missouri
Mennonite Church (1525) Pennsylvania
Methodist (1784) Maryland
Moravian Church (1735) Pennsylvania
Orthodox Church in America (1794) New York
Reformed Church in America (1628) New York
Roman Catholic Church (1634) Maryland

In spite of the guarantee of religious freedom granted under the constitution, there was a great deal of prejudice against certain sects. Jews, Mormons, and Catholics were routinely discriminated against. The teachings of Joseph Smith, founder of the Church of Jesus Christ of Latter-day Saints in 1830, so angered his neighbors in upstate New York that Smith and his followers were forced to leave their New York farms for Ohio. From Ohio, prejudice and discrimination prompted their move to Missouri, then to Illinois in the 1840s. The Mormons founded the town of Nauvoo and worked to build a self-sufficient community united by faith. By 1844, Nauvoo was the largest town in Illinois. It boasted clean streets lined with neat brick houses and was sustained by successful farms, factories, and shops.

Intolerance followed the Mormons even to Nauvoo, and in 1844, Joseph Smith was killed by an angry mob. Brigham Young, the new leader, realized his community needed a new home where it could be safe. He'd read about a valley located between the Rocky Mountains and the Great Salt Lake and decided his people would be able to live in peace in such an isolated place. Moving 15,000 people promised to be a logistical nightmare, and the next several years were devoted to careful planning to ensure success.

NAMING

AMERICA WAS NOW a hodgepodge of people of differing nationalities. Each group that entered the country brought its culture, language, and names. While the languages were generally abandoned in favor of English, names from the cultural groups continued to be used and were added to the general pool from which parents drew the names of their children. The most popular names continued to be those taken from the Bible.

The countries listed after each name below indicate the primary places of origin, not the etymological root. As people became Americanized, names were commonly shared among cultural groups. However, apart from new arrivals to the country, the use of the more foreign-sounding names, such as the Scandinavian Solveig, the French Guillaume, and the Germanic Heinrich, tended to be restricted to people whose nationalites matched the names' origins.

FEMALE NAMES

Abelia (breath) English.
Abelone (of Apollo) **Abellona** Scandinavian.
Abigail (father of exaltation) **Abbey** English.
Abijah (the Lord is father) English.
Abishag (wise) English.
Adah (adornment) English.
Adalheid (nobility) German, Scandinavian.
Adelaide (nobility) English, French.
Adele (noble) **Adela** English, French, German.
Adeline (nobility) English, French.
Adria (from Hadrianus) English.
Agatha (good) **Agata, Agathe** English, French, German, Scandinavian.
Agnes (chaste, pure) **Agna, Agnus** English, French, German, Scandinavian.
Agnethe (chaste, pure) German.
Aileen (?) Irish.
Ailsa (elf victory) Scandinavian.
Alana (O child; ?, perhaps *handsome; rock*) **Alane, Alanna, Alannah, Alanne, Allana** Irish.
Alethea (truth) **Alethea, Aletheia, Alithea** English.
Alexandra (defender of mankind) English, German, Scandinavian.
Alexina (defender of mankind) Scottish.
Alfreda (elf counselor) English, German.
Alice (nobility) **Alyce** English, French.
Alicia (nobility) English, Scandinavian.
Alickina (defender of mankind) Scottish.
Aline (noble) English.
Alison (noble one) English.
Althea (wholesome) English.
Amalia (work) **Amalie, Amelia** English, French, German, Scandinavian.
Amana (established) English.
Amata (love) English.
Amicia (?, possibly *friendship*) **Amice** English.
Amity (friendship) **Amyte** English.
Amma (grandmother) Scandinavian.
Amy (beloved) English.
Anabella (grace, full of grace, mercy + beautiful) **Anabelle, Annabella** English, French, German, Spanish.
Anastasia (resurrection) English, German.
Andrea (womanly) English.
Angela (an angel) English.
Angelica (angelic) English.
Angie (angel, like an angel) English.
Anne (grace, full of grace, mercy) **Ann, Anna** English, French, German, Scandinavian, Spanish.
Anneliese (grace, mercy + God is my oath) **Annelise** German, Scandinavian.
Annette (little Anne) English, French, German, Scandinavian.
Annfrid (beautiful eagle) Scandinavian.
Annie (grace, full of grace, mercy) English.
Annis (chaste, pure) **Annice, Annys** English.

Ann Mary (grace, full of grace, mercy + sea of bitterness or sorrow) English.
Antigone (of contrary birth) English.
Anthea (flowery) English.
Antonia (?, *priceless, of inestimable worth* are folk definitions) English, French, German, Scandinavian.
Aphrah (dust) **Aphra** English.
Apphia (increasing) English.
Appolonia (of Apollo) **Appolina** English.
Arabella (?, perhaps *eagle* or *hearth*) **Arabel, Arabell, Orabel** English.
Arminel (strength) English.
Arna (eagle) Scandinavian.
Artemisia (belonging to Artemis) English.
Asa (a god) Scandinavian.
Asenath (?, perhaps *thornbush*) English.
Aslaug (consecrated to God) Scandinavian.
Aspasia (welcome) English.
Asta (love) Scandinavian.
Astrid (beautiful goddess) German, Scandinavian.
Atarah (crown) English.
Athalia (the Lord is exalted) English.
Aud (riches, prosperity) Scandinavian.
Audra (noble strength) **Audie** English.
Audrey (noble strength) **Awdry; Audie** English.
Aurelia (golden) **Aurelie** English, French.
Aurora (the dawn) **Aurore** English, French.
Averil (boar battle) **Averell, Everild** English.
Avice (?) **Aveza, Avis, Avise** English, German.
Avila (?) German.
Azubah (forsaken) English.
Baptista (a baptizer) English, German.
Bathsheba (daughter of the oath, daughter of Sheba) English.
Bathshua (daughter of riches, daughter of Shua) English.
Beata (happy) English, French, German, Scandinavian.
Beatrice (bringer of joy) **Beatrix** English, French, German, Scandinavian.
Belinda (?, perhaps *snake*) English.
Bella (beautiful) English.
Benedicta (blessed) **Benedicte, Benedikta** English, French, German, Scandinavian.
Benet (blessed) **Bennet, Bennitt** English.
Berenice (bringer of victory) English, French.
Bernardine (bold as a bear) German, French, Scandinavian.
Bertha (bright) English, French, German, Scandinavian.
Bess (God is my oath) **Bessie** English.
Beth (God is my oath) English.
Betsy (God is my oath) **Betsey** English.
Betty (God is my oath) English.
Beulah (married) English.
Biddy (strength) English, Irish.
Bilhah (bashful, faltering) English.
Birgit (strength) **Birgitta, Birgitte, Brigitte** German, Scandinavian.

Bithiah (daughter of Jehovah) **Bethia** English.
Blanch (white) **Blanche** English, French.
Brenda (sword) Irish.
Bridget (strength) **Brigit** Irish, German, Scandinavian.
Carla (full-grown, a woman) German, Scandinavian.
Carlotta (full-grown, a woman) Spanish.
Carol (full-grown, a woman) **Carola, Carole** English, French, German, Scandinavian.
Caroletta (full-grown, a woman) English.
Caroline (full-grown, a woman) **Carrie, Lina** English, French, German, Scandinavian.
Cassandra (?) English, French.
Cathalina (pure, unsullied) Scandinavian, Spanish.
Catherine (pure, unsullied) **Catharine** English, French.
Cecile (blind, dim-sighted) **Cecilia** English, French, German, Scandinavian.
Celia (blind, dim-sighted) Scandinavian.
Charis (grace) English.
Charissa (grace) English.
Charity (charity, benevolence) English.
Charlotte (full-grown, a woman) **Charlotta** English, French, German, Scandinavian.
Charmian (a little joy) English.
Chloe (blooming, verdant) English, French.
Chloris (green) English, French, German.
Christa (a Christian) Scandinavian.
Christabel (?, probably *beautiful Christ*) **Christabell** English.
Christiana (a Christian, a follower of Christ) English, French, German, Scandinavian.
Christine (a Christian, a follower of Christ) **Christina, Khristina, Khristine, Kristina, Kristine; Chris, Chrissie, Christy, Kris, Kristy** English, French, German, Scandinavian.
Christmas (born at Christmastime) English.
Chyna (China) English.
Cicely (blind, dim-sighted) **Cecily, Cicily, Sisley, Sycillie** English.
Clare (bright, clear, famous) **Claire** English, French, German, Scandinavian.
Clarinda (bright, clear, famous) English.
Clarissa (bright, clear, famous) **Clarice, Claricia** English, French, German.
Claude (lame) French.
Claudette (little Claude *lame*) French, German.
Claudia (lame) English, German, Scandinavian.
Cleare (clear) English.
Clemence (clement, mild) **Clemencia, Clemency** English.
Clementine (clement, mild) English, German.
Clorinda (green, verdant) English.
Comfort (comfort, care) English.
Constancy (constant) **Constance, Constanze** English, German.
Cordelia (?, perhaps *daughter of the sea*) **Cordula** English, German.
Corinna (maiden) **Corinne** English, French.
Cornelia (a horn) English, French, German, Scandinavian.
Cynthia (of Kynthos) English.

Dagmar (splendid day; day maid) German, Scandinavian.
Dagna (new day) Scandinavian.
Damaris (?, possibly *heifer*) English.
Dania (God is my judge) Scandinavian.
Deborah (a bee) **Debra, Debrah** English, German.
Delia (from Delos) English.
Delilah (delicate) English.
Denise (of Dionysus) English, French.
Desire (desire, want) English.
Diana (divine) **Diane** English, French.
Dina (judged) **Dinah** English.
Donna (world ruler) Scottish.
Dorcas (gazelle) English.
Dorothea (gift of God) English, French, German, Scandinavian.
Drusilla (?) English.
Dulcibella (sweet + beautiful) **Dulcibell** English.
Dulcie (sweet) English.
Ebba (strong as a wild boar) German, Scandinavian.
Eden (delight) English.
Edith (prosperous in war) **Edyth** English, French, German, Scandinavian.
Eleanor (light, torch, bright) **Eleonore, Elianor, Elinor, Elleanor** French, German.
Elisabet (God is my oath) **Ailsa, Betje, Eliesabet, Elsa, Liese, Lis, Lisa, Lisabet** Scandinavian.
Elisabeth (God is my oath) **Elizabeth, Elsbeth, Elspeth, Lisabet, Lisabeth, Lisbeth; Bess, Bessie, Beth, Betti, Betty, Elise, Eliza, Ellie, Elsa, Else, Elsie, Ilsa, Liese, Lisa, Lise, Lisette, Liza, Lizzie, Lizzy** English, French, German.
Eliza (God is my oath) English.
Eliza Ann (God is my oath + grace, full of grace, mercy) English.
Elke (nobility) Scandinavian.
Ellen (light, torch, bright) **Elen** English.
Eloisa (hale, hearty) **Eloise** English, French.
Emelie (rival, trying to equal or excel) English, French, German, Scandinavian.
Emeline (strength; work) **Emmeline** English.
Emeraud (an emerald) English.
Emerlee (strength; work) English.
Emilia (strength; work) English.
Emily (strength; work) English.
Emma (strength; work) **Em** English, French, German, Scandinavian.
Emmanuelle (God is with us) French.
Erika (eternal ruler) **Erica** German, Scandinavian.
Esmeralda (emerald) English.
Esther (myrtle; star) **Ester** English, French, German, Scandinavian.
Ethel (noble) English, German.
Ethelinda (noble + tender, soft; a snake) English.
Eugenia (well-born, noble) **Eugenie** English, French, German, Scandinavian.
Eulalia (fair speech) **Eulalie** English, French, German, Scandinavian.

Eunice (good victory) English, French, German, Scandinavian.

Euphemia (fair speech) **Euphemie** English, French.

Eustacia (steadfast; happy harvest) English.

Eve (life) **Eva** English, French, German.

Eveline (?) **Evelina, Evelyn** English, German.

Everet (boar hard) English.

Faith (faith, trust) English.

Fanny (from France, a Frank) English.

Felice (lucky, happy) **Felicie** English, French, German, Scandinavian.

Felicity (happiness) **Felicite** English, French.

Finella (white shoulders) **Fenella, Finola, Fionola** Irish. Anglicized form of Fionnaghuala.

Fiona (white, fair, clear, transparent) Irish.

Flavia (yellow) English.

Flora (a flower) **Flore** French, German, Scandinavian, Spanish.

Florence (a blooming) **Florenz, Florinda** English, French, German.

Frances (a Frank, a freeman) English, French, German.

Freya (lady, mistress, noblewoman) **Freja** Scandinavian.

Friede (ruler of peace; gentle peace) **Freda, Frida, Frieda** German.

Gabriela (God is my strength) **Gabriele, Gabrielle** English, German, French, Spanish.

Gail (father of exaltation) English.

Georgina (earth worker, farmer) **Georgiana** English, French.

Gertrude (spear strength) English, German.

Gillian (youth, downy) **Jillian** English.

Gisela (pledge) **Gisele** German, Scandinavian.

Glenna (mountain valley) English.

Grace (grace, mercy) English.

Greer (vigilant, watchful) Scottish.

Gretchen (a pearl) German, Scandinavian.

Gretel (a pearl) German.

Gwyneth (blessed) Welsh.

Hannah (grace, full of grace, mercy) **Hanna, Hanne** English, French, German, Scandinavian.

Harriet (home ruler) English.

Hedda (war) Scandinavian.

Heidi (nobility; battle protector) German.

Helah (rust) English.

Helen (light, torch, bright) **Helena, Helene** English, French, German, Scandinavian.

Helge (prosperous, successful; blessed, holy) **Helga** German, Scandinavian.

Hephzibah (she is my delight) **Hepzibah, Hepsie** English.

Hermia (of Hermes) English.

Hermione (of Hermes) English.

Hester (myrtle; star) English.

Hilda (battle) German, Scandinavian.

Honor (honor, esteem) **Hanora, Honora, Honore, Honoria, Honour** English, French.

Hope (hope, expectation) English.

Hosannah (save pray) **Hosanna** English.

Hughina (heart, mind, spirit) Scottish.

Huldah (weasel) English.

Humility (humbleness) English.

Ida (work, labor) German.

Ideny (work, labor) **Idona, Idonea, Idonia, Idony** English, German, Scandinavian.

Inga (Ing, a Norse fertility god) **Inge** German, Scandinavian.

Ingrid (beautiful Ing) German, Scandinavian.

Irene (peace) **Irena** French, German, Scandinavian.

Isabel (God is my oath) **Isabell, Isabella, Isobel** English, French, Spanish.

Ismenia (?) English.

Jacoba (supplanting, seizing by the heels) **Jacobina** English.

Jacqueline (supplanting, seizing by the heels) **Jacklyn** English, French.

Jael (mountain goat) English.

Jamesina (supplanting, seizing by the heels) **Jamie** Scottish.

Jane (God is gracious) English.

Jane Olivia (God is gracious + olive tree) English.

Janet (God is gracious; little Jane) **Jennet** English.

Janna (God is gracious) **Janne** Dutch.

Jean (God is gracious) **Jeane, Jeanne** English, French.

Jecoliah (the Lord prevails) English.

Jemima (pure) English.

Jerioth (curtains) English.

Jeromia (sacred name) English.

Jerushah (a possession) English.

Jessie (little Janet *God is gracious*; gift) English.

Joan (God is gracious) English.

Johanna (God is gracious) **Joanna** English, German, Scandinavian.

Jonna (God is gracious) Danish.

Josepha (he shall add) **Josefa** French, German, Scandinavian, Spanish.

Joy (joy, happiness) English.

Joyce (merry, happy) English.

Judith (praised) **Judit, Judy** English, French, German, Scandinavian.

Julia (youth, downy) **Julie** English, French, German, Scandinavian, Spanish.

Juliana (youth, downy) English, Scandinavian.

Juliet (youth, downy) **Juliette** English.

Justina (right, just) English.

Kaatje (little Katherine *pure, unsullied*) Norwegian.

Karen (pure, unsullied) Danish.

Karita (charity, affection) Scandinavian.

Karla (woman) **Carla** Scandinavian.

Karolina (woman) **Caroline, Karoline; Carrie, Karrie** Scandinavian.

Katherine (pure, unsullied) **Catherine, Katarina, Katarine, Katerina, Katerine, Katharina, Katherin, Katrine, Katryn; Cathy, Kaethe, Kate, Kathe, Kathy, Katie, Katja, Katrien, Kitty** English, German, Scandinavian.

Keitha (?, perhaps *the wind* or *wood*) Scottish.

Kenna (born of fire; comely, handsome) Scottish.

Kerenhappuch (horn of antimony) **Keren** English.

Keturah (incense) English.

Kezia (cassia) English.
Klara (bright, clear, famous) **Clara** Scandinavian.
Laetitia (happiness) **Letitia** English.
Laila (night, dark beauty) Scandinavian.
Laufeia (leafy island) Scandinavian.
Laura (laurel) **Lora** English, French, German, Scandinavian.
Laurana (from Laurentum) English.
Laurence (from Laurentum) **Laurencia, Laurentia** French.
Lavinia (from Latium) **Lavina** English.
Leah (weary) English.
Lena (light, torch, bright) German, Spanish.
Leslie (small meadow, small clearing, small woods) English.
Letitia (happiness, gladness) **Lettice** English.
Lexine (defender or helper of mankind) Scottish.
Lillian (lily) **Lilian, Lily** English, French, German.
Lisa (God is my oath) English, German, Scandinavian.
Lisabet (God is my oath) **Lisbet, Lysbet** English, German, Scandinavian.
Liv (life) Scandinavian.
Lois (?) English.
Loretta (from Laurentum) **Lauretta** English.
Louise (famous in war) **Louisa** English, French, German, Scandinavian.
Love (love) English.
Lucia (light) English, German, Scandinavian, Spanish.
Lucilla (light) English.
Lucinda (light) English.
Lucy (light) English.
Lydia (Lydian woman) **Lyddia** English, German.
Mabel (lovable) **Mabella, Mabill** English.
Madeline (from Magdala) English, French.
Madge (a pearl) English.
Magda (from Magdala) German, Scandinavian.
Magdalen (from Magdala) **Magdalena, Magdalene, Magdelyn; Maggie** English, German, Scandinavian.
Maggie (a pearl) English.
Mahala (tenderness) English.
Mahalath (a lute, a lyre) English.
Mai (sea of bitterness or sorrow; a pearl) Scandinavian.
Malene (from Magdala) Danish.
Marah (bitterness) English.
Marcella (of Mars, warlike) English, German.
Marcia (of Mars, warlike) **Marcie** English.
Margaret (a pearl) **Margareta, Margaretha, Margarethe, Margrethe, Margriet, Marguerite, Margit, Margery, Margarey** English, German, Scandinavian.
Maria (sea of bitterness or sorrow) **Marie** English, French, German, Scandinavian, Spanish.
Mariel (sea of bitterness or sorrow) French, German.
Marina (of Mars; of the sea) English, German.
Marion (sea of bitterness or sorrow) English.
Marjorie (a pearl) **Margery** English.
Marta (a pearl) Danish.
Martha (lady, mistress) **Marthe** English, German, French, Scandinavian.
Martina (of Mars, warlike) Scandinavian.

Mary (sea of bitterness or sorrow) English.
Mary Ann (sea of bitterness or sorrow + grace, full of grace, mercy) **Mariann** English.
Matilda (strength in battle) **Mathilda** English, French, German, Scandinavian.
Maud (battle strength) English, German.
Maura (great, large; dark-skinned, a Moor) English.
Maureen (sea of bitterness or sorrow) **Maurene, Maurine** English, Irish.
Mehetabel (God makes happy) English.
Melanie (dark, black) English, French, German.
Melicent (work + strength) **Milesent** English.
Melissa (a bee) English.
Melody (a melody) English.
Meraude (of the sea) English.
Mercy (mercy, compassion) English.
Meriall (sea bright) **Meryall** English.
Mia (sea of bitterness or sorrow) Danish, Swedish.
Mikaela (Who is like God?) Swedish.
Mildred (mild strength) English.
Millicent (work strength) **Melicent, Melisande, Mellicent, Milicent, Millesant** English, German.
Minerva (the goddess of wisdom, skill, and invention) English.
Miranda (worthy to be loved) English.
Miriam (sea of bitterness or sorrow) English.
Molly (sea of bitterness or sorrow) **Moll** English.
Monica (?) **Monika** English, German, Scandinavian.
Monique (?) French.
Morna (beloved) **Myrna** Scottish.
Naamah (sweetness) English.
Naomi (my joy, my delight) English.
Narcissa (?, inspired by Narcissus, a mythological youth who was transformed into a narcissus) English.
Natalie (natal day; born at Christmastime) French.
Neilina (champion; a cloud) Scottish.
Nel (horn) Dutch.
Nell (light, torch, bright) **Nelly** English.
Nelleke (horn) Dutch.
Nellie (horn) Scandinavian.
Netta (champion; a cloud) Scottish.
Nicole (victory of the people) **Nicol** English, French, German.
Nicolette (little Nicole *victory of the people*) French.
Nilsine (victory of the people) Swedish.
Noelle (born at Christmas) **Noel** French.
Noemie (pleasant, beautiful) French.
Nora (a woman from the north; honor, esteem) English.
Oceanus (of the ocean) English.
Oddveig (spear woman) Scandinavian.
Odette (prosperity, riches) French, German, Scandinavian.
Ola (ancestor's relic) Scandinavian.
Olaug (dedicated to the ancestors) Scandinavian.
Olga (holy) German, Scandinavian.
Olive (the olive tree) **Olivia** English.
Olympia (of Olympus) **Olympe** English, French.

Onora (honor) English.
Ophelia (help, succor) **Ophelie** English, French.
Ophrah (a fawn) English.
Orabell (?) **Orable, Oriabel** English.
Oriana (to rise) English.
Oriane (to rise; golden) French.
Osanna (save now, save pray) English.
Parnell (a rock) English.
Patience (patience, forebearance) English.
Patricia (a patrician, an aristocrat) English, German.
Peg (a pearl) **Peggy** English.
Penelope (a bobbin) English, German.
Pentecost (fiftieth [day]) English.
Percy (from Percy, Normandy) English.
Perdita (lost) English.
Pernilla (a rock) **Pernille** Danish, Swedish.
Perpetua (perpetual, eternal) English.
Persis (Persian woman) English.
Petra (a rock) German, Scandinavian.
Petronel (a rock) **Peternel** English.
Petronilla (a rock) Scandinavian.
Philadelphia (brotherly love) English.
Philippa (lover of horses) English, French.
Philomena (beloved) **Philomene** English, French.
Phoebe (bright, shining) **Phebe, Phebeus** English.
Pia (pious, devout) Scandinavian.
Pleasance (pleasant) English.
Precilla (former, ancient) **Priscilla** English.
Prisca (former, ancient) English.
Prothesia (?) English.
Prudence (prudent) English.
Rachel (ewe) **Rachael, Rachell** English, French, German.
Rae (doe) Scandinavian.
Ragnhild (battle decision) Scandinavian.
Ranveig (housewife) Scandinavian.
Rebecca (noose) **Rabecca, Rebecka, Rebekah, Rebekka** English, French, German, Scandinavian.
Renate (reborn) **Renatus** English, German, Scandinavian.
Renee (reborn) French.
Rhoda (a rose) English.
Richenda (little Richard *stern king*) English.
Rinda (?) Scandinavian.
Robina (bright with fame) Scottish.
Rona (mighty power) Scandinavian.
Rosabel (beautiful rose) **Rosabella** English, Spanish.
Rosalie (rose garland) English, French.
Rosalind (horse or fame + gentle, tender or serpent) **Rosalinde** English, German.
Rosamond (horse protection) **Rossamond** English, German.
Rose (a rose) **Rosa** English, French, Spanish.
Roseanna (rose + grace, full of grace, mercy) **Roseann, Roseanne, Rosanna, Rose Ann** English.
Rosemarie (rose + sea of bitterness or sorrow; dew of the sea) Scandinavian.
Rosemary (rose + sea of bitterness or sorrow) English.
Rosetta (little Rose) English.

Rowena (famous friend) English.
Roxane (dawn of day) French.
Runa (secret lore) Scandinavian.
Ruth (friend, companion) **Ruthe** English, French, German.
Sabina (Sabine woman) **Sabine** English.
Sally (princess) English.
Salome (peace) English, French.
Sandra (defender of mankind) **Saundra** English, French, German, Scandinavian.
Sapphira (beautiful) English.
Sarah (princess) **Sara** English, French, German, Scandinavian.
Sarah Ann (princess + grace, full of grace, mercy) English.
Saskia (?) Dutch.
Selina (the moon) **Selene, Selinah** English.
Seraphine (burning one, angel) French.
Sheena (God is gracious) Scottish.
Sibylla (fortune-teller, prophetess) **Sibella, Sibilla** Scandinavian.
Sidonia (linen cloth) **Sidonie, Sidony** English.
Signy (new victory) Scandinavian.
Silvia (wood) English.
Simone (heard) French.
Sixten (victory stone) Scandinavian.
Solange (yearly; solemn, religious) French.
Solveig (house of strength) **Solvej, Solvig** Norwegian.
Sophia (wisdom) **Sofia, Sophie** English, French, German.
Sorcha (bright) Irish.
Stephanie (a crown, garland) French.
Sunniva (gift of the sun) Scandinavian.
Susan (lily, rose) **Suzan** English.
Susanna (lily, rose) **Susannah, Susanne, Susanney, Suzanna, Suzannah, Suzanne** English, French, German, Scandinavian.
Svanhild (battle swan) Scandinavian.
Sybil (fortune-teller, prophetess) **Sybell, Sybill, Sybilla, Sybille** English, French, German.
Sylvia (the woods) **Sylvie** French, Scandinavian.
Synnove (gift of the sun) Danish, Swedish.
Tabitha (roe, gazelle) English.
Tacy (hold peace, be silent) English.
Tamar (palm, a date palm) **Tamara** English.
Teodora (God's gift) Scandinavian.
Tessa (harvester) **Tess** English.
Theodora (God's gift) **Theo** English.
Theodosia (God-given) **Theo** English.
Theresa (harvester) **Teresa, Therese; Tess, Tessa** English, French, Spanish.
Thomson (little Tom *a twin*) **Thamasin, Thomasin, Tomson** English.
Thora (Thor) Scandinavian.
Tiffeny (Epiphany, manifestation of God) **Tyffany** English.
Tilda (battle) German, Scandinavian.
Torunn (loved by Thor) Scandinavian.
Tova (beautiful Thor) Scandinavian.
Trudie (spear strength) **Trudy** German.

Tryphena (delicate, dainty) English.
Ulla (will, determination) Scandinavian.
Ulrike (noble ruler) **Ulrika** German, Scandinavian.
Unity (united) English.
Unn (love) Scandinavian.
Ursula (she-bear) **Urselah** German, Scandinavian.
Valentine (strong, healthy) **Valentina** English, Spanish.
Valerie (strong, healthy) French, German.
Vara (?) Scandinavian.
Venetia (blessed) English.
Veronica (true image) **Veronika** German, Scandinavian.
Veronique (true image) French.
Victoria (victory) **Viktoria** German, Scandinavian.
Viola (violet) **Viole** French.
Violet (violet-colored) **Violette** English, French.
Vita (life) Scandinavian.
Vivian (alive) **Viviane, Vivianne, Vivien, Vivienne** English, French, German, Scandinavian.

Wanda (?, perhaps *stem, young tree; a Wend, an old Slavic people*) German.
Wilfreda (resolute peace) German.
Wilhelmina (resolute protector) English, German, Scandinavian.
Willa (resolute protector) German.
Wilma (resolute protector) German.
Winifred (blessed peace) **Winnifred, Winnie** English, German.
Yolande (?, possibly *violet*) French.
Yvette (little archer) French, German, Scandinavian.
Yvonne (archer) French, German, Scandinavian.
Zephyrine (the west wind) French.
Zeresh (gold, splendor) English.
Zillah (shade) English.
Zilpah (?) English.
Zipporah (a little bird) English.
Zoe (live) French, German, Scandinavian.

MALE NAMES

Aaron (exalted) English, German.
Abel (breath) English, French, German.
Abner (the father is a light) English.
Abraham (father of a multitude) English, German, Scandinavian.
Abram (father of exaltation) English.
Absalom (father of peace) **Absalon** English.
Adalard (noble and strong) French.
Adalbert (noble and bright) **Adelbert** German.
Adalrich (noble ruler) German.
Adam (man of the red earth) English, French, German, Scandinavian.
Adelulf (noble wolf) English.
Adolphe (noble wolf) **Adolf** French, German, Scandinavian.
Adrian (man from Hadrianus) **Adrien** English, French, German, Scandinavian.
Aeneas (praiser) English.
Aidan (little fire) Irish.
Ake (?, possibly *ancestor; agate; blameless*) Scandinavian.
Aksel (the father is peace) **Axel** Scandinavian.
Alain (?, perhaps *handsome; rock*) **Allain** French.
Alan (?, perhaps *handsome; rock*) **Allan, Allen** English.
Alard (noble and strong) **Allard** French.
Alarik (ruler of all) Scandinavian.
Alasdair (defender of mankind) **Alastair, Alaster, Alisdair, Alistair, Alister, Allaster** Scottish.
Alberic (elf ruler) English.
Albert (bright through nobility) English, French, German, Scandinavian.
Alberto (bright through nobility) Spanish.
Albin (white) French.
Aldred (old counsel) English.
Alduin (old friend) French.

Aldus (old) English.
Aldwin (old friend) English.
Alex (defender, defender of mankind) English, French, German, Scandinavian.
Alexander (defender of mankind) **Alexandre; Alec, Alick, Sander** English, German.
Alexis (defender) German.
Algernon (mustached) English, French.
Alick (defender) **Alec** Scottish.
Aloysius (famous in war) English, Scandinavian.
Alphonse (noble and ready) French.
Ambrose (immortal) **Ambroise** French.
Amedee (love of God) French.
Amias (?, perhaps *friendship*) **Amyas** English, French.
Amiel (industrious) English, French.
Amos (borne, a burden) English.
Amund (awe, fear; edge, point + protector) Scandinavian.
Anatole (sunrise, daybreak) French.
Anders (manly) Scandinavian.
Andor (eagle + Thor) Scandinavian.
Andre (manly) French.
Andrew (manly) **Dande, Dandy, Tandy** English.
Angus (one, choice, preeminent) **Gus** Irish, Scottish.
Anker (harvester) Scandinavian.
Anselme (divine helmet) French.
Anthony (?, *priceless, of inestimable worth* is a folk definition) **Antony, Tony** English.
Antoine (?, *priceless, of inestimable worth* is a folk definition) French.
Anton (?, *priceless, of inestimable worth* is a folk definition) German.
Antonius (?, *priceless, of inestimable worth* is a folk definition) Dutch.

Ara (eagle) French.

Archibald (genuinely bold, genuinely brave) **Archebald** English, German, Scottish.

Arend (eagle power) **Aren** German, Scandinavian.

Aristide (best) French.

Armand (soldier, warrior) **Armond** French.

Armin (soldier, warrior) German.

Arnbjorn (eagle bear) **Armbjorn** Scandinavian.

Arne (eagle) **Aren** Scandinavian.

Arno (eagle) French.

Arnold (eagle ruler) German.

Arsene (male, virile) French.

Art (a bear) Irish, Scottish, Welsh.

Arthur (?) English, French.

Arvid (eagle tree) Scandinavian.

Asa (healer) English.

Asmund (God is protector) Scandinavian.

Athelstan (noble stone) **Athestan** English.

Auberi (elf ruler) **Aubry** French.

Aubert (noble and bright) French.

Auguste (great, venerable) **August; Gus** French, German.

Augustin (great, venerable) **Gus** French.

Augustus (great, venerable) **Gus** English, French.

Aurele (gold) French.

Aurelien (golden) French.

Austin (great, venerable) English.

Averil (boar battle) English.

Aylmer (nobly famous) English.

Aylwin (elf friend) English.

Azariah (whom Jehovah helps) English.

Baird (a poet) Scottish.

Baldric (bold ruler) French.

Baldwin (bold friend) English, French, German.

Balthasar (?) English.

Baptist (a baptiser) **Baptiste** English, French.

Barclay (from Berkeley *birch meadow*) English.

Bardolph (bright wolf) **Bardolf** English, French.

Barnabas (son of exhortation) English.

Barnabe (son of exhortation) **Barnaby; Barney** French.

Bartel (son of Talmai *hill, mound, furrows*) **Bertel** Dutch, German.

Barthelemy (son of Talmai *hill, mound, furrows*) French.

Bartholomaus (son of Talmai *hill, mound, furrows*) **Bartholomeus** Dutch, German.

Bartholomew (son of Talmai *hill, mound, furrows*) English.

Basil (kingly) **Basile, Bazil, Bazille** English.

Bastien (man from Sebasta) French, German.

Beavis (beautiful) **Beves, Bevis** English, French.

Bellamy (beautiful friend) French.

Bendt (blessed) Scandinavian.

Benedict (blessed) **Benedick, Benedikt, Benedikte** English, German, Scandinavian.

Benjamin (son of the right hand) **Ben** English, French, German, Scandinavian.

Bennet (blessed) English.

Berend (strong as a bear) **Bernd** German.

Berg (mountain) German.

Bernhard (bold as a bear) **Bernard, Barnard** English, French, German.

Bernt (bold as a bear) Scandinavian.

Berold (bear rule) **Berolt** English.

Bertil (bright) Scandinavian.

Bertin(bright friend) English.

Bertram (bright raven) **Bertran** English, French, German, Scandinavian.

Beringer (bear spear) French.

Bertin (bright friend) French.

Birger (helper) Swedish.

Bjorn (bear) **Bjarne** Norwegian, Swedish.

Blaise (deformed, stuttering) **Blaize, Blase, Blaze** English, French.

Bo (a householder) Scandinavian.

Bonaventure (good travels) French.

Brian (force, strength; valor; steep, high) **Bryan** Irish.

Brice (?) French.

Broder (brother) Scandinavian.

Bruce (from Brus, France) English.

Bruno (brown) English, French, German, Scandinavian.

Caesar (blue gray; hairy) **Cesar** English, Spanish.

Caleb (dog; faithful) English.

Calum (dove) Scottish.

Cameron (crooked nose) Scottish.

Camille (?; virgin of unblemished character) French.

Campbell (crooked mouth) Scottish.

Carl (a man, freeman) **Karl** English, German, Scandinavian.

Caspar (treasure master) **Casper, Kaspar, Kasper** Scandinavian.

Cecil (blind, dim-sighted) French.

Charles (full-grown, a man) English, French.

Chauncey (belonging to Chancey, France) **Chauncy** English, French.

Christian (a Christian, a follower of Christ) English, French, German, Scandinavian.

Christoph (bearing Christ) **Christophe** German.

Christopher (bearing Christ) **Christoffer, Kristoffer; Chris, Kester, Kit** English.

Claud (lame) **Claude** English, French.

Claus (victory of the people) German.

Clement (gentle, mild) French.

Colin (dove) Irish, Scottish.

Colin (little Nicholas *victory of the people*) English.

Comfort (comfort, care) English.

Conall (strength; wisdom; high; wolf, dog) Irish, Scottish.

Connell (wisdom, high-mighty) **Connel** Irish, Scottish.

Connor (wisdom, counsel, strength + aid; hound) **Conor** Irish.

Conrad (bold counsel) French, German.

Constant (constant, steadfast) English, French.

Constantine (constant, steadfast) English, French.

Conway (hound of the plain) Irish.

Corneille (horn) French.

Cornelius (a horn) **Cornelis, Corneleus** English.

Craig (rugged rocks; dweller by the crag) Scottish.
Crispin (curled) English, French.
Cuthbert (known and bright) English.
Cyprian (from Cyprus) **Cyprien** English, French.
Cyriack (lordly) English.
Cyril (lordly) **Cyrille** English, French.
Cyrus (lord) English.
Damian (tamer) **Damien** English, French.
Dana (a Dane) Scandinavian.
Daniel (judged by God) English, French, German, Scandinavian, Spanish.
Darby (from the settlement by the deer) English.
David (beloved) English, French, German, Scandinavian, Spanish.
Dennis (belonging to Dionysus) **Denis, Denys** English, French, German.
Derek (ruler of the people) German.
Diederik (ruler of the people) German.
Dierk (ruler of the people) Scandinavian.
Dieter (ruler of the people) German.
Dietrich (ruler of the people) German.
Dirk (ruler of the people) German, Scandinavian.
Dominic (belonging to a lord, belonging to the Lord) **Dominik** English, German.
Dominique (belonging to a lord, belonging to the Lord) French.
Donald (world ruler) English.
Donatien (given by God) French.
Donnal (world ruler) Irish, Scottish.
Dougal (dark-haired stranger) Irish, Scottish.
Douglas (black, dark + blue, green, gray) English.
Drew (manly) English.
Dudley (from Dudda's lea) English.
Duff (dark, black) Scottish.
Duncan (brown warrior) Scottish.
Durand (enduring, lasting) **Durant** English, French.
Easter (born at Easter) English.
Ebenezer (stone of help) English.
Eberhard (strong as a wild boar) German.
Eden (delight) English.
Edgar (wealthy spear) English.
Edmond (wealthy protection) **Edmund** English, French, German, Scandinavian.
Edvard (wealthy guardian) Scandinavian.
Edward (wealthy guardian) **Eduard** English, French, German.
Edwin (wealthy friend) English, German.
Egon (point of a sword) German.
Eilert (brave with the spear) Scandinavian.
Eilif (immortal) Norwegian.
Einar (lone warrior) Scandinavian.
Eleazar (God has helped) English.
Eli (high, ascent) English.
Elias (Jehovah is God) English.
Elijah (Jehovah is God) English.
Elisha (God is salvation) English.
Elkanah (God created) English.

Ellery (alder tree) English, German.
Elmer (nobly famous) English.
Elof (lone descendant) Swedish.
Emanuel (God with us) **Emmanuel** English, Scandinavian.
Emery (ruler of strength) French, German.
Emile (rival, trying to equal or excel) **Emil** French, German, Scandinavian.
Emilien (rival, trying to equal or excel) French.
Enoch (dedicated) English.
Eoghan (lamb; youth; well-born) Irish.
Ephraim (very fruitful) English.
Erasmus (loved, desired) English.
Erik (eternal ruler) **Eirik, Eric** French, German, Scandinavian.
Erlend (foreigner, stranger) **Erland** Scandinavian.
Ernest (earnest, resolute) **Ernst** English, French.
Esau (hairy) English.
Eskel (sacrificial cauldron of a god) Scandinavian.
Eubule (he of good counsel) English.
Eugene (well-born) English, French.
Eusebius (pious) English.
Eustace (steadfast; happy in harvest) **Eustache** English, French.
Evan (youth; God is gracious) Welsh.
Evelyn (?) English.
Everard (strong as a boar) **Everhart, Evert** Dutch, English, French.
Everitt (strong as a boar) **Everet, Everett, Everit, Evert** English.
Ewan (youth) **Ewen** Scottish.
Ewould (lawful rule) Dutch.
Eyvind (island of the Wend) Scandinavian.
Ezekiel (God strengthens) English.
Ezra (help) English.
Faas (resolute counsel) Dutch.
Fabian (a bean) **Fabien** English, French, German.
Farquhar (dear man) Scottish.
Fearghas (man of valor) **Fargus, Fergus** Irish, Scottish.
Felix (lucky) English, French, German.
Ferdinand (peace; journey; youth, life + courage; venture, risk; ready) French.
Fernando (peace; journey; youth, life + courage; venture, risk; ready) Spanish.
Festus (?) English.
Filbert (very bright) French.
Filip (lover of horses) Scandinavian.
Fingall (fair-haired stranger) **Fingal** Irish.
Finlay (fair-haired warrior) Irish.
Finn (from Finland) Scandinavian.
Fiske (fish) Swedish.
Flemming (a Flemming) Scandinavian.
Florence (a blooming) English.
Florent (blossoming) **Florentin** French.
Florian (flowery) English, French, German, Scandinavian.
Floris (blossoming) Dutch.
Forbes (a field) Scottish.
Francis (a Frank, a freeman) English, French.

Francisco (a Frenchman) Spanish.
Francois (French) French.
Frank (a Frank) German.
Franz (a Frenchman) German.
Franziskus (a Frenchman) **Franciscus** German.
Fraser (a Frisian) English.
Frederic (ruler of peace) **Frederick, Frederik, Fredrick, Fredrik; Fred, Freddy** English, Scandinavian.
Friederich (peaceful king) **Friedrich** German.
Friedhelm (peace helmet) German.
Fulbert (very bright) English.
Fulton (the fowl enclosure; a chicken coop) English.
Gabriel (God is strength) **Gabrial** English, French, German, Scandinavian.
Gamaliel (the Lord is recompense) English.
Garrett (spear rule) **Garett, Garit, Garitt** English.
Garrick (spear; brave with the spear) **Garek** German.
Garth (yard, enclosure) Scandinavian.
Gascon (?, possibly *guest, stranger; from Gascony*) French.
Gaspard (treasure master) French.
Gaston (?, possibly *guest, stranger; from Gascony*) English, French.
Gauvain (battle hawk) French.
Gavin (battle hawk) English.
Gedaliah (made great by Jehovah) English.
Gene (well-born, noble) English.
Geoffrey (district; traveler; pledge + peace) **Geffrey, Jeffery, Jeffrey** English.
Geoffroi (district; traveler; pledge + peace) French.
George (earth worker, farmer) **Georg, Georges** English, French, German, Scandinavian.
Gerald (spear rule) **Gerold, Gerolt** English, French, German.
Gerard (brave with the spear) French, Scandinavian.
Gerhard (brave with the spear) German, Norwegian, Swedish.
Gerlach (spear sport) German, Scandinavian.
Germayne (a German) **Germain** English, French.
Gershon (expulsion, stranger) **Gershom** English.
Gervais (servant of the spear) English, French.
Gideon (hewer) English.
Giffard (give + bold, fierce) English.
Gilbert (bright pledge) **Gib, Gil** English, French, German.
Giles (goatskin shield of Zeus; a protection) **Gillis** English, French.
Gillespie (servant of the bishop) Scottish.
Gillies (servant of Jesus) Scottish.
Gilroy (servant of the red-haired lad) Scottish.
Godfried (peace of God) Scandinavian.
Godfry (peace of God) **Godfrey** French.
Godric (powerful God) English.
Godwin (friend of God) English.
Goldwin (friend of gold) English.
Gottfried (peace of God) German.
Graham (from Grantham) **Graeme, Grahame** English.
Grant (great, large) Scottish.
Gregoire (vigilant, watchful) French.
Gregor (vigilant, watchful) German, Scandinavian, Scottish.

Gregory (vigilant, watchful) English.
Griffin (like a griffin, monstrous) English.
Guillaume (resolute protector) French.
Gunnar (war, strife, battle) Scandinavian.
Gunther (bold in war) French, German, Scandinavian.
Gustaf (staff of the Goths) **Gustav** Scandinavian.
Guy (a guide, leader) English, French, German.
Guyon (a guide, leader) French.
Haakon (chosen son) **Hakan, Hakon** Scandinavian.
Hagen (chosen son) Danish.
Halsten (rock stone) Swedish.
Hamilton (from the blunt hill) English.
Hamlet (little house) **Hamlett, Hamnet** English.
Hamon (little house) English.
Hans (God is gracious) **Hannes** German, Scandinavian.
Harald (home ruler) **Harold** German, Scandinavian.
Harry (home ruler) English.
Haward (high guardian) Scandinavian.
Hector (holding fast) English, French.
Heinrich (home ruler) German.
Helmut (courageous protector) German.
Hendrik (home ruler) **Henrik** German, Scandinavian.
Henning (home ruler) Danish.
Henry (home ruler) English, French.
Herbert (army bright) **Harbert, Heribert** English, German.
Herman (warrior, soldier) **Hermann** English, German.
Hezekiah (God strengthens) English.
Hilary (cheerful) **Hilaire, Hilarie** English, French.
Hiram (exalted brother) English.
Hjalmar (warrior's helmet) Scandinavian.
Horatio (?) English.
Hosanna (save pray) English.
Hosea (salvation) English.
Hubert (bright heart) English, French, German, Scandinavian.
Hugh (heart, mind, soul) **Hugo** English, French, German, Scandinavian.
Humphrey (warrior of peace) English.
Iain (God is gracious) **Ian** Scottish.
Ingmar (famous Ing) Scandinavian.
Ingram (Ing's raven; angel raven) English, Scandinavian.
Ingvar (Ing's warrior) Scandinavian.
Ira (watchful) English.
Irving (from the west river) English.
Isaac (laughter) **Isak, Isaak, Izaac, Izaak** English, French, German, Scandinavian.
Isaiah (God is salvation) English.
Israel (contender with God) English.
Ivar (archer, bow warrior) **Iver, Ivor** Scandinavian.
Ives (archer) **Ivo, Yvo** English.
Jabez (height) English.
Jack (God is gracious) **Jackey** English.
Jacob (supplanting, seizing by the heels) **Jakob** English, French, German, Scandinavian.
Jacques (supplanting, seizing by the heels) French.
James (supplanting, seizing by the heels) English.
Jan (God is gracious) **Janne, Jens, Jon, Jons** Scandinavian.

Japheth (enlargement) **Japet, Japeth** English.
Jared (descending) English.
Jason (healer) English.
Jasper (treasure master) English.
Jean (God is gracious) French.
Jean-Baptiste (God is gracious + a baptizer; John the Baptist) French.
Jean-Michel (God is gracious + Who is like God?) French.
Jedaiah (invoker of Jehovah) **Jed** English.
Jedidiah (beloved of Jehovah) **Jed** English.
Jeffrey (peaceful district; traveler of peace; pledge of peace) **Jeffery** English.
Jeremiah (God will uplift) **Jeremias** English, Scandinavian.
Jeremie (God will uplift) **Jeremy** English, French.
Jeroen (holy name) Dutch.
Jerome (holy name) English, French.
Jesimiel (God sets up) English.
Jesper (treasure master) Danish.
Jesse (gift) English.
Jethro (excellence) English.
Joachim (God will establish) **Joachin, Joakim** English, Scandinavian.
Jock (God is gracious) Scottish.
Joel (the Lord is God) English, French.
Johann (God is gracious) German.
Johannes (God is gracious) German, Scandinavian.
John (God is gracious) **Johnny** English.
Jonas (dove) **Jonah** English.
Jonathan (God has given) **Jon** English.
Joost (just, lawful) Dutch.
Jordan (a flowing down) **Jordaan, Judd** English, Dutch.
Jorg (earth worker, farmer) German.
Jorgen (earth worker, farmer) Dutch, Swedish.
Jorn (earth worker, farmer) German.
Joseph (he shall add) **Josef; Joe** Dutch, English, German.
Joshua (God is salvation) **Jozua; Josh** English.
Josiah (the Lord supports) English.
Julian (youth, downy) **Julien** English, French, German.
Julius (youth, downy) English.
Justin (just) **Justyn** English, French.
Justus (just) German.
Juvenal (youth) French.
Kaspar (treasure master) French.
Keir (dark-complexioned) Irish.
Keith (?, perhaps *the wind*; *wood*) Scottish.
Kennet (handsome, comely) Scandinavian.
Kenneth (handsome, comely) English.
Kenrick (royal rule) English.
Kenward (brave guardian) **Kenard** English.
Kernan (little black-haired one) Irish.
Kester (bearing Christ) Scottish.
Kieran (little dark one) Irish.
Kirk (church) Scottish.
Knut (knot) Scandinavian.
Konrad (wise counsel) French, German, Scandinavian.
Laban (white) English.

Lambert (bright land) English, French, German, Scandinavian.
Lance (land) French.
Lars (man from Laurentum) Scandinavian.
Laurance (from Laurentum) **Laurence, Lawrence** English.
Lazarus (whom God helps) English.
Leif (what is remaining, relic; beloved) Scandinavian.
Lemuel (devoted to God) English.
Lennart (brave as a lion) Scandinavian.
Leo (lion) English, French, German, Scandinavian.
Leon (lion) French.
Leonard (bold as a lion) English, French.
Leonhard (bold as a lion) German.
Leopold (bold people) French, German.
Levi (joining) English.
Levin (dear friend) English.
Lionel (little lion) English, French.
Lorens (man from Laurentum) **Lorenz** German, Scandinavian.
Louis (famous in war) **Lewis** English, French, German.
Luc (light; man from Lucania) **Luke** English, French.
Lucas (light; man from Lucania) **Lukas** English, Scandinavian.
Lucian (light; man from Lucania) **Lucien** English, French.
Lucius (light; man from Lucania) English.
Ludovic (famous in war) Scandinavian.
Ludwig (famous in war) French, German.
Lyell (lion) **Lyel** English.
Maarten (of Mars, warlike) Dutch.
Magnus (great, large) French, German, Scandinavian, Scottish.
Malachi (my messenger) English.
Malcolm (servant of Saint Columba) Scottish.
Manfred (peace of man) English, French, German, Scandinavian.
Manus (great, large) Scandinavian.
Marc (?, perhaps *of Mars; manly; soft, tender*) **Mark** English, French.
Marcel (of Mars, warlike) French.
Marco (?, perhaps *of Mars; manly; soft, tender*) Spanish.
Marcus (?, perhaps *of Mars; manly; soft, tender*) **Markus** English, German, Scandinavian.
Martin (of Mars, warlike) **Marten** English, French, German, Swedish.
Matheus (gift of God) **Mathiu, Matteus, Mattheus, Matthews** English, German, Scandinavian.
Matthew (gift of God) **Matheu** Dutch, English.
Matthias (gift of God) **Mathis** English, German.
Mauger (spear grinder) English.
Maurice (a Moor) **Meurisse** English, French.
Maurits (a Moor) Scandinavian.
Max (greatest) German.
Maxwell (large spring; large stream) English.
Maynard (strong and hardy) English, French.
Meinhard (strong and hardy) German.
Meshach (agile) English.
Micah (Who is like God?) English.

Michael (Who is like God?) **Michel, Mikael, Mikel** English, German, Scandinavian.

Michel (Who is like God?) French.

Michiel (Who is like God?) Dutch.

Micky (Who is like God?) **Mick** English.

Miles (?, perhaps *mild, peaceful; merciful*) English.

Milo (?, perhaps *mild, peaceful; merciful*) **Milon** English, French.

Moise (drawn out of the water) French.

Montgomery (from Monte Goumeril) English.

Mordecai (worshiper of Marduk) English.

Morgan (sea bright) Welsh.

Morris (dark, swarthy, a Moor) English.

Morten (of Mars; warlike) Norwegian.

Moses (drawn out of the water) English.

Murdoch (mariner) Scottish.

Murphy (sea warrior) Irish, Scottish.

Murray (from Moray *beside the sea*) Scottish.

Nathan (gift) **Nate** English.

Nathanael (gift of God) **Natanael, Nathaniel** English, French, German, Scandinavian.

Nehemiah (comforted by Jehovah) English.

Neil (champion; a cloud) **Neal, Neill, Nial, Niall, Niel, Niell** Irish, Scottish.

Neville (from the new town) **Nevell, Nevil** English.

Nicholas (victory of the people) **Nikolas, Nikolaus; Nicol, Nicoll, Nichol, Coll** English, French, German, Scandinavian.

Noah (rest, comfort) English.

Noel (born at Christmas) French.

Norbert (north bright) German.

Norman (northman) English.

Obadiah (servant of God) English.

Odo (wealth) English, French, German, Scandinavian.

Ola (ancestor's relic) **Ole** Norwegian, Swedish.

Oliver (olive tree) English, German.

Olivier (olive tree) French.

Olof (ancestor's relic) **Olaf, Olav, Olov, Oluf** Scandinavian.

Osanne (hosannah) French.

Osbern (god bear) **Osborn** English, Scandinavian.

Osbert (god bright) French.

Oscar (God's spear) **Oskar** English, German, Scandinavian.

Osmond (God's protection) **Osmund** English, French.

Oswald (God's power) English, German.

Otto (rich) German.

Owen (well-born) **Own** Welsh.

Paddy (a patrician, an aristocrat) **Pady** Irish.

Parlan (son of Talmai *hill, mound, furrows*) Scottish.

Pascal (Easter, born at Easter) English.

Pat (a patrician, an aristocrat) **Patt** English, Irish.

Patrick (a patrician, an aristocrat) English, German, Irish.

Patterson (son of Peter *a rock, a stone*) English.

Paul (small) English, French, German, Scandinavian.

Paulin (small) English, French, German.

Paulo (small) Spanish.

Pearse (a rock, a stone) English.

Percy (from Percy, Normandy) **Percey** English.

Peter (a rock, a stone) English, French, German, Scandinavian.

Philip (lover of horses) **Philipp, Phillip** English, French, German.

Phineas (oracle) English.

Pierre (a rock, a stone) French.

Quintin (fifth) English.

Rafe (counsel wolf) English.

Ragnar (warrior of decision) Scandinavian.

Rainier (wise army) French.

Ralph(counsel wolf) English, German.

Ramsey (from Ram's island) Scottish.

Randolph (shield wolf) **Randolf, Randulf, Ranulf** English, French, German, Scandinavian.

Ranfred (counsel peace) French.

Raul (counsel wolf) French, German.

Raymund (counsel protection) **Raimund** English, French, German.

Regin (judgment, decision) Scandinavian.

Reginald (judgment power) English.

Reid (red, ruddy) **Read** Scottish.

Reinhard (brave counsel) German.

Renfred (counsel might) English.

Reuben (behold, a son!) English.

Reynard (counsel hard) English, French.

Raynold (powerful protection) **Rainald, Raynald, Renold, Reynold** English.

Ricardo (stern king) Spanish.

Richard (stern king) **Rikard** English, French, German, Scandinavian.

Robert (bright with fame) **Rob, Robb** English, French, German, Scandinavian.

Roberto (bright with fame) Spanish.

Roderick (famous king) **Roddy** English.

Rodolphe (wolf fame) **Rudolf, Rudolph, Rudolphe** French, German.

Roger (famous with the spear) **Rogier, Rodger** English, French, German.

Roland (famous land) **Rolland** English, French, German, Scandinavian.

Rolf (famous wolf) French, German, Swedish.

Ross (dweller on the promontory or peninsula; red, rust-colored) Scottish.

Roth (famous king) Scandinavian.

Roy (red-haired, ruddy-complexioned) Scottish.

Rurik (famous king) Scandinavian.

Rutger (famous spear) Dutch.

Samson (the sun) **Sansom, Sanson** English, French.

Samuel (heard of God) English.

Sander (defender of mankind) **Sandre** English, French, German, Scandinavian.

Sandy (defender of mankind) Scottish.

Saul (asked for) English.

Scott (an Irishman, a Scot) English.

Sebastian (man from Sebastia) **Sebastien** English, French, German, Scandinavian.

Seth (appointed) English.
Severin (severe, strict) French.
Shane (God is gracious) Scottish.
Shaw (dweller at a wood or grove) Scottish.
Shem (renowned) English.
Siegfried (powerful peace) German.
Sigge (victory, conquest) Scandinavian.
Sigmund (victorious protection) **Siegmund** French, German, Scandinavian.
Sigurd (guardian of victory) German, Scandinavian.
Silas (ask for) English.
Silvester (a wood, a forest) English.
Simon (heard) **Simeon** English, French, Scandinavian.
Sinclair (from Saint Clair) Scottish.
Solomon (peaceful) English.
Soren (apart) Danish.
Sorley (mariner, sailor) Scottish.
Spiro (to breathe, to blow) French.
Stanislav (government is glory) German.
Steen (stone) Danish.
Stein (stone) Norwegian.
Steinar (stone warrior) Scandinavian.
Sten (stone) Swedish.
Stephan (a crown, a garland) **Stefan, Steffan, Steffen** Scandinavian.
Stephen (a crown, a garland) English, Scandinavian.
Steven (a crown, a garland) Dutch, English.
Stewart (steward, keeper of the animal enclosure) English.
Svein (strong, youth) **Sveinn, Sven, Svend, Svends** Scandinavian.
Swain (stong, able, wise) Scandinavian.
Sylvester (of the woods) **Sylvestre** French, German.
Talbot (pillager, bandit; lampblack) English, French.
Teague (a poet) Scottish.
Terrence (soft, tender) **Terance** English.
Terrick (ruler of the people) French.
Theodore (gift of God) **Theodoor, Theodor; Theo** Dutch, English, German.
Theodoric (ruler of the people) **Theo** English.
Thomas (a twin) **Thomaas, Tomas** English, French, German, Scandinavian.
Thompson (son of Thom *a twin*) English.

Thor (thunder) **Thore** Scandinavian.
Thurstan (Thor's stone) **Torsten** English, German.
Timothy (honor, respect) **Timothee** English, French.
Titus (?, possibly *to honor*) English.
Toal (people mighty) Scandinavian.
Tobias (God is good) English, German.
Tristan (tumult, sadness) **Tristram** English, French.
Tycho (hitting the mark) **Tyge, Tyko** Scandinavian.
Ulf (wolf) German, Scandinavian.
Uriah (God is light) English.
Valdemar (famous ruler) **Waldemar** Scandinavian.
Valentine (healthy, strong) **Valentin** English, French, German, Scandinavian.
Valery (to be strong) **Valere** French.
Valient (valiant, brave) English.
Victor (victor, winner) **Viktor** French, German.
Vidkun (wide experience) Scandinavian.
Vincent (conquering) English, French, German, Scandinavian.
Virgil (youthful, flourishing) English.
Vital (vital, life-giving) German.
Vivien (alive) French.
Von (hope) Scandinavian.
Walden (to rule) German.
Waldo (to rule) German.
Walter (ruler of an army) English, German, Scandinavian.
Werner (protecting army) **Verner, Warner** German, Scandinavian.
Wilfred (desire for peace) English, German, Scandinavian.
Wilhelm (resolute protector) **Willelm, Willem** German, Scandinavian.
William (resolute protector) English.
Winfred (blessed peace) English.
Winston (from Winston *friend's town*) English.
Wolf (wolf) German.
Wolfgang (traveling wolf) German.
Yves (archer) French.
Yvon (archer) French.
Zachariah (God remembers) **Zacharias, Zachary** English.
Zebedee (God bestows) English.
Zebulun (to carry, to exalt) English.
Zephaniah (the Lord has hidden) English.

SURNAMES

As stated in the previous chapter, immigrant groups brought their naming traditions with them to America. Among the British, French, and Germans, surnames were hereditary, but many Scandinavians still used generational-changing patronymics. Once the Scandinavians reached America, their patronymical surnames became hereditary. Among the Dutch, however, farm names, rather than the patronymics, tended to become the hereditary surname.

Before education became widespread, names everywhere were in a state of flux. One person might spell his name Smythe, and another, Smith. Upon arrival in America, many foreigners chose to translate their names into English. The German Schmidt, for example, became Smith, the Swedish Bjork became Birch, and the Dutch Apfel became Apple. Registrars with little education or knowledge of foreign languages, often altered the spelling of a name to fit the sounds of the English language. Thus, Roggenfelder became Rockefeller. Irish names were spelled in so many different ways, they're almost impossible to sort out. It wasn't until social programs were instated in the twentieth century that stricter rules came into play and the spellings became frozen. Listed below are only the most common forms.

Aagard (dweller in the yard by the river) **Aagaard** Norwegian.

Abbott (an abbot, one from the abbot's household) English.

Ahrens (dweller at the sign of the eagle) Dutch.

Albin (white) **Albyn** English.

Alford (from Alford *the old ford*) English.

Almand (German) **Allmand** English, German.

Almquist (elm twig) **Almkuist** Swedish, German.

Amour (love) French.

Ancel (serving maid) French.

Anders (manly) Scandinavian.

Appleby (from Appleby *the apple tree farm*) English.

Archer (bowman, archer) English.

Arenson (son of Aren *eagle rule*) Norwegian.

Arkin (little Arke *eternal ruler*) Norwegian.

Aronson (son of Aron *lofty mountain*) **Arons** Swedish.

Artaud (brave rule) French.

Arvidson (son of Arvid *man of the people*) **Arvidsson** Swedish.

Ashburner (charcoal maker) English.

Atkinson (son of Atkin *little Adam;*) English.

Aubert (noble and bright) French.

Avenier (grower or seller of oats) French.

Avery (elf ruler) English.

Axelson (son of Axel *divine reward*) Swedish.

Ballou (from Bellou) French.

Barbe (the bearded one, the mustached one) French.

Barker (a bark stripper, a tanner) English.

Barnelby (son of consolation) English.

Barnes (dweller at the barn; child, bairn) English, Scottish.

Barraud (bear might) **Barratt** French.

Barry (descendant of Bearach *spearlike*; dweller at the village by the border; from the rampart) Irish.

Base (the short one) English.

Bastard (a bastard, an illegitimate person) French.

Bastien (from Sebastia) French.

Bate (little Bartholomew *son of Talmai*) English.

Baud (bold) **Bault** French.

Beauchamp (fair field) French.

Beaufoy (beautiful beech tree) French.

Beauregard (beautiful place) French.

Beckman (dweller near the brook) Dutch.

Bedford (from Bedford *Bedica's ford*) English.

Beecher (dweller near the beech tree) English.

Belcher (pretty face) English.

Bell (dweller at the sign of the bell; beautiful, handsome; God is my oath) English.

Benjamin (son of the right hand) French, English.

Benoît (blessed) French.

Benning (son of Benna) English.

Benton (from the town of the bent grass) English.

Berle (water parsnips) French.

Berquist (mountain twig) **Bergquist** Swedish.

Bertelot (little Bartholomew) English.

Bettencourt (from Betto's farm) French.

Billard (sword brave) French.

Birch (birch) English.

Bird (a bird) **Byrd** English.

Bjork (birch) Swedish.

Bjorklund (birch grove) Swedish.

Bjornson (son of Bjorn *bear*) **Bjornsen** Norwegian.

Blanche (white) French.

Blauvelt (dweller near the blue [flax] field) Dutch.

Blomberg (flower mountain) **Bloomberg** Swedish.

Blomgren (flower branch) **Bloomgren** Swedish.

Blomquist (flower twig) **Bloomquist** Swedish.

Blondeau (blond, fair-complexioned) French.

Bloom (flower) Swedish.

Bode (an officer of the court; town crier) Dutch.

Boer (a farmer) Dutch.

Bonnin (little good one) French.

Booz (the angry man; dweller near the cattle stall) **Boos, Booze, Boozer** Dutch.

Borg (dweller near the castle or stronghold) **Borge** Norwegian, Swedish.

Borgman (a money lender; castle man) Dutch.

Bose (dweller in the woods; quarrelsome) Dutch.

Bourk (a fort, stronghold) English.

Bourton (from Bourton *the settlement of the boor, peasant; the settlement by the cattle stall; the settlement near the stronghold; the settlement near the hill*) English.

Bouvier (cattle drover, a herdsman) French.

Bowyer (a maker or trader of bows) English.

Boyle (descendant of Baoghall, ?, perhaps *peril, danger* or *pledge*) Irish.

Brady (spirited) Irish.

Brent (from the high place)

Brigham (from the homestead by the bridge) English.

Brinkman (dweller on or near the grassy hill) **Brinkmann** Dutch.

Broberg (bridge mountain) Swedish.

Bromley (dweller at the broom thicket) English.

Brooks (dweller at the brook) **Brookes** English.

Broughton (from the settlement near the brook; from the settlement near the castle) English.

Buchanan (little small one) Scottish.

Buck (a buck; dweller near the beech tree) English.

Buckler (a buckle maker) English.

Bullman (a bull herder) English.

Bullocke (like a bullock) English.

Burger (from Burg *fortification, stronghold*) Dutch, German.

Burgis (a freeman of a borough) English.

Burnell (the dark one) French.

Burns (dweller at the burnt house) English.

Burr (a person difficult to shake off, one who sticks like a burr; an irritating person) English.

Buxton (Bucca's stone) English.

Campbell (crooked mouth) Scottish.

Carlsen (son of Carl *man*) **Carlson** Norwegian, Swedish.

Carr (dweller at a marsh, rock, or fort) Scottish.

Carroll (descendant of Cearbhall *champion, warrior*) Irish.

Carson (son of Car *a marsh; a fort; a rock; care, anxiety*) Scottish.

Casey (descendant of Cathasach *watchful*) Irish.

Cassen (little Cass *vain*) English.

Cazenove (from the new house) French.

Chambers (a chamber attendant) English.

Charron (a maker of carts) French.

Charter (a carter, a maker, seller or driver of carts) English.

Chenault (dweller near the irrigation channel) French.

Chesne (dweller near the oak tree) French.

Chittingden (from Chittenden *Citta's valley*) English.

Classen (son of Clas *victory of the people*) **Claassen, Clasen, Clausen** Norwegian, Swedish.

Clay (dweller near a clayey place) English.

Cole (victory of the people) English.

Collier (a charcoal burner, a seller of coal or charcoal) English.

Collins (son of Colin [Nicholas] *victory of the people*; descendant of Coileán *whelp, pup*) English, Irish.

Connolly (descendant of Conghal *conflict*) **Connelly** Irish.

Connor (descendant or son of Conchobhar *wisdom, counsel, strength; hound lover*) Irish.

Courtier (agent, broker) French.

Courtis (courteous) English.

Craft (dweller near the small, enclosed field) English.

Crockett (the little crooked, deformed person) English.

Crofts (dweller near the small, enclosed field) English.

Cronkhite (an invalid, an ill person) Dutch.

Crosby (from the farm near the cross) English.

Crosse (dweller near the cross) English.

Cunningham (dweller at the royal manor) Scottish.

Dalton (from Dalton *the settlement in the dale*) English.

Daly (descendant of Dálach *assembly*) Irish.

Delacroix (of the cross) French.

Denton (from the settlement in the valley) English.

Dickinson (son of little Dick *stern king*) English.

Dixon (son of Dick *stern king*) English.

Doherty (descendant of Dochartach *the hurtful one*) Irish.

Donnelly (descendant of Donnghal *brown + valor*) Irish.

Donovan (descendant of Donndubhán *little dark brown one*) Irish.

Douglass (son of Douglas *black, dark + blue green, gray*) Scottish.

Doyle (descendant of Dughbhall *dark-haired stranger*) Irish.

Drake (dweller at the sign of the drake or dragon) English.

Draper (a clothier) English.

Edmundson (son of Edmond *wealthy protector*) English.

Elbert (noble and bright) English.

Ellsworth (from Elle's homestead) English.

Farrell (descendant of Fearghal *man of valor*) Irish.

Fenton (from Fenton *the settlement in the fen*) English.

Filmore (very famous) **Fillmore** English.

Fitzgerald (son of Gerald *spear rule*) Irish, English, French.

Fitzpatrick (son of Patrick *a patrician, an aristocrat*) Irish, English.

Flower (an arrow maker, a flower) English.

Fox (dweller at the sign of the fox) English.

Freeman (a free man) English.

Gallagher (descendant of Gallchobhar *foreign help*) Irish.

Gardner (a gardener) English.

Garrard (brave with the spear) English.

Garret (brave with the spear) English.

Gascoigne (a native of Gascony) English, French.

Geffrey (district; traveler; pledge + peace) English.

Gibbins (son of Gibbin [Gilbert] *bright pledge*) **Gibbons** English.

Gladwell (dweller at the clear spring) English.

Goddard (God + firm) English.

Goddin (little good one) English.

Godfrey (God peace) English.

Gore (dweller at a gore, a three-cornered piece of land) English.

Graham (dweller at the gray land or enclosure) English, Scottish.

Grange (dweller at a barn, granary, or farmhouse) English.

Griffin (descendant of Gríobhtha *like a griffin, monsterlike; red, ruddy*) English.

Grubb (coarse, rough) English.

Gullifer (wolf army) English.

Gurney (from Gournay, France) English.

Hackett (little Hack *cutter; high kin; hook*) English.

Hagstrom (pasture stream; willow stream) **Haggstrom** Swedish.

Hamilton (belonging to Hamela's estate; the enclosure of the mutilated person) English.

Hampton (from Hampton *village on the rich pasture land; the high village*) English.

Harding (warrior, hero, brave) English.

Hardy (bold, hardy, hearty) English.

Harrington (from Harrington *the settlement of Here*) English.

Hartley (from Hartley *the hart lea*) English.

Hayes (descendant of Aodha *fire*) Irish.

Hazell (dweller near the hazel tree) English.

Healy (from the high lea) English.

Hibbins (son of Hibbin *chief bright*) English.

Higgins (descendant of Uigín) Irish.

Holdsworth (from Holdsworth *Hold's farm*) English.

Holloway (dweller at the hollow way or path) English.

Houlgrave (dweller at the grove in the hollow) English.

Houston (from Hugh's *heart, mind* town) **Huston** English.

Hubbard (bright heart) English.

Huckle (little Huck [Hugh] *heart, mind, spirit*) English.

Hudson (son of Hud *hood*) English.

Hull (Hugh *heart, mind, spirit*) English.

Hunt (a hunter) English.

Hunter (a hunter) English.

Hurd (a herdsman) English.

Ireland (from Ireland) English.

Jarman (a German) English.

Jay (chatterer, like a jay bird) English.

Jennings (son of Jenning [little Jean *God is gracious*]) English.

Jervas (servant of the spear) English.

Johnston (son of John *God is gracious*) English.

Julyan (youth, downy-bearded) English.

Kane (descendant of Cathán *little battle*) Irish.

Kavanagh (little handsome one, little gentle one) Irish.

Keane (descendant of Cathán *little battle*) Irish.

Kelly (war, strife) Irish.

Kelso (chalk heights) Scottish.

Kemp (champion, warrior, soldier) **Kimp** English.

Kendall (from Kendal *the dale of the River Kent*) English.

Kennedy (ugly head, ugly chief) Irish.

Kilborne (from Kilbourne *cold stream*) English.

Kimball (from the royal hill) **Kemball, Kemble, Kimble** English.

Kinderslie (from Kinnersley *Cyneheard's lea*) English.

Kingston (from Kingston *the king's royal residence*) English.

Knox (dweller on the hilltop) Scottish.

Lake (dweller near the lake) English.

Lambe (dweller at the sign of the lamb) **Lamb** English.

Lane (dweller in the lane) English.

Lawson (son of Law [Laurence] *man from Laurentum*) English.

Leary (a calf, calf herder) Irish.

Lee (dweller near the meadow, clearing, or woods) English.

Leech (dweller by the water; physician) English.

Lewis (famous in war) English.

Livingstone (stone of Leofing *beloved son*) Scottish.

Lock (dweller by the enclosure or stronghold) English.

Lombard (long beard) **Lumbard** English.

Lord (lord, patron) English.

Lovett (little wolf) English.

Lowe (dweller at a hill; lion) English, German.

Lowenstein (lions' stone) German.

Lowenthal (lions' valley) German.

Lynch (sailor, mariner) English.

McCarthy (son of Cárthagh *loving*) Irish.

McDermott (son of Diarmaid *without injunction, a freeman*) Irish.

McHenry (son of Henry *home ruler*) Irish.

McKenna (son of Cionaed *comely, handsome*) Irish.

McLaughlin (son of Lochlann *land of the lochs*) Irish.

McMahon (son of Mathghamhain *a bear*) Irish.

McNamara (son of Conmara *hound of the sea*) Irish.

Madison (son of Mad *gift of God*) **Madisen, Madsen, Madson** Danish.

Magee (son of Aodh *fire*) Irish.

Maguire (son of Uidhar *dun-colored*) Irish.

Mahony (son of Mathghamhain *a bear*) Irish.

Makepeace (a peacemaker, mediator) English.

Mallion (little monk) Irish.

Manning (son of Mann *servant, vassal*) English.

Manzer (from Mansergh *Mann's land*) English.

Marbury (from the fortified place by the lake) English.

Mason (a stone mason) English.

May (man, warrior, kinsman; young girl, maid) English.

Melton (from Melton *the settlement by the mill; the middle settlement*) English.

Mercer (a storekeeper, haberdasher) English.

Metcalfe (dweller at a meadow croft) English.

Michelson (son of Mikkel *Who is like God?*) **Michelson, Mickelson, Mikkelsen, Mikkelson** Danish, Norwegian.

Middleton (from Middleton *the middle settlement*) English.

Midwinter (born at Christmas) English.

Millard (dweller near the millet field; a miller; dear and strong) English.

Molineux (from Molineaux *little mills*) French.

Moloney (descendant of Maoldhomhnaigh *servant or devotee of the church*) **Maloney** Irish.

Moran (descendant of Morán *little large one, little great one*) Irish.

Morgan (sea bright) English.

Morish (dark-skinned) English.

Mosher (dweller by the swamp) **Moshier** German.

Mueller (a miller) German.

Mulder (a miller, a grinder of grain) Dutch.

Mullan (descendant of Maolán *little bald one*) Irish.

Murray (sea warrior; from the sea marsh) Scottish.

Murrell (dark-colored) English.

Naismith (a knife smith) **Naysmith** English.

Nelme (at the elm) English.

Nelson (son of Nel *victory of the people*) **Neilsen, Neilson, Nelsen** Scandinavian.

Nesbitt (from Nesbit or Nesbitt) **Naisbet, Naisbit, Nesbit** English.

Neville (from the new town) English.

Newton (from Newton *the new town*) English.

Norton (from Norton *the northern settlement*) English.

Okeley (from Oakley *the oak woods*) English.

O'Brien (descendant of Brian *force, strength, valor*; *high, hill; kingly*) Irish.

O'Connell (descendant of Conghal *wisdom, strength, desire*) Irish.

O'Donnell (descendant of Domhnall *world ruler*) Irish.

Oram (dweller at the enclosure by the riverbank) English.

Osgood (divine goodness) English.

O'Sullivan (descendant of Suileabhan *white eyes*) Irish.

Page (a young male attendant) English.

Parkins (son of Parkin [little Peter] *rock, stone*) English.

Partridge (dweller at the sign of the partridge) English.

Pasteur (a shephard) French.

Paterson (son of Peter *rock, a stone*) **Patterson** Scottish, English.

Payne (rustic, pagan, heathen) English.

Pennington (from Pennington *settlement of the Penna family*) **Penington** English.

Perry (son of Harry *home ruler*; dweller near the pear tree; wanderer; little Peter *rock*) Welsh, English.

Pierce (a rock, a stone) English.

Pike (a pike man; woodpecker; a tall, thin person) English.

Pinckney (from Picquigny, France) English, French.

Plant (dweller at a plantation or grove) English.

Poe (dweller at the sign of the peacock; a proud or gaudily dressed man) English.

Porcher (a swineherd) English.

Prichard (son of Richard *stern king*) Welsh.

Profit (a prophet) English.

Quaile (dweller by the hazel tree) **Quail, Quale, Quill** Irish.

Quinby (from the queen's manor) English.

Quincy (from Quincay, France) English, Scottish.

Quinlan (descendant of Caoindealbhan *graceful shape*) Irish.

Quinn (descendant of Conn *wisdom, intelligence, reason*) Irish.

Randolph (shield wolf) **Randolf** English.

Ravenhill (dweller at the raven's hill) English.

Read (red-haired) **Reade** English.

Regan (descendant of Riagán *little king*) Irish.

Reilly (descendant of Raghallach *valiant, warlike*) Irish.

Richardson (son of Richard *stern king*) English.

Roberts (son of Robert *bright with fame*) English.

Robinson (son of Robin *bright with fame*) English, Scottish.

Rosenthal (rose valley) German.

Rourke (descendant of Ruarc *little friend*) Irish.

Ryan (descendant of Rian or Riaghan *kingly*) Irish.

Saint Clair (from Saint Clair *bright, clear, famous*) English.

Sampson (the sun) English.

Sandford (from Sandford *the sandy ford*) English.

Sands (dweller at the sands) English.

Scott (an Irishman, a Scot) English.

Seaborne (victory bear; victorious warrior) English.

Seward (victory protection) English.

Shambrook (from Sambrook *the sandy brook*) English.

Shay (dweller near a thicket) English.

Shea (descendant of Seaghdha *hawklike, majestic*) Irish.

Short (short in stature) English.

Showell (from Showell *the dark well*) English.

Skeete (swift, quick; shooter, archer) English.

Small (small, little) English.

Sommerfeld (summer field) German.

Somner (a summoner) English.

Spicer (a dealer in spices) English.

Stafford (from Stafford *the landing place ford*) English.

Stanford (from Stanford *the stone ford*) English.

Stein (dweller near the rock) **Steen** Dutch.

Stevens (son of Steven *crown, garland*) English.

Stewart (a steward, keeper of the animal enclosure) English, Scottish.

Stowe (dweller near the holy place) English.

Stringer (maker of string or cord) English.

Studley (from Studleigh, Studley *the stud lea*) English.

Sullivan (descendant of Suileabhan *white-eyes*) Irish.

Swartz (dark, black) **Swarts, Swartz, Swarz** German.

Swayne (swineherd; servant) English.

Sweeney (son of Suibhne *pleasant, well-going*) Irish.

Swynden (from Swindon *dweller at the swine hill*) English.

Symmons (son of Simmon *heard*) English.

Tainter (tinter, dyer) English.

Tankard (gracious counsel) English.

Tawyer (a preparer of leather) English.

Terrell (Thor ruler) English.

Thomas (a twin) English.

Thoreau (strong as a bull; descendant of little Thore *gift of God*) French.

Thorpe (from Thorp, Thorpe *the farmstead or small village*) English.

Throgmorton (from Throckmorton) English.

Timmerman (a carpenter) Dutch, German.

Travis (dweller at the crossroads) **Traverse** English.

Trott (beloved, dear, friend) **Tratt** English.

Tyler (a tiler, a maker or seller of tiles) English.

Vogel (bird) **Vogle** Dutch, German.

Vogler (bird-catcher) German.

Waller (a wall maker, mason, bricklayer) English.

Wallington (from Wallington *settlement of the Wealh family*) English.

Wallis (a Welshman) English, Welsh.

Waltz (descendant of Walzo *ruler, manager*) **Walz** German.

Ward (guard, watchman) English.

Washington (from Washington *the settlement of Hwaes*) English.

Webster (a female weaver) English.

Wheeler (a maker or seller of wheels) English.

Whelan (descendant of Faolán *little wolf*) Irish.

Whitman (white-haired man, fair-complexioned man) English.

Whitney (from Whitney *Hwita's island*) English.

Whitton (from Whitton *the white farm; Hwita's farm*) English.

Wilkinson (son of Wilkin [William] *resolute protector*) English.

Wingfield (from Wingfield *Winga's field; Winne's field; Wynna's field*) English.

Winke (friend) English.

Wright (a carpenter) **Write** English.

Wrigley (dweller at the ridge meadow) English.

Wylde (wild, savage) English.

Yeager (a hunter) German.

Yeomans (son of the yeoman) English.

Yonge (young) English.

Young (young; heather) English, Swedish.

Zander (defender of mankind) German.

Zimmerman (a carpenter) German.

Chapter Three

THE WESTWARD MOVEMENT THROUGH THE CIVIL WAR
[1845–1865]

THIS TIME PERIOD covers just twenty years, but with the exception of the years spent gaining independence, those twenty years may have impacted this country more than any other. The battle cry was no longer "Liberty or death," but "Go west, young man" and "Westward Ho!" Thousands heeded the cry, and with Americans now pushing westward at a tremendous rate, steps were taken to protect them from those whose homelands they were invading. In addition, this period of time saw staggering numbers of immigrants entering the country. Their arrival and subsequent influence substantially affected the political, social, and religious makeup of the United States.

POLITICS

IN 1818, THE United States and Great Britain agreed to share the Oregon Territory and allowed people living there to retain all rights given them by their country of citizenship. But because 50,000 Americans lived there by 1860, popular opinion was that the territory should belong solely to the United States. At the same time, more Americans were moving into Texas and desire for annexation was strong.

The election of 1844 had an effect on the way the continental United States are today. Presidential candidates were Henry Clay, a well-known politician and one-time Speaker of the House, and James K. Polk, a little-known candidate who believed Texas, New Mexico, California, and Oregon should be part of the United States. Polk won the election and set out to fulfill his promise of a nation that existed from sea to shining sea.

The first step toward that goal was the annexation of Texas. Since Mexico hadn't even recognized Texan independence, it wasn't about to let go of its territory. President of the Republic of Texas, Sam Houston, signed a treaty of annexation in 1844, but the Senate refused to ratify it for fear of a war with Mexico. It was only after Houston's bluff of allying Texas with Britain that Congress passed a joint resolution admitting Texas into the Union in 1845. After Mexico turned down Polk's offer of $30 million for New Mexico and California, America stood on the brink of war. Mexico was prepared to defend its territory, and the Americans were determined that Mexico should not stand in the way of Manifest Destiny.

In January 1846, Polk ordered General Zachary Taylor to set up military posts on the western side of the

Rio Grande, ostensibly to guard against Mexican invasion of Texas. As Mexico considered that area part of New Mexico, its army was sent to oust the Americans. Armed confrontation between Taylor's forces and the Mexican army came in April. Polk claimed that Mexico had spilled American blood on American soil and persuaded Congress to declare war.

By November 1847, American troops and pushed the Mexican army all the way back to Mexico City. Like the Texans at the Alamo, a group of courageous young Mexican soldiers fought to the death at Chapultepec, a fort just outside the city. Afterward, there was nothing left but to sign the Treaty of Guadalupe Hidalgo. Under the terms of the treaty, the United States gained more than 500,000 square miles of Mexican territory, including all of California and New Mexico, in exchange for $15 million.

Though the Mexican War lasted less than two years, it was viewed by many to be nothing less than naked aggression and unjust territorial expansion. Abraham Lincoln's first speech in the House of Representatives was against U.S. involvement in Mexico, and Ulysses S. Grant, who fought as a lieutenant in the war, later called it "one of the most unjust ever waged by a stronger against a weaker nation."

Meanwhile, Polk was also attempting to annex Oregon in violation of the treaty with Britain. War with Britain seemed likely, but a compromise was reached in 1846. Oregon was divided at latitude 49°N. Britain got all lands north of that line, and the United States got all lands south. The country's dreams of Manifest Destiny had come true.

That fulfillment, however, propelled the issue of slavery to the fore and the country now had to decide whether it was going to allow slave labor in its newly acquired lands. The Oregon Territory had been admitted to the Union as a slave-free zone, and California requested admittance as a slave-free state in 1849. Proslavery forces did not want slaves kept out of another state, especially one as large as California. The debate was bitterly fought by both sides and even led to a new political party called the Free Soil Party. It appeared that a compromise would be the only solution to the problem.

Under the terms of the Compromise of 1850, California was admitted as a free state; Texas, New Mexico, and Utah retained the right to allow slavery should they so desire; slavery and the slave trade was outlawed in the District of Columbia; and a strict Fugitive Slave Law was enacted that provided slave owners with federal assistance in capturing escaped slaves. The Fugitive Slave Law provoked the greatest outrage, for no black person was safe. All a slave owner needed was an affidavit stating the person was his. Special courts were set up to hear the cases of accused fugitive slaves, but the burden of proving status was upon the accused fugitive, who wasn't allowed a jury trial and who wasn't allowed to defend himself. Worse, judges were awarded ten dollars for each black sent back into slavery and only five dollars for each accused to be set free. It was a system begging for abuse. Northern blacks who'd been free for years were subject to seizure and transport to the southern states. Citizens who provided assistance to escaped slaves were subject to heavy fines and imprisonment. Riots broke out immediately among both free black and abolitionists, and thousands of blacks fled to Canada out of fear they would be captured and sent into slavery.

It was outrage over such an abominable law that prompted Harriet Beecher Stowe to pen *Uncle Tom's Cabin,* the novel that was to have the most influence over the nation since Thomas Paine's *Common Sense* spurred the fight for independence. Sales reached an astonishing 300,000 copies in the year following its printing in 1852. Sales worldwide reached 1.5 million, and a play based on the book appeared on stages across the country and around the world. *Uncle Tom's Cabin* personalized the issue of slavery to northerners and encouraged stronger resistance to the institution. Reaction in the South was directly opposite. There, Harriet Beecher Stowe was vilified as a liar and a threat to the southerner's way of life.

In 1854, opponents and proponents of slavery squared off again when Congress passed a bill allowing

Kansas to decide for itself whether it would allow slavery and considered establishing a government for the Nebraska Territory. It was suggested that Nebraska be divided into the Nebraska Territory and the Kansas Territory, and that each be allowed to decide for itself the issue of slavery. Most southerners supported the Kansas-Nebraska Act for they believed slavery would be recognized in the territories; most northerners bitterly opposed it, not only on moral grounds, but on economic grounds as well. Fighting over the issue led to the deaths of more than 200 people.

Since Congress was incapable of solving the issue of slavery, people looked to the Supreme Court to make a decision and restore social harmony. In 1857, the court ruled on the famous Dred Scott case. Dred Scott was a slave who lived with his owner in Missouri for several years before moving with him to Illinois and later to Wisconsin Territory, where slavery was illegal. When Scott's owner died, antislavery forces helped him file a suit for his freedom. They argued that because Scott lived in a slave-free territory, he should be a free man. A Saint Louis county court agreed and granted his freedom. The case went to the Missouri supreme court and the lower court's ruling was overturned. Dred Scott, his wife, and children were remanded into slavery.

When the case made it to the Supreme Court on appeal, abolitionists hoped the higher court would see the injustice of the Missouri court's ruling. Antislavery activists couldn't have been more surprised when the court made its ruling. Each point was devastating. Free or slave, blacks weren't considered citizens of the United States and therefore had no standing before the court. Further, the court ruled that Scott had never ceased to be a slave and was therefore the property of his owner, the same as a mule or a horse. The third point stated that because slaves were property, their owners were protected under the fifth ammendment; the federal government had no right to deprive citizens of their property, nor could they tell states they could not allow slavery. In one fell swoop, the court wiped away all the compromises made over the issue of slavery. Southerners rejoiced at the court's ruling. Antislavery activists became more defiant and many more north-erners joined the emancipation movement.

In 1854, the issue of slavery prompted the formation of another political party: the Republicans. The main goal of the Republican party was to keep slavery out of the western states and territories. A few Republicans, like Abraham Lincoln, sincerely wanted to see the end of slavery in the South and elsewhere. However, unlike other antislavery groups, the majority of Republicans were fighting for economic reasons, not for reasons of human rights. True, they wanted no slaves out West, but they also wanted *no blacks* out West. Prejudice was strong against all minority groups, and the primary fight was to keep jobs in the hands of white men.

The march toward civil war was hastened with the 1860 presidential campaign. During the Democratic convention, Democrats found themselves split between southern Democrats who wished to allow slavery in the territories and northern Democrats who were just as adamantly opposed to the idea. In the end, two candidates were nominated. Southern Democrats chose John Breckinridge, and northern Democrats chose Senator Stephen Douglas, a man who believed the territories should decide the slavery issue. Another party formed, the Constitutional Union party, and they chose John Bell, a moderate Whig who just wanted to keep the Union together. The Republican candidate was Abraham Lincoln, a lawyer and staunch abolitionist.

Before the election, the governor of South Carolina wrote to other southern governors to impress upon them that if Lincoln won the presidency, it would be the duty of the southern states to secede from the Union. The feeling that civil war was imminent was never so strong. Sure enough, Lincoln carried the northern votes and the southern votes had no effect on the election.

In December 1860, South Carolina became the first state to make good on its threat of seccession. By the first of February, six other states followed suit: Alabama, Florida, Georgia, Louisiana, Mississippi, and Texas.

They renamed themselves the Confederate States of America, and their first president was Jefferson Davis of Mississippi. Eight slave states chose not to secede.

Lincoln took office on March 4, 1861. Ironically, he was given the oath of office by Supreme Court Chief Judge Roger Taney, the same judge who handed down the infamous Dred Scott decision. Lincoln was faced with a terrible dilemma. He felt the Confederate states could not lawfully secede from the Union. They had already started taking over federal forts, federal buildings, and the postal service in those states because they were perceived as a threat from a foreign country. The Union held only Fort Sumter, off the coast of South Carolina, and three forts off the coast of Florida. Lincoln now had to make the fateful decision of whether to allow the Confederates to take federal property or to defend that property. He also had the other slave-holding states to consider. If Lincoln started a war, would those states also secede? In the end, he said there would be no war unless the South started it: "In your hands, my dissatisfied fellow countrymen, and not in mine, is the momentous question of civil war. . . . You can have no conflict without being yourselves the aggressors."

Knowing supplies were running low at the Union forts, Lincoln sent a message to the governor of South Carolina, notifying him that a ship carrying food would be going to Fort Sumter. The governor wanted the fort for himself, however, because of its strategic location and because it guarded Charleston Harbor. In April, the Confederates requested that the fort surrender. The Union commander refused, and the Confederates opened fire. A day later, Union troops ran out of ammunition and were forced to surrender the fort. The Civil War had begun.

The Civil War lasted four, long, bloody years, during which time more Americans were killed than in any other war or conflict fought before or since. In the early days, both sides were convinced of the justness of their causes and rallied around their respective flags. Young men proudly joined the armed forces and marched off to a war none believed would last for more than a couple of months. Four of the remaining eight slave states joined the Confederacy: Arkansas, North Carolina, Tennessee, and Virginia. The last state, Virginia, was divided in its loyalties, and when the state seceded, the westerners formed their own government and joined the Union as West Virginia. Delaware quickly sided with the Union. Maryland, Kentucky, and Missouri eventually remained with the Union.

Neither side was prepared to fight a war, and Jefferson Davis announced the popular feeling of the southerners. "All we ask," he said, "is to be left alone." Considering the events leading to war, that was not a realistic option.

It was an uneven battle from the beginning. Although the South had the advantage of fighting a defensive war and had men accustomed to hunting and eager to defend their homes, it had neither the manpower nor the infrastructure to win a war. There were only nine million people living in the South, and a full third or more were slaves. As the economy was run on agriculture, there was very little industrialization, few roads, and fewer railroads that often went from one place to another but connected to nothing. Nearly all its manufactured goods came from the North, which manufactured 90 percent of all goods in the states. This alone was devastating, for without an adequate source for military or domestic supplies, the Confederate states were seriously at risk for failing in their quest for victory. Their fears were realized when Lincoln ordered a naval blockade of the southern ports to cut off European trade.

The North, on the other hand, had four times as many men, a strong navy that was enhanced by a large fleet of merchant vessels, and it had the resources of a nation behind it to support its forces. The North also had 70 percent of the nation's rail roads, which allowed for quick transportation of troops, artillery, and supplies.

In spite of the Union's advantages, they suffered from a lack of leadership. Most of the good generals came from the South and had resigned their oaths to the Union to support the Confederate cause. This left a serious dearth of qualified men to lead the Union troops, a problem quickly realized after the crushing defeat at the Battle of Bull Run and the defeat at the Battle of Ball's Bluff that resulted in the loss of 1,900 Union troops. Congress extended the period of military duty from three months to two years and passed the first income tax law in 1861 to help pay for the war expense.

In 1862, Lincoln issued the Emancipation Proclamation, which was to have several effects. First, it served to make the Confederates resolve to see the war through. It also convinced Britain and France not to back the Confederacy, and it affected they way northerners felt toward the war. When the fight was for the preservation of the Union, volunteers abounded. But the Proclamation ignited fears that all those freed slaves would come north and take jobs held by whites. In spite of raising the payment given to enlisted men from $100 to $300, the number of volunteers fell off drastically, and the president was forced to draft all men from the ages of twenty to forty-five. Those wealthy enough were allowed the option of paying $300 to escape military duty or hired people to serve in their places.

By 1863, hopes that the war would soon end were fading on both sides. Casualties were extremely high, conditions in the camp hospitals were atrocious, some Confederates were so ill-equipped as to be fighting in bare feet, and the blockade was causing starvation throughout the South.

In June 1863, Union and Confederate soldiers encountered one another at the small Pennsylvania town of Gettysburg. Both sides quickly formed up to fight. It was a horrible, bloody battle that left 40,000 dead or wounded. A cemetery was dedicated to the fallen that November, and it was here that Lincoln gave his now-famous Gettysburg Address. At the time, the short speech was regarded as a total failure: "We here highly resolve that these dead shall not have died in vain—that this nation, under God, shall have a new birth of freedom—and that government of the people, by the people, for the people, shall not perish from the earth."

Ulysses S. Grant was chosen in 1864 to command the Union forces and lead the country to victory. Grant's plan was brutal but effective: Destroy the South's ability to keep fighting. That meant destroying the food sources. General Philip Sheridan was ordered into the Shenandoah Valley to carry out a scorched earth policy, and General William Tecumseh Sherman was ordered to follow the same policy in Georgia. Not only did Union troops destroy crops and livestock, they ruined everything that could be of use to Confederate troops. In September 1864, the city of Atlanta was burned. General Robert E. Lee dug in at Petersburg and was beseiged there for nine months. He was finally forced to surrender in April 1865. The South and its people were totally devastated. The Civil War was finally over.

With the South destroyed, the United States government was now faced with the daunting challenge of reconstruction. Many in the North were still so angry at the South that compassion was difficult to find; it was common opinion that the southerners were reaping their just rewards. Southerners, on the other hand, despised the northerners for the destruction of their homeland. Lincoln realized the necessity of restoring the Union and was determined to bring the South back into the family of states. His plan for reconstruction was fairly lenient, calling for southern states to agree to the abolition of slavery and to reestablish new state governments once 10 percent of their voters swore oaths of loyalty to the United States. Unfortunately, Lincoln's plan was never realized. He was assassinated on April 14, 1865.

Vice President Andrew Johnson became president and put forth his own plan calling for a majority of voters in each state to swear oaths of loyalty to the United States and demanding that each southern state ratify the Thirteenth Amendment banning slavery. In December 1865, the Thirteenth Amendment became part of the Constitution, and President Johnson approved the new governments of the southern states.

SOCIETY

THERE WAS SO much happening in the country during this twenty-year time period that the constraints of this book allow but the briefest sketch of American society. The North and the South were taking different paths, and the westward movement was taking society in yet another direction.

Many societal changes are the result of increased population, and it was no different with U.S. society during this time period. Between the years 1840 to 1850, the population exploded when more than six million people immigrated to the United States. Millions disembarked at the ports of New England, and it was to those states that the majority settled. A few Irish had immigrated to escape oppression and religious persecution, but the Great Potato Famine spurred immigration to astounding levels when more than a million Irish were sent to the United States to escape starvation.

In Ireland, governmental repression had reduced the Irish to a largely unskilled people. The majority were desperately poor farmers who knew little beyond the simplest farming techniques. After arriving in the United States, most Irish settled in big cities like New York and Pittsburgh, where the women obtained work as domestic servants and the men sought jobs requiring few skills. Many ended up working in the more dangerous professions that others passed by.

In the New England states, the economy recovered from the depression of 1837, and industry and trade were again thriving. New factories were being built, and new towns were being established. There was a dark side to this growth, however. So many immigrants meant more people trying to enter the workforce, and competition for jobs became fierce. Factory owners were quick to exploit the situation in the name of profits. Labor-saving machinery allowed the replacement of skilled, higher-paid American workers with unskilled foreign workers and women and children, all of whom worked longer hours for lower wages and in increasingly poor conditions. As wages went down and unemployment went up, poverty became a pressing problem. Cities like New York became so overcrowded and so horribly dirty that many people were persuaded to take their chances away from the eastern seaboard.

Black Americans were much better off in the northeastern states than they were in the South, but they still had a harder time assimilating into American society than did European immigrants. Most chose to live in larger cities such as Newark, New York, Philadelphia, and Pittsburgh where there was greater diversity. Nonetheless, prejudice and discrimination kept them in the poorest section of the cities, at the lowest levels of the workforce, and in the lowest-paying jobs.

The impact of the emancipation was quickly felt in the northern cities. Thousands of blacks migrated north, and population in the cities' black neighborhoods exploded, growing nearly six times faster than white communities. This was the birth of the urban ghetto. Living conditions were atrocious. Entire families, and sometimes even more than one family, lived in one- or two-room apartments that were without electricity, toilets, or running water.

In the North Central states, which include the Dakotas, Nebraska, Minnesota, Iowa, Wisconsin, Illinois, Indiana, Michigan, and Ohio, the last battles between whites and Native Americans were being fought. Indians were pushed steadily westward onto unfamiliar lands, and their ability to obtain food and provide for themselves was greatly hampered by white hunters, trappers, and horse thieves. Pleas to the United States government to prevent hunters and others from taking the Indians' primary food sources were met with indifference. The government's response was to tell the Indians to give up hunting and take up farming—something completely foreign to these groups' way of life.

The last of the great tribes had been forced out of the Upper Midwest, and the area was ripe for settlement. Many workers made their way to the Midwest, where conditions were less crowded and competition less severe. Soon, thousands of immigrants were heading directly for the Midwest rather than the large cities of the eastern seaboard.

The majority of German immigrants were peasant farmers or skilled craftsmen who had faced severe discrimination by political, religious, and social institutions in their homeland. By 1860, two-thirds of German immigrants had settled in the farm states of the Midwest. They accepted lower wages than did native-born Americans, but they generally were able to easily find work in their established professions.

Those of the Irish immigrants who chose not to settle on the East Coast usually made their way to the Midwest. A few of the more skilled found employment as craftsmen, construction workers, and factory workers; a few bought farms. English immigrants to the Midwest were easily assimilated into American society, and because of their skill and experience with machinery, they found employment in better, higher-paying jobs in construction and manufacturing. Soaring prices in Canada prompted large numbers of Canadians to emigrate across the border into the Upper Midwest. Like the English, Canadians had no trouble fitting into American society and easily found work as farm hands or lumberjacks.

Nearly 40,000 Scandinavians immigrated during this twenty-year period to escape political turmoil in their homelands; most settled in the Midwest. The Scandinavians were very successful farmers, and at least half of those who immigrated chose to continue that profession in America. Others found work in lumber mills and in factories producing furniture and agricultural machinery.

Czech immigrants began arriving in the Midwest during the 1850s and settled in tightly knit groups in larger towns like Chicago. When enough people of other nationalities entered a Czech neighborhood, the group moved on and established themselves in a new area. Czechs tended to keep their native language and traditions for a longer period of time than did other immigrant groups.

In 1845, life in the South had barely changed. The economy hinged on important cash crops like cotton, sugar, and rice that were used worldwide. In fact, about 60 percent of the world's supply of cotton was grown in the southern United States. Little industry had developed, and though some saw this as shortsighted and a problem, the more wealthy southerners tended to invest their money in land and slaves rather than in new factories. The South, then, was dependent upon the North for nearly all its goods. It was a condition that caused extreme problems during the course of the Civil War.

By 1860, there were about two million white families in the South, but only about one in forty were planters with at least twenty slaves. The rest primarily were small farmers with very few, if any, slaves, and the very poor who owned neither land nor slaves. The planters, known as the "cottonocracy," were few in number, but they controlled southern politics and society. They lived very much like European aristocracy, constructing huge homes and entertaining on a grand scale. Though they took their responsibilities toward their families and farms seriously, overseers took care of the daily operations of their plantations.

The majority of those with small holdings had no slaves because they couldn't afford them, not because they didn't believe in slavery. There were some small landowners who had one or two slaves, but unlike the planters who kept themselves above daily toil, economic circumstances forced small farmers to work alongside their slaves in all aspects of farming.

At the bottom rung of white society were the very poor. These people usually rented the land they toiled upon for a portion of whatever crops they managed to grow. Some lived on small pieces of land far back in the hills and wooded areas. In addition to raising a few crops, the poor often kept very small herds of cattle and pigs but were barely able to sustain themselves and their families.

There were at least 200,000 free blacks in the South at the beginning of this time and nearly 488,000 on the eve of Civil War. Most were descendants of slaves freed during and after the American Revolution or mulatto immigrants from the Caribbean. Southern life was extremely difficult for free blacks, who suffered harsh discrimination. The slave states resented the free blacks' presence, for it was believed they routinely encouraged slaves to rebel or escape. In addition, one of the arguments justifying slavery was that blacks were unable to take care of themselves. Free blacks who survived on their own damaged that argument. In order to discourage free blacks from remaining in the South, states passed discriminatory and oppressive laws against them. Not only did it become illegal for them to travel, it even became illegal for free blacks to reside in some states.

Approximately four million blacks were slaves. Most were agricultural workers who toiled in the fields of the South's farms and plantations. The average workday was fourteen hours in the summer, ten hours in the winter, and eighteen hours during harvest. Even children were put to work doing chores at a very young age. Laws known as the slave codes governed almost every aspect of the slaves' lives. Slaves were not allowed to travel without a pass, they were not allowed to assemble in groups of more than three persons, they were not allowed to buy or sell goods, they could not ride on horses without express permission of the master, they could not carry arms, they were not allowed to bring any type of charges against their owners, and it was illegal for slaves to learn to read or write. In addition, any slave who willfully harmed a white person was faced with the death penalty, as were slaves who willfully damaged crops.

Though it was quite common for slave families to be separated, many were kept together on the larger plantations, both to enlarge the workforce by producing children and to keep them content so they were less likely to escape. For the slaves, family life became a buffer against the hardships and uncertainty prevalent in their lives, and steps were taken to protect their tight-knit group and keep the masters ignorant about what went on in the slave quarters.

In the 1845 Southwest, various Indian tribes were encouraged to continue their raids on the Mexicans in Texas and New Mexico. Three years later, the war with Mexico was over, and those areas became U.S. territories, but the Indians, not understanding the difference in ownership, continued to harass the area. After government troops were sent in to confront the tribes, the Comanche and Kiowa were relocated to reservation land in Oklahoma. The Utes remained behind in the mountain passes of Colorado, Utah, and New Mexico, and while they regularly attacked Mexican villages and other Indian tribes, they rarely came into contact with whites.

People of Mexican heritage were one of the largest ethnic groups in the southwestern states during this period of time, but they weren't the only ones besides the whites and Native Americans. Many people of Asian descent came to make their fortune in the California gold fields before returning home to China. The Chinese on the West Coast encountered as much prejudice and discrimination as did immigrants on the East Coast. Most resentment was caused by fear that the Chinese, who worked for lower wages than everyone else, would cause wages to go down for white workers, though prejudice also stemmed from the strangeness of their language, manner of dress, and culture.

The Northwest was territory still largely unsettled by whites, but discoveries of gold in the early 1860s brought scores of miners to the area. In the Pacific Northwest, lumber rather than gold spurred settlement in the 1830s and continued to draw enough settlers that the United States formed the Oregon Territory in 1848 and divided it in 1853 to organize the Washington Territory.

In the mid-1800s, people began working for social reform. Women's rights, better working conditions, an improved educational system, and better treatment of the mentally ill were favored causes, but the major social issue of the time was slavery. The Mexican War was so strongly protested because many thought annexing Texas would lead to an extension of slavery. Citizens in the northern states called for an end to the institution, and antislavery activists went on the offensive. An underground railroad was formed by a network of abolitionists to help runaway slaves reach freedom in the North. Many abolitionists were women, and as they worked to achieve emancipation for the slaves, they realized they occupied much the same position under the law and united on their own quest for equal rights.

The Civil War had the biggest effect on the United States. It was truly a war of brother against brother, and countless lives were shattered as a result. A few people in the North profited greatly from the war, such as farmers who fed the troops and factory owners who clothed the soldiers and built the machinery of war.

The South, however, was devastated. It had a small population to begin with, but after the war, there were even fewer men to support the families left behind. Many lost everything they had, especially after the implementation of the "total war" policy. The cities of Atlanta, Charleston, Richmond, and Savannah were utterly destroyed, two-thirds of the railroad tracks were twisted and useless, banks had closed, and depositers lost their savings. Plantations were either totally destroyed or in a state of semiruin, bridges were demolished, factories, mills, and cotton gins were burned, crops were burned, and even fences had been ripped out and destroyed. In some areas, every house, barn, cabin, and shed were burned to the ground. Millions were homeless, jobless, and without any means to support themselves or their families. In addition, the nearly four million slaves were now freedmen without jobs or property, and they were completely uneducated.

The United States was now faced with its most monumental task: reconstruction of the South. One of the first things Congress did was establish the Freedmen's Bureau to provide food, clothing, and medical care for the former slaves. The bureau also set up schools and provided teachers to educate freed slaves and established four universities for the higher education of black students.

RELIGION

THERE WERE MANY active denominations and religions in the United States by midcentury. The six organizations to have the largest congregations were the Methodists, Baptists, Presbyterians, Catholics, Congregationalists, and Episcopalians.

Four new churches were organized during this twenty-year time frame. The Lutheran Church—Missouri Synod was formally established in 1847; the Christian Reformed Church in North America was organized in 1857; the Seventh-day Adventists organized in 1863, and the Greek Orthodox Archdiocese of North and South America was established in 1864.

Some of the most important schisms in the nation's churches happened as a result of the slavery issue. For many years, whites believed they were God's chosen people and that God had given them dominion over people of color. This argument was supported by many of the southern churches who further argued that the right to hold slaves was clearly established in the scriptures. For many years, a person's belief in the institution of slavery was a kind of litmus test for every young man applying for admission as a minister into such organizations as the Methodists and Baptists. In time, northerners revised their opinions on the slavery issue, and the northern churches became outspoken in their condemnation of the institution. The issue effectively divided the southern churches from their northern counterparts.

Southern whites firmly believed that they were doing blacks a service by holding them in bondage and converting them to Christianity. Great numbers of preachers were hired by slave owners to give the slaves moral instruction and to teach them that disodbedience was a sin. By doing this, not only did the owners believe rebellion was less likely to occur, they also believed they were doing their Christian duty by their slaves.

Slaves, on the other hand, did not interpret the preacher's message as the owners did. Rather, they compared themselves to the Israelites who had been in bondage in Egypt and believed that they, the slaves, were God's chosen people, not the masters who had enslaved them. This belief gave the slaves the inner strength needed to survive and gave them the hope that their slavery would end as the Israelites' did. The slaves' faith also gave them the courage to hold secret religious meetings of their own in defiance of the law.

NAMING

DURING THIS TIME period, the number of immigrants entering the United States soared. Over 1,000,000 Irish arrived; over 1,000,000 Canadians; nearly 1,000,000 Germans; perhaps 300,000 to 400,000 English; 100,000 French; 100,000 Swedes; 40,000 Chinese; 20,000 Dutch; and 3,700 Danes. People also immigrated from several other countries, and the pool of names in the United States was greatly enriched. Unfortunately, prejudice was so strong that children born to immigrants were often given English forms of names rather than traditional names from their parents' countries.

Bible names continued to be popular, but many of the more unusual fell by the wayside. The common biblical names that had been in widespread use among the different cultural groups continued to be used. Examples are: Mary/Maria/Marie; Anne/Anna/Hannah; John/Jon/Juan/Jean/Sean; David; Daniel; etc.

Another interesting trend occurred with the westward movement, which could have been inspired by the spirit of adventure and the excitement of new beginnings. Whatever the reason, many new coinages were formed during the long trip west. Elements of native names were incorporated in these names, as were words referring to things or experiences seen along the trail. Traditional names were still popular, of course, but there was also a new spirit of creativity when it came to naming children. The advent of the railroad encouraged the trend, and many children were given names of whistle-stops passed along the route.

Free blacks often chose names that were somewhat unique, classical, or had aristocratic sounds. This was one way of affirming their self-worth while living in a prejudicial society. Some slave masters gave their slaves classical names, such as Polonius and Amaryllis, but names like Mingo, Joe, and Glory were probably more common. Also typical was to name a slave for the month in which he or she was born or acquired, as January, April, and July. Very few truly African names remained in use in the black population.

One of the first things blacks did after the emancipation was change their names. Their original names had more than likely been given them by their masters or mistresses, so taking a new name was reflective of their newfound control over their own lives and their new status as freedmen, and a personal rejection of their lives as slaves. Many chose traditional names as a way to put themselves on the same level as other Americans, and others chose names that were a bit more creative, possibly as a way to illustrate the great change in their lives.

FEMALE NAMES

Abbey (monastery, convent)
Abelia (breath)
Abigail (father of exaltation) **Abbey**
Acadia (village, place of plenty)
Ada (nobility)
Adah (adornment)

Adalheid (nobility)
Adelaide (nobility) **Adelaida**
Adele (noble) **Adela**
Adeline (nobility) **Adelina**
Adria (from Hadrianus)
Adriana (from Hadrianus)

Agatha (good) **Agata, Agathe**
Agnes (chaste, pure) **Agna, Agnus**
Agnethe (chaste, pure)
Aileen (?)
Alana (O child; ?, perhaps *handsome; rock*) **Alane, Alanna, Alannah, Alanne, Allana**
Alberta (noble and bright)
Alena (of Magdala)
Alethea (truth) **Aletheia, Alithea**
Alexa (defender of mankind)
Alexandra (defender of mankind) **Alexa**
Alexia (defender)
Alexina (defender of mankind)
Alfreda (elf counselor)
Alice (nobility) **Alyce**
Alicia (nobility)
Aline (noble)
Alison (noble one)
Alke (nobility)
Allegra (cheerful, merry) **Alegra**
Alma (soul)
Althea (wholesome)
Ama (water)
Amada (beloved) **Amadia**
Amalia (work) **Amalie, Amelia**
Amana (established)
Amanda (lovable)
Amaryllis (a flower name; a conventional name for a shepherdess in pastoral poetry)
Amicia (?, possibly *friendship*) **Amice**
Amity (friendship) **Amyte**
Amy (beloved)
Anabella (grace, full of grace, mercy + beautiful) **Anabelle, Annabella**
Anastasia (resurrection)
Andrea (womanly)
Angela (an angel)
Angelica (angelic) **Angelika**
Angie (angel, like an angel)
Anita (grace, full of grace, mercy)
Anne (grace, full of grace, mercy) **Ana, Ann, Anna**
Anneliese (grace, mercy + God is my oath) **Annelise**
Annemarie (grace, mercy + sea of bitterness or sorrow)
Annette (little Anne)
Annfrid (beautiful eagle)
Annie (grace, full of grace, mercy)
Annis (chaste, pure) **Annice, Annys**
Ann Mary (grace, full of grace, mercy + sea of bitterness or sorrow)
Anita (little Ana *grace, full of grace, mercy*)
Antigone (of contrary birth)
Anthea (flowery)
Antonia (?, *priceless, of inestimable worth* is a folk definition)
Aphrah (dust) **Aphra**
Aphrodite (the goddess of love and beauty)
Apphia (increasing)

Appolonia (of Apollo) **Appolina**
April (second, latter; born in April)
Arabella (?, perhaps *eagle* or *hearth*) **Arabel, Arabell, Orabel**
Ariela (lion of God)
Arminel (strength)
Arna (eagle)
Artemisia (belonging to Artemis)
Asa (a god)
Asenath (?, perhaps *thornbush*)
Aspasia (welcome)
Asta (love)
Astrid (beautiful goddess)
Atarah (crown)
Athalia (the Lord is exalted)
Aud (riches, prosperity)
Audra (noble strength) **Audie**
Audrey (noble strength) **Awdry; Audie**
Aurelia (golden) **Aurelie**
Aurora (the dawn) **Aurore**
Averil (boar battle) **Averell, Everild**
Avice (?) **Aveza, Avis, Avise**
Avila (?)
Awinita (young deer) Cherokee.
Azubah (forsaken)
Baptista (a Baptist)
Barbara (foreign woman)
Beata (happy)
Beatrice (bringer of joy) **Beatrix**
Belinda (?, perhaps *snake*)
Bella (beautiful)
Benedicta (blessed) **Benedicte, Benedikta**
Benet (blessed) **Bennet, Bennitt**
Berenice (bringer of victory)
Bernardine (bold as a bear)
Bertha (bright)
Bess (God is my oath) **Bessie**
Beth (God is my oath)
Betsy (God is my oath) **Betsey**
Betty (God is my oath)
Beulah (married)
Biddy (strength)
Birgit (strength) **Birgitta, Birgitte, Brigitte**
Bithiah (daughter of Jehovah) **Bethia**
Blanch (white) **Blanche**
Brenda (sword)
Bridget (strength) **Brigit**
Caledonia (from Caledonia, from Scotland)
Camille (virgin of unblemished character) **Camila, Camilla**
Caridad (charity)
Carina (affection, love)
Carla (full-grown, a woman)
Carlotta (full-grown, a woman)
Carmen (vineyard, orchard)
Carol (full-grown, a woman)
Carola (full-grown, a woman)

Carole (full-grown, a woman)
Caroletta (full-grown, a woman)
Caroline (full-grown, a woman) **Carolina; Carrie, Lina**
Cassandra (?)
Cathalina (pure, unsullied)
Catherine (pure, unsullied) **Catharina, Catharine, Catherina**
Cecile (blind, dim-sighted)
Cecilia (blind, dim-sighted)
Celia (blind, dim-sighted)
Charis (grace)
Charissa (grace)
Charity (charity, benevolence)
Charlotte (full-grown, a woman) **Charlotta**
Charmian (a little joy)
Chloe (blooming, verdant)
Chloris (green)
Christa (a Christian)
Christabel (?, probably *beautiful Christ*) **Christabell**
Christiana (a Christian, a follower of Christ)
Christine (a Christian, a follower of Christ) **Christina, Cristina, Khristina, Khristine, Kristina, Kristine; Chris, Chrissie, Christy, Kris, Kristy**
Christmas (born at Christmastime)
Chula (fox) Muskogean.
Chyna (China)
Cicely (blind, dim-sighted) **Cecily, Cicily, Sisley, Sycillie**
Clare (bright, clear, famous) **Claire, Clara**
Clarimond (bright protection)
Clarinda (bright, clear, famous)
Clarissa (bright, clear, famous) **Clarice, Claricia**
Claude (lame)
Claudette (little Claude *lame*)
Claudia (lame)
Cleare (clear)
Clemence (clement, mild) **Clemencia, Clemency**
Clementine (clement, mild)
Clorinda (green, verdant)
Comfort (comfort, care)
Constancy (constant) **Constance, Constanze**
Consuelo (consolation)
Cordelia (?, perhaps *daughter of the sea*) **Cordula**
Corinna (maiden) **Corinne**
Cornelia (a horn)
Cressida (?)
Cynthia (of Kynthos)
Dagmar (splendid day; day maid)
Dagna (new day)
Dahlia (a dahlia flower) **Dalia**
Damaris (?, possibly *heifer*)
Damiana (tame, gentle)
Dania (God is my judge)
Danielle (God is my judge) **Daniella, Danniela, Danniella**
Daphne (a laurel or bay tree)
Davida (beloved)
Deana (a dean)

Deborah (a bee) **Debora, Debra, Debrah**
Delfina (from Delphi; the delphinium flower)
Delia (from Delos)
Delicia (delicious)
Delilah (delicate)
Denise (of Dionysus)
Desire (desire, want)
Diane (divine) **Diana**
Dido (?) In Roman mythology, Dido was the princess of Tyre, the founder and queen of Carthage.
Dina (judged) **Dinah**
Dionisa (of Dionysus)
Dolores (sorrows)
Donna (world ruler)
Dorcas (gazelle)
Doris (Dorian woman)
Dorothea (gift of God) **Dorotea**
Dove (a dove)
Drusilla (?)
Dulcibella (sweet and beautiful) **Dulcibell**
Dulcie (sweet) **Dulce**
Easter (born on Easter)
Ebba (strong as a wild boar)
Eden (delight)
Edith (prosperous in war) **Edyth**
Eleanor (light, torch, bright) **Eleonor, Eleonora, Eleonore, Elianor, Elinor, Elleanor**
Electra (the shining one)
Elena (light, torch, bright)
Elisabeth (God is my oath) **Elizabeth, Elsbeth, Elspeth, Lisabet, Lisabeth, Lisbeth; Bess, Bessie, Beth, Betti, Betty, Elise, Eliza, Ellie, Elsa, Else, Elsie, Elsy, Ilsa, Liese, Lisa, Lise, Lisette, Liza, Lizzie, Lizzy**
Eliza (God is my oath)
Eliza Ann (God is my oath + grace, full of grace, mercy)
Elke (nobility)
Ellen (light, torch, bright) **Elen**
Ellis (nobility)
Eloisa (hale, hearty) **Eloise**
Elvira (?, perhaps *amiable, friendly*)
Emelie (rival, trying to equal or excel) **Emelia**
Emeline (strength; work) **Emmeline**
Emeraud (an emerald)
Emerlee (strength; work)
Emilia (strength; work)
Emily (strength; work)
Emma (strength)
Emmanuelle (God is with us)
Enriqua (home ruler)
Erika (eternal ruler) **Erica**
Erma (strength)
Erna (capable)
Ernesta (earnest, resolute)
Ernestine (earnest, resolute)
Esmeralda (emerald)
Esperanza (hope, expectation)

Estella (a star)
Esther (myrtle; star) **Ester**
Ethel (noble)
Ethelinda (noble + tender, soft; a snake)
Eugenia (well-born, noble) **Eugenie**
Eulalia (fair speech) **Eulalie**
Eunice (good victory)
Euphemia (fair speech) **Euphemie, Eufemia**
Eustacia (steadfast; happy harvest)
Evangelina (good news, the Gospel)
Eve (life) **Eva**
Eveline (?) **Evelina, Evelyn**
Everet (boar hard)
Faith (faith, trust)
Fanny (from France, a Frank)
Faustina (bringer of good luck)
Felice (lucky, happy) **Felicie**
Felicity (happiness) **Felicite**
Finella (white shoulders) **Fenella, Finola, Fionola** Anglicized form of Fionnaghuala.
Fiona (white, fair, clear, transparent)
Flavia (yellow)
Flora (a flower) **Flore**
Florence (a blooming) **Florencia, Florenz, Florinda**
Frances (a Frank, a freeman)
Francisca (a Frenchwoman) **Franziska**
Freya (lady, mistress, noblewoman) **Freja**
Friede (ruler of peace; gentle peace) **Freda, Frida, Frieda**
Gabriela (God is my strength) **Gabriele, Gabrielle**
Gail (father of exaltation)
Gay (joyous, lighthearted) **Gae, Gaye**
Gemma (gemstone, jewel)
Genesee (beautiful valley)
Georgina (earth worker, farmer), Georgiana
Gertrude (spear strength) **Gerta, Trudie**
Gillian (youth, downy) **Jillian**
Gina Originally a short form of names ending in -gina, such as Georgina.
Gisela (pledge)
Giselle (pledge) **Gisele**
Gladys (lame)
Glenna (mountain valley)
Grace (grace, mercy)
Graciela (agreeable, pleasantness)
Greer (vigilant, watchful)
Gretchen (a pearl)
Gretel (a pearl)
Guadalupe (valley of the wolf)
Gwyneth (blessed)
Hannah (grace, full of grace, mercy) **Hanna, Hanne**
Harmonia (harmony)
Harriet (home ruler)
Hazel (hazel tree)
Hebe (youth)
Hedda (war)
Heidi (nobility; battle protector)

Helah (rust)
Helen (light, torch, bright) **Helena, Helene**
Helge (prosperous, successful; blessed, holy) **Helga**
Heloise (hale, hearty)
Hephzibah (she is my delight) **Hepzibah, Hepsie**
Hermia (of Hermes)
Hermione (of Hermes)
Hester (myrtle; star)
Hilda (battle)
Honor (honor, esteem) **Honora, Honore, Honoria, Honour, Hanora**
Hope (hope, expectation)
Hortense (a gardener) **Hortencia**
Hosannah (save pray) **Hosanna**
Hughina (heart, mind, spirit)
Huldah (weasel)
Humility (humbleness)
Hyacinth (bluebell, hyacinth)
Ida (work, labor)
Ideny (work, labor) **Idona, Idonea, Idony**
Idonia (of good disposition)
Imelda (entire battle)
Imogen (?, perhaps *girl, maiden*)
Ines (chaste, pure, sacred)
Inga (Ing, a Norse fertility god) **Inge**
Ingrid (beautiful Ing)
Inola (black fox) Cherokee.
Irene (peace) **Irena**
Iris (the iris flower; rainbow)
Isabel (God is my oath) **Isabela, Isabell, Isabella, Isobel**
Ismenia (?)
Jacoba (supplanting, seizing by the heels) **Jacobina**
Jacqueline (supplanting, seizing by the heels) **Jacklyn**
Jael (mountain goat)
Jamesina (supplanting, seizing by the heels) **Jamie**
Jane (God is gracious)
Jane Olivia (God is gracious + olive tree)
Janet (God is gracious; little Jane) **Jennet**
Janna (God is gracious) **Janne**
Jasmine (jasmine) **Jasmin, Jazmin**
Jean (God is gracious) **Jeane, Jeanne**
Jecoliah (the Lord prevails)
Jemima (pure)
Jerioth (curtains)
Jeromia (sacred name)
Jerushah (a possession)
Jessica (gift; God is gracious)
Jessie (little Janet *God is gracious*; gift)
Joan (God is gracious)
Johanna (God is gracious) **Joanna**
Jonna (God is gracious)
Josepha (he shall add) **Josefa**
Joy (joy, happiness)
Joyce (merry, happy)
Juana (God is gracious)
Juanita (little Juana *God is gracious*)

Judith (praised) Judit, Judy
Julia (youth, downy) Julie
Juliana (youth, downy)
Juliet (youth, downy) Juliette
Julyann (July, the seventh month + grace, full of grace, mercy)
June (the sixth month, born in June)
Justina (right, just)
Kaatje (little Katherine *pure, unsullied*)
Kalliope (beautiful voice)
Karen (pure, unsullied)
Karita (charity, affection)
Karla (woman) Carla
Karolina (woman) Caroline, Karoline; Carrie, Karrie
Katherine (pure, unsullied) Catherine, Katarina, Katarine, Katerina, Katerine, Katharina, Katherin, Katrine, Katryn; Cathy, Kaethe, Kate, Kathe, Kathy, Katie, Katja, Katrien, Kitty
Keitha (?, perhaps *the wind* or *wood*)
Kenna (born of fire; comely, handsome)
Kerenhappuch (horn of antimony) Keren
Keturah (incense)
Kezia (cassia)
Klara (bright, clear, famous) Clara
Laetitia (happiness) Letitia
Laila (night, dark beauty)
Laufeia (leafy island)
Laura (laurel) Lora
Laurana (from Laurentum)
Laurence (from Laurentum) Laurencia, Laurentia
Laureola (from Laurentum)
Lavinia (from Latium) Lavina
Leah (weary)
Leila (dark beauty, dark as night)
Lena (light, torch, bright)
Leslie (small meadow, small clearing, small woods)
Letitia (happiness, gladness) Laticia, Leticia
Lettice (happiness)
Lexine (defender or helper of mankind)
Lillian (lily) Lilian, Liliana; Lily
Linda (beautiful)
Lisa (God is my oath)
Lisabet (God is my oath) Lisbet, Lysbet
Litonya (hummingbird) Litonia
Liv (life)
Lois (?)
Lorena (from Lorraine)
Loretta (from Laurentum) Lauretta
Louise (famous in war) Louisa, Luisa
Love (love)
Lucia (light)
Lucilla (light)
Lucinda (light)
Lucy (light)
Lydia (Lydian woman) Lyddia
Mabel (lovable) Mabill

Mabella (lovable)
Madeline (from Magdala)
Madge (a pearl)
Magda (from Magdala)
Magdalen (from Magdala) Magdalena, Magdalene, Magdelyn; Maggie
Maggie (a pearl)
Mahala (tenderness)
Mahalath (a lute, a lyre)
Mai (sea of bitterness or sorrow; a pearl)
Malene (from Magdala)
Manuela (God with us) Manuella
Marah (bitterness)
Marcella (of Mars, warlike)
Marcia (of Mars, warlike) Marcie
Margareta (a pearl) Margaret, Margaretha, Margarethe, Margarita, Margrethe, Margriet, Marguerita, Marguerite, Margit, Margery, Margarey
Maria (sea of bitterness or sorrow) Marie
Mariana (of Mars; sea of bitterness or sorrow + grace, full of grace, mercy)
Mariel (sea of bitterness or sorrow)
Marina (of Mars; of the sea)
Marion (sea of bitterness or sorrow)
Marjorie (a pearl) Margery
Marta (a pearl)
Martha (lady, mistress) Marthe
Martina (of Mars, warlike)
Mary (sea of bitterness or sorrow) Moll, Molly
Mary Ann (sea of bitterness or sorrow + grace, full of grace, mercy) Mariann
Matilda (strength in battle) Mathilda
Maud (battle strength)
Maura (great, large; dark-skinned, a Moor)
Maureen (sea of bitterness or sorrow) Maurene, Maurine
May (a pearl; sea of bitterness or sorrow; born in May)
Maya (goddess of increase; industrious, hardworking)
Mehetabel (God makes happy)
Melanie (dark, black)
Melicent (work + strength) Milesent
Melissa (a bee)
Melody (a melody)
Meraude (of the sea)
Mercedes (mercy)
Mercy (mercy, compassion)
Meriall (sea bright) Meryall
Mia (sea of bitterness or sorrow; Who is like God?)
Mikaela (Who is like God?)
Mildred (mild strength)
Millicent (work strength) Melicent, Melisande, Mellicent, Milicent, Millesant
Minerva (the goddess of wisdom, skill, and invention)
Miranda (worthy to be loved)
Miriam (sea of bitterness or sorrow)
Molly (sea of bitterness or sorrow)

Monday (born on Monday)
Monica (?) **Monika**
Monique (?)
Morna (beloved) **Myrna**
Naamah (sweetness)
Nancy (grace, full of grace, mercy)
Nanny (grace, full of grace, mercy)
Naomi (my joy, my delight)
Narcissa (?, inspired by Narcissus, a mythological youth who was transformed into a narcissus flower)
Natalie (natal day; born at Christmastime) **Natalia**
Neilina (champion; a cloud)
Nel (horn)
Nell (light, torch, bright) **Nelly**
Nelleke (horn)
Nellie (horn)
Netta (champion; a cloud)
Nicey (nice, friendly)
Nicole (victory of the people) **Nicol**
Nicolette (little Nicole *victory of the people*)
Nilsine (victory of the people)
Noelle (born at Christmas) **Noel**
Noemie (pleasant, beautiful)
Nora (a woman from the north; honor, esteem)
Oceanus (of the ocean) **Oceana**
Oddveig (spear woman)
Odette (prosperity, riches)
Odile (prosperity, riches) **Odila**
Ola (ancestor's relic)
Olathe (beautiful) Shawnee.
Olaug (dedicated to the ancestors)
Olga (holy)
Olive (the olive tree)
Olivia (the olive tree)
Olympia (of Olympus) **Olympe**
Onora (honor)
Ophelia (help, succor) **Ophelie**
Ophrah (a fawn)
Orabell (?) **Orable, Oriabel**
Oriane (to rise; golden)
Orpah (a fawn, a forelock)
Oriana (to rise)
Osanna (save now, save pray)
Paloma (dove)
Parnell (a rock)
Patience (patience, forebearance)
Patricia (a patrician, an aristocrat) **Pat, Patty**
Peg (a pearl) **Peggy**
Penelope (a bobbin)
Pentecost (fiftieth [day])
Percy (from Percy, Normandy)
Perdita (lost)
Pernilla (a rock) **Pernille**
Perpetua (perpetual, eternal)
Persis (Persian woman)

Petra (a rock)
Petronel (a rock) **Peternel**
Petronilla (a rock)
Philadelphia (brotherly love)
Philippa (lover of horses)
Philomena (beloved) **Philomene**
Phyllis (a leaf) **Phillis, Phylis**
Phoebe (bright, shining) **Phebe, Phebeus**
Pia (pious, devout)
Pleasance (pleasant)
Precilla (former, ancient) **Priscilla**
Precious (priceless, dear)
Princess (a princess)
Prisca (former, ancient)
Prothesia (?)
Prudence (prudent)
Queen (a queen) **Queena**
Queenie (a queen)
Rachel (ewe) **Rachael, Rachell**
Rae (doe)
Ragna (advice, counsel)
Ramona (wise protection)
Raquel (ewe) **Racquel**
Rebecca (noose) **Rabecca, Rebecka, Rebekah, Rebekka**
Renate (reborn) **Renatus**
Renee (reborn)
Rhoda (a rose)
Richenda (little Richard *stern king*)
Rina Originally a short form for names ending in *-rina,* such as Sabrina.
Rinda (?)
Rita (a pearl)
Robina (bright with fame)
Rona (mighty power)
Rosa (a rose)
Rosabel (beautiful rose)
Rosalie (rose garland)
Rosalind (horse or fame + gentle, tender, or serpent) **Rosalinde**
Rosamond (horse protection) **Rossamond**
Rose (a rose) **Rosa**
Roseanna (rose + grace, full of grace, mercy) **Rosana, Rosanna, Rose Ann, Rose Anne**
Rosemarie (rose + sea of bitterness or sorrow; dew of the sea)
Rosemary (rose + sea of bitterness or sorrow)
Rosetta (little Rose) **Rosita**
Rowena (famous friend)
Roxane (dawn of day)
Runa (secret lore)
Rut (friend, companion)
Ruth (friend, companion) **Ruthe**
Sabina (Sabine woman) **Sabine**
Salina (the moon)
Sally (princess)

Salome (peace)
Sandra (defender of mankind) **Saundra**
Sapphira (beautiful)
Sarah (princess) **Sara**
Sarah Ann (princess + grace, full of grace, mercy)
Sarey (princess)
Saskia (?)
Selina (the moon) **Selene, Selinah**
Seraphine (burning ones, angels)
Sharon (a plain, a flat area)
Sheena (God is gracious)
Sibylla (fortune-teller, prophetess) **Sibella, Sibilla, Sybil**
Sidonia (linen cloth) **Sidonie, Sidony**
Signy (new victory)
Sigrun (victory + secret lore)
Silvia (wood)
Simone (heard)
Solange (yearly; solemn, religious)
Soledad (solitude)
Solveig (house of strength) **Solvej, Solvig**
Sophia (wisdom) **Sofia, Sophie**
Sorcha (bright)
Stephanie (a crown, garland)
Sunniva (gift of the sun)
Susan (lily, rose) **Suzan**
Susanna (lily, rose) **Susannah, Susanne, Susanney, Suzanna, Suzannah, Suzanne**
Svanhild (battle swan)
Sybil (fortune-teller, prophetess) **Sybell, Sybill, Sybilla, Sybille**
Sylvia (the woods)
Sylvie (the woods)
Synnove (gift of the sun)
Tabitha (roe, gazelle)
Tacy (hold peace, be silent)
Talise (beautiful water) Creek.
Talula (leaping water) **Tallula, Tallulah, Talulah** Choctaw.
Taluta (scarlet) **Talutah** Sioux.
Tamar (palm, a date palm) **Tamara**
Teodora (God's gift)
Tessa (harvester) **Tess**
Theodora (God's gift) **Theo**
Theodosia (God-given) **Theo**
Theophila (God's friend) **Theo**
Theresa (harvester) **Teresa, Therese; Tess, Tessa**
Thirza (acceptance, pleasantness) **Thyrza**
Thomson (little Tom *a twin*) **Thamasin, Thomasin, Tomson**

Thora (Thor)
Tiffeny (Epiphany, manifestation of God) **Tyffany**
Tilda (battle)
Tina (a Christian, a follower of Christ)
Tirzah (acceptance, pleasantness)
Torunn (loved by Thor)
Tova (beautiful Thor)
Troth (fidelity, good faith)
Trudie (spear strength) **Trudy**
Tryphena (delicate, dainty)
Ulla (will, determination)
Ulrike (noble ruler) **Ulrika**
Unity (united)
Unn (love)
Ursula (she-bear) **Urselah**
Valentine (strong, healthy) **Valentina**
Valerie (strong, healthy)
Vara (?)
Venetia (blessed)
Venus (the loved one, beloved)
Veronica (true image) **Veronika**
Veronique (true image)
Victoria (victory) **Viktoria**
Viola (violet) **Viole**
Violet (violet-colored) **Violette**
Vita (life)
Vivian (alive) **Viviane, Vivianne, Vivien, Vivienne**
Wanda (?, perhaps *stem, young tree; a Wend, an old Slavic people*)
Wauna (snow geese calling as they fly) Miwok.
Wilfreda (resolute peace)
Wilhelmina (resolute protector)
Willa (resolute protector)
Wilma (resolute protector)
Winifred (blessed peace) **Winnifred, Winnie**
Winona (eldest daughter) **Wenona**
Yolande (?, possibly *violet*) **Yolanda**
Yvette (little archer)
Yvonne (archer)
Zenaida (of Zeus)
Zephyrine (the west wind)
Zeresh (gold, splendor)
Zillah (shade)
Zilpah (?)
Zipporah (a little bird)
Zoe (live)
Zoraida (captivating woman)
Zuleka (fair) **Zuleica**

MALE NAMES

Aaron (exalted)
Abel (breath)
Abner (the father is a light)
Abraham (father of a multitude)
Abram (father of exaltation)
Absalom (father of peace) **Absalon**
Adalard (noble and strong)
Adalbert (noble and bright) **Adelbert**
Adalrich (noble ruler)
Adam (man of the red earth)
Adelulf (noble wolf)
Adolphe (noble wolf) **Adolf**
Adrian (man from Hadrianus) **Adrien**
Aeneas (praiser)
Aidan (little fire)
Ake (?, possibly *ancestor; agate; blameless*)
Aksel (the father is peace) **Axel**
Alain (?, perhaps *handsome; rock*) **Allain**
Alan (?, perhaps *handsome; rock*) **Allan, Allen**
Alard (noble and strong) **Allard**
Alarik (ruler of all)
Alasdair (defender of mankind) **Alastair, Alaster, Alisdair, Alistair, Alister, Allaster**
Alberic (elf ruler)
Albert (bright through nobility)
Albin (white)
Aldred (old counsel)
Alduin (old friend)
Aldus (old)
Aldwin (old friend)
Alex (defender, defender of mankind)
Alexander (defender of mankind) **Alexandre; Alec, Alick, Sander**
Alexis (defender)
Algernon (mustached)
Alick (defender) **Alec**
Aloysius (famous in war)
Alphonse (noble and ready)
Ambrose (immortal) **Ambroise**
Amedee (love of God)
Amias (?, perhaps *friendship*) **Amyas**
Amiel (industrious)
Amos (borne, a burden)
Amund (awe, fear; edge, point + protector)
Anatole (sunrise, daybreak)
Anders (manly)
Andor (eagle + Thor)
Andra (manly)
Andre (manly)
Andrew (manly) **Dande, Dandy, Tandy**
Angus (one, choice, preeminent) **Gus**
Anker (harvester)
Anketil (god's kettle, sacrificial cauldron) **Anchitel**
Anselme (divine helmet)

Anthony (?, *priceless, of inestimable worth* is a folk definition) **Antony; Tony**
Antoine (?, *priceless, of inestimable worth* is a folk definition)
Anton (?, *priceless, of inestimable worth* is a folk definition)
Antonius (?, *priceless, of inestimable worth* is a folk definition)
April (the fourth month, born in April)
Ara (eagle)
Archibald (genuinely bold, genuinely brave) **Archebald**
Aren (eagle rule)
Arend (eagle power)
Aristide (best)
Armand (soldier, warrior) **Armond**
Armin (soldier, warrior)
Arnbjorn (eagle bear) **Armbjorn**
Arne (eagle) **Aren**
Arno (eagle)
Arnold (eagle ruler)
Arsene (male, virile)
Art (a bear)
Arthur (?)
Arvid (eagle tree)
Asa (healer)
Asmund (God is protector)
Athelstan (noble stone) **Athestan**
Auberi (elf ruler) **Aubry**
Aubert (noble and bright)
August (the eighth month, born in August)
Auguste (great, venerable) **August; Gus**
Augustin (great, venerable) **Gus**
Augustus (great, venerable) **Gus**
Aurele (gold)
Aurelien (golden)
Austin (great, venerable)
Averil (boar battle)
Aylmer (nobly famous)
Aylwin (elf friend)
Azariah (whom Jehovah helps)
Baird (a poet)
Baldric (bold ruler)
Baldwin (bold friend)
Balthasar (?)
Baptist (a baptiser) **Baptiste**
Barclay (from Berkeley *birch meadow*)
Bardolph (bright wolf) **Bardolf**
Barnabas (son of exhortation)
Barnabe (son of exhortation) **Barnaby, Barney ep Barry** (spearlike)
Bartel (son of Talmai *hill, mound, furrows*) **Bertel**
Barthelemy (son of Talmai *hill, mound, furrows*)
Bartholomaus (son of Talmai *hill, mound, furrows*) **Bartholomeus**
Bartholomew (son of Talmai *hill, mound, furrows*)
Basil (kingly) **Basile, Bazil, Bazille**

Bastien (man from Sebasta)
Beavis (beautiful) **Beves, Bevis**
Bellamy (beautiful friend)
Bendt (blessed)
Benedict (blessed) **Benedick, Benedikt, Benedikte**
Beniemen (son of the right hand) **Beniemim**
Benjamin (son of the right hand) **Ben**
Bennet (blessed)
Berend (strong as a bear) **Bernd**
Berg (mountain)
Beringer (bear spear)
Bernhard (bold as a bear) **Bernard, Barnard**
Bernt (bold as a bear)
Berold (bear rule) **Berolt**
Berry (a berry)
Bertil (bright)
Bertin (bright friend)
Bertram (bright raven) **Bertran**
Billy (resolute protector)
Birger (helper)
Bjorn (bear) **Bjarne**
Blaise (deformed, stuttering) **Blaize, Blase, Blaze**
Bo (a householder)
Bonaventure (good travels)
Brian (force, strength; valor; steep, high) **Bryan**
Brice (?)
Broder (brother)
Bruce (from Brus, France)
Bruno (brown)
Buster (man, boy)
Caesar (blue gray; hairy) **Cesar**
Caleb (dog; faithful)
Calum (dove)
Cameron (crooked nose)
Camille (?; virgin of unblemished character)
Campbell (crooked mouth)
Carl (a man, freeman) **Karl**
Caspar (treasure master) **Casper, Kaspar, Kasper**
Cato (wise one)
Cecil (blind, dim-sighted)
Charles (full-grown, a man)
Chauncey (belonging to Chancey, France) **Chauncy**
Chester (camp of the legions) **Chet**
Christmas (born at Christmas)
Christian (a Christian, a follower of Christ)
Christoph (bearing Christ) **Christophe**
Christopher (bearing Christ) **Christoffer, Kristoffer; Chris, Kester, Kit**
Clarence (from the Clare *bright, shining, clear* family)
Claud (lame) **Claude**
Claus (victory of the people)
Clayborne (dweller near the clay banks) **Clayborn; Clay**
Clayton (from the clay town) **Clay**
Cleanthes (?)
Clement (gentle, mild)

Cleveland (from the hilly land)
Clifford (dweller near the ford by the cliff) **Cliff**
Clifton (from the town by the cliff) **Cliff**
Clinton (from the settlement by the cliff) **Clint**
Coleman (a coal man, a seller of coal) **Cole**
Colin (dove)
Comfort (comfort, care)
Conall (strength; wisdom; high; wolf, dog)
Connell (wisdom, high-mighty) **Connel**
Connor (wisdom, counsel, strength + aid; hound) **Conor**
Conrad (bold counsel)
Constant (constant, steadfast)
Constantine (constant, steadfast)
Conway (hound of the plain)
Corneille (horn)
Cornelius (a horn) **Cornelis, Corneleus**
Craig (rugged rocks; dweller by the crag)
Crispin (curled)
Crispus (curly, curly-haired)
Cuthbert (known and bright)
Cyprian (from Cyprus) **Cyprien**
Cyriack (lordly)
Cyril (lordly) **Cyrille**
Cyrus (lord)
Damian (tamer) **Damien**
Dana (a Dane)
Daniel (judged by God)
Darby (from the settlement by the deer)
David (beloved)
Denmark (from Denmark)
Dennis (belonging to Dionysus) **Denis, Denys**
Derek (ruler of the people)
Diederik (ruler of the people)
Dierk (ruler of the people)
Dieter (ruler of the people)
Dietrich (ruler of the people)
Dirk (ruler of the people)
Dominic (belonging to a lord, belonging to the Lord) **Dominik**
Dominique (belonging to a lord, belonging to the Lord)
Donald (world ruler)
Donatien (given by God)
Donnal (world ruler)
Dougal (dark-haired stranger)
Douglas (black, dark + blue, green, gray)
Drew (manly)
Dudley (from Dudda's lea)
Duff (dark, black)
Duncan (brown warrior)
Durand (enduring, lasting) **Durant**
Dwight (the white one)
Easter (born at Easter)
Ebenezer (stone of help)
Eberhard (strong as a wild boar)
Eden (delight)
Edgar (wealthy spear)
Edmond (wealthy protection) **Edmund**

Edvard (wealthy guardian)
Edward (wealthy guardian) **Eduard**
Edwin (wealthy friend)
Edzard (brave with the spear)
Egil (point of a sword)
Egon (point of a sword)
Eilert (brave with the spear)
Eilif (immortal)
Einar (lone warrior)
Eleazar (God has helped)
Eli (high, ascent)
Elias (Jehovah is God)
Elijah (Jehovah is God)
Elisha (God is salvation)
Elkanah (God created)
Ellery (alder tree)
Elmer (nobly famous)
Elof (lone descendant)
Emanuel (God with us) **Emmanuel**
Emery (ruler of strength)
Emile (rival, trying to equal or excel) **Emil**
Emilien (rival, trying to equal or excel)
Enoch (dedicated)
Eoghan (lamb; youth; well-born)
Ephraim (very fruitful)
Erasmus (loved, desired)
Erik (eternal ruler) **Eirik, Eric**
Erlend (foreigner, stranger) **Erland**
Ernest (earnest, resolute) **Ernst**
Esau (hairy)
Eskel (sacrificial cauldron of a god)
Eubule (he of good counsel)
Eugene (well-born)
Eusebius (pious)
Eustace (steadfast; happy in harvest) **Eustache**
Evan (youth; God is gracious)
Evelyn (?)
Everard (strong as a boar) **Everhart, Evert**
Everitt (strong as a boar) **Everet, Everett, Everit, Evert**
Ewan (youth)
Ewould (lawful rule)
Eyvind (island of the Wend)
Ezekiel (God strengthens)
Ezra (help)
Faas (resolute counsel)
Fabian (a bean) **Fabien**
Farquhar (dear man)
Fearghas (man of valor) **Fergus**
Felix (lucky)
Ferdinand (peace; journey; youth, life + courage; venture, risk; ready)
Fergus (man of valor) **Fargus**
Festus (?)
Filbert (very bright)
Filip (lover of horses)
Fingall (fair-haired stranger) **Fingal**

Finlay (fair-haired warrior)
Finn (from Finland)
Fiske (fish)
Flemming (a Flemming)
Florence (a blooming)
Florent (blossoming)
Florentin (blossoming)
Florian (flowery)
Floris (blossoming)
Forbes (a field)
Francis (a Frank, a freeman)
Francois (French)
Frank (a Frank)
Franz (a Frenchman)
Franziskus (a Frenchman) **Franciscus**
Fraser (a Frisian)
Frederic (ruler of peace) **Frederick, Frederik, Fredrick, Fredrik; Fred, Freddy**
Friederich (peaceful king) **Friedrich**
Friedhelm (peace helmet)
Frode (knowing, wise)
Fulbert (very bright)
Fulton (the fowl enclosure; a chicken coop)
Gabriel (God is strength) **Gabrial**
Gamaliel (the Lord is recompense)
Garrett (spear rule) **Garett, Garit, Garitt**
Garrick (spear; brave with the spear) **Garek**
Garth (yard, enclosure)
Gascon (?, possibly *guest, stranger; from Gascony*)
Gaspard (treasure master)
Gaston (?, possibly *guest, stranger; from Gascony*)
Gauvain (battle hawk)
Gavin (battle hawk)
Gedaliah (made great by Jehovah)
Gene (well-born, noble)
Gentry (upper-class, nobleman)
Geoffrey (district; traveler; pledge + peace) **Geffrey, Jeffery, Jeffrey**
Geoffroi (district; traveler; pledge + peace)
George (earth worker, farmer) **Georg, Georges**
Gerald (spear rule) **Gerold, Gerolt**
Gerard (brave with the spear)
Gerhard (brave with the spear)
Gerlach (spear sport)
Germayne (a German) **Germain**
Gershon (expulsion, stranger) **Gershom**
Gervais (servant of the spear)
Gideon (hewer)
Giffard (give + bold, fierce)
Gilbert (bright pledge) **Gib, Gil**
Giles (goatskin shield of Zeus; a protection) **Gillis**
Gillespie (servant of the bishop)
Gillies (servant of Jesus)
Gilroy (servant of the red-haired lad)
Godfried (peace of God)
Godfry (peace of God) **Godfrey**

Godric (powerful God)
Godwin (friend of God)
Goldwin (friend of gold)
Gottfried (peace of God)
Graham (from Grantham) **Graeme, Grahame**
Grant (great, large)
Gregoire (vigilant, watchful)
Gregor (vigilant, watchful)
Gregory (vigilant, watchful)
Griffin (like a griffin, monstrous)
Guillaume (resolute protector)
Gunnar (war, strife, battle)
Gunther (bold in war)
Gustaf (staff of the Goths) **Gustav**
Guy (a guide, leader)
Guyon (a guide, leader)
Haakon (chosen son)
Hagen (chosen son) **Hakan, Hakon**
Haldor (Thor's rock)
Halsten (rock stone)
Hamilton (from the blunt hill)
Hamlet (little house) **Hamlett, Hamnet**
Hamon (little house)
Hannibal (?)
Hans (God is gracious) **Hannes**
Harald (home ruler) **Harold**
Harry (home ruler)
Haward (high guardian)
Hector (holding fast)
Heinrich (home ruler)
Helmut (courageous protector)
Hendrik (home ruler) **Henrik**
Henning (home ruler)
Henry (home ruler)
Herbert (army bright) **Harbert, Heribert**
Herman (warrior, soldier) **Hermann**
Hezekiah (God strengthens)
Hilary (cheerful) **Hilaire, Hilarie**
Hiram (exalted brother)
Hjalmar (warrior's helmet)
Horatio (?)
Hosanna (save pray)
Hosea (salvation)
Hubert (bright heart)
Hugh (heart, mind, soul) **Hugo**
Humphrey (warrior of peace)
Iain (God is gracious) **Ian**
Ingmar (famous Ing)
Ingram (Ing's raven; angel raven)
Ingvar (Ing's warrior)
Ira (watchful)
Irving (from the west river)
Isaac (laughter) **Isak, Isaak, Izaac, Izaak**
Isaiah (God is salvation)
Israel (contender with God)
Ivar (archer, bow warrior) **Iver, Ivor**

Ives (archer) **Ivo, Yvo**
Jabez (height)
Jack (God is gracious) **Jackey**
Jacob (supplanting, seizing by the heels) **Jakob**
Jacques (supplanting, seizing by the heels)
James (supplanting, seizing by the heels)
Jan (God is gracious) **Janne, Jens, Jon, Jons**
January (of Janus; born in January)
Japheth (enlargement) **Japet, Japeth**
Jared (descending)
Jason (healer)
Jasper (treasure master)
Jean (God is gracious)
Jean-Baptiste (God is gracious + a baptizer; John the Baptist)
Jean-Michel (God is gracious + Who is like God?)
Jedaiah (invoker of Jehovah) **Jed**
Jedidiah (beloved of Jehovah) **Jed**
Jeffrey (peaceful district; traveler of peace; pledge of peace) **Jeffery**
Jeremiah (God will uplift) **Jeremias**
Jeremie (God will uplift) **Jeremy**
Jermaine (a German)
Jeroen (holy name)
Jerome (holy name)
Jesimiel (God sets up)
Jesper (treasure master)
Jesse (gift)
Jethro (excellence)
Joachim (God will establish) **Joachin, Joakim**
Jock (God is gracious)
Joel (the Lord is God)
Johann (God is gracious)
Johannes (God is gracious)
John (God is gracious) **Johnny**
Jonas (dove) **Jonah**
Jonathan (God has given) **Jon**
Joost (just, lawful)
Jordan (a flowing down) **Jordaan, Judd**
Jorg (earth worker, farmer)
Jorgen (earth worker, farmer)
Jorn (earth worker, farmer)
Joseph (he shall add) **Josef; Joe**
Joshua (God is salvation) **Jozua; Josh**
Josiah (the Lord supports)
Julian (youth, downy) **Julien**
Julius (youth, downy)
July (the seventh month)
Justin (just) **Justyn**
Justus (just)
Juvenal (youth)
Kaspar (treasure master)
Keir (dark-complexioned)
Keith (?, perhaps *the wind*; *wood*)
Kennet (handsome, comely)
Kenneth (handsome, comely)
Kenrick (royal rule)

Kenward (brave guardian) **Kenard**
Kernan (little black-haired one)
Kester (bearing Christ)
Kieran (little dark one)
King (king, ruler)
Kirk (church)
Knut (knot)
Konrad (wise counsel)
Laban (white)
Lambert (bright land)
Lance (land)
Lars (man from Laurentum)
Laurance (from Laurentum) **Laurence, Lawrence**
Lazarus (whom God helps)
Leif (what is remaining, relic; beloved)
Lemuel (devoted to God)
Lennart (brave as a lion)
Leo (lion)
Leon (lion)
Leonard (bold as a lion)
Leonhard (bold as a lion)
Leopold (bold people)
Levi (joining)
Levin (dear friend)
Lionel (little lion) English, French.
Lorens (man from Laurentum) **Lorenz**
Louis (famous in war) **Lewis**
Luc (light; man from Lucania) **Luke**
Lucas (light; man from Lucania) **Lukas**
Lucian (light; man from Lucania) **Lucien**
Lucius (light; man from Lucania)
Lucky (lucky, fortunate)
Ludovic (famous in war)
Ludwig (famous in war)
Luke (light; man from Lucania)
Lyell (lion) **Lyel**
Maarten (of Mars, warlike)
Magnus (great, large)
Malachi (my messenger)
Malcolm (servant of Saint Columba)
Manfred (peace of man)
Manus (great, large)
Marc (?, perhaps *of Mars; manly; soft, tender*) **Mark**
Marcel (of Mars, warlike)
Marcus (?, perhaps *of Mars; manly; soft, tender*) **Markus**
Mark (soft, tender; manly; warlike)
Martin (of Mars, warlike) **Marten**
Matheus (gift of God) **Mathiu, Matteus, Mattheus, Matthews**
Matthew (gift of God) **Matheu**
Matthias (gift of God) **Mathis**
Mauger (spear grinder)
Maurice (a Moor) **Meurisse**
Maurits (a Moor)
Max (greatest)
Maxwell (large spring; large stream)

Maynard (strong and hardy)
Meinhard (strong and hardy)
Meshach (agile)
Micah (Who is like God?)
Michael (Who is like God?) **Michel, Mikael, Mikel**
Michiel (Who is like God?)
Micky (Who is like God?) **Mick**
Miles (?, perhaps *mild, peaceful; merciful*)
Milo (?, perhaps *mild, peaceful; merciful*) **Milon**
Moise (drawn out of the water)
Montgomery (from Monte Goumeril)
Mordecai (worshiper of Marduk)
Morgan (sea bright)
Morris (dark, swarthy, a Moor)
Morten (of Mars; warlike)
Moses (drawn out of the water)
Murdoch (mariner)
Murphy (sea warrior)
Murray (from Moray *beside the sea*)
Nathan (gift) **Nate**
Nathanael (gift of God) **Natanael, Nathaniel**
Ned (wealthy guardian)
Nehemiah (comforted by Jehovah)
Neil (champion; a cloud) **Neal, Neill, Nial, Niall, Niel, Niell**
Neville (from the new town) **Nevell, Nevil**
Nicholas (victory of the people) **Nikolas, Nikolaus; Nicol, Nicoll, Nichol, Coll**
Noah (rest, comfort)
Noel (born at Christmas)
Norbert (north bright)
Norman (northman)
Obadiah (servant of God)
Odo (wealth)
Ola (ancestor's relic) **Ole**
Oliver (olive tree)
Olivier (olive tree)
Olof (ancestor's relic) **Olaf, Olav, Olov, Oluf**
Osanne (hosannah)
Osbern (god bear) **Osborn**
Osbert (god bright)
Oscar (God's spear) **Oskar**
Osmond (God's protection) **Osmund**
Oswald (God's power)
Otto (rich)
Owen (well-born) **Own**
Paddy (a patrician, an aristocrat) **Pady**
Parlan (son of Talmai *hill, mound, furrows*)
Pascal (Easter, born at Easter)
Pat (a patrician, an aristocrat) **Patt**
Patrick (a patrician, an aristocrat)
Patterson (son of Peter *a rock, a stone*)
Paul (small)
Paulin (small)
Pearse (a rock, a stone)
Percy (from Percy, Normandy) **Percey**
Peter (a rock, a stone)

Philip (lover of horses) **Philipp, Phillip**
Phineas (oracle)
Pierre (a rock, a stone)
Prince (a prince)
Quintin (fifth)
Rafe (counsel wolf)
Ragnar (warrior of decision)
Rainier (wise army)
Ralph (counsel wolf)
Ramsey (from Ram's island)
Randolph (shield wolf) **Randolf, Randulf, Ranulf**
Ranfred (counsel peace)
Raul (counsel wolf)
Raymund (counsel protection) **Raimund**
Regin (judgment, decision)
Reginald (judgment power)
Reid (red, ruddy) **Read**
Reinhard (brave counsel)
Renfred (counsel might)
Reuben (behold, a son!)
Reynard (counsel hard)
Raynold (powerful protection) **Rainald, Raynald, Renold, Reynold**
Richard (stern king) **Rikard**
Robert (bright with fame) **Rob, Robb**
Roderick (famous king) **Roddy**
Rodney (from Hróda's *fame* island)
Rodolphe (wolf fame) **Rudolf, Rudolph, Rudolphe**
Roger (famous with the spear) **Rogier, Rodger**
Roland (famous land) **Rolland**
Rolf (famous wolf)
Roscoe (from the woods of the red deer)
Ross (dweller on the promontory or peninsula; red, rust-colored)
Roth (famous king)
Roy (red-haired, ruddy-complexioned)
Rufus (red, red-haired)
Rurik (famous king)
Russell (red-haired) **Russ**
Rutger (famous spear)
Samson (the sun) **Sansom, Sanson, Sam**
Samuel (heard of God) **Sam**
Sander (defender of mankind) **Sandre**
Sandy (defender of mankind)
Saul (asked for)
Scott (an Irishman, a Scot)
Sebastian (man from Sebastia) **Sebastiaan, Sebastien**
Seth (appointed)
Severin (severe, strict)
Shane (God is gracious)
Shaw (dweller at a wood or grove)
Shem (renowned)
Siegfried (powerful peace)
Sigge (victory, conquest)
Sigmund (victorious protection) **Siegmund**
Sigurd (guardian of victory)

Silas (ask for)
Silver (silver, silver-haired)
Silvester (a wood, a forest)
Simon (heard) **Simeon**
Sinclair (from Saint Clair)
Siward (victory protection)
Solomon (peaceful)
Soren (apart)
Sorley (mariner, sailor)
Spiro (to breathe, to blow)
Stanislav (government is glory)
Steen (stone)
Stein (stone)
Steinar (stone warrior)
Sten (stone)
Stephan (a crown, a garland) **Stefan, Steffan, Steffen, Stephane, Stephen, Steven**
Stewart (steward, keeper of the animal enclosure)
Svein (strong, youth) **Sveinn, Sven, Svend, Svends**
Swain (stong, able, wise)
Sylvester (of the woods) **Sylvestre**
Talbot (pillager, bandit; lampblack)
Teague (a poet)
Tecumseh (goes through one place to another [a shooting star]) Shawnee.
Ted (God's gift)
Terrence (soft, tender) **Terance**
Terrick (ruler of the people)
Theodore (gift of God) **Theodoor, Theodor; Ted, Teddy, Theo**
Theodoric (ruler of the people) **Theo**
Thomas (a twin) **Thomaas, Tomas**
Thompson (son of Thom *a twin*)
Thor (thunder) **Thore**
Thurstan (Thor's stone) **Torsten**
Timothy (honor, respect) **Timothee**
Titus (?, possibly *to honor*)
Toal (people mighty)
Tobias (God is good)
Tristan (tumult, sadness) **Tristram**
Tycho (hitting the mark) **Tyge, Tyko**
Ulf (wolf)
Uriah (God is light)
Valdemar (famous ruler) **Waldemar**
Valentine (healthy, strong) **Valentin**
Valery (to be strong) **Valere**
Valient (valiant, brave)
Victor (victor, winner) **Viktor**
Vidkun (wide experience)
Vincent (conquering)
Virgil (youthful, flourishing)
Vital (vital, life-giving)
Vivien (alive)
Von (hope)
Walden (to rule)
Waldo (to rule)

Walter (ruler of an army)
Werner (protecting army) **Verner, Warner**
West (west, from the west)
Wilfred (desire for peace)
William (resolute protector) **Vilhelm, Wilhelm, Willelm, Willem**
Winfred (blessed peace)
Winston (from Winston *friend's town*)

Wolf (wolf)
Wolfgang (traveling wolf)
Yves (archer)
Yvon (archer)
Zachariah (God remembers) **Zacharias, Zachary**
Zebedee (God bestows)
Zebulun (to carry, to exalt)
Zephaniah (the Lord has hidden)

SURNAMES

The pool of surnames in the United States was greatly enlarged due to increased immigration. Although some first names fell to the wayside, hereditary surnames were here to stay.

Abel (breath) English, German.
Aberdeen (from Aberdeen *the confluence of the Dee and Don rivers*) Scottish.
Adler (dweller at the sign of the eagle) German.
Albertson (son of Albert *noble and bright*) English, German.
Albrecht (noble and bright) German.
Alemander (a German) German.
Altmann (old servant) German.
Andres (manly) German.
Arenbeck (dweller near the eagle brook) German.
Aschbrenner (a maker of potash, an ashburner) German.
Bach (dweller near the brook) German.
Bachmann (dweller near the brook) German.
Bader (a barber, a surgeon) German.
Baer (dweller at the sign of the bear; bearlike) German.
Baier (from Bavaria) **Bayer** German.
Balderson (son of Balder *bold army*) English.
Ballmann (the bold man) German.
Bamberg (from Bamberg) German.
Barris (son of Barry *from Barry, France; traffic, commerce*) English.
Bartel (son of Talmai *hill, mound, furrows*) German.
Bauer (a farmer, tiller of the soil) German.
Baum (dweller near the tree) German.
Baumann (dweller near the tree) German.
Baumgarten (dweller near the orchard) German.
Becker (baker, a breadmaker) German.
Behrens (dweller near the sign of the bear) German.
Berg (dweller near the mountain) German.
Bergmann (dweller near the mountain) German.
Bernhardt (bold as a bear) German.
Beveridge (from Beveridge *the beaver marsh*) English.
Blewitt (little bluebird) **Blewett** English.
Bluett (little bluebird) French.
Blumberg (from the flower mountain) German.
Blumenstein (from the flower stone) German.
Blumenthal (from the flower valley) German.
Boardman (dweller at a small farm or cottage) English.
Bouchier (butcher) French.

Bradberry (from Bradbury *the broad hill; the broad stronghold; Brada's stronghold*) **Bradburry, Bradbury** English.
Braddock (dweller at a gorge) Irish, Scottish.
Brandt (dweller on the burnt land) German.
Brauer (a brewer of beer) German.
Braun (brown) German.
Brenna (raven) Irish.
Breyer (from Brey) German.
Brinkmann (dweller on the grassy hill) German.
Brydon (from Bredon, Breedon *the broad hill*) English.
Burmeister (a farmer) German.
Busch (dweller near the bush; dweller near the sign of the bush) German.
Cahill (descendant of Cathal *battle mighty*) Irish.
Carl (a man) German.
Carney (warrior, soldier) Irish.
Caroll (warrior, champion) **Carrol, Carroll** Irish.
Cherry (beloved, dear; dweller at or near the cherry trees) English.
Coates (dweller at the small cottages) **Coats** English.
Coffee (victorious) Irish.
Cohen (a priest) **Cohn** German, Hebrew.
Conway (hound of the plain) Irish.
Constantine (constant, steadfast) English, French.
Copeland (from Copeland *the hilltop land*) English.
Costello (proud face) Irish.
Coulson (son of Cole *victory of the people*) English.
Crane (dweller at the sign of the crane) English.
Craven (from Craven *a cleft*) English.
Creed (?, possibly *the creed*) English.
Creswell (from Cresswell *the watercress spring*) English.
Crockett (the little crooked one) English.
Cullen (whelp, pup; handsome) Irish.
Cushman (?, perhaps *maker of cuish, thigh armor*) English.
Cussack (from Cussac, France) **Cusack, Cusak, Cussak** French.
Dahl (dweller in the valley) German, Norwegian.
Dahlmann (dweller in the valley) German.
Dalrymple (from Dalrymple *the field of the crooked pool*) Scottish.

Denham (from Denham *the valley enclosure; Dene's settlement*) English.

Desmond (South Munster) Irish.

Devlin (the plasterer or dauber; from Dublin *dark pool*; descendant of Doibhilin *?*) Irish.

Diamond (seller of diamonds; day protection) English.

Dietz (people) German.

Dorsey (dark one) Irish.

Dowling (brown spear) Irish.

Drummond (dweller at the ridge) **Drumand, Drumman** Irish, Scottish.

Eckhardt (brave with the sword) **Eckardt** German.

Eichmann (dweller near the oak tree) German.

Einstein (a stone mason) German.

Ervin (sea friend; from Irvine *the green river*) English, Scottish.

Erwin (sea friend) English.

Eustace (steadfast) English.

Everard (strong as a boar) English.

Fagan (little voice) Irish.

Featherstone (from Featherstone *FeaÐer's stone*) English.

Fee (raven) Irish.

Feeney (little raven) **Feeny** Irish.

Feldmann (dweller in the field) German.

Ferris (a rock, a stone) Irish.

Ferguson (son of Fergus *man of valor*) English, Irish, Scottish.

Finnegan (fair-complexioned) **Finagan, Finegan, Finnigan** Irish.

Fitzgerald (son of Gerald *spear rule*) English, French, Irish.

Fitzgibbons (son of Gibbon *bright pledge*) English, Irish.

Fitzgill (son of Gill *bright pledge*) English, Irish.

Fitzpatrick (son of Patrick *an aristocrat, a patrician*) English, Irish.

Fitzsimmons (son of Simmons *heard*) English, Irish.

Flynn (red-haired, ruddy-complexioned) **Flynne** Irish.

Fogarty (an exiled person) Irish.

Foley (descendant of Foghlaidh *plunderer*) Irish.

Forbes (from Forbes *the field place*) Scottish.

Friedmann (man of peace) German.

Frost (born during the time of frost; a forest warden) English, Welsh.

Galvin (descendant of Gealbhan *bright white*) Irish.

Gannan (fair-haired) **Gannon** Irish.

Garrity (son of Aireachtach *an assemblyman*) Irish.

Gebhardt (gift + bold, brave, a generous person) German.

Geist (spirit, ghost) German.

Gillan (little servant, little disciple) **Gillen, Gillon** Irish.

Gillespie (servant of the bishop) Scottish.

Gilligan (descendant of the little servant or disciple) Irish.

Gleason (little green one) **Gleeson** Irish.

Gorman (little blue one) Irish.

Griffin (dweller at the sign of the griffin; like a griffin) **Griffan, Griffen** English.

Griffiths (son of Griffith *red, ruddy; a prince*) Welsh.

Hagen (dweller in the grove) German.

Halloran (descendant of Allmhuran *stranger from across the sea*) Irish.

Hanley (descendant of Ainleach *handsome, fair*) Irish.

Hanlon (descendant of Anluan *noble warrior*) **Hanlin** Irish.

Hanrahan (grandson of Annadh *delay*) Irish.

Harkin (red, freckled) Irish.

Harkness (dweller near the temple on the headland) English, Scottish.

Hartmann (the strong, brave man) German.

Hemingway (dweller at Heming's way, road) English.

Hemphill (from Hempshill, Hemede's hill) English.

Hennessey (descendant of Aonghus *one, choice, preeminent*) **Henessy, Hennessy** Irish.

Herritt (ruler of an army; little Henry *home ruler*) English, Irish.

Hewitson (son of Hewitt [Hugh] *heart, mind, spirit*) English.

Higginbottom (dweller in Higgin's valley) English.

Highland (dweller at the high land) **Hyland** English.

Hoffmann (a worker at the large farm) German.

Hurley (from Hurley *homestead in a corner*) English.

Hussey (dweller near the holly grove) English, Scottish.

Hutton (from Hutton *settlement on the bluff*) English.

Irvine (from Irvine *the green river*) **Irvin** Scottish.

Isaac (laughter) English.

Ivory (from Ivry, France) English.

Jacoby (supplanting, seizing by the heels) German.

Jaeger (a hunter) German.

Jantzen (son of Jan *God is gracious*) Dutch, German.

Jung (young) German.

Jungmann (the young servant) German.

Kane (descendant of Cathan *warrior*) Irish.

Kaufmann (the merchant) German.

Kearns (soldier) Irish.

Keating (?, possibly from the Welsh Cethyn) Irish.

Keefe (descendant of Caomh *gentle, lovable*) Irish.

Keegan (son of Egan *little fiery one*) Irish.

Keenan (little handsome one) Irish.

Kehoe (son of Eochaidh *horseman*) **Keough** Irish.

Keith (from Keith *?*) Scottish.

Keller (worker in the celler) German.

Kelly (son of Ceallach *war, warrior*) **Kelley** Irish.

Keown (son of Eoghan *youth; well-born, noble*) Irish.

Kessler (a maker or seller of kettles) German.

Kiernan (son of Tighearnan *little lord*; dark-complexioned; descendant of Cearnachan *little victorious one*) Irish.

Killen (descendant of Cillín *church*) Irish.

Killian (descendant of Cillín *church*) Irish.

Killigan (descendant of the little servant or disciple) Irish.

Killpatrick (servant or disciple of Saint Patrick) Irish.

Kilmartin (servant or disciple of Saint Martin) Irish.

Kilroy (servant or disciple of Ruadh *red-haired*) Irish.

Klaas (victory of the people) Dutch, German.

Koch (a cook) German.

Koe (like a jackdaw) Irish.

Koehler (a coal worker) German.

Lacy (from Lassy *Latius' estate*) **Lacey** French, English, Irish.

Laird (a lord, landlord) Scottish.

Lamb (dweller at the sign of the lamb; like a lamb) English.

Lancaster (from Lancaster *the camp on the River Lune*) English.

Lawler (a mumbler) Irish.

Lazarus (God has helped) English.

Leeson (son of Lece *gladness, happiness*; son of Lee *a wood, a clearing*) English.

Lehmann (a feudal tenant) German.

Lemon (beloved man; dear one, sweetheart) **Lemmon** English.

Lennon (son of the servant of Finnan *little fair one*; son of the servant of Adamnan *little Adam*) Irish.

Lennox (from Lennox *many elms*) Scottish.

Leslie (from Leslie *the holly woods*) Scottish.

Levi (joining) **Levy** Hebrew, German.

Lipinski (dweller near the linden tree) Polish.

Lowenstein (from Lowenstein *lion's stone*) **Loewenstein** German.

Ludlow (from Ludlow *hill of the people; hill of the prince*) English.

Maas (dweller near the Meuse River) Dutch, German.

Mackey (son of Aodh *ardor*) Irish.

Maddock (goodly) Welsh.

Maddox (son of Maddock *goodly*) Welsh.

Magill (son of the servant or disciple) Irish.

Malone (the servant or disciple of Saint John) Irish.

McAdoo (son of Cudabh *black hound*) Irish.

McAfee (son of Dubhshithe *black one of peace*) Irish.

McAndrew (son of Andrew *manly*) Irish, Scottish.

McArdle (son of Árdghal *high valor*) Irish.

McAvery (son of Avery *elf ruler*) Irish, Scottish.

McBaine (son of Bain *white, fair*; son of Beatha *life*) Irish, Scottish.

McBride (son of Bride [Bridget] *strength*) Irish.

McBrien (son of Brian *force, strength; valor; high; kingly*) Irish.

McCarthy (son of Carthach *loving*) Irish.

McCartney (son of Carthannach *the kind one*) Irish.

McClelland (son of the servant of Fillan *wolf*) Irish.

Mauer (a mason) German.

Meier (a servant, an overseer, a farmer) **Meyer** German.

Moeller (a miller) **Mueller** German.

Neumann (the new man) German.

Oppenheimer (from Oppenheim) German.

Otto (rich) German.

Pabst (a priest, priestlike) German.

Paulsen (son of Paul *small*) German, Scandinavian.

Peabody (dweller at the sign of the peacock) English, German.

Pfeiffer (a piper) **Pfeifer** German.

Reichert (stern king) **Reiker** German.

Reuter (a tiller of the soil) German.

Ritter (a knight) German.

Rosenbaum (rose bush) German.

Rosenberg (rose mountain) German.

Rosenthal (rose valley) German.

Rothschild (dweller near the sign of the red shield) German.

Rudolph (famous wolf) German.

Sachs (from Saxony) German.

Sauer (one with a sour disposition) German.

Schaeffer (a shepherd) German.

Schiff (a sailor) German.

Schilling (shield friend) German.

Schmidt (a smith) German.

Schneider (a tailor) German.

Schrader (a tailor) German.

Schultz (a sheriff, a magistrate) **Schulz** German.

Schuster (a cobbler) German.

Schwartz (black-haired) German.

Stein (dweller near the stone) Dutch, German, Swiss.

Steinbeck (dweller near the stony brook) German.

Vogel (dweller at the sign of the bird) German.

Voigt (a steward) German.

Vrooman (the wise man) Dutch.

Wagner (a wagon maker, a wagoneer) German.

Wahl (dweller near the wall) German.

Weiland (from Weilan) German.

Werner (protecting army) German.

Winkler (dweller near the shop) German.

Ximenes (from Ximena) Spanish.

Yung (young) German.

Zacher (God remembers) German.

Zander (defender of mankind) German.

Zeller (from Zell) German.

Zeman (a gentleman) German.

Ziegler (a maker of bricks or tiles; a tiler, a bricklayer) **Zeigler** German.

Zuber (dweller by the little stream) German.

Chapter Four

RECONSTRUCTION THROUGH WORLD WAR II
[1865–1945]

POLITICS

ANDREW JOHNSON TOOK over leadership of the country following Lincoln's assassination. He was born into a poor southern family and had worked as a tailor to support himself before entering politics. Because he had been raised in the South, many felt he would be the perfect person to reunite the Union. (Northern supporters liked him because of his dislike of the Southern Cottonocracy.) But while Johnson didn't believe in slavery, he also didn't believe in allowing equal rights for those newly freed. It was an issue destined to become the center of a bitter fight during the first few years following the Civil War.

In order to obtain readmittance to the Union, former Confederate states agreed to the Thirteenth Amendment abolishing slavery. Southern legislatures found their ways around the Amendment by passing "black codes" designed to keep former slaves from their civil rights and to keep them in virtually the same state as slavery. This was unacceptable to those who had fought for emancipation and expected to see former slaves take their rightful place in society.

The black codes also angered a group within Republican party called the Radical Republicans. They were successful in getting Congress to pass a Civil Rights Act over Johnson's veto in July 1866, then wrote the Fourteenth Amendment to guarantee a person's civil rights under the Constitution of the United States. Congress then refused to readmit any southern state to the Union unless it passed the Fourteenth Amendment. After the "sinful ten" states refused to comply, Congress passed a Reconstruction Act in 1867 (again over Johnson's veto), instituting martial law and sending in troops to guarantee ex-slaves' freedom. According to the act, southern states were not to be admitted to the Union until they wrote new constitutions that were true to the Constitution of the United States. Additionally, the act gave all males over the age of twenty-one the right to vote, except for convicted criminals and those who had fought in the "rebellion." As that meant that all soldiers who had fought for the Confederacy were ineligible to vote, the Act was bitterly opposed but ultimately agreed to. Though federal troops remained in the South for ten years, most of the states had been readmitted to the Union by the end of 1869.

President Johnson refused to sign the Reconstruction Act because he believed it was the states' duty to see to the welfare of the people, not the federal government's. Thaddeus Stevens, the outspoken leader of the Radical Republicans, knew the southern states hadn't cared for their black populations in the past, and he had no faith that they would do so in the future. The two men became mortal enemies over the issue. Johnson accused Stevens of being a traitor and publicly declared he should be hanged; Stevens called for Johnson's impeachment as a "moral necessity" after the president went on a speaking tour during which he ranted about the actions of Congress. The impeachment trial came down to one vote, that of Edmund Ross, a newly elected senator from Kansas. Ross realized that while Johnson had been unpresidential and his ideas prejudicial, the president had not committed the high crimes or misdemeanors required for impeachment. Ross voted in Johnson's favor.

In 1870, the Fifteenth Amendment to the Constitution was passed, guaranteeing voting rights to all black men. Whereas before southern politics had been in the hands of rich white planters, it was now a more democratic affair. Blacks were quickly elected to office by their counterparts. During the years of the Reconstruction, sixteen Blacks served as United States congressmen and more than six hundred had been elected to state legislatures. For the next several years, the Republicans supervised the legislatures of the southern states to ensure their compliance with the civil rights acts. That supervision was eventually relaxed, and southern whites began working through hate groups such as the Ku Klux Klan and political groups like the Democrat Party to terrorize blacks and to work to reverse the laws granting equality.

Ulysses S. Grant was elected president in 1868. Though he was a great war hero and an honest and honorable man, Grant was not as capable as a political leader. He appointed friends and acquaintances to administrative posts and government jobs, and many took advantage of his trusting ways to bilk the American people out of millions of acres of public lands and multimillions of dollars worth of resources. Discontent spread as people grew tired of governmental corruption and the social problems of the South.

Both sides of the presidential election of 1876 ran their campaigns on the issues of corruption and dishonesty in government. Democrat candidate Samuel Tilden, governor of New York, won the popular majority but fell one vote short in the electoral college. A compromise was made between the Republicans and the Democrats whereby the Democrats would give Republican nominee Rutherford B. Hayes the presidency if he pulled federal troops out of the South. The deal was made, the Reconstruction effort ended, and the Democrats resumed control of politics in the South.

Within a few years, blacks had lost nearly all they had gained. They were denied of their civil rights and regularly terrorized by secret societies such as the Ku Klux Klan. Laws were passed segregating blacks and whites in schools, cemeteries, restaurants, streetcars and trains, theaters, and even hospitals. By the late 1880s, white conservatives were manipulating elections by first establishing a poll tax, then requiring literacy tests requiring voters to read a difficult part of the Constitution and explain its meaning. This effectively kept poor and uneducated blacks from being able to vote. But because it also kept poor whites from voting, grandfather clauses were added making eligible for voting any person whose father or grandfather had been eligible to vote on January 1, 1867. Since blacks in the South had not yet received the right to vote by that date, there was no way they could vote now. Reconstruction led to some of the greatest amendments to the Constitution, but it failed in its goal to remake southern society into one in which people of all races could live in harmony.

James Abram Garfield won the 1880 presidential election, but he barely had time to get his administration under way when he was shot on July 2, 1881, by Charles Guiteau, a disgruntled office seeker. Garfield died a month and a half later, on September 19, 1881; his vice president, Chester Alan Arthur, was sworn in as president. Arthur lost in the next election to Grover Cleveland, one of the few presidents to marry while in office.

Benjamin Harrison won the next presidential election, and six more states were added to the Union during his term in office. He also signed several important bills, including the Sherman Silver Purchase Act, which directed the treasury to purchase 4,500,000 ounces of silver each month at the regular market value and to pay for it with treasury notes redeemable in either gold or silver. Harrison won the Republican nomination for another presidential term but lost in the election to former Democrat president, Grover Cleveland.

In 1893, the Cleveland administration was faced with a financial panic precipitated by the Treasury's massive silver purchases through the Sherman Silver Purchase Act. Those purchases resulted in a decline in the nation's gold reserves almost to the point that it would be necessary to put the country on a silver standard; debts would have to be repaid in silver dollars that were worth only sixty cents. The Panic of 1893 was so severe that Cleveland immediately repealed the Sherman Silver Purchase Act over the objections of those in Congress who were supported by distressed constituents from the West, including debtors and silver mine owners. The repeal caused the Democrat party split into two wings: the "gold wing" of the East and the "silver wing" of the West.

Republican William McKinley won the next presidential election. The country soon experienced an upturn in its economic health. Poor harvests in Europe helped raise prices of American produce to a point where farmers were now able to profit, and the discovery of gold in Alaska helped restore the nation's depleted gold reserves. The Republic of Hawaii was annexed to the United States in 1898.

The most important event during McKinley's administration was the war with Spain. The push to annex Cuba had diminished after the island was no longer considered potential slave territory, but Spain's poor adminstration of the island put American financial investments there at serious risk. After the battleship *Maine* was blown up in Havana harbor in February 1898, the U.S. government was given an excuse to intervene. McKinley demanded Spain withdraw from Cuba, and war was announced on April 21 to facilitate that end. Four months later, Spain was ready for peace, and the treaty signed in Paris transfered to the United States the Spanish possessions of the Philippines, Puerto Rico, Guam, and the administration of Cuba. Forces fighting for Philippine independence were forcefully put down in a brutal war that lasted from 1899 to 1905.

McKinley was reelected to a second term. While welcoming guests to the 1901 Pan-American Exposition in Buffalo, New York, the president was shot by an anarchist named Leon Czolgosz. William McKinley died eight days later.

Vice President Theodore Roosevelt assumed the presidency. He was just forty-three years old and the youngest man ever to hold the office. He was reelected in 1904 to a second term. The United States emerged as a world power during Roosevelt's years in office. Cuba was granted independence after ceding Guantánamo to the United States for use as a military base and agreeing to arbitrary American intervention in its affairs. As the United States had other territories in the Caribbean and Pacific, a canal crossing Central America was planned to protect those interests. In 1903, the opportunity to build the canal arose when the province of Panama, under the protection of the U.S. navy, withdrew from Columbia.

In 1904, the Roosevelt Corollary to the Monroe Doctrine gave the United States the right to intervene anywhere in Latin America when local officials were unable to maintain law and order. Under the authority of the Roosevelt Corollary, U.S. armed forces intervened on behalf of American investors and businessmen in Santo Domingo in 1905; in Cuba from 1906 to 1909; in Nicaragua in 1909; in Mexico in 1911; and in Haiti in 1915. Roosevelt also successfully mediated peace between Russia and Japan and won the Nobel Peace Prize in 1905 for his efforts. He was the first American to win a Nobel Prize.

Domestically, Roosevelt followed a progressive policy in which he fought political corruption and illegal business practices. He established the Department of Commerce and Labor, signed a bill regulating railroad rates, and signed the Meat Inspection Act and the Pure Food and Drugs Act of 1906. In 1907, Roosevelt signed an order excluding the admission of Japanese laborers to the country following an outcry about the problem of immigrant workers taking American jobs.

William Howard Taft, a giant of a man, was groomed for the presidency by Roosevelt, and he ended up keeping many of Roosevelt's policies in place after winning the presidential election of 1908. In September 1909, Taft set aside three million acres of oil-rich land, including Teapot Dome in Wyoming, for conservation purposes.

Taft had such mixed results in carrying out Roosevelt's policies that he came under fire from progressives and ended up losing the support of Roosevelt himself. Taft won the Republican nomination for president over Roosevelt, prompting the ex-president to split from the party and organize a new political party called the Progressive Party or the Bull Moose Party. With the Republican vote split, Democrat Woodrow Wilson won the election.

Woodrow Wilson was a two-term president who accomplished a great deal, both domestically and in his foreign policy. He saw to the ratification of the Sixteenth Amendment, which imposed a graduated income tax on Americans, formed the Federal Trade Commission, signed the Federal Reserve Act of 1913 to revolutionize banking, provided federal aid to maintain the nation's roadways, and granted woman's suffrage. Additionally, a treaty was signed in 1916 with Denmark whereby the Virgin Islands were sold to the United States; they became a U.S. territory on January 1, 1917.

War broke out in Europe again, but there was little incentive for the United States to get involved until the German embargo of the British Isles threatened American trade with Great Britain. Wilson warned the Germans not to interfere with American interests, but after they sank four American ships, the United States joined the allied countries of France, Russia, and Great Britain as an associate power and declared war on Germany. In 1918, Wilson put forth a peace plan that was accepted by the Germans.

In January 1920, the Eighteenth Amendment, prohibiting the sale of alcohol, was ratified, and on August 26, woman's suffrage was granted with the signing of the Twenty-ninth Amendment. Wilson's term in office ended in 1921, and he died three years later.

The next president was Republican Warren Gamaliel Harding. During his term in office, the country wound down from the war. The military was demobilized, railroads were transfered back to private ownership, tariffs were raised to their highest levels to protect American industries and produce, and a move was made toward monopolistic practices. Harding presided over a decade of advancement and great prosperity, but members of his administration became embroiled in the Teapot Dome scandal. Illegal practices within the Veterans' Bureau and the Justice Department tainted his last year in office. Warren G. Harding died suddenly on August 2, 1923, in San Francisco, leaving the presidency to Calvin Coolidge.

Coolidge dealt with the scandals and returned the presidency to a state of dignity it was sorely lacking. Secretary of the Interior, Albert B. Fall, became the first Cabinet member in U.S. history to go to jail when he was convicted for leasing part of the naval oil fields of Teapot Dome to private enterprise.

Calvin Coolidge won the 1924 election. He managed to reduce the national debt by $2 billion in just three years and was the favorite for the Republican ticket in 1928, but he announced he had no wish to run for reelection, and fellow Republican Herbert Hoover was elected.

At the Republican convention, Hoover stated, "We in America today are nearer the final triumph over poverty than ever before in the history of the land." Little did he know that just a year later, in September 1929, the stock market would soar to an all-time high when over six million shares were sold, then crash the next day to send the world economy into chaos and usher in the Great Depression. Within a year's time, a run on the banks ended with 1,300 banks closing their doors and millions of depositers losing their deposits.

With unemployment rising to between 4.5 and 5 million, Hoover inaugurated several work programs but steadfastly refused to provide the unemployed with direct aid. In 1930, the immigration of foreign workers was prohibited to keep jobs in American hands. By 1932, Hoover had to agree that getting out of the Depression would be accomplished only with governmental assistance. He created the Reconstruction Finance Corporation to make loans to institutions and businesses to stimulate the job market. It was too little too late. Hoover lost in the next presidential election to Franklin Delano Roosevelt.

Roosevelt's first term in office was spent administering his New Deal program that offered benefits to farmers and the unemployed. Among the New Deal agencies were the Civilian Conservation Corps, the Federal Emergency Relief Administration, the Works Progress Administration, the Agricultural Adjustment Administration, and the Farm Security Administration.

In May 1935, the Works Progress Administration began putting millions of Americans to work building roads, bridges, buildings, parks, and airfields. In August of the same year, the Social Security Act was passed. By 1936, Roosevelt's New Deal program was under attack for misuse of funds and inefficiency, and it appeared to all that he would lose the election to the Republican nominee, Alfred Landon. Roosevelt ended up winning the election, went on to a third and, in spite of failing health, won a fourth term, becoming the first president to break the "no third term" tradition. Roosevelt was also the first president to use the radio for "fireside chats" in communicating the state of the presidency and country, and events surrounding World War II, to the American people.

The years of 1938 and 1939 were spent enlarging the war machine in the face of increased European facism. The top-secret Manhattan Project to develop an atomic weapon helped to further that end and was to play an important role in the next decade.

World War II officially commenced in September when Great Britain, Australia, and New Zealand formally declared war on Hitler. After a German U-boat sunk an American merchant ship in May 1941, Roosevelt issued a declaration of unlimited national emergency but stayed out of the war until the Japanese attacked Pearl Harbor on December 7, 1941. That event shocked the country into immediate action. In January 1942, all aliens in the United States were ordered to register with the government. Two months later, anti-Japanese hysteria led to the forced removal of 110,000 Japanese Americans (75,000 of whom were American citizens) from their homes. There was surprisingly little public outcry to protest such an unbelievable occurrence wherein entire families were loaded onto trains and sent inland to detention camps where they were confined for three years. People lost their homes, their businesses, and their status within their communities. It would take another fifty years before the government admitted its mistake in treating American citizens in such a manner.

The remaining years of Roosevelt's presidency were spent dealing with the war effort. In June 1944, the GI Bill was signed to provide financial aid to veterans, and by the end of the year, it appeared that the war on the European front was entering its final phase. In a February meeting at Yalta, Roosevelt met with Churchill and Stalin. The ailing president had three items on his agenda: The scheduling of a meeting of the United Nations to establish a permanent international organization; persuading the Soviets into an alliance with the United States against Japan, and to make a decision about Poland. Franklin Delano Roosevelt never made it to that meeting. He suffered a massive cerebral hemorrhage while vacationing in Georgia with his longtime mistress, Lucy Rutherford, and died on April 12, 1945.

Though the American people were unaware of the president's failing health before his last election, Washington insiders knew and they weren't comfortable with the thought that then–vice president Henry Wallace might end up as president. Harry S. Truman was chosen to run on the ticket with Roosevelt. Truman had huge shoes to fill after Roosevelt's death. He not only had to take the place of a beloved and respected man and a great world leader, he had to oversee the final phase of the most devastating war in world history.

A day after Roosevelt's death, British and American forces liberated Belsen and Buchenwald, bringing Nazi atrocities to light. The meeting in San Francisco took place as scheduled, with representatives of fifty nations in attendance to draw up the constitution of the United Nations organization and to organize the Security Council in which the United States, Britain, France, China, and the U.S.S.R. would be permanent members. Less than a week later, Dachau was liberated by U.S. forces and Hitler committed suicide; the Germans signed an unconditional surrender on May 7, 1945.

Though the war in Europe was over, fighting continued in the Pacific and Korea. In March, a massive bombing campaign was initiated on Japan. Tons of bombs were dropped on Tokyo and resulting firestorms killed more than 120,000 people. On May 5, a Japanese balloon dropped a bomb over Oregon, killing a woman and five children. This was the first time during the war that civilians were killed on the U.S. mainland, and it aroused tremendous anti-Japanese sentiment.

On August 6, the *Enola Gay* dropped its deadly cargo on Hiroshima. More than 80,000 people were killed in the atomic blast and firestorms, many developed deadly radiation poisoning, and more than 60 percent of the city was destroyed. Three days later, a second atomic bomb was dropped on Nagasaki, killing 40,000 civilians. On August 15, Japanese Emperor Hirohito broadcast a message to his people announcing Japan's unconditional surrender. The document was signed aboard the *Missouri* on September 2, 1945. So ended the most devastating world war known to mankind. American casualties numbered over a million, and it's estimated that 55,000,000 civilians and military personnel died worldwide.

SOCIETY

THE YEARS BETWEEN the close of the Civil War and the close of World War II were ones in which American society underwent massive industrialization and saw some of its greatest achievements. The United States went from being a country of farmers to a nation leading the world in technological advancements.

These achievements included a number of new inventions that were of great benefit and led to a much better quality of life. Electric fans and air conditioners made life a little more bearable during sweltering summers; electric heaters helped during the winters. Indoor plumbing and the electrical appliances that were invented, like the electric stove and washing machine, must have seemed like godsends. Modern bicycles offered cheap alternative transportation and were much easier to care for than a horse. The wireless telegraph, the telephone, the zipper, and the vacuum cleaner were all invented during this time period. They certainly made life much easier, but the one invention to really alter the American way of life was the horseless carriage; the country's love affair with its automobiles continues to this day.

Such an amazing transformation to society was carried out on the backs of millions of workers, twenty million of whom were just off the boat from Europe. Since there just wasn't enough room in the cities of the East for such huge numbers of people, many were persuaded to try their luck out West. Though most who went West were single white men or families, the Homestead Act was worded in such a way that single women were allowed to file claims as well as men.

Large numbers of southern blacks went west in search of better opportunities than what were left for them in the South. Black homesteaders had a more difficult time of it than did whites, mostly because they were practically penniless when they started out, but by organizing and pooling their resources, they were able to help one another. At the beginning of the Civil War, just over six hundred Blacks lived in Kansas. After the turn of the century, more than 50,000 were residing in the state.

The same type of growth occurring in the western states resulted in a number of problems. Chief among them was the "Indian situation." The Indians were guaranteed land west of the ninety-fifth meridian as a permanent home, but railroads were soon built across those lands, disrupting the great herds of buffalo and bringing in a record number of settlers. The Indians didn't just stand by and let the settlers take their land. They defended it the best they could. The U.S. Army stepped in, and from 1865 to 1891, their primary objective was to protect white homesteaders and push the Indians onto smaller and smaller reservations. The resulting Indian wars lasted until the final massacre at Wounded Knee in 1890 where more than two hundred Sioux men, women, and children lost their lives.

The resistance was over, yet the U.S. government was not finished with the Indians. The Bureau of Indian Affairs was formed to oversee daily operation of the reservations, but most of the white agents appointed by the government were crooks. The agents were in charge of buying food, clothing, and all the other items needed to sustain the Indians. What usually happened was that the agents illegally diverted large portions of the supplies to white settlers, leaving the Indians with the barest necessities. Food supplies were often spoiled and blankets were issued that were contaminated with smallpox. Deaths far exceeded births, and by 1910, the native population in the United States had fallen to less than 250,000.

Conditions on the reservations were deplorable, and little was done until Roosevelt's presidency, when a cultural anthropologist and Commissioner of Indians, John Collier, called for major reforms. Part of those reforms included taking children from their homes and placing them in boarding schools to educate them and teach them to fit into American society. These children had their Indian names taken from them and were forbidden to speak their native languages. This resulted in a tremendous loss of culture; the languages of many tribes were lost in just a few years. Living conditions did improve, however, and for the first time in many years, the birth rate surpassed the death rate, and the Native American population began to rise.

America had a virtually open door during this time period. Millions were immigrating, and a significant problem appeared shortly after the turn of the century when it became known that some countries were scouring their jails and asylums and sending their undesirables to the United States. In 1910, an amendment to the 1907 Immigration Act banned the admission of anarchists, criminals, paupers, and people with diseases. In 1924, a new law restricted immigration to 2 percent of any nationality present in the United States in 1890. The Japanese were still excluded from immigration; Canadians and Mexicans were not affected by the law.

World War II created a new American society—one in which women worked outside their homes to support their families and their country. Everybody, even children, chipped in to help the war effort. Patriotism was at an all-time high, as was anti-Nazi, and anti-Communist sentiment.

RELIGION

IMMIGRATION PLAYED A large role in the development of religion during this time period. The Roman Catholic Church had the greatest increase in membership when 4,791,000 Catholics immigrated during the years from 1881 to 1910. The Jews were another group to benefit from immigration. In 1890, there were only 533 Jewish synagogues in the United States Just fifteen years later, there were well over 1,000 congregations. By the 1930s, the number had grown threefold and continued to increase as Jews fled severe persecution and Nazi terrorism in Europe.

As cities grew and America became more urbanized, a number of new organizations arose. Included in these were the Salvation Army, which made its appearance in the United States in 1880 and was active in nearly every large city ten years later. The Church of Christ, Scientist made its formal debut in 1879 and spread quickly through the cities. It was known as the "religion of the comfortable" for its appeal to those not interested in the traditional messages of established churches.

At the end of World War I, a great pacifist movement arose within religious institutions and was particularly strong within the country's colleges and universities, including those that were denominational institutions. They based their beliefs in large part on the Bible verse in Matthew that says, ''. . . resist not evil: but whosoever shall smite thee on they right cheek, turn to him the other also.'' After the atrocities of World War II were made public, many ended up revising their view of total pacifism and were forced to admit that the defeat of the Axis powers was necessary for justice to be served and for lasting peace to be achieved.

At the same time, the Fundamentalist movement began with the publication of a series of books that set forth five fundamentals of Christian truths. Fundamentalists were generally quite strict and traditional in their beliefs, and fought against what they saw as the modernism of Christianity where scientific information was welcomed to explain the mysteries of religion.

NAMING

As in the previous time period, immigration had the greatest influence on the names found in America. Over thirty million people from all parts of the globe entered the United States, making the country truly a nation of nations, and each person added his or her name to the general pool to be drawn from in the future. Most often, however, the native name was Americanized by dropping the diacritical marks, or it was exchanged for an American or English version. For example, the Polish names Laurencjusz and Andżelika were changed to Laurence and Angelica, respectively.

Czech names probably posed the most difficulty for Americans for their unusual spellings and pronunciations, but Czechs were also one of the groups most likely to try to hang on to their native names. Nonetheless, Americans had little patience for the difficult names and were quick to change their Czech neighbors' names for them. It didn't take long for a Czech name like Štěpán to become the more familiar Stephen.

There were also immigrant groups that didn't exchange their names for English ones. German immigrants to the lower Mississippi valley commonly changed their names to French forms, but those who settled in the valleys of North Carolina, Tennessee, and in the Shenandoah often used Scottish and Irish forms of their names. Swedes found their neighbors had difficulty pronouncing names beginning with the letter combinations Bj, Hj, and Kj. To make the names simpler for American tongues, the *j* was usually discarded.

Literature influenced the names found in this time period. The name Janice, for example, was popularized by Paul Leicester Ford's novel *Janice Meredith* (1899). Lorna was an invention of novelist R. D. Blackmore for the heroine of his novel *Lorna Doone* in 1864, and Thelma was a coinage of author Marie Corelli for the Norwegian heroine of her novel *Thelma* (1887). By far the most influential work of fiction was Margaret Mitchell's *Gone with the Wind*, which was published in 1936 and made into a motion picture in 1939. Since many of the characters' names were invented by the author, it's easy to tell just when they became used as personal names. Some of the names attributed to *Gone with the Wind* are Bonnie, Careen, Scarlett, and Rhett. The book also helped popularize Tara as a feminine name.

The advent of motion pictures prompted prospective parents to name their children not only after the characters in the movies, but also after the actors. Vivien Leigh's surname became quite a popular feminine name after her Academy Award. Greer Garson, Ginger Rogers, Spencer Tracy, and Claudette Colbert all lent their names to fashion.

Late in the nineteenth century, a number of feminine names were invented that were based on both flower names and jewel names. Pansy, Daisy, Fern, and Myrtle, and Ruby, Garnet, and Opal are examples. The names of the months April, May, June, and July were increasingly used, both as first names and as middle names. Less invention was seen in male names, but the use of surnames as first names increased.

FEMALE NAMES

Aarona (the exalted one) **Arona**
Abbey (monastery, convent)
Abelia (breath)
Abiela (God is my father)
Abigail (father of exaltation) **Abbey**
Abila (the beautiful)
Abilene (a plain)
Acacia (a thorny tree)
Acadia (village, place of plenty) Micmac.
Ada (nobility)
Adah (adornment)
Adalheid (nobility)
Adama (man of the red earth)
Adelaide (nobility) **Adelaida**
Adele (noble) **Adela**
Adeline (nobility) **Adaline, Adelina**
Adina (ornament, adornment)
Adira (strong, powerful)
Adria (from Hadrianus)
Adriana (from Hadrianus)
Adsila (blossom) Cherokee.
Aemilia (rival, trying to equal or excel)
Agalia (brightness, joy)
Agatha (good) **Agata, Agathe**
Agna (chaste, pure) **Aghna**
Agnella (chaste, pure)
Agnes (chaste, pure) **Agnese, Agnus**
Agnethe (chaste, pure)
Aida (helper, aide)
Aideen (?)
Aiko (child of love) Japanese.
Aileen (?)
Ajalon (place of gazelles)
Akako (red) Japanese.
Alaina (light, torch, bright)
Alana (O child; ?, perhaps *handsome; rock*) **Alane, Alanna, Alannah, Alanne, Allana**
Alba (white)
Alberta (noble and bright)
Albina (little white one)
Albinka (white)
Aleen (?)
Alena (of Magdala)
Alessa (defender of mankind)
Alessandra (defender of mankind)
Alessia (defender)
Aleta (nobility)
Alethea (truth) **Aletheia, Alithea**
Alexa (defender of mankind)
Alexandra (defender of mankind) **Alexa**
Alexia (defender)
Alexina (defender of mankind)
Alfreda (elf counselor)
Alice (nobility) **Alyce**

Alicia (nobility)
Aline (noble)
Alison (noble one)
Aliyah (to ascend) **Aliya**
Alke (nobility) **Alka**
Allegra (cheerful, merry) **Alegra**
Alma (soul; all good)
Aloisia (?, possibly *famous in war*)
Alona (oak tree) **Allona, Allonia, Alonia**
Alonza (noble and ready)
Alpha (ox, leader; first)
Altea (healer)
Althaea (healer)
Althea (wholesome)
Alvera (elf army)
Ama (water) Cherokee.
Amada (beloved) **Amadia**
Amalia (work) **Amalie, Amelia**
Amana (established; faithful)
Amanda (lovable)
Amara (unfading; bitter, sour)
Amaranthe (unfading) **Amaranth**
Amaryllis (?)
Ambrosia (immortal)
Amelina (work)
Amicia (?, possibly *friendship*) **Amice**
Amiela (people of God)
Amity (friendship) **Amyte**
Amma (servant; grandmother)
Amora (love)
Amy (beloved)
An (peace) Chinese.
Anabella (grace, full of grace, mercy + beautiful) **Anabelle, Annabella**
Anarosa (grace, mercy + a rose)
Anastasia (resurrection)
Anatolia (sunrise, daybreak)
Andrea (womanly)
Andreana (womanly)
Angela (an angel)
Angelica (angelic) **Angelika**
Angie (angel, like an angel)
Angusina (one, choice, preeminent)
Aniela (an angel)
Anita (grace, full of grace, mercy)
Anitra Coinage of Henrik Ibsen (1828–1906) given to an Eastern princess in *Peer Gynt.*
Annabel (?, perhaps *eagle; hearth; lovable; joy*; also, *grace, mercy + beautiful*) **Annabell, Annabelle**
Anne (grace, full of grace, mercy) **Ana, Ann, Anna**
Anneliese (grace, mercy + God is my oath) **Annelise**
Annella (grace, full of grace, mercy)
Annemarie (grace, mercy + sea of bitterness or sorrow)

Annette (little Anne)
Annfrid (beautiful eagle)
Annie (grace, full of grace, mercy)
Annis (chaste, pure) **Annice, Annys**
Ann Mary (grace, full of grace, mercy + sea of bitterness or sorrow)
Antigone (of contrary birth)
Anthea (flowery)
Antoinette (?, *priceless, of inestimable worth* is a folk definition)
Antonia (?, *priceless, of inestimable worth* is a folk definition) **Antonie**
Aphrah (dust) **Aphra**
Aphrodite (the goddess of love and beauty)
Apphia (increasing)
Appolonia (of Apollo) **Apolline, Appolina**
April (second, latter; born in April)
Arabella (?, perhaps *eagle* or *hearth*) **Arabel, Arabell, Orabel**
Ardith (prosperous in war)
Arella (angel, messenger) **Arela**
Aria (air; lion)
Ariadne (very holy one)
Arianne (very holy one) **Arianna, Arienna, Arienne**
Ariela (lion of God)
Ariza (cedar panels)
Arizona (little springs)
Arlene American coinage.
Arminel (strength)
Arna (eagle)
Artemis (the Greek goddess of the moon and hunting)
Artemisia (belonging to Artemis)
Artia (?)
Asa (a god)
Asako (child born in the morning) Japanese.
Asela (little burro) **Acela, Asalia, Azela, Azelia**
Asenath (?, perhaps *thornbush*)
Aslaug (consecrated to God) **Aslog**
Aspasia (welcome)
Asta (love)
Aster (a star; the aster flower)
Astrid (beautiful goddess)
Atarah (crown)
Athalia (the Lord is exalted) **Athaliah**
Athanasia (immortal)
Athene (Greek goddess of wisdom, skill, and warfare)
Aud (riches, prosperity) **Aude**
Audny (riches, prosperity)
Audra (noble strength) **Audie**
Audrey (noble strength) **Awdry; Audie**
Augusta (great, venerable)
Augusteen (great, venerable)
Aura (aura, air) **Aure**
Aurabelle (aura, air + beautiful) **Aurabell, Aurbell, Aurbelle**
Aurelia (golden) **Aurelie**
Aurora (the dawn) **Aurore**

Aveline (?)
Avellina (place of hazelnut trees)
Averil (boar battle) **Averell, Everild**
Avice (?) **Aveza, Avis, Avise**
Avila (?)
Awinita (young deer) Cherokee.
Ayalah (deer, gazelle) **Ayala**
Ayumi (pace, walk) Japanese.
Azami (a thistle flower) Japanese.
Azizah (strong) **Aziza**
Azubah (forsaken)
Baptista (a Baptist)
Barbara (foreign woman)
Beata (happy)
Beatrice (bringer of joy) **Beatrix**
Becca (noose)
Belinda (?, perhaps *snake*)
Bella (beautiful) **Bell, Belle**
Belva (beautiful view) **Belvah**
Benedicta (blessed) **Benedicte, Benedikta**
Benet (blessed) **Bennet, Bennitt**
Berdine (bright maiden)
Berenice (bringer of victory) **Berneece**
Bernadean (bold as a bear)
Bernadette (bold as a bear) **Bernette**
Bernardine (bold as a bear)
Berneen (bold as a bear)
Berta (bright)
Bertha (bright) **Berthe**
Bess (God is my oath) **Bessie**
Beth (God is my oath)
Bethel (house of God)
Betsy (God is my oath) **Betsey**
Betty (God is my oath)
Beulah (married)
Beverley (dweller near the beaver stream) **Beverly, Bev**
Bianca (white, fair)
Biddy (strength)
Bidelia (strength)
Billie (resolute protector) **Billy**
Billie Jo (resolute protector + he shall add)
Birdie (a bird)
Birgit (strength) **Birgitta, Birgitte**
Bithiah (daughter of Jehovah) **Bethia**
Blair (dweller on the plain)
Blanch (white) **Blanche**
Blanka (white) **Blanca**
Blossom (a blossom, flower)
Bonita (beautiful)
Bonnie (beautiful, good-natured, cheerful) **Bonny**
Bracha (blessing)
Brenda (sword)
Bridget (strength) **Brigit**
Brigitte (strength) **Brigida, Brigitta**
Calandra (beautiful one) **Kalandra; Callie, Kallie**
Caledonia (from Caledonia, from Scotland) **Callie**

Camille (virgin of unblemished character) **Camila, Camilla, Kamilla**
Careen twentieth-century coinage.
Caridad (charity)
Carina (affection, love)
Carla (full-grown, a woman)
Carlotta (full-grown, a woman)
Carmen (vineyard, orchard)
Carol (full-grown, a woman) **Carole**
Carola (full-grown, a woman)
Caroletta (full-grown, a woman)
Caroline (full-grown, a woman) **Carolina; Carrie, Lina**
Cassandra (?)
Cathalina (pure, unsullied)
Catherine (pure, unsullied) **Catharina, Catharine, Catherina**
Cecile (blind, dim-sighted)
Cecilia (blind, dim-sighted)
Celeste (celestial, heavenly)
Celia (blind, dim-sighted)
Charis (grace)
Charissa (grace)
Charity (charity, benevolence)
Charlene (full-grown, a woman) twentieth-century.
Charlotte (full-grown, a woman) **Charlotta**
Charmian (a little joy)
Chevonne (God is gracious)
Chloe (blooming, verdant)
Chloris (green)
Christa (a Christian)
Christabel (?, probably *beautiful Christ*) **Christabell**
Christiana (a Christian, a follower of Christ)
Christine (a Christian, a follower of Christ) **Christina, Cristina, Khristina, Khristine, Kristina, Kristine; Chris, Chrissie, Christy, Kris, Kristy**
Christmas (born at Christmastime)
Chula (fox)
Chyna (China)
Cicely (blind, dim-sighted) **Cecily, Cicily, Sisley, Sycillie**
Clara Belle (bright, clear, famous + beautiful) **Clara Bell, Clarabell, Clarabelle**
Clare (bright, clear, famous) **Claire, Clara**
Clarimond (bright protection)
Clarinda (bright, clear, famous)
Clarissa (bright, clear, famous) **Clarice, Claricia**
Claude (lame)
Claudette (little Claude *lame*)
Claudia (lame)
Cleare (clear)
Clemence (clement, mild) **Clemencia, Clemency**
Clementine (clement, mild)
Clorinda (green, verdant)
Clotilde (famous in battle) **Clotilda**
Colette (victory of the people)
Colleen (girl) twentieth century.
Comfort (comfort, care)
Constancy (constant) **Constance, Constanze**

Consuelo (consolation)
Coralie (coral; maiden)
Cordelia (?, perhaps *daughter of the sea*) **Cordula**
Corinna (maiden) **Corinne**
Cornelia (a horn)
Creda (?)
Cressida (?)
Crimson (brilliant red)
Crystal (clear, brilliant)
Cynthia (of Kynthos)
Dagmar (splendid day; day maid)
Dagna (new day)
Dahlia (a dahlia flower) **Dalia**
Daisy (a daisy flower)
Damaris (?, possibly *heifer*)
Damiana (tame, gentle)
Dana (God is my judge)
Dania (God is my judge)
Danielle (God is my judge) **Daniella, Danniela, Danniella**
Danika (morning star)
Daphne (a laurel or bay tree)
Darlene (darling) twentieth century.
Davida (beloved)
Davina (beloved)
Dawn (daybreak)
Deana (a dean)
Deborah (a bee) **Debora, Debra, Debrah**
Deirdre (?)
Delfina (from Delphi; the delphinium flower)
Delia (from Delos)
Delicia (delicious)
Delilah (delicate)
Della (a dell, a small valley or glen; nobility)
Denise (of Dionysus)
Desire (desire, want)
Diane (divine) **Diana**
Dido (?) In Roman mythology, Dido was the princess of Tyre, the founder and queen of Carthage.
Dina (sea warrior; famous king; judged) **Dinah**
Dionisa (of Dionysus)
Dixie (the southern states, the Confederacy) **Dixy**
Dolly (gift of God; sorrows)
Dolores (sorrows) **Dolly**
Dominica (belonging to a lord; of the Lord)
Donelle (world ruler)
Donna (world ruler)
Donoma (the sun is there) Omaha.
Dora (gift)
Dorcas (gazelle)
Doreen (little gift)
Doris (Dorian woman)
Dorothea (gift of God) **Dorotea, Dorothy; Dollie, Dolly, Dot, Dottie**
Dorren (sullen)
Dove (a dove)

Drusilla (?)
Dulcibella (sweet and beautiful) **Dulcibell**
Dulcie (sweet) **Dulce**
Dusana (spirit, soul) **Dushana**
Earlene (an earl) **Earline, Erlene, Erline**
Easter (born on Easter)
Ebba (strong as a wild boar)
Eden (delight)
Edith (prosperous in war) **Edyth**
Edmee (love, esteem)
Edna (rejuvenation, delight)
Edwina (prosperous friend)
Effie (?)
Eileen (?) **Eilene**
Eleanor (light, torch, bright) **Eleonor, Eleonora, Eleonore, Elianor, Elinor, Elleanor**
Electra (the shining one)
Elena (light, torch, bright)
Elisabeth (God is my oath) **Elizabeth, Elsbeth, Elspeth, Lisabet, Lisabeth, Lisbeth; Bess, Bessie, Beth, Betti, Betty, Elise, Eliza, Ellie, Elsa, Else, Elsie, Elsy, Ilsa, Liese, Lisa, Lise, Lisette, Liza, Lizzie, Lizzy**
Eliza (God is my oath)
Eliza Ann (God is my oath + grace, full of grace, mercy)
Elke (nobility)
Ella (foreign, other; light)
Ellen (light, torch, bright) **Elen**
Ellis (nobility)
Eloisa (hale, hearty) **Eloise**
Elsie (God is my oath)
Elvira (?, perhaps *amiable, friendly*)
Emelie (rival, trying to equal or excel) **Emelia**
Emma (strength; work) **Em**
Emeline (strength; work) **Emmeline**
Emeraud (an emerald)
Emerlee (strength; work)
Emilia (strength; work)
Emily (strength; work)
Emma (strength)
Emmanuelle (God is with us)
Enriqua (home ruler)
Erika (eternal ruler) **Erica**
Erma (strength)
Erna (capable)
Ernesta (earnest, resolute)
Ernestine (earnest, resolute)
Esmeralda (emerald)
Esperanza (hope, expectation)
Estella (a star) **Estelle**
Esther (myrtle; star) **Ester**
Ethel (noble)
Ethelinda (noble + tender, soft; a snake)
Ethelyne (nobility) **Etheleen, Ethelene, Etheline**
Etta Short form of any names ending in the diminutive suffix *-etta*.
Eufemia (well-spoken) **Euphemia**

Eugenia (well-born, noble) **Eugenie**
Eulalia (fair speech) **Eulalie**
Eunice (good victory)
Eustacia (steadfast; happy harvest)
Evangelina (good news, the Gospel) **Evangeline**
Eve (life) **Eva**
Eveleen (life)
Eveline (?) **Evelina, Evelyn**
Everet (boar hard)
Evette (archer)
Fabiola (a bean)
Faith (faith, trust)
Fanny (from France, a Frank)
Faustina (bringer of good luck)
Faye (fairy) **Fae, Fay**
Felice (lucky, happy) **Felicie**
Felicity (happiness) **Felicite**
Fern (a fern)
Fidelma (?)
Finella (white shoulders) **Fenella, Finola, Fionola**
Fiona (white, fair, clear, transparent)
Flavia (yellow)
Fleur (a flower)
Fleurette (little flower)
Flora (a flower) **Flore**
Florence (a blooming) **Florencia, Florenz, Florinda**
France (from France)
Frances (a Frank, a freeman)
Francine (little French one)
Francisca (a Frenchwoman) **Franziska**
Frederica (peace ruler) **Frederika**
Freya (lady, mistress, noblewoman) **Freja**
Friede (ruler of peace; gentle peace) **Freda, Frida, Frieda**
Fujiko (child of the wisteria) Japanese.
Gabriela (God is my strength) **Gabriele, Gabrielle**
Gail (father of exaltation)
Garnet (the garnet gemstone)
Gay (joyous, lighthearted) **Gae, Gaye**
Gaynel (joyous, lighthearted + light)
Gaynor (white, fair, blessed)
Gemma (gemstone, jewel)
Genesee (beautiful valley)
Genevieve (?, possibly *tribal woman*)
Georgeanne (earth worker, farmer + grace, mercy) **Georgeann, Georgiana**
Georgette (earth worker, farmer)
Georgia (earth worker, farmer)
Georgina (earth worker, farmer)
Geri Originally a pet form of names beginning with *Ger-*.
Gertrude (spear strength) **Gerta, Trudie**
Gillian (youth, downy) **Jillian**
Gina Originally a short form of names ending in *-gina,* such as Georgina.
Ginger (spicy, red-haired)
Gisela (pledge)
Giselle (pledge) **Gisele**

Gladys (lame)
Glenna (mountain valley)
Glenys (pure, holy)
Gloria (glory)
Golda (golden)
Goldie (golden)
Grace (grace, mercy)
Graciela (agreeable, pleasantness)
Greer (vigilant, watchful)
Gretchen (a pearl)
Gretel (a pearl)
Guadalupe (valley of the wolf)
Gwen (white, fair, blessed)
Gwenda (blessed and good)
Gwendolen (fair brows)
Gwyneth (blessed)
Hamako (child of the shore) Japanese.
Hanako (flower child) Japanese.
Hannah (grace, full of grace, mercy) **Hanna, Hanne**
Harmonia (harmony)
Harriet (home ruler) **Harriette**
Haruko (spring child) Japanese.
Hazel (hazel tree)
Hebe (youth)
Hedda (war)
Heidi (nobility; battle protector)
Helah (rust)
Helen (light, torch, bright) **Helena, Helene**
Helge (prosperous, successful; blessed, holy) **Helga**
Heloise (hale, hearty)
Henriette (home ruler) **Henrietta**
Hephzibah (she is my delight) **Hepzibah, Hepsie**
Hermia (of Hermes)
Hermione (of Hermes)
Hester (myrtle; star)
Hilda (battle)
Honey (honey, sweetness)
Honor (honor, esteem) **Honora, Honore, Honoria, Honour, Hanora**
Hope (hope, expectation)
Hortense (a gardener) **Hortencia**
Hosannah (save pray) **Hosanna**
Hughina (heart, mind, spirit)
Huldah (weasel) **Hulda**
Humility (humbleness)
Hyacinth (bluebell, hyacinth)
Ida (work, labor)
Ideny (work, labor) **Idona, Idonea, Idony**
Idonia (of good disposition)
Ikuko (sustaining child) Japanese.
Ilona (light, torch, bright)
Ima (present, now) Japanese.
Imako (present child) Japanese.
Imelda (entire battle)
Imogen (?, perhaps *girl, maiden*) **Imogene**
Ines (chaste, pure, sacred)

Inga (Ing, a Norse fertility god) **Inge**
Ingrid (beautiful Ing)
Inola (black fox) Cherokee.
Irene (peace) **Irena**
Iris (the iris flower; rainbow)
Isabel (God is my oath) **Isabela, Isabell, Isabella, Isabelle, Isobel**
Ismenia (?)
Ivy (the ivy plant, a creeping vine)
Jacoba (supplanting, seizing by the heels) **Jacobina**
Jacqueline (supplanting, seizing by the heels) **Jacklyn**
Jael (mountain goat)
Jamesina (supplanting, seizing by the heels) **Jamie**
Jane (God is gracious)
Jane Olivia (God is gracious + olive tree)
Janet (God is gracious; little Jane) **Jennet**
Janice (God is gracious)
Janna (God is gracious) **Janne**
Jasmine (jasmine) **Jasmin, Jazmin**
Jean (God is gracious) **Jeane, Jeanne**
Jeannette (little Jean *God is gracious*)
Jeannine (little Jean *God is gracious*) **Janine**
Jecoliah (the Lord prevails)
Jemima (pure)
Jennifer (fair lady) Twentieth century.
Jerioth (curtains)
Jeromia (sacred name)
Jerushah (a possession)
Jessica (gift; God is gracious)
Jessie (little Janet *God is gracious*; gift)
Jethra (abundance, excellence)
Joan (God is gracious)
Jocelin (from the tribe of the Gauts) **Joscelin**
Joelle (the Lord is God)
Johanna (God is gracious) **Joanna**
Jonna (God is gracious)
Jordana (descending, a flowing down)
Josee (he shall add) **Josie**
Josepha (he shall add) **Josefa**
Joy (joy, happiness)
Joyce (merry, happy)
Juana (God is gracious)
Juanita (little Juana *God is gracious*)
Judith (praised) **Judit, Judy**
Julia (youth, downy) **Julie**
Juliana (youth, downy)
Juliet (youth, downy) **Juliette**
July (born in July)
Julyann (July, the seventh month + grace, full of grace, mercy)
June (the sixth month, born in June)
Justina (right, just) **Justine**
Kaatje (little Katherine *pure, unsullied*)
Kai (forgiveness) Japanese.
Kaiko (child of forgiveness) Japanese.
Kalliope (beautiful voice)

Kameko (tortoise child) Japanese.

Kaneko (double accomplished child) Japanese.

Karen (pure, unsullied) **Karin**

Karita (charity, affection)

Karla (woman) **Carla**

Karolina (woman) **Caroline, Karoline; Carrie, Karrie**

Katherine (pure, unsullied) **Catherine, Katarina, Katarine, Katerina, Katerine, Katharina, Katherin, Katrina, Katrine, Katryn; Cathy, Kaethe, Kate, Kathe, Kathy, Katie, Katja, Katrien, Kitty**

Kay A pet form of names beginning with the letter *K*.

Keiko (child of reverence) Japanese.

Keitha (?, perhaps *the wind* or *wood*)

Kenna (born of fire; comely, handsome)

Kerenhappuch (horn of antimony) **Keren**

Kerry (black-haired; pure, unsullied)

Keturah (incense)

Kezia (cassia)

Kichi (lucky, fortunate) Japanese.

Kimiko (child without equal) Japanese.

Kinuko (child of silk) Japanese.

Klara (bright, clear, famous) **Clara**

Kyla (narrow)

Kyoko (mirror) Japanese.

Laetitia (happiness) **Letitia**

Laila (night, dark beauty)

Lala (tulip)

Lana (?)

Laufeia (leafy island)

Laura (laurel) **Lora**

Laurana (from Laurentum)

Laurence (from Laurentum) **Laurencia, Laurentia**

Laureola (from Laurentum)

Lavinia (from Latium) **Lavina**

Leah (weary)

Lei (open-hearted, honest) Chinese.

Leigh (dweller in the meadow or woods) **Lee**

Leila (dark beauty, dark as night)

Lena (light, torch, bright)

Leona (lion)

Leslie (small meadow, small clearing, small woods)

Letitia (happiness, gladness) **Laticia, Leticia**

Lettice (happiness)

Levana (white)

Lexine (defender or helper of mankind)

Li (plum) Chinese.

Lida (Lydian woman)

Lilith (of the night) In ancient Semitic folklore, Lilith was a night demon and vampire that lived in desolate places. Medieval Jewish folklore says Lilith was the first wife of Adam, before Eve. She was turned into a demon for disobeying Adam and went around menacing infants and small children at night.

Lillian (lily) **Lilian, Liliana; Lily**

Lilly (a lily)

Linda (beautiful)

Ling (delicate) Chinese.

Lisa (God is my oath)

Lisabet (God is my oath) **Lisbet, Lysbet**

Litonya (hummingbird darting) **Litonia** Miwok.

Liv (life)

Lois (?)

Lorena (from Lorraine)

Loretta (from Laurentum) **Lauretta**

Lorna Invention of R. D. Blackmore for his character in *Lorna Doone* (1864).

Louise (famous in war) **Louisa, Luisa**

Love (love)

Luba (love)

Lucia (light)

Lucilla (light)

Lucinda (light)

Lucretia (riches, wealth)

Lucy (light)

Ludmilla (lover of people, beloved people) **Ludmila**

Lura (laurel; a lure; light)

Lutheria (famous in war)

Lydia (Lydian woman) **Lyddia**

Mabel (lovable) **Mabill**

Mabella (lovable)

Madeline (from Magdala)

Madge (a pearl)

Maeve (?)

Magda (from Magdala)

Magdalen (from Magdala) **Magdalena, Magdalene, Magdelyn; Maggie**

Maggie (a pearl)

Mahala (tenderness)

Mahalath (a lute, a lyre)

Mahalia (fatlings, a calf, a kid)

Mai (sea of bitterness or sorrow; a pearl)

Malene (from Magdala)

Malvina (smooth brow)

Manuela (God with us) **Manuella**

Marah (bitterness) **Mara**

Marcella (of Mars, warlike)

Marcia (of Mars, warlike) **Marcie**

Margareta (a pearl) **Margaret, Margaretha, Margarethe, Margarita, Margrethe, Margriet, Marguerita, Marguerite, Margit, Margery, Margarey**

Margot (a pearl)

Maria (sea of bitterness or sorrow) **Marie**

Mariam (sea of bitterness or sorrow)

Marian (sea of bitterness or sorrow)

Mariana (of Mars; sea of bitterness or sorrow)

Mariel (sea of bitterness or sorrow)

Mariko (ball child) Japanese.

Marilyn (sea of bitterness or sorrow + lake) twentieth century.

Marina (of Mars; of the sea)

Marion (sea of bitterness or sorrow)

Marjolaine (sweet marjoram)

Marjorie (a pearl) **Margery**

Marta (a pearl)
Martha (lady, mistress) **Marthe**
Martina (of Mars, warlike) **Martine**
Mary (sea of bitterness or sorrow)
Mary Ann (sea of bitterness or sorrow + grace, full of grace, mercy) **Mariann**
Mary Kay (sea of bitterness or sorrow + a pet form of names beginning with the letter *K*)
Matilda (strength in battle) **Mathilda, Matilde**
Maud (battle strength)
Maura (great, large; dark-skinned, a Moor)
Maureen (sea of bitterness or sorrow) **Maurene, Maurine**
Mavis (the song thrush)
Maxie (greatest)
Maxine (greatest)
May (a pearl; sea of bitterness or sorrow; born in May)
Maya (goddess of increase; industrious, hardworking)
Mehetabel (God makes happy)
Mei (beautiful) Chinese.
Megan (pearl)
Melanie (dark, black)
Melicent (work + strength) **Milesent**
Melissa (a bee)
Melody (a melody)
Meraude (of the sea)
Mercedes (mercy)
Mercy (mercy, compassion)
Meredith (sea protector)
Meriall (sea bright) **Meryall**
Merry (cheerful, happy)
Mia (sea of bitterness or sorrow; who is like God?)
Michaiah (Who is like God?)
Mikaela (Who is like God?)
Mildred (mild strength) **Millie**
Millicent (work strength) **Melicent, Melisande, Mellicent, Milicent, Millesant; Millie**
Min (quick; sensitive) Chinese.
Minerva (the goddess of wisdom, skill, and invention)
Ming (shining; tomorrow) Chinese.
Miranda (worthy to be loved)
Miriam (sea of bitterness or sorrow)
Missy (who is like God?; a young woman)
Molly (sea of bitterness or sorrow)
Monday (born on Monday)
Moneka (earth, soil) Sioux.
Monica (?) **Monika**
Monique (?)
Moreen (little great one)
Moriya (teacher) **Mariah, Moriah**
Morna (beloved)
Muriel (bright sea)
Myrna (affection, beloved)
Naamah (sweetness)
Nadia (hope) twentieth century.
Nancy (grace, full of grace, mercy)
Nanny (grace, full of grace, mercy)

Naomi (my joy, my delight)
Narcissa (?, inspired by Narcissus, a mythological youth who was transformed into a narcissus flower)
Natalie (natal day; born at Christmastime) **Natalia**
Neilina (champion; a cloud)
Nekoma (grandmother) Chippewa.
Nel (horn)
Nell (light, torch, bright) **Nelly**
Nelleke (horn)
Nellie (horn)
Nesta (chaste, pure, sacred)
Netta (champion; a cloud)
Nettie (light; a short form of names ending in -*nette*)
Niccola (victory of the people)
Nicey (nice, friendly)
Nicole (victory of the people) **Nicol**
Nicolette (little Nicole *victory of the people*)
Nilsine (victory of the people)
Nina (grace, full of grace, mercy)
Noelle (born at Christmas) **Noel**
Noemie (pleasant, beautiful)
Nonie (light)
Nora (a woman from the north; honor, esteem)
Norberta (brightness of the north)
Noreene (little Nora *light*)
Norma (a northman)
Oceanus (of the ocean) **Oceana**
Oddveig (spear woman)
Odette (prosperity, riches)
Odile (prosperity, riches) **Odila**
Ola (ancestor's relic)
Olathe (beautiful) Shawnee.
Olaug (dedicated to the ancestors)
Olga (holy)
Olive (the olive tree)
Olivia (the olive tree)
Olympia (of Olympus) **Olimpia, Olympe**
Onora (honor)
Opal (an opal gemstone)
Ophelia (help, succor) **Ophelie**
Ophrah (a fawn)
Oriane (to rise; golden) **Oriana**
Orpah (a fawn, a forelock)
Orabell (?) **Orable, Oriabel**
Oriana (to rise)
Osanna (save now, save pray)
Paloma (dove)
Pansy (a pansy flower)
Parnell (a rock)
Patience (patience, forbearance)
Patricia (a patrician, an aristocrat) **Pat, Patty**
Pearl (a pearl)
Peg (a pearl) **Peggy**
Penelope (a bobbin)
Pentecost (fiftieth [day])
Peony (the peony flower)

Percy (from Percy, Normandy)
Perdita (lost)
Pernilla (a rock) **Pernille**
Perpetua (perpetual, eternal)
Persis (Persian woman)
Petra (a rock)
Petronel (a rock) **Peternel**
Petronilla (a rock)
Petunia (a petunia flower)
Philadelphia (brotherly love)
Philippa (lover of horses)
Philomena (beloved) **Philomene**
Phoebe (bright, shining) **Phebe, Phebeus**
Phyllis (a leaf) **Phillis, Phylis**
Pia (pious, devout)
Pilar (pillar, column)
Pleasance (pleasant)
Polly (sea of bitterness or sorrow)
Poppy (the poppy flower)
Precilla (former, ancient) **Priscilla**
Precious (priceless, dear)
Princess (a princess)
Prisca (former, ancient)
Prothesia (?)
Prudence (prudent)
Queen (a queen) **Queena**
Queenie (a queen)
Quilla (a quill, a hollow stalk)
Rachel (ewe) **Rachael, Rachell**
Rae (doe)
Ragna (advice, counsel)
Ramona (wise protection)
Raquel (ewe) **Racquel**
Rayna (song of the Lord) **Raina**
Rebecca (noose) **Rabecca, Rebecka, Rebekah, Rebekka**
Regina (queen) **Regine**
Renate (reborn) **Renatus**
Renee (reborn)
Rhoda (a rose)
Richenda (little Richard *stern king*)
Rina Originally a short form for names ending in *-rina,* such as Sabrina.
Rinda (?)
Rita (a pearl)
Robina (bright with fame)
Rolanda (famous land)
Rona (mighty power)
Rosa (a rose)
Rosabel (beautiful rose)
Rosaleen (little rose)
Rosalia (rose)
Rosalie (rose garland)
Rosalind (horse or fame + gentle, tender or serpent) **Rosalinde**
Rosamond (horse protection) **Rossamond**

Rose (a rose) **Rosa**
Roseanna (rose + grace, full of grace, mercy) **Rosana, Rosanna, Rose Ann, Rose Anne**
Rosemarie (rose + sea of bitterness or sorrow; dew of the sea)
Rosemary (rose + sea of bitterness or sorrow)
Rosetta (little Rose) **Rosita**
Rowena (famous friend)
Roxane (dawn of day)
Ruby (a ruby gemstone)
Runa (secret lore)
Rut (friend, companion)
Ruth (friend, companion) **Ruthe**
Sabina (Sabine woman) **Sabine**
Sachiko (child of bliss) Japanese.
Sadie (princess)
Salina (the moon)
Sally (princess)
Salome (peace)
Samantha (name of God) Originated in the southern United States.
Sandra (defender of mankind) **Saundra**
Sandy (defender; sandy) **Sandi, Sandie**
Sapphira (beautiful; sapphire) **Saphira**
Sarah (princess) **Sara**
Sarah Ann (princess + grace, full of grace, mercy)
Sarey (princess)
Sasha (defender of mankind) Twentieth century.
Saskia (?)
Scarlet (bright red) **Scarlett**
Selda (gravel, stone)
Selina (the moon) **Selene, Selinah**
Seraphine (burning one, angel)
Sharon (a plain, a flat area)
Sheena (God is gracious)
Sheryle Twentieth century coinage.
Sibylla (fortune-teller, prophetess) **Sibella, Sibilla, Sybil**
Sidonia (linen cloth) **Sidonie, Sidony**
Signy (new victory)
Sigrid (beautiful victory)
Sigrun (victory + secret lore)
Silver (silver)
Silvia (wood)
Simone (heard)
Solange (yearly; solemn, religious)
Soledad (solitude)
Solveig (house of strength) **Solvej, Solvig**
Sophia (wisdom) **Sofia, Sophie**
Sorcha (bright)
Stella (a star)
Stephanie (a crown, garland)
Suki (fond of) Japanese.
Sunniva (gift of the sun)
Susan (lily, rose) **Suzan**
Susanna (lily, rose) **Susannah, Susanne, Susanney, Suzanna, Suzannah, Suzanne**

Svanhild (battle swan)

Sybil (fortune-teller, prophetess) **Sybell, Sybill, Sybilla, Sybille**

Sylvia (the woods) **Sylvie**

Synnove (gift of the sun)

Tabitha (roe, gazelle)

Tacy (hold peace, be silent)

Talise (beautiful water)

Talula (leaping water) **Tallula, Tallulah, Talulah**

Tamako (jewel child) Japanese.

Tamar (palm, a date palm) **Tamara**

Tamiko (people child) Japanese.

Tamsin (a twin)

Tara (a hill)

Teodora (God's gift)

Tessa (harvester) **Tess**

Thea (truth; flowery; goddess)

Thelma Invention of Marie Corelli for the Norwegian heroine in *Thelma* (1887).

Theodora (God's gift) **Theo**

Theodosia (God-given) **Theo**

Theophila (God's friend) **Theo**

Theresa (harvester) **Teresa, Terese, Therese; Tess, Tessa**

Thirza (acceptance, pleasantness) **Thyrza**

Thomson (little Tom *a twin*) **Thamasin, Thomasin, Tomson**

Thora (Thor)

Tiffeny (Epiphany, manifestation of God) **Tyffany**

Tilda (battle)

Timothea (honoring God)

Tina (a Christian, a follower of Christ)

Tirzah (acceptance, pleasantness)

Torunn (loved by Thor)

Tova (beautiful Thor)

Tovah (good, pleasing)

Troth (fidelity, good faith)

Trudie (spear strength) **Trudy**

Tryphena (delicate, dainty)

Ulla (will, determination)

Ulrike (noble ruler) **Ulrika**

Umeko (plum child) Japanese.

Unity (united)

Unn (love)

Ursula (she-bear) **Urselah**

Valentine (strong, healthy) **Valentina**

Valerie (strong, healthy)

Vanessa An invention of satirist Jonathan Swift (1667–1745).

Vanessa is a partial anagram of Swift's friend, Esther Vanhomrigh.

Vara (?)

Vaunda Contemporary coinage.

Venetia (blessed)

Venus (the loved one, beloved)

Vera (faith)

Verena (true)

Verity (truth, reality)

Verna (dweller among the ferns; of Vernon)

Veronica (true image) **Veronika**

Veronique (true image)

Victoria (victory) **Viktoria**

Viola (violet) **Viole**

Violet (violet-colored) **Violette**

Virginia (springlike, flourishing)

Vita (life)

Vivian (alive) **Viviane, Vivianne, Vivien, Vivienne**

Wanda (?, perhaps *stem, young tree; a Wend, an old Slavic people*)

Wauna (snow geese calling as they fly) Miwok.

Wilfreda (resolute peace)

Wilhelmina (resolute protector)

Willa (resolute protector)

Wilma (resolute protector)

Winifred (blessed peace) **Winnifred, Winnie**

Winona (eldest daughter) **Wenona**

Xanthe (yellow, golden)

Xenia (hospitality)

Yolande (?, possibly *violet*) **Yolanda**

Yvette (little archer)

Yvonne (archer)

Zanna (lily, rose)

Zelda (happiness, joy; ?, perhaps *companion*)

Zenaida (of Zeus)

Zephyra (the west wind)

Zephyrine (the west wind)

Zeresh (gold, splendor)

Zillah (shade)

Zilpah (?, possibly *a dropping*)

Zipporah (a little bird)

Zoe (live)

Zoraida (captivating woman)

Zsa Zsa (God is my oath)

Zuleka (fair) **Zuleica**

MALE NAMES

Aaron (exalted)

Abel (breath)

Abner (the father is a light)

Abraham (father of a multitude)

Abram (father of exaltation)

Absalom (father of peace) **Absalon**

Adalard (noble and strong)

Adalbert (noble and bright) **Adelbert**

Adalrich (noble ruler)

Adam (man of the red earth)

Adelulf (noble wolf)

Adolphe (noble wolf) **Adolf**

Adrian (man from Hadrianus) **Adrien**

Aeneas (praiser)

Aidan (little fire)

Ake (?, possibly *ancestor; agate; blameless*)

Akira (intelligent, smart) Japanese.

Aksel (the father is peace) **Axel**

Alain (?, perhaps *handsome; rock*) **Allain**

Alan (?, perhaps *handsome; rock*) **Allan, Allen**

Alard (noble and strong) **Allard**

Alarik (ruler of all)

Alasdair (defender of mankind) **Alastair, Alaster, Alisdair, Alistair, Alister, Allaster**

Alberic (elf ruler)

Albert (bright through nobility)

Albin (white)

Aldred (old counsel)

Alduin (old friend)

Aldus (old) English.

Aldwin (old friend)

Alex (defender, defender of mankind)

Alexander (defender of mankind) **Alexandre; Alec, Alick, Sander**

Alexis (defender)

Algernon (mustached)

Alick (defender) **Alec**

Aloysius (famous in war)

Alphonse (noble and ready)

Ambrose (immortal) **Ambroise**

Amedee (love of God)

Amias (?, perhaps friendship) **Amyas**

Amiel (industrious)

Amos (borne, a burden)

Amund (awe, fear; edge, point + protector)

Anatole (sunrise, daybreak)

Anders (manly)

Andor (eagle + Thor)

Andra (manly)

Andre (manly)

Andrew (manly) **Dande, Dandy, Tandy**

Angus (one, choice, preeminent) **Gus**

Anker (harvester)

Anketil (god's kettle, sacrificial cauldron) **Anchitel**

Anselme (divine helmet)

Anthony (?, *priceless, of inestimable worth* is a folk definition) **Antony, Tony**

Antoine (?, *priceless, of inestimable worth* is a folk definition)

Anton (?, *priceless, of inestimable worth* is a folk definition)

Antonius (?, *priceless, of inestimable worth* is a folk definition)

April (the fourth month, born in April)

Ara (eagle)

Archibald (genuinely bold, genuinely brave) **Archebald; Archie**

Archie (genuinely bold, genuinely brave)

Aren (eagle rule)

Arend (eagle power)

Aristide (best)

Arlan (foreigner, stranger) **Arland, Arlen**

Armand (soldier, warrior) **Armond**

Armin (soldier, warrior)

Arnbjorn (eagle bear) **Armbjorn**

Arne (eagle) **Aren**

Arnel (eagle strength)

Arno (eagle)

Arnold (eagle ruler)

Arsene (male, virile)

Art (a bear)

Arthur (?)

Arvid (eagle tree)

Asa (healer)

Ashton (from the ash tree settlement)

Asmund (God is protector)

Athelstan (noble stone) **Athestan**

Auberi (elf ruler) **Aubry**

Aubert (noble and bright)

August (the eighth month, born in August) **Auguste; Gus**

Augustin (great, venerable) **Gus**

Augustus (great, venerable) **Gus**

Aurele (gold)

Aurelien (golden)

Austin (great, venerable)

Averil (boar battle)

Aylmer (nobly famous)

Aylwin (elf friend)

Azariah (whom Jehovah helps)

Baird (a poet)

Baldric (bold ruler)

Baldwin (bold friend)

Balthasar (?)

Bannock (exiled, banished) **Banick**

Baptist (a baptiser) **Baptiste**

Barclay (from Berkeley *birch meadow*)

Bardolph (bright wolf) **Bardolf**

Barnabas (son of exhortation)

Barnabe (son of exhortation) **Barnaby, Barney**

Barry (spearlike)

Bartel (son of Talmai *hill, mound, furrows*) **Bertel**

Barthelemy (son of Talmai *hill, mound, furrows*)

Bartholomaus (son of Talmai *hill, mound, furrows*) **Bartholomeus**

Bartholomew (son of Talmai *hill, mound, furrows*)

Basil (kingly) **Basile, Bazil, Bazille**

Bastien (man from Sebasta)

Beau (handsome)

Beavis (beautiful) **Beves, Bevis**

Bellamy (beautiful friend)

Bendt (blessed)

Benedict (blessed) **Benedick, Benedikt, Benedikte**

Beniemen (son of the right hand) **Beniemin**
Benjamin (son of the right hand) **Ben**
Bennet (blessed) **Bennett; Benny**
Benny Short form of names beginning with *Ben-*.
Bentley (from the clearing overgrown with bent grass)
Benton (from the settlement by the bent grass)
Berend (strong as a bear) **Bernd**
Berg (mountain)
Beringer (bear spear)
Bernhard (bold as a bear) **Bernard, Barnard**
Bernt (bold as a bear)
Berold (bear rule) **Berolt**
Berry (a berry)
Bert Short form of names beginning with *Bert-*.
Bertil (bright)
Bertin (bright friend)
Bertram (bright raven) **Bertran**
Billy (resolute protector)
Birchall (dweller near the hall by the birch trees)
Birger (helper)
Bishop (a bishop)
Bjorn (bear) **Bjarne**
Blair (dweller on the plain)
Blaise (deformed, stuttering) **Blaize, Blase, Blaze**
Bo (a householder)
Bonaventure (good travels)
Boyd (son of the yellow-haired one)
Braden (dweller near the broad valley)
Bradford (dweller near the broad ford) **Brad**
Brandon (dweller near the brushwood hill; prince) **Brendon**
Breece (?)
Brennan (descendant of Braoin *sorrow, sadness*; burned hand, a lawbreaker) **Brennand, Brennen**
Brenner (keeper of the hounds; burner of charcoal)
Brett (a Breton)
Brian (force, strength; valor; steep, high) **Bryan**
Brice (?)
Brock (a badger; a young deer; from the brook)
Broder (brother)
Brody (from Brodie *a ditch*; black; son of Bruaideadh *fragment*)
Bruce (from Brus, France)
Bruno (brown)
Buck (a male deer)
Buford (from the ford by the bees) **Buferd**
Burchel (?)
Burton (settlement near the stronghold) **Burt**
Buster (man, boy)
Byron (at the cow sheds)
Cade (lumpy, rotund; an orphaned animal; maker or seller of casks or barrels; one with the physique of a barrel)
Caesar (blue gray; hairy) **Cesar**
Caleb (dog; faithful)
Calum (dove)
Calvin (little bald one)
Cameron (crooked nose)
Campbell (crooked mouth)

Camille (?; virgin of unblemished character)
Carl (a man, freeman) **Karl**
Carlton (from the settlement of freemen) **Carl**
Cary (?, possibly *to move, stir, movement*) **Carey**
Casey (descendant of Cathasach *vigilant, watchful*)
Caspar (treasure master) **Casper, Kaspar, Kasper**
Cato (wise one)
Cecil (blind, dim-sighted)
Cedric An invention of Sir Walter Scott for a character in *Ivanhoe* (1819).
Charles (full-grown, a man)
Chauncey (belonging to Chancey, France) **Chauncy**
Chester (camp of the legions) **Chet**
Christmas (born at Christmas)
Christian (a Christian, a follower of Christ)
Christoph (bearing Christ) **Christophe**
Christopher (bearing Christ) **Christoffer, Kristoffer; Chris, Kester, Kit**
Clarence (from the Clare *bright, shining, clear* family)
Clark (a clerk)
Claud (lame) **Claude**
Claus (victory of the people)
Clayborne (dweller near the clay banks) **Clayborn, Clay**
Clayton (from the clay town) **Clay**
Cleanthes (?)
Clement (gentle, mild)
Cleveland (from the hilly land)
Clifford (dweller near the ford by the cliff) **Cliff**
Clifton (from the town by the cliff) **Cliff**
Clinton (from the settlement by the cliff) **Clint**
Clive (dweller near the cliff or bank of a river)
Clyde (?, a Scottish river name)
Coleman (a coal man, a seller of coal) **Cole**
Colin (dove; victory of the people)
Comfort (comfort, care)
Conall (strength; wisdom; high; wolf, dog)
Connell (wisdom, high-mighty) **Connel**
Connor (wisdom, counsel, strength + aid; hound) **Conor**
Conrad (bold counsel)
Constant (constant, steadfast)
Constantine (constant, steadfast)
Conway (hound of the plain)
Corneille (horn)
Cornelius (a horn) **Cornelis, Corneleus**
Craig (rugged rocks; dweller by the crag)
Crispin (curled)
Crispus (curly, curly-haired)
Curtis (courteous) **Curt**
Cuthbert (known and bright)
Cyprian (from Cyprus) **Cyprien**
Cyriack (lordly)
Cyril (lordly) **Cyrille**
Cyrus (lord)
Dale (dweller in the dale)
Damian (tamer) **Damien**
Dana (a Dane)

Dane (a Dane)
Daniel (judged by God) **Dan**
Darby (from the settlement by the deer)
Darrell (from the town of Airelle) **Darel, Darell, Deral**
Darren (?)
David (beloved)
Dean (a dean)
Delbert (leader of the people + bright, famous) **Del**
Denmark (from Denmark)
Dennis (belonging to Dionysus) **Denis, Denys**
Derek (ruler of the people)
Dewey (beloved)
Dick (stern king)
Diederik (ruler of the people)
Dierk (ruler of the people)
Dieter (ruler of the people)
Dietrich (ruler of the people)
Dirk (ruler of the people)
Dominic (belonging to the Lord) **Dominik**
Dominique (belonging to the Lord)
Donald (world ruler) **Don**
Donatien (given by God)
Donnal (world ruler)
Dorian Invention of Oscar Wilde (1854–1900) for his character in *The Portrait of Dorian Gray*.
Dougal (dark-haired stranger)
Douglas (black, dark + blue, green, gray) **Doug**
Drew (manly)
Duane (little dark one) **Dewayne, Dwayne**
Dudley (from Dudda's lea)
Duff (dark, black)
Duke (a duke)
Duncan (brown warrior)
Durand (enduring, lasting) **Durant**
Dwight (the white one)
Eamon (wealthy protector)
Earl (an earl)
Easter (born at Easter)
Ebenezer (stone of help)
Eberhard (strong as a wild boar)
Eden (delight)
Edgar (wealthy spear)
Edmond (wealthy protection) **Edmund**
Edvard (wealthy guardian)
Edward (wealthy guardian) **Eduard**
Edwin (wealthy friend)
Edzard (brave with the spear)
Egil (point of a sword)
Egon (point of a sword)
Eilert (brave with the spear)
Eilif (immortal)
Einar (lone warrior)
Eldon (from Ella's hill)
Eleazar (God has helped)
Elfred (wise counselor)
Elgin (true nobility)

Eli (high, ascent)
Elias (Jehovah is God)
Elijah (Jehovah is God)
Elisha (God is salvation)
Elkanah (God created)
Ellery (alder tree)
Ellis (Jehovah is God; God is salvation)
Elmer (nobly famous)
Elof (lone descendant)
Emanuel (God with us) **Emmanuel**
Emery (ruler of strength)
Emile (rival, trying to equal or excel) **Emil**
Emilien (rival, trying to equal or excel)
Emmet (of Emma) **Emmett, Emmit, Emmitt**
Engrom (from the grassland enclosure)
Ennis (dweller on an island or riparian meadow)
Enoch (dedicated)
Eoghan (lamb; youth; well-born)
Ephraim (very fruitful)
Erasmus (loved, desired)
Erik (eternal ruler) **Eirik, Eric**
Erlend (foreigner, stranger) **Erland**
Ernest (earnest, resolute) **Ernst**
Errol (?, perhaps *to wander*) **Erroll**
Esau (hairy)
Eskel (sacrificial cauldron of a god)
Ethan (strength, firmness, long-lived)
Eubule (he of good counsel)
Eugene (well-born)
Eusebius (pious)
Eustace (steadfast; happy in harvest) **Eustache**
Evan (youth; God is gracious)
Evelyn (?)
Everard (strong as a boar) **Everhart, Evert**
Everitt (strong as a boar) **Everet, Everett, Everit, Evert**
Ewan (youth)
Ewould (lawful rule)
Eyvind (island of the Wend)
Ezekiel (God strengthens)
Ezra (help)
Faas (resolute counsel)
Fabian (a bean) **Fabien**
Farquhar (dear man)
Fearghas (man of valor) **Fergus**
Felix (lucky)
Ferdinand (peace; journey; youth, life + courage; venture, risk; ready)
Fergus (man of valor) **Fargus**
Festus (?)
Filbert (very bright)
Filip (lover of horses)
Fingall (fair-haired stranger) **Fingal**
Finlay (fair-haired warrior)
Finn (from Finland)
Fiske (fish)
Flemming (a Flemming)

Florence (a blooming)
Florent (blossoming)
Florentin (blossoming)
Florian (flowery)
Floris (blossoming)
Floyd (gray)
Forbes (a field)
Forrest (dweller or worker in the forest)
Francis (a Frank, a freeman)
Francois (French)
Frank (a Frank)
Franklin (a freeman) **Frank**
Franz (a Frenchman)
Franziskus (a Frenchman) **Franciscus**
Fraser (a Frisian)
Fred (elf counselor; ruler of peace)
Frederic (ruler of peace) **Frederick, Frederik, Fredrick, Fredrik; Fred, Freddy**
Friederich (peaceful king) **Friedrich**
Friedhelm (peace helmet)
Frode (knowing, wise)
Fulbert (very bright)
Fulton (the fowl enclosure; a chicken coop)
Gabriel (God is strength) **Gabrial**
Galen (calm)
Gamaliel (the Lord is recompense)
Garfield (dweller near the triangular field)
Garrett (spear rule) **Garett, Garit, Garitt**
Garrick (spear; brave with the spear) **Garek**
Garth (yard, enclosure)
Garvin (spear friend)
Gary (spear of battle)
Gascon (?, possibly *guest, stranger; from Gascony*)
Gaspard (treasure master)
Gaston (?, possibly *guest, stranger; from Gascony*)
Gauvain (battle hawk)
Gavin (battle hawk)
Gedaliah (made great by Jehovah)
Gene (well-born, noble)
Gentry (upper-class, nobleman)
Geoffrey (district; traveler; pledge + peace) **Geffrey, Jeffery, Jeffrey**
Geoffroi (district; traveler; pledge + peace)
George (earth worker, farmer) **Georg, Georges**
Gerald (spear rule) **Gerold, Gerolt**
Gerard (brave with the spear)
Gerhard (brave with the spear)
Gerlach (spear sport)
Germayne (a German) **Germain**
Gershon (expulsion, stranger) **Gershom**
Gervais (servant of the spear)
Gideon (hewer)
Giffard (give + bold, fierce)
Gilbert (bright pledge) **Gib, Gil**
Giles (goatskin shield of Zeus; a protection) **Gillis**
Gillespie (servant of the bishop)

Gillies (servant of Jesus)
Gilroy (servant of the red-haired lad)
Glen (dweller in the glen, dweller in the mountain valley)
Godfried (peace of God)
Godfry (peace of God) **Godfrey**
Godric (powerful God)
Godwin (friend of God)
Goldwin (friend of gold)
Gordon (from Gordon)
Gottfried (peace of God)
Graham (from Grantham) **Graeme, Grahame**
Grant (great, large)
Granville (from the great or large town)
Gregoire (vigilant, watchful)
Gregor (vigilant, watchful)
Gregory (vigilant, watchful)
Griffin (like a griffin, monstrous)
Guillaume (resolute protector)
Gunnar (war, strife, battle)
Gunther (bold in war)
Gustaf (staff of the Goths) **Gustav**
Guy (a guide, leader)
Guyon (a guide, leader)
Haakon (chosen son)
Hagen (chosen son) **Hakan, Hakon**
Haldor (Thor's rock)
Halfert (defender of the rock)
Halsten (rock stone)
Hamilton (from the blunt hill)
Hamlet (little house) **Hamlett, Hamnet**
Hamon (little house)
Hannibal (?)
Hans (God is gracious) **Hannes**
Harald (home ruler) **Harold**
Harley (from the hares' woods)
Haro (wild boar's first son) Japanese.
Harry (home ruler)
Harvey (battle-worthy)
Haward (high guardian)
Hector (holding fast)
Heinrich (home ruler)
Helmut (courageous protector)
Hendrik (home ruler) **Henrik**
Henning (home ruler)
Henry (home ruler)
Herbert (army bright) **Harbert, Heribert**
Herman (warrior, soldier) **Hermann**
Hezekiah (God strengthens)
Hilary (cheerful) **Hilaire, Hilarie**
Hiram (exalted brother)
Hiroshi (generous) Japanese.
Hjalmar (warrior's helmet)
Horatio (?)
Hosanna (save pray)
Hosea (salvation)
Howard (heart brave; high warden; high guardian; ewe herd)

Hubard (bright heart) **Hubbard**
Hubert (bright heart)
Hugh (heart, mind, soul) **Hugo**
Humphrey (warrior of peace)
Iain (God is gracious) **Ian**
Ike (laughter)
Ingmar (famous Ing)
Ingram (Ing's raven; angel raven)
Ingvar (Ing's warrior)
Ira (watchful)
Irving (from the west river)
Isaac (laughter) **Isak, Isaak, Izaac, Izaak**
Isaiah (God is salvation)
Israel (contender with God)
Ivar (archer, bow warrior) **Iver, Ivor**
Ives (archer) **Ivo, Yvo**
Jabez (height)
Jack (God is gracious) **Jackey**
Jackson (son of Jack) **Jack**
Jacob (supplanting, seizing by the heels) **Jakob**
Jacques (supplanting, seizing by the heels)
Jake (supplanting, seizing by the heels)
James (supplanting, seizing by the heels)
Jan (God is gracious) **Janne, Jens, Jon, Jons**
January (of Janus; born in January)
Japheth (enlargement) **Japet, Japeth**
Jared (descending) **Jarod, Jarrod**
Jason (healer)
Jasper (treasure master)
Jean (God is gracious)
Jean-Baptiste (God is gracious + a baptizer; John the Baptist)
Jean-Michel (God is gracious + Who is like God?)
Jedaiah (invoker of Jehovah) **Jed**
Jedidiah (beloved of Jehovah) **Jed**
Jeffrey (peaceful district; traveler of peace; pledge of peace) **Jeffery**
Jeremiah (God will uplift) **Jeremias**
Jeremie (God will uplift) **Jeremy**
Jermaine (a German)
Jeroen (holy name)
Jerome (holy name)
Jesimiel (God sets up)
Jesper (treasure master)
Jesse (gift)
Jethro (excellence)
Joachim (God will establish) **Joachin, Joakim**
Jock (God is gracious)
Joel (the Lord is God)
Johann (God is gracious)
John (God is gracious) **Johnny**
Jonas (dove) **Jonah**
Jonathan (God has given) **Jon**
Joost (just, lawful)
Jordan (a flowing down) **Jordaan; Judd**
Jorg (earth worker, farmer)
Jorgen (earth worker, farmer)

Jorn (earth worker, farmer)
Joseph (he shall add) **Josef; Joe**
Joshua (God is salvation) **Jozua; Josh**
Josiah (the Lord supports)
Julian (youth, downy) **Julien**
Julius (youth, downy)
July (the seventh month)
Justin (just) **Justyn**
Justus (just)
Juvenal (youth)
Kanji (tin) Japanese.
Kaspar (treasure master)
Keir (dark-complexioned)
Keith (?, perhaps *the wind*; *wood*)
Kelly (war, strife)
Kelvin (A Scottish river name) Used from the 1920s.
Ken (the same) Japanese.
Kenji (second son) Japanese.
Kennet (handsome, comely) **Ken**
Kenneth (handsome, comely) **Ken**
Kenrick (royal rule)
Kenward (brave guardian) **Kenard**
Kernan (little black-haired one)
Kester (bearing Christ)
Kieran (little dark one)
King (king, ruler)
Kirk (church)
Knut (knot)
Koji (child, little) Japanese.
Konrad (wise counsel)
Laban (white)
Lambert (bright land)
Lance (land)
Lars (man from Laurentum)
Laurance (from Laurentum) **Laurence, Lawrence**
Lazarus (whom God helps)
Lee (dweller in the meadow or woods)
Leif (what is remaining, relic; beloved)
Leland (dweller near the clearing or fallow land)
Lemuel (devoted to God)
Lennart (brave as a lion)
Leo (lion)
Leon (lion)
Leonard (bold as a lion) **Lennard**
Leopold (bold people)
LeRoy (the king)
Lester (a dyer; from Leicester)
Levi (joining)
Levin (dear friend)
Lionel (little lion)
Lloyd (gray)
Lorens (man from Laurentum) **Lorenz**
Louis (famous in war) **Lewis**
Lovell (a wolf cub)
Luc (light; man from Lucania) **Luke**
Lucas (light; man from Lucania) **Lukas**

Lucian (light; man from Lucania) **Lucien**
Lucius (light; man from Lucania)
Lucky (lucky, fortunate)
Ludovic (famous in war)
Ludwig (famous in war)
Luke (light; man from Lucania)
Lundy (?)
Lyell (lion) **Lyel**
Lyndon (dweller near the lime tree hill)
Maarten (of Mars, warlike)
Magnus (great, large)
Malachi (my messenger)
Malcolm (servant of Saint Columba)
Manfred (peace of man)
Manus (great, large)
Marc (?, perhaps *of Mars; manly; soft, tender*) **Mark**
Marcel (of Mars, warlike)
Marcus (?, perhaps *of Mars; manly; soft, tender*) **Markus**
Mark (soft, tender; manly; warlike)
Marshall (a horse servant, a groom; a farrier; a marshal)
Martin (of Mars, warlike) **Marten**
Marvin (sea hill, eminent marrow; clear lake)
Matheus (gift of God) **Mathiu, Matteus, Mattheus, Matthews**
Matthew (gift of God) **Matheu**
Matthias (gift of God) **Mathis**
Mauger (spear grinder)
Maurice (a Moor) **Meurisse**
Maurits (a Moor)
Max (greatest)
Maxwell (large spring; large stream)
Maynard (strong and hardy)
Meinhard (strong and hardy)
Melvin (?, perhaps *council protector*) **Melvyn; Mel**
Merrill (sea bright)
Mervin (sea hill, eminent marrow) **Mervyn**
Meshach (agile)
Micah (Who is like God?)
Michael (Who is like God?) **Michel, Mikael, Mikel**
Michiel (Who is like God?)
Micky (Who is like God?) **Mick**
Miles (?, perhaps *mild, peaceful; merciful*)
Milo (?, perhaps *mild, peaceful; merciful*) **Milon**
Milton (from the mill town) **Milt**
Mitchell (who is like God?) **Mitch**
Moise (drawn out of the water)
Montgomery (from Monte Goumeril)
Mordecai (worshiper of Marduk)
Morgan (sea bright)
Morris (dark, swarthy, a Moor)
Morten (of Mars; warlike) **Morton**
Moses (drawn out of the water)
Murdoch (mariner)
Murphy (sea warrior)
Murray (from Moray *beside the sea*)
Myron (myrrh)
Nathan (gift) **Nate**

Nathanael (gift of God) **Natanael, Nathaniel; Nate**
Ned (wealthy guardian)
Nehemiah (comforted by Jehovah)
Neil (champion; a cloud) **Neal, Neill, Nial, Niall, Niel, Niell**
Neville (from the new town) **Nevell, Nevil**
Nicholas (victory of the people) **Nikolas, Nikolaus; Nicol, Nicoll, Nichol, Coll**
Nick (victory of the people)
Noah (rest, comfort)
Noel (born at Christmas)
Nolan (descendant of Nuallan *shout*)
Norbert (north bright)
Norman (northman)
Norris (northerner; nurse)
Norval (from the northern town) **Norvall, Norvel, Norvell, Norvil, Norvill, Norville**
Obadiah (servant of God)
Odo (wealth)
Ola (ancestor's relic) **Ole**
Oliver (olive tree)
Olivier (olive tree)
Olof (ancestor's relic) **Olaf, Olav, Olov, Oluf**
Orson (bear cub)
Orville (?) Possibly a French place name or an invention of novelist Fanny Burney for her hero in *Evelina* (1778).
Osanne (hosannah)
Osbern (god bear) **Osborn**
Osbert (god bright)
Oscar (God's spear) **Oskar**
Osmond (God's protection) **Osmund**
Oswald (God's power)
Oswin (friend of the gods) **Ozzie**
Otto (rich)
Owen (well-born) **Own**
Paddy (a patrician, an aristocrat) **Pady**
Parish (dweller at the parish)
Parker (a park keeper, a gamekeeper)
Parlan (son of Talmai *hill, mound, furrows*)
Parnell (little Peter *rock, stone*)
Pascal (Easter, born at Easter)
Pat (a patrician, an aristocrat) **Patt**
Patrick (a patrician, an aristocrat) **Pat**
Patterson (son of Peter *a rock, a stone*)
Paul (small)
Paulin (small)
Pearse (a rock, a stone)
Percy (from Percy, Normandy) **Percey**
Perry (dweller by the pear tree)
Peter (a rock, a stone)
Philip (lover of horses) **Philipp, Phillip**
Phineas (oracle)
Pierre (a rock, a stone)
Piers (a rock, a stone)
Prince (a prince)
Quentin (fifth) **Quintin**
Quincy (fifth; from Cuinchy, Normandy)

Rafe (counsel wolf)
Ragnar (warrior of decision)
Rainier (wise army)
Ralph (counsel wolf)
Ramsey (from ram's island; from the raven's island)
Rand (shield wolf)
Randall (shield wolf)
Randolph (shield wolf) **Randolf, Randulf, Ranulf**
Ranfred (counsel peace)
Raul (counsel wolf)
Raymond (counsel protection) **Raimund, Raymund**
Raynold (powerful protection) **Rainald, Raynald, Renold, Reynold**
Reed (red) **Read, Reid**
Reese (ardor) **Reece, Rees**
Regin (judgment, decision)
Reginald (judgment power)
Reid (red, ruddy) **Read**
Reinhard (brave counsel)
Renfred (counsel might)
Reuben (behold, a son!)
Reynard (counsel hard)
Richard (stern king) **Rikard**
Riley (dweller near a rye field) **Reilly**
Robert (bright with fame) **Rob, Robb**
Roderick (famous king) **Roddy**
Rodney (from Hróda's *fame* island)
Rodolphe (wolf fame) **Rudolf, Rudolph, Rudolphe**
Roger (famous with the spear) **Rogier, Rodger**
Roland (famous land) **Rolland**
Rolf (famous wolf)
Rollo (famous wolf)
Ronald (ruler of judgment) **Ron, Ronny**
Roscoe (from the woods of the red deer)
Ross (dweller on the promontory or peninsula; red, rust-colored)
Roth (famous king)
Roy (red-haired, ruddy-complexioned)
Royce (Roy's son)
Rufus (red, red-haired)
Rurik (famous king)
Russell (red-haired) **Russ**
Ruston (from Rust's estate) **Russ, Rusty**
Rusty (red-haired, ruddy-complexioned)
Rutger (famous spear)
Samson (the sun) **Sansom, Sanson, Sam**
Samuel (heard of God) **Sam**
Sander (defender of mankind) **Sandre**
Sandy (defender of mankind)
Saul (asked for)
Scott (an Irishman, a Scot)
Sean (God is gracious)
Sebastian (man from Sebastia) **Sebastiaan, Sebastien**
Seth (appointed)
Severin (severe, strict)
Shane (God is gracious)
Shaw (dweller at a wood or grove)

Shem (renowned)
Shilo (he who is to be sent, the Messiah)
Shiro (fourth son) Japanese.
Sidney (from Saint Denis; dweller on the wide, riverside meadow; dweller on the wide island)
Siegfried (powerful peace)
Sigge (victory, conquest)
Sigmund (victorious protection) **Siegmund**
Sigurd (guardian of victory)
Silas (ask for)
Silver (silver, silver-haired)
Silvester (a wood, a forest)
Simon (heard) **Simeon**
Sinclair (from Saint Clair)
Siward (victory protection)
Solomon (peaceful)
Soren (apart)
Sorley (mariner, sailor)
Spencer (dispenser of provisions, a butler or steward)
Spiro (to breathe, to blow)
Stanislav (government is glory)
Stanley (dweller near the stony clearing) **Stan**
Stein (stone) **Steen, Sten**
Steinar (stone warrior)
Stephan (a crown, a garland) **Stefan, Steffan, Steffen, Stephane, Stephen, Steven**
Stewart (steward, keeper of the animal enclosure) **Stuart**
Svein (strong, youth) **Sveinn, Sven, Svend, Svends**
Swain (stong, able, wise)
Sylvester (of the woods) **Sylvestre**
Talbot (bandit; lampblack)
Taro (firstborn son) Japanese.
Teague (a poet)
Ted (God's gift)
Terrence (soft, tender) **Terance**
Terrick (ruler of the people)
Thaddeus (God's gift; praised) **Tad**
Theodore (gift of God) **Theodoor, Theodor; Ted, Teddy, Theo**
Theodoric (ruler of the people) **Theo**
Thomas (a twin) **Thomaas, Tomas**
Thompson (son of Thom *a twin*)
Thor (thunder) **Thore**
Thurstan (Thor's stone) **Torsten**
Timothy (honor, respect) **Timothee**
Titus (?, possibly *to honor*)
Toal (people mighty)
Tobias (God is good) **Toby**
Tomi (rich, prosperous) Japanese.
Travis (one who passes through a gate or crosses a bridge or river)
Tristan (tumult, sadness) **Tristram**
Troy (from Troyes, Normandy)
Tycho (hitting the mark) **Tyge, Tyko**
Tyler (a tiler; a maker or seller of tiles)
Ulf (wolf)
Uriah (God is light)

Valdemar (famous ruler) **Waldemar**
Valentine (healthy, strong) **Valentin**
Valery (to be strong) **Valere**
Valient (valiant, brave)
Vaughn (small, little) **Vaughan**
Verne (dweller among the ferns)
Vernon (from Vernon *alder tree grove*)
Victor (victor, winner) **Viktor**
Vidkun (wide experience)
Vincent (conquering)
Virgil (youthful, flourishing)
Vital (vital, life-giving)
Vivien (alive)
Von (hope)
Wade (to go; dweller near a ford)
Walden (to rule)
Waldo (to rule)
Wallace (a Welshman)
Walter (ruler of an army)
Ward (a guard, watchman, warden)
Wayne (a wagoner)
Webster (a weaver of cloth)
Werner (protecting army) **Verner, Warner**
Wesley (dweller at the western wood or clearing) **Wes**

West (west, from the west)
Wilfred (desire for peace) **Will**
Willard (resolutely brave) **Will**
William (resolute protector) **Vilhelm, Wilhelm, Willelm, Willem; Bill, Billy, Will, Willy**
Winfred (blessed peace)
Winston (from Winston *friend's town*)
Wolf (wolf)
Wolfgang (traveling wolf)
Woodrow (dweller near the hedgerow by the wood, dweller in the row of houses by the wood)
Wyatt (little Guy *guide, leader*)
Wystan (battle stone)
Yancy (a Yankee, an Englishman)
Yukio (snow boy) Japanese.
Yves (archer)
Yvon (archer)
Zachariah (God remembers) **Zacharias, Zachary; Zac, Zack**
Zane (God is gracious)
Zebedee (God has bestowed) **Zeb**
Zebulun (to carry, exalt) **Zeb**
Zeke (God strengthens)
Zephaniah (the Lord has hidden)
Zinan (second son) Japanese.

SURNAMES

Just as immigration brought a number of foreign first names to the United States, so did it bring surnames. In fact, there was probably a greater influence on the surnames found in this country than on first names, for surnames were hereditary and weren't readily put aside for American names. That isn't to say the names didn't undergo some type of alteration, however. Illiterate immigrants filing through Ellis Island were often uncertain how to spell their last names. In such cases, immigration officials merely made phonetical approximations of names when registering immigrants. Diacritical marks were quickly omitted from surnames, thus changing their pronunciation and in some cases, even the definition of the names.

Greek immigrants who had to first transliterate their names from the Greek alphabet to the English were more likely to shorten their last names or translated them into English. Alexopoulos, for example, became Alex, and Ioannou (son of John) was translated into Johnson. In Greece, a male child assumed the surname of the father and a female child assumed her father's name in the genitive case. Upon marriage, women changed their middle names to their husbands' first names and assumed his surname in the genitive case. After Greeks immigrated to the United States, these traditions were discarded in favor of the American system of name giving.

Many Irish immigrants had already dropped the Mac and O prefixes from their names in the face of governmental oppression in Ireland, and few added the prefixes back onto their names when they arrived in America. It was only after people regained a measure of pride in their heritage that they attempted to replace the prefixes. In some cases, Mac prefixes were added to names that traditionally only had O prefixes, and O prefixes were incorrectly added to names that were traditionally Mac forms. In addition, because centuries of English oppression prompted many Irish to adopt English names, please also note that many of the names of English origin belonged to Irish immigrants.

Slaves were generally given the same last names as their masters for identification purposes. One of the first things a newly freed slave did was change his or her name, and a number of reasons affected the choice of a new surname. Some chose the names of famous individuals, such as Washington or Lincoln, others chose names reflective of their craft and future occupations, such as Carpenter, Green (a gardener), Mason, Porter, or Smith, or names reflective of coloring, such as Browne or Black. There were some who chose names like Liberty, Freeman, or Justice to commemorate their victory over slavery. There were many, however, who continued to use the surname of their masters, and this was especially true of mulattos and those who wished to take advantage of whatever popularity or familiarity those names might have had.

Aarsen (son of Arthur) Dutch.

Aberdeen (from Aberdeen *the confluence of the rivers Dee and Don*) Scottish.

Ackroyd (dweller at the oak clearing) English.

Acland (from Acland *Acca's lane*) English.

Agnes (chaste, pure, sacred) **Agnus** Irish.

Aiken (little Adam *man of the red earth*) **Aikin** English.

Ahlstrand (dweller near the alder shores) Swedish.

Ackridge (dweller at the oak tree ridge) English.

Alcock (little Allan *?*) English.

Alcorn (from Alchorne) English.

Alemander (a German) German.

Alepin (from the old Pictish name *Ailpean*) **Alpine** Scottish.

Allison (son of Alice *noble one*; son of Ellis *God is salvation*) English, Scottish.

Amundson (son of Amund *awe, fear; edge, point + protector*) French.

Andre (manly) French.

Annis (pure, chaste) English.

Apostol (apostle) French.

Applegard (from Applegarth *the apple orchard*) English.

Arch (dweller at an arch or vault) English.

Archbald (genuinely bold, genuinely brave) **Archbold** Scottish.

Arnaud (eagle power) **Arnault** French.

Arntsen (son of Arnt *eagle power*) Scandinavian.

Arrowkeeper Native American.

Arrowood Native American.

Arthur (?) **Arther** English, Irish.

Ashburn (from Ashbourne *the ash tree brook*) English.

Ashcroft (dweller at the ash tree farm) English.

Ashley (from Ashley *the ash woods*) English.

Ashmore (dweller at the ash tree moor) English.

Aubrey (elf ruler) English, French, Irish.

Auld (old) Scottish, Irish.

Ayers (heir) English.

Bagster (female baker) English.

Bailiss (son of the bailiff) English.

Baird (poet, bard) Scottish.

Balderson (son of Balder *bold army*) English.

Balfour (from Balfour *the village by the pasture*) Scottish.

Bancroft (dweller near the bean farm) English.

Bann (slayer) English.

Bannan (descendant of Banan *white*) **Bannon** Irish.

Bannigan (?) Irish.

Barnacle (from Barnacle *?, possibly* Beornheah's Wall) English.

Barris (son of Barry *from Barry, France; traffic, commerce*) English.

Bearpaw Native American.

Bechtold (bright forest) German.

Bernal (bold as a bear) Spanish.

Berryman (servant in the manor house) English.

Bigdrum Native American.

Bird (a bird) English, Native American.

Birdsall (from Birdsall *the recess where birds existed*) English.

Birmingham (from Birmingham *settlement of Breme's family*) English.

Blanks (a fair complexion, white-haired) English.

Block (dweller at the sign of the block; built like a block) English.

Blue (a bluish complexion) English.

Boice (dweller at or near the woods; boy, young male servant) English.

Bolan (little poet) **Boland** Irish.

Boylan (descendant of Baoghallan *danger*) **Boyland** Irish.

Bradley (from Bradley *the broad lea*) English.

Branagan (little Bran *raven*) **Branigan, Brannigan** Irish.

Brannan (little Bran *raven*) **Branan, Branand** Irish.

Brenan (little Bran *raven*) **Brenann** Irish.

Brien (force, strength; valor; high; kingly) Irish.

Bristol (from Bristol *the site of the bridge*) English.

Buchanan (little small one) Scottish.

Buckhorn Native American.

Buckskin Native American.

Bushyhead Native American.

Cafferty (?) Irish.

Caffery (Gafradh [Geoffrey] *district; traveler; pledge + peace*) **Caffrey** Irish.

Callaghan (little warrior) **Calahan, Callahan** Irish.

Canning (white-haired) Irish.

Cannon (white-haired) Irish.

Cano (white-haired) Spanish.

Carberry (charioteer) Irish.

Casas (house) Spanish.

Casey (descendant of Cathasch *vigilant, watchful*) Irish.

Cassidy (bent, curly, twisted lock of hair; love, esteem) Irish.

Castillo (from Castilla) Spanish.

Castle (dweller near the castle) English.

Castro (dweller near the military camp) Portuguese, Spanish.

Cathir (battle man, warrior) Irish.

Caulfield (dweller at the cold field; dweller at the cabbage field) English.

Cavanagh (little handsome one) **Cavanaugh** Irish.

Chapin (maker or seller of low shoes) French.

Cheevers (son of Cheever *goatherder*; *like a goat*) English.

Climbingbear Native American.

Cochran (from Cochrane) Welsh, Irish.

Coldweather Native American.

Colon (dove) Spanish.

Comingdeer Native American.

Conklin (chieftain) Dutch.

Coogan (a drink, draught) Irish.

Cooney (dweller at the sign of the rabbit; rabbitlike) English.

Cosgrove (from Cosgrove *Cole's grove*) English.

Cowell (from Cowell *the cow hill*) English.

Creek Killer Native American.

Crow Native American.

Cunningham (dweller at the royal manor) English.

Curran (little hero) Irish.

Dagnall (from Dagnall *Dægga's hall*) English.

Darby (without injunction, a freeman) Irish.

Daylight Native American.

Deer-In-Water Native American.

Delaney (dark, black + healthy, whole) Irish.

Delgado (slender, thin) Portuguese, Spanish.

Demonte (from the hill) French.

Dempsey (proud) Irish.

Dermitt (without injunction, freeman) Irish.

Donnelly (brown warrior) **Donnely** Irish.

Donohoe (brown warrior; strong warrior) Irish.

Dorch (from Thuringia) German.

Downes (dweller at the down or hill) English.

Drywater Native American.

Favre (smith, carpenter) French.

Feather Native American.

Federico (king of peace) Italian.

Fishinghawk Native American.

Fivekiller Native American.

Floating Ice Native American.

Flores (flower) Spanish.

Forked Tail Native American.

Fourkiller Native American.

Fugere (steward, overseer) German.

Gallego (from Galacia) Spanish.

Garza (brave with the spear) Spanish.

Gennrich (home ruler) German.

Goingsnake Native American.

Goingwolfe Native American.

Gomez (son of Gomesano *path; man*) Spanish.

Gonzalez (a smith, a metalworker; son of Gonzalo *battle elf*) **Gonzales** Spanish.

Grabowski (from Grabow *the birch tree*) Polish.

Graybeard Native American.

Greenleaf Native American.

Greenup (dweller near the green valley) English.

Greer (son of Gregor *vigilant, a watchman*) Scottish.

Gutierrez (battle sword) Spanish.

Herrera (from the ironworks) Spanish.

Hild (battle) German.

Hinojosa (grower or seller of fennel; from Hinojosa *place where fennel grows*) Spanish.

Hollister (dweller near the holly trees) English.

Kalinski (snowball tree) Polish.

LaLonde (from Lalonde *the grove*) French.

Lampe (land bright) German.

Latimer (interpreter) French.

Leary (a calf, calf herder) Irish.

Legg (leg) English.

Lemoine (the monk) **Le Moine** French.

Linden (dweller near the linden tree) Swedish.

Lindberg (linden tree mountain) Swedish.

Lukin (man from Lucania) Croatian, Russian.

Mac Cabe (son of the abbot) **Mackabe** Irish, Scottish.

Mc Cormick (son of Cormac *chariot*) **Mccormick** Irish.

Mac Cracken (son of Carrachan *rough-faced*) **Maccracken** Irish.

Mc Duff (son of Dubh *black, dark*) **Mcduff** Irish.

Mc Gill (son of Gille *servant, disciple*) **Mcgill** Irish.

Mc Ginnis (son of Angus *one, choice, preeminent*) **Mcginnis** Irish, Scottish.

Mac Goldrick (son of Goldrick *gold ruler*) **Macgoldrick** Irish.

Mack (son) Irish, Scottish.

Mac Nally (son of Failgeach *poor*) **Macnally** Irish.

Macteague (son of Teague *poet, philospher*) **Mac Tague, Mac Teague** Irish.

Maitland (discourteous, rude) French.

Manson (son of Magnus *great, large*; *son of the servant*) **Mansen**

Merritt (a tenant farmer) French.

Moreno (dark-haired) Portuguese, Spanish.

Music (composer, a player of music) Italian.

Omann (fearsome protector; great-grandfather protector) Scottish.

Parrish (dweller at the parish) English.

Pascual (born during Easter) French.

Pellecchia (fur coat) Italian.

Perez (rock, stone) Spanish.

Piccinini (little one) Italian.

Quist (twig) Swedish.

Ramirez (counsel fame) Spanish.

Ramos (dweller near the woods) Portuguese, Spanish.

Reyes (king) Spanish.

Rivera (from the river) Spanish.

Rodriguez (famous ruler) Portuguese, Spanish.

Romero (a Roman; a pilgrim to Rome) Italian, Spanish.

Rooney (red, red-haired) Irish.

Ruiz (famous ruler) Spanish.

Sams (son of Sam *heard*) English.

Sanchez (sacred) Portuguese, Spanish.

Santiago (from Santiago *Saint James*) Portuguese, Spanish.

Santos (holy) Portuguese, Spanish.

Scriven (scribe, clerk) English.
Shutte (dweller at a narrow lane) English.
Silva (dweller in the woods) Portuguese, Spanish.
Soto (dweller in the grove) Spanish.
Tebout (people bold) English.
Teesdale (dweller in the valley of the trees) English.
Tobin (little Tobias *God is good*) English.
Torres (?, possibly *dweller near the tower*) Spanish.

Trout (beloved, deer, friend) English.
Vanderpool (dweller near the pond) Dutch.
Van Patten (from Putten *well, pool*) Dutch.
Vaughan (small) **Vaughn** Welsh.
Vennell (dweller at the small street or alley) **Vennall, Venel**
Whelan (little wolf) Irish.
Wynne (white, fair, blessed) Welsh.
Yeager (a hunter) German.

Chapter Five

CONTEMPORARY AMERICA
[1945–PRESENT]

POLITICS

THE END OF World War II saw not only the beginning of the Korean War, but the beginning of the Cold War. On September 8, 1945, U.S. troops landed in southern Korea; the Soviets were to occupy the northern part of the country. This arrangement was to be temporary until elections could be held, but as time wore on, the United States and the Soviets found themselves siding with the people of southern and northern Korea, respectively.

In Eastern Europe, elections that the allied powers hoped would establish democratic governments showed a decided turn toward socialism. The Soviet Union began to be surrounded by socialist governments, and it was feared that the rest of Europe would follow. In March 1946, Churchill addressed an audience at Fulton College, saying, "An Iron Curtin has descended across the continent" allowing "police government" to rule Eastern Europe. Fear of Soviet power and the strength of the Iron Curtin was to play a major role in U.S. foreign and domestic policy, and it resulted in the space race and new defense systems.

In 1947, the president proposed a new foreign policy to combat Communism. Truman declared, "I believe it must be the policy of the United States to support free peoples who are resisting subjugation by armed minorities or by outside pressures." Known as the Truman Doctrine, the plan put $400 million in military aid and American advisers into the countries of Greece and Turkey. An additional $12 billion was pumped into France and other European countries; the Soviets declined the aid on behalf of its satellite states. As a humanitarian gesture, the Marshall Plan certainly helped the countries rebuild, but behind the gesture was the hope that it would rebuild European capitalism to contain Communism. Ten countries banded together with the United States and Canada to form the North Atlantic Treaty Organization which served as a joint military force for the anti-Communist countries in Europe.

The paranoia against Communism that spread through American society after the close of World War I quickly intensified. Truman established loyalty boards to seek out Communist sympathizers in the federal government. Thousands of federal employees were investigated, and many careers were ruined in this modern-day witch hunt that found little evidence of subversive activities. In October 1947, the House Un-American Activities Committee, led by Sen. Joseph McCarthy, directed its look into American society itself when it began investigating the alleged Communist infiltration of Hollywood.

In 1948, the first clash between Communist and anti-Communist forces in Europe occurred when the Soviets blockaded non-Communist parts of Berlin and prevented British and American supply trains from entering. The Allies responded with a counterblockade and by air-dropping 2.3 tons of food and coal into West Berlin. The seige ended in September 1949, but American fears of Communism continued, especially in the face of the millions of Chinese who were now united under the Communist fist of Mao Tse-tung and Chou En-lai.

In June of 1949, fears of Communism and a ''Red Invasion'' reached such a peak that the president announced a crackdown on those who spread false rumors and promised to dismiss anyone within the executive branch that contributed to the hysteria.

The arms race began in 1950 when Truman directed the Atomic Energy Commission to work on producing the hydrogen bomb—a bomb far more destructive than anything released over Japan. Tensions were also heating up in Korea, and on June 25, 90,000 North Korean troops poured over the thirty-eighth parallel. The next day, Truman authorized U.S. air and naval forces to assist South Korean troops. The United Nations Security Council adopted a resolution on armed intervention in Korea, and the United States found itself at war once again. Instead of fighting the despised Nazis, the country was now fighting its most terrifying enemies, the Communist Chinese and the Soviet-backed North Koreans.

Truman left the Korean problem to Dwight D. Eisenhower, the winner of the 1952 presidential election. On July 27, 1953, the United Nations and North Korean officials signed a truce that ended the war. Conditions of the truce included the establishment of a demilitarized zone separating North and South Korea along the thirty-eighth parallel. U.S. Forces remained in South Korea to ensure peace and provide military aid; economic aid to the country continued.

During the Korean War, the United States had also been supporting the French in Indochina. A conference was called in Geneva to negotiate a peace between the French and Vietnamese, and by July, an agreement was reached to divide the area into Communist North Vietnam and a nationalist South Vietnam. Both the United States and South Vietnam refused to sign the agreement, and because a number of Viet Cong remained in South Vietnam to pursue their Communist agenda, the United States decided to keep military advisers in the country.

Eisenhower and his vice president, Richard Nixon, were elected to a second term in 1956. In May 1958, the North American Air Defense Command (NORAD) was established between the United States and Canada. Less than a year later, Alaska was admitted to the Union as the forty-ninth state; Hawaii followed in August 1959 as the fiftieth state.

The United States next found itself being threatened by the tiny nation of Cuba when Castro signed an economic pact with the Soviet Union and began receiving arms and military personel from Soviet bloc countries. The United States responded by cutting Cuban sugar imports by 95 percent, then severing diplomatic relations with the country.

In 1960, John F. Kennedy became the first Catholic and the youngest man ever elected to office of president of the United States. In his inaugural address, he uttered the famous words, "Ask not what your country can do for you, but what you can do for your country." One of his first acts as President was the creation of the Peace Corps, which gave idealistic young Americans the chance to serve their country.

Meanwhile, the CIA was following through with an Eisenhower administration plan to secretly train and equip 1,400 anti-Castro Cubans to carry out an invasion of Cuba. On April 17, the anti-Castro force landed at the Bay of Pigs. The result was disastrous; over 1,000 were taken prisoner. In the ensuing fallout, Castro suggested an exchange of Bay of Pig prisoners for 500 U.S. tractors. The deal was rejected, and five months later, the United States had to agree to help pay a $60 million ransom for the release of the prisoners. In January 1962, the United States declared an unrestricted trade embargo with the island nation, and in December, the prisoners were exchanged for $53 million worth of medicine, medical equipment, and baby food, and $2.9 million in cash. Looking back, the government should have settled for the 500 tractors.

In 1961, the Kennedy administration sent additional military advisers and the first U.S. troops to Vietnam. Within two years' time, the number of advisers swelled from 1,000 to 16,000. In December 1961, Specialist 4 James Davis was killed by the Viet Cong. He was the first American casualty in what would become known as the Vietnam Conflict.

In November 1963, President Kennedy and his wife, Jacqueline, traveled to Texas to drum up support for the 1964 presidential campaign. His stops in San Antonio and Houston went well, but his advisers knew Dallas was a political uncertainty and urged the President not to go there. Kennedy felt confident enough of his popularity to ignore the warning. On November 22, 1963, both President Kennedy and Texas Governor John Connally were shot during their motorcade ride. President Kennedy died soon afterward in a Texas hospital and Vice President Lyndon B. Johnson was sworn in on Air Force One with a stunned and bloodied Jackie Kennedy looking on.

Just hours had passed when Lee Harvey Oswald was captured and arrested for the president's murder. Two days later, while being transfered to a safer jail, Oswald was shot by Dallas nightclub owner Jack Ruby. Conspiracy theories about who was behind the assassination abounded, and over thirty years later, it is still a hotly debated topic.

Lyndon Johnson knew Americans were tiring of the unending violence, and he made the renewal of social order a cornerstone of his 1964 presidential campaign. Central to his idea of a better society was his belief in putting an end to the cycle of poverty through job training and economic opportunities for the poor and for oppressed minorities, and to imbue the American people with a new respect for the environment. Johnson initiated his program for the establishment of a "Great Society" by forming the Office of Economic Opportunity and by signing the Civil Rights Act of 1964 to ban racial and religious discrimination. After the elections, a Voting Rights Act was passed, the Head Start program was begun, the Job Corps was formed, and Medicaid and Medicare programs were established.

Unfortunately for Johnson, the horrors of the Vietnam War were to overshadow his domestic policy. In March 1965, the first combat troops were sent to Vietnam to protect the air force base at Danang. In July, American troops in Vietnam were increased to 125,000, and in the United States, 35,000 young men a month were drafted to support the war effort, spurring a significant antiwar movement in the nation's colleges and universities.

By 1967, the war had really heated up. The United States was conducting massive bombing raids from bases in Thailand, and peace discussions with North Vietnam had stalled over the issue of the withdrawl of U.S. troops. In May 1967, an eighteen-member International Tribunal on War Crimes met in Stockholm to review charges of U.S. atrocities in Vietnam. Eight days later, the Tribunal found the United States guilty of the crimes of aggression and "widespread, systematic and deliberate" bombing of civilian targets. At home, Johnson came under attack for his policy on Vietnam and an eight-hour parade in New York in support of U.S. troops was overshadowed by increased antiwar protests.

A year later, a war-weary President Johnson agreed to a unilateral cessation of the bombing of North Vietnam, called for peace talks with the Viet Cong, then announced his decision not to run for reelection. Four days later, on April 4, 1968, Martin Luther King was assassinated, touching off widespread rioting across the country. It seemed as if things couldn't possibly get any worse, but just a month later, presidential candidate Robert Kennedy was assassinated following victories in the California and South Dakota primaries.

Richard Nixon won the 1968 presidential election over Democratic opponent Hubert Humphrey. American troops in Vietnam numbered nearly 550,000 and the death toll stood at nearly 34,000. President Nixon was well aware that antiwar sentiment wasn't merely a student protest but extended throughout the American population as casualties and war atrocities were reported on the nightly news. The effort to turn the war over to the South Vietnamese started in June when 814 returning servicemen became the first wave of a 25,000-troop withdrawl from Vietnam.

Releasing American POWs and bringing American servicemen and -women home was described as a top priority of the Nixon administration, but the president had secretly okayed the bombing of Cambodia and deployed nearly 30,000 troops to the area. His public announcement of the Cambodia situation was the reason for the riot at Kent State University that resulted in deaths of four unarmed students at the hands of Ohio National Guardsmen.

June 1972 heralded the beginning of the end for President Nixon when five men, all employed by the Committee to Reelect the President, were arrested for burglarizing the offices of the Democratic National Committee at the Watergate office complex in Washington, D.C. President Nixon denied any prior knowledge of the incident. The military draft ended and by August, the last of the combat troops were withdrawn from Vietnam. Soon afterward, Secretary of State Henry Kissinger traveled to South Vietnam to work on a peace plan, and just two weeks before the presidential election, Kissinger announced that peace was imminent. These events helped the president win reelection in a landslide victory over Democrat George McGovern.

In April of 1973, Richard Nixon's presidency began to crumble. He made his gravest mistake when he addressed the nation on the Watergate affair and took responsibility for the actions of his aides but denied any personal knowledge of the cover-up. During a Senate Watergate committee investigation, the president was implicated in the cover-up, and it was discovered that that all Oval Office conversations were taped; the President refused to turn over the tapes, claiming they held privileged executive information. To make matters worse, Vice President Spiro Agnew resigned in October, following charges of tax evasion. Days later, the Oval Office tapes were turned over to the special prosecutor and were found to have an eighteen-minute gap. Public outrage turned to cries for impeachment.

In December, Gerald Ford assumed the office of vice president. Nixon appeared to be weathering his political storm, but he lost support during the ensuing months of investigations. In July 1974, the House Judiciary Committee opened impeachment hearings and recommended the adoption of three articles of impeachment, charging abuse of power, obstruction of justice, and contempt of Congress. On August 9, 1974, President Richard Nixon resigned his office and Gerald Ford was sworn in as president. A month later, Ford incurred a storm of protest and criticism when he granted Nixon a full pardon.

Ford held the office of president for two years before losing the 1976 presidential election to Jimmy Carter. His inability to curb the severe unemployment and inflation caused by the OPEC oil embargo of the early '70s, the stigma of Watergate, and his pardon of President Nixon no doubt led to his defeat.

Carter was faced with the same economic and political problems as Ford. In September 1994, Ford had proposed giving Vietnam-era draft dodgers and deserters amnesty in exchange for two years' public service work. His idea was rejected by bitter military veterans and by organized exile groups. Carter's first major presidential act involved the same issue. In January 1977, the president granted full amnesty to the 10,000 men who had dodged the draft; his action was roundly condemned by veterans' groups.

Carter's greatest achievement was his role in bringing together Middle Eastern leaders and his work to bring about a lasting peace between them. Carter's worst crisises came from that same region. In November 1979, 500 Iranian militants stormed the American embassy in Teheran and took ninety hostages to exchange for the shah. The president ordered the deportation of Iranian students and froze Iranian assets in U.S. banks; military attempts to rescue the hostages several months later ended in disaster.

James Earl Carter was an honorable person but possibly too nice for the difficult job of president. In spite of his success in helping to bring peace to the Middle East, he had not succeeded in bringing down double-digit inflation or interest rates, nor had he been able to resolve the hostage situation in Iran in a timely manner. America was ready for new leadership, and in November 1980, Jimmy Carter lost the presidency to Ronald Reagan. In what some saw as an omen for the new administration's future successes, the hostages in Iran were released just minutes after Reagan was sworn in.

During the presidential campaign, Ronald Reagan promised to reduce inflation, cut taxes, reduce government deficits, and agressively rebuild the nation's defenses against outside threat. Inflation and unemployment continued unabated until increased competition among oil-producing nations resulted in a drop in oil prices that spurred economic recovery in the United States.

On March 30, 1981, Reagan was the victim of an assassination attempt. Though shot in the chest, he made a remarkable recovery, and it seemed yet again that the president was blessed with extraordinary good luck. Even when his administration was plagued by scandals of corruption and illegal dealings, he seemed to emerge unscathed, earning the nickname the Teflon President.

The 1984 presidential primary was a historical occasion as Geraldine Ferraro became the first woman on the ticket as a Democrat Party candidate for vice president. Nonetheless, Reagan and Bush ended up winning the election with a record 525 electoral college votes and 59 percent of the popular vote.

In 1986, the fight against the production of nuclear weapons and the fear that they might actually be used led thirty-five nations to organize a communications network for the verification and notification of military maneuvers to lessen the chances of accidental warfare. In 1987, the United States and U.S.S.R. signed the IMF treaty that called for the destruction of all U.S. and Soviet nuclear missles. People were more than ready for world peace and U.S. and U.S.S.R. relations began to thaw considerably.

Though Reagan had successfully brought down inflation, unemployment, interest rates, and oversaw great technological advancements, he was unable to bring down the high budget deficits that plagued the nation. His last year in office was marred by the Iran-Contra scandal, where it was revealed that the United States had secretly sold weapons to Iran in exchange for U.S. hostages being held in Lebanon, and that the profits had been funneled illegally and just as secretly to Nicaraguan contras in violation of Congress.

Though many were somewhat disillusioned with the president, he and his programs were still popular enough that many Americans felt the vice president could do just as good a job. In November 1988, George Bush became the first sitting vice president since 1836 to win the presidential election.

Unfortunately for Bush, he inherited several problems from the Reagan administration, including huge budget and trade deficits. He also had to deal with the government bail-out of failed savings and loan institutions. From the end of the Cold War to his military success in Kuwait, George Bush proved to be quite capable in the area of foreign policy. But many also felt he was ignoring significant domestic problems. The American people were growing more liberal in their social views, and they were increasingly finding themselves at odds with the conservative views held by the president.

In the 1992 election, the more liberal Bill Clinton was elected president; he won a second term in 1996. Some believed the candidacy of H. Ross Perot, who ran as an independent, divided the Republican vote and thereby ensured that the presidency went to Clinton. Others believed he won by promising everything to everyone.

Regardless, the new president made history by appointing record numbers of women and minorities to important positions within his administration. Clinton worked to create a more open and accepting social environment by attempting to more fully integrate minority groups into American society. Civil rights, individual rights, gay rights, rights for the disabled—all became issues to rally around. This new stand for individual rights and freedoms gave birth to terms like ''politically correct'' and ''empowerment'' that quickly became the catch-phrases of the '90s.

Clinton overturned the restrictions on abortion that had been imposed under the Reagan and Bush administrations, and he oversaw a great deal of legislation, such as the Family and Medical Leave Act, the ''motor-voter'' bill, and the Brady Bill, which dealt with the purchase of weapons. In spite of his successes in domestic policy, the Clinton administration was plagued with scandals and political snafus from the start. He denied a twelve-year affair with another woman, then later reluctantly admitted to it; a botched ATF raid on a suspected White Supremacist's cabin in the woods resulted in the deaths of a woman, a youngster, and an agent; another botched ATF operation at the Branch Dividian compound in Waco, Texas resulted in a fifty-one-day seige of the compound and the fiery deaths of seventy-two cult members, including seventeen children; the Clintons' long-time friend and deputy White House counsel, Vincent Foster, committed suicide in a northern Virginia park; the unending federal probe into the Whitewater Development Co.; allegations of sexual misconduct by the president; and charges that Clinton obstructed justice and lied under oath about his extramarital relationships.

The United States seems to have developed a different set of values since the time Richard Nixon had impeachment proceedings brought against him for lying. It remains to be seen whether Bill Clinton will be able to weather his political storm.

SOCIETY

THE YEARS FOLLOWING World War II were ones of prosperity and a return to normalcy. Soldiers came home to resume their head-of-the-household status, and many women were again relegated to the position of housewife and mother. In what came to be known as the ''baby boom,'' more than 76,000,000 children were born from the years 1946 to 1964.

With families growing at a tremendous pace, there was a corresponding amount of residential building going on, as was the development of what became known as the suburbs. The first suburban housing development, the dream of William Levitt, was Levittown on Long Island. Levitt's experiment was an overwhelming success, and from 1948 to 1958, more than thirteen million new homes were built for Americans moving from crowded cities to the suburbs.

It was also at the beginning of this time period that American society began its love affair with technology.

TVs began appearing in every household, as did modern washers, dryers, ranges, and dishwashers. Tape recorders, electric blankets, instamatic cameras, microwave ovens, vinyl LPs, and the first situation comedy all appeared before 1950. Americans' love of science fiction blossomed at the same time, especially after 1947, when the first UFO was sighted in the United States.

For the first time since the Reconstruction, civil rights became an issue important to all Americans. On February 2, 1948, President Truman presented his civil rights package to Congress, calling for an end to segregation and discrimination in the workplace. Though Southern Democrats united to oppose Truman's plans, in July 1948, the president signed an executive order barring segregation in the armed forces and bringing an end to racial discrimination in the federal government. In 1954, the Supreme Court ruled that racial segregation in public schools was unconstitutional and ordered desegregation to proceed with "all deliberate speed," a phrase that would be interpreted very differently by different groups.

When Rosa Parks refused to give up her bus seat to a white man in Montgomery, Alabama, in 1955, she had no idea her moment of defiance would change American society. Her arrest prompted the blacks of Montgomery to unite under the leadership of a young Martin Luther King, Jr., and boycott the Montgomery city bus service. The retaliatory measures perpetrated by the community's white population brought the issue of racism, prejudice, and discrimination into the headlines. Soon, blacks from across the country united to demand their civil rights and the modern Black Movement was born.

Anti-Communism had been strong in American society since World War I, but it reached near fever pitch in the '40s and resulted in the House Un-American Activities Commission that was relentless in its search for Communist sympathizers within American society. In the '50s, the Soviets announced they were sharing nuclear materials and scientific information with other Communist countries, and a rerun of the hysteria of the '40s grabbed Americans. People now began to fear attack from Communist China or the Soviets. When the Cuban Missile Crisis heated up, the fear was so strong that millions of Americans constructed bomb shelters to protect their families in the case of nuclear war.

The '50s were years in which the space race accelerated. Scientific research resulted in a number of new inventions and technologies that imbued Americans with feelings of superiority and gave then a renewed sense of pride in the country and its achievements. The first electric power from nuclear energy was produced in 1951; the first live creatures (four monkeys) were sent into orbit in the same year; the first thermonuclear tests were conducted in the Marshall Islands (A year later, the United States agreed to pay $2 million to Japan for damages resulting from the test, which included injuries to twenty-two fishermen and the death of another due to radioactive ash.); the first nuclear-powered submarine was launched in 1954; and the first satellite, *Explorer I*, was sent into orbit in 1958.

Though the Soviets were the first to put a man into orbit on April 12, 1961, Alan B. Shepard, Jr., became the first man to make it into space on May 5, 1961. From there on, American and Soviet achievements in space would continue during the race for the moon. Americans were the first and only humans to make it to the lunar surface. The Soviets chose to concentrate their energies on the construction and deployment of a space station. In the new spirit of cooperation and friendship, space research and exploration has become more of a global venture. Many shuttle flights carry crew members from other countries, and the United States and Russians now often work together on space missions.

At the end of the 1950s, many young people lost the need to conform to society's rule. In 1957, Jack Kerouac's book, *On the Road,* inspired many of America's young people to join the beatnik movement. Central to beatnik culture was the abandonment of conformity and social convention, which manifested itself in a vagabond lifestyle, strange clothing, foul language, and widespread use of drugs and alcohol.

The words "generation gap" took on a whole new meaning in the 1960s. Men and women who had lived through the Depression and the sacrifice of World War II found it difficult to relate to the young people of the '60s with their long, unkempt hair and weird clothes (and sometimes no clothes!), their liberal attitudes and contempt for authority, and their lack of respect for their government. Even the music of the nation's young people was difficult for many older citizens to appreciate. It was too wild, too raw, and too loud compared with the tunes from the first half century.

Soon after John F. Kennedy assumed office, he signed the executive order that created the Peace Corps. At first, those who joined the Peace Corps were mostly altruistic young people who shared a desire to help the poor, or the adventurous who thought traveling overseas would be fun. But, as the Vietnam war heated up and the draft began, it quickly became a sought-after alternative to serving in the military.

In 1961, a series of "Freedom Rides" were undertaken in the South to challenge segregationist practices on public transportation, prompting the Kennedy administration to send in 600 armed U.S. marshals to protect the riders. Two busloads of freedom riders made the trip from Alabama to Jackson, Mississippi, without incident, but once there, Jackson police arrested twenty-seven riders after the riders attempted to use segregated washrooms.

The issue of civil rights and antiwar crusades dominated the social scene of the 1960s. In February 1960, four black college students refused to leave a Woolworth's lunch counter after being refused service. The incident prompted a number of "sit-ins" that became a favored tool of college students to bring their issues to light. People soon began taking a more aggressive stand on civil rights. Hate crimes increased, and a number of black churches were burned to terrorize blacks and to discourage them from voting. Race riots broke out at the University of Mississippi after U.S. marshals escorted James Meredith, the first black to register for admission, to the campus.

Rather than terrorizing blacks back into submission, such activities merely added fuel to the growing black civil rights campaign led by Martin Luther King. In 1963, more than 200,000 people assembled in Washington, D.C. to demand black civil rights and equal rights for all under the Constitution of the United States. The gathering culminated in King's famous "I Have a Dream" speech that galvanized both blacks and sympathetic whites to fight for equality. White radicals retaliated with bombings and assassinations of black leaders. In 1964, Malcolm X announced the formation of a new group of black activists who took a more militant stance against white supremacism. In June 1964, President Johnson signed the Civil Rights Act, banning racial and religious discrimination.

Race riots continued throughout the '60s, as did increasing tensions between the black movement's more militant and antiviolence members. Added to the social turmoil was the women's movement. Televised reports of women burning their bras as a symbolic gesture against male domination were watched on television news along with live coverage of race riots, antiwar demonstrations, and the toll of military casualties in Vietnam. Never before were so many people confronted with so many terrible images. In addition to televised reports from Vietnam, the images of starving children in Biafra were haunting reminders of the inhumanity of man against man.

The war with Vietnam spurred intense antiwar sentiments within large sectors of American society. None, however, so vocally protested the war as the nation's college and university students. Draft cards were burned, antiwar demonstrations were carried out in major cities, and in the coming months, two Quakers and a member of the Catholic Worker movement burned themselves to death in a symbolic gesture.

There were many achievements during the 1960s that had a profound effect on American society. Medical research paid off in the discovery of new vaccines to prevent diseases like polio, measles, and the mumps;

cardiologist J. R. Jude introduced external cardiac massage to save the lives of heart attack victims; the first heart transplants were performed; the link between cigarette smoking and cancer was made; and the first *in vitro* fertilization of human egg cells was successfully carried out. One of the most positive experiences of the 1960s, and even of history, occurred on July 20, 1969, when Neil Armstrong became the first human to set foot on the moon and imortalize the words: "One small leap for a man, one giant leap for mankind."

The turbulent '60s seemed to have wrung all it could out of the American people. By the end of the Vietnam War, many were again ready for a return to a more settled society. Scientific, medical, and technological advancements continued and got an even more eager welcome during the oil crisis of the '70s. And with the nation drowning in garbage and gasping in smog-filled air, environmentalism became the next social issue to tackle. The philosophy of recycling was taught in the nation's schools and recycling efforts were started around the country. Acid rain became a hotly debated topic, as did global warming and the greenhouse effect, and the destruction of the Amazon rain forest. In general, most people in the United States now have a sense of environmental awareness and understand the role environmental health plays on society, but there are still bitter arguments about the best way to balance a healthy environment with the realities of progress and growth.

RELIGION

FOLLOWING WORLD WAR II, representatives from 135 church organizations from forty countries met in Amsterdam to form a World Council of Churches. Rather than working for a unified world church, the council was formed to bring together the world's Christians to discuss world issues and to work to spread Christianity to all corners of the world. Missing from the Amsterdam meeting were the Roman Catholics, the Russian Orthodox, the Southern Baptists, and the Missouri Synod Lutherans.

A renewed interest in religion was sparked in 1947 when a shepherd boy found several scrolls of papyrus and leather in a cave near Jericho. The "Dead Sea Scrolls" as they came to be known, were versions of the Old Testament and other religious writings of a Jewish sect called the Essenes and were dated from 100 B.C. to 70 A.D.

Religion managed to work its way out of the confines of church walls shortly thereafter. Billy Graham was one of the most successful in bringing religion out into the open where it could be celebrated freely and enthusiastically. His evangelical meetings grew larger and larger, until huge stadiums and sports arenas were necessary to seat all his followers. Graham and other religious leaders like him were quick to recognize the potential of television, and they used that medium with great effectiveness to convert people and to obtain monetary support.

In 1958, many of the nation's churches began allowing women to serve as ministers. In June 1962, the Supreme Court, in a six to one decision, ruled that the recitation of a prayer in New York public schools was unconstitutional and a violation of the separation of Church and state.

Just as the '60s were years of social experimentation, so were they years of religious experimentation. There was a marked increase in Satanism, Wicca, and off-beat groups like Timothy Leary's League of Spiritual Discovery, which declared itself a religion based on the "sacramental" use of marijuana, peyote, LSD, and other drugs. The Beatles' association with their Indian guru led others to seek out Eastern religions, and the number of people dropping everything to join religious cults was significant. Few who actually experienced the sixties can forget the "Moonies," who frequented airports and other public places with their flowers and requests for monetary donations.

In the '70s, cult leader Jim Jones persuaded hundreds to follow him to create Jonestown, a new cult compound in Guyana. The people spent several years toiling to sustain the community and just as many years being brainwashed by a deranged and fanatical Jones, who directed several mock-mass-suicide trials. In 1978, Jones convinced cult members that their lives on earth were threatened and directed them to take part in a mass suicide. With poison-laced Kool-Aid, 911 members took their lives and the lives of their children. The aftermath of the horror of Jonestown was televised, shocking the world and spurring anticult sentiments.

By the 1980s, religious experimentation was drawing to a close. The conservative movement in politics and conservative leanings in society were reflected in increased membership in more traditional religious organizations.

In 1978, Roman Catholics gained a new leader when Karol Cardinal Wojtyla became Pope John Paul II, the first non-Italian Pope since 1523. Unlike many pontiffs of the past, Pope John Paul is a warm and concerned individual and has spent a great deal of time traveling to give public addresses to the world's Catholics. His popularity grew quickly and he is well-respected by Catholics and world leaders alike. On a similar note, Elizabeth Ann Seton was canonized in 1975, becoming the first American-born saint.

Many of America's blacks have converted to Islam over the last decade, and it is that religion that continues to be the fastest growing in the United States.

NAMING

THOUGH THE MORE common Bible names like John, James, Matthew, Hannah, and Mary remain popular, many of the Old Testament names have fallen by the wayside. Abner, Abraham, Hiram, Esther, and Eunice are examples of biblical names that were common at the beginning of the century but are now seldom used. One biblical name that was quite unpopular in the past but has made a strong resurgence in the last few years is the name Noah.

For females, modern naming trends are a significant departure from the traditions of the past. One of the most significant trends is the increased use of surnames for given names. This originated as a southern tradition, but it has since spread across the country. Originally, the eldest female child was given the mother's maiden name as a first or middle name. While this still happens, unrelated surnames are increasingly used. Some of the most popular surnames for females are Ashley, Bailey, Blair, Madison, and Taylor. Another trend is the use of male names for females. Drew, Michael, and Toby are examples.

Flower and gemstone names are still popular choices, but they have also been modernized. Names like Pansy, Primrose, and Violet have been exchanged for names like Daisy, Holly, Ivy, and Willow. Jewel names like Opal, Pearl, and Ruby have seen their popularity wane in favor of names like Amber, Jade, and Chalcedony.

The same surname-as-a-first-name trend applies to males, and most of the popular male names are drawn from that category. Examples are: Blake, Brandon, Cameron, Cody, Hunter, Parker, Tanner, and Taylor. Another trend is the use of vocabulary words as names. Most of the words are descriptive or have nature themes and were very popular in the '60s. Examples are names like Bay, Bear, Buck, Free, Hawk, Ridge, River, Talon, and Trail. Even unusual names like Antelope were used. Place names are another source Americans draw from. Names like Dakota, Dallas, Kodiak, Montana, and Nevada are used more often than ever before.

As these kinds of names became popular, they replaced many of the traditional names that were popular for centuries. Names like Florence, Verna, and Shirley for women, and Albert, Alfred, Bernard, and even Charles for men are regarded as old-fashioned and are rarely used today, though they were quite popular during the first half century.

Besides using surnames as first names, the most popular name trend today is free invention. Parents will often create a new name from elements of other names or will build upon name elements such as *-eesha* or *-tae*. The prefixes *La-* and *Sha-* form the foundations for contemporary names of both sexes, as does the Irish name Sean and its many Americanized variants. America's blacks have led the way in this kind of naming for the last hundred years.

Today, television and movies have a greater impact on the names bestowed upon children than does literature. Actors, sports personalities, and the names of favored characters from television shows and movies are increasingly used. In recent years, cultural stereotypes and influences have meant the death sentence for a number of names. Gay, a very popular name fifty years ago, is rarely used today, and the same is true with the name Bruce. Dorcas fell from grace when the slang term ''dork'' became so popular, and Biddy was quickly abandoned after the word ''biddy'' became a term for a cranky old lady. Fanny lost favor when the name became a common word for a derriere, and the name Elvira is now linked to that black-haired, witchy woman of late night TV.

FEMALE NAMES

Aaliyah (to ascend) **Aliah, Aliya, Aliyah**
Aba (born on Thursday) Ghanaian.
Abana (stony)
Abbey (monastery, convent)
Abelia (breath)
Abigail (father of exaltation) **Abbey**
Abila (the beautiful)
Abilene (a plain)
Acacia (a thorny tree)
Acadia (village, place of plenty) Micmac.
Ada (nobility)
Adah (adornment)
Adelaide (nobility) **Adelaida**
Adele (noble) **Adela**
Adeline (nobility) **Adaline, Adelina**
Adina (ornament, adornment)
Adira (strong, powerful)
Adria (from Hadrianus)
Adriana (from Hadrianus)
Adsila (blossom) Cherokee.
Aemilia (rival, trying to equal or excel)
Aideen (?)
Aiko (child of love) Japanese.
Aileen (?)
Aimee (beloved) **Amie, Amy**
Aisha (life; alive and well) **Aishah, Ayesha, Ayisha** Used mainly from the '60s.
Ajalon (place of gazelles)
Akako (red) Japanese.
Alaina (light, torch, bright)
Alana (O child; ?, perhaps *handsome; rock*) **Alane, Alanna, Alannah, Alanne, Allana**
Alberta (noble and bright)

Aleece (nobility) **Aleese, Alleece**
Aleen (?)
Alena (of Magdala)
Alessa (defender of mankind)
Alessandra (defender of mankind)
Alessia (defender)
Aleta (nobility)
Alethea (truth) **Alethea, Aletheia, Alithea**
Alexa (defender of mankind)
Alexandra (defender of mankind) **Alexa**
Alexia (defender)
Alexina (defender of mankind)
Alfreda (elf counselor)
Alice (nobility) **Alyce**
Alicia (nobility) **Aleesha, Alisha**
Alisha (protected by God)
Alison (noble one) **Allison, Alysson**
Aliyah (to ascend) **Aliya**
Alke (nobility) **Alka**
Allegra (cheerful, merry) **Alegra**
Alma (soul; all good)
Aloisia (?, possibly *famous in war*)
Alona (oak tree) **Allona, Allonia, Alonia**
Alonza (noble and ready)
Alpha (ox, leader; first)
Alsace Taken from the area of Alsace-Lorraine in France.
Althaea (healer)
Althea (wholesome)
Ama (water) Cherokee.
Amalia (work) **Amalie, Amelia**
Amana (established; faithful)
Amanda (lovable)
Amara (unfading; bitter, sour)

Amaranthe (unfading) **Amaranth**
Amaryllis (?)
Amber (a translucent fossil resin; the sky; fabric)
Ambrosia (immortal)
Amicia (?, possibly *friendship*) **Amice**
Amiela (people of God)
Amity (friendship) **Amyte**
Amma (servant; grandmother)
Amora (love)
Amy (beloved)
An (peace) Chinese.
Anabella (grace, full of grace, mercy + beautiful) **Anabelle, Annabella**
Anarosa (grace, mercy + a rose)
Anastasia (resurrection)
Anatolia (sunrise, daybreak)
Andelee Contemporary coinage.
Andrea (womanly)
Andreana (womanly)
Angela (an angel)
Angelica (angelic) **Angelika**
Angie (angel, like an angel)
Aniela (an angel)
Anisha (lord; supreme)
Anita (grace, full of grace, mercy)
Anitra Coinage of Henrik Ibsen (1828–1906) given to an Eastern princess in *Peer Gynt*.
Annabel (?, perhaps *eagle; hearth; lovable; joy*; also, *grace, mercy + beautiful*) **Annabell, Annabelle**
Anne (grace, full of grace, mercy) **Ana, Ann, Anna**
Anneliese (grace, mercy + God is my oath) **Annelise**
Annella (grace, full of grace, mercy)
Annemarie (grace, mercy + sea of bitterness or sorrow)
Annette (little Anne)
Annie (grace, full of grace, mercy)
Annis (chaste, pure) **Annice, Annys**
Antigone (of contrary birth)
Anthea (flowery)
Antoinette (?, *priceless, of inestimable worth* is a folk definition)
Antonia (?, *priceless, of inestimable worth* is a folk definition) **Antonie**
Aphrodite (the goddess of love and beauty)
Appolonia (of Apollo) **Apolline, Appolina**
April (second, latter; born in April)
Arabella (?, perhaps *eagle* or *hearth*) **Arabel, Arabell, Orabel**
Ardith (prosperous in war)
Arella (angel, messenger) **Arela**
Aria (air; lion)
Ariadne (very holy one)
Arianne (very holy one) **Arianna, Arienna, Arienne**
Ariel (lion of God) **Ariela**
Ariza (cedar panels)
Arizona (little springs)
Arlene American coinage. **Arleen, Arline**

Arminel (strength)
Arnett (little eagle) **Arnet, Arnette**
Artemis (the Greek goddess of the moon and hunting)
Artemisia (belonging to Artemis)
Artia (?)
Asako (child born in the morning) Japanese.
Asela (little burro) **Acela, Asalia, Azela, Azelia**
Asenath (?, perhaps *thornbush*)
Ashley (dweller near the ash tree forest)
Asia Borrowed from the name of the continent.
Aspasia (welcome)
Asta (love)
Aster (a star; the aster flower)
Astrid (beautiful goddess)
Athalia (the Lord is exalted) **Athaliah**
Athanasia (immortal)
Athene (Greek goddess of wisdom, skill, and warfare)
Aubrey (elf ruler) **Aubree, Aubri, Aubry**
Audny (riches, prosperity)
Audra (noble strength) **Audie**
Audrey (noble strength) **Awdry; Audie**
Augusta (great, venerable)
Aura (aura, air) **Aure**
Aurabelle (aura, air + beautiful) **Aurabell, Aurbell, Aurbelle**
Aurelia (golden) **Aurelie**
Aurora (the dawn) **Aurore**
Autumn (autumn, fall)
Aveline (?)
Avellina (place of hazelnut trees)
Averil (boar battle) **Averell, Everild**
Avice (?) **Aveza, Avis, Avise**
Awinita (young deer) Cherokee.
Ayalah (deer, gazelle) **Ayala**
Ayumi (pace, walk) Japanese.
Azami (a thistle flower) Japanese.
Azizah (strong) **Aziza**
Azubah (forsaken)
Bailey (administrator; an officer of justice; worker near the castle baile; from the berry clearing)
Baines (from Baines, France; white, fair, pale)
Bambi (female baby) Popularized by the Disney film *Bambi*.
Baptista (a baptiser)
Barbara (foreign woman)
Beata (happy)
Beatrice (bringer of joy) **Beatrix**
Becca (noose)
Belinda (?, perhaps *snake*)
Bella (beautiful) **Bell, Belle**
Belva (beautiful view) **Belvah**
Benedicta (blessed) **Benedicte, Benedikta**
Benet (blessed) **Bennet, Bennitt**
Berdine (bright maiden)
Bernadean (bold as a bear)
Bernadette (bold as a bear) **Bernette**
Bernardine (bold as a bear)
Berneen (bold as a bear)

Berta (bright)

Bertha (bright) **Berthe**

Beryl (beryl, a greem gemstone)

Bess (God is my oath) **Bessie**

Beth (God is my oath)

Bethany (house of figs) **Bethanee, Bethani, Bethanie, Betheny**

Bethel (house of God)

Betsy (God is my oath) **Betsey**

Betty (God is my oath)

Beverley (dweller near the beaver stream) **Beverly, Bev**

Bianca (white, fair)

Billie (resolute protector) **Billy**

Billie Jo (resolute protector + he shall add)

Birdie (a bird)

Birgit (strength) **Birgitta, Birgitte**

Blaine (the groin; angular, thin; a hollow)

Blair (dweller on the plain)

Blanch (white) **Blanche**

Blanka (white) **Blanca**

Blossom (a blossom, flower)

Bobbie (bright with fame)

Bonita (beautiful)

Bonnie (beautiful, good-natured, cheerful) **Bonny**

Brandy (brandy, a distilled liquor) **Brandi, Brandie**

Brenda (sword)

Breqlynn Contemporary.

Brett (a Breton)

Brianna (force, strength; valor; steep, hill; kingly)

Brice (force, strength; valor)

Bridget (strength) **Brigit**

Brigitte (strength) **Brigida, Brigitta**

Brittany (from Brittany, a Breton) **Britt**

Brontë (thunder)

Brook (a brook, a small stream) **Brooke**

Brooklyn Borrowed from the New York City borough. **Brooklin, Brooklinn, Brooklynn**

Brylieva Contemporary.

Bryn Contemporary.

Brynae Contemporary.

Buffy Originated as a pet form of Elisabeth *God is my oath.*

Bunnie (a rabbit) **Bunny**

Cachay Contemporary, possibly influenced by the French *cachet* (distinction, prestige).

Calandra (beautiful one) **Kalandra; Callie, Kallie**

Caledonia (from Caledonia, from Scotland) **Callie**

Cambria Borrowed from Cambria County, Pennsylvania, named for the Cambrian Mountains in Wales.

Cameo (a carving on a shell or gem)

Camika Contemporary.

Camille (virgin of unblemished character) **Camila, Camilla, Kamilla**

Canada (where the heavens rest upon the earth) Borrowed from the name of the country.

Candace (white, pure, sincere) **Candice**

Candra (the moon; luminescent)

Careen twentieth-century coinage.

Carey (full-grown, a woman)

Caridad (charity)

Carina (affection, love)

Carissa (beloved, dear) **Carrie**

Carla (full-grown, a woman) **Carlie**

Carleigh (full-grown, a woman)

Carlotta (full-grown, a woman)

Carmen (vineyard, orchard)

Carol (full-grown, a woman) **Carole**

Carola (full-grown, a woman)

Caroletta (full-grown, a woman)

Caroline (full-grown, a woman) **Carolina; Carrie, Lina**

Carter (a carter, a driver of a cart)

Casey Short form of Cassandra. **Caysi, Kaycee**

Cassandra (?)

Cassidy (clever one, one with the twisted locks of hair; full of love and esteem) **Cassie**

Cathalina (pure, unsullied)

Catherine (pure, unsullied) **Catharina, Catharine, Catherina; Cathy**

Cathy (pure, unsullied)

Cecile (blind, dim-sighted)

Cecilia (blind, dim-sighted)

Celeste (celestial, heavenly)

Celia (blind, dim-sighted)

Chalcedony (a precious stone)

Chanda Contemporary.

Chandra (the moon)

Chandelle (candle)

Chandler (a maker or seller of candles)

Chaney (dweller near the oak wood)

Chantal (boulder, stone)

Chanté Contemporary, possibly after the French *enchanté* (enchanted). **Chantae, Chantay**

Charanne Contemporary.

Charis (grace)

Charisma (an inspiring personality)

Charissa (grace)

Charity (charity, benevolence)

Charlene (full-grown, a woman) **Charlayne, Sharleen, Sharlene**

Charlotte (full-grown, a woman) **Charlotta**

Charmain (a son, verse) **Charmayne, Sharmain, Sharmaine, Sharmayne**

Charmian (a little joy)

Charney (from the island in the River Charn)

Chastity (modesty, purity, virtuousness)

Chelsea (a port of ships) **Chelsie**

Cheney (from the oak wood)

Cheree (darling)

Cheryl Contemporary.

Chevonne (God is gracious)

Cheyenne (unintelligible speakers) Sioux.

Chloe (blooming, verdant)
Chloris (green)
Christa (a Christian)
Christabel (?, probably *beautiful Christ*) **Christabell**
Christiana (a Christian, a follower of Christ)
Christine (a Christian, a follower of Christ) **Christina, Cristina, Khristina, Khristine, Kristina, Kristine; Chris, Chrissie, Christy, Kris, Kristy**
Christmas (born at Christmastime)
Chula (fox) Muskogean.
Chyna (China)
Ciara (black-haired one)
Cicely (blind, dim-sighted) **Cecily, Cicily, Sisley, Sycillie**
Cinnamon (cinnamon spice)
Clare (bright, clear, famous) **Claire, Clara**
Clarinda (bright, clear, famous)
Clarissa (bright, clear, famous) **Clarice, Claricia**
Claudette (little Claude *lame*)
Claudia (lame)
Cleare (clear)
Clementine (clement, mild)
Clover (the clover plant)
Colette (victory of the people)
Colleen (girl)
Constancy (constant) **Constance, Constanze**
Consuelo (consolation)
Coralie (coral; maiden)
Cordelia (?, perhaps *daughter of the sea*) **Cordula**
Corinna (maiden) **Corinne**
Cornelia (a horn)
Courtney (from Courtenay, France)
Cressida (?)
Cricket Originated as a nickname of Christine *a Christian*. Now often given in reference to the insect.
Crimson (brilliant red)
Crystal (clear, brilliant)
Cynthia (of Kynthos)
Dahlia (a dahlia flower) **Dalia**
Daisy (a daisy flower)
Damaris (?, possibly *heifer*)
Damiana (tame, gentle)
Dana (God is my judge)
Danae (the parched or dry one)
Danean Contemporary.
Dania (God is my judge)
Danielle (God is my judge) **Daniella, Danniela, Danniella**
Danika (morning star)
Daphne (a laurel or bay tree)
Darah Contemporary.
Darby (without injunction, a freeman)
Darenda Contemporary.
Darla (darling)
Darlene (darling) **Darline**
Darlonna Contemporary.
Darshelle Contemporary.

Davida (beloved)
Davina (beloved)
Dawn (daybreak)
Deana (a dean)
Deandra (womanly)
Deborah (a bee) **Debora, Debra, Debrah**
Deirdre (?)
Delaney Anglicized form of O'Dubhshláine.
Delani Contemporary.
Delfina (from Delphi; the delphinium flower)
Delia (from Delos)
Delicia (delicious)
Delilah (delicate)
Della (a dell, a small valley or glen; nobility)
Demi (half, not full-sized)
Denise (of Dionysus)
Desire (desire, want)
Desirae (desired, beloved) **Desiray, Desiree, Desirée**
Destiny (fate)
Devon (a poet) **Devin**
Diane (divine) **Diana**
Dido (?) In Roman mythology, Dido was the princess of Tyre, the founder and queen of Carthage.
Dina (sea warrior; famous king) **Deena**
Dina (judged) **Dinah**
Dionne (divine; of Dionysus)
Dixie (the southern states, the Confederacy) **Dixy**
Dolly (gift of God; sorrows)
Dominica (belonging to a lord; of the Lord)
Donelle (world ruler)
Donna (world ruler)
Donoma (the sun is there) Omaha.
Dora (gift)
Doreen (little gift)
Doris (Dorian woman)
Dorothea (gift of God) **Dorotea, Dorothy; Dollie, Dolly, Dot, Dottie**
Dorren (sullen)
Dove (a dove)
Drew (manly)
Drusilla (?)
Duchess (the wife of a duke)
Dulcie (sweet) **Dulce**
Dusana (spirit, soul) **Dushana**
Earlene (an earl) **Earline, Erlene, Erline**
Eartha (the earth)
Easter (born on Easter)
Eden (delight)
Edith (prosperous in war) **Edyth**
Edmee (love, esteem)
Edna (rejuvenation, delight)
Edwina (prosperous friend)
Effie (?)
Egypt Borrowed from the name of the North African country.
Eileen (?) **Eilene**

Elaine (light, torch, bright)
Eleanor (light, torch, bright) **Eleonor, Eleonora, Eleonore, Elianor, Elinor, Elleanor**
Electra (the shining one)
Elena (light, torch, bright)
Elisabeth (God is my oath) **Elizabeth, Elsbeth, Elspeth, Lisabet, Lisabeth, Lisbeth; Bess, Bessie, Beth, Betti, Betty, Elise, Eliza, Ellie, Elsa, Else, Elsie, Elsy, Ilsa, Liese, Lisa, Lise, Lisette, Liza, Lizzie, Lizzy**
Eliza (God is my oath)
Elke (nobility)
Ella (foreign, other; light)
Ellen (light, torch, bright) **Elen**
Ellis (nobility)
Eloisa (hale, hearty) **Eloise**
Elsie (God is my oath)
Emelie (rival, trying to equal or excel) **Emelia**
Emeline (strength; work) **Emmeline**
Emeraud (an emerald)
Emerlee (strength; work)
Emilia (strength; work)
Emily (strength; work)
Emma (strength)
Emmanuelle (God is with us)
Enriqua (home ruler)
Erika (eternal ruler) **Erica**
Erin (Ireland)
Erin (elephant) Yoruban.
Erisha (speech)
Erma (strength)
Ernestine (earnest, resolute)
Esmeralda (emerald)
Esperanza (hope, expectation)
Estella (a star) **Estelle**
Esther (myrtle; star) **Ester**
Ethelyne (nobility) **Etheleen, Ethelene, Etheline**
Eugenia (well-born, noble) **Eugenie**
Eunice (good victory)
Euphemia (fair speech) **Eufemia, Euphemie**
Eustacia (steadfast; happy harvest) **Staci**
Evangelina (good news, the Gospel) **Evangeline**
Eve (life) **Eva**
Eveline (?) **Evelina, Evelyn**
Everet (boar hard)
Evette (archer)
Faith (faith, trust)
Fana (light) Ethiopian.
Farah (happiness) Arabic.
Farrah (beautiful, fair, pleasant) **Ferrah**
Fauna (the animals of a specified time or area)
Faustina (bringer of good luck)
Fawn (a baby deer)
Faye (fairy) **Fae, Fay**
Felice (lucky, happy) **Felicie**

Felicity (happiness) **Felicite**
Fern (a fern)
Ferren Contemporary.
Fidelma (?)
Finella (white shoulders) **Fenella, Finola, Fionola**
Fiona (white, fair, clear, transparent)
Flora (a flower) **Flore**
Florida (abounding in flowers)
Folawn Contemporary.
Frances (a Frank, a freeman)
Francine (little French one)
Francisca (a Frenchwoman) **Franziska**
Frederica (peace ruler) **Frederika**
Fujiko (child of the wisteria) Japanese.
Gabriela (God is my strength) **Gabriele, Gabrielle**
Gail (father of exaltation) **Gayle**
Garcelle (little spear)
Garnet (the garnet gemstone)
Gay (joyous, lighthearted) **Gae, Gaye**
Gaynel (joyous, lighthearted + light) **Gay**
Gaynor (white, fair, blessed) **Gay**
Gemma (gemstone, jewel)
Genesee (beautiful valley)
Geneva (juniper berry)
Genevieve (?, possibly *tribal woman*)
Georgeanne (earth worker, farmer + grace, mercy) **Georgeann, Georgiana**
Georgette (earth worker, farmer)
Georgia (earth worker, farmer)
Geri Originally a pet form of names beginning with *Ger-*.
Gillian (youth, downy) **Jillian**
Gina Originally a short form of names ending in -*gina*, such as Georgina.
Ginger (spicy, red-haired)
Gisela (pledge)
Giselle (pledge) **Gisele**
Glenna (mountain valley)
Glenys (pure, holy)
Gloria (glory)
Golda (golden)
Goldie (golden)
Grace (grace, mercy)
Graciela (agreeable, pleasantness)
Greer (vigilant, watchful)
Gretchen (a pearl)
Gretel (a pearl)
Gwen (white, fair, blessed)
Gwendolen (fair brows)
Gwyneth (blessed)
Haidee Coinage of Byron for a character in the poem *Don Juan*.
Halley (dweller at the gathering place meadow)
Halima (gentle)

Hamako (child of the shore) Japanese.
Hanako (flower child) Japanese.
Hannah (grace, full of grace, mercy) **Hanna, Hanne**
Harmonia (harmony)
Haruko (spring child) Japanese.
Hayley (dweller in the remote valley)
Heather (heather, plants of the heath family)
Heidi (nobility; battle protector)
Helen (light, torch, bright) **Helena, Helene**
Hermia (of Hermes)
Hermione (of Hermes)
Hilary (cheerful, merry) **Hillary, Hillery**
Hollis (dweller at the holly trees)
Holly (the holly tree)
Honey (honey, sweetness)
Honor (honor, esteem) **Honora, Honore, Honoria, Honour, Hanora**
Hope (hope, expectation)
Humility (humbleness)
Hunter (a hunter)
Hyacinth (bluebell, hyacinth)
Ideny (work, labor) **Idona, Idonea, Idony**
Idonia (of good disposition)
Ikuko (sustaining child) Japanese.
Ilesha (lord of the earth)
Ilona (light, torch, bright)
Ima (present, now) Japanese.
Imako (present child) Japanese.
Imelda (entire battle)
India Borrowed from the name of the Asian subcontinent.
Indiana (of India)
Ines (chaste, pure, sacred)
Ingrid (beautiful Ing)
Inola (black fox) Cherokee.
Irene (peace) **Irena**
Iris (the iris flower; rainbow)
Isabel (God is my oath) **Isabela, Isabell, Isabella, Isabelle, Isobel**
Ivy (the ivy plant, a creeping vine)
Jackie (God is gracious)
Jacqueline (supplanting, seizing by the heels) **Jacklyn**
Jade (jade, stone of the side [from the belief that it cured pains in the side])
Jael (mountain goat)
Jakeisha Contemporary. **Jackeesha, Jakeesha; Jackie**
Jamae Contemporary.
Jameeka Contemporary. **Jamika, Jamikah**
Jamie (supplanting, seizing by the heels) **Jaymie**
Jane (God is gracious)
Janeal Contemporary.
Janet (God is gracious; little Jane) **Jennet**
Janice (God is gracious) **Janis, Janys**
Janna (God is gracious) **Janne**

Jasmine (jasmine) **Jasmin, Jazmin**
Jean (God is gracious) **Jeane, Jeanne**
Jeannette (little Jean *God is gracious*)
Jeannine (little Jean *God is gracious*) **Janine**
Jennifer (fair lady)
Jerri Feminine form of Jerry, a pet form of names beginning with *Jer-*.
Jessica (gift; God is gracious)
Jessie (little Janet *God is gracious*; gift)
Jewel (gem)
Jill (youth, downy)
Joan (God is gracious)
Joanna (God is gracious)
Jocelin (from the tribe of the Gauts) **Joscelin**
Jody (praised) **Jodi, Jodie**
Joelle (the Lord is God)
Joey (he shall add)
Johanna (God is gracious) **Joanna**
Jonna (God is gracious)
Jordana (descending, a flowing down)
Josee (he shall add) **Josie**
Joy (joy, happiness)
Joyce (merry, happy)
Juana (God is gracious)
Juanita (little Juana *God is gracious*)
Judith (praised) **Judit; Judy**
Julia (youth, downy) **Julie**
Juliana (youth, downy)
Juliet (youth, downy) **Juliette**
June (the sixth month, born in June)
Juniper (the juniper shrub) **June**
Justina (right, just) **Justine**
Kai (forgiveness) Japanese.
Kaiko (child of forgiveness) Japanese.
Kalliope (beautiful voice)
Kameko (tortoise child) Japanese.
Kaneesha Contemporary. **Kaneisha**
Kaneko (double-accomplished child) Japanese.
Karen (pure, unsullied) **Karin**
Karita (charity, affection)
Karla (woman) **Carla**
Karolina (woman) **Caroline, Karoline; Carrie, Karrie**
Katherine (pure, unsullied) **Catherine, Katarina, Katarine, Katerina, Katerine, Katharina, Katherin, Katrina, Katrine, Katryn; Cathy, Kaethe, Kate, Kathe, Kathy, Katie, Katja, Katrien, Kitty**
Kay A pet form of names beginning with the letter *K*.
Kayla Contemporary.
Kayleigh Contemporary. **Kaylee, Kayli**
Keiko (child of reverence) Japanese.
Keitha (?, perhaps *the wind* or *wood*)
Kelby (dweller at the farm by the spring)
Kelsey (victory ship)
Kendall (a spring)

Kendra (chief hero; high summit; child of Henry; royal rule)
Kenitra Contemporary.
Kenna (born of fire; comely, handsome)
Kenya Borrowed from the East African country of the same name.
Kerry (black-haired; pure, unsullied)
Kessie (born fat) Ghanaian.
Kezia (cassia)
Kiana Contemporary. **Kianna, Kyana, Kyanna**
Kiara Contemporary.
Kichi (lucky, fortunate) Japanese.
Kiley (graceful, beautiful)
Kimana (butterfly) Shoshone.
Kimberley (?, second element of the name is *wood, clearing, meadow*)
Kimiko (child without equal) Japanese.
Kinuko (child of silk) Japanese.
Klara (bright, clear, famous) **Clara**
Kyesha Contemporary.
Kyla (narrow)
Kyoko (mirror) Japanese.
Lacy (from the town Lacy, France; lacy, delicate) **Lacey, Laci**
Laetitia (happiness) **Letitia, Laticia, Leticia, Lettice**
Laila (night, dark beauty)
Lala (tulip)
Lana (?)
Lani (sky, heaven, heavenly, spiritual, divine) Hawaiian.
Lannette (from the small lane)
Laree Contemporary.
Larissa (?, perhaps *cheerful*) **Larisa**
Lark (a lark, songbird)
Latasha Contemporary.
Latifa (gentle, kind) **Lateefa, Lateefah, Latifah**
Laura (laurel) **Lora**
Laurana (from Laurentum)
Laurence (from Laurentum) **Laurencia, Laurentia**
Laureola (from Laurentum)
Lavinia (from Latium) **Lavina**
Leah (weary)
Lei (open-hearted, honest) Chinese.
Lei (flower garland) Hawaiian.
Leigh (dweller in the meadow or woods) **Lee**
Leila (dark beauty, dark as night)
Leilani (heavenly lei) Hawaiian.
Lena (light, torch, bright)
Leona (lion)
Leslie (small meadow, small clearing, small woods)
Levana (white; moon; light)
Lexine (defender or helper of mankind)
Li (plum) Chinese.
Lilith (of the night) In ancient Semitic folklore, Lilith was a night demon and vampire that lived in desolate places. Medieval Jewish folklore says Lilith was the first wife of Adam, before Eve. She was turned into a demon for disobeying Adam and went around menacing infants and small children at night.

Lillian (lily) **Lilian, Liliana; Lily**
Lilly (a lily)
Linda (beautiful)
Lindsay (from Lindsay *the lake colony*) **Lynsey**
Ling (delicate) Chinese.
Linnea After the name of Swedish botanist Karl von Linné. **Linea, Linae, Lynnae**
Lisa (God is my oath)
Lisabet (God is my oath) **Lisbet, Lysbet**
Litonya (hummingbird darting) **Litonia** Miwok.
Liv (life)
Lois (?)
Lorena (from Lorraine)
Loretta (from Laurentum) **Lauretta**
Lorna Invention of R. D. Blackmore for his character in *Lorna Doone* (1864).
Lorraine (famous in war) **Laraine, Larraine, Loraine**
Louise (famous in war) **Louisa, Luisa**
Love (love)
Lucia (light)
Lucilla (light)
Lucinda (light)
Lucretia (riches, wealth)
Lucy (light)
Lura (laurel; a lure; light)
Lutheria (famous in war)
Lydia (Lydian woman) **Lyddia**
Lynette (shapely; lake; flaxen-haired) **Lynett, Lynnett, Lynnette**
Lynn (lake) **Lynne**
Mabel (lovable) **Mabill**
Mabella (lovable)
Madeline (from Magdala)
Madge (a pearl)
Madison (son of Mad *gift of God*)
Madonna (my lady)
Maeve (?, perhaps *joy; great, large; mead*)
Magdalen (from Magdala) **Magdalena, Magdalene, Magdelyn; Maggie**
Maggie (a pearl)
Mahala (tenderness)
Mahalia (fatlings, a calf, a kid)
Mai (sea of bitterness or sorrow; a pearl)
Malaea (sea of bitterness or sorrow) **Malia** Hawaiian.
Malaika (an angel) Swahili.
Malene (from Magdala)
Mallory (the unlucky one)
Malvina (smooth brow)
Manuela (God with us) **Manuella**
Maraea (sea of bitterness or sorrow) Hawaiian.
Marah (bitterness) **Mara**
Marcella (of Mars, warlike)
Marcia (of Mars, warlike) **Marsha**
Marcie (of Mars, warlike)

Margareta (a pearl) **Margaret, Margaretha, Margarita, Margrethe, Marguerita, Marguerite, Margit, Margery, Margarey**

Margot (a pearl) **Margeaux, Margo**

Maria (sea of bitterness or sorrow) **Marie**

Mariam (sea of bitterness or sorrow)

Marian (sea of bitterness or sorrow)

Mariana (of Mars; sea of bitterness or sorrow)

Mariel (sea of bitterness or sorrow)

Mariko (ball child) Japanese.

Marilee (sea of bitterness or sorrow + woods, clearing)

Marilyn (sea of bitterness or sorrow + lake)

Marina (of Mars; of the sea)

Marion (sea of bitterness or sorrow)

Marisol (sea of bitterness + solitude)

Marissa (sea of bitterness or sorrow) **Marisa**

Marjolaine (sweet marjoram)

Marjorie (a pearl) **Margery**

Markea Contemporary.

Marlene Contraction of Mary Magdalene. **Marleen, Marlena**

Martha (lady, mistress) **Marthe**

Marti (of Mars, warlike)

Martina (of Mars, warlike) **Martine**

Mary (sea of bitterness or sorrow)

Mary Ann (sea of bitterness or sorrow + grace, full of grace, mercy) **Mariann**

Mary Kay (sea of bitterness or sorrow + a pet form of names beginning with the letter *K*)

Mason (a stone mason)

Maura (great, large; dark-skinned, a Moor)

Maureen (sea of bitterness or sorrow) **Maurene, Maurine**

Maxie (greatest)

Maxine (greatest)

May (a pearl; sea of bitterness or sorrow; born in May) **Mae**

Maya (goddess of increase; industrious, hardworking)

Mei (beautiful) Chinese.

Megan (pearl)

Melanie (dark, black)

Melissa (a bee)

Melody (a melody)

Meraude (of the sea)

Mercedes (mercy)

Mercy (mercy, compassion)

Meredith (sea protector)

Meriall (sea bright) **Meryall**

Merry (cheerful, happy)

Mia (sea of bitterness or sorrow; Who is like God?)

Michael (Who is like God?)

Michaiah (Who is like God?)

Mikaela (Who is like God?)

Millicent (work strength) **Melicent, Melisande, Mellicent, Milicent, Millesant; Millie**

Min (quick; sensitive) Chinese.

Ming (shining; tomorrow) Chinese.

Miranda (worthy to be loved)

Miriam (sea of bitterness or sorrow)

Missy (Who is like God?; a young woman)

Misty (foggy, misty) **Mistie**

Molly (sea of bitterness or sorrow)

Monday (born on Monday)

Moneka (earth, soil) Sioux.

Monica (?)

Monika (quiet)

Monique (?)

Montana (mountainous) Borrowed from the state of the same name.

Moreen (little great one)

Morgan (sea circle, sea bright)

Moriya (teacher) **Mariah, Moriah**

Morna (beloved)

Muriel (bright sea)

Myrna (affection, beloved)

Naamah (sweetness)

Nadia (hope)

Nadine (hope)

Nancy (grace, full of grace, mercy)

Naomi (my joy, my delight)

Narcissa (?) Inspired by the narcissus flower.

Natalie (natal day; born at Christmastime) **Natalia**

Nekoma (grandmother) Chippewa.

Nell (light, torch, bright) **Nellie, Nelly**

Nevada (snowy) Borrowed from the state of the same name.

Nia Contemporary.

Nicole (victory of the people) **Nichole, Niccola, Nicola**

Nicolette (little Nicole *victory of the people*)

Nikeesha Contemporary. **Nikisha, Kikkisha; Nikki**

Nina (grace, full of grace, mercy)

Noelle (born at Christmas) **Noel**

Noemie (pleasant, beautiful)

Nonie (light)

Nora (a woman from the north; honor, esteem)

Noreene (little Nora *light*)

Norma (a woman from the north)

Oceana (of the ocean)

Odette (prosperity, riches)

Olathe (beautiful) Shawnee.

Olga (holy)

Olivia (the olive tree)

Olympia (of Olympus) **Olimpia, Olympe**

Oneida (standing rock)

Opal (an opal gemstone)

Ophelia (help, succor) **Ophelie**

Ophrah (a fawn)

Oriane (to rise; golden) **Oriana**

Orpah (a fawn, a forelock)

Orabell (?) **Orable, Oriabel**

Oriana (to rise)

Osanna (save now, save pray)

Pacifica (to pacify, to make peace)
Paige (a page, a boy attendant)
Paloma (dove)
Pamela Sixteenth-century coinage of the poet Sir Philip Sidney (1554–1586).
Pansy (a pansy flower)
Paradise (heaven, a place of perfection and great beauty)
Parnell (a rock)
Parrish (dweller near the parish)
Patience (patience, forbearance)
Patricia (a patrician, an aristocrat) **Pat, Patty**
Paula (small)
Pauline (small)
Pearl (a pearl)
Peg (a pearl) **Peggy**
Penelope (a bobbin)
Penny (a bobbin; a penny)
Peony (the peony flower)
Pepper (the pepper spice; a lively personality)
Percy (from Percy, Normandy)
Pernilla (a rock) **Pernille**
Petra (a rock)
Petronel (a rock) **Peternel**
Petronilla (a rock)
Philadelphia (brotherly love)
Philippa (lover of horses)
Phyllis (a leaf) **Phillis, Phylis**
Phoebe (bright, shining) **Phebe, Phebeus**
Pia (pious, devout)
Pilar (pillar, column)
Piper (one who plays the pipe)
Pleasance (pleasant)
Polly (sea of bitterness or sorrow)
Poppy (the poppy flower)
Prairie (a plain, a large grassland)
Precilla (former, ancient) **Priscilla**
Precious (priceless, dear)
Princess (a princess)
Queen (a queen) **Queena, Queenie**
Quilla (a quill, a hollow stalk)
Quinn (wisdom, reason, intelligence)
Rachel (ewe) **Rachael, Rachell**
Rae (doe)
Rain (rain, precipitation) **Raine, Rayn**
Ramona (wise protection)
Raquel (ewe) **Racquel**
Raven (a large blackbird)
Ravenna (a large blackbird; a borrowing of the name of a northern Italian commune)
Rayna (song of the Lord) **Raina**
Reba (noose)
Rebecca (noose) **Rabecca, Rebecka, Rebekah, Rebekka**
Regina (queen) **Regine**
Renate (reborn) **Renatus**
Renee (reborn)
Reva (restored to health; young girl)

Rhiannon (great queen)
Rhoda (a rose)
Rhonda (good lance)
Richenda (little Richard *stern king*)
Riley (dweller by the rye field) **Reilly**
Rina Originally a short form for names ending in *-rina,* such as Sabrina.
Rinda (?)
Rita (a pearl)
Robin (bright with fame)
Rolanda (famous land)
Rona (mighty power)
Rosa (a rose)
Rosalie (rose garland)
Rosalind (horse or fame + gentle, tender or serpent) **Rosalinde**
Rosamond (horse protection) **Rossamond**
Rose (a rose) **Rosa**
Roseanna (rose + grace, full of grace, mercy) **Rosana, Rosanna, Rose Ann, Rose Anne**
Rosemarie (rose + sea of bitterness or sorrow; dew of the sea)
Rosemary (rose + sea of bitterness or sorrow)
Rosetta (little Rose) **Rosita**
Rowena (famous friend)
Roxane (dawn of day)
Royce (son of Roy *red-haired*)
Ruby (a ruby gemstone)
Ruth (friend, companion) **Ruthe**
Sachiko (child of bliss) Japanese.
Sabrina (?)
Sadie (princess)
Saffron (the saffron spice, bright orange yellow color)
Sage (the sage herb)
Sahara (desert)
Salina (the moon)
Sally (princess)
Salome (peace)
Samantha (name of God) **Sam, Sammie**
Sandra (defender of mankind) **Saundra**
Sandy (defender; sandy) **Sandi, Sandie**
Sapphira (beautiful; sapphire) **Saphira**
Sarah (princess) **Sara**
Sarah Ann (princess + grace, full of grace, mercy)
Sasha (defender of mankind)
Savannah (a treeless plain) **Savanna**
Scarlet (bright red) **Scarlett**
Scout (a scout)
Selda (gravel, stone)
Selina (the moon) **Selene, Selinah**
Seraphine (burning one, angel)
Serenity (calmness, tranquillity)
Shaena (beautiful)
Shaina (God is gracious)
Shan (God is gracious)

Shanay Contemporary. **Shanae, Shanai**
Shannah (lily, rose) **Shanna**
Shannon (old, wise)
Sharon (a plain, a flat area)
Shasta Borrowed from the mountain of the same name in northern California.
Shaun (God is gracious) **Shawn**
Shauna (God is gracious) **Shawna, Shonna**
Shaundra Contemporary, influenced by both Saundra and Shauna.
Sheena (God is gracious)
Shelby (a willow grove)
Shelly (dweller on the clearing near the ledge)
Sheridan (peaceful)
Sherry (fortified Spanish wine; darling)
Sheryle Twentieth-century coinage. **Cheryl, Sheryl**
Shirley (bright meadow) **Shirlee**
Shona (crimson)
Shoshannah (a lily, a rose)
Sibylla (fortune-teller, prophetess) **Sibella, Sibilla, Sybil**
Sierra (mountain)
Signy (new victory)
Silver (silver)
Silvia (wood)
Simone (heard)
Skye (sky) **Sky**
Skyla (sky)
Solange (yearly; solemn, religious)
Soledad (solitude)
Sondya (wisdom, skill)
Sophia (wisdom) **Sofia, Sophie**
Spencer (dispenser of provisions, a butler)
Spring (springtime)
Stacy (resurrection) **Stacey**
Star (a star)
Stella (a star)
Stephanie (a crown, garland) **Steffanie**
Stevie (a crown, garland)
Stormy (inclement weather)
Suki (fond of) Japanese.
Summer (born in the summer)
Sunniva (gift of the sun)
Sunny (shining, happy, bright personality)
Susan (lily, rose) **Suzan**
Susanna (lily, rose) **Susannah, Susanne, Susanney, Suzanna, Suzannah, Suzanne**
Sybil (fortune-teller, prophetess) **Sybell, Sybill, Sybilla, Sybille**
Sylvia (the woods) **Sylvie**
Synnove (gift of the sun)
Tabitha (roe, gazelle)
Tacy (hold peace, be silent)
Talise (beautiful water) Creek.
Talula (leaping water) **Tallula, Tallulah, Talulah** Choctaw.
Tamako (jewel child) Japanese.

Tamara (palm, a date palm) **Tami, Tammy**
Tamiko (people child) Japanese.
Tamisha Contemporary.
Tamsin (a twin)
Tanya (?)
Tara (a hill)
Taren Contemporary. **Taryn**
Tawny (a soft, brownish yellow color) **Tawnee, Tawney**
Taylor (a tailor)
Tempest (stormy)
Terra (the earth)
Thea (truth; flowery; goddess)
Thelma Invention of Marie Corelli for the Norwegian heroine in *Thelma* (1887).
Theresa (harvester) **Teresa, Terese, Therese; Tess, Tessa**
Thomson (little Tom *a twin*) **Thamasin, Thomasin, Tomson**
Tiara (a crown)
Tiffany (Epiphany, manifestation of God) **Tiffeny, Tyffany**
Timothea (honoring God) **Timmi**
Tina (a Christian, a follower of Christ)
Tishra Contemporary.
Tivian Contemporary.
Toby (the Lord is good)
Tonda Contemporary.
Tova (beautiful Thor)
Tovah (good, pleasing)
Tracy (place of Thracius) **Tracie, Tracey**
Treasure (wealth of riches)
Trena (third child) **Trenia**
Tricia (a patrician, an aristocrat)
Trudie (spear strength) **Trudy**
Tuesday (the third day of the week, Tiu's day)
Tupper (ram)
Twyla (double-threaded) **Twila, Twilah**
Tyana Contemporary.
Ulrike (noble ruler) **Ulrika**
Umeko (plum child) Japanese.
Una (remember) Hopi.
Unity (united)
Ursula (she-bear) **Urselah**
Valentine (strong, healthy) **Valentina**
Valerie (strong, healthy)
Vanessa An invention of satirist Jonathan Swift (1667–1745). Vanessa is a partial anagram of Swift's friend, Esther Vanhomrigh.
Vara (?)
Vaunda Contemporary coinage.
Velvet (luxurious, soft cloth)
Vené Contemporary.
Venetia (blessed)
Venus (the loved one, beloved)
Vera (faith)
Verena (true)
Verity (truth, reality)
Verna (dweller among the ferns; of Vernon)
Veronica (true image) **Veronika**

Veronique (true image)
Vianna Contemporary.
Victoria (victory) **Viktoria; Torie**
Viola (violet) **Viole**
Violet (violet-colored) **Violette**
Virginia (springlike, flourishing)
Vita (life)
Vivian (alive) **Viviane, Vivianne, Vivien, Vivienne**
Wanda (?, perhaps *stem, young tree; a Wend, an old Slavic people*)
Wallace (a Welshman)
Wauna (snow geese calling as they fly) Miwok.
Wednesday (the fourth day of the week, Woden's day)
Whitney (Hwita's island)
Wilhelmina (resolute protector) **Willie**
Willa (resolute protector) **Willie**
Willow (a willow tree; gracefully slender and lithe)
Wilma (resolute protector)
Winifred (blessed peace) **Winnifred; Winnie**
Winona (eldest daughter) **Wenona** Sioux.
Wynne (white, fair, blessed) **Wynn**
Xenia (hospitality)

Yasmin (jasmine) **Yasmeen, Yasmina**
Yolande (?, possibly *violet*) **Yolanda**
Yolanna Contemporary.
Yolondra Contemporary.
Yvelle (little archer)
Yvette (little archer)
Yvonne (archer)
Zalika (well-born, noble) **Zeleka**
Zan (mankind)
Zandra (mankind) **Xandra; Xandi, Dandie, Zandi, Zandie, Zandy**
Zanna (lily, rose; God is gracious)
Zea (ripened grain)
Zelda (happiness, joy; ?, perhaps *companion*)
Zenaida (of Zeus)
Zephyra (the west wind)
Zephyrine (the west wind)
Zhané Contemporary.
Zoe (live)
Zoraida (captivating woman)
Zsa Zsa (God is my oath)
Zuleka (fair) **Zuleica**

MALE NAMES

Aaron (exalted)
Abel (breath)
Abram (father of exaltation)
Ace (excellent, first in quality)
Adalard (noble and strong)
Adam (man of the red earth)
Addison (son of Addy)
Adlai (refuge of the Lord)
Adrian (man from Hadrianus) **Adrien**
Aeneas (praiser)
Aidan (little fire)
Ake (?, possibly *ancestor*; *agate*; *blameless*)
Akira (intelligent, smart) Japanese.
Aksel (the father is peace) **Axel**
Alain (?, perhaps *handsome; rock*) **Allain**
Alan (?, perhaps *handsome; rock*) **Allan, Allen**
Alard (noble and strong) **Allard**
Alarik (ruler of all)
Alasdair (defender of mankind) **Alastair, Alaster, Alisdair, Alistair, Alister, Allaster**
Albert (bright through nobility)
Albin (white)
Alden (old friend; half-Dane)
Aldwin (old friend)
Alex (defender, defender of mankind) **Alec**
Alexander (defender of mankind) **Alexandre; Alec, Alick, Sander**
Alexis (defender)
Alphonse (noble and ready)

Alton (old town)
Ambrose (immortal) **Ambroise**
Anatole (sunrise, daybreak)
Anders (manly)
Andre (manly)
Andrew (manly)
Andor (eagle + Thor)
Andre (manly)
Andrew (manly) **Dande, Dandy, Tandy**
Angus (one, choice, preeminent) **Gus**
Anselme (divine helmet)
Anthony (?, *priceless, of inestimable worth* is a folk definition) **Antony, Tony**
Antoine (?, *priceless, of inestimable worth* is a folk definition)
Anton (?, *priceless, of inestimable worth* is a folk definition)
Antonius (?, *priceless, of inestimable worth* is a folk definition)
Ara (eagle)
Arcell Contemporary.
Archer (an archer, a bowman)
Archie (genuinely bold, genuinely brave)
Aren (eagle rule)
Arend (eagle power)
Aristide (best)
Arlan (foreigner, stranger) **Arland, Arlen**
Armand (soldier, warrior) **Armond**
Armin (soldier, warrior)
Arne (eagle) **Aren**
Arnel (eagle strength)

Arno (eagle)
Arnold (eagle ruler)
Arsenio (male, virile)
Art (a bear)
Arthur (?)
Arun (exalted; enlightened; reddish brown)
Arvid (eagle tree)
Asa (healer; restlessness)
Ashby (from the village near the ash trees)
Ashton (from the ash tree settlement)
Asmund (God is protector)
Auberi (elf ruler) **Aubry**
Aubert (noble and bright)
Aubrey (elf ruler)
Augustus (great, venerable) **Gus**
Aundray Contemporary.
Austin (great, venerable)
Averil (boar battle) **Averill**
Aylwin (elf friend)
Bailer (ax maker) **Bailor, Baylor**
Bailey (administrator; worker at the outer court of a castle; savior)
Baird (a poet)
Baldwin (bold friend)
Balthasar (?)
Banner (a flag, a banner; a bearer of the banners)
Bannock (exiled, banished) **Banick**
Barclay (from Berkeley *birch meadow*)
Barnabe (son of exhortation) **Barnaby, Barney**
Baron (a baron, nobleman)
Barry (spearlike)
Bartel (son of Talmai *hill, mound, furrows*) **Bertel**
Bartholomew (son of Talmai *hill,mound, furrows*)
Bastien (man from Sebasta)
Bay (a bay, an indentation in the shoreline)
Bear (a bear)
Beau (handsome)
Beavis (archer) **Beves, Bevis**
Beck (dweller near the brook)
Bellamy (beautiful friend)
Benedict (blessed) **Benedick, Benedikt, Benedikte**
Benjamin (son of the right hand) **Ben**
Bennet (blessed) **Bennett; Benny**
Benny Short form of names beginning with *Ben-*.
Benson (son of Ben) **Ben, Benny**
Bentley (from the clearing overgrown with bent grass)
Benton (from the settlement by the bent grass)
Berg (mountain)
Beringer (bear spear)
Berlin Borrowed from the German city of the same name.
Bernard (bold as a bear) **Barnard**
Bert Short form of names beginning with *Bert-*.
Bertin (bright friend)
Bevan (God is gracious)
Billy (resolute protector)
Birchall (dweller near the hall by the birch trees)

Bishop (a bishop)
Bjorn (bear) **Bjarne**
Blaine (son of the disciple of Blaan *yellow* or Blane *the lean*)
Blair (dweller on the plain)
Blaise (deformed, stuttering) **Blaize, Blase, Blaze**
Blake (black, dark-complexioned)
Bo (a householder)
Booker (a scribe, a writer of books)
Boyd (son of the yellow-haired one)
Braden (dweller near the broad valley)
Bradford (dweller near the broad ford) **Brad**
Bram (father of a multitude)
Brandon (dweller near the brushwood hill; prince) **Brendon**
Breck (freckled)
Breece (?)
Brennan (descendant of Braoin *sorrow, sadness*; burned hand, a law-breaker) **Brennand, Brennen**
Brenner (keeper of the hounds; burner of charcoal)
Brett (a Breton)
Brevin Contemporary.
Brian (force, strength; valor; steep, high) **Bryan**
Brice (?)
Brock (a badger; a young deer; from the brook)
Broder (brother)
Brody (from Brodie *a ditch*; black; son of Bruaideadh *fragment*)
Bruce (from Brus, France)
Bruno (brown)
Buck (a male deer)
Burke (a fort, a stronghold)
Burton (settlement near the stronghold) **Burt**
Buster (man, boy)
Byron (at the cow sheds)
Cabot (small head)
Cade (lumpy, rotund; an orphaned animal; maker or seller of casks or barrels; one with the physique of a barrel)
Cain (smith, craftsman)
Calder (the stream through the woods; a breaking out of water)
Caldwell (the cold spring or well)
Cale (thin, slender)
Caleb (dog; faithful)
Callister (son of Alister *defender of mankind*)
Calum (dove)
Calvin (little bald one)
Camas (sweet, the camas plant)
Cameron (crooked nose)
Campbell (crooked mouth)
Cardell (goldfinch)
Carl (a man, freeman) **Karl**
Carlton (from the settlement of freemen) **Carl**
Carrick (rock)
Carson (son of Carr *a mossy place; a rock fort*)
Carter (a cart driver)
Cary (?, possibly *to move, stir, movement*) **Carey**
Case (a dwelling place)
Casey (descendant of Cathasach *vigilant, watchful*)
Caspar (treasure master) **Casper, Kaspar, Kasper**

Cato (wise one)
Cecil (blind, dim-sighted)
Cedric An invention of Sir Walter Scott for a character in *Ivanhoe* (1819).
Chad (?)
Channing (Cana's son)
Charles (full-grown, a man)
Chase (dweller at the hunting ground)
Chauncey (belonging to Chancey, France) **Chauncy**
Chester (camp of the legions) **Chet**
Christian (a Christian, a follower of Christ)
Christoph (bearing Christ) **Christophe**
Christopher (bearing Christ) **Christoffer, Kristoffer; Chris, Kester, Kit**
Clancy (ruddy warrior)
Clarence (from the Clare *bright, shining, clear* family)
Clark (a clerk)
Claud (lame) **Claude**
Claus (victory of the people)
Clayborne (dweller near the clay banks) **Clayborn, Clay**
Clayton (from the clay town) **Clay**
Cleanthes (?)
Clellen (son of the servant of Fillan *little wolf*)
Clement (gentle, mild)
Cleveland (from the hilly land)
Clifford (dweller near the ford by the cliff) **Cliff**
Clifton (from the town by the cliff) **Cliff**
Clinton (from the settlement by the cliff) **Clint**
Clive (dweller near the cliff or bank of a river)
Clyde (?, a Scottish river name)
Cody (son of Odo *wealthy*)
Colby (from Koli's homestead)
Cole (coal; dark-skinned)
Coleman (a coal man, a seller of coal) **Cole**
Colin (dove; victory of the people)
Colt (a young male horse)
Colter (keeper of the colt herd)
Colton (from Cola's homestead) **Colt**
Coltrin Contemporary.
Comfort (comfort, care)
Conall (strength; wisdom; high; wolf, dog)
Connell (wisdom, high-mighty) **Connel**
Connor (wisdom, counsel, strength + aid; hound) **Conor**
Conrad (bold counsel)
Conway (hound of the plain)
Cooper (a maker or seller of barrels)
Corbett (little raven)
Cordell (marker and seller of rope) **Cord**
Corey (a cauldron, a seething pool, a hollow; spear)
Cornell (rook, crow)
Corridon (a spear)
Craig (rugged rocks; dweller by the crag)
Cramer (shopkeeper, peddler)
Cruz (cross)
Cullen (son of Cuileann *holly*)
Curtis (courteous) **Curt**

Cyprian (from Cyprus) **Cyprien**
Cyril (lordly) **Cyrille**
Cyrus (lord)
Dack (day)
Dakota (allies, to be thought of as friends)
Dale (dweller in the dale)
Dallas (from Dallas *the waterfall field*)
Dalton (from the village in the valley)
Damian (tamer) **Damien**
Dana (a Dane)
Dane (a Dane)
Daniel (judged by God) **Dan**
Dante (lasting, enduring)
Darby (from the settlement by the deer)
Darcy (from Arcy, France)
Daren (born at night) Nigerian.
Darien (?) **Darian**
Darius (?, possibly *kingly*)
Darrell (from the town of Airelle) **Darel, Darell, Deral**
Darren (?)
David (beloved)
Davis (son of Davie *beloved*)
Dean (a dean)
Delaney (?, possibly *healthy, whole*)
Delbert (leader of the people + bright, famous) **Del**
Denmark (from Denmark)
Dennis (belonging to Dionysus) **Denis, Denys**
Deontae Contemporary. **Deantae, Deanté, Diontae**
Derek (ruler of the people)
Devin (poet) **Devon**
Dick (stern king)
Dirk (ruler of the people)
Dominic (belonging to the Lord) **Dominik**
Donald (world ruler) **Don**
Donatien (given by God)
Donnal (world ruler)
Douglas (black, dark + blue, green, gray) **Doug**
Doyle (descendant of the dark one)
Drake (dragon; male duck)
Drew (manly)
Duane (little dark one) **Dewayne, Dwayne**
Dudley (from Dudda's lea)
Duff (dark, black)
Dugan (little black one)
Duke (a duke)
Duncan (brown warrior)
Durand (enduring, lasting) **Durant**
Dustin (?, possibly *Thor's stone*)
Dusty (full of dust)
Dwight (the white one)
Dylan (?, possibly *sea*)
Eamon (wealthy protector)
Earl (an earl)
Eden (delight)
Edgar (wealthy spear) **Ed**
Edison (son of Eadie or Edie *prosperity, wealth*) **Ed, Eddy**

Edmond (wealthy protection) **Edmund; Ed, Eddy**
Edward (wealthy guardian) **Eduard; Ed, Eddy**
Edwin (wealthy friend) **Ed, Eddy**
Egon (point of a sword)
Einar (lone warrior)
Eldon (from Ella's hill)
Eli (high, ascent)
Elias (Jehovah is God)
Elijah (Jehovah is God)
Elisha (God is salvation)
Elkanah (God created)
Ellery (alder tree)
Elliot (Jehovah is God)
Ellis (Jehovah is God; God is salvation)
Emanuel (God with us) **Emmanuel**
Emerson (son of Emery *ruler of strength*)
Emery (ruler of strength)
Emilien (rival, trying to equal or excel)
Emmet (of Emma) **Emmett, Emmit, Emmitt**
Engrom (from the grassland enclosure)
Ennis (dweller on an island or riparian meadow)
Enoch (dedicated)
Eoghan (lamb; youth; well-born)
Ephraim (very fruitful)
Erasmus (loved, desired)
Erik (eternal ruler) **Eirik, Eric**
Erlend (foreigner, stranger) **Erland**
Ernest (earnest, resolute) **Ernst**
Errol (?, perhaps *to wander*) **Erroll**
Esau (hairy)
Eskel (sacrificial cauldron of a god)
Ethan (strength, firmness, long-lived)
Eugene (well-born)
Eustace (steadfast; happy in harvest) **Eustache**
Evan (youth; God is gracious)
Evander (manly)
Everard (strong as a boar) **Everhart, Evert**
Everest (son of Everett *strong as a boar*)
Everett (strong as a boar) **Everet, Everit, Everitt, Evert**
Ewan (youth)
Eyvind (island of the Wend)
Ezekiel (God strengthens)
Ezra (help)
Fabian (a bean) **Fabien**
Farquhar (dear man)
Farrell (man of valor) **Ferrell**
Fearghas (man of valor) **Fergus**
Felix (lucky)
Fergus (man of valor) **Fargus**
Festus (?)
Finch (a small songbird)
Finlay (fair-haired warrior)
Finn (from Finland)
Fiske (fish)
Fleetwood (creek wood)

Flemming (a Flemming)
Fletcher (an arrow maker)
Floyd (gray)
Forbes (a field)
Forrest (dweller or worker in the forest)
Foster (foster parent, nurse; officer in charge of a forest, a forest worker; a maker of scissors)
Fox (a fox)
Francis (a Frank, a freeman)
Francois (French)
Frank (a Frank)
Franklin (a freeman) **Frank**
Fraser (a Frisian)
Fred (elf counselor; ruler of peace)
Frederic (ruler of peace) **Frederick, Frederik, Fredrick, Fredrik; Fred, Freddy**
Free (liberated, without restraint)
Gabriel (God is strength) **Gabrial; Gabe**
Galen (calm)
Garen Contemporary.
Gareth (?)
Garfield (dweller near the triangular field)
Garrett (spear rule) **Garett, Garit, Garitt**
Garrick (spear; brave with the spear) **Garek**
Garth (yard, enclosure)
Garven (little Garbh *rough*)
Garvin (spear friend)
Gary (spear of battle)
Gascon (?, possibly *guest, stranger; from Gascony*)
Gaspard (treasure master)
Gaston (?, possibly *guest, stranger; from Gascony*)
Gauvain (battle hawk)
Gavin (battle hawk)
Gene (well-born, noble)
Gentry (upper-class, nobleman)
Geoffrey (district; traveler; pledge + peace) **Geffrey, Jeffery, Jeffrey; Geoff, Jeff**
George (earth worker, farmer) **Georg, Georges**
Gerald (spear rule) **Gerold, Gerolt**
Gerard (brave with the spear)
Germayne (a German) **Germain**
Gervais (servant of the spear)
Gideon (hewer)
Giffard (give + bold, fierce)
Gilbert (bright pledge) **Gib, Gil**
Giles (goatskin shield of Zeus; a protection) **Gillis**
Gillespie (servant of the bishop)
Gilroy (servant of the red-haired lad)
Glen (dweller in the glen, dweller in the mountain valley) **Glenn**
Godfry (peace of God) **Godfrey**
Godwin (friend of God)
Gordon (from Gordon)
Graham (from antham) **Graeme, Grahame**
Grant (great, large)

Granville (from the great or large town)
Gregoire (vigilant, watchful) **Greg**
Gregor (vigilant, watchful) **Greg**
Gregory (vigilant, watchful) **Greg**
Griffin (like a griffin, monstrous)
Gunnar (war, strife, battle)
Gunther (bold in war)
Guy (a guide, leader)
Guyon (a guide, leader)
Hagen (chosen son) **Hakan, Hakon**
Haldor (Thor's rock)
Halsten (rock stone)
Hamilton (from the blunt hill)
Hammond (chief protector)
Hamon (little house)
Hannibal (?)
Hans (God is gracious) **Hannes**
Harald (home ruler) **Harold**
Harley (from the hares' woods)
Haro (wild boar's first son) Japanese.
Harry (home ruler)
Harvey (battle-worthy)
Haward (high guardian)
Hawk (a hawk, a falcon)
Hayes (dweller near the hedged enclosure)
Heath (a heath, a moor)
Hector (holding fast)
Hendrik (home ruler) **Henrik**
Henry (home ruler)
Herbert (army bright) **Harbert, Heribert**
Herman (warrior, soldier) **Hermann**
Hezekiah (God strengthens)
Hiatt (dweller at the high gate
Hilary (cheerful) **Hilaire, Hilarie**
Hiram (exalted brother)
Hiroshi (generous) Japanese.
Holt (dweller near a wooded hill)
Horatio (?)
Howard (heart brave; high warden; high guardian; ewe herd)
Hoyce (spirit, mind)
Hoyte (heart, mind, spirit)
Hubard (bright heart) **Hubbard**
Hubert (bright heart)
Hugh (heart, mind, soul) **Hugo**
Humphrey (warrior of peace)
Hunter (a hunter, a huntsman)
Iain (God is gracious) **Ian**
Ike (laughter)
Ingram (Ing's raven; angel raven)
Ira (watchful)
Irving (from the west river)
Isaac (laughter) **Isak, Isaak, Izaac, Izaak**
Isaiah (God is salvation)
Israel (contender with God)
Ivar (archer, bow warrior) **Iver, Ivor**

Ives (archer) **Ivo, Yvo**
Ivory (tusk)
Jack (God is gracious) **Jackey**
Jackson (son of Jack) **Jack**
Jacob (supplanting, seizing by the heels) **Jakob**
Jacques (supplanting, seizing by the heels)
Jake (supplanting, seizing by the heels)
Jalen Contemporary.
Jamar Contemporary.
James (supplanting, seizing by the heels)
Jamison (son of Jamie *supplanting, seizing by the heels*)
Jan (God is gracious) **Janne, Jens, Jon, Jons**
Jared (descending) **Jarod, Jarrod**
Jason (healer)
Jasper (treasure master)
Jathan Contemporary.
Jedidiah (beloved of Jehovah) **Jed**
Jeffrey (peaceful district; traveler of peace; pledge of peace) **Jeffery**
Jeremiah (God will uplift) **Jeremias**
Jeremie (God will uplift) **Jeremy**
Jermaine (a German)
Jeroen (holy name)
Jerome (holy name)
Jesimiel (God sets up)
Jesper (treasure master)
Jesse (gift)
Jethro (excellence)
Jevin Contemporary.
Joachim (God will establish) **Joachin, Joakim**
Jock (God is gracious)
Joe (he shall add)
Joel (the Lord is God)
John (God is gracious) **Jon, Johnny**
Jonas (dove) **Jonah**
Jonathan (God has given) **Jon**
Jordan (a flowing down) **Jordaan; Judd**
Jorg (earth worker, farmer)
Jorgen (earth worker, farmer)
Jory (to flow down, descend)
Joseph (he shall add) **Josef; Joe**
Joshua (God is salvation) **Jozua; Josh**
Josiah (the Lord supports)
Judd (to flow down, descend)
Judge (a judge)
Julian (youth, downy) **Julien**
Julius (youth, downy)
July (the seventh month)
Junior (younger)
Justin (just) **Justyn**
Justus (just)
Juvenal (youth)
Kadin Contemporary.
Kamal (lotus; perfection)
Kaniel (a reed; a spear)
Kanji (tin) Japanese.

Keefe (handsome, noble)
Keenan (little ancient one)
Kefir (lion cub)
Keir (dark-complexioned)
Keiran (little dark one)
Keith (?, perhaps *the wind; wood*)
Kelby (dweller at the farmstead by the stream)
Kelland (from the swampy land)
Kellen (from the swamp)
Keller (companion dear; tavernkeeper; storekeeper)
Kelly (war, strife)
Kelsey (victory ship)
Kelvin (A Scottish river name)
Kemper (soldier, warrior)
Ken (the same) Japanese.
Kendall (a spring)
Kenji (second son) Japanese.
Kenner (connoisseur)
Kennet (handsome, comely) **Ken**
Kenneth (handsome, comely) **Ken**
Kenrick (royal rule)
Kent (rim, edge, border; white, bright)
Kenward (brave guardian) **Kenard**
Kenya Borrowed from the African country of the same name.
Kenyon (rabbit; white-haired, fair-haired)
Kernan (little black-haired one)
Kerry (black-haired)
Kester (bearing Christ)
Kevin (handsome, comely)
Kevlin Contemporary.
Kez Contemporary.
Kieran (little dark one)
King (king, ruler)
Kipp (a pointed hill)
Kirby (from the church settlement)
Kirk (church)
Kit (bearing Christ)
Kivi (dweller by the stone)
Knut (knot)
Kodiak (island)
Koji (child, little) Japanese.
Konrad (wise counsel)
Kylar (wild boar)
Kyle (narrow, a sound, a strait)
Laban (white)
Lacroix (of the cross)
Lake (a lake, an inland body of water)
Lamar (famous land)
Lambert (bright land)
Lamond (the lawyer) **Lamont**
Lance (land)
Land (land)
Landis (from the swampy place)
Lando (country, land)
Lane (a lane, a narrow country road)
Langston (from Langstone *long stone*)

Larell Contemporary.
Larnell Contemporary.
Lars (man from Laurentum)
Laurance (from Laurentum) **Laurence, Lawrence**
Lawyer (a lawyer, one who is trained in the law)
Lazarus (whom God helps)
Leander (lion man)
Lee (dweller in the meadow or woods)
Leif (what is remaining, relic; beloved)
Leland (dweller near the clearing or fallow land)
Lemuel (devoted to God)
Lennart (brave as a lion) **Lenny**
Lennier Contemporary.
Lennox (from the place of the elms)
Leo (lion)
Leon (lion)
Leonard (bold as a lion) **Lennard**
LeRoy (the king)
Lester (a dyer; from Leicester)
Levi (joining)
Levin (dear friend)
Lindsey (from the linden tree wetland)
Lionel (little lion)
Lloyd (gray)
Logan (dweller at the little hollow)
Londo (fame of the land)
Lonzo (noble and ready)
Loren (man from Laurentum)
Louis (famous in war) **Lewis**
Lovell (a wolf cub)
Luc (light; man from Lucania) **Luke**
Lucas (light; man from Lucania) **Lukas**
Lucian (light; man from Lucania) **Lucien**
Lucius (light; man from Lucania)
Lucky (lucky, fortunate)
Luke (light; man from Lucania)
Luther (famous in war)
Lyell (lion) **Lyel**
Lyle (dweller on the isle)
Lyndon (dweller near the lime tree hill)
Mac (son)
MacAllister (son of Alister *defender of mankind*) **McAllister**
MacDonald (son of Donald *world ruler*)
MacKenzie (son of Coinneach *fair one, handsome*) **McKenzie**
Magnus (great, large)
Malachi (my messenger)
Malcolm (servant of Saint Columba)
Manfred (peace of man)
Manus (great, large)
Marc (?, perhaps *of Mars; manly; soft, tender*) **Mark**
Marcel (of Mars, warlike)
Marcus (?, perhaps *of Mars; manly; soft, tender*) **Markus**
Mark (soft, tender; manly; warlike)
Marland (dweller at the famous land)
Marshall (a horse servant, a groom; a farrier; a marshal)
Martin (of Mars, warlike) **Marten**

Marvin (sea hill, eminent marrow; clear lake)
Mason (a stone mason)
Mateo (gift of God)
Matthew (gift of God) **Matt**
Matthias (gift of God) **Mathis; Matt**
Mauger (spear grinder)
Maurice (a Moor) **Meurisse**
Max (greatest)
Maxwell (large spring; large stream)
Maynard (strong and hardy)
McAllister (son of Allister *defender of mankind*) **Mac**
McKinley (son of Cinfaoladh *learned leader, skilled leader*) **Mac**
Melvin (?, perhaps *council protector*) **Melvyn; Mel**
Merrill (sea bright)
Mervin (sea hill, eminent marrow) **Mervyn**
Michael (Who is like God?) **Michel, Mikael, Mikel**
Micky (Who is like God?) **Mick**
Miles (?, perhaps *mild, peaceful; merciful*)
Milo (?, perhaps *mild, peaceful; merciful*) **Milon**
Milton (from the mill town) **Milt**
Mitchell (Who is like God?) **Mitch**
Montana (mountainous)
Montgomery (from Monte Goumeril)
Mordecai (worshiper of Marduk)
Morgan (sea bright)
Morris (dark, swarthy, a Moor)
Morten (of Mars; warlike) **Morton**
Moses (drawn out of the water)
Muir (dweller near the moor)
Murdoch (mariner)
Murphy (sea warrior)
Murray (from Moray *beside the sea; sailor*)
Myron (myrrh)
Nathan (gift) **Nate**
Nathanael (gift of God) **Natanael, Nathaniel; Nate**
Ned (wealthy guardian)
Neil (champion; a cloud) **Neal, Neill, Nial, Niall, Niel, Niell**
Nelson (son of Neil *champion, cloud*; son of Nell *light, torch, bright*)
Nevada (snowy)
Neville (from the new town) **Nevell, Nevil**
Nevin (little bone; servant of the disciple of the saint)
Niall (champion, cloud)
Nicholas (victory of the people) **Nikolas, Nikolaus; Nicol, Nicoll, Nichol, Coll**
Nick (victory of the people)
Nile Borrowed from the African river of the same name.
Noah (rest, comfort)
Noel (born at Christmas)
Nolan (descendant of Nuallan *shout*)
Norman (northman)
Norris (northerner; nurse)
Norval (from the northern town) **Norvall, Norvel, Norvell, Norvil, Norvill, Norville**
Odo (wealth)

Olof (ancestor's relic) **Olaf, Olav, Olov, Oluf**
Olsen (son of Olaf *ancestor's relic*)
Omar (prosperous, thriving; eloquent)
Oren (fir tree; eagle)
Orson (bear cub)
Orville (?, possibly a French place name or an invention of novelist Fanny Burney for her hero in *Evelina* (1778).
Osbern (god bear) **Osborn**
Osbert (god bright)
Oscar (God's spear) **Oskar**
Osmond (God's protection) **Osmund**
Oswald (God's power)
Oswin (friend of the gods) **Ozzie**
Otto (rich)
Owen (well-born)
Pardee (?)
Parish (dweller at the parish)
Parker (a park keeper, a gamekeeper)
Parlan (son of Talmai *hill, mound, furrows*)
Parnell (little Peter *rock, stone*)
Pat (a patrician, an aristocrat) **Patt**
Patrick (a patrician, an aristocrat) **Pat**
Patterson (son of Peter *a rock, a stone*)
Paul (small)
Paulin (small)
Payton (from Pægan's settlement)
Pearse (a rock, a stone)
Pepper (the pepper spice; a lively personality)
Percy (from Percy, Normandy) **Percey**
Perry (dweller by the pear tree)
Peter (a rock, a stone)
Philip (lover of horses) **Philipp, Phillip**
Phoenix (bright red)
Pierce (a rock, a stone)
Pierre (a rock, a stone)
Piers (a rock, a stone)
Porter (a porter, a carrier)
Powell (son of Howell *eminent, prominent, conspicuous*)
Prentice (apprentice) **Prentis**
Prescott (from the priest's cottage)
Preston (from the priest's village)
Price (son of Rhys *ardor*)
Prince (a prince)
Quentin (fifth) **Quintin**
Quincy (fifth; from Cuinchy, Normandy)
Quinn (counsel, advice)
Rafe (counsel wolf)
Rainier (wise army)
Ralph (counsel wolf)
Ramsey (from ram's island; from the raven's island)
Rand (shield wolf)
Randall (shield wolf) **Randy**
Randolph (shield wolf) **Randolf; Randy**
Raphael (God has healed)
Rashad (good judgment)
Raul (counsel wolf)

Ray (counsel protection)
Raymond (counsel protection) **Raimund, Raymund; Ray**
Raynold (powerful protection) **Rainald, Raynald, Renold, Reynold**
Reed (red) **Read, Reid**
Reese (ardor) **Reece, Rees**
Regin (judgment, decision)
Reginald (judgment power)
Reid (red, ruddy) **Read**
Renfred (counsel might)
Reuben (behold, a son!)
Rex (king)
Reynard (counsel hard)
Rhys (ardor) **Reece, Rees, Reese**
Richard (stern king) **Rikard**
Ridge (a long, narrow crest of a hill or mountain)
Riley (dweller near a rye field) **Reilly**
River (a river)
Robert (bright with fame) **Rob, Robb**
Rocky (stony, full of rocks)
Roderick (famous king) **Roddy**
Rodney (from Hróda's *fame* island) **Rod**
Rogan (red-haired)
Roger (famous with the spear) **Rogier, Rodger**
Roland (famous land) **Rolland**
Rolf (famous wolf)
Rollo (famous wolf)
Roman (a Roman)
Ronald (ruler of judgment) **Ron, Ronny**
Roscoe (from the woods of the red deer)
Ross (dweller on the promontory or peninsula; red, rust-colored)
Roth (famous king)
Rowan (little red-haired one; dweller at or near the rowan tree)
Roy (red-haired, ruddy-complexioned)
Royce (Roy's son)
Ruddick (robin red-breast)
Russell (red-haired) **Russ**
Ruston (from Rust's estate) **Russ, Rusty**
Rusty (red-haired, ruddy-complexioned)
Rutger (famous spear)
Samson (the sun) **Sansom, Sanson, Sam**
Samuel (heard of God) **Sam**
Sander (defender of mankind) **Sandre**
Sanders (defender of mankind; son of Sander *defender of mankind*)
Sandy (defender of mankind)
Saul (asked for)
Sawyer (a cutter of timber)
Scott (an Irishman, a Scot)
Scout (a scout)
Sean (God is gracious) **Shawn**
Sebastian (man from Sebastia) **Sebastiaan, Sebastien**
Seth (appointed)
Shad (?, possibly *Aku's command*)
Shane (God is gracious)

Shaw (dweller at a wood or grove)
Shawnel (God is gracious)
Shea (descendant of Seaghdha *learned; majestic*) **Shay, Shaye**
Shelby (from the farm at the hall)
Sheldon (from the ledge on the hill)
Shem (famous; name)
Sheridan (peaceful; seeker)
Sherman (a shearer or cutter)
Sherwin (to shear the wind; a fleet-footed runner)
Shilo (he who is to be sent, the Messiah)
Shiro (fourth son) Japanese.
Sidney (from Saint Denis; dweller on the wide, riverside meadow; dweller on the wide island)
Silas (ask for)
Silvester (a wood, a forest)
Simon (heard) **Simeon**
Sinclair (from Saint Clair)
Skye (the sky) **Sky**
Skylar Contemporary.
Sloane (warrior, soldier) **Sloan**
Smokey (having the color of smoke, smoky)
Solomon (peaceful)
Sonny (son, youngster)
Soren (apart)
Spencer (dispenser of provisions, a butler or steward)
Spiro (to breathe, to blow)
Stanley (dweller near the stony clearing) **Stan**
Stephan (a crown, a garland) **Stefan, Steffan, Steffen, Stephane, Stephen, Steven**
Stewart (steward, keeper of the animal enclosure) **Stuart**
Stoddard (a keeper of horses)
Storm (an atmospheric disturbance)
Svein (strong, youth) **Sveinn, Sven, Svend, Svends**
Swain (stong, able, wise)
Sylvester (of the woods) **Sylvestre**
Talbot (bandit; lampblack)
Talon (the sharp claw of a bird of prey)
Tandie Contemporary.
Tanier Contemporary.
Tanner (a tanner of hides)
Tannis Contemporary.
Tannon Contemporary.
Taro (firstborn son) Japanese.
Taylor (a tailor)
Teague (a poet)
Ted (God's gift)
Teegan (little poet)
Teger Contemporary.
Telfor (a worker of iron)
Terrence (soft, tender) **Terance**
Terrick (ruler of the people)
Thaddeus (God's gift; praised) **Tad**
Theodore (gift of God) **Theodoor, Theodor; Ted, Teddy, Theo**
Theodoric (ruler of the people) **Theo**
Thomas (a twin) **Thomaas, Tomas**

Thompson (son of Thom *a twin*)
Thor (thunder) **Thore**
Thurstan (Thor's stone) **Torsten**
Timothy (honor, respect) **Timothee**
Titus (?, possibly *to honor*)
Tobias (God is good) **Toby**
Todd (a fox)
Tomi (rich, prosperous) Japanese.
Tonio (?, *priceless, of inestimable worth* is a folk definition) **Tony**
Tony (?, *priceless, of inestimable worth* is a folk definition)
Trace (a mark; to follow the trail of something)
Trail (a path)
Travis (one who passes through a gate or crosses a bridge or river)
Trent (stream, current)
Trevor (prudent, discreet)
Trey (third)
Tristan (tumult, sadness) **Tristram**
Trout (a trout, a type of fish)
Troy (from Troyes, Normandy)
Tucker (a fuller of cloth)
Tully (people mighty)
Tupper (ram)
Turk (a Turk)
Tycho (hitting the mark) **Tyge, Tyko**
Tyler (a tiler; a maker or seller of tiles) **Ty**
Tyson (firebrand)
Ulysses (hater)
Uriah (God is light)
Valery (to be strong) **Valere**
Valient (valiant, brave)
Van (of, from)
Vance (dweller near or at the winnowing fan; dweller near a small hill)
Vaughn (small, little) **Vaughan**
Verlin (springlike, flourishing)
Verne (dweller among the ferns)
Vernon (from Vernon *alder tree grove*)
Victor (victor, winner) **Viktor**
Vincent (conquering)
Virgil (youthful, flourishing)
Von (hope)
Wade (to go; dweller near a ford)

Walden (to rule)
Waldo (to rule)
Walker (a cleaner, fuller, and thickener of cloth)
Wallace (a Welshman)
Walter (ruler of an army)
Ward (a guard, watchman, warden)
Warren (dweller near the game preserve)
Wayne (a wagoner)
Webb (weaver)
Webster (a weaver of cloth)
Werner (protecting army) **Verner, Warner**
Wesley (dweller at the western wood or clearing) **Wes**
West (west, from the west)
Wilfred (desire for peace) **Will**
Willard (resolutely brave) **Will**
William (resolute protector) **Vilhelm, Wilhelm, Willelm, Willem; Bill, Billy, Will, Willy**
Winfred (blessed peace)
Winston (from Winston *friend's town*)
Wolf (wolf)
Woodrow (dweller near the hedgerow by the wood, dweller in the row of houses by the wood)
Wyatt (little Guy *guide, leader*)
Wystan (battle stone)
Xander (defender of mankind)
Xavier (from the new house)
Yale (one who yields, one who pays)
Yancy (a Yankee, an Englishman)
Young (young, junior)
Yukio (snow boy) Japanese.
Yves (archer)
Yvon (archer)
Zachariah (God remembers) **Zacharias, Zac, Zack**
Zachary (God remembers) **Zackary, Zackery; Zac, Zack, Zak**
Zack (God remembers)
Zander (defender of mankind)
Zane (God is gracious)
Zebedee (God has bestowed) **Zeb**
Zebulun (to carry, exalt) **Zeb**
Zebedee (God bestows)
Zebulun (to carry, to exalt)
Zeke (God strengthens)
Zephaniah (the Lord has hidden)
Zinan (second son) Japanese.

SURNAMES

Aagard (dweller in the yard by the river) **Aagaard** Norwegian.
Aarsen (son of Arthur) Dutch.
Abelson (son of Abel *breath*) English.
Abdallah (servant of Allah) Arabic.
Abernathy (from Abernethy *the narrow opening*) **Abernethy** Scottish.
Abrams (son of Abram *father is exalted*) English.

Acevedo (dweller near the holly tree) Spanish.
Acosta (long coast) Spanish.
Adair (dweller near the oak tree ford) Scottish.
Aguilar (place of the eagles) Spanish.
Aguilera (place of the eagles) Spanish.
Akins (dweller near the strait of Akin, Scotland) Scottish, English.

Albano (white) Italian.

Alvarado (from the white place) Spanish.

Alvarez (son of Alva *white*) Spanish.

Ameche (friend) Italian.

Ames (son of Ame *friend; work ruler*; son of the uncle) English.

Amour (love) French.

Anaya (brother) French, Spanish.

Andersen (son of Anders *manly*) **Anderson, Andersson, Andresen** English, Scandinavian.

Andre (manly) **Andres** French.

Arbuckle (from Arbuckle *the height of the shepherd*) Scottish.

Arendt (eagle rule) Norwegian.

Arkin (little Arke *eternal ruler*) Norwegian.

Armstrong (strong arms) **Armstrang** Scottish, English.

Arndt (eagle power) Danish.

Arnold (eagle power) English.

Aronson (son of Aron *lofty mountain*) **Arons** Swedish.

Artaud (brave rule) French.

Ashby (from the settlement where the ash trees grew) English.

Ashe (dweller near the ash tree) **Ash** English.

Atchinson (son of Ache *sword*) English.

Atkinson (son of Atkin *little Adam*) English.

Austin (great, venerable) **Austen** English, Scottish.

Avenier (grower or seller of oats) French.

Avery (elf ruler; bold as a wild boar) English.

Axelson (son of Axel *divine reward*) Swedish.

Ayala (from the grassy slope) Spanish.

Bacheler (young knight, novice in arms) **Bachelor** English.

Bachrach (from Bacharach, Germany) German.

Bacon (side of bacon; seller of bacon) English.

Baggio (toad) Italian.

Bailey (a bailiff, a steward) **Baily** English, Scottish.

Bain (dweller near the River Bain *straight*) English.

Baine (an attendant at a bathhouse) French.

Ballew (from Bellou, France) French.

Bambrick (dweller near the footbridge) English.

Banfield (dweller near the bean field) English.

Banner (flag bearer) English.

Barbarossa (red beard) Italian.

Barfield (from the border field) English.

Barnett (little Bernard *brave as a bear*) **Barnet** English.

Baron (a baron, a nobleman) English.

Barraud (bear might) **Barratt** French.

Barrett (bear rule) English.

Barry (descendant of Bearach *spearlike*; dweller at the village by the border; from the rampart) Scottish, Irish.

Barrington (from Bara's settlement) English.

Bassett (the little short, fat one) French.

Bastien (from Sebastia) French.

Bates (stout, heavy; son of Bate [Bartholomew] *son of Talmai*) English.

Bear Native American.

Bear Killer Native American.

Beard (bearded; from Beard *bank*) English.

Beare (dweller near the grove; bearlike; dweller near the sign of the bear) English.

Beatty (little Bartholomew *son of Talmai*; little Beatrice *bringer of blessings*) English, Scottish.

Becker (dweller near the brook; maker of bread) English, German.

Beckett (dweller near the brook; little bee) **Beckitt** English.

Beckford (from Beckford) English.

Beecham (dweller at the beech enclosure; fair field) English.

Belcher (beautiful face, pretty face) English.

Bellamy (dear friend, beautiful friend) French.

Bellarosa (beautiful rose) Italian.

Benedetto (blessed) **Benedetti** Italian.

Benes (blessed) Czech, Slovakian.

Bennett (blessed) **Bennet** English.

Berkowitz (son of Berko *blessed*) **Berkowicz** Polish, Ukranian.

Berquist (mountain twig) **Bergquist** Swedish.

Bettencourt (from Betto's farm) French.

Bigfeather Native American.

Big Head Native American.

Big Leggins Native American.

Billings (from Billing *Billa's people*; from Billinge *sword*) English.

Bird Tail Native American.

Bishop (a bishop, a member of the bishop's entourage) English.

Blackburn (dweller near the black stream; dweller near the clear stream; from Blackburn) English, Scottish.

Black Fox Native American.

Blacktooth Native American.

Blue Eagle Native American.

Bobbitt (stammerer; a haughty, pompous person) **Bobbett** French.

Bober (dweller at the sign of the beaver; beaverlike) Czech, Slovakian.

Boccaccio (ugly mouth) Italian.

Bochenek (dweller near the sign of the bread loaf) Polish.

Body (from Bod *meadow*) Hungarian.

Boileau (drinker of water, a teetotaler) **Boilleau** French.

Bolger (a maker of leather bags) English.

Bollinger (from Bollingen, Switzerland) German, Swiss.

Bolton (from Bolton *enclosed settlement*) **Boltin** English, Scottish.

Bond (a bondsman, a peasant; householder, freeman) English.

Bonelli (the small good man) **Bonello** Italian.

Bonnell (from the house by the stream) Scottish.

Bono (good) Italian.

Booker (a copier of books; dweller near the beech tree) English.

Borden (from the swine pasture hill) English.

Bowen (son of Owen *youth; well-born*) Welsh.

Boyd (yellow-haired) Irish.

Boyer (maker or seller of bows; a cattle herder) English, French.

Bradbury (dweller near the fort made of boards) English.

Bravebird Native American.

Brennan (descendant of little Bran *raven*) **Brennen** Irish.

Brenner (a burner of charcoal) English.

Brewster (female brewer of beer) English.

Briggs (dweller near the bridge) Scottish, English.

Broken Canoe Native American.

Brodie (son of Bruaideadh *fragment*) Irish.

Brodie (from the muddy place) Scottish.

Brodie (one with an unusual beard) German.

Brody (from Brody) Russian.

Brogan (little Brog *sorrowful*) Irish.

Bryant (descendant of Brian *force, strength; valor; steep, high; kingly*) Irish.

Buchanan (little small one) Scottish.

Buffington (?, possibly an American form of Bovingdon *upon the hill* or Bovington *Bōfa's settlement*) English.

Bullfrog Native American.

Burkhardt (dweller in the strong fortress) **Burkhart** German.

Bush (dweller near the bush or near the sign of the bush) **Busch, Busche** English, German.

Burnett (from Burnett *the burnt place*) English.

Butler (bottle maker; keeper of the bottles; keeper of the wine casks) English.

Calder (dweller near the River Calder *violent stream*) English.

Caldwell (dweller near the cold stream) English.

Camus (snub-nosed) French.

Candiotti (from Candia, Crete) Italian.

Canfield (from Canfield *Cana's field*) English.

Cannon (a clergyman of a cathedral or large church; servant of the canon) **Canon** English.

Capone (?, possibly *rooster*) Italian.

Cardoza (from the place where thistles grew) Spanish.

Carruthers (dweller near the stronghold of Ruther) Welsh.

Carson (son of Car *a marsh; a fort; a rock; care, anxiety*) English.

Case (dweller at the manor farm; from Case, France) English.

Cashman (a cashier) English.

Castello (from the fortress) Spanish.

Catalano (from Catalan, Spain) Italian.

Catterson (son of Cater or Catter *caterer, purveyor*) English.

Chang (constantly; mountain; drawing a bow) Chinese, Korean.

Chapa (dweller at the evergreen oak grove; cloak, cap) Basque, Spanish.

Chen (to attend, to arrange) Chinese.

Cheng (journey; to complete) Chinese.

Cheung (sedate) Chinese.

Childs (a young knight; a young attendant; son of Cilda *child*) **Child, Childe** English.

Chin (true; to increase; to grasp) Chinese, Korean.

Ching (?) Chinese.

Chism (from Chisholm *gravelly island*) English, Scottish.

Cho (to draw a bow; to establish) Chinese.

Choi (tortoise) Chinese.

Chong (hanging bell) **Chung** Chinese.

Chow (everywhere) Chinese.

Christmas (born on Christmas) English.

Chu (bamboo; to bless; deep red) Chinese.

Chun (stupid, foolish; clumsy) Chinese.

Ciccolo (descendant of Cicco [Francisco] *a freeman*) Italian.

Ciccone (big Cicco [Francisco] *a freeman*) Italian.

Claxton (from Clac's settlement) English.

Clearwater Native American.

Cleary (descendant of Cleireach *clerk, cleric*) **Clery** Irish.

Clementi (merciful, mild) **de Clemente** Italian.

Climbing Bear Native American.

Coggins (dweller in the bowl-shaped valley) English.

ColdWeather Native American.

Comerford (from Comberford *Combra's ford*) English.

Conrad (wise counsel) German.

Corrado (wise counsel) Italian.

Cortez (court, town) Spanish.

Coulter (a keeper of colts, a colt herd) **Colter** English.

Craig (dweller near the crag) **Craige** Scottish, English.

Crawford (from Crawford *the ford by the crows*) English, Scottish.

Crews (dweller near the cross; nimble, lively) English.

Crisp (curly-haired) English.

Crosby (from Crosby *the village of the cross*) **Crosbie, Crossby** English, Scottish.

Cruz (cross) Spanish, Portuguese.

Crying Bear Native American.

Crying Bird Native American.

Crying Fawn Native American.

Crying Snake Native American.

Currier (a leather dresser) English.

Cutler (maker, seller, or repairer of knives) English.

Dailey (descendant of Dálach *assembly*) **Daily** Irish.

D'Alessandro (son of Alesandro *defender or helper of mankind*) Italian.

Dallas (from Dallas *the place on the plain,* Scotland) Scottish.

Danek (from Denmark) German.

Danforth (from Denford *the ford in the valley*) English.

D'Angelo (the son of Angelo *angel*) Italian.

Daniels (son of Daniel *God is my judge*) Welsh, English.

Danielson (son of Daniel *God is my judge*) English.

Danner (dweller near the fir tree) German.

Danziger (from Danzig *the Dane's town,* Poland) **Danzig** German.

Darby (a freeman, without injunction) Irish.

Dawes (son of Daw [David] *beloved*; like a jackdaw) **Daw, Dawe** Welsh.

Dawson (son of Daw [David] *beloved*) English.

Dean (a dean, a member of the dean's staff; dweller at the valley) **Deane** English.

Dearborn (dweller near the stream used by wild animals) English.

De Bartolo (the son of Bartolo *son of Talmai*) Italian.

De Boer (a farmer) Dutch.

De Carlo (the son of Carlo *man, a freeman*) Italian.

Diaz (the son of Diago *supplanting, seizing by the heels*) Spanish.

Dietrich (ruler of the people) **Diederich, Diedrich, Dietrich, Dietrick** German.

Dietz (son of Diet *people*) **Dietsch, Dietze** German.

Diggins (son of Diggin [Richard] *stern king*) English.

Di Maggio (son of Maggio *born during the month of May*) Italian.

Dinwoodie (from Dinwoodie *the hill with the shrubs*) **Dinwiddie** Scottish.

Disney (from Isigny, France) English.

DiVito (son of Vito *life*) Italian.

Dix (son of Dick *stern king*) English.

Dixon (son of Dick *stern king*) **Dickson** English.

Dorman (the dear man; a doorman) English.

Dow (dark-complexioned) Irish.

Drennan (son of Draighnean *blackthorn*) Irish.

Dubes (dove; one who raised and sold feather-legged pigeons) French.

Durward (doorkeeper, keeper of the gate) English.

Eades (the son of Ead *wealth, prosperity*) **Eads** English.

Eagle (descendant of Aegel *noble*; dweller at the sign of the eagle; an eagle) English, Native American.

Eaglefeather (an eagle feather) Native American.

Eastman (from the east) English.

Easton (from Easton *the eastern settlement*) English.

Economos (a steward) Greek.

Eden (son of Ead *wealth, prosperity*) **Edens** English.

Edwards (son of Edward *wealthy guardian*) Welsh.

Eger (descendant of Agilhard *brave with the sword*) English, German.

Eisenberg (from Eisenberg *iron mountain*) German.

Eisenhower (an iron cutter; a miner of iron; a maker of eisenhauers, a blade capable of cutting an iron nail) German.

Endicott (dweller at the end cottage) English.

English (an Englishman) English.

Ennis (dweller on an island or riparian meadow; son of Aonghus *one, choice, preeminent*) **Ennes** English, Irish.

Eppstein (from Eppstein *Eppo's stone,* Germany) **Epstein** German.

Erhardt (eternally strong) **Erhard, Erhart** German.

Erskine (from Erskine *the green ascent*) Scottish.

Espinosa (from the thorny thicket) Spanish.

Esposito (exposed; a foundling) Italian.

Estrada (dweller near the paved road) Spanish.

Ettinger (from Oettingen, Bavaria) German.

Evanoff (son of Evan *youth; well-born*) Russian.

Evans (son of Evan *youth; well-born*) Welsh.

Everybodytalksabout Native American.

Exposita (exposed; a foundling) Spanish.

Faber (a metalsmith) **Fabre, Favre, Fevre** French.

Factor (a manager of a business or estate) **Facktor** German.

Fairbanks (dweller near the ridge where bulls, sheep, or boars were found) English.

Fairfax (blond-haired) English.

Farka (dweller at the sign of the wolf; wolflike) **Farkas, Farkash** Hungarian.

Fast Horse Native American.

Fernandez (son of Fernando *peace; journey; youth, life + courage; venture, risk; ready*) **Fernandes** Spanish.

Fife (from Fife) **Fyfe** Scottish.

Figueroa (place of fig trees) Spanish.

Fiore (dweller near the flower patch) **Fiori** Italian.

Fisher (catcher or seller of fish) **Fischer** English, German.

Flanagan (descendant of little Flann *red*) **Flanigan, Flannagan, Flannigan** Irish.

Flannery (descendant of Flannabhra *red eyebrows*) Irish.

Florek (little Flor *flowering, a blooming*) Polish.

Fontana (dweller near the spring) **Fontano** Italian.

Forgets Nothing Native American.

Fox (like a fox) English, Native American.

Franco (free) Spanish.

Fu (teacher) Chinese.

Fujii (dweller near the river where wisteria grew) Japanese.

Fujikawa (dweller near the river where wisteria grew) Japanese.

Fujimoto (dweller near the river where wisteria grew) Japanese.

Fullerton (from Fullerton *the settlement of the bird catchers*) English.

Furman (a ferryman) **Fuhrman, Fuhrmann** German.

Gabor (God is my strength) Hungarian.

Gabriel (God is my strength) French, English.

Gage (a pledge) English.

Galbraith (a foreigner; a stranger from Briton) **Galbreth** Scottish.

Gallagher (descendant of Gallchobhar *foreign help*) Irish.

Galloway (from Galloway *the white hill face*) **Gallaway** Scottish.

Galvin (white, bright) **Galvan** Irish.

Gannon (grandson of the fair-haired one) Irish.

Garcia (spear rule) Spanish.

Garner (warrior of protection) English.

Garofalo (dweller near the place where soapwort grew) Italian.

Gates (dweller near the gate or gap in the hills) English.

Geiger (a violinist) German.

Gelman (a moneychanger; cashier) German.

Genario (descendant of Genaro *January, of Janus*) Italian.

Genero (son-in-law) Italian.

Genovese (from Genova *head of the water*) Italian.

Gentry (a nobleman) English.

Givens (son of Gibbons [Gilbert] *bright pledge*) Scottish, English.

Glenn (dweller in the valley) **Glen** Welsh.

Goldwater (gold water, usually a translation of the German Goldwasser) American.

Goodman (the good man; master of the house) English.

Gore (dweller near the triangular piece of land) English.

Gould (the golden-haired one) English.

Grant (the large man) English, Scottish, French.

Grinnell (from Grindle *the green hill*) English.

Groome (a groom, a young servant) **Groom** English.

Gunn (war) Scottish.

Guy (a guide, leader) English, French.

Hacker (cultivator of the soil with a hack; a maker of hacks) English.

Hahn (dweller at the sign of the cock) **Hahne** German.

Hammond (home; chief protector) **Hammon, Hammonds, Hammons** English.

Hayakawa (early river) Japanese.

Henley (from Henley *the high woods, the high meadow; the hen's woods*) English.

Henslee (dweller in or near the hens' woods) **Hensley** English.

Hernandez (son of Hernando *peace; journey; youth, life + courage; venture, risk; ready*) Spanish.

Hesse (from Hesse *the hooded people*) **Hess** German.

Hicks (son of Hick [Richard] *stern king*) English.

Hilliard (dweller at the hill enclosure) English.

Hinshaw (dweller at the deer woods; dweller at the back woods) English.

Hodgins (son of Hodge [Roger] *famous with the spear*) **Hodgin** English.

Hodgkins (son of Hodgkin [Roger] *famous with the spear*) **Hodgkin** English.

Hoffman (worker at a large farm) **Hoffmann** German.

Hofstetter (from Hofstetter) German, Swiss.

Hohman (the tall man) **Homan, Homann, Hohmann** German.

Holbrook (from Holbrook *the stream in the deep hollow*) English.

Hollis (dweller near the holly tree) English.

Holt (dweller near or in the woods) **Holte** English.

Honeycutt (from Huncote *Huna's cottage*) English.

Hong (from the Hong dynasty) China.

Hoover (a feudal tenant) German.

Hoskins (son of Oskin [pet form of names beginnng with Os-] *a god*) **Hoskin** English, Welsh.

Housden (from Houston, Scotland) Scottish.

Howell (eminent) **Howel** Welsh.

Hummingbird Native American.

Husak (dweller near the sign of the gander) Czech, Slovakian.

Hutchinson (son of Hutch [Hugh] *heart, mind, spirit*) **Hutcheson, Hutchison** Scottish, English.

Hynes (a servant) **Hynds** English.

Ianson (son of Ian *God is gracious*) Scottish.

Inman (an innkeeper) **Inmon** English.

Innes (from Innes *island*) **Innis** Scotland.

Inoue (well, good + upper) Japanese.

Ippolito (freer of horses) Italian.

Iredale (from Airedale) **Iredell** English.

Irons (?, possibly from Airaines *brass,* France) English, Scottish.

Ivanov (son of Ivan *God is gracious*) Russian.

Ivory (from Ivry, France; bow warrior; worker of ivory) English.

Izzi (snail-like; dweller near the oak tree) **Izzo** Italian.

Jacobi (supplanting, seizing by the heels) **Jacoby, Jakobi, Jakoby** French, German.

Jacobs (son of Jacob *supplanting, seizing by the heels*) English, Welsh.

Jaeger (a hunter of game) **Jager** German.

Jaffee (descendant of Jaffe [Japheth] *increase*) **Jaffe, Jaffey** Hebrew.

Jakubowski (son of Jacob *supplanting, seizing by the heel*) Polish.

Janda (descendant of Yan [John] *God is gracious*) Czech, Slovakian.

Janicke (little Jahn *God is gracious*) **Janicki** German, Polish.

Janik (little Jan *God is gracious*) Polish.

Jardin (dweller at or near the garden) **Jarden, Jardine** French, Scottish.

Jaros (young) **Jarosz** Polish, Ukranian.

Jarvis (servant of the spear) English.

Jaworski (from Jaworow *maple tree,* Poland) Polish.

Jaye (a chatterer, like a jaybird; dweller at the sign of the jay) **Jay** English.

Jenner (an engineer, an operator of a war machine) Scottish.

Jennings (son of Jen *God is gracious*) English.

Jessen (son of Jesse *gift*) Danish.

Jessup (Joseph *he shall add*) **Jessop** English.

Jewell (the Lord is God) English.

Jewett (little Julius *youth, downy-bearded*) **Jewitt** English.

Jimenez (descendant of the house of Simon *heard*) Spanish.

Joffe (the beautiful person; descendant of Jaffe [Japheth] *increase*) **Joffee** Hebrew.

Joffre (God's peace) **Joffrey, Jofre** French.

Jonas (dove) Hebrew.

Joslyn (Jocelin *tribe of the Gauts*) **Joslin, Josselyn, Josslin** English.

Kafka (dweller at the sign of the bird) Czech, Slovakian.

Kagan (rabbi, teacher) **Kagen** Russian, Polish.

Kallen (dweller at the sign of the cock) German.

Kallio (dweller near the cliff) Finnish.

Kaminsky (dweller near the boundary marker) **Kaminski** Polish, Russian.

Kaplan (a chaplain) **Kaplin** German, Polish.

Karlinsky (son of little Karl *man*) Russian.

Karras (dark-complexioned) **Karas** Greek.

Kawasaki (dweller near the river on the headland) Japanese.

Keating (Anglicized form of Céitinn [*?*]) Irish.

Kent (from Kent *rim, edge* or *white, bright*) English.

Ketchum (from Caecca's homestead) **Ketcham** English.

Kincaid (from Kincaid *the head of the pass*) **Kinkaid** Scottish.

Kingsbury (from Kinsbury *the king's fort*) English.

Kingsley (from Kingsley *from the king's woods*) **Kinsley** English.

Kirkland (dweller on or near the church's land) Scottish.

Kirsch (grower or seller of cherries; dweller at the sign of the cherries) **Kirsh** German.

Knapp (dweller on top of the hill; from Knapp *hilltop*) **Knap** English.

Knowles (dweller near the small knoll) English, Scottish.

Kostner (one in charge of the church's sacristy) **Costner** German.

Kravitz (a tailor of outer garments) **Kravets, Kravets, Kravis, Kravits** Eastern European.

Krentz (from Krantz *wreath*) **Krenz** German.

Laing (the long or tall man) Scottish.

Lamar (from La Mare *the pool, the pond*) French.

Lambert (land bright) English.

Lancaster (from Lancaster *the Roman camp on the Lune River*) English.

Landau (from Landau *the meadowland*) German.

Landon (from Langdon *the long hill*) English.

Landreth (from Lanreath *court of justice*) English, Scottish.

Latham (from Latham *at the barns*) English.

Lau (lion) German.

Le (pear tree) Chinese.

LeBlanc (blond-haired, white-haired, light-complexioned) French.

Leland (from Leyland *the fallow land*; dweller near the fallow land) English.

Leone (lion; lionlike; dweller near the sign of the lion) Spanish, Greek.

Leslie (from Leslie *the gray fort*) **Laslie, Lesley, Lesslie** Scottish.

Li (plum; black) Chinese, Korean.

Lin (forest) Chinese.

Lind (dweller near the linden tree) English, Swedish.

Ling (forest) Chinese.

Linvill (from Linivilla, France) **Linville** French.

Lipton (from Lepton *the settlement in the abyss*) English.

Liska (dweller at the sign of the fox; foxlike) Czech, Slovakian.

Little (small, short) English.

Liu (willow; battle-ax) Chinese.

Llewellyn (lionlike) **Llewellin, Luellen** Welsh.

Lockhart (strong stronghold; dweller at or near the castle) English, Scottish.

Loeb (from Lôbau *dear meadow*) German.

Logan (dweller at or near the little hollow) **Login** Scottish.

Lomax (from Lomax *the flat land by the pool*) English.

Longo (tall) **Longi** Italian.

Lopez (the son of Lupe *wolf*) Spanish.

Lorton (from Lorton) English.

Lovell (little wolf; little love) English.

Lowe (dweller at the sign of the lion; a lion, lionlike) German.

Lowell (dweller at the sign of the wolf) English.

Lowenthal (from the lion's valley) German.

Lundgren (grove branch) Swedish.

Lupino (dweller at the sign of the wolf) **Luppino** Italian.

Ly (glass, cup; small quantity) Vietnamese.

Lytton (from Litton *the settlement on the rough stream*) English.

McFadden (son of Padin [Patrick] *patrician, an aristocrat*) Irish.

Makes Room for Them Native American.

Maldonado (son of Donald *world ruler*) Spanish.

Malenkov (son of the little man) Russian.

Mangan (descendant of Mongan *little hairy one*) **Mangin** Irish.

Man Killer Native American.

Mann (a servant, vassal) **Man** English, German.

Marchetti (little Marco *of Mars, warlike*) Italian.

Marco (of Mars; warlike) **Marcoe** Italian.

Marek (of Mars; warlike) Polish.

Margulies (descendant of Margaret *a pearl*) **Margolis, Margulis** Russian, Ukranian.

Marian (sea of bitterness or sorrow) **Marion, Merian** English, French.

Marino (of the sea) Italian, Spanish.

Marlowe (from Marlow *lake remains*; dweller at the hill by the lake) **Marlow** English.

Martin (of Mars, warlike) English, French.

Martinez (son of Martin *of Mars, warlike*) Spanish.

Marzano (belonging to Mars) Italian.

Marzec (born in March) Polish.

Matlock (from Matlock *the oak tree meeting place*) English.

Matos (dweller near the cultivated trees) Portuguese.

Matsumoto (from Matsumoto *original pine tree*) Japanese.

Medicine Crow Native American.

Mendez (descendant of Mendel *knowledge, wisdom*) **Mendes** Spanish, Portuguese.

Mendoza (cold mountains) **Mendosa** Spanish, Portuguese.

Mercado (marketplace) Spanish.

Mercurio (the god Mercury) Spanish.

Merrell (sea bright) **Merrill** English.

Messina (from Messina) Italian.

Metzger (butcher) German.

Meyer (light) Hebrew.

Mikos (Who is like God?) Greek.

Milam (from Mileham *the mill village*) English.

Milewski (from Milew) Polish.

Milford (from the mill by the ford) English.

Minkus (little Minkus *remember*) Lithuanian.

Minsky (from Minsk) Russian.

Minter (minter of money) English.

Miranda (from Miranda *the admired place*) **Mirando** Spanish, Portuguese.

Mitchell (Who is like God?) **Mitchel** English.

Mitchum (from the great homestead) **Mitcham, Mitchem** English.

Moliere (dweller near the quarry) French.

Molina (a mill) Spanish.

Monahan (descendant of Manachan *little monk*) Irish.

Monk (a monk) English.

Monroe (dweller near the River Roe; dweller near the red swamp) **Monro** Scottish.

Montoya (horse pasture) Spanish.

Moody (brave, spirited) **Moodie** English.

Moore (descendant of Mordha *majestic*; dweller near a moor)

Morales (dweller near the mulberry tree) Spanish.

Moreau (from Moreau *a Moor*) French.

Morelli (descendant of little More [Amore, *love*], [Mauro, *a Moor*]; small dark man) Italian.

Moreno (dark-skinned) Spanish.

Mork (dweller near the mork, unenclosed land owned jointly) Norwegian.

Morrison (son of Morris *dark-skinned, a Moor*) English, Scottish.

Mosher (dweller by the swamp) **Moshier** German.

Moskovitz (son of Mosko [Moses] *drawn out of the water*) Czech, Slovakian.

Moy (plum flower) Chinese.

Moyers (son of the steward) **Moyer** Irish.

Muir (dweller at or near the moor) Scottish.

Muirhead (from Muirhead *the head of the moor*) Scottish.

Mulder (a miller, a grinder of grain) Dutch.

Munday (born on Monday) **Mundy** English.

Munoz (son of Muno *hill*) **Muniz, Muñiz, Muñoz** Spanish.

Murillo (from Murillo de Rio de Leza, Spain) Spanish.

Muskie (strong, masculine) Czech, Slovakian.

Mussolini (gnatlike) Italian.

Muszynski (from Muszyn *fly*) Polish.

Myers (an overseer; head servant; a farmer) **Meier, Myer** German.

Myles (descendant of Miles [?]) English.

Nakamura (middle village) Japanese.

Nagel (a nail maker) **Naegel, Nagle, Nagler** German.

Nagy (the big man) Hungarian.

Nance (from Nance *valley*) English.

Napoleon (from Neapolis *new city*) **Napoleone** Italian.

Navarro (from the plain among the hills) Spanish.

Needham (from the poor or needy homestead) English.

Neiman (a stranger, newly arrived man) German.

Nemec (dumb, mute; a German who didn't know the Slavic language) Czech, Slovakian.

Ness (dweller on the promontory or peninsula; dweller on the marshy ground) English, Scottish.

Newby (from the new settlement) English.

Newkirk (dweller near the new church) Scottish.

Newton (from the new town) Scottish, English.

Ng (crow) Chinese.

Ngo (?, possibly *stupid, dim-witted; violent, reckless; undisciplined*) Vietnamese.

Nguyen (?, possibly *to swear, to pray; the origin, source*) Vietnamese.

Nixon (son of Nick *victory of the people*) **Nickson** English.

Nogales (dweller near the walnut tree) Spanish.

Novak (a stranger, a newcomer) **Novack, Novacek** Czech, Slovakian.

Nunez (son of Nuno) **Nuñez** Spanish.

Nye (dweller on the island) English.

Oakley (from the oak woods) English.

Oates (son of Odo *rich*) English.

Oberlin (from Oberlind *upper linden tree*) German.

O'Brien (descendant of Brian *force, strength, valor; high, hill; kingly*) **O'Brien, O'Bryan** Irish.

O'Callaghan (descendant of Ceallachan *war, strife*) **O'Callahan** Irish.

O'Connell (descendant of Conall *wisdom, strength, desire*) Irish.

O'Day (descendant of Deaghadh *good luck*) **O'Dea** Irish.

O'Donnell (descendant of Donnell *world ruler*) Irish.

Odell (from Odell *hill of mustard plants*) English.

Ogden (dweller in the oak valley) **Ogdon** English.

O'Grady (descendant of Grada *noble*) Irish.

O'Hara (descendant of Eaghra *bitter*) Irish.

Oldenburg (from the old fort) **Oldenburger** German.

Ondrus (descendant of Andrew *manly*) Czech, Slovakian.

Orlando (famous land) Italian.

Ortega (dweller at the sign of the grouse; grouselike) Spanish.

Ortis (son of Ordono *fortunate*) Portuguese.

Ortiz (son of Ordono *fortunate*) Spanish.

Ostrom (from the island stream) Swedish.

Ostrowski (dweller on a river island) Polish.

O'Sullivan (descendant of Sullivan *white eyes*) Irish.

Overman (dweller near the riverbank; overseer of a coal mine) English.

Owens (son of Owen *youth; well-born*) Welsh.

Owsley (dweller near the stream in the woods or meadow) English.

Pacelli (little Pace [Bonapace] *good peace*) Italian.

Padget (a page, a young male servant) **Padgett, Padgitt** English, French.

Paterson (son of Peter *rock, a stone*) **Patterson** Scottish, English.

Paulson (son of Paul *small*) Danish, English, Norwegian, Swedish.

Payton (from Peyton *Paega's settlement*) English.

Peebles (from Peebles *the assembly place*) **Peeples** Scottish.

Pena (large rock) **Peña** Spanish.

Peterson (son of Peter *a rock, a stone*) **Petersen** Welsh, English, Danish, Swedish.

Petroski (descendant of Peter *rock, stone*) Polish.

Petrov (son of Petr *rock, stone*) **Petroff** Russian.

Pheasant Native American.

Piazza (dweller near the square) **Piazzi** Italian.

Picard (from Picardy *pike men*) **Pickard** French.

Piccolo (a small child) **Piccoli** Italian.

Pinkerton (from Pinkerton, Scotland) Scottish.

Pinsky (from Pinsk *foam*) **Pinsky** Russian, Ukranian, Polish.

Pitt (dweller near the hole or hollow) **Pitts** English.

Pointer (maker of laces for fastening clothes) **Poynter** English.

Polinski (dweller on or near a field) Polish.

Porter (a porter) English.

Potema (a martyr) Polish.

Potts (short form of Philipot [Philip] *lover of horses*) **Pot, Pott** English.

Preble (from Prevelles, France) **Prebble** English.

Priest (a priest; priestlike) **Pries, Priess** English.

Prosser (son of Rosser *famous with the spear*) Welsh.

Pulaski (from Pulawy, Poland) Polish.

Pullman (dweller near the pool) English.

Purcell (dweller at the sign of the young pig; like a little pig) **Pursell** English.

Putz (dweller near the well or spring) German.

Quaile (dweller by the hazel tree) **Quail, Quale, Quill** Irish.

Quinby (from the queen's manor) English.

Quincy (from Quincay, France) French.

Quinlan (descendant of Caoindealbhan *graceful shape*) Irish.

Quinn (descendant of Conn *wisdom, intelligence, reason*) Irish.

Quintana (village) Spanish.

Rabinowitz (son of the rabbi) Eastern European, Russian.

Rafferty (son of Robhartach) Irish.

Raines (counsel; dweller near the boundary line; dweller at the sign of the frog; froglike) **Raynes** English.

Rakowski (dweller at the sign of the crab; a crabber) Polish.

Ramirez (son of Ramon *wise protector*) Spanish.

Ramos (branch) Spanish.

Randolph (shield wolf) **Randolf** English.

Ranieri (wise army) **Rainere** Italian.

Rankin (little Randal *shield wolf*) **Ranken, Rankine** English.

Rappaport (the physician from Porto, Italy) **Rapaport, Rappeport, Rappoport** Italian.

Raskin (descendant of Rashe [little Rachel]) Russian, Polish.

Reagan (little king) **Reagen, Reagin** Irish.

Red Bear Native American.

Red Cloud Native American.

Red Tomahawk Native American.

Rees (ardor) **Reese** Welsh.

Reeves (one appointed to supervise a lord's tenants) **Reeve** English.

Regan (little king) Irish.

Reis (giant) **Reiss** German.

Remington (from Rimington *settlement on the rim*) English.

Remus (protector) English.

Renfrow (from Renfrew *the flowing brook*) **Renfrew, Renfro** Scottish.

Rhys (ardor) Welsh.

Ricardo (stern king) Spanish, Portuguese.

Ricci (home ruler) **Ricca** Italian.

Riccio (curly-haired) Italian.

Rice (ardor) Welsh.

Richards (stern king) **Richard** English.

Rickert (from the Dutch Rijkert [Richard] *stern king*) English.

Rifkin (son of Rifka *a snare*) Russian, Ukranian.

Rigby (from Rigbi *homestead on the ridge*) English.

Riggs (dweller on the ridge) **Rigg** English, Scottish.

Ripley (from Ripley *the long, narrow meadow or wood*) English.

Ruiz (son of Ruy [Rodrigo] *famous ruler*) Spanish.

Ryan (descendant of Rian or Riaghan *kingly*) Irish.

Sabatino (born on the Sabbath) **Sabatano, Sabatini** Italian.

Sage (the wise person) English.

Salazar (from the manor house) Spanish.

Salerno (from Salerno, Italy) Italian.

Salinas (from the salt mine) Spanish.

Sandoval (from the fallow ravine) Spanish.

Santangelo (from Sant Angelo *saint angel*) Italian.

Santelli (the little saint) **Santilli, Santillo** Italian.

Santiago (St. James) Spanish.

Santos (of the saints) Spanish, Portuguese.

Santucci (little saint) Italian.

Sato (a village) Japanese.

Scarpelli (maker and seller of shoes)

Schaeffer (a shepherd) **Schaefer, Schafer, Schaffer, Shafer, Shaffer** German.

Schultz (sheriff; a steward) **Schultze, Schulze** German.

Shivers (a goatherd) **Shiver, Shivver** French.

Sibley (prophetess, fortune teller) English.

Sikora (from Sikora *titmouse*; like a titmouse) Polish.

Sikorski (from Sikora *titmouse*) Polish.

Silva (from the woods) Spanish, Portuguese.

Simpson (son of Sim *heard*) English.

Sims (son of Sim *heard*) **Simms** English.

Six Killer Native American.

Slezak (from Silesia *the bad land*) Czech, Slovakian.

Soukup (a trader, merchant) Czech, Polish, Slovakian.

Spector (inspector) Used by Jewish teachers in old Russia. Russian.

Spence (dispenser of provisions) English, Scottish.

Squirrel Native American.

Standing Bear Native American.

Standing Man Native American.

Stearns (stern, austere) English.

Steeves (son of Steeve *crown, garland*) **Steeve** English.

Steffen (crown, garland) **Steffan, Steffens** English.

Stetson (son of Stith)

Stillsmoking (one who smokes a lot) Native American.

Stocks (dweller near the tree stump; dweller near the post; from Stoke *the dwelling place*) English.

Suslov (like a gopher) Russian.

Sussman (a sweet man) **Susman** German.

Swanson (son of Swan *servant*) **Swenson** Swedish.

Sweitzer (from Switzerland) **Switzer** German.

Swift Hawk Native American.

Sorensen (severe, strict) **Sorenson**

Sousa (from the salty place) **Souza** Portuguese.

Tabor (a small drum, one who played the tabor) **Taber** English.

Taggart (son of the priest) **Taggert** Scottish.

Talcott (dweller in front of the cottage) English.

Talfer (cutter of iron) **Talfor, Telfer, Telford** English.

Tanaka (from the middle rice field) Japanese.

Tanner (a maker or seller of leather) English.

Tarkington (from Torkington *settlement of Turec*) English.

Tarrant (from Tarrant *trespasser*; dweller near the River Tarrant) English.

Tenney (pet form of Dennis *of Dionysus*) **Tenny** English.

Terence (?, possibly *soft, tender*) **Terance** English.

Thatcher (a thatcher, one who thatches roofs) **Thacher, Thacker** English.

The Thunderer Comes With Noise Of Thunder Native American.

Tibon (generous, noble; wolf) Spanish.

Tiffany (born on Epiphany Day, January 6; manifestation of God) English.

Tilley (from Tilley *branch*; from Tilly *linden tree*) **Tilly** English.

Timson (son of Tim *honoring God*) English.

Torres (dweller near the tower) Spanish.

Tovar (from Tovar *sandstone quarry*) Spanish.

Townsend (dweller at the end of the town) **Townshend** English.

Trujillo (from Trujillo *the citadel of Julian*) **Trujilo** Spanish.

Tucker (a cleaner and thickener of cloth) English.

Udell (from Yewdale *the valley of yews*) English.

Ulrich (wolf ruler) **Ullrich, Ullrick** German, English.

Umansky (from Uman *settlement of the wise one* in the Ukraine) Russian, Ukranian.

Unsworth (from Unsworth *Hund's settlement*) English.

Urbanski (son of Urban *city dweller*) Polish.

Vaccaro (cow herder) Italian.

Valdez (from Valdes) Spanish.

Valente (valiant, brave) **Valenti** Italian.

Valentini (strong, healthy) **Valentino** Italian.

Valkoinen (light-complexioned) Finnish.

Van Gelder (from the county of Gelder) Dutch.

Van Patten (from Putten *pool*) Dutch.

Varga (a shoemaker) Hungarian.

Vargas (from the steep hill) Spanish, Portuguese.

Vasquez (a shepherd; a Basque) **Vazquez** Spanish.

Vedder (father's brother; a male cousin) **Vetter** German.

Vega (dweller in the meadow) Spanish.

Velasquez (slow, weak) Spanish.

Ventura (good luck; a foundling) Italian.

Viles (the old man) English.

Villareal (from the royal villa) **Villarreal** Spanish.

Voight (a steward, an overseer) **Voigt, Voit** German.

Voorhies (dweller in front of the town of Hess) **Voorhees** Dutch.

Wade (dweller near the shallow ford) English.

Wagner (a wagon driver; a maker of wagons) English, German.

Wainwright (a maker of wagons) English.

Waite (a watchman) English.

Wakefield (from Wakefield *field where plays were performed*) English.

Walcott (from Walcot *the peasant's cottage*) English.

Walking Stick Native American.

Walkley (from Walkley *the Welshman's meadow or woods*) English.

Wang (yellow; prince) Chinese.

Warnock (little Warin *protection*) English.

Weller (dweller near the well) English.

Whipple (from Whimple *the white stream*) English.

White Bull Native American.

White Eagle Native American.

White Hat Native American.

Wick (dweller at the dairy farm) English.

Wiggs (son of Wigg *war, warrior*) English.

Wilbur (beloved stronghold) English.

Wolf (dweller at the sign of the wolf; wolflike) **Wolfe** English, German, Native American.

Wong (wide seas) Chinese.

Wray (from the isolated place) English.

Wright (a carpenter, a workman) English.

Xavier (from the new house) Spanish.

Xenos (a stranger) Greek.

Ximena (from Ximena *place of Simon or Jimena*) Spanish.

Yalowitz (dweller near the juniper tree) Ukranian.

Yamamoto (mountain + origin, dweller at the mountain) Japanese.

Yamashita (mountain + below, dweller below the mountain) Japanese.

Yarnell (eagle strength) **Yarnall** English.

Yee (I, first person singular) Chinese.

Yellow Wolf Native American.

Yonan (God is gracious) German.

Young Bear Native American.

Yost (fighter) German.

Zabel (dweller at the sign of the sable; like a sable; trapper or seller of sables) Czech, Slovakian, Polish.

Zachary (God remembers) English.

Zagorski (dweller beyond the hill) Polish.

Zahara (from Zahara *desert*) Spanish.

Zajak (dweller at the sign of the rabbit; rabbitlike) **Zajik** Czech, Slovakian, Polish, Ukranian.

Zaleski (dweller beyond the woods) Polish.

Zaremba (a swordsman) Polish.

Zidek (a little Jew) Polish.

Zielinski (from Zielinsk *the green place*) Polish.

Zieman (man of victory) **Ziemann** German.

Zuber (dweller by the creek) German, Swiss.

[BIBLIOGRAPHY]

Ardagh, John. *Ireland and the Irish: Portrait of a Changing Society.* London: Hamish Hamilton; Penguin, 1994.

Arthur, William. *An Etymological Dictionary of Family and Christian Names.* New York: Sheldon, Blakeman & Co., 1857.

Bailey, Anthony. *A Walk Through Wales.* New York: HarperCollins Publishers, 1992.

Baird, Charles W. *Huguenot Emigration to America.* 2 vols. Baltimore: Regional Publishing Company, 1966.

Bancroft, George. *History of the United States of America, from the Discovery of the Continent.* New York: Appleton, c. 1882–1886.

Beckett, J. C. *The Making of Modern Ireland, 1603–1923.* New York: Knopf, 1966.

Blankenship, Bob. *Cherokee Roots.* 2 vols. Cherokee, North Carolina: Cherokee Roots Publishing, 1994.

Blevins, Winfred. *Dictionary of the American West.* New York: Facts on File, 1993.

The Book of Saints: A Dictionary of Servants of God Canonised by the Catholic Church. Compiled by the Benedictine Monks of Saint Augustine's Abbey, Ramsgate. New York: Macmillan and Co., 1944.

Bottigheimer, Karl S. *Ireland and the Irish: A Short History.* New York: Columbia University Press, 1982.

Bowyer, Bell. *The Irish Troubles: A Generation of Violence, 1967–1992.* New York: St. Martin's Press, 1993.

Boyer, Carl (ed.). *Ship Passenger Lists. New York and New Jersey (1600–1825).* 4 vols. Newhall, California: Boyer, 1978.

Briggs, Asa. *A Social History of England.* New York: Viking Press, 1984.

Burner, David, Robert D. Marcus, and Emily S. Rosenberg. *America: A Portrait in History.* Englewood Cliffs, New Jersey: Prentice-Hall, 1974.

Butterfield, Roger Place. *The American Past. A History of the United States from Concord to Hiroshima, 1775–1945.* New York: Simon & Schuster, 1966.

Cahill, Thomas. *How the Irish Saved Civilization: The Untold Story of Ireland's Heroic Role from the Fall of Rome to the Rise of Medieval Europe.* New York: Nan A. Talese, Doubleday, 1995.

Cairns, John Campbell. *France.* Englewood Cliffs, New Jersey: Prentice-Hall, 1965.

Calthrop, Dion Clayton. *English Costume, 1066–1820.* London: A. & C. Black, 1907.

Cameron, Viola Root. *Emigrants from Scotland to America 1774–1775.* Baltimore: Genealogical Publishing Co., 1980.

Campbell, James. *Invisible Country: A Journey Through Scotland.* New York: New Amsterdam, 1990.

Cassidy, Frederic, and Richard Ringler. *Bright's Old English Grammar and Reader.* New York: Holt, Rinehart, & Winston, 1974.

Charbonneau, Claudette, and Patricia Slade Lander. *The Land and People of Norway.* New York: HarperCollins, 1992.

Chessex, Pierre. *Origine des Noms de Personnes: Sens et Origine des Prenoms, des Noms de Famille et des Surnoms.* Geneva: Slatkine, 1983.

Coghlan, Ronan, Ida Grehan, and P.W. Joyce. *Book of Irish Names: First, Family, and Place Names.* New York: Sterling Pub. Co., 1989.

Coldham, Peter Wilson. *The Complete Book of Emigrants.* 3 vols. Baltimore: Genealogical Publishing Co., 1987.

The Complete Romances of Chretien de Troyes. Translated by David Staines. Bloomington, Indiana: Indiana University Press, 1990.

Cottle, Basil. *The Penguin Dictionary of Surnames.* Harmondsworth, England: Penguin, 1967.

Daiches, David (ed.). *A Companion to Scottish Culture.* New York: Homes & Meier Publishers, 1982.

Davies, John. *A History of Wales.* London and New York: Allen Lane / Penguin Press, 1993.

De Breffny, Brian. *Irish Family Names: Arms, Origins, and Locations.* Dublin: Gill and Macmillan, 1982.

Directory of Scottish Settlers in North America. 6 vols. Baltimore: Genealogical Publishing Co., 1985.

Dockstader, Frederick J. *Great North American Indians.* New York: Van Nostrand Reinhold, 1977.

Dolan, J. R. *English Ancestral Names: The Evolution of the Surname from Medieval Occupations.* New York: C. N. Potter, 1972.

Drain, Thomas A. *A Sense of Mission: Historic Churches of the Southwest.* San Francisco: Chronicle Books, 1994.

Durant, Will, and Ariel Durant. *The Age of Louis XIV; A History of European Civilization in the Period of Pascal, Moliere, Cromwell, Milton, Peter the Great, Newton, and Spinoza: 1648–1715.* New York: Simon & Schuster, 1963.

Durant, Will. *The Reformation: A History of European Civilization from Wyclif to Calvin, 1300–1564.* New York: Simon and Schuster, 1957.

Earle, Alice Morse. *Home Life in Colonial Days.* Williamstown, Massachusetts: Corner House, 1975.

Ellis, Steven. *Tudor Ireland: Crown, Community, and the Conflict of Cultures, 1470–1603.* London: Longman, 1985.

Ewen, C. L'estrange. *A History of Surnames of the British Isles.* Baltimore: Genealogical Publishing Co., 1968.

Filby, P. William, and Mary K. Meyer (eds.). *Passenger and Immigration Lists Index.* 4 vols. Detroit: Gale Research Co., 1985.

Foster, R. F. *Modern Ireland 1600–1972.* New York: Penguin Books, 1989.

Fox, Edward W. *Atlas of European History.* New York: Oxford University Press, 1957.

Fraser, Antonia. *Cromwell, the Lord Protector.* New York: Knopf, 1973.

———. *King James VI of Scotland, I of England.* New York: Knopf, 1975.

———. *The Lives of the Kings and Queens of England.* Ed. by Antonia Fraser. New York: Knopf, 1975.

Fucilla, Joseph G. *Our Italian Surnames.* Baltimore: Genealogical Publishing Co., 1987.

A Genealogical History of the Milesian Families of Ireland. Compiled and edited by Heraldic Artists Limited. Dublin: Heraldic Artists Limited, 1968.

Glazier, Ira A. (ed.). *The Famine Immigrants. Lists of Irish Immigrants Arriving at the Port of New York 1846–1851.* 7 vols. Baltimore: Genealogical Publishing Co., 1983.

Goubert, Pierre. *The Course of French History.* New York: F. Watts, 1988.

Grenham, John. *The Clans and Families of Ireland: The Heritage and Heraldry of Irish Clans and Families.* Secaucus, New Jersey: Wellfleet Press, 1993.

Grimble, Ian. *Scottish Clans and Tartans.* New York: Tudor Pub. Co., 1973.

Guérard, Albert Léon. *France; A Modern History 1880–1959.* Ann Arbor, Michigan: University of Michigan Press, 1969.

Guy, John. *Tudor England.* Oxford and New York: Oxford University Press, 1988.

Hallam, Elizabeth. *Domesday Book Through Nine Centuries.* New York: Thames and Hudson, 1986.

Hallam, Elizabeth (ed.). *The Plantagenet Chronicles.* New York: Crescent Books, 1995.

Hamilton, E. N. *Bible Names.* San Francisco: John Howell, 1940.

Hamilton, Ronald. *The Visitor's History of Britain.* Boston: Houghton Mifflin, 1964.

Hanks, Patrick, and Flavia Hodges. *A Dictionary of First Names.* Oxford and New York: Oxford University Press, 1990.

Hanley, Clifford. *The Scots.* New York: Times Books, 1980.

Harrison, Henry. *Surnames of the United Kingdom.* Baltimore: Genealogical Publishing Co., 1969.

Herda, D. J. *Ethnic America,* 6 vols. Brookfield, Connecticut: Millbrook Press, 1991.

Holmes, Martin Rivington. *Elizabethan London.* New York: F. A. Praeger, 1969.

Hook, J. N. *Family Names: How Our Surnames Came to America.* New York: Macmillan; Collier Macmillan, 1982.

———. *Family Names: The Origins, Meanings, Mutations, and History of More Than 2,800 American Names.* New York: Collier Books; Collier Macmillan, 1983.

Hughes, Charles. *How You Got Your Name: The Origin and Meanings of Surnames.* London: Phoenix House, 1961.

Innes of Learney, Sir Thomas. *The Tartans of the Clans and Families of Scotland.* Edinburgh: Johnston and Bacon, 1971.

Jacob, P. L. *France in the Middle Ages: Customs, Classes and Conditions.* New York: Ungar, 1963.

Jenner, Michael. *Scotland Through the Ages.* London: Joseph, 1987.

Johnson, Douglas W. J. *A Concise History of France.* New York: Viking Press, 1971.

Jones, Colin. *The Cambridge Illustrated History of France.* Cambridge: Cambridge University Press, 1994.

Jones, George F. *German-American Names.* Baltimore: Genealogical Publishing Co., 1990.

Jones, Gwyn. *A History of the Vikings.* Oxford and New York: Oxford University Press, 1984.

Jordan, Jerry Wright. *Cherokee by Blood.* 5 vols. Bowie, Maryland: Heritage Books, Inc., 1990.

Kaminkow, Jack, and Marion Kaminkow. *Emigrants from England to America 1718–1759*. Baltimore: Magna Carta Book Company, 1981.

Kaufman, Rosalie. *The Queens of England*. Boston: Estes and Lauriat, 1887.

Kee, Robert. *Ireland: A History*. Boston: Little, Brown, 1982.

Kirkham, E. Kay. *Our Native Americans and Their Records of Genealogical Value*. 2 vols. Logan, Utah: The Everton Publishers Inc., 1984.

Kolatch, Alfred J. *Complete Dictionary of English and Hebrew First Names*. Middle Village, New York: J. David Publishers, 1984.

———. *Dictionary of First Names*. New York: Perigee Books, 1990.

———. *The Name Dictionary; Modern English and Hebrew Names*. New York: J. David, 1967.

Kurelek, William. *They Sought a New World: The Story of European Immigration to North America*. Montreal: Tundra Books, 1985.

Labarge, Margaret Wade. *Medieval Travellers*. New York: W. W. Norton, 1983.

Landon, Michael. *Erin and Britannia: the Historical Background to a Modern Tragedy*. Chicago: Nelson-Hall, 1981.

Lanier, Sidney (ed.). *Knightly Legends of Wales:The Mabinogion*. New York: Scribner, 1901.

Lecky, William Edward Hartpole. *A History of England in the Eighteenth Century*. New York: AMS Press, 1968.

———. *A History of Ireland in the Eighteenth Century*. New York: AMS Press, 1969.

Lepthien, Emilie U. *The Cherokee*. Chicago: Children's Press, 1985.

Levenson, Dorothy. *Homesteaders and Indians*. New York: F. Watts, 1971.

Lunt, W. E. *History of England*. New York: Harper & Brothers, 1945.

Mackie, J. D. *A History of Scotland*. Harmondsworth and New York: Penguin, 1978.

Mackie, R. L. *A Short History of Scotland*. New York: Praeger, 1963.

Maclean, Fitzroy. *A Concise History of Scotland*. New York: Viking Press, 1970.

MacLysaght, Edward. *More Irish Families*. Blackrock, Co. Dublin: Irish Academic Press, 1982.

———. *The Surnames of Ireland*. Dublin: Irish Academic Press, 1985.

MacManus, Seumas. *The Story of the Irish Race: A Popular History of Ireland*. New York: Devin-Adair Co., 1944.

Martell, Hazel. *The Vikings and Jorvik*. New York: Dillon Press, 1993.

Martine, Roderick. *Scottish Clan and Family Names: Their Arms, Origins, and Tartans*. Edinburgh: Mainstream Pub., 1992.

Matheson, Sir E. *Special Report on Surnames in Ireland*. Baltimore: Genealogical Publishing Co., 1968.

McCormick, Anita Louise. *Native Americans and the Reservation in American History*. Springfield, New Jersey: Enslow Publishers, 1996.

McGee, Thomas D'Arcy. *A History of the Irish Settlers in North America from the Earliest Period to the Census of 1850*. Baltimore: Genealogical Publishing Co., 1980.

Meyer, Kathleen Allan. *Ireland, Land of Mist and Magic*. Minneapolis: Dillon Press, 1983.

Moberg, Vilhelm. *A History of the Swedish People*. New York: Pantheon, 1972.

Moncreiffe, Sir Iain. *The Highland Clans: The Dynastic Origins, Chiefs and Background of the Clans Connected with Highland History and of Some Other Families*. New York: C. N. Potter, 1967.

Morris, Jan. *The Matter of Wales: Epic Views of a Small Country*. Oxford and New York: Oxford University Press, 1984.

O'Ballance, Edgar. *Terror in Ireland: The Heritage of Hate*. Novato, California: Presidio Press, 1981.

O'Corráin, Donnchadh, and Fidelma Maguire. *Gaelic Personal Names*. Dublin, 1981.

O'Laughlin, Michael C. *The Complete Book of Irish Family Names*. Kansas City, Missouri: Irish Genealogical Foundation, 1986.

O'Malley, Padraig. *The Uncivil Wars: Ireland Today*. Boston: Houghton Mifflin, 1983.

Paxson, Frederic L. *History of the American Frontier, 1763–1893*. Boston and New York: Houghton Mifflin Co., 1924.

Pine, L. G. *The Highland Clans*. Rutland, Vermont: Charles E. Tuttle, 1972.

———. *They Came with the Conqueror: A Study of the Modern Descendants of the Normans*. New York: Putnam, 1955.

Porter, Donald Clayton. *Cherokee*. Toronto and New York: Bantam Books, 1984.

Price, Roger. *A Concise History of France*. Cambridge: Cambridge University Press, 1993.

Puckett, Newbell Niles. *Black Names in America*. Boston: G. K. Hall & Co., 1975.

Reaney, P. H. *A Dictionary of British Surnames*. London: Routledge & Kegan Paul, 1958.

Rees, William. *Historical Atlas of Wales, from Early to Modern Times*. London: Faber and Faber, 1959.

Ridley, Jasper Godwin. *Henry VIII*. New York: Viking, 1985.

———. *The Tudor Age*. Woodstock, New York: Overlook Press, 1990.

Ritchie, J. N. G. *Scotland: Archaeology and Early History*. London: Thames and Hudson, 1981.

Robb, H. Amanda, and Andrew Chesler. *Encyclopedia of American Family Names*. New York: HarperCollins, 1995.

Roberts, J. M. *History of the World*. New York: Oxford University Press, 1993.

Ross, Stewart. *Elizabethan Life*. London: B. T. Batsford, 1991.

Rowse, A. L. *Eminent Elizabethans*. Athens: University of Georgia Press, 1983.

Ryan, Kathleen Jo, and Bernard Share. *Irish Traditions*. New York: H. N. Abrams, 1985.

Scally, Robert James. *The End of Hidden Ireland: Rebellion, Famine and Emigration*. New York: Oxford University Press, 1995.

Scandinavia Past and Present. 3 vols. Odense, Denmark: Arnkrone, 1959.

Schroeder, Noel (ed.). *Foxe's Book of English Martyrs: Reformation Heroes Who Paid the Price for Our Religious and Political Freedoms*. Waco, Texas: Word Books, 1981.

Schwartz, Richard. *Daily Life in Johnson's London*. Madison, Wisconsin: University of Wisconsin Press, 1983.

Seaman, L. C. B. *A New History of England, 410–1975*. Brighton, Sussex: Harvester Press Ltd., 1982.

Singman, Jeffrey L. *Daily Life in Chaucer's England*. Westport Connecticut: Greenwood Press, 1995.

———. *Daily Life in Elizabethan England*. Westport, Connecticut: Greenwood Press, 1995.

Smith, Elsdon C. *New Dictionary of American Family Names*. New York: Harper & Row, 1973.

———. *The Story of Our Names*. New York: Harper, 1950.

Smout, T. C. *A History of the Scottish People 1560–1830*. New York: Charles Scribner's Sons, 1969.

Somerset Fry, Plantagenet. *The History of Scotland*. London: Routledge & Kegan Paul, 1982.

Stenton, Frank M. *Anglo-Saxon England*. Oxford and New York: Oxford University Press, 1971.

Stewart, George R. *American Given Names*. New York: Oxford University Press, 1979.

Strickland, Agnes. *Lives of the Queens of England, from the Norman Conquest: Compiled from Official Records and Other Authentic Documents, Private As Well As Public*. Philadelphia: J. B. Lippincott, 1893.

Sutton, Ann, and Richard Carr. *Tartans: Their Art and History*. New York: Arco Pub., 1984.

Taylor, A. J. P. *English History, 1914–1945*. New York: Oxford University Press, 1965.

Tepper, Michael (ed.). *Passengers to America. A Consolidation of Ship Passenger Lists from the New England Historical and Genealogical Register*. Baltimore: Genealogical Publishing Co., 1978.

Terry, Ted. *American Black History: Reference Manual*. Tulsa, Oklahoma: Myles Pub., 1991.

Thomas, George. *My Wales*. London: Century, 1986.

Thomas, Hugh. *A History of the World*. New York: Harper & Row, 1979.

Tomkeieff, Olive. *Life in Norman England*. New York: Putnam, 1966.

Tournier, Paul. *The Naming of Persons*. New York: Harper and Row, 1975.

Vanberg, Bent. *Of Norwegian Ways*. Minneapolis: Dillon Press, 1970.

Van de Weyer, Robert. *Celtic Fire: The Passionate Religious Vision of Ancient Britain and Ireland*. New York: Doubleday, 1991.

Weekley, Ernest. *Jack and Jill: A Study in Our Christian Names*. New York: Dutton, 1940.

———. *The Romance of Names*. New York: E. P. Dutton & Co., 1914.

———. *Surnames*. New York: Dutton, 1937.

White, Deborah G. *Let My People Go: African-Americans, 1804–1860*. New York: Oxford University Press, 1995.

Whitelock, Dorothy. *The Beginnings of English Society*. Harmondsworth, England: Penguin, 1952.

Williams, E. Neville. *Life in Georgian England*. London: B. T. Batsford, 1962.

Williamson, David. *Debrett's Kings and Queens of Europe*. Topsfield, Massachusetts: Salem House, 1988.

Wilson, Woodrow. *A History of the American People*. New York: Harper & Brothers, 1902.

Withycombe, E. G. *The Oxford Dictionary of English Christian Names*. Oxford: Clarendon Press, 1977.

Woods, Richard. *Hispanic First Names*. Westport, Connecticut: Greenwood Press, 1984.

Woulfe, Patrick. *Irish Names and Surnames*. Kansas City, Missouri: Irish Genealogical Foundation, 1992.

Yoder, Don (ed.). *Rhineland Emigrants. Lists of German Settlers in Colonial America*. Baltimore: Genealogical Publishing Co., 1985.

Yonge, Charlotte. *History of Christian Names*. London: Macmillan & Co., 1884.

Zimmerman, Gary J., and Marion Wolfert. *German Immigrants: Lists of Passengers Bound from Bremen to New York 1847–1854*. Baltimore: Genealogical Publishing Co., 1987.